A HISTORY OF GRAPHIC DESIGN

Philip B. Meggs

VNR VAN NOSTRAND REINHOLD COMPANY
New York Cincinnati Toronto London Melbourne

Library of Congress Catalog Card Number 82-2826
ISBN 0-442-26221-3 (cloth)

Printed in the United States of America

Designed by Paul Chevannes

Published by Van Nostrand Reinhold Company Inc.
135 West 50th Street
New York, NY 10020

Fleet Publishers
1410 Birchmount Road
Scarborough, Ontario MIP 2E7, Canada

Van Nostrand Reinhold Australia Pty. Ltd.
480 Latrobe Street
Melbourne, Victoria 3000, Australia

Van Nostrand Reinhold Company Limited
Molly Millars Lane
Wokingham, Berkshire, England RG11 2PY

16 15 14 13 12 11 10 9 8 7 6 5 4 3 2 1

Library of Congress Cataloging in Publication Data

Meggs, Philip B.
A history of graphic design.

Bibliography: p.
Includes index.
1. Printing, Practical—History. 2. Graphic arts—History. I. Title.
Z244.5.M42 686.2′09 82-2826
ISBN 0-442-26221-3 AACR2

Acknowledgments

Several hundred people generously provided the author with information, assistance, pictorial material, and reproduction permissions. Unfortunately, it is not possible to thank each one of them here. The assistance and kindness of a number of people have been so crucial to this effort that I wish to express deep and sincere gratitude.

At the Library of Congress, Elaina Millie of the Poster Collection and Katheleen Hunt of the Rare Book and Special Collections Division provided invaluable information and courteous assistance beyond normal expectations. Robert Coates of the Museum of Modern Art Design Study Center and Susan Reinhold of the Reinhold-Brown Poster Galleries generously shared research materials. At the Virginia Commonwealth University Libraries, Arts Librarian Joan Muller and Janet Dalberto of Collections Development made remarkable contributions to my research. Dr. Robert Godwin-Jones assisted in the translation of numerous German and French materials. Continuing support has been provided by Dr. Murry N. DePillars.

I am indebted to family members of several deceased twentieth century graphic designers for research materials and reproduction permissions. Hattula Moholy-Nagy clarified several issues and provided materials by her father, Laszlo Moholy-Nagy. Mrs. Carla Binder provided research materials and reproduction permission for work by her husband, Joseph Binder. Mrs. Dorothy M. Beall, wife of Lester Beall, was generous in her contributions. Material by Alvin Lustig was made available through the courtesy of Elaine Lustig Cohen.

George Nan provided insights and help on photographic matters. Cathleen Crone assisted in the preparation of photography, and Jerry Bates assisted in the preparation of graphic materials, including several reconstructions of material that would not otherwise have been available.

1. the creative process is not performed by the skilled hand alone, or by the intellect alone, but must be a unified process in which "head, heart, and hand play a simultaneous role."

2. I quote the Japanese saying, "first acquire an infallible technique and then open yourself to inspiration."

3. the human being as a manifestation of the supreme spirit or the source of life "performs what he is given to do." in the consciousness of I of myself can do nothing the artist becomes a transparency through which the creative principle operates.

herbert bayer
16 march 1979

Charlene Cosby and Margaret Hill typed (and retyped) the manuscript. In addition, Margaret Hill provided invaluable administrative and logistical support over several years. My editor at Van Nostrand Reinhold, Wendy Lochner, guided this manuscript through its critical final stages. Thanks for other editorial work to Jeanette Mall, Doreen Eckstein, Martina D'Alton, Marilyn Houston, and Louise Richardson.

My understanding of the modern movements of twentieth-century art has been greatly informed by Richard Carlyon. John T. Hilton contributed immeasurably to my comprehension of the humanist and social role of design activities. Robert C. Carter generously shared research materials and his understanding of the Bauhaus era, and Mallory Callan's insights into the genesis of the modern design movement have proven invaluable. Professor Han Schroeder was most helpful in providing information about the *De Stijl* movement, particularly Rietveld's Schroeder house.

Research leading to publication of this book was made possible by the generous support of a Design Fellowship from the Design Arts Program of the National Endowment for the Arts, a Federal agency. Likewise, a Faculty Grant-in-Aid research grant from Virginia Commonwealth University was critical to my pictorial and bibliographic research. Without the spiritual and intellectual support of my wife, Libby Phillips Meggs, this book could have been neither conceived nor carried to completion.

Any errors and omissions in this work are solely the responsibility of the author, and those who have been so generous in their support share none of the blame for the inevitable shortcomings of this book.

Photographs by Nadar are copyright Arch. Phot, Paris/SPADEM/VAGA, New York, 1982, and are reproduced by permission.

Max Ernst's collage from *Une Semaine De Bonte* is reproduced by courtesy of Dover Publications, Inc., from the 1976 republication of the 1934 limited edition by Editions Jeanne Bucher, Paris.

Selected works by El Lissitzky are reprinted from *El Lissitzky* by Sophie Lissitzky-Kuppers; copyright 1967, Verlag Der Kunst Dresden, publisher.

Selected designs by Jan Tschichold are reprinted from *Jan Tschichold: Typographer* by Ruari McLean; copyright 1975 by Ruari McLean, by permission of David R. Godine, Publisher, Inc., Boston, Massachusetts.

Designs by H. N. Werkman are reproduced from the 1978 publication, *Hendrik Werkman, The Next Call,* by Jan Martinet, through the courtesy of the publisher, uitgeverij Reflex, Utrecht, The Netherlands.

Material designed by Ladislav Sutnar for Sweet's is reproduced by permission of the copyright holder, Sweet's Division, McGraw-Hill Information Systems Company.

Material from *Observations,* copyright 1959 by Richard Avedon and Truman Capote under the provisions of the International Copyright Union, is reprinted by permission of Simon & Schuster, a Division of Gulf and Western Corporation.

Pages from *Westvaco Inspirations* are reprinted by courtesy of Westvaco Corporation.

Designs by John Heartfield for *Neue Jugend* and *AIZ* are reprinted from *Montage: John Heartfield* by Eckhard Siepmann, copyright 1977, by permission of the publisher, Elefanten Press Verlag GMBH, West Berlin.

Foreword

There is a German word, *zeitgeist,* that does not have an English equivalent. It means the spirit of the time, and refers to the cultural trends and tastes that are characteristic of a given era. The immediacy and the ephemeral nature of graphic design, combined with its link with the social, political, and economic life of its culture, enable it to more closely express the zeitgeist of an epoch than many other forms of human expression. Ivan Chermayeff, a noted designer, has said: the design of history is the history of design.

Since prehistoric times, people have searched for ways to give visual form to ideas and concepts, to store knowledge in graphic form, and to bring order and clarity to information. Over the course of history, these needs have been filled by various people including scribes, printers, and artists. It was not until 1922, when the outstanding book designer William Addison Dwiggins coined the term "graphic designer" to describe his activities as an individual who brought structural order and visual form to printed communications, that an emerging profession received an appropriate name. However, the contemporary graphic designer is the heir to a distinguished ancestry. Sumerian scribes who invented writing, Egyptian artisans who combined words and images on papyrus manuscripts, Chinese block printers, medieval illuminators, and fifteenth-century printers and compositors who designed early European printed books all become part of the rich heritage and history of graphic design. By and large, this is an anonymous tradition, for the social value and aesthetic accomplishments of graphic designers, many of whom have been creative artists of extraordinary intelligence and vision, have not been sufficiently recognized.

History is in large measure a myth, because the historian looks back over the great sprawling network of human struggle and attempts to construct a web of meaning. Oversimplification, ignorance of causes and their effects, and the lack of an objective vantage point are grave risks for the historian. When we attempt to record the accomplishments of the past, we do so from the vantage point of our own time. History becomes a reflection of the needs, sensibilities, and attitudes of the chronicler's time as surely as it represents the accomplishments of bygone eras. As much as one might strive for objectivity, the limitations of individual knowledge and insights ultimately intrude.

The concept of art for art's sake, a beautiful object that exists solely for its aesthetic values, did not develop until the nineteenth century. Before the Industrial Revolution, the beauty of the forms and images that people made were linked to their function in human society. The aesthetic qualities of Greek pottery, Egyptian hieroglyphics, and medieval manuscripts were totally integrated with useful values; art and life were unified into a cohesive whole. The din and thunder of the Industrial Revolution turned the world upside down in a process of upheaval and technological progress that continues to accelerate at an ever-quickening pace. By jolting the arts and crafts from their social and economic roles, the machine age created a gulf between people's material life and their sensory and spiritual needs. Just as voices call for a restoration of humanity's unity with the natural environment, there is a growing awareness of the need to restore human and aesthetic values to the man-made environment and mass communications. The design arts—architectural, product, fashion, interior, and graphic design—offer one means for this restoration. Once more a society's shelter, artifacts, and communications might bind a people together. The endangered aesthetic and spiritual values might be restored. A wholeness of need and spirit, reunited through the process of design, can contribute in great measure to the quality and raison d'être of life in urban societies.

This chronicle of graphic design was written in the belief that if we understand the past, we will be better able to continue a cultural legacy of beautiful form and effective communication. If we ignore this legacy, we run the risk of becoming buried in the mindless morass of a commercialism whose molelike vision ignores human values and needs as it burrows forward into darkness.

Contents

PART I

PROLOGUE: *The evolution of graphic communications from prehistoric times until the invention of movable typography*

1

The Invention of Writing

It is not known precisely when or where the biological species of conscious, thinking people, *Homo sapiens,* emerged. The search for our prehistoric origins continues to push back into time the early innovations of our ancestors. It is believed that we evolved from a species that lived in the southern part of Africa. They ventured out onto the grassy plains and into caves as the forests slowly disappeared in that part of the world. In the tall grass, these early humanoids began to stand erect. Perhaps this was done to watch for predators in the tall grass, or to ward off enemies by increasing their apparent size and even holding branches as weapons. In any event, the hand developed a magnificent ability to carry food and hold objects. Found near Lake Turkana in Kenya, a nearly three-million-year-old stone that had been sharpened into an implement proves the thoughtful and deliberate development of a technology, a tool. Early shaped stones may have been used to dig for roots or to cut away flesh from dead animals for food. While we can only speculate about the use of early tools, we know that they mark a major step in the human species' immense journey from primitive origins toward a civilized state. A number of quantum leaps provided the capacity to organize a community and gain some measure of control over human destiny. Speech, the ability to make sounds in order to communicate with one another, was an early skill developed by the species in the long evolutionary trail from its archaic beginnings. Writing is the visual counterpart of speech. Marks, symbols, pictures, or letters drawn or written upon a surface, or *substrate,* became a graphic counterpart of the spoken word or unspoken thought. The limitations of speech are the fallibility of human memory and an immediacy of expression that cannot transcend time and place. Until the present electronic age, the spoken word vanished without a trace; the written word remained. The invention of writing brought the luster of civilization to people and made it possible to preserve hard-won knowledge, experiences, and thoughts.

The development of writing and visible language had its earliest origins in simple pictures, for a close connection exists between the drawing of pictures and the marking of writing. Both are natural ways of communicating ideas, and primitive man used pictures as an elementary way to record and transmit information.

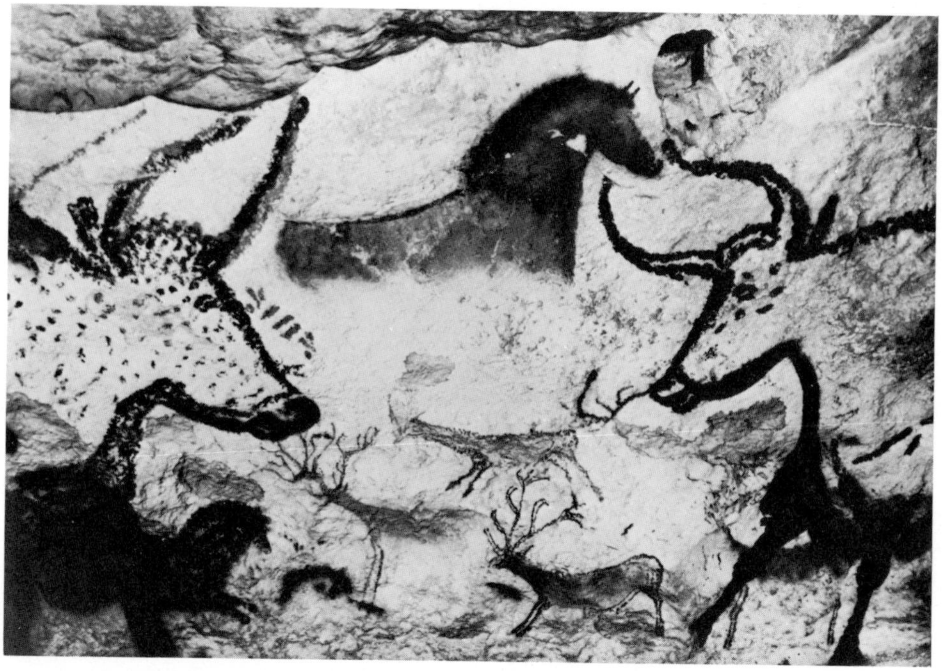

Cave painting from Lascaux, c. 15,000–10,000 B.C. Random placement and shifting scale signify prehistoric people's lack of structure and sequence in recording their experiences. *Courtesy of the French Tourist Office.*

Prehistoric visual communications

From the early Paleolithic until the Neolithic periods (35,000 B.C. to 4000 B.C.), early people in Africa and Europe left paintings in caves, including the famous Lascaux caves in southern France. A black made from charcoal and a range of warm tones, from light yellows through red-browns, made from red and yellow ochers formed the palette of pigments, mixed with fat as a medium. Images of animals were drawn and painted upon the walls of these former subterranean water channels occupied as a refuge by prehistoric men and women. Perhaps the pigment was smeared onto the walls with a finger, or a brush was fabricated from bristles or reeds. This was not the beginning of art as we know it. Rather, it was the dawning of visual communications, because these early pictures were made for survival and were created for utilitarian and ritualistic purposes. The presence of what appears to be spear marks in the sides of some of these animal images indicates that they might have been used in magical rites designed to gain power over animals and success in the hunt. Or perhaps they were teaching aids to instruct the young on the process of hunting as a cooperative group effort. Abstract geometric signs including dots, squares, and other configurations are intermingled with the animals in many cave paintings. Whether they represent man-made objects or are proto-writing is not known. It will never be known with any certainty, because they were made before the beginning of history—the 5,000-year period during which people have recorded in writing a chronicle of their knowledge of facts and events. The animals painted on the cavès are *pictographs*—elementary pictures or sketches to represent the things depicted.

Throughout the world, from Africa to North America to the islands of

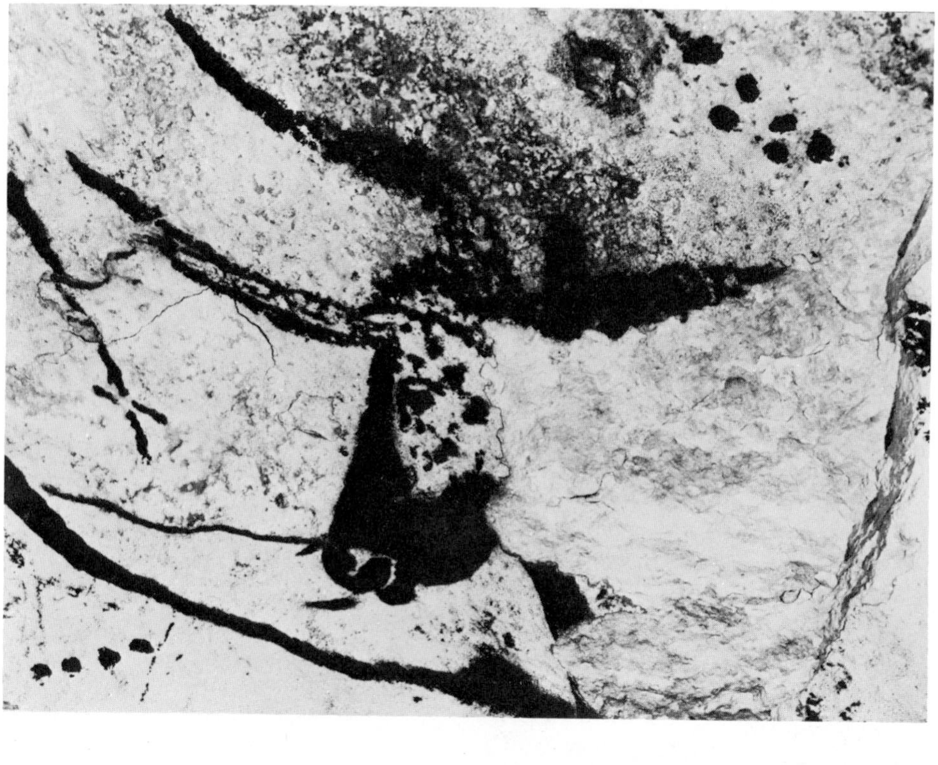

Bull's head, cave-painting detail from Lascaux, c. 15,000–10,000 B.C. The lifelike proportion and animated eye indicate careful observation and drawing skill. Note the dots and geometric form to the left. *Courtesy of the French Tourist Office.*

New Zealand, prehistoric man has left numerous *petroglyphs,* which are carved or scratched signs or simple figures on rock. Many of the petroglyphs are pictographs, and some may be *ideographs,* or symbols to represent ideas or concepts.

A high level of observation and memory is evidenced in many prehistoric drawings. In an engraved reindeer antler found in the cave of Lorthet in southern France, the scratched drawings of deer and salmon are remarkably accurate. Even more fascinating, however, are two diamond-shaped forms with interior marks. The early pictographs evolved in two ways. First, they were the beginning of pictorial art. The objects and events of the world were recorded with increasing fidelity and exactitude as the centuries passed. Second, pictographs also evolved into writing. The images, whether the original pictorial form was retained or not, ultimately became symbols for spoken-language sounds.

The Paleolithic artist developed a tendency toward simplification and stylization. Figures became increasingly abbreviated and were expressed with a minimum number of lines. By the late Paleolithic period, some petroglyphs and pictographs had been reduced to the point of almost resembling letters.

Found carved and sometimes painted on rocks throughout the western portion of the United States, these petroglyphic figures, animals, and signs are similar to those found all over the world.

The cradle of civilization

Until recent discoveries indicated that early peoples in Thailand may have practiced agriculture and manufactured pottery at an even earlier date, archaeologists had long believed that the ancient land of Mesopotamia, "the land between rivers," was the cradle of civilization. Between the Tigris and Euphrates Rivers, which flow from the mountains of eastern Turkey across the land that is now Iraq and into the Persian Gulf, there lies a flat, once-fertile plain whose wet winters and hot, dry summers proved very attractive to early man. It was here that man ceased his restless nomadic wanderings and established a village culture. Around 8000 B.C. wild grain was planted, animals were domesticated, and agriculture began. By the year 6000 B.C., objects were being hammered from copper; the Bronze Age was ushered in about 3000 B.C. when copper was alloyed with tin to make durable tools and weapons, and the wheel was invented.

The leap from village culture to high civilization occurred after the arrival upon the scene of the Sumerian people near the end of the fourth millennium B.C. The origin of the Sumerians remains a great mystery. Before 3000 B.C., they had settled in the lower part of the fertile crescent. As vital as the technologies developed in Mesopotamia were for the future of the human race, the Sumerians' contribution to social and intellectual progress had even more impact upon the future. The Sumerians invented a system of gods, headed by a supreme deity named Anu, who was the god of the heavens. An intricate system of god-man relationships was developed. The city emerged, with the necessary social order for large numbers of people to live together. But of the numerous inventions in Sumer that launched man onto the path of civilization, the invention of writing brought about an intellectual revolution that had a vast impact upon social order, economic progress, and technological and cultural developments.

The history of Mesopotamia records waves of invaders who flooded onto the fertile plain and conquered the peoples living there. The culture

Engraved drawing on a deer antler, c. 15,000 B.C. This prehistoric image is shown in a cast made by rolling the antler onto clay. The geometric forms imply an early symbol-making ability. *Musée des Antiquities Nationales, St. Germain-en-Laye, France.*

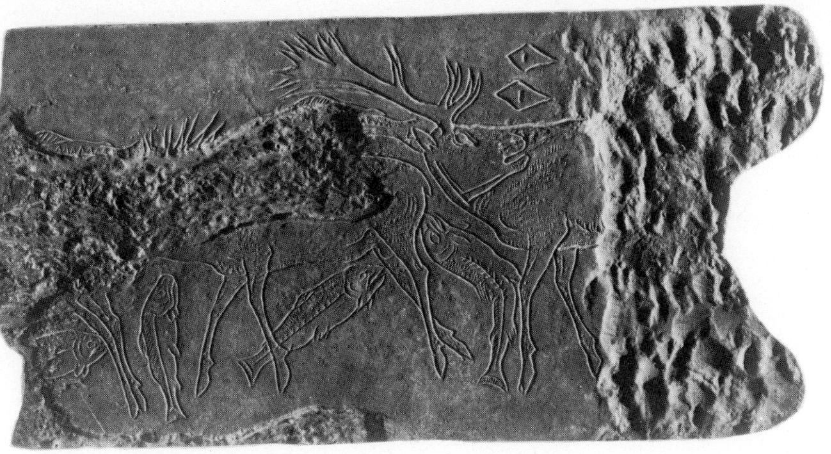

established by the Sumerians conquered the invaders in turn, and the sequence of ruling peoples adopted and developed civilization. The peoples who dominated Mesopotamia during its long history include Akkadians, Assyrians, Babylonians, and Chaldeans. Persians from the west and Hittites from the north also conquered the area and spread Mesopotamian civilization beyond the fertile crescent.

The invention of writing

Religion dominated life in the Mesopotamian city-state, just as the massive ziggurat, a stepped temple compound, dominated the city. These vast, multistory complexes were built of brick and towered over the area. Inside, priests and scribes wielded enormous power as they controlled the inventories of the gods and the King, and ministered to the magical and religious needs of the people. Writing may have evolved because this temple economy had a desperate need for record keeping. The temple chiefs must have consciously sought a system for setting down information.

In human memory, time can become a blur, and important facts are sometimes forgotten. Who delivered their taxes in the form of crops? How much food was stored, and was it adequate to meet community needs before the next harvest? How much seed must be held until planting time to ensure that the next crop would be an abundant one, and how much could be used for human and animal food? An accurate continuum of knowledge became imperative if the temple priests were to be able to maintain the order and stability necessary in the city-state. One theory holds that the origin of visible language evolved from the need to identify the contents of sacks and pottery containers used to store food. Small clay tags were made that identified the contents with a pictograph and the amount in an elementary decimal numbering system, inspired by the ten fingers on a person's hands.

Alabaster relief from the palace of King Tiglath-Pileser III at Nimrud, c. 500 B.C. In this bas-relief, two Assyrian scribes compile lists of the spoils of war upon clay tablets with their styli as the former are listed by the official on the left. *The British Museum, London.*

Early Sumerian pictographic tablet, c. 3100 B.C. This "archaic" pictographic script contained the seeds for the development of writing. Information is structured by horizontal and vertical division into zones. *Musée de Louvre, Paris.*

The earliest written records are tablets from the city of Uruk, which apparently list commodities by pictographic drawings of objects, accompanied by numerals and personal names inscribed in orderly columns. An abundance of clay in Sumer made it the logical material for record keeping, and a reed stylus sharpened to a point was used to draw the fine, curved lines of the early pictographs. Beginning in the top right-hand corner of the tablet, they were written in careful vertical columns. The clayey mud tablet was held in the left hand, and pictographs were scratched in the surface with the wooden stylus. The inscribed tablet was dried in the hot sun or baked rock-hard in a kiln.

This writing system underwent an evolution over several centuries. A *grid system* was developed to contain writing in horizontal and vertical spatial divisions. Sometimes the scribe's hand would smear the writing as it moved across the tablet. Around 2800 B.C. the scribes turned the pictographs on their sides and began to write in horizontal rows from left to right and top to bottom. This made writing easier, and it made the pictographs less literal. About three hundred years later, writing speed was increased by replacing the sharp-pointed stylus with a triangular-tipped one. This stylus was pushed into the clay instead of being dragged through it. The characters were now composed of a series of wedge-shaped strokes rather than of a continuous line drawing. This innovation radically altered the nature of the writing; pictographs evolved into an abstract sign writing called *cuneiform* (from the Latin for "wedge-shaped").

While the graphic form of Sumerian writing was evolving, its ability to record information was expanding. From the first stage, when picture-symbols represented animate and inanimate objects, signs became ideographs and began to represent abstract ideas. The symbol for sun, for example, began to represent ideas such as "day" and "light." As early scribes developed their written language so that it would function in the same way as their speech, the need to represent spoken sounds that were not easily depicted arose. Adverbs, prepositions, and personal names could not often be adapted to pictographic representation. Picture-symbols began to represent the sound of the object depicted instead of the object itself. Cuneiform became rebus writing; pictures became *phonograms*, or graphic symbols for sounds. The highest development of cuneiform was its use of abstract signs to represent syllables, which are sounds made of combinations of more elementary sounds.

Cuneiform was an awesome writing system to master even after the Assyrians simplified it into only five hundred and sixty signs. Youngsters destined to become scribes began their schooling at the *edubba* or tablet

The Blau monument, early Sumerian. This etched and carved shale artifact from the third quarter of the fourth millennium B.C. is the oldest extant artifact combining images and writing. *The British Museum, London.*

This clay tablet demonstrates how the Sumerian symbols for star (which also meant heaven or god), head, and water evolved from early pictographs (3100 B.C.). The latter were turned on their side by 2800 B.C. and evolved into the early cuneiform writing by 2500 B.C.

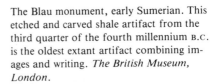

house before the age of ten and worked from sunrise to sunset every day, with only six days off a month. Professional opportunities in the priesthood, estate management, accounting, medicine, and government were reserved for these elect. Writing took on important magical and ceremonial qualities. The general public held those who could write in awe, and it was believed that death occurred when a divine scribe etched one's name in a mythical Book of Fate.

The knowledge explosion made possible by writing was astounding. Libraries were organized and contained thousands of tablets about religion, mathematics, history, law, medicine, and astronomy. Thousands of commercial contracts and records remain, and literature sprang up as poetry, myths, hymns, epics, and legends were recorded on the clay tablets. Writing fostered a deep sense of history, and tablets chronicled with meticulous exactitude the events that occurred during the reign of each monarch.

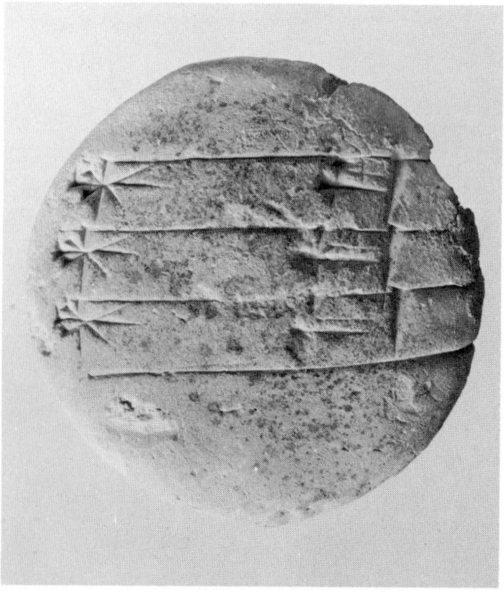

Sumero-Akkadian exercise tablet, third millennium B.C. On this rare surviving tablet, a student in the *edubba* practiced writing the words *God Urash* three times. *The Metropolitan Museum of Art, New York, purchase, 1886.*

Cuneiform tablet, c. 2100 B.C. This clay tablet lists expenditures of grain and animals. *The Metropolitan Museum of Art, New York.*

Stele bearing the Code of Hammurabi, c. 1930–1880 B.C. Above the densely textured law code, King Hammurabi is shown on a mountaintop with the seated sun god Shamash, who orders the king to write down the laws for the people of Babylon. A graphic image of divine authority as the source for the code becomes powerful visual persuasion. *Musée de Louvre, Paris.*

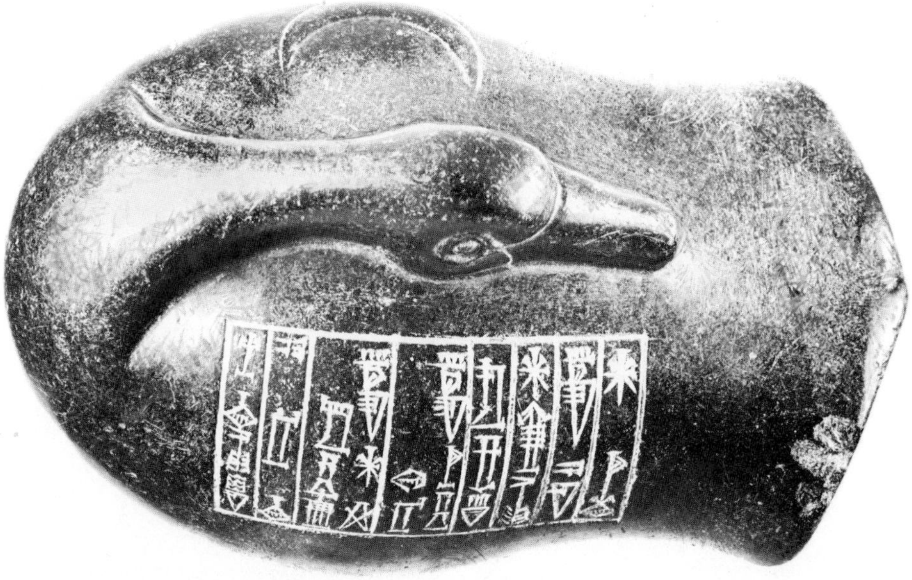

Black stone duck weight, c. 3000 B.C. The cuneiform inscription states that this weight is dedicated to the god Nanna by the King of Ur, and confirms a weight of five *minas*. Each Mesopotamian *mina* weighed about 0.559 kilograms, or 18 ounces. *Courtesy of the Iraq Museum, Bagdad.*

Writing enabled society to stabilize itself under rule and law. Measurements and weights were standardized and guaranteed by written inscription. Law codes, such as the Code of Hammurabi, dating from the period 1930–1880 B.C., spelled out crimes and their punishment, thus establishing social order and justice. The Code of Hammurabi is written in careful cuneiform on a 2.44-meter (8-foot) tall *stele,* or slab, of irregular but carefully polished stone. The stele contains two hundred eighty-two laws gridded in twenty-one columns. Steles with Hammurabi's reformed law code were erected in the main temple of Marduk at Babylon and in other cities. Written in a precise style, harsh penalties were expressed with clarity and brevity. Some of these commandments include: "a thief stealing from a child is to be put to death"; "a physician operating on a slightly wounded man with a bronze scalpel shall have his hands cut off"; and "a builder who builds a house that falls and kills the owner shall be put to death."

Visual identification

Two natural by-products of the rise of village culture were the ownership of property and the specialization of trades or crafts. Both made visual identification necessary. Cattle brands and proprietary marks were developed so that ownership could be established, and the maker of pottery or other objects could be identified if problems developed or if superior quality inspired repeat purchases. A means of identifying the author of a clay cuneiform tablet, certifying commercial documents and contracts and proving the authority of religious and royal proclamations, was needed. The fascinating Mesopotamian cylinder seals, which provided a forgery-proof method of sealing documents and proving their authenticity, were developed. In use for over three thousand years, these small cylinders had images and writing etched into their surface. When they were rolled across the damp clay tablet, a raised impression of the depressed design, which became a "trademark" for the owner, was formed. Because the image carved into the round stone appeared on the tablet as a raised flat design, it was virtually impossible to duplicate or counterfeit. Many had a hollow perforation running through them so that they could be worn by the owner on a string around his neck or wrist.

The widely traveled Greek historian Herodotus (c. 500 B.C.) wrote that the Babylonians all wore a cylinder seal on a cord around their wrists like a bracelet. Prized as an ornament, status symbol, and unique personal signature, cylinder seals were even used to mark a damp clay seal on the door when the household was away to indicate whether burglars had entered the premises. Seal cutters developed great skill and a refined sense of design. The earliest seals were engraved with simple pictures of kings, a line of cattle, or mythic creatures. Later, more narrative images developed; for instance, one god would present a man (probably the seal's owner) to another god, or a man would figure prominently in fighting a battle or killing a wild

animal. In the later Assyrian period, north of Mesopotamia, a more stylized and heraldic design approach developed. Stories of the gods were illustrated and animals were shown engaged in battle.

The last glory of Mesopotamian civilization occurred during the long reign of King Nebuchadnezzar (d. 562 B.C.) in the city-state of Babylon. But, in 538 B.C., after less than a century of great power, during which Babylon became the richest city in the world, with a population reaching perhaps a million people, Babylon and Mesopotamia fell to the Persians. The Mesopotamian culture began to perish as it became a province of Persia, then Greece and Rome. By the birth of Christ, great cities such as Babylon were abandoned, and the ziggurats had fallen into ruins. The dawning of visible language, the magnificent gift to the future of mankind that was writing, passed forward to the Phoenicians, who reduced the formidable complexity of cuneiform to simple phonetic signs.

Hittite cylinder seal, undated. Thought to portray a ritual, possibly with a sacrificial offering on the right, this seal combines decorative ornament with figurative images. It has both a "rolled" image on the side and a stamped image on the bottom. *Museum of Fine Arts, Boston, Henry Lillie Pierce Residuary Fund.*

Detail of the Code of Hammurabi, c. 1800 B.C. Whether pressed into clay or carved into stone as shown here, Mesopotamian scribes achieved a masterful control and delicacy in their writing and arrangement of the strokes in the partitioned space. *Musée de Louvre, Paris.*

Mesopotamian cylinder seals, c. 1880–1550 B.C. The diversity of cylinder-seal design ranged from the highly structured and figurative to the random and abstract. *The Metropolitan Museum of Art, New York, Cesnol Collection, purchased by subscription, 1874–76.*

Persian stamp seal, c. 500 B.C. Incised into a precious pale blue quartz called chalcedony in a gold mount, this seal, with its symmetrical design of a pair of heraldic beasts locked in combat, probably belonged to a member of the royal family or the high priesthood. *Museum of Fine Arts, Boston, gift of Mr and Mrs. Donald P. Edgar.*

2

Graphic Communications in Ancient Egypt

THE NILE RIVER COURSES 6,689 kilometers (4,157 miles) through the northwest corner of Africa toward the Mediterranean Sea. The basin of this ancient river—the planet's longest—has yielded stone implements that are one hundred thousand years old. The early flint-implement inhabitants lived in a warm, moist climate, but thousands of years ago the region began to grow more arid. Deserts slowly crept toward the narrower Nile River, and twenty thousand years ago the area that became Egypt had become a vast sandy desert devoid of life except for the lush flood plain clinging to each side of the river. Perhaps it was five or six thousand years ago that agriculture began in the Nile Valley. The early tillers of the soil deified this great river whose cycle of floods nourished their crops and animals.

By the time King Menes unified the land of Egypt and formed the First Dynasty around the year 3100 B.C., a number of inventions from the Sumerians in Mesopotamia had reached the Egyptians. Included were the cylinder seal, architectural designs of brick, a number of decorative design motifs, and the fundamentals of writing. Unlike the Sumerians, who evolved their pictographic writing into the abstract cuneiform, the Egyptians retained their picture-writing system, called *hieroglyphics* (Greek for "sacred carving" after the Egyptian for "the god's words"), for almost three and a half millennia. The earliest known hieroglyphs date from about 3100 B.C., and the last written hieroglyphic inscription known was carved in 394 A.D., many decades after Egypt had become a Roman colony.

Ivory tablet of King Zet, First Dynasty. This five-thousand-year-old tablet is perhaps the earliest known example of the Egyptian pictographic writing that evolved into hieroglyphics. It was found in ruins at the ancient sacred city of Abydos. *Courtesy of the Egyptian Antiquities Museum, Cairo.*

Egyptian hieroglyphs

For nearly fifteen centuries, men looked with fascination upon Egyptian hieroglyphs without understanding their meaning. The last people to use this language system were fourth-century A.D. Egyptian temple priests, and they were so secretive that Greek and Roman scholars of the era believed that this amazing writing was nothing more than magical symbols for sacred rites. In August of 1799, Napoleon's troops were digging a foundation for an addition to the fortification in the Egyptian town of Rosetta that they were occupying. A black slab was unearthed bearing an inscription in two languages and three scripts: Egyptian hieroglyphics, Egyptian demotic script, and Greek. This decree had been written in 197 or 196 B.C. after a great council of Egyptian priests met to commemorate the ascension of Pharaoh Ptolemy V (born c. 210 B.C.) to the throne of Egypt nine years earlier. It was realized that the inscription was probably the same in the three languages, and efforts to translate it began. In 1819, Dr. Thomas Young (1773–1829) proved that the direction in which the glyphs of living creatures faced was the direction from which hieroglyphics should be read and that the cartouche for Ptolemy occurred several times.

The major deciphering of the Rosetta Stone hieroglyphs was done by Jean François Champollion (1790–1832). He realized that some of the signs were alphabetic, some were syllabic, and some were determinatives (signs that determined how the preceding glyphs should be interpreted). Realizing that the hieroglyphs often functioned as phonograms and not simply pictographs, Champollion was able to meticulously sound out the names Ptolemy and Cleopatra. This breakthrough happened in 1822 after Champollion had been given a photograph of an obelisk (a tall, totemlike Egyptian monument bearing an inscription). As Champollion studied the photograph, he was stunned to see the cartouches of both Ptolemy and Cleopatra, which he had recognized earlier. Champollion assigned sounds to the three glyphs found in both words: p, o, and l. Then he patiently sounded out the others until he had a dozen hieroglyphic translations. Armed with this new knowledge, he proceeded to decipher the cartouche for Alexander. Champollion gathered all the cartouches he could find from the Greco-Roman era and quickly translated eighty, building a large vocabulary of glyphs in the process. After his death at the age of forty-two, Champollion's *Egyptian Dictionary* and an *Egyptian Grammar* were both published. He had made such progress toward translating hieroglyphics that the Egyptologists who followed during the course of the nineteenth century were able to unlock the mysteries of Egyptian history and culture that had been silently preserved in this beautiful graphic-language system.

When the early Egyptian scribes were confronted with difficult words to express in visual form, they probably devised a rebus, using pictures for sounds, to write the desired word. At the same time, they designated a pictorial symbol for every consonant sound and combination of consonants in their speech. Even though they never developed signs for the connecting vowel sounds, combining the various glyphs formed a skeletonized form of every word. By the time of the New Kingdom (1570–1085 B.C.), this remarkably efficient writing system had over seven hundred hieroglyphs, over one hundred of which remained strictly visual pictographs or word-pictures. The remainder had become phonograms. Because the Egyptian language contained so many homonyms (such as, for example, a *pool* of water and the game of *pool*), determinatives were used after these words to insure that the reader correctly interpreted the word. *Hinew,* for example, could mean a liquid measure or neighbors. In the former

The Rosetta Stone, c. 197–196 B.C. From top to bottom, the concurrent hieroglyphic, demotic, and Greek inscriptions provided the key to the secrets of ancient Egypt. *The British Museum, London, Department of Egyptian Antiquities.*

case, it was followed by the glyph for beer pot; in the latter, by glyphs for a man and a woman.

The ancient Egyptians had an extraordinary sense of design, and they were sensitive to the remarkable decorative and textural qualities of their hieroglyphs. This monumental visible language system was everywhere. Hieroglyphs were carved into stone as raised images or incised relief, and color was often applied. These covered the inside and exterior of temples and tombs. Furniture, coffins, clothing, utensils, buildings, and jewelry all bore hieroglyphs having both decorative and inscriptional purpose. Frequently, magical and religious values were ascribed to certain hieroglyphs. The hieroglyph *ankh* was a cross surmounted by a loop and had modest origins as the symbol for a sandal strap. Due to the phonetic similarity, it gained meaning as a symbol for life and immortality and was widely used as a sacred emblem throughout the land.

The design flexibility of hieroglyphics was greatly increased by the choice of writing direction. One started from the direction in which the living creatures were facing, and the lines could be written horizontally or vertically. The designer of an artifact or manuscript had four choices: left to right horizontally; left to right in vertical columns; right to left horizontally; and right to left in vertical columns. Sometimes, as demonstrated in the schematic of the sarcophagus of Aspalta, these design possibilities were combined in one work.

Cartouche of Sesostris I, c. 1950 B.C. The cartouche—as shown in this example etched on iridescent mother of pearl—is a bracketlike plaque containing the glyphs for an important name. *Museum of Fine Arts, Boston, Harvard-MFA Expedition.*

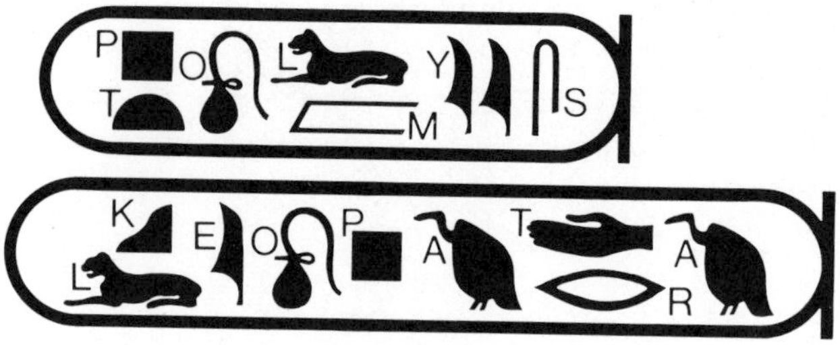

Alphabet characters have been applied beside each hieroglyph in the cartouches of Ptolemy and Cleopatra to demonstrate the approximate phonetic sounds deciphered by Champollion.

These Egyptian hieroglyphs illustrate the rebus principle. Words and syllables are represented by pictures of objects and by symbols whose names are similar to the word or syllable to be communicated. These hieroglyphs mean bee, leaf, sea, and sun. As rebuses (using the English language) they could also mean belief and season.

Offering Niche of the Lady Sat-tety-lyn, Sixth Dynasty. In contrast to the raised images in the lower registers, these hieroglyphs are carved into the surface and are contained in a mathematical grid of carved lines. *Museum of Fine Arts, Boston, purchased from Services des Antiques Egypt.*

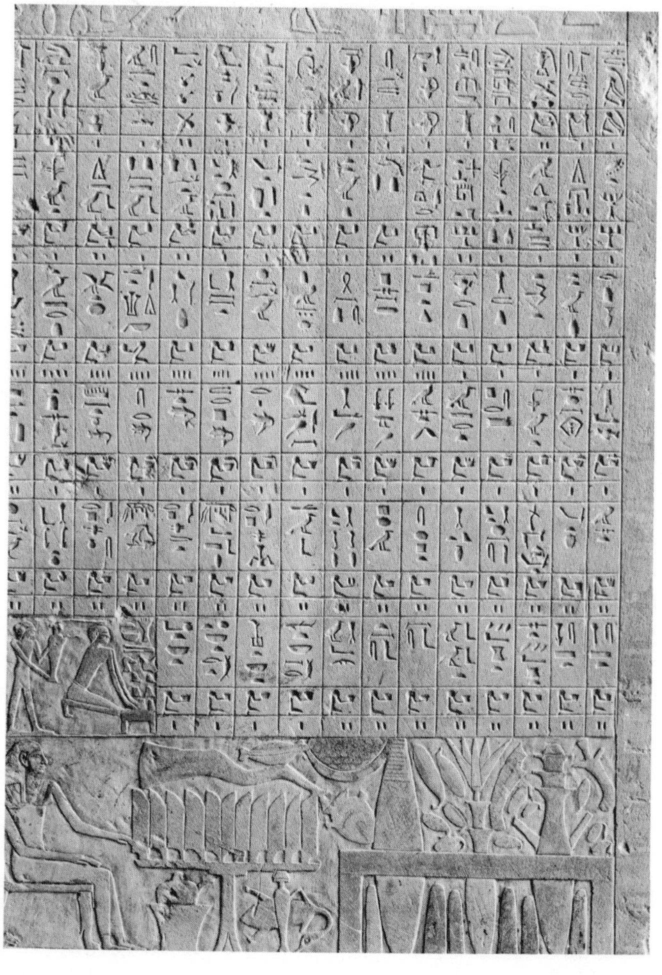

Hieroglyphic praise to Sesostris I c. 1971–1928 B.C. In this beautiful carved relief, some of the pictographs become detailed pictorial sculpture. Sesostris I's cartouche is seen at the bottom, left of center. *Hirmer Fotoarchiv, Munich.*

Sarcophagus of Aspalta, King of Ethiopia c. 593–568 B.C. This detail of the designs scribed into this granite sarcophagus demonstrates the flexibility of hieroglyphics. *Museum of Fine Arts, Boston, Harvard-MFA Expedition.*

Papyrus and writing

In Egypt a major forward step in visual communications was the development of papyrus, a paperlike substrate for writing manuscripts. In ancient times the *Cyperus papyrus* plant grew along the Nile in shallow marshes and pools, and the Egyptians made extensive use of this plant. A 5-meter (about 15-foot) root about as thick as a man's wrist lies along the bottom of the shallows. Smaller feeder roots are sunk into the mud, and 2-meter (about $6\frac{1}{2}$-foot) long stems grow up above the water. Papyrus flowers were used for garlands at the temples, and the root was used for fuel and utensils. From the stem, the Egyptians made sails, mats, cloth, rope, sandals, and most importantly, the paperlike substrate called papyrus.

In his *Natural History,* Roman historian Pliny the Elder (23–79 A.D.) tells how papyrus was made. After peeling away the rind, the inner pith of the stems was cut into longitudinal strips and laid side by side. A second layer of strips was then laid on top of the first layer at right angles to it. These two layers were joined by being soaked in the Nile River and then pressed or hammered until they were a single sheet. Apparently, the glutinous sap of the papyrus stem acted as an adhesive. After drying the sheets in the sun, an ivory or stone polisher was used to smooth the sheet. If flaws such as spots, stains, or spongy areas appeared, the sheet would be peeled apart and remade. Eight different grades were made for uses ranging from royal proclamations to daily accounting. The finished sheet had an upper surface of horizontal fibers called the *recto* and a bottom surface of vertical fibers called the *verso.* The tallest papyrus sheets measured 49 centimeters ($19\frac{1}{2}$ inches), and up to twenty sheets would be pasted together and rolled into a scroll with the recto side facing inward.

As in Sumer, knowledge was power, and the scribes gained significant authority in Egyptian society. Learning to read and write the complex language took many years, and the profession of scribe was highly respected and enjoyed many privileges, not the least of which was exemption from taxation.

The wooden palette used by the scribe was a trademark, for to carry this slab of wood identified one as being able to read and write. The example shown is 32.5 centimeters ($12\frac{3}{4}$ inches) long. One end has at least two depressions to hold black, red, and sometimes other ink cakes. With a gum solution as a binder, carbon was used to make black ink and ground red ocher to make red ink. These were dried into cakes not unlike contemporary watercolors, then a wet brush would be rubbed onto the cake to return the ink to a liquid state for writing. A slot in the middle of the palette held the brushes which were made from rush stems. The stem's tip was cut on an angle and was chewed by the scribe to separate the fibers into a brush.

Holding the scroll with his left hand, the scribe would begin at the outer right-hand edge and write a column of hieroglyphs from top to bottom, writing column after column as shown in the detail of the *Book of the Dead* of Tuthmosis III. This hieroglyphic book handwriting evolved from the monumental form. The scribes simplified the inscriptional hieroglyphs to a quickly drawn gesture instead of a carefully constructed picture.

By 1500 B.C., a cursory *hieratic* (from the Greek for "priestly") script, a kind of penstroke simplification of the hieroglyphic book hand, was developed by the priests for religious writings. The earliest hieratic script was different from the hieroglyphs only in that the use of a rush pen instead of a pointed brush produced more abstract characters with a terse, angular quality. An even more abstract script called *demotic* (from the Greek word for "popular") came into secular use by the year 400 B.C. for commercial and legal writing. The hieroglyph for scribe was a pictorial image of the very early brush-holder, palette, and sack of ink. The characters accompanying the photograph of these artifacts show this evolution. Hieratic and demotic scripts supplemented rather than replaced hieroglyphs, which continued in use for religious and inscriptional purposes.

Detail from the *Book of the Dead* of Tuthmosis III, c. 1450 B.C. Written hieroglyphics were simplified, but they maintained their pictographic origin. *Museum of Fine Arts, Boston, gift of Horace L. Meyer.*

Egyptian scribe's palette with an inscription in hieratic script. *Museum of Fine Arts, Boston, gift of C. Granville Way Hay Collection.*

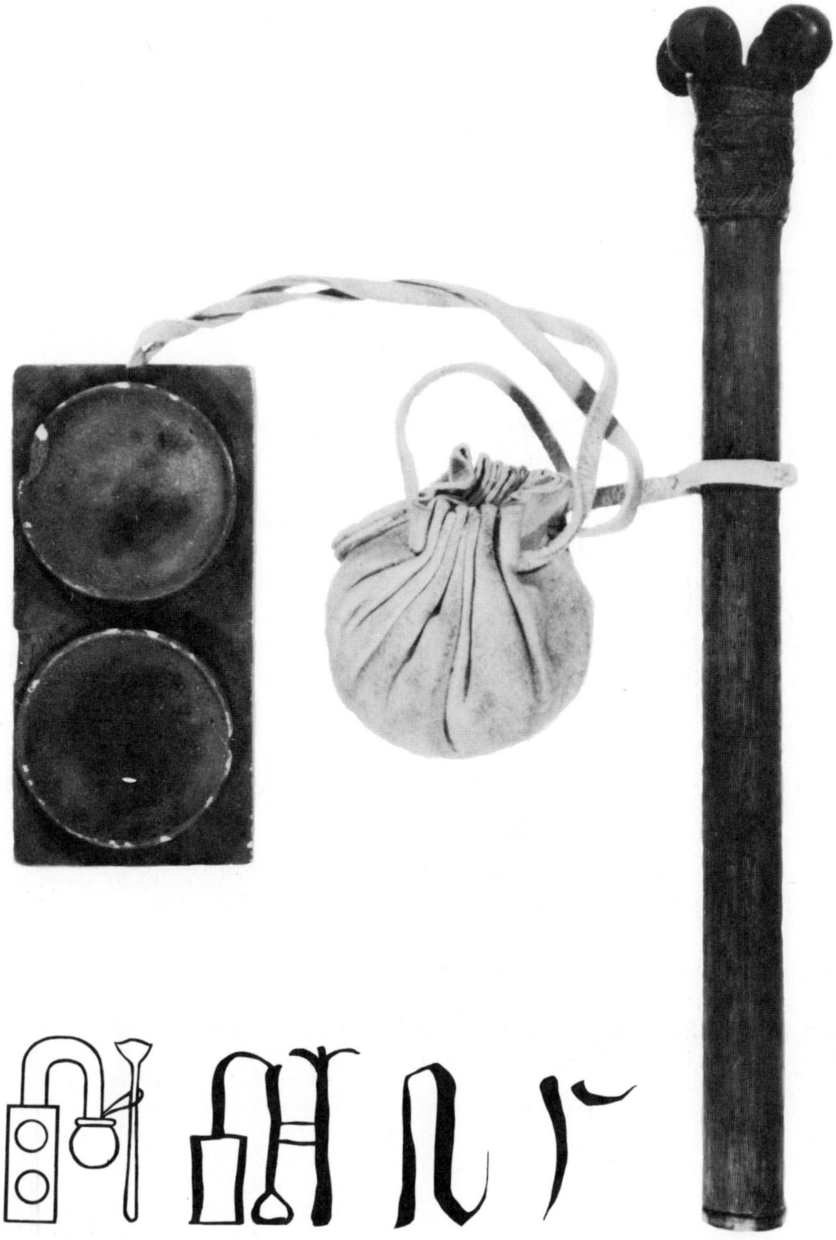

The hieroglyph for scribe depicted the Old Kingdom palette, the drawstring sack for dried ink cakes, and a reed brush holder. The changes in this glyph demonstrate the evolutionary process (from left to right): hieroglyphic, 2700 B.C.; hieroglyphic manuscript hand, c. 1500 B.C.; hieratic script, c. 1300 B.C.; and demotic script, c. 400 B.C. *Staatliche Museen zu Berlin, East Germany.*

The first illustrated manuscripts

The Egyptians were the first people to produce illustrated manuscripts in which words and pictures combine to communicate information. A preoccupation with death and a strong belief in the afterlife compelled the Egyptians to evolve a complex mythology about one's journey into the afterlife. Mythology was early man's way to deal with natural phenomena and other unknown aspects of life and the world. By inventive myth and legend, the inexplicable could be explained and faced. A final judgment would ultimately allow the deceased either to be admitted into the company of the gods or suffer eternal damnation. The prayer of every man was that he would be cleansed of sin and be found worthy at the final judgment. Scribes and artists were commissioned to prepare funerary papyri called *The Chapters of Coming Forth by Day.* A nineteenth-century scholar named them *The Book of the Dead,* and this name is generally used today.

The Book of the Dead was a logical evolution of the need for funerary texts. Beginning with the pyramid of Unas (c. 2345 B.C.), the walls and passages of the pyramids were covered with the *Pyramid Texts* of hieroglyphic writings including myths, hymns, and prayers relating to the godlike Pharaoh's life in the afterworld. This practice was followed by the *Coffin Texts.* All surfaces of the wooden coffin and/or stone sarcophagus were covered with writings carved into the surface, and often illustrated with pictures of possessions for the afterlife. Thus, high officials and noblemen could now enjoy the benefits of the funerary texts even though the cost of a pyramid was beyond their means.

The dawning of the New Kingdom around 1580 B.C. saw papyrus manuscripts come into use for funerary texts. Even citizens of fairly limited means could afford to have at least simple papyri to accompany them on the journey into the Underworld. From pyramid to coffin to papyri: this evolution toward cheaper and more widespread use of funerary texts paralleled the increasingly democratic and secular aspect of Egyptian life.

The Book of the Dead was written in a first-person narrative by the deceased and placed in the tomb to help triumph over the dangers of the Underworld. The artists who illustrated *The Book of the Dead* papyrus were called upon to foretell future events that would occur after the subject died and entered the afterlife. Magical spells could enable the deceased to turn into powerful creatures; passwords to enter various states of the Underworld were provided; and the protection of the gods was sought. Wonderful futures are illustrated in various *Books of the Dead*. One might dwell in the Fields of Peace, ascend into the heavens to live as a star, travel the sky with the sun god, Re, in his solar boat, or help Osiris rule the underworld.

The journey into the Underworld is depicted as a chronological narrative. The final judgment is shown in the *Papyrus of Ani* (c. 1420 B.C.). Ani, a royal scribe, temple accountant, and grainery manager from Thebes, and his wife Thuthu approach the scales where the jackal-headed god Anubis, keeper of the dead, prepares to weigh Ani's heart against a feather symbolizing truth to see if he is "true of voice" and free from sin. Thoth, the ibis-headed scribe of the gods and keeper of the magical arts, is poised with a scribe's palette to write the verdict. To the right, the monster Ammit, the devourer of the dead, stands poised for action should Ani fail to pass the moment of judgment. An imaginative visual symbol, Ammit has the head of a crocodile, the torso of a lion, and the hindquarters of a hippopotamus. A register across the top shows twelve of the forty-two gods who sit in judgment. Addressing each god in turn, a "negative confession" denies a host of sins: "I have not done evil; I have not stolen; I have not killed people; I have not stolen food. . . ." After making this negative confession, Ani spoke to his heart: "Set now thyself to bear witness against me. Speak not against me in the presence of the judges, cast not your weight against me before the Lord of the Scales." Upon being found virtuous, Ani is presented to Osiris, Lord of the Underworld, then his soul spends the night after death traveling into the Underworld. On the following morning, he arrives at his "coming forth by day."

Vignette from the Papyrus of Nekht, c. 1250 B.C. Standing between their house and ornamental pool, this military scribe and his wife worship Osiris and the goddess Maat. Note how the pool is shown as a flat projection, and note the "windcatchers" on the roof of the house. *The British Museum, London, Department of Egyptian Antiquities.*

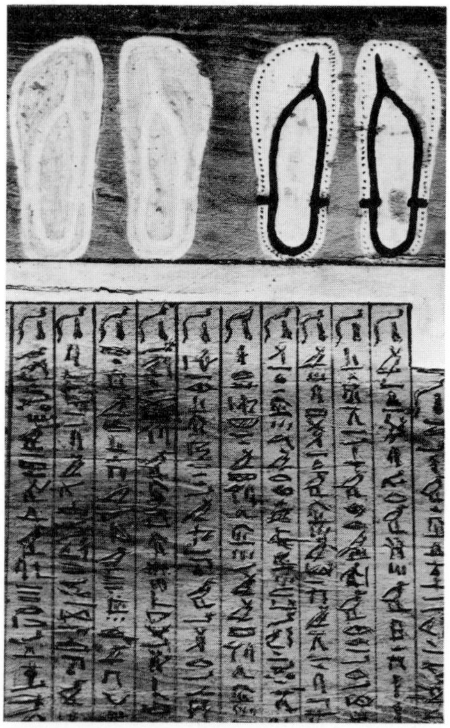

Detail, the coffin of Diehurty-Matcht's wife, Twelfth Dynasty. Portions of the Coffin Text are shown on the inside of this wooden coffin. The registers of pictorial images, including these two pairs of sandals, could become real food, objects, and clothing in the afterlife. *Museum of Fine Arts, Boston, Harvard-MFA Expedition.*

Detail from the Papyrus of Hunefer, c. 1370 B.C. Hunefer and his wife are worshiping the Gods of Amenta. The sun-god Re bears an *ankh* symbol on his knee, and Thoth holds the *udjat,* the magical protective "sound eye" of the god Horus. *British Museum, London, Department of Egyptian Antiquities.*

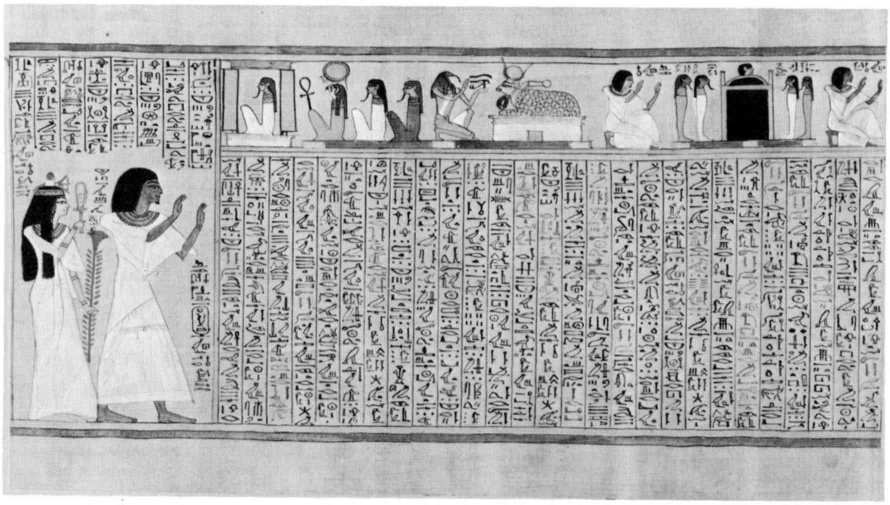

The Final Judgement from the Papyrus of Ani, c. 1420 B.C. The illustrator chose the suspenseful moment as Anubis adjusts the balance of the scales and everyone present awaits the fateful judgment. *British Museum, London, Department of Egyptian Antiquities.*

A consistent design format evolved for the illustrated Egyptian papyri. One or two horizontal bands, usually colored, ran across the top and bottom of the manuscript. Vertical columns of writing separated by ruled lines were written from right to left. Images were inserted adjacent to the text illustrated. Often, images stood on the lower horizontal band, and the columns of text hung down from the top horizontal band. Frequently, a horizontal friezelike register will run along the top of a sheet. Sometimes, a sheet was divided into rectangular zones to separate text and images. The functional integration of text and image was aesthetically pleasing, for the dense texture of the brush-drawn hieroglyphs contrasted handsomely with the illustration's open spaces and flat planes of color. In the earlier *Books of the Dead,* the scribe designed the manuscript. If it was to be illustrated, blank areas were left which the artist would fill in as best he could. The vignettes gradually became more important and dominated the design. The artist would draw these illustrations first. Then, the scribe would write the manuscript, trying to avoid awkward blank spaces and sometimes writing in the margins if the illustrator did not leave adequate room for the text. Excellent artists were retained to create the images, but the scribes who did this work were not scholars. Often, passages were omitted for purposes of layout or through poor workmanship. The manuscript illustrations were drawn in simplified contour lines using black or brown ink, then flat color was applied using white, black, brown, blue, green, and sometimes yellow pigments. Perhaps the extensive use of luminous blue and green together in the papyri is a response to the intense blue of the Nile and the rich green of the foliage along its banks, a cool streak of life winding through vast reaches of desert.

Wall paintings and papyri shared the same vocabulary of design conventions. These are shown clearly in the dry fresco wall painting of a fowling scene from the Tomb of Nakht at Thebes. Men had darker skin color than women, and important persons were shown in larger scale than less important persons. The human body was drawn as a two-dimensional schematic. The frontal body has arms, legs, and head in profile. The stylized eye reads simultaneously as both profile and frontal image. The concern for design regularity and geometry is seen in the repetition of papyrus plants, which are reduced to simplified symbols. Action is frozen. Even though the flatness is maintained, the Egyptian artists were capable of sensitive observation and recording of details, as shown in the birds flying up from the papyrus swamp.

One could commission a funerary papyrus, or purchase a stock copy and have one's name filled in the appropriate places. The buyer could select the number and choice of chapters, the number and quality of illustrations, and the length. Excepting the 57-meter (185-foot) long great Turin Papyrus, *The Book of the Dead* scrolls ranged from 4.6 meters (15 feet) to 27.7 meters (90 feet) long and

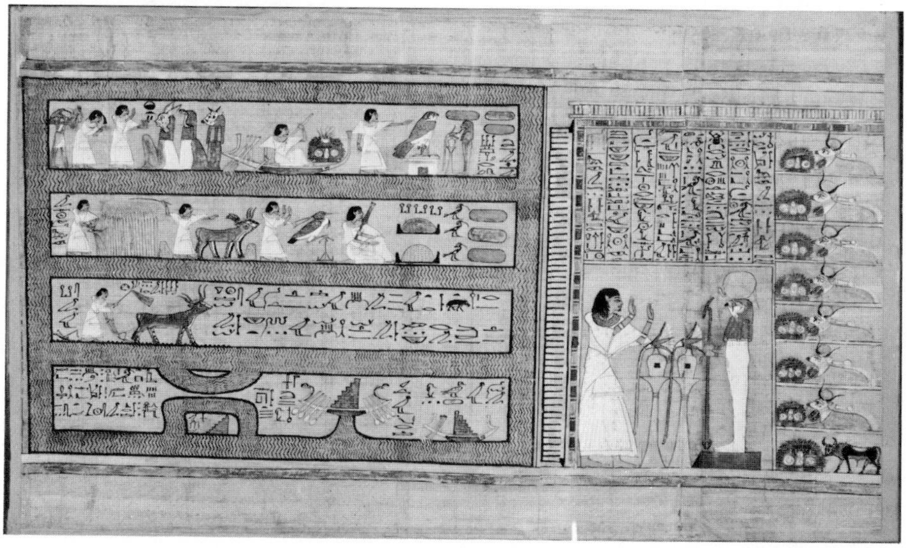

The *Fields of Peace* from the Papyrus of Ani, c. 1420 B.C. The idyllic afterworld is illustrated as a series of registers depicting Ani's activities in the afterlife. A blue, decorative pattern area represents a series of irrigation canals. *British Museum, London, Department of Egyptian Antiquities.*

were from 30 centimeters (about 12 inches) to 45 centimeters (about 18 inches) tall. Toward the final collapse of the Egyptian culture, *The Book of the Dead* consisted often merely of sheets of papyrus, some of which were only a few inches square.

Fowling in the Marshes, fresco painting from the Tomb of Nakht, c. 1450 B.C. Armed with throw-sticks, Egyptians ventured into the Nile delta area on light boats to hunt birds. *The British Museum, London, Department of Egyptian Antiquities.*

"heart-scarab" was placed over the heart of a mummy with its wrappings. Its engraved undersurface had a brief plea to the heart not to act as a hostile witness in the Hall of Justice of Osiris.

The majestic Egyptian culture survived for over three thousand years. Hieroglyphics, papyrus, and illustrated manuscripts are its visual-communications legacy. Along with the accomplishments of Mesopotamia, these innovations triggered the development of alphabet and graphic communications in Phoenicia and the Greco-Roman world.

Scarab of Ikhnaton and Nefertiti, c. 1370 B.C. This 6-centimeter (2.4-inch) scarab bears the cartouche of Ikhnaton on the side shown. The engraved hieroglyphs of the flat bottom were etched with a bronze needle. *Museum of Fine Arts, Boston, Helen and Alice Colburn Fund.*

Visual identification

The Egyptians used cylinder seals and proprietary marks on items such as pottery very early in their history. The seals certainly were inherited from the Sumerians, and the proprietary marks may also have been. A uniquely Egyptian contribution that expressed love of natural form and decoration was the scarab seal. From prehistoric times, the scarab beetle was venerated in ancient Egypt as being sacred or magical. In the Twelfth Dynasty, carved scarab emblems were commonly used as identification seals. These oval stones, usually of a glazed steatite, were sculpted likenesses of the scarab beetle. Because steatite was soft enough for carving but also held up well under the heat needed to apply a glaze, it became the stone of choice for the scarabs. The flat underside, engraved with a hieroglyphic inscription, was used as a seal. Sometimes, the scarab was mounted as a signet ring. Every Egyptian of any standing had a personal seal. Interestingly, very little evidence of scarabs actually being used for sealing has survived. Possibly the communicative function was secondary to the scarab's value as talisman, ornament, and symbol of resurrection. The scarab beetle was connected with the creator sun god, Kheper, and the scarab was sometimes depicted rolling the sun across the sky just as the living scarab or dung beetle was seen forming a ball of dung and rolling it across the sand to its burrow to be eaten over the following days. The ancient Egyptians mistakenly believed that the scarab beetle laid its eggs in this ball, and felt that the life cycle of the scarab represented the daily rebirth of the sun. A scarab called a

3

The Chinese Contribution

Civilization seemingly sprang from nothing along the banks of the Tigris and Euphrates Rivers in Mesopotamia and along the course of the Nile River in Egypt. The origins of the splendid civilization that developed in the vast ancient land of China are shrouded in similar mystery. Legend suggests that by the year 2000 B.C. a culture was evolving in virtual isolation from the western pockets of civilization. Among the many innovations of the ancient Chinese, some proved to change the course of human events. There is evidence that the Chinese invented the compass, which made exploration and seafaring possible; gunpowder, which fueled that warlike aspect of man's nature and changed the nature of war, was used by the Chinese for fireworks instead of weapons; and Chinese calligraphy, an ancient writing system, is used today by more people than any other visual language system. Paper, a magnificent and economical substrate for transmitting information, and printing, the duplication of words and images, made possible the wide communication of thought and deed. The adoption of these Chinese inventions became the means that allowed Europeans to set forth and conquer the world. The compass directed the early explorers across the seas and around the globe. Firearms enabled them to subjugate the native populations of Africa, Asia, and the Americas. Printing on paper became the method for spreading European language, culture, religion, and law throughout the world.

Chinese calligraphy

Chinese calligraphy is a form of purely visual art. It is not an alphabetical language, and every symbol is composed of a number of differently shaped lines within an imaginary square. Legend holds that calligraphy was invented about 1800 B.C. by Ts-ang Chieh, who was inspired to invent writing by contemplating the clawmarks of birds and footprints of animals. Ts-ang Chieh proceeded to develop elementary pictographs of things in nature. Each image was highly stylized and composed of a minimum number of lines, but they are easily deciphered. The Chinese sacrificed the realism found in hieroglyphs for more abstract designs. Aesthetic considerations seem to have interested the Chinese from the early beginnings of their writing. Simple nouns were developed first, and the language slowly matured and became enriched as characters were invented to express feelings, actions, colors, sizes, and types. Chinese calligraphic characters are *logograms,* graphic characters or signs that represent an entire word. (The sign *$,* for instance, is a logogram to represent the word "dollar.") Ideographs and phonetic loans—borrowing the sign of a similar-sounding word—were developed, but calligraphy was never broken down into syllable signs, like cuneiform, or alphabetic signs for elementary sounds. Therefore, there is no direct relationship between the spoken and written Chinese language. Both are independent systems for conveying thought; a sound from the mouth to the ear, and a sign from the hand to the eye. Learning the total vocabulary of forty-four thousand characters was the sign of great wisdom and scholarship.

The earliest known Chinese calligraphy seems to be closely bound to the art of divination, which is an effort to foretell future events through communication with the gods or long-dead ancestors. This ancient writing—as in hieroglyphics and cuneiform—was pictographic. Dating from the eighteenth century before Christ, Chinese pictographs are found incised on tortoise shells and large animals' flat shoulder bones, called "oracle bones," which contain communications between the living and the dead. When one wished to consult an exalted ancestor or a god, the royal diviner was asked to inscribe the message on a polished animal bone. The diviner pushed a red-hot metal bar into a hole in the inscribed bone, and the heat produced an intricate web of cracks. The diviner could read these cracks, which were believed to be a message from the dead. This earliest pictographic writing has been called *bone-and-shell* script. It was followed by inscriptions on bronze vessels, called *bronze script.* Answers received from gods and ancestors during the divination were carved on permanent materials to preserve them. Ceremonial containers, used to hold food offerings for ancestor worship, had inscriptions carved all over the inside. Bronze script had more studied and regular forms than bone-and-shell script.

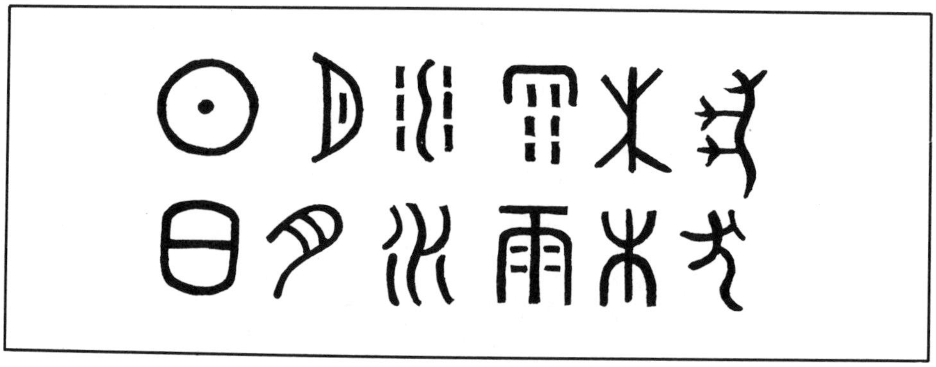

The top row of pictographs are bone-and-shell script attributed to the legendary Ts'ang Chieh. The lower row shows the same words from Li Ssu's unified bronze script, which was called *small-seal style.* From left to right: sun, moon, water, rain, wood, and dog.

Artists in different places developed different writing styles until Chinese calligraphy was unified under the powerful Emperor Shih Huang Ti (259–210 B.C.). During his reign, Confucian scholars were buried alive and their books burned. Thousands of lives were sacrificed building the Great Wall of China to protect the emperor and his empire. But he also unified the Chinese people into one nation and unified their writing by royal decree. Prime minister Li Ssu (c. 280–208 B.C.) was charged with designing the new writing style. This third phase in the design evolution of Chinese calligraphy is called the *small-seal style.* All the lines are drawn in thicker, more even strokes. More curves and circles are used in this graceful flowing style, which is much more abstract than the earlier two styles. Each character is neatly balanced and fills its imaginary square primly.

The final step in the evolution of Chinese calligraphy is called *k'ai-shu* or *regular style* and has been in continuous use for nearly two thousand years. In regular style, every line, dot, and nuance of the brush can be controlled by the sensitivity and skill of the calligrapher. An infinite range of design possibilities exists within every word. Structure, composition, shape, stroke thickness, and the relationship of strokes to each other and to the white spaces surrounding them are design factors determined by the writer. Regular-style calligraphy has an abstract beauty that rivals humanity's highest attainments in art and design. Indeed, it is considered to be the highest art form in China, more important, even, than painting. Oriental painting and calligraphy have close bonds. Both are executed with ink on paper or silk using gestured strokes of the brush.

The evolution of Chinese calligraphy can be traced from its pictographic origins through one of the early characters; for example, the prehistoric character for the three-legged pot called a *li* which is now the word for "tripod." The *li* was an innovative product design, for the black discolorations on some surviving examples indicate that it stood in the fire to heat its contents rapidly. In the oracle-bone script, it was an easily recognized pictograph. In the 1000 B.C. bronze script, this character had evolved into a simpler form. The k'ai-shu or regular-style script character echoes the three-part bottom and flat top of the earlier forms.

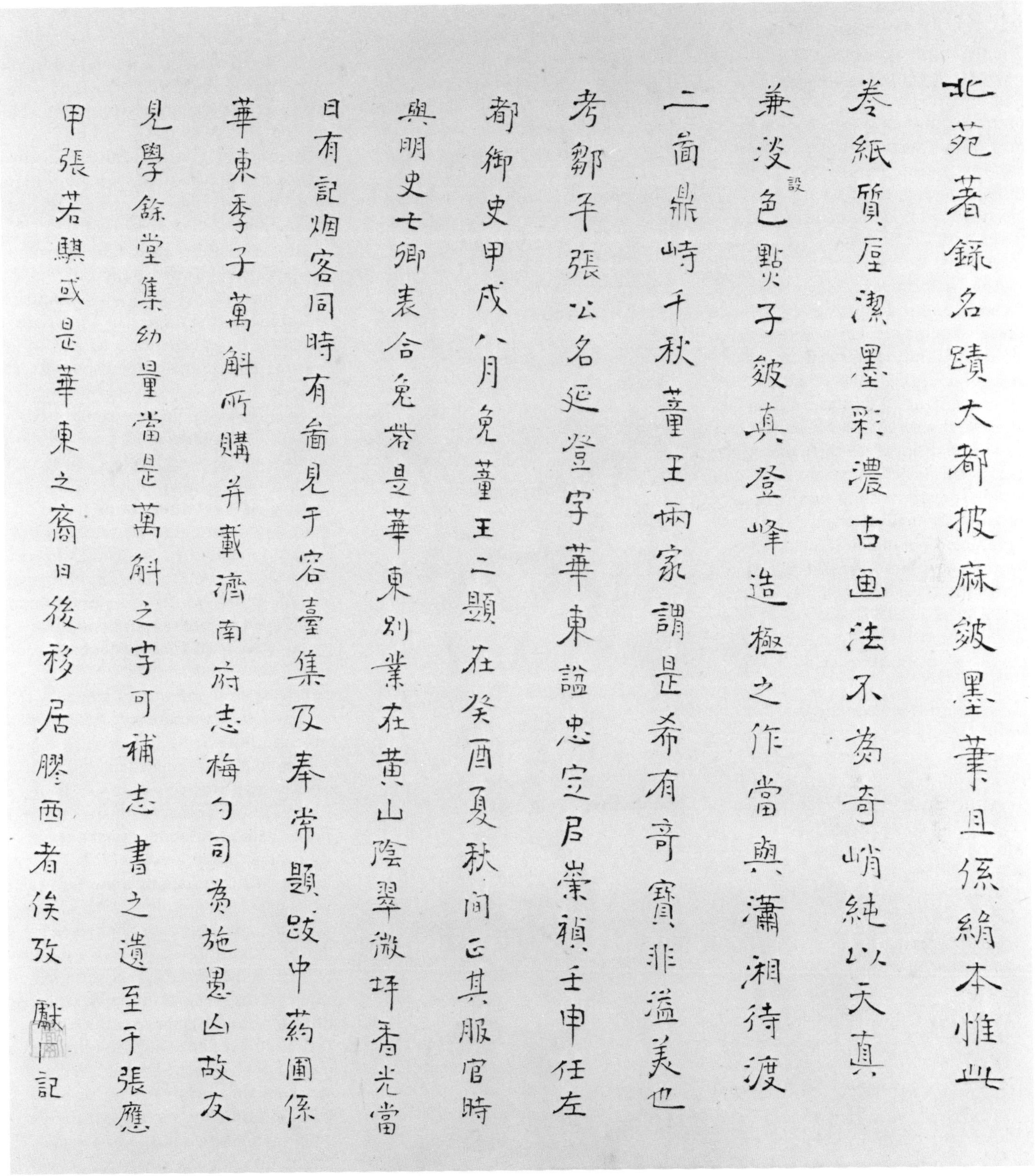
北苑著錄名蹟大都披麻皴墨筆且係絹本惟此
卷紙質匡潔墨彩濃古畫法不為奇峭純以天真
兼設色點子皴真登峰造極之作當與瀟湘待渡
二圖鼎峙千秋董王兩家謂是希有奇寶非溢美也
考鄒平張公名延登字華東謚忠定君崇禎壬申任左
都御史甲戌八月免董王二題在癸酉夏秋間正其服官時
與明史七卿表合免歸是華東別業在黃山陰翠微坪香光當
日有記烟客同時有圖見于容臺集及奉常題跋中葯圃係
華東季子萬斛所購并載濟南府志梅勺司為施愚山故友
見學餘堂集紉量當是萬斛之字可補志書之遺至于張應
甲張若騏或是華東之裔日後移居膠西者俟攷 獻記

As this Sung Dynasty example shows, *k'ai-shu* or regular style calligraphy allows the writer to use the full gestural potential of the brush. *Museum of Fine Arts, Boston.*

The painting of bamboo from the *Album of Eight Leaves* by Li Fang-Yin (1695–1754) shows how the vividly descriptive brushstrokes with a bamboo brush join calligraphy and painting, poem and illustration, into a unified communication. Nature is the inspiration for both, and every stroke and dot is given the energy of a living thing. Children begin their early training by drawing bamboo leaves and stems with the brush to learn the basic strokes.

Spiritual states and deep feelings can be expressed in calligraphy. Thick, languid strokes become mournful, and poems written in celebration of spring have a light exuberance. Once a master calligrapher was asked why he dug his ink-stained fingers so deeply into the hairs of his brush. He replied that only then could he feel the *tao* (cosmic spirit that operates throughout the universe in animate and inanimate things) flow from his arm, into the brush, and onto the paper.

Li (three-legged pottery vessel), late neolithic period. The evolution of the calligraphic character *Li* stemmed from this pot: oracle bone pictograph, bronze script, 1000 B.C., and *k'ai-shu* or regular style, 200 B.C. *Photograph: The Asia Society, New York.*

Calligraphy was said to have bones (authority and size), meat (the proportion of the characters), blood (the texture of the fluid ink), and muscle (spirit and vital force). The exuberance of master calligrapher Chu Yun-Ming's *Eight Immortals of the Wine Cup* shows just how dynamic and inventive calligraphy could be with broad strokes thrusting down the page in contrast to lively, delicate strokes of smaller characters.

The invention of paper

Dynastic records attribute the invention of paper to the eunuch and high governmental official Ts'ai Lun, who reported his invention to Emperor Ho in 105 A.D. Whether Ts'ai Lun invented paper, perfected an earlier invention, or patronized its invention is not known. He was, however, deified as the god of the papermakers.

In earlier times the Chinese wrote on bamboo slats or wooden strips using a bamboo pen with a dense and durable ink, the origins of which are obscure. Lampblack or soot was deposited on a dome-shaped cover over a vessel of oil with several burning wicks. The lampblack was collected, mixed thoroughly with a gum solution using a mortar and pestle, then molded into sticks or cubes. For writing, it is returned to the liquid state by rubbing it in water on an inking stone. The strips of wood were used for short messages; 23-centimeter (about 9-inch) pieces of bamboo tied together with leather strips or silk string were used for longer communications. Although these substrates were abundant and easy to prepare, they were heavy. After the invention of woven silk cloth, it too was used as a writing surface. However, it was very costly.

Ts'ai Lun's process for making paper continued almost unchanged until papermaking was mechanized in nineteenth-century England. Natural fibers, including mulberry bark, hemp fishnets, and rags were soaked in a vat of water and beaten into a pulp with pounding mortars. A vatman dipped a framelike mold with a screen bottom into the pulp solution, taking just enough of the solution onto the mold for the sheet of paper. With skill and split-second judgment, the vatman raised the mold from the vat while oscillating and shaking it to cross and mesh the fibers as the water drained through the bottom of the mold. Then the paper was counched, or pressed onto a woolen cloth to which it adhered while it dried. The mold was free for immediate reuse. The counched sheets were stacked, pressed, and then hung to dry. The first major improvement in the process was the use of starch sizing or gelatin to stiffen and strengthen the paper and increase its ability to absorb the ink.

In its early decades some ancient Chinese often considered paper to be a cheap substitute for silk or bamboo, but as time went on its light weight, economical manufacture, and versatility overcame all reservations. The coarse, long-fibered quality of this early paper caused no problems because the hair brush, invented many centuries earlier, was the primary writing instrument. Scrolls for writing were made by gluing together sheets of paper, sometimes delicately stained slate blue, lemon yellow, or a pale, warm yellow. These were rolled onto dowels of sandalwood or ivory, which were sometimes tipped with jade or amber. In addition to writing, the Chinese used their new material as wrapping paper, wailpaper, toilet paper, and napkins.

Li Fang-Yin, from the *Album of Eight Leaves,* number six, 1744. The design of the total space, with the bamboo bending out into the open space in contrast to the erect column of writing, is exquisite. *Museum of Fine Arts, Boston, Keith McLeod Fund.*

Chu-Yun-Ming, handscroll with poem, *Eight Immortals of the Wine Cup,* eighth century A.D. The imaginative powers for inventive design were unleashed in the writing of this poem. *Museum of Fine Arts, Boston, Helen S. Coolidge Fund.*

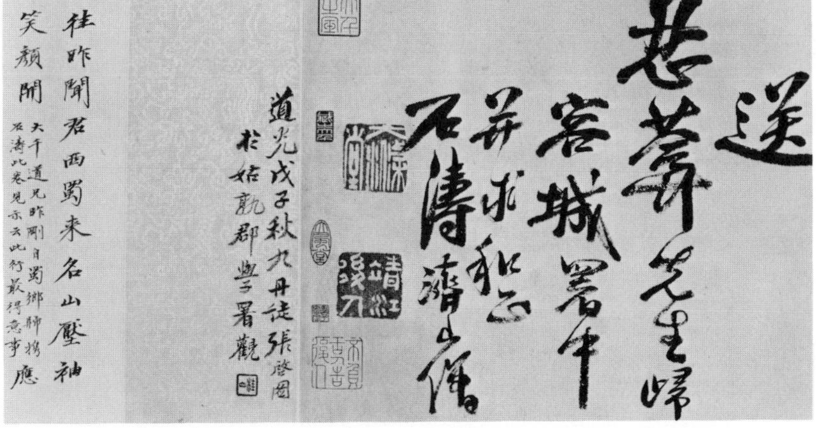

Tao Chi (1630–c. 1707 A.D.), *Mountain and River Landscape,* detail of scroll. The visual design qualities of calligraphy—from delicate and lacy to thunderous and bold—are contrasted in this scroll. *Museum of Fine Arts, Boston, Keith McLeod Fund.*

The discovery of printing

Printing, the second most important invention in human history after writing, was invented by the Chinese. This was *relief printing:* the spaces around an image on a flat surface are cut away; the remaining raised surface is inked; and a sheet of paper is placed over the surface and rubbed to transfer the inked image to it. Two hypotheses have been advanced about the invention of printing. One theory is that the use of engraved seals to make identification imprints evolved into printing. As early as the third century B.C., seals or stamps were used to make impressions in soft clay.

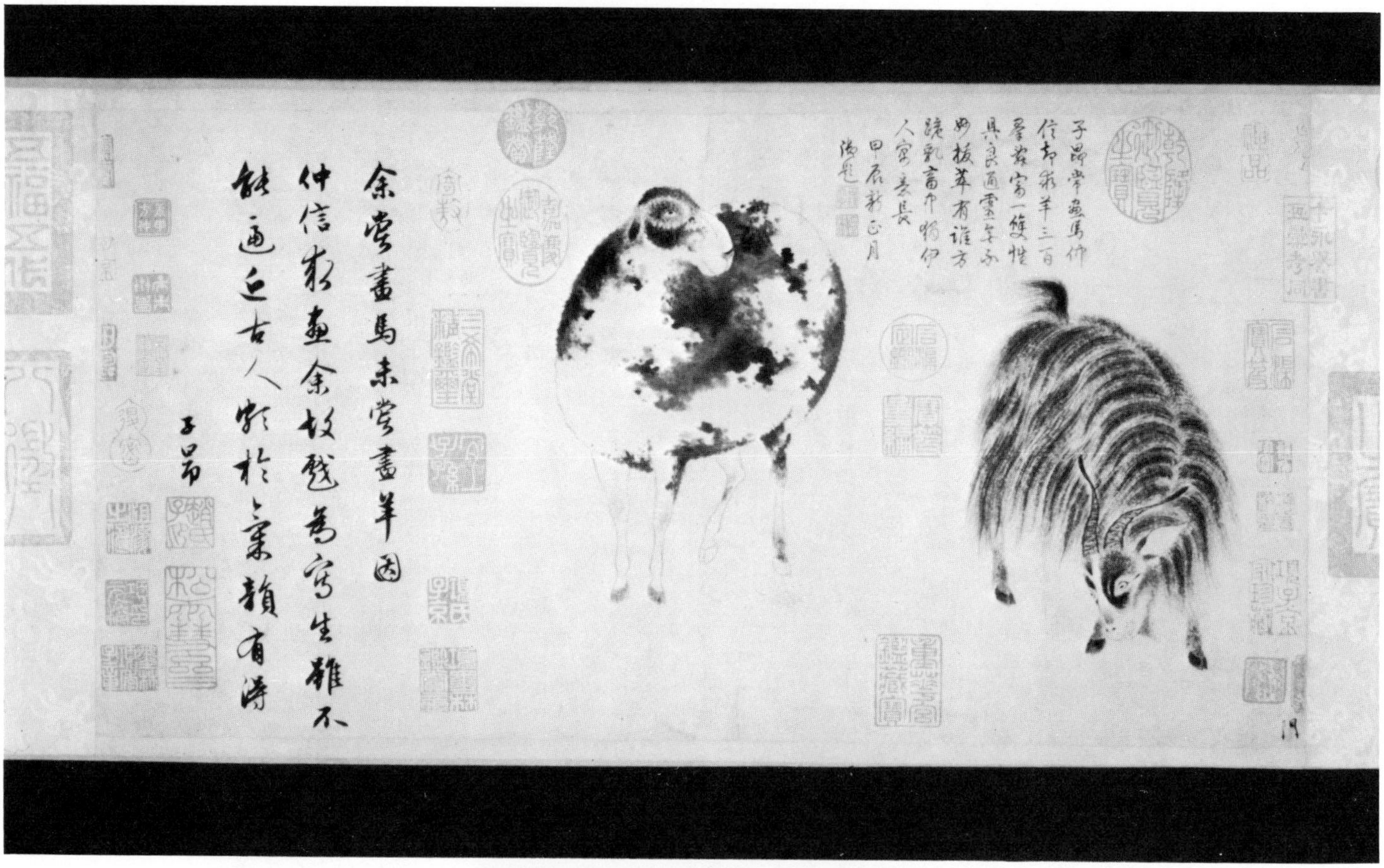

Yuan Chao Meng-fu, painting of a goat and a sheep, fourteenth century A.D. Note the two kinds of chops imprinted on this painting: white characters reversed from a solid ground, and solid characters surrounded by a white ground. *Freer Gallery of Art, Washington, D.C.*

Often, bamboo or wood strips bearing writing were wrapped in silk, which was then sealed with clay that bore an impression.

During the Han dynasty (third century A.D.), seals called chops were made by carving calligraphic characters into a flat surface of jade, silver, gold, or ivory. The flat surface was inked by pressing it into a paste-like red ink made from cinnabar, then the chop was pressed onto a substrate to form an impression similar in method to present-day rubber stamps. The impression was a red shape with white characters. Around 500 A.D., chops came into use on which the artisan had cut away the negative area surrounding the characters, so that the characters could be printed in red surrounded by white paper. The fundamental technique for block printing was now available.

Chinese chop, c. 1500 A.D. As this example, carved in yellow field stone shows, the chop is beautiful at both ends. The identification stamp was inscribed into the bottom of a small decorative sculpture. *Museum of Fine Arts, Boston.*

The second theory about the origins of printing focuses on the early Chinese practice of making inked rubbings from inscriptions carved in stone. Beginning in 165 A.D., Confucian classics were carved into stone to insure an accurate, permanent record. The disadvantages of these stone "books" were their weight and the space required. One historical work required thirteen acres for storage of the tablets spaced in the environment like rows of tombstones. Soon, copies of these inscriptions were pulled by making ink rubbings. A damp sheet of thin paper was laid on the stone. Using a stiff brush, the paper was pressed into the depressions of the inscription. Then, an inked cloth pad was lightly rubbed over the surface to produce an ink image from the incised inscription. Although the ink is applied to the top of the paper rather than to the relief image, the process is related to relief printing.

As early as the second century A.D., rubbings were also made from stone relief sculptures carved as offering shrines and tombs. In a sense, these reliefs were closer to painting than to sculpture for the figures crowding the complex designs are handled as flat silhouettes with linear detail and little effort to create spatial depth. In retrospect, these votive and tomb carvings resemble neither sculp-

Buddhist dedicatory stela, c. 562 A.D. This votive limestone tablet illustrates the early Chinese practice of rendering inscriptions with time-defying permanence and accuracy by carving them on stone. *Museum of Fine Arts, Boston, Otis Norcross Fund.*

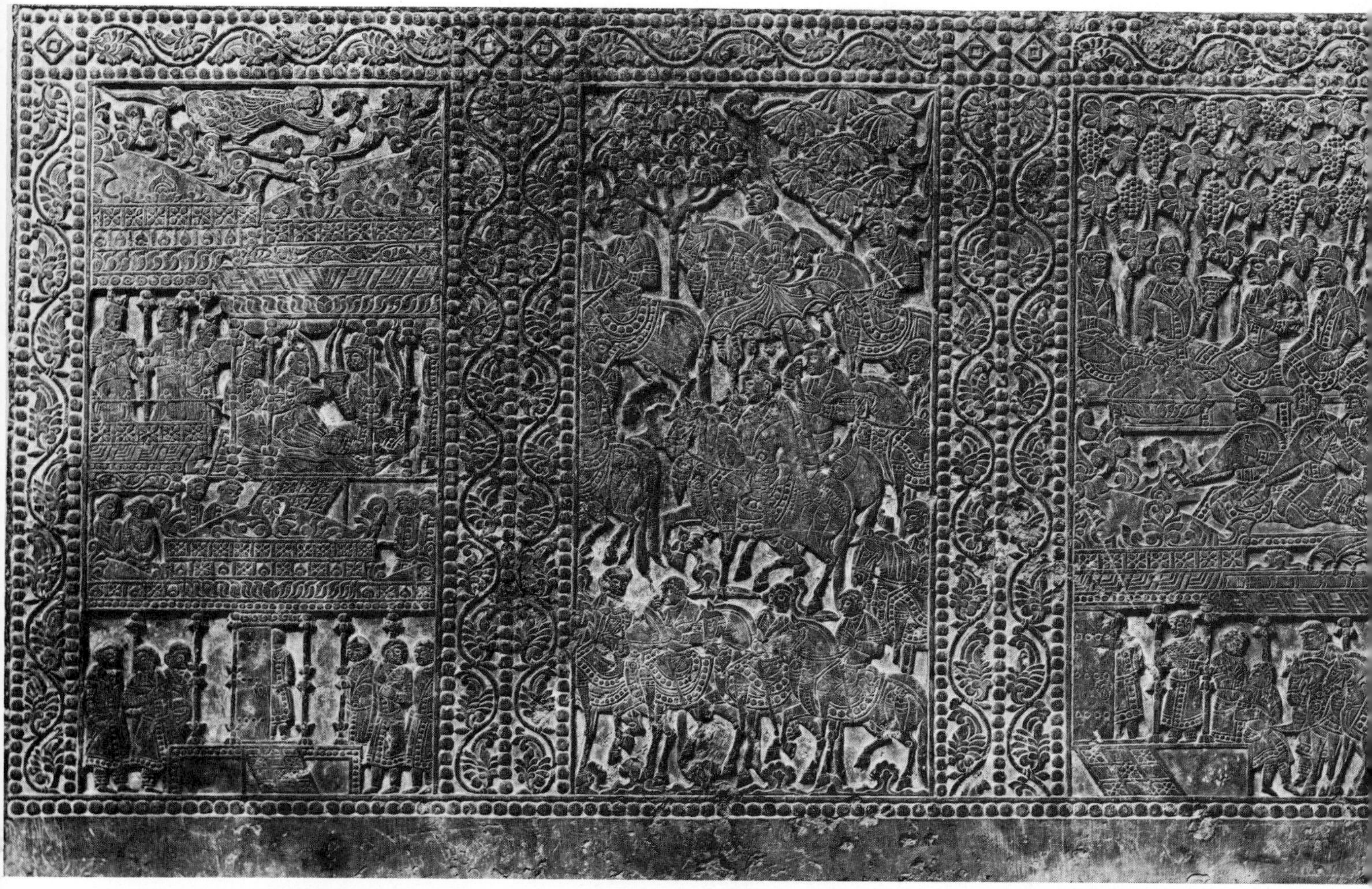

ture nor painting as much as they do a relief woodblock printing plate!

Whether relief printing evolved from chops, rubbings from stone inscriptions, or a synthesis of both techniques is not known. Just who invented relief printing and when or where it began remain a mystery. The route is marked by undated relics: printed fabrics, stencil pictures, and thousands of stamped impressions of the Buddha figure. By the time the earliest existing datable relief printing was produced, around 770 A.D., the technique had been well developed. Using a brush and ink, the material to be printed is prepared on a sheet of thin paper. Calligraphy is written, and images are drawn. The blockcutter applies this thin page to the smooth wooden block, with the image side down, after wetting the surface with a paste or sizing. When the paste or sizing is thoroughly dry, the paper is carefully rubbed off. A faint inked imprint of the image, which is now reversed, remains on the surface of the block.

Working with amazing speed and accuracy, the blockcutter carves away the surface around the inked image, leaving it in high relief. The printer inks the raised surface, applies a sheet of paper over it, then rubs the back of the paper with a rubber or stiff brush to transfer the ink to the page, which is then lifted from the block. So efficient is this method that a skilled printer can pull over two hundred impressions per hour.

During the eighth century, Chinese culture and the Buddhist religion were exported to Japan, and the earliest surviving datable printing was produced there. Mindful of the terrible smallpox epidemic three decades earlier, the Japanese Empress Shōtoku decreed that one million copies of Buddhist *dhāranī* ("charms") be printed and placed inside one million miniature pagodas about 11.5 centimeters ($4\frac{1}{2}$ inches) tall. Buddha had advised his followers to write seventy-seven copies of a *dhāranī* and place them in a pagoda, or place each one in a small clay

Chinese relief tomb sculpture and rubbing, Tang Dynasty (c. 618–907 A.D.). Illustrative images from the life of the deceased are captured in stone and with ink on paper. *Museum of Fine Arts, Boston, gift of Denman Waldo Ross.*

pagoda. This would lengthen one's life and eventually lead to paradise. Empress Shōtoku's efforts failed, for she died about the time the charms were being distributed, rolled up in their little three-story wooden pagodas. But the sheer number produced, combined with their sacred value, enabled numerous copies to survive to this day.

The oldest surviving printed manuscript is the *Diamond Sūtra.* It consists of seven sheets of paper pasted together to form a scroll 16 feet (4.9 meters) long and 12 inches (30.5 centimeters) high. Six sheets of text convey Buddha's revelations to his elderly follower Subhuti; the seventh is a complex linear woodcut illustration of the Buddha and his disciples. Buddha decreed that whoso-

ever repeats this text shall be edified. Apparently one Wang Chieh responded to the Buddha's charge, for the final lines of text declare that he made the *Diamond Sūtra* for wide free distribution to honor his parents on the date equivalent to 11 May 868 A.D. The excellence of the printing indicates that the craft had advanced to a high level by the time it was produced.

During the early ninth century A.D., the Chinese government began to issue paper certificates of deposit to merchants who deposited metal currency with the state. When a critical provincial shortage of iron money developed shortly before the year 1000, paper money was designed, printed, and used in lieu of metal coins. The government took control of its production, and millions of notes per year were printed. Soon there was inflation and devaluation, followed by efforts to restore confidence: money was printed on perfumed paper of high silk content; some money was printed on colored paper; and the penalty for counterfeiting was death. China became the first society in which ordinary people had daily contact with printed images. In addition to paper money, religious block prints bearing religious images and texts received wide distribution.

During the tenth century, the Chinese prime minister Fêng Tao became deeply concerned when errors in the Confucian classics came to light, and he felt that new master texts should be made. Lacking the resources needed for extensive cutting of stone inscriptions, Fêng Tao turned to the rapidly developing block printing method for this monumental task. With the great scholars as editors and a famous calligrapher to oversee the

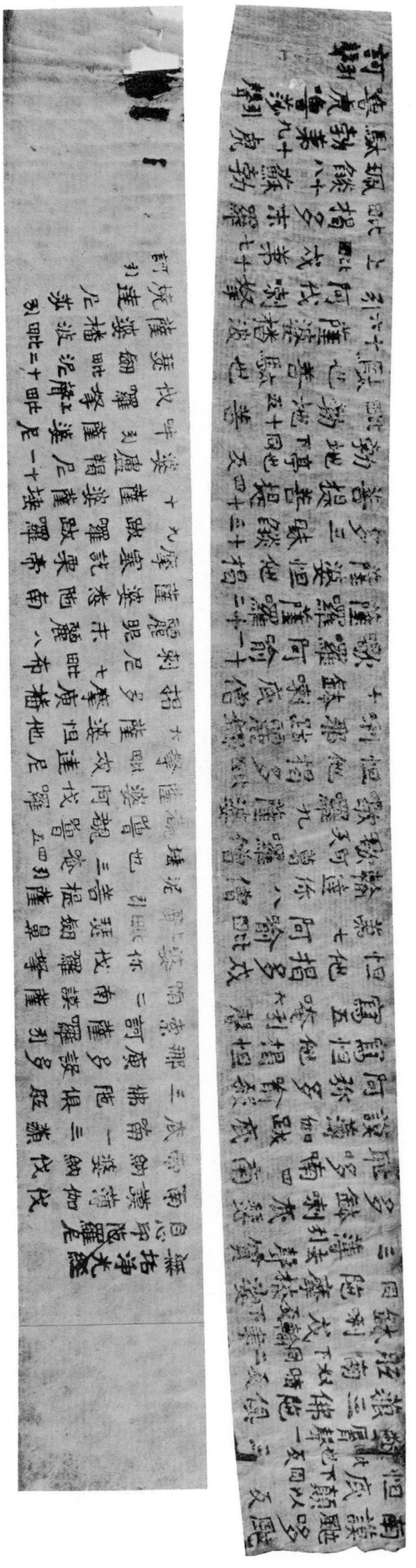

Dhāraṇī Buddhist charms, c. 770 A.D. Rolled up and inserted in little pagodas, these earliest surviving specimens of relief printing had the text printed in Chinese calligraphy on one side and in Sanskrit on the other. *Museum of Fine Arts, Boston, bequest of Miss E. S. Bates, Ross Collection.*

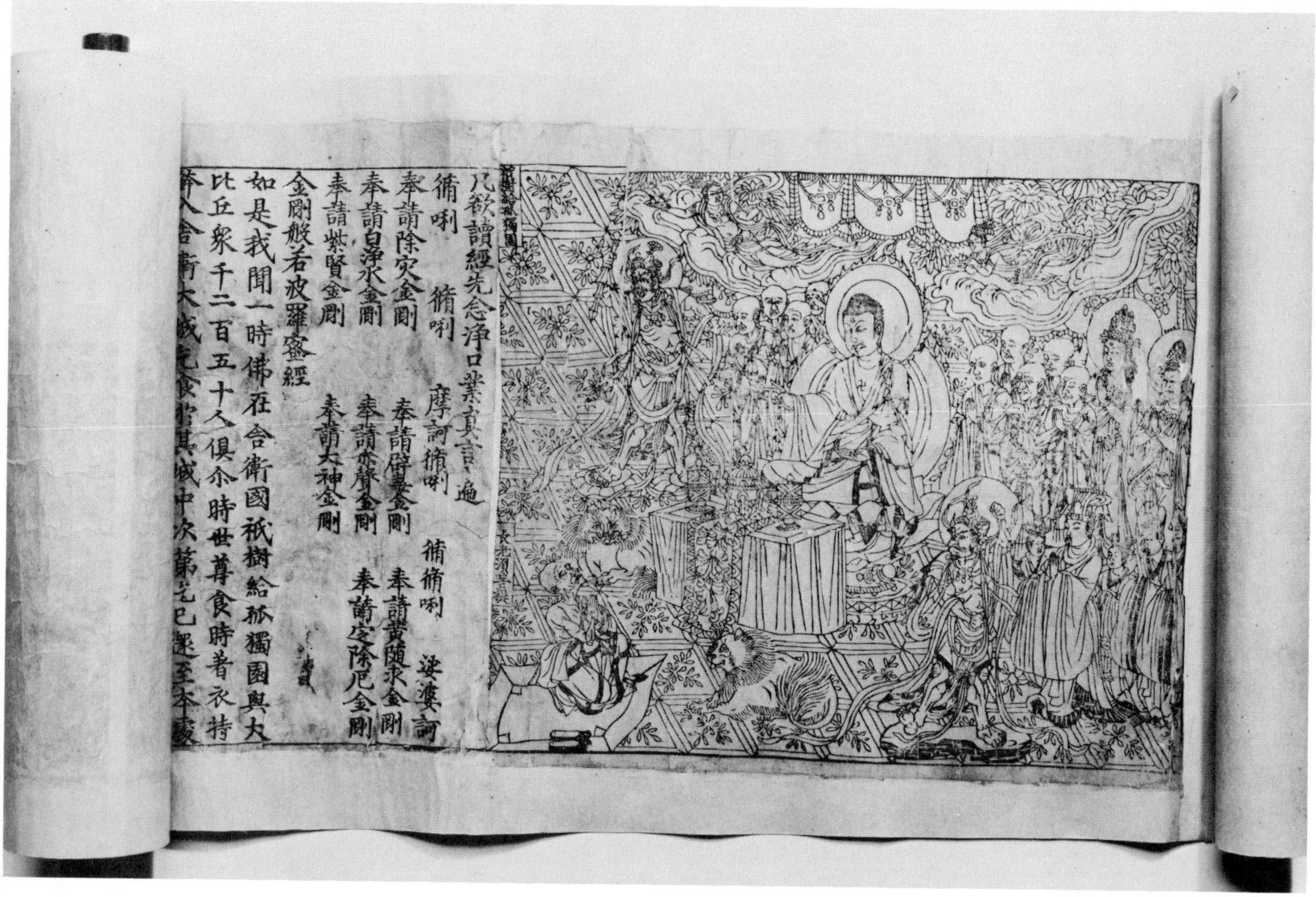

The *Diamond Sutra,* 868 A.D. Wang Chieh sought spiritual improvement by commissioning the duplication of the *Diamond Sutra* by printing; the wide spread of knowledge was almost incidental. *The British Library, London.*

writing of the master copies, the one hundred thirty volumes of the nine Confucian classics with their commentaries took twenty-one years from 932–953 A.D. Not spreading knowledge to the masses, but authenticating the texts was the goal. Fêng Tao took a fairly obscure craft and thrust it into the mainstream of Chinese civilization.

The scroll was replaced with paged formats in the ninth or tenth century. First, folded books that opened accordion-style were developed. These resembled scrolls that were folded, like a railroad timetable, instead of rolled. In the tenth or eleventh century, stitched books were developed. Two pages of text were printed from one block. Then, the sheet was folded down the middle with the unprinted side of the sheet facing inward and the two printed pages facing out. Sequences of these folded and printed sheets were gathered and sewn to make a codex-style book. The pages from the *Pen ts-ao* medical herbal are assembled in this fashion. Illustrations and calligraphy are used for headings. A graphic design used to separate the text into sections is shown in the center of the right-hand page.

Another early form of Chinese graphic design and printing was playing cards. These "sheet dice" were first printed on heavy paper cards about the time that paged books replaced manuscript scrolls.

A benchmark in block printing—reproducing beautiful calligraphy with perfection—was established in China by 1000 A.D. and has never been surpassed. The calligrapher was listed with the author and printer in the colophon. State printers were joined by private printers as histories and herbals, science and political science, poetry and prose were carved onto blocks of wood and printed. The quiet revolution that printing wrought upon Chinese intellectual life brought about a renaissance of learning and culture just as surely as Johann Gutenberg's invention of movable type in the west did over five hundred years later in Europe.

The invention of movable type

Instead of cutting each calligraphic character and every page of writing that was to be printed from a woodblock, Pi Sheng (1023–1063 A.D.) developed printing from movable and reusable type. These independent calligraphic characters were cut from thin clay, then heated over a straw fire to make hard earthenware type. A wax coating was placed onto an iron

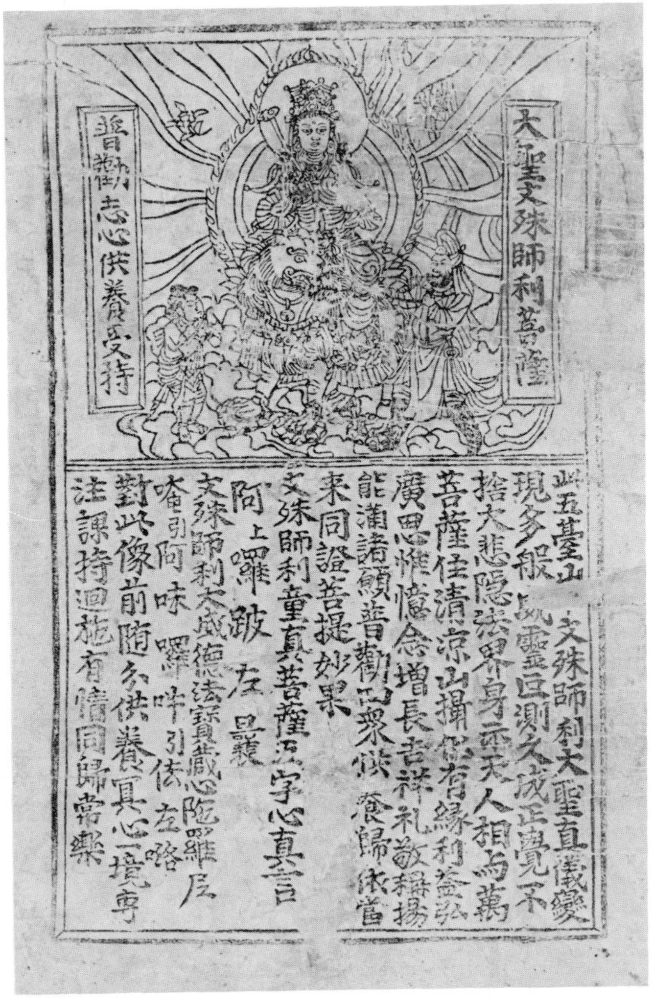

Chinese woodblock print, c. 950 A.D. This 31-by-20-centimeter (12½-by-7½-inch) printed sheet bearing an illustration and text was presented to pay for a vow at a Buddhist shrine. *Museum of Fine Arts, Boston, John Ware Willard Fund.*

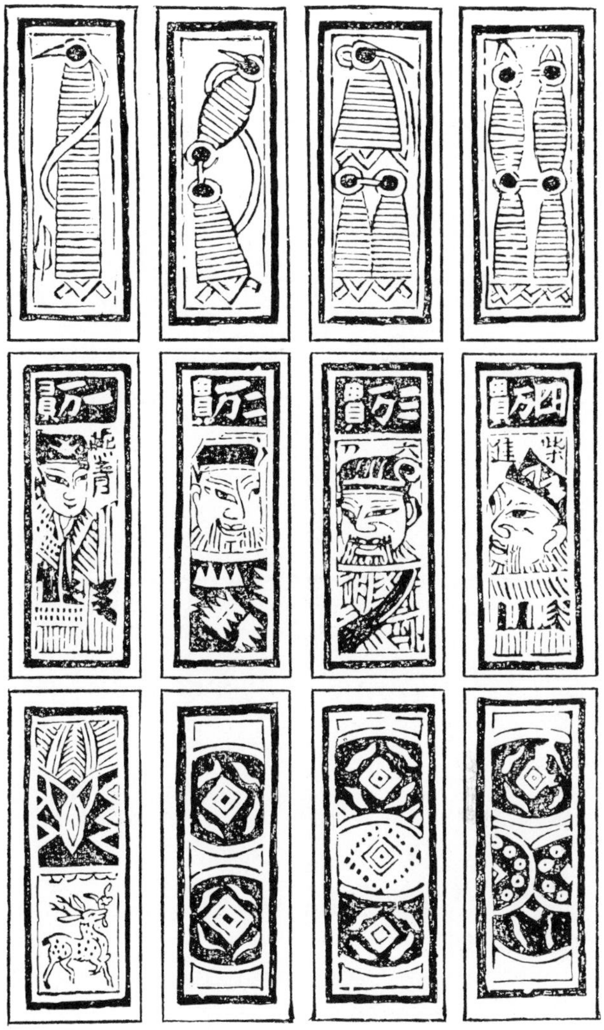

Chinese playing cards, undated. Many of the design conventions used here—numerical sequences of images signifying the suits and the depiction of royalty—survive in playing cards to this day.

form, and the type characters were set upon it. The full form was placed over the fire to soften the wax, then a flat board was pressed down over the type characters to make sure that all were equally raised above the surface of the form. Thus set, the type was printed exactly like woodblocks. After the printing was complete, the form was heated again to loosen the wax so that the characters could be filed in wooden cases. Since calligraphy is not alphabetical, the types were organized according to rhymes. The large number of characters in oriental languages made filing and retrieving the characters difficult. Later the Chinese cast letters in tin and cut them from wood, but movable type never replaced the handcut woodblock as a printing method in the Orient.

A notable effort to print from bronze movable type began in Korea under government sponsorship in the year 1403 A.D. Characters cut from beechwood were pressed into a trough filled with fine sand to make a negative impression. A cover with holes was placed over the impression and molten bronze was poured into it. After the bronze cooled, a type character was formed. These were, of course, less fragile than Pi Sheng's earthenware types.

It is curious that movable type should first be invented in cultures whose language systems numbered—not in the hundreds—but in the thousands of characters. With a total of over forty-four thousand characters, it is not surprising that movable type never came into widespread use. One interesting effort to simplify sorting and setting types was the invention of a revolving "lazy susan" table with a spinning tabletop 2.13 meters (7 feet) in diameter. The compositor could sit at this table and rotate it to bring the section with the needed character around to him.

The Chinese contribution to the evolution of visual communications was formidable. During the western world's thousand-year retreat into the medieval "dark ages," China's invention of paper and printing spread slowly westward, and arrived in Europe just as that continent was rising from its long night to awaken into a renaissance of learning and culture.

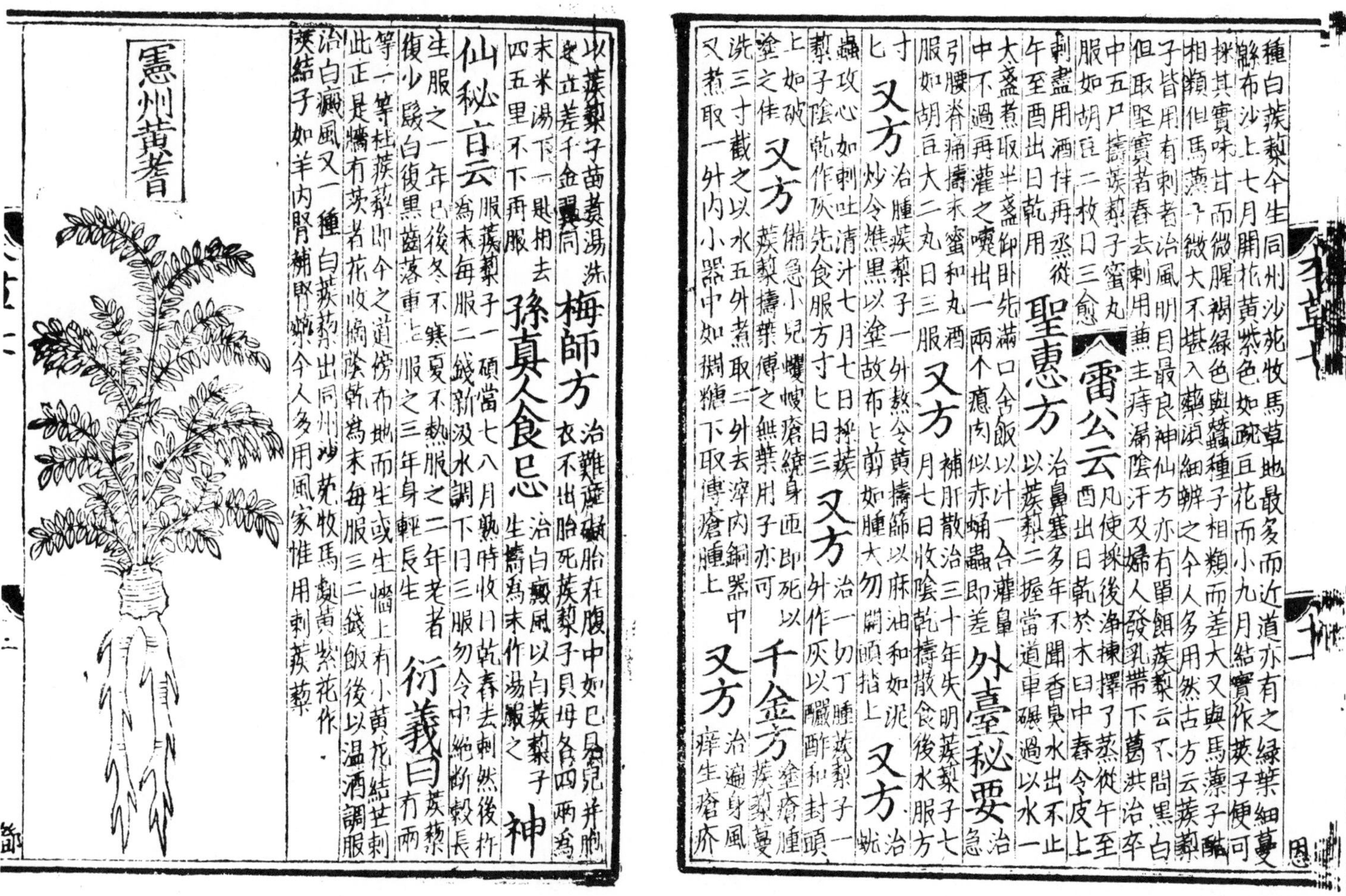

Pages from the *Pen ts'ao,* 1249 A.D. In this illustrated woodblock book on Chinese herbal medicine, a generous top margin and ruled lines bring order to the page. *Library of Congress, Washington, D.C.*

Chinese movable types, c. 1300 B.C. This group of carved wood types ranges in size from about 1.25 to 2.5 centimeters (½ to 1 inch) in height. *Metropolitan Museum of Art, gift of Paul Pelliot, 1924.*

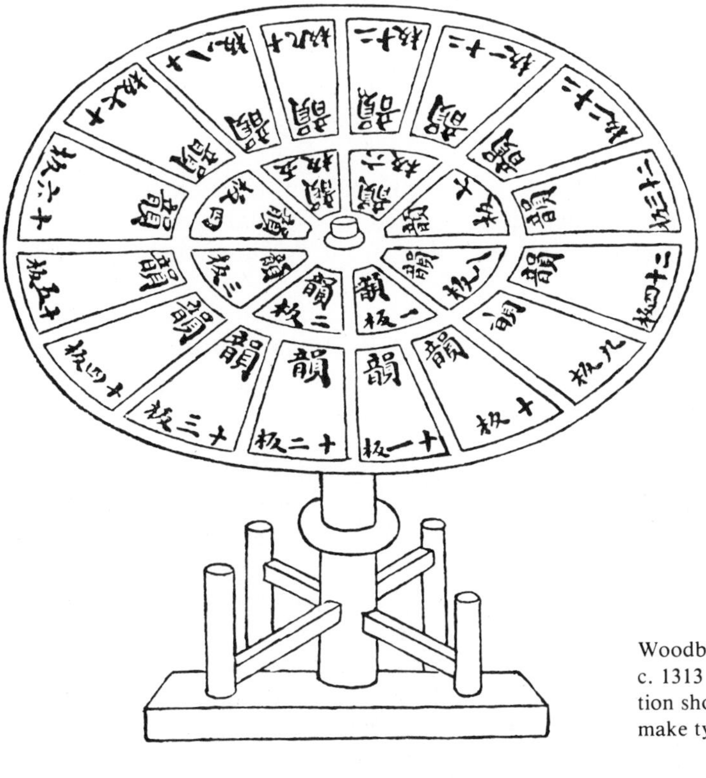

Woodblock image of a revolving typecase, c. 1313 A.D. This quaintly stylized illustration shows the revolving case designed to make typesetting more efficient.

4

The Alphabet

EARLY VISUAL LANGUAGE SYSTEMS including cuneiform, hieroglyphs, and Chinese calligraphy contained a built-in complexity. In each, pictographs had become rebus writing, ideographs, logograms, or even a syllabary. But these early writing systems remained unwieldy and required long, hard study to master. The number of individuals who gained literacy was small. Their access to knowledge enabled them to gain great power in the early cultures. The invention of the *alphabet* (from the first two letters of the Greek alphabet, *alpha* and *beta*) represents a major step forward in human communications. An alphabet is a series of simple visual symbols that stand for elementary sounds. They can be connected and combined to make a visual configuration for any and every sound, syllable, and word uttered by the human mouth. The hundreds of signs and symbols required by cuneiform and hieroglyphs were replaced by twenty or thirty easily learned elementary signs. Various theories have been advanced about the origins of the alphabet, but the inventor of this magnificent idea remains unknown. Theories naming cuneiform, hieroglyphs, prehistoric geometric signs, and early Cretan pictographs as the source of the alphabet have been advanced. Some scholars even wonder if the alphabet was invented by a brilliant genius, independent of the existing writing systems.

Cretan pictographs

The Minoan civilization that existed on the Mediterranean island of Crete ranks behind only Egypt and Mesopotamia in its early level of advancement in the ancient western world. Picture symbols were in use as early as 2800 B.C. Short pictographic inscriptions have been found that were written as early as 2000 B.C. About one hundred thirty-five surviving pictographs include figures, arms, and other parts of the body; animals; plants; and some geometric symbols. By 1700 B.C. these pictographs seem to have yielded to linear script writing, a precursor to the spoken Greek language.

One of the most extraordinary relics of the Minoan civilization is the Phaistos Disk, which was unearthed on Crete in 1908. Lacking precedent or parallel, the modest, flat clay disk has pictographic and seemingly alphabetic forms imprinted on both sides in spiral bands. Typelike stamps were used to carefully impress each character into the wet clay; thus the principle of movable type was used in a western culture as early as 2000 B.C. Just what the inscriptions say, who made them, and whether the stamps or types were used to make messages upon papyrus or other perishable substrates may never be known. The Phaistos disk remains one of the great mysteries in the history of graphic design and communications. Some scholars have speculated that it may have originated from some location other than Crete, but there is no evidence to support or reject this theory.

Phaistos Disk, c. 2000 B.C. This 16.5 centimeters (6½ inches) in diameter terra cotta disk bears two hundred forty-one signs, including a man in a plumed headdress, a hatchet, an eagle, a carpenter's square, an animal skin, and a vase. *Herakleion Museum, Crete.*

The Phoenician alphabet

The earliest known alphabetical writings come from the ruins of ancient Phoenicia, a culture that developed in what is now Lebanon and parts of Syria and Israel. Situated on the Mediterranean Sea between the Egyptian and Mesopotamian civilizations, the Phoenicians absorbed influences and ideas from both. During the second millennium B.C., the Phoenicians developed as a seafaring and merchant society with settlements throughout the Mediterranean world. The Phoenician city-states exported pine and cedar woods from Lebanon, fine linens woven in their city-states of Byblos and Tyre, metal and glass work, wine, salt, and dried fish. In exchange, they received precious metals and gems, papyrus, ostrich eggs, ivory, silk, spices, and horses. Their sailing ships were the fastest and best engineered in the ancient world. They invented a beautiful deep crimson dye which was so costly that wearing purple robes became a mark of royalty. This dye was made from a secretion extracted from a Mediterranean mollusk called *Purpura* in Latin, from which the English word "purple" derives. But the Phoenician contributions of commerce, ships, and dye fade in comparison to their major contribution to human civilization, the phonetic alphabet.

Geography has wielded great influence upon the affairs of man. Even the development of the alphabet may be an act of geography, for the Phoenician city-states where the alphabet apparently developed had become the hub of the ancient world. Their location on the western shores of the Mediterranean Sea enabled Phoenicia to become the crossroads of international trade. During the second half of the second millennium B.C., the Phoenicians received cuneiform from Mesopotamia in the west, and Egyptian hieroglyphics and scripts from the south. It is probable that the Phoenicians, sailors that they were, had knowledge of the Cretan pictographs and scripts and may have been influenced by them. Faced with this range of visible languages, it is not surprising that they started experimenting with alternative possibilities. They seemed to have preferred cuneiform written on clay tablets to the hieroglyphics written on papyrus, leather, or stone. Cylinder seals were used to sign their clay tablets. Apparently Phoenician ethnic pride and their practical nature made them want a writing system for their own northern Semitic speech, and evidence of a number of localized experiments have been unearthed.

Around the year 1500 B.C., Semitic workers in Egyptian turquoise mines in the Sinai desert area designed an achrophonic adaptation of hieroglyphs. In this mostly undeciphered *Sinaitic script,* a pictorial symbol or hieroglyph for an object was used for the initial sound of the name of the object.

Clay tablets written in a true Semitic alphabetical script using thirty characters to represent elementary consonant sounds have been unearthed in the ruins of the ancient city of Ugarit. At first glance, this writing looks like cuneiform. The signs are written with wedge-shaped marks resembling cuneiform because a similar stylus is used. This *Ras Shamra script* has no vowels, and its "alphabetical order"—the sequence in which the letters are memorized—is the same as the later Phoenician and Greek alphabets.

It is believed that the alphabet was born in the oldest of the Phoenician city-states, Byblos. The Greeks named papyrus *byblos* because it was exported through the port of Byblos. The English word "Bible" derives from Byblos from the Greek phrase meaning "the [papyrus] book." As early as 2700 B.C., cedarwood was being shipped to Egypt from Byblos, and by 1200 B.C. Byblos had become the dominant Phoenician city-state. A writing script developed there is called *sui generis*. It used pictographic signs devoid of any remaining pictorial meaning. The stone and bronze documents, written about 2000 B.C. and having a syllabary of over a hundred characters, were a major step on the road to an alphabet.

The writing system exported by the Phoenicians that conquered the world is a totally abstract and alphabetical system of twenty-two characters that was in use by 1500 B.C. One of the oldest datable inscriptions in the Phoenician alphabet is found on the limestone sarcophagus of the Byblos King Ahiram (c. 1000 B.C.) This sarcophagus is supported by four carved lions and has relief figures carved on the sides, ends, and lid top. A lengthy inscription is carved along the side of the lid. It is believed that the right-to-left writing style of the Phoenicians developed because stonemasons carved inscriptions by holding a chisel in the left hand and a hammer in the right. The Phoenitic or northern Semitic script was also written on papyrus with a brush or pen. Unfortunately, Phoenician literature written on papyrus in this early alphabet has perished including, for instance, one Byblos author's nine-book work on mythology.

The theory that Cretan pictographs may have inspired some characters of the Phoenician alphabet is demonstrated in this illustration.

Ras Shamra script, c. 1500 B.C. Used for bureaucratic and commercial documents, myths and legends, the Ras Shamra script, reducing cuneiform to a mere thirty-two characters, has—oddly enough—only been found in Ugarit. *The British Museum, London.*

Archaic Greek votive wheel, c. 525 B.C. A dedication to Apollo is clearly legible through the medium green patina of this 16 centimeters (6¼ inches) in diameter metal wheel used for worship purposes. *Museum of Fine Arts, Boston, William Amory Gardiner Fund.*

Early Phoenician alphabet, c. 1500 B.C. The twenty-two letters of the first alphabetical system include some characters that have retained an identity through thirty-five centuries.

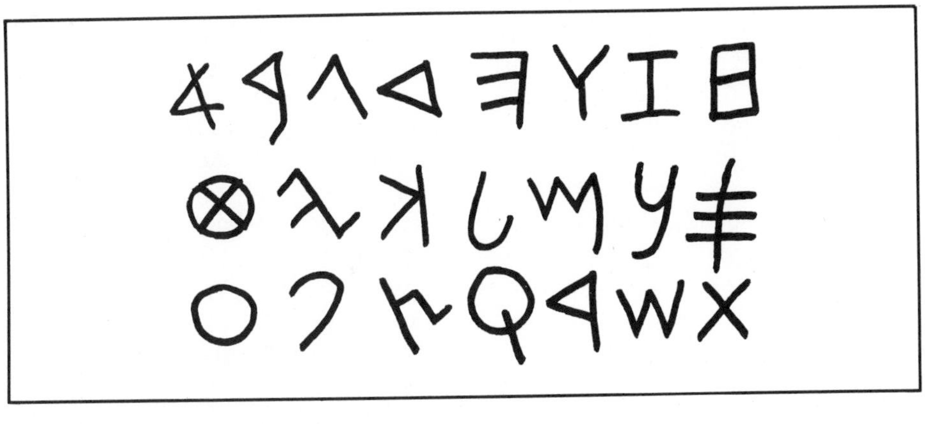

The alphabet that has survived from Phoenicia is the historical beginning of the alphabet, but it probably descended from an earlier, lost prototype design. It is likely that the same protoalphabet that produced the Phoenician alphabet evolved into Hebrew and Arabic alphabets elsewhere in the region. The graphic forms of the Hebrew alphabet are squared bold letters with the horizontal strokes thicker than the vertical ones. Basically, the Hebrew alphabet is the twenty-two consonant letters of the ancient northern Semitic alphabet.

The Arabic visible language of curving calligraphic gestures contains the twenty-two original sounds of the Semitic alphabet, plus six additional characters at the end. Both of these functional and beautifully designed letter systems are still written from right to left in the manner of their early origins.

Just as the invention of printing launched a quiet revolution in Chinese culture, the alphabet written on papyrus slowly turned western society upside down. Easy to write and learn, this system of simple signs for elementary sounds made literacy available to large numbers of people. The alphabet is a democratic or people's writing in contrast to the theocratic writing of the temple priests of Mesopotamia and Egypt. Scribes and priests lost their monopoly on written knowledge, and their political power and influence was shattered. Secular and military leaders came to the fore as leaders of the classical world of Greece and Rome.

The Greek alphabet

Greek civilization laid the foundation for most of the accomplishments of the western world. Science, philosophy and democratic government all developed in this ancient land. Art, architecture, and literature are a priceless part of the Greek heritage. And the Greeks adopted the alphabet and vastly developed its beauty and utility.

The date when the Phoenician alphabet was taken up by the ancient Greeks and spread through their city-states has been put from before 1000 B.C. to as late as 700 B.C. The oldest inscriptions date from the eighth century B.C., but the Greek alphabet, occupying a supreme position in the evolution of graphic communication, may have developed earlier. The Greeks took the Phoenician or northern Semitic alphabet and changed five consonants to vowels, which are connecting sounds that join consonants to make words. These have evolved into the present letters, *a, e, i, o,* and *u.* When vowel sounds are spoken, the breath channel is not constricted or blocked enough to create an audible friction. It is not known for certain who transported the alphabet from Phoenicia to Greece, but both mythology and tradition, which, in the ancient world, frequently became scrambled with oral history, point toward Cadmus of Miletus (dates unknown). According to various ancient accounts, Cadmus invented history or created prose or designed some of the letters of the Greek alphabet. These alleged accomplishments raise the possibility that Cadmus may have brought the alphabet to Greece.

In an enigmatic parallel, early Greek mythology reports that Cadmus, King of Phoenicia, set forth to find his sister Europa after she was abducted by Zeus. During his journey, King Cadmus killed a dragon that had slain his traveling companions. On the advice of Athena, he planted the dragon's teeth like seeds, and from them, an army of fierce men sprang forth. Tradition holds that King Cadmus brought the alphabet to Greece. Perhaps myth and oral history hint at a blinding truth! The power of Cadmus to raise armies from nowhere could, in fact, be because he commanded the alphabet. Troop movements, scouting reports, and orders to the field could be delivered by writing. Power came, not from Cadmus' ability to plant dragon's teeth, but from his ability to raise and direct armies using the alphabet as an information and communication tool which was as advanced in the ancient world as instantaneous electronic communications are today.

Perhaps Cadmus' story is a myth, and traders from Byblos and Tyre brought the alphabet to Greece and other Mediterranean areas. Local Greek areas adapted the alphabet to their own needs, then two versions—the Chalcidian in the west and the Ionic in the east—became dominant. Near the end of the fifth century B.C., Athens officially adopted the Ionic version which became standard throughout Greece. Writing was part of a Greek cultural renaissance that came on the heels of a dark and troubled age. The Dorian invasions, occurring until 1100 B.C., brought waves of migrant peoples into the Greek peninsula. Instability continued for some time before the Golden Age of ancient Greece blossomed in this mountainous land surrounded by languid cerulean oceans.

The period around 700 B.C. is significant in the development of Greek culture. Homer's epic poems, the *Odyssey* and *Iliad,* had been composed, and architects had begun to build in stone. On pottery the human figure was starting to appear as a major subject, and large freestanding sculpture was only decades away. The city-state of Athens, cradle of representative government, had organized the towns of the Attica region into a unified political unit and was moving toward the establishment of an aristocratic republic with elected archons—the nine chief magistrates first voted into one-year terms in 683 B.C. During this period the alphabet came into increasing use in Greek city-states.

From a graphic-design standpoint, the Greeks took the cockeyed Phoenician characters and converted them into art forms of great harmony and beauty. The written form, as shown in *The Persians* by Timotheus, has a visual order and balance as the letters march along a baseline in an even repetition of form and space. The letters and their component strokes are somewhat standardized because a system of horizontal, vertical, curved, and diagonal strokes is used. In the inscriptional form, such as the fifth-century B.C. *Votive Stella with Four Figures,* the letters became symmetrical geometric constructions of timeless beauty. Stonecarvers took imaginative liberties with letterform design while still maintaining the basic structure of the twenty-four character alphabet that had stabilized by the classical period and is still in use in Greece today. In this inscription, letterforms including the *E* and *M* are based on a square, *A* is constructed from an equilateral triangle, and the design of the *O* is a near perfect circle.

Initially, the Greeks adopted the Phoenician style of writing from right to left. Later, they developed a writing method called *boustrophedon,* which has been compared to plowing a field with an ox, for every other line reads in the opposite direction. Line one will read from right to left, then the characters do an aboutface, and line two reads from left to right. The lines alternate direction in this manner, and the reader can scan the text with a continuous back and forth eye movement, unhindered by the need to return to the beginning of the column to read each line. Finally, the Greeks adopted the left to right reading movement that has continued to this day in western civilization. From their classical alphabet, the Greeks developed more expeditious cursive and uncial scripts for everyday writing on wood and other soft writing materials such as wax and clay.

The Golden Age of Athens (c. 500 B.C.) was the high point of Greek culture. Democracy or "people rule" was practiced. Aristotle called democracy "a state where freemen and the poor, being in a majority, are invested with the power of the State." The vote of the majority became law. Visual communications played a secondary role in the oral culture of the Greek city-state. All citizens could attend the popular assembly and vote, and all elected officials were responsible to it. The orator who could speak persuasively to the assembly, the actor, and the lecturer were paramount in these city-states, where the total population including the surrounding countryside seldom exceeded ten thousand people. The historian or poet who wrote rather than spoke was less seriously regarded.

The alphabet played a role in democracy; it enabled the use of allotment tokens when selecting citizens by lot for public service. Secret voting by jurors was possible through the use of metal ballots with alphabet inscriptions. The freedom and equality of Greek citizens did not extend to a concept of equality for all people. The system was, in fact, based on slavery because slave labor freed citizens to devote their time and energy to public affairs.

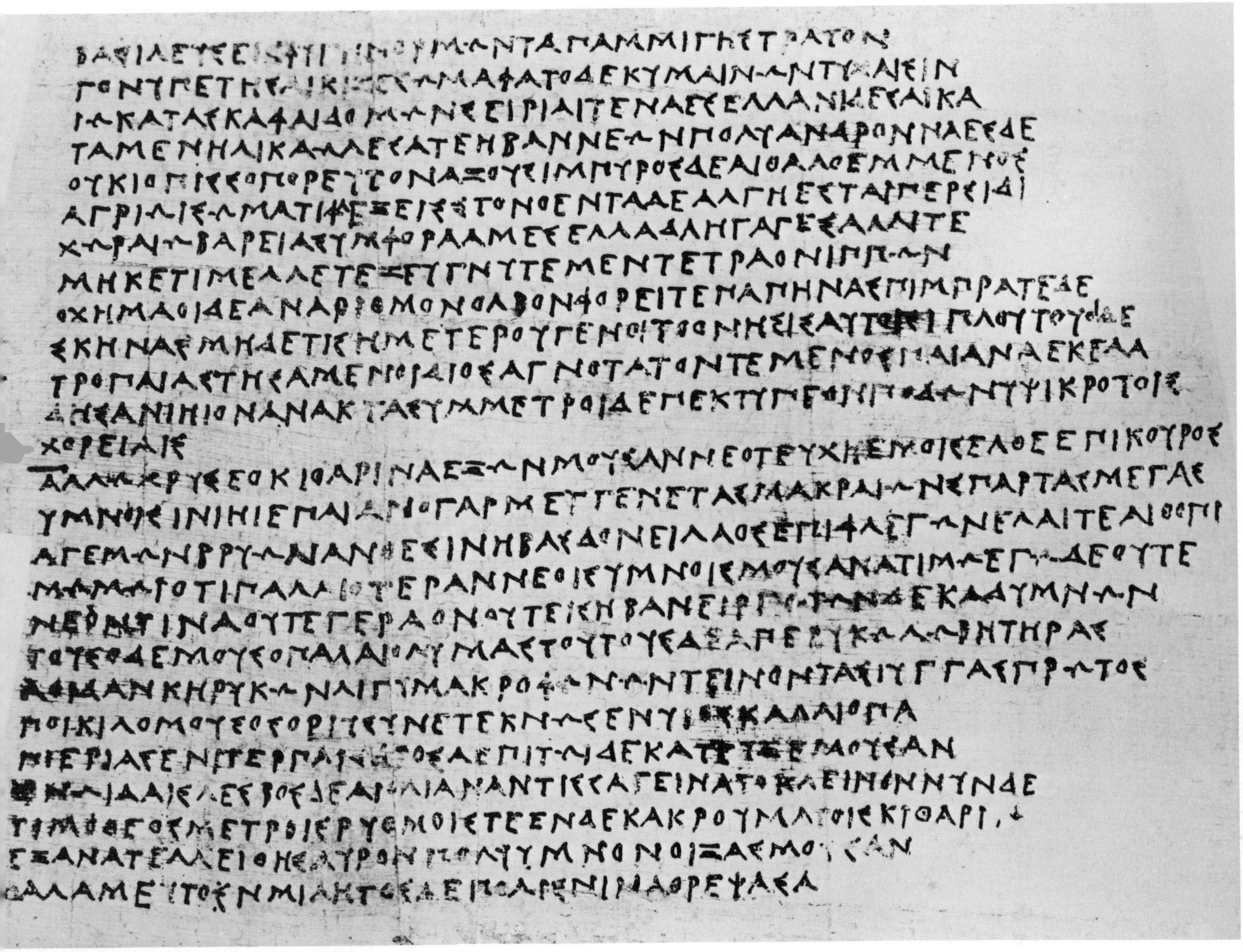

Timotheus, *The Persians,* papyrus manuscript, fourth century B.C. This excellent example of the Greek alphabet shows the symmetrical form and even visual rhythm that evolved. These qualities made the Greek alphabet the prototype for subsequent developments. *Staatliche Museen zu Berlin, East Germany.*

Votive stella with four figures, fifth century B.C. The design excellence of Greek inscriptions is clearly shown in this fragment. By using a three-sided square with a central dot for the *E* and a *V*-shaped horizontal in the *A,* the designer engaged in a personal inventiveness with form. *Museum of Fine Arts, Boston, gift of Mrs. C. A. Cummings.*

To authorize and endorse documents, wealthy Greek citizens used signature seals which could be stamped into wax or clay. Exquisite designs were engraved into the flat, oval bottom of a translucent precious stone called chalcedony, which is a pale blue or gray variety of quartz. Animals were a favorite motif. The refined forms, harmonious balance, and wholeness that we associate with Greek sculpture were achieved in these small (about 2-centimeter, or $\frac{3}{4}$-inch) devices used to impress a personal identification.

From the Macedonian city-state of Pella at the top of the Greek peninsula, Alexander the Great (356–323 B.C.) smashed the power of the Persian Empire and carried Hellenistic culture throughout the ancient world, including Egypt, Mesopotamia, and India. Reading and writing had become more important by the time of Alexander because the expansion of information and knowledge exceeded the ability of an oral culture to contain it. Alexander formed libraries, a major one being in the colonial outpost of Alexandria in Egypt and housing several hundred thousand scrolls.

The format design of the papyrus scroll was usually 10.5 meters (about 35 feet) long, 24 centimeters (9 or 10 inches) high, and, when rolled, 4 to 6 centimeters (about $1\frac{1}{2}$ to $2\frac{1}{4}$ inches) in diameter. The text layout was in flush-left-edge, random-right-edge columns about 8 centimeters (3 inches) wide, with generous 2.5-centimeter (about 1-inch) margins between them. Unfortunately, most of the great storehouse of knowledge and culture compiled by the Greek civilization has been lost due to the fragile nature of papyrus scrolls and the dampness of the Greek climate. Only thirty thousand scrolls remain. Of the three hundred thirty plays by the great Greek playwrights, for instance, only forty-three have survived. After Alexander's death in Babylon at the age of thirty-two, his generals split his empire into separate Hellenistic kingdoms. Greek civilization and its alphabet now became an influence throughout the world. The Greek alphabet fathered the Etruscan, Latin, and Cyrillic alphabets, and through these ancestors, it became the grandfather of alphabet systems used throughout the world today.

Base for a statue of Arsinoe Philadelphos, third century B.C. In the hands of the Greeks, the alphabet evolved a clarity of form and a clear differential between the various letterforms. Note the subtle tapering of the strokes. *The Metropolitan Museum of Art, New York, Cesnola Collection.*

Greek wooden tablet with uncials, 326 A.D. The rounded uncials allowed an *A* to be made with two strokes instead of three and an *E* to be made with three strokes instead of four. *Museum of Fine Arts, Boston, Hay Collection.*

Greek allotment tokens, c. 450–430 B.C. In the Greek city-state, some public officials were elected, and others were selected by lot. These tokens were used in the selection process. *Agora Excavations, American School of Classical Studies, Athens.*

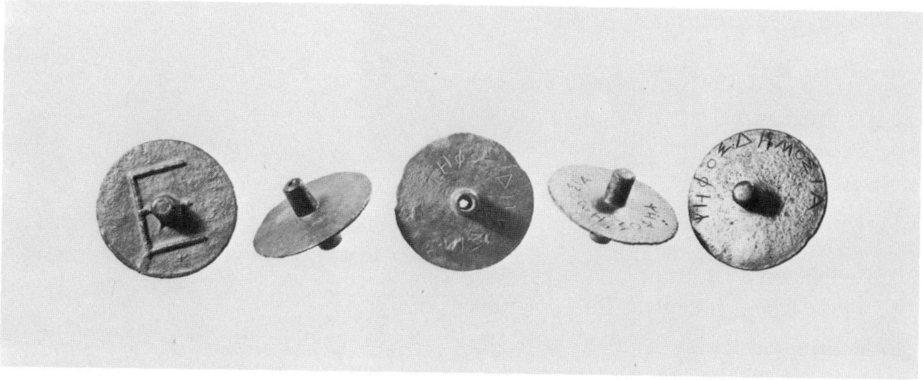

Greek juror's ballots, fourth century B.C. A juror voted not guilty with a ballot having a solid hub, and a hollow-hubbed ballot was used to cast a guilty vote. *Agora Excavations, American School of Classical Studies, Athens.*

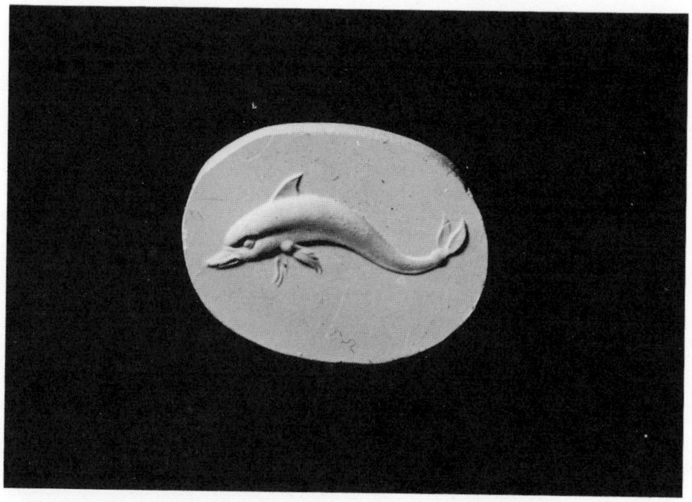

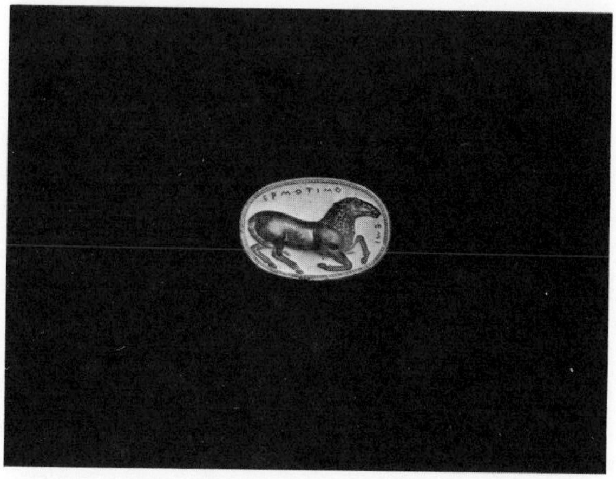

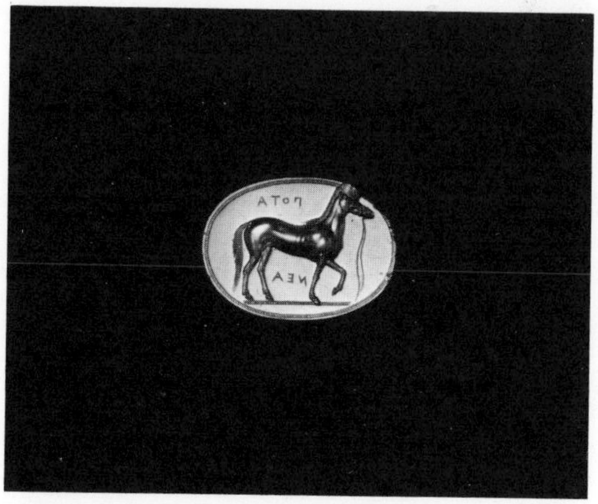

Greek signature seals, fifth century B.C. The leaping dolphin was photographed from a plaster impression made from the seal. A heron standing on one leg, a ewe rising from the ground, and a racehorse with broken reins are reproduced from the actual small carvings. *Museum of Fine Arts, Boston: race horse, H. L. Pierce Fund; others, Francis Bartlett Donations.*

The Latin alphabet

The rise of Rome from a small village to the great imperial city that ruled the known world, and the awesome collapse of this mighty empire, constitutes one of the great sagas of history. Perhaps as early as 750 B.C., Rome existed as a humble village on the Tiber River in central Italy. By the first century A.D., the Roman Empire stretched from England in the north to Egypt in the south, and from Spain in the west to the Persian Gulf at the base of the ancient land of Mesopotamia in the east.

From a farm near Rome, the great poet Horace (65–8 B.C.) wrote that "Captive Greece took Rome captive." After the Roman conquest of Greece, scholars and whole libraries were packed and moved to Rome. The Romans captured Greek literature, art, and religion, adapted them to the conditions of Roman power and confidence, and spread them throughout the vast Roman Empire.

The Roman alphabet came from Greece by way of the ancient Etruscans, an early people who dominated the Italian peninsula during the early first millennium B.C. After the letter *G* was designed by one Spurius Carvilius (c. 250 B.C.) to replace the Greek letter *Z* which was of little value to the Romans, the Latin alphabet contained twenty-one letters: *A, B, C, D, E, F, G, H, I, K, L, M, N, O, P, Q, R* (which evolved as a variation of *P*), *S, T, V, X.* Following the Roman conquest of Greece during the first century B.C., the Greek letters *Y* and *Z* were added to the end of the Latin alphabet to accommodate Greek words containing these sounds that were being borrowed by the Romans. Three additional letters were added to the alphabet during the Middle Ages to arrive at the twenty-six letters of the contemporary English alphabet. The *J* is an outgrowth of *I*, which was lengthened in fourteenth-century manuscripts to indicate use with consonant force, particularly as the first letter of some words. Both *U* and *W* are variants of *V*, which was being used for two sounds in medieval England. At the beginning of the tenth century, *U* was designed to represent the soft vowel sound in contrast to the harder consonant sound of *V*. The *W* began as a ligature, which is a joining of two letters. In twelfth-century England two *V* letterforms were joined into *VV* to represent "double U."

Etruscan Bucchero vase, seventh or sixth century B.C. A prototype of the educational toy, this toy jug in the shape of a rooster bears an inscription of the Etruscan alphabet. *The Metropolitan Museum of Art, Fletcher Fund, 1924.*

Rome took great pride in its imperial accomplishments and conquests, and created monumental letterform designs for architectural inscriptions celebrating victories and generals. Roman inscriptions were designed to have great beauty and permanence. The simple geometric lines of the *capitalis monumentalis* ("monumental capitals") were drawn in thick and thin strokes, with organically unified straight and curved lines. Each letterform was designed to become one form rather than merely the sum of its parts. Careful attention was given to the shapes of spaces inside the letters and between the letters. A Roman inscription becomes a sequence of linear geometric forms adapted from the square, triangle, and circle. Combined into an inscription, these letterforms mold the negative shapes around and between them into a measured graphic melody of spatial forms. An eternal wholeness is achieved.

Much debate has centered on the elegant serifs, which are small lines extending from the ends of the major strokes of a letterform. One theory holds that the serifs were originally

Carved inscription from the base of Trajan's column, c. 114 A.D. Located in Trajan's forum in Rome, this masterful example of capitalis monumentalis gives silent testimony to the ancient Roman dictum, "The written word remains." *(Photograph: James Mosley)*

SENAT
CAESARI·DIVI·NERVAE·F
TRAIANO·AVG·GERM·DAC
MAXIMO·TRIB·POT·XVII
AD DECLARANDVM
MONS ET LOCVS TAN

chisel marks made by the "cleanup" strokes as the stonemason finished carving a letter. Others argue that the inscriptions were first drawn on the stone with a flat signwriter's brush, and that the signwriter gave a short gesture before lifting the brush to sharpen the termination of the stroke. Regardless of which tool initiated the serif as a design element, we do known that the original letters were drawn on the stone with a brush. The shapes and forms defy mathematical analysis or construction with a T-square and compass. A letter found several times on an inscription will have subtle differences in width and proportion. In some inscriptions, lines with more letters will have both the letterforms and the negative spaces between them slightly condensed to accommodate the information. This represents an artistic judgment by the brushwriter rather than a measured

Detail, inscription on a tomb along the Appian Way, Rome. The controlled calligraphic drawing of the forms onto the stone with the brush combine with the precision of the stonemason's craft to create letterforms of majestic proportion and harmonious form. *(Photograph: James Mosley)*

calculation. Some Roman inscriptions even contain minute particles of red paint that have adhered to the stone through the centuries, leaving little doubt that the letters were painted. Monumental capitals were carved as a wedge-shaped trough. The edges of the letterforms were not sharp 90-degree angles with the flat surface of the stone; rather, a more gentle angled taper created a shallower edge that resisted chipping and wearing.

The Roman written hand took several design styles. The most important is the *capitalis quadrata* ("square capitals"). Written carefully and slowly with a flat pen, square capitals had stately proportions and outstanding legibility. The space between lines and letters was generous, but there was no space left between words. The letters were written between two horizontal baselines, and the *F* and *L* extended slightly above this line. The letter designs are amazingly similar to the letters we call *capitals* today. The flat pen was held at a slant or cant angle to the horizontal line and produced pronounced thick and thin strokes. Serifs were added with the pen and strengthened the ends of the strokes. Square capitals were widely used from the second century A.D. until the fifth century A.D.

The *capitalis rustica* ("rustic capitals") were used during the same period. These extremely condensed letterforms saved space. Parchment and papyrus were expensive, and rustic capitals enabled the writer to squeeze half again as many rustic capitals on the page in comparison to square capitals. The flat-nibbed pen or brush was held in an almost vertical position when writing rustic capitals. The thin verticals create a staccato beat contrasting with a textured pattern of the elliptical round and arched diagonal strokes. Occasional horizontal forms function as accents. One interesting design element is the lack of a horizontal stroke on the letter *A*. Rustic capitals were written quickly, but they are hard to read.

From the ruins of Pompeii and Herculaneum, we have learned that Roman brushwriters wrote notices,

Wall writing from Pompeii, first century A.D. This inscription is one of over sixteen hundred messages ranging from passages from Virgil to crude obscenities that were preserved under more than 3.6 meters (12 feet) of volcanic ash. *(Photograph: James Mosley)*

political campaign material, and advertising announcements on exterior walls using both square capitals and rustic capitals. In addition to wall writing, poster messages were painted on reusable panels which were set up in the streets. Placards and picture signboards were executed by professional letterers. Trademarks were widely used to identify the firm or place of origination of handcrafted products. Commercial records, documents of state, and literature were written on a variety of substrates. Papyrus from Egypt was supplemented by wood, clay, flat pieces of metal, and wax tablets held in wooden frames upon which writing was scratched with a stylus. The flat end of this stylus was used to erase the writing in the soft wax so that the tablet could be used again.

Around 190 B.C., the use of *parchment* as a substrate for writing came into common use. Tradition holds that Ptolemy V (ruled c. 205–181 B.C.) of Alexandria and King Eumenes II (ruled 197–160 B.C.) of Pergamum were engaged in a fierce library-building rivalry, and Ptolemy placed an embargo on papyrus shipments to prevent Eumenes from continuing his

rapid production of scrolls. Parchment, a writing surface made from the skins of domestic animals—particularly calves, sheep, and goats—was invented to overcome the embargo. These refined leather sheets are made by first washing the skin and removing all hair or wool. Then, the skin is stretched tightly on a frame and scraped to remove all traces of hair or flesh. After being whitened with chalk, it is smoothed with pumice. Larger, more durable and flexible than papyrus sheets, parchment had a smoother surface and became very popular as a writing surface. The highest quality of parchment is called *vellum* and is made from the smooth skins of newborn calves.

A revolutionary format design called the *codex* began to supplant the scroll (called a *rotulus*) in Rome and Greece, beginning about the time of Christ. Parchment was gathered in signatures of two, four, or eight sheets. These were folded, stitched, and combined into codices with pages like a modern book. The parchment codex had several advantages over the papyrus scroll. The clumsy process of unrolling and rolling scrolls to look up information yielded to the quick process of opening a codex to the desired page. Papyrus was too fragile to be folded into pages, and the vertical strips on the back of a papyrus scroll made writing on both sides impractical. Since both sides of the parchment pages in a codex could be used for writing, storage space and material costs both dropped.

During the rise of Christianity, from after 1 A.D. until around 400 A.D., scrolls and codices were used side by side. The durability and permanence of the codex appealed to Christians because their writings were viewed as sacred words from God. With a whole pantheon of gods and little clear distinction between god and man, pagan scholars were less inclined to revere their religious writings. Traditionally, pagan writings were on scrolls. Christians were involved in comparative study of different texts, particularly the Gospels. It is easy to have several codices open on a table, but virtually impossible to have several scrolls unrolled for comparative reference. Christians sought the codex format to alienate themselves from the pagan scroll; pagans clung to their scrolls in resistance to Christianity. Graphic format became a symbol of religious belief during the late decades of the Roman Empire. The world outlook of Christianity, which sought universality and the conversion of all peoples, elevated books and writing to far greater importance than their previous role in the ancient world.

Christianity was adopted as the state religion of Rome in 325 A.D. by the Emperor Constantine (d. 337 A.D.). The Roman legions which had once persecuted Christians now began to carry a monogram of Christ into battle as a symbol of salvation.

The collapse of the Roman Empire was as dramatic as its rise from humble origins. In the first century A.D., Rome began to experience hostile actions from tribal peoples (called "Barbarians" by the Greeks) living beyond the Danube and Rhine Rivers. In 325 A.D., Emperor Constantine moved the capital from Rome to the Greek town of Byzantium (later renamed Constantinople), located astride the mouth of the Black Sea. Quite naturally, this weakened the strength of the western provinces, and the warlike Huns began to put great pressure against Rome's border neighbors. In 360 A.D. the Visigoths were allowed to settle west of the Danube inside the Roman Empire after their defeat by the Huns. Two years later the Visigoths killed the Emperor Valens (c. 328–378 A.D.) and two-thirds of his army in a pivotal battle. The Empire was permanently divided in half in 395 A.D., and Rome itself was sacked by the Visigoths in 410 A.D. The Emperor moved his court to Ravenna, which became the capital of the western Roman Empire. Then, in 476 A.D., Ravenna fell to the Barbarians and became the capital of an Ostrogothic Kingdom. This marked the final dissolution of the Roman Empire. Even as the Barbarians were filtering into the Roman Empire and destroying it, they were being converted to the Christian religion. But Rome left a legacy that includes its architecture, engineering, law, language, and literature. The grandeur of Roman society informed many aspects of later human culture, and its alphabet became the design form for visible languages in the western world.

5

The Medieval Manuscript

THE COLLAPSE OF THE ROMAN EMpire was followed by an era of dislocation and uncertainty in the West. After the Empire split into two portions, with capitals in Byzantium (Constantinople) and Rome, the eastern half of the Roman Empire thrived as the sophisticated Byzantine society. The western portion saw the light of civilization flicker and almost vanish. The thousand-year Dark Ages of the medieval period lasted from the fall of Rome in the fifth century A.D. until the Renaissance of the fifteenth century. Cities in the western half of the Roman Empire degenerated and became small villages; officials left their duties and moved to their country estates; government and law ceased to exist. Trade and commerce slumped and almost became nonexistent, for travel became extremely dangerous. The regional languages, customs, and geographic divisions of Europe started to form in isolated areas during this Dark Age. The general population languished in illiteracy, poverty, and superstition. A feudal society was established where land-owning noblemen had dictatorial power over the peasants who toiled in the fields. But the centuries following the fall of Rome saw Barbarian and Roman influences combine to produce a rich and colorful design vocabulary in the arts and crafts. There was nothing "dark" about the crafts of the medieval period, including the making of books.

The knowledge and learning of the classical world was almost completely lost. The Christian belief in sacred religious writings became the primary impetus for the preservation of books. Christian monasteries became the centers of cultural, educational, and intellectual activities. The preservation of knowledge within the monastery included the making of *illuminated manuscripts,* which in the strictest sense, are handwritten books that have been embellished with gold or silver. However, the term has come to mean any handwritten book that was decorated, illustrated, and produced during the medieval period. For the medieval Christian, the sacred writings had great meaning. The use of graphic and illustrative embellishment to expand the word visually became very important, and the illuminated manuscripts were produced with extraordinary care and design sensitivity.

Illuminated manuscript production was costly and time consuming. Parchment or vellum took hours to prepare and a large volume might require the skins of two to three hundred sheep. Black ink for lettering was prepared from fine soot or lampblack. Gum and water were mixed with sanguine or red chalk to make a red ink used for headings and paragraph marks, and irongall (a mixture of iron sulfate and oak apples, which are oak galls caused by wasp larvae) was used to make a brown ink. Mineral, animal, and vegetable substances were used to make colors for the illustrations. A vibrant, deep blue was made from lapis lazuli. This precious mineral was only mined in Afghanistan, and yet it found its way to monasteries as far away as Ireland. Gold, and less frequently silver, was applied in two ways. Sometimes it was ground into a powder and mixed into a gold paint. This left a slightly grainy surface, so the preferred method of application was to hammer the gold into a fine sheet of gold leaf, which was applied over an adhesive ground. Burnishing for texture, punching, and tooling with metalworking tools were sometimes used for design effects. The dazzling luminosity of the gold leaf when it caught and reflected light spawned the term *illuminated manuscript*. The book covers were wooden boards usually covered with leather. Decorative patterns were applied by tooling the leather, and important liturgical manuscripts often had precious jewels, gold- and silverwork, enameled designs, or ivory carving on the covers.

During the early medieval era, nearly all books were created in the monastic *scriptorium,* or writing room. Christian scriptures were the most important works produced. The head of the scriptoria was the *scrittori,* a well-educated scholar who understood Greek and Latin. He functioned as an editor and art director with overall responsibility for the design and production of the manuscripts. A *copisti* was a production letterer who spent his days bent over a writing table penning page after page in a trained lettering style. A number of colophons inform us that the work of the copisti was difficult and tiring. The *colophon* of a manuscript or book is an inscription, usually at the end, containing facts about the production. Often the scribe, designer, or later, printer, is identified. In the colophon of one illuminated manuscript, a scribe named George declared that "As the sailor longs for a safe haven at the end of his voyage, so does the writer for the last word." Another scribe, Prior Petris, described writing as a terrible ordeal for the entire body that "dims your eyes, makes your back ache, and knits one's chest and stomach together . . ." The reader was then advised to turn the pages carefully and to keep his finger far from the text. The *illuminator* or illustrator was an artist responsible for the execution of ornament and image in visual support of the text. The word was supreme, and the scrittori controlled the scriptorium. He would lay out the pages to indicate where illustrations were to be added after the text was written. Sometimes this was done with a light sketch, but often a note jotted in the margin told the illustrator what to draw in the space.

The illustration and ornamentation were not mere decoration. The monastic leaders were mindful of the educational value of pictures and ability of ornament to create mystical and spiritual overtones. Most illuminated manuscripts were small enough to fit into a saddlebag. This portability enabled manuscripts to transmit knowledge and ideas from one region to another and one time period to another. Manuscript production over the thousand-year course of the medieval era created a vast vocabulary of graphic forms, page layouts, illustration and lettering styles, and techniques. Regional isolation and difficult travel caused innovation and influences to spread very slowly, so identifiable regional design styles emerged. Some of the more distinctive schools of manuscript production can be ranked as major innovations in graphic design.

The classical style

In classical antiquity, the Greeks and Romans designed and illustrated manuscripts, but none have survived. The Egyptian *Book of the Dead* was probably an influence, and the fabulous Greek library at Alexandria, where late Egyptian culture met early classical culture, probably contained many wonderful, illustrated manuscripts that are now lost. This great library reportedly housed seven hundred thousand scrolls when it was destroyed by fire at the time of Julius Caesar (100–44 B.C.). In the few fragments of illustrated scrolls that survive, the layout approach uses numerous small illustrations drawn in a crisp, simple style and inserted throughout the text. The frequency with which these appear creates a cinematic graphic sequence not unlike the contemporary comic book.

The invention of parchment, which was so much more durable than papyrus, and the codex format, which could take thicker paint because it did not have to be rolled, opened new possibilities for design and illustration. Literary references refer to manuscripts on vellum, illustrated with a portrait of the author as a *frontispiece*.

The earliest extant illuminated manuscript from the late antique and early Christian era is the *Vatican Virgil.* Created in the late fourth century or early fifth century A.D., this volume contains two of the three great poems of Publius Vergilius Maro (70–19 B.C.). Virgil was the greatest Roman poet. The *Vatican Virgil* contains his *Georgics,* a didactic poem on farming and country life, and the *Aeneid,* an epic narrative about the Trojan Aeneid who left the flaming

The *Vatican Virgil.* The death of Laocoön, early fifth century A.D. The vibrant red of Laocoön's cape creates a focal point and echoes the bright red border framing the illustration. *The Vatican Library, Rome.*

ruins of Troy and set out to found a new city in the west. A consistent graphic design approach is used. The text is lettered in crisp rustic capitals, with one wide column on each page. Illustrations are framed in bright bands of color, frequently red, and are the same width as the text column. These are placed at the top, middle, or bottom of the page to be adjacent to the passage illustrated. There are six full-page illustrations. The illustrator neatly lettered the name of the major figures upon the illustration in the manner of present-day political cartoonists.

The *Vatican Virgil* is completely Roman and pagan in its conception and execution. The lettering is Roman, and the illustrations echo the rich colors and illusionistic space of the wall frescoes preserved at Pompeii. The demise of Laocoön, a priest who was punished by death for profaning the temple of Apollo, is shown in a sequence within one image. On the left, Laocoön calmly prepares to sacrifice a bull at the temple of Poseidon, oblivious to the approach of two serpents in the lake at the upper left-hand corner. On the right, Laocoön and his two young sons are attacked and killed by the serpents.

This pictorial and historical style of book illustration, so similar to late Roman painting and combined with rustic capitals, represents the *classical style.* It was used in many of the earliest Christian manuscripts and surely was the book-design style of the late Roman Empire.

As early as the third century A.D., a dazzling design effect was achieved in early Christian manuscripts by dyeing parchment a deep and costly purple color. Lettering was executed in silver or gold to produce some of the most elegant pages in the history of graphic design. These monastic graphic artists were severely reprimanded by St. Jerome (c. 347–420 A.D.) who, in his preface to a manuscript Book of Job, blasted the practice as a useless and wasteful extravagance.

UNCIALS
semi-uncials

The evolution of writing styles was a continuing search for simpler and faster letterform construction and writing ease. Two important new writing styles came into prominence during the course of the late antique and early Christian period. Both were primarily used within the Christian church from the fourth until the ninth century A.D. and have retained this association. As mentioned earlier, the *uncials* (so named because they were written between two guidelines that are one *uncia* [the Roman inch] apart) were actually invented by the Greeks as early as the third century B.C. In the Greek wooden tablet from 326 A.D. shown in Chapter 3, the primary characteristics of uncials are seen. Uncials are rounded, freely drawn majuscule letters more suited to rapid writing than either square capitals or rustic capitals. The curves reduced the number of strokes required to make many letterforms, and the number of angular joints—which have a tendency to clog or close up with ink—was significantly reduced. Certain letters in the uncial style threaten to develop ascenders or descenders, but the design remains that of a majuscule letter. A step toward the development of minuscules (small or "lower case" letterforms) was the *semi-uncial* or *half-uncial.* Four guidelines instead of two were used, and strokes were allowed to soar above and sink below the two principal lines, creating true ascenders and descenders. The pen was held flatly horizontal to the baseline, which gave the forms a strong vertical axis. Half-uncials were easy to write and had increased legibility because the visual differentiation between letters was improved. Although some half-uncials appeared in the third century A.D., it was not until the late sixth century A.D. that the style began to flourish.

Celtic book design

The period from the collapse of Rome until the eighth century was a time of migration and upheaval throughout Europe as different ethnic tribes fought for territory. These unsettled times were the blackest decades of the medieval era. Wandering hordes of Germanic Barbarians did not invade the island of Ireland tucked in the far corner of Europe, and the Celts living there enjoyed relative isolation and peace. In the early fifth century A.D., the legendary St. Patrick and other missionaries began to rapidly convert the Celts to Christianity. In a bizarre melding of culture and religion, pagan temples were converted to churches and Celtic ornaments were applied to chalices and bells brought to Ireland by the missionaries. Celtic design is abstract and extremely complex. Geometric linear patterns weave, twist, and fill a space with thick visual textures. Bright, pure colors are used in close juxtaposition. This Celtic craft tradition of intricate, highly abstract decorative patterns was applied to book design in the monastic scriptoria, and a new concept and image of the book emerged. A series of gospel books containing the four narratives

The Book of Durrow, the lion, symbol for Mark, c. 680 A.D. Reflecting a pagan and barbarian ancestory, this symbolic lion has a head of red dots; body stripes, tail, and feet in intense yellow contour lines; and a body of red and green diamond shapes. *Trinity College Library, Dublin.*

The Book of Durrow, the man, symbol of Matthew, c. 680 A.D. As flat as a Cubist painting and constructed from simple geometric forms, this figure, facing the opening of the Gospel of St. Matthew, wears a checkered pattern of red, yellow, and green squares and tile-like patterned textures. *Trinity College Library, Dublin.*

of the life of Christ, which are the first four books of the New Testament of the Christian Bible, represent the height of the Celtic style. Written and designed around 680 A.D., the *Book of Durrow* is the earliest fully designed and ornamented Celtic book. The *Lindisfarne Gospels,* written by Eadfrith, Bishop of Lindisfarne, before 698 A.D., represents the full flowering of the Celtic style. The masterwork of the epoch is the *Book of Kells,* created in the scriptorium at the island monastery of Iona around 800 A.D. Countless hours of work were lavished upon individual pages whose vibrant color and form is in stunning contrast to the stark reclusive environment and rule of silence found in the monastic scriptorium.

Ornament was used in three ways. Ornament frames or borders were created to enclose portraits of the apostles and other full-page illustrations. Opening pages of each gospel and other important passages were singled out for illumination, particularly by the design of ornate initials. Full pages of decorative design called *carpet pages* were bound into the manuscript. This name developed because the densely packed design has the intricate patterning associated with oriental carpets. As a carpet page from the *Lindisfarne Gospels* shows, a cross or other geometric motif becomes an organizing form that brings structure to the interlaces and lacertines filling the space. The *interlace* is a two-dimensional decoration formed by a number of ribbons or straps woven into a complex, usually symmetrical design. It is evident that drafting instruments were used to construct many of the designs in Celtic manuscripts. Interlaces created by animal forms were called *lacertines*. Most of the forms were either invented from imagination or based on earlier models. Careful observation of nature was not required of the Celtic designer or illustrator.

Large initials on the opening pages grew bigger in newer books as the decades passed. The need to integrate these initials with the rest of the text was a challenging design problem that was beautifully resolved in the scriptoria. In the opening page of the Gospel of Saint Mark in the *Book of Durrow,* the first letters of the word "Initium" create a large monogram thrusting down the page. A graphic principle called *diminuendo,* which is the decreasing scale of graphic information, is operative in this page design. The large, double initial is followed in decreasing size by a smaller initial, the last four letters of the first word, the next two words, and the text. This descending scale unites the large initial to the text. Red *S*-shaped lines or dots align each line of text to the initial and further unify the elements. The red-dot pattern transforms the first three words into rectangles and contours the first letters of each verse. A thoughtful and harmonious design system is created. These red dots were used profusely, and watercolor washes were often used to fill in the negative areas inside and between letters. Sometimes pigments were handled thickly and opaquely; at other times they were as thin and translucent as enamel.

The Lindisfarne Gospels, carpet page facing the opening of St. Matthew, c. 698 A.D. A mathematical grid buried under swirling lacertine birds and quadrupeds brings structure to the textured areas, and a red, contoured cross with white circular "buttons" brings timeless stability to one of the most animated pages in the history of design. *The British Library, London.*

One of the most important moments in the Gospels occurs when the name of Christ is first mentioned in the eighteenth verse of the first chapter of Matthew. The writer announces that "Now the birth of Christ was on this wise . . ." Upon arriving at the word "Christ," the illuminator created a graphic explosion using the monogram *XPI*. This monogram—used to write Christ in manuscripts—is called the *Chi-Rho* after the first two letters of the Greek word for Christ, Chi (*X*) and Rho (*P*). The Chi-Rho in the *Book of Kells* is composed of shimmering color and intricate convoluted form, blossoming over a whole page. Amidst the intricate patterns of spirals and lacertines, the artist has drawn thirteen human heads. At the base of the plunging descender of the *X*, two cats and two mice calmly watch as two other mice tug at a wafer. An otter holds a salmon in another niche at the base of the monogram.

In the Celtic manuscript, a radical design innovation is the practice of leaving a space between words to enable the reader to separate the string of letters into words more quickly. The half-uncial script of late antique codices journeyed to Ireland with the early missionaries and was transformed into the *scriptura scottica,* or insular script, as it is now called. These half-uncials became the national letterform style in Ireland and are still used for special writings and as a type style. Starting with the half-uncial, the Celts subtly redesigned the alphabet to suit their visual traditions. Written with a slightly angled pen, the full, rounded charac-

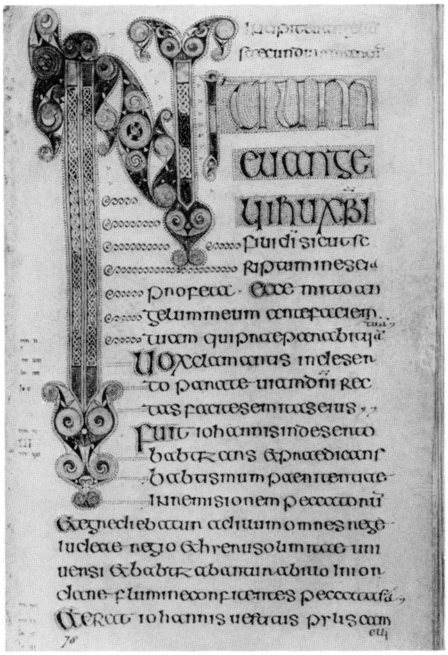

The Book of Durrow, opening page, the Gospel of Saint Mark, c. 680 A.D. Linked into a ligature, an *I* and an *N* become an artform of interlaced threads and coiling spiral motifs in a black, yellow, red, and white color scheme. *Trinity College Library, Dublin.*

The Book of Kells, the Chi-Rho initial page, c. 795–806 A.D. Three letters of the alphabet are transformed to convey a transcendental spiritual expression of deep religious faith. *Trinity College Library, Dublin.*

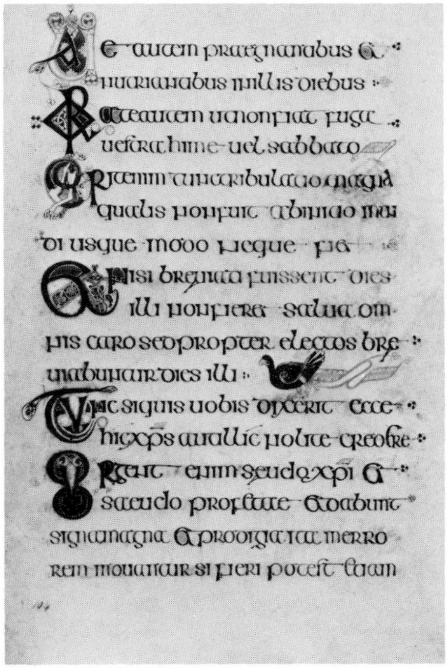

The Book of Kells, text page with ornamental initials, c. 795–806 A.D. The incredible originality of the hundreds of illustrated initials is suggested by the variety of imaginative forms in the six initials on this one page. *Trinity College Library, Dublin.*

ters have a strong bow with ascenders bending to the right. A heavy triangle perches at the top of ascenders, and the horizontal stroke of the last letter of the word, particularly an *e* or *t*, zips out into the space between words. The text page from the *Book of Kells* shows how carefully the insular script was lettered. Characters are frequently joined at the waistline or the baseline.

Ironically, beautiful carefully lettered half-uncials convey a text that is careless and incorrect and that contains numerous misspellings and misreadings. Even so, the *Book of Kells* is the zenith of Celtic illumination. Its noble design has generous margins, huge initial letters, and far more full-page illustrations than any other Celtic manuscript. Over twenty-one hundred ornate capitals make every page a visual delight. Here and there through the course of its three hundred thirty-nine leaves a sentence blooms into a full page of illumination. The magnificent Celtic school of manuscript design ended abruptly

The Book of Kells, symbols of the Gospel authors, c. 795–806 A.D. Winged and stylized almost to abstraction, Matthew's man, Mark's lion, Luke's ox, and John's eagle float in four rectangles wrapped in a densely ornamented frame. *Trinity College Library, Dublin.*

before the *Book of Kells* was completed. In 795 A.D. northern raiders made their first appearance on the Irish coast, and a period of intense struggle between the Celts and the Vikings followed. Both Lindisfarne and Iona, seats of two of the greatest scriptoria in medieval history, were destroyed. When the invading Northmen swarmed over the island of Iona where the *Book of Kells* was being completed in the monastery scriptorium, escaping monks took it to Kells and continued to work on it there. It can only be guessed whether or not majestic illuminated manuscripts were lost, or what magnificent volumes might have been designed had peace and stability continued for the Celts of Ireland.

The Caroline graphic renewal

When Charlemagne (742(3)–814), King of the Franks since 768 and the leading ruler of central Europe, rose from prayer in St. Peter's Cathedral

Portrait of Saint John from the *Coronation Gospels,* late eighth century. Rejecting the flat patterns of earlier medieval illumination, the Caroline illuminators embraced illusionistic painting techniques. *Kunsthistorisches Museum, Vienna.*

in Rome on Christmas Day, 800 A.D., Pope Leo III (d. 816) placed a crown on his head, and declared him emperor of what became known as the Holy Roman Empire. The whole of central Europe was united under Charlemagne in an empire that was neither Roman nor particularly holy. Nevertheless, it attempted to recapture the grandeur and unity of the Roman Empire in a Germanic and Christian federation. In addition to restoring the concept of empire to the West, Charlemagne introduced the feudal system in an effort to bring order to chaotic medieval society.

Although by some reports he was illiterate except to sign his name, Charlemagne fostered a revival of learning and the arts. England of the 700s had seen much intellectual activity, and Charlemagne recruited the English scholar Alcuin of York (c. 732–804) to come to his palace at Aachen and establish a palace school. Except for the Celtic pattern-making tradition, book design and illumination had sunk to an inept low in most of Europe. Illustrations were poorly drawn and composed, and writing had become localized and undisciplined in the hands of poorly trained scribes. Many manuscripts were difficult, if not impossible, to read. Charlemagne mandated reform by royal edict in 789. At the court in Aachen, a *turba scriptorium* ("crowd of scribes," as Alcuin called them) was assembled to prepare master copies of the important religious texts. Then books and scribes were dispatched throughout Europe to disseminate the reforms.

Standardization of page layout, writing style, and decoration was attempted. The alphabet was successfully reformed. For a model, the ordinary writing script of the late antique period was selected and molded into an ordered uniform script called *Caroline minuscule.* Ideas from this late Roman cursive script were combined with some of the Celtic innovations in their insular script, including the use of four guidelines, ascenders, and descenders. The Caroline minuscule is the forerunner of our contemporary lowercase or small-letter alphabet. This clear set of letterforms was practical and easy to write. Characters were set apart instead of joined, and the number of ligatures was reduced. Much writing had become a slurred scrawl; the new alphabet restored legibility. The Caroline minuscule became the standard throughout Europe for a time, but as the decades passed, various areas veered toward a regional style. Roman capitals were studied and adopted for headings and initials of great beauty. These were not calligraphic, but carefully drawn and built up with more than one stroke. The use of a dual alphabet was not fully developed in the sense that we use capital and small letters today, but a process in that direction had begun. In addition to graphic reforms, the court at Aachen reformed sentence and paragraph structure and punctuation. The Caroline revival of scholar-

caroline minuscules

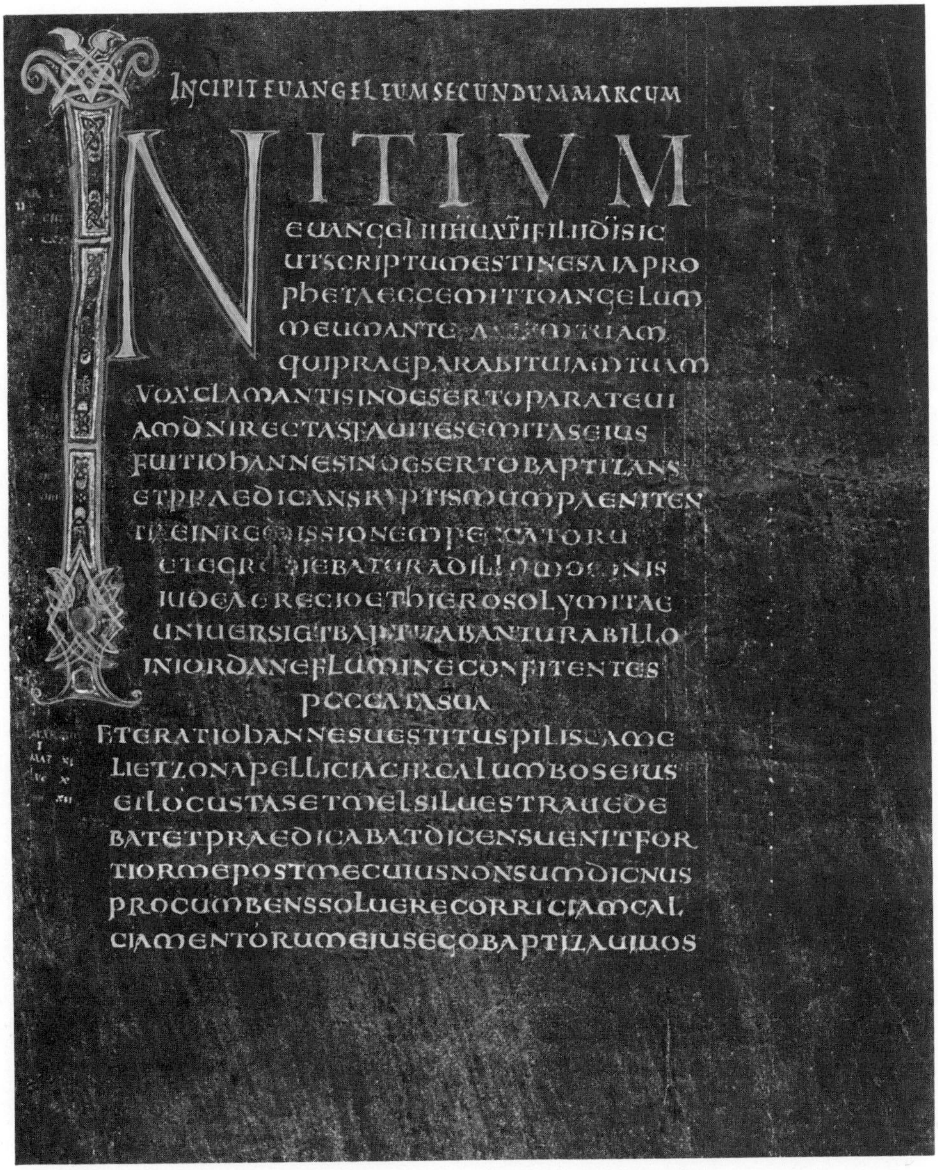
INCIPIT EUANGELIUM SECUNDUM MARCUM
INITIUM

Opening page to the gospel of St. Mark from the *Coronation Gospels,* late eighth century. A perfection of craft, beautiful and luxurious materials, and an understated harmony of layout combine to make the *Coronation Gospels* a rare masterpiece of the bookmaking art. *Kunsthistorisches Museum, Vienna.*

ship and learning stayed a serious loss of human knowledge and writings that had been occurring through the early medieval period.

When early manuscripts from the late antique period and the Byzantine culture were imported for study, illuminators were shocked and stunned when they saw the naturalism and illusion of deep space of the illustrations. The two dimensional, decorative style suddenly seemed passé in the face of this "picture-window" style where space moved back into the page from a decorative frame, and clothes seemed to wrap the forms of a living human figure. Lacking the skill or basic knowledge of the antique artists, Caroline illuminators began to copy these images with sometimes uneven results. The classical heritage was revived as accurate drawing and illusionistic techniques were mastered by some illuminators. Figurative imagery and ornament, which had been scrambled together in earlier medieval illumination, became separate and distinct design elements.

In a manuscript book such as the *Coronation Gospels,* designed and produced at the court of Charlemagne in the late eighth century, a dignified classical elegance emerges. In the beginning of each gospel, the figure of the author sits in a natural landscape on a page of deep crimson stained parchment. The facing page is stained a deep purple and has gold lettering. These two facing pages are unified by their exactly equal margins. The initial letters echo Roman monumental capitals, and the text appears to be closely based on the insular script of Ireland. Furthermore, supplementary materials including chapter lists, introductory words, and prefaces are lettered in rustic capitals. Whether this book was designed, lettered, and illuminated by scribes brought in from Italy, Greece, or Constantinople is not known. The creators of this book had a precocious understanding of both the lettering styles and painting techniques of classical culture. (Legend claims that in the year 1000 Emperor Otto III (980–1002) of the Holy Roman Empire journeyed to Aachen, and while he was there he opened the tomb of Charlemagne and found the Emperor seated on a throne with the *Coronation Gospels* on his lap.)

Spanish pictorial expressionism

On the Spanish peninsula, surrounded by oceans and isolated from the rest of Europe by mountains, the scriptoria did not experience the initial impact of the Caroline renewal. In 711 A.D., a Moorish army under the Arab governor of Tangier crossed the Straits of Gibraltar and smashed the Spanish army. Even the Spanish King was among the missing-in-action. Moorish settlers brought an Islamic presence that mingled with Christian traditions to create unique manuscript designs during the medieval period.

A number of Islamic design ideas filtered into Spanish Christian manuscripts. Flat shapes of intense color were used. Sometimes they were sprinkled with stars, rosettes, polygons, or garlands in optically active contrasting colors. Flat, schematic drawing had prominent outlines. The two-dimensional aggressive color created a frontal intensity that obliterated any hint of atmosphere or illusion. A pagan tradition of totemlike animals dates back through Islamic northern Africa to Persia to ancient Mesopotamia, and these ghastly creatures reared their frightful heads in Spanish illumination. Decorative frames enclosed most illustrations with intricate patterns evoking the richly colored geometric designs applied to Moorish architecture in tilework, and molded and chiseled decorations.

Great delight was taken in designs of intricate geometry and intense pure color. In the commemorative labyrinth from Pope Gregory's *Moralia in Iob* (*Commentary on Job*) of 945 A.D., the scribe Florentius designed a *labyrinth page* bearing the words "Florentius indignum memorare" which modestly asks the reader to "remember the unworthy Florentius." The humility of Florentius' message is incongruous with the dazzling graphic treatment and his decision to put his full-page labyrinth opposite the monogram of Christ. The labyrinth arrangement of commemorative messages dates to ancient Greece and Rome and was quite popular in medieval manuscripts.

For the medieval faithful, life on earth was but a prelude to eternal salvation, if the individual could triumph in the battle between good and evil being raged on earth. Supernatural explanations were still assigned to natural phenomena that were not understood; eclipses, earthquakes, plague, and famine were seen as dire warnings and punishments. It was believed that a terrible destruction awaited the earth, and this tragic end was encouraged by the Biblical Book of Revelation which foretold a horrible doomsday. Revelation suggested a

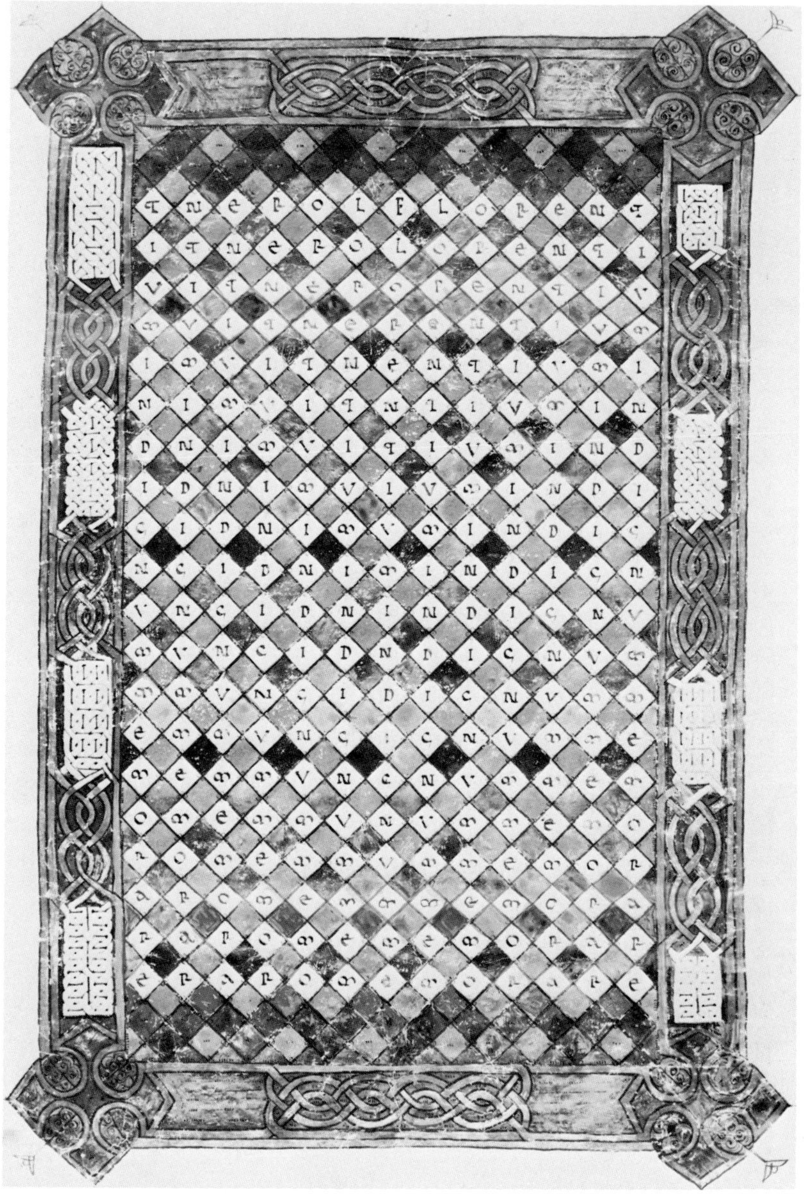

Commemorative labyrinth from *Moralia in Iob,* 945 A.D. Starting in the center of the top line, the inscription reads down, left, and right establishing a labyrinth of letterforms. The checkered diamonds are bright yellow, red, orange, and purple. *Biblioteca Nacional, Madrid.*

date, "When the thousand years had expired . . . ," as a likely time for the last judgment. This led many individuals to consider the year 1000 A.D. as the probable end of the world, and concern mounted as the year drew nigh. A number of interpretations of Revelation were written. Most potent and widely read was *The Commentary of Beatus on the Apocalypse of Saint John the Divine.* The monk Beatus (730–798 A.D.) of Liebana in northern Spain wrote this harrowing interpretation in 776 A.D. In numerous copies penned and illustrated throughout Spain, graphic artists were called upon to give visual form to the fearful events of the end of the world. The monastic dictum, *Pictura est laicorum literatura* ("The picture is the layman's literature"), evidences the concern for conveying information to the illiterate citizenry that prompted the creation of illustrations. Combining Christian prophecy with Moorish design influences, they succeeded admirably. Revelation is laced with rich, imaginative imagery, and in designing copies of Beatus' commentary, scrittori gave pictures an importance that rivaled the text. Full-page illustrations appeared frequently.

The twenty-three surviving copies of Beatus' commentary represent a high-water mark of graphic expressionism. Over sixty different passages have been illustrated in the surviving copies. Stark, symbolic imagery challenged the artist's mind as Beatus' interpretation of this prophecy was visualized. This is the most forceful interpretation of the Apocalypse in graphic art before Albrecht Dürer's intricate woodcut illustrations in the early 1500s.

On New Year's Eve, 999 A.D., people all over Europe gathered to await the final judgment. It is reported that many spent the night naked on their cold rooftops waiting for the end. When nothing happened, new interpretations of the "thousand years" phrase were made, and manuscript copies of Beatus' *Commentary* continued to be produced. In the masterful *Beatus of Fernando and Sancha* of 1047 A.D., the scribe and illuminator Facundus drew schematic figures acting out the final tragedy in a hot and airless space created by flat horizontal bands of pure hue. The thick color is bright and clear. Chrome yellow, cobalt blue, red ocher, and intense green are slammed together in jarring contrasts. The Four Horsemen of the Apocalypse, which are traditionally war, famine, pestilence, and death, ride forth in front of blue, yellow, orange, and tan stripes to unleash their terror upon the world.

A passage in Revelation tells that "the fourth angel sounded, and the third part of the sun was smitten, and the third part of the moon, and the third part of the stars, so as the third part of them was darkened, and the day shown not for a third part of it, and the night likewise." (Rev. 8:12.) The illuminator pushed the angel to the left in a space structured with bands of intense blue, yellow, and red. The sun (labeled "sol") and the moon (labeled "luna") are pie-charts that are one-third white and two-thirds red to illustrate that one-third had fallen away. Finally, a sinister eagle flies into the space screaming "Woe, woe, woe to those who dwell on the earth . . . ." Angel and eagle bear wings with feathers as sharp and menacing as daggers. As an iconic symbol, the angels in the *Beatus* illustrations are worlds away from the pure white angel of hope found in later Christian imagery. Inspired by the words from the Apocalypse, "I am the alpha and the omega, the beginning and the end," Facundus designed the first page of the *Beatus of Fernando and Sancha* as a huge illuminated *A* (alpha, the first letter of the Greek alphabet), and the last page as a huge illuminated *O* (omega, the last letter of the Greek alphabet).

During the early eleventh century A.D., the balance of power in Spain swung away from the Moors and toward the Christians. Communications with other European countries improved, and Spanish graphic design tilted toward the continental mainstream that developed from the Caroline style. The expressionistic style that filled Bibles, commentaries, and most especially the *Commentary of Beatus* faded from fashion.

The Four Horsemen of the Apocalypse from *The Beatus of Fernando and Sancha,* 1047 A.D. Unlike the usual interpretations, Beatus' commentary saw the first horseman—being crowned by an angel—as an envoy of God whose arrows pierce the heart of nonbelievers. The demon at lower right is bright blue against an orange background. *Biblioteca Nacional, Madrid.*

The fourth angel from *The Beatus of Fernando and Sancha,* 1047 A.D. Wings, tail, and trumpet bring a lively counterpoint of angles to the static bands of color. *Biblioteca Nacional, Madrid.*

Late medieval illuminated manuscripts

The Romanesque period, c. 1000–1150, was a period of renewed religious fervor and even stronger feudalism. Christendom was united in a vigorous effort to conquer the Holy Land through the Crusades. Monasticism reached its peak, and large liturgical books including Bibles, Gospels, and Psalters were produced in the booming scriptoria. For the first time, a universal design style seemed possible as visual ideas traveled back and forth on the pilgrimage routes. The illusionistic revival of the Caroline era was replaced by a new emphasis on linear drawing and a willingness to distort figures to meld with the overall design of the page. The representation of deep space became less important, and figures were placed against backgrounds of gold leaf or textured patterns.

During the middle of the twelfth century, the Romanesque period developed into the Gothic period, which lasted from 1150 until the Renaissance of European culture which began in fourteenth-century Italy. This transitional period saw the power of the feudal lords constrained by reasonable laws. The towns and villages began to grow into cities. Agriculture yielded to international trade as the foundation of political power, and money replaced land as the primary measure of wealth. Europe was slowly rousing from its long centuries of slumber and was preparing to move into a glorious renaissance. Particularly in France and England, monarchy was established by powerful noblemen, and this enabled relatively stable central governments to emerge. Uncertainty and fear had been the daily companions of medieval peoples for centuries. During the Gothic period, the social and economic environment became more predictable, replacing the wildly inconsistent conditions that still prevailed in Romanesque times.

During the 1200s, the rise of the universities created a demand for books that expanded the market. Of the hundred thousand residents of Paris, for example, twenty thousand were students who had flocked to the city to attend the university. Literacy was on the rise.

The Book of Revelation had a surge of unexplained popularity in England and France during the 1200s. A scriptorium at St. Albans with high artistic standards seems to have figured prominently in this development. At least ninety-three copies of the *Apocalypse* survive from this period. The horror and anxiety of the earlier Spanish editions is replaced with a straight forward naturalism anchored in this world rather than a future one.

textur

The *Douce Apocalypse,* written and illustrated around 1265, is one of the many masterpieces of the Gothic style. Each of a hundred illustrated pages (three are now missing) has an illustration at the top with two columns of beautifully lettered text below. The scribe used the *textur* style of lettering, which looks like a picket fence with its rigid repetition of verticals capped with pointed serifs. This style was quite functional, for all the vertical strokes in a word were drawn first, then the scribe would add the serifs and other strokes needed to transform the group of verticals into a word. Rounded strokes are almost eliminated, and the letters and the spaces between them are condensed in an effort to save space on the precious parchment. The overall effect is one of a dense black texture. On every page, an open square is left in the upper left-hand corner for an initial, but these were never added. Illustrations that were drawn but never painted show an even line of great sensitivity and decisiveness. The illustrations are divided into segments by elaborate framing. In the illustration for the last passage of the seventh chapter of Revelation, the triumphant white-robed multitude who survived the great tribulation are shown surrounding a very human-looking God with his Lamb. St. John's soft blue robe and rust brown cloak set the tone for a mellow palette of blues, greens, reds, browns, grays, and yellows.

The *Douce Apocalypse* is one of a new breed of picture books that established the graphic design approach of the fifteenth-century woodblock books after printing came to Europe. The scribe and illuminator are not known; in fact, scholars have argued over whether the *Douce Apocalypse* was created in England or France. This blurring of national origin evidences the trend toward an *international Gothic style,* which pervaded the late Gothic period. It is characterized by elongated figures that rise upward in a vertical movement, often wearing elegant fashionable costumes or flowing robes. It is a style of increasing naturalism. Even though the figures are pulled upward, there is a conviction of solid, almost monumental weight and an expression of human dignity. Elements from the national styles of various countries were combined, and increased commissions for private books, particularly from royal patrons, enabled scribes and illuminators to travel and disseminate artistic conventions and techniques.

Liturgical books of the late medieval era contained incredible designs. The *Ormesby Psalter,* designed and produced during the early 1300s in England, is a stunning example. Its generous 33.6-centimeter (about 13 ½-inch) height allows for illustrated capital initials containing biblical scenes with gold-leaf backgrounds. The large text is written in the textur writing style, which was sometimes called black letter in England. The text area is surrounded by an intricate frame filled with decorative patterns,

The multitude worshiping God from the *Douce Apocalypse,* c. 1265. In many of the images, St. John, the roving reporter of the final doom, is shown at the left of the scene peering curiously into the rectangular image. *The Bodleian Library, Oxford.*

Ost hec uidi turbam mag
nam quam dinumerare
nemo poterat ex omnib; gentibus
et tribub; ⁊ p̄plis et linguis. stan
tes ante thronum in conspectu
agni amicti stolis albis ⁊ palme
in manib; eorum. et clamabant
uoce magna dicentes. Salus deo
nostro qui sedet super thronum et
agno. Et omnes angli stabant i
circuitu throni ⁊ ceciderunt ⁊ adora
uerunt deum dicentes. amen. Ben
dictio ⁊ claritas ⁊ sapiencia ⁊ gra
rum actio. honor ⁊ uirtus ⁊ fortitu
do deo nr̄o in scl'a scl'orum. amen.

Et respondens unus de senioribus
dicens michi. Hii sunt qui amic
ti stolis albis qui sunt ⁊ unde ue
nerunt. Et dixit illi. Dn̄e mi tu
scis. Et dixit m̄. Hii sunt q̄ ue
nerūt ex magna tribulatione sto
las suas ⁊ deallbauerunt eas ī san
guine agni. Ideo sunt ante thro
num dei ⁊ seruiunt ei die ac noc
te. in templo eī. Et qui sedet super
thronum habitabit super eos. Nō
esurient neq; sicient amplius n; ca
det s' eos sol nec ullus estus. qm̄ agnus
qui ī medio troni ē reget eos ⁊ deducet
illos ad fontes aq̄rum ⁊ absterget d's om̄em
lacrimam ab oculis eorum.

8 [E]t cum aperuisset sigillum
septimum factum est silen
cium in celo quasi media hora. Et
uidi septem angelos stantes in
conspectu dei et date sunt illis sep
tem tube. Apertio septimi sigilli ad nati
uitatem pertinet xpi. Sed querendum nobis est cur in septimo et non in quinto lo
co ponatur. In genesi scriptum est quia sex diebus
fecit deus cuncta que ex celo et terra originem sum
pserunt. septimo autem requieuit. Ideirco uocauit
diem septimum sabbatum. id est requiem.
Quid est autem requies nostra
nisi xpc. Non inconuenienter ergo
in septima sigilli apertione nati
uitas xpi ponitur. quia ipse requies
omnium sanctorum que per sep
timum diem figuratur. et cetera.

Et quia in ea que in natiuitate xpi gesta sunt
spiritalem intelligentiam optinent. Septimum
sigillum xpc aperuit cum ea que per significationem
gesta sunt doctoribus ecclesie per inspirati
onem spiritus sancti manifestauit. Fac
tum est silencium in celo quasi
media hora. per silencium pax que
ab octouiano augusto xpo nascen
te per uniuersum orbem facta est
designatur. Media autem hora silen
cium factum est. quia pax
quam ecclesia in initio fidei apud paganos habuit
pauco tempore mansit. Nam a nerone imperato
re interrupta est et petro pauloque interfectis prece
pit omnes perse
qui xpianos. Et uidi septem an
gelos stantes in conspectu dei et da
te sunt illis septem tube. Or
do istorum septem angelorum in
sequentibus est. Nam sicut predictum est et cetera.

capital initials, and rich marginalia which are thought to be visual clues suggesting appropriate parables and stories to the priest after he completes the scriptural reading to the congregation. The page illustrated has an owl/horse conferring with a man/snail at the top. At the bottom, a demon smugly watches a betrothal. The young maiden eagerly reaches for the falconer's engagement ring; the symbolic cat and mouse below the couple hint that someone is being victimized. The everyday life of the people had found its way into the margins of religious books. Some historians have seen this as an indication of the first promise of the coming humanism of the Renaissance with its concern for the quality of human life on earth.

The Christian faith did not have a monopoly on illuminated manuscripts, for parallel graphic traditions evolved among followers of the Hebrew and Islamic religions. Hebrew illuminated manuscripts are rare, but the ones that have survived are jewels of graphic design. In the *Darmstadt Haggādāh,* a dense black calligraphy and dominance of browns and other earth tones give a weighty elegance to the volume. The large, decorated initials become focal points for the pages. Drawings of figures, animals, and birds are executed with great sensitivity.

Perhaps even more than Christians and Jews, people of the Muslim faith are devoted to their sacred books. The relationship of calligraphy to the Prophet Mohammed's Koran made calligraphy the Islamic world's major artform. The finest Muslim manuscripts were designed during the sixteenth century. In the Persian Empire (centered in the present country of Iran), the ruling Shahs patronized the creation of shimmering pages of great beauty and intricacy. The production of illuminated manuscripts for private use had become increasingly important. By the late medieval period of the early 1400s, the *Book of Hours* had become the most popular book. This private devotional book contained religious texts for each hour of the day, prayers, and calendars listing the days of important Saints. The pinnacle of the illuminated book was reached in the early fifteenth century when a passionate lover of beautiful books, the French nobleman and brother of King Charles V, Jean, Duc de Berry (1340–1416), who owned a vast portion of central France, installed the Limbourg brothers of Dutch origin in his castle to establish a private scriptorium. Little is known about the brief lives of Paul, Herman, and Jean Limbourg. It is believed that all three were born after 1385. Sons of a Dutch wood sculptor, all three apprenticed as goldsmiths, then probably trained at an important Paris scriptorium after 1400. The Duc de

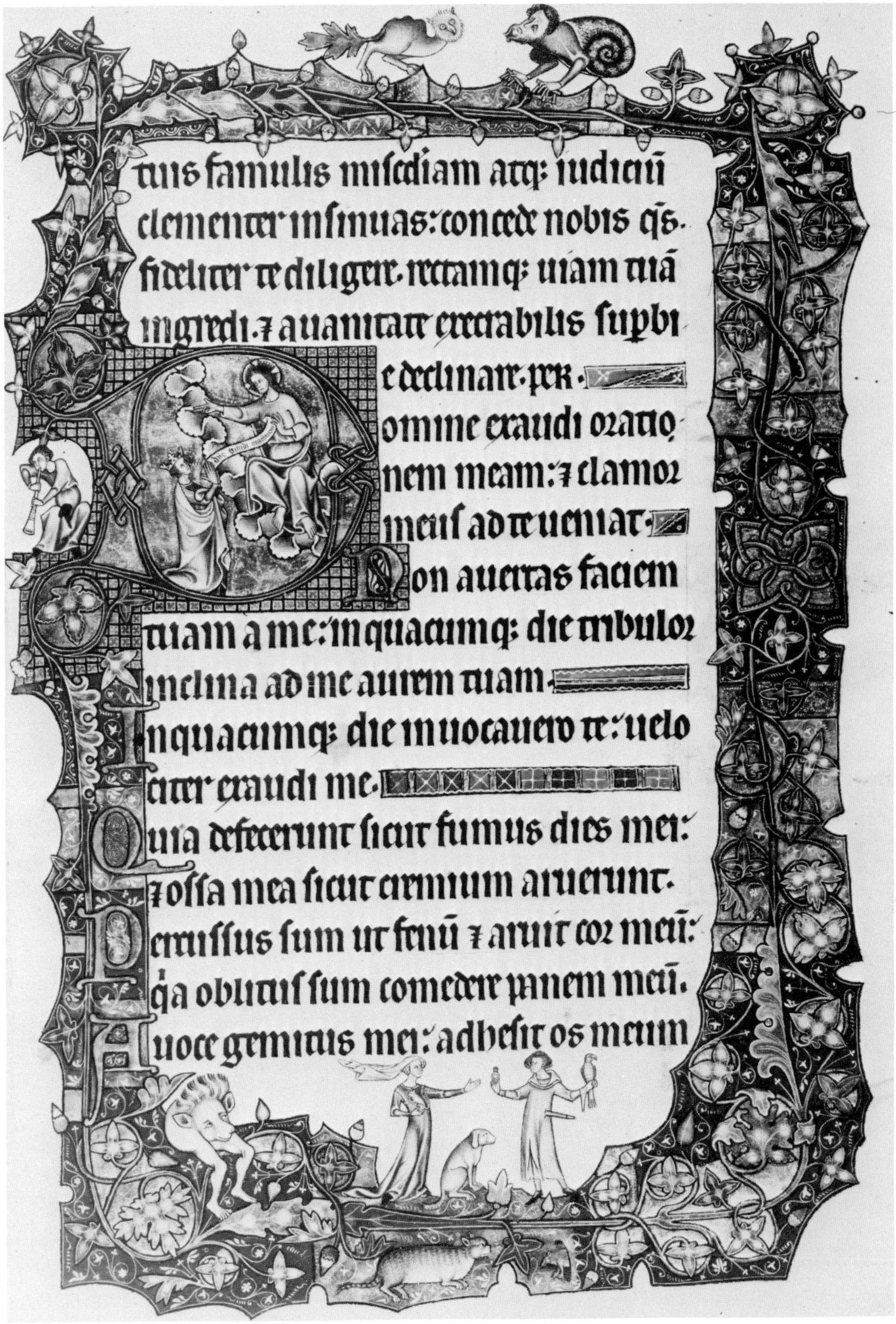

Page from the *Ormesby Psalter,* c. early fourteenth century. A bright red and blue color scheme dominates the ornaments and illustrations of this and other late-Gothic English manuscripts. *The Bodleian Library, Oxford.*

Berry employed Paul Limbourg in 1408 to head his workshop. Paul was probably the designer responsible for layout and page design.

The Duc de Berry, whose library of one hundred fifty-five books including fourteen Bibles and fifteen *Books of Hours,* owned one of the largest private libraries in the world at that time. He followed the design and execution of each page with keen interest. Apparently a close rapport developed between patron and designer/illustrators, for on New Year's Day of 1411 the Limbourg brothers gave the Duc a bogus book consisting of a wooden block bound in white velvet and locked with an enameled clasp decorated with the Duc's coat of arms.

In the early fifteenth century, the Limbourgs were the avant-garde of the evolution toward the interpretation of visual experience. The Gothic tendency toward abstraction and stylized presentation was reversed. The Limbourgs sought a convincing realism. Atmospheric perspective was used to push planes and volumes back in deep space, and a consistent effort toward linear perspective was made. The Limbourgs' exceptional gifts of observation combined with remarkable painting skill to enable them to propel book design and illustration to its zenith. There is a strong sense of mass and volume, and in some illustrations, highlights and cast shadows are created by a single light source.

The Limbourg brothers' masterpiece is *Les Tres Riches Heures du Duc de Berry* which was produced between 1413 and 1416. The first twenty-four pages are an illustrated calendar. Each month has a double-page spread with an genre illustration relating to seasonal activities of the month on the left-hand page and a calendar of the saints' days on the right-hand page. Each month's miniature painting is crowned with a graphic astronomical chart depicting constellations and the phases of the moon. The winter farm scene for February includes a cutaway building with people warming themselves by the fire. The calendar page lists the saints' days and uses vibrant red and blue inks for the lettering. A pencil grid structure establishes the format containing the information.

In the pages with prayers and scriptures, layouts are built around illustrations contained in gold outlines. Circular extensions to the rectangular illustrations were a favorite design device. On many pages, a mere four lines of text are lettered in two columns aligned under the illustrations. Decorated initials spin off whirling acanthus foliage which is sometimes accompanied by angels, animals, or flowers in the generous margins. Ap-

Page from the *Darmstadt Haggādāh*, c. 1420. This masterpiece of Hebrew illumination has exquisitely drawn birds and animals, well-formed calligraphy in the Hebrew alphabet, and superb initials contained in earth-toned plaques. *Courtesy, Hessische Landes- und Hochschulbibliothek, Darmstadt.*

Pages from a Persian manuscript Koran, c. sixteenth century. This Islamic manuscript has the intricate floral and geometric patterns with interlocked positive and negative areas associated with architectural decorations and carpets designed in Muslim countries. *Museum of Fine Arts, Boston, Ross Collection.*

prentices were kept busy grinding colors on a marble slab with a muller. The medium was water mixed with arabic or tragacanth gum as a binder to adhere the pigment to the vellum and preserve the image. The Limbourg brothers used a palette of ten colors plus black and white. These included cobalt and ultramarine blue and two greens, one made from a carbonate of copper, the other from iris leaves. Gold-leaf and gold-powder paint were used in profusion. The minute detail achieved implies that a magnifying lens might have been used for painting detail.

The Limbourg brothers did not live to complete this masterpiece, for all three died before February of 1416, and the Duc de Berry died on 15 July 1416, perhaps the victims of a terrible epidemic or plague which is believed to have swept through France that year. The inventory of the Duc de Berry's library taken after his death indicates that half his books were religious works, and a third were history books, with geography, astronomy, and astrology volumes rounding out the collection. During the same years that the Limbourgs were working on their great graphic designs, a new means of visual communication—woodblock printing—was appearing in Europe. The invention of movable type in the West was but three decades away. The production of illuminated manuscripts continued through the fifteenth century and even into the early decades of the sixteenth century, but this thousand-year-old craft dating back to antiquity was doomed to eventual extinction with the coming of the typographic book.

The Limbourg Brothers, The Annunciation from *Les Tres Riches Heures du Duc de Berry,* 1413–16. Bearing a white lily and a scroll containing his message, the angel Gabriel calls upon the Virgin Mary in her Gothic chapel. *Musée Conde, Chantilly. (Photograph: Giraudon)*

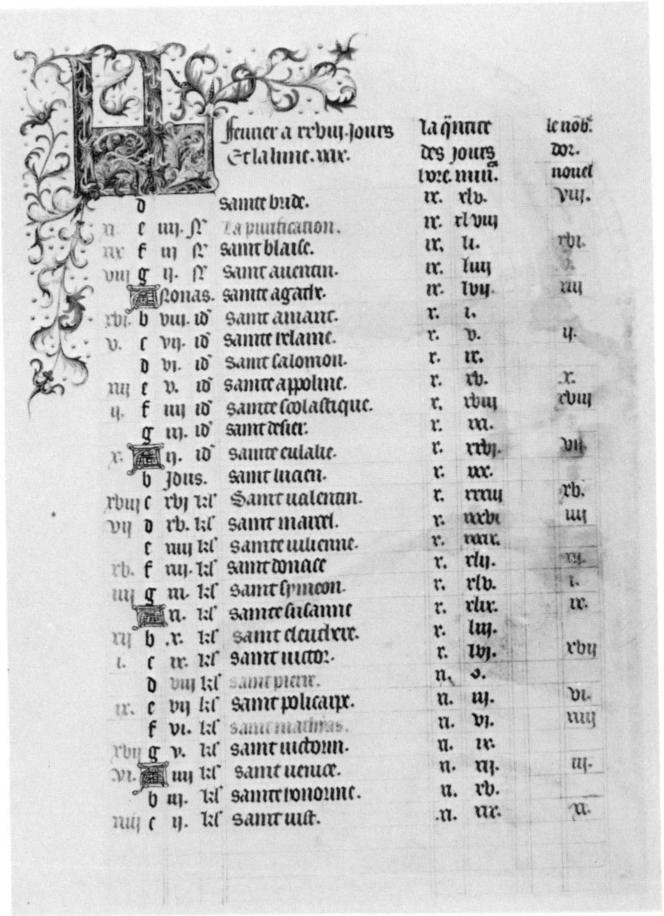

Feurier a xxviij jours
Et la lune xxix.

The Limbourg Brothers, February pages from *Les Tres Riches Heures du Duc de Berry,* 1413–16. Both pictorial and written information are presented with clarity indicating a high level of observation and visual organization. *Musée Conde, Chantilly. (Photograph: Giraudon)*

PART II

ORIGINS: *The origins of printing and typography in Europe and the design of the printed page*

6

Printing Comes to Europe

Xylotypography is the technical term for the relief printing from a raised surface that originated in the Orient. *Typography* is the term for printing through the use of independent, movable, and reusable bits of metal, each of which has a raised letterform on its top. This dry definition belies the immense potential for human dialogue and the new horizons for graphic design, that were unleashed by this extraordinary invention in the mid-1400s by a restless German experimenter whose portrait and signature are lost to the relentless passage of time. Some historians have declared the invention of typography to be the most important advance in civilization after the creation of writing. Writing gave the human family a means of storing, retrieving, and documenting knowledge and information that transcended time and place. Typographic printing allowed the economical and multiple production of alphabet communication. Knowledge spread rapidly, and literacy increased as a result of this remarkable invention.

Several factors created a climate in Europe that made typography feasible. The demand for books had become insatiable as Europe was slowly aroused from the medieval era into the Renaissance. The emerging literate middle class and students in the rapidly expanding universities had snatched the monopoly on literacy from the clergy, creating a vast new market for reading material. The slow and expensive process of bookmaking had changed little in one thousand years. A simple two-hundred-page book required four or five months' labor by a scribe, and the twenty-five sheepskins needed for the parchment were even more expensive than his labor.

In 1424 the university at Cambridge had only one hundred twenty-two manuscript books in its library, and the library of a wealthy nobleman whose books were his most prized and sought-after possessions would probably number less than two dozen volumes. The value of a book was equal to the value of a farm or vineyard. The steady growth of demand had led independent merchants to develop an assembly-line division of labor with specialists trained in lettering, decorative initialing, gold ornamentation, proofreading, and binding. Even this exploding production of manuscript books was unable to meet the demand.

Papermaking had completed a long, slow journey from China to Europe, so a plentiful substrate was available. Over six hundred years passed before papermaking, which spread westward following caravan routes from the Pacific Ocean to the Mediterranean Sea, reached the Arab world. After repelling a Chinese attack on the city of Samarkand in 751 A.D., the Arab occupation forces captured some Chinese papermakers. Abundant water and bountiful crops of flax and hemp enabled Samarkand to become a papermaking center, and the craft spread to Baghdad, Damascus, and reached Egypt by the tenth century. From there, it spread across North Africa and was introduced into Sicily in 1102 and into Spain by the Moors during the middle of the twelfth century. By 1276 a paper mill was established in Fabriano, Italy. Troyes, France, had a paper mill in 1348. Without paper, the speed and efficiency of printing would have been useless.

The watermark, a translucent emblem produced by pressure from a raised design on the mold and visible when the sheet of paper is held to the light, was first used in Italy in 1282. The origin of this design device is unknown. Trademarks for paper mills, individual craftsmen, and perhaps religious symbolism were early uses. As successful marks were imitated, they began to be used as a designation for sheet and mold sizes and paper grade. Mermaids, unicorns, animals, flowers, and heraldic shields were frequent design motifs.

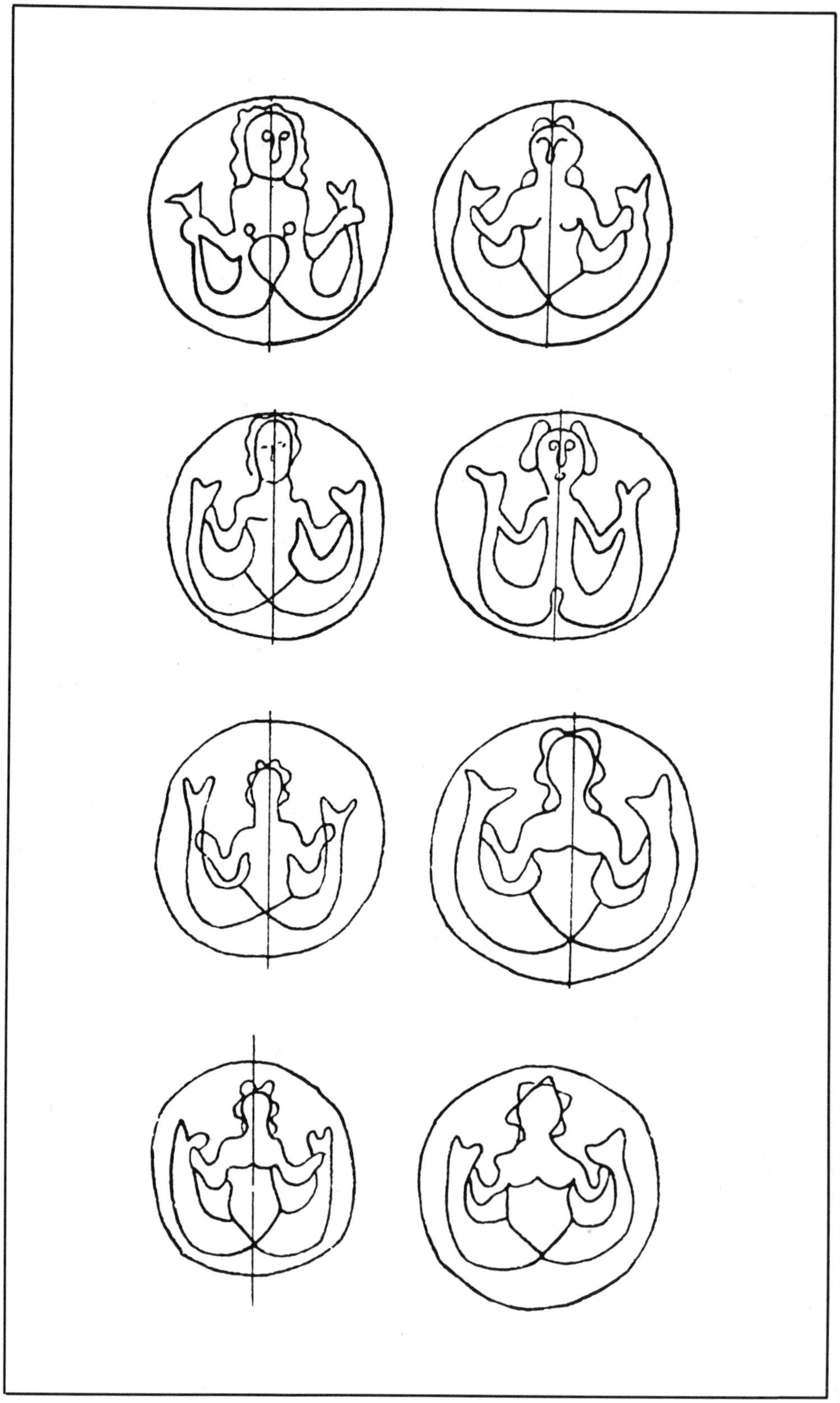

French watermark designs, fifteenth century. These mermaid designs were produced by bent wire attached to the mold used in making paper.

Early European block printing

The origins of woodblock printing in Europe are shrouded in mystery. Because the Crusades had opened Europe to an eastern influence, relief printing arrived on the heels of paper; playing cards and religious-image prints were early manifestations. Circumstantial evidence implies that, like paper, relief printing from woodblocks had also spread westward from China. By the early 1300s pictorial designs were being printed on textiles in Europe. Card playing was popular, and in spite of being outlawed and denounced by zealous churchmen, this pastime stimulated a thriving underground block-printing industry, probably before 1400.

In 1415 the Duke of Milan played cards with images painted on ivory plates by famous artists, and Flemish nobles used engraved silver plates. Throughout Europe, the working class gathered in taverns and by the roadside to play with grimy cards that were block-printed and stenciled on coarse paper. The first graphic designs to move into an illiterate culture, these cards are the earliest manifestation of printings' democratizing ability in Europe, for the games of kings could now become the games of peasants and craftsmen. As these cards introduced the masses to symbol recognition, sequencing, and logical deduction, their intrinsic value transcended idle entertainment.

The first known European block printing with a communications function were devotional prints of saints ranging from small images that will fit in a person's hand to larger images of 25 by 35 centimeters (about 10 by 14 inches). Image and lettering were cut from the same block of wood. These early graphic designs evolved into the *block books,* which were woodcut picture books with religious subject matter and brief text. Each page was cut from a block of wood and printed as a complete word and picture unit. Since most of the few surviving copies were printed in the Netherlands after 1460, it is not known whether the block book preceded the typographic book. Drawn in a simplified illustration style, with the visual elements dominant as in contemporary comic books, the block book was used for religious instruction of illiterates. This form gradually declined during the fifteenth century as literacy increased. Common subjects included the Apocalypse, a forewarning of the final doom and destruction of the

Jack of Diamonds, woodblock playing card, c. 1400. The flat, stylized design conventions of playing cards have changed little in over five hundred years. Visual signs to designate the suits began as the four classes of medieval society. Hearts symbolized the clergy; spades (derived from *spada,* "sword," in Italy) stood for the nobility; the leaflike club represented the peasantry; and diamonds signified the burghers.

Woodblock print of St. Christopher, 1423. The unknown illustrator depicted the legendary saint, a giant who carried travelers safely across a river, bearing the infant Christ. The inscription below reads: "In whatsoever day thou seest the likeness of St. Christopher/In that same day thou wilt at least from death no evil blow incur/ 1423." One of the earliest dated European block prints, this image has an effective use of changing contour-line width to show form. The relative scale of the three peasants is absurd.

Blockprint of The Annunciation, undated. The black area between the angel and Virgin becomes an effective focal point and serves to unify the two figures. The scroll, with a Latin inscription, serves the same communicative function as a "talk balloon." (The upper left-hand corner of this print is missing.)

Block-book page from *The Story of the Blessed Virgin,* 1400s. This page attempts to justify the Immaculate Conception by a series of "logical" parallels: If the light of Venus' temple cannot be extinguished, if the moon is reflected in water, if a person can be changed into stone, and if man can be painted on stone, why should not the Blessed Virgin be able to generate?

Letter *K* from a Grotesque Alphabet, c. 1464. This page from a twenty-four page, abecedarium block-book presented each letter of the alphabet by composing figures into the shape of the letter.

Ex Libris design for Johannes Knabensberg, c. 1450s. One of the earliest extant bookplates, it bears an inscription, "Hans Igler that the hedgehog may kiss you." (Igler, his nickname, derives from the Germanic *hedgehog*.) Apparently the inscription threatens the potential thief.

world. *Ars Moriendi* (art of dying) advised one on the preparation and meeting of the final hour. In a Europe that had been decimated by the great cycles of plague, called the black death, which claimed one-fourth of the population during the fourteenth century and caused a thousand villages to either totally vanish or be critically depopulated, death was an ever present preoccupation.

In the *Ars Moriendi* shown, eleven illustrations depict the temptation of the devil and the comfort of the angel on subjects such as faith, impatience, vainglory, and the final hour of death. Thirteen pages are block-print text. While the apparent raison d'être of the *Ars Moriendi* was to help people meet death, it must be considered as one of the first examples of printed propaganda (dissemination of ideas, information, arguments, or allegations to help or injure a cause, person, or institution), for it urges the dying to put aside the desire to provide for one's family and to will the estate to the church. *Biblia Pauperum* (bible of the poor) was a compendium of events in the life of Christ including testimony about how Old Testament prophecy was fulfilled.

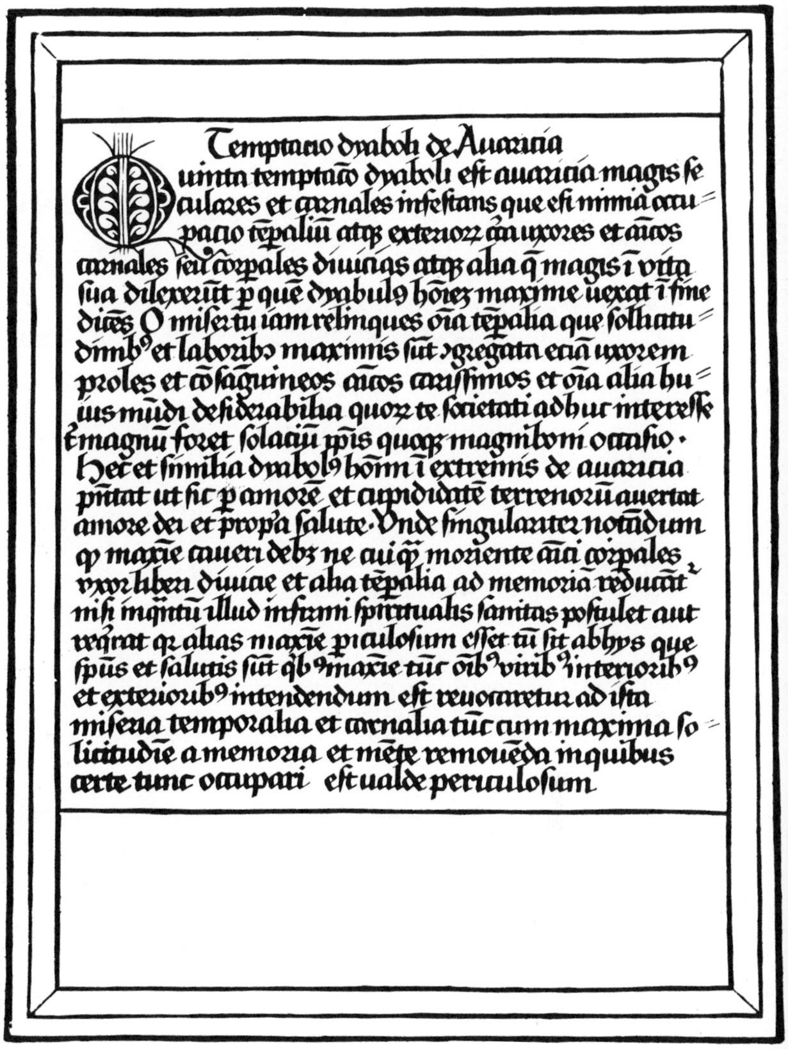
Temptacio dyaboli de Auaricia
Quinta temptacio dyaboli est auaricia magis se
culares et carnales infestans que est nimia occu=
pacio tepalium atque exteriorum quantum uxores et amicos
carnales seu corporales diuicias atque alia q magis i vita
sua dilexerunt p quem dyabulus hoiem maxime uexat i fine
dicens O miser tu iam relinques oia tepalia que sollicitu=
dinib9 et laboribus maximis sunt congregata eciam uxorem
proles et consanguineos amicos carissimos et oia alia hu=
ius mundi desiderabilia quorum te societati adhuc interesse
magnum foret solacium ipsis quoque magni boni occasio ·
Hec et similia dyabol9 homini i extremis de auaricia
pmitat ut sic p amore et cupiditate terrenorum auertat
amore dei et propria salute · Unde singulariter notandum
q maxime caueri debz ne cuiquam moriente amici corporales
vxor liberi diuicie et alia tepalia ad memoriam reducantur
nisi inquantum illud infirmi spiritualis sanitas postulet aut
requirat quia alias maxime periculosum esset tum sit ab hys que
spus et salutis sunt qb9 maxime tunc oib9 virib9 interiorib9
et exteriorib9 intendendum est reuocaretur ad ista
miseria temporalia et carnalia tunc cum maxima so=
licitudine a memoria et mente remouenda in quibus
certe tunc occupari est ualde periculosum

Pages from *Ars Moriendi,* 1466. In the illustration, a tight montage effect is achieved by juxtaposing the deathbed scene with a view of the subject's estate. One demon urges, "Provide for your friends," while the other advises, "Attend to your treasures." The densely textured text page suggests that one's earthly goods should be given to the church. *Library of Congress, Washington, D.C., Rosenwald Collection.*

Most block books contained from thirty to fifty leaves. In addition to hand coloring and the use of stencils to apply flat areas of color to textile, playing card, and later block-book woodcuts, some fifteenth century prints exist where woodblocks were used to print paste or gum, sprinkled with tinsel (minute sparkling fragments of metal), incrustation (minute quartz crystals with color), or flocking (powdered wool). These were used as design elements to bring a vibrant tactile quality and luminosity to the image. The earliest block books were printed with a hand rubber in brown or gray ink; later versions were printed in black ink on a printing press. Because the hand rubber created too much indention to allow double-sided printing, the earliest block books are only printed on one side of the paper. Each double-page spread was followed by two blank pages which were usually pasted together to preserve the visual flow of images and text. While the monastic designer might also cut his own woodblock, in the secular world the distinction between *designer* and *cutter* (*formschneider*) was vigorously upheld by trade guilds. The cutters who worked from the designer's ink layout on either paper or woodblock were often members of carpentry guilds.

Movable typography in Europe

With the availability of paper, relief printing from woodblocks, and the growing demand for books, the mechanization of book production by means such as movable type was sought by printers in Germany, the Netherlands, France, and Italy. In Avignon, France, goldsmith Procopius Waldfoghel was involved in the production of "alphabets of steel" around 1444, but with no known results. The Dutchman Laurens Janszoon Coster of Haarlem allegedly explored the concept of movable type by cutting out letters or words from his woodblocks for reuse. The judgment of history, however, is that Johann

Gensfleisch zum Gutenberg (c. 1387–1468) of Mainz, Germany, brought together the complex systems and subsystems necessary to print a typographic book around the year 1550. The third son of the wealthy Mainz patrician Friele Gensfleisch, Johann Gutenberg apprenticed as a goldsmith, developing the metalworking and engraving skills necessary for making type. In September 1428, he was exiled from Mainz for his leadership role in a power struggle between the landed noblemen and the burghers of the trade guilds who sought a greater political voice. He relocated in Strasbourg, one hundred miles to the southwest, and became a successful and prosperous gem cutter and metalworker.

Early in 1438, Gutenberg formed a contractual partnership with Strasbourg citizens Andreas Dritzehen (who had received gem-cutting training from Gutenberg) and Andreas Heilmann (who owned a paper mill). He agreed to teach them a secret process for making mirrors to sell at an Aachen pilgrimage fair the following year. Mirrors were rare and difficult to manufacture. Molten lead was poured over glass and formed a reflective surface when it cooled. The difficulty was preventing the glass from cracking from the heat. When the fair was postponed until 1440, Gutenberg entered a new five-year contract to teach his partners another secret process.

When Dritzehen died in late 1438, his brothers Georg and Claus sued Gutenberg for either admission to the partnership or a refund. On 12 December 1439, the court ruled in Gutenberg's favor because his original contract specified that only one hundred florins would be paid to any partner's heirs. The record of this trial shows conclusively that Gutenberg was involved in printing. Several witnesses mention that the partners owned a press; woodturner Conrad Saspach testified that he had constructed the press. Testimony mentions type, a stock of lead and other metals, and a mysterious four-piece instrument secured by double hand-screws (probably a type mold). Goldsmith Hans Dünne testified that as early as 1436 he had sold Gutenberg one hundred guilders' worth of material "solely for that which belonged to printing." In the mid-1440s Gutenberg moved back to Mainz, where he resolved the technical, organizational, and production problems that had plagued earlier typographic printing efforts. He had labored for ten years before his first printing and twenty years before printing the forty-two-line Bible. Typographic printing did not grow directly out of block printing because wood was too fragile. Block printing was advantageous for the Chinese

Page from a *Biblia Pauperum,* 1465. In this typical layout, a crosslike architectural structure brings order to a complex page. Bible verses appear in the upper corners; David and three other prophets are above and below with a quotation from each on a scroll. Across the center, the creation of Eve, the Crucifixion of Christ, and Moses striking the rock are shown. The unknown Dutch or German designer of this visual teaching aid packed enough material for a complete sermon on each page. *Library of Congress, Washington, D.C., Rosenwald Collection.*

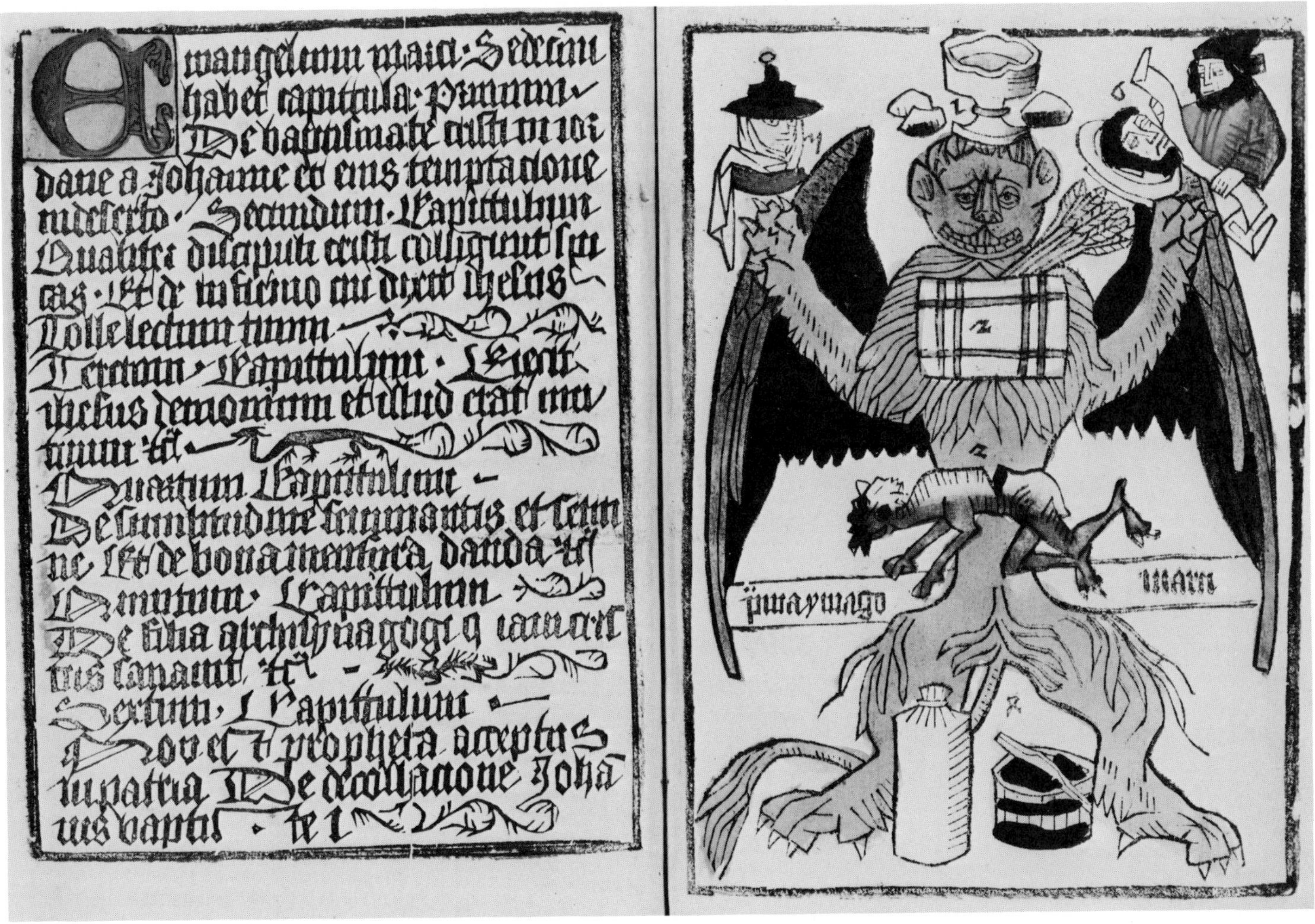

Pages from *Ars memorandi per figuras Evangelistarum,* c. 1470. Fluid washes of watercolor were applied to the block prints in this design, rich in symbolic imagery. *Library of Congress, Washington, D.C., Rosenwald Collection.*

because alignment between characters was not critical and sorting over five thousand basic characters was untenable. By contrast, the need for exact alignment and the modest alphabet system of about two dozen letters made the printing of text material from independent, movable and reusable type highly desirable in the West.

A number of steps were necessary in the creation of typographic printing. A style of letter had to be selected. Gutenberg made the obvious choice of the square, compact textur lettering style commonly used by German scribes of his day. Early printers sought to compete with calligraphers by imitating their work as closely as possible. This "picket fence" style of block letter with no subtle curves was so well developed by Gutenberg that the characters in the forty-two-line Bible are hardly distinguishable from good calligraphy. Next each character in the font—small and capital letters, numbers, punctuation, ligatures—had to be engraved into the top of a steel bar to make a punch. This punch was then driven into a matrix of softer copper or brass to make a negative impression of the letterform.

The key to Gutenberg's invention was the type mold used for casting the individual letters. Each character had to be plane parallel in every direction and the exact same height. Gutenberg's two-part type mold, which adjusted to accept matrixes for narrow characters (*i*) as well as wide ones (*m*), solved the need for casting large volumes of type made to critical tolerances. Type required a metal soft enough to cast but hard enough to hold up for thousands of impressions. It must not expand and contract when it was melted, poured into the type mold, then returned to a solid state as it cooled. As a metalsmith, Gutenberg had learned that antimony would expand when it cooled from a liquid to a solid state, in contrast to most metals which contract when cooled. He developed a unique alloy of 80 percent lead, 5 percent tin, and 15 percent antimony to maintain a constant mass throughout the process of manufacturing type. Gutenberg needed as many as fifty thousand single pieces of type in use at a time, so the speed, accuracy, and economy achieved by this type mold and its casting process were critical. The type was stored in compartmented cases and pulled out letter by letter to set the lines. After a page was printed, the type was returned to the compartments letter by letter.

The medieval block printer used a thin watery ink made from oak gall.

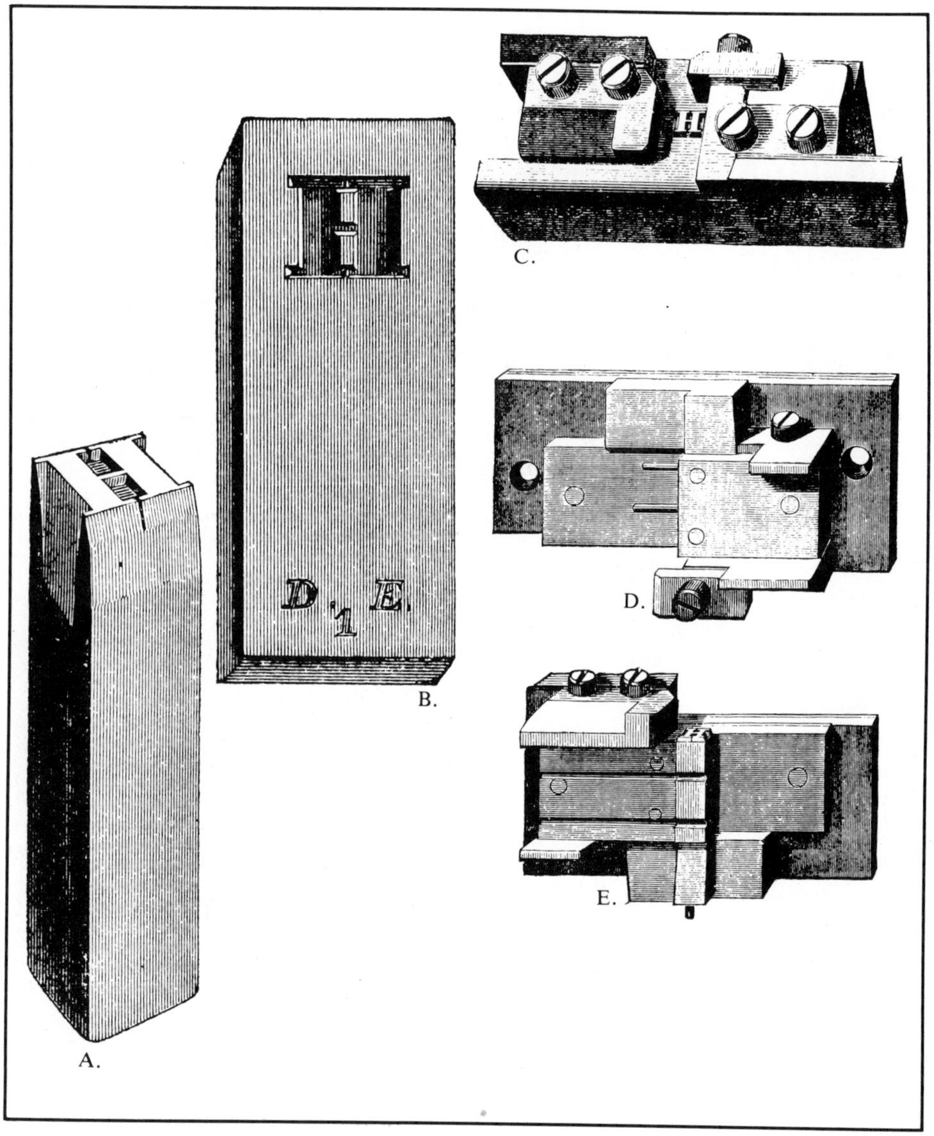

These early 19th Century engravings show Gutenberg's system for casting type. A steel punch is used to stamp an impression of the letterform into a softer brass matrix. After the matrix is slipped into the bottom of the two-part type mold, the mold is filled with the molten lead alloy to cast a piece of type. After the lead alloy cools, the type mold is opened and the type is removed.
A. Punch
B. Matrix
C. Type Mold (with matrix removed to show a newly cast *H*.)
D. & E. Type Mold (opened so that the newly cast *H* can be removed.)

Since the woodblock could absorb excess moisture, this ink worked fine, but it would run off or puddle on metal type. Gutenberg used boiled linseed oil colored with lampblack, which produced a thick, tacky ink that could be smoothly applied. To ink type, a dollop of ink was placed on a flat surface and smeared with a soft leather ball, coating the ball's bottom. The ball was then daubed onto the type to apply an even coating of ink.

A strong, sturdy press capable of sufficient force to pressure the ink from the type onto the paper surface was needed. Ample prototypes existed in presses used in making wine, cheese, and baling paper, and Gutenberg adapted their design, which was based on a large screw lowering and raising a plate, to printing. Gutenberg's press and system were used for four hundred years with moderate improvements. These included a frisket to protect margins and other unprinted areas, modification of the screw to lessen the energy needed to print, and a quick release feature so that less energy was needed to lift the plate than to lower it. Eventually, a mechanical linkage replaced the screw. This precision machine, sometimes underrated, allowed tremendous printing speed and consistent quality in comparison to the hand-rubbing method of the Orient and early European block printers.

Among the assorted surviving examples of early typographic design and printing—a German poem on the Last Judgment, four calendars, and a

Jost Amman, woodcut illustrations for *Ständebuch* ("Book of Trades"), 1568. This little book presented over a hundred occupations, from the Pope to the scissors sharpener. Amman's crisp illustrations were accompanied by prolific poet Hans Sachs' descriptive rhymes. The occupations of the graphic arts are shown here.
A. The parchment maker is shown scraping animal skins to produce a smooth surface after they have been washed, stretched, and dried.
B. The papermaker lifts his mold out of the vat as he forms each sheet by hand.
C. The typefounder is depicted pouring the melted lead into the type mold to cast a character. The foreground basket is filled with newly cast type.
D. One printer is shown removing a newly printed sheet from the press while the other one inks the type. In the background, compositors are shown setting type at typecases.
E. The designer is illustrated as he draws an image in preparation for a woodcut or copper engraving. (This is probably Amman's self-portrait.)
F. The woodblock cutter carefully cuts the drawing or design into a block of wood.
G. The illuminator, who applied gold leaf and color—originally to manuscripts—continued his craft on the typographically printed page.
H. Bookbinders are presented as one collates the pages of a volume by hand. The other prepares a book for the application of the covers.

A.

B.

C.

D.

E.

F.

G.

H.

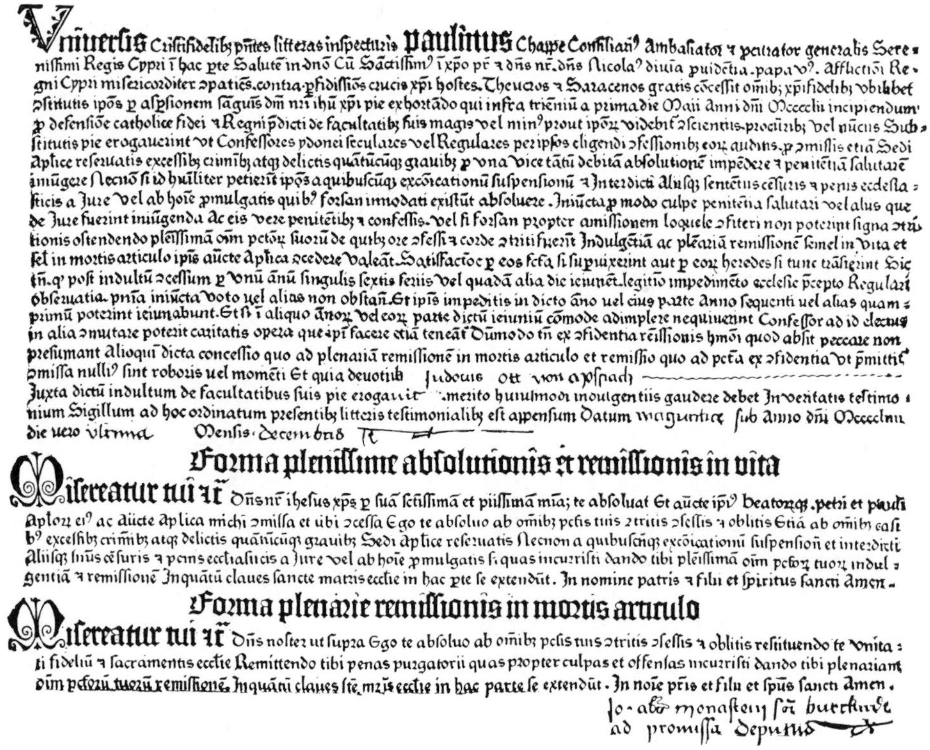
Forma plenissime absolutionis et remissionis in vita

Forma plenarie remissionis in mortis articulo

Johann Gutenberg, thirty-one-line *Letters of Indulgence,* c. 1454. The written additions in this copy indicate that on the last day of December 1454, one Judocus Ott von Apspach was pardoned of his sins.

number of editions of a *Latin Grammar* by Donatus—the earliest *dated* specimens are the 1454 "Letters of Indulgence" issued in Mainz. Pope Nicholas V issued this pardon of sins to all Christians who had given money to support the war against the Turks. Apparently the agents selling manuscript copies early in 1454 learned of Gutenberg's work and realized the value of printing this letter in quantity. Seven editions in two styles were ordered during 1454 and 1455.

Because the relentless expenses of research and development were a constant drain on Gutenberg's financial resources, in 1450 he found it necessary to borrow eight hundred guilders from Johann Fust (c. 1400–1460), a wealthy Mainz burgher and merchant, to continue his work. The printing equipment was offered as collateral. At some point, Gutenberg conceived the idea of printing a Bible. Around 1452 he had to borrow another eight hundred guilders from Fust "for their common profit" establishing a partnership "in the production of books."

A heroic effort was required to produce this first typographic book, which is also one of the finest examples of the printer's art. The large 30-by-40.5 centimeter ($11\frac{3}{4}$ by 16-inch) pages have two columns of type with a generous 2.9 centimeter ($\frac{3}{4}$ inch) margin between them. The first nine pages have forty lines per column, the tenth page has forty-one lines per column, and the rest have forty-two lines per column. It is not known whether Gutenberg followed a manuscript like this or whether he began a forty-line Bible, then increased the number of lines per column for economy. With one thousand two hundred eighty-two pages in a two-volume work, the increase of two lines per column saved an additional sixty pages. This fantastic project began with two presses, which were increased to six presses. With lines of about thirty-three characters, each page had over two thousand five hundred characters set from a font of two hundred ninety different characters. The generous number of alternate characters and ligatures enabled Gutenberg to achieve the richness and variety of the manuscript page. For further enrichment, blank spaces were left for decorative initials to be drawn in later by a scribe. A rigorous justification of the columns was possible because Latin words could be abbreviated freely by up to six letters by the use of abbreviation symbols above the words. The edition of two hundred ten copies consisted of one hundred eighty on paper and thirty on fine vellum requiring five thousand carefully prepared calfskins.

In 1455, as work neared completion, Fust suddenly sued Gutenberg for two thousand twenty-six guilders in payment of loans and interest. On 6 November 1455, the courts ruled in favor of Fust with the requirement that he appear at the local monastery and swear before God that he was paying interest on some of the money he had loaned Gutenberg. Fust appeared and fulfilled the edict of court by taking the oath. Gutenberg did not attend. Instead, he sent two friends to beg Fust to give him more time. Fust found himself in possession of Gutenberg's printing equipment and all work in progress; on the eve of completion of the immensely valuable forty-two-line Bible which would have enabled him to pay all debts, Gutenberg was locked out of his printing shop.

Fust immediately entered into an agreement with Peter Schoeffer (d. 1502), who was Gutenberg's skilled assistant and foreman. An artist/designer experienced as an illuminator and manuscript dealer and a scribe at the University of Paris in 1449, Schoeffer quite possibly played a key role in the format development and type design for the forty-two-line Bible. If so, he may have been the first graphic and typeface designer. With Fust as business manager and Schoeffer in charge of printing, the firm of Fust and Schoeffer became the most important printing firm in the world and established a hundred-year family dynasty of printers, publishers, and booksellers, for Schoeffer married Fust's daughter, Christina, around 1467. The new partnership's first venture was the completion of the forty-two-line Bible. Since one of the forty-seven surviving copies bears a

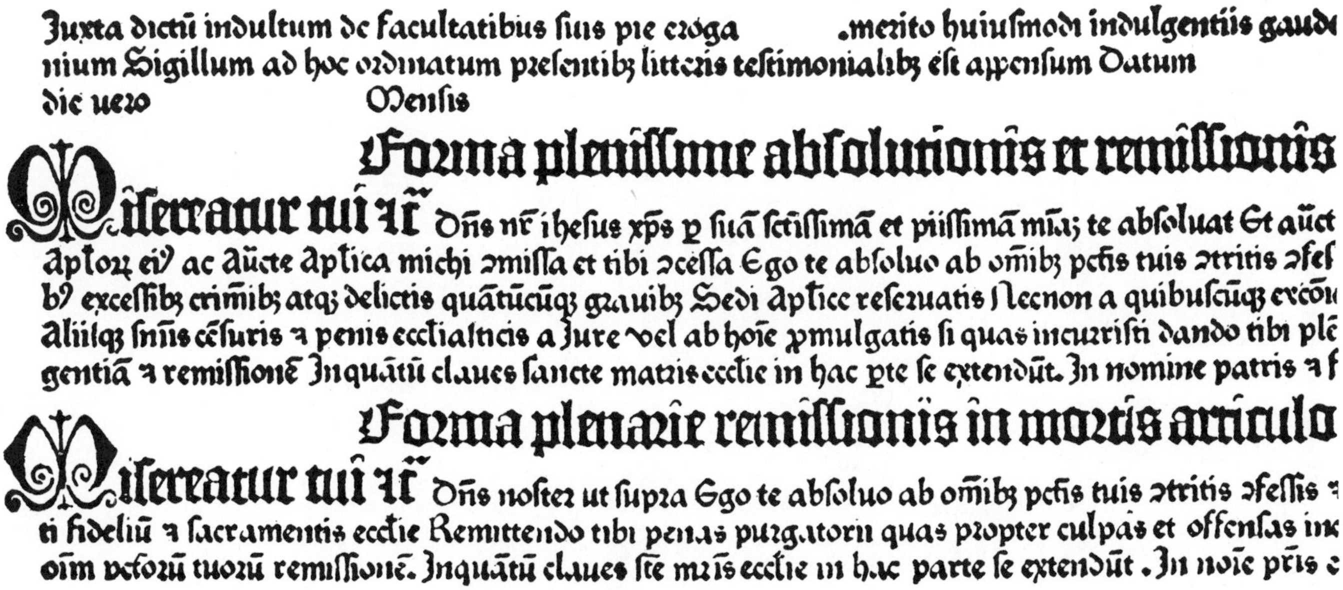

Juxta dictũ indultum de facultatibus suis pie eroga .merito huiusmodi indulgentiis gaude
nium Sigillum ad hoc ordinatum presentib; litteris testimonialib; est appensum Datum
die uero Mensis

Forma plenissime absolutionis et remissionis

Misereatur tui ꝛc Dñs nr̃ ihesus xp̄s p suã sctissimã et piissimã mĩa; te absoluat Et auct
aplo2 ei9 ac auc̃te aplica michi cõmissa et tibi cõcessa Ego te absoluo ab omib; pctis tuis ctritis cõfes
b9 excessib; crimib; atq; delictis quãtucũq; grauib; Sedi aplice reseruatis Necnon a quibuscũq; excõi
Aliisq; sniis cẽsuris 7 penis ecclialticis a Jure vel ab hoie pmulgatis si quas incurristi dando tibi plẽ
gentiã 7 remissionẽ Inquãtũ claues sancte matris ecclie in hac pte se extendũt. In nomine patris 7 f

Forma plenarie remissionis in mortis articulo

Misereatur tui ꝛc Dñs noster ut supra Ego te absoluo ab omib; pctis tuis ctritis cõfessis 7
ti fideliũ 7 sacramentis ecclie Remittendo tibi penas purgatorii quas propter culpas et offensas inc
oim pctorũ tuorũ remissionẽ. Inquãtũ claues sce mris ecclie in hac parte se extendũt. In noie pris 7

Johann Gutenberg, detail of the thirty-one-line *Letters of Indulgence,* c. 1454. These first dated, printed documents are also the first typographic materials to have blanks so that names and dates can be filled in later.

marginal notation that the hand rubrication, which is the application of red-ink initials and titling by a scribe, was completed on 24 August 1456, we can presume that Fust acquired a nearly complete production when he foreclosed.

Sales of the forty-two-line Bible were brisk as Fust traveled widely to distribute them. An early author relates that Fust carried a parcel of Bibles to Paris and attempted to sell them as manuscripts. The forty-two-line Bible had no title page, no page numbers, or other innovations to distinguish it from handmade manuscripts. Both Gutenberg and his customers probably wanted it this way. After the French observed the number and conformity of the volumes, they decided that witchcraft was involved. To avoid indictment and conviction, Fust was forced to

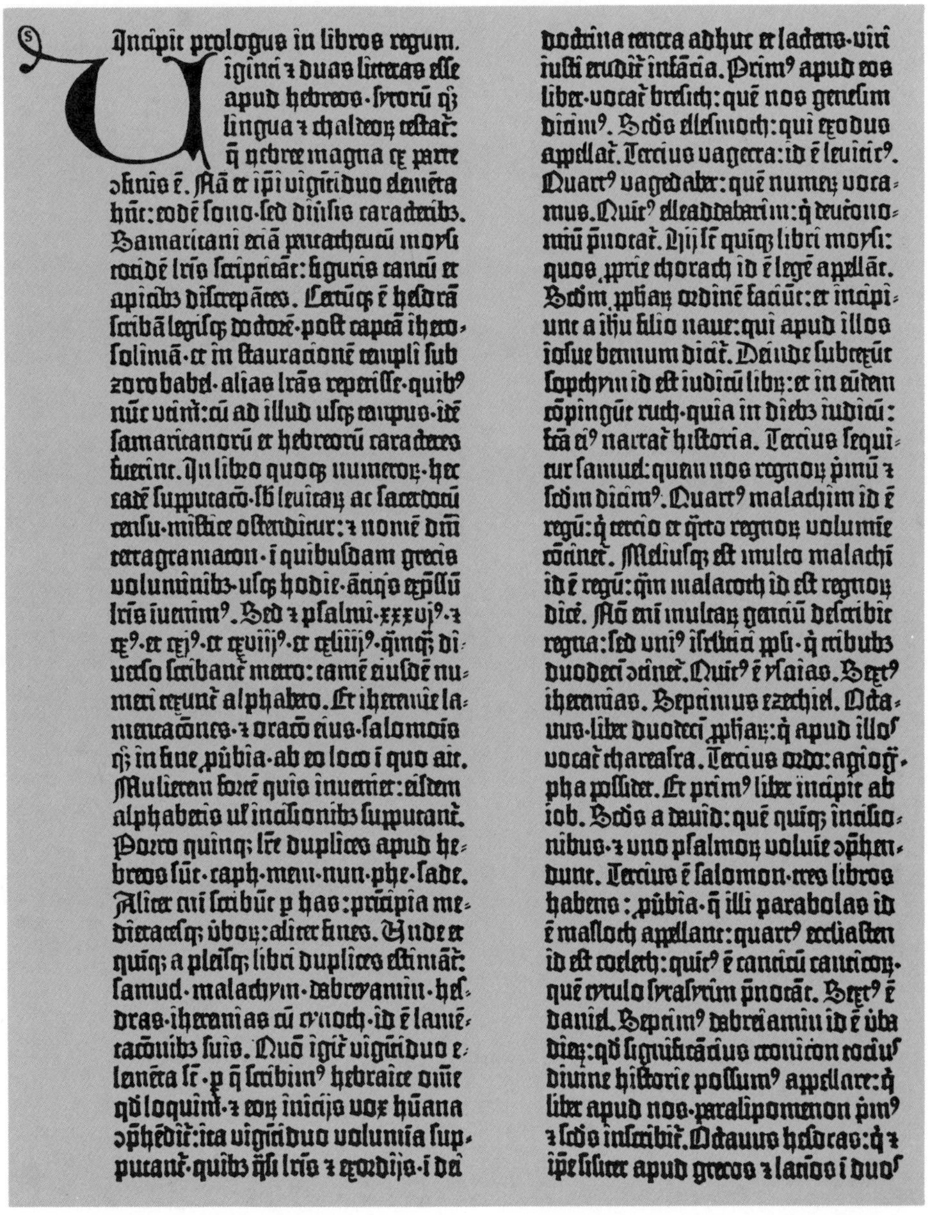

Incipit prologus in libros regum.
Viginti et duas litteras esse
apud hebreos · syrorũ q;
lingua 7 chaldeo2 testatur:
q̃ hebree magna ex parte
cõfinis ē. Nã et ipi uiginti duo elementa
hñt: eodē sono · sed diuersis caracterib;.
Samaritani etiã pentatheucũ moysi
totidē lrīs scriptitãt: figuris tantũ et
apicib; discrepãtes. Certũq; ē esdrã
scribã legisq; doctorē · post captã ihero-
solimã · et instauracionē templi sub
zorobabel · alias lrās repperisse · quib9
nūc utimr: cũ ad illud usq; tempus idē
samaritanorũ et hebreorũ caracteres
fuerint. In libro quoq; numero2 · hec
eadē supputacio · sb leuitaru ac sacerdotũ
censu · mistice ostenditur: 7 nomē dñi
tetragramaton · i quibusdam grecis
uoluminib; · usq; hodie · antiqs expssũ
lrīs inuenim9. Sed 7 psalmi · xxxvj9 · 7
cx9 · et cxj9 · et cxviij9 · et cxliiij9 · quãq; di-
uerso scribant metro: tamē eiusdē nu-
meri texunt alphabeto. Et iheremie la-
mentacões · 7 oracõ eius · salomonis
q; in fine puerbia · ab eo loco i quo ait.
Mulierem fortē quis inueniet: eisdem
alphabetis ul incisionib; supputant.
Porro quinq; lrē duplices apud hebreos sūt · caph · mem · nun · phe · sade.
Aliter enī scribūt p has: principia me-
dietatesq; uerbo2: aliter fines. Unde et
quinq; a plerisq; libri duplices estimant:
samuel · malachim · dabreiamin · hel-
dras · iheremias cũ cynoth · id ē lamē-
tacõib; suis. Quõ igit uiginti duo e-
lementa sūt · p q̃ scribim9 hebraice oē
qd loquimr · 7 eo2 inicijs uox hūana
cõphēdit: ita uiginti duo uolumina supputant · quib; q̃si lrīs 7 exordijs · i dei
doctrina tenera adhuc et lactens · uiri
iusti eruditur infancia. Prim9 apud eos
liber · uocatur bresith: quē nos genesim
dicim9. Secūdus ellesmoth: qui exodus
appellatur. Tercius uagecra: id ē leuiticus.
Quart9 uagedaber: quē numeros uoca-
mus. Quint9 elleaddabarim: q̃ deutrono-
miũ pnotatur. Hij sūt quinq; libri moysi:
quos pprie thorath id ē legē appellãt.
Secūm pphetarũ ordinē faciūt: et incipi-
unt a ihũ filio naue: qui apud illos
iosue bennum dicitur. Deinde subtexũt
sophtim id est iudicũ librũ: et in eūdem
cõpingũt ruth · quia in diebus iudicũ
facta ei9 narratur historia. Tercius sequi-
tur samuel: quem nos regno2 primū 7
scdm dicim9. Quart9 malachim id ē
regũ: q̃ tercio et quarto regno2 uolumie
cõtinetur. Meliusq; est multo malachī
id ē regũ: q̃m malacoth id est regno2
dicē. Nõ enī multa2 gentiũ describit
regna: sed uni9 israhelitici ppli · q̃ tribub;
duodecim cõtinetur. Quint9 ē ysaias. Sext9
iheremias. Septimus ezechiel. Octauus · liber duodecim pphetarũ: q̃ apud illos
uocatur thareasra. Tercius ordo: agiogra-
pha possidet. Et prim9 liber incipit ab
iob. Scds a dauid: quē quinq; incisio-
nibus · 7 uno psalmo2 uolumie cõphen-
dunt. Tercius ē salomon · tres libros
habens: puerbia · q̃ illi parabolas id
ē masloth appellant: quart9 ecclesiasten
id est coeleth: quint9 ē canticũ canticorũ
quē titulo sirasirim pnotant. Sext9 ē
daniel. Septim9 dabreiamin id ē uba
dierũ: qd significancius cronicon totius
diuine historie possum9 appellare: q̃
liber apud nos · paralipomenon prim9
7 scds inscribitur. Octauus esdras: q̃ 7
ipe similiter apud grecos 7 latinos i duos

Johann Gutenberg, page from the Gutenberg Bible, 1450–55. The superb typographic legibility and texture, generous margins, and excellent presswork make this first printed book a canon of quality that has seldom been surpassed.

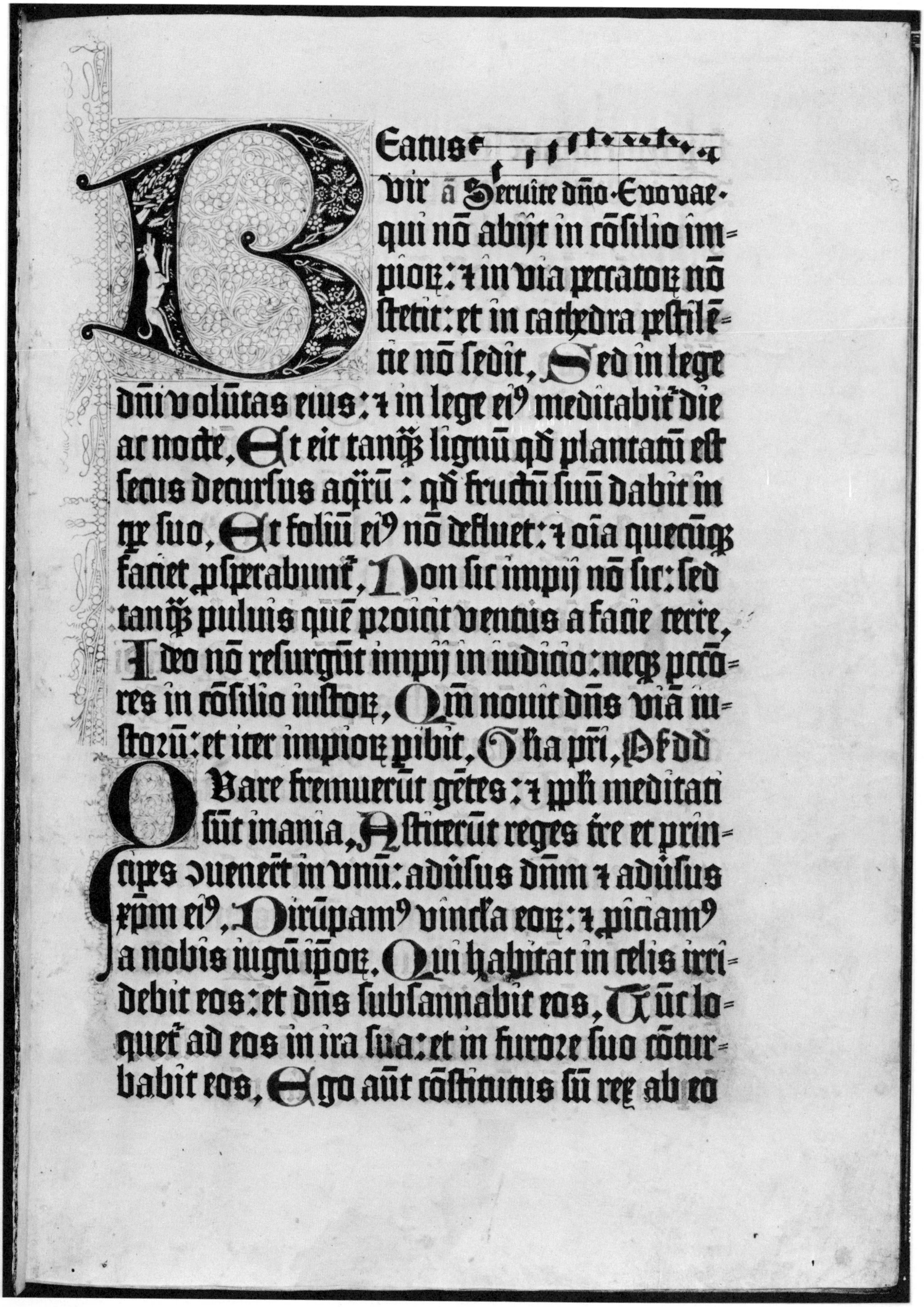
Beatus
vir Seruite dn̄o. Euouae.
qui nō abiit in cōsilio impioꝝ: ⁊ in via peccatoꝝ nō
stetit: et in cathedra pestilē-
tie nō sedit. Sed in lege
dn̄i volūtas eius: ⁊ in lege eiꝰ meditabit̄ die
ac nocte. Et erit tanq̄ lignū qd̄ plantatū est
secus decursus aq̄rū: qd̄ fructū suū dabit in
tp̄e suo. Et foliū eiꝰ nō defluet: ⁊ oīa quecūq̄
faciet ꝓsperabunt̄. Non sic impii nō sic: sed
tanq̄ puluis quē proicit ventus a facie terre.
Ideo nō resurgūt impii in iudicio: neq̄ pcc̄o-
res in cōsilio iustoꝝ. Qm̄ nouit dn̄s viā iu-
storū: et iter impioꝝ ꝑibit. Gl̄a pri. Euouae
Quare fremuerūt gētes: ⁊ pp̄li meditati
sūt inania. Astiterūt reges t̄re et prin-
cipes ꝯuenerūt in vnū: aduSus dn̄m ⁊ aduSus
xp̄m eiꝰ. Dirūpamꝰ vincla eoꝝ: ⁊ ꝓiciamꝰ
a nobis iugū ipsoꝝ. Qui habitat in celis irri-
debit eos: et dn̄s subsannabit eos. Tūc lo-
quet̄ ad eos in ira sua: et in furore suo cōtur-
babit eos. Ego aūt cōstitutus sū rex ab eo

reveal his secret. It has been claimed that this event is the basis for the popular story, related by several authors, of the German magician Dr. Faustus (Johann Faust in an early version), who grew dissatisfied with the limits of human knowledge and sold his soul to the devil in exchange for knowledge and power.

On 14 August 1457, Fust and Schoeffer published a magnificent *Psalter in Latin* with a monumental 30.5 by 43.2 centimeter (12-by-17-inch) page size. The large red and blue initials were printed from two-part metal blocks which were either inked separately, reassembled, and printed with the text in one press impression or stamped after the text was printed. These famous decorated two-color initials were a major innovation. The *Psalter in Latin* was also the first book to bear a printer's trademark and imprint, printed date of publication, and colophon. A translation of the colophon reads: "This book of the Psalms, decorated with beautiful capitals, and with an abundance of rubrics, has been fashioned thus by an ingenious invention of printing and stamping without use of a pen. And to the worship of God it has been diligently brought to Completion by Johann Fust, a citizen of Mainz, and Peter Schoeffer of Gernsheim, in the year of Our Lord 1457, on the eve of the Feast of the Assumption."

Peter Schoeffer, printer's trademark, 1457. Fust and Schoeffer's *Psalter in Latin* was the first book to be printed with a printer's mark to identify the printer. The double crests are thought to symbolize the two printers.

Jan Fust and Peter Schoeffer, *Psalter in Latin,* edition of 1459. The typographic vitality and elegance of the red and blue initials rivaled the most beautiful of manuscript pages. *Pierpont Morgan Library, New York.*

Jan Fust and Peter Schoeffer, page from *Rationale divinorum officiorum,* 1459. The innovative small type is combined with wonderfully intricate printed red and blue initials that evidence the early printer's efforts to mimic the design of the manuscript book. *The Library of Congress, Washington, D.C., Rosenwald Collection.*

Another important innovation appeared in Fust and Schoeffer's 1459 edition of *Rationale divinorum officiorum.* This long volume explaining religious ceremonies was the first typographic book that used a small-size typestyle to conserve space and increase the amount of text on each page. This achieved significant economy in the amount of presswork, ink, and parchment needed to print the edition.

Other major works included a beautiful Latin Bible, 1462, and an edition of Cicero's *De officiis,* 1465, which was the first printing of a classic from antiquity. Typography spurred the interest in ancient Greek and Roman culture. As knowledge of the ancient world began to exist alongside knowledge of the medieval era, the fusion became a catalyst for the creation of the modern world.

During a 1466 Paris trip to sell books, Johann Fust died, probably of plague. Peter Schoeffer and his associate Conrad Henkis, who married Fust's widow the year after Fust died, continued this highly successful printing business producing broadsheets, books, and pamphlets.

While Fust and Schoeffer were selling Bibles and printing Psalters, Johann Gutenberg, who, like most innovators, was running a heartbeat ahead of his time, drifted into bankruptcy and in 1458 defaulted on interest payments for a 1442 loan. Although he was sixty years of age and down and out, he had perfected his craft and completed his research. It is believed that, with financial support from Mainz citizen Dr. Conrad Homery, Gutenberg was able to establish a new printing shop. Some scholars view him as the printer of the thirty-six-line Bible, a late 1450s reprint of the forty-two-line Bible with similar but less refined type. His *Catholicon,* an encyclopedic dictionary, was published in 1460 with a colophon—perhaps in Gutenberg's own words—stating that the work was published "with the protection of the Almighty, at whose will the tongues of infants become eloquent and who often reveals to the lowly what he hides from the wise." On 17 January 1465, Archbishop Adolf of Mainz appointed Gutenberg courtier with the rank of nobleman, entitling him to clothing, keep, and "twenty matter of corn and two fudder of wine each year." The flyleaf of a book owned by a Mainz priest bears an inscription that "the honorable Master Johann Gutenberg died 3 February 1468." Based on prior agreements, Dr. Homery petitioned the courts for ownership of the "forms, letters, instruments, tools, and other things pertaining to the work of printing" that belonged to the late Gutenberg. On 26 February 1468, the archbishop transferred possession to Dr. Homery, who promised to keep this equipment in Mainz and give first preference to Mainz citizens in the event of future sale.

For a brief few years, printing was centered in Mainz as Schoeffer and Fust, Gutenberg, and former apprentices who had established their own firms were located there. Ironically, the swift spread of printing was created by a bloody conflict. German princes and lords were involved in power struggles which erupted into full-scale war. Leading an army of eight hundred horsemen and several thousand foot soldiers, Adolf of Nassau descended upon Mainz in 1462 and sacked the town. Plundering and looting brought trade and commerce to a halt. Warnings from other towns in Adolf's path enabled many Mainz merchants and craftsmen to load everything possible on wagons and

The Master of the Playing Cards, *The Three of Birds,* c. 1450. Masterful design and placement of the images in the space enhanced the sureness of drawing and use of line for tonal effects. *Bibliotheque Nationale, Paris.*

carts and scatter like seeds in the wind. Many younger printers and apprentices did not return. Rather, presses were soon established as far away as France and Italy.

Copperplate engraving

During the same time and in the same section of Europe that Johann Gutenberg invented movable type, an unidentified artist called the Master of the Playing Cards created the earliest known copperplate engravings. *Engraving* is printing from an image that is incised or cut into the printing surface. To produce a copperplate engraving, a drawing is scratched into a smooth metal plate. Ink is applied into the depressions, the flat surface is wiped clean, and paper is pressed against the plate to receive the ink image. The Master of the Playing Card's finest work is a set of playing cards using birds, animals, and wild men as images. The quality of his drawing suggests that he probably trained as an artist rather than as a goldsmith. The masterful execution implies that these playing cards were designed and engraved by someone who had already mastered engraving, not someone struggling to perfect a new graphic technique.

Scholars have speculated that Johann Gutenberg, in addition to inventing typographic printing, may have been involved in the research and development of copperplate engraving. Images by the Master of the Playing Cards have now been associated with Mainz illuminators, including artists associated with Gutenberg's printing works during the 1450s. The links that bind these early researchers into printing together are illustrations of birds, animals, flowers, and figures that are duplicated in the engraved playing cards, an illuminated Bible produced in Mainz during the early 1450s, and the illumination added to a surviving copy of the forty-two-line Bible.

This circumstantial evidence has raised an exciting possibility: was Johann Gutenberg striving to perfect the printing—not just of scribe's lettering—but the magnificent ornamentation and illustration of the medieval manuscript as well? Was engraving pioneered as a means to print illustrations onto the typographic pages, which could then be handcolored? Did Gutenberg explore using engraving plates as molds to cast relief versions, so that illustrations could be printed with type? These provocative questions, still without definite answers, indicate that Gutenberg's research might have carried the printed book in a different direction from its subsequent development. But when Johann Gutenberg's world came crashing down in 1455, and he was locked out of his printing shop, research into these possibilities ended.

The Master of the Playing Cards or his follower, *Vine Ornament with Two Birds,* c. 1440–50. This design is one of the earliest copperplate engravings. Its designer has achieved a remarkable overall design pattern and convincing form using linear shading. *National Gallery of Art, Washington, D.C., Rosenwald Collection.*

7

The German Illustrated Book

THE LATIN WORD *Incunabula* means "cradle" or "baby linen." Its connotations of birth or beginning caused seventeenth-century writers to adopt it as a name for the historical period that ranges from Gutenberg's invention of typography until the end of the century. (This date is completely arbitrary; this chapter traces the logical continuation of the Incunabula period into the early 1500s.) Printing's rapid spread is evidenced by the fact that by 1480, twenty-three northern European towns, thirty-one Italian towns, seven French towns, six Spanish and Portuguese towns, and one English town had presses. By 1500, printing was practiced in over one hundred forty towns. It is estimated that the printers of the Incunabula produced over thirty-five thousand editions for a total of nine million books. In 1450, Europe's monasteries and libraries housed a mere fifty thousand volumes. In addition, a vast array of ephemera—including religious tracts, pamphlets, and broadsides—was produced for free distribution or sale. Broadsides, or broadsheets, are single-leaf pages printed on one side. Printed posters, advertisements, and newspapers evolved from the broadside. Four years after printing came to Venice, a dismayed scribe complained that the city was "stuffed with books." The boom in this new craft led to overproduction and proliferation of firms. From the ranks of over one hundred printing firms established in Venice before 1490, only ten survived until the end of the century.

Printing was resisted in some quarters. The scribes in Genoa, Italy, banded together and demanded that the town council forbid printing in that town. They argued that greedy printers were threatening their livelihood. The council did not support the petition, and within two years Genoa joined the mushrooming list of towns with printers. Parisian illuminators filed suits in the courts in a vain attempt to win damages from printers who were engaged in unfair competition that caused the demand for manuscript books to decline. Some bibliophiles maintained that type was inferior to calligraphy and unworthy of their libraries. In 1492 a cardinal, who later became Pope Julius II, ordered scribes to handletter a copy of a typographic book for his library. But typographic printing reduced the cost of books to a fraction of their earlier cost and turned the serious shortage of books (and the knowledge they contained) into an abundance. The tide of progress could not be stayed, and manuscript production slowly declined. The philosopher Alfred N. Whitehead once observed that a major technical advance is a process that wrecks the society in which it occurs. Typography, the major communications advance between the invention of writing to that of electronic mass communications in the twentieth century, played a pivotal role in the social, economic, and religious upheavals that occurred during the fifteenth and sixteenth centuries. The modern nation developed as a result of the vigorous spirit of nationalism that swept over Europe and led to the American and French revolutions of the late eighteenth century. In addition to being a powerful vehicle to spread ideas about the rights of man and the sovereignty of the people, printing stabilized and unified languages. People all across France, for example, were reading the same material in the French language, which formerly had many provincial idiosyncrasies of spelling and grammar. The French, English, and German tongues became typographic mass media that communicated to audiences of unprecedented size with one voice.

Illiteracy, the inability to read and write, began a long steady decline. Literacy was of limited value to a medieval peasant who had no hope of gaining access to books. But tumbling book prices, the beginnings of popular writing such as romantic novels, and the proliferation of the ever-present broadsheet made reading desirable and increasingly necessary for the Renaissance townspeople. The medieval classroom had been a scriptorium of sorts where each student penned his own book. Typography radically altered education. Learning became an increasingly private, rather than communal, process. Human dialogue, extended by type, began to take place on a global scale that bridged time and space. Gutenberg's invention was the first mechanization of a skilled handicraft. As such, it set into motion, over the next three hundred years, the machinations that would lead to the industrial revolution.

The Renaissance innovators altered our perception of information by creating two visual systems. Painting evoked illusions of the natural world on flat surfaces through such means as the single light source and light and shadow modeling, the fixed viewpoint and linear perspective, and atmospheric perspective. Typography created an ordering of information and space that was sequential and repeatable. It led man toward linear thought and logic, and a categorization and compartmentalization of information that formed the basis for empirical scientific inquiry. It developed the individualism that has been a dominant aspect of western society since the Renaissance.

As edition after edition of the Bible was published, increased study led men throughout Europe to formulate their own interpretations instead of relying on religious leaders as the locus of truth. This led directly to the Reformation, which shattered Christianity into hundreds of sects. After Martin Luther (c. 1483–1546) posted his ninety-five theses for debate on the door of Castle Church in Wittenberg, Germany, on 31 October 1517, his friends passed copies to printers. By December his proclamation had spread throughout central Europe. Within a few months, thousands of people all over Europe knew his views. Without typography, it is doubtful that the Protestant movement of the Reformation era could have happened. Both Luther and Pope Leo X used printed broadsides and tracts in a theological dispute before a mass audience of the entire continent.

By the end of the Incunabula, presses had been established throughout Europe, but very few of these printers contributed to the development of graphic design. Most were content to print copies of manuscripts or earlier printed editions. Except that the press replaced the copisti in producing the running text, the same division of labor found in the scriptorium continued. Except for the multicolor printing of Fust and Schoeffer's *Psalter In Latin,* rubrication, decoration, and illumination in early Incunabula books were almost always by hand. Perhaps the difficulties of multicolor printing made it more expensive, or maybe enough political pressure was generated by the rubricators and illuminators to allow them to continue their crafts on typographic books.

Design innovation took place in Germany, where woodcut artists and typographic printers collaborated to develop the illustrated book and broadsheet. In Italy, the letterstyles and format design inherited from illuminated manuscripts gave way to a design approach unique to the typographic book. Early printers followed the manuscript custom of putting the title and author at the top of the first page, in the same size and style of lettering as the text. A short space was skipped, then *Incipit* ("Here Begins") launched the book. In 1463 Fust and Schoeffer printed the first title page. The title page became an expressive vehicle for graphic design. Early in the Incunabula, a printed *ex libris,* or bookplate, that could be pasted into the front of a book to identify the owner, was developed. As printing spread from Mainz, so did the use of the printer's trademark as a visual identifier. Block printers and woodcarvers, like the scribes and illuminators, feared typographic printing as a serious threat to their livelihood. But the Incunabula's passing decades saw marked increases in the use of woodblock illustrations in typographic books, which increased the demand for blocks and the illustrators' stature. Also, woodcut artists were often called upon to make *exemplars* or layouts for illustrated books and broadsides.

Manuscript books have been discovered with editorial notes, marginal notes to indicate where typeset pages ended, inky fingerprints, and sketches for woodblocks. These indicate their use as a layout and manuscript for printed books. In one such manuscript, the scribe's colophon is scratched out, and in the printed book, is replaced by a typeset one.

The development of the illustrated book

The earliest typographic book with woodcut illustrations was *Der Ackerman aus Böhmen (The Farmer from Böhmen),* printed by Albrecht Pfister of Bamberg around 1460 using Gutenberg's type and five woodblocks. Augsburg and Ulm, centers for woodblock playing card and religious print production, became centers for illustrated books. In the 1470s Günther Zainer (d.1478) established a press in Augsburg, and his relative Johann Zainer established one about 70 kilometers (43 miles) to the east at Ulm. Both were scribes and illuminators who had learned printing at Strassbourg.

Günther Zainer met resistance from the Augsburg woodcutter's guild when he wanted to illustrate his books with woodblocks. A 1471 agreement allowed Zainer to use woodblock illustrations as long as he commissioned them from members of the guild. His first illustrated books used a rounded Gothic type and woodblocks set into a type column of the same width. By 1475, his illustrated books, including *Spiegel des menschlichen Lebens (The Mirror of Life),* which analyzes the positive and negative aspects of various careers, used woodcuts with textured areas and some solid blacks. This introduced a greater tonal range to the page design. Fortune smiled upon Günther Zainer, for the sale of over thirty-six thousand books printed in over a hundred editions enabled him to become one of Augsburg's most

Gunther Zainer (printer), illustration from *Spiegel des menschlichen Lebens,* 1475. In this illustration of a voice instructor, the triangular pattern on the tile floor introduces a lively tonal contrast.

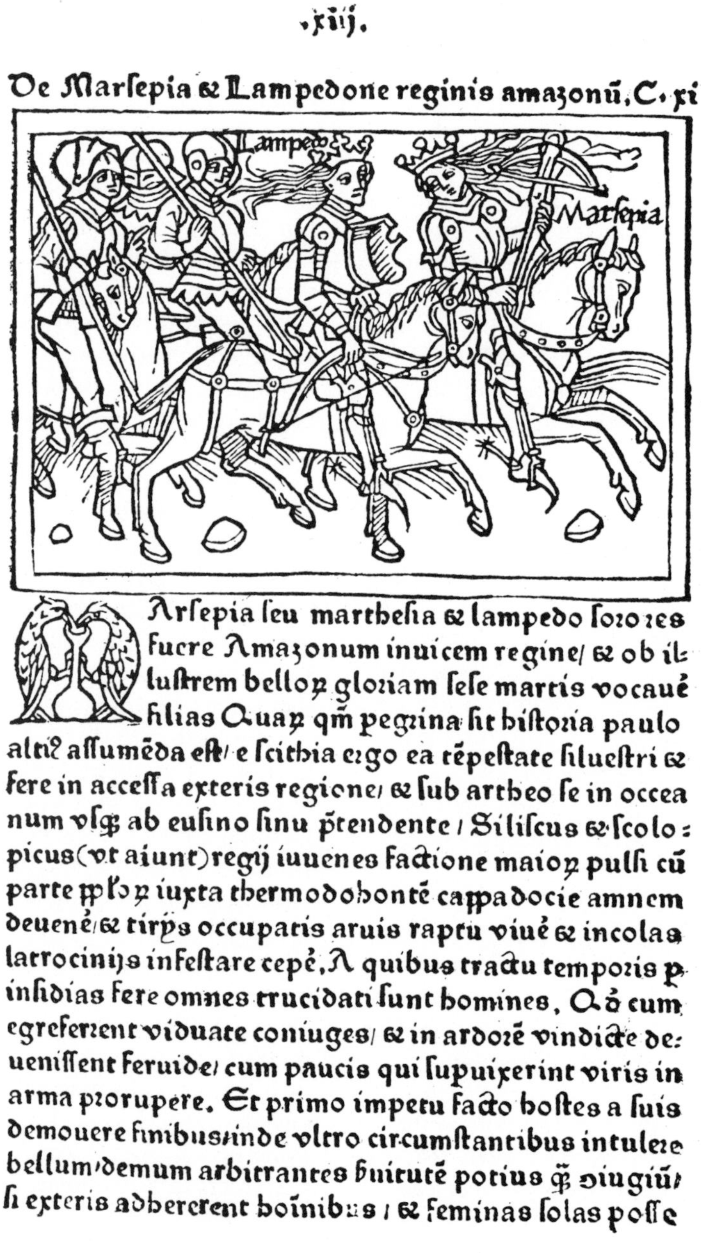
.xiij.

De Marsepia & Lampedone reginis amazonũ. C. xi

Arsepia seu marthesia & lampedo sorores fuere Amazonum inuicem regine/ & ob illustrem bellorũ gloriam sese martis vocauẽ filias Quarũ qm peregrina sit historia paulo altius assumẽda est/ e scithia ergo ea tẽpestate siluestri & fere inaccessa exteris regione/ & sub artheo se in occeanum vsq ab eusino sinu ptendente / Siliscus & scolopicus (vt aiunt) regij iuuenes factione maiorũ pulsi cũ parte ppl'orũ iuxta thermodohontẽ cappadocie amnem deuenẽ/ & tirpis occupatis aruis raptu viuẽ & incolas latrocinijs infestare cepẽ. A quibus tractu temporis p insidias fere omnes trucidati sunt homines. Quo cum egreferent viduate coniuges/ & in ardorẽ vindicte deuenissent feruide/ cum paucis qui supuixerint viris in arma prorupere. Et primo impetu facto hostes a suis demouere finibus/ inde vltro circumstantibus intulere bellum/ demum arbitrantes huiutẽ potius q̃ coniugiũ/ si exteris adhererent hominibus / & feminas solas posse

Johann Zainer, page from *De mulieribus claris* by Boccaccio, 1473. In this book about famous women, the woodcuts are all designed in rectangles the width of the type column and dropped in flush to it. *Library of Congress, Washington, D.C., Rosenwald Collection.*

prominent and affluent citizens.

In Ulm, Johann Zainer used eighty woodcuts in his 1473 edition of *De mulieribus claris (Of Famous Women)* by Boccaccio. These illustrations have a very even line weight, and the capital initials are printed rather than added later by hand. These are wonderful little woodblock letters formed by birds, snakes, and plants. Woodcuts were used over and over in different books. For example, the two hundred woodcuts in Johann Zainer's 1476 Aesop's *Vita et fabulae* appear again in the edition by Ulm printer Anton Sorg four years later. Many of these illustrations are not completely enclosed with rectangular borders, which allows white space to flow from the wide margins into the pictures. Simple outline initials extend this light design effect. Typographic paragraph marks leave nothing for the rubricator in this volume; the printed book was becoming independent of the manuscript.

Unusually small fonts were designed for Johann Froben's 1491 Bible. With 11.5-by-17-centimeter ($4\frac{1}{2}$-by-$6\frac{5}{8}$-inch) page and only 6.4 centimeters thick ($2\frac{1}{2}$ inches), Froben's Bible pushed miniaturization to the threshold of legibility in the minute references to other passages that were printed along with the biblical text.

At Cologne, Henrich Quentell (d. 1501) printed a Bible whose illustrations had a significant impact on the approach to sacred subjects for generations. Ironically, either financial exigencies or poor planning resulted in almost all of the woodcuts being in the first half of the volume. Two outstandingly well-designed books were printed at Mainz by Peter Schoeffer. In 1485 a herbal entitled *Gart der Gesundheit (Garden of Health)* by Dr. Joannes de Cuba included many blocks drawn directly from nature. Herbals were medicine books that date from ancient Greece and contain formulas for medicines from the plant world.

The first illustrator to be identified as such in a book is Erhard Reuwich, for his work in *Peregrinationes in montem Syon (Travels in Mount Syon),* printed with Schoeffer's types

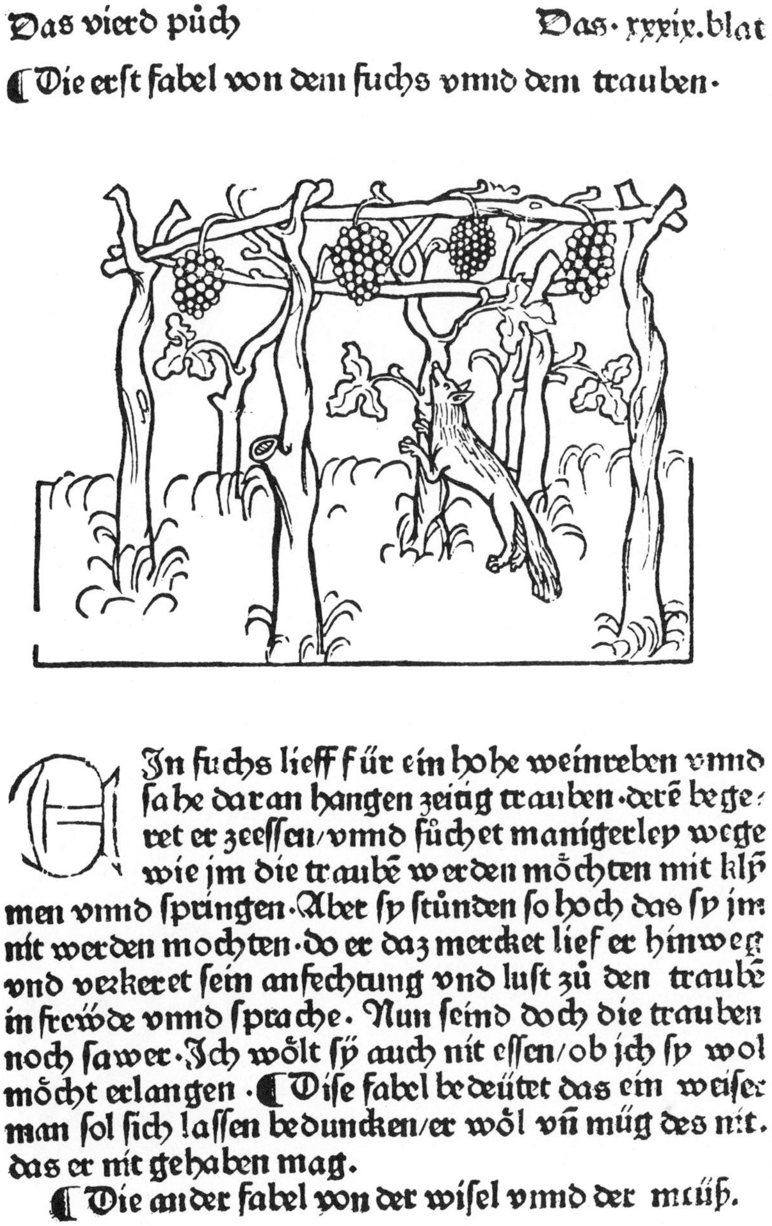
Das vierd pűch Das · xxxix. blat ·

¶ Die erst fabel von dem fuchs vnnd dem trauben·

EIn fuchs lieff für ein hohe weinreben vnnd ſahe daran hangen zeitig trauben·derē bege⸗ ret er zeeſſen/vnnd ſůchet manigerley wege wie jm die traubē werden möchten mit klī men vnnd ſpringen·Aber ſy ſtůnden ſo hoch das ſy jm nit werden mochten·do er daz mercket lief er hinweg vnd verkeret ſein anfechtung vnd luſt zů den traubē in frewde vnnd ſprache· Nun ſeind doch die trauben noch ſawer·Jch wölt ſÿ auch nit eſſen/ob jch ſy wol möcht erlangen ·¶ Diſe fabel bedeütet das ein weiſer man ſol ſich laſſen beduncken/er wöl vñ müg des nit. das er nit gehaben mag.

¶ Die ander fabel von der wiſel vnnd der müß.

Anton Sorg, page from Aesop's *Vita et fabula,* c. 1479. Sorg used a wider column width than Zainer's earlier version of Aesop's *Fables* and tried to compensate for the lack of alignment between the woodcut and the type column by a margin of white space above and below the illustration. *Library of Congress, Washington, D.C., Rosenwald Collection.*

in 1486. Reuwich was a careful observer of nature who introduced cross-hatch illustration in this volume, which had fold-out illustrations, including a view of Venice that stretches out almost 1.5 meters (4 feet, 9 inches). The author of this interesting narrative, Bernardus de Breidenbach, traveled to the Holy Land and took Reuwich along to illustrate his writing.

Because printing required a huge capital investment and large trained labor force, it is not surprising that Nuremberg, which had become central Europe's prosperous center of commerce and distribution, housed Germany's most esteemed printer by the end of the century. Anton Koberger (c.1440–1513) printed over two hundred editions, including fifteen Bibles, at his printing firm, which was staffed by a hundred craftsmen operating twenty-four presses. As a bookseller, he owned sixteen shops and had agents throughout Europe. By the 1490s, most printers had trouble selling large books and abandoned the huge format of the liturgical

Erhard Reuwich (illustrator), page from *Peregrinationes in montem Syon,* 1486. With his accurate observations and brilliant illustrations, Reuwich launched pictorial journalism. *Pierpont Morgan Library, New York.*

Bibles. They adopted smaller page sizes that were more convenient and economical for the private customer. Koberger, however, continued to publish and sell large books. As a printer working in concert with master illustrators, he produced three masterpieces. The 1491 *Schatzbehalter,* a religious treatise, contains ninety-two full-page woodcuts by the painter and woodcut illustrator Michael Wolgemuth (1434–1519).

Published in German and Latin versions in 1493, the six-hundred-page *Liber Chronicarum (Nuremberg Chronicle)* by Dr. Hartmann Schedel is an ambitious history of the world from the dawn of creation until 1493. One of the masterpieces of Incunabula graphic design, the Nuremberg Chronicle has one thousand eight hundred nine woodcut illustrations in its complex, carefully designed 47.5-by-32.7 centimeter (18¾-by-12⅞-inch) pages. The exemplars (a handmade model layout and manuscript text used as a guide for the woodcut illustrations, typesetting, page design, and makeup) for both editions survive and provide rare insight into the design and production process. The publishers contracted Michael Wolgemuth and his stepson, Wilhelm Pleydenwurff (d. 1494), to create the exemplars, draw the illustrations, and cut, correct, and

Georg Alt, title page for the index to the *Nuremberg Chronicle,* 1493. This dazzling calligraphy reads, "Registry [index] for this Book of Chronicles with illustrations and portraits from the initiation of the world." The design for this woodblock is attributed to Alt (c. 1450–1510), a scribe who assisted Hartmann Schedel in lettering the Latin exemplar and translated the Latin manuscript into German for that version. *The Library of Congress, Washington, D.C., Rosenwald Collection.*

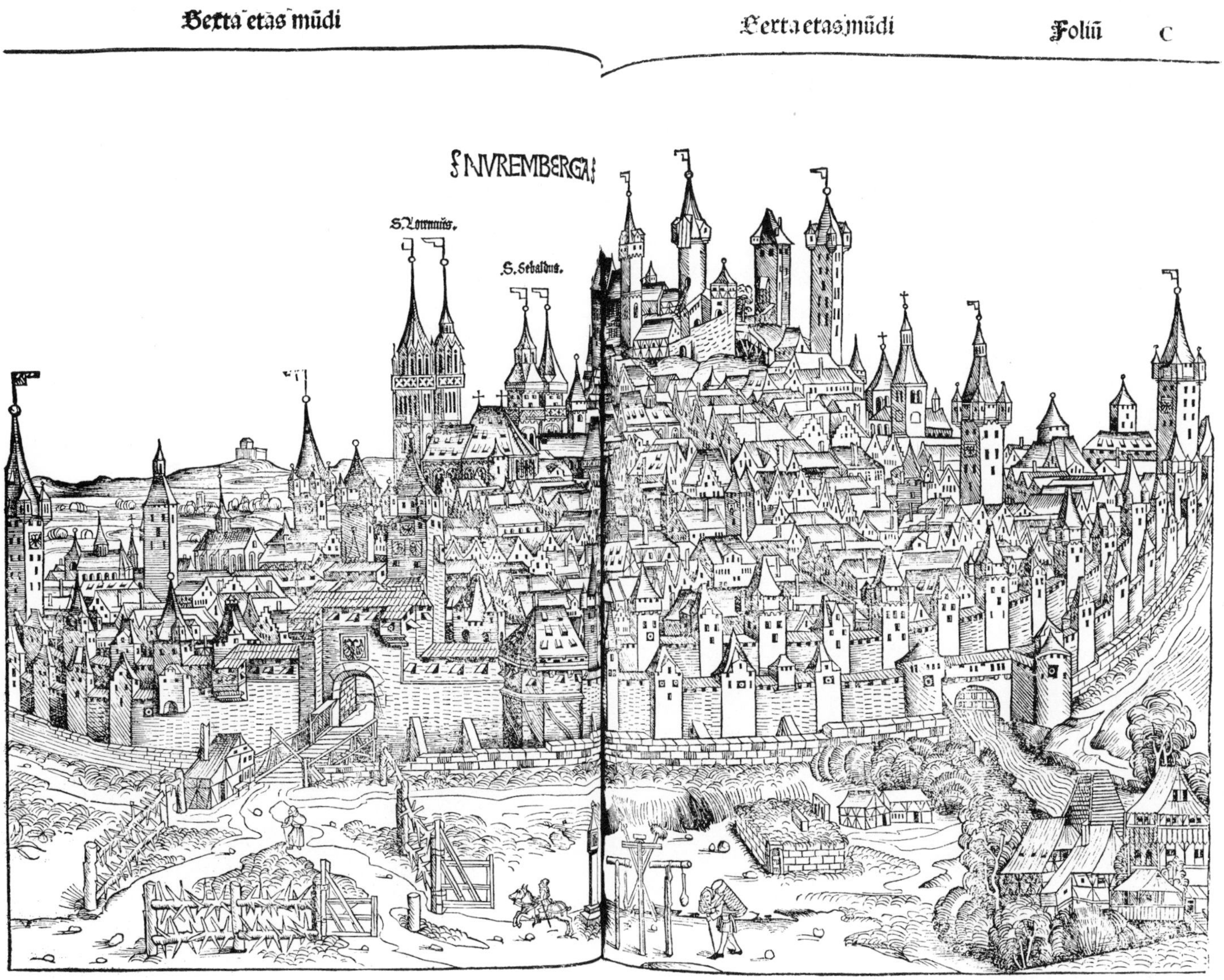

Anton Koberger, pages from the *Nuremberg Chronicle,* 1493. Alive with a staccato repetition of Gothic towers and rooftops, this illustration's expansive quality is enhanced by its size. *Library of Congress, Washington, D.C., Rosenwald Collection.*

prepare the woodblocks for printing. Also, one or the other had to be present at the printshop during typesetting and printing. For this work the artists were paid a one-thousand-guilder advance and guaranteed one-half of the net profits.

Because many woodcuts were used several times, only six hundred forty-five different woodcuts were required. For example, five hundred ninety-eight portraits of popes, kings, and other historical personages were printed from ninety-six blocks.

Koberger's contract required him to: order and pay for paper, as good as or better than the sample he had supplied; print the book according to the exemplars in an acceptable type style; maintain the security of a locked room for the project; and provide a workroom for Wolgemuth and Pleydenwurff. Koberger was paid four guilders for every ream (five hundred sheets) of four-page sheets printed. During the months of production, Koberger could bill the publishers periodically for portions of the book that had been printed and gathered into twelve-page, three-sheet signatures.

The exemplars or layouts for the *Nuremberg Chronicle* are the work of several "sketch artists" and numerous scribes, whose lettering in the exemplar has the same character count as the typefont to ensure an accurate conversion. The variety and diversity of page layouts range from a full double-page illustration of the city of Nuremberg to unillustrated type pages. On some pages, woodcuts are inserted into the text; on others, woodcuts are lined into horizontal columns. Rectangular illustrations are placed under or above type areas. Just when the layout threatens to become repetitious, the reader is jolted by an unexpected page design. The dense texture and rounded strokes of

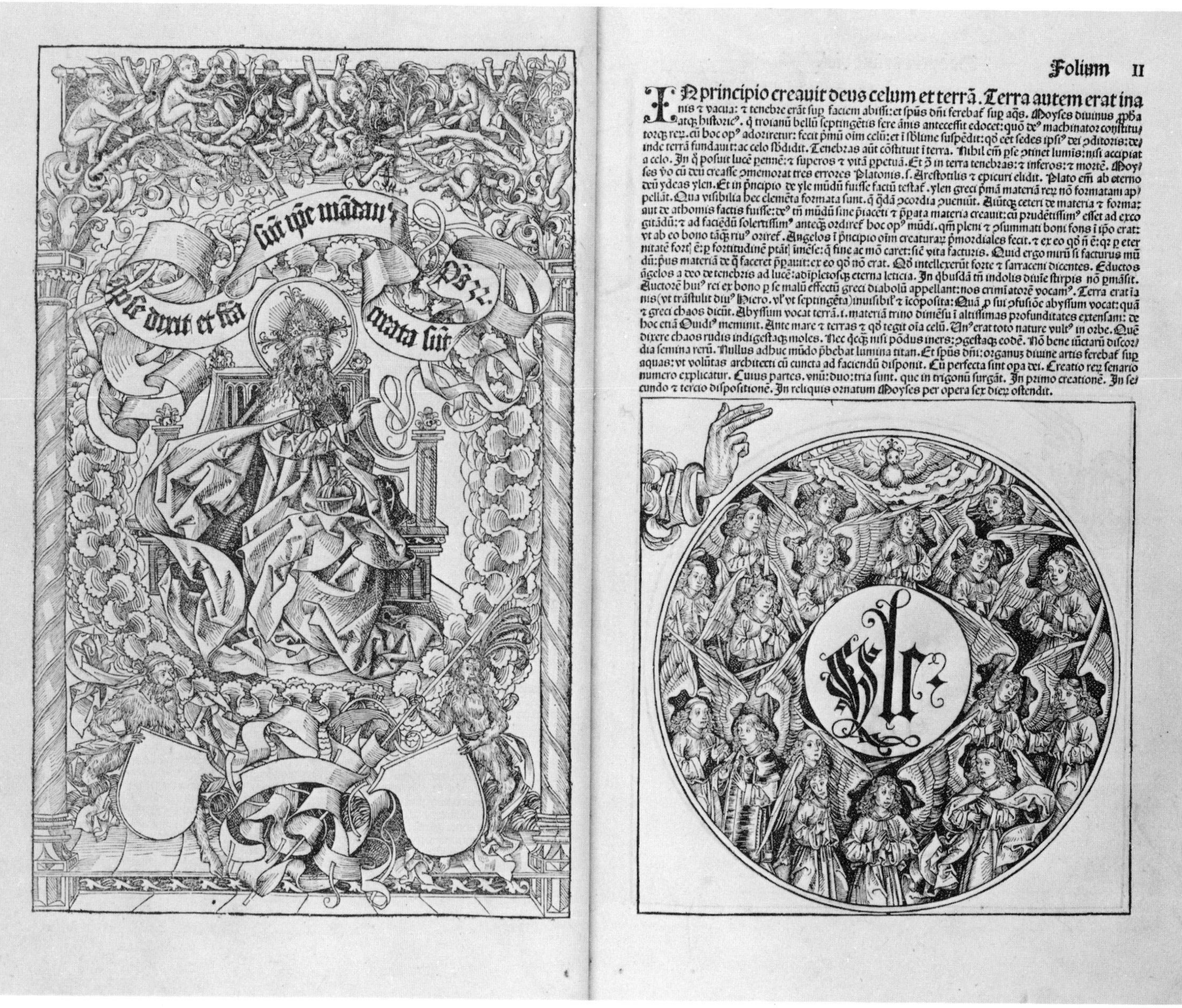

Koberger's sturdy Gothic types contrast handsomely with the tones of the woodcuts. The illustrators' imaginations enabled them to create unseen monstrosities, unvisited cities, awful tortures; and to express the story of creation in graphic symbols.

Koberger was godfather to Albrecht Dürer (1471–1528), whose goldsmith father apprenticed him to Michael Wolgemuth for almost four years beginning in 1486. Perhaps the young Dürer, who grew up three houses down the street in Nuremburg from Wolgemuth's home and studio, assisted in the layout and illustration for the *Nuremberg Chronicle.*

In 1498, publication of Latin and German editions of *The Apocalypse,* which contains Dürer's monumental sequence of fifteen woodcuts illustrating St. John's Revelation, brought the twenty-seven-year-old graphic artist and painter fame throughout Europe. This thirty-two-page book with 44.5-by-30.5-centimeter (17e-k-by-12-inch) pages has fifteen layouts with two columns of Koberger's gothic type on the left, facing one of Dürer's illustrations on the right. Dürer's *Apocalypse* has an unprecedented emotional power and graphic expressiveness. Volume and depth, light and shadow, texture and surface are created by black ink on white paper which becomes a metaphor for light in a turbulent world of awesome powers.

Anton Koberger, pages from the *Nuremberg Chronicle,* 1493. The raised hand of God in the initial illustration becomes a visual theme appearing over the next several pages that chronicle the biblical story of creation. *Library of Congress, Washington, D.C., Rosenwald Collection.*

The colophon reads, "Printed by Albrecht Dürer." Given his prodigious volume of prints, we may assume that he had a press in his workshop. Since the types used are Koberger's, we don't know if Dürer acquired set type from his godfather and printed the *Apocalypse,* printed the blocks and sent the sheets to Koberger's shop for typographic im-

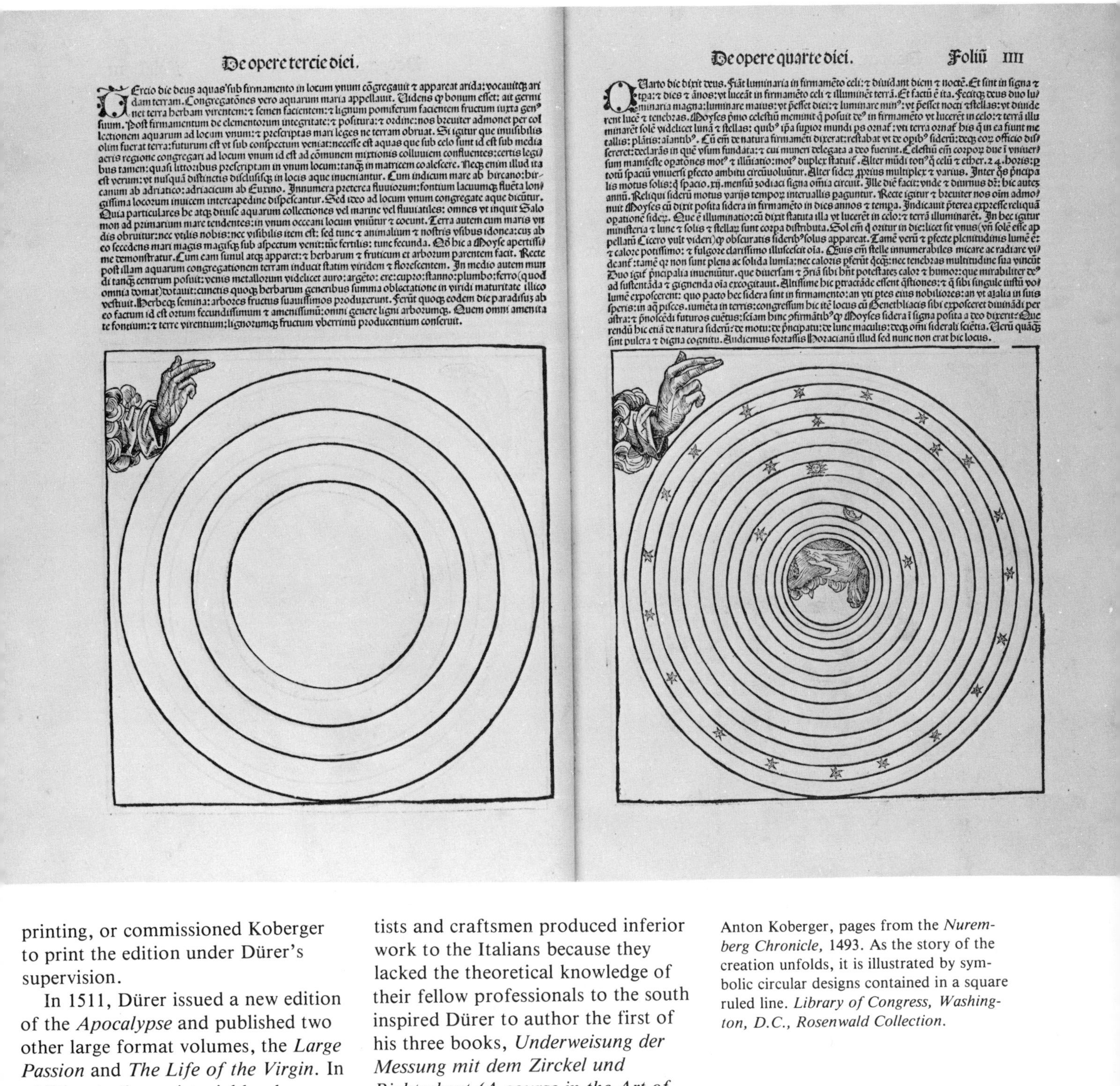

Anton Koberger, pages from the *Nuremberg Chronicle,* 1493. As the story of the creation unfolds, it is illustrated by symbolic circular designs contained in a square ruled line. *Library of Congress, Washington, D.C., Rosenwald Collection.*

printing, or commissioned Koberger to print the edition under Dürer's supervision.

In 1511, Dürer issued a new edition of the *Apocalypse* and published two other large format volumes, the *Large Passion* and *The Life of the Virgin.* In addition to these pictorial books, Dürer illustrated several broadsheets.

Trips to Venice for six months at age twenty-three and for one and a half years when he was thirty-four enabled Dürer to absorb the painting theory and technique as well as the humanist philosophy of the Italian Renaissance. Dürer became a major influence in the cultural exchange that saw the Renaissance spirit filter into Germany. His feeling that German artists and craftsmen produced inferior work to the Italians because they lacked the theoretical knowledge of their fellow professionals to the south inspired Dürer to author the first of his three books, *Underweisung der Messung mit dem Zirckel und Richtscheyt (A course in the Art of Measurement with Compass and Ruler)* in 1525. The first two chapters are theoretical discussions of linear geometry and two-dimensional geometric construction. The third chapter explains the application of geometry to architecture, decoration, engineering, and letterforms. Dürer's beautifully proportioned Roman capitals with clear instructions for their construction made a significant contribution to the evolution of alphabet design. This book also presents his modular system for textur, the German manuscript hand. It begins with a lowercase *i* which is composed of six stacked squares with the top and bottom units tilted to form the serifs. From this construction Dürer proceeds to build an entire alphabet. The fourth chapter covers the construction of geometric solids,

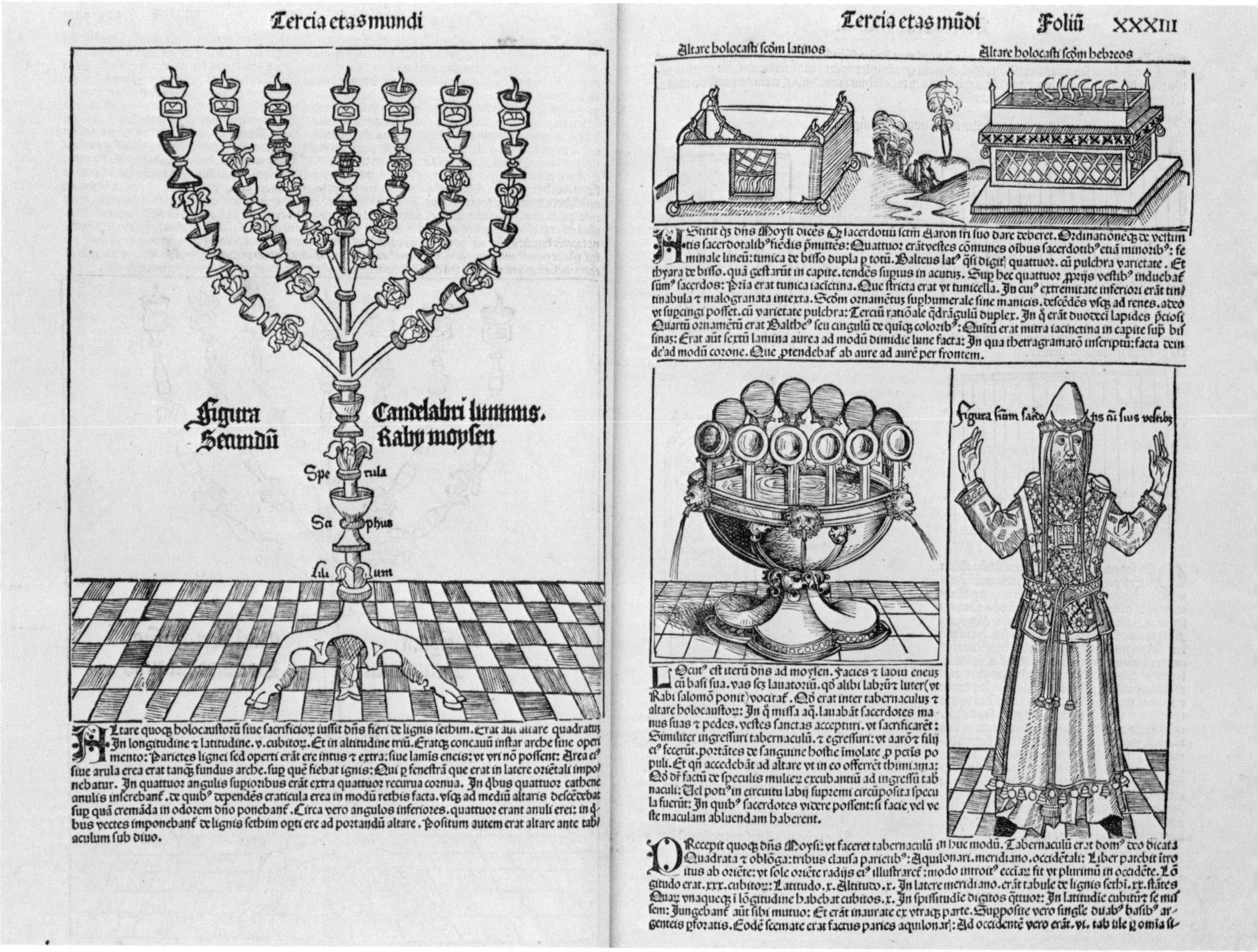

Anton Koberger, pages from the *Nuremberg Chronicle,* 1493. This complex layout is ordered by the use of rules around the illustrations. These convert the silhouette images into rectangles which can be tightly fitted with the rectangles of type. *Library of Congress, Washington, D.C., Rosenwald Collection.*

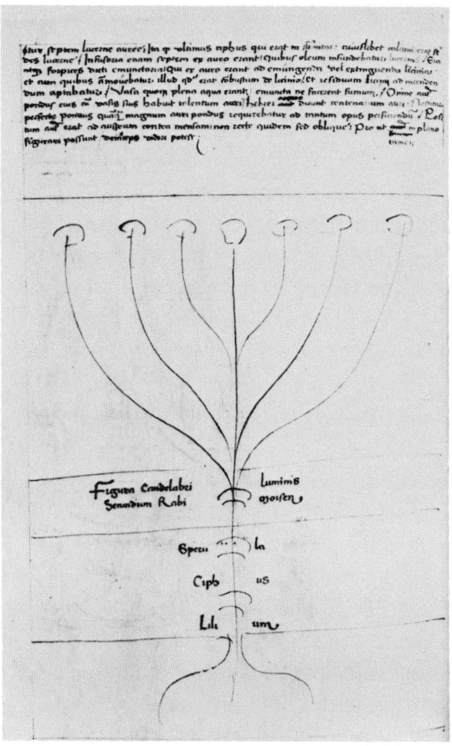

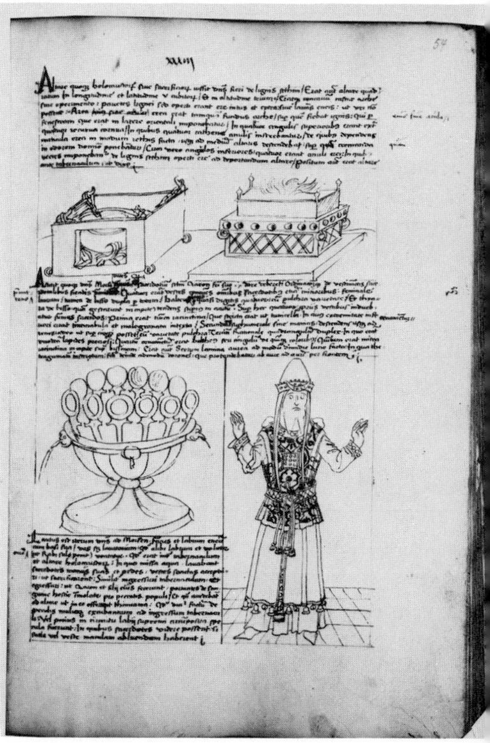

Studio of Michael Wolgemuth and Wilhelm Pleydenwurff, pages from the *Nuremberg Chronicle,* Latin exemplar, pre-1493. This layout and manuscript provided guidance for the compositors, although liberties were taken in the final layout. These woodblocks are among a small number that were not created for this volume, but had been used by Koberger earlier. *Stadtbibliothek, Nuremberg.*

Theodoricus Ulsenius Phrisius Medicus Universis litterarum Patronis in Epidimicam scabiem que passim toto orbe grassatur vaticiniū dicat.

LICHNICA GENESIS

Nup iāditā scabiē mutabile vulgȝ
Clamat: & arbitrio docte stipēdia turbe
Murmurat āguicomā crines scalpēre Megera
En: ait: ignote nemo succurrere pesti
Nemo salutiferā novit conferre medelam
Inde neces dū nostra rotat corda Empiricis
Impunes pagit medicorum contrio discors.
Talibus ut crucior ppl'i clamoribus: ecce
Fessa soporiferā deposcūt membra quietem
Libera mens clarum speculatur in ethere phebū
Visus adesse deus qualis Cumea sacerdos
Intonat Eneadū dū fortia corda remollit:
Non ego retrogrados flecto giramine gressus
Roscida signifero quāquā soror evolat arcu
Sed certis metā gradibus pverto: eandem
Ipse deū medius: moderator lucis & auctor
Carminis inocuasque freqns depromo sagittas
Plectra lyramque gero laur' mihi tpa nectit.
Ne tamē insontem pergat lacerare Camenā
Neu Parnasicolas solito depravet honore
Vulgus iners: ventosa cohors: arcana recludā
Que sinit Altitonās facta atque infecta deorum
Pandere Apollineā & cunctis pstare salutem
Mun' utrūque meum ē herbis ac carmine sano:
Vidimus [illegible] Mavortis nup in aula
Stare patrem natoque satis male succensentē
Quod nimis hūano generi indulgere putaret
[illegible] Jubar & vitalis numē olympi
[illegible]eminas falcēque pigram psepe levantem:
Scilicet ille pcax Genius Jovis altera cura
Sanguie spumabit nimio. ven' improba luxu
Sordilego monstrisque ferēt turbarier orbem:
Eurystheus dū magnus adest dūque atria tētat
Dura novercales Moesor [illegible] pdidit iras
Aeria: luce minor Chyrius quos Chelifer ambit
Utrosque nepa none libramina Sphere:
Hic ubi cōgressum statuūt ubi pocula ponūt
Nectaris ambrosii: scelus ē laudare nocentes:
Falcifer ambiguū genitis miscere venenum
Cogitat & sancta Gradivi sedius in ede
Frangere: maiorum liceat meminisse nefanda:
Protinus igniuomā tumor deferturr ad aram
Nigraque corrigere flamina psonat hydre
Notia continuo meditatus prelia Mavors
Ista licent: iratus ait: Sic spernimur istis
Numinibus pigris: & nostra altaria squallēt
Sulfure: dū tetricas imergit thure cucullas
Hocibelle gen' dū clausa murmurat umbra:
Victaque hec pauca fremēs: in dāna maiplos
Evocat: & celeres frustra retinente Minerva

Urget equos: bilemque ciet: calcantur arista
Almaque vitali frauadatur munere Ceres
Leditur omne gen' divū neque te bone Iacche
Libera simplicitas vitato flamine mundū
Miscuerint superi: supos culpare quis ausit [illegible]
Semina dira mali corrupto slēmate pendent
Postera pgenies vix ulli chara priorum.
Haud secus ac silicis cussu scintilla relabens
Crescit in immensum: teneros depasc[illegible] [illegible]
Sulfur edax picto qz obnubilat omnia [illegible]
Hinc pestes hinc fata pluūt potentia [illegible] [illegible]
Martia nōnūeris scatuit germania [illegible]
Ni videat natura fugat: dissensio circh.
Quāta volubilibus tanta ē discordia fi[illegible] [illegible]
Cernere sub medias: viresque adimit resum[illegible]
Ausa diu tentare nihil sub pondere tanto
Deficiat: levo ventris cui meta recessu
Per vada secalē pallenti corde lienem
Harmoniā distenta premit: rostra parocis
Emicat: hinc bullas vermis inde papillas
Diiaculat ovans Mentagrā viscida Lich[illegible]
Feda lues spurco primū contagia pen[illegible]
Custos sic bñ nota Cano: nova [illegible]
Nemo putet celo quod sedet mens nesci[illegible]
Ethereo timidos quo sirit liber [illegible]
Fusca bicorporeū de cardine bestia [illegible]
Ulcera sulfuree vibrabat acumine caude
Oriona fugans pestis monumenta [illegible]:
At quis forte roget que sit medicina [illegible]
Est locus alacr [illegible] in ethe[illegible]
Piniferumque solum Musis non ulcim[illegible].
Sive Helycō seu Nysa place: [illegible] [illegible]
Aonios iterum latices: ubi Phi[illegible] [illegible]
Luserat ista Jatrus: flava P[illegible] [illegible]
Qua secat in scopes: Silvas [illegible] [illegible]
Collis: ubi eoos inter notiss[illegible] [illegible]
Menia: Virgineo [illegible] gens [illegible]:
Hic Geni' deposcat opē mea [illegible] [illegible]
Asclepium Figulumque dabo cmō digna [illegible]
Sacra locet: placabo deos & munuscula po[illegible]
Antidotūque feram vitus cinaceat [illegible]
Me duce sic mēbris mox satisfet humor [illegible]
Innocu': scabrasque trahet purgamine sordes [illegible]
Cuthi' hec. Ast Mnemosyne mēdosa repellit
Sōnia: huic morum labentis ante ruinas
Quest' erā: ah qriēs suspirās inqt amena ē
Phillirīdū vitiata man': quid vedere p quo
Nōne vidēs Astrea fugit: quid secla culpant
Quid quereris dforme cahos: dū tpa volu[illegible]
Maxima dum veteres [illegible] [illegible] figuras.

Insigni Archyatrie studio Sacrum:

Si mihi turpe putas medico cōponere v'sus
Et Musis operam carminibusque dare
Nullaque Pegasei tanqz sit gloria fontis
Metraque sint studijs inferiora meis
Falleris: Ille meas primus qui tradidit artes
Quique salutiferam condidit auctor opē
Inter Pierides cythara crepitāte sorores
Phebus divino pollice ducit ebur.
Sic lustrat celos: sic clara poemata fingit
Irradiatque novē flamina docta deas:

Nurnberge Calendis Sextilibus
1496

Albrecht Dürer, broadside, 1496. The text, a poem by Frisian Doctor Ulsenius, warns about the dangers of syphilis. Dürer centered the illustration between two columns of type with a headline above and descriptive material in the white space below. A victim, standing below a zodiac chart and between Nuremberg's symbolic shields, brings graphic intensity to the message.

Albrecht Dürer, *The Four Horsemen of the Apocalypse,* 1498. Poised at a historical watershed as the medieval epoch waned to the light of the German Renaissance, Dürer simultaneously achieved the spiritual power of the former and the artistic mastery of the latter.

Albrecht Dürer, title page for *The Life of the Virgin,* 1511. Dürer's mature work achieved a mastery in the use of line as tone. A linear sunburst effect surrounds "The Virgin in Glory" with a dazzling luminosity seldom achieved with black ink on white paper. The triangular shape of the title above the illustration echoes the angular lines radiating from the figures, and the text below repeats the horizontal sky tone below the figures.

linear perspective, and mechanical aids to drawing.

The illustrated book *De Symmetria Partium Humanorum Corpum (Treatise on Human Proportions),* which first appeared in Nuremberg shortly after Dürer's death in 1528, shared Dürer's tremendous knowledge of drawing, the human figure, and the advances of Italian Renaissance artists with German painters and graphic artists.

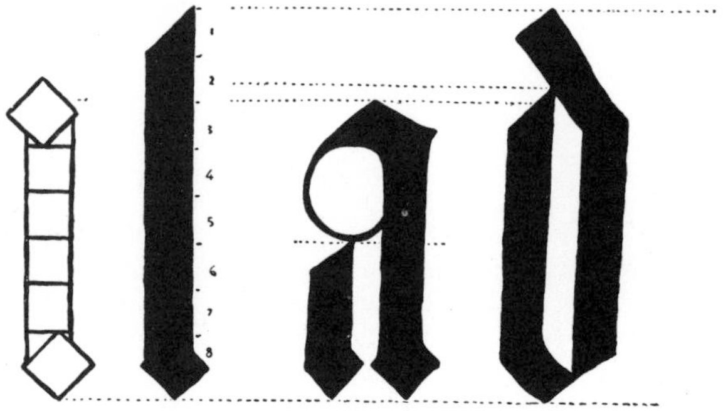

Albrecht Dürer, page from *Underweisung der Messung,* 1525. This diagram illustrates Dürer's modular system for constructing a gothic alphabet.

EPITOME IN DIVAE PARTHENICES MARI
AE HISTORIAM AB ALBERTO DVRERO
NORICO PER FIGVRAS DIGES
TAM CVM VERSIBVS ANNE
XIS CHELIDONII

Quisquis fortunæ correptus turbine.perfers
Quam tibi iacturam fata sinistra ferunt.
Aut animæ delicta gemis.Phlegethontis & ignes
Anxius æternos corde tremente paues.
Quisquis & vrgeris iam iam decedere vita
Alterius:migrans:nescius hospitij.
Huc ades:auxilium:pete:continuoq; rogabo
Pro te:quem paui lacte:tuliq; sinu.
Ille deus rerum mihi subdidit astra:deosq;.
Flectitur ille meis O homo supplicijs.

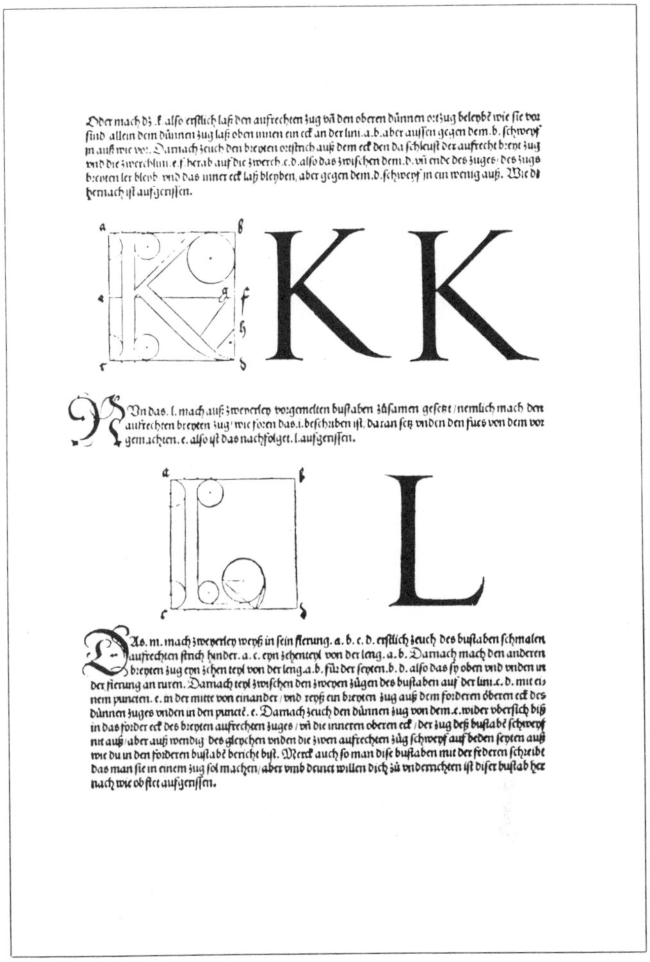

Oder mach dz .k. also erstlich laß den aufrechten zug vñ den oberen dünnen ortzug beleybē wie sie vor sind allein dem dünnen zug laß oben innen ein eck an der lini.a.b.aber aussen gegen dem.b. schweyf jn auß wie vor. Damach zeuch den breyten ortstrich auß dem eck den da schleust der aufrecht breyt zug vnd die zwerchlini.e.f. herab auf die zwerch.c.d.also das zwischen dem.d. vñ ende des zuges/des zugs breyten ler bleyb vnd das inner eck laß bleyben, aber gegen dem.d. schweyf jn ein wenig auß. Wie dz hernach ist aufgerissen.

Nun das. l. mach auß zweyerley vorgemelten bustaben zůsamen gesetzt/nemlich mach den aufrechten breyten zug/wie foren das.i. beschriben ist, daran setz vnden den fues von dem vor gemachten. e. also ist das nachfolget. l. aufgerissen.

L

Das. m. mach zweyerley weyß in sein fierung. a. b. c. d. erstlich zeuch des bustaben schmalen aufrechten strich hinder. a. c. eyn zehenteyl von der leng. a. b. Darnach mach den anderen breyten zug eyn zehen teyl von der leng.a.b. für der seyten.b. d. also das sy oben vnd vnden in der fierung an ruren. Darnach teyl zwischen den zweyen zügen des bustaben auf der lini.c. d. mit eynem puncten. e. in der mitte von einander/vnd reyß ein breyten zug auß dem forderen öberen eck des dünnen zuges vnden in den punctē. e. Darnach zeuch den dünnen zug von dem.e.wider vbersich biß in das forder eck des breyten aufrechten zuges/vñ die inneren oberen eck/der zug deß bustabē schweyf nit auß/aber außwendig des gleychen vnden die zwen aufrechten züg schweyf auf beden seyten auß wie du in den forderen bustabē bericht byst. Merck auch so man dise bustaben mit der federen schreibt das man sie in einem zug sol machen/aber vmb deiner willen dich zů vnderrichten ist diser bustab her nach wie ob stet aufgerissen.

Albrecht Dürer, page from *Underweisung der Messung,* 1525. Relating each letter to the square, Dürer worked out a construction method using a one-to-ten ratio of the heavy stroke to the height. This is the approximate proportion of the Trajan alphabet, but Dürer did not base his designs on any single source.

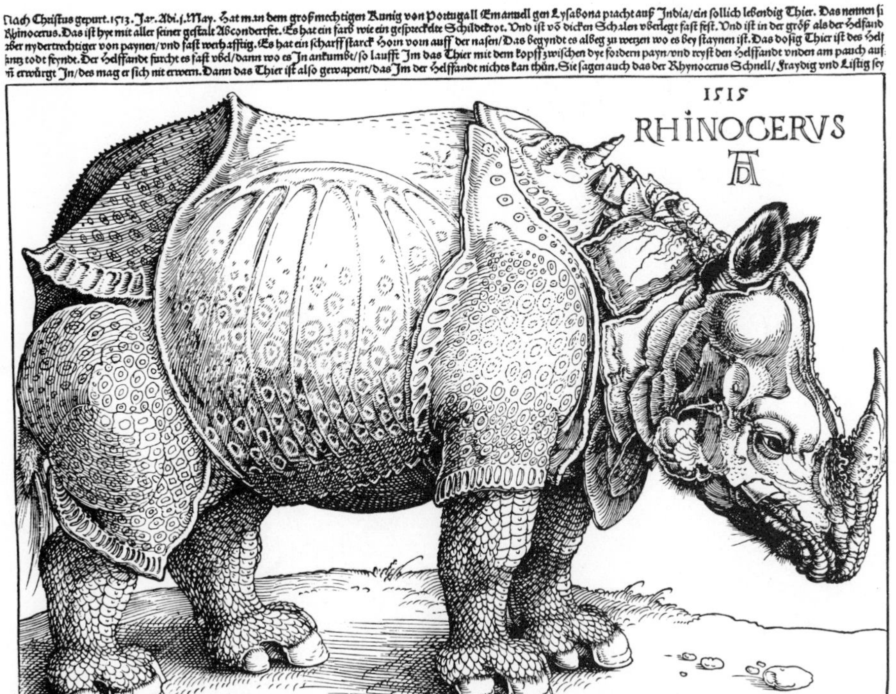

Nach Christus gepurt.1513.Jar.Adi.1.May. Hat man dem großmechtigen Kunig von Portugall Emanuell gen Lysabona pracht auß India/ein sollich lebendig Thier. Das nennen si Rhinocerus.Das ist hye mit aller seiner gestalt Abcondertfet.Es hat ein farb wie ein gespreckelte Schildtkrot.Vnd ist vō dicken Schalen vberlegt fast fest.Vnd ist in der größ als der Helfand aber nydertrechtiger von paynen/vnd fast werhafftig.Es hat ein scharff starck Horn vorn auff der nasen/Das begyndt es albeg zu wetzen wo es bey staynen ist.Das dosig Thier ist des Helfantz todt feyndt.Der Helffandt furcht es fast vbel/dann wo es Jn ankumbt/so laufft Jm das Thier mit dem kopff zwischen dye fordern payn/vnd reyst den Helffandt vnden am pauch auf vñ erwürgt Jn/des mag er sich nit erwern.Dann das Thier ist also gewapent/das Jm der Helffandt nichts kan thůn.Sie sagen auch das der Rhynocerus Schnell/Fraydig vnd Listig sey

Albrecht Dürer, broadside, 1515. Dürer developed his woodcut illustration from a sketch and description sent from Spain, after the first rhinoceros in over a thousand years arrived in Europe. The text was undoubtedly carefully edited so that the five lines of metal type form a perfect rectangle of tone that aligns with the woodcut border. This broadside was so popular that at least eight editions went out of print.

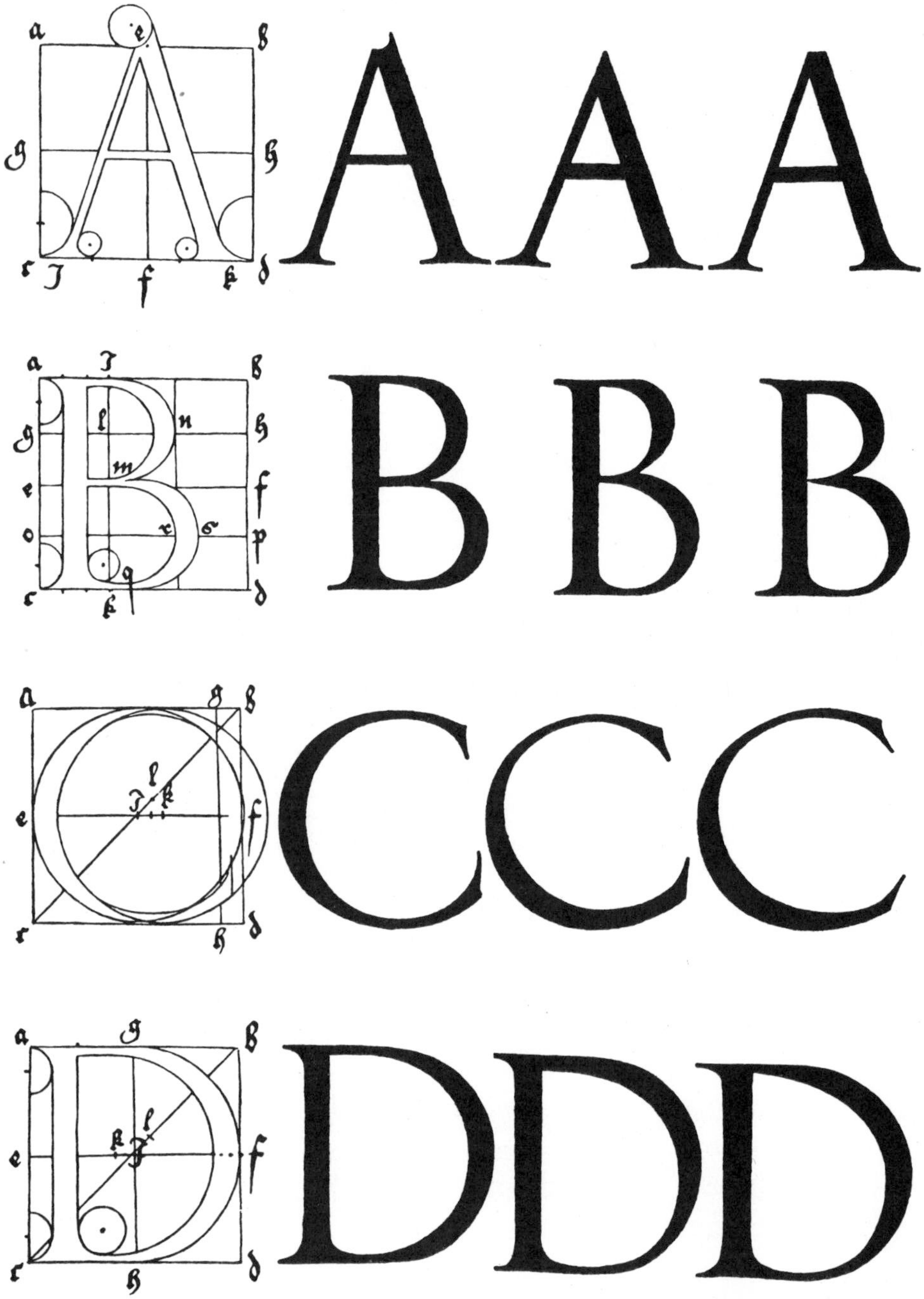

Albrecht Dürer, page from *Underweisung der Messung,* 1525. Dürer presented variations for each character in the alphabet. Recognizing the value of art and perception over geometry, Dürer advised his readers that certain construction faults could only be corrected by a sensitive eye and trained hand.

Albrecht Dürer, page from *Underweisung der Messung,* 1525. This mechanical aid in drawing, explained by Dürer, consists of a frame device for drawing foreshortened perspective views of objects.

Albrecht Dürer, woodcut from *De Symmetria Partium Humanorum Corporum,* 1532. To assist his fellow artists, Dürer offers a "through-the-looking-grid" device as an aid to drawing. *The Metropolitan Museum of Art, New York, gift of Felix M. Warburg, 1918.*

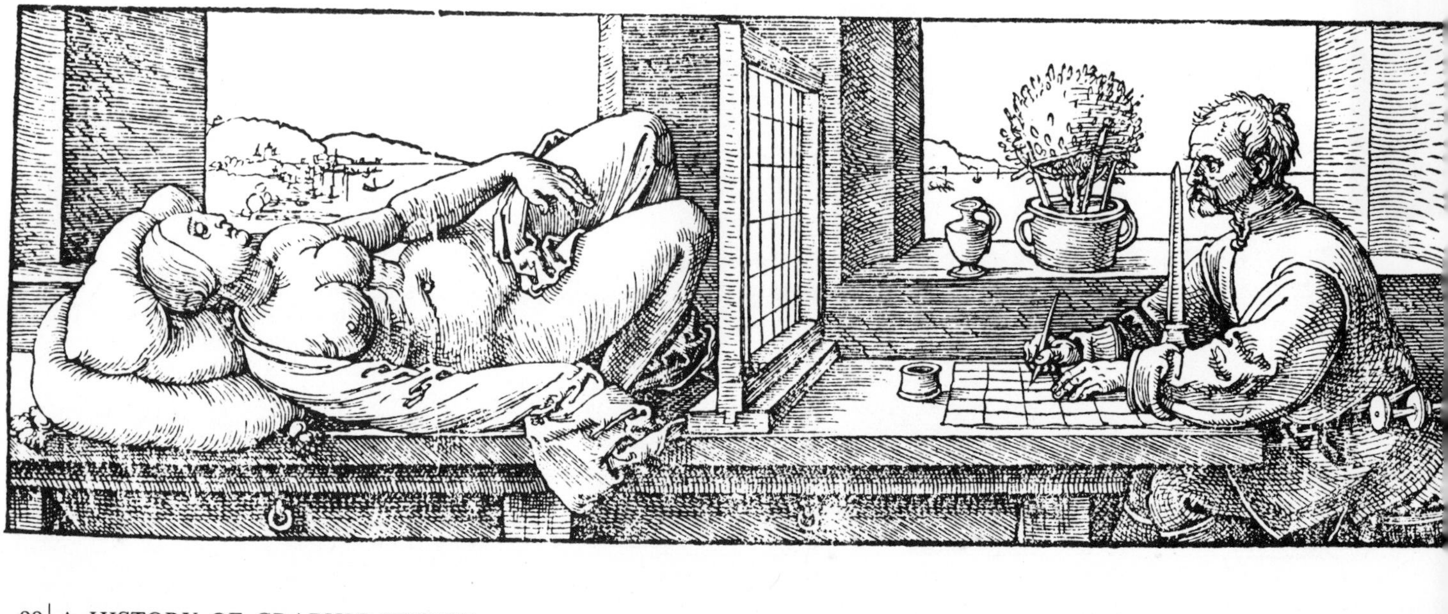

36

Unfalo dem was nicht zuuil
Khein schalkheit als Ich sagen wil
Es was in rechter winterzeit
Darinn gewonnlich vil schne leit
Ging Unfalo zum Helden dar
Sprach/herr Ich sage Euch fürwar
Dort steet in der aw vil wildpret
So ferr Ir darzu ein lust het

So möcht Ir daraus schiessen wol
Ein Jeger mit Euch ziehen sol
Der weyset Euch die rechten strass
Tewrdannck sprach/so beuelcht Im/das
Er sich von stundan mach gerecht
Unfalo vordert einen knecht
Und nam den an ein heimlich ort
Sprach gesell merckh auf meine wort
Eylunds hin auf das gepirg lauff
Unnd schaw mit allem fleys darauf
Wann der Held Tewrdannckh wirt reyten
Unnden für an des pergs leyten
So mach von schnee einen pallen
Unnd lass den gmach herab fallen
Das daraus werd ein leenen gross
Dieselb den Helden zutodt stoss
Ist sach das du darinn fleyssig
Bist/bey glauben Ich dir versprich
Dich reich unnd selig zumachen
Derselb knecht begundt zulachen
Sprach/herr khein fleys will Ich darinn sparn
Das solt Ir durch die tat erfarn
Tewrdannck der reyt mit dem Jeger
Suchend das wilpret im leger

Johann Schoensperger (printer), pages from *Teuerdank,* 1517. The flamboyant calligraphic gestures are appropriate for this romantic novel about chivalry. The swashes are carefully placed to animate the pages in the layout of the book. *Library of Congress, Washington, D.C.*

One of Dürer's former students, Hans Schäufelien, was commissioned to design the illustrations for Pfintzing's *Teuerdank,* an adventure of chivalry and knighthood that was printed by Johann Schoensperger the Elder at Nuremberg in 1517. Commissioned by Emperor Maximilian to commemorate his marriage to Mary of Burgundy, this lavish book required five years in production time. The types for *Teuerdank,* designed by court calligrapher Vincenz Rockner, were one of the earliest examples of the Gothic style known as *fraktur.* Some of the rigid, angular straight lines found in textur letterforms were replaced with flowing curved strokes. In comparing the design qualities of Rockner's fraktur with Gutenberg's textur, one might almost say that flowers and vines are now growing on the picket fence to soften the overall effect.

Rockner carried this design quality even further in a heroic effort to duplicate the gestural freedom of the pen. As many as eight alternate characters were designed and cast for each letterform. These had sweeping calligraphic flourishes, some of which flowed deep into the surrounding space. Other printers insisted that these ornamental letterforms had to be printed from woodblocks, for they refused to believe that it was possible to achieve these effects with cast metal types. (An inverted *i* in the 1517 edition, however, conclusively proves that metal types were used to print *Teuerdank.)*

Technically speaking, a *broadside* is a single leaf of paper printed on one side only. When both sides are printed, the usual designation is a *broadsheet.* When the printed sheet is folded, a pamphlet, tract—and later, a newspaper—is the result. This ubiquitous and ephemeral form of graphic communications became a major means for information dissemination from the invention of printing until the middle of the nineteenth century. Content ranged from announcements of deformed births and natural phenomena to portraits of famous secular and religious leaders. Festivals and fairs were advertised, and the sale of lottery tickets and indulgences were announced. Political causes and religious beliefs were expounded, and invasions and disasters were proclaimed. The design of a broadside was often the task of the compositor, who organized the space and made typographic decisions while setting the type. Woodblock illustrations were commissioned from artists. Once available, a given woodblock might appear in a number of broadsides, or be sold, or loaned to another printer.

During the early decades of the sixteenth century, Basel joined Nuremberg as an important center for book design and printing. Basel, which became a part of Switzerland in 1501, had its first printer as early as 1467 when Bertold Ruppel, an early associate of Gutenberg, established his press there. The Basel style of graphic design—with dense typography and a heavy use of classical initials, borders, headpieces, and tailpieces—was quite influential until Italian book design became an important inspiration after 1500. Johann Froben (1460–1527) came to this sophisticated college town from his native Bavaria to attend the University of Basel, then began to print there in 1491. Froben became Basel's leading printer and attracted the outstanding humanist scholar of the Northern Renaissance, Desiderius Erasmus (1466–1543), to Basel. For eight years beginning in 1521, Erasmus worked with Froben as author, editor, and advisor on matters of scholarship. Unlike most of his German contemporaries, Froben favored hearty, solid roman types instead of gothics.

A twenty-three-year-old painter, Hans Holbein the Younger (1497–1543), arrived in Basel from Augsburg in the autumn of 1519, was received as a master in the *Zum Himmel* guild, and was engaged by Froben to illustrate books. His border designs were sculptural and complex and often included a scene from the Bible or classical literature. His prolific designs for headpieces, tailpieces, and several sets of illustrated initials ranged from the humorous (peasants chasing a fox), to the genre (dancing peasants and playing children), to a morbid series of initials depicting the Dance of Death.

Ein Frag an eynen Müntzer/wahin doch souil Geltz kumme das man alltag müntzet: Antwort des selben Müntzers/Von dreyen Feinden vnnsers Geltz/wa wir nit acht darauff haben/werden wir den Seckel zum Gelt an.

Wann wir hetten rechten glauben
Gott vnd gemainen nutz vor augen

Recht Elen/darzů maß vnd gwicht
Gůt frid vñ auch gleich Recht vñ Ghricht

Einerlay Müntz vnd kain falsch Gelt
So stünd es wol in aller welt.

Frag an den Müntzer.

Antwort des müntzers

Der Erste Feindt.

Der Ander Feindt.

Der Dritt Feindt.

Jorg Breu the Elder (1480–1537) (illustrator), *Announcement of an Indulgence,* 1530. The traditional elements of the advertisement—headline, rectangular image, body-copy—were codified early in the evolution of graphic design.

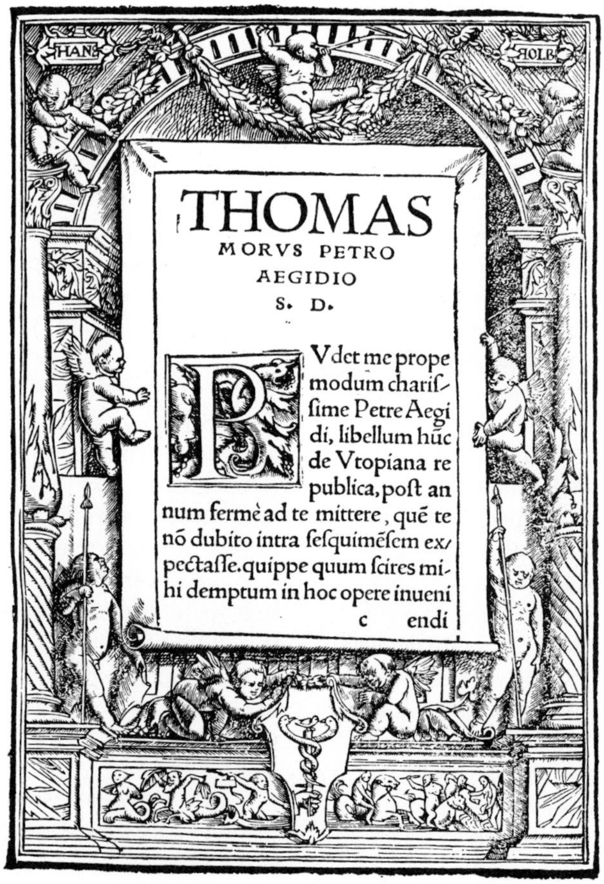
THOMAS
MORVS PETRO
AEGIDIO
S. D.

PVdet me prope modum charissime Petre Aegidi, libellum hũc de Vtopiana republica, post annum fermè ad te mittere, quẽ te nõ dubito intra sesquimẽsem expectasse. quippe quum scires mihi demptum in hoc opere inueni c endi

Johann Froben (printer) and Hans Holbein (illustrator), title page for Sir Thomas More's *Utopia,* 1518. Complex of image and tone, this title-page design unifies the typography to the illustration by placing it on a hanging scroll. *Library of Congress, Washington, D.C., Rosenwald Collection.*

In ſudore vultus tui veſceris pane
tuo.
GEN. III.
Ipſe tibi multo panem ſudore parabis,
Præbebit victum nec niſi cultus ager.
Poſt varios vſus rerum vitæq; labores
Finiet ærumnas Mors violenta tuas.
Homo natus de muliere, breui viuens tempo
re, repletur multis miſeriis: qui quaſi flos
egreditur, & cõteritur, & fugit velut vmbra.
IOB XIIII.
Omnis homo veniẽs grauida mulieris ab aluo
Naſcitur ad varijs tempora plena malis.
Flos citò marceſcens velu decedit, & ille
Sic perit, & tãquã corporis vmbra fugit.

Joannes Frellonius (printer) and Hans Holbein the Younger (illustrator), pages from *Imagines Mortis* ("The Dance of Death"), 1547. The terror of a child suddenly taken from his home by death is in striking contrast to the modest size (6.65 centimeters or 2 $\frac{5}{8}$ inches) of the illustrations and the understated elegance of Frellonius' typography. *Toledo Museum of Art, Toledo.*

Before leaving for England in 1526, Holbein was probably already working on his greatest graphic work, the forty-one woodcuts illustrating *Imagines Mortis (The Dance of Death).* The first edition of this little book was printed in Lyons, France, by K. and M. Treschsel in 1538. This is not surprising; Lyons is about 300 kilometers (180 miles) southwest of Basel, and printers in the two towns were enjoying a lively exchange. Types, woodcut borders, and illustrations from Basel were on many Lyons presses, and Lyons printers often produced editions for their busy Basel counterparts. The Dance of Death, a procession in which skeletons or corpses escort the living to their graves, was a major theme in the visual arts as well as music, drama, and poetry. This use of art as an ominous reminder to the unfaithful of the inevitability of death originated in the fourteenth century when the great waves of the plague swept over Europe. By separating the procession into individual scenes, Holbein was able to intensify the suddenness and personal tragedy of death. Numerous editions were printed from the blocks engraved by Hans Lutzelburger after Holbein's drawings.

After Froben's death, Johann Oporinus became Basel's leading printer. His masterpiece is the enormous six hundred sixty-seven-page folio, *De humani corporis fabrica,* by the brilliant founder of modern anatomy from Brussels, Andreas Vesalius (1514–1564). This important book was illustrated by full-page woodcuts of remarkable clarity and accuracy by artists working from dissected corpses under Vesalius' supervision. Many of the anatomical figures are gracefully posed in landscapes. Oporinus set Vesalius' turgid, wordy text in closely set pages of roman type with precise page numbers, running heads, marginal notes in delicate italic type, and no paragraph indications. A curious note of humor is introduced by illustrated, square initials that break up the text. In them, *cherubs* curiously examine bones, circumcise one of their little friends, and perform a dissection on a

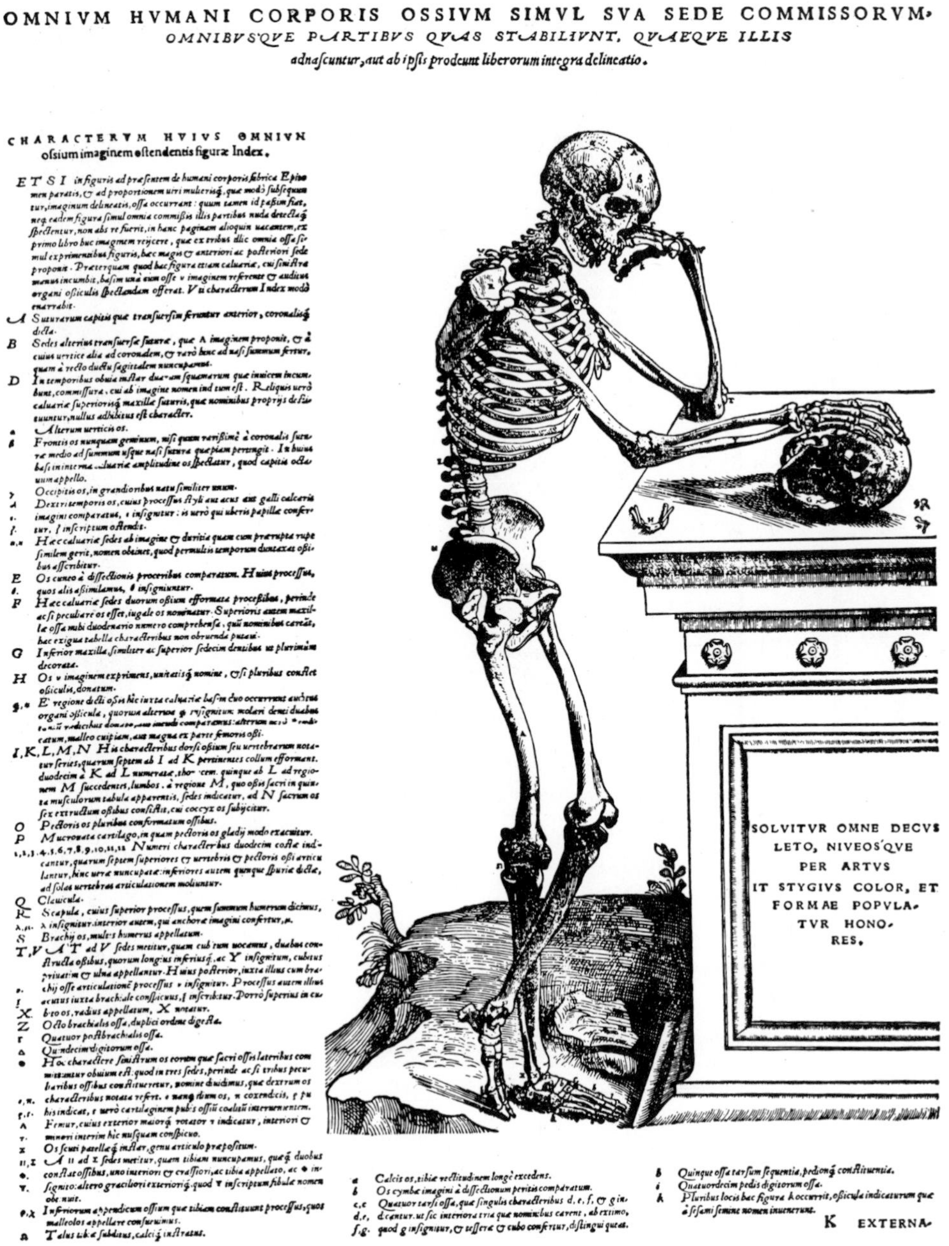

Johann Oporinus (printer), page from *De humani corporis fabrica,* 1543. Anatomical illustrations of skeletons and muscles in natural poses appear in pages of italic captions set in three columns to the page.

wild boar. If imitation is the sincerest form of flattery, *De humani corporis fabrica* ranks as a great book, for it was pirated, translated, reprinted, copied, and abridged by printers all across Europe. In fact, King Henry VIII of England ordered the production of an English pirated edition in 1545. Its carefully executed, copperplate-engraved illustrations—copied from the original woodcut title page and illustrations—mark this copy as the first successful book with engraved illustrations.

As Martin Luther pressed his breach with the Catholic Church that began in 1517, his presence at the university in Wittenberg brought importance to the graphics produced there. Luther found a fast friend and follower in the artist Lucas Cranach the Elder (1472–1553), who had been called to Wittenberg by the electors of Saxony. In addition to his studio with a number of well-trained assistants, Cranach operated a printing office, a bookshop, and a paper mill, and even found time to serve as mayor of Wittenberg twice. He turned his considerable energy to the Reformation by portraying the Reformers and their cause in books and broadsides. When Luther traveled to Worms for his celebrated trial in 1512, his portraits by Cranach filled the town on printed matter proclaiming his beliefs. And yet, Cranach regularly accepted commissions for Madonnas and Crucifixions from Catholic clients, and many of the woodcuts he produced for the Luther Bible were also used in a subsequent Catholic edition. A most effective example of propaganda is Cranach's work for the *Passional Christi und Antichristi,* printed by Grunenberg in 1521. Inspired by Luther, graphic contrast is achieved on facing pages as scenes from the life of Christ and biting depictions of the papacy are juxtaposed. Both of Cranach's sons, Hans Cranach (d. 1537) and Lucas Cranach the Younger (1515–1586), joined their father's studio; few examples of Hans' work remain, but the younger son continued to work in the family style for many years after his father's death. The epitaph on Lucas Cranach the Elder's tomb honors him as *pictor celerrimus*—the swiftest of painters!

Typography spreads from Germany

Italy, which was at the forefront of Europe's slow transition from the medieval world into a cultural and commercial revival, sponsored the first printing press to be set up outside of Germany. Although fifteenth-century Italy was a political patchwork of city-states, monarchies, republics, and papal domains, it was at the zenith of its wealth and splendid patronage of the arts and architecture in the Renaissance. In 1465, Cardinal Turrecremata of the Benedictine monastery at Subiaco invited two printers, Conrad Sweynheym (d. 1477) of Mainz, who had been employed by Peter Schoeffer, and Arnold Pannartz (d. 1476) of Cologne,

Jhesus ist eyn weytten wegk gangen / ist er müd worden.
an. 4. Der mir will nach folgen / der nem seyn Creutz vff
vnd folge mir. Mathei 16.
at ym seyn Creutze selbest getragen vnd ist zu der stell die
arie gnant wirdt / gangen. 19.

Antichristi.
Antichristus.
Das capittel Si quis suadente vñ der gleychen zeygt gnug an
wie gerne der Bapst das Creutz der wyderwertigkeyt duldet/so
er alle die ihenen/die handt an die pfaffen an legē vormaladeyet
vñ dem teuffel gibt Vnd alßo ouch tregt der Bapst das Creutz
das ymen getauffte Christen vff yren achsselen tragen mussen.

Warhafftige Abcontrafactur D. Martini Lutheri
seligen/Durch welchen Gott / als durch seinen sonderlichen darzu erwelten
werckzeug/das lauter vnd klar Liecht seines heiligen Euangelij / wider an rechten vnd seligen tag /
zu diesen letzten zeiten bracht hat / Gott gebe das wir dafür danckbar
sein vnd darbey bleiben / Amen.
Zu Wittemberg bey Jörg Formschneider.

Above: Grunenberg (printer) and Lucas Cranach the Elder (illustrator), pages from *Passional Christi und Antichristi,* 1521. In a biting visual contrast of travel, Christ labors under the weight of his cross while the Pope travels in style in a sedan chair. *Library of Congress, Washington, D.C., Rosenwald Collection.*

Above, right: Lucas Cranach the Younger, broadside, 1551. This commemorative portrait of Martin Luther bears the identification of the illustrator (Cranach's flying snake device) and the block cutter, a craftsman named Jörg, who is identified typographically above the date.

Below: Hans Lufft (printer) and Lucas Cranach the Younger (illustrator), pages from Auerswald's *Ringer-Kunst,* 1539. In this how-to-do-it book on the art of wrestling, Lufft printed Cranach's eighty-seven woodcuts without the usual border. This enables them to move dynamically on the page. The centered captions above and thick rule below restore balance in this predominantly pictorial book. *Toledo Museum of Art, Toledo.*

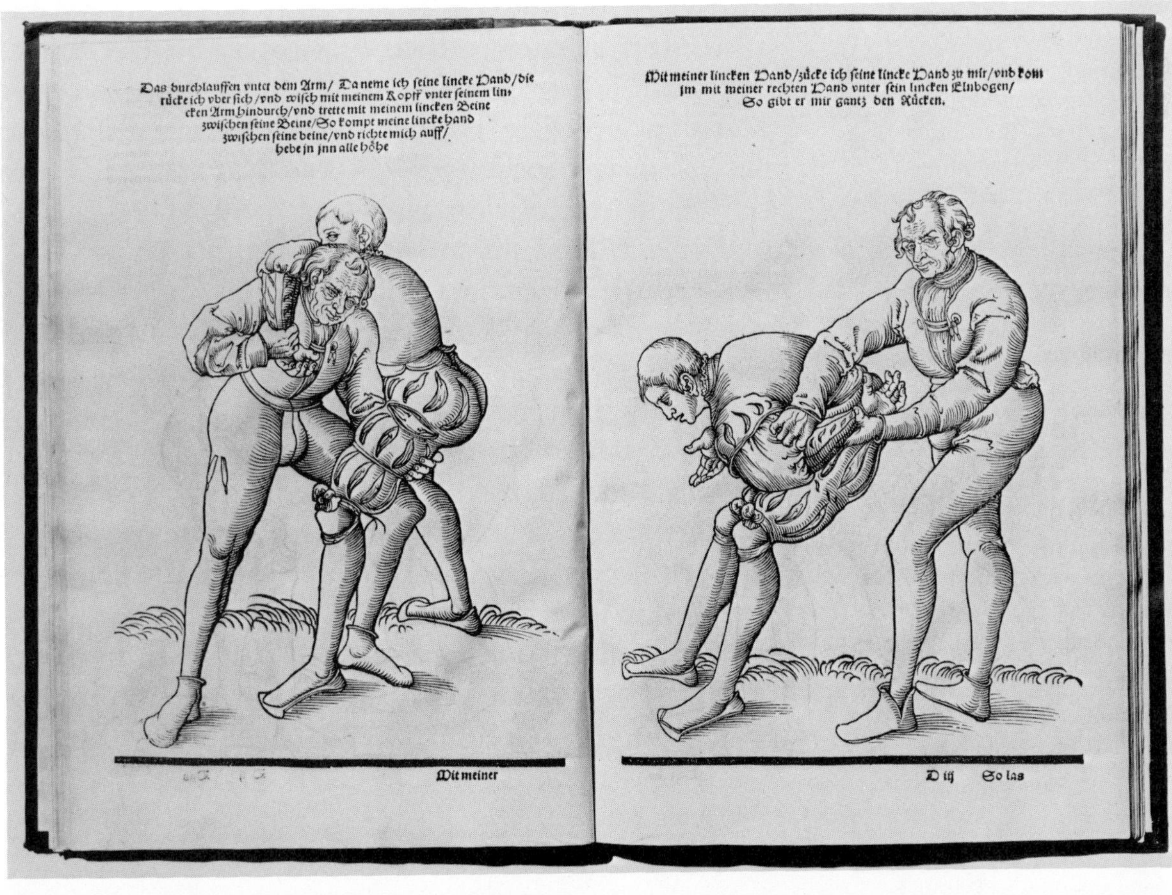

to Subiaco to establish a press. The Cardinal wished to publish Latin classics and his own writings.

The types designed by Sweynheym and Pannartz marked the first step toward roman-style typography based on the humanistic writing that had been developed by Italian scribes. These scholars had discovered copies of lost Roman classics written in ninth-century Caroline minuscules. They mistakenly thought that authentic Roman writing had been discovered in contrast to the black, medieval writing that they erroneously believed to be the writing style of the barbarians who had destroyed Rome. Sweynheym and Pannartz created a typographic "double alphabet" by combining the capital letters of ancient Roman inscriptions with the rounded minuscules that had evolved in Italy from the Caroline minuscule. They tried to unify these contradictory alphabets by adding serifs to some of the minuscule letters and redesigning others. After three years in Subiaco, Sweynheym and Pannartz moved to Rome where they designed a more fully roman alphabet that became the prototype for the roman alphabets still in use today. By 1473 the partnership had printed over fifty editions, usually in press runs of two hundred seventy-five copies. Ten Italian cities also had printers publishing Latin classics, and the market could not absorb the sudden supply of books. The partnership of Sweynheym and Pannartz suffered a financial collapse and was dissolved.

Early volumes printed in Italy continued the pattern of the early German printed books. Initials, folios, headings, and paragraph marks were not printed. Space was left for these to be rubricated by a scribe with red ink. Often, a small letter would be printed in the space left for an illuminated initial to tell the scribe what initial to draw. In many volumes from the Incunabula, the paragraph marks were not drawn in red in the spaces provided. Eventually, the blank space alone indicated a paragraph.

After apprenticing in the English textile trade, William Caxton (c. 1421–1491) left his native land for

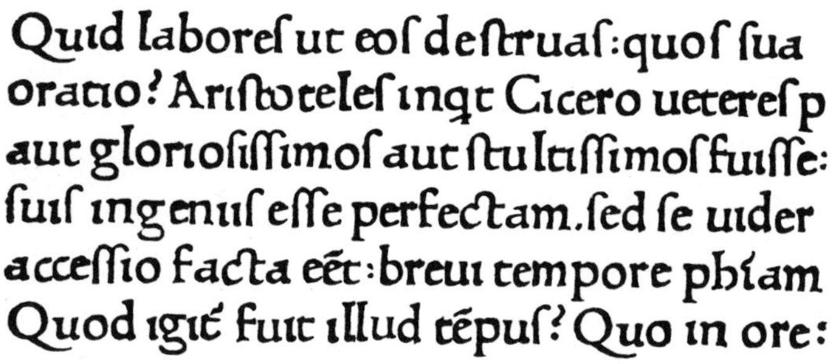
Quid laboreſ ut eoſ deſtruaſ:quoſ ſua
oratio? Ariſtoteleſ inqt Cicero ueteres p
aut glorioſiſſimoſ aut ſtultiſſimoſ fuiſſe:
ſuiſ ingeniiſ eſſe perfectam.ſed ſe uider
acceſſio facta eēt:breui tempore phiam
Quod igit̄ fuit illud tēpuſ? Quo in ore:

Conrad Sweynheym and Arnold Pannartz, detail from *Lactantu . . .*, 1468. The second typeface of Sweynheym and Pannartz, designed after they moved to Rome, is shown actual size.

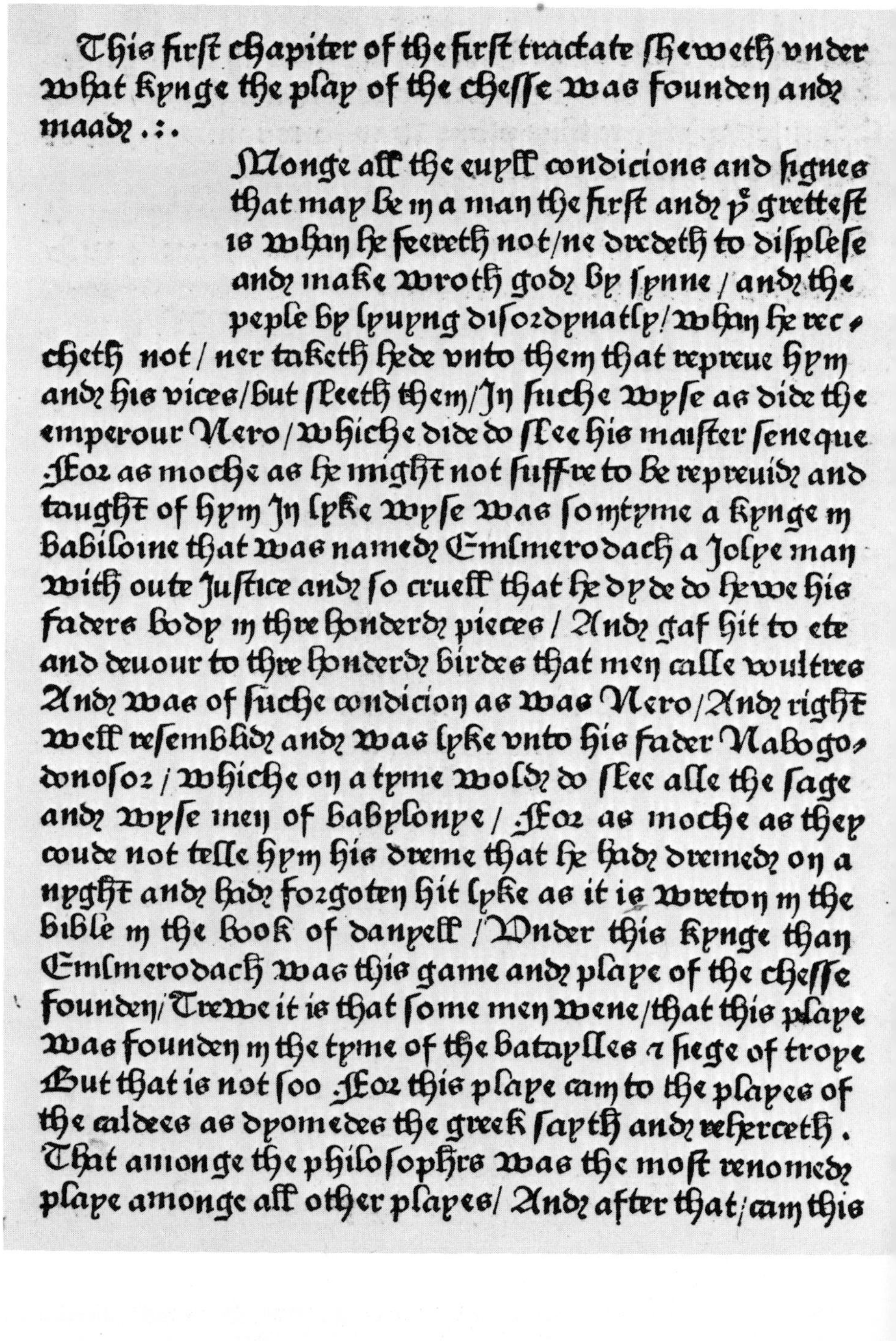
This first chapiter of the first tractate ſheweth vnder
what kynge the play of the cheſſe was founden and
maad .:.
Monge all the euyll condicions and ſignes
that may be in a man the first and ye grettest
is whan he feereth not/ne dredeth to diſpleſe
and make wroth god by ſynne / and the
peple by lyuyng diſordynatly/whan he rec-
cheth not / ner taketh hede vnto them that repreue hym
and his vices/but ſleeth them/In ſuche wyſe as dide the
emperour Nero/whiche dide do ſlee his maiſter ſeneque
For as moche as he might not ſuffre to be repreuid and
taught of hym In lyke wyſe was ſomtyme a kynge in
Babiloine that was named Emlmerodach a Jolye man
with oute Juſtice and ſo cruell that he dyde do hewe his
faders body in thre honderd pieces / And gaf hit to ete
and deuour to thre honderd birdes that men calle wultres
And was of ſuche condicion as was Nero/And right
well reſemblid and was lyke vnto his fader Nabogo-
donoſor / whiche on a tyme wold do ſlee alle the ſage
and wyſe men of babylonye / For as moche as they
coude not telle hym his dreme that he had dremed on a
nyght and had forgoten hit lyke as it is wreton in the
bible in the book of danyell /Vnder this kynge than
Emlmerodach was this game and playe of the cheſſe
founden/Trewe it is that ſome men wene/that this playe
was founden in the tyme of the batayles & ſiege of troye
But that is not ſoo For this playe cam to the playes of
the caldees as dyomedes the greek ſayth and reherceth .
That amonge the philoſophres was the moſt renomed
playe amonge all other playes/ And after that/cam this

William Caxton and Colard Mansion, page from *The Game and Playe of the Chesse*, c. 1476. The kinky, jerky type used by Caxton ushered the era of the typographic book into the British nation. *Library of Congress, Washington, D.C., Rosenwald Collection.*

the textile center of Bruges in the Netherlands where he prospered. In the early 1470s, he spent a year and a half in Cologne where he translated the *Recuyell of the Histories of Troy* from French into English, and learned printing. On returning to Bruges, he enlisted the help of the illuminator and calligrapher Colard Mansion, and in 1475 Caxton's translation became the first typographic English language book. In the epilogue to the third part, Caxton tells the reader that "my pen is worn, my hand is weary and shaky, my eyes are dimmed from too much looking at white paper"; thus he "practiced and learned at great expense how to print it."

After printing an English translation of *The Game and Playe of the Chesse* (1476) and two or three French language books, the partners separated. Mansion remained in Bruges and printed twenty-seven editions before 1484, when he was forced to flee the city to escape his creditors. Caxton moved his types and press across the English Channel and established the first press on English soil. He had printed the first book in English; now he printed the first book in England, at the Sign of the Red Pail in Westminster.

The first of about ninety books that he published in Westminster was *The Dictes or Sayenges of the Phylosophers.* Nearly all the existing English literature up to the fifteenth century, including Chaucer's *Canterbury Tales* and Sir Thomas Malory's *Morte d'Arthur,* was published by Caxton. He is a pivotal figure in the development of a national English language, for his typographic work stabilized and unified the constantly changing, diverse dialects in use throughout the islands. Primarily a scholar and translator, Caxton contributed little to the evolution of graphic design and printing. This is a polite way of saying that his work had a crude vigor devoid of graphic elegance or refinement. Woodcut illustrations from his volumes have a brash forcefulness and awkward drawing, and the workmanship of his printing is inferior to continental printing of the same period.

William Caxton, printer's trademark, after 1477.

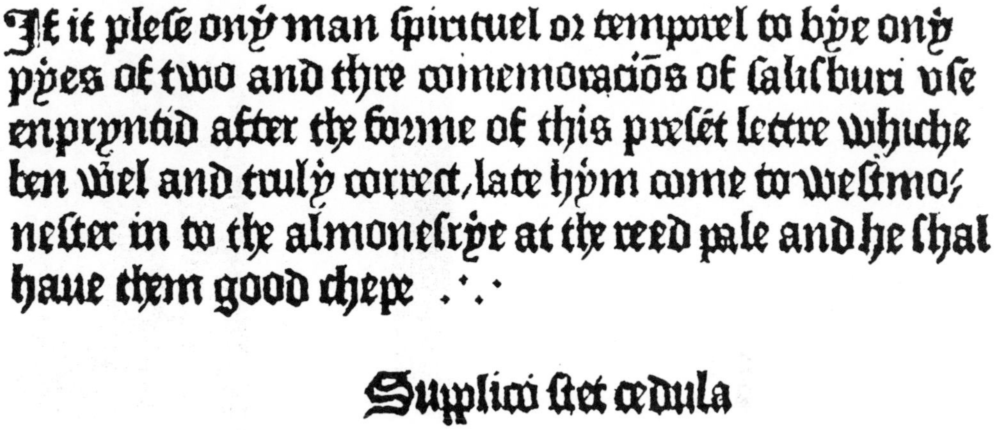

If it plese ony man spirituel or temporel to bye ony pyes of two and thre comemoracios of salisburi vse enpryntid after the forme of this presēt lettre whiche ben wel and truly correct, late hym come to westmo/nester in to the almonesrye at the reed pale and he shal haue them good chepe .·.

Supplico stet cedula

William Caxton, advertising poster/handbill, 1477. Because a copy of this announcement for "Pyes of Salisbury Use" in a Manchester, England library bears a handwritten request, "Pray, do not pull down the advertisement," we can conclude that this is possibly the first printed English language poster.

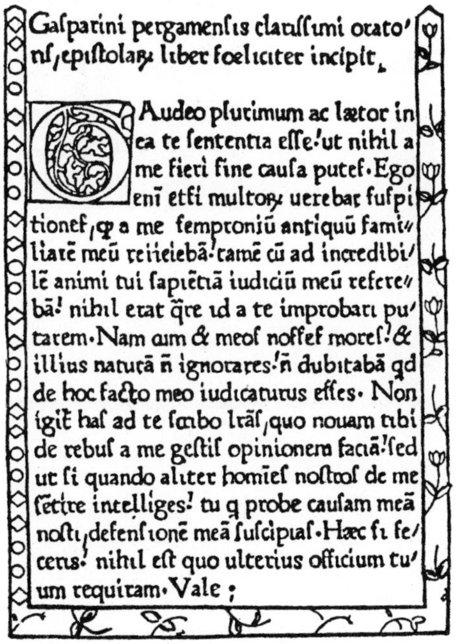

Gasparini pergamensis clarissimi orato/ris epistolarum liber foeliciter incipit.

Audeo plurimum ac laetor in ea te sententia esse: ut nihil a me fieri sine causa putes. Ego enim etsi multorum uerebar suspitiones, quae a me sempronium antiquum familiarem meum reiiciebam: tamen cum ad incredibilem animi tui sapientiam iudicium meum referebam: nihil erat quare id a te improbari putarem. Nam cum & meos nosses mores: & illius naturam non ignorares: non dubitabam quod de hoc facto meo iudicaturus esses. Non igitur has ad te scribo litteras, quo nouam tibi de rebus a me gestis opinionem faciam: sed ut si quando aliter homines nostros de me sentire intelliges: tu quam probe causam meam nosti, defensionem meam suscipias. Haec si feceris: nihil est quo ulterius officium tuum requiram. Vale;

Michael Freiburger, Ulrich Gering, and Martin Kranz, first page of *Letters* by Gaspari, 1470. In this first book printed in Paris, the ornamental woodcuts and rude roman typography are harbingers of the golden era of French typography that bloomed after the turn of the century.

After Caxton's death, his foreman, Wynkyn de Worde, continued his work and published nearly four hundred titles over the following four decades.

Printing came to France in 1470 when three German printers—Michael Freiburger, Ulrich Gering and Martin Kranz—were sponsored by the Prior and the Librarian of the Sorbonne to establish a press there. At first they used a roman letter, inspired by Italian types, and reprinted classics, but after they lost their Sorbonne sponsorship in 1473, they began to print with Gothic types that were more familiar to their French audience. The inevitable competition appeared before long. Nowhere else in Europe did block printers and typographic printers join forces in an attempt to duplicate the design of illuminated manuscripts as in France. Late Gothic illumination was the zenith of French art at that time, and early French printing surrounded its Gothic type and woodcut illustrations with modular blocks that filled the space with flowers and leaves, birds and animals, patterns, and portraits. Jean Dupré printed France's first outstanding typographic book, St. Augustine's *La Cité de Dieu,* in 1486. Philippe Pigouchet's *Horae (Book of Hours)* (1485–1515) established the graphic excellence of this popular form. He appears to have introduced the *criblé* technique, in which the black areas of a woodblock are punched with white dots, giving the page a lively tonality.

Spain also received three German printers, who arrived in Valencia in 1473 under the auspices of a major, German import-export firm. The Spanish design sense, which favored dark masses balancing decorative detail, influenced their graphic design, particularly their large woodblock title pages. A particular masterpiece of Spanish typographic design is Arñao Guillen de Brocar's *Polyglot Bible* of 1514–17. Composed of correlated texts in multiple languages, this massive research project drew scholars from all over Europe to the University of Alcalá de Henares. The printer had to design a page format to accommodate five simultaneous typographic presentations.

Christopher Columbus discovered the New World in 1492, and a spice-laden but badly leaking vessel, *Victoria,* limped back to Portugal with the seventeen survivors of Ferdinand Magellan's expedition to circumnavigate the globe in 1522. An energetic competition by European nations to colonize new territory began. A missionary zeal for converting the natives in the colonies to Christianity characterized this expansion. On Columbus' second voyage, a Roman Catholic priest was on board. In 1539 the Franciscan archbishop in Mexico, Juan de Zumarraga, made arrangements to establish the first printing press in the New World for the instruction and conversion of the Indians. A Spanish printer in Seville had attempted to print a bilingual catechism in Spanish and the Nahuatl language of the Mexican Indians, but serious difficulties were encountered. An Italian printer, Giovanni Paoli (Juan Pablos in Spanish), contracted to sail to Mexico, establish a press, and remain for a decade. His first works are lost to history; the earliest known survivor is the 1540 *Manual de Adultos,* which was published a century before the first printing press was established in British North America.

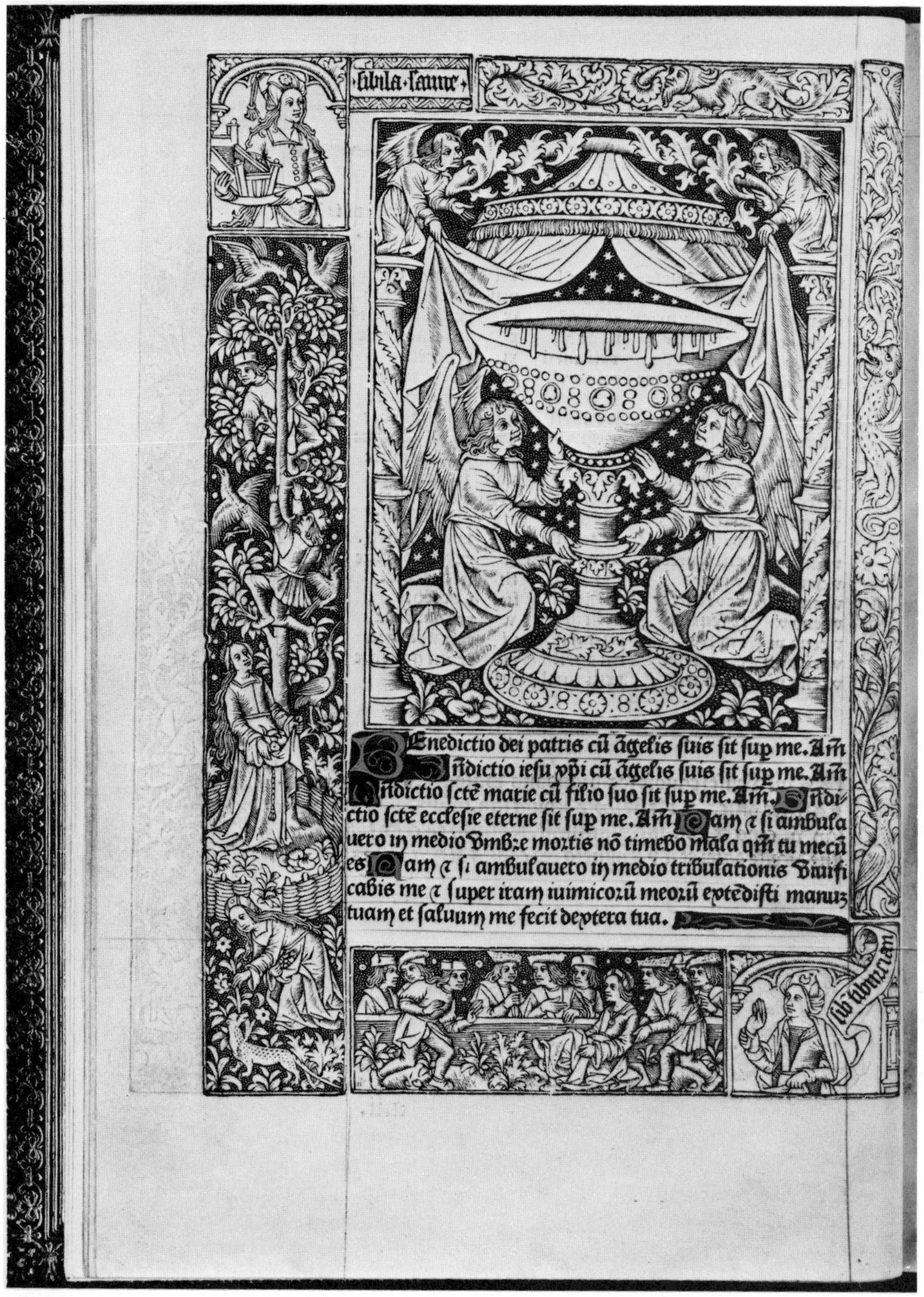

Philippe Pigouchet, page from *Horae Beatus Virginis Mariae,* 1498. The dense complexity of illustration, typography, and ornaments compressed into the space is typical of Pigouchet's design style. *Library of Congress, Washington, D.C., Rosenwald Collection.*

Arñao Guillen de Brocar, page from the *Polyglot Bible,* 1514–17. The grid system developed for this volume used uneven columns to compensate for the different running lengths of the different languages. *Pierpont Morgan Library, New York.*

Diego de Gumiel, title page for *Aureum Opus,* 1515. The title almost becomes an afterthought in this title page. The use of white on black woodblocks and heraldic imagery is typical of early Spanish graphic design.

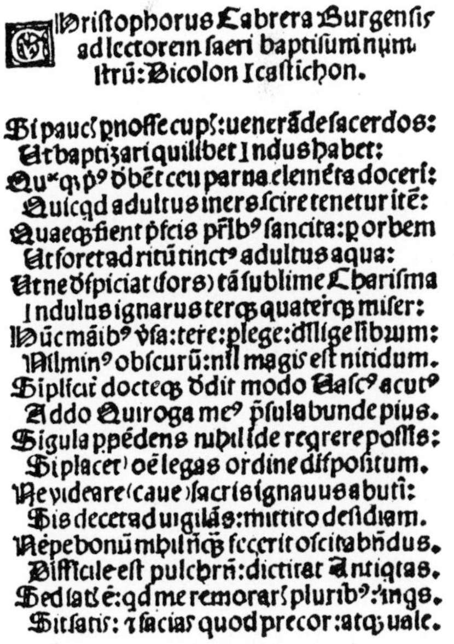

Giovanni Paoli, page from *Manual de Adultos* by Juan de Zumarraga, 1540. In this earliest extant book printed in America, Paoli established a handsome rhythm by indenting every other line.

8

Renaissance Graphic Design

THE WORD *RENAISSANCE* MEANS "revival" or "rebirth." Originally, this term was used to denote the period that began in the fourteenth and fifteenth centuries in Italy when the classical literature of ancient Greece and Rome was revived and read anew. Frequently, however, the word is used to encompass the period marking the transition from the medieval world to the modern world. In the history of graphic design, the renaissance of classical literature and the work of the Italian humanists are closely bound to an innovative approach to book design. Type design, page layout, ornaments, illustration, and even the total design of the book were all rethought by Italian printers and scholars. The prototype roman alphabet designs of Sweynheym and Pannartz might be considered the first tentative step toward a unique, Renaissance design style. The flowering of a new approach to the design of the book that was independent of the German illustrated book started in Venice and continued there during the last three decades of the fifteenth century.

Graphic design of the Italian Renaissance

It was not Florence, where the wealthy Medicis scorned printing as inferior to manuscript books, but Venice—the center of commerce and Europe's gateway to trade with the eastern Mediterranean nations, India, and the Orient—which led the way in Italian typographic book design. A Mainz goldsmith, Johannes de Spira (d.1470), was given a five-year monopoly on printing in Venice, publishing his first book, *Epistolae ad Familiares* by Cicero, in 1469. His innovative and handsome roman type cast off some of the gothic qualities found in the fonts of Sweynheym and Pannartz, and he claimed that it was an original invention. In partnership with his brother, Vindelinus, de

rodiaĩ artibus certius.Quid Apollonii ſ
cleatius poſſit ĩueniri?Cum igitur eos o
grȩcorum cõmentariis ſunt relicta artis
certisq; rationis legibus emendaſſe: no
illos imitatorem eorum extitiſſe. quipp
ſtudiis litterarum ,ppter inopiam ſcript

Johann de Spira (type design) and Vindelinus de Spira (printer), typography from Priscianus' *Opera,* 1470. The vertical stress and sharp angles of gothic type that remained as a design feature in the types of Sweynheym-Pannartz yielded to a more organic unity of horizontal, vertical, and rounded forms. *Library of Congress, Washington, D.C.*

Spira's 1470 edition of *De Civitate Dei* was the first typographic book with printed page numbers. Vindelinus de Spira inherited his brother's press—but not the exclusive right to printing in Venice—upon Johannes de Spira's untimely death.

Nicolas Jenson (c.1420–1480), from France, who had been Master of the Royal Mint of Tours, was a highly skilled cutter of dies used for striking coin. He established Venice's second press shortly after de Spira's death. In 1458 King Charles VII of France had sent Jenson to Mainz to learn printing. It has been said that Jenson chose not to return to France after Louis XI ascended to the French throne in 1461. Jenson's fame as one of history's greatest typeface designers and punch cutters rests on the types used in Eurebius' *De Praeparatione Evangelica,* which was the full flowering of roman type design.

Part of the lasting influence of Jenson's fonts is their extreme legibility, but it was his ability to design the spaces between the letters and within each form to create an even tone throughout the page that places the mark of genius on his work. During the last decade of his life, Jenson designed outstanding Greek and Gothic fonts and printed approximately one hundred and fifty books that brought him financial success and artistic renown. The characters in Jenson's fonts aligned more perfectly than those of any other printer of his time.

The Renaissance had a love for floral decoration. Wildflowers and vines were applied to furniture, architecture, and the manuscript. The book continued to be a collaboration

ab hoc opere perſpicere licet.Quod ille ideo ſu
apud gentiũ præclaros philoſophia uiros nobi
paternamq; deorũ religionem catholicæ uerita
partim accuſãtibus ſuum propoſitum reſpond
uiribus ſuis uoluit cõfirmare.Itaq; ĩ duas uniu

Nicolas Jenson, from Eurebius' *De Praeparatione Evangelica,* 1470. In this first book set in Jenson's roman type, we find that—relative to the Gutenberg forty-two-line Bible—the tone and texture is lighter, letterforms are wider, and ascenders and descenders go higher and lower in proportion to the *x*-height (the height of the lower case *x,* which is a standard typographic measurement). *Library of Congress, Washington, D.C.*

Laurentius de Rubeis, printer's mark, 1482. This orb and cross was designed in the town of Ferrara located about 90 kilometers (55 miles) southwest of Venice.

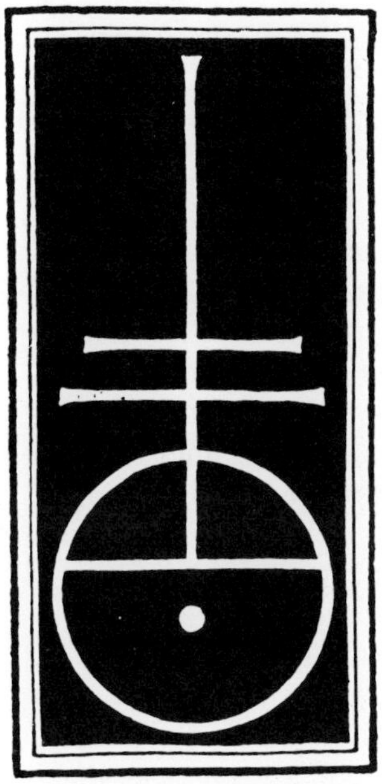

Attributed to Nicolas Jenson, mark for The Society of Venetian Printers, 1481. One of man's oldest symbols, the orb-and-cross motif is found in a chamber of Cheop's pyramid at Giza, where it was hewn into stone as a quarry mark. In Jenson's time it symbolized that "God shall reign over earth."

Pere Miguel, printer's mark, 1494. Dozens of Incunabula printers adopted an orb-and-cross mark. Miguel worked in Barcelona, Spain.

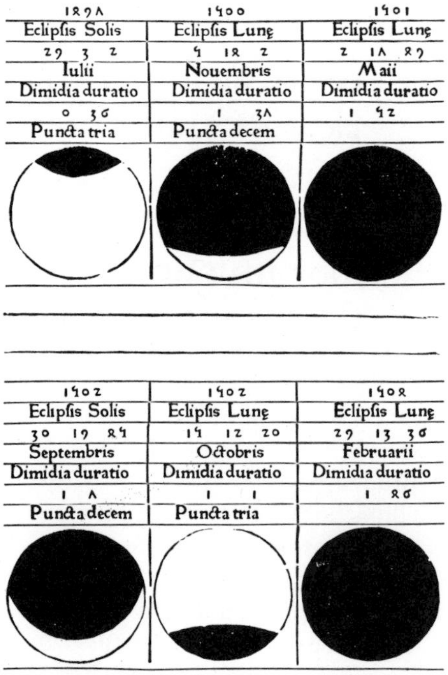

1498	1500	1501
Eclipsis Solis	Eclipsis Lunę	Eclipsis Lunę
29 3 2	5 14 2	2 18 49
Iulii	Nouembris	Maii
Dimidia duratio	Dimidia duratio	Dimidia duratio
0 36	1 38	1 52
Puncta tria	Puncta decem	

1502	1502	1504
Eclipsis Solis	Eclipsis Lunę	Eclipsis Lunę
30 19 45	15 12 20	29 13 36
Septembris	Octobris	Februarii
Dimidia duratio	Dimidia duratio	Dimidia duratio
1 8	1 1	1 46
Puncta decem	Puncta tria	

Erhard Ratdolt, Peter Loeslein, and Bernhard Maler, page from *Calendarium* by Regiomontanus, 1476. A grid system of metal rules brings order and legibility to the record of past and future solar and lunar eclipses. *Library of Congress, Washington, D.C., Rosenwald Collection.*

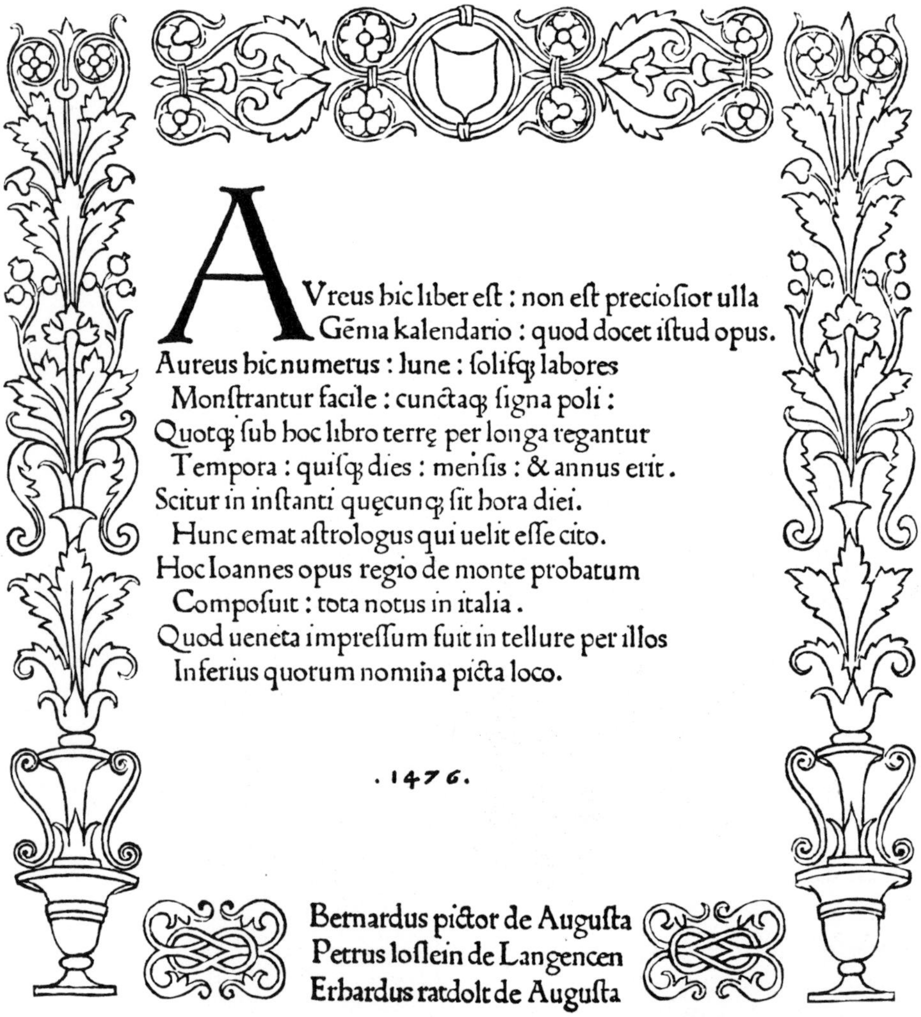

AVreus hic liber est : non est preciosior ulla
Gēma kalendario : quod docet istud opus.
Aureus hic numerus : Lune : solisq; labores
Monstrantur facile : cunctaq; signa poli :
Quotq; sub hoc libro terrę per longa regantur
Tempora : quisq; dies : mensis : & annus erit.
Scitur in instanti quęcunq; sit hora diei.
Hunc emat astrologus qui uelit esse cito.
Hoc Ioannes opus regio de monte probatum
Composuit : tota notus in italia.
Quod ueneta impressum fuit in tellure per illos
Inferius quorum nomina picta loco.

. 1476 .

Bernardus pictor de Augusta
Petrus loslein de Langencen
Erhardus ratdolt de Augusta

Erhard Ratdolt, Peter Loeslein, and Bernhard Maler, title page for *Calendarium* by Regiomontanus, 1476. The title and author are identified in verse describing the book. The date and printers' names in Latin appear below.

between a typographic printer—in the Incunabula period typography was sometimes called "artificial writing"—and the illuminator who added initials and ornaments. The logical evolution was to print everything on a printing press. Erhard Ratdolt (1442–1528) achieved significant design innovations toward this goal. A master printer from Augsburg, Germany, Ratdolt worked in Venice from 1476 until 1486. Working closely with his partners, Bernhard Maler and Peter Loeslein, Ratdolt's 1476 *Calendarium* by Regiomontanus had the first complete title page used to identify the book. It was printed the same year that the author, an astronomer and mathematician named Johann Müller (1436–1476), who called himself Regiomontanus, was assassinated during a return visit to Rome where he had advised Pope Sixtus IV on calendar reform. In addition to the innovative title page, *Calendarium* contained sixty diagrams of solar and lunar eclipses printed in yellow and black. Fear and superstition were being swept away as scientists began to understand natural phenomena, and printers disseminated this knowledge. Eclipses moved from black magic to predictable fact. In the rear of the book, there is a three-part mathematical wheel for calculating the solar cycles.

Yet another innovation by Ratdolt is the use of woodcut borders and initials as design elements. These decorative designs include naturalistic forms inspired by western antiquity and more patterned forms derived from the eastern Islamic cultures. Partner Bernhard Maler (also called Pictor) was probably the designer of these borders. Both fine-line ornaments and reversed designs (white forms on a solid background) were used. Sometimes, these were printed in red ink. A three-sided woodcut border used on the title page for a number of Ratdolt's editions became a kind of trademark. It is used in the title page of Euclid's *Geometriae elementa* of 1482. This geometry book's format design uses a large outer margin about half as wide as the text column width. Small geometric figures, whose sheer delicacy of line represent a technical breakthrough, are placed in these margins adjacent to the supporting text.

When Ratdolt decided to leave Venice and return to his native Augsburg, he publicized his return by issuing the first printer's type specimen sheet. This showed his range of typographic sizes and styles. Ratdolt remained an active printer until his death at age eighty-one. The innovations of Ratdolt and his partners during his decade in Venice were not immediately adopted by other Vene-

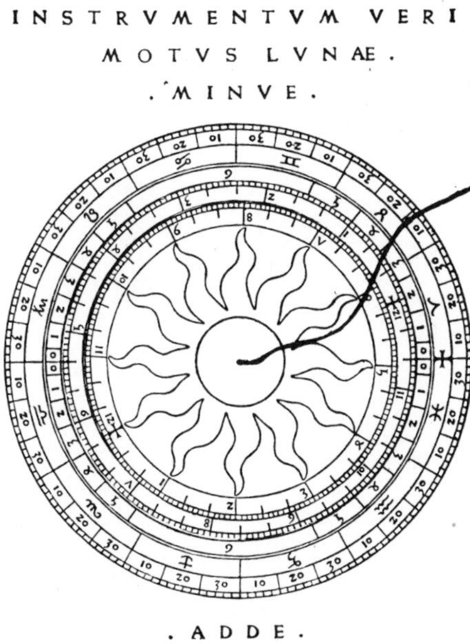

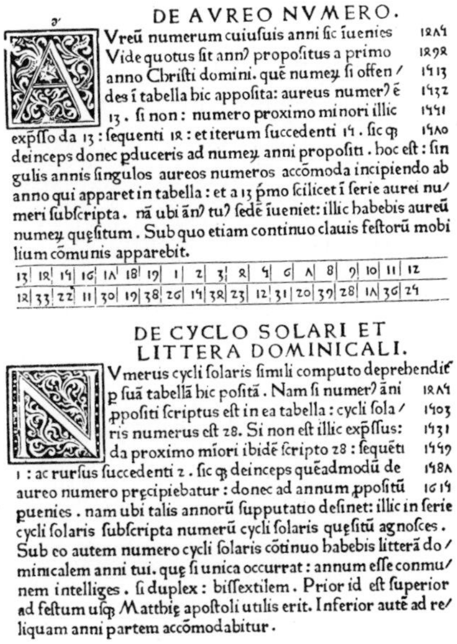
DE AVREO NVMERO.

Vreũ numerum cuiusuis anni sic iuenies Vide quotus sit anni propositus a primo anno Christi domini. quẽ numerũ si offendes ĩ tabella hic apposita: aureus numerus ẽ 13. si non: numero proximo minori illic expsso da 13: sequenti 12: et iterum succedenti 14. sicq deinceps donec pduceris ad numerũ anni propositi. hoc est: singulis annis singulos aureos numeros accõmoda incipiendo ab anno qui apparet in tabella: et a 13 pmo scilicet ĩ serie aurei numeri subscripta. nã ubi ãnus tuus sedẽ iueniet: illic habebis aureũ numerũ quęsitum. Sub quo etiam continuo clauis festorũ mobilium cõmunis apparebit.

DE CYCLO SOLARI ET LITTERA DOMINICALI.

Vmerus cycli solaris simili computo deprehendit p suã tabellã hic positã. Nam si numerus ãni ppositi scriptus est in ea tabella: cycli solaris numerus est 28. Si non est illic expssus: da proximo mĩori ibidẽ scripto 28: sequẽti 1: ac rursus succedenti 2. sicq deinceps queãdmodũ de aureo numero pręcipiebatur: donec ad annum ppositũ pueneris. nam ubi talis annorũ supputatio desinet: illic in serie cycli solaris subscripta numerũ cycli solaris quęsitũ agnosces. Sub eo autem numero cycli solaris cõtinuo habebis litterã dominicalem anni tui. quę si unica occurrat: annum esse communem intelliges. si duplex: bissextilem. Prior id est superior ad festum usq Matthię apostoli utilis erit. Inferior autẽ ad reliquam anni partem accõmodabitur.

Erhard Ratdolt, Peter Loeslein, and Bernhard Maler, pages from *Calendarium* by Regiomontanus, 1476. The three-part diagram on the left is similar in structure to a contemporary proportion wheel. The two top circles are printed on heavy paper, cut out, and mounted over the larger woodcut with tape and a string. This may be the first "die-cut" and hand tip-in graphic material in a printed book. *Library of Congress, Washington, D.C., Rosenwald Collection.*

Erhard Ratdolt, Peter Loeslein, and Bernhard Maler, title page for Euclid's *Geometriae elementa,* 1482. A dazzling "white-on-black" design brackets the text, and incredibly fine line diagrams in the wide margin visually define Euclid's terms. *Library of Congress, Washington, D.C., Rosenwald Collection.*

Attributed to Bernhard Maler, title page for *Vita di Sancti Padri,* c. 1500. A simple geometric structure brings order to a title page that is laden with decoration. The borders, printed in black, frame a white circle and square which contain the printer's medallion and title printed in red.

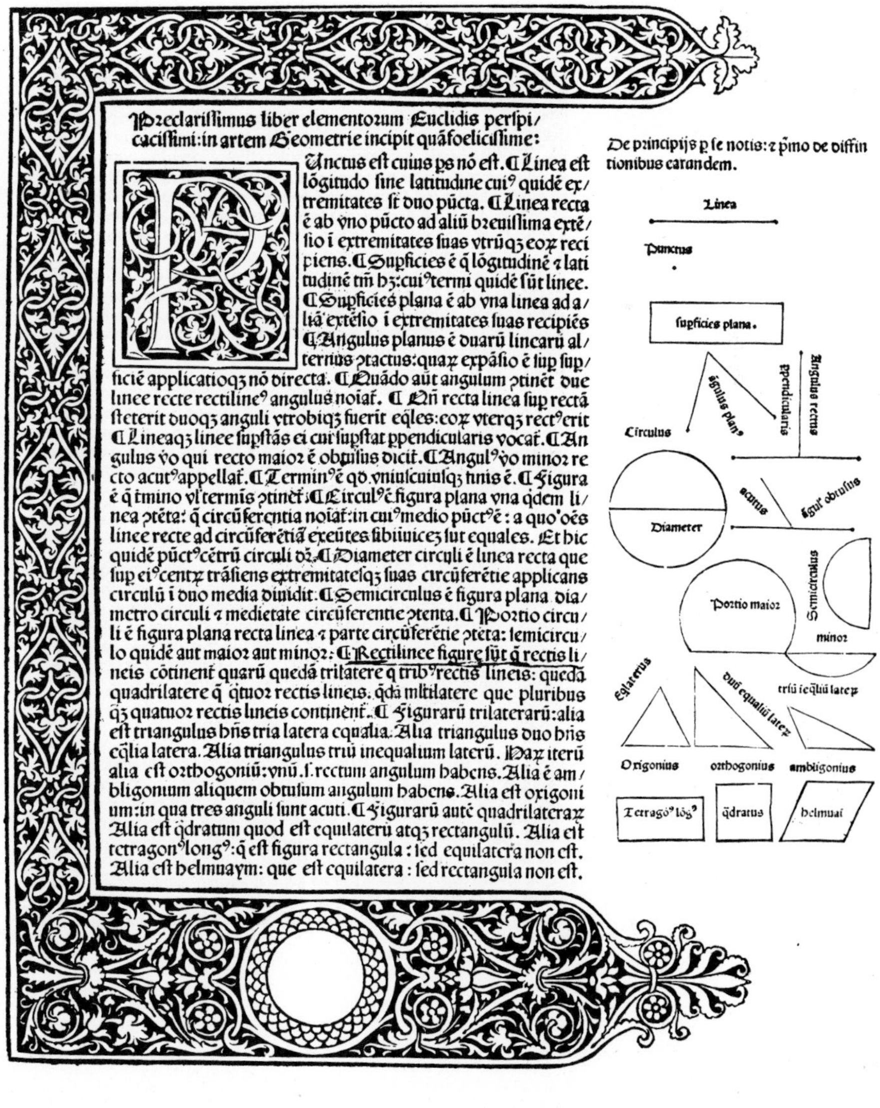
Preclarissimus liber elementorum Euclidis perspicacissimi: in artem Geometrie incipit quãfoelicissime:

Punctus est cuius ps nõ est. Linea est lõgitudo sine latitudine cuius quidẽ extremitates sũt duo pũcta. Linea recta ẽ ab vno pũcto ad aliũ breuissima extẽsio ĩ extremitates suas vtrũq3 eorum recipiens. Supficies ẽ q̃ lõgitudinẽ 7 latitudinẽ tm̃ hz: cui termi quidẽ sũt lineę. Supficies plana ẽ ab vna linea ad aliã extẽsio ĩ extremitates suas recipiẽs. Angulus planus ẽ duarũ linearũ alterius ptactus: quarum expãsio ẽ sup supficiẽ applicatioq3 nõ directa. Quãdo aũt angulum ptinẽt due lineę recte rectilineus angulus noiat. Qñ recta linea sup rectã steterit duoq3 anguli vtrobiq3 fuerit eqles: eorum vterq3 rectus erit. Lineaq3 linee supstãs ei cui supstat ppendicularis vocat. Angulus vo qui recto maior ẽ obtusus dicit. Angulus vo minor recto acutus appellat. Terminus ẽ qd vniuscuiusq3 finis ẽ. Figura ẽ q̃ tmino vl termis ptinet. Circulus ẽ figura plana vna qdem linea ptẽta: q̃ circũferentia noiat: in cuius medio pũctus ẽ: a quo oẽs linee recte ad circũferẽtiã exeũtes sibiinuicẽ sut equales. Et hic quidẽ pũctus cẽtrũ circuli dr. Diameter circuli ẽ linea recta que sup eius centrum trãsiens extremitatesq3 suas circũferẽtie applicans circulũ ĩ duo media diuidit. Semicirculus ẽ figura plana diametro circuli 7 medietate circũferentie ptenta. Portio circuli ẽ figura plana recta linea 7 parte circũferẽtie ptẽta: semicirculo quidẽ aut maior aut minor. Rectilinee figure sũt q̃ rectis lineis cõtinent quarũ quedã trilatere q̃ trib rectis lineis: quedã quadrilatere q̃ qtuor rectis lineis. qdã mltilatere que pluribus q3 quatuor rectis lineis continent. Figurarũ trilaterarũ: alia est triangulus hñs tria latera equalia. Alia triangulus duo hñs eqlia latera. Alia triangulus triũ inequalium laterũ. Harum iterũ alia est orthogoniũ: vnũ.s. rectum angulum habens. Alia ẽ ambligonium aliquem obtusum angulum habens. Alia est oxigonium: in qua tres anguli sunt acuti. Figurarũ autẽ quadrilaterarum Alia est q̃dratum quod est equilaterũ atq3 rectangulũ. Alia est tetragonus longus: q̃ est figura rectangula: sed equilatera non est. Alia est helmuaym: que est equilatera: sed rectangula non est.

De principijs p se notis: 7 pmo de diffinitionibus earundem.

tian printers. The full flowering of graphic decoration in the printed book did not begin until the turn of the century.

The *Ars Moriendi* was a best seller during the fifteenth century. At least sixty-five editions including manuscripts, blockbooks, and typographic books were produced before 1501. An edition published on 28 April 1478 by the Italian printers Giovanni and Alberto Alvise in Verona is believed to be the first design that used *printers' flowers* (fleurons), which are decorative elements cast like type. The Verona *Ars Moriendi* used these as graphic elements in the title-page design and as fillers in short lines that left blank

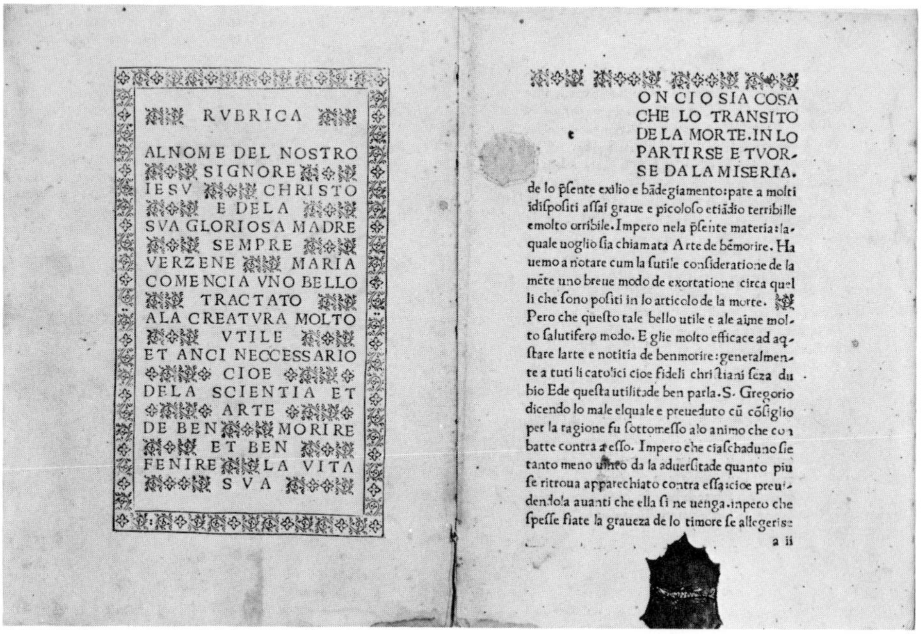
RVBRICA

ALNOME DEL NOSTRO SIGNORE IESV CHRISTO E DELA SVA GLORIOSA MADRE SEMPRE VERZENE MARIA COMENCIA VNO BELLO TRACTATO ALA CREATVRA MOLTO VTILE ET ANCI NECCESSARIO CIOE DELA SCIENTIA ET ARTE DE BEN MORIRE ET BEN FENIRE LA VITA SVA

ONCIOSIA COSA CHE LO TRANSITO DE LA MORTE.IN LO PARTIRSE E TVORSE DA LA MISERIA. de lo pſente exilio e bādegiamento:pare a molti idiſpoſiti aſſai graue e picoloſo etiādio terribille emolto orribile. Impero nela pſēte materia:laquale uoglio ſia chiamata Arte de bēmorire. Ha uemo a notare cum la ſutile conſideratione de la mēte uno breue modo de exortatione circa quel li che ſono poſiti in lo articolo de la morte. Pero che queſto tale bello utile e ale aime molto ſalutifero modo. E glie molto efficace ad aqſtare larte e notitia de benmorire:generalmente a tuti li catolici cioe fideli chriſtiani ſeza dubio Ede queſta utilitade ben parla. S. Gregorio dicendo lo male elquale e preueduto cū cōſiglio per la ragione fu ſottomeſſo alo animo che con batte contra a eſſo. Impero che ciaſchaduno ſie tanto meno uīto da la aduerſitade quanto piu ſe ritroua apparechiato contra eſſa:cioe preuedendola auanti che ella ſi ne uenga.impero che ſpeſſe fiate la graueza de lo timore ſe allegeriſe:

a ii

Giovanni and Alberto Alvise, title page and first text page from *Ars Moriendi,* 1478. The vocabulary of graphic design possibilities was expanded by the design and casting of metal decorative ornaments which could be composed as part of the page along with type. *Library of Congress, Washington, D.C.*

areas in the text blocks.

Quite possibly, a printer identified as Johannes Nicolai de Verona, who printed a manual on warfare entitled *De re militari* by Roberto Valturio in 1472, was Giovani Alvise. If so, he scored an earlier design innovation; the light contour style of woodblock illustration used in *De re militari* initiated the fine-line style that became popular in Italian graphic design during the later decades of the fifteenth century.

A fascinating manuscript copy of *De re militari* shows the relationship between the typographic book and the manuscript books which were used as exemplars or layouts. This manuscript book is written in semi-Gothic script, but has marginal corrections in a

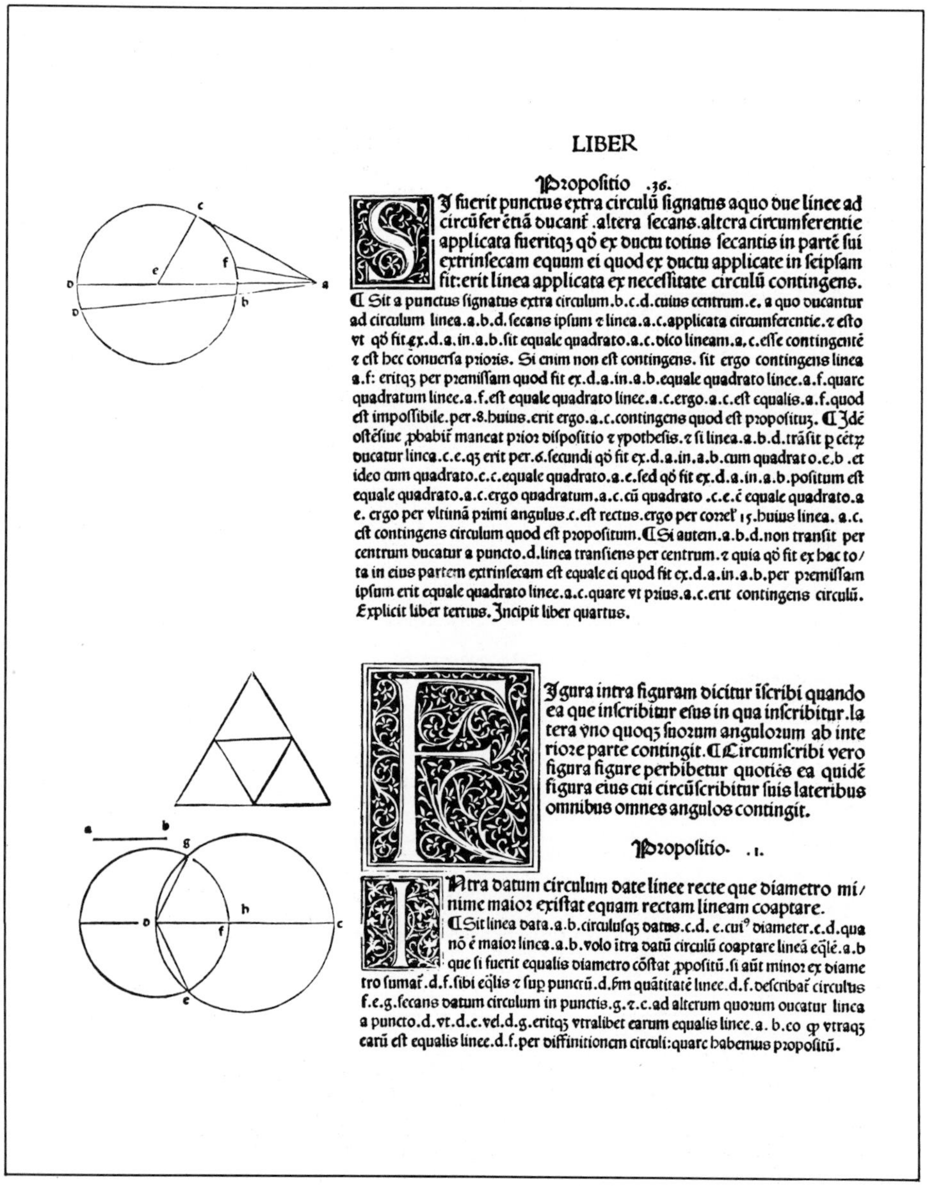
LIBER

Propoſitio .36.

Si fuerit punctus extra circulū ſignatus aquo due linee ad circūferētiā ducant̄ .altera ſecans.altera circumferentie applicata fueritq3 qḋ ex ductu totius ſecantis in partē ſui extrinſecam equum ei quod ex ductu applicate in ſeipſam fit:erit linea applicata ex neceſſitate circulū contingens.

Figura intra figuram dicitur iſcribi quando ea que inſcribitur eius in qua inſcribitur.latera vno quoq3 ſuorum angulorum ab interiore parte contingit. Circumſcribi vero figura figure perhibetur quotiēs ea quidē figura eius cui circūſcribitur ſuis lateribus omnibus omnes angulos contingit.

Propoſitio. .1.

Intra datum circulum date linee recte que diametro minime maior exiſtat equam rectam lineam coaptare.

Erhard Ratdolt, Peter Loeslein, and Bernhard Maler, page from Euclid's *Geometriae elementa,* 1482. The wide outer margin is maintained throughout the book for explanatory diagrams. Two sizes of initial letters denote sections and subsections. *Library of Congress, Washington, D.C., Rosenwald Collection.*

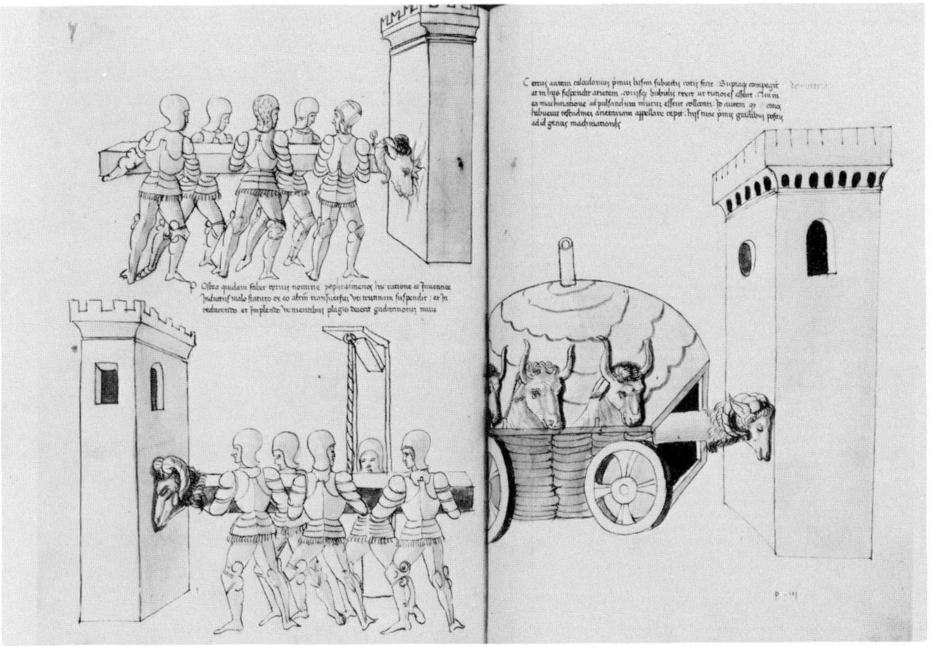

Manuscript book of Roberto Valturio's *De re militari,* undated. Freely drawn in brown pen and ink, the illustrations have brown and ochre washes applied. *Library of Congress, Washington, D.C., Rosenwald Collection.*

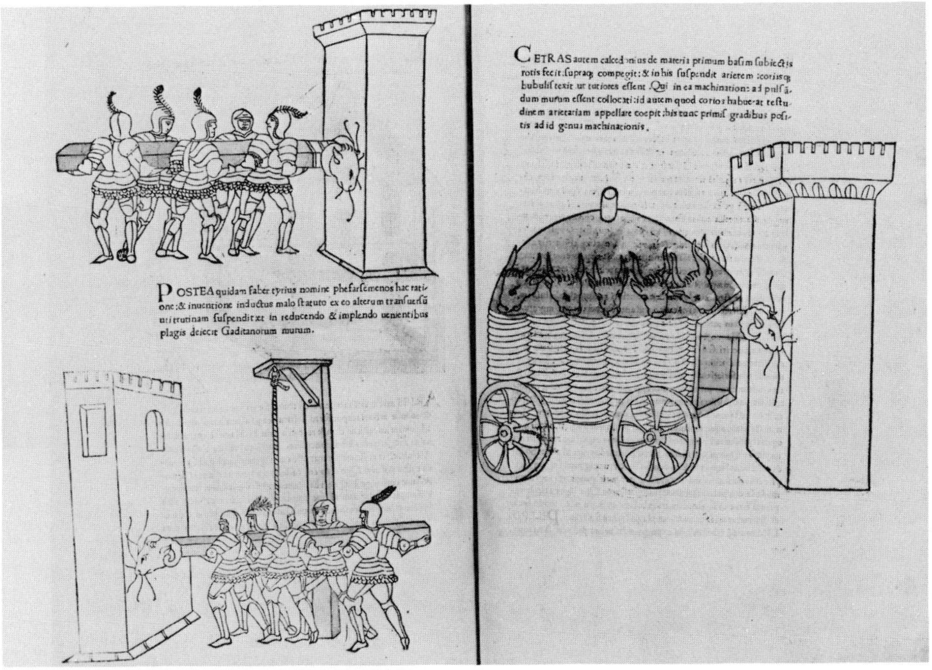

Joannes Nicolai of Verona (printer), pages from Roberto Valturio's *De re militari,* 1472. Detail and gestural line quality are lost in the translation from manuscript original to printed volume, but the basic layout remains the same. *Library of Congress, Washington, D.C., Rosenwald Collection.*

roman hand. Because these corrections are incorporated by the printer, it is believed that this manuscript version was corrected by the author. Then, it was used as corrected copy by the compositors, as a layout by the blockcutters, and as a guide for page design and makeup by the pressman.

This extraordinary book, a manual on warfare, is a compendium of the latest techniques and devices (many imaginary) for scaling walls, catapulting missiles, ramming fortifications, and torturing enemies. The page designs are unique. The text is set in a tight column with wide outer margins, and the freely shaped images sprawl across the pages in dynamic asymmetrical layouts. In the spread showing battering rams, the repetition of the towers and rams' heads gives the pages a lively visual rhythm.

Medieval Christianity fostered a belief that the value of human life was primarily its effect on God's judgment after death. A turning away from medieval beliefs toward a new concern for human potential and value characterized Renaissance *humanism,* a philosophy of human dignity and worth that defined man as capable of using reason and scientific inquiry to achieve both an understanding of the world and self-meaning. This new spirit was accompanied by a renewed study of classical writings from Greek and Roman cultures. An important humanist and scholar of the Italian Renaissance, Aldus Manutius (1450–1515), established a printing press in Venice at age forty-five to realize his vision: he would publish the major works of the great thinkers of the Greek and Roman world. Important scholars and skilled technical personnel were recruited to staff his Aldine Press, which rapidly became known for its editorial authority and scholarship. From 1494 until 1498, a five-volume edition of Aristotle was published.

A most important member of the Aldine staff was Francesco da Bologna, surnamed Griffo (1450–1518). Manutius called this brilliant typeface designer and punch cutter to Venice, where Griffo cut Roman, Greek, Hebrew and the first italic types for Aldine editions. His initial project in Venice was a roman face for *De Aetna* by Pietro Bembo in 1495. Griffo researched pre-Caroline scripts to produce a roman type that was less artistic but more authentic than Jenson's designs. This style survives today as the book text face Bembo.

While the German Incunabula closed with Koberger and Dürer creating a technical and artistic masterpiece in *The Apocalypse,* in Italy Aldus Manutius ended the epoch with his 1499 edition of Fra Francesco

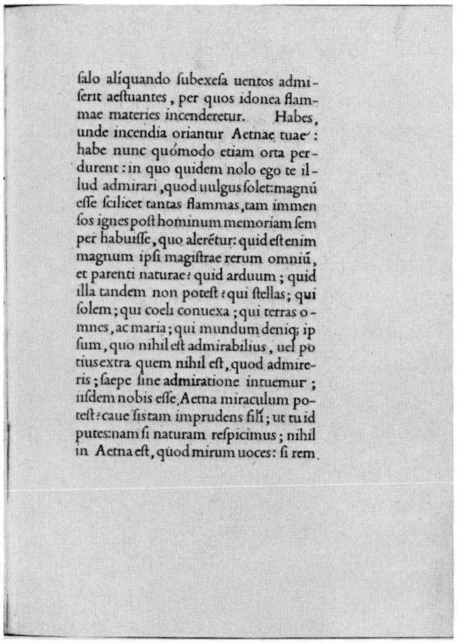

ſalo aliquando ſubexeſa uentos admi-
ſerit aeſtuantes, per quos idonea flam-
mae materies incenderetur. Habes,
unde incendia oriantur Aetnae tuae:
habe nunc quómodo etiam orta per-
durent: in quo quidem nolo ego te illud admirari, quod uulgus ſolet: magnú
eſſe ſcilicet tantas flammas, tam immen
ſos ignes poſt hominum memoriam ſem
per habuiſſe, quo alerétur: quid eſt enim
magnum ipſi magiſtrae rerum omniú,
et parenti naturae? quid arduum; quid
illa tandem non poteſt? qui ſtellas; qui
ſolem; qui coeli conuexa; qui terras o-
mnes, ac maria; qui mundum deniq; ip
ſum, quo nihil eſt admirabilius, uel po
tius extra quem nihil eſt, quod admire-
ris; ſaepe ſine admiratione intuemur;
iiſdem nobis eſſe Aetna miraculum poteſt? caue ſis tam imprudens fili; ut tu id
putes: nam ſi naturam reſpicimus; nihil
in Aetna eſt, quod mirum uoces: ſi rem.

Aldus Manutius, page from Pietro Bembo's *De Aetna,* 1495–96. As the model for Garamond in the sixteenth century, this typeface became the prototype for two centuries of European typographic design. *Pierpont Morgan Library, New York.*

Colonna's *Hypnerotomachia Poliphili (The Strife of Love in a Dream* or *The Dream of Poliphilus).* This romantic fantasy tells of young Poliphilus' wandering quest for his lover, who had taken a vow to preserve her chastity, which takes him through classical landscapes and architectural environments. A celebration of paganism, with erotic overtones and a few explicit illustrations, it probably escaped scandal only because of its high cost and limited Venetian audience.

This masterpiece of graphic design achieved an elegant harmony of typography and illustration that has seldom been equaled. The communicative coordination of the illustrations with the text and the exceptional design integration of images and typography, indicate that the printer, type designer, author, and artist worked in close collaboration. The name of the artist who designed the one hundred sixty-eight delicate linear illustrations is lost to history. Griffo designed new capitals for use with the Bembo lowercase. These capitals were based on the most precise research

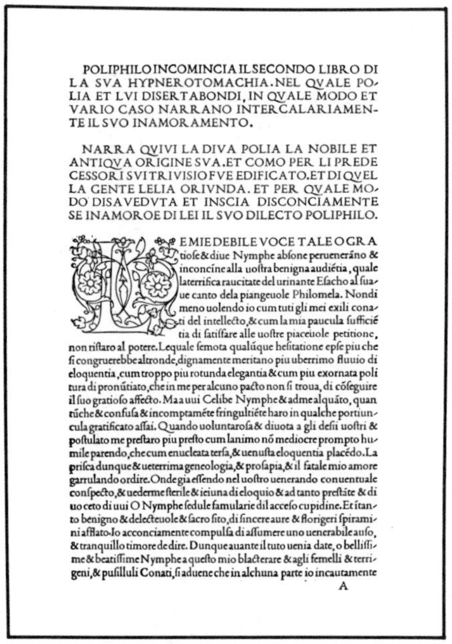

POLIPHILO INCOMINCIA IL SECONDO LIBRO DI LA SVA HYPNEROTOMACHIA. NEL QVALE POLIA ET LVI DISERTABONDI, IN QVALE MODO ET VARIO CASO NARRANO INTERCALARIAMENTE IL SVO INAMORAMENTO.

NARRA QVIVI LA DIVA POLIA LA NOBILE ET ANTIQVA ORIGINE SVA. ET COMO PER LI PREDECESSORI SVI TRIVISIO FVE EDIFICATO. ET DI QVELLA GENTE LELIA ORIVNDA. ET PER QVALE MODO DISAVEDVTA ET INSCIA DISCONCIAMENTE SE INAMOROE DI LEI IL SVO DILECTO POLIPHILO.

TEMIE DEBILE VOCE TALE O GRAtioſe & diue Nymphe abſone peruenerãno & inconcíne alla uoſtra benigna audiétia, quale la terrifica raucitate del urinante Eſacho al ſuaue canto dela piangeuole Philomela. Nondimeno uolendo io cum tuti gli mei exili conati del intellecto, & cum la mia paucula ſufficiétia di ſatiſſare alle uoſtre piaceuole petitione, non riſtaro al potere. Lequale ſemota qualúque heſitatione epſe piu che ſi congruerebbe altronde, dignamente meritano piu uberrimo fluuio di eloquentia, cum troppo piu rotunda elegantia & cum piu exornata politura di pronútiato, che in me per alcuno pacto non ſi troua, di cóſeguire il ſuo gratioſo affecto. Ma a uui Celibe Nymphe & adme alquáto, quantúche & confuſa & incomptaméte fringultiéte haro in qualche portiuncula gratificato aſſai. Quando uoluntaroſa & diuota a gli deſii uoſtri & poſtulato me preſtaro piu preſto cum lanimo nó mediocre prompto humile parendo, che cum enucleata terſa, & uenuſta eloquentia placédo. La priſca dunque & ueterrima geneologia, & proſapia, & il fatale mio amore garrulando ordire. Onde gia eſſendo nel uoſtro uenerando conuentuale conſpecto, & uederme ſterile & ieiuna di eloquio & ad tanto preſtáte & diuo ceto di uui O Nymphe ſedule famularie dil acceſo cupidine. Et itanto benigno & delecteuole & ſacro ſito, di ſincere aure & florigeri ſpiramini afflato. Io acconciamente compulſa di aſſumere uno uenerabile auſo, & tranquillo timore de dire. Dunque auante il tuto uenia date, o belliſſime & beatiſſime Nymphe a queſto mio blacterare & agli femelli & terrigeni, & puſilluli Conati, ſi aduene che in alchuna parte io incautamente

A

Aldus Manutius, typographic page from *Hypnerotomachia Poliphili,* 1499. The texture of the headings (set in all capitals), the text typography, and the outline initial have a subtle yet beautiful contrast. The one-line intervals of space separating the information into three areas introduces light and order into the page. *Library of Congress, Washington, D.C., Rosenwald Collection.*

and study of Roman inscriptions available and used the one-to-ten (stroke weight-to-height) proportion advanced by leading mathematicians of the era whose search for mathematical laws of proportion included a study of Roman inscription lettering. Griffo made his lowercase ascenders taller than the capitals to correct an optical color problem—the tendency of capitals to appear too large and heavy in a page of text—that had plagued earlier Roman fonts. Griffo's typefaces became the model for the talented French type designers who perfected these letterforms during the following century. Exquisite chapter headings in capitals that are the same size as the text, large outline initials surrounded by stylized floral ornamentation, and an overall lightness to the page—combined with generous margins, beautiful paper, and meticulous presswork—excited printers and designers throughout Europe. *Poliphili* was Manutius' only illustrated book. After it was published the Aldine staff turned their attention to scholarly editions.

In 1501, Manutius addressed the need for smaller, more economical books by publishing the prototype of the "pocket book." This edition of Virgil's *Opera* had a 7.7-by-15.4-centimeter (3e-f-by-6-inch) page size and was set in the first italic type font. Between the smaller size type and the narrower width of italic characters, a 50-percent gain in the number of characters in a line of a given measure was achieved over Jenson's fonts and Griffo's type for *De Aetna.* Italic was closely modeled on the *cancelleresca* script, a slanted handwriting style which was finding favor among scholars who liked its writing speed and informality. On 14 November 1502, Manutius was granted a monopoly on Greek publishing and italic printing by the Venetian government, and shortly thereafter Griffo and Manutius quarreled and separated. Manutius wished to protect his huge investment in type design and production; Griffo found that he could not sell his original and popular typeface designs to other printers. With the parting of ways of this printer-publisher and his brilliant staff designer, graphic-design innovation in Venice ended.

Until his death in 1515, Manutius published numerous classical editions in the small format and italics of Virgil's *Opera.* These made the Aldine Press logo—a dolphin and anchor inspired by one of the illustrations in *The Dream of Poliphilus*—famous throughout Europe. Griffo returned to Bologna, where he vanished from the historical record after being charged for the murder of his son-in-law, who was bludgeoned with an iron bar in 1516.

The typographic book came to Italy from Germany as a manuscript book printed with types. A series of design innovations including the title page, roman and italic type, printed page numbers, woodblock and cast metal ornaments, and innovative approaches to the layout of illustrations with type, enabled the Italian printers

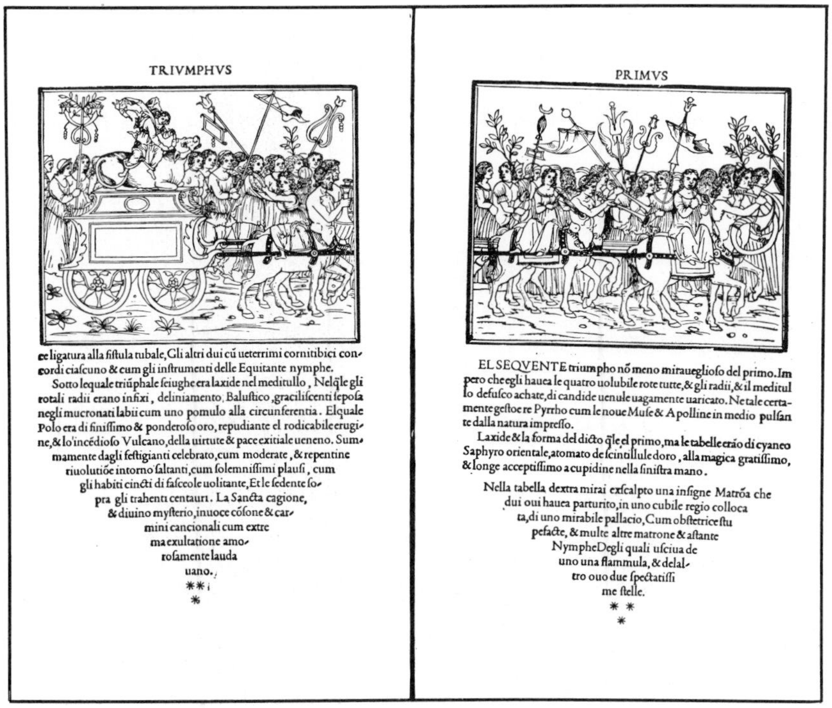

TRIVMPHVS

ee ligatura alla fiſtula tubale, Gli altri dui cũ ueterrimi cornitibici concordi ciaſcuno & cum gli inſtrumenti delle Equitante nymphe.

Sotto lequale triũphale ſeiughe era laxide nel meditullo, Nelq̃le gli rotali radii erano infixi, deliniamento Baluſtico, graciliſcenti ſepoſa negli mucronati labii cum uno pomulo alla circunferentia. Elquale Polo era di finiſſimo & ponderoſo oro, repudiante el rodicabile erugine, & lo incẽdioſo Vulcano, della uirtute & pace exitiale ueneno. Summamente dagli feſtigianti celebrato, cum moderate, & repentine riuolutiõe intorno ſaltanti, cum ſolemniſſimi plauſi, cum gli habiti cincti di faſceole uolitante, Et le ſedente ſopra gli trahenti centauri. La Sancta cagione, & diuino myſterio, inuoce cõſone & carmini cancionali cum extrema exultatione amoroſamente laudauano.

PRIMVS

EL SEQVENTE triumpho nõ meno miraueglioſo del primo. Impero che egli hauea le quatro uolubile rote tutte, & gli radii, & il meditullo defuſco achate, di candide uenule uagamente uaricato. Ne tale certamente geſtoe re Pyrrho cum le noue Muſe & Apolline in medio pulſante dalla natura impreſſo.

Laxide & la forma del dicto q̃le el primo, ma le tabelle erão di cyaneo Saphyro orientale, atomato de ſcintillule doro, alla magica gratiſſimo, & longe acceptiſſimo a cupidine nella ſiniſtra mano.

Nella tabella dextra mirai exſcalpto una inſigne Matrõa che dui oui hauea parturito, in uno cubile regio collocata, di uno mirabile pallacio, Cum obſtetrice ſtupefacte, & multe altre matrone & aſtante Nymphe Degli quali uſciua de uno una flammula, & delaltro ouo due ſpectatiſſime ſtelle.

Aldus Manutius, illustrated spread from *Hypnerotomachia Poliphili,* 1499. The exquisite symmetry of each page is emphasized by the shaped type that tapers down to Griffo's light ornaments. The illustrations of the triumphant pagan procession are actually two parts of a continuous image; this unifies the spread. *Library of Congress, Washington, D.C., Rosenwald Collection.*

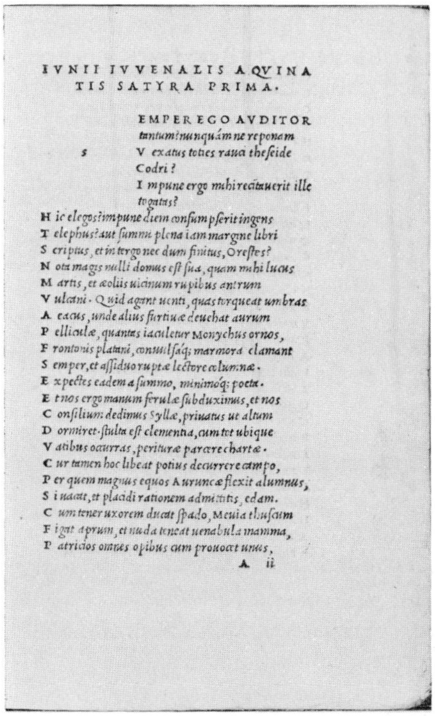

IVNII IVVENALIS AQVINATIS SATYRA PRIMA.

EMPER EGO AVDITOR tantum? nunquám ne reponam
V exatus toties rauci theſeide Codri?
I mpune ergo mihi recitauerit ille togatas?
H ic elegos? impune diem conſumpſerit ingens
T elephus? aut ſummi plena iam margine libri
S criptus, et in tergo nec dum finitus, Oreſtes?
N ota magis nulli domus eſt ſua, quam mihi lucus
M artis, et æoliis uicinum rupibus antrum
V ulcani. Quid agant uenti, quas torqueat umbras
A eacus, unde alius furtiuæ deuehat aurum
P elliculæ, quantas iaculetur Monychus ornos,
F rontonis platani, conuulſaq; marmora clamant
S emper, et aſſiduo ruptæ lectore columnæ.
E xpectes eadem a ſummo, minimóq; poeta.
E t nos ergo manum ferulæ ſubduximus, et nos
C onſilium dedimus Syllæ, priuatus ut altum
D ormiret. ſtulta eſt clementia, cum tot ubique
V atibus occurras, perituræ parcere chartæ.
C ur tamen hoc libeat potius decurrere campo,
P er quem magnus equos Auruncæ flexit alumnus,
S i uacat, et placidi rationem admittitis, edam.
C um tener uxorem ducat ſpado, Meuia thuſcum
F igat aprum, et nuda teneat uenabula mamma,
P atricios omnes opibus cum prouocet unus,

A ii

Aldus Manutius, page from Juvenal and Persius, *Opera,* 1501. This was one of the first books using Griffo's new italic type. Note the unfilled space for a rubricated initial, the letterspaced, all-capital heading, and the capital roman letter at the beginning of each line. *Pierpont Morgan Library, New York.*

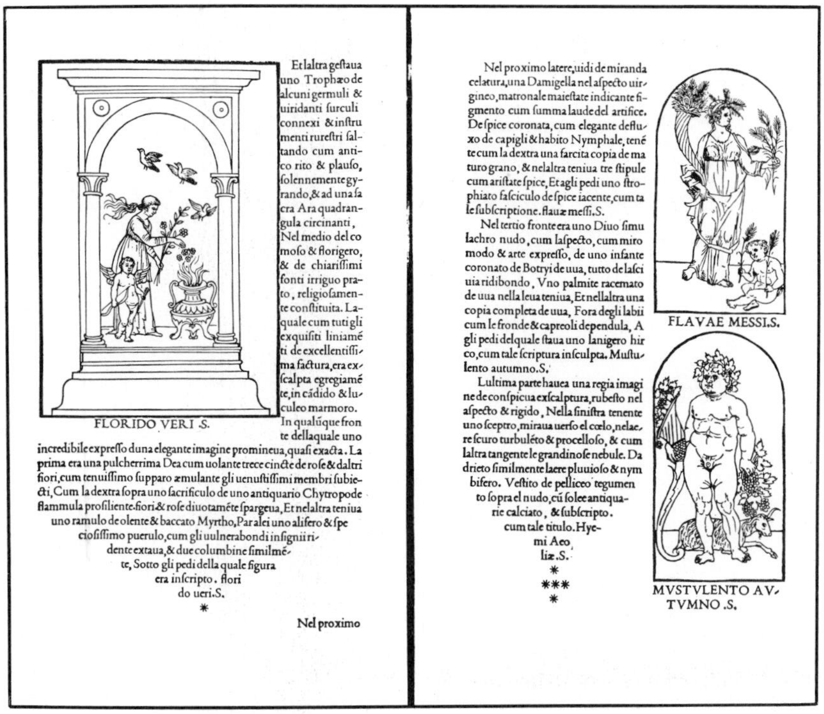

Et laltra geſtaua uno Trophæo de alcuni germuli & uiridanti ſurculi connexi & inſtrumenti rureſtri ſaltando cum antico rito & plauſo, ſolennemente gyrando, & ad una ſacra Ara quadrangula circinanti, Nel medio del comoſo & florigero, & de chiariſſimi fonti irriguo prato, religioſamente conſtituita. Laquale cum tuti gli exquiſiti liniamẽti de excellentiſſima factura, era exſcalpta egregiamẽte, in cãdido & luculeo marmoro. In qualũque fronte dellaquale uno incredibile expreſſo duna elegante imagine promineua, quaſi exacta. La prima era una pulcherrima Dea cum uolante trece cincte de roſe & daltri fiori, cum tenuiſſimo ſupparo æmulante gli uenuſtiſſimi membri ſubiecti, Cum la dextra ſopra uno ſacrificulo de uno antiquario Chytropode flammula proſiliente. fiori & roſe diuotamẽte ſpargeua, Et nelaltra teniua uno ramulo de olente & baccato Myrtho, Par alei uno alifero & ſpecioſiſſimo puerulo, cum gli uulnerabondi inſignii ridente extaua, & due columbine ſimilmẽte, Sotto gli pedi della quale figura era inſcripto. floridoueri.S.

FLORIDO VERI .S.

Nel proximo

Nel proximo latere, uidi de miranda celatura, una Damigella nel aſpecto uirgineo, matronale maieſtate indicante figmento cum ſumma laude del artifice. De ſpice coronata, cum elegante defluxo de capigli & habito Nymphale, tenẽte cum la dextra una farcita copia de maturo grano, & nelaltra teniua tre ſtipule cum ariſtate ſpice, Et agli pedi uno ſtrophiato faſciculo de ſpice iacente, cum tale ſubſcriptione. flauæ meſſi.S.

Nel tertio fronte era uno Diuo ſimulachro nudo, cum laſpecto, cum miro modo & arte expreſſo, de uno infante coronato de Botryi de uua, tutto de laſciuia ridibondo, Vno palmite racemato de uua nella leua teniua, Et nellaltra una copia completa de uua, Fora degli labii cum le fronde & capreoli dependula, A gli pedi delquale ſtaua uno lanigero hirco, cum tale ſcriptura inſculpta. Muſtulento autumno.S.

Lultima parte hauea una regia imagine de conſpicua exſcalptura, rubeſto nel aſpecto & rigido, Nella ſiniſtra tenente uno ſceptro, miraua uerſo el cœlo, nelaere ſcuro turbulẽto & procelloſo, & cum laltra tangente le grandinoſe nebule. Da drieto ſimilmente laere pluuioſo & nymbifero. Veſtito de pelliceo tegumento ſopra el nudo, cũ ſolee antiquarie calciato, & ſubſcripto. cum tale titulo. Hyemi Aeoliæ.S.

FLAVAE MESSI.S.

MVSTVLENTO AVTVMNO .S.

Aldus Manutius, illustrated spread from *Hypnerotomachia Poliphili,* 1499. The asymmetrical balance is unusual for its time. The arched borders of the two illustrations on the right echo the arch form in the illustration on the left. This repetition of shape increases the unity of the layout. *Library of Congress, Washington, D.C., Rosenwald Collection.*

of the Renaissance to pass on to posterity the basic format of the typographic book as we know it today.

Aldus Manutius, printer's trademark, c. 1500.

Italian writing masters

Ironically, the inevitable decline in manuscript writing that followed on the heels of typographic printing occurred while new opportunities opened for master calligraphers almost as a side effect of printing. The rapid growth of literacy created a huge demand for writing masters to teach this fundamental skill, and the attendant expansion of government and commerce created a demand for expert calligraphers to draft important state and business documents. The first of many sixteenth-century writing manuals was created by Italian master calligrapher, printer, and type designer Lodovico Arrighi (d. c. 1527). His small volume of 1522, entitled *La Operina da imparare di scrivere littera cancellaresca,* was a brief course using magnificent examples to teach the cancelleresca script. Arrighi's masterful writing was meticulously cut onto woodblocks by engraver Ugo da Carpi. Arrighi's directions were so clear and simple that the reader could learn this hand in a few days. *La Operina . . . cancellaresca* sounded the deathknell for the scriptorium as an exclusive domain for the few who could write; it rang in the era of the writing master and public writing skill. A follow-up 1523 volume entitled *Il Modo de temperare le penne* presented a dozen handwriting styles. Among those influenced by Arrighi, Giovanni Battista Palatino (c.1515–c.1575) produced the most complete and widely used writing manuals of the sixteenth century.

The Renaissance in Italy began to fade with the sack of Rome in 1527 by the combined forces of the Holy Roman Emperor Charles V and his Spanish allies. One of the victims of this outrage appears to be Lodovico Arrighi. He was working in Rome at the time and then vanishes from the historical record without a trace.

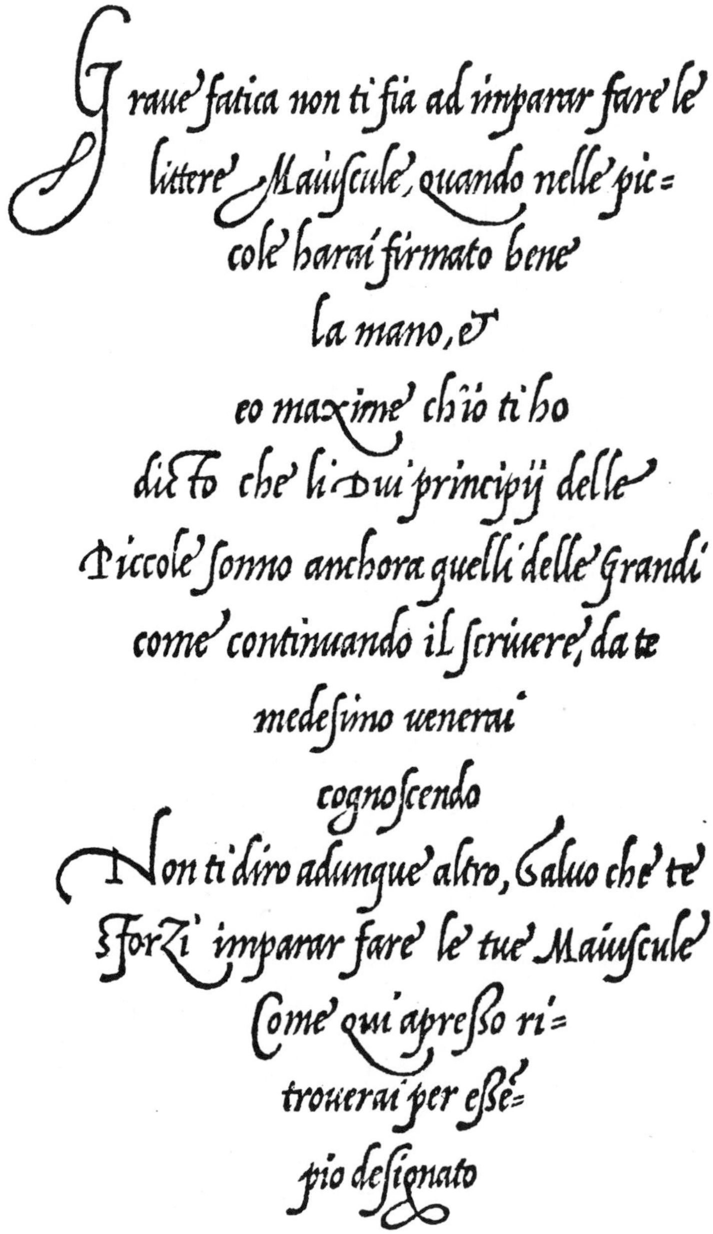
Graue fatica non ti fia ad imparar fare le
littere Maiuscule, quando nelle pic=
cole harai firmato bene
la mano, et
eo maxime chio ti ho
ditto che li dui principij delle
Piccole sonno anchora quelli delle Grandi
come continuando il scriuere, da te
medesimo uenerai
cognoscendo
Non ti diro adunque altro, saluo che te
sforzi imparar fare le tue Maiuscule
Come qui apresso ri=
trouerai per esse=
pio designato

Lodovico Arrighi, page from *La Operina da imparare di scrivere littera cancellaresca,* 1522. The ample spaces between lines in Arrighi's brilliant writing leave room for the plumelike ascenders waving to the right in elegant counterpoint to the descenders sweeping gracefully to the left. *Library of Congress, Washington, D.C., Rosenwald Collection.*

Innovation passes to France

Filled with glorious dreams of romantic conquest and empire, the French king Charles VIII (1470–1498) crossed into Italy with a vast army in 1494 and attempted to gain control of the Kingdom of Naples. This began an absurd effort by French kings, over the next fifty years, to conquer Italy. Although vast outlays of money and men gained little except fleeting glory, the cultural vitality of the Italian Renaissance was imported to France. Francis I (1494–1547) ascended to the French throne on 1 January 1515 and began his spectacular reign. Under his patronage, the French Renaissance flowered as he gave generous support to humanists, authors, and visual artists.

This cultural epoch was a fertile one for graphic design and printing, and the sixteenth century has become known as "the golden age of French typography." The initial design impetus was imported from Venice. Henri Estienne (d. 1520) was one of the early French scholar-printers who become enthusiastic about Aldus' *Poliphilus*. Soon books printed in roman types, with title pages and initials inspired by the Venetians, were sprouting all over Paris. Estienne's untimely death left his wife with three young sons. The widowed mother quickly married Estienne's foreman, Simon de Colines (d. 1546), who ran the family business until his stepson, Robert Estienne (1503–1559), was able to take over in 1526. At this time, Simon de Colines opened his own firm. Robert Estienne became a brilliant printer of scholarly works in Greek, Latin, and Hebrew. His growing reputation as a publisher of great books, including a major Latin dictionary, enabled young Estienne to join his stepfather as one of the leading figures in this grand period of book design and printing.

Censorship became an increasingly difficult problem during the 1500s as church and state sought to maintain their authority and control. Propagating ideas, not pressing inked type onto paper, was the main purpose of the scholar-printers who often found their quest for knowledge and critical study in conflict with religious leaders and the royalty. In spite of war and censorship, however, the humanist spirit took hold in France and produced both excellent scholarship and a graceful school of graphic design. The leading printers produced books of fine proportions, outstanding legibility, beautiful typography, and elegant ornamentation. Two brilliant graphic artists, Geoffroy Tory (1480–1533), and a typeface designer and punchcutter, Claude Garamond (c.1480–1561), created visual forms that were embraced by printers for two hundred years.

The phrase "renaissance man" is

CONTENTA.

¶CONTINETVR HIC ARISTOTELIS CA-
stigatissime recognitum opus metaphysicū a Clarissimo prin-
cipe Bessarione Cardinale Niceno latinitate fœlici-
ter donatum/xiiij libris distinctum: cum adiecto
in xij primos libros Argyropyli Byzantij in-
terpretamēto/rarū proculdubio & hactenus desideratū opus. Deus optimus
qui sub nomine ipsius entis in hoc
opere celebratur: hoc ipsū fa-
ciat ad sui & laudem &
cognitionem om-
nibus studijs
proficu-
um.

THEOPHRASTI metaphysicorum liber I

ITEM METAPHYSICA
introductio: quatuor
dialogorum li-
bris elu-
cida-
ta.

¶Venale habetur hoc eximium Aristotelis opus apud Henricum Stepha-
num e regione scholæ Decretorum. ex cuius officina accuratissime recognitū
prodijt Anno CHRISTI qui summum ens entium existit MDXV.
vicesima die mensis Octobris.

Henri Estienne, title page for Aristotle's *Metaphysics,* 1515. By setting the type in geometric shapes, Estienne achieved a distinctive graphic design with minimal means.

BIBLIA

HEBRAEA, Chaldæa, Græca & Latina nomina virorum, mulierum, populorum, idolorum, vrbium, fluuiorum, montium, cæterorumque locorum quæ in Bibliis leguntur, restituta, cum Latina interpretatione.

Locorum descriptio è Cosmographis.

INDEX prætcrea rerum & sententiarum quæ in iisdem Bibliis continentur.

HIS accesserunt schemata Tabernaculi Mosaici, & Templi Salomonis, quæ præeunte Francisco Vatablo Hebraicarum literarum Regio professore doctissimo, summa arte & fide expressa sunt.

PARISIIS
EX OFFICINA ROBERTI STEPHANI TYPOGRAPHI REGII.
M. D. XL.

CVM PRIVILEGIO REGIS.

Robert Estienne, title page for a Bible, 1540. As with many printers' marks of the era, Estienne's olive tree with a branch falling off became a pictorial illustration.

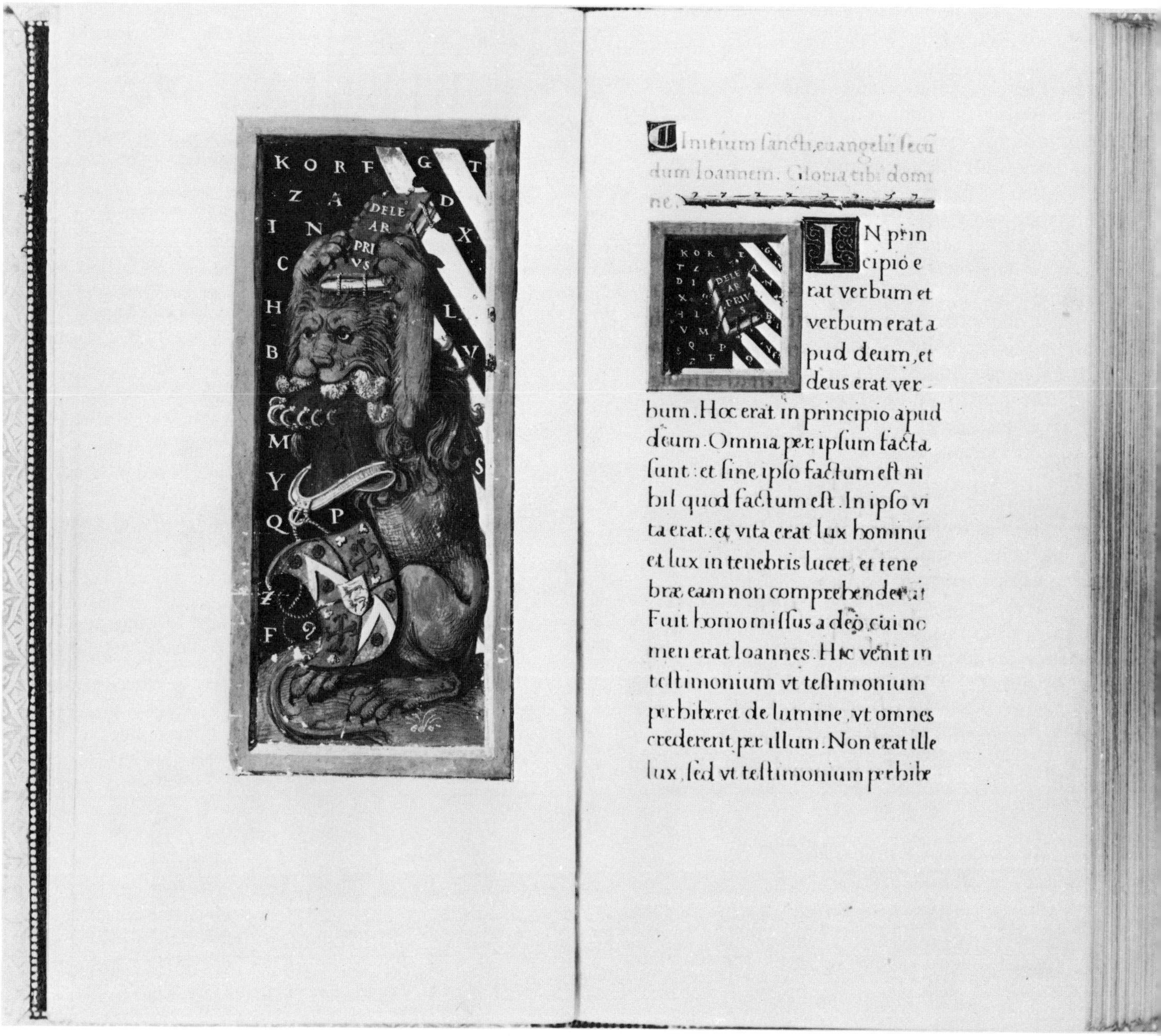

Geoffroy Tory, pages from *Les Heures de Jean Lallement,* 1506. In this manuscript book, twenty-five-year-old Tory used the roman letterforms that he developed in Italy. Gold roman capitals are in front of a striking blue field with red and white stripes. *Library of Congress, Washington, D.C., Rosenwald Collection.*

often used to identify a unique individual of genius whose wide-ranging activities in various philosophic, literary, artistic, or scientific disciplines result in important contributions to more than one field. Such a person was Geoffroy Tory. His range of accomplishments is staggering: professor, scholar, and translator; poet and author; publisher, printer, and bookseller; calligrapher, designer, illustrator, and engraver. He translated, edited, and often published Latin and Greek texts. As a reformer of the French language, he introduced the apostrophe, the accent, and the cedilla. In the graphic arts, he played a major role in importing the italianate influence. Then, he proceeded to develop a uniquely French Renaissance style of book design and illustration.

Born of humble means in Bourges, Tory's brilliance captured the attention of leading citizens in that city, who made it possible for him to journey to Italy for study at the universities in Rome and Bologna. Returning to France in 1505, Tory became a lecturer in philosophy at the University of Paris, sometimes worked as a reader at Henri Estienne's printing office, and was active as a scribe and illuminator. His boundless enthusiasm for the visual forms of the Italian Renaissance included a deep love for roman letterforms. Tory's lettering in the 1506 manuscript book, *Les Heures de Jean Lallemant,* is a light roman with long ascenders and descenders. The background of the armorial fron-

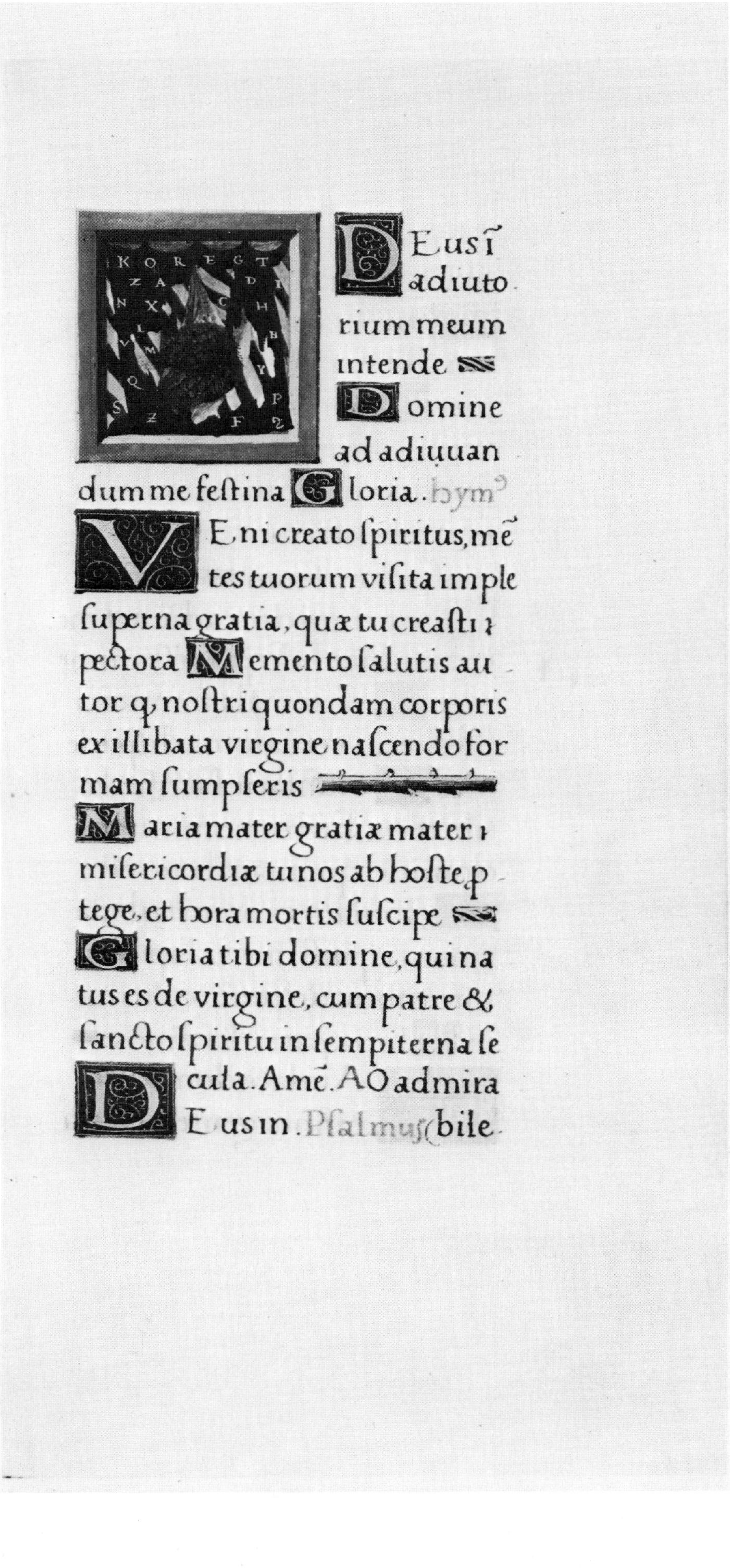
D Eus ĩ
adiuto
rium meum
intende
D omine
ad adiuuan
dum me feſtina G loria. hym
V Eni creato ſpiritus, mẽ
tes tuorum viſita imple
ſuperna gratia, quæ tu creaſti ĩ
pectora M emento ſalutis au
tor q, noſtri quondam corporis
ex illibata virgine naſcendo for
mam ſumpſeris
M aria mater gratiæ mater ĩ
miſericordiæ tu nos ab hoſte p
tege, et hora mortis ſuſcipe
G loria tibi domine, qui na
tus es de virgine, cum patre &
ſancto ſpiritu in ſempiterna ſe
cula. Amẽ. AO admira
D Eus in. Pſalmus bile

tispiece and forty vignettes are decorated with orderly rows of the twenty-three letterforms of the Latin alphabet. Some scholars believe that Tory designed early roman types used by Henri Estienne and Simon de Colines.

After a period of publishing with Simon de Colines, Tory made a second extended trip to Italy from 1516 until 1518 to improve his abilities as an artist and designer. Upon returning to Paris, Tory seems to have turned first to manuscript illumination for his livelihood, which quickly yielded to the design and engraving of woodblocks commissioned by printers. After Simon de Colines' 1520 marriage to Henri Estienne's widow, he began to commission borders, floriated letters, trademarks, and an italic typeface from Tory. It was this collaboration between the master printer and graphic artist that established the new open, lighter style.

In sixteenth-century France, engravers were usually booksellers. In keeping with this tradition, Tory opened a Parisian bookselling firm on the Petit Pont at the sign of the *Pot Cassé* (''broken urn'') where he illustrated, published, bound, and—for several years—printed books. Tory sought out excellent craftsmen and trained them in his approach to book design, which chased the dense, claustrophobic page layout and heavy, Gothic typography from French printing. The symbolic origin of the *Pot Cassé* trademark, which quickly became a symbol for the fresh winds of the French Renaissance, is poignant. On 25 August 1522 Tory's ten-year-old daughter Agnes died suddenly. The devastated father wrote and published a poem in her memory. At the end of the text, the first engraving of the Pot Cassé appears. This shattered antique urn, chained to a closed, locked book and bearing the inscription ''non plus'' (no longer, or nothing more), seems to symbolize the tragic death of his daughter. This interpretation is strengthened by the small winged figure in the upper right-hand corner, a detail that had been cut away from the woodblock by the time this same cut was used in a book published by Tory a year later.

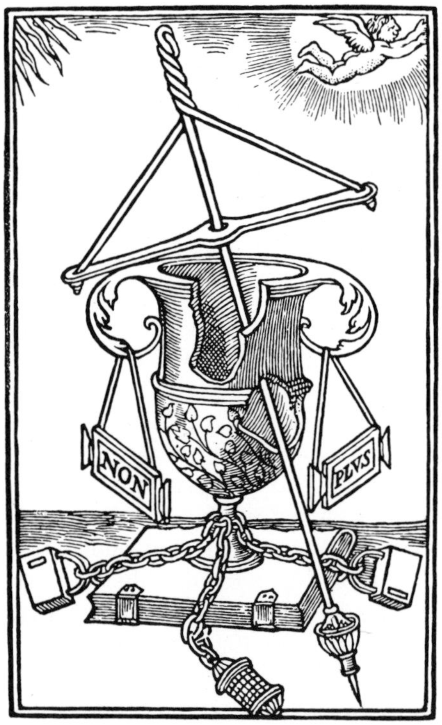

Geoffroy Tory, Pot Cassé emblem, 1524. Later, Tory explained that the broken jar symbolized one's body, the toret or auger symbolized fate, and the book held shut by three padlocked chains signified the book of a life after it is shut by death.

Nothing captured the imagination of French printers as did several series of initials designed by Tory. Roman capitals constructed with the proportions presented later in *Champ Fleury* are set into black squares that come alive with meticulous floral designs and *criblé.* Along with matching printer's ornaments and headpieces,

Geoffroy Tory, pages from *Horae ad usum Romanum,* 1531. This layout from Tory's book of hours demonstrates the delicate lightness of his woodcut borders and illustrations. The bird becomes a powerful accent of black. *Library of Congress, Washington, D.C., Rosenwald Collection.*

Geoffroy Tory, capital from a series of criblé initials, c. 1526. Engraved for Robert Estienne, this alphabet of roman capitals brought elegance and "color" to the pages of books printed at Estienne's press.

LE SEGOND LIVRE.

LE TRIVMPHE DAPOLLO ET DESES MVSES.

a

Trium-phe Dapollo, & ſens moral dicelluy. Franceſco Petracha.

OR voyez doncques le beau triumphe Dapollo, auec ſes Muſes & autres dames compaignes qui nous monſtrent a loeuil commant au moyen des bonnes lettres & Sciences tout homme en bien vſant peut paruenir a conſomme hõneur & immortalite de ſon nom. Si a ce propos on deſiroit en veoir plus a plain, quon ſen aille eſbatre a lire aux Triũphes de meſſer Franceſco Petrarcha, & on trouuera au Triũphe de Renõmee commãt les Poetes, les Philoſophes, & les Orateurs par leur ſtudieuſe vertus, cõbien quilz ſoiẽt piecza morts corporellement, viuent ſpirituellement, & viuront pluſque nulz autres tant vertueulx ayent ilz peu eſtre.

La goute dor. Iupiter, Acriſius, Danae, Moly. Homere.

IE porrois cy adiouxter dauãtage, & approprier, pareillement moraliſer La goute dor en la quelle, ſelon les Poetes & Philoſophes anciens Iupiter ſe tranſmua pour deſcendre du Ciel en Terre en la tour de Acriſius Roy de Grece, & pere de la belle Danae. Semblablement ie porrois auſſi eſcrire de lherbe & verge mercurialle nõmee en Grec Moly. De la quelle Homere faict menſion “ en ſon Odiſſee, au dixieſme liure, mais laiſſant ces choſes a rumyner aux bons eſperits, Ie paſſeray oultre, & viendray a proportiõner & deſcrire toutes noz lettres Attiques & Abecedaires lune apres lautre ſelon leur ordre vulgaire. Et pour y commancer, auec laide de Dieu, Il me ſouuient que iay piecza dit cy deſſus, que toutes noſdites lettres Attiques ſont faictes & participantes de le I. & de le O. & que I. & A. auoient eſte fantaſiez en la fleur dun lis ayant couleur de pourpre, quon dit en Paris Liſſamble, & que Dioſcoride, ſemblablement ſon tranſlateur Florentin nõme Marcel virgile, appellent Hyacinthus. que le langage vulgaire Italien nõme & dit Hyacintiol, ien fays cy presvng deſeing au quel le A. eſt aſſis ſus vng dit Liſſambe en quadrature & rotondite pareillement eſt faict de le I. multiplie en triangle, ou ſi voules autrement dire, dittez que le A, eſt faict de trois I, aſſis & logez lun ſus lautre, en prenãt de chacun ce quil conuient a former vng A parfaict, comme pouuez veoir au dit deſeing enſuyuant, au quel iay faict le A, noir, & le reſte des trois I, Ie lay laiſſe en blanc comme choſe ſuperabundante du dit A. Le deſeing eſt tel quil ſenſuyt.

Liſſãbe. Dioſcoride, Marcel Virgile, Hyacinthiol.

LE SEGOND LIVRE. FEVIL.XXX.

b

BACCHVS CERES ET VENVS SONT ICY MENEZ CAPTIFZ

VEla donques comme iay dit, commant le I, eſt le modele & proportion aux lettres Attiques, Ceſt a ſcauoir, a celles qui ont iambes droittes. Nous verrons de le O. ou nous ferons le B. qui eſt de le I. & de le O. entendu quil a iambe & panſe qui denote briſeure.

EN ceſt endroit louuant noſtre ſeigneur Dieu, Ie feray fin a noſtre Segond liure, au quel auons ſelon noſtre petit entendement demonſtre lorigie des lettres Attiques & auõs voulu ſuader & prier, la quelle choſe encores prions, que quelques bons eſperits ſeuertuaſſent a mettre noſtre langue francoiſe par reigle, afin quen peuſſions vſer honneſtement & ſeurement a coucher par eſcript les bonnes Sciences, quil nous fault mendier des Hebreux, des Grecs, & des Latins, & que ne pouuons auoir ſans grans couſts / fraiz / & deſpens de temps & dargent.

LA FIN DV SEGOND LIVRE.

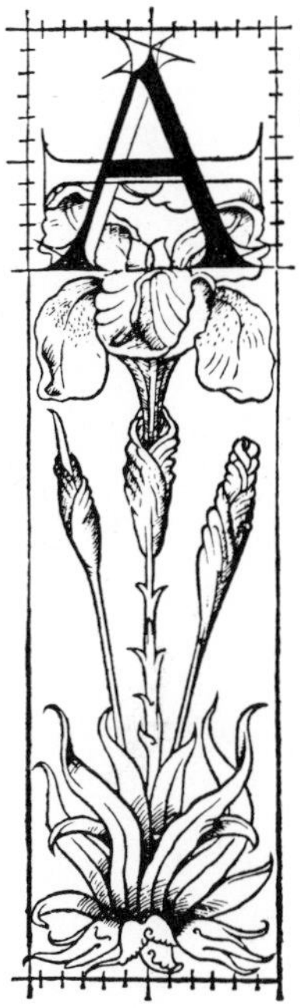

Ordõnãce de le A, faict de trois I. ſus la fleur du Liſſãbe.

Notez bien icy, & entendez.

these initials were the perfect accompaniment for the lighter new roman types by Garamond.

Tory's influence gained momentum in 1525, when he initiated a series of *Horae* (Book of Hours), printed for him by Simon de Colines, that set the style for the era. It was a new clarity of thought, an innovative attitude toward form, and a precise harmony of the various elements—text, capital initials, borders, and illustrations—that mark the 1525 *Horae* as a milestone in graphic design. The patchwork quilt of woodblocks filling the space of early Books of Hours became passé. A light, delicate effect is achieved in the complex illustrations and ornamental borders because Tory used a fine contour line with air flowing around and within his graceful curves. The texture and tone of these visual elements echo the typographic lightness. Tory selected a size and weight of initial that added just the right darker accent, and he used outline initials with his headings. He cut the woodblocks for these borders and illustrations himself. The creative momentum in publishing and graphic design had now passed to France, and King Francis I honored Tory's contribution by naming him *imprimeur du roi* ("printer to the king") in 1530.

Geoffroy Tory, pages from *Horae in laudem Virgin Marie,* 1541. A set of border components, filled with plant and animal motifs, are combined and recombined throughout the book. The open line quality facilitates the application of color by hand. The crowned *F* in the bottom center of the left-hand page is an homage to King Francis I. *Library of Congress, Washington, D.C., Rosenwald Collection.*

Tory's *Champ Fleury* (subtitled *The art and science of the proper and true proportions of the attic letters, which are otherwise called antique letters, and in common speech roman letters*), first published in 1529, was his most important and influential work. It consists of three books. In the first, he attempted to establish and order the French tongue by fixed rules of pronunciation and speech. The second discusses the history of roman letters and compares their proportions with the ideal proportions of the human figure and face. Errors in Albrecht Dürer's letterform designs in the recently published *Underweisung der Messung* are carefully analyzed, then Dürer is forgiven his errors because he is a painter. Painters—according to Tory—rarely understand the proportions of well-formed letters.

Geoffroy Tory, pages from *Champ Fleury,* 1529. This double-page spread discusses how the Roman philosophers, poets, and orators live in spirit through the power of the Roman letters, illustrated by woodcuts of mythological subjects about which we have knowledge through the alphabet. The final paragraph of this "second book" introduces the "third book," the construction of roman letters, with an illustration showing the construction of an *A* from three *I*s.

The third and final book offers instructions in the geometric construction of the twenty-three letters of the Latin alphabet on background grids of one hundred squares. Finally, it closes with Tory's designs for thirteen other alphabets including Greek, Hebrew, Chaldean, and his extraordinary fantasy style made of handtools.

Champ Fleury is a personal book written in a rambling conversational style with frequent digressions into Roman history and mythology. And yet its message about the Latin alphabet came through loud and clear to a generation of French printers and punch cutters, and Tory became the most influential graphic designer of his century.

During the 1530s and 1540s, Robert Estienne achieved a wide reputation as a great printer renowned for the scholarship and intellectual acumen that he brought to the editorial process. During the same time, Colines earned a similar reputation based on the elegance and clarity of his book designs. Illustrated title pages, typographic arrangements, ornaments and borders, and fine presswork contributed to this reputation.

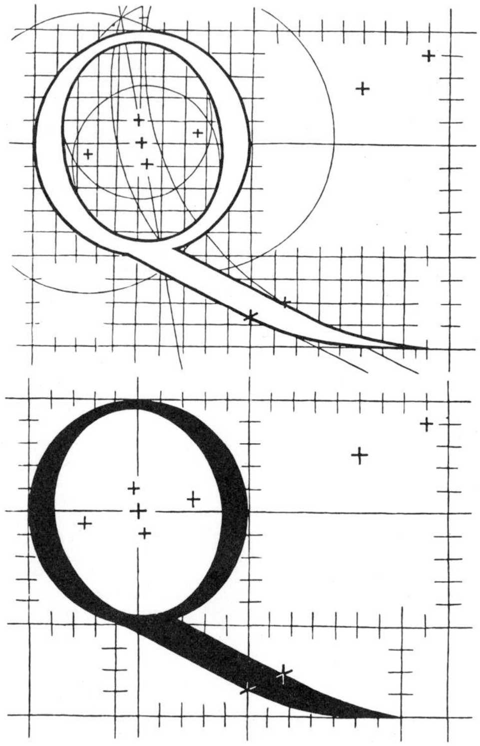

Geoffroy Tory, construction of the letter *Q* from *Champ Fleury,* 1529. Tory used five compass centers in his effort to construct geometrically an ideal roman *O,* and he used an additional two compass centers to add a tail for the *Q.*

Claude Garamond was the first punch cutter to work independently of printing firms. His roman typefaces were designed with such perfection that French printers in the sixteenth century were able to print books of extraordinary legibility and beauty. Garamond is credited, by the sheer quality of his fonts, with a major role in eliminating Gothic styles from compositor's cases all over Europe, except in Germany. Around 1510, Garamond apprenticed as a punch cutter under Antoine Augereau. Just how much credit for the evolution of roman type should to go Augereau, whose religious beliefs led him to the gallows in 1534; Geoffroy Tory, with whom Garamond worked about 1520; and Garamond himself is somewhat muddled. Perhaps these three Frenchmen, all of whom developed a passionate love for roman letterforms designed by Griffo, each had a hand in the struggle to perfect roman fonts.

Around 1430, Garamond established his independent type foundry to sell to printers cast type ready to distribute into the compositor's case. This was a first step away from the "scholar-publisher-typefounder-printer-bookseller," all in one, that began in Mainz some eighty years earlier. The fonts Garamond cut during the 1540s achieved a mastery of visual form, a snugness of fit that allowed closer wordspacing, and a harmony of design between capitals, lowercase, and italic. These types permit books such as the French language *Poliphili,* printed by Jacques Kerner in 1546, to maintain their status as benchmarks of typographic beauty and readability to this day.

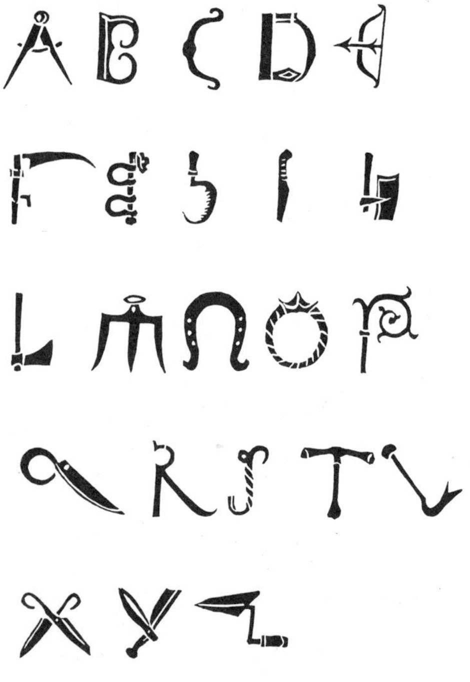

Geoffroy Tory, fantastic alphabet from *Champ Fleury,* 1529. The thirteen alphabets concluding this book (Hebrew, Greek, Persian, and so on) included this whimsical sequence of pictorial letterforms composed of tools. *A* is a compass, *B* is a fusy (steel used to strike a flint to start a fire), and *C* is a handle.

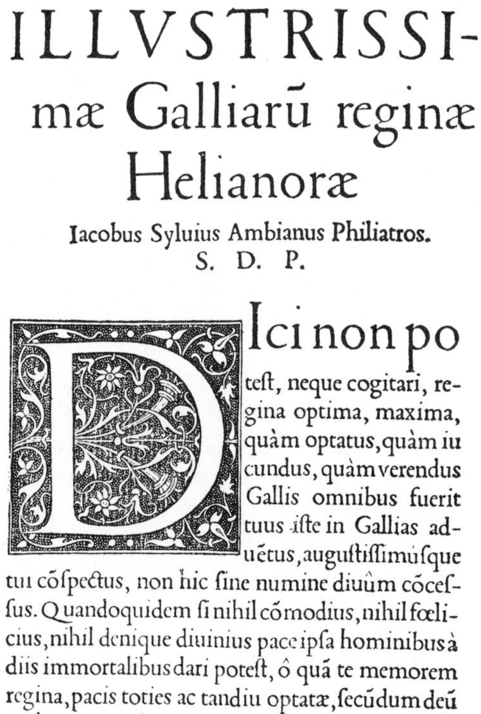

ILLVSTRISSI-
mæ Galliarũ reginæ
Helianoræ
Iacobus Syluius Ambianus Philiatros.
S. D. P.

DIci non po
teſt, neque cogitari, re-
gina optima, maxima,
quàm optatus, quàm iu
cundus, quàm verendus
Gallis omnibus fuerit
tuus iſte in Gallias ad-
uẽtus, auguſtiſſimúſque
tui cõſpectus, non hic ſine numine diuûm cõceſ-
ſus. Quandoquidem ſi nihil cõmodius, nihil fœli-
cius, nihil denique diuinius pace ipſa hominibus à
diis immortalibus dari poteſt, ô quã te memorem
regina, pacis toties ac tandiu optatæ, ſecũdum deũ
author, pacis alumna, pacis vinculum, faxit deus,
adamãtinum. Quos tibi triumphos vniuerſa de-
a.ii.

Robert Estienne, opening page from *Illustrissimae Galliaru reginae Helianorae,* 1531. It is believed that the types used in this book are made from Claude Garamond's first type punches and matrices. *Houghton Library, Harvard University, Cambridge, Mass.*

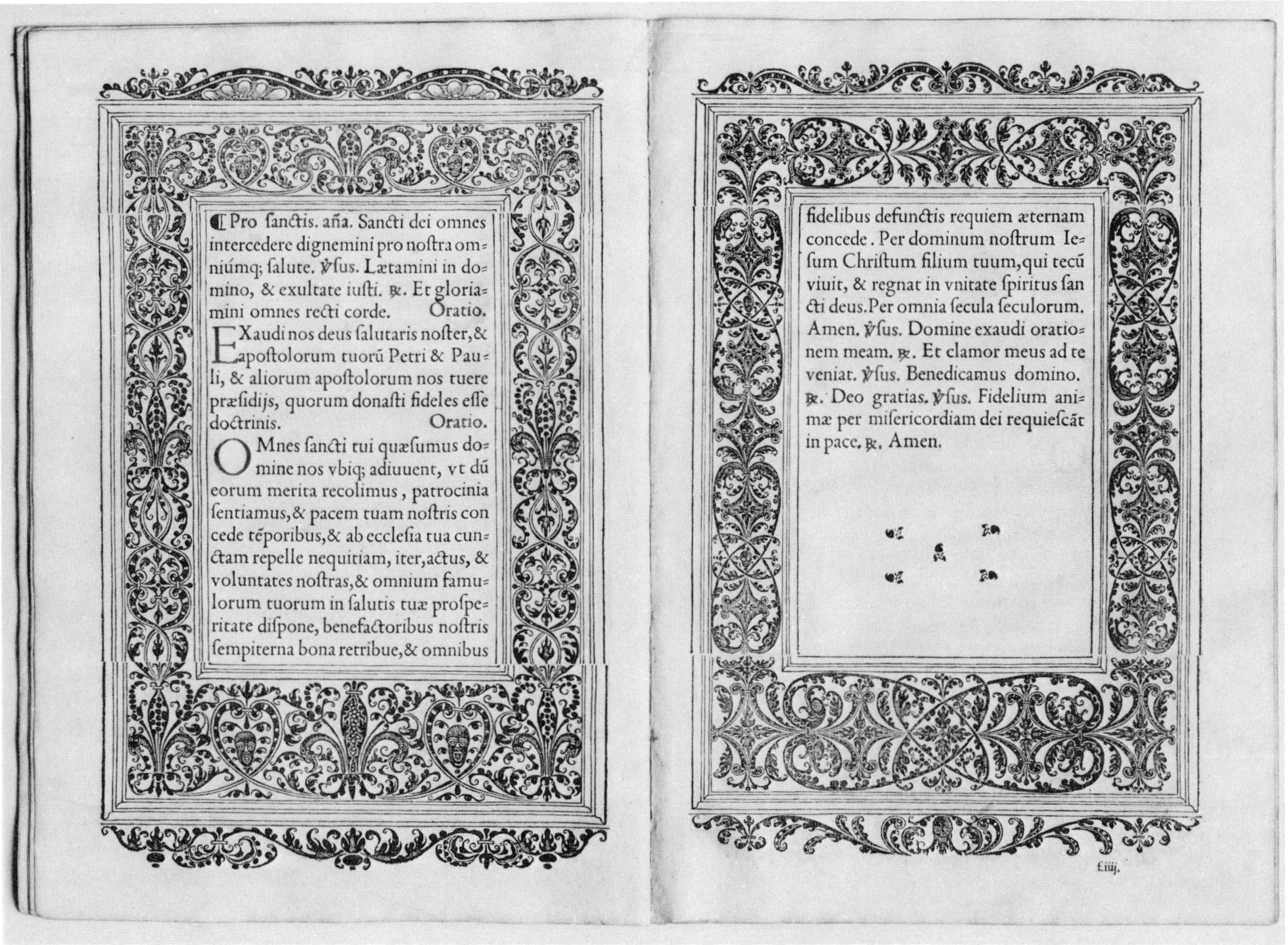

¶ Pro ſanctis. aña. Sancti dei omnes intercedere dignemini pro noſtra omniumq; ſalute. ℣ſus. Lætamini in domino, & exultate iuſti. ℟. Et gloriamini omnes recti corde. Oratio.

Exaudi nos deus ſalutaris noſter, & apoſtolorum tuorũ Petri & Pauli, & aliorum apoſtolorum nos tuere præſidijs, quorum donaſti fideles eſſe doctrinis. Oratio.

Omnes ſancti tui quæſumus domine nos vbiq; adiuuent, vt dũ eorum merita recolimus, patrocinia ſentiamus, & pacem tuam noſtris con cede tẽporibus, & ab eccleſia tua cunctam repelle nequitiam, iter, actus, & voluntates noſtras, & omnium famulorum tuorum in ſalutis tuæ proſperitate diſpone, benefactoribus noſtris ſempiterna bona retribue, & omnibus

fidelibus defunctis requiem æternam concede. Per dominum noſtrum Ieſum Chriſtum filium tuum, qui tecũ viuit, & regnat in vnitate ſpiritus ſancti deus. Per omnia ſecula ſeculorum. Amen. ℣ſus. Domine exaudi orationem meam. ℟. Et clamor meus ad te veniat. ℣ſus. Benedicamus domino. ℟. Deo gratias. ℣ſus. Fidelium animæ per miſericordiam dei requieſcãt in pace. ℟. Amen.

f.iiij.

Simon de Colines (printer) and Geoffroy Tory (designer), pages from a Book of Hours, 1543. This dense border design projects its own graphic qualities and is no longer a schematic for the application of color by hand. *The Metropolitan Museum of Art, New York.*

The influence of writing as a model diminished in Garamond's work, for typography was evolving a language of form rooted in the processes of making steel punches, casting metal type, and printing instead of imitating forms created by hand gestures with an inked quill on paper. Old age did not treat Garamond kindly, and he was desperately poor when he died at age eighty-one. His widow sold his punches and matrixes. No doubt this contributed to the wide use of his fonts, which remained a major typographic influence until the late 1700s.

Oronce Finé (1494–1555) was a mathematics professor and author whose abilities as a graphic artist complemented his scientific publications. In addition to illustrating his mathematics, geography, and astronomy books, Finé became interested in book ornament and design. His contemporaries had equal admiration for his contributions to science and graphic arts. He worked closely with printers, notably Simon de Colines, in the design and production of his books. Also, he made an excellent contribution as an editor and designer involved in numerous other titles. While Tory's inspiration is evident, Finé's mathematical construction of his ornaments and the robust clarity of his graphic illustration are the work of an innovative graphic designer.

During the 1540s, Robert Estienne was caught up in the turmoil of the Reformation. The protection King Francis I (1494–1547) provided for his "dear printer" ended with the king's death, and Estienne's work as a scholar and printer of "pagan language" Latin, Greek, and Hebrew Bibles incurred the wrath of Catholic theologians at the Sorbonne, who suspected that he was a heretic. After a 1549 visit to Geneva, Switzerland, to meet Protestant Reformation leader John Calvin (1509–1564), Estienne began careful preparations to move his printing firm to that city the following year. In choosing to relocate in Switzerland, Estienne was mindful of the fate of Étienne Dolet (1509–1546), whose two-volume *Commentarii linguage Latinae* had made a major contribution to classical scholarship. On three occasions officials' displeasure with the books Dolet published had caused him to be imprisoned. Finally, he was accused of atheism, tried, and condemned by the Sorbonne Theological Faculty. On

Simon de Colines, title page for *De natura stirpium libri tres,* 1536. The typography is surrounded by an illustration, perhaps by Oronce Finé, that takes great liberties with natural scale and perspective to create a joyous interpretation of the natural bounty of the earth's flora. This volume is widely regarded as being one of the most beautifully designed and printed books of the sixteenth century.

3 August 1546, thirty-seven-year-old Dolet was burned at the stake, and his books were used to fuel the flames. Ironically, his first work, *Cato christianus,* had been a profession of his Christian creed.

Comparison of the editions of *Poliphili* printed by Jacques Kerver during the middle of the sixteenth century with Manutius' 1499 edition shows just how rapidly the French Renaissance printers expanded the range of graphic design. Manutius produced his *Poliphili* with one size of roman type and used capitals as his only means of emphasis; Kerver called upon a large range of roman and italic type sizes in designing his pages. Manutius used a set of ornamental initials and little starlike ornaments; Kerver selected from an elegant stock of headpieces, tailpieces, and printers' flowers to embellish the printed page. The illustrations in Manutius' *Poliphili* use a monotone contour line; Kerver's illustrator achieved a broad range of tonal effects. And, a fully developed title page in the Kerver editions set the tone for his volume.

As was true with illuminated manuscripts, the earliest typographic books in each European country had an identifiable national style. Garamond-derived type fonts and Tory-inspired initials and ornaments began to be available to printers throughout France, the Low Countries, Germany, Switzerland, and Italy. The unified structure and tone of the French book produced during the golden age of French typography was admired throughout the continent. Printers began to emulate the light elegance and ordered clarity of Parisian books. As a result, the first international style of typographic design flourished as the dominant graphic theme of the sixteenth century.

After Paris, the next major center of printing in France was Lyons. Most of the forty printers there churned out routinely designed material such as popular romances for the commercial market using Gothic type. In 1542 Jean de Tournes (1504–1564) opened his firm in Lyons and began to use Garamond types with initials and ornaments designed by Tory. But de Tournes was not content to imitate Parisian graphic design. He retained his fellow Lyonese, Bernard Salomon, to design headpieces, arabesques, *fleurons* (printers' flowers), and woodblock illustrations. The excellent book design of these collaborators was further enhanced when they were joined by a Parisian type designer working in Lyons, Robert Granjon (d. 1579), who married Salomon's daughter Antoinette.

The most original of the designers inspired by Garamond's roman faces, Granjon created delicate italic fonts which had beautiful italic capitals with swashes. Books set in italic lowercase had been using regular capitals. Granjon attempted to add a fourth major style—in addition to Gothic, roman, and italic—when he designed and promoted the *caractères de civilité,* a typographic version of the French secretarial writing style then in vogue. The distinctive appearance of these typefaces with flamboyant cursive ascenders was insufficient compensation for their poor legibility. Therefore, *civilité* was just a passing fancy. The fleurons designed by Granjon were modular and could be put together in endless combinations to make headpieces, tailpieces,

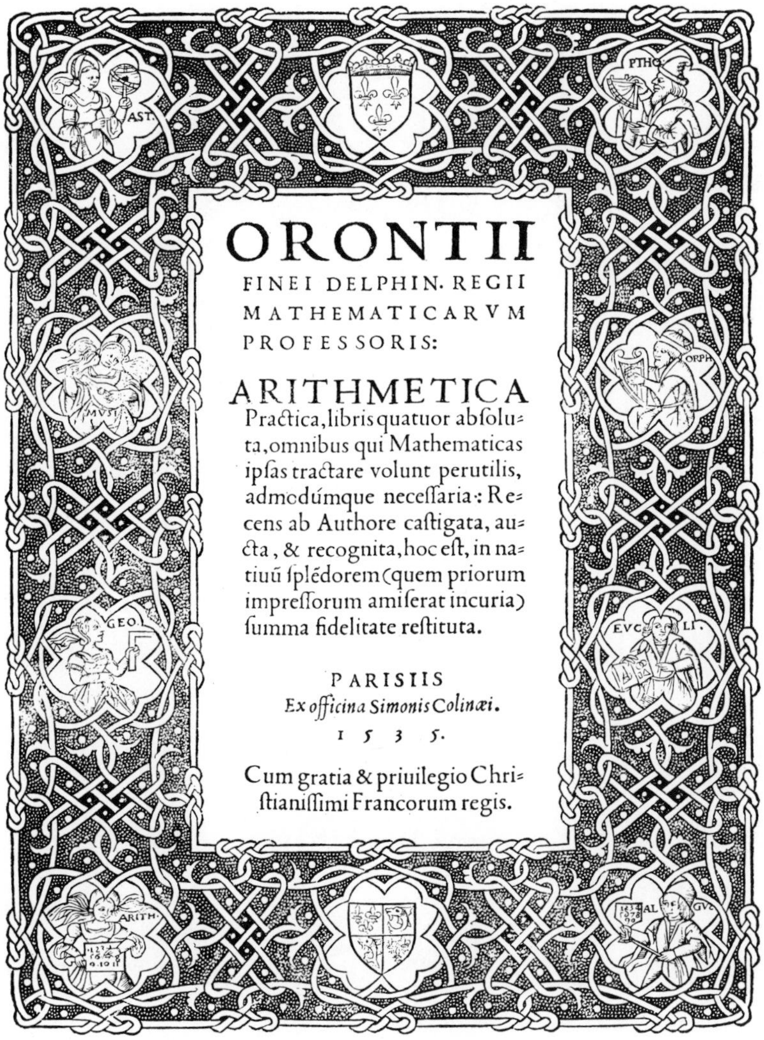
ORONTII
FINEI DELPHIN. REGII
MATHEMATICARVM
PROFESSORIS:
ARITHMETICA
Practica, libris quatuor absoluta, omnibus qui Mathematicas ipsas tractare volunt perutilis, admodúmque necessaria: Recens ab Authore castigata, aucta, & recognita, hoc est, in natiuũ splẽdorem (quem priorum impressorum amiserat incuria) summa fidelitate restituta.
PARISIIS
Ex officina Simonis Colinæi.
1 5 3 5.
Cum gratia & priuilegio Christianissimi Francorum regis.

Simon de Colines (printer) and Oronce Finé (designer), title page for Oronce Finé's *Arithmetica,* 1535. In this title-page border, Finé used carefully measured strapwork, symbolic figures representing areas of knowledge, and a criblé background. De Colines' exquisite typography combines with this border to create a masterpiece of Renaissance graphic design. *Library of Congress, Washington, D.C.*

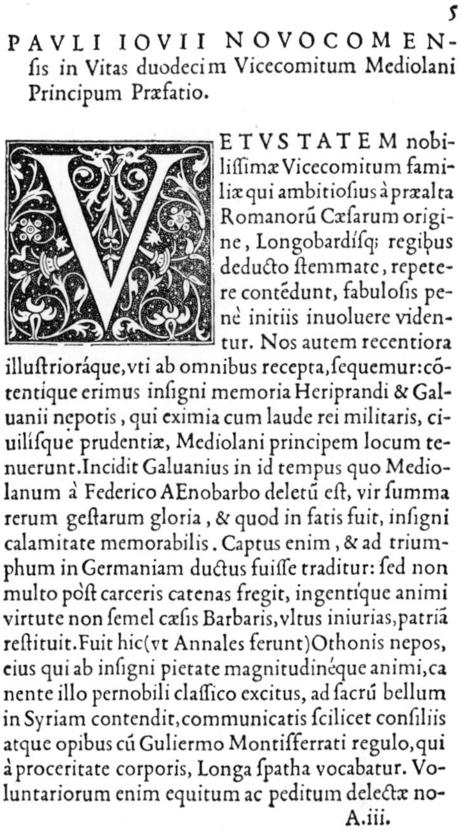
5
PAVLI IOVII NOVOCOMENsis in Vitas duodecim Vicecomitum Mediolani Principum Præfatio.

VETVSTATEM nobilissimæ Vicecomitum familiæ qui ambitiosius à præalta Romanorũ Cæsarum origine, Longobardísq; regibus deducto stemmate, repetere contẽdunt, fabulosis penè initiis inuoluere videntur. Nos autem recentiora illustrioráque, vti ab omnibus recepta, sequemur: cõtentíque erimus insigni memoria Heriprandi & Galuanii nepotis, qui eximia cum laude rei militaris, ciuilísque prudentiæ, Mediolani principem locum tenuerunt. Incidit Galuanius in id tempus quo Mediolanum à Federico AEnobarbo deletũ est, vir summa rerum gestarum gloria, & quod in fatis fuit, insigni calamitate memorabilis. Captus enim, & ad triumphum in Germaniam ductus fuisse traditur: sed non multo pòst carceris catenas fregit, ingentíque animi virtute non semel cæsis Barbaris, vltus iniurias, patriã restituit. Fuit hic (vt Annales ferunt) Othonis nepos, eius qui ab insigni pietate magnitudinéque animi, canente illo pernobili classico excitus, ad sacrũ bellum in Syriam contendit, communicatis scilicet consiliis atque opibus cũ Guliermo Montisferrati regulo, qui à proceritate corporis, Longa spatha vocabatur. Voluntariorum enim equitum ac peditum delectæ no-
A.iii.

Robert Estienne, page from Paolo Giovio's *Vitae duodecim Vicecomitum Mediolani Principum,* 1549. Estienne used Garamond's roman fonts and Geoffroy Tory's initials in this book. Headings are set in one line of capitals and two lines of lower case.

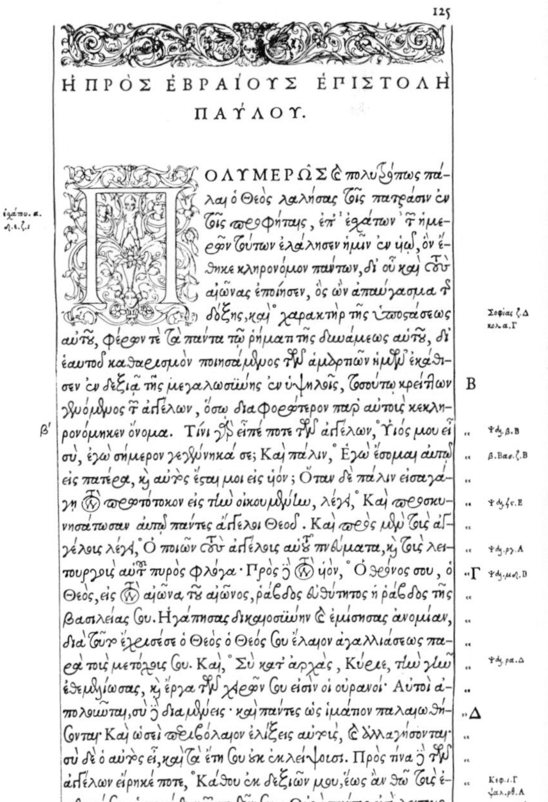
125
Η ΠΡΟΣ ΕΒΡΑΙΟΥΣ ΕΠΙΣΤΟΛΗ ΠΑΥΛΟΥ.

ΠΟΛΥΜΕΡΩΣ καὶ πολυτρόπως πάλαι ὁ Θεὸς λαλήσας τοῖς πατράσιν ἐν τοῖς προφήταις, ἐπ' ἐσχάτων τῶν ἡμερῶν τούτων ἐλάλησεν ἡμῖν ἐν υἱῷ, ὃν ἔθηκε κληρονόμον πάντων, δι' οὗ καὶ τοὺς αἰῶνας ἐποίησεν, ὃς ὢν ἀπαύγασμα τῆς δόξης, καὶ χαρακτὴρ τῆς ὑποστάσεως αὐτοῦ, φέρων τε τὰ πάντα τῷ ῥήματι τῆς δυνάμεως αὐτοῦ, δι' ἑαυτοῦ καθαρισμὸν ποιησάμενος τῶν ἁμαρτιῶν ἡμῶν ἐκάθισεν ἐν δεξιᾷ τῆς μεγαλωσύνης ἐν ὑψηλοῖς, τοσούτῳ κρείττων B γενόμενος τῶν ἀγγέλων, ὅσῳ διαφορώτερον παρ' αὐτοὺς κεκληρονόμηκεν ὄνομα.
β′ Τίνι γὰρ εἶπέ ποτε τῶν ἀγγέλων, Υἱός μου εἶ σύ, ἐγὼ σήμερον γεγέννηκά σε; Καὶ πάλιν, Ἐγὼ ἔσομαι αὐτῷ εἰς πατέρα, καὶ αὐτὸς ἔσται μοι εἰς υἱόν; Ὅταν δὲ πάλιν εἰσαγάγῃ τὸν πρωτότοκον εἰς τὴν οἰκουμένην, λέγει, Καὶ προσκυνησάτωσαν αὐτῷ πάντες ἄγγελοι Θεοῦ. Καὶ πρὸς μὲν τοὺς ἀγγέλους λέγει, Ὁ ποιῶν τοὺς ἀγγέλους αὐτοῦ πνεύματα, καὶ τοὺς λειτουργοὺς αὐτοῦ πυρὸς φλόγα· Γ Πρὸς δὲ τὸν υἱόν, Ὁ θρόνος σου, ὁ Θεός, εἰς τὸν αἰῶνα τοῦ αἰῶνος, ῥάβδος εὐθύτητος ἡ ῥάβδος τῆς βασιλείας σου. Ἠγάπησας δικαιοσύνην καὶ ἐμίσησας ἀνομίαν, διὰ τοῦτο ἔχρισέ σε ὁ Θεὸς ὁ Θεός σου ἔλαιον ἀγαλλιάσεως παρὰ τοὺς μετόχους σου. Καί, Σὺ κατ' ἀρχάς, Κύριε, τὴν γῆν ἐθεμελίωσας, καὶ ἔργα τῶν χειρῶν σου εἰσὶν οἱ οὐρανοί· Αὐτοὶ ἀπολοῦνται, σὺ δὲ διαμένεις· καὶ πάντες ὡς ἱμάτιον παλαιωθήσονται· Δ Καὶ ὡσεὶ περιβόλαιον ἑλίξεις αὐτούς, καὶ ἀλλαγήσονται· σὺ δὲ ὁ αὐτὸς εἶ, καὶ τὰ ἔτη σου οὐκ ἐκλείψουσι. Πρὸς τίνα δὲ τῶν ἀγγέλων εἴρηκέ ποτε, Κάθου ἐκ δεξιῶν μου, ἕως ἂν θῶ τοὺς ἐχθρούς σου ὑποπόδιον τῶν ποδῶν σου; Οὐχὶ πάντες εἰσὶ λειτουρ-

Robert Estienne, page from a Greek New Testament, 1550. The great scholar-printer designed the pages of his Greek volumes using, once again, graphic material created by punch cutter Claude Garamond and engraver Geoffroy Tory.

Comment ilz ſignifioient Dieu.

Pour ſignifier dieu ilz paignoient vng oeil pource que ainſi que loeil veoit & regarde ce qui eſt audeuant de luy dieu veoit conſidere & congnoit toutes choſes.

Jacques Kerver (printer), page from *Hora pollo,* 1543. An unsettling Surrealism springs from the woodblock illustrations in this small volume where eyes and disembodied feet float in the sky. *Library of Congress, Washington, D.C., Rosenwald Collection.*

HYPNEROTOMACHIE, OV

Diſcours du ſonge
DE POLIPHILE,
Deduiſant comme Amour le combat à l'occaſion de Polia.

Soubz la fiction de quoy l'aucteur monſtrant que toutes choſes terreſtres ne ſont que vanité, traicte de pluſieurs matieres profitables, & dignes de memoire.

Nouuellement traduict de langage Italien en Francois.

A PARIS.
Pour Iaques Keruer à la Licorne, Rue S. Iaques.

M. D. LXI.

Jacques Kerver, title page from *Poliphili,* 1561. A satyr and a nymph eyeing each other amidst an abundant harvest clue the reader to the pagan adventures within the book. *Library of Congress, Washington, D.C., Rosenwald Collection.*

ornaments, and borders. Garamond's type designs were so beautiful and legible that for two hundred years, from about 1550 until the mid-1700s, most typeface designers followed Granjon by merely refining and altering Garamond's forms.

On 1 March 1562, a conflict between French troops and a Reformed church congregation ended in a massacre. This began four decades of religious wars that effectively ended the innovation of the golden age of French typography. Many Huguenot (French Protestant) printers fled to Switzerland, England, and the Low Countries to escape religious strife, censorship, and rigid trade laws. Just as the momentum for innovative graphic design had moved from Italy to France, it now passed from France into the Low Countries, especially the cities of Antwerp and Amsterdam.

A serious arm injury in the early 1550s ended the outstanding bookbinding career of Christophe Plantin (1514–1589). Thus he changed his career to printing in mid-life, and the Netherlands found its greatest printer. Plantin was born in a rural French village near Tours, apprenticed as a bookbinder and bookseller in Caen, then set up shop in Antwerp at age thirty-five. While de Tournes' dedication to quality and unsurpassed design standards have led many authorities to proclaim him the sixteenth century's "best printer," Plantin's remarkable management sense and publishing acumen could earn him the same accolade for different reasons. Classics and Bibles, herbals and medicine books, music and maps—a full range of printed matter—poured from what became the world's largest and strongest publishing house. Even Plantin got into trouble during this dangerous time

LIVRE PREMIER DE

Comment ilz arriuerent en l'Iſle Cytherée, la BEAVTE DE LAQVELLE EST ICY DESCRITE,

enſemble la forme de leur barque: & comme au deſcendre vindrent au deuant d'eulx, pluſieurs Nymphes, pour faire honneur à Cupido leur maiſtre.

VOguans donc en ceſte maniere, non pas de la borde ou artimõ, mais auec les aëlles de cupido, qu'il auoit eſtendues au vent, comme dict eſt. Polia & moy conformes en voluntez, tous deux deſirans paruenir au lieu determiné pour noſtre beatitude au plus grand aiſe qu'onq̃s ſens humain peuſt ſentir, & langue dire, ſouſpirans de doulceur par amour embrazée: & eſchauffez cõme le pot bouillant à trop grand feu, lequel ſe reſpend par deſſus, arriuames au port de la ſaincte iſle Cytherée, en la barque de Cupido, qui n'eſtoit eſtiuée ny chargée de laytage, mais branlante ſur les vndes, & faicte comme ſ'enſuyt.

Des quatre parties les deux eſtoiẽt employées l'vne en la poupe, l'autre en la proe, & les deux autres à la mizane, ou elle eſtoit plus large d'vne tierce partie Les poſtices auoient deux piedz de haulteur ſur la couuerture, & les bancs vn pied & demy. La carene & les coſtieres eſtoiẽt couuertes de lames d'or: laquelle ſortoit ſur la proe, & ſur la poupe eſleuée en forme de croſſe, & ſe replioit en façon d'vn rouleau, au rond duquel y auoit vn riche ornement de perles. Du reply partoit vn fueillage courant ſur le plan du ſiege, faict de fin or, & taillé apres le naturel. L'eſpoiſſeur de ſes rouleaux faiſoit la largeur du Paleſcalme, du meſme metal, cizelé d'vne frize de quatre doigtz de large, garnie de pierrerie, & les ſcalmes d'Ebene. Tout le corps du nauire ſi biẽ faict, que lon n'y euſt ſceu veoir vne ioincture, ains ſembloit eſtre d'vne piece, ſans calfietter par deſſus, ſinon de la compoſition que i'ay par cy deuãt deduicte. C'eſtoit la miſtiõ dont il eſtoit pegé ou eſpalmé, & la peincture de deſſus eſtoient Arabeſques d'or moulu.

Ce lieu

LES FABLES

Honorer Dieu auſſi bien en proſperité qu'en aduerſité.

Qui en ſa vie à Dieu ne fait honneur,
Quãd la mort viẽt, ou quelque maladie,
Dieu l'habãdõne, & point n'y remedie:
Pour biẽ ou mal fault louer tel ſeigneur.

Jean de Tournes and Guillaume Gazeau (printers) and Bernard Salomon (illustrator), page from Aesop's *Fables,* 1547. This delightful miniature book is one of the first collaborations between de Tournes and woodcut illustrator Bernard Salomon. (Reproduced approximately actual size.)

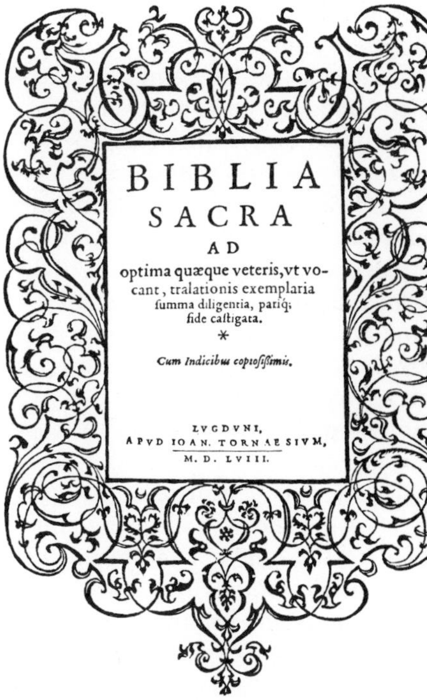

BIBLIA SACRA AD optima quæque veteris, vt vocant, tralationis exemplaria ſumma diligentia, pariq; fide caſtigata.

Cum Indicibus copioſiſſimis.

LVGDVNI, APVD IOAN. TORNAESIVM, M. D. LVIII.

for printers. While he was in Paris in 1562, his staff printed a heretical tract, and his assets were seized and sold. He recovered much of the money, however, and within two years was reorganized and going strong. Plantin's design style was a more ornamented, weightier adaptation of French typographic design. Granjon was called to Antwerp for a period as type designer in residence. Plantin loved Granjon's fleurons and

Jacques Kerver, typographic page from *Poliphili,* 1561. Bracketed by white space, Kerver's heading uses three sizes of type with capitals and lower case, all capitals, and italic to bring variety to the design. *Library of Congress, Washington, D.C., Rosenwald Collection.*

Jean de Tournes, title page for a Bible, 1558. This delicate, open arabesque border is typical of the innovative design style developed by de Tournes and his associates in Lyons.

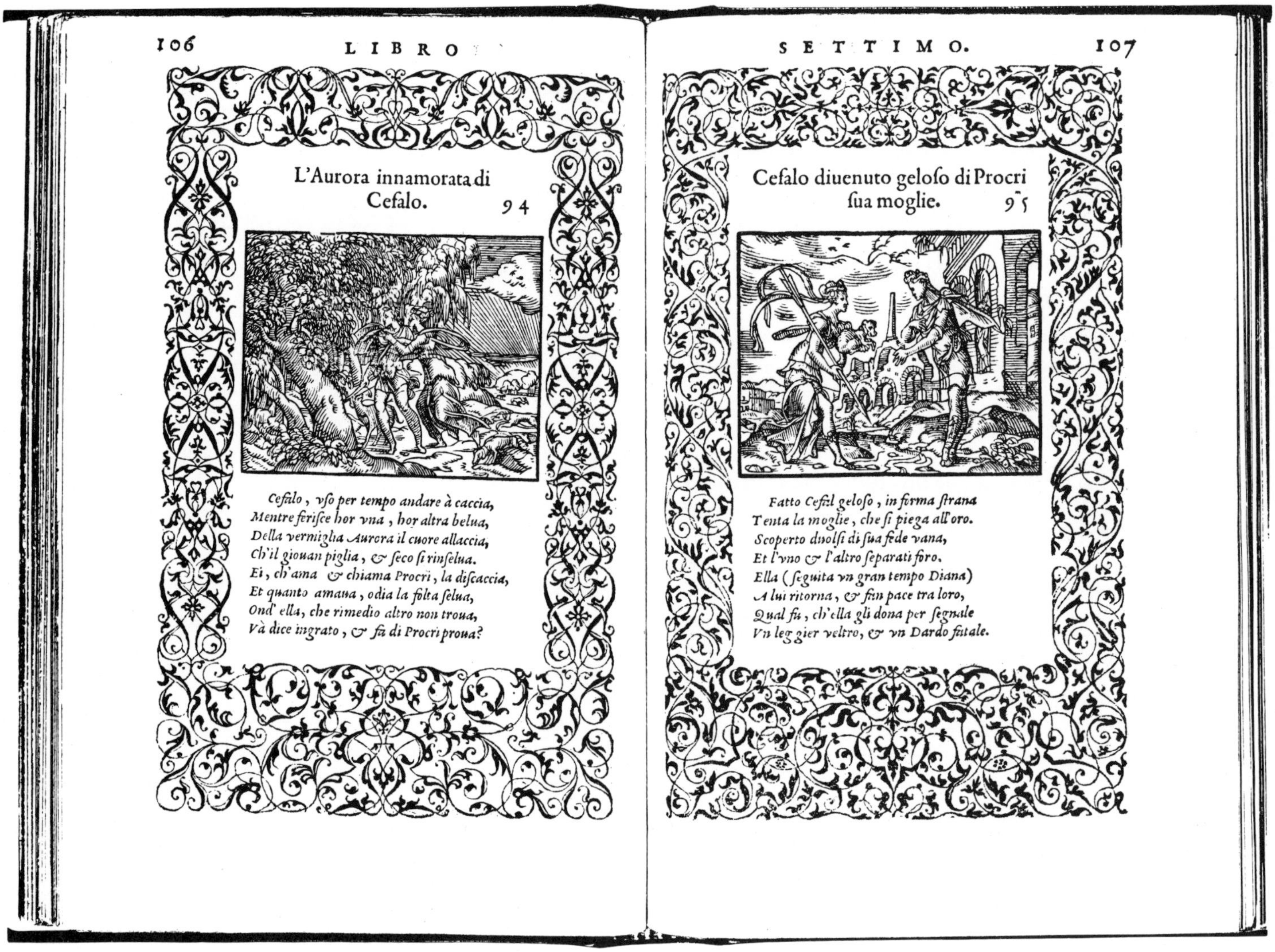
106 LIBRO
L'Aurora innamorata di Cefalo. 94
Cefalo, vso per tempo andare à caccia,
Mentre ferisce hor vna, hor altra belua,
Della vermiglia Aurora il cuore allaccia,
Ch'il giouan piglia, & seco si rinselua.
Ei, ch'ama & chiama Procri, la discaccia,
Et quanto amaua, odia la folta selua,
Ond' ella, che rimedio altro non troua,
Và dice ingrato, & fa di Procri proua?
SETTIMO. 107
Cefalo diuenuto geloso di Procri sua moglie. 95
Fatto Cefal geloso, in forma strana
Tenta la moglie, che si piega all'oro.
Scoperto duolsi di sua fede vana,
Et l'vno & l'altro separati foro.
Ella (seguita vn gran tempo Diana)
A lui ritorna, & fan pace tra loro,
Qual fu, ch'ella gli dona per segnale
Vn leggier veltro, & vn Dardo fatale.

Jean de Tournes (printer) and Bernard Salomon (illustrator), pages from Ovid's *La Vita er Metamorfoseo,* 1559. Three tonal qualities—Salomon's spectacular border designs, his denser illustrations, and Granjon's italics that echo the flowing curves of the borders—are used by de Tournes with just the right amount of white space to make this a masterpiece of Renaissance book design. *Metropolitan Museum of Art, New York.*

used them in profusion, particularly in his ever-popular emblem books. Plantin published fifty emblem books, which contained illustrated verses or mottos for moral instruction or meditation. At the estate sales of Colines and Garamond, Plantin secured numerous punches and types. Under the patronage of King Phillip II of Spain, Plantin published the second of the great Polyglot Bibles from 1569–1572. This eight-volume work almost bankrupted him when the promised patronage was slow to materialize.

The use of copperplate engravings, instead of woodcuts, to illustrate his books was Plantin's main design contribution. He commissioned masters of this flourishing printmaking medium to design title pages and to illustrate books. Soon engraving was

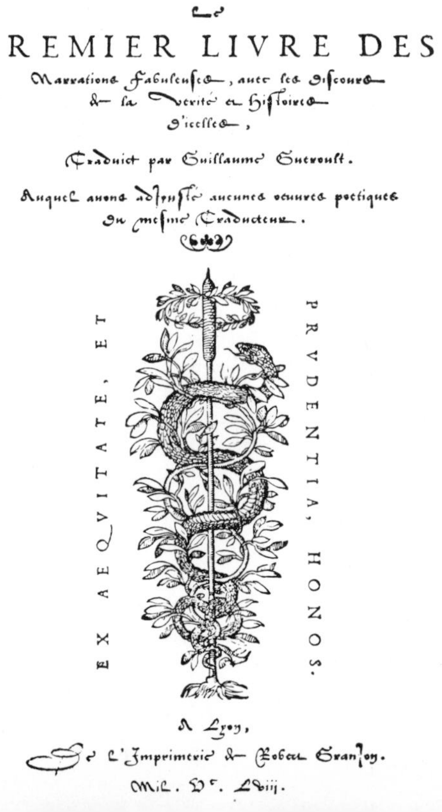

Robert Granjon, title page for *Le Premier Livre des Narrations Fabuleuses,* 1558. The script letterforms are Granjon's *caracteres de civilité* (characters of civilty), which were used for the entire text of this one-hundred twenty-page book. The serpent device, elegantly bracketed by the motto in roman capitals, is Granjon's trademark.

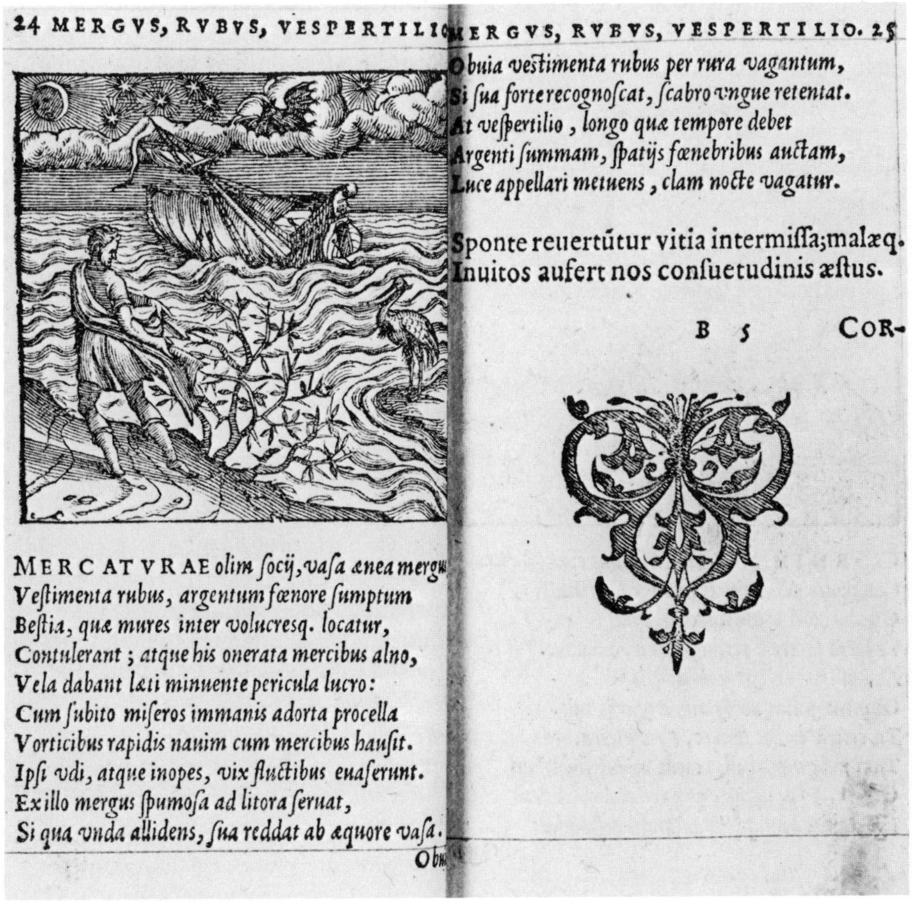
24 MERGVS, RVBVS, VESPERTILIO. MERGVS, RVBVS, VESPERTILIO. 25

MERCATVRAE olim socij, vasa ænea mergus,
Vestimenta rubus, argentum fœnore sumptum
Bestia, quæ mures inter volucresq. locatur,
Contulerant; atque his onerata mercibus alno,
Vela dabant læti minuente pericula lucro:
Cum subito miseros immanis adorta procella
Vorticibus rapidis nauim cum mercibus hausit.
Ipsi udi, atque inopes, vix fluctibus euaserunt.
Ex illo mergus spumosa ad litora seruat,
Si qua vnda allidens, sua reddat ab æquore vasa.
Obui-

Obuia vestimenta rubus per rura vagantum,
Si sua forte recognoscat, scabro vngue retentat.
At vespertilio, longo quæ tempore debet
Argenti summam, spatijs fœnebribus auctam,
Luce appellari metuens, clam nocte vagatur.

Sponte reuertũtur vitia intermissa; malæq.
Inuitos aufert nos consuetudinis æstus.

B 5 COR-

Christophe Plantin, pages from *Centvm fabvlae ex antiqvis* by Gabriello Faerno, 1567. By the late 1500s, an abundant stock of fonts, ornaments, and illustration material enabled printers, including Plantin, to produce handsome volumes in the Renaissance style economically. *Library of Congress, Washington, D.C., Rosenwald Collection.*

Christophe Plantin, title page for *Centvm fabvlae ex antiqvis* by Gabriello Faerno, 1567. Dignified and architectural, this title page is typical of the Plantin house style. *Library of Congress, Washington, D.C., Rosenwald Collection.* (bottom left)

Christophe Plantin, page from the *Polyglot Bible,* 1569–72. A double-page format, with two vertical columns over a wide horizontal column, contained the Hebrew, Latin, Aramaic, Greek, and Syriac translations of the Bible. *Pierpont Morgan Library, New York.*

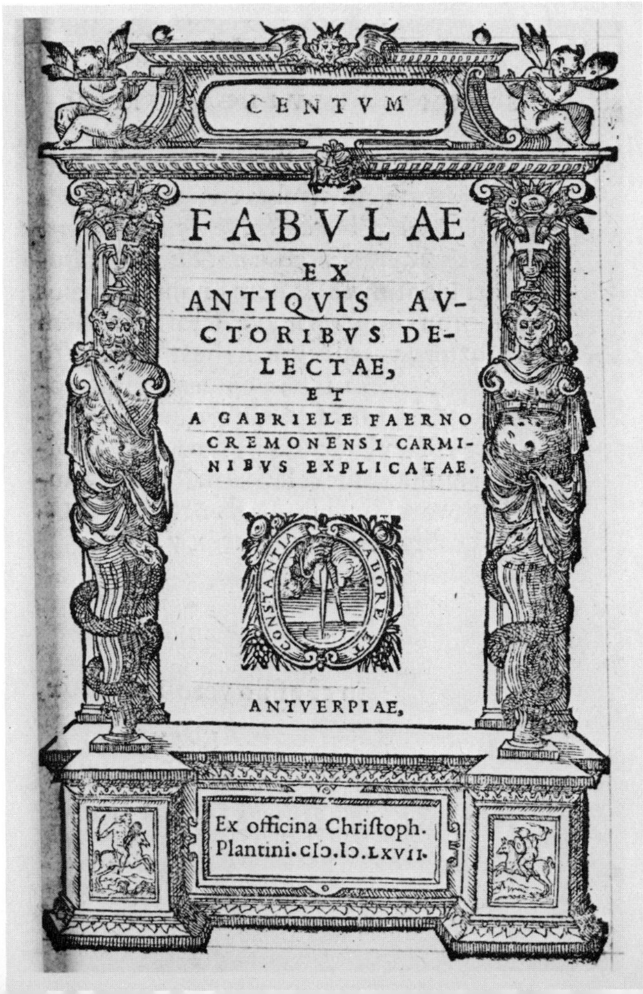
CENTVM
FABVLAE
EX
ANTIQVIS AVCTORIBVS DELECTAE,
ET
A GABRIELE FAERNO CREMONENSI CARMINIBVS EXPLICATAE.

ANTVERPIAE,
Ex officina Christoph. Plantini. CIↃ.IↃ.LXVII.

GENESIS. Translat.B.Hierony. Noe.

21 Et deleuit omnem substantiam quæ erat super terram, ab homine vsque ad pecus, tam reptile, quàm volucres cæli: & deletæ sunt de terra. Remansit autem solus Noe, & qui cum
24 eo erant in arca. Obtinueruntq; aquæ terrã centum quinquaginta diebus. CAP. VIII.
1 A Recordatus autem Deus Noe, cunctorumque animantium, & omnium iumentorum quæ erant cum eo in arca: adduxit spiritum super terram, & imminutæ sunt aquæ:
2 Et clausi sunt fontes abyssi, & cataractæ cæ-
3 li: & prohibitæ sunt pluuiæ de cælo. Reuersæque sunt aquæ de terra, euntes & redeuntes: & cœperunt minui pòst centum quinquagin
4 ta dies. Requieuitque arca mense septimo, vicesimoseptimo die mensis super montes Ar-
5 meniæ. At verò aquæ ibant & decrescebãt vsque ad decimum mensem. Decimo enim mense, prima die mensis, apparuerunt cacu-
6 mina montium. Cumque transissent quadraginta dies, aperiens Noe fenestram arcæ
7 quam fecerat, Dimisit coruum, qui egrediebatur & reuertebatur, donec siccarẽtur a-
8 quæ super terram. Emisit quoque colum-
B bam post eũ, vt videret si iam cessassent aquæ
9 super faciem terræ. Quæ cùm non inuenisset vbi requiesceret pes eius, reuersa est ad eum in arcam. Aquæ enim erant super vniuersam terram. Extenditque manum suam, & ap
10 prehensam intulit in arcã. Expectatis autẽ vltra septẽ diebus aliis, rursum dimisit columbã
11 ex arca. At illa venit ad eũ ad vesperã, portans ramũ oliuæ virentibus foliis in ore suo. Intellexit ergo Noe quòd cessassent aquæ super terrã.
12 Expectauitq; nihilominus septẽ alios dies, & emisit colũbã, quæ nõ est reuersa vltra ad eũ.
13 Igitur sexcentesimo primo anno, primo men
C se, prima die mensis, imminutæ sunt aquæ super terram. Et aperiens Noe tectum arcæ, aspexit, viditque quòd exiccata esset superfi-
14 cies terræ. Mense secundo, septimo & vicesi-
15 mo die mẽsis, arefacta est terra. Locutus est au
16 tẽ De' ad Noe, dicens: Egredere de arca tu, & vxor tua, filij tui, & vxores filiorũ tuorũ tecũ.

replacing the woodcut as the major technique for graphic images throughout Europe. After Plantin's death, his son-in-law John Moretus continued the firm, which remained in the family until 1876, when the town of Antwerp purchased it and turned this amazing house and printing firm into a unique museum of typography and printing, containing two presses dating from Plantin's time.

The seventeenth century

After the remarkable progress in graphic design that took place during the brief decades of the Incunabula, and the exquisite typography and book design of the Renaissance, the seventeenth century was a relatively quiet time for graphic design innovation. Punches, matrices, and woodblocks from the 1500s were widely available, so there was little incentive for printers to commission new graphic materials. Book design and printing were characterized by a business-as-usual attitude. An awakening of literary genius occurred during the seventeenth century. Immortal works by gifted authors, including the British playwright and poet William Shakespeare (1564–1616) and the Spanish novelist, playwright, and poet Miguel de Cervantes Saavedra (1547–1616), were widely published. Unfortunately, similar innovation was lacking in the graphic arts. There were no important new layout approaches or typefaces to provide a distinctive format for outstanding new literature.

The oldest surviving newspaper dates from early in the century. This was the *Avisa Relation oder Zeitung* printed in the German town of Augsburg on a regular basis in 1609. Others followed in many German cities and other European countries. England, for example, had its first two-page "running news" publications, called *corantos,* in 1621.

Printing came to the North American colonies during this century. A British locksmith named Stephen Daye (c.1594–1668) contracted with a wealthy dissenting clergyman, Reverend Jesse Glover, to sail with him to the New World to establish a printing press in the colonies. Glover died during the sea voyage in the autumn of 1638 and was buried at sea. Upon arrival in Cambridge, Massachusetts, Glover's widow assisted Daye in setting up the printing office. The first printing was done in early 1639, and the first book to be designed and printed in the English American colonies was *The Whole Book of Psalmes* (now called *The Bay Psalm Book*) of 1640. As the title page with its dominant word "whole" and border of cast metal printer's flowers demonstrates, the design and production of this volume was diligent but understandably lacking in refinement. Stephen's son Matthew, who was second in charge and had apprenticed in a Cambridge, England, printing shop before sailing to America, probably did the typesetting and took responsibility for the design of the broadsides, books, and other matter produced at this press. In spite of strong censorship and a stamp tax on both newspapers and advertising, printing grew steadily in the colonies. By 1775, there were about fifty printers in the thirteen colonies, and they fueled the revolutionary fever that was brewing. Just as printing had hurled Europe toward the Protestant Reformation during its early decades, it now pushed the American colonies toward revolution.

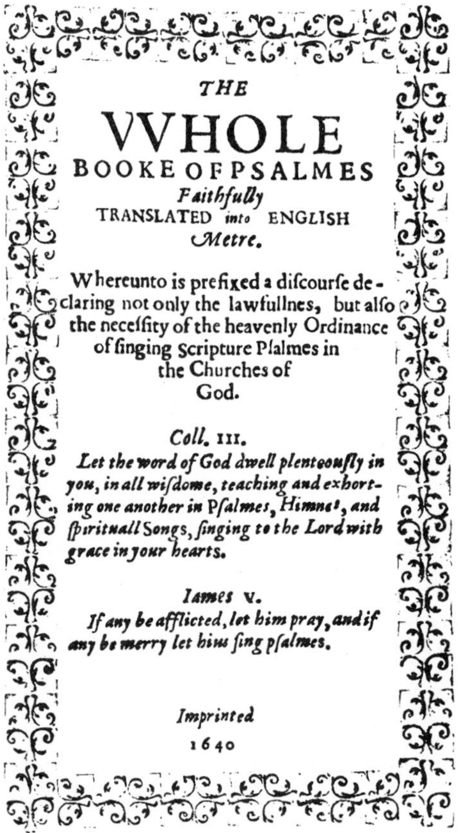
THE
VVHOLE
BOOKE OF PSALMES
Faithfully
TRANSLATED *into* ENGLISH
Metre.
Whereunto is prefixed a discourse declaring not only the lawfullnes, but also the necessity of the heavenly Ordinance of singing Scripture Psalmes in the Churches of God.
Coll. III.
Let the word of God dwell plenteously in you, in all wisdome, teaching and exhorting one another in Psalmes, Himnes, and spirituall Songs, singing to the Lord with grace in your hearts.
Iames V.
If any be afflicted, let him pray, and if any be merry let him sing psalmes.
Imprinted
1640

Stephen and Matthew Daye, title page for *The Whole Book of Psalmes,* 1640. In the title typography, a rich variety is achieved by combining three type sizes and using all capitals, all lower case, and italics to express the importance and meaning of the words.

The copperplate engraving continued to grow in popularity as technical refinements greatly increased its range of tone, textures, and detail. Independent engraving studios were established, as shown in the combined etching and engraving by Abraham Bosse (1602–1676) illustrating the plate printers in his printing shop. In addition to commissions for copperplate engravings to be bound into books as illustrations, these studios produced engravings for hanging on the wall. This enabled persons who were unable to afford oil paintings to have images in their homes. Broadsheets, advertising cards, and other printed ephemera were produced by the engraving studios. The wonderful imagination that was sometimes displayed is seen in the set of engravings called *The Trades,* originally created by N. de Larmessin in 1690. The tools or products of each trade were turned into lavish costumes on the figures. The nature of engraving—scratching fine lines into metal—encouraged the development of script letterforms of extreme fineness and delicacy.

During the seventeenth century, the Netherlands prospered as a mercantile and seafaring nation whose cultural attainment included the master artists Rembrandt and Vermeer. During this century, books became an important export commodity as a result of the accomplishments of yet another family dynasty of printers, founded by Louis Elzevir (1540–1617). Their handy and practical little volumes had solid, legible Dutch types surrounded by economically narrow margins and featured engraved title pages. Compe-

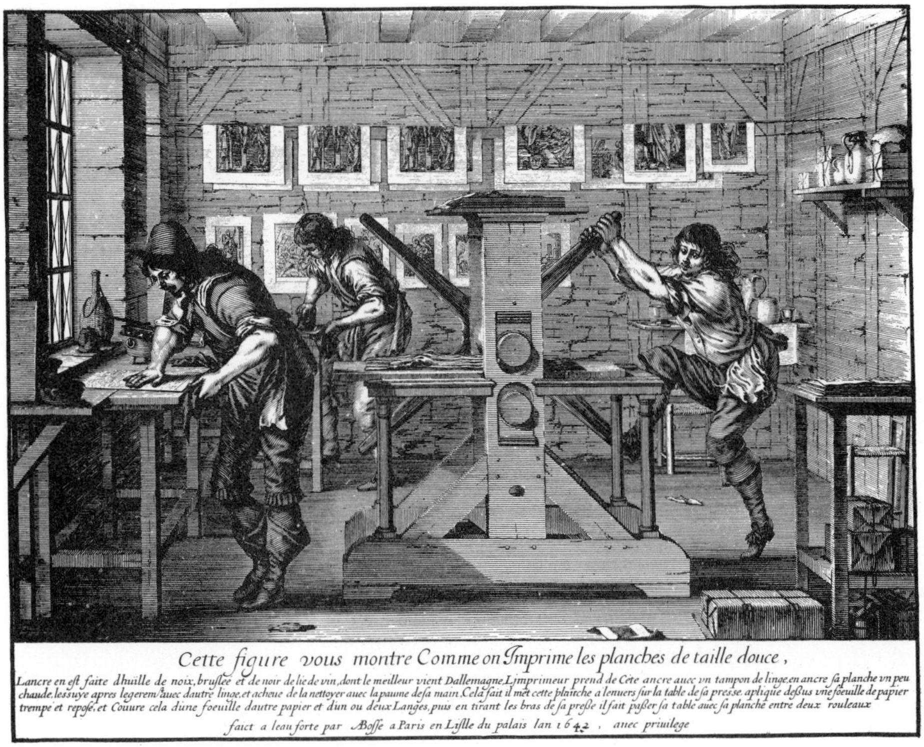

Cette figure vous montre Comme on Imprime les planches de taille douce,
Lancre en est faite dhuille de noix, bruslee et de noir de lie de vin, dont le meilleur vient Dallemagne. Limprimeur prend de Cete ancre auec vn tampon de linge, en ancre sa planche vn peu chaude, lessuye apres legerem^t auec dautre linge, et acheue de la nettoyer auec la paume de sa main. Cela fait il met cette planche a lenuers sur la table de sa presse, aplique dessus vne foeuille de papier trempe et repose, et Couure cela dune foeuille dautre papier et dun ou deux Langes, puis en tirant les bras de sa presse il fait passer sa table auec sa planche entre deux rouleaux
faict a leau forte par Bosse a Paris en Lisle du palais lan 1642, auec priuilege

Abraham Bosse, *Printing Shop—The Plate Printer,* 1642. A convincing range of lights and darks is built from scratched lines. *The Metropolitan Museum of Art, New York, Rogers Fund.*

tent editing, economical prices, and convenient size enabled the Elzevirs to pioneer an expansion of the book-buying market. The format design of their volumes was amazingly consistent, leading one prominent printing historian to declare that if you have seen one, you have seen them all! Elzevir's five sons and his nephews carried the family business from Leyden to Utrecht and Amsterdam. Editors were hired for Dutch, English, French, German, and Latin books that were exported throughout Europe. Many of their types were designed by the great Dutch designer and punchcutter, Christoffel van Dyck. Designed to resist the wear and tear of printing, his types had stubby serifs with heavy bracketing (the connecting curve that unifies the serif to the main stroke of the letter) and the hairline elements are fairly stout. Van Dyck's matrices and types were used continuously until 1810, when the fashion for the extreme thicks and thins of modern style types led the Haarlem foundry which owned these to thoughtlessly melt them down to reuse the metal.

After N. de Larmessin, *"Habit de Rotisseur,"* from *The Trades,* 1690. A stately symmetry and somber demureness intensify the outrageous humor of this image. *The Metropolitan Museum of Art, New York, Elisha Whittelsey Collection.*

COMMENTARIORUM
JOANNIS CALVINI
IN
E U A N G E L I U M
SECUNDUM JOANNEM

P R Æ F A T I O

Magnificis Dominis, Syndicis, Senatuique
Genevenſi, Dominis ſuis vere obſervandis Joan. Calvinus *Spiritum prudentiæ & fortitudinis, proſperumque gubernationis ſucceſſum à Domino precatur.*

QUoties in mentem venit illa Chriſti ſententia, qua tanti æſtimat quod hoſpitibus colligendis impenditur humanitatis officium, ut in ſuas rationes acceptum ferat, ſimul occurrit quam ſingulari vos honore dignatus ſit, qui urbem veſtram non unius vel paucorum, ſed commune Eccleſiæ ſuæ hoſpitium eſſe voluit. Semper apud homines profanos non modo laudata, ſed una ex præcipuis virtutibus habita fuit hoſpitalitas: ac proinde in quibus extremam barbariem ac mores prorſus efferatos damnare vellent, eos ἀξένους, vel (quod idem valet) inhoſpitales vocabant. Laudis autem veſtræ longe potior eſt ratio, quod turbulentis hiſce miſeriſque temporibus Dominus vos conſtituit quorum in fidem præſidiumque ſe conferrent pii & innoxii homines, quos non ſæva minus quam ſacrilega Antichriſti tyrannis è patriis ſedibus fugat ac diſpellit. Neque id modo, ſed ſacrum etiam apud vos domicilium nomini ſuo dicavit, ubi pure colatur. Ex his duobus quiſquis minimam partem vel palam reſcindere, vel furtim auferre conatur, non hoc agit modo ut nudatam præcipuis ſuis ornamentis urbem veſtram deformet, ſed ejus quoque ſaluti maligne invidet. Quamvis enim quæ Chriſto & diſperſis ejus membris præſtantur hic pietatis officia, caninos impiorum latratus provocent, merito tamen hæc vobis una compenſatio ſatis eſſe debet quod è cælo Angeli & ex omnibus mundi plagis filii Dei benedi-

Jan Jacob Schipper, page from Calvin's *Commentary,* 1667. Using types designed by Christoffel van Dyck, Schipper's mixture of sizes, letterspacing, and leading in the heading material is an exemplary representation of the Baroque sensibility.

9

An Epoch of Typographic Genius

DURING THE LATE 1500S AND early 1600s, innovation in graphic design and printing declined. Louis XIII of France, under the influence of his prime minister, Cardinal Richelieu, established the *Imprimerie Royale* ("royal printing office") at the Louvre in 1640 in an effort to restore the earlier quality. In 1692, Louis XIV, who had a strong interest in printing, ordered the establishment of a committee of scholars to develop a new type whose letters were to be designed by "scientific" principles. Headed by mathematician Nicolas Jaugeon, the academicians studied all previous alphabets and writers on type design.

To construct the new roman capital letters, a square was divided into a grid of sixty-four units, then each of these squares was divided into thirty-six smaller units for a total of two thousand three hundred four tiny squares. Italics were constructed on a similar parallelogram. The refined designs that were developed had less of the calligraphic properties inspired by the chisel and flat pen; a mathematical harmony was achieved by measurement and drafting instruments. However, these designs were not merely mechanical constructions, for ultimately the final decisions were made by the eye.

This Romain du Roi, as the new typeface was called, had increased contrast between thick and thin strokes; sharp horizontal serifs; and an even balance to each letterform. The master alphabets were engraved as large copperplate prints by Louis Simonneau (1654–1727). Philippe Grandjean (1666–1714) cut the punches for the reduction in size from the master alphabets to text type. The minute refinement on a two-thousand-three-hundred-four-square grid proved absolutely worthless when reduced to text-size types; the delicacy of Grandjean's meticulous punch cutting and his aesthetic judgments became as important as the committee's lengthy deliberations and Simon-

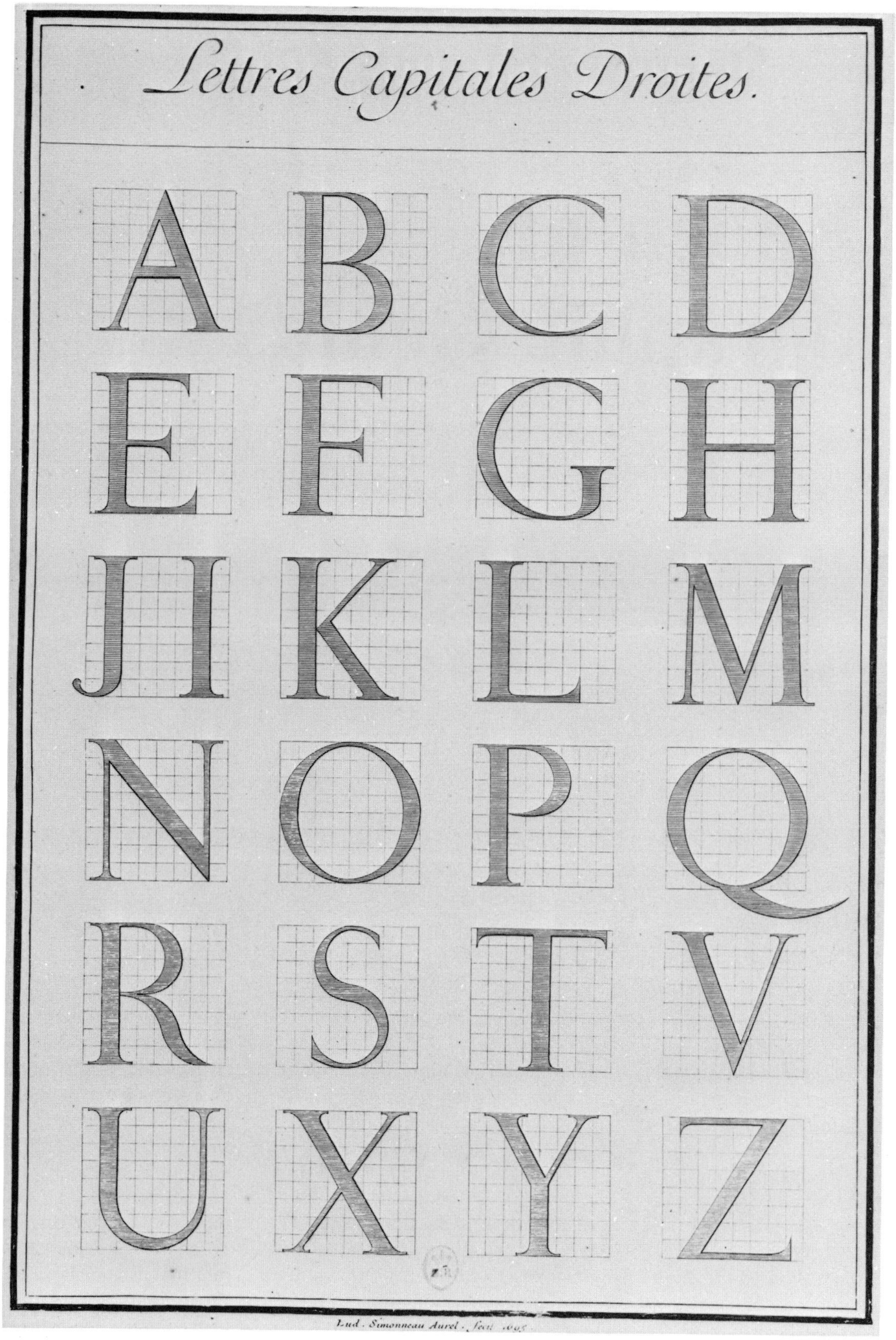

Louis Simonneau, master alphabets for the *Romain du Roi,* 1695. These copper plate engravings were intended to establish graphic standards for the new alphabet. *Bibliotheque Nationale, Paris.*

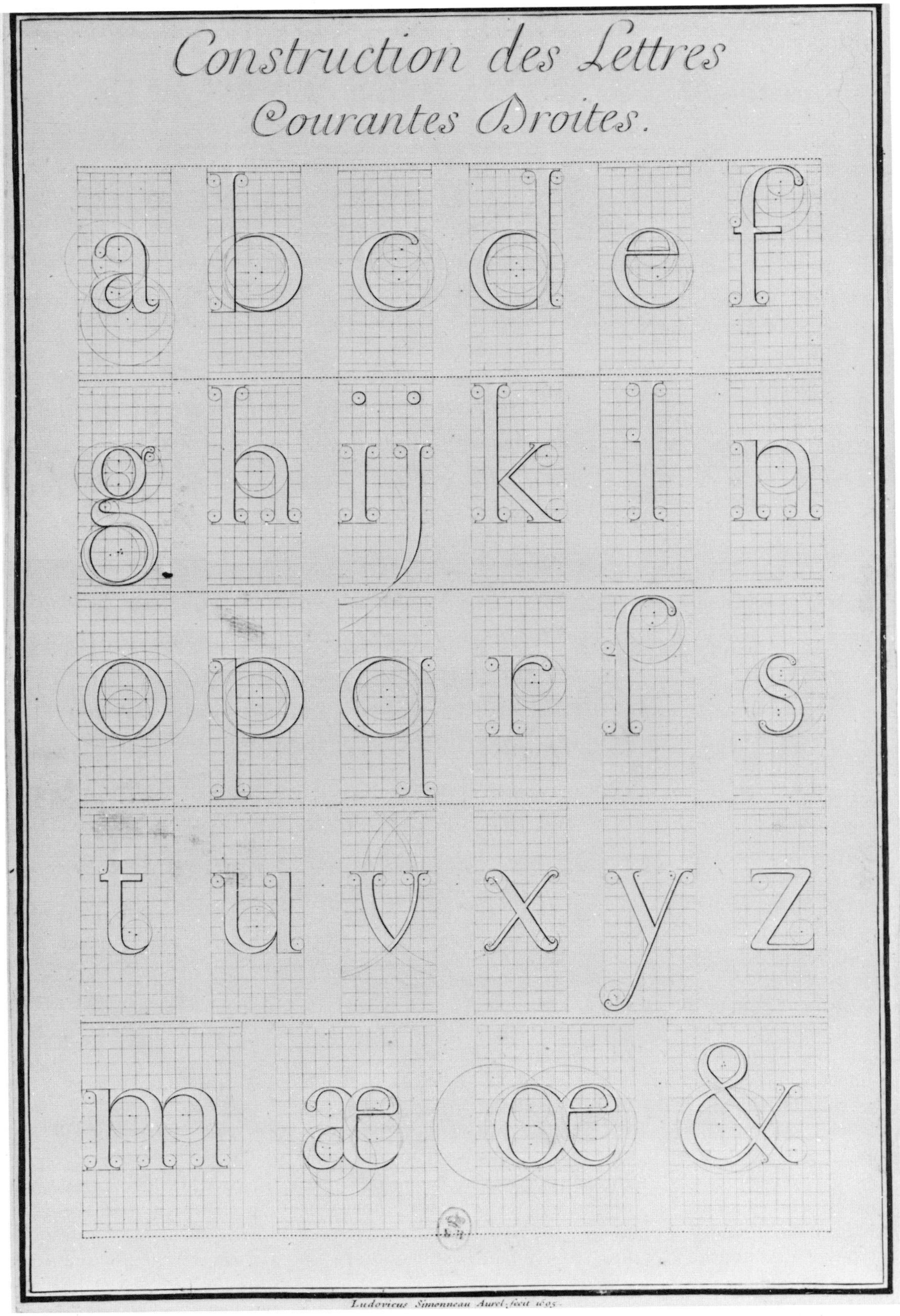
Construction des Lettres
Courantes Droites.
Ludovicus Simonneau Aurel. fecit 1695.

neau's meticulous engravings as a source for the new typestyle.

Types designed for the Imprimerie Royale were for use only by that office for royal printing. Other use constituted a capital offense. Other typefounders quickly cut types with similar characteristics, but they made sure the designs were sufficiently different to ensure that their fonts were not confused with Imprimerie Royale fonts.

In 1702 the *Médailles* folio was the first book to use the new types. As the first important shift from the Venetian tradition of Old Style roman type design, the Romain du Roi initiated a category of types called *transitional roman*. These break with a tradition of calligraphic qualities, bracketed serifs, and relatively even stroke weights of Old Style fonts. The Romain du Roi (as William Morris observed in the late nineteenth century) saw the calligrapher replaced by "the engineer" as the dominant typographic influence.

PREMIERE PARTIE

LES ÉPOQUES.

PREMIERE ÉPOQUE

ADAM OU LA CREATION.

Premier age du Monde.

L'intention principale de Bossuet est de faire observer dans la suite des temps celle de la religion et celle des grands Empires. Après avoir fait aller ensemble selon le cours des années les faits qui regardent ces deux choses, il reprend en particulier avec les réflexions nécessaires premièrement ceux qui nous font entendre la durée perpétuelle de la religion, *et enfin ceux qui nous découvrent les* causes des grands changements arrivés dans les empires.

La première époque vous présente d'abord un grand spectacle : Dieu qui crée le ciel et la terre par sa parole, et qui fait l'homme à son image. C'est par où commence Moïse, le plus ancien

Philippe Grandjean, specimen of *Romain du Roi,* 1702. Compared to Old Style roman fonts, the crisp geometric quality and increased contrast of this first transitional typeface are clearly evident. The small spur on the center of the left side of the lower case *l* is a device used to identify types of the Imprimerie Royale.

Graphic design of the Rococo era

The fanciful French art and architecture that flourished from about 1720 until around 1770 is called *Rococo.* Florid and intricate, Rococo ornament is composed of *S-* and *C*-curves with scrollwork, tracery, and plant forms derived from nature, classical art, oriental, and even medieval sources. This lavish expression of the era of French King Louis XV (1710–1774) found its strongest graphic design impetus in the work of Pierre Simon Fournier le Jeune (1712–1768), the youngest son of a prominent family of printers and typefounders. At age twenty-four Fournier le Jeune established an independent type design and foundry operation after studying art and apprenticing at the Le Bé foundry operated by his older brother, where he had cut decorative woodblocks and learned punchcutting.

In the eighteenth century type measurement was chaotic, for each foundry had its own type sizes, and nomenclature varied. In 1737 Fournier le Jeune pioneered standardization when he published his first Table of Proportions. The *pouce* (a now obsolete French unit of measure slightly longer than an inch) was divided into twelve lines, each of which was divided into six points. Thus, his Petit-Romain size was one line, four points, or about equal to contemporary ten-point type; his Cicero size was two lines, or similar to contemporary twelve-point type.

Fournier le Jeune published his first specimen book, *Modèles de Caractères de l'Imprimerie,* shortly before his thirtieth birthday in 1742. It presented four thousand six hundred characters. Over a six-year period, he had both designed and cut punches for all of these by himself. His roman styles were transitional forms inspired by the Romain du Roi of 1702. However, his variety of weights and widths innovated the idea of a "type family" of fonts that are visually compatible and can be mixed. He personally designed and set the more complex pages, which were richly garlanded with his exquisite typographic flowers that could be used singly or multiplied for unlimited decorative effect. His explorations into casting enabled him to cast single, double, and triple ruled lines up to 35.5 centimeters (about 14 inches) and to offer the largest metal type (equivalent to contemporary eighty-four- and one-hundred-eight-point sizes) yet made. His decorative types—outline, shaded, flowered, and exotic—worked remarkably well with his roman fonts, ornaments, and rules.

Printing has been called "the artillery of the intellect." It might be said that Fournier le Jeune stocked the arsenals of Rococo printers with a complete design system (roman, italic, script, and decorative type styles, rules, and ornaments) of standardized measurement whose parts integrated both visually and physically. Since French law now prevented a type founder from printing, Fournier le Jeune delivered made-up pages to Jean Joseph Barbou, the printer of his *Modèles des Caractères.* His nephew, Jean Gerard Barbou, was closely associated with Fournier le Jeune. In addition to publishing all of Fournier le Jeune's other books, the younger Barbou produced volumes of exceptional Rococo design combining Fournier le Jeune's decorative types and copperplate engravings by Charles Eisen (1720–1778), who specialized in illustrations of graceful intricacy and sensual intimacy in vogue with royalty and the wealthy. Add the talents of the engraver Pierre Philippe Choffard (1730–1809), who specialized in ornate tailpieces and spot illustrations, and the results are book designs such as Jean La Fontaine's *Contes et nouvelles en vers* of 1762. In a small number of copies for a special audience, the coy romantic escapades in Eisen's engravings were replaced with other versions depicting explicit sexual conduct. In the *éditions de luxe,* the typefounder, printer, and illustrator combined their talents to project the psychology of the Rococo era: extravagant, sensuous, and pastoral; a joyous fantasyland oblivious to the misery and growing militancy of the poverty-stricken masses. These wildly popular books remained in vogue until the French Revolution of 1789 brought the monarchy and Rococo era tumbling down.

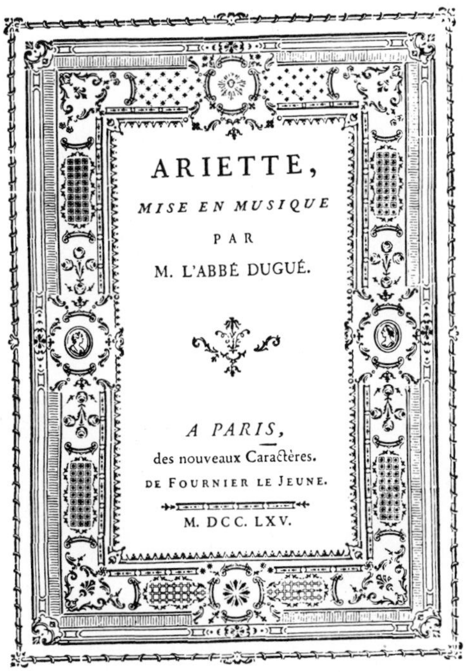

ARIETTE,
MISE EN MUSIQUE
PAR
M. L'ABBÉ DUGUÉ.

A PARIS,
des nouveaux Caractères.
DE FOURNIER LE JEUNE.
M. DCC. LXV.

Pierre Simon Fournier le Jeune, title page for *Ariette, Mise en Musique,* 1756. Vast numbers of floral, curvilinear, and geometric ornaments were needed to construct designs like this, which set the standard of excellence of the Rococo period.

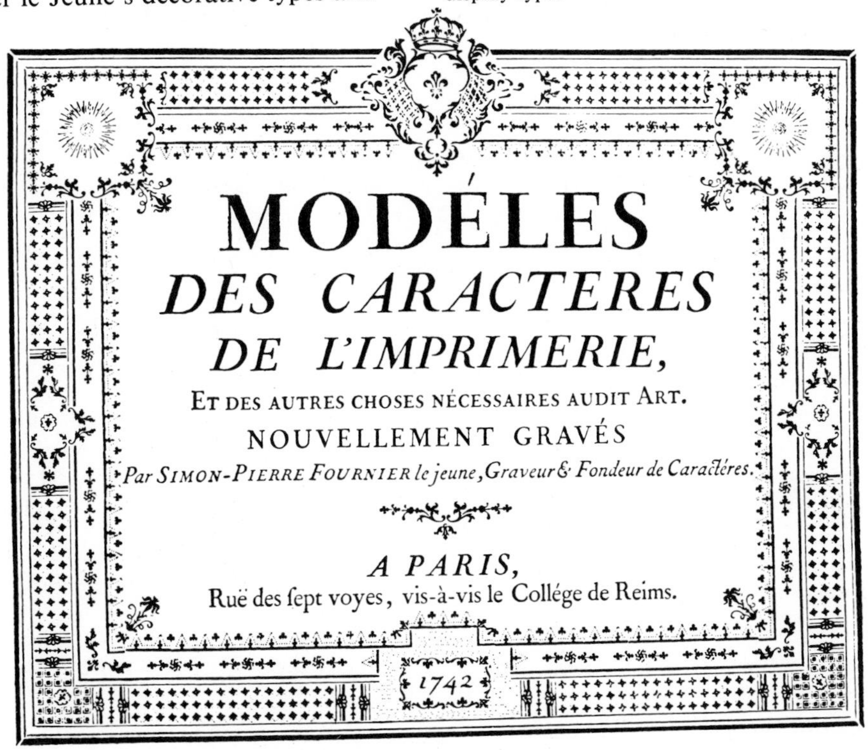

MODÉLES
DES CARACTERES
DE L'IMPRIMERIE,
ET DES AUTRES CHOSES NÉCESSAIRES AUDIT ART.
NOUVELLEMENT GRAVÉS
Par SIMON-PIERRE FOURNIER le jeune, Graveur & Fondeur de Caractères.
A PARIS,
Ruë des ſept voyes, vis-à-vis le Collége de Reims.
1742

Pierre Simon Fournier le Jeune, title page for *Modèles des Caractères de l'Imprimerie,* 1742. Here, Fournier had an opportunity to demonstrate to printers the ornate graphic design possibilities that were possible using his printer's flowers and rules. Note the sharp serifs and contrast between thick and thin strokes of his display type.

Fournier le Jeune planned a four-volume *Manuel Typographique* for many years, but only produced two volumes: *Type,* its cutting and founding, 1764; and *Type Specimens* (originally planned as volume four), 1768. An improved measurement system, based on the *point* (instead of the line and point), was introduced. He did not live to complete the other two volumes, on printing and on the great typographers' lives and work. Although his crowning achievement, the *Manuel Typographique,* was only half completed, Fournier le Jeune made more typographic innovations and had a greater impact on graphic design than any other person of his era.

While even the most extravagant designs of Fournier le Jeune and his followers maintained the vertical and horizontal alignment that is part of the physical nature of metal typography, engravers were free to take tremendous liberties with form. Basically, an engraving is a drawing made with a graver instead of a pencil as the drawing tool and a copperplate instead of a sheet of paper as the substrate. Because this free line was

LE BÂT.

UN peintre étoit, qui jaloux de sa femme,
Allant aux champs, lui peignit un baudet
Sur le nombril, en guise de cachet.
Un sien confrere amoureux de la Dame,
La va trouver, & l'âne efface net,
Dieu sçait comment ; puis un autre en remet,
Au même endroit, ainsi que l'on peut croire.
A celui-ci, par faute de mémoire,
Il mit un Bât ; l'autre n'en avoit point.
L'époux revient, veut s'éclaircir du point.
Voyez, mon fils, dit la bonne commere ;
L'âne est témoin de ma fidélité.
Diantre soit fait, dit l'époux en colere,
Et du témoin, & de qui l'a bâté.

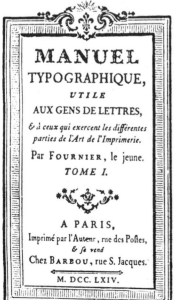

MANUEL
TYPOGRAPHIQUE,
UTILE
AUX GENS DE LETTRES,
& à ceux qui exercent les différentes parties de l'Art de l'Imprimerie.
Par FOURNIER, le jeune.
TOME I.

A PARIS,
Imprimé par l'Auteur, rue des Postes,
& se vend
Chez BARBOU, rue S. Jacques.
M. DCC. LXIV.

N°. XXXVI. 34

CICÉRO, PETIT ŒIL.

LE Directeur à la mode, semblable au Médecin, flatte, console, encourage, entretient la délicatesse & la sensibilité sur soi-même ; il n'ordonne que de petits remèdes benins, & qui se tournent en habitude. On ne fait que tournoyer dans un petit cercle de vertus communes, au-delà desquelles on ne passe jamais généreusement.

Certains Dévots n'aiment jamais tant Dieu que lorsqu'ils ont obtenu leurs satisfactions temporelles ; ils ne prient jamais mieux que quand l'esprit & la chair sont contens & qu'ils prient ensemble.

MANUEL
TYPOGRAPHIQUE.

PREMIÈRE PARTIE.

LA GRAVURE,
OU TAILLE DES POINÇONS.

POUR être un bon Graveur de Caractères, il faut être Typographe, c'est-à-dire, savoir tous les détails du méchanisme de la Fonderie & de l'Imprimerie, afin d'y assujétir son travail. Maitre de l'art, le Graveur doit tout prévoir dans la fonte & dans l'impression. C'est par-là que les Simon de Colines, les Garamond, les
A

Des faits éloignés de nos yeux
Ces Caractères nous instruisent,
Et par cet Art ingénieux,
Tous les talens s'immortalisent.

an ideal medium for expressing the florid curves of the Rococo sensibility, engraving flourished throughout the 1700s. Delicate detail and fine lines made this medium much prized for labels, business cards, and announcements. Writing masters of the period developed flamboyant pen-and-ink flourishes which translated well into engraving. Typical of this collaboration is the title page for George Shelley's *The Second Part of Natural Writing.* Shelley's compendium of virtuoso writing styles was faithfully translated into the printed medium by George Bickham.

As engravers became increasingly skillful, they even began to produce books independent of the typographic

Joseph Gerard Barbou, pages from *Contes et nouvelles en vers* by Jean La Fontaine, 1762. To adorn a poem about a painter's romantic interlude with his subject, Barbou used Eisen's etching of the event, a topical tailpiece by Choffard, and Fournier le Jeune's ornamented type. *Library of Congress, Washington, D.C., Rosenwald Collection.*

Ch. Eisen inv. delin. 1770. C. Baquoy Sculp.

XI. BAISER.

L A M O R S U R E.

Thaïs, quel folâtre caprice
Contre moi semble t'exciter?
Eh, quoi! tu ris de ta malice,
Et te plais à la répéter?
Tu comptes donc pour rien, cruelle,
Ces traits pénétrans, enflammés,
Que l'enfant aîlé, ton modèle,
Dans mon cœur a tous enfermés?

F iv

Lambert and Delalain (printers) and Charles Eisen (illustrator), page from *Les Baisers* by Claude Joseph Dorat, 1770. Rococo book design reflected the elegance and luxury of the wealthy through its ornamental type and images. *Library of Congress, Washington, D.C., Rosenwald Collection.*

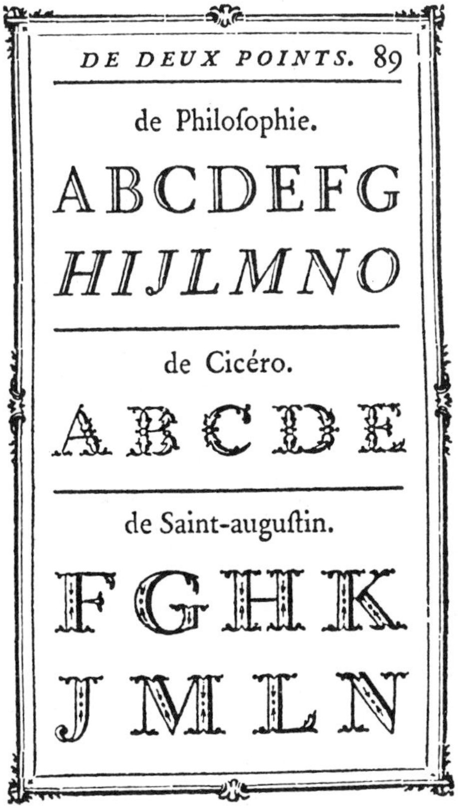

DE DEUX POINTS. 89

de Philosophie.

ABCDEFG

HIJLMNO

de Cicéro.

ABCDE

de Saint-augustin.

FGHK

JMLN

Pierre Simon Fournier le Jeune, specimen page of decorative types, 1768. Within each of Fournier's ornamental display letterforms, there is the structure of a well-proportioned roman letter.

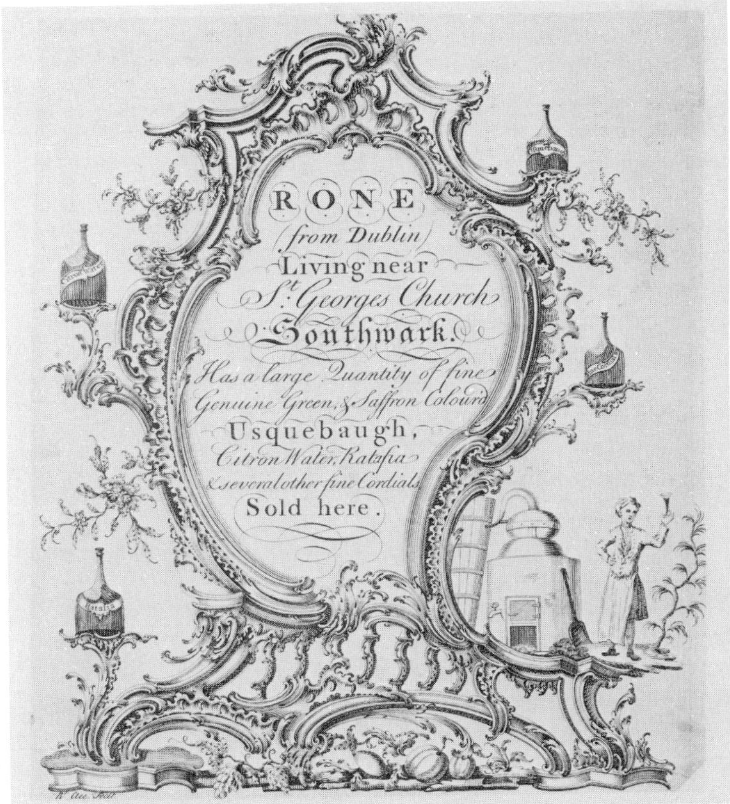

Pierre Simon Fournier le Jeune, pages from *Manuel Typographique,* 1764 and 1768. In addition to showing the design accomplishments of a lifetime, Fournier's type manual is a masterwork of Rococo design.

Robert Clee, trade card for a liquor dealer, eighteenth century. The design of copperplate engraved trade cards used extravagantly ornate border configurations and florid scripts. *The Metropolitan Museum of Art, New York.*

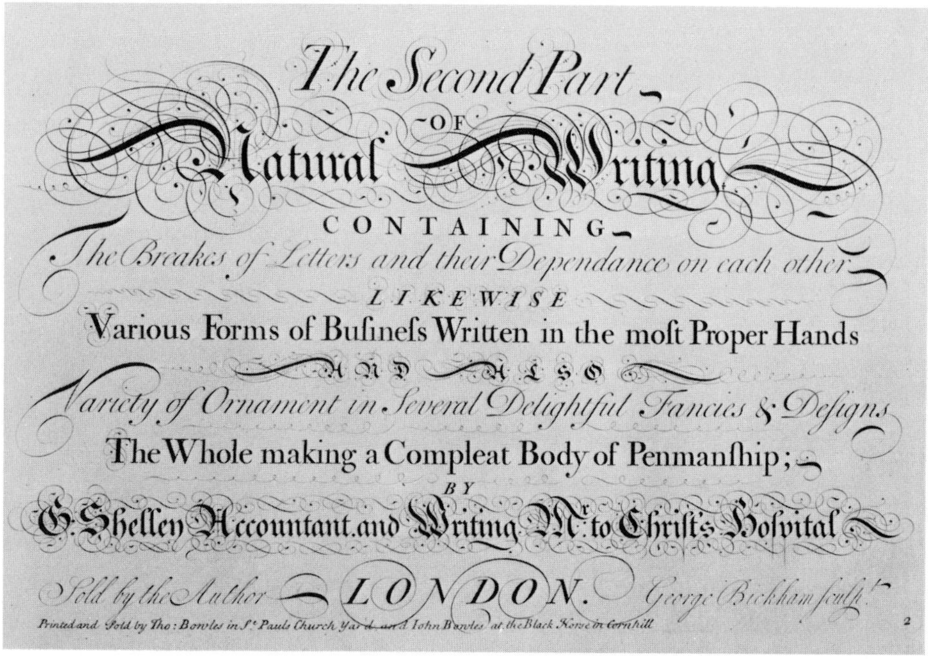

The Second Part
OF
Natural Writing,
CONTAINING
The Breakes of Letters and their Dependance on each other
LIKEWISE
Various Forms of Buſineſs Written in the moſt Proper Hands
AND ALSO
Variety of Ornament in Several Delightful Fancies & Deſigns
The Whole making a Compleat Body of Penmanſhip;
BY
G. Shelley Accountant and Writing Mr. to Chriſt's Hoſpital
Sold by the Author LONDON. George Bickham ſculp.
Printed and Sold by Tho: Bowles in St. Pauls Church Yard and John Bowles at the Black Horse in Cornhill
2

George Shelley (designer) and George Bickham (engraver), title page for *The Second Part of Natural Writing,* c. 1709. Writing master Shelley designed the title page for his book as an opulent demonstration of his writing styles, ornaments, and "delightful fancies." *The Metropolitan Museum of Art, New York, Harris Brisbane Dick Fund, 1929.*

printers by hand-engraving both illustrations and text. Englishman John Pine (1690–1756) was one of the best. His books, including the 1737 *Opera* of Horatii, were sold by subscription before publication, and a list naming each subscriber was engraved in script in the front of the volume. Because serifs and thin strokes of letterforms were reduced to the delicate scratch of the engraver's finest tool, the contrast in the text material was dazzling and inspired imitation by typographic designers. As each letter was inscribed by hand, the text has a slight vibration giving it a handmade quality instead of a mechanical uniformity.

Pine's book design and production shared his time with his position as chief engraver of seals for the king of England and production of large portfolios of etchings. One extraordinary set printed in 1753 depicts the 1588 defeat of the Spanish Armada in jumbo 52-by-36-centimeter (20 ½-by-14 ¼-inch) prints. These naval clashes were printed from two copperplates using black and blue-green ink. The effect is not unlike a subtle duotone.

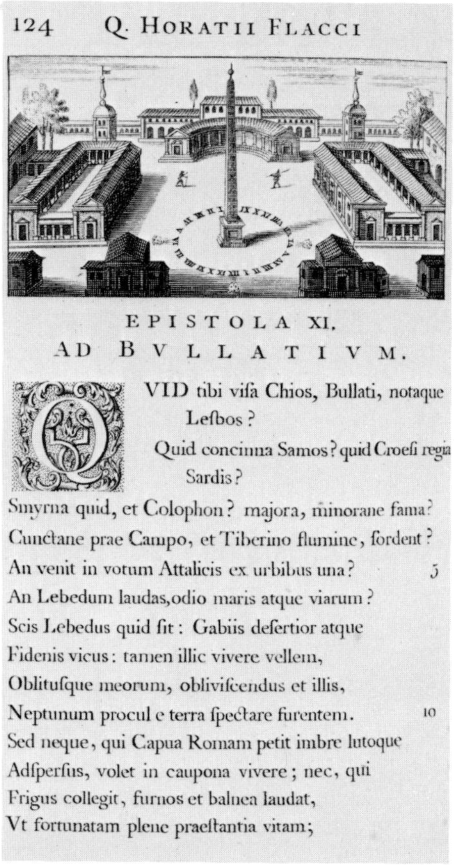

124 Q. HORATII FLACCI

EPISTOLA XI.
AD BVLLATIVM.

QVID tibi viſa Chios, Bullati, notaque Leſbos?
Quid concinna Samos? quid Croeſi regia Sardis?
Smyrna quid, et Colophon? majora, minorane fama?
Cunctane prae Campo, et Tiberino flumine, ſordent?
An venit in votum Attalicis ex urbibus una? 5
An Lebedum laudas, odio maris atque viarum?
Scis Lebedus quid ſit: Gabiis deſertior atque
Fidenis vicus: tamen illic vivere vellem,
Oblituſque meorum, obliviſcendus et illis,
Neptunum procul e terra ſpectare furentem. 10
Sed neque, qui Capua Romam petit imbre lutoque
Adſperſus, volet in caupona vivere; nec, qui
Frigus collegit, furnos et balnea laudat,
Vt fortunatam plene praeſtantia vitam;

John Pine, page from Horatii's *Opera,* Volume II, 1737. The illustration and text were hand-engraved upon a copper printing plate and printed in one pass through the press. *Library of Congress, Washington, D.C.*

Caslon and Baskerville

For over two and a half centuries after the invention of movable type, England had looked to the continent for typography and design leadership. Civil war, religious persecution, harsh censorship, and government control of printing had created a climate that was not conducive to graphic innovation. Upon ascending to the throne in 1660, Charles II had demanded that the number of printers be reduced to twenty "by death or otherwise."

Type and design ideas were imported across the English channel from Holland until a native genius emerged in the person of William Caslon (1692–1766). After apprenticing to a London engraver of gunlocks and barrels, young Caslon opened his own shop and added silver chasing and the cutting of gilding tools and letter stamps for bookbinders to his repertoire of engraving skills. The printer William Bowyer encouraged Caslon to take up type design and founding, which he did in 1720 with almost immediate success. His first commission was an Arabic font for the Society for Promoting Christian Knowledge. This was closely followed by the first size of Caslon Old Style with italic in 1722, and his reputation was made. For the next sixty years, virtually all English printing used Caslon fonts, and these types followed English colonialism around the globe. Printer Benjamin Franklin (1706–1790) introduced Caslon into the American colonies where it was used extensively, including the official printing of the Declaration of Independence by a Baltimore printer.

Caslon's type designs were not particularly fashionable or innovative. They owed their tremendous popularity and appeal to an outstanding legibility and sturdy texture that make them "comfortable" and "friendly to the eye." Beginning with the Dutch types of his day, Caslon increased the contrast between thick and thin

DOUBLE PICA ROMAN.

Quouſque tandem abutere, Catilina, patientia noſtra ? quamdiu nos etiam furor iſte tuus eludet ? quem ad finem ſeſe effrenata jac-

ABCDEFGHJIKLMNOP

Double Pica Italick.

Quouſque tandem abutere, Catilina, patientia noſtra ? quamdiu nos etiam furor iſte tuus-eludet ? quem ad finem ſeſe effrenata jac-

ABCDEFGHJIKLMNO

GREAT PRIMER ROMAN.

Quouſque tandem abutêre, Catilina, patientia noſtra ? quamdiu nos etiam furor iſte tuus eludet ? quem ad finem ſeſe effrenata jactabit audacia ? nihilne te nocturnum præſidium palatii, nihil urbis vigiliæ, nihil timor populi, nihil con-

ABCDEFGHIJKLMNOPQRS

Great Primer Italick.

Quouſque tandem abutêre, Catilina, patientia noſtra ? quamdiu nos etiam furor iſte tuus eludet ? quem ad finem ſeſe effrenata jactabit audacia ? nihilne te nocturnum præſidium palatii, nihil urbis vigiliæ, nihil timor populi, nihil con-

ABCDEFGHIJKLMNOPQR

William Caslon, specimens of Caslon roman and italic, 1734. The straightforward practicality of Caslon's design made them the dominant roman style throughout the British empire far into the nineteenth century.

strokes by making the thick elements slightly thicker. This was in direct opposition to fashion on the continent, which was embracing the lighter texture of the Romain du Roi. Caslon's fonts have a variety of design giving them an uneven, rhythmic texture that adds to their visual interest and appeal. The Caslon foundry continued under his heirs and operated until the 1960s.

William Caslon worked in a tradition of Old Style roman typographic design that had begun over two hundred years earlier during the Italian Renaissance. This tradition was bolted by John Baskerville (1706–1775), an innovator who broke the prevailing rules of design and printing in fifty-six editions produced at his Birmingham, England, press. Baskerville was involved in all facets of the bookmaking process. He designed, cast, and set type, improved the printing press, conceived and commissioned new papers, and designed and published the books he printed. This native of rural Worcestershire, who had "admired the beauty of letters" as a boy, moved to Birmingham as a young man and became established as a master writing teacher and stonecutter. While still in his thirties, Baskerville became a manufacturer of japanned ware. These frames, boxes, clock cases, candlesticks, and trays were made from thin sheet metal, often decorated with hand-painted fruit and flowers, and finished with a hard, brilliant varnish. Manufacturing earned Baskerville a fortune, and he built an estate, Easy Hill, near Birmingham. Around 1751, he returned to his first love, the art of letters, and began to experiment with printing. As an artist who wanted to control all aspects of book design and production, he sought graphic perfection and was able to invest the time and resources necessary to achieve his goals. He was assisted by John Handy, a punch cutter, and William Martin, an apprentice who later became his foreman. Baskerville's type designs, which bear his name to this day, represent the zenith of the transitional style bridging the gap between Old Style and modern type design. His letters possessed a new elegance and lightness. In comparison with earlier designs, his types are wider, and the weight contrast between thick and thin strokes is increased. Placement of the thickest part of the letter is different. The treatment of serifs is new. The serifs flow smoothly out of the major strokes and terminate as refined points. His italic fonts most clearly show the influence of master handwriting.

As a book designer in a period of intricate, engraved title pages and illustrations, and generous use of printer's flowers, ornaments, and decorated initials, Baskerville opted for the pure typographic book. Generous margins and a liberal use of space between letters and lines were used around his magnificent alphabets. To maintain an elegant purity of typographic design, an unusually large percentage of each press run was rejected, and he melted down and recast his type after each printing.

Baskerville's improvements for his four presses, built in his own workshops, focused on perfect alignment between the inch-thick brass platen and the smooth, stone press bed. The packing behind the sheet of

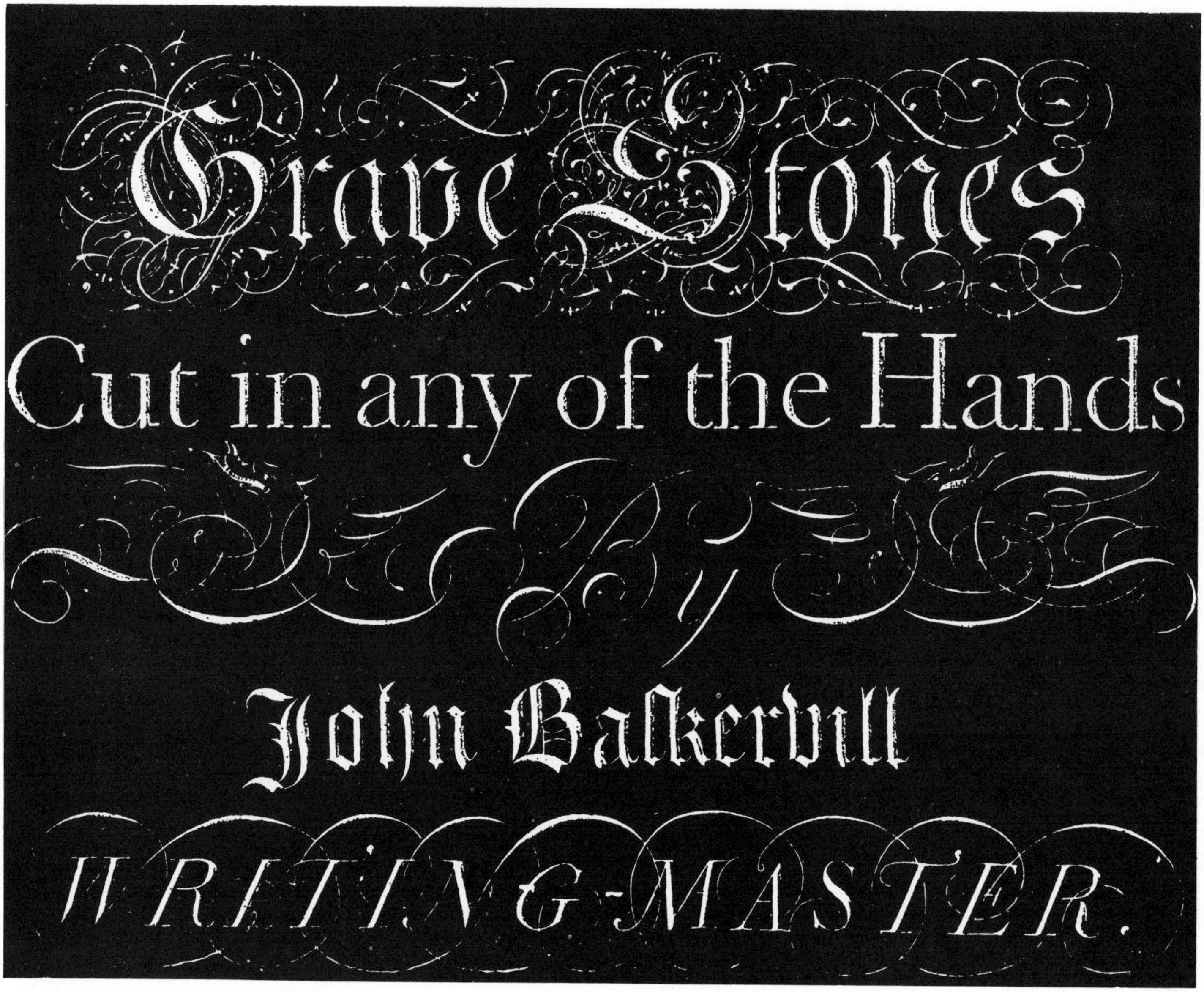
Grave Stones
Cut in any of the Hands
By
John Baskervill
WRITING-MASTER.

John Baskerville, *The gravestone slate,* undated. This demonstration stone showed potential customers young Baskerville's carving skill and range of lettering styles. *Reference Library, Local Studies Department, Birmingham Public Library, Birmingham, England.*

paper being printed was unusually hard and smooth. As a consequence, he achieved even, overall impressions.

Trial and error led to the development of an ink composed of boiled linseed oil which was aged for several months after black or amber resin had been added. Then, a fine lampblack—acquired from "glass pinchers' and solderers' lamps"—was ground into it. The resin added a sheen to this unusually dense black ink whose luster bordered on purple.

The smooth, glossy surface of the paper in Baskerville's books had not been seen before. This quality was achieved by using hot-pressed wove paper. Before Baskerville's *Virgil,* books were printed on laid paper, which has a textural pattern of horizontal lines. This pattern is created in manufacture by wires that form the screen in the papermaker's mold. This wire screen had close parallel wires supported by larger wires running at right angles to the thinner wires. The wove paper manufactured for Baskerville was formed by a mold having a much finer screen made of wires woven in and out like cloth. The texture from wire marks was virtually eliminated from this wove paper.

All handmade papers have a coarse surface. When paper was moistened before printing on a hand press, it became even coarser. Baskerville's desire for elegant printing led him to hot-press the paper after it was printed to produce a smooth, refined surface. How he hot-pressed or calendered his paper is controversial because early sources give conflicting reports. One version reports that Baskerville designed and constructed a smoothing press with two copper rollers 21.6 centimeters (8½ inches) in diameter and almost a meter (39 inches) long. A second version explains that Baskerville employed a woman and a litle girl to operate a pressing or glazing machine that worked in a manner not unlike iron-

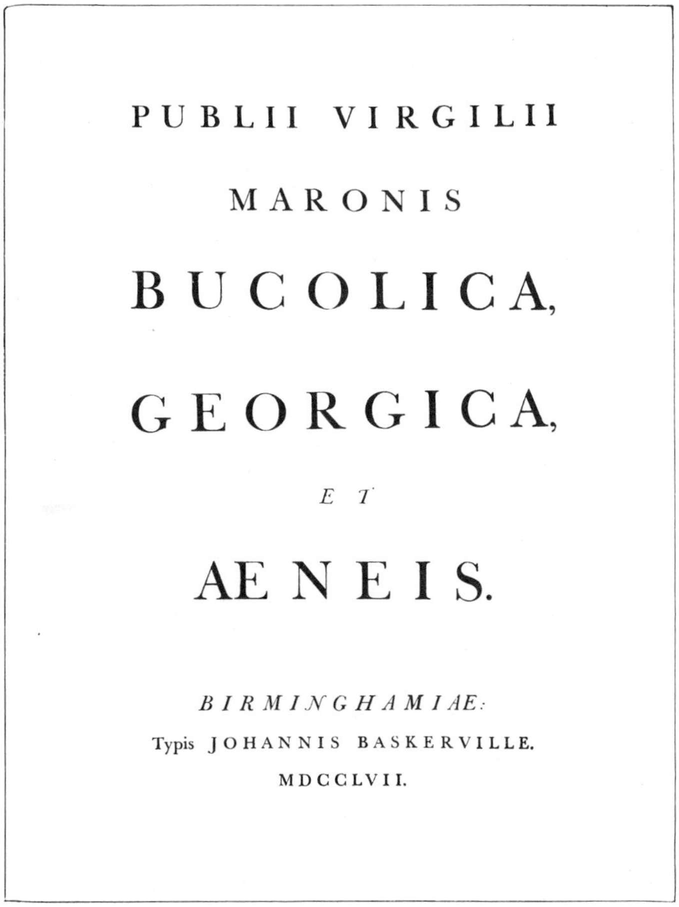
PUBLII VIRGILII

MARONIS

BUCOLICA,

GEORGICA,

ET

AENEIS.

BIRMINGHAMIAE:

Typis JOHANNIS BASKERVILLE.

MDCCLVII.

John Baskerville, title page for the *Virgil,* 1757. Baskerville reduced the design to letterforms symmetrically arranged and letterspaced; he reduced content to author, title, publisher, date, and city of publication. Economy, simplicity, and elegance resulted.

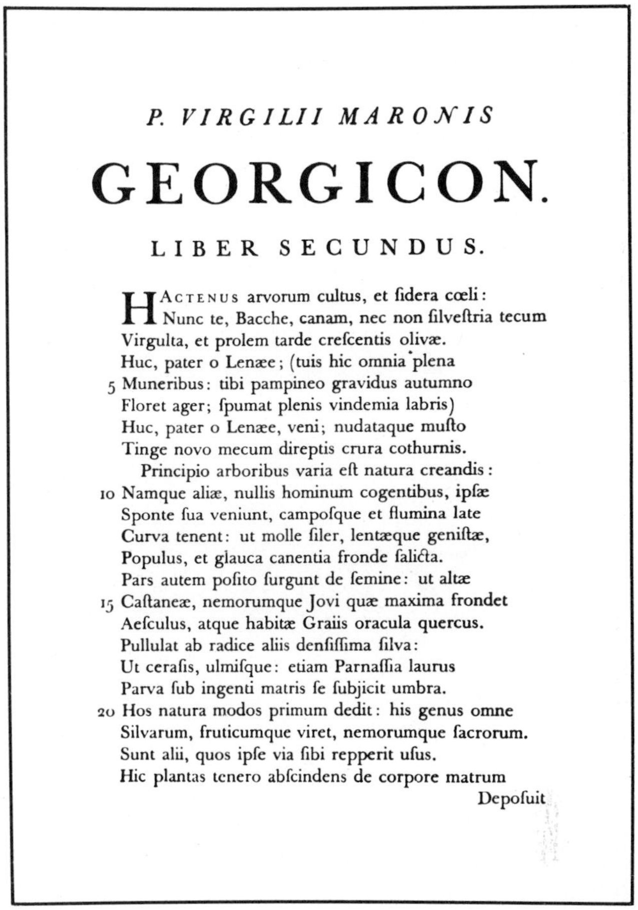
P. VIRGILII MARONIS

GEORGICON.

LIBER SECUNDUS.

Hactenus arvorum cultus, et ſidera cœli:
Nunc te, Bacche, canam, nec non ſilveſtria tecum
Virgulta, et prolem tarde creſcentis olivæ.
Huc, pater o Lenæe; (tuis hic omnia plena
Muneribus: tibi pampineo gravidus autumno
Floret ager; ſpumat plenis vindemia labris)
Huc, pater o Lenæe, veni; nudataque muſto
Tinge novo mecum direptis crura cothurnis.
Principio arboribus varia eſt natura creandis:
Namque aliæ, nullis hominum cogentibus, ipſæ
Sponte ſua veniunt, campoſque et flumina late
Curva tenent: ut molle ſiler, lentæque geniſtæ,
Populus, et glauca canentia fronde ſalicta.
Pars autem poſito ſurgunt de ſemine: ut altæ
Caſtaneæ, nemorumque Jovi quæ maxima frondet
Aeſculus, atque habitæ Graiis oracula quercus.
Pullulat ab radice aliis denſiſſima ſilva:
Ut ceraſis, ulmiſque: etiam Parnaſſia laurus
Parva ſub ingenti matris ſe ſubjicit umbra.
Hos natura modos primum dedit: his genus omne
Silvarum, fruticumque viret, nemorumque ſacrorum.
Sunt alii, quos ipſe via ſibi repperit uſus.
Hic plantas tenero abſcindens de corpore matrum
Depoſuit

John Baskerville, sectional heading page from the *Virgil,* 1757. The stately order of Baskerville's page design results from the harmony of elements and the spatial intervals that separate them.

ing clothes. Yet another version declares that as each page was removed from the press, it was sandwiched between two highly polished heated copperplates which expelled moisture, set the ink, and created the smooth, glossy surface. Since Baskerville closely guarded his innovations, we can only guess which one (or all) of these methods were employed. Realizing the potential market for mirror-smooth writing paper, he used his process to develop a steady stationery business through booksellers.

The net result of this effort was books of dazzling contrast, simplicity, and refinement. Professional jealousy caused Baskerville's critics to dismiss him as an "amateur," although his work set a high standard of quality. Some of his critics argued that reading Baskerville type hurt their eyes because it was so sharp and contrasty. Benjamin Franklin, who admired Baskerville, wrote him a letter relating that he, Franklin, had torn the foundry name from a Caslon specimen sheet, told an acquaintance who was complaining about Baskerville's type that it was Baskerville's specimen sheet, and asked the man to point out the problems. The victim of Franklin's whimsy proceeded to pontificate on the problems, complaining that just looking at it was giving him a headache.

While Baskerville met with indifference and even hostility in the British Isles, the design of his type and books became important influences on the continent as the Italian Giambattista Bodoni (1740–1813) and the Didot family in Paris became enthusiastic about his work.

The imperial designs of Louis René Luce

An imperial and stately graphic design style was achieved by another type designer and punch cutter at the Imprimerie Royale, Louis René Luce (d. 1773). During the three decades from 1740 until 1770, Luce designed a series of types that were narrow and condensed, with serifs as sharp as spurs. Engraved borders were being widely used in graphic designs, and these required a second printing. Luce created a large series of letterpress borders, ornaments, trophies, and other devices of impressive variety and excellent printing quality. These were designed with a mechanistic perfection that projects an air of imperial authority. Cast in modular sections, these ornaments were then assembled into the desired configuration by the compositor. The density of line in Luce's ornaments was carefully planned to be visually compatible with his typefaces and often had an iden-

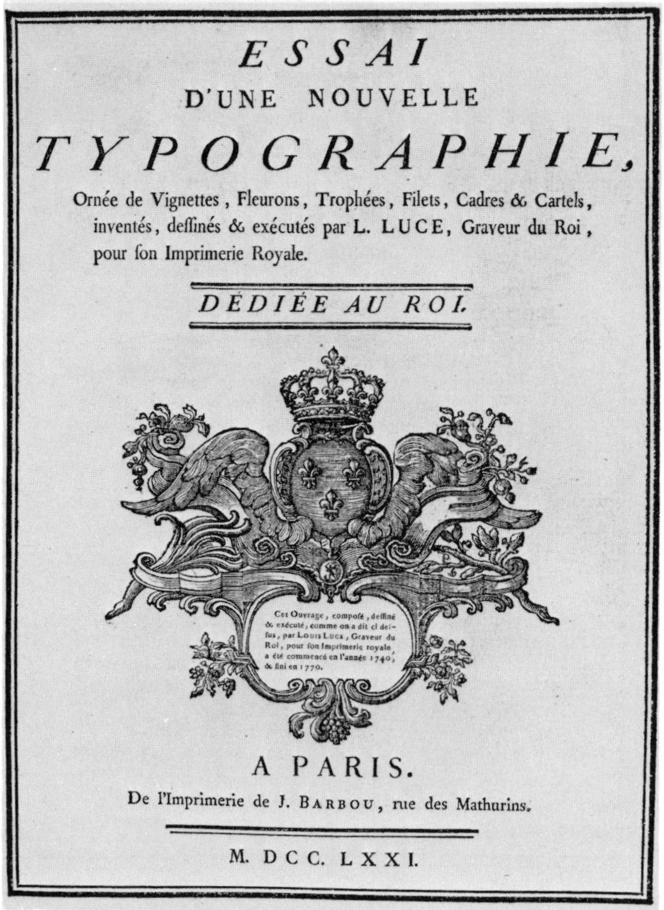

ESSAI
D'UNE NOUVELLE
TYPOGRAPHIE,

Ornée de Vignettes, Fleurons, Trophées, Filets, Cadres & Cartels, inventés, deſſinés & exécutés par L. LUCE, Graveur du Roi, pour ſon Imprimerie Royale.

DÉDIÉE AU ROI.

Cet Ouvrage, composé, deſſiné & exécuté, comme on a dit ci deſſus, par Louis Luce, Graveur du Roi, pour ſon Imprimerie royale a été commencé en l'année 1740, & fini en 1770.

A PARIS.

De l'Imprimerie de J. BARBOU, rue des Mathurins.

M. DCC. LXXI.

Louis René Luce (designer) and Jean Joseph Barbou (printer), title page from *Essai d'une Nouvelle Typographie,* 1771. By replacing the floral lushness of Rococo design with a more rigorous design feeling, Luce pointed toward the Modern style of Bodoni and the Didots. *Library of Congress, Washington, D.C., Rosenwald Collection.*

Louis René Luce (designer) and Jean Joseph Barbou (printer), ornaments page from *Essai d'une Nouvelle Typographie,* 1771. These meticulously constructed cornices and borders express the authority and absolutism of the French monarchy. *Library of Congress, Washington, D.C., Rosenwald Collection.*

tical weight so that they would look as if they belonged together in a design. In 1771, Luce published his *Essai d'une Nouvelle Typographie (Essay on the New Typography)* with ninety-three plates presenting the range of his design accomplishments. Mindful of the power of his patron, King Louis XV, Luce's layout for the first of eleven foldout, hypothetical graphic designs showing his ornaments and types in use is a "Frontispiece for a history of the King." Both Fournier le Jeune and Luce died before the French Revolution tore apart the world they lived in and served, the *ancien régime* of the French monarchy. The majestic design styles in architecture, interiors, and graphics patronized by royalty lost all social relevance in the world of democracy and equality that emerged from the chaos of revolution. Perhaps the ultimate irony occurred in 1790, when Romain du Roi typefaces commissioned by Louis XIV were used to print radical political tracts in support of the French Revolution.

The modern style

The son of a poor printer, Giambattista Bodoni was born in Saluzzo in northern Italy. As a young man, he traveled to Rome and apprenticed at the Propaganda Fide, the Catholic press that printed missionary materials in native tongues for use around the globe. Bodoni learned punch cutting, but his interest in living in Rome declined after his mentor, Ruggeri—who was the director—committed suicide. Shortly thereafter, Bodoni left the Propaganda Fide with the idea of journeying to England and perhaps working with Baskerville.

While visiting his parents before leaving Italy, twenty-eight-year-old Bodoni was asked to take charge of the Stamperia Reale, the official press of Ferdinand, Duke of Parma. Bodoni accepted the charge and became the private printer to the court. He printed official documents and publications desired by the Duke, in addition to projects conceived and initiated by Bodoni. His initial design influence was Fournier le Jeune, whose foundry supplied type and ornaments to the Stamperia Reale after Bodoni took charge. The quality of Bodoni's design and printing, even though scholarship and proofreading were sometimes lacking, created a growing international reputation. In

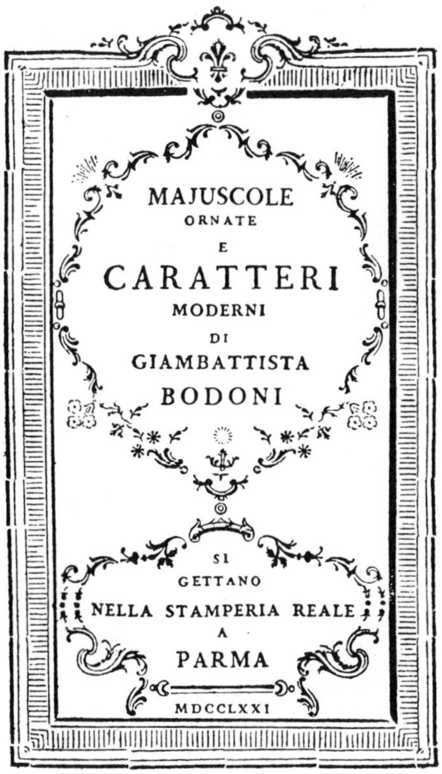
MAJUSCOLE
ORNATE
E
CARATTERI
MODERNI
DI
GIAMBATTISTA
BODONI
SI
GETTANO
NELLA STAMPERIA REALE
A
PARMA
MDCCLXXI

Giambattista Bodoni, title page from *Saggio tipografico,* 1771. The tremendous influence of Fournier le Jeune upon Bodoni's earlier work is evident in this page design.

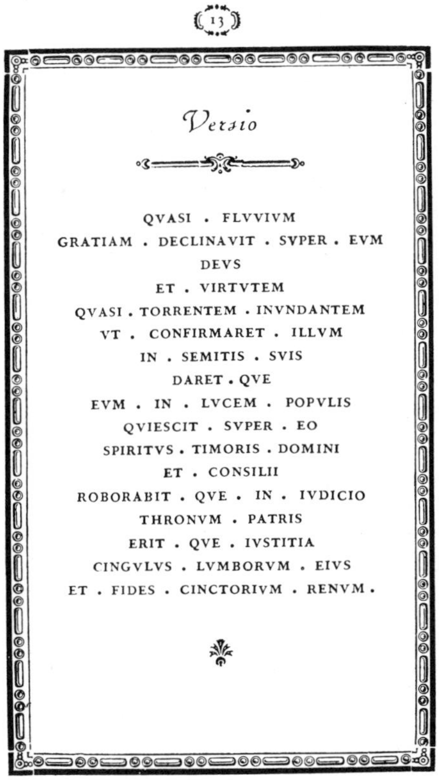
13

Versio

QVASI . FLVVIVM
GRATIAM . DECLINAVIT . SVPER . EVM
DEVS
ET . VIRTVTEM
QVASI . TORRENTEM . INVNDANTEM
VT . CONFIRMARET . ILLVM
IN . SEMITIS . SVIS
DARET . QVE
EVM . IN . LVCEM . POPVLIS
QVIESCIT . SVPER . EO
SPIRITVS . TIMORIS . DOMINI
ET . CONSILII
ROBORABIT . QVE . IN . IVDICIO
THRONVM . PATRIS
ERIT . QVE . IVSTITIA
CINGVLVS . LVMBORVM . EIVS
ET . FIDES . CINCTORIVM . RENVM .

Giambattista Bodoni, page from *Pel battesimo d.S.A.R. Ludovico,* 1774. Moving away from Fournier le Jeune's influence, Bodoni began to favor more geometric ornaments and white space. *Library of Congress, Washington, D.C., Rosenwald Collection.*

1790, the Vatican invited Bodoni to Rome to establish a press for printing the classics there, but the duke countered with an offer of expanded facilities, greater independence, and the privilege of printing for other clients. Bodoni elected to remain in Parma.

At about the same time, the cultural and political climate was changing. Politically, the revolt against the French monarchy led to a total rejection of the lush styles so popular during the reigns of Louis XV and XVI. To fill the formal void, architects, painters, and sculptors enthusiastically embraced the classical forms of Greek and Roman antique art which were captivating the public by the 1790s. Excavations, mostly at Herculaneum, Pompeii, and around Rome, fueled the mania. Graphic design required another language of form to replace the seemingly outmoded Rococo style. It was Bodoni who took a leadership role in evolving new typefaces and page layout.

The term *modern,* which defines a new category of roman type, was first used by Fournier le Jeune in his *Manuel Typographique* to describe the design trends that culminated in Bodoni's mature work. The initial impetus was the thin, straight serifs of Grandjean's Romain du Roi commissioned by Louis XIV, followed by engraved graphic designs by artists including Pine. Next came the letterforms and page layouts of Baskerville, particularly his practice of making the light strokes of his characters thinner to increase the contrast between thicks and thins. Also, Baskerville's rejection of ornament and his generous use of space were factors. Another trend, the design of narrower, more condensed letterforms, gave type a taller and more geometric appearance. Finally, all of these evolutionary trends were encouraged by a growing sensibility for a lighter typographic tone and texture, and this new fashion reinforced the other trends.

In 1791 Bodoni redesigned the roman letterforms with a more mathematical, geometric, and mechanical appearance. He reinvented the serifs by making them hairlines that formed sharp right angles with the upright strokes. There is no tapered flow of the serif into the upright stroke as in Old Style roman. The thin strokes of his letterforms were trimmed to the same weight as the hairline serifs, creating a brilliant sharpness and a dazzling contrast that had not been seen before. Bodoni defined his design ideal as cleanness, good taste, charm, and regularity. This regularity—the standardization of units—was a concept of the emerging industrial era of the machine. Bodoni decided that the letters in a type font should be created through combinations of a very limited number of identical units. This standardization of forms that could be measured and constructed marked the death of calligraphy and writing as the wellspring for type design and the end of the imprecise cutting and casting of earlier type design. Bodoni's precise, measurable, and repeatable forms expressed the vision and spirit of the machine age. It is noteworthy that as Bodoni was constructing alphabets of interchangeable parts, American inventor Eli Whitney was assembling firearms of interchangeable parts in his New Haven, Connecticut, factory, foreshadowing the mass-production techniques soon to revolutionize western society.

In Bodoni's page layouts, the borders and ornaments of the earlier decorative style that had brought international fame to the Stampera Reale were cast aside for a severe economy of form and efficiency of function. The severe purity of Bodoni's late graphic design style has affinities with twentieth-century functional typography. Open, simple page design with generous margins, wide letter and line spacing, and large areas of white space became his hallmark. Lightness was increased by using a smaller *x*-height and longer ascenders and descenders. In some fonts, letters were cast on oversized metal so the type could not be set solid. As a result, these fonts always had the appearance of generous leading. Like a majority of books of his time, most of the three hundred forty-five books that Bodoni published were new editions of Greek and Roman classics. Critics hailed Bodoni's volumes like the great Roman poet Virgil's *Opera* as the typographic expression of Neoclassicism and a return to "antique virtue." This is surprising, for Bodoni was breaking new ground. Bodoni designed about three hundred fonts of type and planned a monumental specimen book presenting this work. After his death his widow, Signora Bodoni, and foreman, Luigi Orsi, persisted with the project and published the two-volume *Manuale Tipografico* in 1818. This monumental celebration of the aesthetics of letterforms and homage to Bodoni's genius is a milestone in the history of graphic design.

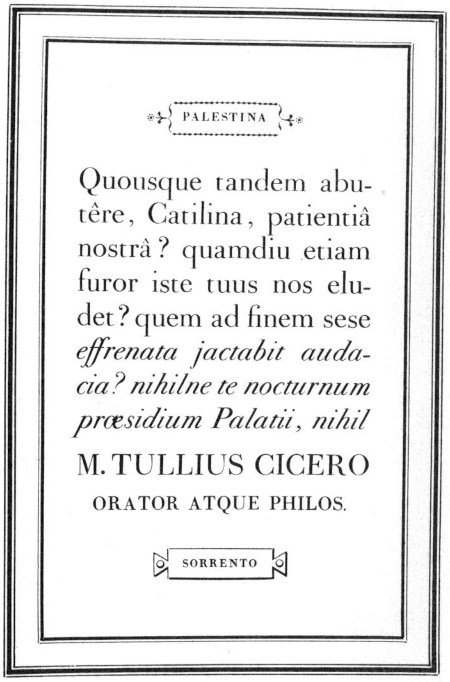
PALESTINA

Quousque tandem abutêre, Catilina, patientiâ nostrâ? quamdiu etiam furor iste tuus nos eludet? quem ad finem sese *effrenata jactabit audacia? nihilne te nocturnum præsidium Palatii, nihil*

M. TULLIUS CICERO

ORATOR ATQUE PHILOS.

SORRENTO

Giambattista Bodoni, page from *Manuale Tipografico,* 1818. The crisp clarity of Bodoni's letterforms are echoed by the *scotch rules*. Composed of double and triple thick-and-thin elements, these rules and borders echo the weight contrasts of Bodoni's modern types.

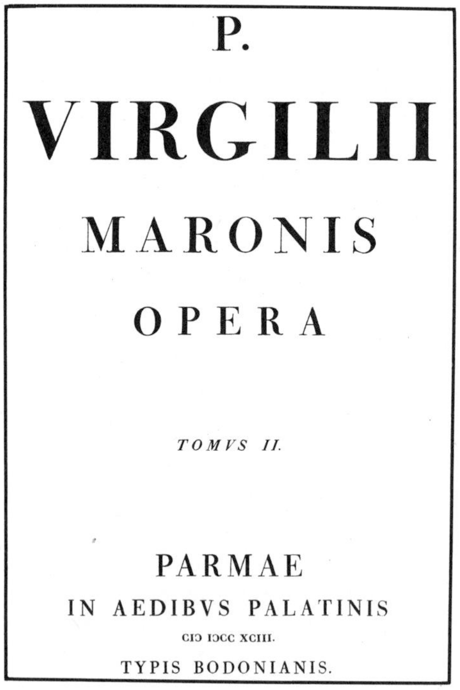
P.

VIRGILII

MARONIS

OPERA

TOMVS II.

PARMAE

IN AEDIBVS PALATINIS

CIↃ IↃCC XCIII.

TYPIS BODONIANIS.

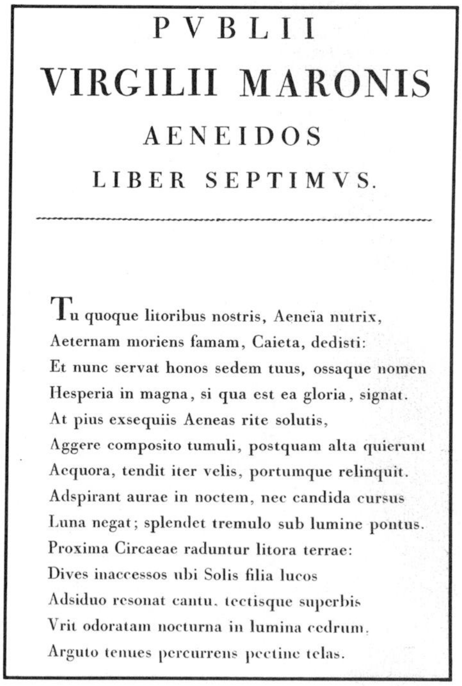
PVBLII

VIRGILII MARONIS

AENEIDOS

LIBER SEPTIMVS.

Tu quoque litoribus nostris, Aeneïa nutrix,
Aeternam moriens famam, Caieta, dedisti:
Et nunc servat honos sedem tuus, ossaque nomen
Hesperia in magna, si qua est ea gloria, signat.
At pius exsequiis Aeneas rite solutis,
Aggere composito tumuli, postquam alta quierunt
Aequora, tendit iter velis, portumque relinquit.
Adspirant aurae in noctem, nec candida cursus
Luna negat; splendet tremulo sub lumine pontus.
Proxima Circaeae raduntur litora terrae:
Dives inaccessos ubi Solis filia lucos
Adsiduo resonat cantu, tectisque superbis
Vrit odoratam nocturna in lumina cedrum,
Arguto tenues percurrens pectine telas.

Giambattista Bodoni, title page and section-heading page for Virgil's *Opera,* Volume II, 1793. In graphic designs so pure and simple, every adjustment of letterspace and line space becomes critical to the overall design harmony. *Library of Congress, Washington, D.C., Rosenwald Collection.*

In 1872, the citizens of Saluzzo honored their native son by erecting a statue of Bodoni. Ironically, they carved his name in the base in Old Style roman letters!

A family dynasty of printers, publishers, papermakers, and typefounders began in 1713 when Françoise Didot (1689–1757) established his printing and bookselling firm in Paris. One of his major works is the twenty-volume travels of the famous novelist Abbé Prévost, published in 1747. The family line that made the greatest contribution begins with François' son, François Ambroise Didot (1730–1804), who published a series of French classics by order of King Louis XVI. In 1780 he introduced into France a highly finished, smooth paper of wove design modeled after the paper commissioned by Baskerville in England. The Didot typefoundry's constant experimentation led to *maigre* (thin) and *gras* (fat) type styles similar to the condensed and expanded fonts of our time. Around 1785, François Ambroise revised Fournier's typographic measurement system and created the point system used in France today. François Ambroise realized that the Fournier scale was subject to shrinkage after being printed on moistened paper, and even Fournier's metal master had no standard for comparison. Therefore, François Ambroise adopted the official *pied de roi,* divided into twelve French inches, as his standard. Then each inch was divided into seventy-two points. Didot discarded the traditional nomenclature for various type sizes (Cicero, Petit-Romain, Gros-Text, and so on) and identified them with the measure of the metal type body in points (ten point, twelve point, and so on). The Didot system was adopted in Germany, where it was revised by Hermann Berthold in 1879 to work with the metric system. In 1886, the Didot system—revised to suit the English inch—was adopted as a standard point measure by American typefounders, and England adopted the point system in 1898. The fonts brought out around 1775 by Françoise Ambroise are the first to possess the

AVIS

AUX SOUSCRIPTEURS

DE

LA GERUSALEMME

LIBERATA

IMPRIMÉE PAR DIDOT L'AÎNÉ

SOUS LA PROTECTION ET PAR LES ORDRES

DE MONSIEUR.

LES ARTISTES choisis par MONSIEUR pour exécuter son édition de LA GERUSALEMME LIBERATA demandent avec confiance aux souscripteurs de cet ouvrage un délai de quelques mois pour en mettre au jour la premiere livraison. Il est rarement arrivé qu'un ouvrage où sont entrés les ornements de la gravure ait pu être donné au temps préfix pour lequel il avoit été promis : cet art entraîne beaucoup de difficultés qui causent des retards forcés; et certainement on peut regarder comme un empêchement insurmontable les jours courts et obscurs d'un hiver long et rigoureux. D'ailleurs la quantité d'ouvrages de gravure proposés actuellement par

François Ambroise Didot, prospectus for Tasso's *La Gerusalemme Liberata,* 1784. Designed at the Didot foundry, the typeface used in this announcement for a forthcoming romantic novel is the first presentation of a true Modern style letterform. Straight hairline serifs, extreme contrast between thick and thin strokes, and construction on a vertical axis are the characteristics that mark this break with transitional letterforms.

Didot touch, a lighter, more geometric quality similar in feeling to the evolution occurring in Bodoni's designs under Baskerville's influence.

François Ambroise had two sons: Pierre l'aîné Didot (1761–1853), who took charge of his father's printing office; and Firmin Didot (1764–1836), who succeeded his father as head of the Didot type foundry. Firmin's notable achievements included the invention of *stereotyping*. This process is casting a duplicate of a relief printing surface by pressing a molding material (damp paper pulp, plaster, or clay) against it to make a matrix. Molten metal is poured into the matrix to form the duplicate printing plate. Stereotyping made longer press runs possible.

After the Revolution, the French government honored Pierre l'aîné by granting him the printing office formerly used by the Imprimerie Royale at the Louvre. There he gave the neoclassical revival of the Napoleonic era its graphic design expression in a series of *éditions du Louvre*. These magnificent classics included Virgil (1798), Horace (1799), Racine (1801–1805), and Aesop (1802). The lavish margins set off Firmin Didot's modern typography which is even more mechanical and precise than Bodoni's. The engravings of flawless technique and sharp value contrast were designed by various artists working in the Neoclassical manner of the painter Jacques Louis David (1748–1825). In seeking to imitate nature in her most perfect form, these artists created figures as ideally modeled as Greek statues who are frozen in shallow picture boxes. A seldom equaled, though brittle, perfection is achieved.

Bodoni and the Didots were rivals and kindred spirits. Comparisons and speculation about who innovated and who followed become inevitable. They shared common influences and the same cultural milieu. In the opinion of this writer, their influence upon each other was mutually reciprocal, for Bodoni and the Didots attempted to push the modern style farther than the other. In so doing, each pushed the aesthetics of contrast, mathematical construction, and neoclassical refinement to the ultimate possible level. Bodoni is credited with greater skill as a designer and printer, but the Didots possessed greater scholarship. Bodoni proclaimed that he sought only the magnificent and did not work for common readers. In addition to their extravagant folio editions, the Didots used their new

Girodet inv.
A. Urb. Massard sculp.
Ille agmine longo
Tandem inter pateras et levia pocula serpens
Libavitque dapes, rursusque innoxius imo
Successit tumulo, et depasta altaria liquit.

AENEIDOS

LIBER QUINTUS.

INTEREA medium Aeneas jam classe tenebat
Certus iter, fluctusque atros Aquilone secabat,
Mœnia respiciens, quæ jam infelicis Elissæ
Collucent flammis. Quæ tantum accenderit ignem
Causa latet; duri magno sed amore dolores
Polluto, notumque furens quid femina possit,
Triste per augurium Teucrorum pectora ducunt.
Ut pelagus tenuere rates, nec jam amplius ulla
Occurrit tellus, maria undique et undique cœlum;
Olli cæruleus supra caput adstitit imber,
Noctem hiememque ferens; et inhorruit unda tenebris.
Ipse gubernator puppi Palinurus ab alta:
Heu! quianam tanti cinxerunt æthera nimbi?
Quidve, pater Neptune, paras? Sic deinde locutus,
Colligere arma jubet, validisque incumbere remis;
Obliquatque sinus in ventum, ac talia fatur:
Magnanime Aenea, non, si mihi Juppiter auctor

Pierre l'âîné Didot (printer), pages from Virgil's *Bucolica, Georgica, et Aeneis,* 1798. This double-page spread shows the splendid perfection, lavish margins, and cool understatement of Neoclassical graphic design. *Library of Congress, Washington, D.C., Rosenwald Collection.*

LE QUINZE.

Cette épitre se trouve en tête de mon édition in-folio des œuvres de Boileau, en deux volumes, tirée seulement à 125 exemplaires, dont Sa Majesté a daigné agréer la dédicace.

AU ROI.

SIRE,

D'un monarque guerrier, l'un de tes fiers aïeux,
Despréaux a chanté le courage indomptable,
La marche menaçante et le choc redoutable,
Les assauts, les combats, et les faits merveilleux.
LOUIS, applaudis-toi d'un plus heureux partage.
Plus beau, plus fortuné, toujours cher à la paix,
Ton règne ami des lois doit briller d'âge en âge;
Tous nos droits affermis signalent tes bienfaits.
Le ciel t'a confié les destins de la France:
Qu'il exauce nos vœux, qu'il veille sur tes jours!
De ta carrière auguste exempte de souffrance
Que sa bonté pour nous prolonge l'heureux cours!

Pierre Didot, page from *Nouveaux Caractères,* 1819. The similarities in the design of letterforms and pages by the Didot family and Bodoni are striking.

stereotyping process to produce much larger editions of economical books for a broader audience. A year after the *Manuale Typografico* appeared, the 1819 *Spécimen des Nouveaux Caractères . . . de P. Didot l'aîné* was published in Paris.

The illuminated printing of William Blake

During the waning years of the eighteenth century, an unexpected counterpoint to the severe typography of Bodoni and the Didots is found in the *illuminated printing* of the visionary English poet and visual artist, William Blake (1757–1827). After serving an engraving apprenticeship and studying at the Royal Academy, Blake opened a printing shop at age twenty-seven, where he was assisted by his younger brother Robert. After Robert's untimely death three years later, Blake told his friends that Robert appeared to him in a dream and told him of a way to print both his poems and illustrations as relief etchings without typography. Blake began to publish books of his poetry, and each page was printed as a monochrome etching combining word and image. Then, Blake and his wife either handcolored each page with watercolor or printed colors, handbound each copy in paper covers, and sold them at modest prices. The lyrical fantasy, glowing swirls of color, and imaginative vision that Blake achieved in his poetry and accompanying designs represent an effort to transcend the material of graphic design and printing to achieve a spiritual expression. The title page from *Songs of Innocence* shows how Blake integrated letterforms into illustrations. The swirls of foliage that spin from the serifs of the letters become leaves for the tree; small figures frolic among these letters that are set against a vibrant sky.

William Blake, title page for *Songs of Innocence,* 1789. A joyful rainbow of color animates the sky of the title page in Blake's volume of gentle lyrics capturing the wonder of childhood. *Library of Congress, Washington, D.C., Rosenwald Collection.*

The epoch closes

British national pride led to the establishment of the Shakespeare Press in 1786 to produce editions of splendor to rival the folio volumes of Paris and Parma. The state of English printing was such that a printing house, typefoundry, and ink manufactory had to be established to produce work of the desired quality. Punch-cutter William Martin (d. 1815), former apprentice to Baskerville and brother of Baskerville's foreman Robert Martin, was called to London to design and cut types "in imitation of the sharp and fine letter used by the French and Italian printers." His types combined the majestic proportions of Baskerville with the sharp contrasts of modern fonts. William Bulmer (1757–1830) was chosen by publishers John and Josiah Boydell and George and W. Nicol to print, in nine volumes, *The Dramatic Works of Shakespeare,* 1792–1802. These were followed by a three-volume edition of Milton.

As a boy in Newcastle, Bulmer had a close friend in Thomas Bewick (1753–1828), who is called the father of wood engraving. After apprenticing to engraver Ralph Beilby and learning to engrave sword blades and door plates, Bewick turned his attention to the wood engraving of illustrations. His "white-line" technique employed a fine graver to achieve delicate tonal effects by cutting across the grain on woodblocks of Turkish boxwood instead of with the grain on the blocks of softer wood used in creating woodcuts. Publication of his *General History of Quadrupeds* in 1790 brought renown to Bewick and his techniques, which became a major illustration method in letterpress printing until the advent of photomechanical halftones nearly a century later.

Bulmer used Martin's types and Bewick's wood engravings together in a series of volumes, including *Poems by Goldsmith and Parnell* in 1795 and William Somerville's *The Chase* of 1796, in which the clean, spacious design of Bodoni and Didot was tempered by a traditional English legibility and warmth. These gentle volumes might be called a lyrical envoi of a three-and-a-half-century period of graphic design and printing that began with Gutenberg in Mainz. Printing had been a handicraft, and graphic design had involved the layout of metal type and related material with illustrations printed from handmade blocks. The eighteenth century closed with stormy political revolutions in France and the American colonies. England was the nucleus for the gathering forces of the vast upheavals of the Industrial Revolution. The sweeping changes ushered in by the conversion of an agrarian, rural society with handicraft manufacture to the industrial society of machine manufacture shook western civilization to its very foundations. All aspects of the human experience, including visual communications, were transformed by profound and irrevocable changes.

Thomas Bewick, "Old English Hound" from the *General History of Quadrupeds,* 1790. Bewick achieved his dazzling tonal range by combining "white-line-on-black" techniques—much like drawing in chalk on a blackboard—with a more usual "black-line-on-white" treatment in the lighter tonal areas.

Thomas Bewick, "The Yellow Bunting" from *British Birds,* 1797. "Sticking to nature as closely as he could," Bewick achieved a tonal range and accuracy of drawing which set the standard of excellence for wood-engraved illustrations.

In Albion's isle, when glorious Edgar reign'd,
He, wisely provident, from her white cliffs
Launch'd half her forests, and, with numerous fleets,
Cover'd his wide domain: there proudly rode,
Lord of the deep, the great prerogative
Of British monarchs. Each invader bold,
Dane and Norwegian, at a distance gazed,
And, disappointed, gnash'd his teeth in vain.
He scour'd the seas, and to remotest shores
With swelling sails the trembling corsair fled.
Rich commerce flourish'd; and with busy oars
Dash'd the resounding surge. Nor less, at land,
His royal cares; wise, potent, gracious prince!
His subjects from their cruel foes he saved,

Thomas Bewick (engraver) and William Bulmer (printer), page from William Somerville's *The Chase,* 1796. Simplicity becomes exquisite, for the paper, type, printing, and engravings all reflect a perfection of craft. *Library of Congress, Washington, D.C.*

PART III

THE INDUSTRIAL REVOLUTION: *The impact of industrial technology upon visual communications*

10

Typography for an Industrial Age

ALTHOUGH IT MIGHT BE SAID THAT the Industrial Revolution first occurred in England during the period from 1760 until 1840, it is a radical process of social and economic change rather than a historical period of time. A major impetus for this conversion from an agricultural society into an industrial one was energy. Until James Watt (1736–1819) perfected the steam engine, which was deployed rapidly starting in the 1780s, animal- and manpower were the primary sources of energy. During the course of the nineteenth century, the amount of energy generated by steam increased a hundredfold. During the last three decades of the century, electricity and gasoline-fueled engines further expanded productivity. A factory system with machine manufacturing and divisions of labor was developed. New materials, particularly iron and steel, became available.

Masses of people left a subsistence existence living on the land and sought employment in the factories. Cities grew rapidly, and there was a wider distribution of wealth. Political power shifted away from the aristocracy and toward capitalist manufacturers, merchants, and even the working class. The growing scientific knowledge was applied to manufacturing processes and materials, and man's sense of dominion over nature and faith in the ability to exploit the earth's resources to satisfy material wants and needs created a heady confidence.

The capitalist replaced the landowner as the most powerful force in western countries, and capital investment in machines for mass manufacture became the basis for change in industry after industry. A spiraling production cycle was created. Demand from a rapidly growing urban population with increased buying power stimulated technological improvements. In turn, this enabled mass production, which increased availability and lowered costs. The cheaper, more abundant merchandise now available stimulated a mass market and even greater demand. Graphics played an important role in marketing factory output. This cycle of industrial supply and demand became the force behind the relentless progress of industrial developments.

The giddy developments of the Industrial Revolution were not without their social costs. Workers who traded overpopulated rural areas for urban factories worked thirteen-hour days for miserable wages and lived in filthy, unsanitary tenements. This huge work force of men, women, and children often suffered from shutdowns caused by earlier overproduction, depressions, economic panics, business and bank failures, and the loss of jobs to newer technological improvements. On measure, however, the overall standard of living of people in Europe and America improved dramatically over the course of the nineteenth century. Critics of the new industrial age cried that civilization was shifting from an interest in humanist values toward a preoccupation with material goods, and that people were losing their communion with nature and aesthetic and spiritual values.

The greater degree of equality that sprang from the French and American Revolutions led to increased public education and literacy. The audience for reading matter expanded accordingly, and this unsettled period of fluid change was characterized by greater importance and availability of graphic communications. As with other commodities, technology lowered unit costs and increased the production of printed materials. In turn, the greater availability created an insatiable demand, and the era of mass communications dawned.

Handicrafts almost completely vanished. The unity of design and production, in which a craftsman designed and fabricated a chair, for example, or a printer was involved in all aspects of his craft from the design of typefaces and layout of the printed page to the actual printing of books and broadsheets, ended. Over the course of the nineteenth century, the specialization of the factory system fractured graphic communications into separate design and production components. The nature of visual information was profoundly changed. The range of typographic sizes and styles of letterforms exploded. The invention of photography—and later, the means to print photographic images—expanded the meaning of visual documentation and pictorial information. Color lithography put sensual and colorful printing into every home in a democratic revolution that enabled the aesthetic experience of colorful images to pass from the privileged few to the whole society. This dynamic, exuberant, and often chaotic century witnessed a staggering parade of new technologies, imaginative forms, and expanded applications of graphic design.

Innovations in typography

Many authorities of typography and printing history have deplored the Pandora's box of typographic design unleashed by the Industrial Revolution. In doing so, they fail to recognize the shifting social and economic role of typographic communication. Before the nineteenth century, dissemination of information, primarily through the medium of the book, had been the dominant function. The faster pace and mass communications needs of an increasingly urban and industrialized society produced a rapid expansion of jobbing printers, advertising, and posters. Larger scale, greater visual impact, and a different kind of tactile and expressive character were demanded, and the book typography that had slowly evolved from handwriting did not fulfill these needs.

It was no longer enough for the twenty-six letters of the alphabet to function only as phonetic symbols. The industrial age required that these signs be transformed into abstract visual forms projecting powerful concrete shapes of strong contrast and large size from the billboards. At the same time, letterpress printers were under increasing competitive pressure from lithographic printers where skilled craftmen rendered plates directly from an artist's sketch and produced images and letterforms limited only by the artist's imagination. The letterpress printers turned to the typefounders to expand their design possibilities, and the founders were only too happy to comply. The early decades of the nineteenth century saw an outpouring of new type designs without precedence.

As in many other aspects of the Industrial Revolution, England played a pivotal role and major design innovations were achieved by London typefounders. In a sense, it might almost be said that the first William Caslon was grandfather of this revolution. In addition to his heirs, two of his former apprentices who were dismissed for leading a workers' revolt, Joseph Jackson (1733–1792) and Thomas Cotterell (d. 1785), became successful type designers and founders in their own right. Apparently Cotterell began the trend of sand casting large, bold display letters as early as 1765, when his specimen book displayed, in the words of one of his amazed contemporaries, a "proscription, or posting letter, of great bulk and dimension, as high as the measure of twelve *lines of pica*!" (about 5 centimeters or 2 inches).

The idea of larger and fatter letters was embraced by other founders, and type grew steadily bolder by the decade. This led to the invention of *fat faces,* a major category of type design innovated by Cotterell's pupil and successor, Robert Thorne (d. 1820) and first shown by him in 1803. Basically, a fat-face typestyle is a roman face whose contrast and weight has been increased by expanding the thickness of the heavy strokes to a proportion of one to two and a half or even one to two relative to the height of the capitals. These bulldozer bold fonts were only the beginning, as Thorne's Fann Street Foundry began a lively competition with William Caslon IV (1781–1869) and Vincent Figgins (1766–1844). The full range of Thorne's accomplishment as a type designer was documented after his death when William Thorowgood—who was not a type designer,

ABC

Thomas Cotterell, twelve-line pica, letterforms, c. 1765. These display letters, shown actual size, seemed gigantic to eighteenth-century compositors who had been used to setting handbills and broadsides using types that were rarely even half this size.

punch-cutter, or printer, but used money won in a lottery to offer the top bid when Thorne's Fann Street Foundry was auctioned after Thorne's death—published the one-hundred-thirty-two-page book of specimens that had been typeset and was ready to go onto the press when Thorne died.

One of Joseph Jackson's apprentices, Vincent Figgins, stayed with him and took full charge of his operation during the three years preceding Jackson's death from scarlet fever in 1792. Figgins failed in his efforts to purchase his master's foundry because William Caslon III offered the highest bid. Undeterred, Figgins established his own typefoundry and quickly built a reputation for quality type design and mathematical, astronomical, and other symbolic material numbering in the hundreds of sorts. By the turn of the century, Figgins had designed and cast a complete range of romans and had begun to produce scholarly and foreign faces. The rapid tilt in typographic design taste toward modern style romans and new jobbing styles after the turn of the century seriously affected him. But he rapidly responded and his 1815 printing specimens showed a full range of modern styles, *antiques* (Egyptians)—the second major innovation of nineteenth-century type design—and numerous jobbing faces including "three-dimensional" fonts.

Having a bold machinelike feeling, these antiques were characterized by slablike rectangular serifs, an evenness of weight throughout the form, and short ascenders and descenders. In Thorowgood's 1821 specimen book of Thorne's type, the name *Egyptian*—which continues to be used for this style—was used for the slab-serif fonts shown. Perhaps the fascination for all aspects of ancient Egyptian culture, which was intensified by Napoleon's 1798–99 invasion and occupation, inspired this name. It may be that design similarities were seen between the chunky geometric alphabets and the visual qualities of some Egyptian artifacts. As early as the 1830s, a variation of Egyptian, having slightly bracketed serifs and increased contrast between thicks and thins, was called Ionic. In 1845 William Thorowgood and Company copyrighted a modified Egyptian called Clarendon. Similar to the Ionics, these letterforms were condensed Egyptians with stronger contrasts between thick and thin strokes and somewhat lighter serifs.

Robert Thorne, Fat Face types, 1821. Although the dated record of these designs is William Thorowgood's 1 January 1821 publication of *New Specimen of Printing Types, late R. Thorne's,* it is generally thought that Thorne designed the first Fat Faces in 1803.

MINT
main.

Quousque tandem abutere,
Catilina, patientia nostra ?
quamdiu nos etiam furor is
te tuus eludet ? quem after
CONSTANTINOPLE
£1234567890

Two Lines Pica, Antique.

ABCDEFGHIJ
KLMNOPQR
STUVWXYZ&,:;.-
£1234567890

Vincent Figgins, Two Lines Pica, Antique, 1815. The inspiration for this highly original design, first shown by Figgins, is not known. Whether Figgins, Thorne, or an anonymous sign painter first invented this style is another mystery surrounding the sudden appearance of slab-serif letterforms.

Quosque tandem abu-
tere Catilina patientia
FURNITURE 1820

Quosque tandem abutere Catilina
patientia nostra? quamdiu nos
W. THOROWGOOD.

Robert Thorne, Egyptian type designs, 1821. Comparison with Figgins' design reveals subtle differences. Thorne based this lower case on the structure of Modern style letters, but he radically modified the weight and serifs.

Quousque tandem abu-
tere, Catilina, patientia
nostra? quamdiu nos e-
tiam furor iste tuus elu-
det? quem ad finem sese
effrenata jactabit auda-
cia? nihilne te noctur-
num præsidium palatii,
nihil urbis vigiliæ, nihil
ABCDEFGHIJKLMN
ABCDEFGHIJKLMNOPQR
£ 1234567890

Henry Caslon, Ionic type specimen, mid-1840s. Bracketing refers to the curved transition from the main strokes of a letterform to its serif. Egyptian type replaced the bracket with an abrupt angle; Ionic type restored a slight bracket.

Figgins' 1815 specimen book also presented the first nineteenth-century version of Tuscan-style letters. This style, characterized by serifs that are extended and curved, was put through an astounding range of variations during the nineteenth century, often with bulges, cavities, and ornaments.

It seemed that the English typefounders were trying to invent every possible design permutation by modifying forms or proportions and applying all manner of decoration to their alphabets. In 1815, Vincent Figgins showed styles that projected the illusion of three dimensions and appeared as bulky objects rather than two-dimensional signs. This device proved to be very popular and specimen books began to show perspective clones for every imaginable style. An additional variation was the depth of shading, which ranged from pencil-thin shadows to deep perspectives. Realizing that every device—perspective, outline, reversing, expanding, contracting—could multiply each style into a kaleidoscope of design possibilities, the designers proliferated styles with boundless enthusiasm.

The third major typographic innovation of the early 1800s, *sans-serif* type, whose most obvious characteristic is the absence of serifs, made its modest debut in an 1816 specimen book issued by William Caslon IV. Buried among the decorative display fonts of capitals in the back of the book, one line of medium-weight monoline serifless capitals proclaimed "W CALSON JUNR LETTER-FOUNDER." It looked a lot like an Egyptian face with the serifs removed, which is probably how Caslon IV designed it. The name—Two Lines English Egyptian—Caslon adopted for this style tends to support the theory that it had its origins in an Egyptian style. (English denoted a type size roughly equivalent to today's fourteen-point;

Quousque tandem abutere Catilina, patientia nostra ? quamdiu nos etiam furor iste tuus eludet ? quem ad finem sese effrenata jactabit audacia ? nihilne te nocturnum præsidium palatii, nihilne urbis vigiliæ, nihil timor populi, nihil consensus bonorum omnium, nihil hic munitissimus habendi senatus locus, nihil horum

£1234567890

SALES BY PUBLIC AUCTION.

Robert Besley (designer, with Thorowgood), specimen of the first Clarendon, 1845. An even more subtle adaptation of Ionic than Ionic was of Egyptian, Clarendon styles were wildly popular after their introduction. When the three-year patent expired, numerous imitations and piracies were issued by other founders.

HER

HER

THIN

The top two specimens are typical Tuscan styles with ornamental serifs, and demonstrate the diversity of expanded and condensed widths produced by nineteenth-century designers. The bottom specimen is an Antique Tuscan with slab-serifs that have been curved and slightly pointed. Note the care given to the design of the negative shapes that surround the letters.

FIVE LINES PICA, IN SHADE.

ABCDEFGH
IJKLMNOP
RSTUVWX.

V. FIGGINS.

Vincent Figgins, Five Lines Pica, In Shade, 1815. The first three-dimensional or perspective fonts were Fat Faces. Perhaps designers were seeking to compensate for the lightness of the thin strokes, which tended to reduce the legibility of Fat Faces at a distance.

thus, Two Lines English indicated a display type of about twenty-eight points). Sans serif, which became so important to twentieth-century graphic design, had a tentative beginning. The inelegant early sans serifs were primarily used for subtitles and descriptive material under sledgehammer bold fat faces and Egyptians.

In the early 1830s several typefounders introduced new sans-serif styles. Each designer and foundry seems to have invented a name: Caslon used Doric, Thorowgood called his fonts grotesques, Blake and Stephenson named their version sans-surryphs, and in the United States the Boston Type and Stereotype Foundry asserted independence from the British origins by naming its first American sans serif faces Gothics. Perhaps the rich black color of these display types seemed similar to the density of Gothic types. But it was Vincent Figgins, who dubbed his 1832 specimen sans serif, in recognition of the font's most apparent feature, and the name stuck.

German printers had a strong interest in sans serifs, and by 1830 the Schelter and Giesecke foundry had issued the first sans-serif fonts with a lowercase alphabet. By mid-century serifless alphabets were seeing increased use. At the end of the century, the German firm of Berthold began designing a "family" of ten sans-serifs styles which were variations upon one original design. The first of these Akzidenz Grotesque faces (called Standard in the United

MR. CO. NO. &c. –,;:.'!
ABCDEFGHIJKLNMOPQRSTUVX
WYZÆŒ!

VINCENT FIGGINS,
LETTER FOUNDER,
17, WEST STREET, SMITHFIELD,
LONDON.

Vincent Figgins, Two-Line Pearl, Outline, 1833. In outline and open fonts, a contour line of even weight encloses the alphabet shape that usually appears black.

MOLDER

William Thorowgood, Six-line Reversed Egyptian Italic, 1828. Types which appeared white against a printed black background enjoyed a brief popularity during the middle decades of the nineteenth century, then went almost completely out of fashion.

W CASLON JUNR LETTERFOUNDER

William Caslon IV, Two-line English Egyptian, 1816. This specimen quietly introduced what was to become a major resource for graphic design.

TWO-LINE GREAT PRIMER SANS-SERIF.

TO BE SOLD BY AUCTION,
WITHOUT RESERVE;
HOUSEHOLD FURNITURE,
PLATE, GLASS,
AND OTHER EFFECTS.
VINCENT FIGGINS.

Vincent Figgins, Two-line Great Primer Sans-serif, 1832. Both the name and wide use of sans-serif typography were launched by the awkward black display fonts in Figgins' 1832 *Specimens of Printing Types.*

ABCDEFGHIJKLMNOPQRSTUVWXYZ
abcdefghijklmnopqrstuvwxyz

ABCDEFGHIJKLMNOPQRSTUVWXYZ
abcdefghijklmnopqrstuvwxyz

ABCDEFGHIJKLMNOPQRSTUVWXYZ
abcdefghijklmnopqrstuvwxyz

ABCDEFGHIJKLMNOPQRSTUVWX
abcdefghijklmnopqrstuvwxyz

Akzidenz Grotesque (Standard) typestyle, 1898–1906. In addition to the four weights shown here, Berthold released three expanded and three condensed variations. This graphically unified family of faces enabled printers to achieve contrast and emphasis with a single family, but the message was lost on most turn-of-the-century designers and printers accustomed to mixing contradictory styles together.

States) was issued in 1898. The anonymous craftsmen who designed these forms achieved a remarkable harmony and clarity that became the basis for the sans-serif types of the post-World War II era.

The Wood Type Poster

As the size of display types crept upward, problems magnified for both printer and founder. In casting, it was difficult to keep the metal in a liquid state while pouring, and uneven cooling often created slightly concave printing surfaces. Many printers found large metal types to be prohibitively expensive, brittle, and heavy. For example, a wide twelve-line capital might weigh as much as five hundred grams (about 1.1 pounds). It is easy to imagine the problems in setting, handling, storing, and shipping that resulted. An American printer named Darius Wells (1800–1875) began to experiment with handcarved wooden types while recovering from a serious illness, and in 1827 he invented a lateral router that enabled the economical mass manufacture of types for display printing. Durable, lighter, and costing less than half as much as large metal types, wood type rapidly overcame printers' initial objections and had a significant impact on poster and broadsheet design. Beginning in March of 1828, when Wells launched the wood type industry with his first specimen sheets, American wood type manufacturers imported type design ideas from Europe and exported wood type. Soon, however, European countries began to develop their own wood type manufactories, and American firms began to create innovative decorative alphabets by mid-century.

After William Leavenworth (1799–1860) combined the pantograph with the router in 1834, new styles could be introduced so easily that customers were invited to send a drawing of one letter of a desired new style; the manufactory offered to design and produce the entire font based on the sketch without an additional charge for design and pattern drafting.

Paul Gavarni (1804–1866), *An afficheur at work,* 1845. The famous French illustrator and cartoonist lampooned the proliferation of posters by showing an *afficheur* ("poster hanger") pasting his posters over competitive messages.

CHESNUT STREET THEATRE
PRICES OF ADMISSION.
SUMMER SEASON
PLEASING ENTERTAINMENTS!
OPERATIC
GEMS
AND
GENTEEL COMEDIES
SIGN'R STRINI
MRS. ADA KING,
MR. EDWARD WARDEN
SATURDAY EVENING, June 17, 1854
THE SECRET
MRS. DUPUIS.
MRS. ADA KING
After which, CAVATINA from the Opera of Cinderella by Signor STRINI
PERFECTION!
Or, The Maid of Munster.
KATE O'BRIEN, with Songs,
MRS. ADA KING
IRISH LION!
MR. LYSANDER THOMPSON,
The Celebrated Comedian,

The impetus of this new display typography and the increasing demand for public posters by clients ranging from traveling circuses and vaudeville troupes to clothing stores and the new railroads led to poster houses specializing in letterpress display material. In the eighteenth century, job printing had been a sideline of the newspaper and book printers. The design of handbills, wood-type posters, and broadsheets at the poster houses did not involve a graphic designer in the twentieth century sense. The compositor, often in consultation with the client, selected and composed the type, rules, ornaments, and wood-engraved or metal-stereotyped stock illustrations which filled the typecases. Armed with this infinite typographic range of sizes, styles, weights, and novel ornamental effects, the design philosophy was to use it! The need to lock all the elements tightly on the press enforced a horizontal and vertical stress onto the design; this became the basic organizing principle.

Design decisions were pragmatic. Long words or copy dictated condensed type, and short words or copy were set in expanded fonts. Important words were given emphasis through the use of the largest available type sizes. There was a practical side to the extensive mixing of styles in job printing because many fonts, each having a limited number of characters, were available at the typical print shop. Wood and metal types were used together freely. In the avalanche of nineteenth-century ephemera printed by letterpress, a surprising number of well-designed posters and handbills were produced among the more typical workaday compositions. The typographic poster houses that developed with the advent of wood

Brown's Steam-power Job Printing Establishment, wood type poster, 1854. By letterspacing lines to be flush left and right, centering the type, and creating a rhythm of horizontals moving down the space, the compositor managed to bring order to a combination of novelty, sans-serif, slab-serif, Fat Face, and Modern styles.

Printer's proof, 1888. Proofed on tissue-thin, translucent paper, with pale blue stripes for checking alignments, this poster for a Leap Year Ball is typical of the job printing produced by letterpress printers in small towns and provincial centers all across Europe and America.

Two-Line English Ornamented, No. 2.
FORESHADOW
Two-Line English Ornamented, No. 7.
BARE IONIC COLUMN
Two-Line English Ornamented, No. 8.
DELIGHTING
Two-Line English Ornamented, No. 9.
MARBLEIZED
Two-Line Great Primer Tuscan Open.
INTERLINING
Two-Line Great Primer Antique Shaded.
FRINGED
Two-Line Great Primer Tuscan.
INK-LIMNING
Two-Line Great Primer Ornamented.
MELODIOUS
Two-Line Great Primer Ornamented, No. 3.
MELONS
Two-Line Great Primer Ornamented, No. 4.
RIGHT STRIPE
Two-Line Great Primer Ornamented, No. 5.
ROPE ONIONS
Two-Line Great Primer Ornamented, No. 6.
BLENDING
Two-Line English Ornamented, No. 10.
ANGULAR
Two-Line English Ornamented, No. 11.
GEMMED EYE
Two-Line English Ornamented, No. 12.
MAGNIFICENT
Two-Line English Ornamented, No. 13.
HANDSOMER
Two-Line English Ornamented, No. 15.
SUPERNACULUM
Three-Line Small Pica Ornamented.
CAMELOPARDIANAS
Two-Line Great Primer Gothic Shaded, No. 2.
WATER-IMAGED
Two-Line Great Primer Ornamented, No. 8.
DIAMONDS
Two-Line Great Primer Ornamented, No. 10.
OCCIDENT
Two-Line Great Primer Ornamented, No. 11.
ELABORATE
Two-Line Great Primer Ornamented, No. 12.
ENTWINING
Two-Line Great Primer Ornamented, No. 13.
EFFULGENCE
MACKELLAR, SMITHS & JORDAN. 474 SANSOM STREET, PHILADELPHIA.

MacKellar, Smith, and Jordan, page from *Book of Specimens,* 1881. The two dozen styles of type on this page suggest the bewildering range of possibilities available to the nineteenth-century designer of printing.

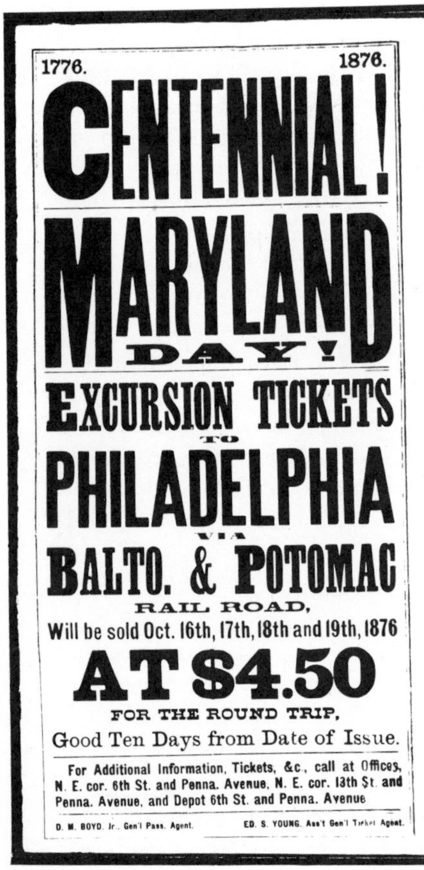

Handbill for an excursion train, 1876. To be bolder than bold, the compositor used heavier letterforms for the initial letter of important words. Oversized terminal letterforms are used effectively with condensed and extended styles in the phrase, "Maryland Day!" *Courtesy, Virginia Historical Society, Richmond, Virginia.*

type began to decline after 1870 as improvements in lithographic printing resulted in more pictorial and colorful posters by that process. Also, the importance of traveling entertainment shows—a mainstay among their clients—declined. The growth of magazines and newspapers with space advertising, and the legislative restrictions on posting began to shift commercial communications away from posted notices. The unique graphic design form of the letterpress poster houses, alive with typographic variety and textural richness, had almost vanished by the end of the century.

A revolution in printing

The printing presses used by Baskerville and Bodoni were remarkably similar to the first one used by Gutenberg over three centuries earlier. It was inevitable that the relentless progress of the Industrial Revolution would radically alter printing. Inventors sought to apply mechanical theory and metal parts to the hand press to increase its efficiency and the size of its impression. In 1772, Wilhelm Haas of Basel introduced the first metal parts, but their use was forbidden by the guilds. Several improvements in the hand press to make it stronger and more efficient culminated in Lord Stanhope's invention of a printing press constructed completely of cast iron parts in 1800. The metal screw mechanism required approximately one-tenth the manual force needed to print on a wooden press, and Stanhope's press enabled a doubling of the paper sheet size which could be printed. William Bulmer's printing office installed and experimented with Lord Stanhope's first successful prototype. These innovations served to improve a partially mechanized handicraft. The next step was to convert printing into a high-speed factory operation.

Far more crucial, however, were the accomplishments of Friedrich Koenig, a German printer who arrived in London around 1804 and presented his plans for a steam-powered printing press to major London printers. Finally receiving financial support from Thomas Bensley in 1807, Koenig obtained a patent in March, 1810, for his press which produced its first production trial—three thousand sheets for the *Annual Register*—during April, 1811. This press printed four hundred sheets per hour in comparison to the hourly output of two hundred fifty sheets on the Stanhope hand press. Koenig's first powered press was designed much like a hand press connected to a steam engine. Other innovations included a method of inking the type by rollers instead of the hand inking balls. The horizontal movement of the type forms in the bed of the machine and the movement of the *tympan* and *frisket* were automated. This press was a prelude to Koenig's development of the stop-cylinder steam-powered press, which enabled much faster operation. In this design, the type form was on a flat bed which moved back and forth beneath a cylinder. During the printing phase, the cylinder rotated over the type, carrying the sheet to be printed. It stopped while the form moved from under the cylinder to be inked by rollers. While the cylinder was still, the pressman fed a fresh sheet of paper onto the cylinder.

John Walter II of *The Times* in London commissioned Koenig to build two double-cylinder steam-powered presses. These were capable of printing one thousand one hundred

This engraved illustration depicts the printing press of all-iron parts invented in England by Charles, third Earl of Stanhope.

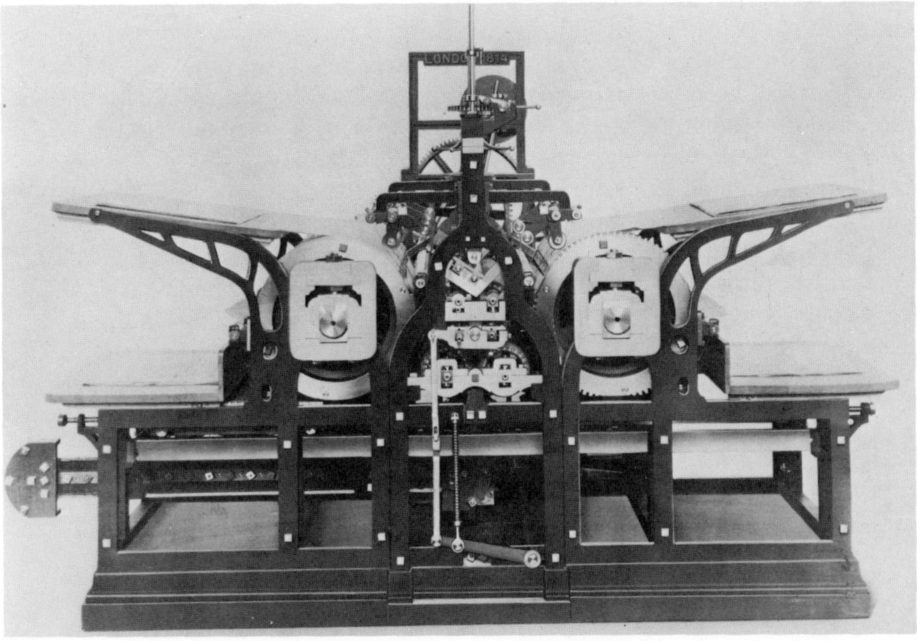

The first steam-powered cylinder press, 1814. Koenig's invention caused the speed of printing to skyrocket while the price dropped considerably. *Courtesy of* The Times *of London.*

impressions an hour on sheets of paper that were 90 centimeters (35 ½ inches) long and 56 centimeters (22 inches) wide. Fearing the sabotage which often destroyed new machinery when workers felt their jobs were endangered, Walter had the new presses moved to Printing House Square in absolute secrecy. The employees who had threatened Koenig and his invention were directed to wait for news from the continent on the fateful morning of 29 November 1814. At six o'clock, Walter entered the press room to announce that "*The Times* is already printed—by steam." That day's edition informed its readers that "Our Journal of this day presents to the public the practical result of the greatest improvement connected with printing since the discovery of the art itself. The reader of this paragraph now holds in his hand one of the many thousand impressions of *The Times* newspaper, which were taken off last night by a mechanical apparatus." An immediate savings resulted in the composing room, for *The Times* had been typesetting a duplicate of each edition so the two hand presses could print each page. Also, the news could be printed to reach subscribers several hours earlier.

In 1815, William Cowper obtained a patent for a printing press using curved stereotyped plates wrapped around a cylinder. This press achieved two thousand four hundred impressions per hour, and it could be used to print one thousand two hundred sheets on both sides. In 1827 *The Times* commissioned Cowper and his partner Ambrose Applegath to develop a four-cylinder steam-powered press using curved stereotyped plates made rapidly from *papier-mâché* molds. This press printed four thousand sheets per hour—on both sides.

All across Europe and North America, book and newspaper printers began to retire their hand presses and replace them with steam-powered ones. The Industrial Revolution had caught up with the printer; the Applegath and Cowper steam-powered multiple-cylinder press produced thirty-two impressions for every one printed on the Stanhope hand press. The cost of printing began to plunge downward as the size of editions soared upward. By the 1830s, printing began its incredible expansion as newspaper, book, and jobbing printers proliferated. While early printers served the relatively limited needs of the church and scholars, this conveyor of literacy now served all facets of society.

The value of high speed, steam-powered printing would have been limited without an economical and abundant source of paper. A young clerk in the Didot paper mill in France, Nicolas-Louis Robert, developed a prototype for a paper-making machine in 1798, but political turmoil in France prevented him from perfecting it. In 1801, English patent two thousand four hundred eighty-seven was granted to John Gamble for "an invention for making paper in single sheets without seam or joining from one to twelve feet and upwards wide, and from one to forty-five feet and upwards in length." In 1803, the first production paper machine was operative at Frogmore, England. This machine, which was similar to Robert's prototype, poured a suspension of fiber and water in a thin stream upon a vibrating wire-mesh conveyor belt. As long as the supply of pulp was maintained and the conveyor belt continued to move and shake, an unending sheet of paper could be manufactured. The rights were acquired by Henry and Sealy Fourdrinier, who invested their fortune financing and promoting what is called the Fourdrinier machine to this day. Ironically, although the Fourdrinier brothers perfected the paper-making machine and gave the world economical and abundant paper, they ruined themselves financially in the process. With machine-manufactured paper printed on high speed, steam-powered presses, a new era of knowledge and education dawned. There was a global spread of words and pictures, and the age of mass communications arrived.

11

Photography, the New Communications Tool

THE MAKING OF PICTORIAL IMAGES and the preparation of printing plates for reproducing pictorial images remained a handwork process until the invention of photography and its application to graphic production. A series of inventions through the course of the nineteenth century swept the production and reproduction of images forward into the machine age.

The concept behind the device used for making images by photochemical processes, the *camera obscura* (Latin for "dark room"), was known in the ancient world as early as the time of Aristotle in the fourth century B.C. A camera obscura is a darkened room or chamber with a small opening or lens in one side. Light rays passing through this aperture are projected onto the opposite side and form a picture of the bright objects outside. Artists have used the camera obscura as an aid to drawing for centuries. Around 1665, small, portable boxlike camera obscuras were developed.

When mirrors or additional lenses are incorporated into a camera obscura to project the image onto a plane surface so that it can be traced, it is called a *camera lucida* (Latin for "light chamber"). As the only additional element necessary to "fix" or make permanent the image projected into a camera lucida was a light sensitive material capable of capturing this image, it is not surprising that the early inventors of photography used their camera obscuras as the basis for their experiments.

The inventors of photography

Photography and graphic communications have been closely linked beginning with the first experiments to capture an image of nature with a camera. Joseph Niepce (1765–1833), the Frenchman who first produced a photographic image, began his experiments by seeking an automatic means for transferring drawings onto printing plates. As a lithographic printer of popular religious images, Niepce depended on his son, Isadore, to make transfer drawings onto lithographic stones. Isadore was drafted into the army, and the father did not have the drawing skills necessary to continue this work. Niepce was a restless experimenter, and he searched for a way to make plates other than by drawing. In 1822, Niepce coated a pewter sheet with a light-sensitive asphalt, called bitumen of Judae, which hardens when exposed to light. Then a drawing which had been oiled to make it transparent was contact printed to the pewter using sunlight. Niepce washed the pewter plate with lavender oil to remove the parts not hardened by light, then he etched it with acid to make an incised copy of the original. Niepce called his invention *heliogravure* ("sun engraving"). A photographically etched printing plate made from an engraving of Cardinal d'Amboise and subsequently used for printing marked the dawning of photogravure.

In 1826 Niepce had an exciting idea. By putting one of his pewter plates in the back of his camera obscura and pointing it out the window, could he not make a picture directly from nature? The earliest extant photograph is a pewter sheet that Niepce exposed all day. After removing it from the camera obscura that night and washing it with lavender oil, a hazy image of the sunlit buildings outside his workroom window was captured. Niepce continued his research with light-sensitive materials, including silver-coated copper. He became very guarded when a theatrical performer and painter who had participated in the invention of the diorama, Louis Jacques Daguerre (1799–1851), contacted him. Daguerre

As this early nineteenth-century portable camera obscura demonstrates, the optical principles for photography were well understood and used by artists as a drawing aid. *George Eastman House, Rochester, N.Y.*

Joseph Niepce, photolithographic print of Cardinal d'Ambroise, c. 1822. This routine portrait print is the first image printed from a plate that was created by the photochemical action of light, rather than by the human hand. *Gernsheim Collection, Humanities Research Center, The University of Texas at Austin.*

had been conducting similar research, and after Niepce warmed to him, the two men became friends and began to share ideas until Niepce died of a stroke in 1833.

Daguerre persevered, and on 7 January 1839 his perfected process was presented to the French Academy of Sciences. The members marveled at the clarity and minute detail of his *daguerreotype* prints and the incredible accuracy of the images. In his perfected process, a highly polished silver-plated copper sheet was sensitized by placing it, silver side down, over a container of iodine crystals. After the rising iodine vapor combined with the silver to produce light-sensitive silver iodide, the plate was placed in the camera and exposed to light coming through the lens, to produce a latent image. The visible image was formed by placing the exposed plate over a dish of heated mercury. After the mercury vapors formed an alloy with the exposed areas of silver, the unexposed silver iodide was removed and the image was fixed with a salt bath. The bare metal appeared black in areas where no light had struck it. The luminous, vibrant image was a bas-relief of mercury and silver compounds that varied in density in direct proportion to the amount of light that had struck the plate during exposure. In one giant leap, the technology of the Industrial Revolution had caught up with creating pictorial images. Cries of fraud were stilled after the French government acquired Daguerre's process and the Academy of Sciences made it available to the public. In one early year, a half million daguerreotypes were made in Paris.

Daguerreotypes had limitations, for each plate was a one-of-a-kind image of predetermined size, and the process required meticulous polishing, sensitizing, and development. The polished surface had a tendency to produce glare, and unless it was viewed at just the right angle, the image had a curious habit of reversing itself and appearing as a negative.

In parallel research, an Englishman, William Henry Fox Talbot (1800–1877), pioneered the

Joseph Niepce, the first photograph from nature, 1826. Looking out over the rear courtyard of the Niepce home, the light and shadow patterns formed by (from left to right) a wing of the house, a pear tree, the barn roof in front of the low bakehouse with its chimney, and another wing of the house are seen. *Gernsheim Collection, Humanities Research Center, The University of Texas at Austin.*

Louis Jacque Daguerre, *Paris Boulevard,* 1839. In this early daguerreotype, the wagons, carriages, and pedestrians were not recorded because the slow exposure could only record stationary objects. On the lower left-hand street corner, a man stopped to have his boots polished and became the first person ever to be photographed. *Bavarian National Museum, Munich.*

process that became the basis for both photography and the use of photomechanical platemaking in printing. While sketching in the Lake Como region of Italy in 1833, Talbot became frustrated with his lack of drawing ability and the difficulties of recording the beautiful fleeting image of the landscape. He thought "how charming it would be if it were possible to cause these natural images to imprint themselves durably, and remain fixed upon the paper." Talbot knew that silver nitrate was a light-sensitive chemical, and after returning that fall to his estate, Lacock Abbey, he began a series of experiments with paper treated with silver compounds. In his early explorations, he would float paper in a weak brine solution, let it dry, then treat it with a strong solution of silver nitrate to form an insoluble light-sensitive silver-chloride compound in the paper. When he held a piece of lace or a leaf tight against the paper with a pane of glass and exposed it in sunlight, the paper around the object would slowly darken. Washing this image with a salt solution or potassium iodide would fix it somewhat by making the unexposed silver compounds fairly insensitive to light.

Talbot called these images, made without a camera, *photogenic drawings;* today we call images made by manipulating the light striking photographic paper with objects *photograms.* This technique has been valuable to twentieth-century graphic designers in their quest for form. During the course of his 1835 experiments, Talbot combined his new techniques with a microscope to produce the first microphotographs. Plant cross-sections so small that they could not be studied with the naked eye were photographed. Talbot began to use his treated paper in the camera obscura to create minute photographic images which had light areas rendered dark and dark areas appearing light. Also, these images were mirror images of nature. About one of his early pictures he once wrote, "I believe this to be the first instance on record of a house having painted its own portrait."

William Henry Fox Talbot, *View toward Lecco, 6 October 1833.* Able only to capture the basic lines of the landscape in his camera obscura drawings, Talbot was inspired to begin research toward the invention of photography. *Royal Photographic Society, London.*

William Henry Fox Talbot, cameraless shadow picture of flowers, 1839. By sandwiching the flowers between his photographic paper and a sheet of glass and exposing the light-sensitive emulsion to sunlight, Talbot invented the *photogram. The Metropolitan Museum of Art, New York, Harris Brisbane Dick Fund, 1936.*

Having satisfied his initial scientific curiosity, Talbot let his research drop and turned to other interests for almost three years until the sudden international hullabaloo over Daguerre spurred him to action. Talbot rushed his work to London, and on 31 January 1839, three weeks after Daguerre stunned the world with his announcement, Talbot presented a hastily prepared report, "Some Account of the Art of Photogenic Drawing," to the Royal Society.

Upon learning about the research of Daguerre and Talbot, the eminent astronomer and chemist Sir John Herschel (1792–1871) tackled the problem. In addition to duplicating Talbot's results, he innovated the use of sodium thiosulfate to fix or make permanent the image by halting the action of light. On 1 February 1839, he shared this knowledge with Talbot. Both Daguerre and Talbot adopted this means of fixing the image in their processes. During February, Talbot solved the problem of the reversed image by contact printing his reverse images to another sheet of his sensitized paper in sunlight. Herschel named the reversed image a *negative* and called the contact print restoring the values of nature a *positive.* These terms and Hershel's later name for Talbot's invention, *photography* (from the Greek *photos graphos,* meaning "light drawing") have been adopted throughout the world.

Late in 1840 Talbot achieved a further breakthrough and was able to increase the light sensitivity of his paper, expose a latent image, then physically develop it after it was removed from the camera. He called his new process *calotype* (from the Greek *kalos typos,* meaning "beautiful impression"). Later he adopted the name *talbotype* at the suggestion of his friends. In 1844 Talbot began publishing his book, *The Pencil of Nature,* in installments for subscribers. There were twenty-four photographs mounted into each copy by hand. In the foreword, he expressed a desire to present "some of the beginnings of the new art." Each photograph was presented opposite a text explaining the picture and forecasting future uses of the new medium. As the first volume completely illustrated with photographs, *The Pencil of Nature* was a milestone in the history of the book.

The crystal clarity of daguerreotypes was superior to the softness of calotype images. To make a positive calotype print, a sheet of the light-sensitive paper was tightly sandwiched underneath the calotype negative and placed in bright sunlight.

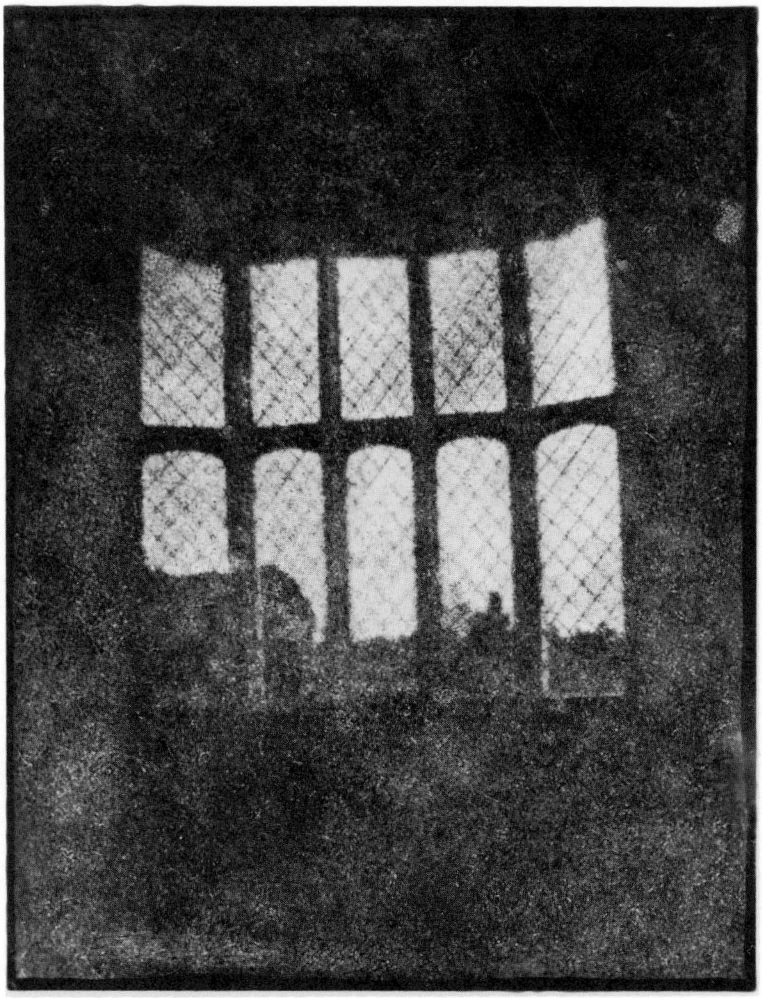

William Henry Fox Talbot, Print from the first photographic negative. The sun provided the light source to contact print the negative to another sheet of sensitized paper, producing this positive image of the sky and land outside the windows. *Courtesy, Science Museum, London.*

William Henry Fox Talbot, the first photographic negative, 1835. This image was made on Talbot's light-sensitive paper in the camera obscura, which pointed toward the leaded glass windows in a large room of his mansion, Lacock Abbey. *Courtesy, Science Museum, London.*

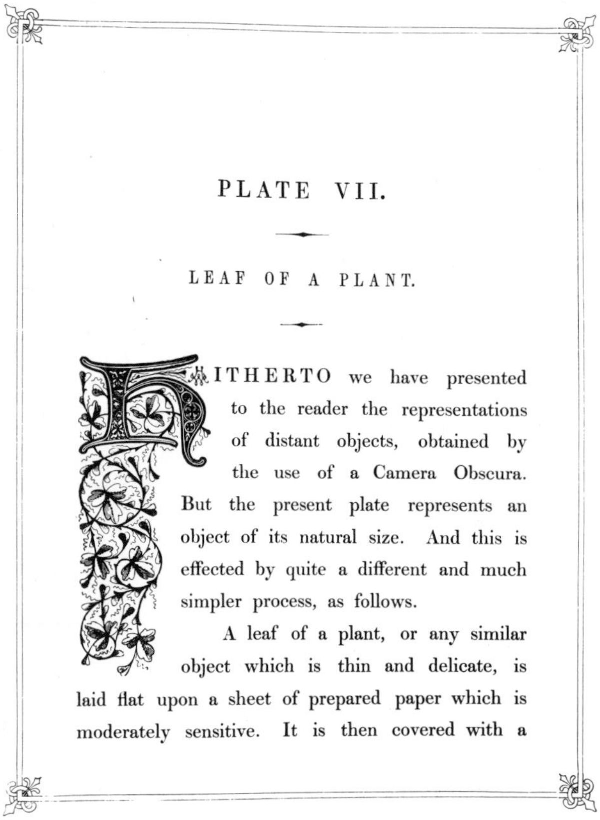

PLATE VII.

LEAF OF A PLANT.

HITHERTO we have presented to the reader the representations of distant objects, obtained by the use of a Camera Obscura. But the present plate represents an object of its natural size. And this is effected by quite a different and much simpler process, as follows.

A leaf of a plant, or any similar object which is thin and delicate, is laid flat upon a sheet of prepared paper which is moderately sensitive. It is then covered with a

Pages from Talbot's *The Pencil of Nature,* 1844. This first book to be illustrated entirely with photographs had original prints mounted onto the printed page. Plate VII is a photogram. (The use of Modern style type with ornate initials is typical of early Victorian book design.)

Because the sun's rays were diffused by the fibers of the paper negative, the positive print was slightly blurred. But because a negative could be exposed to other light-sensitive materials to make an unlimited number of prints and could later be enlarged, reduced, and used to make photo-process printing plates, Talbot's invention radically altered the course of both photography and graphic design. In photography's earliest decades, however, Daguerre's process was dominant because Talbot's potpourri of exclusive patents slowed the spread of his methods for a time.

While the softness of calotypes was not without character, having a textural quality similar to charcoal drawing, a search for a suitable vehicle to adhere light-sensitive material to glass for negatives of extreme detail and for positive lantern slides was underway. Many substances, including the slime left by snails, were explored before Abel Niepce de Saint Victor (1805–1870), nephew of Joseph Niepce, invented the albumen process in which a glass plate is coated with beaten egg white containing potassium/iodine compounds which could then be sensitized with silver nitrate.

This slow process was replaced by the wet collodiom process announced by the English sculptor Frederick Archer (1813–1857) in the March 1850 *Chemist.* By candlelight in a darkroom, a clear viscous liquid collodion—made of pyroxyline (guncotton) dissolved in alcohol and ether and sensitized with iodine compounds—is poured over a glass plate, immersed in a bath of silver nitrate, and exposed and developed in the camera while still wet. Archer's wet-plate collodion process was adopted by photographers throughout the world. Archer did not patent his process, and because it enabled much shorter exposure times than daguerreotypes and calotypes, it almost completely replaced them by the mid-1850s.

For economical portraiture, Archer and his friend P. W. Fry devised an interesting modification. Sir John Herschel had observed that when a negative is viewed by reflection against a black background it appeared to be a positive; by backing an underexposed negative with black velvet or paper, this phenomenon was used to produce the very popular *ambrotype* portraits. When the collodion material was coated on black lacquered metal, the portrait was called a *tintype.* Ambrotypes and tintypes were produced by the tens of

An ambrotype was a photographic negative whose positive-negative character was reversed by placing black cloth or paper behind it to make the clear areas of the negative black, while the emulsion's opaque surface reflected light to take on the quality of a dull, positive print. *George Eastman House, Rochester, N.Y.*

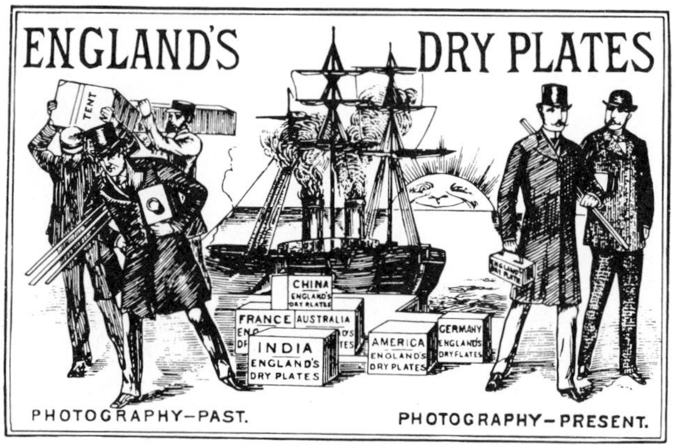

Advertisement for dry plates, c. 1884. The dry plate's important advantage—an end to the need to haul a clumsy portable darkroom and lab for preparing and processing plates—is graphically illustrated in this ad.

Advertisement for the Kodak camera, c. 1889. George Eastman's camera, so simple that "anyone can use it who can wind a watch," played a major role in making photography "every man's art form."

thousands, and citizens of modest means could have their image fixed for immortality for the first time in history.

The scope of photography was seriously limited by the need to prepare a wet plate immediately before making the exposure and develop it immediately afterwards. Innovations by many experimenters finally led to the commercial manufacture of gelatin emulsion dry plates by several firms in 1877. The three-decade heyday of the collodion wet plate rapidly yielded to the dry-plate method after 1880.

The application of photography to printing

Beginning in the 1840s, the rising level of wood engraving that started with Thomas Bewick fostered more frequent and effective use of images in editorial and advertising communications. Because wood-engraving blocks were type high and could be locked into a letterpress and printed with type, while copperplate and steel engraving or lithographs had to be printed as a separate press run, wood engraving dominated book, magazine, and newspaper illustration. However, the preparation of wood-engraved

Illustration of Moss' photographic department from *Scientific American,* 1877. When this major science journal reported on the rise of photoengraving, it revealed that, unknown to its readers, thousands of photoengravings had been used side by side with hand engravings during the 1870s with no recognizable differences. *Pioneer Moss Photoengraving, New York, N.Y.*

printing blocks was very costly, and numerous inventors and tinkerers continued the search begun by Niepce to find an economical and reliable photoengraving process for preparing printing plates. Inventors tended to keep their innovations top secret instead of patenting them. Once a patent became a matter of record, competitors would start looking for a loophole that would allow them to get around the inventor's legal rights. This has made identification of the first inventor of the many techniques difficult.

In 1871, John Calvin Moss of New York pioneered a commercially feasible photoengraving method for translating line artwork into metal letterpress plates. A negative of the original illustration was made on a copy camera suspended from the ceiling by a rope to prevent vibration. In a highly secret process, a negative of the original art was contact printed to a metal plate coated with a light-sensitive gelatin emulsion, then etched with acid. To preserve his secret method, only Mrs. Moss and two other trusted women employees were taught the process. After hand tooling for refinement, the metal plate was mounted on a type-high block of wood. The gradual implementation of photoengraving cut the cost and time required to produce printing blocks, and achieved greater fidelity to the artist's original image.

Close on the heels of Moss, the Frenchman Firmin Gillot perfected his *gillotage* method for the photographic transfer of planographic images into letterpress plates. In 1875, his son Charles opened Paris' first photorelief printing firm.

Before it was possible to print photographs, photography was used as a research tool in developing wood-engraved illustrations. The documentary reality of photography aided the illustrator in his studio in capturing current events. During the 1860s and 1870s, wood engravings drawn from photographs became prevalent in mass communications. An example is found in the photograph, "Freedmen on the Canal Bank in Richmond," attributed to Matthew Brady. Arriving in Richmond, Virginia, shortly after the evacuation and destruction by fire of most of the business district on 2 April 1865 when the Union forces broke through the Confederate defenses of the city, Brady turned his camera upon a group of former slaves who suddenly found themselves to be freedmen. A moment in time was preserved; a historical document to aid man in his understanding of his history was formed with the timeless immediacy of photography.

Attributed to Matthew Brady, photograph, *Freedmen on the Canal Bank at Richmond,* 1865. The photographer supplied the visual evidence needed by the illustrator to document an event. *Valentine Museum, Richmond, Virginia.*

John Macdonald, wood engraving, *Freedmen on the Canal Bank at Richmond.* The tonality of the photographer's image was reinvented in the visual syntax of wood-engraved line. *Valentine Museum, Richmond, Virginia.*

Stephen H. Horgan, experimental photoengraving, 1880. This first halftone printing plate to reproduce a photograph in a newspaper heralded the potential of photography in visual communications. *George Eastman House, Rochester, N.Y.*

A SCENE IN SHANTYTOWN, NEW YORK.
REPRODUCTION DIRECT FROM NATURE.

Since the means to reproduce this image was not yet available, *Scribner's* magazine turned to an illustrator to reinvent the image in the language of the wood engraving so that it could be reproduced. It was reprinted in *Scribner's Popular History of the United States* in 1876. This book was issued on the Centennial of the founding of the United States and drew heavily from editorial and illustrative material from the magazine.

The passionate search for a way to print photographs on printing presses continued. Experimentors, beginning with Talbot, realized that, if a photographic printing plate that could print the subtle nuances of tone found in a photograph was to be invented, a method to separate continuous tones into dots of varying sizes was necessary. Then, tones could be achieved in spite of the even ink application of the relief press. During the 1850s, Talbot experimented with gauze as a way to break up tones.

Many individuals worked on the problem and contributed to the evolution of this process. An 1857 French patent protected a single-direction line screen produced by scratching a series of horizontal lines in an opaque background. The solution came with a major breakthrough occurring on 4 March 1880, when the *New York Daily Graphic* printed the first reproduction of a photograph with a full tonal range in a newspaper. Entitled *A Scene in Shantytown,* it was printed from a crude *halftone screen* invented by Stephen H. Horgan. The screen broke the image into a series of minute dots whose varying sizes created tones. Values from pure white paper to solid black ink were simulated by the amount of ink printed in each area of an image.

A mechanically ruled pattern of horizontal and vertical lines on film was used by Frederick E. Ives to print halftones in 1885. The amount of light that could pass through each little square formed by the lines determined how big that dot would be. The sum of all these dots made an image that gave the illusion of continuous tones. In 1893 brothers Max and Louis Levy produced consistent commercial halftones using etched glass screens. A ruling machine was used to scribe parallel lines in an acid-resist coating on optically clear glass. After acid was used to etch the ruled lines into the glass, the indented lines were filled with an opaque material, and two sheets of this ruled glass were sandwiched, face to face, with one set of lines running horizontally and the other set running vertically. Superb halftone images could be made from the Levys' screens, and the era of photographic reproduction had arrived.

Printing full-color images was an important goal. The first photomechanical color illustrations were printed by the Paris magazine *L'Illustration* in the 1881 Christmas issue. Complicated and time-consuming, photomechanical color separation remained experimental until the end of the century. During the 1880s and '90s, photomechanical reproduction was in the air, and technology began to rapidly eliminate the "middle man." The highly skilled craftsmen who transferred artists' designs into handmade printing plates witnessed the death of their craft, forcing early retirements and occupational changes. Years of apprenticeship and professional practice were suddenly rendered obsolete by the click of a camera. Up to a week had been required to prepare a complex wood engraving; the photographic processes reduced the time from art to printing plate to one or two hours with greatly reduced costs.

Defining the medium

During the same decades that eager inventors were expanding the technical boundaries of the new photographic medium, the image-making potential was being explored by artists and adventurers. In photography's first years, just pointing the camera to capture an image was sufficiently magical to satisfy most needs. An early effort to introduce design concerns into photography began in May of 1843 when the Scottish painter David Octavius Hill (1802–1870) decided to immortalize the four hundred seventy-four ministers who withdrew their congregations from the Presbyterian Church and formed the Free Church of Scotland. Hill badly needed portraits as reference materials for this giant group portrait, so he teamed up with Edinburgh photographer Robert Adamson (1821–1848), who had been making calotypes for about a year. Using 40-second exposures, Hill posed their subjects in sunlight using all the compositional skill and figurative knowledge gained in two decades of portraiture. The resulting calotypes were lauded as superior to Rembrandt's paintings. Hill and Adamson created landscape photographs that echoed the visual order found in landscape paintings of the period. When a Newhaven minister began a campaign for improved fishing boat design to lessen job dangers for his parishioners, Hill and Adamson made photographs to document the problems. This was probably the first use of photography as visual communications to inform an audience.

David O. Hill and Robert Adamson, *Reverend Thomas H. Jones,* c. 1845. The painter's attention to lighting, characterization, placement of hands and head, and composition within the rectangle replaced the "mug-shot" sensibility of earlier photographers. *George Eastman House, Rochester, N.Y.*

When Julia Margaret Cameron (1815–1879) received a camera and the equipment for processing collodion plates as a forty-ninth-birthday present from her daughter and son-in-law, the note said, "It may amuse you, Mother, to photograph." From 1864 until 1874, this homely wife of a high British Civil Servant extended the artistic potential of photography through portraiture that recorded "faithfully the greatness of the inner man as well as the features of the outer man." Converting a chicken coop into a studio and her coal bin into a darkroom, Cameron produced portraits that have been hailed by scientists, writers, and artists as a major contribution to images expressing the human condition.

A lively contribution to photography was made by the Frenchman F. T. Nadar (1820–1910). This freelance writer looked for a more lucrative livelihood after marrying, in the early 1850s. He hesitated when a friend told him about a photography setup that was for sale, because he did not want to betray his artist friends. Portraits and other visual documentary matter provided artists with their principal income, and photography was already eroding it. Nadar's portraits of writers, actors, and artists have a direct and dignified simplicity and provide an invaluable historical record.

In 1858, Nadar made the first aerial photographs from a captive balloon. The two-story car of his 1863 gas balloon could hold forty-nine people and contained both a darkroom and a printing press for printing leaflets to be distributed from the air. On its third descent, the anchors failed to hold, and the balloon dragged Nadar, tangled in the ropes, over French farmland for several hours. He broke both legs, and rejected ballooning. Nadar pioneered artificial light photography by using gas illumination to photograph the ancient catacombs and extensive sewers under Paris. In 1886, the first photographic interview was published in *Le Journal Illustré.* A series of twenty-one photographs were made by Nadar's son Paul as Nadar interviewed the eminent hundred-year-old scientist Marie Eugene Chevreul. The elderly man's expressive gestures accompanied his answers to Nadar's questions.

The ability of photography to provide a historical record and define human history for forthcoming generations was dramatically proven by the prosperous New York studio photographer, Matthew Brady (c. 1823–1896). He spent his entire hundred-thousand-dollar fortune to send a corp of photographic teams to document every phase of the American Civil War. With assistants including Alexander Gardner (1821–1882) and Timothy O'Sullivan (1840–1882), Brady set out with a handwritten card from the President—"Pass Brady–A. Lincoln,"—a white duster, and a straw hat to record the war. From Brady's photography wagons, called "What-sit" by the Union troops, a great national trauma was etched forever in the collective memory by the thin unblinking photographic emulsion. Battlefield photographs joined artist's sketches as reference materials for wood-engraved magazine and newspaper illustrations.

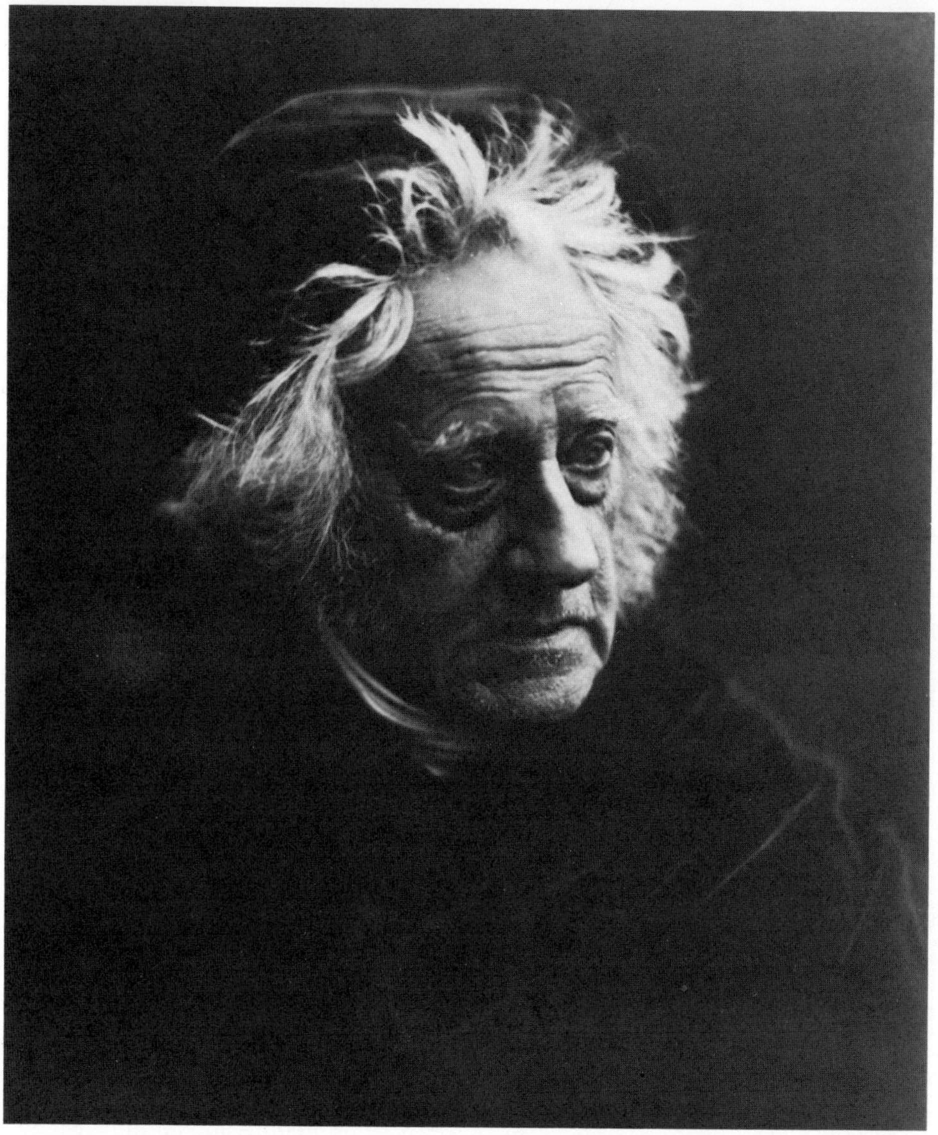

Julia Margaret Cameron, *Sir John Herschel,* 1867. Moving beyond descriptive imagery, Cameron's compelling psychological portraits revealed the inner being of her subjects. *George Eastman House, Rochester, N.Y.*

After the Civil War, photography became an important documentary and communications tool in the exploration of new territory and the opening of the American West. Photographers including Tim O'Sullivan were hired by the Federal government to accompany expeditions into the wild, unexplored western territories. From 1867 until 1869, O'Sullivan accompanied the Geological Exploration of the Fourth Parallel beginning in western Nevada. Returned to the East and translated into illustrations for reproduction, images of the West inspired the great migratory wanderlust that conquered all of North America.

One of the expedition photographers, Eadweard Muybridge (1830–1904), settled in San Francisco after photographing Yosemite and Alaska. An entrepreneur of the Central Pacific Railway, Leland Stanford, commissioned Muybridge to document whether or not a trotting horse lifted all four feet off the ground simultaneously; a twenty-five-thousand-dollar wager rested on the outcome. While working on the problem, Muybridge became interested in photographing a horse's stride at regular intervals. Success came in 1877 and 1878, when a battery of twenty-four cameras—facing an intense white background in the dazzling California sunlight—was equipped with rapid drop shutters that were slammed down by springs and rubber bands as a trotting horse broke threads attached to the shutters. The simultaneity of time and space were arrested on a graphic surface. The development of motion-picture photography, the kinetic medium of changing light passing through a series

Nadar, *Sarah Bernhardt*, 1859. The famous actress took Paris by storm and became a major subject for the emerging French poster. *George Eastman House, Rochester, N.Y.*

Paul Nadar, *Nadar Interviewing Chevreul*, 1886. The words spoken by the one-hundred-year-old chemist were recorded below each photograph to produce a visual-verbal record of the interview. *George Eastman House, Rochester, N.Y.*

Honoré Daumier (1808–1879), "Nadar elevates photography above the art of Lithography," c. 1870. The famous French cartoonist and social commentator lampooned Nadar's gas-balloon aerial photography. Note the number of photography signs in the Parisian streets below. *The Metropolitan Museum of Art, New York, Harris Brisbane Dick Fund, 1926.*

Matthew Brady, *Dunker Church and the Dead,* 1862. Made in the aftermath of the Battle of Antietam, this photograph shows how visual documentation took on a new level of authenticity with the arrival of photography. So fearsome was the fighting, with charges and countercharges through the lush Virginia land, that in one nearby cornfield "the green corn that grew upon it looked as if it had been struck by a storm of bloody hail." *Library of Congress, Washington, D.C.*

of still photographs joined by the human eye through the persistence of vision, was the logical extension of Muybridge's innovation.

Nineteenth-century inventors like Talbot, documentarists like Brady, and visual poets like Cameron had a significant collective impact upon graphic design. By the arrival of the twentieth century, photography was becoming an increasingly important tool in the reproduction of graphic design. New technologies radically alter existing ones, and both graphic techniques and illustration changed dramatically. Photography—the visual truth at 1/125 of a second—asserts an authority as document, unmatched by other image-making processes. As photomechanical reproduction replaced handmade plates, illustrators gained a new freedom of expression. Photography gradually pushed the illustrator away from factual document toward fantasy and fiction. The textural and tonal properties of the halftone image changed the visual appearance of the printed page.

Eadweard Muybridge, *The Horse in Motion,* 1878. Sequence photography indicated that graphic images could record time and space relationships, and the notion of moving images became a possibility. *George Eastman House, Rochester, N.Y.*

Timothy H. O'Sullivan, *Sand Dunes near Sand Springs, Nevada,* 1867. The virgin territory of the American West was documented by expedition photographers. O'Sullivan's photography wagon—isolated by the almost Oriental space of the sand dunes—becomes a symbol of these lonely journeys over vast distances. *George Eastman House, Rochester, N.Y.*

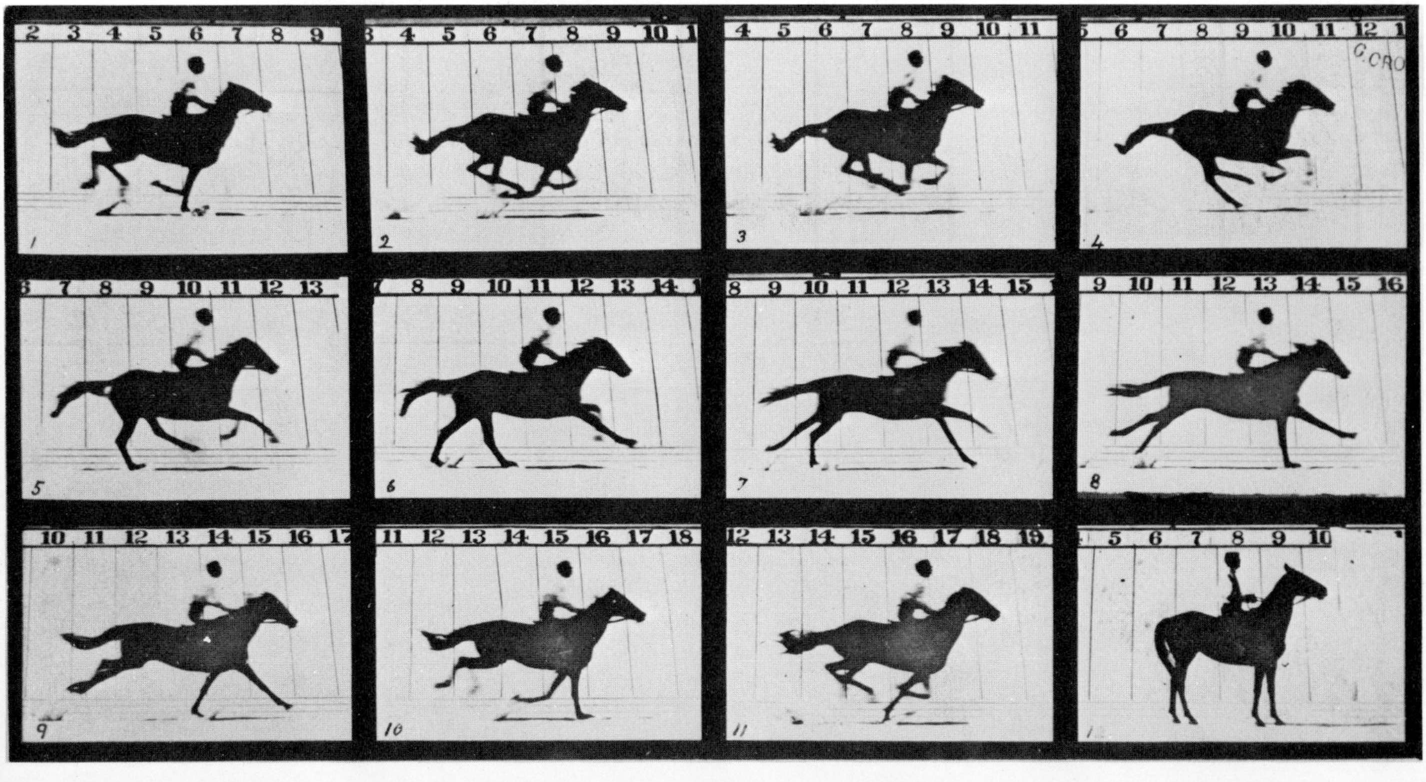

12

Popular Graphics of the Victorian Era

THE LONG REIGN OF VICTORIA (1819–1901), who became Queen of the United Kingdom of Great Britain and Ireland in 1837, spanned two-thirds of the nineteenth century and is called the Victorian Era. This was a time of strong moral and religious beliefs, proper social conventions, and optimism. "God's in his heaven, all's right with the world" was a popular motto. The Victorian period was an era in search of a style. Aesthetic confusion led to a number of often contradictory design styles and philosophies mixed together in a helter-skelter fashion. A taste for the Gothic, which suited the pious Victorians, was fostered by the English architect A. W. N. Pugin (1812–1852), who designed the ornamental details of the British House of Parliament. The first nineteenth-century designer to articulate a philosophy, Pugin defined design as a moral act which achieved the status of art through the designer's ideals and attitudes. Although he said that he looked to earlier periods—particularly Gothic—not for *style,* but for a *principle,* the net result of Pugin's influence was a wide mimicking of Gothic architecture, ornament, and letterforms.

Popular narrative and romantic painting of the Victorian Era was closely linked with the graphic pictorialism of chromolithographers including Louis Prang (1824–1909). Prang often commissioned art and held competitions to acquire subjects for use in his printed images. The English designer, author, and authority on color, Owen Jones (1809–1874), became a major design influence at mid-century. During his mid-twenties, Jones traveled to Spain and the Near East and made a systematic study of

Title page, 1844. This title page demonstrates the eclectic confusion of the Victorian era. Medieval letterforms, Baroque plant forms, and geometric interlaces are combined into a dense symmetrical design.

N.°
The
Pencil of Nature
by
H. Fox Talbot
F.R.S.
LONGMAN, BROWN, GREEN AND LONGMANS.
LONDON. 1844.

Islamic design. Jones introduced Moorish ornament to western design in his 1842–45 book, *Plans, Elevations, Sections, and Details of the Alhambra.* His main influence was through his widely studied 1856 book of large color plates, *The Grammar of Ornament.* This catalog of design possibilities from eastern and western cultures, "savage" tribes, and natural forms became the nineteenth-century designer's bible of ornament. The Victorian love of complexity and fussiness was expressed by "gingerbread" woodwork applied to domestic architecture, ornate extravagant embellishments on manufactured products from silverware to large furniture, and ornate borders and lettering in graphic design.

Sweetness and piety embraced traditional values of home, religion, and patriotism in graphic images and designs that captured and conveyed the values of an era. Sentimentality, nostalgia, and a canon of idealized beauty were expressed by images of children, maidens, puppies, and flowers. The production medium for this outpouring of Victorian popular graphics was *chromolithography,* an innovation of the Industrial Revolution that enabled thousands of copies of colorful naturalistic images to be printed.

Diecut and embossed Valentine, c. 1890. The intricacy of the design and its production demonstrates the high craftsmanship of the designer, diemaker, and pressman.

The development of lithography

Lithography (from the Greek, literally "stone printing") was invented by Aloys Senefelder (1771–1834) of Bavaria in 1796. An author, Senefelder was seeking a cheap way to print his own dramatic works and was experimenting with etched stones and metal reliefs. One day his mother called out a laundry list for him before he went out. Lacking a handy sheet of paper in his workroom, Senefelder wrote the list with a grease pencil on a flat printing stone. Suddenly, it dawned upon him that the stone could be etched away around the grease pencil writing and made into a printing plate. Senefelder began a series of experiments that culminated in the invention of lithographic printing. The image to be printed is neither raised, as in relief printing, nor incised, as in intaglio printing. Rather, it is formed on the flat plane of the printing surface.

Lithography is based on the simple, chemical principle that oil and water do not mix. An image is drawn on a flat stone surface with an oil-based crayon, pen, or pencil. Water is spread over the stone to moisten all areas except the oil-based image, which repels the water. Then an oil-based ink is rolled over the stone, adhering to the image but not to the wet areas of the stone. A sheet of paper is placed over the image and a printing press is used to transfer the inked image onto the paper. In the early 1800s, Senefelder began experimenting with multicolor lithography, and in his 1819 book he predicted that one day this process would be perfected to allow reproduction of paintings. German printers spearheaded the development of color lithography, and the French printer Godefroy Engelmann named the process *chromolithographie* in 1837. In the earliest chromolithographs, one plate, usually printed in black, established the image, and other plates put flat color or tints behind it.

The Boston school of chromolithography

American chromolithography began in Boston, and several outstanding practitioners there innovated a school of lithographic realism that achieved technical perfection and naturalistic convincing imagery of compelling realism. By 1840, English lithographers were producing color book illustrations. One of them, William Sharp (b. 1803), introduced chromolithography to America. Sharp

William Sharp, *Reverend F. W. P. Greenwood,* chromolithograph, 1840. Printed from two or perhaps three lithographic stones, the image is constructed much like a duotone. Apparently tan, flesh, and gray tones come together and combine to produce this image which launched chromolithography in America. *Smithsonian Institution, Washington, D.C.*

was a London painter and drawing teacher who opened a lithography shop in 1829. He emigrated to Boston in the late 1830s, intent upon establishing steady commissions as a portrait painter. In 1840, Sharp was retained by the Congregation of Kings Chapel to create the first chromolithograph in America. This was a portrait of their minister, the Reverend F.W.P. Greenwood. Dark gray, tan, and flesh-tone inks were printed from two or three stones. When these separate colors were overprinted, a muted naturalistic color range emerged. From these humble beginnings, American chromolithography was born. During the next quarter century, Sharp applied his subtle crayon drawing style to sheet music cover designs, portraits, floral plates, and book illustrations. Sharp's intent was to reproduce the painted image as closely as possible.

In 1846, the American inventor and mechanical genius Richard M. Hoe (1812–1886) perfected the rotary lithographic press, which was nicknamed the "lightning press" because it increased lithographic production sixfold relative to the flat-bed presses then in use. This innovation proved to be an important boost in lithography's competition with letterpress and released the floodgates of lithography. Economical color printing, ranging from art reproductions for middle-class parlors to advertising graphics of every description, poured from the presses in millions of impressions each year.

The next major innovator of chromolithography in Boston was John H. Bufford (d. 1870), a masterful draftsman whose crayon-style images achieved a stunning realism. After training in Boston and working in New York, Bufford returned to Boston in 1840. He became the first American lithographer not associated with Sharp to experiment with chromolithography beginning in 1843. Specializing in art prints, posters, covers, and book and magazine illustrations, Bufford often used five or more colors. The meticulous tonal drawing of his black stone always became the master plate. Working from an original master drawing for an edition such as the Swedish Song Quartet poster, for example, the precise tonal drawing was duplicated on a lithographic stone. Then, separate stones were prepared to print the flesh tones, reds, yellows, blues, and slate-gray background color. Browns, grays, and oranges were created when these five stones were overprinted in perfect registration. The color range of the original was separated in component parts, then reassembled in printing.

In 1864, Bufford's sons entered his firm as partners. The senior Bufford maintained artistic direction responsibilities until his death in 1870. The hallmark of Bufford designs was meticulous and convincing tonal drawing. A major graphic design concern of this firm was the integration of image and lettering into a unified design. In the Swedish Song Quartet poster, the arcs of the words move gracefully in the space above the carefully composed seven members of this musical group. The large capital letters in the name are placed adjacent to the heads of the three standing women to establish a visual relationship between word and image.

In their political campaign graphics, such as the poster for Grover Cleveland and Thomas A. Hendricks in the 1884 presidential campaign, a rich vocabulary of patriotic motifs including eagles, flags, banners, columned frames, and Liberty clothed in the flag were used to establish a patriotic tone. The Bufford firm folded in 1890. The two decades after the founders' death were a period of declining quality, cut-rate pricing, and emphasis on cheap novelties. The Cleveland and Hendricks poster is atypical of the later period; it recaptures both the style and the quality of John Bufford's finer work.

Lithography maintained a German heritage. Both the highly skilled craftsmen who prepared the stones for printing and the excellent Bavarian lithographic stones were exported from Germany to nations all around the world. The four decades from 1860 until 1900 were the heyday of chromolithography; it became the predominant printing medium. Popular graphics of the Victorian Era found its most prolific innovator in a German emigrant to America, Louis Prang, whose work and influence were international.

After mastering the complexities of his father's fabric-printing business, twenty-six-year-old Prang arrived in America in 1850 and settled in Boston. His knowledge of printing chemistry, color, business management, designing, engraving, and printing was of great value when he formed a chromolithography firm with Julius Mayer in 1856. Initially, Prang designed and prepared the stones, and Mayer did the printing on a single hand press. The popularity of Prang's colorful work provided the impetus for growth, and there were seven presses when Prang bought Mayer's share of the firm and named it L. Prang and Co. in 1860.

In addition to art reproductions and Civil War maps and scenes, Prang put vivid color into the lives of every citizen through the production of literally millions of album cards called *scrap*. Collecting these "beautiful art bits" was a major Victorian pastime, and Prang's wildflowers, butterflies, children, animals, and birds became the ultimate expression of the period's love for sweetness, nostalgia, and traditional values.

Prang followed closely in the tradition of Sharp and Bufford, for his meticulously drawn, naturalistic images were duplicated as precisely as possible. Prang has been called "The Father of the American Christmas Card" for his pioneering work in

J. H. Bufford's Sons, Lithography, *The Swedish Song Quartett,* poster, c. 1867. In this masterful example of the Boston style of chromolithographic realism, the near-photographic lithographic crayon drawing glows with the bright underprinted yellows and reds of the folk costumes.

S. S. Frizzall (artist) and J. H. Bufford's Sons (printers), poster for the Cleveland and Hendricks presidential campaign, 1884. The loose style of the flags and other symbolic imagery framing the candidates emphasizes the extreme realism of the portraits. *Library of Congress, Washington, D.C., Poster Collection.*

graphics for holiday celebrations. He had begun to produce Christmas images suitable for framing in the late 1860s, then he published a Christmas card for mailing in England in 1873. His first American Christmas card was designed the following year. Typical images of these first Christmas cards were Santa Claus, reindeer, and Christmas trees. A full line of designs followed, and Easter, birthday, Valentine, and New Years cards were produced yearly by L. Prang and Company during the early 1880s. Prang sometimes used as many as forty stones for one design. Part of the exceptional quality of his firm's work was the fact that Bufford's master black plate was dropped in favor of a slow building and heightening of the image through the use of many plates bearing subtle colors.

The album chromolithographs evolved into the advertising trade card in the 1870s. Prang's claim that he invented this graphic form does not hold up, for copperplate engravers of the eighteenth century produced large numbers of illustrated advertising cards. Certainly, however, Prang's distribution of twenty to thirty thousand business cards with floral designs at the 1873 Vienna International Exhibition helped to popularize the use of chromolithographic trade cards for advertising. Unlike many of his competitors who jumped into the field, Prang seldom identified his firm on advertising materials, making identification of L. Prang & Company trade cards difficult. Competition was fierce, and Prang was constantly developing new ideas to stay ahead of imitators who were undercutting his prices by using fewer stones for similar designs.

Prang made a lifelong contribution to art education after he started to teach his daughter art in 1856. Unable to find quality, nontoxic art materials for children, Prang began to manufacture and distribute watercolor sets and crayons. Finding a complete lack of competent educational materials for teaching industrial artists, fine artists, and children, Prang devoted tremendous energy to developing and publishing art-instruction books. On two occasions, Prang ventured into magazine publishing. *Prang's Chromo* was a popular art journal first published in 1868, and *Modern Art Quarterly,* published from 1893 until 1897, showed Prang's ability to continue to grow and explore new artistic possibilities in his old age.

Arthur W. Dow (1857–1922), *Modern Art* poster, c. 1890. The simplified, painterly quality of this poster, commissioned by Louis Prang to promote his 1890s art magazine, indicates how Prang's sensibilities were not locked into the Victorian era, but kept pace with developments in art. *Library of Congress, Washington, D.C., Poster Collection.*

The design language of chromolithography

From Boston, chromolithography quickly spread to other major cities, and by 1860 about sixty chromolithography firms employed eight hundred people. A phenomenal growth put chromolithographers in every American city, and by 1890 over eight thousand people were employed by seven hundred lithographic printing firms. The album page (overleaf) shows the diversity of chromolithographs produced by Prang and his competitors. Pasted around a nursery catalogue cover, clockwise from the top left, are: a thread company card with nine babies clustered behind the label; a diecut friendship card; an album card from one of Prang's bird series; a trade card for Hunt's remedy, which is advertised on the back as a cure to restore proper healthy action to the kidney, liver, and bowels when all else fails; an early Christmas card; lions from a pack of jungle animal album cards; two clowns performing acrobatics with a spool of the advertiser's thread; a diecut figure from a sheet of stickers; two patriotic little girls appearing on behalf of a cod liver oil tonic; and a beautifully printed image of a loving mother, daughter, and cat drenched in Victorian sweetness. Sold in bulk, this last card enabled the merchant or manufacturer to imprint an advertising message on the back.

Letterpress printers and admirers of fine typography and printing were appalled by the design language that emerged with the growth of lithography. Design was done on the artist's drawing board instead of the compositor's metal press bed. Without traditions and lacking the constraints of letterpress, chromolithograph designers could invent any letterform that suited their fancy and allow lettering to run in angles and arcs or flow right over images. In addition, the lithographer had an unlimited palette of bright vibrant color, the likes of which had never been seen in printed communications. It is little wonder that chromolithography began to drive letterpress posters from the market.

The vitality of this revolution in graphics grew from the talented artists who created original designs, frequently working in watercolor, and the highly skilled craftsmen who traced the original art onto the stones. These disciplined workers interpreted the design by making five, ten, twenty, or even more separate stones whose colors would come together in perfect registration, magically to create hundreds or even thousands of glowing duplicates of the original. The name of the lithography firm that produced the design, rather than the graphic artists or craftsmen who

This album page shows the range of graphic ephemera collected by Victorian children.

created it, appeared on the work. Therefore, the names of many innovators who defined the medium by bringing an original vision to chromolithography are lost to history. Among the firms around the nation which attained a high level of Victorian design, Schumacher and Ettlinger Lithography of New York, The Strobridge Litho. Company and the Krebs Lithographing Company in Cincinnati, and A. Hoen and Company of Baltimore and Richmond created engaging graphic designs.

Schumacher & Ettlinger, Lithographers, stock advertising trade card, undated. By printing these in great quantity, with a blank area for the client to imprint an advertising message, the lithographer was speculating that business firms would like the designs offered.

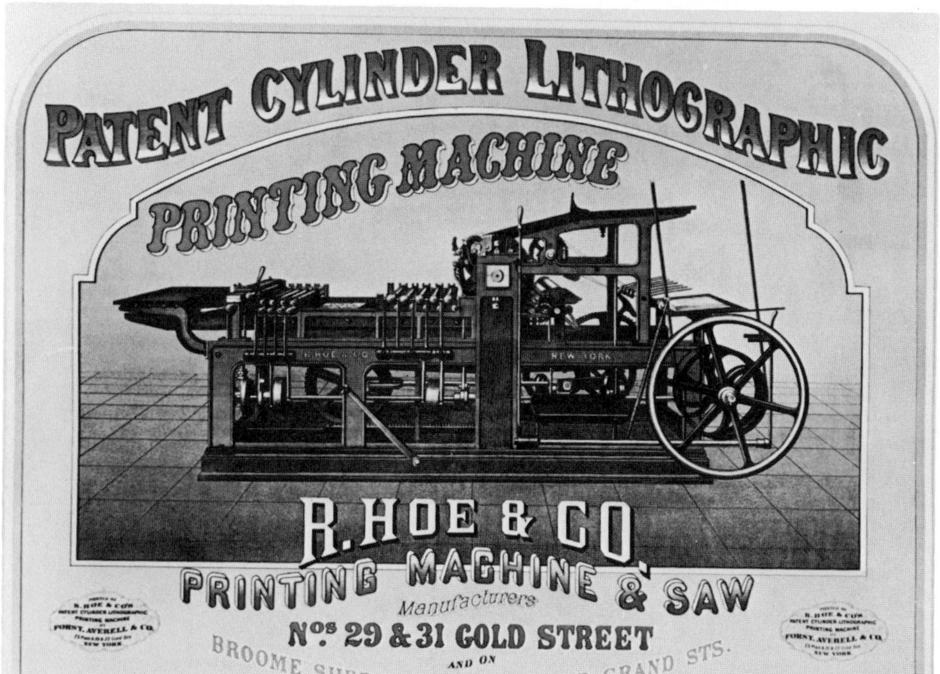

Forst, Averell & Co., poster for the Hoe printing press, 1870. In addition to publicizing the press that made mass editions of chromolithographs possible, this poster demonstrates new design possibilities: lines of lettering seem elastic and even overlap the picture, split founts and graduated color are used on lettering and in the illustration's background, and ruled borders are free to notch and curve at will.

Schumacher and Ettlinger's art staff was particularly skilled at combining imagery with Victorian ornament. The ''peacock'' trade card demonstrates the integration of illustration with decorative patterns not unlike material found in the *Grammar of Ornament.* The upper left-hand corner of this design is being peeled away to reveal a geometric pattern underneath. Trompe-l'oeil devices such as this delighted nineteenth-century graphic artists. In the 1888 premium booklet, *Our Navy,* commissioned by the Allen & Ginter Company, a montage effect is achieved through the use of complex ornaments and ribbons that become compositional devices and unify the layouts by tying disparate elements together.

In Cincinnati, the Strobridge Litho. Company became internationally famous for the quality of its chromos, particularly the large posters created for circuses and other theatrical traveling entertainments. The graphic clarity of designs by the Strobridge art department—which combined convincing pictorial images with simple and legible lettering, often placed on brightly colored shapes or bands across the top of the image—found great favor with producers of entertainment spectaculars. The Strobridge firm continued to produce chromolithographs, particularly for circuses, well into the twentieth century.

A high design standard was also maintained by the firm of Adolph Krebs (b. 1833). One of the finest designs by this firm is the poster for the 1883 Cincinnati Industrial Exposition. The Victorian passion for allegory inspired a mythic scene in front of the exhibition hall. An allegorical figure representing the ''Queen City,'' as Cincinnati loved to call herself, accepts machinery, agricultural products, and manufactured goods from symbolic figures representing the various states participating in the exhibition.

Schumacher & Ettlinger, Lithographers, cover and pages from *Our Navy* premium booklet, 1888. Contrasting sizes and perspectives combine with ornaments that move forward and backward in space to create complex illusions.

Label design, for the numerous and newly coined brand names identifying products, was an important use of chromolithography. A. Hoen of Baltimore and Richmond counted labels as one of its specialties. The rapidly growing tobacco industry provided A. Hoen's art staff with dozens of names like Indian Queen, Cora, Comet, Crusader, Black Swan, Golden Eagle, and Tiger Brand which needed graphic interpretation. Fantasy and the exotic were used to bring drama to ordinary products.

By the mid-1890s, the golden era of chromolithography was coming to a close. Changing public tastes and the development of photoengraving was making the use of chromolithography from hand-prepared stones obsolete. Perhaps the end of the chromolithographic era can be marked by the year 1897, when Louis Prang—mindful of the revolution that was occurring in tastes and technology—merged his firm with Clark Taber & Company, a printing firm specializing in the new photographic-process reproduction of artwork. By contrast, the famous art reproduction firm of Currier & Ives continued to print graphic expressions of outmoded Victorian sentiment by stone lithography and went bankrupt shortly after the turn of the century.

The Strobridge Litho. Company, *The Original Black Crook,* theatrical poster, c. 1881. The idealized young woman, floral motif, and curvilinear scroll suggest the Victorian roots from which Art Nouveau sprang a decade later.

Krebs Lithographing Company, poster for the Cincinnati Industrial Exposition, 1883. Glowing with a rich palette of yellow and golden tones, this poster expresses a buoyant optimism in industrial progress. *Library of Congress, Washington, D.C., Poster Collection.*

A. Hoen & Company, company masthead, undated. The sign on the Baltimore headquarters reveals that A. Hoen & Company were lithographers, engravers, and steam-power printers sharing space with a wood-engraving and job-printing firm, J. D. Ehlers & Company. *Smithsonian Institution, Washington, D.C.*

A. Hoen and Company, label for *Comet* Tobacco, 1880s. Nineteenth-century manufacturers loved to display their buildings, and the designer accommodated with a giant comet flaming above the client's facilities. *Courtesy of Viginia Historical Society, Richmond, VA.*

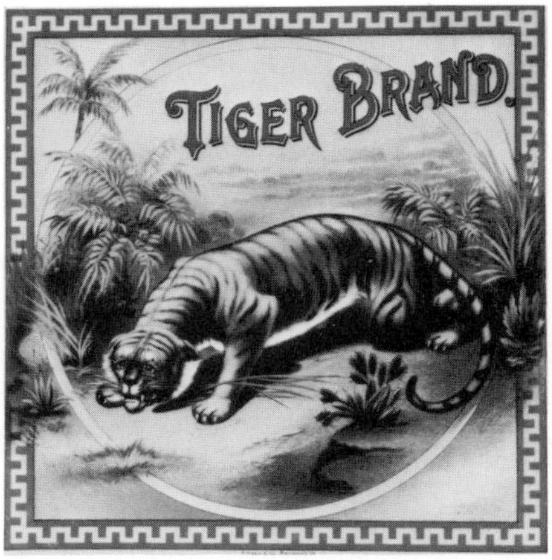

A. Hoen and Company, label for *Tiger Brand* tobacco, 1880s. A yellow circle in a red and yellow square border is dissolved by the illustration, which overlaps these borders. *Courtesy of Virginia Historical Society, Richmond, VA.*

A. Hoen and Company, label for *Cora* tobacco, 1880s. Intense red, yellow, and blue are used in the Victorian framing above and below the illustration. *Courtesy of Virginia Historical Society, Richmond, VA.*

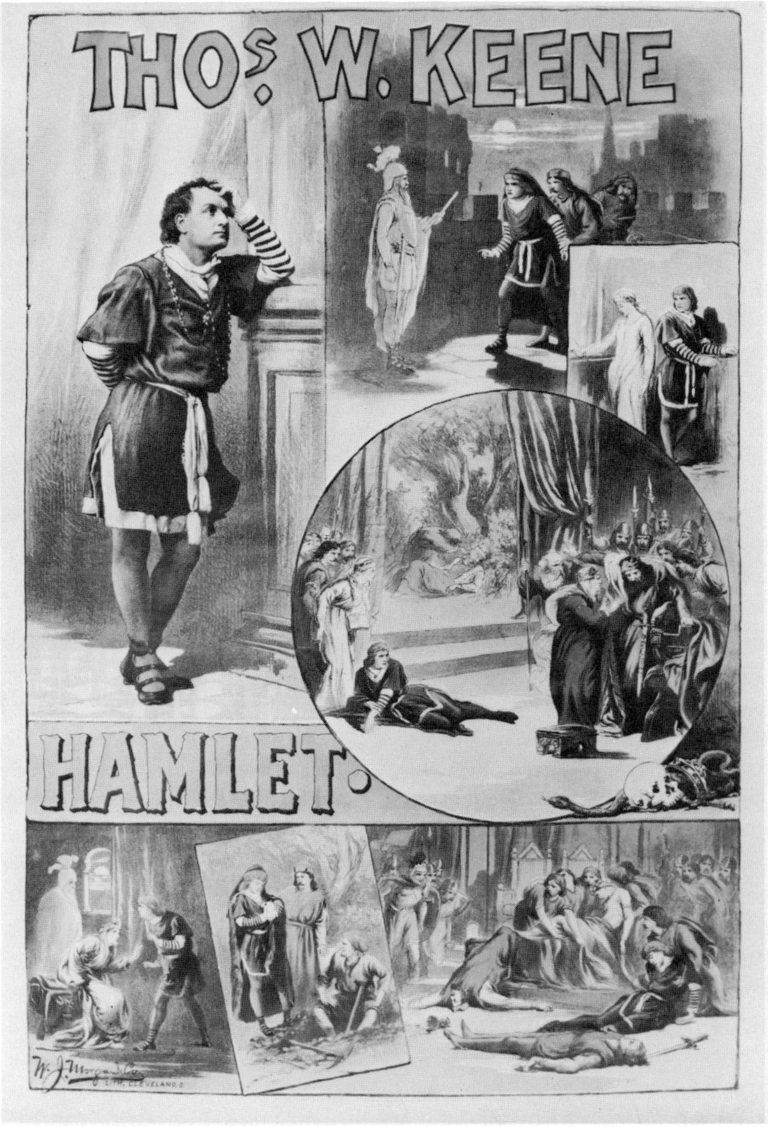

W. J. Morgan and Co., Cleveland, lithographic theater poster, 1884. Graphic designers developed a complex montage or collage effect by combining many images with shifting scale, perspective planes, and depth during the heyday of chromolithography. *Library of Congress, Washington, D.C., Poster Collection.*

The battle on the signboards

Poster for *L'Algerie,* c. 1845. In this poster for a book describing life in Algeria, the use of a large central figure dominating the space is typical of posters produced by Rouchon. *Bibliotheque Nationale, Paris.*

The ascendency of the letterpress poster and broadsheet was challenged in the middle of the nineteenth century by a more visual and pictorial poster. Lithography was the graphic medium allowing a more illustrative approach to public communication. During the late 1840s, posters from the French printing firm of Rouchon, who acted as an art director and adviser to book publishers, theatrical producers, and fashion houses, pioneered the graphic impact that could be achieved by simplification. Rouchon commissioned design from leading artists of his day, including Paul Baudry (1828–1886). A stencil process was used to print flat planes of color that combined to construct a stylized representational image. An unusual design quality of Rouchon posters was the unprecedented use of bright, often violently contrasting colors that caused these images seemingly to leap from the billboards in striking contrast to the more typical graphic designs of the period.

The letterpress printers responded to competition from the fluid and colorful lithographs, beginning to be pasted on the signboards by mid-century, with heroic and ingenious efforts to extend their medium. Witness, for example, the 344-centimeter (11-foot) long multicolored woodcut poster designed by Joseph Morse of New York for the Sands, Nathan and Company Circus in 1856. The enormous wooden blocks were printed in sections to be assembled by the poster hangers. In his work from the 1860s, James Reilley of New York would design ingenious ways to increase the pictorial impact of the letterpress poster. The 1866 poster for John O'Brien's Consolidated Six Shows is an excellent example of Reilley's imaginative design solutions.

Another approach was the "if you can't beat them join them" philosophy. In France, letterpress poster houses and lithographers collaborated. In these graphic "piggyback" designs, each medium did what it could do best, for colorful lithographic illustrations were pasted onto large woodtype posters. A masterpiece of the genre is the 1871 *Cirque D'Hiver* ("Winter Circus") poster of which only one copy survives. The Morris Pere et Fils printing firm commissioned a lithographer, Emile Levy, to illustrate an acrobatic dance act called *Les Papillons* (The Butterflies). The spectacular finale of this crowd-thrilling act featured two young female performers—one black and one white—being hurled through the air. Levy illustrated them as surreal butterfly women. An important designer in the development of lithographic posters in France was Jules Chéret (1836–1932), who carried the poster from his complex Victorian early style all the way into the twentieth century and became one of the major innovators of the Art Nouveau style.

In England, the 1871 poster for a play, *The Woman in White,* at the Olympic Theatre, is considered to be one of the first British visual posters.

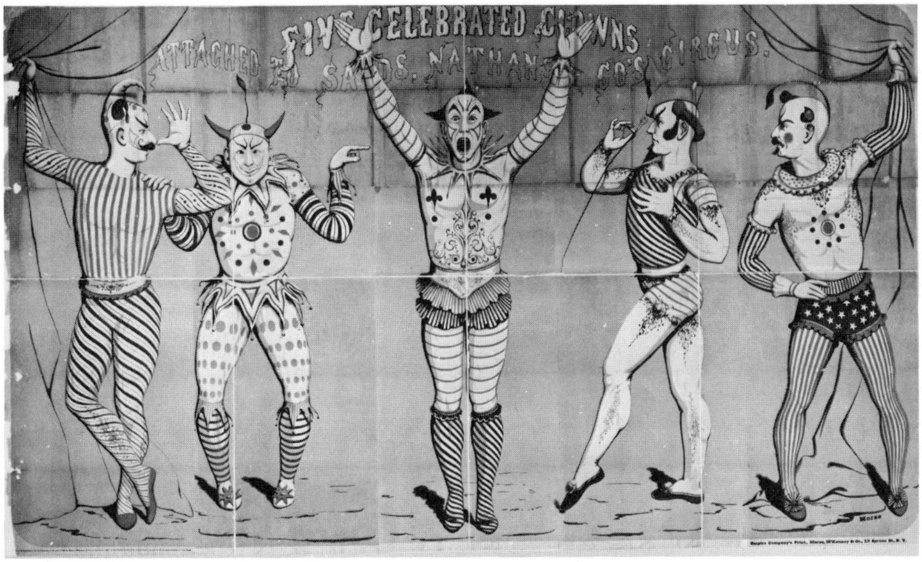

The wood engraving was executed by W. H. Hooper after the design of the painter-illustrator Frederick Walker (1840–1875). The only poster by Walker, it created a stir throughout London when the dramatic boldness of its dominant image appeared among the typographic messages jostling for the passerby's attention. This is a watershed design: it marked the beginning of the visual poster in England at the same time that it signaled the final glory of relief or letterpress posters. In the long run, the writing was on the wall for the magnificent wood-type posters that turned walls and fences into typographic collages throughout the first half of the nineteenth century.

Joseph Morse, colored woodcut poster, 1856. The heroic scale—262 by 344 centimeters (11 by $8\frac{1}{2}$ feet)—allowed the presentation of life-sized figures on the billboards. The pictorial images in this early circus poster dominate the headline, *Five Celebrated Clowns Attached to Sands, Nathan Co.'s Circus,* which is pushed into the background behind the clowns. *Library of Congress Washington, D.C., Poster Collection.*

Victorian graphics printed by chromolithography were the prototypes for a new visual language that would burst upon Europe during the last years of the century.

James Reilley (printer and engraver), poster for John O'Brien's Circus, 1866. Several wood engravings are pieced together to create an endless circus parade weaving down the poster.

Morris Père and Fils (typographic printers) and Emile Levy (lithographer), *Cirque D'Hiver,* poster, 1871. The soft pastel colors of the lithograph charmed the viewer and the bold wood type hammered the message home. *Musée Carnavalet, Paris.*

Frederick Walker, theater poster, 1871. This jumbo-sized wood engraving has a fluid, calligraphic quality in the drawing of the clothing in contrast to the rectangular forms of the door frame and lettering.

Randolph Caldecott, illustration from *Hey Diddle Diddle,* c. 1880. Oblivious to the outlandish elopement, Caldecott's dancing dinnerware moves to a driving musical rhythm.

Images for children

Before the Victorian era, western countries had a tendency to treat children as "little adults." The Victorians developed a more doting and tender attitude toward their offspring, and this was expressed through the development of *toy books,* colorful picture books for preschool children. Three English illustrators achieved good page design, excellent pictorial composition, and a restrained use of color in their work. Standards and an approach to children's graphics were established, and their influence still lingers.

Most of the earliest toy books were not dated, so just who pioneered this graphic form is not clear. It is generally acknowledged, however, that Walter Crane (1845–1915) was one of the earliest and the most influential designers of children's picture books. Apprenticed as a wood engraver as a teenager, Crane was twenty years old in 1865 when his *Railroad Alphabet* was published. A long series of his toy books broke with the traditions of printed material for children. Earlier graphics for children insisted on a didactic or moral purpose, and always either taught or preached to the young. Crane sought only to entertain. He was the first to be influenced by the Japanese woodblock and introduced it into western art. He had acquired some Japanese prints from a British sailor in the late 1860s and was inspired by the use of flat color and flowing contours. This unprecedented design quality in his work produced a tremendous volume of commissions to design tapestries, stained glass windows, wallpaper, and fabrics. Crane remained on the design scene well into the twentieth century. He played an important role in the Arts and Crafts Movement and had a significant impact upon design and art education.

While Crane entertained children, Randolph Caldecott (1846–1886) set forth to amuse them. As a bank clerk in his twenties, Caldecott developed a passion for drawing and took evening lessons in painting, sketching, and modeling. He learned anatomy by dissecting birds and animals. A steady stream of freelance assignments encouraged him to move to London and turn professional at the age of twenty-six. He possessed a devastating sense of the absurd, and his ability to slightly exaggerate movement and the facial expressions of both people and animals brings his work to life. Caldecott created a world where dishes and plates are personified, cats make music, children are at the center of society, and adults become servants. His humor and lively drawing became a major prototype for children's books and animated films.

Kate Greenaway's (1846–1901) expressions of the childhood experience captured the imagination of the Victorian era, although her work was static and humorless in comparison to Caldecott's. As a poet and illustrator, Greenaway created a modest small world of childhood happiness; as a book designer, she sometimes pushed her graceful sense of page layout to innovative levels. White space, silhouetting of images, and asymmetrical balance combine with a soft color sense to create pages of great charm.

The clothes Greenaway designed for her models had a major influence on children's fashion design. Walter Crane, however, complained that

Bowl away! bowl away!
Fast as you can;
He who can fastest bowl,
He is my man!
Up and down, round about,—
Don't let it fall;
Ten times, or twenty times,
Beat, beat them all!

Kate Greenaway, page from *Under the Window,* 1879. The use of white space and asymmetrical composition were design innovations without immediate precedent.

Kate Greenaway, page from *Under the Window,* 1879. Often Greenaway would leave out the background as a means of simplifying the page design and focusing on the figures.

Up you go, shuttlecocks, ever so high!
Why come you down again, shuttlecocks—why?
When you have got so far, why do you fall?
Where all are high, which is highest of all?
KG

Greenaway "overdid the big bonnet, and her little people are almost lost in their clothes." In the thousands of little pictures created by Greenaway, childhood became an idealized fantasy world. This led one child psychologist to denounce her for creating "a false and degenerate race of children in art," but the Victorian love of sentiment and idealization made Greenaway an internationally famous graphic artist whose books are still in print.

The rise of editorial and advertising design

Brothers James (1795–1869) and John (1797–1875) Harper, using modest savings and their father's offer to mortgage the family farm if necessary, established a New York printing firm in 1817. Their younger brothers Wesley (1801–1870) and Fletcher (1807–1877) joined the firm in 1823 and 1825, respectively. Eighteen-year-old Fletcher Harper was made the firm's editor when he became a partner, and the firm's own publishing ventures grew dramatically over the decades. By mid-century, Harper and Brothers had become the largest printing and publishing firm in the world. In the role of senior editor and manager of publishing activities, Fletcher Harper shaped graphic communications in America for a half century.

Inventive book design was not a concern for most publishing firms in America and Europe, including Harper and Brothers, during most of the nineteenth century. With the rapid expansion of the reading public, and the economies resulting from new technologies, publishers focused on large editions at modest prices. Modern-style fonts, usually second-rate derivatives of Bodoni and Didot designs, were composed in workaday page layouts.

During the 1840s, Harper and Brothers launched a monumental project that was destined to become the finest achievement of graphic design and book production to date in the young country's history. *Harper's Illuminated and New Pictorial Bible,* printed on presses especially designed and built for its production, contained sixteen hundred wood engravings from illustrations by Joseph A. Adams. Its publication in fifty-four installments of twenty-eight pages each was heralded by a carefully orchestrated advertising campaign. Each segment was handsewn and bound in heavy paper covers printed in two colors. During the preliminary preparations for this work, Adams invented an electrotyping process. This involved pressing the wood engraving into wax to make a mold, which was dusted with graphite to make it electroconductive, then an electrodeposit of metal (usually copper) was made in the mold. The resulting thin shell was backed with lead, and this harder printing surface enabled Harper to publish fifty thousand copies in installments. A hardbound edition of twenty-five thousand copies with handtooled gold gilding on morocco leather binding was bound and sold after the series of installments was completed. The format consisted of two columns of text with a central margin bearing annotations. Illustrations included large images the width of two columns contained in ornate Victorian frames and hundreds of spot illustrations dropped into the text. Every chapter opened with an illuminated initial.

The firm opened the era of the pictorial magazine in 1850 when the one-hundred-forty-four-page *Harper's New Monthly Magazine* began publication with serialized English fiction and numerous woodcut illustrations created for each issue by the art staff. The monthly magazine was joined by a weekly periodical that functioned as a newsmagazine, *Harper's Weekly,* in 1857. *Harper's Bazar* (sic) for women was founded in 1867, and the youth audience was addressed with *Harper's Young People* in 1879. *Harper's Weekly* billed itself as "a journal of civilization" and developed an elaborate division of shop labor for the rapid production of woodblocks for printing cartoons and graphic reportage based on drawings from artist/correspondents, including Thomas Nast (1840–1902).

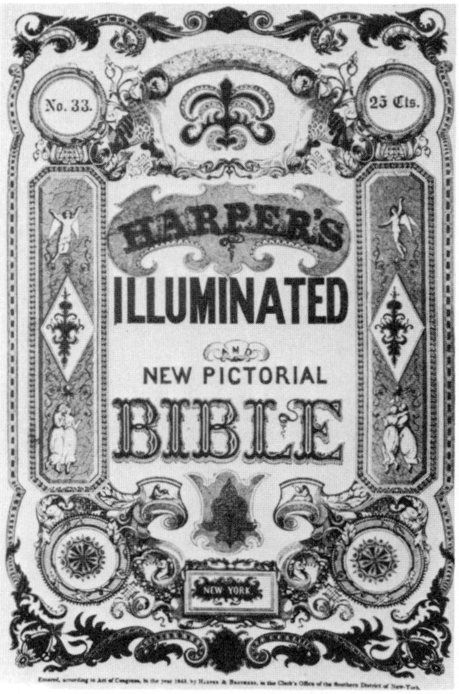

Joseph A. Adams, cover design, installment thirty-three of *Harper's Illuminated and New Pictorial Bible,* 1844. This two-color engraving achieves the pomp and grandeur of Victorian design. Extravagant floral elements soften the architectonic symmetrical structure.

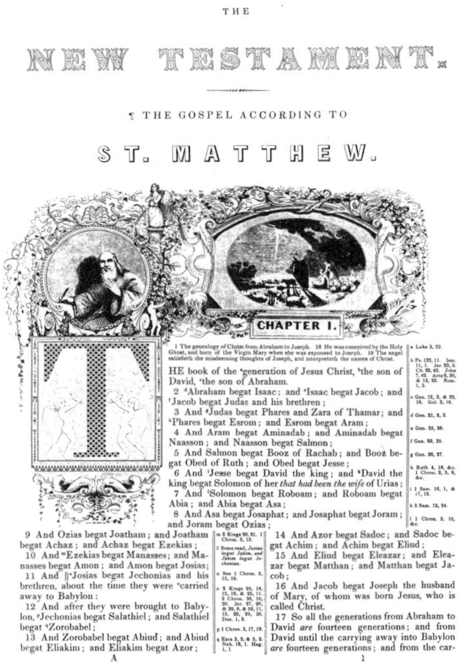
THE

NEW TESTAMENT.

THE GOSPEL ACCORDING TO

ST. MATTHEW.

CHAPTER I.

1 The genealogy of Christ from Abraham to Joseph. 18 He was conceived by the Holy Ghost, and born of the Virgin Mary when she was espoused to Joseph. 19 The angel satisfieth the misdeeming thoughts of Joseph, and interpreteth the names of Christ.

THE book of the generation of Jesus Christ, the son of David, the son of Abraham.
2 Abraham begat Isaac; and Isaac begat Jacob; and Jacob begat Judas and his brethren;
3 And Judas begat Phares and Zara of Thamar; and Phares begat Esrom; and Esrom begat Aram;
4 And Aram begat Aminadab; and Aminadab begat Naasson; and Naasson begat Salmon;
5 And Salmon begat Booz of Rachab; and Booz begat Obed of Ruth; and Obed begat Jesse;
6 And Jesse begat David the king; and David the king begat Solomon of her *that had been the wife* of Urias;
7 And Solomon begat Roboam; and Roboam begat Abia; and Abia begat Asa;
8 And Asa begat Josaphat; and Josaphat begat Joram; and Joram begat Ozias;
9 And Ozias begat Joatham; and Joatham begat Achaz; and Achaz begat Ezekias;
10 And Ezekias begat Manasses; and Manasses begat Amon; and Amon begat Josias;
11 And ‖Josias begat Jechonias and his brethren, about the time they were carried away to Babylon:
12 And after they were brought to Babylon, Jechonias begat Salathiel; and Salathiel begat Zorobabel;
13 And Zorobabel begat Abiud; and Abiud begat Eliakim; and Eliakim begat Azor;
14 And Azor begat Sadoc; and Sadoc begat Achim; and Achim begat Eliud;
15 And Eliud begat Eleazar; and Eleazar begat Matthan; and Matthan begat Jacob;
16 And Jacob begat Joseph the husband of Mary, of whom was born Jesus, who is called Christ.
17 So all the generations from Abraham to David *are* fourteen generations; and from David until the carrying away into Babylon *are* fourteen generations; and from the car-

A 1

Joseph A. Adams, page from *Harper's Illuminated and New Pictorial Bible,* 1846. In the first page of the Old and the New Testaments, the two-column format with a central margin for annotation was disrupted by centering the first few verses. *Library of Congress, Washington, D.C.*.

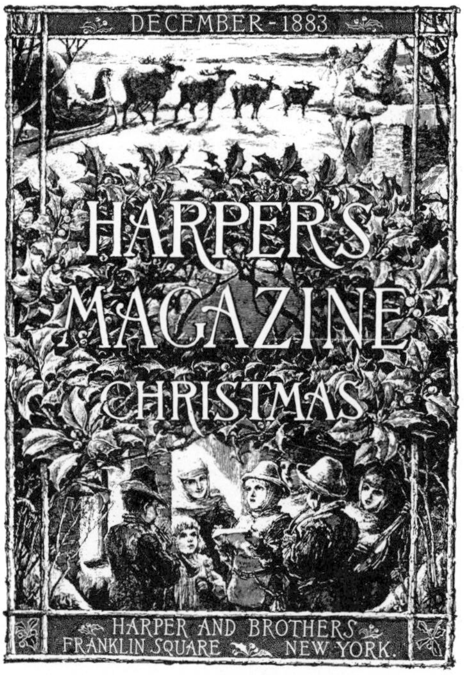

Richard G. Tietze, poster for *Harper's Magazine,* 1883. An impressionist quality is achieved in an illustration that is divided into three zones, with the middle holly area providing a background for the message while separating the images. *Library of Congress, Washington, D.C., Poster Collection.*

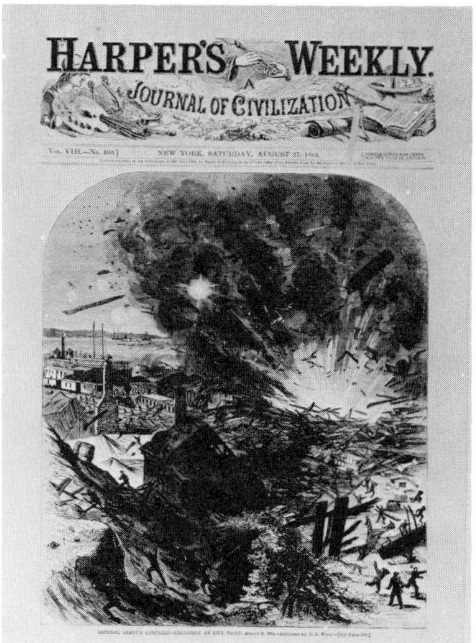

After A. H. Wald, cover for *Harper's Weekly,* 1864. Engraved after a sketch from a "visual journalist" in the field, this cover is a forerunner of the newsmagazine coverage of current events.

Nast, a precociously talented artist, had switched from public school to art school after the sixth grade and began his career as a four-dollar-per-week staff illustrator for *Leslie's Weekly* when he was fifteen years old. Fletcher Harper hired him when he was twenty-two to make battlefield sketches during the Civil War. The power of his work was such that President Abraham Lincoln called Nast "the best recruiting sergeant . . ." and General Ulysses S. Grant declared that Nast had done as much as anyone to bring the conflict to a close. Public response to Nast's work was a major factor in propelling the circulation from one hundred thousand to three hundred thousand copies per issue.

After the war, Nast remained with *Harper's Weekly* where he would draw his images directly on the woodblock in reverse for the craftsmen to cut. His deep social and political concerns led him to strip away detail and introduce symbols and labels for increased communicative effectiveness in his work. He has been called the "Father of American Political Cartooning." The graphic symbols Nast popularized and focused include a number of important images: Santa Claus, John Bull (as a symbol for England), the Democratic donkey, the Republican elephant, Uncle Sam, and Columbia (a symbolic female signifying democracy that became the prototype for the Statue of Liberty).

The potential of visual communications was demonstrated when Nast took on the governmental corruption of the political boss William Marcy Tweed, who controlled New York politics from infamous Tammany Hall. Tweed exclaimed that he did not care what the papers wrote, because voters couldn't read, but "they could sure see them damn pictures." Nast's relentless graphic attack culminated in an election day, double-page cartoon of the "Tammany tiger" loose in the Roman Coliseum, devouring liberty, while Tweed as the Roman emperor, surrounded by his elected officials, presided over the slaughter. The opposition won the election.

Thomas Nast, political cartoon from *Harper's Weekly,* 1872. As pressure against Tweed mounted, Nast depicted the political boss and his ring as "A Group of Vultures Waiting for the Storm to 'Blow Over.—Let Us *Prey*.'"

After Fletcher Harper died in 1877, a more conservative editorial staff took over the magazine, leading Nast to declare that "policy always strangles individuals." So effective were Nast's graphics for the Republican Party that President Theodore Roosevelt appointed him Consul General to Ecuador. Nast died of yellow fever six months after his arrival in that tropical country.

Charles Parsons became the art editor of Harper and Brothers in 1863, and his efforts contributed to a higher standard of pictorial images in the publications. Parsons had a superb eye for young talent, and the illustrators he brought along included a master of pen-and-ink drawing, Edwin Austin Abbey (1852–1911); the creator of beautiful young women and square-jawed men who established a canon of perfection in the mass media that endured for decades, Charles Dana Gibson (1867–1944); and a teenaged wood engraver who joined Harper's staff in 1876 and became loved for his pen-and-ink drawings of animals and rural American folk, Arthur B. Frost (1851–1928).

Among the many illustrators encouraged by Parsons, Howard Pyle (1835–1911) had the broadest influence. Pyle's own work and his remarkable gifts as a teacher made him the major force that launched the period called the "Golden Age of American Illustration." Spanning the decades from the 1890s until the 1940s, this period saw visual communications in America dominated by the illustrator. The art editors of magazines primarily selected the illustrators whose work would dominate a rather routine typographic format, and advertising layouts were often guides for the illustrator so that he would know how much room to

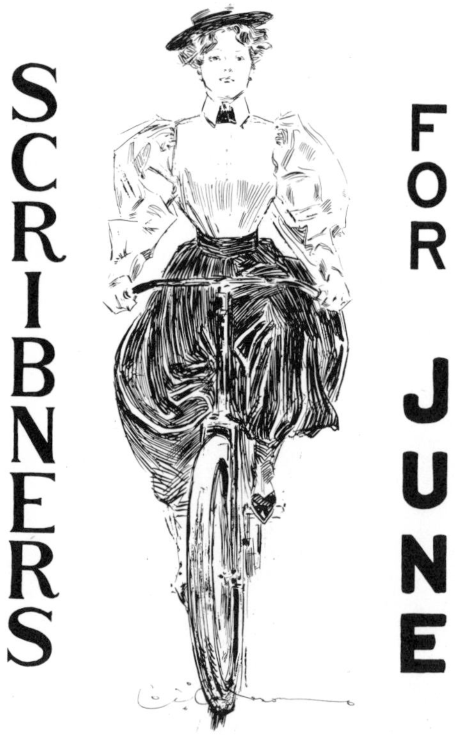

Charles Dana Gibson, poster for *Scribner's,* 1895. Although the exquisite beauty of the "Gibson Girls" was captured with extraordinary facility, economy, and control, Gibson was completely unconcerned with the design of type and image as a cohesive whole. In this poster, the printer added type to the left and the right of the figure in incompatible typefaces. *Library of Congress, Washington, D.C., Poster Collection.*

leave for the type, which was often *pub-set* (composed by the publication and locked into the letterpress chase to be printed with the plates for the illustration). During his long and illustrious career, Pyle published over three thousand three hundred illustrations and two hundred texts, ranging from simple children's fables to his monumental four-volume legend of King Arthur. The meticulous research, elaborate staging, and historical accuracy of Pyle's work inspired a younger generation of graphic artists who carried forward the tradition of realism in America. The impact of photography, the new communications tool, upon graphic illustration can be traced in Howard Pyle's career, which evolved with the new reproduction technologies. He was a surprising forty-one years old when he received his first illustration commission from *Scribner's Monthly* in 1876. Like nearly all magazine and newspaper illustration of the time, it was an ink line drawing which was turned over to a wood engraver to be cut into a relief block which could be locked in place with type and printed by letterpress.

A decade later, in 1887, Pyle was fifty-one years old when he received his first commission for a tonal illustration. The new photomechanical halftone process, discussed in the preceding chapter, made possible the conversion of the blacks, whites, and grays in Pyle's oil and gouache painting into minute black dots that were blended by the human eye to produce the illusion of continuous tone. In addition to the impact upon engravers, illustrators were faced with the need to either shift to tonal, painted illustrations instead of pen-and-ink art or face a dwindling market for their work.

Another advance occurred for Pyle in 1893, when the fifty-eight-year-old illustrator created his first two-color illustration. Pink flesh tones and browns were mixed from the limited palette of black, white, and red paint. The image was printed from two halftone plates. One impression was in black ink, and the other—shot with a filter—separated the red tones from the blacks and grays. This plate was inked with a red ink closely matched to Pyle's red paint. Four years later, in 1897, Pyle had passed his sixty-second birthday when he had a first opportunity to apply his spectacular sense of color to a full-color illustration assignment. This image was printed by the developing four-color process system. All of Pyle's full-color illustrations were painted during the fifteen years from 1897 until his death at age seventy-seven in 1911.

Harper's leading competitors in the magazine field were the *Century* magazine (1881–1930) and *Scribner's Monthly* (1887–1939). All three of these major periodicals were printed at the printing firm of Theodore Low De Vinne (1824–1914). De Vinne and his staff gave a quiet, dignified, but rather dry layout to all three. In the *Century,* for example, text was set in two columns of ten-point type, and the wood engravings were dropped in adjacent to the copy discussed. Article titles were merely set in twelve point, all capitals, and centered above the beginning page of the article. De Vinne was dissatisfied with the thin modern typefaces used in this magazine, so he commissioned type designer L. B. Benton to cut a blacker, more readable face that is slightly extended with thicker thin strokes and short slab serifs. Called Century, this unusually legible style is still widely used today.

The rising tide of literacy, plunging production costs, and the growth of advertising revenues pushed the number of newspapers and magazines published in the United States from eight hundred to five thousand between 1830 and 1860. During the 1870s, magazines were being used extensively for general advertising. This additional revenue lowered prices for the readers, which caused even greater circulation increases. Closely bound to the growth of magazines was the development of advertising agencies. In 1841, Volney Palmer of Philadelphia opened what is considered to be the first advertising agency. He sold space for publishers much as a travel agent sells tickets for airlines today, and received a 25 percent commission on his sales. The advertising agency as a consulting firm with an array of specialized skills was pioneered by another Philadelphia advertising agent, N. W. Ayer and Son. In 1875, Ayer gave his clients an open contract, which allowed them access to the real rates publications were charging. Then, the agency received an additional percentage for placing the advertisements. In the 1880s, Ayer established the idea that an advertising agency should provide services clients were not equipped to perform and publishers did not offer, when his firm began to write copy for clients. By the end of the century, Ayer was well on the way toward offering a complete spectrum of services: copywriting, art direction, production, and media selection.

Many of the conventions of persuasive selling were developed during

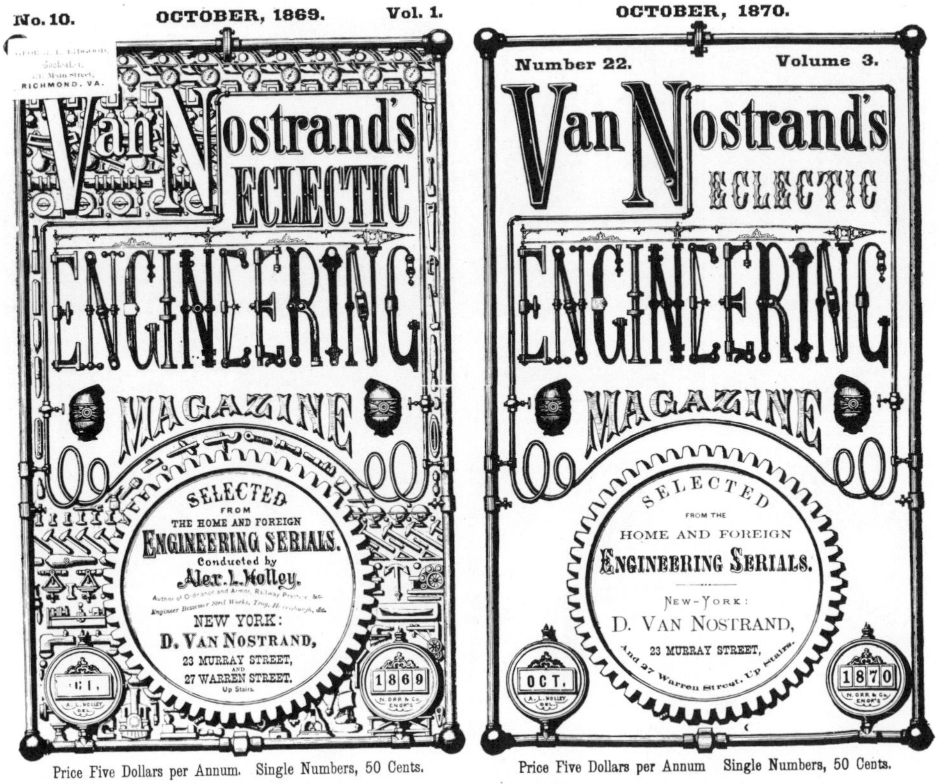

No. 10.
OCTOBER, 1869.
Vol. 1.
Van Nostrand's
Eclectic
Engineering
Magazine
Selected from the Home and Foreign
Engineering Serials.
Conducted by
Alex. L. Holley.
New York:
D. Van Nostrand,
23 Murray Street,
and
27 Warren Street.
Up Stairs.
1869
Price Five Dollars per Annum. Single Numbers, 50 Cents.
OCTOBER, 1870.
Number 22.
Volume 3.
Van Nostrand's
Eclectic
Engineering
Magazine
Selected from the
Home and Foreign
Engineering Serials.
New-York:
D. Van Nostrand,
23 Murray Street,
And 27 Warren Street, Up Stairs.
OCT.
1870
Price Five Dollars per Annum Single Numbers, 50 Cents.

Covers for *Van Nostrand's Eclectic Engineering,* 1869–70. Apparently, a design decision to radically simplify cover format was made between October 1869 and October 1870.

Trademark for Moss Engraving Company, 1872. Graphic complexity and slogans often embellished Victorian trademarks.

the last two decades of the nineteenth century. The page of advertisements from the English and American magazines of the period demonstrate some of these techniques. An aura of glamour and adventure is projected by the exotic hunters in the International Fur Store advertisement. An appeal to self improvement and idealized beauty is conveyed by the ad for Sozodont, which will turn one's teeth into "pearls in the mouth." A demonstration of product excellence in the Brook's Soap ad shows how this product turns pots and pans into bright reflecting mirrors. For Cadbury's Cocoa, the celebrity testimonial is pioneered by none other than Queen Victoria herself enjoying the product in her royal train coach. The design of this page demonstrates the makeup of Victorian advertising pages; printing plates for the various ads are locked together with little concern for a total design. By the end of the century, magazines, including *Cosmopolitan* and *McClure's,* were carrying over a hundred pages of advertisements in every monthly issue. Frequently an engraved illustration would have type set above or below it, and often the prevalent practice of chromolithography to superimpose lettering on top of a pictorial image was adopted.

On 20 June 1877 a new graphic format was launched by the Pictorial Printing Company of Chicago, when the first issue of *The Nickel Library* hit newsstands throughout America. Called nickel novels or story papers, these weekly publications hired graphic artists to design and illustrate action-filled covers interpreting tales of Civil War, Indians, and the western frontier. The typical format was sixteen to thirty-two pages, set with two to four type columns per page. The 20.3-by-30.5-centimeter (8-by-12-inch) page size allowed the artists to create strong visual impact on the news dealer's shelf.

Typical of the many imitators was publisher Frank Tousey's (1876–1902) *Wide Awake Library,* which was eagerly purchased by thousands of young people who followed the weekly adventures written by authors such as Luis P. Senarens (1865–1939). Writing under the pseudonymn "Noname," Senarens drew upon his considerable scientific knowledge to make believable the astounding inventions of young inventor Frank Reade, Jr., whose electric horses, helicopters, airships, and other inventions accurately forecast future technologies. The names of the anonymous artists who created the accompanying graphics are lost to history.

Advertisements, 1880–90. This potpourri of advertisements demonstrates the range of Victorian advertising from small typographic to full-page ads with a dominant pictorial image.

Advertising page from *Century* magazine, 1882. The lettering of *Century*'s heading and the large, top advertisement are excellent examples of the Victorian passion for variety and intricacy in graphic design.

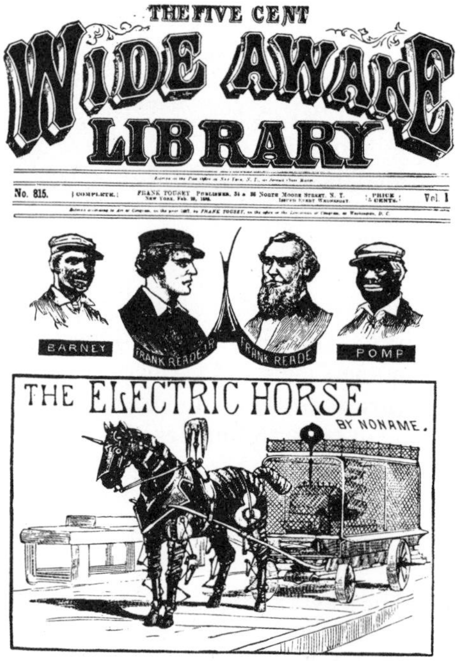

Cover for Frank Tousey's *Wide Awake Library,* 1888. Speculating visually about the form of the new, nineteenth-century graphic artists often wrapped the future in the forms of the past.

The mechanization of typography

Setting type by hand, then redistributing it into the job case remained a slow and costly process. By the middle of the nineteenth century, presses could produce twenty-five thousand copies per hour, but each letter in every word in every book, newspaper, and magazine had to be set by hand. While scores of experimenters attempted to invent the motor car and flying machine, dozens more worked to perfect a machine to compose type. The first patent for a composing machine was registered in 1825. By the time Ottmar Mergenthaler (1854–1899) perfected his *Linotype machine* in 1886, about three hundred machines had been patented in Europe and America, and several thousand patent claims were on file. Millions of dollars were invested in the search for automatic typesetting. Before the Linotype was invented, the high cost and slow pace of composition limited even the largest daily newspapers to eight pages, and books remained fairly precious. Mergenthaler was a German immigrant working in a Baltimore machine shop, who struggled for a decade to perfect his typesetter. On 3 July 1886, the thirty-two-year-old inventor demonstrated his keyboard-operated machine in the office of the *New York Tribune*. Whitelaw Reid, the editor of the *Tribune,* reportedly exclaimed "Ottmar, you've done it! A line o' type." The new machine received its name from this enthusiastic reaction.

Ottmar Mergenthaler demonstrates the Blower Linotype, the first line-casting keyboard typesetter, to editor Whitelaw Reid on 3 July 1886. *Courtesy of the Merganthaler Linotype Company, Melville, N.Y.*

Many earlier inventors had tried to make a machine that would compose metal type mechanically by automating the traditional typecase. Others had tried a typewriter affair that pressed letters into a papier-mâché mold or attempted to transfer a lithographic image into a metal relief. Mergenthaler's brilliant breakthrough involved the use of small brass matrices with female impressions of the letterforms, numbers, and symbols. Ninety typewriter-like keys controlled vertical tubes that were filled with these matrices. Each time the operator pressed a key, a matrix for that character was released. It slid down a chute and was automatically lined up with the other characters in that line. Melted lead was poured into the line of matrices to cast a slug bearing the raised line of type.

In 1880, the New York newspapers offered over one half million dollars in prizes to any inventor who could create a machine that would reduce the compositor's time by 25 to 30 percent; Mergenthaler's Linotype machine could do the work of seven or eight hand compositors! The rapid deployment of the Linotype replaced thousands of highly skilled hand typesetters, and strikes and violence threatened many installations. But the new technology caused an unprecedented explosion of graphic material, creating thousands of new jobs. The three-cent price of an 1880s newspaper, which was too steep for the average citizen, plunged to one or two pennies, while the number of pages multiplied and circulation soared. Book publishing expanded rapidly, with fiction, biographies, technical books, and histories joining the educational texts and literary classics that were being published. The Linotype aided in a revolution in periodicals, and illustrated weeklies including *The Saturday Evening Post* and *Collier's* reached audiences of millions by the turn of the century. Another American, Tolbert Lanston (1844–1913), invented the *Monotype machine,* which cast single characters from hot metal, in 1887. It was a decade before the Monotype was efficient enough to be put into production.

Handset metal type, which was now called *cold type* in contrast to the machine-set *hot type,* faced a dwindling market. Most text type was machine set, and display type was hand set. Devastating price wars and cutthroat competition featured discounts of 50 percent plus another 10 percent for cash payment. Consortiums, such as the 1892 merger of fourteen foundries into the American Type Founders Company, were formed in an effort to stabilize the industry. Design piracy was rampant. Foundries would commission new typeface designs, but competitors would immediately electroplate the new designs, then cast and sell types from the counterfeit matrices.

The popular graphics of the Victorian Era stemmed, not from a design philosophy or artistic convictions, but from the prevalent attitudes and sensibilities of the period. Undaunted by the revolutionary design ideas that developed during the 1890s or by the decline of chromolithography, many conventions of Victorian design continued into the early years of the twentieth century, particularly in commercial promotion.

The Model 5 Linotype became the workhorse of printing with keyboards and matrices in over a thousand languages. *Courtesy of the Mergenthaler Linotype Company, Melville, N.Y.*

13

The Arts and Crafts Movement

As the nineteenth century wore on, the quality of book design and production became a casualty of the Industrial Revolution, with a few notable exceptions, such as the books by the English publisher William Pickering (1796–1854). At age fourteen Pickering apprenticed to a London bookseller and publisher, and at age twenty-four he established his own bookshop, specializing in old and rare volumes. Shortly thereafter this young man, with a deep love of books and outstanding scholarship, began his publishing program. Pickering played an important role in the separation of graphic design from printing production, for he maintained control over the format design, type selection, illustrations, and all other visual considerations. The actual production of his books was commissioned from printers, who worked under Pickering's close supervision. A cordial working relationship between publisher/designer and printer was established by Pickering and Charles Whittingham (1795–1876) of the Chiswick Press. Whittingham's excellent craftsmanship complemented Pickering's demands for quality very nicely. In books of prose and poetry, such as Pickering's fifty-three-volume series of "Aldine Poets," his design sense moved toward classic simplicity. In collaboration with Whittingham, Pickering revived Caslon types, which he loved for their straightforward legibility. Pickering's liturgical books, including the 1844 *Book of Common Prayer,* are some of the finest examples of the revival of Gothic forms that infested the nineteenth century.

In spite of the efforts of Pickering and others, the decline in book design was not checked until late in the century, when there began a renaissance of book design, as a limited-edition art object, and of commercial production. This revival was largely a by-product of the Arts and Crafts Movement, which flourished in England during the last decades of the nineteenth century as a reaction against the social, moral, and artistic confusion of the Industrial Revolution. Design and a return to handicraft were advocated, and the "cheap and nasty" mass-produced goods of the Victorian era were abhorred. The leader of the English Arts and Crafts Movement, William Morris (1834–1896), called for a fitness of purpose, truth to the nature of materials and methods of production, and individual expression by both designer and worker.

The writer and artist, John Ruskin (1819–1900), inspired the philosophy of this movement. Asking how society could "consciously order the lives of its members so as to maintain the largest number of noble and happy human beings," Ruskin rejected the mercantile economy and pointed toward the union of art and labor in service to society, as exemplified in the design and construction of the medieval Gothic cathedral. Ruskin called this the social order which Europe must "regain for her children." A process of separating art and society had, according to Ruskin, begun after the Renaissance. Industrialization and technology caused the severing of art from society to reach a critical stage, isolating the artist. The consequences were eclecticism of historical models, a decline in creativity, and design by engineers without aesthetic concern. Ruskin first advanced the notion that beautiful things were valuable and useful precisely because they were beautiful. From the philosophy of art, Ruskin became concerned for social justice, advocating improved housing for industrial workers, a national education system, and retirement benefits for the elderly.

Among the artists, architects, and designers who embraced a synthesis of Ruskin's aesthetic philosophies and social consciousness, William Morris is a pivotal figure in the history of design. The eldest son of a wealthy wine importer, Morris grew up in a Georgian mansion on the edge of Epping Forest where the near-feudal way of life, ancient churches and mansions, and beautiful English countryside made a profound impression.

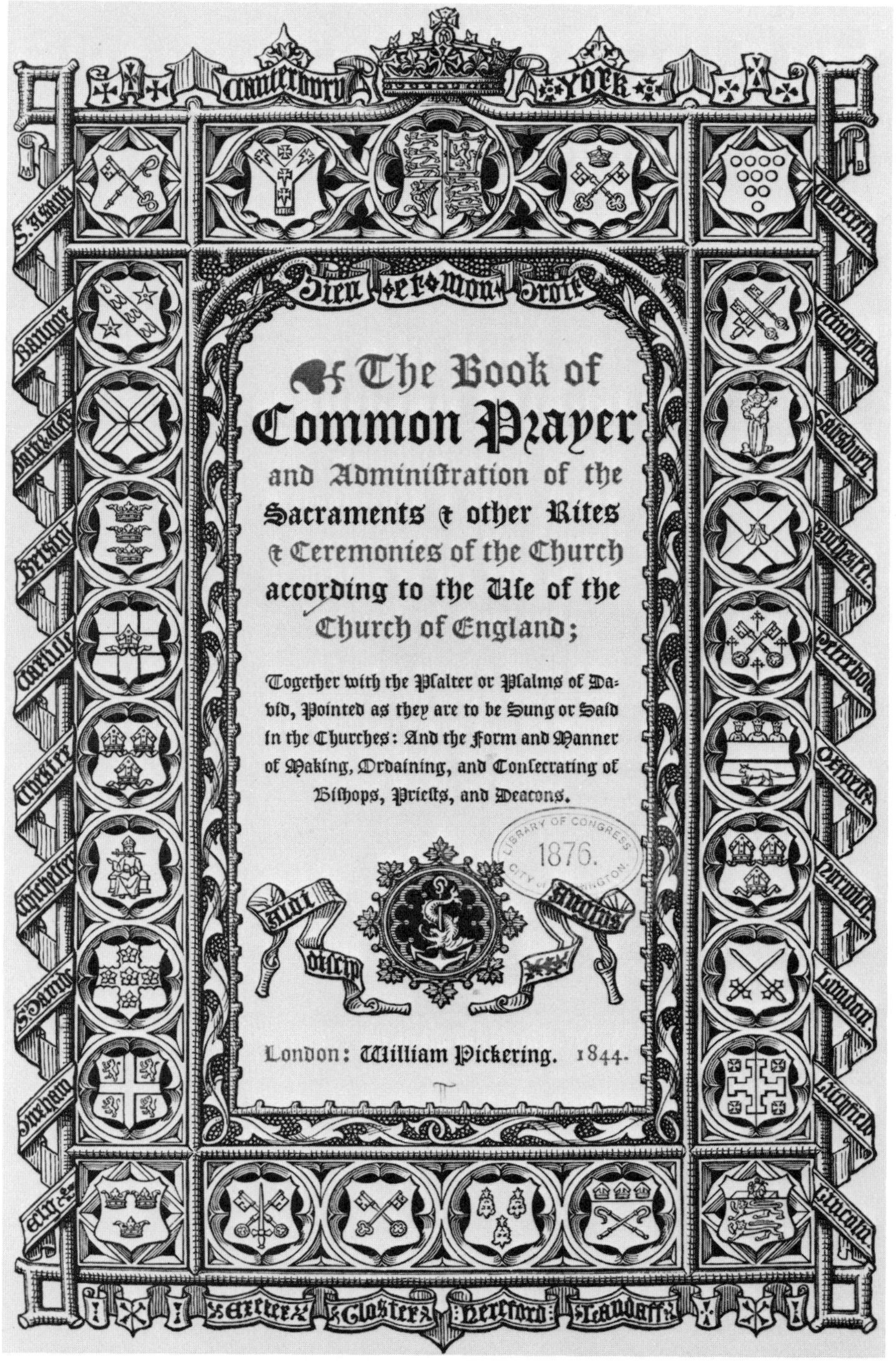
The Book of
Common Prayer
and Administration of the
Sacraments & other Rites
& Ceremonies of the Church
according to the Use of the
Church of England;

Together with the Psalter or Psalms of David, Pointed as they are to be Sung or Said in the Churches: And the Form and Manner of Making, Ordaining, and Consecrating of Bishops, Priests, and Deacons.

London: William Pickering. 1844.

William Pickering, title page for *The Book of Common Prayer,* 1844. The intricacy of Gothic architecture and heraldic devices are convincingly depicted in this red and black title page. *Library of Congress, Washington, D.C.*

In 1853 he entered Exeter College, Oxford, where he began his life-long friendship with Edward Burne-Jones (1833–1898). Both planned to enter the ministry, and their wide reading included medieval history, chronicles, and poetry. Writing became a daily activity for Morris, who published his first volume of poems at age twenty-four. Throughout his career, he produced a steady flow of poetry, fiction, and philosophical writings which filled twenty-four volumes when his daughter May (1862–1938) published his collected works after his death.

While traveling in France on a holiday in 1855, Morris and Burne-Jones decided to become artists instead of clergymen, and after graduation Morris entered the Oxford architectural office of G. E. Street. There, Morris formed a close friendship with young architect Philip Webb (1831–1915), who was his supervisor. Morris found the routine of an architectural office stifling and dull, so in the fall of 1856 he left architecture and joined Burne-Jones in the pursuit of painting. Since Morris' family estate provided an income of nine hundred pounds a month, he could follow his ideas and interests wherever they might lead. The two artists fell under the influence of the Pre-Raphaelite painter Dante Gabriel Rossetti (1828–1882). Morris struggled with his romantic paintings of medieval pageantry but was never fully satisfied with his work. He married his hauntingly beautiful model, Jane Burden, daughter of an Oxford stableman, and, during the process of establishing their home, began to find his design vocation.

Red House, designed for them by Philip Webb, is a landmark in domestic architecture. Rather than stuff rooms in a rectangular box behind a symmetrical façade, the L-shaped plan grew out of functional interior space planning. Here and there the exterior façade darts in or out, in response to interior needs. When it came time to furnish Red House, Morris suddenly discovered the appalling state of Victorian product and furniture design. Over the next several years, he designed and supervised the execution of furniture, stained glass, and tapestries for Red House.

As a result of this experience, Morris joined with six friends in 1861 to establish the art-decorating firm of Morris, Marshall, Faulkner and Company. Growing rapidly, the firm established London showrooms and began to assemble teams of craftsmen that eventually included furniture and cabinetmakers, weavers and dyers, stained glass fabricators, and ceramic and tile makers. Morris proved to be a brilliant two-dimensional pattern designer. He created over five hundred pattern designs for wallpapers, textiles, carpets, and tapestries. A similar number of stained glass win-

J. P. Seddon, cabinet designed for Morris and Company, 1861. Paintings illustrating the honeymoon of the fifteenth-century Italian King René of Anjou by Ford Madox Brown, Edward Burne-Jones, and D. G. Rossetti grace this cabinet. The structure and ornamental carving allude to design from the late medieval era. *The Victoria and Albert Museum, London.*

William Morris, "Pimpernel," wallpaper design, 1876. His close study of botany and drawing fluency enabled Morris to create intricate willowy patterns weaving decorative arabesques of natural forms. *Cooper-Hewitt Museum, New York, The Smithsonian Institution's National Museum of Design.*

dows were created under his supervision. Medieval arts and botanical forms were his main inspirations. The firm reorganized in 1875 as Morris and Company, with William Morris as the sole owner.

Deeply concerned about the problems of industrialization and the factory system, Morris tried to implement Ruskin's ideas. The tastelessness of mass-produced goods and the lack of honest craftsmanship could be addressed by a reunion of art with craft. Art and craft could combine to create beautiful objects, from buildings to bedding. The worker could find joy in his work once again, and the manmade environment—which had declined into industrial cities of squalid, dismal tenements filled with tacky, manufactured goods—could be revitalized. A moral concern over the exploitation of the poor led Morris to embrace socialism. Dismay over the wanton destruction of the architectural heritage motivated him to found the Society for the Protection of Ancient Buildings, called "Anti-Scrape." Disgust at the false and misleading claims of advertising caused him to become involved in the Society for Checking the Abuses of Public Advertising, which confronted offenders directly.

During the 1880s and 1890s, the Arts and Crafts Movement was underpinned by a number of societies and guilds, which sought to establish democratic artistic communities united for the common good. These ranged from exhibition cooperatives to communes based on socialist and religious ideals.

The Century Guild

A twenty-six-year-old architect, Arthur H. Mackmurdo (1851–1942), met William Morris and was inspired by Morris' ideas and accomplishments in applied design. In trips to Italy in 1878 and 1880, Mackmurdo filled his sketchbooks with studies of Renaissance architectural structure and ornament, in addition to extensive drawings of botanical and other natural forms. Back in London, Mackmurdo led a youthful group of artists and designers who banded together in 1882 to establish the Century Guild. The group included designer-illustrator Selwyn Image (1849–1930) and designer-writer Herbert P. Horne (1864–1916). The goal of the Century Guild was "to render all branches of art the sphere, no longer of the tradesman, but of the artist . . ." The design arts were to be elevated to "their rightful place beside painting and sculpture." The group evolved a new design aesthetic as Mackmurdo and his friends, who were about two decades younger than Morris and his associates, incorporated Renaissance and Japanese design ideas into their work. Their graphic designs provide a link from the Arts and Crafts Movement to the floral stylization of Art Nouveau.

Featuring the work of guild members, *The Century Guild Hobby Horse* began publication in 1884 as the first finely printed magazine devoted exclusively to the visual arts. The medieval passions of the Arts and Crafts Movement were reflected in the graphic designs of Image and Horne. However, several designs by Mackmurdo have swirling organic forms that are pure Art Nouveau in their conception and execution. He first explored abstract intertwining floral patterns in an 1881 carved chair back that is now lost. The 1883 title page for his book, *Wren's City Churches,* followed by the Century Guild trademark and *Hobby Horse* graphic designs a year later, appear in retrospect as seminal innovations that

Arthur Mackmurdo, chair, 1881. In developing this decorative pattern, Mackmurdo carefully considered visual design qualities and structural strength. This involvement in construction and ornament became an important characteristic of Art Nouveau. *William Morris Gallery, London.*

Arthur H. Mackmurdo, title page for *Wren's City Churches,* 1883. Mackmurdo's plant forms are stylized into flamelike, undulating rhythms that compress the negative space between them. This establishes a positive and negative interplay between black ink and white paper.

Arthur H. Mackmurdo, design element from the *Hobby Horse,* 1884. The now-lost chair back was similar in design to this ornament. The design is a reversal of the title-page design, for the stylized plant forms, undulating rhythms, animation of the space, and visual tension between positive and negative spaces are created by white forms on a black field instead of black forms on a white field.

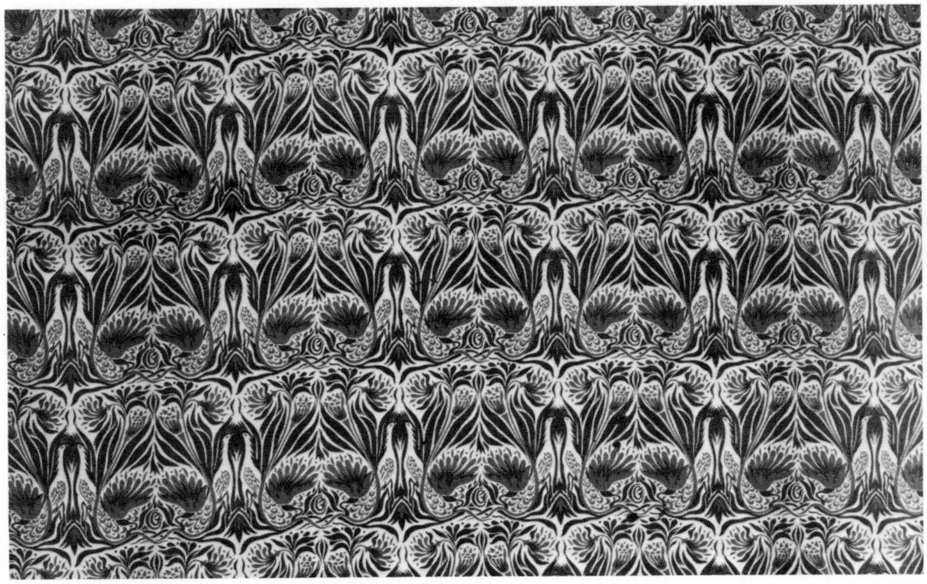

Arthur H. Mackmurdo, "Peacock" design, 1883. Mackmurdo applied forms and images similar to those on his famous title page to this printed cotton fabric. *The Victoria and Albert Museum, London.*

could have launched a movement. But these designs were born before their time; Mackmurdo did not explore this direction further; and Art Nouveau did not explode into a movement until the following decade.

The *Hobby Horse,* which sought to proclaim the philosophy and goals of the Century Guild, was produced with painstaking care under the tutelage of the master printer and typographer at the Chiswick Press, Emery Walker. Its careful layout and typesetting, handmade paper, and intricate woodblock illustrations made it the harbinger of the growing arts-and-crafts interest in typography, graphic design, and printing. In addition to Art Nouveau, Mackmurdo was a forerunner of the private press movement and the renaissance of book design. This private press movement should not be confused with amateur presses. Rather, it was an aesthetic concern for the design and production of beautiful books regaining the design standards, quality materials, and careful workmanship of printing that existed before the Industrial Revolution. The *Hobby Horse* was the first publication in the 1880s to introduce British design and theory to a European audience and to treat printing as a serious design form. Later Mackmurdo related that he showed William Morris a copy of *Hobby Horse* and discussed the difficulties of typographic design including the problems of proportions and margins, letterspacing and leading between lines, choosing paper and typefaces. Reportedly, Morris was filled with enthusiasm about the possibilities of book design as he admired the well-crafted typographic pages, generous margins, wide linespacing, and meticulous printing alive with handcut woodblock illustrations, head and tail pieces, and ornamented capitals. Original etchings and lithographs were printed as fine plates and bound into the quarterly issues.

In an article entitled "On the Unity of Art" in the January 1887 issue of *Hobby Horse,* Selwyn Image passionately argued that all forms of visual expression deserved the status of art. He suggested that "the unknown inventor of patterns to decorate a wall or a water-pot" who "employs himself in representing abstract lines and masses" deserves equal claim to being called an artist as the painter, Raphael, who represented "the human form and the highest human interests." He chided the Royal Academy of Art by recommending that its name be changed to the Royal Academy of Oil Painting because it was so limited relative to the total range of art and design

Arthur H. Mackmurdo, trademark for the Century Guild, 1884. Flame, flower, and initials are compressed and tapered into proto-Art Nouveau forms.

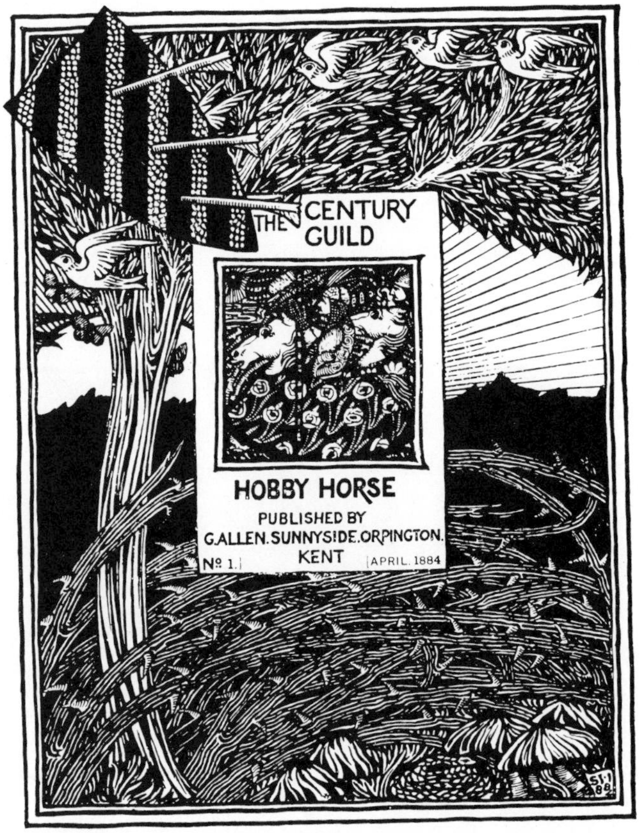

Selwyn Image, title page to *The Century Guild Hobby Horse,* 1884. Packing it with detail, Image designed a "page within a page" that reflects the medieval preoccupation of the Arts and Crafts Movement.

Selwyn Image, Woodcut from the *Hobby Horse,* 1886. The potential of shape and pattern as visual means to express thought and feeling is realized in this graphic elegy for illustrator/engraver Arthur Burgess. A black bird flies toward the sun over mournful down-turned tulips that hover above flamelike leaves.

forms. In perhaps the most prophetic observation of the decade, Image concluded that "For when you begin to realize, that all kinds of invented Form, and Tone, and Colour, are alike true and honorable aspects of Art, *you see something very much like a revolution looming ahead of you* (italics added)."

Although it received ample commissions, the Century Guild disbanded in 1888. Emphasis had been upon collaborative projects, but now the members were becoming more preoccupied with their individual work. Selwyn Image designed typefaces, innumerable illustrations, mosaics, stained glass, and embroidery. Mackmurdo focused on social politics and the development of theories to reform the monetary system. Almost in defiance of the mainstream concern for ornament, Herbert Horne designed books with classic simplicity and restraint. His educational background had included typesetting, and his layouts have a concise sense of alignment, proportion, and balance. In 1900 he moved to Florence, Italy, and devoted seven years to writing a biography of Botticelli.

The Kelmscott Press

A number of groups and individuals concerned with the craft revival combined to form the Art Worker's Guild in 1884. The guild's activities were expanded in 1888 when a splinter group formed the Combined Arts Society, elected Walter Crane as its first president, and planned to sponsor exhibitions. By the October 1888 opening of the first exhibition, the name had been changed to the Arts and Crafts Exhibition Society.

Early exhibitions featured

Herbert Horne, title page for *Poems by Lionel Johnson,* 1895. Symmetry, outline type, letterspacing, and alignment are the design qualities of Horne's work. The outline quality of the letterforms is a perfect companion for the illustration.

Herbert Horne, trademark for The Chiswick Press, c. 1895. Whether the Chiswick Lion is paying homage to the Aldine dolphin, or moving it out of the way, is an amusing ambiguity.

Walter Crane, trademark for the Chiswick Press, c. 1898. The literal and medieval overtones of Crane's version of the Chiswick mark, in contrast to the simplified version by Horne, demonstrates the divergent viewpoints of the period.

demonstrations and lectures. In 1888, these included William Morris on tapestry weaving, Walter Crane on design, and Emery Walker on book design and printing. In his November 15th lecture, Walker showed lantern slides of medieval manuscripts and Incunabula type design. Advocating a unity of design, Walker told his audience that "the ornament, whatever it is, picture or pattern-work, should form part of the page, should be part of the whole scheme of the book." Walker considered book design similar to architecture, for only careful planning of every aspect—paper, ink, type, spacing, margins, illustration, and ornament—could result in a design unity. As Morris and Walker, who were friends and neighbors, walked home together after the lecture that autumn evening, Morris resolved to plunge into typeface design and printing. This was a possibility he had considered for some time, and he began work on his first typeface design that December.

It is not surprising that Morris decided to tackle graphic design and printing, for he had long been interested in books. His library included some magnificent medieval manuscripts and Incunabula volumes. Earlier, Morris had made a number of manuscript books, writing the text in beautifully controlled scripts and embellishing them with delicate borders and initials with flowing forms and soft, clear colors. An 1866 attempt to publish a folio edition of *The Earthly Paradise* failed. Morris had hand-cut woodblocks for thirty-five of Burne-Jones' one hundred illustrations, and the rest were cut by other engravers. The Chiswick Press had proofed specimen pages in Caslon type. But when both the woodblocks and typography evidenced technical defects as press trials began, the project was dropped.

Morris named his first typeface Golden, because his original plan was to print *The Golden Legend* by Voragine as his first book, working from William Caxton's translation. Golden was based on the Venetian

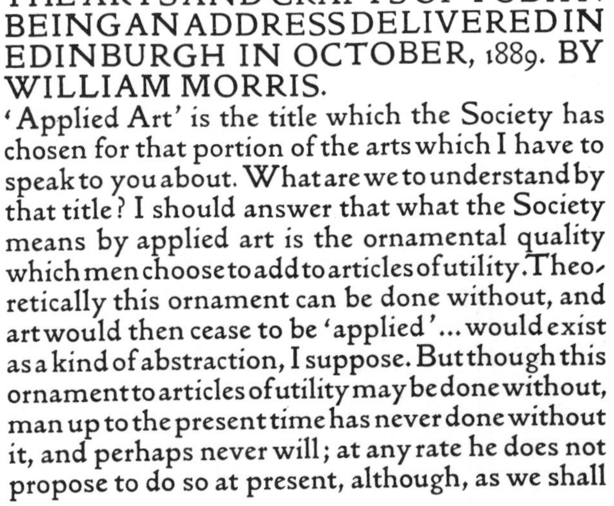
THE ARTS AND CRAFTS OF TODAY. BEING AN ADDRESS DELIVERED IN EDINBURGH IN OCTOBER, 1889. BY WILLIAM MORRIS.

'Applied Art' is the title which the Society has chosen for that portion of the arts which I have to speak to you about. What are we to understand by that title? I should answer that what the Society means by applied art is the ornamental quality which men choose to add to articles of utility. Theoretically this ornament can be done without, and art would then cease to be 'applied'... would exist as a kind of abstraction, I suppose. But though this ornament to articles of utility may be done without, man up to the present time has never done without it, and perhaps never will; at any rate he does not propose to do so at present, although, as we shall

William Morris, Golden typeface, 1888–90. This alphabet design was the inspiration for a renewed interest in Venetian and Old Style typography. Designers, type founders, and printers began to study and use these forms.

William Morris (designer) and Walter Crane (illustrator), title-page spread for *The Story of the Glittering Plain*, 1894. Operating on his compulsion to ornament the total space, Morris created a luminous range of contrasting values. *Library of Congress, Washington, D.C., Rosenwald Collection.*

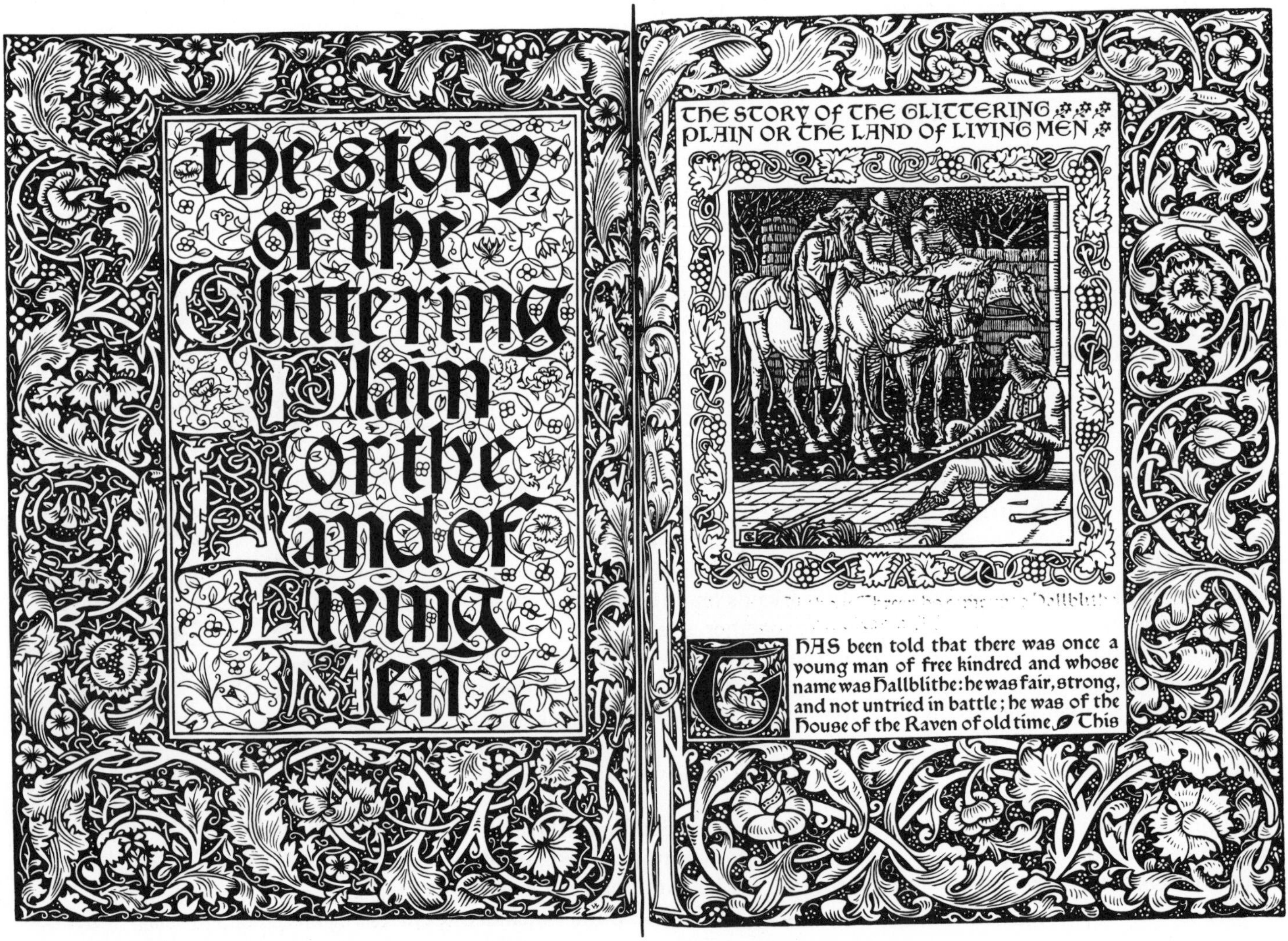

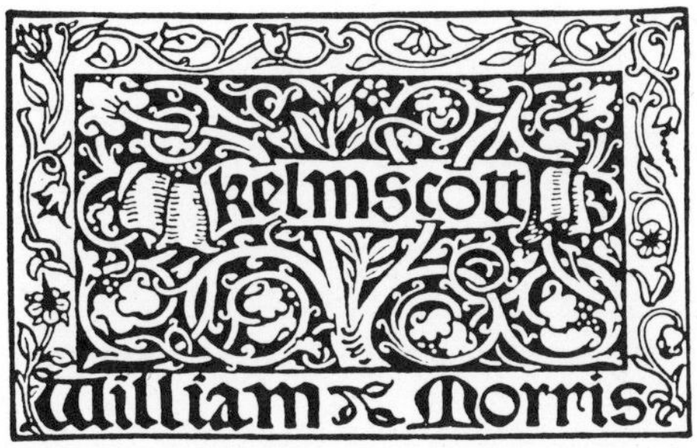

William Morris, trademark for the Kelmscott Press, 1892.

roman faces designed by Nicolas Jenson between 1470 and 1476. Morris studied large photographic prints of Jenson's letterforms, then drew them over and over. Punches were made and revised for the final designs, which captured the essence of Jenson's work but did not slavishly copy it. Typefounding of Golden began in December of 1890. Workmen were hired, and an old handpress rescued from a printer's storeroom was set up in a rented cottage near Kelmscott manor in Hammersmith, which Morris had purchased as a country home. Kelmscott Press' first production was *The Story of the Glittering Plain* by William Morris with illustrations by Walter Crane. Initially twenty copies were planned, but as word of the enterprise spread Morris was persuaded to increase the press run to two hundred paper copies and six on vellum. From 1891 until the Kelmscott Press disbanded in 1898, two years after Morris' death, over eighteen thousand volumes of fifty-three different titles were produced.

Careful study of the Incunabula gothic types of Peter Schoeffer, Anton Koberger, and Günther Zainer informed Morris' design of Troy, a blackletter style whose characters are remarkably legible. Morris made the characters wider than most gothic types, increased the differences between similar characters, and made the curved characters rounder. A smaller version of Troy, called Chaucer, was the last of Morris' three typeface designs. These stirred a renewed interest in Jenson and gothic styles and inspired a number of other versions in Europe and America.

BUT on the morrow the men arose, & the Sea-eagle and his damsel came to Hallblithe; for the other two damsels were departed, and the

Sea-eagle said to him: "Here am I well honoured and measurelessly happy; and I have a message for thee from the King". "What is it?" said Hallblithe; but he deemed that he knew what it would be, and he reddened for the joy of his assured hope. Said the Sea-eagle: "Joy to thee, O shipmate! I am to take thee to the place where thy beloved abideth, & there shalt thou see her, but not so as she can see thee: & thereafter shalt thou go to the King, that thou mayst tell him if she shall accomplish thy desire". Then was Hallblithe glad beyond measure, & his heart danced within him, & he deemed it but meet that the others should be so joyous and blithe with him, for they led him along without any delay, and were glad at his rejoicing: and words failed him to tell of his gladness.

BUT as he went, the thoughts of his coming converse with his beloved curled sweetly round his heart, so that scarce anything had seemed so sweet to him before: & he fell a-pondering what they twain, he and the Hostage, should do when they came together again; whether they should abide on the Glittering Plain, or go back again to Cleveland by the Sea and dwell in the House of the Kindred; and for his part he yearned to behold the roof of his fathers and to tread the meadow which his scythe had swept, and the acres where his hook had smitten the wheat. But he said to himself: "I will wait till I hear her desire hereon". Now they went into the wood at the back of the King's pavilion and through it, and so over the hill, and beyond it came into a land of hills and dales exceeding fair and lovely; and a river wound about the dales, lap-

g 3 85

William Morris (designer) and Walter Crane (illustrator), pages from *The Story of the Glittering Plain,* 1894. Legibility was as important to Morris as decoration, as evidenced in this layout. The border around Crane's illustration was carefully selected to frame the darker illustration in a lighter tone, and generous margins set off the Troy type. *Library of Congress, Washington, D.C., Rosenwald Collection.*

The Kelmscott Press was committed to recapturing the beauty of Incunabula books. Meticulous handprinting, handmade paper, handcut woodblocks, and initials and borders similar to those used by Ratdolt turned the picturesque cottage into a time machine swinging back four centuries into the past. The book became an art form.

The design style of the Kelmscott Press was established in its early books. Decorative borders and initials designed by Morris were engraved on wood by William H. Hooper, (1834–1912), a master craftsman lured from his retirement to work at the press. These have a wonderful visual compatibility with Morris' types and woodblock illustrations cut from drawings by Burne-Jones, Crane, and C. M. Gere. Morris designed six hundred sixty-four blocks for the press, including initials, borders, frames, and title pages. He first lightly sketched the main lines in pencil. Then, armed with white paint and black ink, he worked back and forth, painting the background in black and, over it, the pattern in white. The entire final design would be developed through this fluid process, for Morris believed that meticulous copying of a preliminary drawing squeezed the life from a work.

The outstanding volume from the Kelmscott Press is the ambitious five-hundred-fifty-six-page *The Works of Geoffrey Chaucer*. Four years in the making, the Kelmscott *Chaucer* has eighty-seven woodcut illustrations from drawings by Burne-Jones, and fourteen large borders and eighteen smaller frames around the illustrations cut from designs by Morris. It was printed in black and red in large folio size. An exhaustive effort was required by everyone involved in the project. This edition, forty-two copies on paper and thirteen on vellum, was the final achievement of Morris' career. On 2 June 1896 the bindery delivered the first two copies to the ailing designer. One was for Burne-

Jones, the other for Morris. Four months later, on 3 October, William Morris died at age sixty-two.

The paradox of William Morris is that as he sought refuge in the handicraft of the past, he developed design attitudes that charted the future. His call for workmanship, truth to materials, making the utilitarian beautiful, and fitness of design to function are attitudes adopted by succeeding generations who sought to unify—not art and craft—but art and industry. Morris taught that design could bring art to the working class, but the exquisite furnishings of Morris and Company and the magnificent Kelmscott books were available only to the wealthy.

The extraordinary influence of William Morris and the Kelmscott Press upon graphic design, particularly book design, was not the direct stylistic imitation of the Kelmscott borders, initials, and typestyles. Rather, Morris' concept of the well-made book, his typeface designs of great beauty, and his sense of design unity with the smallest detail relating to the total concept inspired a whole new generation of book designers. Ironically, this crusader for handicraft became the inspiration for a revival of fine book design that lasted well into the twentieth century and filtered into commercial printing. The incredible complexity of Morris' decorations tends to draw attention away from other accomplishments. His books achieved a harmonious whole, and his typographic pages—which form the overwhelming majority of the pages in his books—are conceived and executed with readability in mind. Morris' searching reexamination of earlier typestyles and graphic design history touched off an energetic redesign process that resulted in a major improvement in the quality and variety of fonts available for design and printing.

One final irony is that while Morris was returning to printing methods of the Incunabula, he used initials, borders, and ornaments that were modular, interchangeable, and repeatable. A basic aspect of industrial production was applied to the printed page.

HEREBEGINNETH THE TALES OF CANTERBURY AND FIRST THE PROLOGUE THEREOF

WHAN THAT Aprille with his shoures soote
The droghte of March hath perced to the roote,
And bathed every veyne in swich licour,
Of which vertu engendred is the flour;
Whan Zephirus eek with his swete breeth
Inspired hath in every holt and heeth
The tendre croppes, and the yonge sonne
Hath in the Ram his halfe cours yronne,
And smale foweles maken melodye,
That slepen al the nyght with open eye,
So priketh hem nature in hir corages;
Thanne longen folk to goon on pilgrimages,
And palmeres for to seken straunge strondes,
To ferne halwes, kowthe in sondry londes;
And specially, from every shires ende
Of Engelond, to Caunterbury they wende,
The hooly blisful martir for to seke,
That hem hath holpen whan that they were seeke.
BIFIL that in that seson on a day,
In Southwerk at the Tabard as I lay,
Redy to wenden on my pilgrymage
To Caunterbury with ful devout corage,
At nyght were come into that hostelrye
Wel nyne and twenty in a compaignye,
Of sondry folk, by aventure yfalle
In felaweshipe, and pilgrimes were they alle,
That toward Caunterbury wolden ryde.

William Morris, illustrated page from *The Canterbury Tales,* 1896. Although the sensibility was medieval, the modular and interchangeable quality of the frames, illustration borders, and ornamented initials established continuity in the layouts and reflected the standardization of industrialism.

The private-press movement

Architect, graphic designer, silversmith, and jeweler, the indefatigable Charles R. Ashbee (1863–1942) founded the Guild of Handicraft on 23 June 1888 with three members and only fifty pounds, British sterling, as working capital. Although William Morris was dubious and threw "a great deal of cold water" upon Ashbee's plan, the guild met with unexpected success in its endeavors. Ashbee also founded the School of Handicraft that attempted to unify the teaching of design and theory with workshop experience.

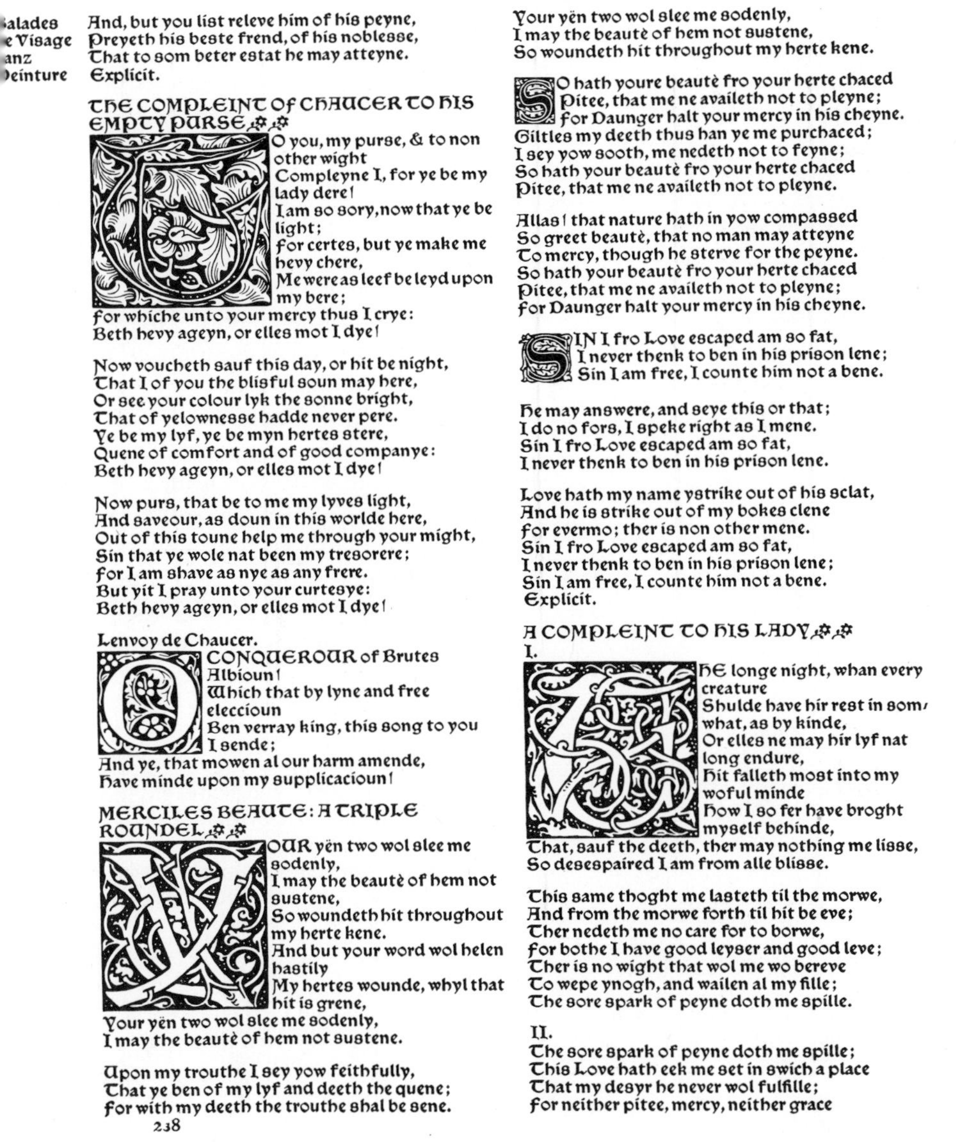
alades e Visage anz einture

And, but you list releve him of his peyne,
Preyeth his beste frend, of his noblesse,
That to som beter estat he may atteyne.
Explicit.

THE COMPLEINT OF CHAUCER TO HIS EMPTY PURSE.

O you, my purse, & to non other wight
Compleyne I, for ye be my lady dere!
I am so sory, now that ye be light;
For certes, but ye make me hevy chere,
Me were as leef be leyd upon my bere;
For whiche unto your mercy thus I crye:
Beth hevy ageyn, or elles mot I dye!

Now voucheth sauf this day, or hit be night,
That I of you the blisful soun may here,
Or see your colour lyk the sonne bright,
That of yelownesse hadde never pere.
Ye be my lyf, ye be myn hertes stere,
Quene of comfort and of good companye:
Beth hevy ageyn, or elles mot I dye!

Now purs, that be to me my lyves light,
And saveour, as doun in this worlde here,
Out of this toune help me through your might,
Sin that ye wole nat been my tresorere;
For I am shave as nye as any frere.
But yit I pray unto your curtesye:
Beth hevy ageyn, or elles mot I dye!

Lenvoy de Chaucer.

O CONQUEROUR of Brutes Albioun!
Which that by lyne and free eleccioun
Ben verray king, this song to you I sende;
And ye, that mowen al our harm amende,
Have minde upon my supplicacioun!

MERCILES BEAUTE: A TRIPLE ROUNDEL.

YOUR yën two wol slee me sodenly,
I may the beautè of hem not sustene,
So woundeth hit throughout my herte kene.
And but your word wol helen hastily
My hertes wounde, whyl that hit is grene,
Your yën two wol slee me sodenly,
I may the beautè of hem not sustene.

Upon my trouthe I sey yow feithfully,
That ye ben of my lyf and deeth the quene;
For with my deeth the trouthe shal be sene.

238

Your yën two wol slee me sodenly,
I may the beautè of hem not sustene,
So woundeth hit throughout my herte kene.

SO hath youre beautè fro your herte chaced
Pitee, that me ne availeth not to pleyne;
For Daunger halt your mercy in his cheyne.
Giltles my deeth thus han ye me purchaced;
I sey yow sooth, me nedeth not to feyne;
So hath your beautè fro your herte chaced
Pitee, that me ne availeth not to pleyne.

Allas! that nature hath in yow compassed
So greet beautè, that no man may atteyne
To mercy, though he sterve for the peyne.
So hath your beautè fro your herte chaced
Pitee, that me ne availeth not to pleyne;
For Daunger halt your mercy in his cheyne.

SIN I fro Love escaped am so fat,
I never thenk to ben in his prison lene;
Sin I am free, I counte him not a bene.

He may answere, and seye this or that;
I do no fors, I speke right as I mene.
Sin I fro Love escaped am so fat,
I never thenk to ben in his prison lene.

Love hath my name ystrike out of his sclat,
And he is strike out of my bokes clene
For evermo; ther is non other mene.
Sin I fro Love escaped am so fat,
I never thenk to ben in his prison lene;
Sin I am free, I counte him not a bene.
Explicit.

A COMPLEINT TO HIS LADY.

I.

THE longe night, whan every creature
Shulde have hir rest in som/what, as by kinde,
Or elles ne may hir lyf nat long endure,
Hit falleth most into my woful minde
How I so fer have broght myself behinde,
That, sauf the deeth, ther may nothing me lisse,
So desespaired I am from alle blisse.

This same thoght me lasteth til the morwe,
And from the morwe forth til hit be eve;
Ther nedeth me no care for to borwe,
For bothe I have good leyser and good leve;
Ther is no wight that wol me wo bereve
To wepe ynogh, and wailen al my fille;
The sore spark of peyne doth me spille.

II.

The sore spark of peyne doth me spille;
This Love hath eek me set in swich a place
That my desyr he never wol fulfille;
For neither pitee, mercy, neither grace

William Morris, text page from *The Works of Geoffrey Chaucer,* 1896. Titles, over two hundred ornamented letters and initial words designed by Morris for this book, marginal captions and line spacing served dual purposes. Beautiful pages of texture and tone were created; the reader finds an order and clarity that make the author's words legible and accessible.

Ashbee sought to restore the holistic experience of apprenticeship, which had been destroyed by the subdivision of labor and machine production. During a decade, about seven hundred students received a dualistic education with practical skill development, supplemented by readings from Ruskin and study of the application of art principles to materials. Able neither to secure state support nor to compete with the state aided technical schools, the School of Handicraft finally closed. The Guild of Handicraft, on the other hand, flourished as a cooperative where workers shared in governance and profits. It was inspired by both socialism and the Arts and Crafts Movement. In 1890, the guild leased Essex House, an old Georgian mansion in what had declined into a grimy and desolate section of industrial London.

After the death of William Morris, Ashbee opened negotiations with the executors of the estate to transfer the Kelmscott Press to Essex House. When it became known that the Kelmscott woodblocks and types were to be deposited in the British Museum with the stipulation that they not be used for printing for a hundred years, Ashbee resolved to hire key personnel from the Kelmscott Press, to purchase the equipment that was available for sale, and to form the Essex House Press. The *Psalter* of 1902 was the design masterpiece of the Essex House Press. The text is in vernacular sixteenth-century English from the c. 1540 translation of Archbishop Thomas Cranmer of Canterbury. Ashbee developed a graphic program for each psalm consisting of a roman numeral, the Latin title in red capitals, an English descriptive title printed in black capitals, an illustrated woodcut initial, and the body of the psalm. Verses are separated by woodcut leaf ornaments printed in red. Ashbee's design for the Essex House type was a curious cross between an Egyptian and a Roman type imbued with a medieval feeling. Awkward calligraphic touches, such as the small swash ascender on the lower case *h, n,* and *m,* give it a curious but engaging quality. Its even stroke weight and unusually large *x*-height provide an interesting texture which is handsome in the mass of text and contrasts effectively with the tone of Ashbee's ever-present woodcut initials.

In 1902, the guild moved to the rural village of Chipping Campden and began the ambitious task of turning the village into a communal society for guild workers and their families. The large costs involved, combined with the expenses of maintaining the guild's retail store on Brook Street in London, forced the guild into deficit finances which led to voluntary bankruptcy in 1907. Many of the craftsmen continued to work independently, and the undaunted Ashbee returned to his architectural practice which had lain fallow during his noble experiments over two decades. Although he was a leading design theorist and follower of the ideals of Ruskin and Morris at the turn of the century, after World War I, Ashbee began to question the belief that industrial manufacturing was of necessity evil, and he began to formulate a design policy relevant to the industrial age. Thus, Ruskin's

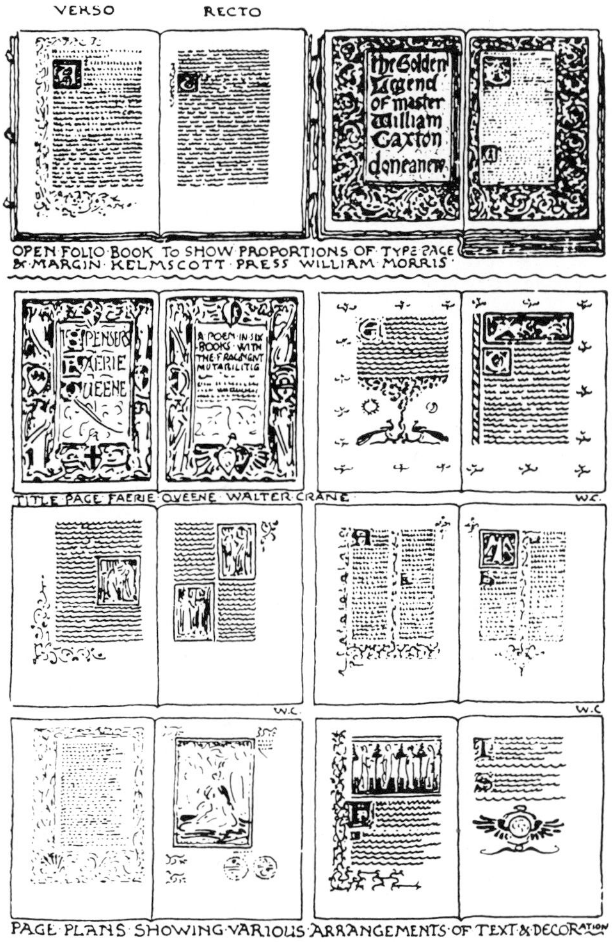

Walter Crane, layout sketches from *The Bases of Design,* 1898. Crane used these sketches to demonstrate the relationship of two pages which form a double-page unit, and how the margins can be used for decorative effect.

follower who went farthest in establishing an idyllic workshop paradise became a major English voice calling for integration of art and industry in a later era.

In 1900, the bookbinder T. J. Cobden-Sanderson (1840–1922) joined Emery Walker in establishing the Doves Press at Hammersmith. They set out to "attack the problem of pure Typography" with the view that "the whole duty of Typography is to communicate to the imagination, without

Charles R. Ashbee, pages from the Essex House *Psalter,* 1902. The figures of the hand-cut woodblock initials, the calligraphic quality of the type, the handmade paper, and hand-press printing combine to re-create the quality and conditions of the Incunabula book.

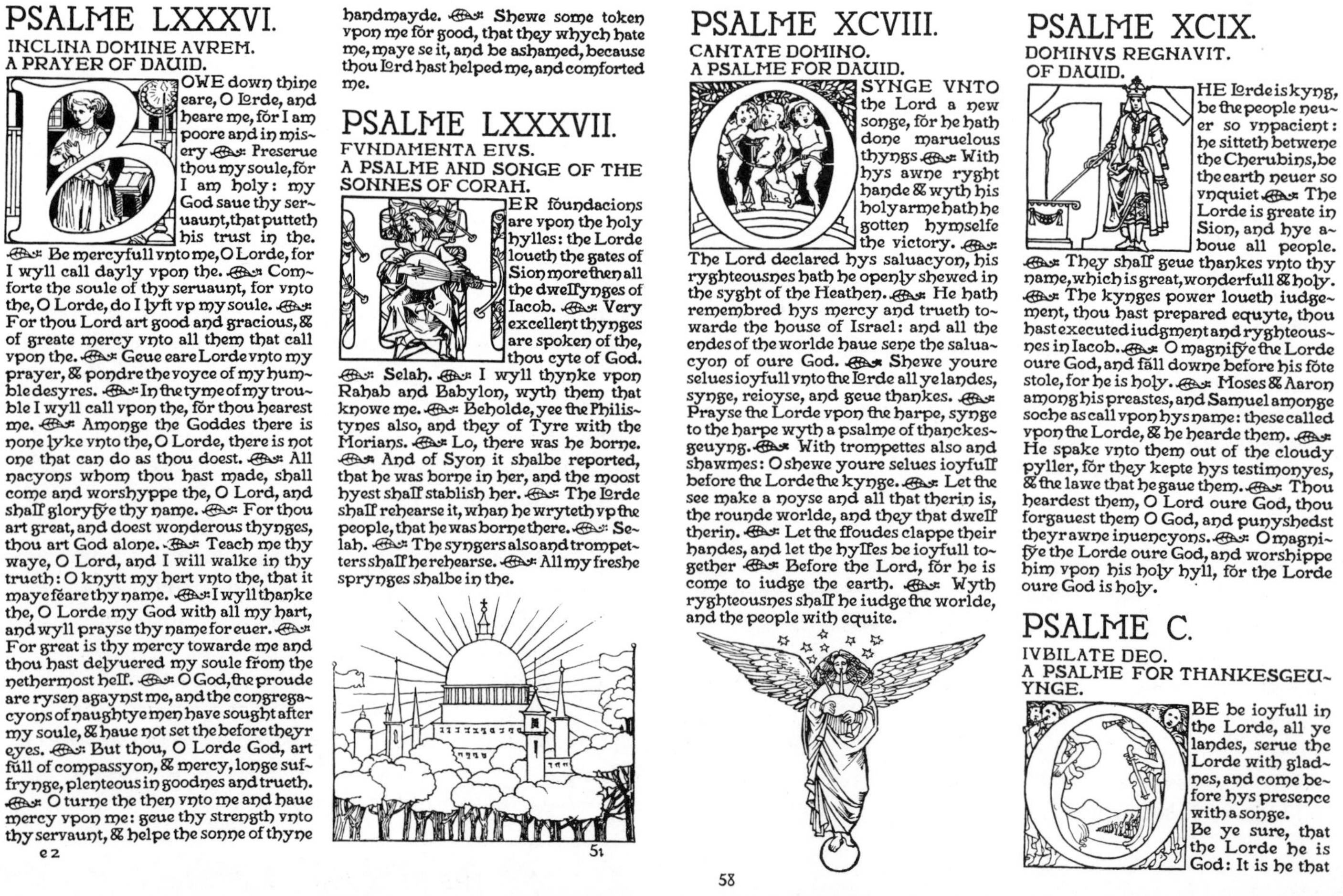

PSALME LXXXVI.

INCLINA DOMINE AVREM.
A PRAYER OF DAUID.

BOWE down thine eare, O Lorde, and heare me, for I am poore and in misery. Preserue thou my soule, for I am holy: my God saue thy seruaunt, that putteth his trust in the. Be mercyfull vnto me, O Lorde, for I wyll call dayly vpon the. Comforte the soule of thy seruaunt, for vnto the, O Lorde, do I lyft vp my soule. For thou Lord art good and gracious, & of greate mercy vnto all them that call vpon the. Geue eare Lorde vnto my prayer, & pondre the voyce of my humble desyres. In the tyme of my trouble I wyll call vpon the, for thou hearest me. Amonge the Goddes there is none lyke vnto the, O Lorde, there is not one that can do as thou doest. All nacyons whom thou hast made, shall come and worshyppe the, O Lord, and shall gloryfye thy name. For thou art great, and doest wonderous thynges, thou art God alone. Teach me thy waye, O Lord, and I will walke in thy trueth: O knytt my hert vnto the, that it maye feare thy name. I wyll thanke the, O Lorde my God with all my hart, and wyll prayse thy name for euer. For great is thy mercy towarde me and thou hast delyuered my soule from the nethermost hell. O God, the proude are rysen agaynst me, and the congregacyons of naughtye men have sought after my soule, & haue not set the before theyr eyes. But thou, O Lorde God, art full of compassyon, & mercy, longe suffrynge, plenteous in goodnes and trueth. O turne the then vnto me and haue mercy vpon me: geue thy strength vnto thy servaunt, & helpe the sonne of thyne

e2

handmayde. Shewe some token vpon me for good, that they whych hate me, maye se it, and be ashamed, because thou Lord hast helped me, and comforted me.

PSALME LXXXVII.

FVNDAMENTA EIVS.
A PSALME AND SONGE OF THE SONNES OF CORAH.

HER foundacions are vpon the holy hylles: the Lorde loueth the gates of Sion more then all the dwellynges of Iacob. Very excellent thynges are spoken of the, thou cyte of God. Selah. I wyll thynke vpon Rahab and Babylon, wyth them that knowe me. Beholde, yee the Philistynes also, and they of Tyre with the Morians. Lo, there was he borne. And of Syon it shalbe reported, that he was borne in her, and the moost hyest shall stablish her. The Lorde shall rehearse it, whan he wryteth vp the people, that he was borne there. Selah. The syngers also and trompetters shall he rehearse. All my freshe sprynges shalbe in the.

51

PSALME XCVIII.

CANTATE DOMINO.
A PSALME FOR DAUID.

O SYNGE VNTO the Lord a new songe, for he hath done maruelous thyngs. With hys awne ryght hande & wyth his holy arme hath he gotten hymselfe the victory. The Lord declared hys saluacyon, his ryghteousnes hath he openly shewed in the syght of the Heathen. He hath remembred hys mercy and trueth towarde the house of Israel: and all the endes of the worlde haue sene the saluacyon of oure God. Shewe youre selues ioyfull vnto the Lorde all ye landes, synge, reioyse, and geue thankes. Prayse the Lorde vpon the harpe, synge to the harpe wyth a psalme of thanckesgeuyng. With trompettes also and shawmes: O shewe youre selues ioyfull before the Lorde the kynge. Let the see make a noyse and all that therin is, the rounde worlde, and they that dwell therin. Let the floudes clappe their handes, and let the hylles be ioyfull together Before the Lord, for he is come to iudge the earth. Wyth ryghteousnes shall he iudge the worlde, and the people with equite.

PSALME XCIX.

DOMINVS REGNAVIT.
OF DAUID.

THE Lorde is kyng, be the people neuer so vnpacient: he sitteth betwene the Cherubins, be the earth neuer so vnquiet. The Lorde is greate in Sion, and hye aboue all people. They shall geue thankes vnto thy name, which is great, wonderfull & holy. The kynges power loueth iudgement, thou hast prepared equyte, thou hast executed iudgment and ryghteousnes in Iacob. O magnifye the Lorde oure God, and fall downe before his fote stole, for he is holy. Moses & Aaron among his preastes, and Samuel amonge soche as call vpon hys name: these called vpon the Lorde, & he hearde them. He spake vnto them out of the cloudy pyller, for they kepte hys testimonyes, & the lawe that he gaue them. Thou heardest them, O Lord oure God, thou forgauest them O God, and punyshedst theyr awne inuencyons. O magnifye the Lorde oure God, and worshippe him vpon his holy hyll, for the Lorde oure God is holy.

PSALME C.

IVBILATE DEO.
A PSALME FOR THANKESGEUYNGE.

OBE be ioyfull in the Lorde, all ye landes, serue the Lorde with gladnes, and come before hys presence with a songe.
Be ye sure, that the Lorde he is God: It is he that

Charles R. Ashbee, emblem for the Essex House Press, c. 1902. This full-page woodcut, which seems to compare the quality work of the Guild of Handicrafts with the bee seeking a flower, sometimes appeared on the colophon page of Ashbee's books.

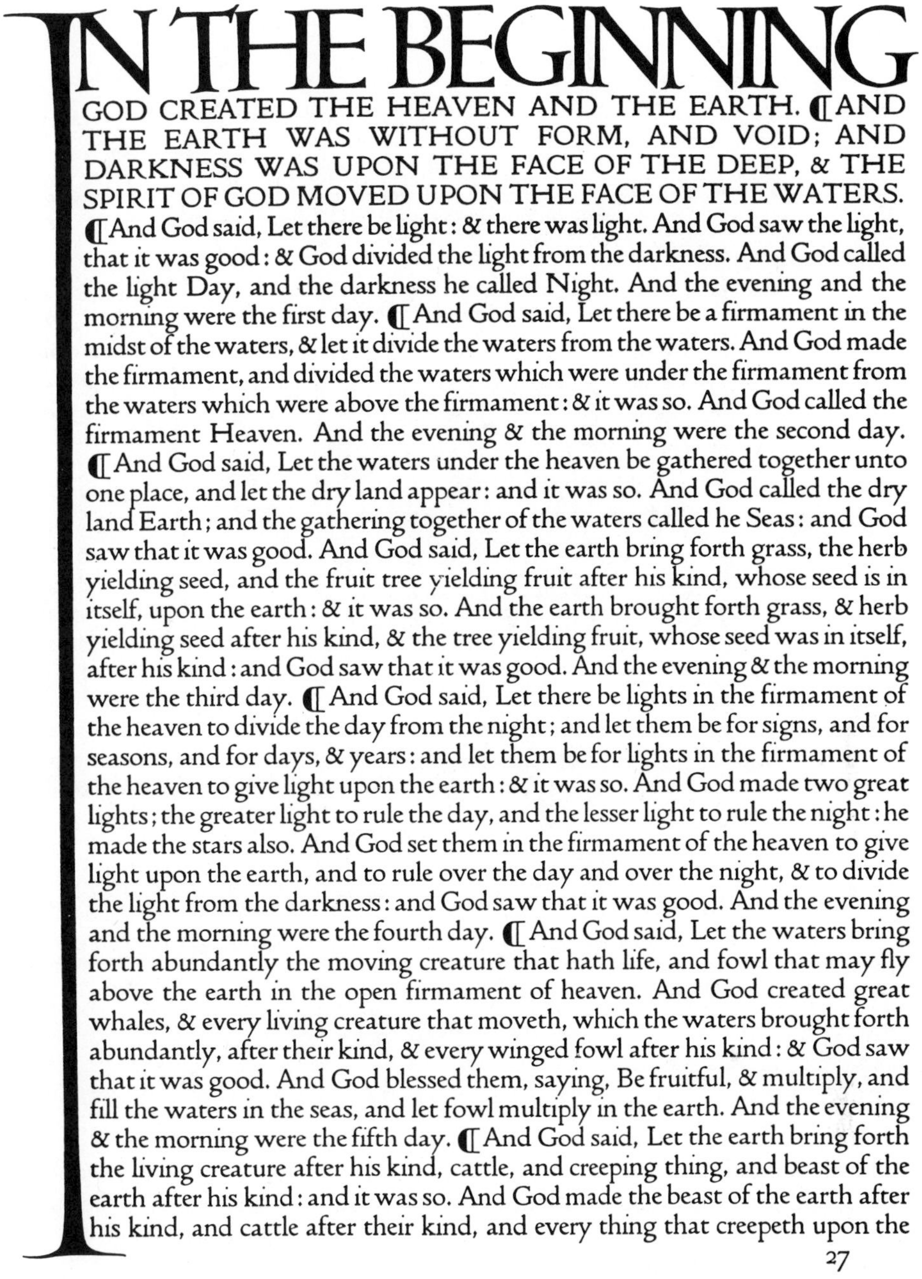

IN THE BEGINNING GOD CREATED THE HEAVEN AND THE EARTH. ¶ AND THE EARTH WAS WITHOUT FORM, AND VOID; AND DARKNESS WAS UPON THE FACE OF THE DEEP, & THE SPIRIT OF GOD MOVED UPON THE FACE OF THE WATERS. ¶ And God said, Let there be light: & there was light. And God saw the light, that it was good: & God divided the light from the darkness. And God called the light Day, and the darkness he called Night. And the evening and the morning were the first day. ¶ And God said, Let there be a firmament in the midst of the waters, & let it divide the waters from the waters. And God made the firmament, and divided the waters which were under the firmament from the waters which were above the firmament: & it was so. And God called the firmament Heaven. And the evening & the morning were the second day. ¶ And God said, Let the waters under the heaven be gathered together unto one place, and let the dry land appear: and it was so. And God called the dry land Earth; and the gathering together of the waters called he Seas: and God saw that it was good. And God said, Let the earth bring forth grass, the herb yielding seed, and the fruit tree yielding fruit after his kind, whose seed is in itself, upon the earth: & it was so. And the earth brought forth grass, & herb yielding seed after his kind, & the tree yielding fruit, whose seed was in itself, after his kind: and God saw that it was good. And the evening & the morning were the third day. ¶ And God said, Let there be lights in the firmament of the heaven to divide the day from the night; and let them be for signs, and for seasons, and for days, & years: and let them be for lights in the firmament of the heaven to give light upon the earth: & it was so. And God made two great lights; the greater light to rule the day, and the lesser light to rule the night: he made the stars also. And God set them in the firmament of the heaven to give light upon the earth, and to rule over the day and over the night, & to divide the light from the darkness: and God saw that it was good. And the evening and the morning were the fourth day. ¶ And God said, Let the waters bring forth abundantly the moving creature that hath life, and fowl that may fly above the earth in the open firmament of heaven. And God created great whales, & every living creature that moveth, which the waters brought forth abundantly, after their kind, & every winged fowl after his kind: & God saw that it was good. And God blessed them, saying, Be fruitful, & multiply, and fill the waters in the seas, and let fowl multiply in the earth. And the evening & the morning were the fifth day. ¶ And God said, Let the earth bring forth the living creature after his kind, cattle, and creeping thing, and beast of the earth after his kind: and it was so. And God made the beast of the earth after his kind, and cattle after their kind, and every thing that creepeth upon the

27

T. J. Cobden-Sanderson and Emery Walker, page from the Doves Press *Bible*, 1903. This book's purity of design and flawless perfection of craft has seldom been equaled. *Library of Congress, Washington, D.C., Rosenwald Collection.*

loss by the way, the thought or image intended to be conveyed by the Author." Books from the Doves Press, including their monumental masterpiece, the 1903 Doves Press Bible, are remarkably beautiful typographic books. Illustration and ornaments were rejected in the approximately fifty volumes produced there. Fine paper, perfect presswork, and exquisite type and spacing were relied upon to produce inspired graphic design. Their five-volume Bible uses a few stunning initials designed by Edward Johnston (1872–1944). This master calligrapher of the Arts and Crafts Movement had been inspired by William Morris and abandoned his medical studies for the life of a scribe. Johnston's study of pen techniques and early manuscripts, and his teaching activities made him a major influence upon the art of letters.

Established in 1895, the Ashendene Press, directed by C. H. St. John Hornby of London, proved to be an exceptional private press. The type designed for Ashendene was inspired by the semi-Gothic types used by Sweynheym and Pannartz in Subiaco. It possessed a ringing elegance and straightforward legibility with modest weight differences between the thick and thin strokes and a slightly compressed letter.

A curious twist in the unfolding of the Arts and Crafts Movement is the case of the American, Elbert Hubbard (1856–1915), who met William Morris in 1894. Hubbard established an arts-and-crafts center called the Roycrofters in East Aurora, New York. Books, inspirational booklets, and his two magazines were wrapped in the look of Kelmscott volumes, and the Roycrofters became a tourist mecca where four hundred employees pro-

AL NOME DEL NOSTRO SIGNORE GESU CRISTO CROCIFISSO E DELLA SUA MADRE VERGINE MARIA.

IN QUESTO LIBRO SI CONTENGONO CERTI FIORETTI, MIRACOLI, ED ESEMPLI DIVOTI DEL GLORIOSO POVERELLO DI CRISTO, MESSER SANTO FRANCESCO, E DALQUANTI SUOI SANTI COMPAGNI, A LAUDE DI GESU CRISTO. AMEN.

CAPITOLO PRIMO. Capitolo i

IN PRIMA E DA CONsiderare che il glorioso Messer Santo Francesco in tutti gli atti della vita sua fu conforme a Cristo benedetto: che come Cristo nel principio della sua predicazione elesse dodici Apostoli, a dispregiare ogni cosa mondana, a seguitare lui in povertade, & nell'altre virtudi; così Santo Francesco elesse dal principio del fondamento dell'Ordine dodici Compagni, possessori dell' altissima povertade, e come uno de' dodici Apostoli di Cristo, riprovato da Dio, finalmente s'impiccò per la gola; così uno de' dodici Compagni di Santo Francesco, ch' ebbe nome Frate Giovanni dalla Cappella, apostatò, e finalmente s'impiccò se medesimo per la gola. E questo agli eletti è grande assempro & materia di umiltade e di timore; considerando che nessuno è certo di dovere perseverare alla fine nella grazia di Dio. E come que' Santi Apostoli furono al tutto maravigliosi di santitade e di umiltade, e pieni

b 1

C. H. St. John Hornby, pages from St. Francis of Assisi's *Legend,* 1922. A liberal use of all-capital type and initial words printed in color brought distinction to Ashendene Press page layout. *Library of Congress, Washington, D.C., Rosenwald Collection.*

duced artistic home furnishings, copperware, leather goods, and printing. When May Morris visited America, she declined an invitation to visit "that obnoxious imitator of my dear father."

Even after Hubbard's untimely death in 1915 aboard the ill-fated Lusitania, the Roycrofters continued until 1938. Hubbard's detractors claim that he tarnished the whole movement, while his defenders counter that the Roycrofters brought beauty into the lives of ordinary people who would not have otherwise had an opportunity to enjoy the fruits of the reaction against industrialism's mediocre products.

Lucien Pissarro (1863–1944) learned drawing from his father, the impressionist painter Camille Pissarro, then apprenticed as a wood engraver and illustrator under the renowned book illustrator Auguste Lepère. Disillusioned with the response to his work in France and learning of a revival of interest in wood-engraved illustrations in England, Pissaro crossed the English Channel to join the movement. Captivated by the Kelmscott books, Pissarro established the Eragny Press (named after the Normandy village where he was born and studied with his father). The design of three- and four-color woodblock illustrations at Hammersmith in 1894 is a unique design feature of Eragny Press books.

Pissarro and his wife collaborated on designing, wood engraving, and printing the books produced at the Eragny Press. His Brook type was also a Jenson-inspired design. Younger than most members of the Arts and Crafts Movement, Pissarro combined the traditional medieval sensibilities of the private press movement with an interest in the blossoming Art Nouveau movement. This proved to be even more true with Charles Ricketts (1866–1931), who founded the Vale Press in 1896. Ricketts spent more time as a consulting graphic designer working in the Art Nouveau style than as a private press operator.

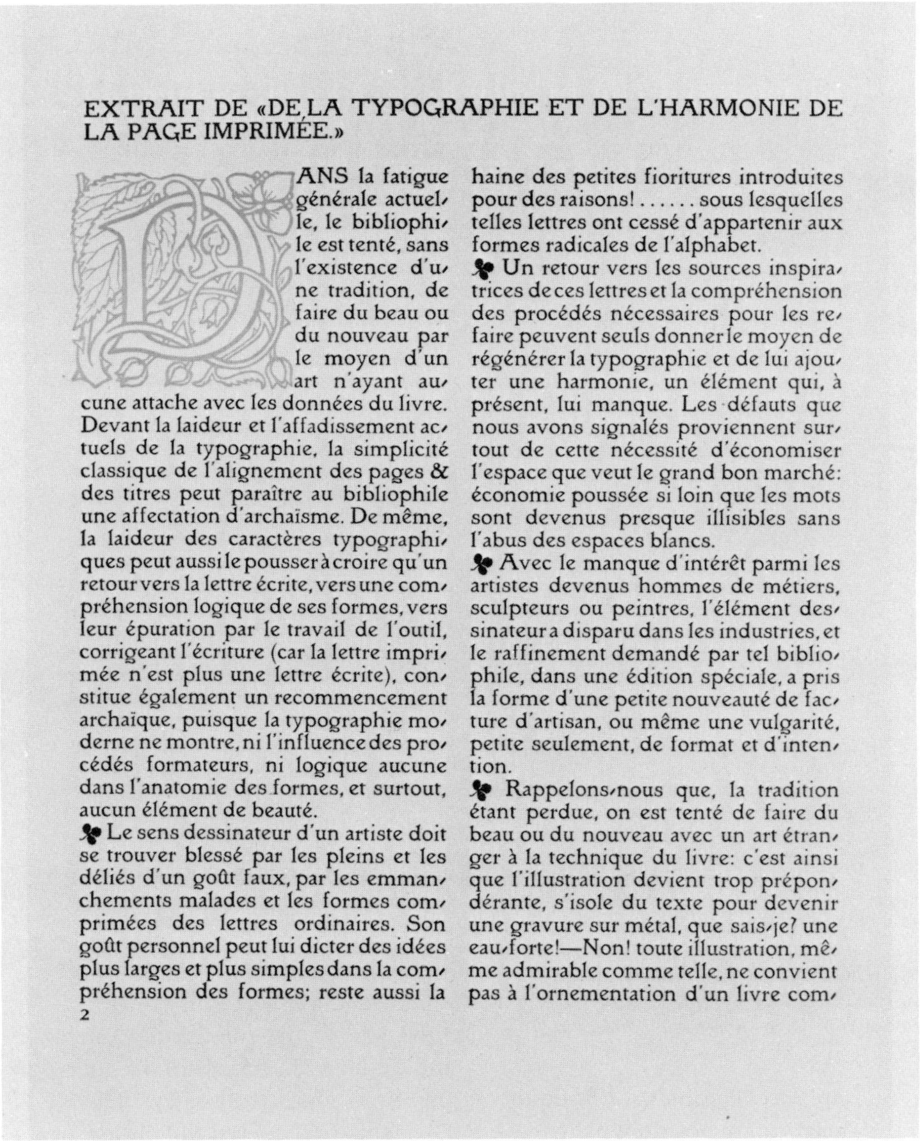

EXTRAIT DE «DE LA TYPOGRAPHIE ET DE L'HARMONIE DE LA PAGE IMPRIMÉE.»

DANS la fatigue générale actuelle, le bibliophile est tenté, sans l'existence d'une tradition, de faire du beau ou du nouveau par le moyen d'un art n'ayant aucune attache avec les données du livre. Devant la laideur et l'affadissement actuels de la typographie, la simplicité classique de l'alignement des pages & des titres peut paraître au bibliophile une affectation d'archaïsme. De même, la laideur des caractères typographiques peut aussi le pousser à croire qu'un retour vers la lettre écrite, vers une compréhension logique de ses formes, vers leur épuration par le travail de l'outil, corrigeant l'écriture (car la lettre imprimée n'est plus une lettre écrite), constitue également un recommencement archaïque, puisque la typographie moderne ne montre, ni l'influence des procédés formateurs, ni logique aucune dans l'anatomie des formes, et surtout, aucun élément de beauté.

❧ Le sens dessinateur d'un artiste doit se trouver blessé par les pleins et les déliés d'un goût faux, par les emmanchements malades et les formes comprimées des lettres ordinaires. Son goût personnel peut lui dicter des idées plus larges et plus simples dans la compréhension des formes; reste aussi la haine des petites fioritures introduites pour des raisons! . . . . . . sous lesquelles telles lettres ont cessé d'appartenir aux formes radicales de l'alphabet.

❧ Un retour vers les sources inspiratrices de ces lettres et la compréhension des procédés nécessaires pour les refaire peuvent seuls donner le moyen de régénérer la typographie et de lui ajouter une harmonie, un élément qui, à présent, lui manque. Les défauts que nous avons signalés proviennent surtout de cette nécessité d'économiser l'espace que veut le grand bon marché: économie poussée si loin que les mots sont devenus presque illisibles sans l'abus des espaces blancs.

❧ Avec le manque d'intérêt parmi les artistes devenus hommes de métiers, sculpteurs ou peintres, l'élément dessinateur a disparu dans les industries, et le raffinement demandé par tel bibliophile, dans une édition spéciale, a pris la forme d'une petite nouveauté de facture d'artisan, ou même une vulgarité, petite seulement, de format et d'intention.

❧ Rappelons-nous que, la tradition étant perdue, on est tenté de faire du beau ou du nouveau avec un art étranger à la technique du livre: c'est ainsi que l'illustration devient trop prépondérante, s'isole du texte pour devenir une gravure sur métal, que sais-je? une eau-forte!—Non! toute illustration, même admirable comme telle, ne convient pas à l'ornementation d'un livre com-

2

Lucien Pissarro, excerpt from *Of Typography and the Harmony of the Printed Page*, c. 1900. Using his legible Brook type which combined roman structure with slab serifs and a few decorative Art Nouveau details, Pissarro's page design typifies the structural unity and workmanship of the private press movement. *Houghton Library, Harvard University, Cambridge, Mass.*

A book-design renaissance

The long-range effect of William Morris was a significant upgrading of book design and typography throughout the world. In Germany, this influence inspired a renaissance of arts-and-crafts activities, wonderful new typefaces, and a significant improvement in book design.

The most important of the German men of letters was Rudolf Koch (1876–1934). This powerful figure was deeply mystical and medieval in his viewpoints. A devout Christian, Koch taught at the Arts and Crafts School in Offenbach am Main, where he led a community of writers, printers, stonemasons, and metal and tapestry workers in a creative community. He regarded the alphabet as a supreme spiritual achievement of humanity. Basing his work on pen-drawn calligraphy, before World War I, Koch sought the medieval experience through the design and lettering of handmade manuscript books. But he did not merely seek to imitate the medieval scribe; he tried to build upon the calligraphic tradition by creating an original, simple expression from his gestures and materials. After the war, Koch turned to handlettered broadsides and handicrafts, then became closely associated with the Klingspor Type Foundry. His type designs ranged from original interpretations of medieval letterforms to unexpected new designs such as the rough-hewn chunky letterforms of his Neuland face.

In America, the last phase of the Arts and Crafts Movement, the revitalization of typography and book design, moved forward in the hands of two young men from the Midwest who fell under the spell of the Kelmscott Press during the 1890s. Inspired for a lifetime of creative work, book designer Bruce Rogers (1870–1956) and typeface designer Frederic W. Goudy (1865–1947) lived long lives filled with a love of books and diligent work that enabled them to carry their exceptional sense of book design and production well into the twentieth century.

Even as a boy in Bloomington, Illinois, Frederic Goudy had a passionate love of letterforms. He later related that he cut over three thousand letters from colored paper and turned the church he attended into a multicolored environment of Biblical passages on the walls. Goudy was working in Chicago as a bookkeeper in the early 1890s when he became involved in printing and publicity. Books from the Kelmscott Press, including their *Chaucer*, and from other private presses at the rare book department of the A.C. McClurg Bookstore, fired Goudy's imagination. He became interested in art, literature and typography on "a higher plane than mere commercialism."

In 1894, Goudy started the Camelot Press with a friend, then left it and returned to bookkeeping the following year when disagreements developed. In 1895, he set up the short-lived Booklet Press, then designed his first typeface during the period of unemployment that followed. Named Camelot, his pencil

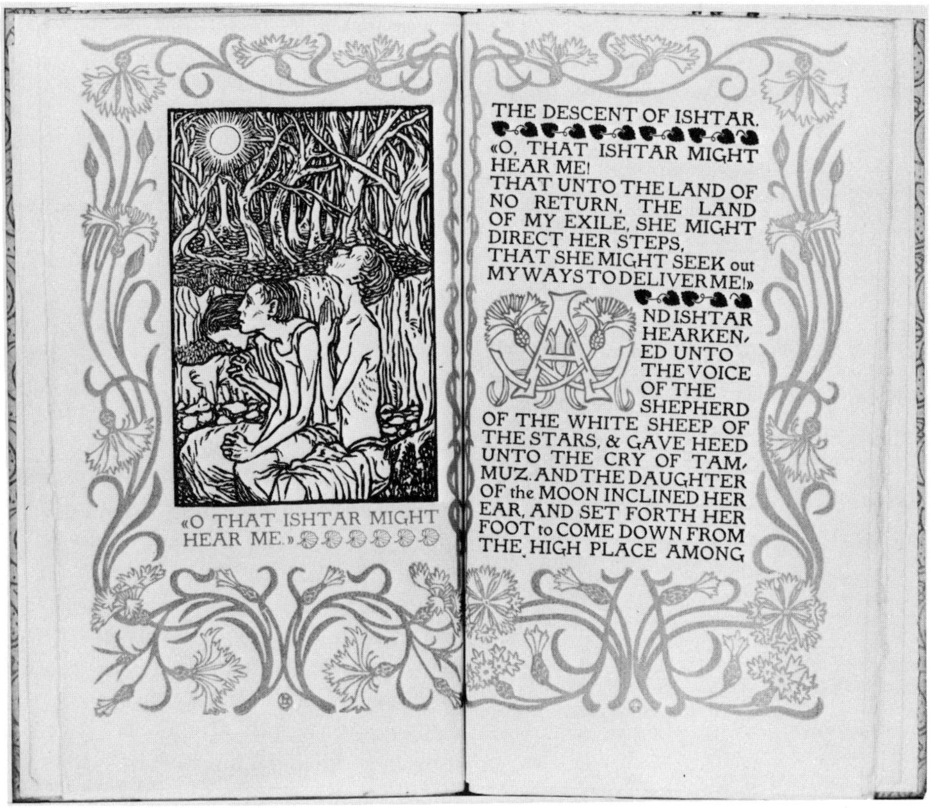

Lucien Pissarro, pages from *Ishtar's Descent to the Nether World,* 1903. The craft and handpress techniques of the private press movement combined with the design qualities of Art Nouveau in many Eragny Press volumes. *Library of Congress, Washington, D.C., Rosenwald Collection.*

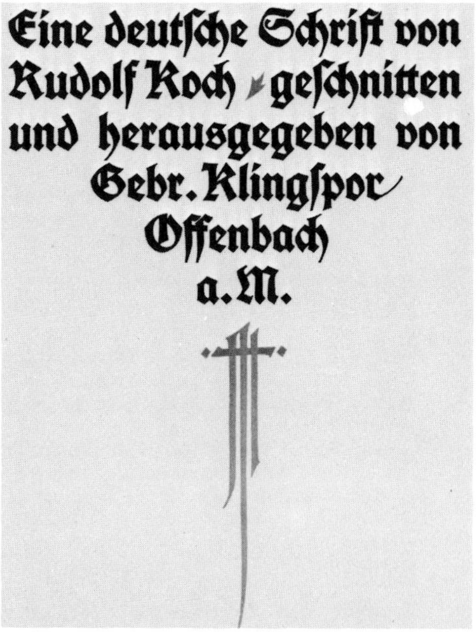

Rudolf Koch, title page demonstrating *Eine deutsche Schrift,* 1910. Koch's gothic revivals achieved unusual legibility, striking typographic color and spatial intervals, and many original forms and ligatures. *Houghton Library, Harvard University, Cambridge, Mass.*

drawing of capitals was mailed to the Dickinson Type Foundry of Boston with an offer to sell the design for five dollars. After a week or two, a check for ten dollars in payment of the design arrived. In 1899, Goudy became a freelance designer in Chicago specializing in lettering and typographic design. Another venture in printing, the Village Press, was modeled on the private press ideal of handicraft.

The Village Press was moved first to Boston then to New York, where a terrible fire completely destroyed it in 1908. That same year marked the end of Goudy's efforts as a printer; he turned his energy to the design, cutting, and casting of typefaces. It was also the year when Goudy began a long association with the Lanston Monotype Company, which commissioned some of his finest fonts. Goudy designed a total of one hundred twenty-two typefaces by his own count, including a few faces that were never produced and counting roman and italic variations as two faces. Even so, this outpouring of designs makes Goudy the most prolific American type designer and, perhaps, second only to Giambattista Bodoni in the sheer volume of designs created. With an amiable and witty personality and wonderful writing ability, Goudy became a link between William Morris and his ideals and the everyday printers. His readable books include *The Alphabet* (1908), *Elements of Lettering* (1921), and *Typologia* (1940). The two journals he edited, *Ars Typographica* and *Typographica,* impacted the course of book design. In 1923 Goudy established the Village Letter Foundry in an old mill on the Hudson River. There he designed types, cut matrices, and cast and sold type. In 1939 a second disastrous fire burned the mill to the ground, destroying about seventy-five of the seventy-four-year-old type designer's original type designs and thousands of matrices. Undaunted, Goudy continued to work until his death at age eighty-two.

A student of Goudy's at the turn of the century named William Addison Dwiggins (1880–1956) proved to be a highly literate book designer who established a house style for the Alfred A. Knopf publishing company and designed hundreds of volumes for this firm. During the early 1920s, Dwiggins first coined the phrase *graphic designer* to describe his professional activities. In 1938, Dwiggins designed one of the most widely used book faces in America, Caledonia.

Albert Bruce Rogers of Lafayette, Indiana, evolved from his Kelmscott roots in the 1890s and became the most important American book designer of the early twentieth century. After graduating from college where he was active as a campus artist, Rogers became a newspaper illustrator in Indianapolis for a time. Dismayed by the ambulance-chasing school of pictorial reportage that included frequent trips to the local morgue, Rogers tried landscape painting, worked for a Kansas railroad, and did book illustrations for an Indianapolis studio in the typical saga of the young man in search of himself. When he was shown Kelmscott books

DENN EINE JEGLICHE KUNST
ODER WERK WIE KLEIN
SIE SEIEN DAS SIND ALLE
SAMT GNADEN UND WIR
KET SIE ALLESAMT DER HEI+
LIGE GEIST ZU NUTZ UND
ZU FRUCHT DER MENSCHEN
+WÄRE ICH NICHT EIN PRIE
STER UND WÄRE UNTER
EINER VERSAMMLUNG+ICH
NÄHME ES FÜR EIN GROSSES
DING DASS ICH SCHUHE MA
CHEN KÖNNTE UND ICH
WOLLTE AUCH GERNE MEIN
BROT MIT MEINEN HÄN
DEN VERDIENEN KINDER
DER FUSS NOCH DIE HAND
DIE SOLLEN NICHT DAS AUGE
SEIN WOLLEN EIN JEGLI
CHER SOLL SEIN AMT TUN
DAS IHM GOTT ZUGEFÜGT.

Rudolph Koch, specimen of *Neuland,* 1922–23. A dense texture is achieved in this intuitively designed typeface with unprecedented capital *C* and *S* forms. The woodcut-inspired ornaments are used to justify this setting into a crisp rectangle. *Courtesy of D. Stempel AG, Frankfurt au Main, Germany.*

by a close friend, J. M. Bowles, his interest immediately shifted toward the total design of books. Bowles was running an art supply store and editing a small magazine called *Modern Art.* Louis Prang became interested in this periodical and invited Bowles to move to Boston and edit what now became an L. Prang and Company periodical. A typographic designer was needed, so Rogers was hired at fifty cents an hour with a twenty-hour-per-week guarantee.

Rogers joined the Riverside Press of the Houghton Mifflin Company in 1896, and designed a number of books with a strong Arts and Crafts influence. In 1900, the Riverside Press established a special department for producing quality limited editions, and Rogers became the designer for the series. Sixty limited editions produced at Riverside over the next twelve years enabled Rogers to emerge as an influential book designer. His work set the tone for the well-designed twentieth-century book. Beatrice Warde wrote that Rogers "managed to steal the Divine Fire which glowed in the Kelmscott Press books, and somehow be the first to bring it down to earth." Rogers applied the ideal of the beautifully designed book to commercial production. He has been called an allusive designer, for his work recalls earlier years and styles. For inspiration, he shifted from Incunabula volumes of Jenson and Ratdolt with their sturdy types and strong woodblock ornaments to the lighter, graceful books of the French Renaissance.

Beginning in 1912, Rogers left the Riverside Press to become a freelance book designer. In spite of some difficult years, Rogers needed freedom to be able to realize his full potential as a graphic artist. His 1915 typeface design, Centaur, is one of the finest of the numerous styles based on the 1470 style by Jenson. It was first used in Rogers' design for the *Centaur* by Maurice de Guerin, which is one of Rogers' most elegant book designs. In 1916, Rogers journeyed to England for an unsuccessful effort to collaborate with Emery Walker and stayed on as a consultant to the Cambridge University Press until 1919. Again from 1928 through 1932, when his comissions included the design of the monumental Oxford Lectern Bible, Rogers worked in England.

Very much an intuitive designer, Rogers possessed an outstanding sense of visual proportion and of "rightness." Design is a decision-making process; the culmination of subtle choices about paper, type, margins, leading between lines, and so on can combine to create either a unity or a disaster. Rogers wrote that "the ultimate test, in considering the employment or the rejection of an element of design or decoration, would seem to be: does it look as if it were *inevitable,* or would the page look as well or better for its omission?" So rigorous were Rogers' design standards that, when he compiled a list of successful books from among the seven hundred he designed, he only selected thirty! The first book on his list was predated by over a hundred earlier ones. While Rogers was a classicist who revived the forms of the past, he did so with a sense of appropriate form for outstanding book

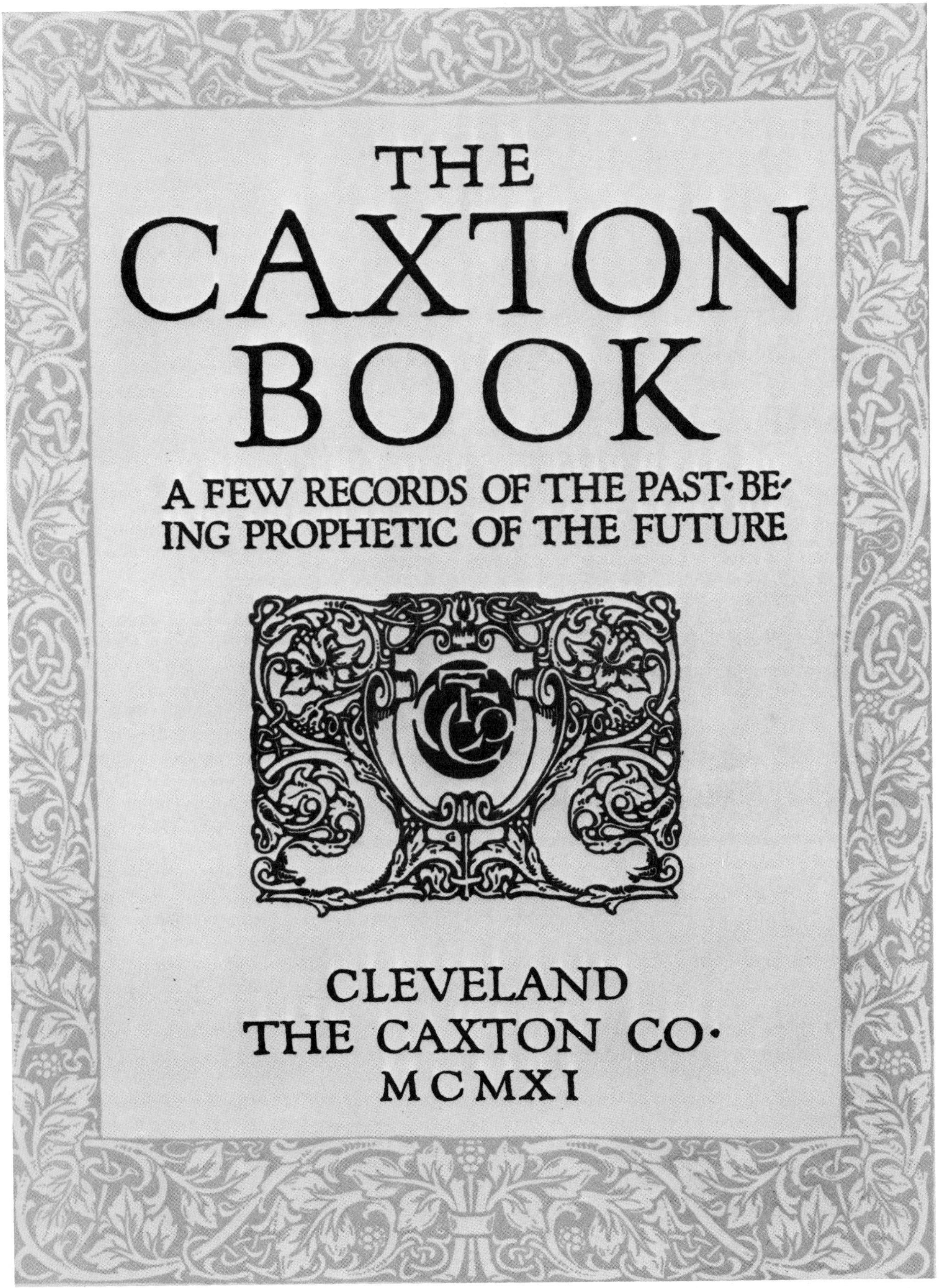
THE
CAXTON
BOOK

A FEW RECORDS OF THE PAST·BE-
ING PROPHETIC OF THE FUTURE

CLEVELAND
THE CAXTON CO·
MCMXI

Frederic Goudy, booklet cover for the Caxton Company, 1911. The decoration is Kelmscott, but the lettering is all Goudy.

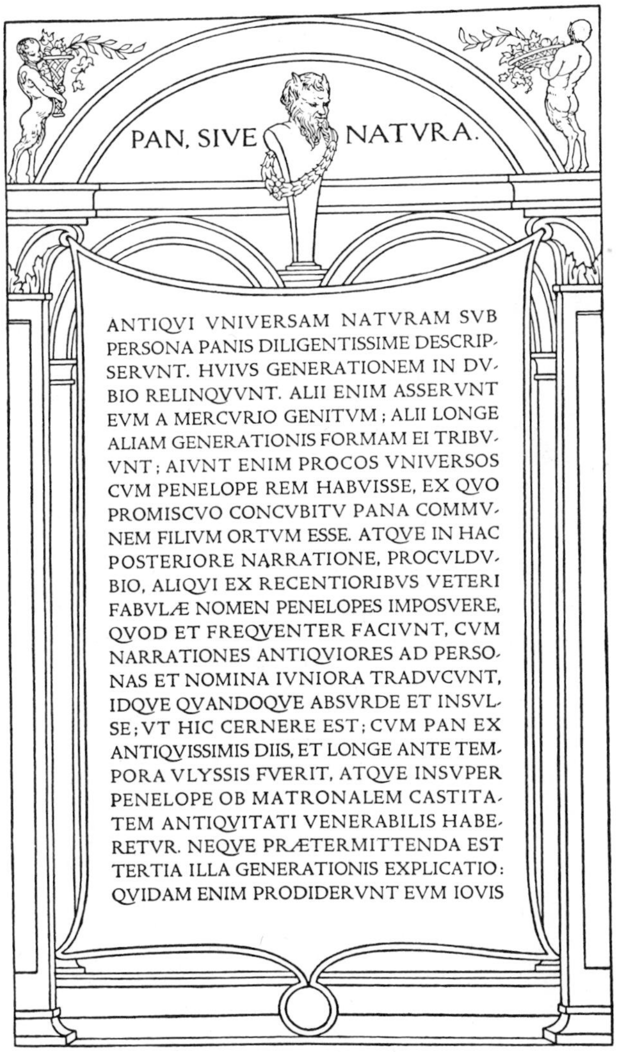
PAN. SIVE NATVRA.

ANTIQVI VNIVERSAM NATVRAM SVB PERSONA PANIS DILIGENTISSIME DESCRIPSERVNT. HVIVS GENERATIONEM IN DVBIO RELINQVVNT. ALII ENIM ASSERVNT EVM A MERCVRIO GENITVM; ALII LONGE ALIAM GENERATIONIS FORMAM EI TRIBVVNT; AIVNT ENIM PROCOS VNIVERSOS CVM PENELOPE REM HABVISSE, EX QVO PROMISCVO CONCVBITV PANA COMMVNEM FILIVM ORTVM ESSE. ATQVE IN HAC POSTERIORE NARRATIONE, PROCVLDVBIO, ALIQVI EX RECENTIORIBVS VETERI FABVLÆ NOMEN PENELOPES IMPOSVERE, QVOD ET FREQVENTER FACIVNT, CVM NARRATIONES ANTIQVIORES AD PERSONAS ET NOMINA IVNIORA TRADVCVNT, IDQVE QVANDOQVE ABSVRDE ET INSVLSE; VT HIC CERNERE EST; CVM PAN EX ANTIQVISSIMIS DIIS, ET LONGE ANTE TEMPORA VLYSSIS FVERIT, ATQVE INSVPER PENELOPE OB MATRONALEM CASTITATEM ANTIQVITATI VENERABILIS HABERETVR. NEQVE PRÆTERMITTENDA EST TERTIA ILLA GENERATIONIS EXPLICATIO: QVIDAM ENIM PRODIDERVNT EVM IOVIS

Bruce Rogers, typographic page of classical typography. Venetian in concept, this design uses a similar weight in the type strokes and frame. The light coming through the all-capitals type makes a value close to the tone of the architectural motif, which further unifies the two elements.

THE CENTAUR. WRITTEN BY MAURICE DE GUÉRIN AND NOW TRANSLATED FROM THE FRENCH BY GEORGE B. IVES.

I Was born in a cavern of these mountains. Like the river in yonder valley, whose first drops flow from some cliff that weeps in a deep grotto, the first moments of my life sped amidst the shadows of a secluded retreat, nor vexed its silence. As our mothers draw near their term, they retire to the caverns, and in the innermost recesses of the wildest of them all, where the darkness is most dense, they bring forth, uncomplaining, offspring as silent as themselves. Their strength giving milk enables us to endure without weakness or dubious struggles the first difficulties of life; yet we leave our caverns later than you your cradles. The reason is that there is a tradition amongst us that the early days of life must be secluded and guarded, as days engrossed by the gods.

My growth ran almost its entire course in the darkness where I was born. The innermost depths of my home were so far within the bowels of the mountain, that I should not have known in which direction the opening lay, had it not been that the winds at times blew in and caused a sudden coolness and confusion. Sometimes, too, my mother returned, bringing with her the perfume of the valleys, or dripping wet from the streams to which she resorted. Now, these her home-comings, although they told me naught of the valleys or the streams, yet, being attended by emanations therefrom, disturbed my thoughts, and I wandered about, all agitated, amidst my darkness. 'What,' I would say to myself, 'are these places to which my mother goes and what power reigns there which summons her so frequently? To what influences is one there exposed,

Bruce Rogers, page from *The Centaur* by Maurice de Guerin, 1915. The headpiece, initial, and page layout echo the wonderful graphic designs of the French Renaissance.

design. As did Frederic Goudy, Rogers lived a long life and was honored for his accomplishments as a graphic designer during his twilight years.

As a result of the interest in typographic history inspired by the Arts and Crafts Movement and the private presses, the first decades of the twentieth century saw many revivals of traditional typeface designs. Garamond, Plantin, Caslon, Baskerville and Bodoni: the typeface designs of past masters were studied, recut, and issued for hand and keyboard composition during the first three decades of the century.

Goudy Old Style
Goudy Old Style Italic
Goudy Catalogue
Goudy Bold
Goudy Extra Bold
Goudy Heavyface
Goudy Handtooled
Goudy Mediaeval

Frederic Goudy, the Goudy family of Old Style fonts captures the feeling of Venetian and French Renaissance typography.

14

Art Nouveau and the Turn of the Century

INTERNATIONAL IN SCOPE, ART Nouveau is a decorative style that thrived during the two decades (c. 1890–1910) that girded the turn of the century. It encompassed all the design arts: architecture, furniture and product design, fashion, and graphics. This design revolution touched all aspects of the man-made environment: posters, packages, and advertisements; teapots, dishes, and spoons; chairs, doorframes, and staircases; factories, subway entrances, and houses.

Art Nouveau's identifying visual quality is an organic plantlike line. Freed from roots or gravity, it can either undulate with whiplash energy or flow with elegant grace as it defines, modulates, and decorates a given space. Vine tendrils, flowers such as the rose and lily, birds (particularly peacocks), and the female form were frequent motifs from which this fluid line was adapted.

To dismiss Art Nouveau as surface decoration is to ignore its pivotal role in the evolution of all aspects of design. Art Nouveau is the "transitional style" that turned from the *historicism* which dominated design for most of the nineteenth century. Historicism is the almost servile use of forms and styles from the past instead of the invention of new forms to express the present. By replacing historicism with innovation, Art Nouveau became the initial phase of the modern movement. It prepared the way for the twentieth century by sweeping this historicizing spirit from design.

Ideas, processes, and forms in twentieth-century art bear witness to this catalytic importance. Modern architecture, graphic and industrial design, surrealism, and abstract art have roots in its underlying theory and concepts. Instead of decorating the structure by applying ornament to the surface of a building or object, as in earlier styles, the basic form and shape of an Art Nouveau design was often governed by, and evolved with, the design of the ornament. This was a new design principle: decoration, structure, and intended function are unified. Because the forms and lines of Art Nouveau were often invented rather than copied from nature or the past, it was a revitalization of the design process that pointed toward abstract art.

During this period, there was a close collaboration between visual artists and writers. The French Symbolist movement in literature of the 1880s and 1890s, with its rejection of realism in favor of the metaphysical and sensuous, was an important influence. This contact led to symbolic and philosophic attitudes by artists. In a skeptical era when scientific rationalism was on the rise and traditional religious beliefs and social norms were under assault, art was seen as a potential vehicle to a much needed spiritual rejuvenation. Birth, life, and death; growth and decay; these became symbolic subject matter. The complexity of this era and movement has allowed contradictory interpretations. Because of its decorativeness, some observers see Art Nouveau as an expression of late nineteenth-century decadence. However, others see it as a reaction against the decadence and materialism of this epoch. This view is a response to Art Nouveau's quest for spiritual and aesthetic values.

Art Nouveau graphic designers and illustrators attempted to make art a part of everyday life. Their fine arts training had educated them about art forms and methods developed primarily for aesthetic considerations. At the same time, they enthusiastically embraced applied art techniques which had evolved with the development of commercial printing processes. As a result, they were able to upgrade significantly the visual quality of mass communications.

The international character of Art Nouveau was expedited by advances in transportation and communications technology. Contact between artists in various nations, primarily through print media, allowed cross-fertilization to take place. The many art periodicals of the 1890s served this purpose while introducing the new art and design to the larger public.

The numerous sources often cited for Art Nouveau are diffuse and wide ranging. They include William Blake's book illustration, Celtic ornament, the Rococo style, the Arts and Crafts Movement, Pre-Raphaelite painting, and Japanese decorative design and woodblock prints. The treaties that resulted from American Commodore Matthew C. Perry's naval expeditions to Japan beginning in 1853 led to the collapse of Japan's traditional isolationist policy and the opening of trade with the west. Japanese art and artifacts began to pour into Europe, and several books on Japanese art and ornament were published during the 1880s. The influence of the Japanese

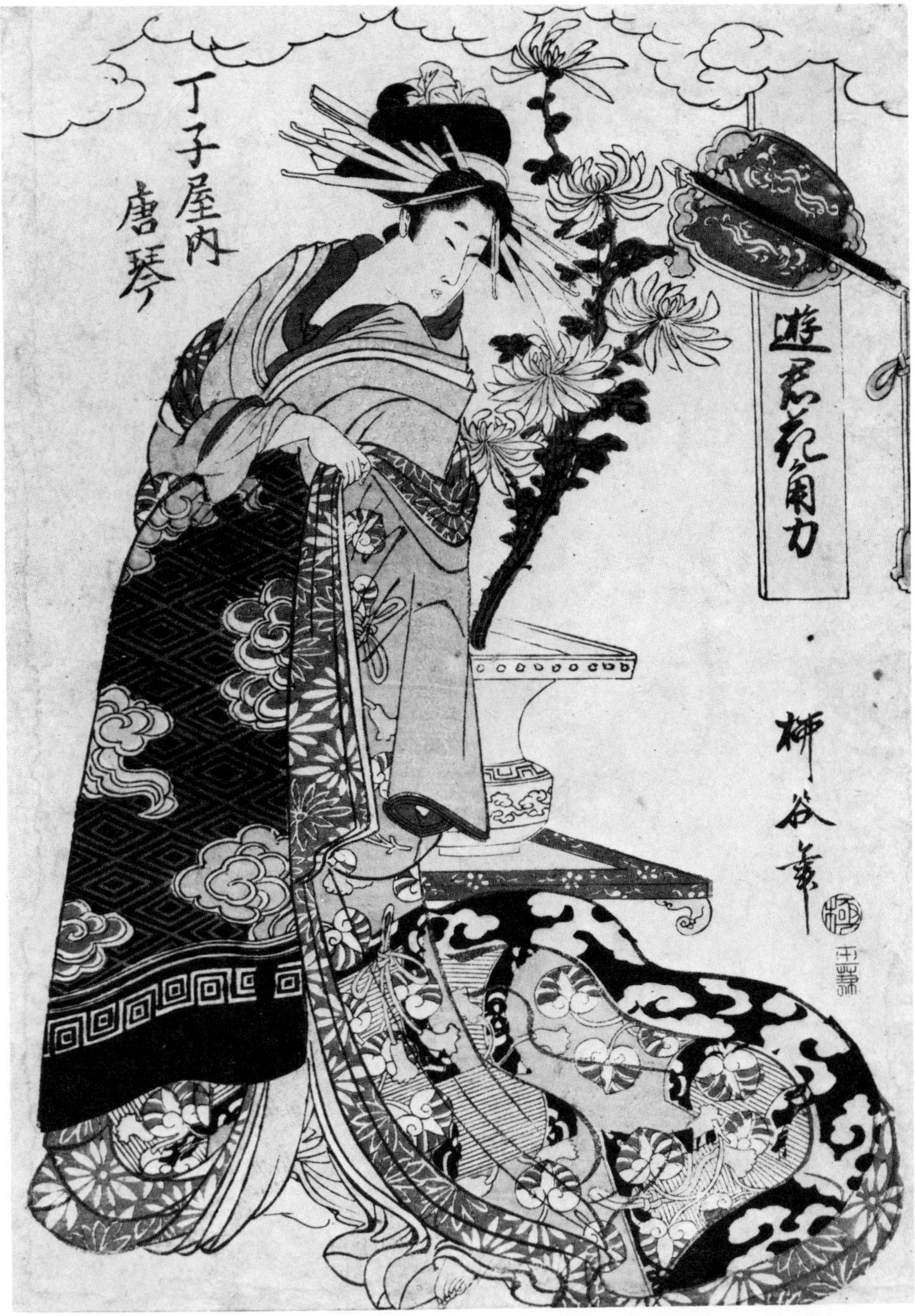

Hishikawa Ryuoku, *Woman Standing Before a Large Pot of Chrysanthemums,* woodblock print, nineteenth century. This print has the qualities that excited nineteenth-century artists and designers: flowing curved contours, flat shapes of color, and decorative patterns. *Virginia Museum, Richmond, Bequest of Mr. Charles B. Samuels, 1941.*

print included calligraphic line drawing, the simplification of natural appearances, flat silhouette shapes and color, and decorative areas of pattern.

Important inspiration came from the painting of the late 1880s, which had fallen under the oriental spell. The swirling forms of Vincent Van Gogh (1853–1890), the flat color and stylized organic contour of Paul Gauguin (1848–1903), and the work of the Nabis group of young artists played a role. The Nabis explored symbolic color and decorative patterns. They concluded that a painting was, first of all, an arrangement of color in two-dimensional patterns.

Jules Chéret, poster for *Orphée aux Enfers,* 1879. In this poster from Chéret's transitional period, the major figures and letterforms become dominant, although the intricate background competes for attention. *Musée de l'Affiches, Paris*

Chéret and Grasset

The transition from Victorian graphics to the Art Nouveau style was a gradual one. Two graphic artists working in Paris, Jules Chéret (1836–1933) and Eugène Grasset (1841–1917), played important roles in the transition.

In 1881 a new French law concerning freedom of the press lifted many censorship restrictions and allowed posters to be attached anywhere except churches, polls, and areas designated for official notices. This new law led to a booming poster industry of designers, printers, and *afficheurs.* The streets became an art gallery for the nation, as even the poorest worker saw the environment transformed by images and color. Respected painters felt no shame at creating advertising posters. The Arts and Crafts Movement was creating a new respect for the applied arts, and Jules Chéret had shown the way. Acclaimed as the father of the modern poster, Chéret was the son of a poor typesetter who paid four hundred francs to secure a three-year lithographic apprenticeship for him at age thirteen. The young teenager spent his weekdays lettering backwards on lithographic stones and his Sundays absorbing art at the Louvre. After completing his apprenticeship, he worked as a lithographic craftsman and renderer for several firms and took drawing classes at the National Drawing School. When he was eighteen, he headed for London but could only find work making catalogue drawings of furniture, so he returned to Paris after six months. He moved into the small attic room of his brother, Joseph, also a lithographer, where they took turns sleeping on the bed and the floor.

These were difficult years for Chéret. He was convinced that pictorial lithographic posters would replace the typographic letterpress posters, which filled the urban environment and only occasionally had small woodcut illustrations, but he could not convince advertisers of this. At the age of twenty-two, he produced a blue-and-brown poster for Offenbach's operetta, *Orphée aux Enfers* (*Orpheus in Hades*). When further commissions were not forthcoming, he returned to London. English color lithography was more advanced, and Chéret soon mastered it. A poster commission for a family of clowns he had befriended was the turning point; it led to label commissions from the philanthropist and perfume manufacturer, Eugene Rimmel. Several years of close association and friendship with Rimmel were marked by extensive design and production experience,

Jules Chéret, poster for *La Biche au Bois,* 1866. Printed in green and black, Chéret's early poster used the multiple-image format so popular in the 1860s. The lettering is a harbinger of the swirling forms of Chéret's mature style. *Musée de l'Affiches, Paris.*

culminating in Rimmel financing Chéret to establish a printing firm in Paris in 1866. The latest English technology and custom-crafted, oversized lithographic stones were purchased, and Chéret was poised to begin the process of running letterpress typography from the signboards. The first poster from his shop was a monochromatic design for the theatrical production *La Biche au Bois* (*The Doe in the Wood*) starring the twenty-two-year-old Sarah Bernhardt. Artist and actress took Paris by storm as Bernhardt became the leading actress of her day and Chéret pioneered the visual poster. His second poster was a color production for the Bal Valentino dance hall. From 1866 until the turn of the century, he produced over one thousand posters.

Chéret's artistic influences included the idealized beauty and carefree lifestyle painted by Watteau and Fragonard, the color luminosity of Turner, and the churning movement of Tiepolo, whose figures expressed energy and movement through twisting torsos and extended limbs. Chéret personally worked directly on the stone, in contrast to the standard practice of commissioning a design from an artist for execution on the stones by craftsmen. During the 1880s he used a black line with the primary colors; red, yellow, and blue. He achieved a graphic vitality with these bright colors, and subtle overprinting allowed an astonishing range of color and effects. Stipple and crosshatch; soft watercolorlike washes, and bold calligraphic chunks of color; scratching, scraping, and splattering; all were used in his work. His typical composition is a central figure or figures in animated gesture, surrounded by swirls of color, secondary figures or props, and bold lettering that often echos the shapes and gestures of the figure. His unending production for music halls and the theater, beverages and medicines, entertainers, and publications transformed the walls of Paris.

In 1881 he sold his printing company to Imprimerie Chaix and became artistic director of this large firm, a move that allowed more time for art and design. In the mornings he drew

Jules Chéret, poster for *Valentino's Ball*, 1872. The lively dynamic figures and efforts to unify words and images visually—hallmarks of Chéret's mature style—are developing. *Jules Chéret Museum, Nice.*

from the model, then spent the afternoons painting at his easel, drawing pastels, and working on his huge lithographic stones.

The beautiful young women he created, dubbed "the Chérette" by an admiring public, were archetypes, not only for the idealized presentation of woman in mass media, but for a generation of French women who used her dress and apparent lifestyle as inspiration. One pundit has dubbed Chéret "the father of women's liberation" because his women introduced a new role model as the Victorian Era gave way to the Gay Nineties. Options for women were still limited, and the proper lady in the drawing room and the tramp in the bordello were stereotyped roles. Into this dichotomy swept the Chérette. Neither prude nor prostitute, these self-assured, happy creatures enjoyed life to the fullest, wearing low-cut dresses, dancing, drinking wine, and even smoking in public. By 1884, some Chéret posters were produced in sizes up to seven feet tall by printing the image in sections to be joined on the wall by the afficheurs. The total annual press runs of his designs were almost two hundred thousand copies. At least eight French printers specialized in posters, and Chéret was joined by a score of other poster designers.

While Chéret preferred the large format, saying that since "a well-made woman is about 150 centimeters, a poster 240 centimeters in length affords ample space for drawing a figure full length," his output ranged from lifesize images to the diminutive.

In 1889, Chéret's contribution was recognized when he received a gold medal at the International Exhibition and enjoyed the acclaim of leading critics reporting on his major one-man show. A petition was circulated which led to Chéret being named to the Legion of Honor by the French government in 1890. He was cited for creating a new branch of art which advanced printing and served the needs of commerce and industry. After the turn of the century Chéret's poster production nearly ceased as he spent more time on pastels and paintings. He retired to Nice, where the Jules Chéret Museum preserving his work opened shortly before his death at the age of ninety-seven.

Jules Chéret, *Loie Fuller* poster, 1893. To capture the dynamics of the American dancer who performed with swirling veils and had taken Paris by storm, Chéret used painterly gestures of color.

Jules Chéret, *Palais de Glace* ("Ice Palace") poster, 1896. Parisian elegance, a carefree grace, and astounding technical mastery were achieved in Chéret's 1890s posters. The figures create a lively play of angles linking the lettering at bottom left and top right.

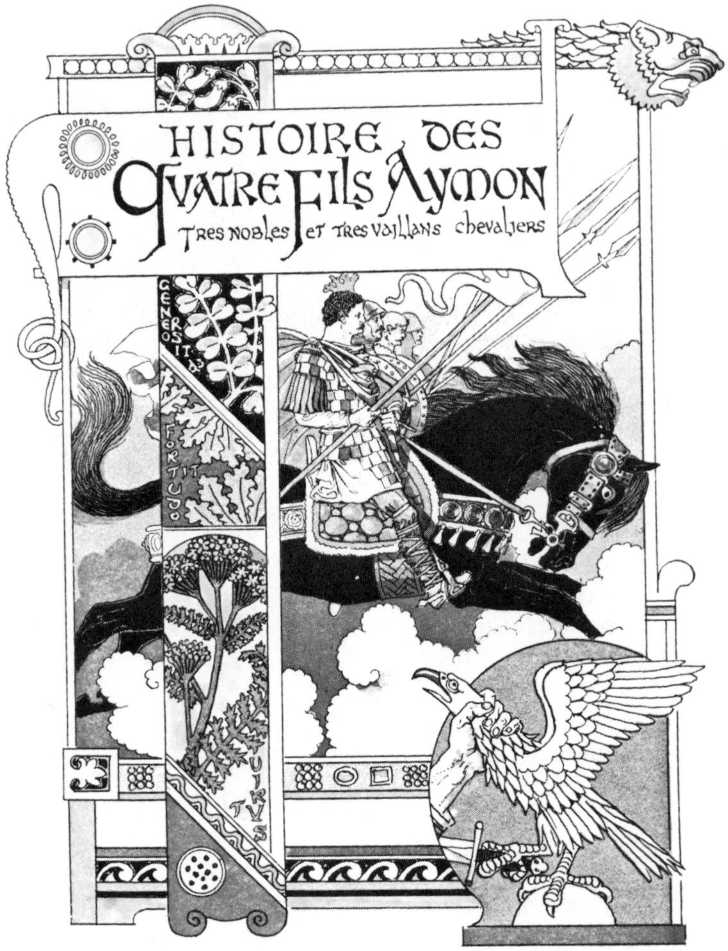

Eugène Grasset, title page for *Histoire des Quartre Fils Aymon,* 1883. Using contour lines that divide the space into zones, Grasset was able to pull together lettering, illustration, and decorative patterns into a total page design. *Houghton Library, Harvard University, Cambridge, Mass.*

Swiss-born Eugène Grasset was the first illustrator/designer to rival Chéret in public popularity. Grasset had studied medieval art intensely, and this influence, mingled with a love of exotic oriental art, reflected strongly in his designs for furniture, stained glass, textiles, and books. A bellwether achievement, both in graphic design and printing technology, is the 1883 publication of *L'Histoire des quatre fils Aymon* which was designed and illustrated by Grasset. It was printed in an aquatint grain, color photo-relief process from plates made by Charles Gillot, who transformed Grasset's line and watercolor designs into subtle full color, printed book illustrations. The artist and platemaker collaborated closely on this two-year project with Grasset working extensively on the plates. The design is important for its total integration of illustrations, format, and typography. Some of Grasset's design ideas that were rapidly assimilated after publication include the decorative borders framing the content, the integration of illustration and text into a unity, and the design of illustrations so that typography is printed over skies and other areas.

In 1886 Grasset received his first poster commission. His willowy maidens, appearing in long flowing robes and static poses, and advertising inks, chocolates, and beer, soon began to grace French streets. He developed a "coloring-book style" of thick black contour drawing and flat areas of color. His figures echo Botticelli and medieval clothing; his stylized, flat cloud patterns reflect his study of Japanese woodblocks. Grasset's formal composition and muted color contrasted strongly to Chéret's informally composed, brightly colored work. In spite of Grasset's tradition-bound attitude, his flowing line, subjective color, and everpresent floral motifs pointed toward French Art Nouveau.

English Art Nouveau

In England the Art Nouveau movement was primarily concerned with graphic design and illustration rather than architectural and product design. Its sources included Gothic art and Victorian painting in addition to those listed earlier. A strong momentum toward an international style was created by the inaugural issue of *The Studio* in April 1893. The first of nearly a dozen upstart European art periodicals of the 1890s, the April issue reproduced the work of Aubrey Beardsley (1872–1898). *The Three Brides* by the Dutch artist Jan Toorop

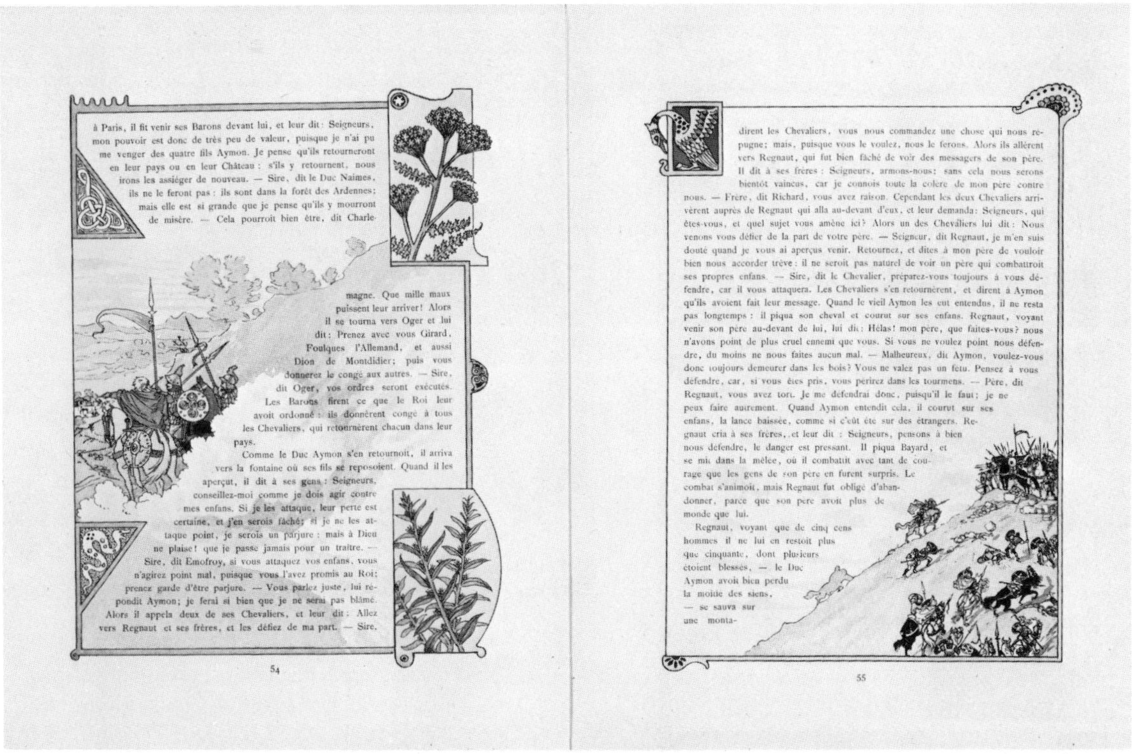

à Paris, il fit venir ses Barons devant lui, et leur dit : Seigneurs, mon pouvoir est donc de très peu de valeur, puisque je n'ai pu me venger des quatre fils Aymon. Je pense qu'ils retourneront en leur pays ou en leur Château : s'ils y retournent, nous irons les assiéger de nouveau. — Sire, dit le Duc Naimes, ils ne le feront pas : ils sont dans la forêt des Ardennes; mais elle est si grande que je pense qu'ils y mourront de misère. — Cela pourroit bien être, dit Charlemagne. Que mille maux puissent leur arriver! Alors il se tourna vers Oger et lui dit : Prenez avec vous Girard, Foulques l'Allemand, et aussi Dion de Montdidier; puis vous donnerez le congé aux autres. — Sire, dit Oger, vos ordres seront exécutés. Les Barons firent ce que le Roi leur avoit ordonné : ils donnèrent congé à tous les Chevaliers, qui retournèrent chacun dans leur pays.

Comme le Duc Aymon s'en retournoit, il arriva vers la fontaine où ses fils se reposoient. Quand il les aperçut, il dit à ses gens : Seigneurs, conseillez-moi comme je dois agir contre mes enfans. Si je les attaque, leur perte est certaine, et j'en serois fâché; si je ne les attaque point, je serois un parjure : mais à Dieu ne plaise! que je passe jamais pour un traître. — Sire, dit Emofroy, si vous attaquez vos enfans, vous n'agirez point mal, puisque vous l'avez promis au Roi; prenez garde d'être parjure. — Vous parlez juste, lui répondit Aymon; je ferai si bien que je ne serai pas blâmé. Alors il appela deux de ses Chevaliers, et leur dit : Allez vers Regnaut et ses frères, et les défiez de ma part. — Sire,

54

dirent les Chevaliers, vous nous commandez une chose qui nous répugne; mais, puisque vous le voulez, nous le ferons. Alors ils allèrent vers Regnaut, qui fut bien fâché de voir des messagers de son père. Il dit à ses frères : Seigneurs, armons-nous; sans cela nous serons bientôt vaincus, car je connois toute la colère de mon père contre nous. — Frère, dit Richard, vous avez raison. Cependant les deux Chevaliers arrivèrent auprès de Regnaut qui alla au-devant d'eux, et leur demanda : Seigneurs, qui êtes-vous, et quel sujet vous amène ici? Alors un des Chevaliers lui dit : Nous venons vous défier de la part de votre père. — Seigneur, dit Regnaut, je m'en suis douté quand je vous ai aperçus venir. Retournez, et dites à mon père de vouloir bien nous accorder trêve : il ne seroit pas naturel de voir un père qui combattroit ses propres enfans. — Sire, dit le Chevalier, préparez-vous toujours à vous défendre, car il vous attaquera. Les Chevaliers s'en retournèrent, et dirent à Aymon qu'ils avoient fait leur message. Quand le vieil Aymon les eut entendus, il ne resta pas longtemps : il piqua son cheval et courut sur ses enfans. Regnaut, voyant venir son père au-devant de lui, lui dit : Hélas! mon père, que faites-vous? nous n'avons point de plus cruel ennemi que vous. Si vous ne voulez point nous défendre, du moins ne nous faites aucun mal. — Malheureux, dit Aymon, voulez-vous donc toujours demeurer dans les bois? Vous ne valez pas un fétu. Pensez à vous défendre, car, si vous êtes pris, vous périrez dans les tourmens. — Père, dit Regnaut, vous avez tort. Je me défendrai donc, puisqu'il le faut; je ne peux faire autrement. Quand Aymon entendit cela, il courut sur ses enfans, la lance baissée, comme si c'eût été sur des étrangers. Regnaut cria à ses frères, et leur dit : Seigneurs, pensons à bien nous défendre, le danger est pressant. Il piqua Bayard, et se mit dans la mêlée, où il combattit avec tant de courage que les gens de son père en furent surpris. Le combat s'animoit, mais Regnaut fut obligé d'abandonner, parce que son père avoit plus de monde que lui.

Regnaut, voyant que de cinq cens hommes il ne lui en restoit plus que cinquante, dont plusieurs étoient blessés, — le Duc Aymon avoit bien perdu la moitié des siens, — se sauva sur une monta-

55

Eugène Grasset, pages from *Histoire des Quartre Fils Aymon,* 1883. Typography that is set in shapes designed around the illustrations combine with illustrations that fade out behind the typography in remarkable page layouts. *Houghton Library, Harvard University, Cambridge, Mass.*

Eugène Grasset, from *Ornaments Typographiques,* c. 1894. During the 1880s, Grasset designed three dozen sets of headpieces, tailpieces, and ornamental initials, which were gathered together in this 1894 printer's specimen book. *Houghton Library, Harvard University, Cambridge, Mass.*

Eugène Grasset, exhibition poster, c. 1894. Quietly demure instead of exuberant, Grasset's figures were the opposite of Chéret's, and the firm contour lines lock the forms into flat color planes in a manner similar to medieval stained glass windows.

(1858–1928) was included in the September issue. The collective influence of these two artists was enormous. Early issues of *The Studio* also included work by Walter Crane and furniture and textiles produced for the department store, Liberty and Company. Crane was an early innovator in the application of Japanese ornamental pattern and Eastern interpretations of nature to the design of surface pattern; Liberty's textiles led the Italians to call Art Nouveau *stile Liberty.*

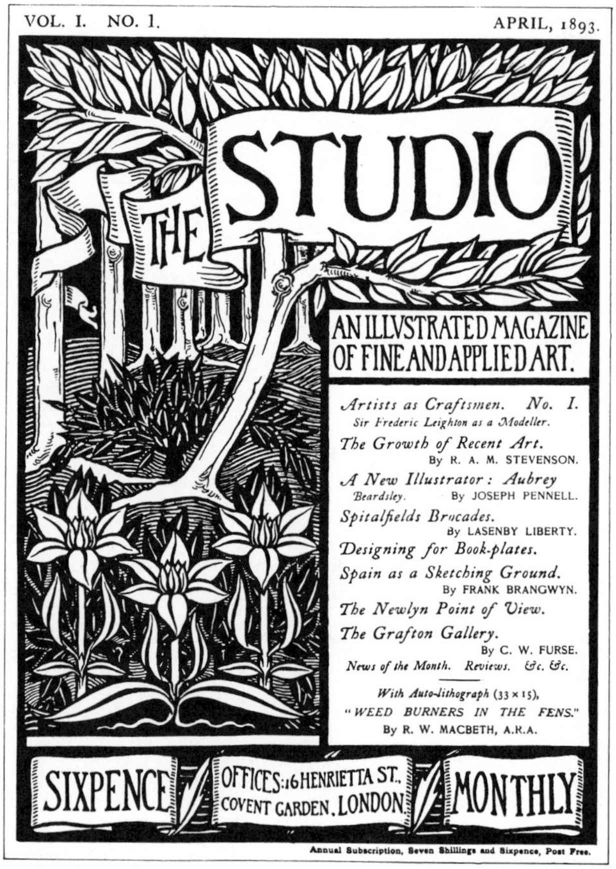

Aubrey Beardsley, *The Studio,* 1893. Beardsley's career was launched when editor C. Lewis Hine featured him on the cover and reproduced eleven of his illustrations in the inaugural issue of *The Studio*. This magazine's first years suffered from dull layout because page after page of two text columns were broken with very small illustrations.

Aubrey Beardsley was the enfant terrible of Art Nouveau with his stunning pen line, vibrant black and white, and shockingly exotic imagery. A strange cult figure, he was furiously prolific for only five years and died of tuberculosis at age twenty-six. He became famous at age twenty when his illustrations for a new edition of Malory's *Mort D'Arthur* began to appear in monthly installments. A strong Kelmscott influence was augmented by strange and imaginative distortions of the human figure and powerful black shapes. Japanese blockprints and William Morris were synthesized into a new style. Beardsley's unique line was preserved by the process-engraving woodblock method which, unlike the handcut block, re-

Jan Toorop, *The Three Brides,* 1893. In this pencil and colored crayon drawing on brown paper, Toorop considered the undulating flow of stylized ribbons of hair to symbolize sound pouring forth from the bells. *Courtesy, Rijksmuseum Kröller-Muller, Otterlo, Holland.*

Aubrey Beardsley, *Mort D'Arthur,* full-page illustration, 1893. This image shows Beardsley's emerging ability to compose contour line, textured areas, and black-and-white shapes into powerful compositions. The contrast between geometric and organic shapes reflects the influence of the Japanese print.

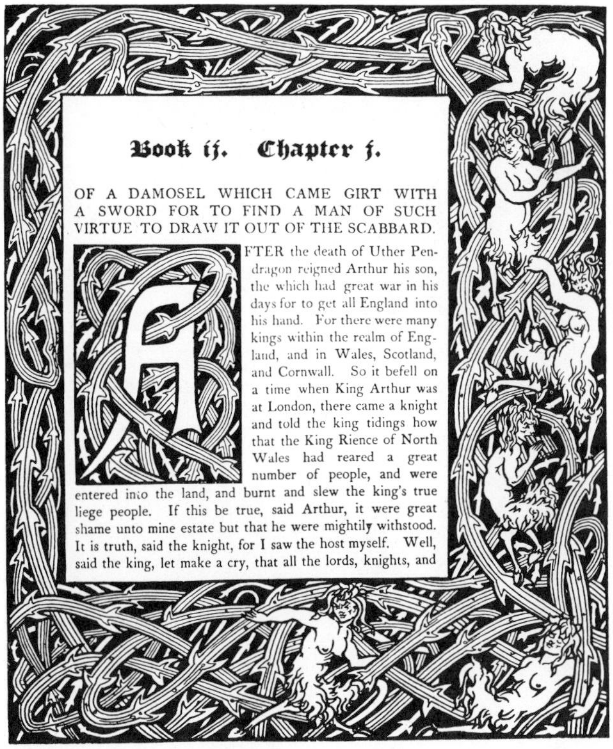
Book ij. Chapter j.

OF A DAMOSEL WHICH CAME GIRT WITH A SWORD FOR TO FIND A MAN OF SUCH VIRTUE TO DRAW IT OUT OF THE SCABBARD.

AFTER the death of Uther Pendragon reigned Arthur his son, the which had great war in his days for to get all England into his hand. For there were many kings within the realm of England, and in Wales, Scotland, and Cornwall. So it befell on a time when King Arthur was at London, there came a knight and told the king tidings how that the King Rience of North Wales had reared a great number of people, and were entered into the land, and burnt and slew the king's true liege people. If this be true, said Arthur, it were great shame unto mine estate but that he were mightily withstood. It is truth, said the knight, for I saw the host myself. Well, said the king, let make a cry, that all the lords, knights, and

Aubrey Beardsley, *Mort D'Arthur,* chapter opening, 1893. William Morris' lyrical bouquets were replaced by rollicking mythological nymphs in a briar border design.

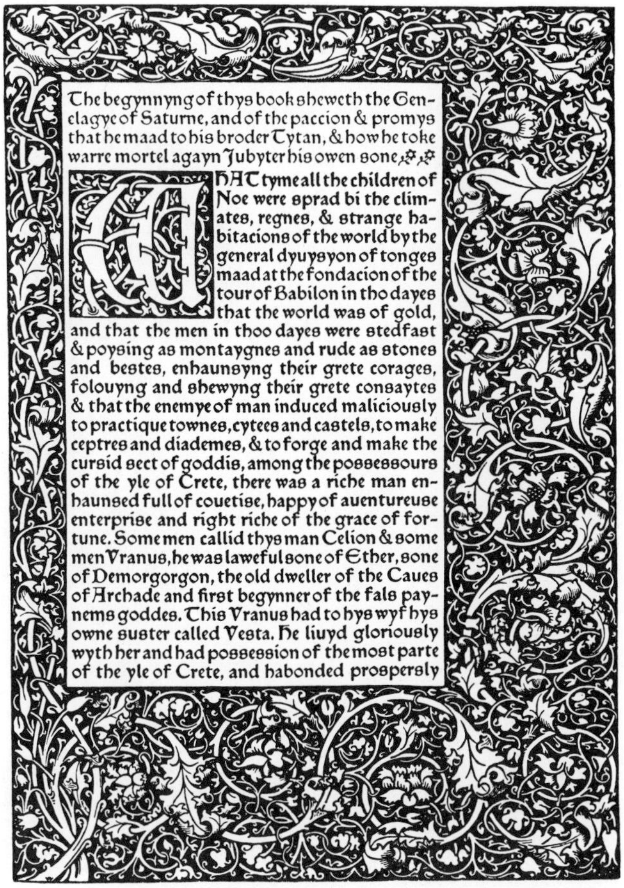
The begynnyng of thys book sheweth the Genelagye of Saturne, and of the paccion & promys that he maad to his broder Tytan, & how he toke warre mortel agayn Jubyter his owen sone.

WHAT tyme all the children of Noe were sprad bi the climates, regnes, & strange habitacions of the world by the general dyuysyon of tonges maad at the fondacion of the tour of Babilon in tho dayes that the world was of gold, and that the men in thoo dayes were stedfast & poysing as montaygnes and rude as stones and bestes, enhaunsyng their grete corages, folouyng and shewyng their grete consaytes & that the enemye of man induced maliciously to practique townes, cytees and castels, to make ceptres and diademes, & to forge and make the cursid sect of goddis, among the possessours of the yle of Crete, there was a riche man enhaunsed full of couetise, happy of auentureuse enterprise and right riche of the grace of fortune. Some men callid thys man Celion & some men Vranus, he was laweful sone of Ether, sone of Demorgorgon, the old dweller of the Caues of Archade and first begynner of the fals paynems goddes. This Vranus had to hys wyf hys owne suster called Vesta. He liuyd gloriously wyth her and had possession of the most parte of the yle of Crete, and habonded prospersly

William Morris, page from *The Recuyell of the Historyes of Troye,* 1892. Comparison of page designs by Morris and Beardsley reveal that the differences reflect a dichotomy of philosophy, lifestyle, and social values.

tained complete fidelity to the original art.

William Morris was so angry when he saw Beardsley's *Mort D'Arthur* that he considered legal action. Beardsley had, to Morris' mind, vulgarized the design ideas of the Kelmscott style by replacing the formal naturalistic borders with more stylized, flat patterns. Burne-Jones' classical woodcut illustrations yielded to dramatic contrasts of black and white shapes. Walter Crane, always ready with an unequivocal viewpoint, declared that Beardsley's *Mort d'Arthur* had mixed the medieval spirit of Morris with a weird "Japanese-like spirit of deviltry and the grotesque," which Crane thought fit only for the opium den.

In spite of Morris' anger, the enthusiastic response to Beardsley's work resulted in numerous commissions. Beardsley was named art editor for *The Yellow Book,* a magazine

Aubrey Beardsley, illustration for Oscar Wilde's *Salome,* 1894. Symbolically, John the Baptist and Salome, who was given his head on a platter by Herod after her dance, are remarkable figures. Graphically, the simplification of details and the dynamic interplay between positive and negative shapes have seldom been equaled.

whose bright yellow cover on London newsstands became a symbol for the new and outrageous. In 1894, Oscar Wilde's *Salomé* received widespread notoriety for the obvious erotic sensuality of Beardsley's illustrations of women. Late Victorian English society was shocked by this celebration of evil, which reached its peak in Beardsley's work for an edition of Aristophanes' *Lysistrata.* Banned by English censors, it was widely circulated on the continent. During the last two years of his life, Beardsley was an invalid. When he could work, a more naturalistic and romantic style was inspired by eighteenth-century French painters such as Antoine Watteau. Even as he lingered toward a tragically early death, Beardsley's lightning influence penetrated the design and illustration of every European country and America.

Aubrey Beardsley, illustration showing "The Ascension of Saint Rosa," 1896. On posters and illustrations Beardsley used color as flat area. Here, for example, the dress is a flat blue and the sky is green. Conventional anatomy and proportion were ignored in figures that often became symbols rather than depictions.

Aubrey Beardsley, illustration for *The Pierrot of the Minute,* 1897. In his later work, Beardsley turned from the celebration of evil toward a more lyrical and romantic style. The flat patterns and dynamic curves of Art Nouveau were replaced with a more naturalistic tonal quality, and dotted contours softened the decisive line of his earlier work.

Beardsley's leading rival among English graphic designers working in the wake of the Arts and Crafts Movement and on the crest of Art Nouveau was Charles Ricketts who maintained a lifelong collaboration with his close friend Charles Shannon (1863–1931). Ricketts began as a wood engraver and received training as a compositor; therefore, his work was based on a thorough understanding of printed production. While Beardsley tended to approach his work as illustrations to be inserted between pages of typography, Ricketts approached the book as a total entity to be designed inside and out, focusing upon a harmony of the parts; binding, end sheets, title page, typography, ornaments, and illustrations which were frequently commissioned from Shannon. Ricketts worked as an engraver and designer for several printing firms before establishing his own studio and publishing firm.

In 1893 Ricketts' first total book design appeared, and the following year he produced his masterful design for Oscar Wilde's exotic and perplexing poem, *The Sphinx.* Although Ricketts owes a debt to Morris, he usually rejected the density of Kelmscott design. Ricketts' page layouts are lighter, his ornaments are more open and geometric, and his designs have a vivid luminosity. The complex intertwining ornament of Celtic design and the flat stylized figures painted on Greek vases which he studied in the British Museum were major inspirations. Like Beardsley, who also studied Greek vase painting, Ricketts learned how to indicate figures and clothing with minimal lines, and flat shapes with no tonal modulation.

In 1896, Ricketts launched the Vale Press. This was not a private press in

Charles Ricketts, binding design for *The Sphinx,* 1894. Stamped in gold upon white vellum, a linear structure evocative of Japanese interiors frames the stunning apparition placed in dynamic balance with the narrator. *Library of Congress, Washington, D.C., Rosenwald Collection.*

the sense of the Kelmscott Press, for Ricketts did not own a press or do his own printing. Rather, he placed his typesetting and presswork with printing firms who labored under his exacting requirements. William Morris was shown Vale Press books during his final illness, and he cried in admiration of the great beauty and design of Ricketts' volumes.

The well-known author Laurence Housman (1865–1959) was active as a book designer at the turn of the century. Arguing that it was as unreasonable to ask book designers always to work with the standard format sizes as it would be to require painters to work only on stretchers of a fixed size and proportion, Housman designed tall, narrow books and square books. His title pages were often unique and unconventional, and his decorative designs were executed with meticulous detail. After the turn of the century, Housman's soaring reputation as a writer, and his failing eyesight closed his graphic design career.

One of the most remarkable moments in the history of graphic design is the brief career of The Beggarstaffs. James Pryde (1866–1941) and William Nicholson (1872–1949) were brothers-in-law who had been close friends since art school. Respected academic painters, they felt it necessary to adopt a pseudonym to protect their fine arts reputations when in 1894 they decided to open an advertising design studio. One of them found a sack of corn in a stable with a hearty old English name, The Beggarstaff Brothers, on it. They adopted the name, dropping "Brothers" from it, and plunged into business. During their brief collaboration (Pryde later wrote that he had become half a poster artist), they developed a new technique later named collage. Cut pieces of paper were moved around, changed, and pasted into position on board. The resulting style of absolutely flat planes of color had sensitive edges "drawn" with scissors. They were immune to the prevalent floral Art Nouveau as they forged this new working method into posters of powerful colored shapes and silhouettes.

Their work was an artistic success but a financial disaster. Unfortunately, they attracted few clients and only a dozen of their designs were printed. Their most famous poster, for Sir Henry Irving's production of *Don Quixote* at the Lyceum Theater, was never printed because Irving decided it was a bad likeness. They only billed him for fifty pounds; he paid them one hundred pounds. Later, this was published in a limited edition, small size for collectors.

When it became economically advisable for Nicholson and Pryde to terminate the partnership, each returned to painting and received some measure of recognition. Nicholson also developed a woodcut style of illustration that maintained some of the graphic economy of Beggarstaff posters. Ironically, the brief months they masqueraded as the Beggarstaffs overshadow their individual accomplishments.

Like Nicholson and Pryde, British painter and illustrator Dudley Hardy (1866–1922) also turned to poster and advertising design. He was instrumental in introducing the graphic pictorial qualities of the French poster to the London billboards during the 1890s.

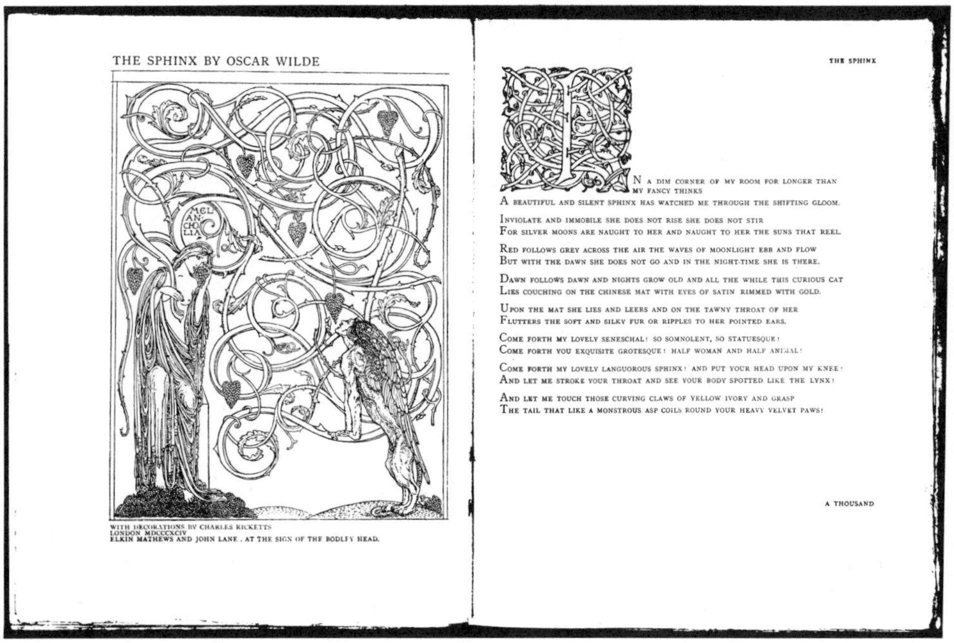

THE SPHINX BY OSCAR WILDE

WITH DECORATIONS BY CHARLES RICKETTS
LONDON MDCCCXCIV
ELKIN MATHEWS AND JOHN LANE . AT THE SIGN OF THE BODLEY HEAD.

THE SPHINX

IN A DIM CORNER OF MY ROOM FOR LONGER THAN MY FANCY THINKS
A BEAUTIFUL AND SILENT SPHINX HAS WATCHED ME THROUGH THE SHIFTING GLOOM.

INVIOLATE AND IMMOBILE SHE DOES NOT RISE SHE DOES NOT STIR
FOR SILVER MOONS ARE NAUGHT TO HER AND NAUGHT TO HER THE SUNS THAT REEL.

RED FOLLOWS GREY ACROSS THE AIR THE WAVES OF MOONLIGHT EBB AND FLOW
BUT WITH THE DAWN SHE DOES NOT GO AND IN THE NIGHT-TIME SHE IS THERE.

DAWN FOLLOWS DAWN AND NIGHTS GROW OLD AND ALL THE WHILE THIS CURIOUS CAT
LIES COUCHING ON THE CHINESE MAT WITH EYES OF SATIN RIMMED WITH GOLD.

UPON THE MAT SHE LIES AND LEERS AND ON THE TAWNY THROAT OF HER
FLUTTERS THE SOFT AND SILKY FUR OR RIPPLES TO HER POINTED EARS.

COME FORTH MY LOVELY SENESCHAL! SO SOMNOLENT, SO STATUESQUE!
COME FORTH YOU EXQUISITE GROTESQUE! HALF WOMAN AND HALF ANIMAL!

COME FORTH MY LOVELY LANGUOROUS SPHINX! AND PUT YOUR HEAD UPON MY KNEE!
AND LET ME STROKE YOUR THROAT AND SEE YOUR BODY SPOTTED LIKE THE LYNX!

AND LET ME TOUCH THOSE CURVING CLAWS OF YELLOW IVORY AND GRASP
THE TAIL THAT LIKE A MONSTROUS ASP COILS ROUND YOUR HEAVY VELVET PAWS!

A THOUSAND

Charles Ricketts, title page for *The Sphinx,* 1894. Ricketts' unconventional title page, dominated by an illustration, is placed on the left rather than the right. The text is set in all capitals. *Library of Congress, Washington, D.C., Rosenwald Collection.*

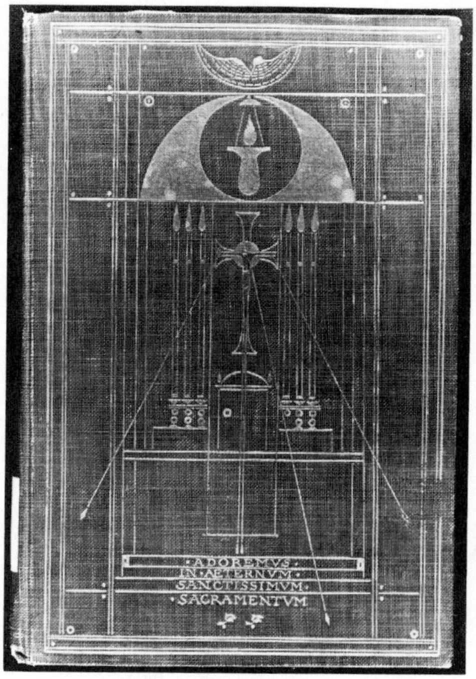

Charles Ricketts, binding design for *Poems of Adoration* by Michael Fields, c. 1900. Christian symbolism is abstracted into elemental forms with rigorous rectangles punctuated with a few well-placed circles and arches.

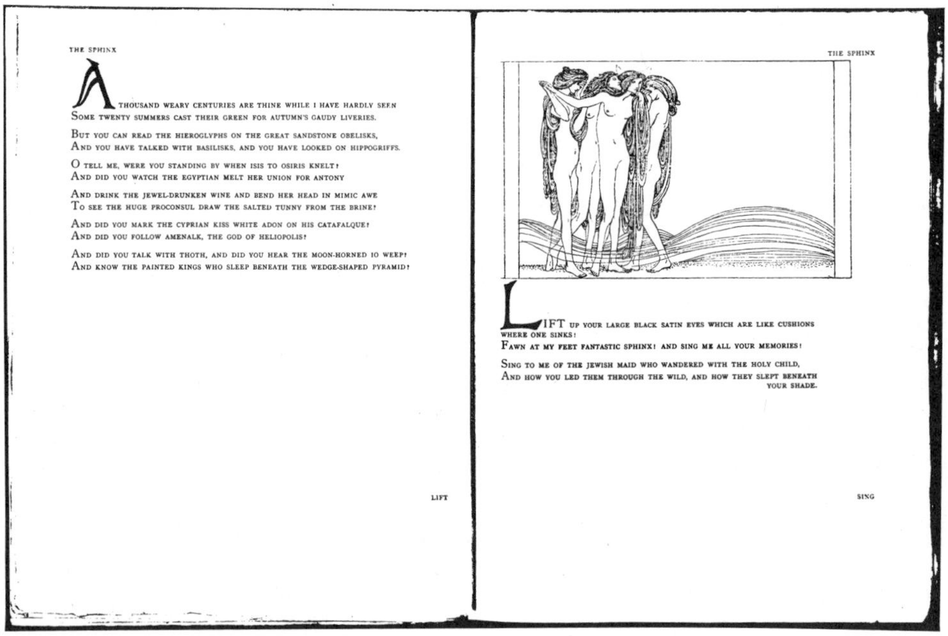

THE SPHINX

A THOUSAND WEARY CENTURIES ARE THINE WHILE I HAVE HARDLY SEEN
SOME TWENTY SUMMERS CAST THEIR GREEN FOR AUTUMN'S GAUDY LIVERIES.

BUT YOU CAN READ THE HIEROGLYPHS ON THE GREAT SANDSTONE OBELISKS,
AND YOU HAVE TALKED WITH BASILISKS, AND YOU HAVE LOOKED ON HIPPOGRIFFS.

O TELL ME, WERE YOU STANDING BY WHEN ISIS TO OSIRIS KNELT?
AND DID YOU WATCH THE EGYPTIAN MELT HER UNION FOR ANTONY

AND DRINK THE JEWEL-DRUNKEN WINE AND BEND HER HEAD IN MIMIC AWE
TO SEE THE HUGE PROCONSUL DRAW THE SALTED TUNNY FROM THE BRINE?

AND DID YOU MARK THE CYPRIAN KISS WHITE ADON ON HIS CATAFALQUE?
AND DID YOU FOLLOW AMENALK, THE GOD OF HELIOPOLIS?

AND DID YOU TALK WITH THOTH, AND DID YOU HEAR THE MOON-HORNED IO WEEP?
AND KNOW THE PAINTED KINGS WHO SLEEP BENEATH THE WEDGE-SHAPED PYRAMID?

LIFT

THE SPHINX

LIFT UP YOUR LARGE BLACK SATIN EYES WHICH ARE LIKE CUSHIONS WHERE ONE SINKS!
FAWN AT MY FEET FANTASTIC SPHINX! AND SING ME ALL YOUR MEMORIES!

SING TO ME OF THE JEWISH MAID WHO WANDERED WITH THE HOLY CHILD,
AND HOW YOU LED THEM THROUGH THE WILD, AND HOW THEY SLEPT BENEATH YOUR SHADE.

SING

Charles Ricketts, pages from *The Sphinx,* 1894. Ricketts' use of white space is as unprecedented as his decision to print the typography in rust and olive green ink. *Library of Congress, Washington, D.C., Rosenwald Collection.*

THE WERE-WOLF
BY CLEMENCE HOUSMAN
WITH SIX ILLUSTRATIONS
BY LAURENCE HOUSMAN

LONDON: JOHN LANE
AT THE BODLEY HEAD
CHICAGO: WAY AND
WILLIAMS 1896

Laurence Housman, title page design for *The Were-Wolf,* 1896. Typical of Housman's unconventional vision, this design has an ornamental Art Nouveau initial and typographic information compressed into three rectangles.

The Beggarstaffs, poster for *Harper's* magazine, 1895. The viewer is invited to fill in the missing contours and shapes to complete the figure in this poster.

The Beggarstaffs, poster for *Don Quixote,* 1896. Cut paper shapes—a black windmill, brown torso, brown horse contour, and light brown head—produced a graphic image whose simplicity and technique were ahead of its time.

The Beggarstaffs, poster design, c. 1895. A radical simplification of the subject, a woman reading, is achieved in a composition of cut and torn, black and red papers arranged and pasted on a white ground.

William Nicholson, illustration from *An Alphabet,* 1897. After Nicholson and Pryde ended their partnership, Nicholson continued his interest in graphic art with bold woodcut illustrations that echoed the simplicity of Beggarstaff posters.

In much of Hardy's strongest work, lettering and figures are placed against simple flat backgrounds.

The development of the French Art Nouveau poster

During the 1880s, Grasset was a regular at Rodolphe Salis' La Chat Noir nightclub, a gathering place for artists and writers that opened in 1881. It was there that he met and shared his enthusiasm for color printing with younger artists in their twenties: Henri de Toulouse-Lautrec (1864–1901), Georges Auriol (1863–1939), and fellow Swiss artist Théophile-Alexandre Steinlen (1859–1923).

Steinlen joined the urban migration that was swelling Europe's cities, for he arrived in Paris at age twenty-two armed with a young wife, a great love of drawing, and a mania for cats. His first Paris commissions were cat drawings for Chat Noir. A prolific illustrator during the 1880s and 1890s, Steinlen's radical political views, Socialist affiliations, and anticleric stance led him toward a social realism depicting poverty, exploitation, and the working class. Often his black-and-white lithographs would have color printed by a stencil process. He

Dudley Hardy, theatrical poster, 1898. The actor and play-title stand out dramatically against the stark black background.

Théophile-Alexandre Steinlen poster for Guillot sterilized milk, 1897. Tender without being overly sentimental, the "slice of life" advertising syndrome of the twentieth century was anticipated by this domestic scene.

experimented with subtle colors overprinted to create additional colors. His vast oeuvre included over two thousand magazine cover and interior illustrations, nearly two hundred sheet music covers, over a hundred book illustration assignments, and three dozen large posters.

Although his first color poster was designed in 1885, his legacy is based on master works of the 1890s. His 305-by-228 centimeter (10-by-7 $\frac{1}{2}$ foot), multipanel poster for Charles Verneau's printing works mirrored in nearly life-sized, environmental scale the pedestrians on adjacent Parisian sidewalks. Remarkable tenderness was displayed in a dairy poster on which

Théophile-Alexandre Steinlen, *La Rue* ("The Street"), 1896. A cross section of Parisian society, a mother and baby, a washer-woman, two workers, Steinlen's daughter Colette with her nanny, a businessman, and sophisticated shoppers promenade a nearly life-sized echo of the adjacent sidewalks.

his hungry cats demand that his daughter Colette share her bowl of milk.

There is an affinity, in the fluid reportorial line and flat color, between the posters and prints of Steinlen and those of his friend and frequent rival for commissions, Toulouse-Lautrec. The debate over which one influenced the other is probably irrelevant, because Steinlen and Lautrec drew inspiration from similar sources and each other. But while Steinlen maintained a naturalistic quality, even Jules Chéret had to concede that Lautrec's 1891 poster, "La Goulue au Moulin Rouge," broke new ground in poster design. A dynamic pattern of flat planes—black silhouettes of spectators, yellow ovals for lamps, and the stark white undergarments of the notorious cancan dancer who performed with transparent or slit underwear—move horizontally across the center of the poster behind the profile of the dancer Valentine, known as "the boneless one" because of the amazing flexibility of his body.

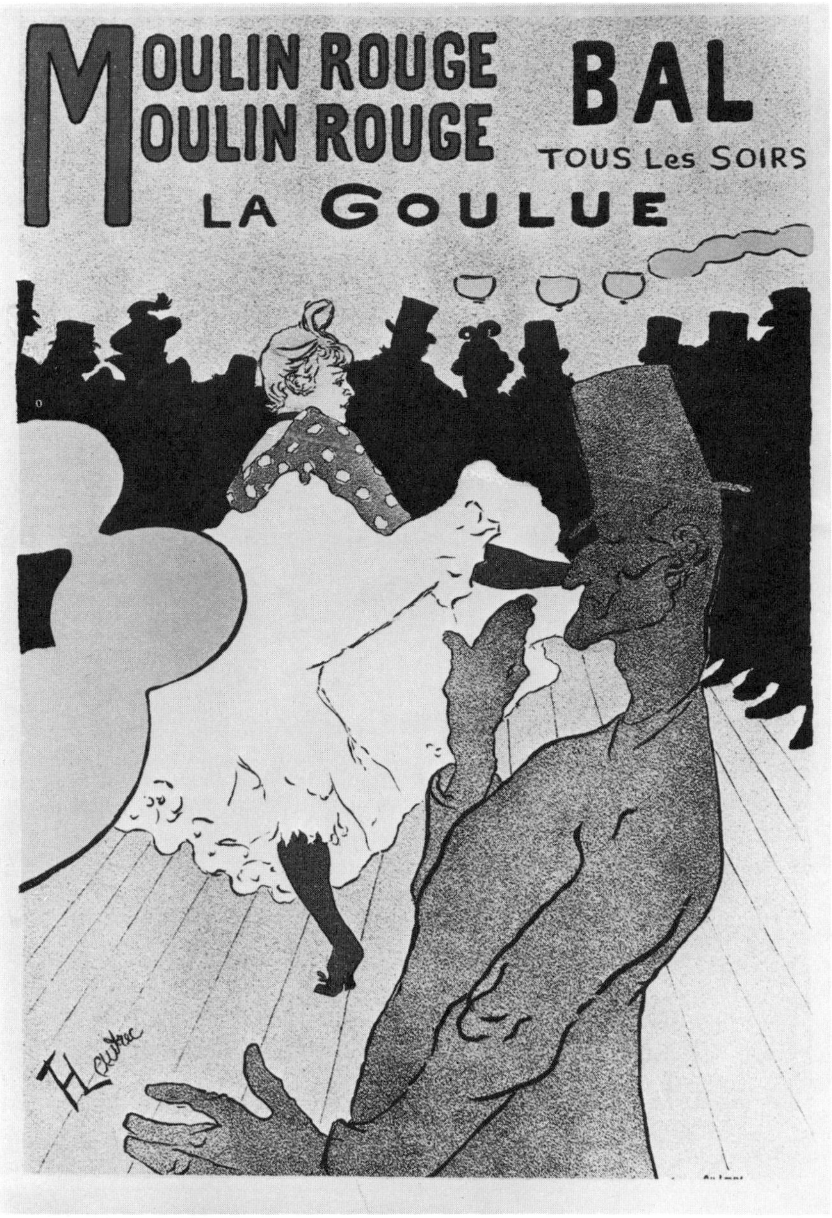

Henri de Toulouse-Lautrec, poster for the Moulin Rouge, 1891. This milestone in graphic design showed that simplified symbolic shape and dynamic pattern could be the material from which expressive and communicative images could be formed.

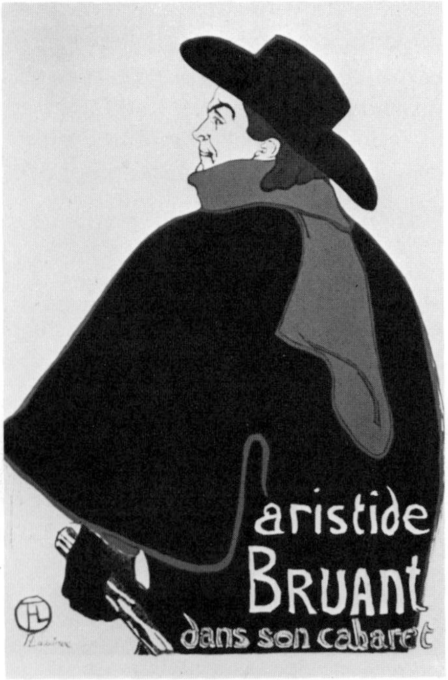

Henri de Toulouse-Lautrec, poster for Aristide Bruant, 1893. The influence of the Japanese print is clearly evident in this image with the flat silhouette, unmodulated color, and stylized curvilinear drawing.

The son of the Count of Toulouse, Henri de Toulouse-Lautrec had turned obsessively to drawing and painting after breaking both hips in an accident at age thirteen. Left crippled, further growth of his legs was stunted. He became a master draftsman in the academic tradition after moving to Paris two years later. Japanese art, Impressionism, and Degas' design and contour excited him. He haunted Paris cabarets and bordellos, watching, drawing, and developing a journalistic, illustrative style that captured the night life of *la belle epoque* ("the beautiful era," a term used to describe glittering late nineteenth-century Paris). Primarily a printmaker, draftsman, and painter, Toulouse-Lautrec only produced thirty-two posters, and a modest number of music and bookcover designs. His command of direct drawing on the lithographic stone was exuberant. His poster commissions were negotiated in the cabarets in the evenings. The next day he would commandeer the Ancourt printing shop. He often worked from memory with no sketches and used an old toothbrush that he always carried to achieve tonal effects with a careful

Henri de Toulouse-Lautrec, poster for Jane Avril, 1893. The gestural expressiveness of Toulouse-Lautrec's direct drawing on the lithographic stone captures the vitality of the dancer. This poster was created from sketches made during a performance.

splatter technique.

The young Czech artist, Alphonse Mucha (1860–1939), had shown remarkable drawing ability when he was growing up in the small Moravian village of Ivancice. After journeying to Paris at age twenty-seven, Mucha spent two years of study supported by a benefactor. This training ended suddenly, and a period of deep poverty ensued. But Mucha gained steady acceptance as a dependable illustrator with strong drawing skills.

On Christmas Eve, 1894, Mucha was dutifully correcting proofs, at the Lemercier's printing company, for a friend who had taken a holiday. Suddenly, the printing firm's manager burst into the room, upset because the famous actress Sarah Bernhardt was demanding a new poster for the play, *Gismonda,* by New Year's Day. Since Mucha was the only artist available, he received the commission. Using the basic pose from Grasset's poster for Bernhardt's "Joan of Arc" and sketches of Bernhardt made at the theater, Mucha elongated Grasset's format, called upon Byzantine mosaics for background motifs, and produced a poster totally different from any of his prior work. Even though the bottom portion of this poster was unfinished because only a week was available for design, printing, and posting, it created an overnight sensation with its life-sized figure, mosaic pattern, and elongated shape. Because of its complexity and muted colors, Mucha's work lacked Chéret's distant impact. But, stepping closer, Parisians were astounded.

On New Year's Day, 1895, as Alphonse Mucha began his meteoric rise, a number of influences throughout Europe were converging

Eugène Grasset, poster for Sarah Bernhardt as Joan of Arc, 1894. The figure, lettering, and background cacophony of clouds and spears are somewhat awkward in their visual relationships, but the theatrical drama and historical period are expressed well.

into what would be labeled l'Art Nouveau. Although Mucha resisted this label, maintaining that art was eternal and could never be new, the further development of his work and of the visual poster are inseparably linked to this diffuse international movement and must be considered as part of its development.

Just as the English Arts and Crafts Movement was a special influence of that country's Art Nouveau, the light and fanciful flowing curves of eighteenth-century French Rococo was a special resource in France. The new art was hailed as *le style moderne* until December 1895, when Samuel Bing, long a dealer in Far Eastern art and artifacts and influential in the growing awareness of Japanese work, opened his new gallery, l'Art Nouveau, to exhibit art and crafts by young artists working in new directions. Bing commissioned the Belgian architect and designer Henri van de Velde (1863–1957) to design his interiors and exhibited painting, sculpture, glasswork, jewelry, and posters by an international group of artists and designers.

Graphic design, more ephemeral and timely than most other art forms, began to codify rapidly toward the floral phase of Art Nouveau as Chéret, Grasset, Toulouse-Lautrec, and especially Mucha incorporated Art Nouveau motifs in their work. From 1895 until 1900, Art Nouveau found its most comprehensive statement in Alphonse Mucha's work. His dominant theme was a central female figure surrounded by stylized forms derived from plants and flowers, Moravian folk art, Byzantium mosaics, and even magic and the occult. So pervasive was his work that by 1900 *le style Mucha* was often used interchangeably with *l'art nouveau.* His women project an archetypal sense of unreality. Exotic and sensuous, yet maidenlike, they express no specific age, nationality, or historical period. His stylized hair patterns became a hallmark of the era in spite of detractors who dismissed this aspect as "noodles and spaghetti."

Sarah Bernhardt had not been pleased with Grasset's Joan of Arc poster or many of the posters for her performances. She felt that Mucha's Gismonda poster expressed her so well graphically that she signed him to a six-year contract for sets, costumes, jewelry, and nine more posters. The sheer volume of Mucha's output was astounding. For example, the one hundred thirty-four lithographs for the book *Ilsée, Princesse de Tripoli,* printed in a limited edition of two hundred fifty-two copies, were produced in three months. In 1904, at the height of his fame, he left Paris for his first American visit. His last major work in the Art Nouveau style was ex-

Alphonse Mucha, *Gismonda* poster, 1894. The line-drawing plate was printed in a muted blue. Subtle greens and golds predominate, and bright golden hair with pink flowers in it and the white word, "Bernhardt," form a focal point. (In this later printing, the "Theatre de la Renaissance" has been removed from the plate and replaced with "American Tour.") *Library of Congress, Washington, D.C., Poster Collection.*

Alphonse Mucha, poster for Cassan Fils printers, c. 1897. A young pressman is distracted by a muse in this poster for an outstanding printer of deluxe artistic and commercial printing. *The Virginia Museum, Richmond.*

Alphonse Mucha, poster for Job cigarette papers, 1898. The warm pinks and brown hair of the figure glow against the deep purple background and icy green letterforms in this vintage example of "le style Mucha." Mucha delighted in filling the total space with animated form and ornament.

ecuted in 1909. When Czechoslovakia regained its status as a free nation in 1917, his time and work were centered there, and his last decades were primarily spent producing *Slav Epic,* a series of twenty large murals depicting the history of his native people. When the Germans partitioned Czechoslovakia in 1939, Mucha was one of the first persons arrested and interrogated by the Gestapo. When he died a few months later, his beloved homeland was once again under foreign domination, and the world was a vastly different place from the brief energetic years when he carried Art Nouveau to its zenith.

Although Emmanuel Orazi (1860–1934) came to prominence as a poster designer in 1884 when he designed a poster for Sarah Bernhardt, it was not until his static style yielded to the influences of Grasset and Mucha a decade later that he produced his best work. His masterpiece is a 1905 poster for La Maison Moderne, a gallery that was competitive with L'Art Nouveau. An extraordinarily sophisticated young lady is posed before a counter bearing objects from the gallery.

La Maison Moderne's logo, centered in the window, is one of many examples of Art Nouveau letterforms applied to trademark design. Other trademarks of Art Nouveau origin, designed for firms such as the American General Electric and Coca-Cola, have been in continuous use since the 1890s.

mütterchen, den Blumen der nahen Trauer. — Und sie erreichten den Palast der Prinzessin, in seiner leichten Anmuth umstrahlt von der sanften Schönheit des Morgens.

Als ob man den sterbenden Gast erwartet hätte, war ein Lager von weissen Lilien in dem grossen Saale bereit, — dort, wo sonst die farbigsten Blumenkronen geleuchtet hatten. Als Jaufré auf dem Bette ruhte, kamen leise, mit heimlichen Schritten, junge Diener mit hellen Augen und Frauen mit verwunderten Blicken und umringten die Prinzessin. Und es kamen ihrer so viele, dass der Saal sie nicht zu fassen vermochte und viele in den Gängen des Parkes bleiben mussten; und auch der Park war nicht weit genug, um sie alle aufzunehmen, und sie standen am Strande bis an die Grenzen der Wüste; denn es fehlte niemand bei diesem Feste der Trauer.

Ferne, ferne Klänge erhoben sich leise, so leise, dass man glaubte,

Alphonse Mucha, illustration from *Ilsée, Princesse de Tripoli,* 1901. This masterful example of Mucha's page design has contour lines printed in dark blue-gray, with light blue-gray, metallic gold, pink, yellow, and brown printed from five other lithographic stones.

Paul Berthon (1872–1909), a student of Grasset, pushed the Art Nouveau style toward softness. He used Grasset's strong contour, stylized Japanese cloud formations, and flowers, but the contour color was muted and blended with the color planes, and the flowers threatened to become repetitive design motifs. Georges de Feure (1868–1928) had studied with Chéret. His wide-ranging design activities included graphics, theatrical design, procelains, and—under the influence of Henri van de Velde—furniture and objects d'art. The forms and shapes in de Feure's *Le Journal des Ventes* poster echo this influence.

Art Nouveau found one of its most complete architectural expressions in the work of Hector Guimard (1867–1942), whose iron and glass entrances and pavilions for the Paris Metro achieved visual expression and were constructed with standardized industrial fabrication methods.

Trademark for General Electric, c. 1890. This design satisfies the requirements of a successful trademark: it is unique, legible, and unequivocal. Therefore, it has survived many decades of changing graphic styles. (A registered trademark of General Electric Company, used by permission.)

In addition to graphics, Mucha designed furniture, carpets, stained glass windows, and manufactured objects. He published pattern books, including *Combinaisons ornementales* in collaboration with Maurice Verneuil (1869–after 1934) and Georges Auriol (1863–1939), that spread the Art Nouveau style.

Emmanuel Orazi, poster for La Maison Moderne, 1905. Drawn in an almost Egyptian profile, this visitor to the gallery shows the elegant influence of Art Nouveau upon fashion design.

Art Nouveau comes to America

British and French graphic art joined forces to invade America. In 1889, and again in 1891 and 1892, *Harper's Bazar* (sic) had commissioned covers from Eugène Grasset. These first presentations of a new approach to

Paul Berthon, poster for *L'Ermitage* magazine, 1900. A soft, mellow quality was achieved, even though Berthon used a strong, rigid line, by printing with inks of limited color or value contrast.

Georges de Feure, poster for *Le Journal des Ventes,* 1897. De Fleure created strong graphic impact by organizing his posters into organic "zones" of light, dark, and middle tones.

Maurice Verneuil, page from *Combinaisons Ornementales,* 1900. In collaboration with Mucha and Georges Auriol, Verneuil designed Art Nouveau ornaments in a style book of possibilities for artists and designers.

graphic design were literally imported, for Grasset's designs were printed in Paris and shipped to New York by boat to be bound onto the magazines.

British born Louis Rhead (1857–1926) studied in England and Paris before emigrating to America in 1883. After eight years in New York

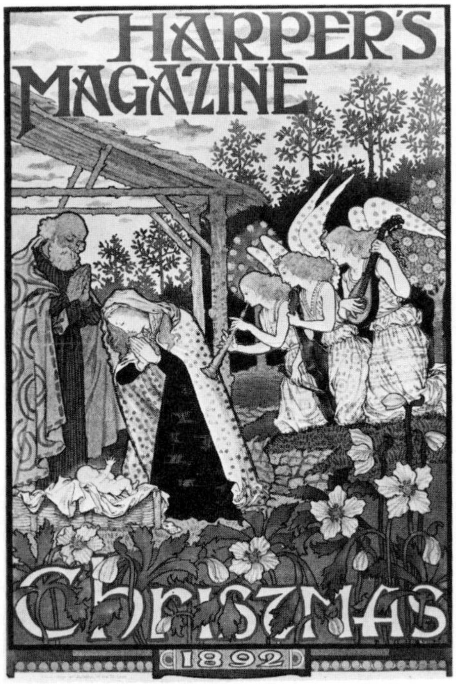

Eugène Grasset, cover for *Harper's Magazine,* 1892. Combining flowing contours and flat color with an almost medieval flavor, Grasset's work captured the American imagination. *Library of Congress, Washington, D.C., Poster Collection.*

Louis Rhead, cover for *Harper's Bazar,* 1894. Dazzling linear patterns animate the background of this cover design. Note the intensity of Rhead's colorful advertisement for Royal Baking Powder on the back cover in contrast to its more typical competitors. *Library of Congress, Washington, D.C., Poster Collection.*

as an illustrator, he returned to Europe for three years and adopted Grasset's style. Upon his return to America, a prolific flow of posters, magazine covers, and illustrations enabled him to join the self-taught American, William H. Bradley (1868–1962) as the two major American practitioners of Art-Nouveau-inspired graphic design and illustration.

The visual poster was first adopted in America by the publishing industry, and colorful placards began to appear at the newsstands advertising the new issues of major magazines including *Harper's, Scribner's,* and the *Century.* New books were also advertised with posters. While Rhead embraced Grasset's willowy maidens, contour line, and flat color, he rejected Grasset's pale colors in favor of vibrant combinations. On occasion, Rhead even used such unexpected combinations as a maiden with red contour lines on her bright blue hair standing before an intense green sky. Rhead's work sometimes mixed a profusion of influences. Decorative patterns left over from Victorian design, forms inspired by the Arts and Crafts Movement, and curving abstract linear patterns are sometimes combined in his designs.

While Rhead adopted the French poster as his model, the uninhibited, energetic and enormously talented Will Bradley was inspired by English sources. After the death of his father from wounds received in the Civil War, nine-year-old Bradley and his mother moved from Massachusetts to Ishpeming, Michigan, to live with relatives. His early training in graphic arts began at age eleven, when be became a *printer's devil* for the *Iron Agitator* (later the *Iron Ore*) newspaper. A printer's devil was a young apprentice and errand boy in a printing office, so named because he often became black with ink from cleaning type and presses. When Bradley was seventeen he used his fifty-dollar savings to go to Chicago and apprentice at Rand-McNally as an engraver. Realizing that engravers didn't design or illustrate, and illustrators and designers didn't engrave, he returned to Ishpeming. But Chicago beckoned again, and he became a typographic designer at the Knight & Leonard printing company when he was nineteen.

Unable to afford art lessons, Bradley became a voracious student of magazines and library books. As with Frederic Goudy and Bruce Rogers, William Morris and his ideals had enormous impact on Bradley. By 1890 his Arts and Crafts inspired pen-and-ink illustrations were bringing regular commissions. In early 1894, Bradley became aware of Aubrey Beardsley's work, which led him toward flat shapes and stylized contour. Bradley's 1894 work for *The Chap Book* and *The Inland Printer* marks the beginning of Art Nouveau in America. His detractors dismissed him as "the American Beardsley," but Bradley used Beardsley's style as a stepping stone to innovative graphic technique and a visual unity of type and image that moved beyond imitation.

Bradley was free spirited in his approach to typographic design and flouted all the prevailing rules and conventions. Type became a design element to be huddled in the corner of

Louis Rhead, cover and page from a poster calender, 1898. Rich contrasts of warm and cool colors and decorative patterns were the qualities that brought originality to Rhead's work. *Library of Congress, Washington, D.C., Poster Collection.*

the space, squeezed into a narrow column, or letterspaced so that lines of many and few letters all became the same length and formed a rectangle.

Inspired by the example of the Kelmscott Press, Bradley moved from Chicago to Springfield, Massachusetts, in late 1894 and established The Wayside Press. He produced books and advertisements and began publication of an art and literary periodical, *Bradley: His Book,* in 1896. Both the magazine and press were critical and financial successes, but the rigors of the job—editor, designer, illustrator, press manager—threatened Bradley's health. The press was sold to the University Press in Cambridge in 1898, and he accepted a position there.

During a visit to the Boston Public Library in 1895, Bradley had studied their collection of books printed in colonial New England. The vigor of this work, with its Old Style Caslon types, wide letterspacing, sturdy woodcuts, and plain rules, inspired a new direction that became known as the Chap Book Style. (Chap books were crudely printed small books formerly sold by traveling peddlers known as chapmen.)

After the turn of the century, Bradley became a consultant to the American Type Founders (ATF), designing typestyles and ornaments. He wrote and designed their series of twelve magazines, *The American Chap-Book.* His demonstration designs using ATF type and ornaments were called "The Printer Man's Joy." His illustration career was swallowed by this passion for type design and layout, and in 1907 thirty-nine year old Bradley became art editor of *Collier's* magazine. The last decades of his long career were significant to the evolution of twentieth-century editorial design.

Outstanding among the designers who responded to Bradley's American interpretation of the Arts and Crafts Movement and British Art Nouveau, Theodore B. Hapgood (b. 1871) created intricate and charming graphic patterns for book and periodical design assignments. He often used the crisp outlines of the Chap Book style in conjunction with decorative patterns reminiscent of William Morris' work.

Ethel Reed (b. 1876) became the first woman in America to achieve national prominence for her work as a graphic designer and illustrator. Born and raised in Massachusetts, she became well known as a book illustrator by age eighteen. For four brief years from 1894 until 1898, she

Will Bradley, covers for *The Inland Printer*, 1894–95. These cover designs show the range of Bradley's graphic vocabulary. Delicate contour line for an overall light effect, complex full tone drawing, and reduction of the image to black and white silhouette masses were all effects that he explored.

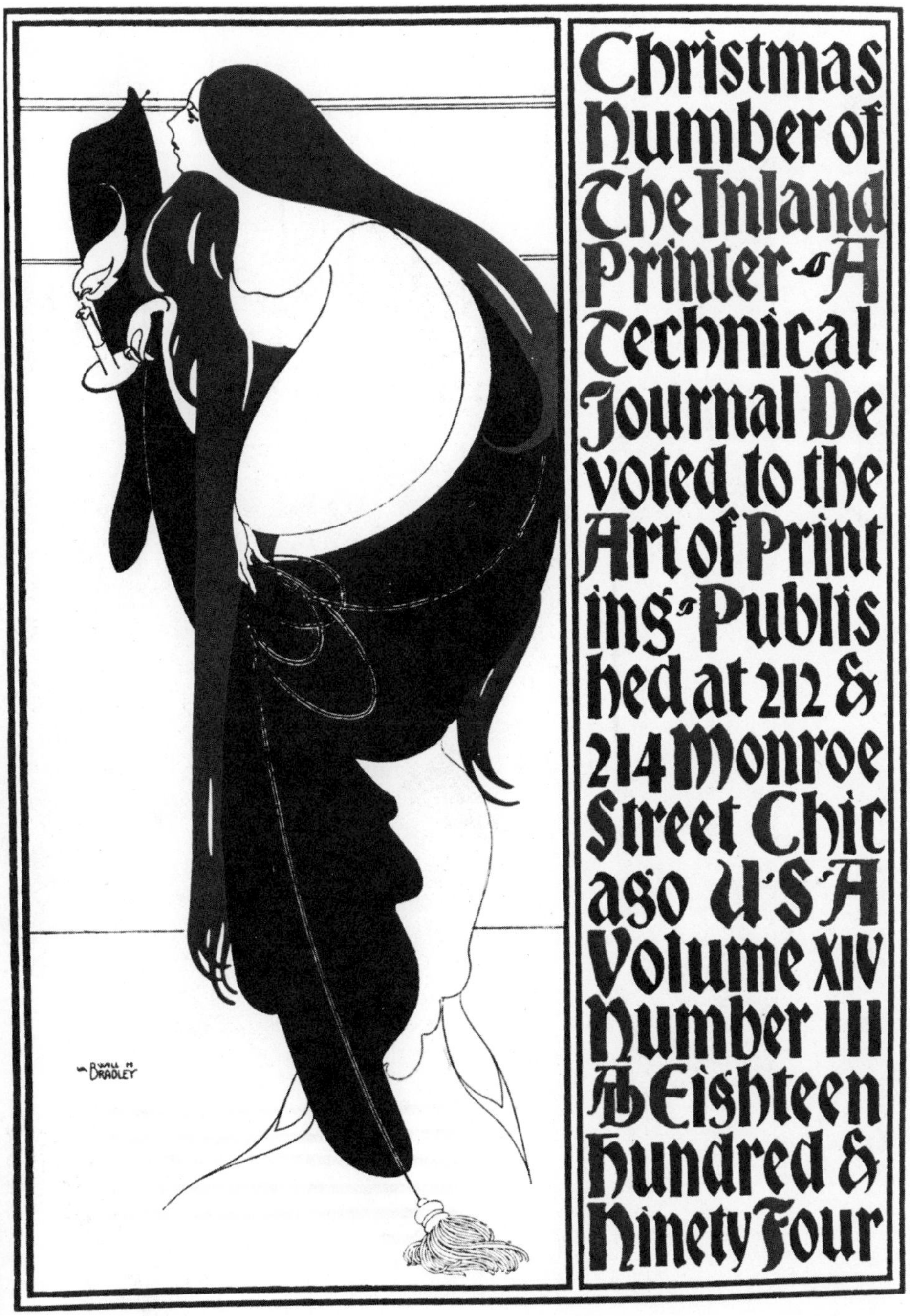
Christmas
Number of
The Inland
Printer A
Technical
Journal De
voted to the
Art of Print
ing Publis
hed at 212 &
214 Monroe
Street Chic
ago U S A
Volume XIV
Number III
AD Eighteen
Hundred &
Ninety Four

Will Bradley, cover for *The Inland Printer,* 1894. A dynamic tension is created between the organic curves and white space of the illustrations in opposition to the squared panel of lettering with its dense texture. American Type Founders acquired rights to these letterforms and issued them as the typeface Bradley.

was active as a poster designer for Boston publishers Copeland & Day, and Lamson, Wolffe and Company. Curiously, Reed's career ends abruptly in 1898, and her life after age twenty-two is a mystery. Perhaps she either married and abandoned her art or met an untimely death. It is unfortunate that such precocious early work did not see further development.

An art director for Harper and Brothers publications from 1891 until 1901, Edward Penfield (1866–1925) enjoyed a reputation rivaling Bradley and Rhead. His monthly series of posters for *Harper's* magazine from 1893 until 1898 portrayed members of the upper class. They were *Harper's* audience, and Penfield frequently depicted them reading or carrying an issue of the magazine. Penfield's first poster for *Harper's* was designed for the January 1894 issue and featured a naturalistic watercolor illustration showing a sophisticated young man purchasing a subscription. During the course of that year, Penfield evolved toward his mature style of contour drawing with flat planes of color. By eliminating the background, Penfield forced the viewer to focus upon the figure and lettering. Penfield drew with a vigorous fluid line, and his flat planes of color were often supplemented by a masterful stipple technique. Inessentials were eliminated, and visual means were used to communicate an idea.

In a whimsical 1894 poster for the July issue, a young lady lights a string of fireworks without even looking at them so preoccupied is she with her reading. The absorbing enjoyment of reading *Harper's* is conveyed. Everyone on a train, including the conductor, is reading *Harper's* in an 1897 cover. This campaign was wildly

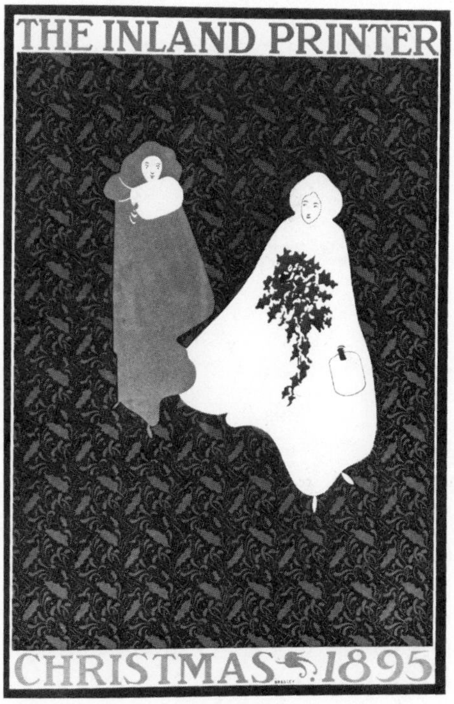
THE INLAND PRINTER
CHRISTMAS 1895

Will Bradley, poster for *The Inland Printer,* 1895. Placed against a green and black pattern, these figures—one, a flat red shape with a white muff; the other, a white shape with her head, green holly, and muff delicately balanced within the shape—almost become pure form.

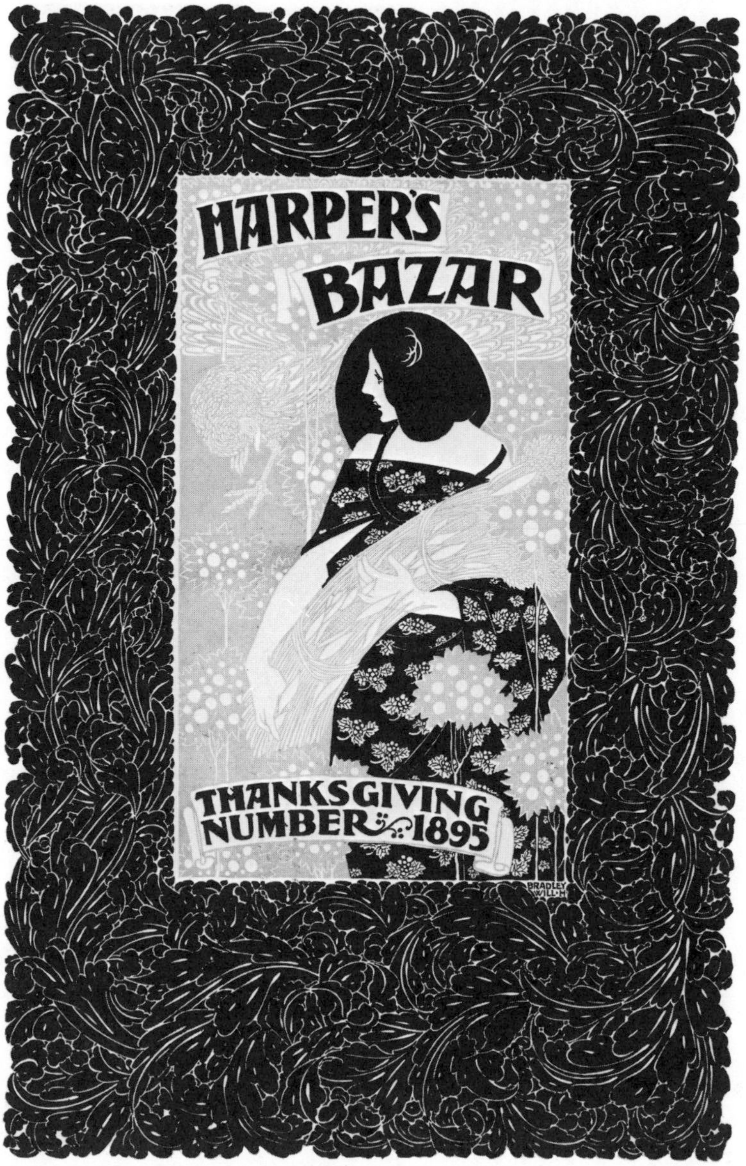

Will Bradley, cover for *Harper's Bazar,* 1895. Printed in a gray-green and olive green, this magazine cover has a density and graphic impact that breaks away from Bradley's English influences. *Library of Congress, Washington, D.C., Poster Collection.*

Will Bradley poster for *The Chap Book,* 1895. Repetition of the figure in a smaller size overlapping the larger figure is a compositional technique enabling Bradley to create a more complex set of visual relationships.

successful in promoting *Harper's,* and competitive publications commissioned imitative designs showing the reading public absorbed in *their* magazines. William Carqueville (1871–1946) created similar posters for *Lippincott's* magazine, including a girl dropping her *Lippincott's* after a young boy startles her with a firecracker for the July 1895 issue. After Carqueville left for Paris to continue his study of art, J. J. Gould was hired to continue the campaign.

Several younger artists of the 1890s poster movement were to become major illustrators for magazines and books during the twentieth century. Maxfield Parrish (1870–1966) was rejected as a student by Howard Pyle, who told young Parrish that there was nothing more that Pyle could teach him, and that he should develop an independent style. Parrish expressed a romantic and idealized view of the world in book, magazine, and advertising illustrations during the first three decades of the twentieth century before turning to painting landscapes for reproduction. Joseph C. Leyendecker (1874–1951) became America's most popular illustrator from the World War I era until the early 1940s. Leyendecker picked up where Gibson left off in creating beautiful young people for the mass media.

Will Bradley, poster for *Bradley, His Book,* 1896. Medieval romanticism, Arts-and-Crafts-inspired patterns, and Art Nouveau are meshed into a compressed, frontal image. *Library of Congress, Washington, D.C., Poster Collection.*

Will Bradley, advertisement for the Ault & Wiborg Ink Company, 1898. White type drops out of an orange plaque glowing against the greenish blue-gray background in this sturdy example of Bradley's "Chap Book" period. *Library of Congress, Washington, D.C., Poster Collection.*

This crude woodcut from the colonial era has the strong black and white contrasts and awkward drawing that inspired Will Bradley to move into the "Chap Book" phase of his career.

Theodore B. Hapgood, cover for *The Inland Printer,* 1896. Geometry brings stability to this decorative design. The seed pods in the central area form an inverted triangle which arrests the meandering arabesques. *Library of Congress, Washington, D.C., Poster Collection.*

Will Bradley, cover design for *The Printer Man's Joy,* 1905. After the turn of the century, Bradley's fascination with colonial printing and woodcuts inspired the shift from Art Nouveau to the bold graphic style typified here.

Will Bradley, cover design for a newspaper, 1899. As with Art Nouveau, Bradley's response to colonial printing was not mere imitation. He responded to the vigor and design concepts of the Chap Book era and interpreted it in a new way.

Ethel Reed, poster for the book, *Miss Traumerei,* 1895. Flat shapes and the flowers overlapping the subject at an angle show how well Reed has absorbed the Japanese compositional ideas passed through contemporary European graphic artists. *Library of Congress, Washington, D.C., Poster Collection.*

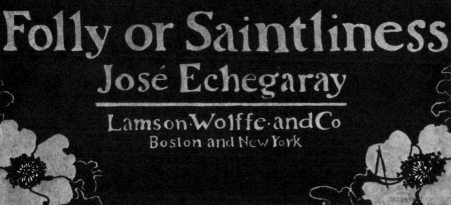

Ethel Reed, poster for the book, *Folly or Saintliness,* 1895. In an imaginative use of three-color printing, the white face with red lips glows against an otherwise black and orange-brown poster. *Library of Congress, Washington, D.C., Poster Collection.*

Edward Penfield, poster for *Harper's,* 1894. Figurative letterforms and the dramatic sense of expectation—the moment before the fireworks begin—create a whimsical concept. *Library of Congress, Washington, D.C., Poster Collection.*

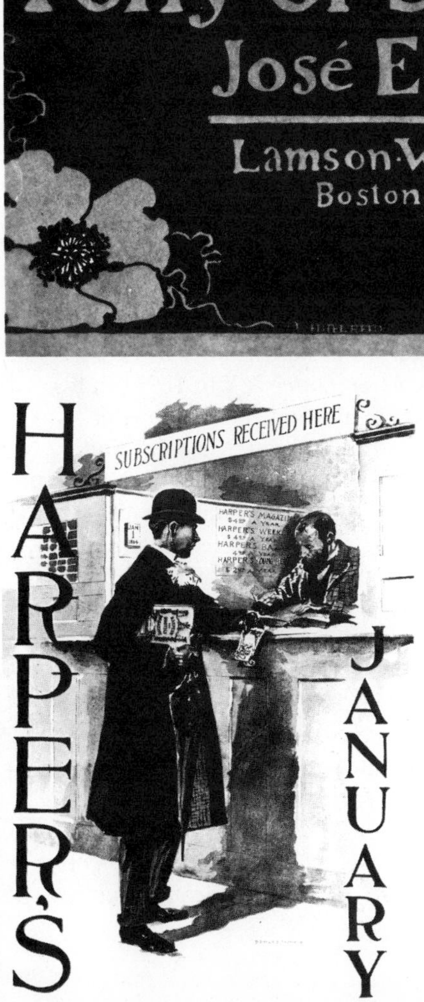

Edward Penfield, poster for *Harper's,* 1894. This image is created by traditional tonal modeling instead of the line and color in Penfield's work later that same year. *Library of Congress, Washington, D.C., Poster Collection.*

Will Carqueville, poster for *Lippincott's,* 1895. Both the style and concept of Penfield's poster for the preceding Fourth of July are imitated. *Library of Congress, Washington, D.C., Poster Collection.*

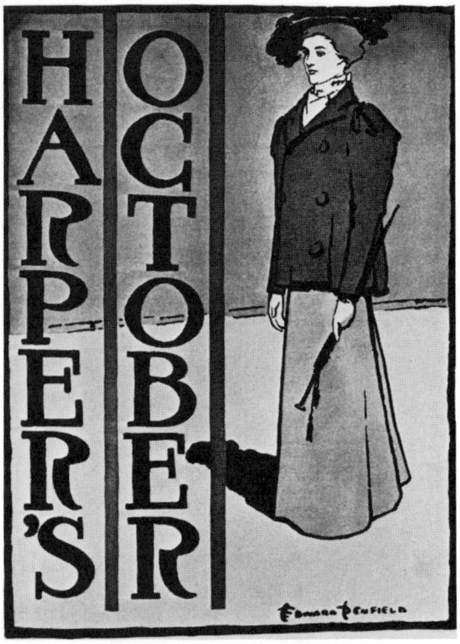

Edward Penfield, poster for *Harper's* 1897. A repetition of verticals—lettering, rules, and figure—create an organization of elements that is unique for its time.

J. J. Gould, poster for *Lippincott's,* 1897. The grainy lithographic crayon quality is the unique distinguishing feature of Gould's designs. *Library of Congress, Washington, D.C., Poster Collection.*

Edward Penfield, poster for *Harper's,* 1897. A visual compression, not unlike that of a telephoto lens in photography, converts five figures overlapping in space into a rhythmic two-dimensional pattern.

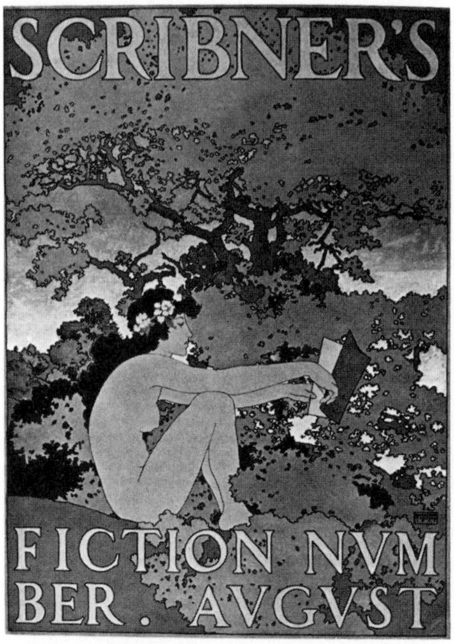

Maxfield Parrish, poster for *Scribner's* magazine, 1897. Parrish created an elegant land of fantasy with his idealized drawing, pristine color, and intricate composition.

Innovation in Belgium

Art Nouveau sprang to life in Belgium during the mid-1890s. Nestled between France and Germany, this small country had experienced the beginnings of creative ferment during the 1880s when the *Cercle des XX* (''Group of Twenty'') formed to enable more progressive art to be exhibited outside the *salon* establishment. By the middle 1890s, Belgian Art Nouveau became a significant force, as evidenced by Jan Toorop's poster for Delftsche Slaolie.

Perhaps the seminal genius of the movement was Belgian architect Baron Victor Horta (1861–1947). His 1892 townhouse for Emile Tassel was unified by tendrilous curvilinear networks unlike anything yet seen in England or on the Continent at that time.

After six years in Paris, Privat Livemont (1861–1936) returned to his native Belgium. This teacher and painter produced nearly three dozen posters strongly inspired by Mucha's idealized women, their tendrilous hair, and lavish ornament. His major innovation was a double contour that separates the figure from the background. The dark contour was outlined by a thick, white band which increased the image's impact when posted on the billboards.

Gisbert Combaz (1869–1941) turned from the practice of law to become an artist and art historian specializing in the Far East. He was a leading member of *La Libre Esthetique,* the organization that evolved from *Cercle des XX* in 1893. In his many exhibition posters for this group, he used intense color and pushed the Art Nouveau arabesque into an almost mechanical, tense line.

The Belgian architect, painter, designer, and educator Henri Clemens van de Velde (1863–1957) was a one-man watershed. He synthesized sources including French Art Nouveau, the English Arts and Crafts Movement, and the Glasgow School into a unified style. After the turn of the century, his teaching and writing (*The Renaissance in Modern Applied Art,* 1901; *A Layman's Sermons on Applied Art,* 1903) became a vital

Jan Toorop, poster for Delftsche Slaolie, 1894. Printed in yellow and lavender, this salad dressing poster becomes almost kinetic in the busy repetition of patterns filling the space. *Library of Congress, Washington, D.C., Poster Collection.*

theoretical source for the development of twentieth-century architecture and design. An example of his theoretical pedagogy is his observation that, when a shadow is cast, it creates a complementary form whose outline is identical to the shadow's outline. He argued that this negative form is as important as the object casting the shadow.

He studied painting in Antwerp and Paris, exploring Post-Impressionist styles, such as Pointillism, then turned to the study of architecture and joined *Cercle de XX*. After 1885, William Morris' example inspired an increasing involvement in design. Interiors, book design, bookbindings, jewelry, and metalwork became major activities. In book design he broke creative ground. His only poster was for a concentrated food product, Tropon, for which he created labeling and advertising. Although van de Velde became an innovator of Art Nouveau, he was far more interested in furthering the philosophy of the Arts and Crafts Movement than in style as an end in itself.

Van de Velde advocated the concept that all branches of art—from painting to graphic design and from industrial design to sculpture—shared a communal language of form and an equality of importance to the human community. Appropriate materials, functional forms, and a unity of visual organization were demanded. He saw ornament not as decoration but as a means of expression that could achieve the status of a work of art.

Privat Livemont, Rajah Coffee poster, 1899. The interplay between the steam from the coffee cup and the product name creates a fascinating interplay of forms.

Henri van de Velde, *Van Nu en Straks* (''Today and Tomorrow''), title page, 1893. In this woodcut graphic, van de Velde combines the Japanese influence and the growing fascination with organic drawing into a churning wave and sun landscape that stops just short of becoming nonfigurative.

Henri van de Velde, *Salutations* book cover, 1893. This boldly abstract design with curvilinear rhythms foretells the coming of Kandinsky and abstract expressionism in the twentieth century. The illustration and lettering are unified by the similarity of forms and line weights. *Houghton Library, Harvard University, Cambridge, Mass.*

Gisbert Combaz, poster for *La Libre Esthetique,* 1898. In this lithograph printed in six flat colors, a turquoise, yellow, and blue peacock struts on an olive green tree with dark green leaves before a brilliant red sky.

Henri van de Velde, Poster for Tropon food concentrate, 1899. Rather than communicate about the product or depict people using it, van de Velde engages the viewer with an extraordinary expression of pure visual form.

Dynamic linear forms embrace their surrounding space and the intervals between them in his work. He did not apply ornament to structure. Rather, ornament was a logical aspect of the total that grew out of construction considerations. Thus, van de Velde's work evolved from forms inspired by plant motifs and symbolic ideas, to an abstract style. When this abstract approach was applied to graphic design, it is not surprising to find that van de Velde is a precursor of twentieth-century painting.

Van de Velde brought a moral imperative to his demand that contemporary work must be modern and express the needs of the day. Machine-made objects had to be true to their manufacturing process instead of trying, deceitfully, to appear handmade. After the Grand Duke of Saxe Weimar called van de Velde to Weimar as art and design advisor in 1902, he reorganized the Weimar Arts and Crafts Institute and the Weimar Academy of Fine Arts. This was a preliminary step toward the formation of the Bauhaus by Walter Gropius in 1919. When World War I broke out, van de Velde returned to his native country. In 1925, the Belgian government, as an expression of their appreciation, named van de Velde, who was then sixty-two, director of the Institut Superieur des Arts Decoratifs in Brussels.

Henri van de Velde, title pages for *Also Sprach Zarathustra,* 1908. In this most monumental of Art Nouveau book designs, a bold drama of expression is achieved by van de Velde in the full-page designs. *Houghton Library, Harvard University, Cambridge, Mass.*

Frank Lloyd Wright and the Glasgow School

During the later years of the 1890s the work of the American architect Frank Lloyd Wright (1867–1959) was becoming known to European artists and designers. Undoubtedly, he was an inspiration for the designers evolving from curvilinear Art Nouveau toward the rectilinear phase. In 1893 Wright began his independent practice. He rejected historicism in favor of a philosophy of "organic architecture" with "the reality of the

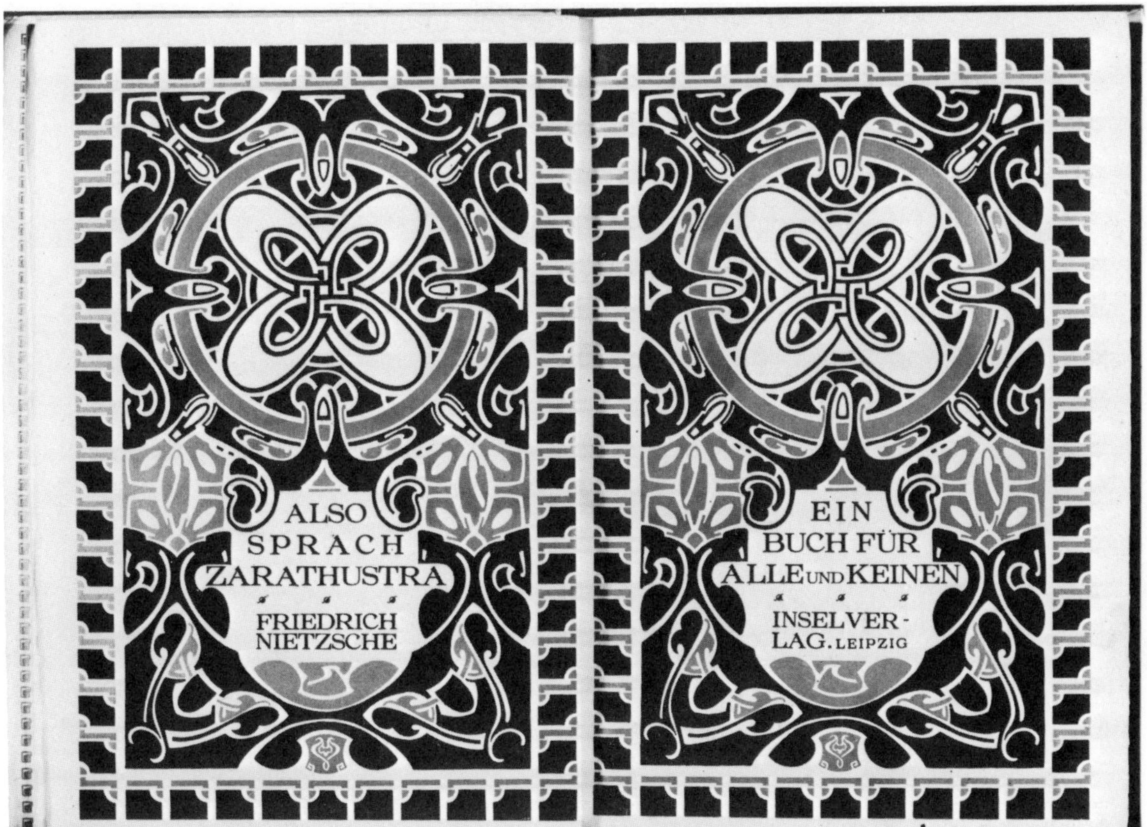

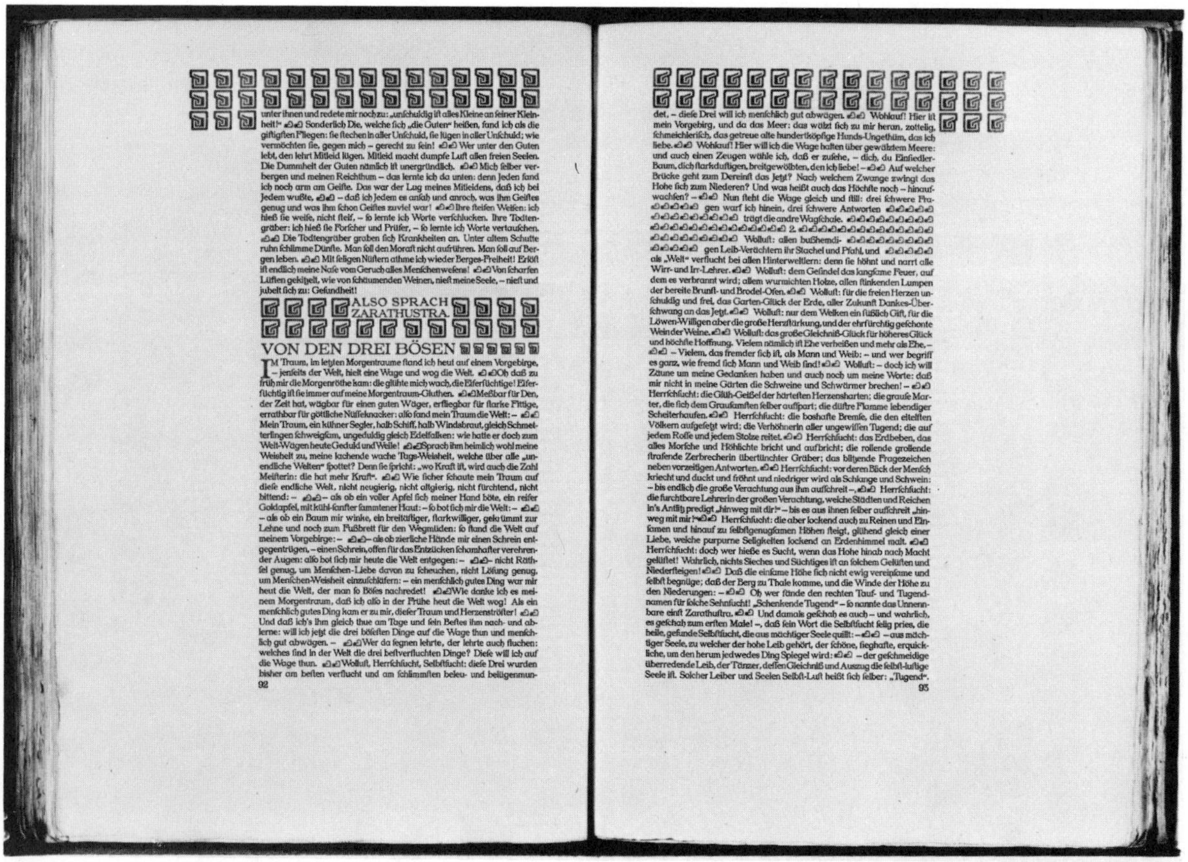

Henri van de Velde, double title page for Friedrich Nietzsche's *Ecce Homo,* 1908. In contrast to the symphonic crescendo of the *Also Sprach Zarathustra* title pages, in this design van de Velde's flowing curves weave the quieter harmony of a string quartet. *Houghton Library, Harvard University, Cambridge, Mass.*

Henri van de Velde, text pages from *Also Sprach Zarathustra,* 1908. Van de Velde's gold ornaments cap each column of type. In the center of the left-hand page, note van de Velde's design for chapter headings. Equally original is the design to mark chapter sections, which is shown high on the right-hand page. *Houghton Library, Harvard University, Cambridge, Mass.*

building'' existing, not in the design of the façade, but in dynamic interior spaces where people lived and worked. Wright looked to Japanese architecture and design for a model of harmony of proportion and visual poetry; in Pre-Columbian architecture and art he found organic ornament restrained by a mathematical repetition of horizontal and vertical spatial divisions.

Periodically during his long career, Wright turned his hand to graphic design. During the winter of 1896–97, Wright collaborated with William H. Winslow in the production of *The House Beautiful* by William C. Gannet. Only ninety copies of this extraordinary book were printed on a handpress using handmade paper at the Auvergne Press. Wright's border designs were executed in a fragile freehand line in a lacy pattern of highly stylized plant forms. His design interests included furniture, graphics, fabrics, wallpapers, and stained-glass windows. At the turn of the century, he was operating at the forefront of the emerging modern movement.

The Studio and its reproductions of work by Beardsley and Toorop had a strong influence on a group of young Scottish artists who became friends at the Glasgow School of Art. This closely knit group was led by Charles Rennie Mackintosh (1868–1928). He was joined by J. Herbert McNair (1868–1955), and two sisters, Margaret Macdonald (1865–1933) and Frances Macdonald (1874–1921). In 1899 McNair married Frances. The following year, Mackintosh and Margaret were wed.

Known as the Glasgow School, and also called the Four Macs, these young collaborators developed a unique style whose lyrical originality and symbolic complexity was celebrated on the Continent, particularly in Vienna, but often ignored in the British Isles. In 1896, the

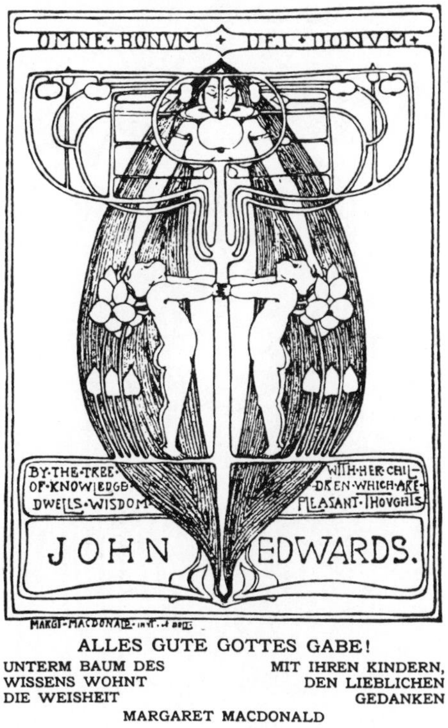

Margaret Macdonald, bookplate design, 1896. Reproduced in *Ver Sacrum* in 1901 as part of an article on the Glasgow group, this design depicts Wisdom protecting her children within the leaflike shelter of her hair before a symbolic tree of knowledge whose linear structure is based on Macdonald's metalwork.

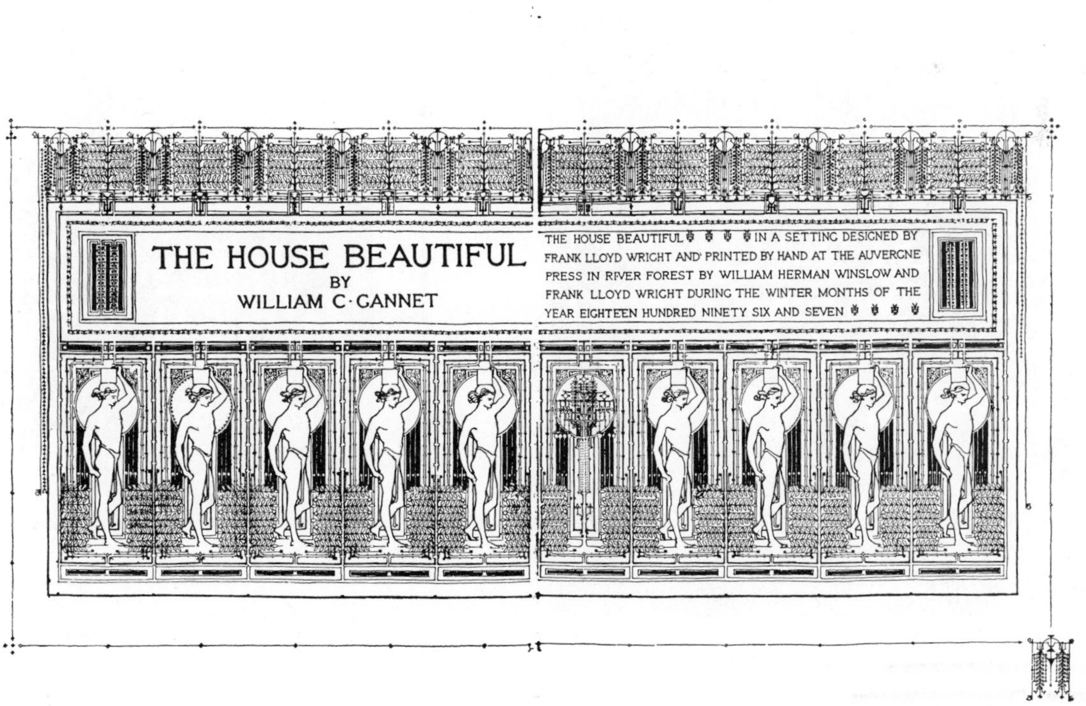

Frank Lloyd Wright, title page for *The House Beautiful,* 1896–97. An underlying geometric structure imposed a strong order upon the intricacy of Wright's textural designs. *Library of Congress, Washington, D.C.*

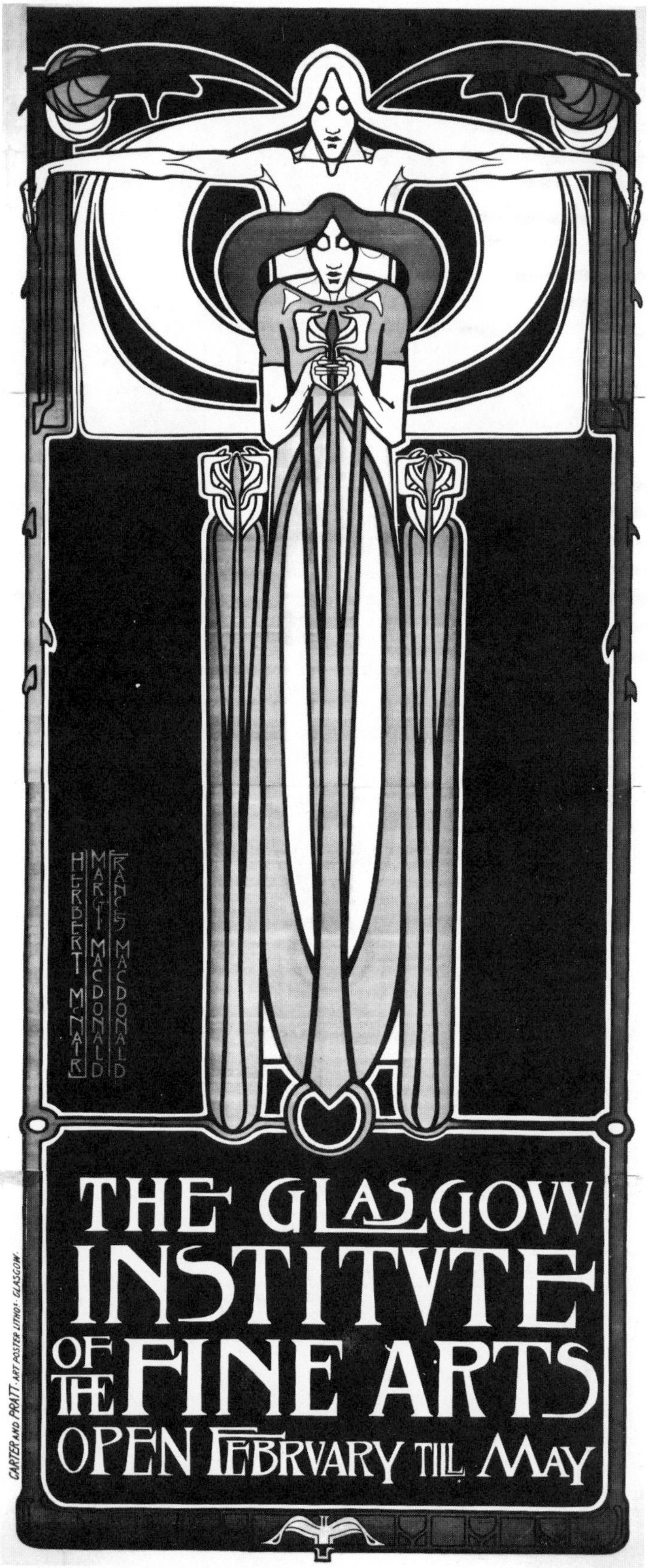

J. Herbert McNair and Margaret and Frances Macdonald, Glasgow Institute of the Fine Arts poster, 1895. The rising verticality and integration of flowing curves and geometric structure illustrate the mature style of the Four Macs. *Library of Congress, Washington, D.C., Poster Collection.*

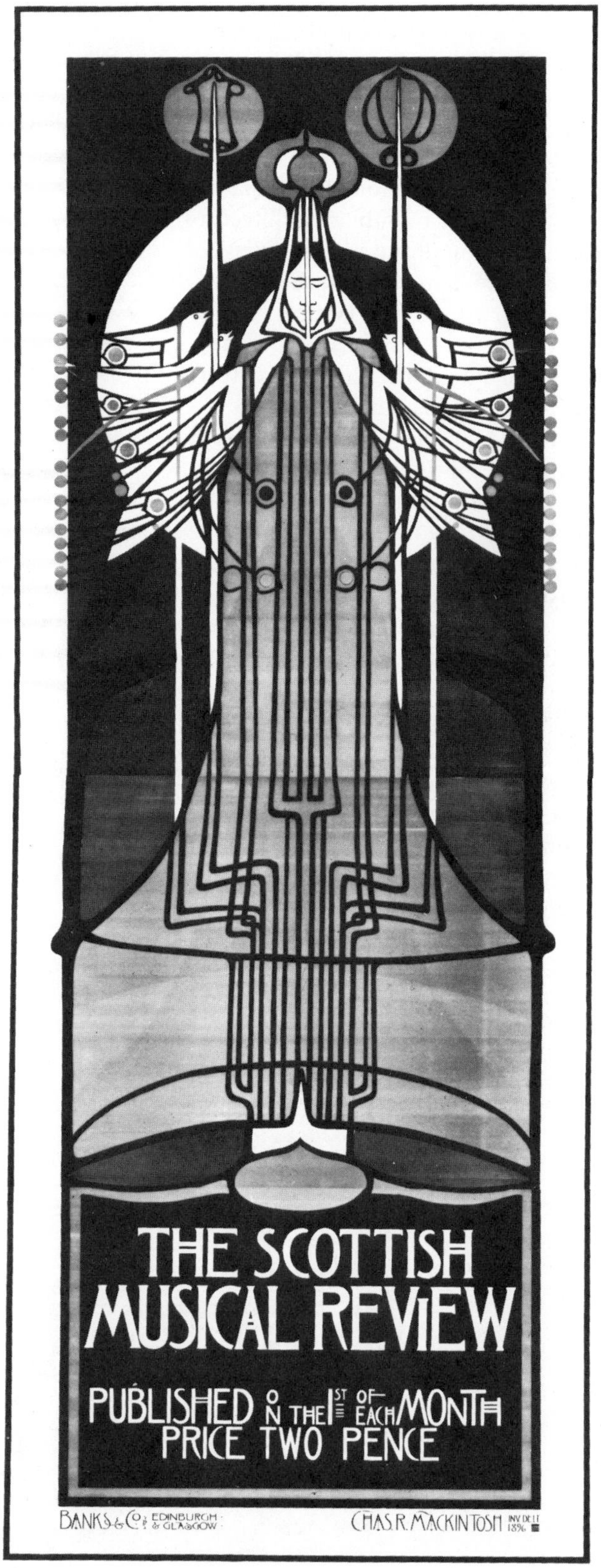

Charles Rennie Mackintosh, poster for The Scottish Musical Review, 1896. In this towering image that rises 2.46 meters (over 8 feet) above the spectator, complex overlapping planes are unified by areas of flat color. The white ring and birds around the figure create a strong focal point. *The Museum of Modern Art, New York.*

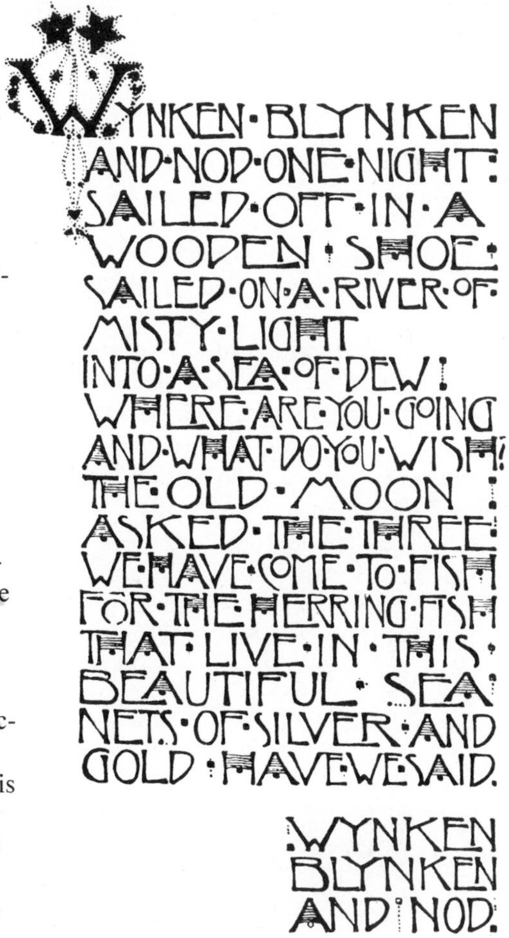
WYNKEN·BLYNKEN
AND·NOD·ONE·NIGHT:
SAILED·OFF·IN·A
WOODEN·SHOE:
SAILED·ON·A·RIVER·OF·
MISTY·LIGHT
INTO·A·SEA·OF·DEW!
WHERE·ARE·YOU·GOING
AND·WHAT·DO·YOU·WISH?
THE·OLD·MOON
ASKED·THE·THREE:
WE·HAVE·COME·TO·FISH
FOR·THE·HERRING·FISH
THAT·LIVE·IN·THIS·
BEAUTIFUL·SEA:
NETS·OF·SILVER·AND
GOLD·HAVE·WE·SAID.
WYNKEN
BLYNKEN
AND·NOD.

Jessie Marion King, lettering for a nursery rhyme, 1898. The proportions, vertical stress created by the high center stroke of the *E* and *F,* multiple horizontal strokes on the *A* and *H,* and multiple dots reflect King's Glasgow schooling.

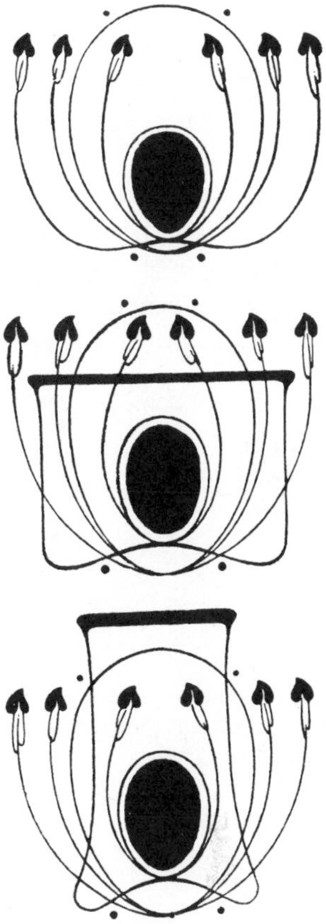

Talwin Morris, page ornaments from the Red Letter Shakespeare series, c. 1908. The name for this small, modestly priced set of Shakespearean plays derives from the two-color printing with the character's names in red. Between the introduction and the play, each volume had a page with a graceful ornament, printed in black with a red oval, from a series by Morris.

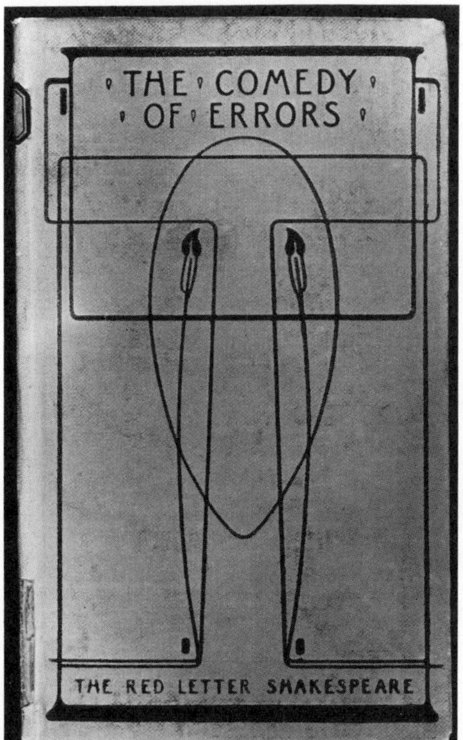
THE COMEDY
OF ERRORS
THE RED LETTER SHAKESPEARE

Talwin Morris, binding for *The Comedy of Errors,* c. 1908. Printed in muted green and red on off-white fabric, the standard format for the Red Letter Shakespeare series is typical of the subtle graphic lyricism achieved by Morris in economical commercial editions.

organizers at the annual Arts and Crafts exhibition invited them to participate. So dismayed were the hosts, however, that no further invitations were extended. But the editor of *The Studio* was so impressed that he visited Glasgow and published two articles in 1897. The German and Austrian movements learned of Glasgow's countermovement to mainstream Art Nouveau through these articles.

The Glasgow School offered a more geometric composition by tempering floral and curvilinear elements with strong rectilinear structure. Mackintosh's main design theme is of rising vertical lines, often with subtle curves at the ends to temper their junction with the horizontals. Narrow right angles, tall slivers of rectangles, and the counterpoint of ovals, circles, and arcs characterize his work. The Macdonald sisters had strong religious beliefs and embraced symbolist and mystical ideas. The confluence of Mackintosh's structure with his wife's world of fantasy and dreams produced an unprecedented transcendental style that has been variously described as feminine, a fairyland fantasy, and a melancholy disquietude.

Their modest graphic design production is uniformly superb. In addition to Mackintosh's notable architectural achievements, it is in the design of objects, chairs, and interiors as total environments that their main accomplishments were realized. Their furniture is simple and basic in design with delicate decorative ornaments. In their interiors, every small detail makes visual reference to the whole. The Four Macs, in their work and their influence on the Continent, became important transitions to the aesthetic of the twentieth century.

Among their followers who developed personal styles inspired by the Glasgow School, Jessie Marion King (1876–1949) developed a medieval, fairy style of illustration, and Annie French (1872–1965) became a prominent London book illustrator.

After working in architectural offices and serving as assistant art director for *Black and White* magazine in London, Talwin Morris (1865–1911) was selected to become art director of the Glasgow publishing firm of Blackie's in 1893, when he answered their want ad in the *London Times.* Shortly after moving to Glasgow, Morris established contact with the Four Macs and was influenced by their ideas. Blackie's was a volume printer of large editions of popular books for the mass market, including novels, reprints, and encyclopedias.

This provided Morris with a forum to apply the geometric spatial division and lyrical organic forms of the Glasgow group to mass communications.

Most of the editions he designed were economically printed. He often developed formats for series that could be used over and over again with subtle variations. The sheer volume of his work was a major factor in introducing the English public to Art Nouveau and preparing them to accept the emerging ideas and visual forms of modern architecture and design.

The Vienna Secession

In Austria, *Sezessionstil,* or the Vienna Secession, came into being on 3 April 1897 when the younger members of the Künstlerhaus, which was the Viennese Creative Artists' Association, resigned in stormy protest. Technically the refusal to allow foreign artists to participate in Künstlerhaus exhibitions was a main issue, but the conflict between tradition versus new ideas emanating from France, England, and Germany lay at the heart of the conflict, and the young artists wanted to exhibit more frequently. Painter Gustav Klimt (1862–1918) was the first president and the guiding spirit who led the revolt.

Architects J. J. Olbrich (1867–1908) and Josef Hoffmann (1870–1956) and artist-designer Koloman Moser (1868–1918) were key members. Like the Glasgow School from which it drew inspiration, *Sezessionstil* became a countermovement to the floral Art Nouveau that flourished in France and Germany.

Talwin Morris, page from *All's Well That Ends Well,* c. 1908. The standard format for the character list in the Red Letter Shakespeare series has this rigorous linear structure printed in red.

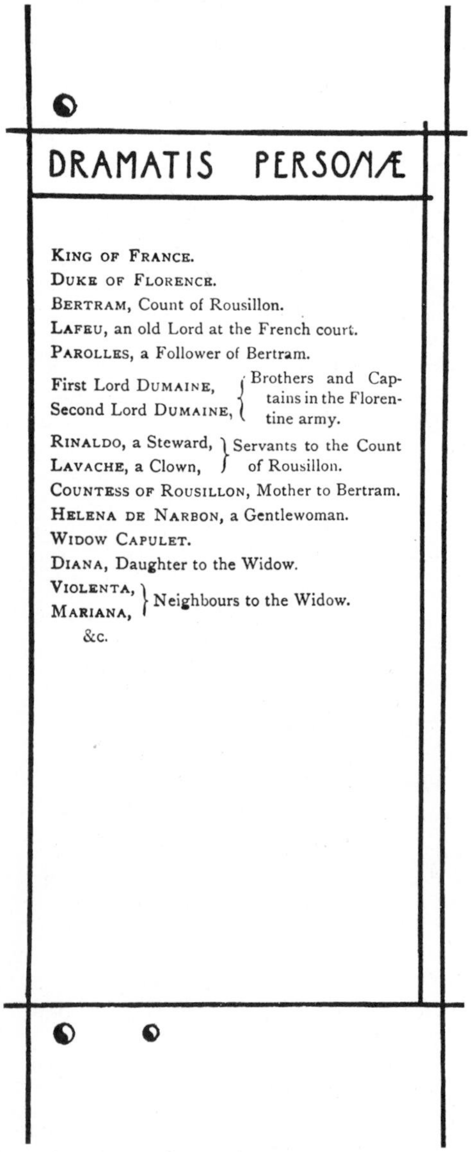

DRAMATIS PERSONÆ

KING OF FRANCE.
DUKE OF FLORENCE.
BERTRAM, Count of Rousillon.
LAFEU, an old Lord at the French court.
PAROLLES, a Follower of Bertram.
First Lord DUMAINE, Second Lord DUMAINE, } Brothers and Captains in the Florentine army.
RINALDO, a Steward, LAVACHE, a Clown, } Servants to the Count of Rousillon.
COUNTESS OF ROUSILLON, Mother to Bertram.
HELENA DE NARBON, a Gentlewoman.
WIDOW CAPULET.
DIANA, Daughter to the Widow.
VIOLENTA, MARIANA, } Neighbours to the Widow.
&c.

Gustav Klimt, poster for the first Vienna Secession exhibition, 1898. From Greek mythology, Klimt illustrated Athena, goddess of the arts, watching Theseus deliver the death blow to the Minotaur, an allegory for the struggle between the Secession and the Künstlerhaus. The trees were overprinted later after the Viennese police were outraged by the male nude. Klimt's use of a large open space in the poster's center is unprecedented.

The examination of benchmark posters for the Vienna Secession's exhibitions demonstrate the group's rapid evolution from the illustrative allegorical style of Symbolist painting, to a French-inspired floral style, to the mature Vienna Secession style. By 1898 the influence of the floral phase of Art Nouveau had been enthusiastically absorbed. In their graphic design, the Viennese preferred clean, legible sans-serif lettering that ranged from flat blocky slabs to fluidly calligraphic forms. For a brief period after 1900, Vienna became the main center for further creative innovation in the final blossoming of Art Nouveau. When the French floral style was rejected, Vienna Secession artists turned toward flat shapes and greater simplicity. Design and craft became increasingly important as this metamorphosis culminated in an emphasis on geometric patterning and modular construction of design. The design language they evolved used squares, rectangles, and circles in repetition and combination. Decoration and the application of ornament depended on similar elements used in parallel nonrhythmic sequence. Their geometry was not mechanical and rigid, but possessed a subtle organic quality.

Along with Julius Klinger (1876–1950), Alfred Roller (1864–1935), and Berthold Loffler (1874–1960), Koloman Moser made major contributions in graphic design. The most beautiful of turn-of-the-century magazines was the Vienna Secession's elegant *Ver Sacrum*

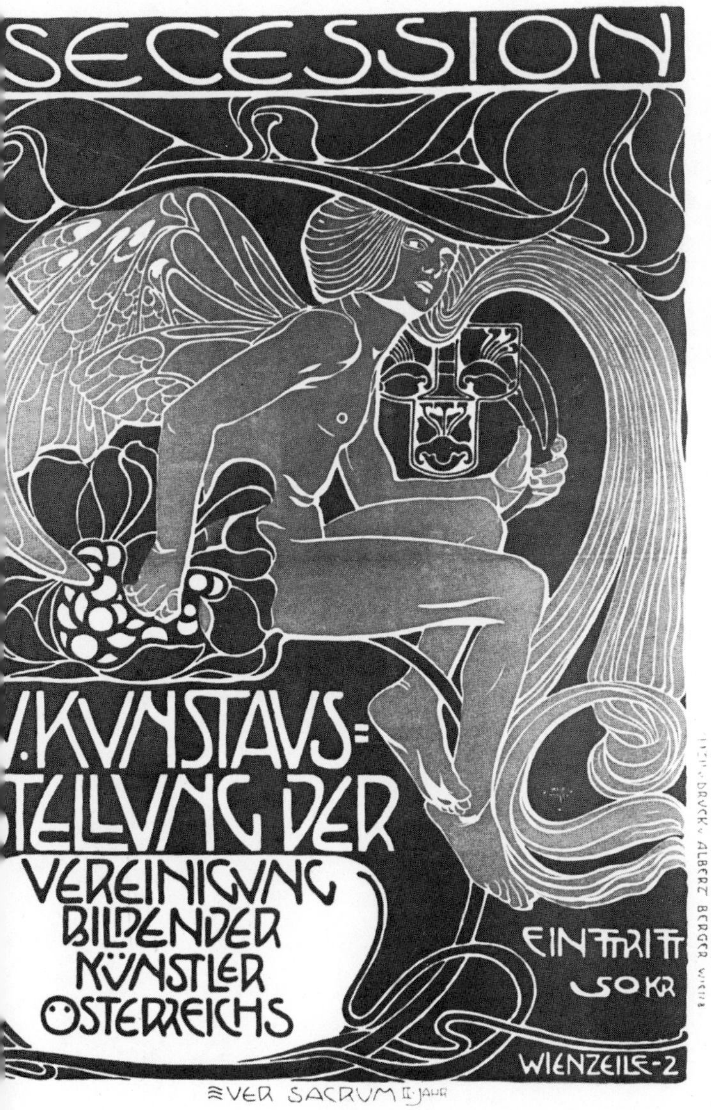

Koloman Moser, fifth Vienna Secession exhibition poster, 1899. The central, idealized figure and swooping floral forms are strongly influenced by French Art Nouveau. The figure is printed in metallic gold-bronze, and the background is olive green. The yellow-tone paper forms the contour lines for a stunning effect.

Koloman Moser, poster advertising Fromme's calendar, 1899. Used by the client with color changes for fifteen years, Moser's design depicting a goddess of personal destiny holding a snake-ring and hour-glass, symbols for the eternal circle of life and the passing of time, continued a mythological orientation but moved toward a flat two-dimensional space.

Koloman Moser, thirteenth Vienna Secession exhibition poster, 1902. In this masterpiece of the mature Vienna Secession style, mathematical patterns of squares and rectangles contrast with the circular forms of the figures and letterforms.

Alfred Roller, poster for the Vienna Secession exhibition, 1902. Two-dimensional geometric patterns form the image in this poster, whose visual qualities anticipate Cubism and Art Deco. *Houghton Library, Harvard University, Cambridge, Mass.*

Alfred Roller, cover design for *Ver Sacrum,* initial issue, 1898. Roller used an illustration of a tree whose growth has destroyed its pot, allowing it to take root in firmer soil, to symbolize the Secesson.

Alfred Roller, cover for *Ver Sacrum,* 1898. A stipple drawing of leaves becomes a frame for the lettering, which sets in a square that gives the impression of a collage element.

Josef Hoffmann, title frame from the premiere issue of *Ver Sacrum,* 1898. Berries, drawn in the free contour style favored by many Secession artists, flow around a plaque that proclaims "Association of Visual Artists of Austria. / Secession."

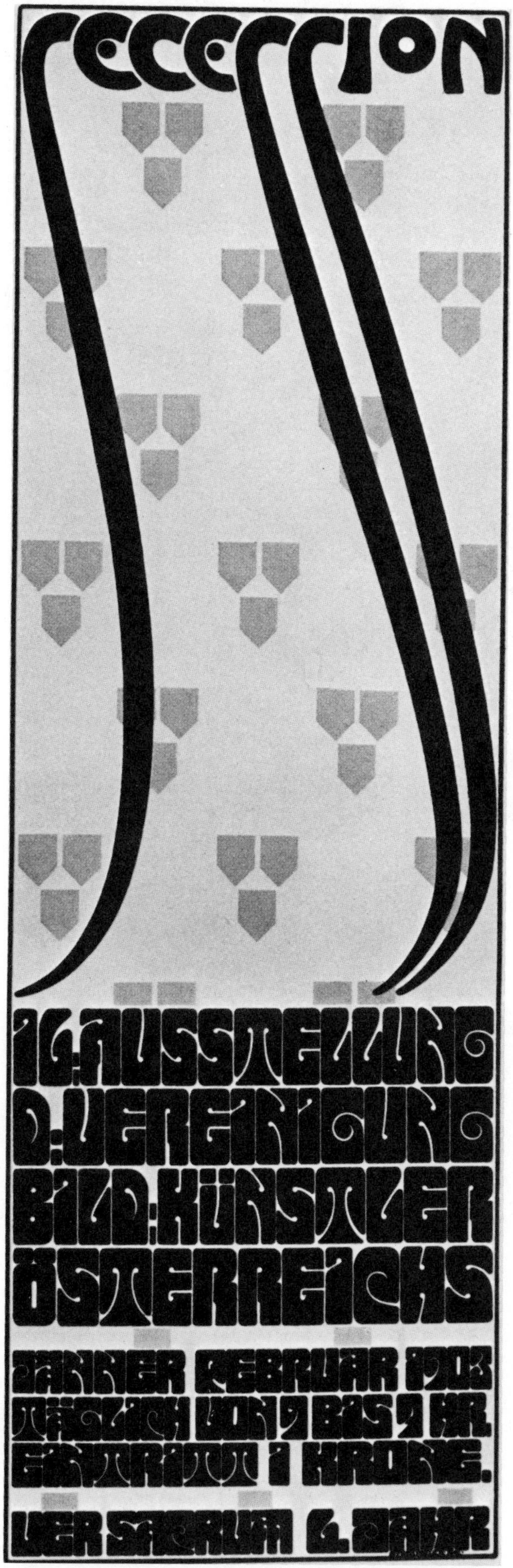

Alfred Roller, sixteenth Vienna Secession poster, 1902. By reducing letterforms to curved-corner rectangles with slashing white curves to define each character, Roller sacrificed legibility in favor of an unprecedented textural density.

Adolf Bohm, page from *Ver Sacrum*, 1898. The lyrical contours of trees reflected on a lake provided an appropriate environment for a poem about autumn trees swaying in the wind.

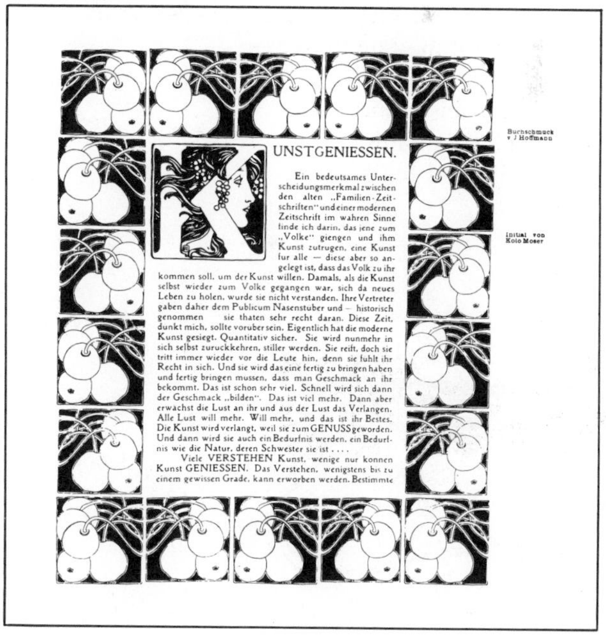

KUNSTGENIESSEN.

Ein bedeutsames Unterscheidungsmerkmal zwischen den alten „Familien-Zeitschriften" und einer modernen Zeitschrift im wahren Sinne finde ich darin, das jene zum „Volke" giengen und ihm Kunst zutrugen, eine Kunst fur alle — diese aber so angelegt ist, dass das Volk zu ihr kommen soll, um der Kunst willen. Damals, als die Kunst selbst wieder zum Volke gegangen war, sich da neues Leben zu holen, wurde sie nicht verstanden. Ihre Vertreter gaben daher dem Publicum Nasenstuber und — historisch genommen sie thaten sehr recht daran. Diese Zeit, dunkt mich, sollte voruber sein. Eigentlich hat die moderne Kunst gesiegt. Quantitativ sicher. Sie wird nunmehr in sich selbst zuruckkehren, stiller werden. Sie reift, doch sie tritt immer wieder vor die Leute hin, denn sie fuhlt ihr Recht in sich. Und sie wird das eine fertig zu bringen haben und fertig bringen mussen, dass man Geschmack an ihr bekommt. Das ist schon sehr viel. Schnell wird sich dann der Geschmack „bilden". Das ist viel mehr. Dann aber erwachst die Lust an ihr und aus der Lust das Verlangen. Alle Lust will mehr. Will mehr, und das ist ihr Bestes. Die Kunst wird verlangt, weil sie zum GENUSS geworden. Und dann wird sie auch ein Bedurfnis werden, ein Bedurfnis wie die Natur, deren Schwester sie ist . . . .

Viele VERSTEHEN Kunst, wenige nur konnen Kunst GENIESSEN. Das Verstehen, wenigstens bis zu einem gewissen Grade, kann erworben werden. Bestimmte

Buchschmuck v J Hoffmann

Initial von Kolo Moser

Josef Hoffmann (border) and Koloman Moser (initial), page from *Ver Sacrum*, 1898. Hoffman's modular berry motif and Moser's figurative initial combine to produce an exquisitely beautiful page.

(*Sacred Spring*), published from 1898 until 1903. With a continuously changing editorial staff, artistic responsibility through a rotating committee of artists, and unpaid contribution of art and design, *Ver Sacrum* was more a design laboratory than a magazine. In 1900 there were only three hundred subscribers and a press run of six hundred copies, but work on *Ver Sacrum* enabled Koloman Moser and his colleagues to develop innovative graphic design as they explored the merger of text, illustration, and ornament into a lively unity. It had an unusual square format. The 1898–99 issues were 28 by 28.5 centimeters (11 by 11 $\frac{1}{4}$ inches), and the 1900–03 issues were reduced to 23 by 24.5 centimeters (9 by 9 $\frac{3}{4}$ inches). *Ver Sacrum*'s unprecedented use of white space in its page layout, combined with the sleek coated stock, gave an aura of quality. Color plates were tipped in, and original etchings and lithographs were bound into the volumes. Sometimes signatures were printed in color combinations including muted brown and blue-gray, blue and green, brown with red-orange, and chocolate with gold. When signatures were bound together, four instead of two colors appeared on the double spreads. The Vienna Secession artists did not hesitate to experiment. A poem is printed in metallic gold ink on translucent paper; a photograph of an interior is printed in scarlet ink; and for one issue, a linear design by Koloman Moser is embossed on silky smooth, coated white stock in what may be the first white-on-white embossed graphic design.

Koloman Moser, cover for *Ver Sacrum,* 1899. A stencil-effect technique for creating images has an affinity, in the reduction of the subject to black and white planes, with high contrast photography.

Alfred Roller, design for a pocket-watch cover, 1900. Night and day are symbolized by two snails. This drawing almost takes on an oriental yin-yang (positive and negative principles in nature) quality.

J. M. Olbrich and Koloman Moser, page from *Ver Sacrum,* 1898. Secession artists took special delight in collaborating on page layouts combining graphics by two or more members. *Houghton Library, Harvard University, Cambridge, Mass.*

VER SACRUM.

Für V. S. gez. v. J. M. Olbrich.

Was hat das „Künstlerhaus" also für die Kunst gethan? Die Kunsthändler leisten mehr. Ein Künstler wie Rumpler, der in dem Einerlei der akademischen Lehrroutine zum Einsiedler geworden war, musste erst durch Miethke wieder „entdeckt" und dem Publicum vorgestellt werden. Alfons Mucha fand bei Artaria ein Unterkommen.

Für V. S. gez. v. Kolo Moser.

LIEBER SPÄT ALS NIE!

Mit dem thatkräftigen Eingreifen des neuen Directors des Österreichischen Museums für Kunst und Industrie, Hofraths v. Scala, hat ein frischer Zug sich geltend gemacht, welcher der Vorläufer einer glücklichen Zukunft zu werden verspricht. Die Weihnachts-Ausstellung bot eine reiche Fülle von Anregungen und das Verdienst, diese dargebotenen Erzeugnisse eines selbständig entwickelten nationalen Stils und Geschmacks uns vor Augen zu führen, ist hoch anzuschlagen. England und Amerika sind die Vorbilder und Chippendale, Sheraton und Tiffany heissen die drei Zauberer, deren Namen hinter jedem Stuhl, Aufsatz oder „favrile" Glas „unsichtbar, sichtbar" auftauchen. Viele von diesen vornehmen Mustermöbeln sind, wie die angehängten Zettel verrathen, bereits in kaufkräftige Hände übergegangen. Die Anregungen scheinen also auf nicht ganz unempfänglichen Boden zu fallen, und das ist der Hauptzweck derselben.

Wir hoffen aber, dass Hofrath v. Scala dabei nicht stehen bleibt. Der erste Schritt ist gethan und hier ist einmal der Anfang nicht, wie gewöhnlich, der schwerste, sondern der leichtere Theil der Arbeit. Die Hauptsache kommt noch! Nicht mehr nachmachen, selbst erfinden, selbst machen, das ist die Lehre, die wir aus dieser Anregung nehmen. „Besinne dich selbst", lautet nun der Wahlspruch. Ein kleines, bescheidenes Möbel, das nicht zur Ausstellung gehört und weitab in einer Ecke steht, wäre recht geeignet, zu solchem Besinnen aufzufordern. Wir meinen den prächtig originellen Bauernstuhl aus der „Schwalm" in Hessen. „Aus dem 19ten Jahrhundert", steht darauf vermerkt. Nun, Ihr Herren, da ist ja etwas! Seht Euch nur an, wie das selbständig gemacht ist. Einen deutschen Stil aus dem 19ten Jahrhundert .... hat man uns doch gesagt, das gäbe es nicht? In allen Stilen arbeiten wir, sind in allen Jahrhunderten zu Hause ≡ nur in unserem nicht. Wir wollen uns das nicht länger sagen lassen, wir wollen es nicht länger mit ansehen, wie Handlanger der Kunst ihre kümmerlichen Flammen aus dem mühsam zusammengetragenen Aschenhäufchen vergangener Stilepochen herausblasen! Das Ragout von anderer Leute Schmaus ist ungeniessbar. Von England und Amerika wollen wir uns gerne zeigen lassen, wie man selbständig wird, wie man von innen heraus arbeitet, wie man sich einen STIL schafft. Dann aber heisst's auch bei uns: „HILF DIR SELBST!"

S.

DREI TOEPFE FUER BLUMEN

Buchschmuck für V. S. gez. v. Kolo Moser.

25

Josef Olbrich, frame for *Ver Sacrum* article title, 1899. The fluid repetition of forms and symmetry of this decorative botanical frame with its dense black color brought lively contrast to the typographic page.

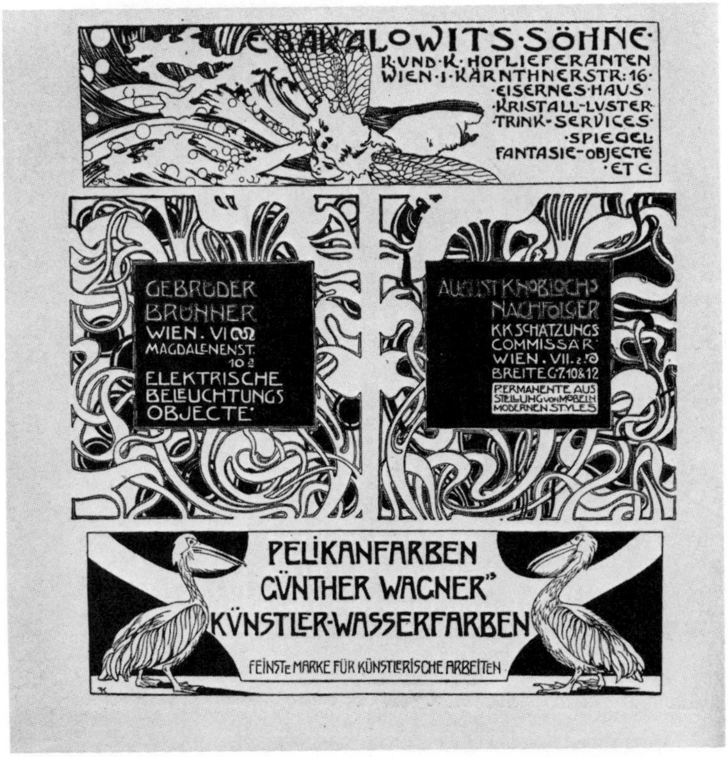

Alfred Roller, Koloman Moser, and Frederick Koenig, inside front cover advertisements for *Ver Sacrum,* 1899. Both the design of each ad and the makeup of the whole page are carefully planned to minimize the graphic clutter and clash usually present when small ads are clustered together. *Houghton Library, Harvard University, Cambridge, Mass.*

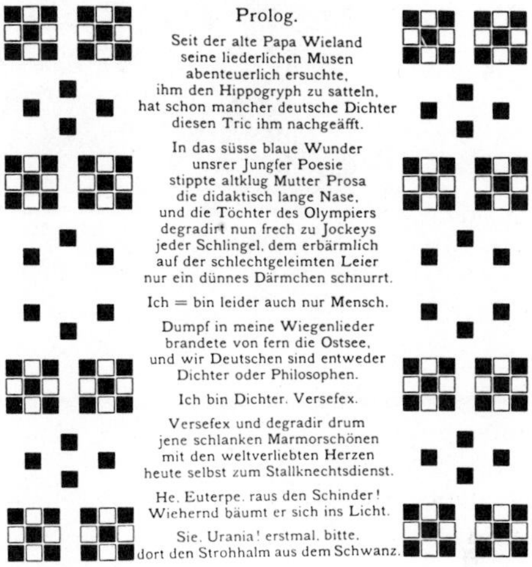

Prolog.

Seit der alte Papa Wieland
seine liederlichen Musen
abenteuerlich ersuchte,
ihm den Hippogryph zu satteln,
hat schon mancher deutsche Dichter
diesen Tric ihm nachgeäfft.

In das süsse blaue Wunder
unsrer Jungfer Poesie
stippte altklug Mutter Prosa
die didaktisch lange Nase,
und die Töchter des Olympiers
degradirt nun frech zu Jockeys
jeder Schlingel, dem erbärmlich
auf der schlechtgeleimten Leier
nur ein dünnes Därmchen schnurrt.

Ich = bin leider auch nur Mensch.

Dumpf in meine Wiegenlieder
brandete von fern die Ostsee,
und wir Deutschen sind entweder
Dichter oder Philosophen.

Ich bin Dichter. Versefex.

Versefex und degradir drum
jene schlanken Marmorschönen
mit den weltverliebten Herzen
heute selbst zum Stallknechtsdienst.

He, Euterpe, raus den Schinder!
Wiehernd bäumt er sich ins Licht.

Sie, Urania! erstmal, bitte,
dort den Strohhalm aus dem Schwanz.

Pickelhering.

Und ist der Hundsfott endlich todt,
dann mengt ihn mir mit Mäusekoth.
So geh es jedem Klexer,
pro Pfund 'n Sechser!

Epitaph.

In des Teufels Paradies
brät er jetzt an einem Spiess;
schlägt rund rum die Riesenwelle,
hier liegt die Pelle.

330

Koloman Moser, pages from *Ver Sacrum,* 1901. As the Prologue and Epitaph demonstrate, Arno Holz's lengthy poem was bracketed with black-and-white patterns of squares which changed on each page. *Houghton Library, Harvard University, Cambridge, Mass.*

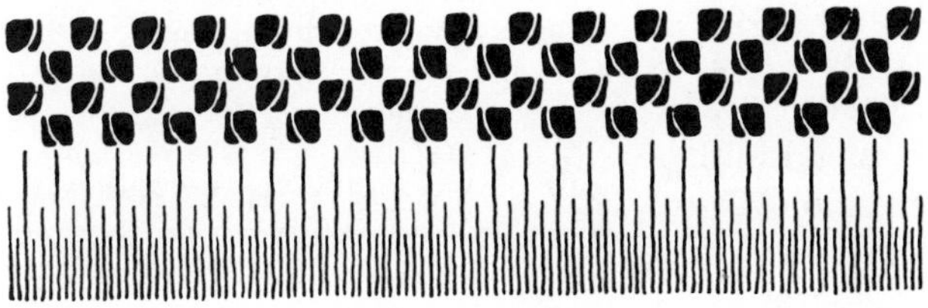

GEORGE MINNE.

MAN hat merkwürdige Sachen in Wien über die Minne=Ausstellung gelesen und gehört; deprimie=rend merkwürdig, grotesk und leider so roh, als wären wir noch in der Zeit der Kreuzzüge. Wo bleibt der berühmte Fortschritt? Man fährt immer schneller,

von Banalem umgeben, wir müssen Banales sehen und thun, so will es unser Erdenlos. Gebenedeit seien die Augen=blicke, wo uns anderes geschieht.

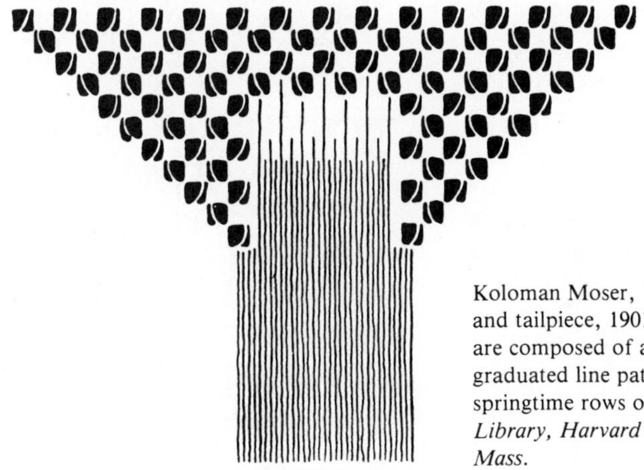

Koloman Moser, *Ver Sacrum* headpiece and tailpiece, 1901. These graphic designs are composed of a checkerboard and graduated line pattern, but they also evoke springtime rows of tulips. *Houghton Library, Harvard University, Cambridge, Mass.*

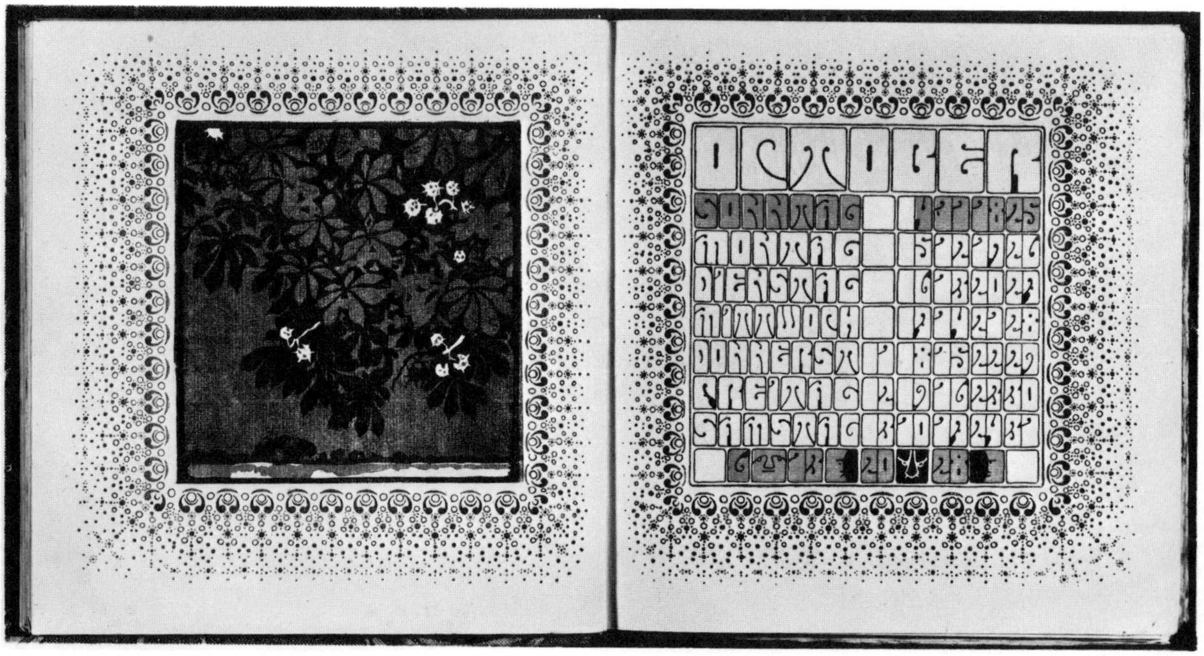

Design aesthetics were so important that advertisers were required to commission their advertising designs from the artists and designers contributing to each issue to insure a visual design unity. The exceptional linear and geometric design elements gracing *Ver Sacrum*'s pages became an important design resource as the Vienna Secession style evolved.

By the turn of the century, both Koloman Moser and Josef Hoffmann had been appointed to the faculty of the Vienna School for Applied Art. Their ideas about clean geometric design, formed when they stripped the Glasgow influence of its virgins, symbolic roses, and mystical overtones, captured the imagination of their students.

Financed by the industrialist Fritz Wärndorfer, the *Wiener Werkstätte* ("Vienna Workshops") were founded in 1903. An outgrowth of *Sezessionstil,* this spiritual continuum of Morris' workshops sought a close union of pure and applied arts in the design of lamps, fabrics, and other objects for everyday use. Originally formed to produce designs by Moser and Hoffmann, the Vienna Workshops flourished and many other collaborators participated. Several buildings were executed as total works of art. Their goal was to offer an alternative to poorly designed mass-produced articles and trite historicism. Function, honesty to materials, and harmonious proportion were important concerns. Decoration was used only when it served these goals and did not violate them. Master carpenters, bookbinders, metalsmiths, and leather workers were employed to work with the designers in the effort to elevate crafts to the standards of fine arts. Moser left the Vienna Workshops in 1907, and his death at age fifty in 1918 cut short the career of one of the great innovators of graphic design. The Vienna Workshops flourished until the Depression Era, when financial difficulties forced their closing in 1932.

All areas of design owe a debt to the polemic Austrian architect Adolf Loos (1870–1933), who roundly condemned both historicism and *Sezessionstil* as he called for a functional simplicity which banished "useless decoration" in any form. Standing alone at the turn of the century, Loos blasted the nineteenth-century love of decoration and horror of empty spaces. To him organic meant not curvilinear but the use of human needs as a standard for measuring utilitarian form. His 1906 Villa Karma, built in Switzerland, forecast the simple geometric forms of the 1920s avant garde. By 1910, the creative momentum in Vienna had passed. But the gulf between nineteenth-century ornament and Art Nouveau on the one hand, and the rational functionalism and geometric formalism of the twentieth century on the other, had been bridged.

Alfred Roller (designer) and Karl Müller (illustrator), *Ver Sacrum* calendar for October 1903. Roller's border has a fairyland exuberance, and the numbers and letterforms are squeezed into rectangles. *Houghton Library, Harvard University, Cambridge, Mass.*

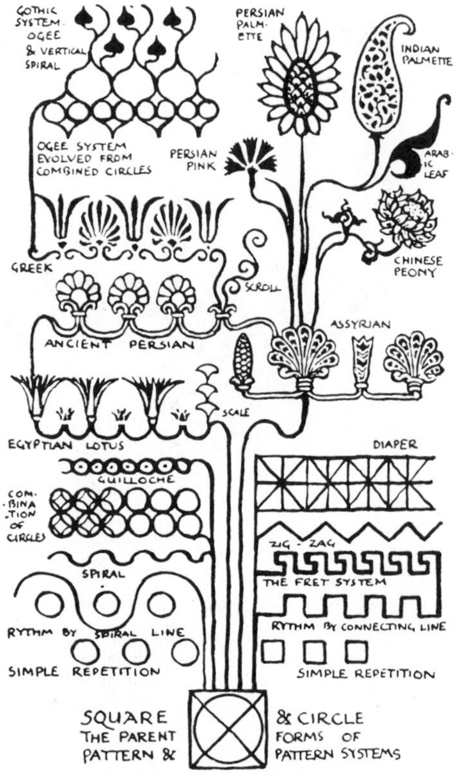

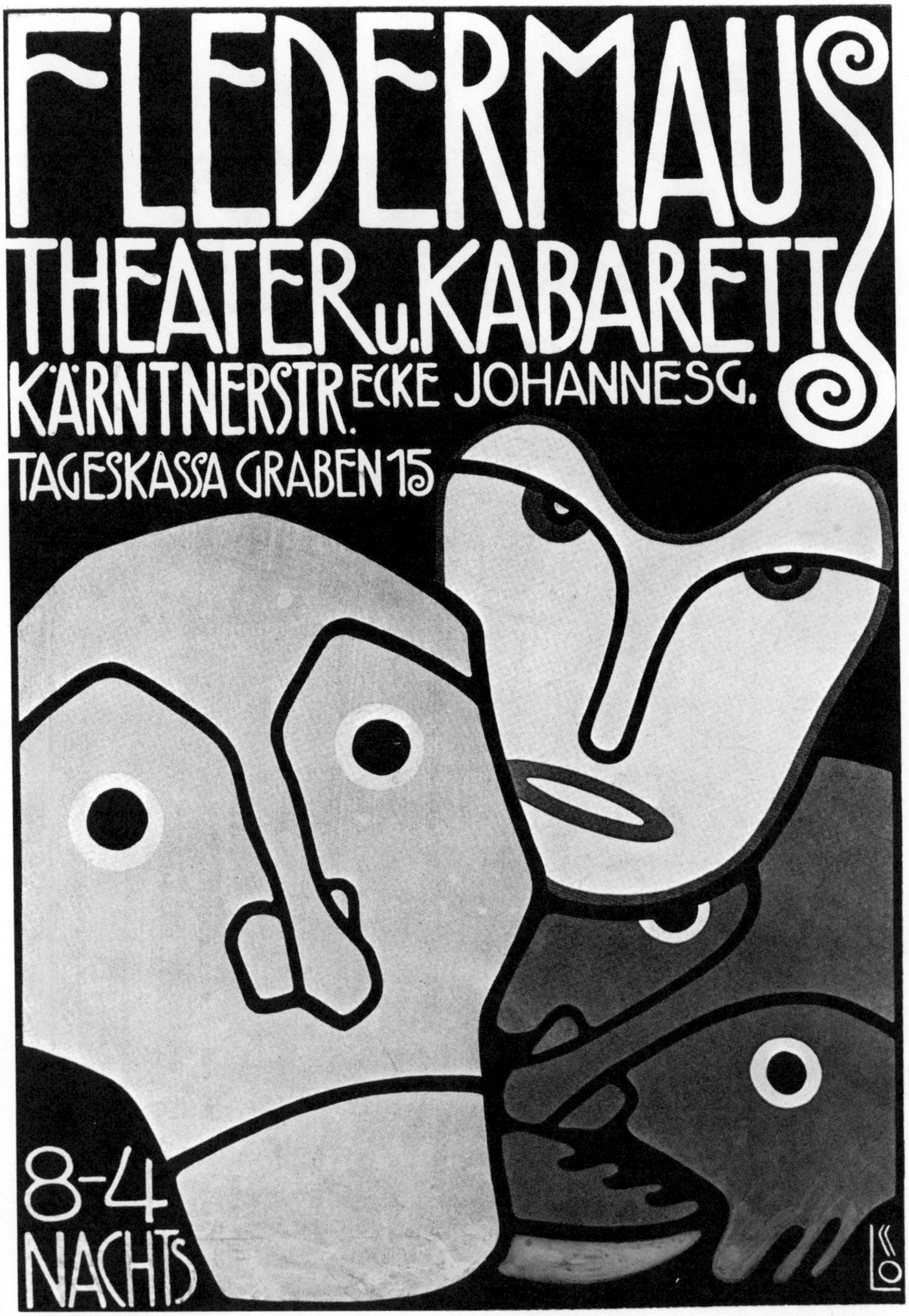

Berthold Loeffler, poster for a theater and cabaret, c. 1907. Loeffler innovated a graphic language of thick contours and geometric features in these masklike faces which glow in intense flat yellow, white, and red against the flat black background.

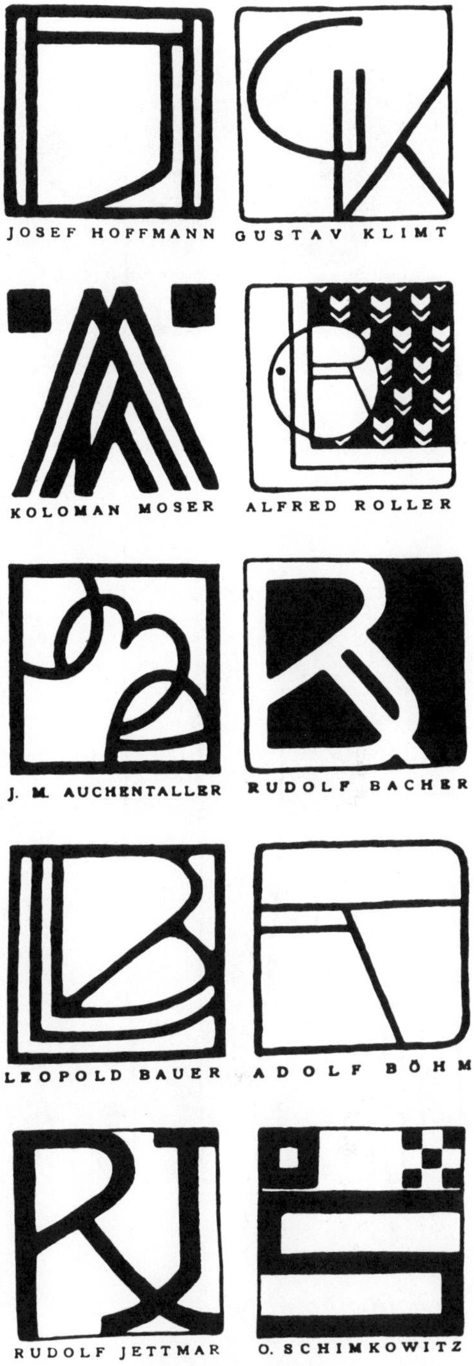

Walter Crane, diagram from *Line and Form,* 1900. In his widely read book, it almost seems, in retrospect, that Crane was predicting the evolution of form toward a geometric purity that was achieved by the Vienna Secession and the post-Cubism avant-garde.

The registered trademark and monogram applied to products of the Vienna Workshops demonstrate the harmony of proportion, lyrical geometry, and clarity of form that characterize designs produced there.

These personal monograms designed by members of the Vienna Secession were included in the catalogue of one of their exhibitions in 1902.

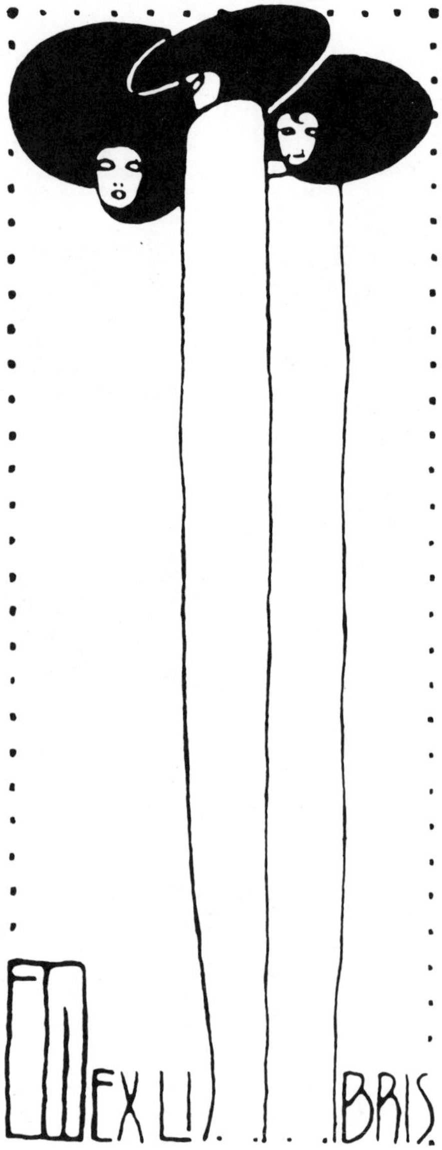

Josef Hoffmann, bookplate design, 1903. In this example from a large series of figure studies, Hoffmann abstracted the human figure to elongated contours and simple shapes to evoke hair or hats.

Josef Hoffmann, Wiener Werkstätte exhibition poster, 1905. A severe geometric pattern was created in blue by a hand-stencil technique after the lettering and two lower rectangles were printed by lithography. The lettering was also used in an advertisement and similar posters with different pattern designs.

Jugendstil and Neue Schlichkeit

Art Nouveau arrived in Germany, where it was called *Jugendstil* ("young style"). This name was adopted from a new periodical called *Jugend* (*Youth*), which began publication at Munich in 1896. From Munich, *Jugendstil* spread to Berlin, Darmstadt, and all over Germany. German Art Nouveau had strong French and British influences, but it still retained strong links to the more traditional academic art that preceded it. The German interest in medieval letterforms—Germany was the only European country that did not replace the textur style types with the roman styles of the Renaissance—continued side by side with Art Nouveau motifs.

During the first year *Jugend* was published, the circulation climbed to thirty thousand copies per week. As it walked a fine line between being an arts magazine and a journal of popular entertainment, *Jugend* soon attracted a readership of one hundred thousand per week.

Jugend used illustrations or Art Nouveau ornaments on virtually every editorial page. Full double-page illustrations, horizontal illustrations across the top of a page, an abundance of spot illustrations, and decorative Art Nouveau designs brought rich variety to a format that was about half visual material and half text. One unprecedented editorial policy was to allow each week's cover designer the latitude to design a masthead to go with the cover design. Over the course of a year, the *Jugend* logo might appear as giant, Medieval black letters, tendrillike Art Nouveau lettering, or just the word *Jugend* set in twenty-four-point typography above the image because that week's designer had ignored the problem of integrating the logo. In the cover design for 14 October 1899 by Hans Christiansen (1866–1945), one of the leading artists associated with *Jugend,*

the simple, sans-serif letterforms are drawn in icy, pale violet with pale pink outlines. The stylized curves of the letterforms pick up the stylized curves of the flat shapes of the image. Christiansen predates the Fauve movement of the early twentieth century in his use of flat planes of bright color.

Another frequent *Jugend* artist was Josef Sattler (1867–1931), who is particularly noted for his work for *Pan* magazine. During its five years of publication (1895–1900), *Pan* provided a forum for the important literature of the period.

Hans Christiansen, cover for *Jugend,* 1899. In a free design of flat colors, Christiansen's pink swans swim in brilliant blue and green water that is reflecting glowing pinks and oranges of the sunset. Remarkably close-valued, this design gains its vitality from contrasting warm and cool hues.

Josef Sattler, *Pan* magazine poster, 1895. The pistil of the flower forms the word *"Pan,"* and the red stamen report that the year is 1895.

Peter Behrens, trademark for Insel-Verlag, 1899. A delightful ship in a circle perches on Art Nouveau waves.

ECKMANN

Geschnitten nach den Entwürfen
des Herrn Professor O. Eckmann

Gesetzlich geschützt!

Rudhard'sche Gießerei
in Offenbach am Main

Dekorative Schrift

Otto Eckmann, title page for *Eckmann-Schriftprobe,* 1901. The title page of Eckmann's book on letterforms uses one of the typefaces that he designed.

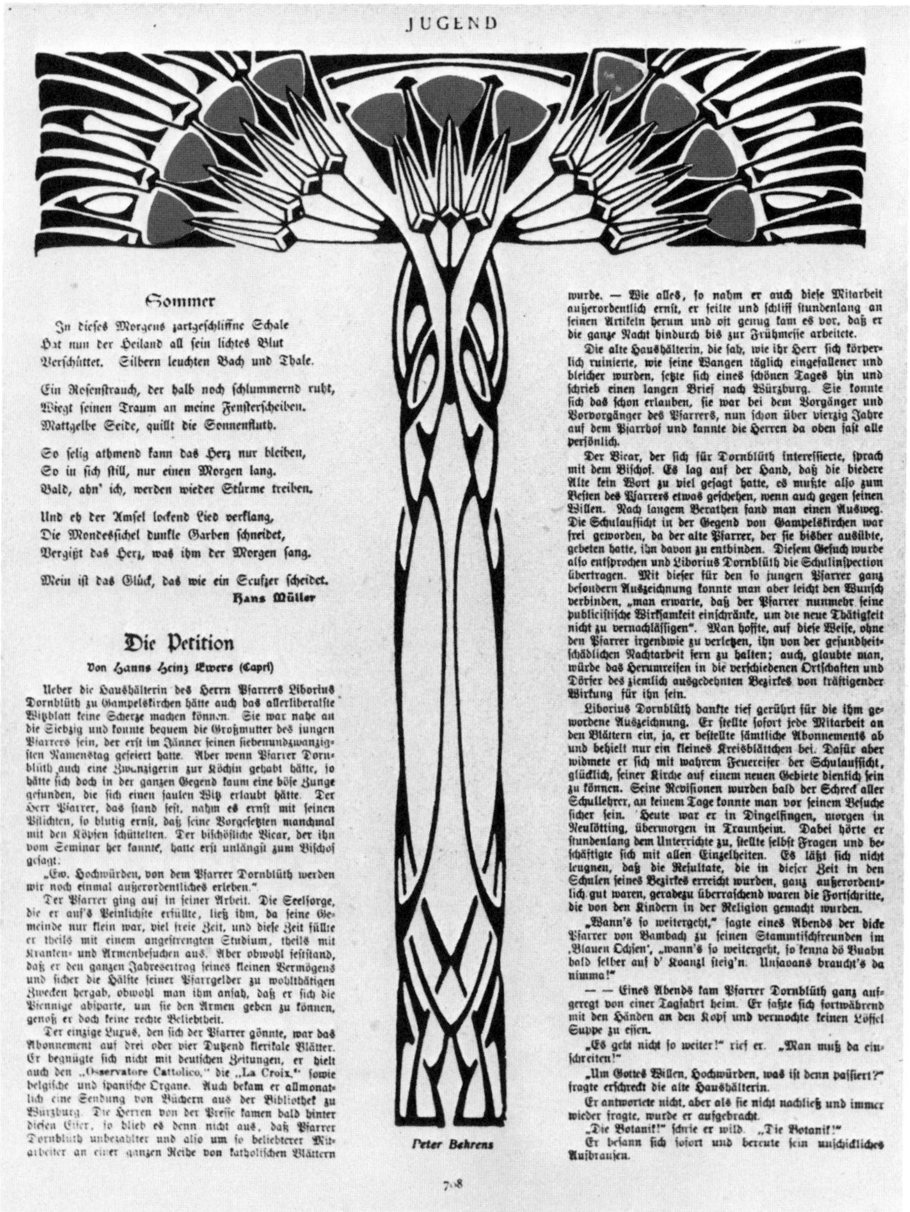

JUGEND

Sommer

In dieses Morgens zartgeschliffne Schale
Hat nun der Heiland all sein lichtes Blut
Verschüttet. Silbern leuchten Bach und Thale.

Ein Rosenstrauch, der halb noch schlummernd ruht,
Wiegt seinen Traum an meine Fensterscheiben.
Mattgelbe Seide, quillt die Sonnenfluth.

So selig athmend kann das Herz nur bleiben,
So in sich still, nur einen Morgen lang.
Bald, ahn' ich, werden wieder Stürme treiben.

Und eh der Amsel lockend Lied verklang,
Die Mondessichel dunkle Garben schneidet,
Vergißt das Herz, was ihm der Morgen sang.

Mein ist das Glück, das wie ein Seufzer scheidet.

Hans Müller

Die Petition

Von Hanns Heinz Ewers (Capri)

Ueber die Haushälterin des Herrn Pfarrers Liborius Dornblüth zu Gampelskirchen hätte auch das allerliberalste Witzblatt keine Scherze machen können. Sie war nahe an die Siebzig und konnte bequem die Großmutter des jungen Pfarrers sein, der erst im Jänner seinen siebenundzwanzigsten Namenstag gefeiert hatte. Aber wenn Pfarrer Dornblüth auch eine Zwanzigerin zur Köchin gehabt hätte, so hätte sich doch in der ganzen Gegend kaum eine böse Zunge gefunden, die sich einen faulen Witz erlaubt hätte. Der Herr Pfarrer, das stand fest, nahm es ernst mit seinen Pflichten, so blutig ernst, daß seine Vorgesetzten manchmal mit den Köpfen schüttelten. Der bischöfliche Vicar, der ihn vom Seminar her kannte, hatte erst unlängst zum Bischof gesagt:

„Ew. Hochwürden, von dem Pfarrer Dornblüth werden wir noch einmal außerordentliches erleben."

Der Pfarrer ging auf in seiner Arbeit. Die Seelsorge, die er auf's Peinlichste erfüllte, ließ ihm, da seine Gemeinde nur klein war, viel freie Zeit, und diese Zeit füllte er theils mit einem angestrengten Studium, theils mit Kranken- und Armenbesuchen aus. Aber obwohl feststand, daß er den ganzen Jahresertrag seines kleinen Vermögens und sicher die Hälfte seiner Pfarrgelder zu wohlthätigen Zwecken hergab, obwohl man ihm ansah, daß er sich die Pfennige absparte, um sie den Armen geben zu können, genoß er doch keine rechte Beliebtheit.

Der einzige Luxus, den sich der Pfarrer gönnte, war das Abonnement auf drei oder vier Dutzend klerikale Blätter. Er begnügte sich nicht mit deutschen Zeitungen, er hielt auch den „Osservatore Cattolico," die „La Croix," sowie belgische und spanische Organe. Auch bekam er allmonatlich eine Sendung von Büchern aus der Bibliothek zu Würzburg. Die Herren von der Presse kamen bald hinter diesen Eifer, so blieb es denn nicht aus, daß Pfarrer Dornblüth unbezahlter und also um so beliebterer Mitarbeiter an einer ganzen Reihe von katholischen Blättern wurde. — Wie alles, so nahm er auch diese Mitarbeit außerordentlich ernst, er feilte und schliff stundenlang an seinen Artikeln herum und oft genug kam es vor, daß er die ganze Nacht hindurch bis zur Frühmesse arbeitete.

Die alte Haushälterin, die sah, wie ihr Herr sich körperlich ruinierte, wie seine Wangen täglich eingefallener und bleicher wurden, setzte sich eines schönen Tages hin und schrieb einen langen Brief nach Würzburg. Sie konnte sich das schon erlauben, sie war bei dem Vorgänger und Vorvorgänger des Pfarrers, nun schon über vierzig Jahre auf dem Pfarrhof und kannte die Herren da oben fast alle persönlich.

Der Vicar, der sich für Dornblüth interessierte, sprach mit dem Bischof. Es lag auf der Hand, daß die biedere Alte kein Wort zu viel gesagt hatte, es mußte also zum Besten des Pfarrers etwas geschehen, wenn auch gegen seinen Willen. Nach langem Berathen fand man einen Ausweg. Die Schulaufsicht in der Gegend von Gampelskirchen war frei geworden, da der alte Pfarrer, der sie bisher ausübte, gebeten hatte, ihn davon zu entbinden. Diesem Gesuch wurde also entsprochen und Liborius Dornblüth die Schulinspection übertragen. Mit dieser für den so jungen Pfarrer ganz besondern Auszeichnung konnte man aber leicht den Wunsch verbinden, „man erwarte, daß der Pfarrer nunmehr seine publicistische Wirksamkeit einschränke, um die neue Thätigkeit nicht zu vernachlässigen". Man hoffte, auf diese Weise, ohne den Pfarrer irgendwie zu verletzen, ihn von der gesundheitschädlichen Nachtarbeit fern zu halten; auch, glaubte man, würde das Herumreisen in die verschiedenen Ortschaften und Dörfer des ziemlich ausgedehnten Bezirkes von kräftigender Wirkung für ihn sein.

Liborius Dornblüth dankte tief gerührt für die ihm gewordene Auszeichnung. Er stellte sofort jede Mitarbeit an den Blättern ein, ja, er bestellte sämtliche Abonnements ab und behielt nur ein kleines Kreisblättchen bei. Dafür aber widmete er sich mit wahrem Feuereifer der Schulaufsicht, glücklich, seiner Kirche auf einem neuen Gebiete dienlich sein zu können. Seine Revisionen wurden bald der Schreck aller Schullehrer, an keinem Tage konnte man vor seinem Besuche sicher sein. Heute war er in Dingelfingen, morgen in Neulötting, übermorgen in Traunheim. Dabei hörte er stundenlang dem Unterrichte zu, stellte selbst Fragen und beschäftigte sich mit allen Einzelheiten. Es läßt sich nicht leugnen, daß die Resultate, die in dieser Zeit in den Schulen seines Bezirkes erreicht wurden, ganz außerordentlich gut waren, geradezu überraschend waren die Fortschritte, die von den Kindern in der Religion gemacht wurden.

„Wann's so weitergeht," sagte eines Abends der dicke Pfarrer von Bambach zu seinen Stammtischfreunden im ‚Blauen Ochsen', „wann's so weitergeht, so kenna dö Buabn bald selber auf d' Koanzl steig'n. Unsavans braucht's da nimma!"

— — Eines Abends kam Pfarrer Dornblüth ganz aufgeregt von einer Tagfahrt heim. Er faßte sich fortwährend mit den Händen an den Kopf und vermochte keinen Löffel Suppe zu essen.

„Es geht nicht so weiter!" rief er. „Man muß da einschreiten!"

„Um Gottes Willen, Hochwürden, was ist denn passiert?" fragte erschreckt die alte Haushälterin.

Er antwortete nicht, aber als sie nicht nachließ und immer wieder fragte, wurde er aufgebracht.

„Die Botanik!" schrie er wild. „Die Botanik!"

Er besann sich sofort und bereute sein unschickliches Aufbrausen.

Peter Behrens

708

Peter Behrens, graphic design for *Jugend,* 1904. A gray and brown structure, evocative of peacock feathers and Egyptian lotus designs, rises above two columns of gothic style type.

Peter Behrens, cover for *Der Bunte Vogel,* 1899. The bold simplicity and use of traditional gothic type are typical of Jugendstil. *Houghton Library, Harvard University, Cambridge, Mass.*

In contrast to the free-wheeling typographic approach of *Jugend,* a literary journal called *Die Insel,* which began publication in Munich in 1899, was the first publication to establish and maintain a uniform, typographic layout style throughout. The design advisor for *Die Insel* was Peter Behrens (1868–1940), one of the finest *Jugendstil* designers. *Die Insel* was not illustrated, but like another literary anthology using Behrens as designer, *Der Bunte Vogel,* it experimented with ornaments and vignettes of abstract design throughout.

The primary German contribution was not *Jugendstil,* however, but the innovations that developed in reaction to it after the turn of the century, as architects and designers, including Otto Eckmann (1865–1902) and Peter Behrens, became influenced by the ideals of the Arts and Crafts Movement, purged of its medieval affections. Behrens had been educated at the Fine Arts School in his hometown of Hamburg. In 1897 he moved to Munich and played an important role in the German arts and crafts renaissance centered there. During 1900 he moved to Darmstadt, and three years later, he was named director of the Dusseldorf School of Arts and Crafts. Perhaps more than any other designer of his time, Behrens deserves recognition as the pivotal innovator in the transition from the floral and decorative sensibilities of the nineteenth century to the simple, functional geometric forms of the twentieth century. An interdisciplinary practitioner of the design arts, Behrens designed buildings, graphics, products, fabrics, and furniture as he moved from one design problem to another with ease. Shortly after the turn of the century, Behrens began to test his *Jugendstil* design approach against a reappraisal of the design needs of the industrial era. For example, in 1900, Behrens designed a book, *Feste des Lebens,* that was set entirely in sans-serif type. This was the first time that a graphic designer expressed the emerging modern sensibility in this manner.

The turning point in his career came in 1907, when Emil Rathenau, general director of Allgemeine Elektricitäts-Gesellschaft (A.E.G.), one of the world's largest electrical manufacturing corporations, called thirty-nine-year-old Behrens to Berlin to take charge of all areas of A.E.G.'s visual image: architecture, industrial,

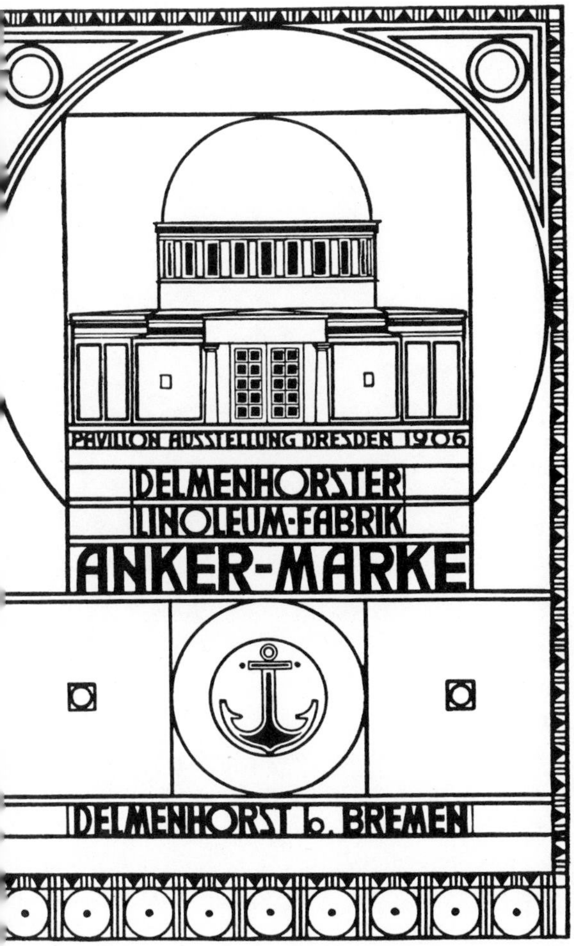

Peter Behrens, brochure cover for Anchor Linoleum, 1906. An exhibition pavilion designed by Behrens was drawn graphically in the same rectangles and circles used to create the cover design and border.

Peter Behrens, specimen sheet of typographic ornaments, 1907. Designed for the Klingspor Foundry, these typographic ornaments demonstrate the tempering of Art Nouveau's floral swirls by geometric measurement.

Peter Behrens, *Quarzlampe* brochure cover, 1908. An architect's concern for harmony of proportion is evidenced in the use of bold rules to divide and define the space. Note the joining of the *L* and *A* in the word *Quarzlampe* to prevent an awkward space in the texture of the lettering.

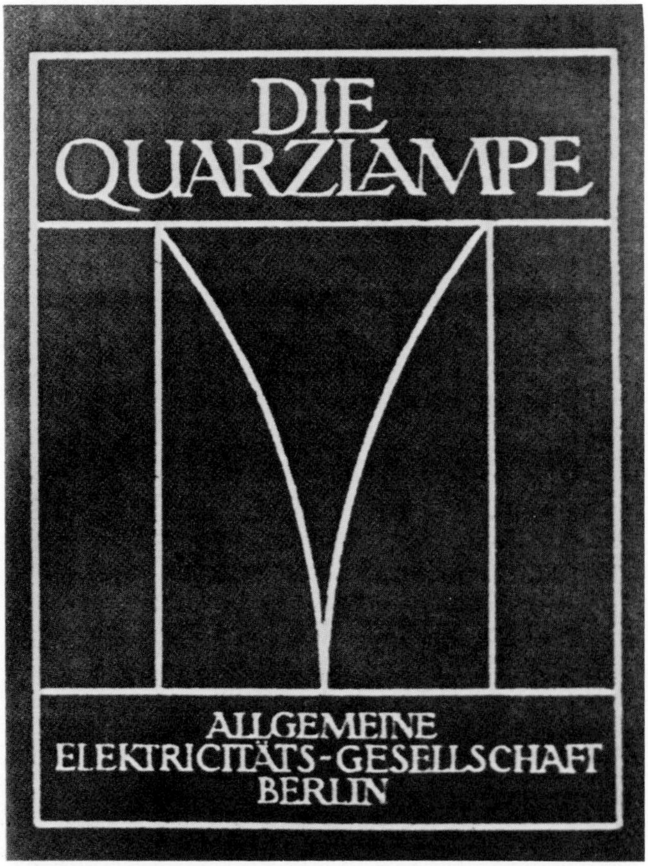

Peter Behrens, Allgemeine Elektricitaets Gesellschaft mark, 1908. This famous honeycomb with the firm's initials was used by Behrens and his staff as the linchpin unifying a consistent graphic communications program.

and graphic design. Rathenau was an unusually astute business executive who realized that industry needed the unifying visual identity and standards of quality that could only be achieved by design. Until this move, Behrens had designed book covers, fabrics, interiors, and so on, that were typical of the time. As he concentrated intensely on design problems for A.E.G., he emerged as a vital force in design.

He is considered to be the first known industrial designer (a visually trained individual charged with the design of the structure, operation, and appearance of mass-manufactured factory products). Electrical appliances including stoves, clocks, and teakettles were designed as logical forms stripped of ornament, for Behrens believed that beauty could grow from expediency. This philosophic reaction against the nineteenth century was called the *Neue Schlichkeit* (''New Objectivity'').

In the realm of architecture, his 1909 turbine factory complex with a glass curtain wall is a benchmark in architectural history. Younger architects who worked in his office include Walter Gropius, Ludwig Mies van der Rohe, and Le Corbusier. Behrens looked to classical art for sources and proclaimed proportion to be the alpha and omega of all visual art and design. To him, the modern movement was seeking a new classical art to express the spirit and conditions of modern times.

Perhaps Behrens' work for A.E.G. is the first coordinated and cohesive corporate design program. Visual identification was consistent in the application of the famous honeycomb logo he designed, type styles used, and the approach to organizing space. As in his three-dimensional work, harmony of proportion became the dominant design criterion.

In Germany, as in Scotland and Austria, innovative designers, who were not content with Art Nouveau, charted new directions in response to personal and societal needs, and laid the groundwork for the new century.

The English art historian Herbert Read once observed that the life of any art movement is like that of a flower. A budding in the hands of a small number of innovators is followed by full bloom. Then, the process of decay begins as the influence becomes diffused and distorted in the hands of imitators who do not understand the driving passions that forged the movement but merely the stylistic manifestations. After the turn of the century, this was the fate of Art Nouveau. Before then, Art Nouveau objects and furniture had been primarily one-of-a-kind or limited edition items. As the graphic design of posters and periodicals brought Art Nouveau to an everwidening circle of admirers, far greater quantities were produced with an inevitable deterioration of design. Manufacturers focused on the bottom line by turning out vast amounts of merchandise and graphics with lower design standards. In some cases, designers were eliminated, and inferior copies of existing work were cheaply produced. Many of the innovators moved on to other directions. Nevertheless, Art Nouveau lingered, slowly declining, until it vanished in the ashes of World War I. Its legacy is a tracery of the dreams and lifestyles of a brief Indian summer in the human saga. Its offspring are twentieth-century designers who adopted, not its style, but its attitudes toward materials, processes, and values.

Peter Behrens, Poster for A.E.G lights, 1910. Behren's quest for a contemporary language of form is realized in this poster. Geometric elements are used to compose the space and symbolize the radiance of light from the electric lamp. A capital *A* and *E* are joined into a ligature in the word *Elektricitaets*.

ALLGEMEINE
ELEKTRICITAETS
GESELLSCHAFT
A·E·G-METALLFADENLAMPE
ZIRKA EIN WATT PRO KERZE

PART IV

THE TWENTIETH CENTURY: *The growth and development of modern graphic design*

15

The Influence of Modern Art

THE FIRST TWO DECADES OF THE twentieth century were a time of incredible ferment and change that radically altered all aspects of the human condition. The social, political, cultural, and economic character of life was caught in fluid upheaval. In Europe, monarchy was replaced by democracy, socialism, and Russian communism. Technology and scientific advances transformed commerce and industry. Transportation was radically altered by the coming of the motorcar (1885) and the airplane (1903). The motion picture (1896) and wireless radio transmission (1895) foretold a new era of human communications. Beginning with the Turkish bloodless revolution and Bulgarian declaration of independence in 1908, the undeveloped areas of the world began to awaken and demand independence. Fought with the destructive weapons of technology, the slaughter during the first of two global wars shook the traditions and institutions of western civilization to their foundations.

Against this turbulence, it is not surprising that the visual arts experienced a series of creative revolutions that questioned their values, systems of organizations, and social role. The traditional objective view of the world was shattered. Representation of external appearances did not fulfill the needs and vision of the European avant-garde that emerged. Elemental ideas of color and form, social protest, and the expression of Freudian and deeply personal emotional states occupied many artists. While some of these modern movements—Fauvism and German Expressionism, for example—had little effect upon graphic design, others—Cubism and Futurism; Dada and Surrealism; de Stijl, Suprematism, and Constructivism—directly impacted upon the graphic language of form and visual communications in this century.

The evolution of twentieth-century typographic design closely relates to modern painting, poetry, and architecture. It might almost be said that a collision between Cubist painting and Futurist poetry spawned twentieth-century graphic design.

Pablo Picasso, *Les Demoiselles D'Avignon*, 1907. The seeds of Cubism are contained in the background spaces that warp and buckle forward toward the picture plane. The personhood of these five figures yields to Picasso's exploration of form and space. *The Museum of Modern Art, New York, Lillie P. Bliss Bequest.*

Cubism

By creating a concept of design independent of nature, Cubism began a new artistic tradition and way of seeing that ended the four-hundred-year-old Renaissance tradition of pictorial art.

The genesis of this movement is the 1907 *Les Demoiselles d'Avignon* by the Spanish painter, Pablo Picasso (1881–1973). Taking clues from the geometric stylizations of African sculpture and Post Impressionist Paul Cézanne (1839–1906), who observed that the painter should "treat nature in terms of the cylinder and the sphere and the cone," this painting was a new approach to handling space and expressing human emotions. The figures are abstracted into geometric planes, and classical norms of the human figure are broken. The spatial illusions of perspective give way to an ambiguous shifting of two-dimensional planes. The seated figure is simultaneously seen from a multiplicity of viewpoints.

Over the next few years, Picasso and his close associate Georges Braque (1881–1963) evolved Cubism as the art movement that replaced rendering appearances with the endless possibilities of invented form. Analytical Cubism is the name given to their work from about 1910–12. During this period, the artists analyzed the planes of the subject matter, often from different points of view, and used these perceptions to construct a painting composed of rhythmic geometric planes. The real subject became the visual language of form used to create a highly structured work of art. Analytical Cubism's compelling fascination grows from the unresolvable tension between the sensual and intellectual appeal of the pictorial structure in conflict with the challenge of interpreting the subject matter.

Juan Gris, *Portrait of Picasso,* 1912. The shimmering planes of Cubism that move forward and backward in shallow space by tonal modulation begin to line up with the orderly arithmetic of a grid in Gris' portrait of his friend. *The Art Institute of Chicago.*

Picasso and Braque introduced paper collage elements into their work in 1912. Collage allowed free composition independent of subject matter and declared the reality of the painting as two-dimensional object. Texture of collage elements could signify objects. For example, Picasso glued oilcloth printed with a chair cane pattern into a painting to represent a chair. Often, letterforms and words from newspapers were incorporated as visual form and for associated meaning.

In 1913, Cubism evolved into what has been called Synthetic Cubism. Drawing upon past observations, the Cubists invented forms that were signs

African mask from the Ivory Coast, undated. Boldly chiseled geometric planes were an exciting revelation for Picasso and his friends. Carved in secrecy and representing awesome spiritual forces, African tribal masks were used in rituals including ancestor worship, puberty, agriculture, and to ward off evil spirits. *Virginia Museum, Richmond.*

Fernand Léger, *The City,* 1919. About this monumental composition of pure, flat planes signifying the geometry, color, and energy of the modern city, Léger observed that "it was advertising that first drew the consequences" of it. *Philadelphia Museum of Art, The A. E. Gallatin Collection.*

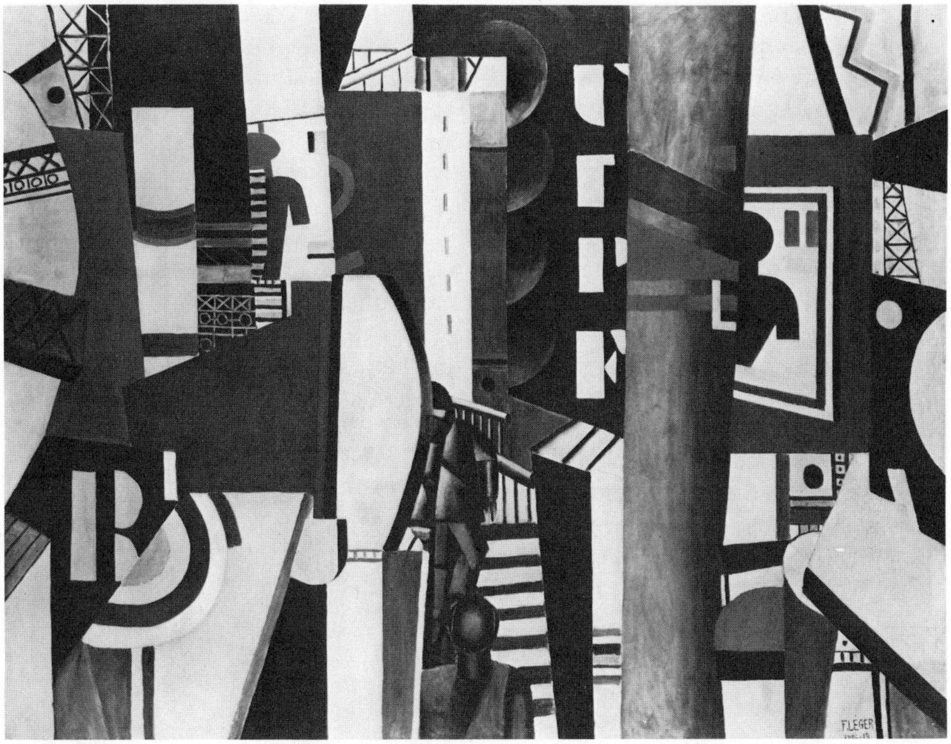

rather than representations of the subject matter. The essence of an object and its basic characteristics, rather than its outward appearance, were depicted.

Juan Gris (1887–1927) was a major painter in the development of Synthetic Cubism. His paintings such as the 1912 *Portrait of Picasso* combined composition from nature with an independent structural design of the picture space. First, he planned a rigorous architectural structure using golden section proportions and a modular composition grid, then he "laid the subject matter" upon this design scheme. Gris was to have a profound influence upon the development of geometric art and design; his paintings are a kind of "halfway house" between an art based on perception and an art realized by the relationships between geometric planes.

Among the artists who clustered around Picasso and Braque and joined the Cubist movement, Fernand Léger (1881–1955) also moved Cubism away from the initial impulses of the founders. From around 1910, Léger took Cézanne's famous dictum about the cylinder, sphere, and cone far more seriously than any other Cubist. Motifs such as nudes in a forest were transformed into a field of colorful stovepipe sections littering the picture plane. Léger might have evolved toward an art of pure color and shape relationships, but his four years of

Georges Braque, *Pitcher and Violin,* 1909. In this breakthrough image on the road to Analytical Cubism, Braque studied the planes of the motif from different vantage points, fractured them, and pulled them forward toward the canvas surface. The planes shimmer vibrantly in ambigious positive and negative relationships one to another. *Kuntsmuseum Basel, Switzerland.*

military service among working class French citizens, and his intensified vision perception that developed during the war, turned him toward a style that was more recognizable, accessible, and populist. He moved closer to his visual experience in paintings like *The City*. Perceptions of the colors, shapes, posters, and architecture of the urban environment—glimpses and fragments of information—are assembled into a composition of brightly colored planes. The letterforms in this painting and in Léger's graphic work for Blaise Cendrar's book *La Fin du Monde* . . . pointed the way toward geometric letterforms. His almost pictographic stylizations of the human figure and objects were a major inspiration for the pictorial modernism that became the major thrust of the revived poster art of the 1920s. Léger's flat planes of color, urban motifs, and the hard-edge precision of his machine forms helped define the modern design sensibility after World War I.

Futurism

"We intend to sing the love of danger, the habit of energy and fearlessness. Courage, audacity, and revolt will be essential elements of our poetry . . . We affirm that the world's magnificence has been enriched by a new beauty: the beauty of speed . . . a roaring car that seems to ride on grapeshot is more beautiful than the *Victory of Samothrace* . . . Except in struggle, there is no more beauty. No work without an aggressive character can be a masterpiece." When these stirring words of the *Manifesto of Futurism* were published in Paris' *La Figaro* on 20 February 1909, Italian poet Filippo Marinetti (1876–1944) established Futurism as a revolutionary movement for all the arts to test their ideas and forms against the new realities of scientific and industrial society. The manifesto voiced enthusiasm for war, the machine age, speed, and modern life. It attacked museums, libraries, moralism, and feminism.

Marinetti and his followers produced an explosive and emotionally charged poetry that defied correct syntax and grammar. In January 1913, Giovanni Papini (1881–1956) began publication of the journal *Lacerba* in Florence, and typographic design was pulled onto the artistic battlefield. The June 1913 issue published Marinetti's article calling for a typographic revolution against the classical tradition. Harmony was rejected as a design quality because it contradicted "the leaps and bursts of style running through the page." On a page, three or four ink colors and twenty typefaces (italics for quick impressions, boldface for violent noises and sounds) could redouble words' expressive power. Free, dynamic, and torpedolike words could be given the velocity of stars, clouds, airplanes, trains, waves, explosives, molecules, and atoms. A new and painterly typographic design called "free typography" and "words in freedom" was born on the printed page.

Since Gutenberg's invention of movable type, most graphic design has had a vigorous horizontal and vertical structure. The Futurist poets cast these constraints to the wind. Freed from tradition, they animated their pages with a dynamic, nonlinear composition achieved by pasting words

Ardengo Soffici, *Bifszf + 18 Simultaneità Chimismi Iirici,* 1915. In this powerful Futurist poem, Soffici contrasts terse verse with clusters of modulating letterforms used as pure visual form. Diagonal rules link the units and create rhythms from page to page.

Filippo Marinetti, *Montagne + Vallate + Strade × Joffre* (Mountains + Valleys + Streets × Joffre") 1915. Like the Futurist painters, the poets tried to communicate the "simultaneity" of perception and experience in modern life. Traditional sentence structure, grammar, and punctuation were abandoned.

Carlo Carrà, *parole in libertà* ("free word composition"), 1914. The Futurist poets believed that the use of different sizes, weights, and styles of type allowed them to weld painting and poetry because the intrinsic beauty of letterforms, mainpulated creatively, transformed the printed page into a work of visual art.

and letterforms in place for photographic reproduction.

On 11 February 1910, five artists who joined Marinetti published the *Manifesto of the Futurist Painters.* Umberto Boccioni (1882–1916), Carlo Carrá (1881–1966), Luigi Russolo (1885–1947), Giacomo Balla (1871–1958), and Gino Severini (1883–1966) declared their intent to: "Destroy the cult of the past . . . Totally invalidate all kinds of imitation . . . Elevate all attempts at originality . . . Regard art critics as useless and dangerous . . . Sweep the whole field of art clean of all themes and subjects which have been used in the past . . . Support and glory in our day-to-day world, a world which is going to be continually and splendidly transformed by victorious Science." The Futurist painters were strongly influenced by Cubism, but they also attempted to express motion, energy, and cinematic sequence in their work. They first used the word *simultaneity* in a visual art context to express concurrent existence or occurrence, such as the presentation of different views in the same work of art.

The *Manifesto of Futurist Architecture* was written by Antonio Sant'Elia (1888–1916). He called for construction based on technology and science, and design for the unique demands of modern life. He declared decoration to be absurd, and used dynamic diagonal and elliptic lines because their emotional power is greater than horizontals and verticals. Tragically, Sant'Elia was killed on the battlefield, but his ideas and visionary drawing influenced the course of modern design, particularly Art Deco. The violent, revolutionary techniques of the Futurists were adopted by the Dadaists, Constructivists, and de Stijl. The publication of manifestos, typographic experimentation, and publicity stunts (on 8 July 1910, eight hundred thousand copies of Marinetti's leaflet, "Against Past-Loving Venice," were dropped from a clock tower onto Venice crowds) were initiated by the Futurists.

The Futurist concept that writing and/or typography could become concrete and expressive visual form has been a sporadic preoccupation of poets dating back at least to the Greek poet Simias of Rhodes (around 33 B.C.). Called *pattern poetry,* this verse often took the shape of objects or religious symbols. In the nineteenth century, the German poet Arno Holz (1863–1929) reinforced intended auditory effects by such devices as omitting capitalizations and punctuation, varying wordspacing to signify pauses, and using more than one punctuation mark for emphasis. Lewis Carroll's *Alice's Adventures in Wonderland* used descending sizes of type and pictorial shape to construct a mouse's tail as part of the mouse's tale.

Filippo Marinetti, poem from *Les mots en liberté* (''The words to freedom''), 1919. The confusion and violent noise and chaos of battle explode above the girl reading her lover's letter from the front. Marinetti's experience in the trenches of war inspired this poem. Noise and speed, two dominant conditions of twentieth-century life, were expressed in Futurist poetry.

Filippo Marinetti, A tumultuous meeting, 1919. Marinetti wrote that a man who has witnessed an explosion does not stop to connect his sentences grammatically. He hurls shrieks and words at his listeners. Marinetti urged that poets also liberate themselves from servitude to grammar to open new worlds of expression.

Filippo Marinetti, Futurist poem. In French, *chair* means *flesh*. Marinetti used mathematical signs to create lyrical equations, and numbers were selected intuitively to express intensities.

CH
ÈÈÈÈÈÈÈèèè
+ Je t'aime + − × 29 caresses + la lune et les ruisseaux
chantent sous les arbres.... paradis de mes bras Viens
chance + − × + −
vanité eeeeeeeeeeeeeee
AI Rrrrrrr
R
3000 par mois +
bague rubis 8000 +
6000 frs. chaussures
Demain chez moi
Suis sérieuse Trois
baisers futuristes
R

The French Symbolist poet Stéphane Mallarmé (1842–1898) published the poem ''Un Coup de Dés'' composed of seven hundred words on twenty pages in a typographic range: capital, lowercase, roman, and italic. Rather than surround a poem with white, empty margins, this ''silence'' was dispersed through the work as part of the meaning. Instead of stringing words in linear sequence like beads, they are placed unexpectedly on the page to express sensations and evoke ideas. Mallarmé was successful in relating typography to the musical score; the placement and weight of words relate to intonation, importance in oral reading, and rhythm.

Another French poet, Guillaume Apollinaire (1880–1918), was closely associated with the Cubists, particularly Picasso, and was involved in a rivalry with Marinetti. Apollinaire had championed African sculpture, defined the principles of Cubist painting and literature, and once observed that ''catalogs, posters, advertisements of all types, believe me, they contain the poetry of our epoch.'' His unique contribution to graphic design was the 1918 publication of a book entitled *Calligrammes,* poems in which the letterforms are arranged to form a visual design, figure, or pictograph. In these poems he explored the potential fusion of poetry and painting, and he attempted to introduce the concept of simultaneity to the time and sequence-bound typography of the printed page.

Guillaume Apollinaire, poem from *Calligrammes,* 1917. Entitled ''It's Raining,'' this poem is composed of letterforms that sprinkle figuratively down the page to relate visual form to poetic content. *Editions Gallimard, Paris.*

Giacomo Balla, *Dynamism of a Dog on a Leash,* 1912. The Futurist painters sought to introduce dynamic motion, speed and energy to the static two-dimensional surface. *Albright-Knox Art Gallery, Buffalo, New York.*

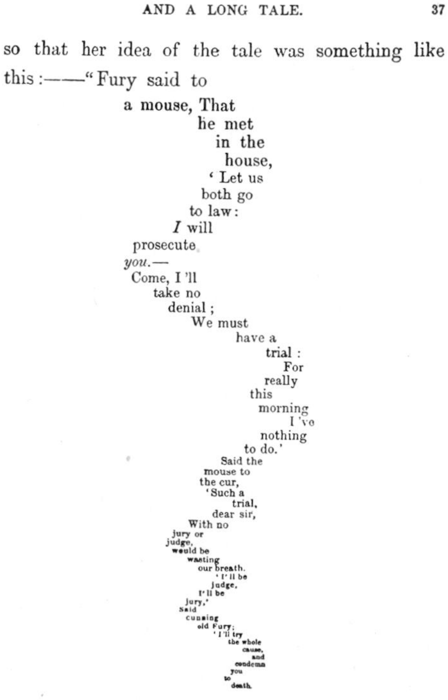

AND A LONG TALE. 37

so that her idea of the tale was something like this:——"Fury said to
a mouse, That
he met
in the
house,
'Let us
both go
to law:
I will
prosecute
you.—
Come, I'll
take no
denial;
We must
have a
trial:
For
really
this
morning
I've
nothing
to do.'
Said the
mouse to
the cur,
'Such a
trial,
dear sir,
With no
jury or
judge,
would be
wasting
our breath.
'I'll be
judge,
I'll be
jury,'
Said
cunning
old Fury:
'I'll try
the whole
cause,
and
condemn
you
to
death.'

Lewis Carroll, typographic image, 1866. Unexpected and totally different from the rest of *Alice's Advertures in Wonderland,* this graphic experiment in figurative typography has received acclaim from both design and literary viewpoints.

Antonio Sant'Elia, drawing for the new city of the future, 1914. Sant'Elia did not survive the war, but his ideas did. These drawings were reproduced with his manifesto in *Lacerba* Volume II, No. 15, on 1 August 1914. After the war many of his ideas about form developed in architecture, product and graphic design. *Comune di Como, Como, Italy.*

Guillaume Apollinaire, poem from *Calligrammes,* 1917. The typography becomes a bird, a water fountain, and an eye in this expressive design. *Editions Gallimard, Paris.*

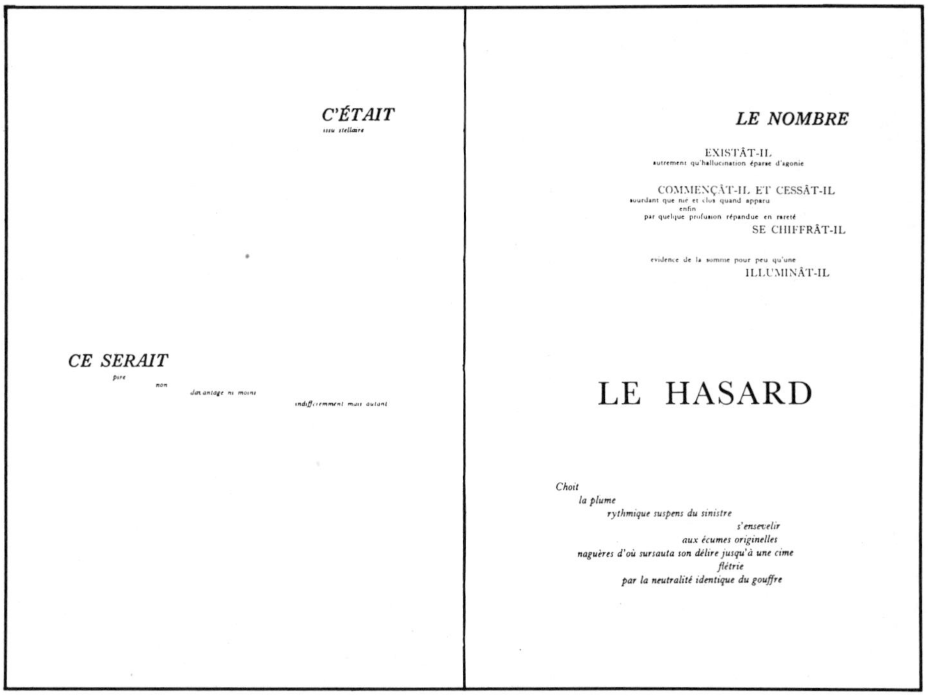
C'ÉTAIT
issu stellaire

CE SERAIT
pire
non
davantage ni moins
indifféremment mais autant

LE NOMBRE
EXISTÂT-IL
autrement qu'hallucination éparse d'agonie
COMMENÇÂT-IL ET CESSÂT-IL
sourdant que nié et clos quand apparu
enfin
par quelque profusion répandue en rareté
SE CHIFFRÂT-IL
evidence de la somme pour peu qu'une
ILLUMINÂT-IL

LE HASARD

Choit
la plume
rythmique suspens du sinistre
s'ensevelir
aux écumes originelles
naguères d'où sursauta son délire jusqu'à une cime
flétrie
par la neutralité identique du gouffre

Stéphane Mallarmé, pages from *Un Coup de Dés* ("A Throw of the Dice"), 1897. Mallarmé anticipated the formal and expressive typographic concerns that emerged in the twentieth century when poets and painters became interested in the creative potential of the printed page.

KARAWANE
jolifanto bambla ô falli bambla
grossiga m'pfa habla horem
égiga goramen
higo bloiko russula huju
hollaka hollala
anlogo bung
blago bung
blago bung
bosso fataka
ü üü ü
schampa wulla wussa ólobo
hej tatta gôrem
eschige zunbada
wulubu ssubudu uluw ssubudu
tumba ba- umf
kusagauma
ba - umf
(1917)
Hugo Ball

Hugo Ball, Dada poem, 1917. Sound and sight poems such as this expressed the Dada desire to replace man's logical nonsense with an illogical nonsense.

Dada

The Dada movement developed spontaneously as a literary movement after the poet Hugo Ball opened the Cabaret Voltaire in Zurich, Switzerland, as a gathering place for independent young poets, painters, and musicians. Dada's guiding spirit was a young Hungarian poet, Tristan Tzara (1896–1963), who edited the periodical *DADA* begining in July 1917. Along with Ball, Hans Arp, and Richard Huelsenbeck, Tzara explored sound poetry, nonsense poetry, and chance poetry. He wrote a steady stream of Dada manifestos and contributed to all major Dada publications and events. Reacting against a world gone mad, Dada claimed to be antiart and had a strong negative and destructive element. Rejecting all tradition, it sought complete freedom. Dadaists did not even agree on the origins of the name Dada, such was the anarchy of this movement. One story says that the movement was randomly named by opening a French dictionary and quickly pointing to a word, "dada," a child's hobby horse. These writers and artists were concerned with shock, protest, and nonsense. They bitterly rebelled against the horrors of the world war, the decadence of European society, shallowness of blind faith in technological progress, and inadequacy of religion and conventional moral codes in a continent in upheaval. Their rejection of art and tradition enabled the Dadaists to enrich the visual vocabulary of Futurism. Their synthesis of spontaneous chance actions with planned decisions allowed them to further rid typographic design of its traditional precepts. Also, Dada continued Cubism's concept of letterforms as concrete visual shapes—not just phonetic symbols.

The French painter Marcel Duchamp (1887–1968) joined the Dada movement and became its most prominent visual artist. Earlier, he had analyzed his subjects as geometric planes under the influence of Cubism. His painting, *Nude Descending the Staircase,* pushed the limits of the static image's ability to record and express motion. To Duchamp, Dada's most articulate spokesman, art and life were both processes of random chance and willful choice. Artistic acts became matters of individual decision and selection. This philosophy of absolute freedom allowed Duchamp to create "ready-made" sculpture, such as a bicycle wheel mounted on a wooden stool, and exhibit "found objects," such as a urinal, as art. The public was outraged when Duchamp painted a mustache on a reproduction of the Mona Lisa. This act was not, however, an attack upon the Mona Lisa. Rather, it was an ingenious assault upon the tyranny of tradition and a public that had lost the humanistic spirit of the Renaissance.

Dada quickly spread from Zurich to other European cities. In spite of the claim that they were not creating art but were mocking and defaming a society that had become insane, several Dadaists produced meaningful visual art that has contributed to graphic design. Dada artists claim to

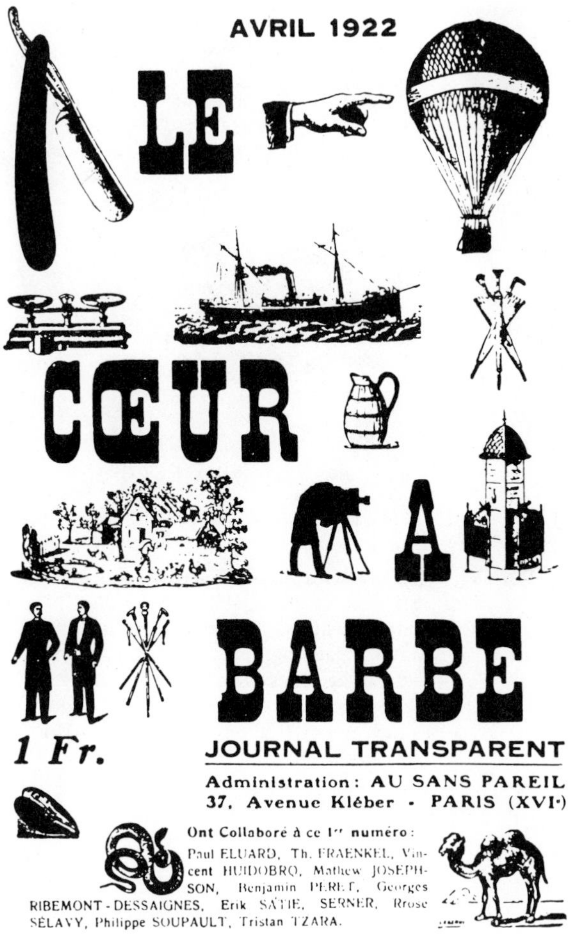

This Dada journal cover for "The Bearded Heart," 1922, shows a casual organization of space as found illustrations are randomly dispersed about the page with no particular communicative intent.

Ilya Zdanevitch, poster for the play, "Party of the Bearded Heart," 1923. A wonderful vitality and legibility results even though Zdanevitch has combined typographic material from over forty fonts.

Marcel Duchamp, *Bicycle Wheel,* 1951. (Third version, after the lost original of 1913.) When an object is removed from its usual context, we suddenly see it with fresh eyes that respond to its intrinsic visual properties. *The Museum of Modern Art, New York, Gift of Sidney and Harriet Janis.*

Marcel Duchamp, *Nude Descending a Staircase,* 1912. Duchamp wrote that this painting was "an organization of Kinetic elements, an expression of time and space through the abstract presentation of motion." *Philadelphia Museum of Art. The Louise and Water Arensberg Collection.*

have invented photomontage, the technique of manipulating found photographic images to create jarring juxtapositions and chance associations. Both Raoul Hausmann (1886–1977) and Hannah Höch (1889–1978) were creating outstanding work in the medium as early as 1918.

Kurt Schwitters (1887–1948) of Hanover, Germany, created a nonpolitical offshoot of Dada that he named Merz, coined from the word *kommerz* ("commerce") in one of his collages. Schwitters gave Merz meaning as the title of a one-man art movement. Beginning in 1919, his Merz pictures were collage compositions using printed ephemera, rubbish, and found materials to compose color against color, form against form, and texture against texture. His complex designs combined Dada's element of nonsense and chance with strong design properties. When he tried to join Club Dada as "an artist who nails his pictures together," he was refused membership for being too bourgeois.

Poetry that played sense against nonsense was an important concern. Schwitters defined poetry as the interaction of elements: letters, syllables, words, sentences. In the early 1920s, Constructivism became an added influence in Schwitters' work after he made contact with El Lissitzky and Théo van Doesburg, who invited Schwitters to Holland to promote Dada. From 1923 until 1932 Schwitters published twenty-four issues of the periodical, *Merz*. Advertising typography was the subject of *Merz* 11. During this time Schwitters ran a successful graphic design studio with Pelikan, manufacturer of office equipment and supplies, as a major client. The city of Hanover employed him as typography consultant for several years. When the German political situation deteriorated in the 1930s, Schwitters spent increasing time in Norway and moved to Oslo in 1937. After Germany invaded Norway in 1940, he fled to the British Isles, where he spent his last years.

In contrast to the artistic and Constructivist interests of Kurt Schwitters, the Berlin Dadaists John Heartfield (1891–1968), Wieland Herzfelde (b. 1896), and George Grosz (1893–1959) possessed vigorous revolutionary political beliefs and oriented many of their artistic activities toward visual communications to raise public consciousness and promote social change.

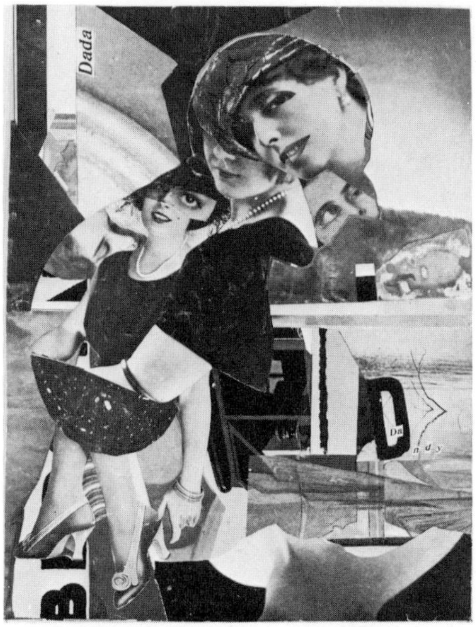

Hannah Höch, *Da—dandy,* collage and photomontage, 1919. Images and materials are recycled with both accidental chance juxtapositions and planned decisions contributing to the creative process.

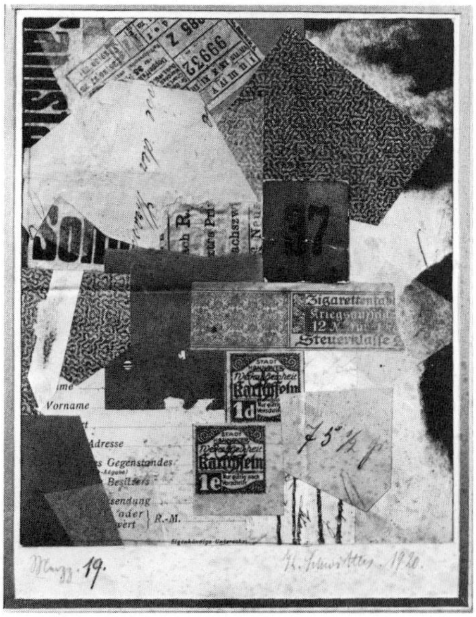
Kurt Schwitters, *Merz Picture 19,* 1920. Material gathered from the streets, alleys, and garbage cans was washed and catalogued according to size and color for use as the raw material of art. *Yale University Art Gallery, New Haven, Conn., Gift of Collection Société Anonyme.*

Kurt Schwitters, Théo van Doesburg, and Kate Steinitz, page from *Die Scheuche Marchen* ("The Scarecrow Marches"), 1922. In this modern fairy tale, type and image are wedded literally and figuratively as the *B* overpowers the *X* with verbiage.

W W
PBD
ZFM
RF RF
TZPF TZPF
MWT
RFMR
RKT PCT
SW SW
KPT
F G
KPT
R Z
KPT
RZL
TZPF TZPF
HFTL

priimiitittii.
priimiitittii tisch
tesch
priimiitittii tesch
tusch
priimiitittii tischa
tescho
priimiitittii tescho
tuschi
priimittii
priimiitittii
priimiitittii too
priimiitittii taa
priimiitittii too
priimiitittii taa
priimiitittii tootaa
priimiitittii tootaa
priimiitittii tuutaa
priimiitittii tuutaa
priimiitittii tuutaatoo
priimiitittii tuutaatoo
priimiitittii tootaatuu
priimiitittii tootaatuu

Kurt Schwitters, *W W priimiitittii,* 1920. The Dada poets separated the word from its language context; these two poems are intended to be seen as pure visual form and read as pure sound. Intuitive, but highly structured typographics grew out of the initial random chance of early Dada poetry.

John Heartfield is an English name adopted by Helmut Herzfelde as a protest against German militarism and the army in which he served from 1914–16. A founding member of the Berlin Dada group in 1919, Heartfield used the harsh disjunctions of photomontage as a potent propaganda weapon and innovated in the preparation of mechanical art for offset printing. The Weimar Republic and the growing Nazi party were his targets in posters, book jackets, political illustrations, and cartoons. His montages are the most urgent in the history of the technique. Heartfield did not take photographs or retouch images but worked directly with glossy prints acquired from magazines and newspapers. Occasionally, he commissioned a needed image from a photographer. Photography was still considered a poor man's art form; his images allowed immediate identification and comprehension by the working class. In 1933, after storm troopers occupied his apartment-studio, Heartfield fled to Prague. In 1938 he learned that he was on a secret Nazi list of enemies, and fled to London. In 1950 he moved to Leipzig, East Germany, where he designed theater sets and posters. Before his death in 1968, he produced photomontages protesting the Vietnam War and calling for world peace. "Unfortunately Still Timely" is the title given to retrospectives of his graphic art.

Heartfield's younger brother, Wieland Herzfelde, was a poet, critic, and publisher who edited the journal *Neue Jugend,* which was designed by Heartfield. After being jailed in 1914 for distributing communist literature, Wieland started the Malik Verlag publishing house, an important avant-garde publisher of Dada, left-wing political propaganda, and advanced literature.

Another charter member of Berlin Dada, the painter and graphic artist George Grosz, was closely associated with the Herzfelde brothers. His biting pen attacked a corrupt society with satire and caricature. He advocated a classless society, and his drawings project an angry intensity of deep political convictions in what he

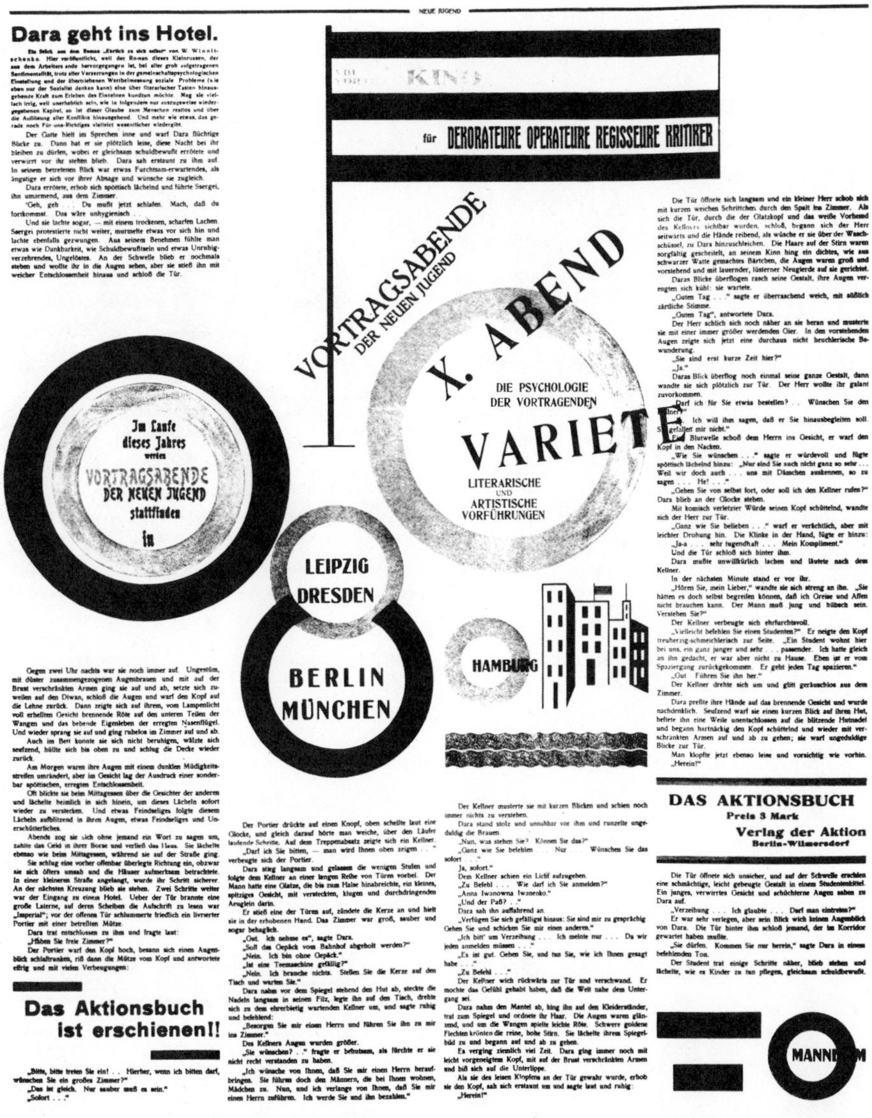
NEUE JUGEND

Dara geht ins Hotel.

für DEKORATEURE OPERATEURE REGISSEURE KRITIKER

VORTRAGSABENDE DER NEUEN JUGEND

X. ABEND

DIE PSYCHOLOGIE DER VORTRAGENDEN

VARIETE

LITERARISCHE UND ARTISTISCHE VORFÜHRUNGEN

Im Laufe dieses Jahres werden VORTRAGSABENDE DER NEUEN JUGEND stattfinden in

LEIPZIG DRESDEN

BERLIN MÜNCHEN

HAMBURG

MANNHEIM

DAS AKTIONSBUCH
Preis 3 Mark
Verlag der Aktion
Berlin-Wilmersdorf

Das Aktionsbuch ist erschienen!!

John Heartfield, page from *Neue Jugend,* 1917. In this radical tabloid paper, Heartfield brought the gray newspaper page to life with a visual vitality of Dadaist origin. *Elefanten Press Galerie, Berlin.*

John Heartfield, yuletime poster, 1934. Under a headline proclaiming "Oh German evergreen, how crooked are your branches," a pathetic Christmas tree symbolizes the pathos of the Third Reich.

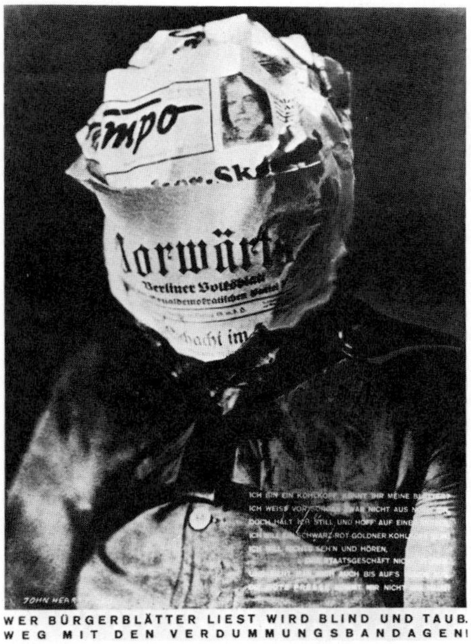

John Heartfield, poster attacking the press, 1930. A surreal visual image, a head wrapped in newspaper, appears over a headline declaring that "whoever reads the bourgeois press turns deaf and blind. Away with these bandages which cause stupidity!"

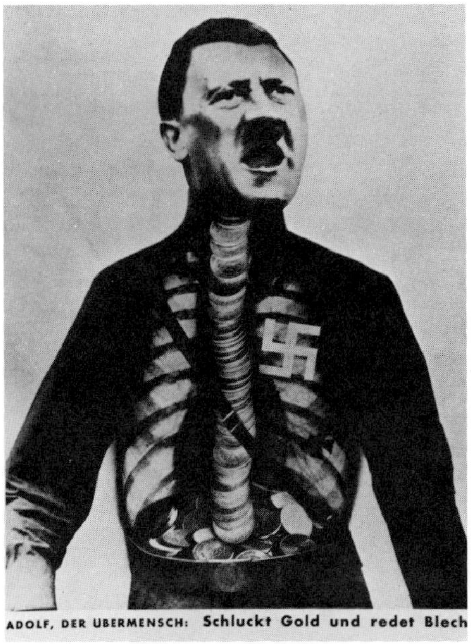

John Heartfield, anti-Nazi propaganda poster, 1935. The headline, "Adolf, the Superman: Swallows gold and talks tin," is visualized by a photomontage x-ray of the Fuhrer showing an esophagus of gold coins.

perceived to be a decadent, degenerate milieu.

Having inherited Marinetti's rhetoric and assault upon all artistic and social traditions, Dada was a major liberating movement that continues to inspire innovation and rebellion. Dada was born in protest against war, and its destructive and exhibitionist activities became more absurd and extreme after the war ended. In 1921 and 1922, controversy and disagreement broke out among its members, and the movement split into factions. André Breton (1896–1966), who was associating with the Dadaists, emerged as a new leader who believed that Dada had lost its relevance and that new directions were necessary. Having pushed its negative activities to the limit, lacking a unified leadership, and with its members facing the new ideas leading to Surrealism, Dada floundered and ceased to exist as a cohesive movement by the end of 1922. Dadaists like Schwitters and Heartfield continued to evolve and produced their finest work after the movement dissolved.

John Heartfield, Cover for *AIZ,* 1934. Weapons are turned into a cathedral to symbolize the mentality of national leaders involved in military expansion and an arms race.

George Grosz, cover for *Der Blutige Ernst,* 1919. Sensitive to the decadence of postwar Germany, Grosz portrayed a couple against a collage of cabaret advertisements.

John Heartfield, theater poster, 1955. Heartfield's late work maintains the compositional and montage ideas of his earlier designs, but the biting social comment often yields to a more gentle communication.

Surrealism

Giorgio de Chirico, *The Departure of the Poet,* 1914. A member of the short-lived Italian Metaphysical School of Painting, de Chirico created a timeless poetry that stops short of the bizarre or supernatural. *Museum of Art, Rhode Island School of Design, Providence, R.I., Anonymous Loan.*

With roots in Dada and the Littérature group of young French writers and poets, Surrealism burst onto the Paris scene in 1924, searching for the "more real than real world behind the real"—the world of intuition, dreams, and the unconscious realm explored by Freud. Apollinaire had used the expression "surreal drama" in reviewing a play in 1917. André Breton, founder of Surrealism, imbued the word with all the magic of dreams, the spirit of rebellion, and the mysteries of the subconscious in his 1924 *Manifesto du Surrealisme: "Surrealism,* noun, masc. pure psychic automatism by which it is intended to express, either verbally or in writing, the true function of thought. Thought dictated in the absence of all control exerted by reason, all aesthetic or moral preoccupations."

Tristan Tzara came from Zurich to join Breton, Louis Aragon (b. 1897), and Paul Eluard (1895–1952). He stirred the group on toward scandal and rebellion. These young poets rejected the rationalism and formal conventions dominating postwar creative activities in Paris. They sought ways to make new truths dawn to reveal "the language of the soul." Surrealism ("superreality" in French) was not a style or a matter of aesthetics. Rather, it was a way of thinking and knowing, a way of feeling, and a way of life. Dada had been negative, destructive, and perpetually exhibitionist; Surrealism professed a poetic faith in man and his spirit. Humanity could be liberated from social and moral conventions. Intuition and feeling could be freed. The writers experimented with stream-of-consciousness writing (automatism) to seek an uninhibited truth.

The impact of the Surrealist poets and writers has been limited to French literary and scholarly circles. It was through the painters that Surrealism affected society and visual communications. While Surrealists often created images so personal that communication became impossible, it also produced images whose feeling, symbols, or fantasy triggered a collective, universal response among large numbers of people.

Breton and his friends had speculated about the possibility of surreal painting. They discovered the work of Giorgio de Chirico (1888–1978) and declared him to be the first Surrealist painter. De Chirico painted hauntingly empty vistas of Italian Renaissance palaces and squares that possess an intense melancholy. Vacant buildings, harsh shadows, deep tilted perspective, and enigmatic images combine to communicate feelings far removed from ordinary experience.

Of the large number of artists who joined the Surrealist movement, several influenced visual communications significantly. The major impact has been on photography and illustration. Max Ernst (1891–1965), a restless German Dadaist who joined Surrealism, innovated a number of techniques that have been adopted in graphic communications. Fascinated by the wood engravings of nineteenth-century novels and catalogues, Ernst reinvented them by using collage techniques to create strange illustrative images. His *frottage* technique involved using rubbings to compose directly on paper. This technique allowed Ernst intuitively to liberate his imagination by suggesting images which could be developed from his rubbings. *Decalcomania,* Ernst's process of transferring images from printed matter to a drawing or painting, enabled him to incorporate a variety of images into his work in unexpected ways. This technique has been used extensively in illustration, painting, and printmaking.

The figurative Surrealist painters have been called naturalists of the imaginary. Space, color, perspective, and figures are rendered in careful naturalism, but the image is an unreal dreamscape. The Belgian Surrealist René Magritte (1898–1967) used jolting and ambiguous scale changes, defied the laws of gravity and light, created unexpected juxtapositions, and maintained a poetic dialogue between reality and illusion, truth and fiction. His prolific body of images inspired many visual communications.

The theatrical Spanish painter, Salvador Dali (b. 1904), influenced graphic design in two ways. His deep perspectives have inspired attempts to bring depth to the flat, printed page; his realistic approach to simultaneity has been used to bring impact to posters and book jackets.

Another group of Surrealist painters, the Emblematics, worked with a purely visual vocabulary. Visual automatism (intuitive stream of consciousness drawing and calligraphy) is used to create spontaneous expressions of inner life in the work of Joan Miró (b. 1893) and Hans Arp (1887–1966). Miró explored a process of metamorphosis through which he intuitively evolved his motifs into cryptic, organic shapes. As early as 1916, Arp explored chance and unplanned harmonies in works like *Squares Arranged According to the Laws of Chance.* The organic, elemental forms and open composition of these two artists have been incorporated into design, particularly during the 1950s.

Max Ernst, collage from *Une Semaine De Bonté,* 1934. Printing techniques obscured the cut edges of Ernst's collages giving them a remarkable unity. His surreal collage concepts have strongly influenced illustration.

René Magritte, *The Blank Signature,* 1965. The Surrealists defied our rational understanding of the world, and their vocabulary of pictorial and symbolic innovations began to seep into the mass media. *Collection of Mr. and Mrs. Paul Mellon.*

Surrealism's impact on graphic design has been diverse. It provided a poetic example of the liberation of the human spirit. It pioneered new techniques and demonstrated how fantasy and intuition could be expressed in visual terms. Unfortunately, the ideas and images of Surrealism have been exploited and trivialized frequently in the mass media.

René Magritte, *The False Mirror,* 1928. The spectator is unable to reconcile the contradiction of image and space; thus, the poetry of the ambiguous haunts the observer long after seeing the painting. *The Museum of Modern Art, New York.*

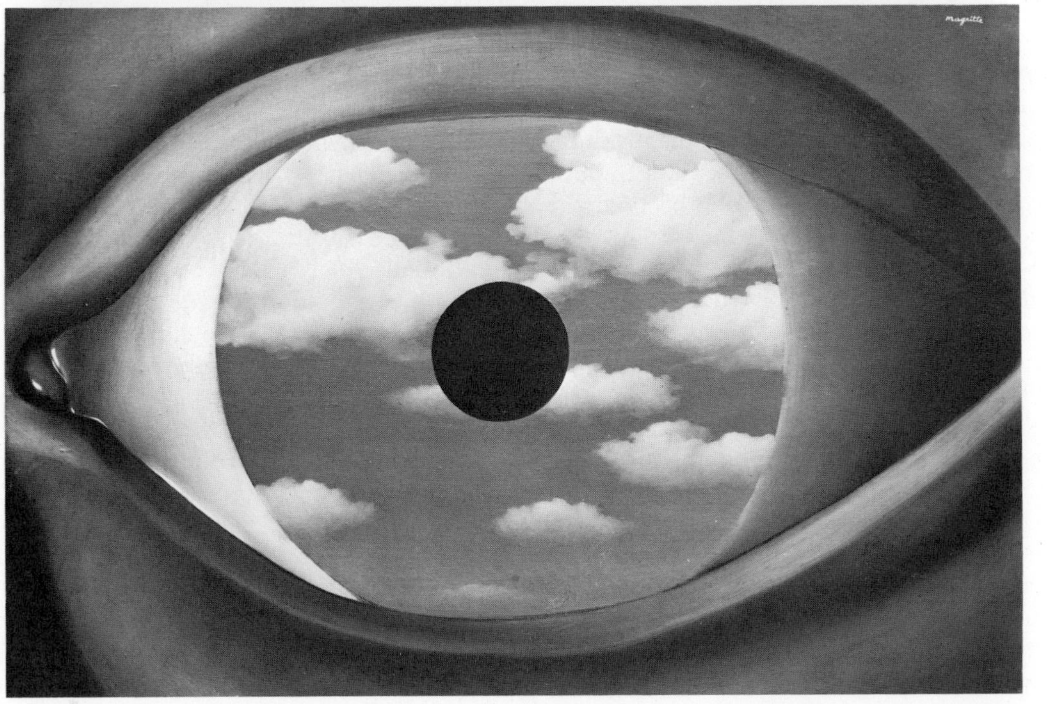

Salvador Dali, *Le Grand Paranoiac,* 1936. The viewer simultaneously sees figures groping in a landscape and a large human head in this oil painting. *Museum Boymans-van Beuningen, Rotterdam.*

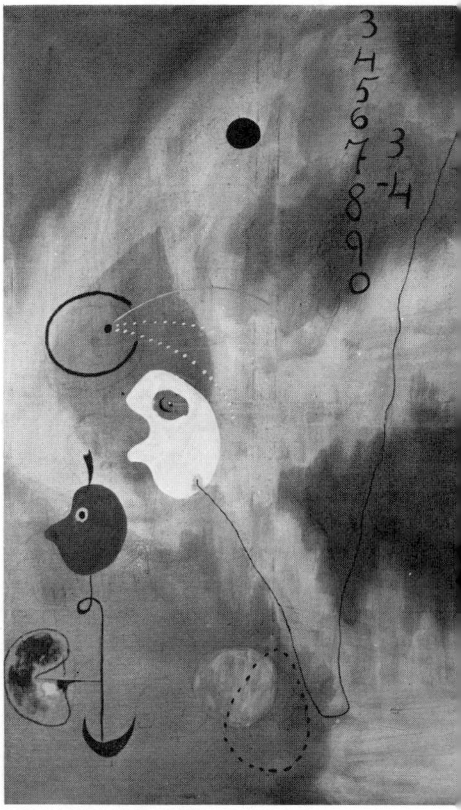

Joan Miró, *Peinture (Dite L'addition),* 1925. Because Miró often worked with little conscious direction of his brush, his work became intuitive, spontaneous expressions of the subconscious mind. *Pierre Matisse Gallery, New York.*

Photography and the Modern Movement

It was inevitable that the new visual language of the modern movements—with a concern for point, line, plane, shape, and texture, and the relationship between these visual elements—would begin to influence photography, just as it had impacted typography in the Futurist and Dadaist approach to graphic design. Photography had been invented as a means to document reality with greater accuracy than painting; in the early twentieth century, painting pulled photography into its new realm of abstraction and design.

Francis Bruguiere (1880–1945) began to explore multiple exposures in 1912 as he pioneered the potential of light recorded on film as a medium for poetic expression. Another photographer who extended his vision into the realm of pure form was Alvin Langdon Coburn (1882–1966). By 1913 his photographs of rooftops and views from tall buildings focused on the pattern and structure found in the world instead of depicting objects and things. Perhaps Coburn's jewellike kaleidoscope patterns, which he called *vortographs* when the series began in 1917, are the first nonobjective photographic images. Coburn praised the beautiful design seen through a microscope, explored multiple exposure, and used prisms to split images into fragments.

The technique used in William Henry Fox Talbot's early "photogenic drawings" was first revived by the photographer and painter Christian Schad (b. 1894) who began making *schadographs* in 1918. String, bits of fabric, and scrap paper were composed into Cubist-like compositions with other flat materials and small objects on photographic paper in the darkroom. Then, an exposure would be made to record the design.

An American artist from Philadelphia, Man Ray (1890–1976), met Marcel Duchamp and fell under the spell of Dada in 1915. Moving to Paris in 1921, Man Ray joined the Surrealists in their evolution from Dada toward a less haphazard investigation of the role played by the unconscious and chance in artistic creation. During the 1920s, he worked as a professional photographer while applying Dada and Surrealism to

Francis Bruguiere, *Light Abstraction,* undated. By cutting and bending paper, Bruguiere composed a photographic composition of forms moving in and out of space. *George Eastman House, Rochester, N.Y.*

Alvin Langdon Coburn, *The Octopus,* 1912. The visual design patterns of shape and tone became Coburn's subject as he viewed the world from unexpected vantage points. *George Eastman House, Rochester, N.Y.*

Man Ray, *Gun with Alphabet Squares,* 1924. In this "rayogram," multiple exposures and a shifting light source transform the photographic record of the gun and stencil letters into a new order of visual form. *Arnold H. Crane Collection, Chicago.*

Man Ray, *Sleeping Woman,* 1929. In this surreal image, the solarization technique is used, not just as a visual technique, but as a means to plumb the psychic experience. *George Eastman House, Rochester, N.Y.*

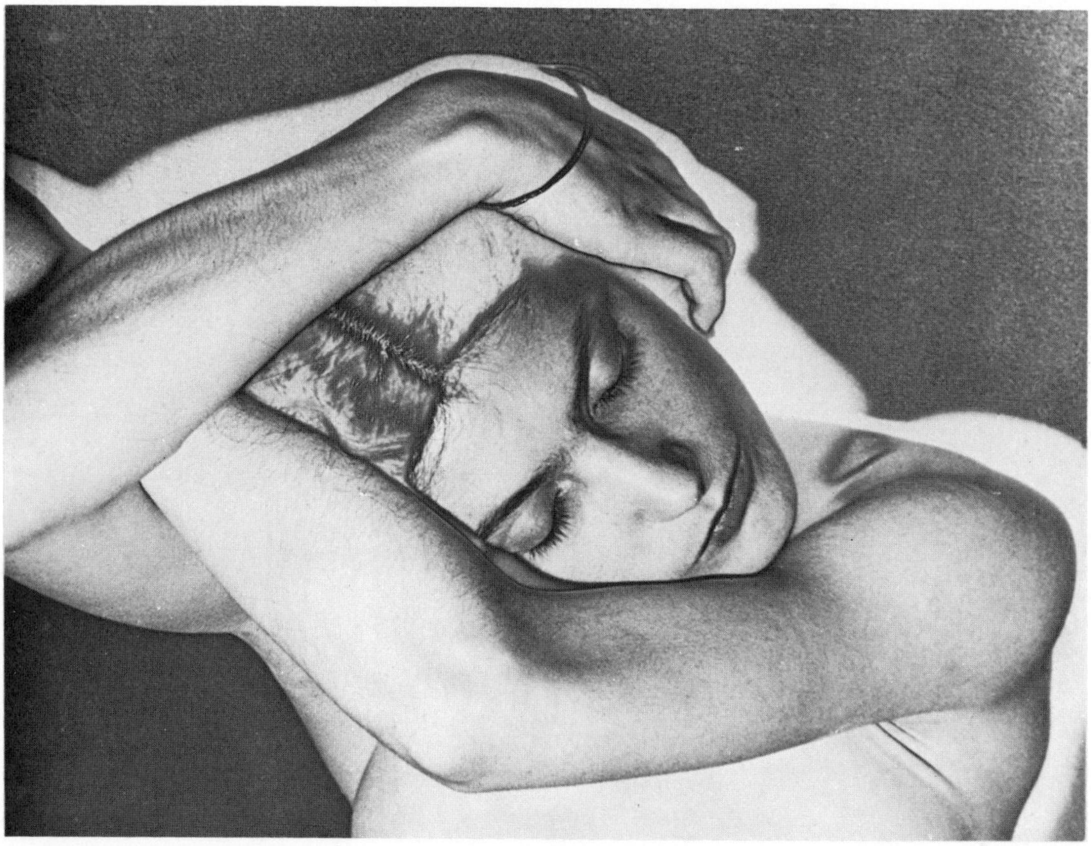

photography using both darkroom manipulation and bizarre studio setups. He was the first photographer to explore the creative potential of *solarization,* the reversal of the tonal sequence in the denser areas of a photographic negative or print, which adds strong black contours to the edges of major shapes. Solarization is achieved by giving a latent or developing photographic image a second exposure to light. Man Ray called his cameraless prints *rayographs.* These were more complex than schadographs for Man Ray made his exposures with moving lights and beams of light. He combined experimental techniques like solarization with the basic technique of placing objects on the photopaper. Distortion, printing through textures, and multiple exposures were also used as Man Ray searched for dreamlike images and new interpretations of time and space.

The concepts, images, and methods of visual organization of Cubism, Futurism, Dadaism, and Surrealism have provided valuable insights and processes for graphic designers. The innovators of these movements, who dared to walk into a no man's land of unexplored artistic possibilities, continue to influence artists to this day.

Man Ray, poster for the London Underground, 1932. Drawing a visual analogy between the London Underground symbol and Saturn, Man Ray propels the trademark into space in an unexpected application of Surrealist dislocation to visual communications. *The Museum of Modern Art, New York, Gift of Bernard Davis.*

16

Pictorial Modernism

The European poster during the first half of the twentieth century is a continuation of the 1890s poster, but its course was strongly affected by the modern art movements and altered by the communication needs of two world wars. Influenced by Cubism and Constructivism, yet cognizant of the need to maintain a pictorial reference if their posters were to communicate persuasively with the general public, graphic designers involved in the poster walked a tightrope between the creation of expressive and symbolic images on the one hand, and their concern for the total visual organization of the picture plane on the other hand. This dialogue between communicative imagery and design form generates the excitement and energy of pictorial modernism.

The Poster in Berlin

In 1898, fifteen-year-old Lucien Bernhard (1883–1972) attended the Munich Flaspalast Exhibition of Interior Decoration and was overwhelmed by what he saw. Returning home "just drunk with color" from this avant-garde design show, Bernhard began to repaint the proper nineteenth-century decor of the Bernhard home while his father was away on a three-day business trip. Walls, ceilings, and even furniture traded drabness for a wonderland of brilliant color. Upon his return home, the elder Bernhard was not amused. Lucien was called a potential criminal and severely rebuked. He ran away from home that very day and never returned. In Berlin, Bernhard was trying unsuccessfully to support himself as a poet when he saw an advertisement for a poster contest sponsored by Priester matches. The prize was two hundred marks (about fifty dollars at the time), so Bernhard, who had excelled at art in high school, decided to enter. His first design showed a checkered tablecloth on a round table, on which

Lucien Bernhard, poster for Priester matches, c. 1905. Color became the visual means that enabled Bernhard to project a powerful message with minimal information. Against a deep brown field, the bright blue letterforms and scarlet matches with yellow tips glow brightly.

Lucien Bernhard, poster for Stiller shoes, 1912. Reducing the message to a flat presentation of the product and the brand name once again, Bernhard achieves impact with color. Against the brown background, dark letterforms, and black shoe, the inside of the shoe is intense red and the front of the heel is bright orange.

was an ashtray with a lighted cigar and box of matches. Feeling that the image was too bare, Bernhard painted scantily clad dancing girls in the background. Later that day, he decided that the image was too complex and painted the girls out. When a friend dropped by and asked if it was a poster for a cigar, Bernhard painted out the cigar. Deciding that the tablecloth and ashtray stood out too prominently, Bernhard painted them out, leaving a pair of matches on a bare table. Because the entries had to be postmarked by midnight on that date, Bernhard hastily painted the word Priester above the matches in blue, wrapped the poster, and sent it off.

Later, Bernhard learned that the jury's immediate reaction to his poster was total rejection. A late arriving juror, Ernst Growald of the Hollerbaum and Schmidt lithography firm, rescued Bernhard's design from the trashcan and tacked it on the wall. Stepping back to study the image, Growald proclaimed, "This is my first prize. Here is a genius." Growald convinced the rest of the jury, and Bernhard's first poster was the now famous Priester matches poster, which reduced communication to one word and two matches.

This self-taught young artist probably did not realize it at the time, but he had moved the visual poster one step further in the process of simplification and reduction of naturalism into a graphic language of shapes. Toulouse-Lautrec had started the process, and the Beggarstaffs had continued it. Bernhard established an approach to the poster using flat color shapes, the product name, and product image. He would repeat this approach over and over during the next two decades. In addition, he designed over three hundred packages for sixty-six products, using similar elementary graphics.

The outstanding Berlin lithography firm of Hollerbaum and Schmidt, recognizing that an important style of German poster art seemed to be developing in the hands of Bernhard and the young poster artists whom he influenced, signed Bernhard and five other graphic designers to an exclusive contract. This farsighted business acumen meant that anyone wishing to commission posters from these artists would have to work with the Hollerbaum and Schmidt printing firm. In addition to Bernhard, the group included Hans Rudi Erdt (1883–1918), Julius Gipkens (b. 1883), and Julius Klinger.

Comparison of the Opel motorcar poster by Erdt and the Stiller shoes poster by Bernhard demonstrates how well Erdt was able to apply the Bernhard formula: flat background color; large, simple image; and product name. Gipkens, like Bernhard, was a self-taught graphic designer who developed a large clientele in Berlin. The fluid, linear drawing of Gipkens' work gave a nervous wiggle to both his lettering and images; this became a stylistic trademark in his work.

Julius Klinger was born and educated in Vienna and had been associated with the Vienna Secession artists. Sensing a better opportunity for graphic design in Germany, Klinger moved to Berlin early in the century, and his style veered from floral Art Nouveau toward decorative two-dimensional shapes of bright, clear color and concise, simple lettering.

Hans Rudi Erdt, poster for the Opel motorcar, 1911. The distinguished motorist projects an image of status.

Julius Gipkens, poster for Heinemann's Wicker Furniture, undated. Less reductive than Bernhard, Gipkens added a dog and checkered cushion to the product and store name. These lend an ambiance of hearth and home.

INNEN-DEKORATION
VERLAG UND REDAKTION

Berthold Type Founders, Block Type, 1910. Early twentieth-century sans-serif typefaces were based on the poster lettering of Lucien Bernhard.

Lucien Bernhard, trademark for Hommel Micrometers, 1912. Every shape and form comprising this figure is based on a part from one of Hommel's products.

During the early years of Bernhard's poster design career, he developed a sans-serif lettering style painted in broad brushstrokes. At first, he did not have any particular concept, but gradually a dense alphabet of unique character developed. This alphabet design impressed a staff member from the Berthold Type Foundry in Berlin, and a typeface design was based on it. When the typeface was released in 1910, Bernhard was quite surprised to see his personal lettering style cast in metal for all the world to use. His sense of simplicity was applied to trademark design. For Hommel Micrometers in 1912, Bernhard constructed a little mechanical man holding one of the client's sensitive measuring devices. For Manoli cigarettes in 1911, Bernhard reduced the trademark to a simple *M* in a circle printed in a second color.

Bernhard was a pivotal innovator. His work might be considered the logical conclusion of the turn-of-the-century poster movement. At the same time, emphasis on reduction, minimalist form, and simplification anticipates the Constructivist movement.

As time went on, Bernhard tackled interior design, then studied carpentry to learn furniture design and construction. This led to a study of architecture, and Bernhard was designing furniture, rugs, wallpapers, and lighting fixtures as well as office buildings, factories, and houses.

A visit to America in 1923 excited Bernhard, and he returned to live in New York. His work was far too modern to gain acceptance in America, and it was five years before he received any poster commissions. During that time he worked as an interior designer. In 1928, Bernhard contracted with the American Type Founders to design new typefaces. A steady stream of new fonts captured the sensibilities of the era.

Lucien Bernhard, trademark for Manoli cigarettes, 1911. A simple *M* in a circle suggests the minimal forms of forthcoming twentieth-century symbols and trademarks.

The poster goes to war

The poster reached the zenith of its importance as a medium of communication during World War I (1914–18). Printing technologies had been perfected, and radio and other electronic means of public communication had not yet come into prominence. In this total global conflict, governments turned to the poster as a major means of propaganda and visual persuasion. Armies had to be recruited, and public morale had to be boosted to maintain popular support for the war effort. In this first conflict fought with the armaments of technology—airplanes, zeppelins, heavy artillery, and tanks—fund-raising drives were used to raise vast amounts of money to finance the destruction and prevent governmental bankruptcy. As resources were diverted to the war effort, public support for conservation and home gardening was required to lessen the risk of acute shortages. Finally, the enemy had to be assailed for his barbarism and threat to civilization.

Posters of the Central Powers (led by Germany and Austria-Hungary) and the Allies (led by France and Great Britain, then joined by the United States in 1917) were radically different. In Germany and Austria-Hungary, a design approach that continued the traditions of the Vienna Secession and Bernhard was dominant. Words and images were integrated, and the essence of the communication was conveyed by simplifying images into powerful shapes and patterns. In expressing this philosophy of design, Julius Klinger observed that the United States flag was the best poster America had.

Klinger's war posters were reduced to simple pictographic war symbols. In his poster for the eighth Bond Drive, eight arrows piercing a dragon remind the citizens that their contributions have helped wound the enemy. Curiously, Bernhard adopted a very gothic approach in a number of his war posters, such as the hand-drawn lithographic poster for the Seventh War Loan. In an almost primeval expression of the ancient Germanic spirit, Bernhard depicts a clenched fist in medieval armor thrusting into the space over the gothic inscription that reads, "This is the way to peace—the enemy wills it so! Thus subscribe to the war loan!"

It fell to others to use the simplicity Bernhard had pioneered in war posters, and Gipkens and Erdt did so. A frequent propaganda device is the destruction of the enemy's symbol or flag. One of the most effective examples of this approach is Cologne designer Otto Lehmann's (b. 1865) poster depicting industrial workers and farmers holding a soldier on their shoulders who is taking down a ripped British flag. It proclaims, "Support

Julius Klinger, poster for the eighth war loan campaign, 1917. The green and black dragon rises through the red eight in this dramatic symbolic poster.

Lucien Bernhard, poster for a war loan campaign, 1915. Both the illustration and the lettering style convey a sharp militaristic feeling in this red and black lithograph. *Library of Congress, Washington, D.C., Poster Collection.*

Hans Rudi Erdt, poster entitled *U-Boats Out!,* c. 1916. After 1916 it became evident that submarine warfare was the only possible way that Germany could break the English blockade. Erdt's powerful visual joining of the large *U* with the U-Boat commander peering through a periscope at the sinking vessel served to celebrate Germany's heroes and rally the public behind them.

our men in field gray. Crush England's might. Subscribe to the war loan."

The Allies' approach to graphic propaganda was more illustrative with literal rather than symbolic imagery used to address propaganda objectives. British posters called upon the need to protect traditional values, the home, and the family. Perhaps the most effective British poster of the war years is the 1915 military recruiting poster by Alfred Leete (1882–1933) showing the popular Lord Horatio Kitchener, British Secretary of War, pointing directly at the viewer. Originally, this image appeared as the 5 September 1914 cover of the *London Opinion* magazine above the headline, "Your country needs you." The Parliamentary Recruiting Committee sought permission to convert it into this powerful frontal eyeball-to-eyeball confrontation that inspired a number of imitations.

Public patriotism ran high when the United States entered the war to "make the world safe for democracy" in "the war to end all wars." Illustrator Charles Dana Gibson offered his services as art director to the division of Pictorial Publicity, a Federal agency that produced over seven hundred posters and other propaganda materials for fifty other governmental agencies. Working without charge, the leading magazine illustrators turned to poster design and grappled with the change in scale from magazine page to poster. Persuasive propaganda replaced narrative interpretations, and suddenly the illustrators had to integrate lettering with the image. James Montgomery Flagg (1877–1960), whose sketchy painting style was widely known, whipped out some forty-six war posters during the year and a half of American involvement in the war, including his American version of the

Julius Gipkens, poster for an exhibition of captured airplanes, 1917. Stark graphic shapes project boldly against the white field. A symbolic eagle sits triumphantly upon the red, white, and blue indicia of a captured allied aircraft.

Otto Lehmann, poster for a war loan campaign, undated. The cluster of figures and dense lettering created a solid base from which the soldier and flag thrust upward into the white space.

Alfred Leete, poster for military recruiting, c. 1915. This printed sheet made eye contact and confronted the spectator.

Kitchener poster. Five million copies of Flagg's "Uncle Sam" poster were printed, making it one of the most widely reproduced posters in history.

The rising star of illustrator Joseph C. Leyendecker received a boost from his popular posters. Painted with a slablike brushstroke, Leyendecker's images have a distinctive appearance. His ability to capture the essence of a subject was emerging. This ability held Leyendecker in good stead after the war, for his three hundred twenty-two covers for *The Saturday Evening Post* and countless advertising illustrations, notably for Arrow Shirts and Collars during the 1920s, captured the essence of the American experience and attitudes during the decades between the world wars.

Honoring one's soldiers and creating a cult around national leaders or symbolic figures was one function of the poster; ridiculing or disparaging the leaders of the enemy forces was another. In Paul Verrees' unusual attempt at humor, which was seldom seen in propaganda posters, the Kaiser is "canned."

James Montgomery Flagg, poster for military recruiting, 1917. Flagg's famous self-portrait masquerading as Uncle Sam has become a mass-media icon. It was reprinted when America entered World War II. *Library of Congress, Washington, D.C., Poster Collection.*

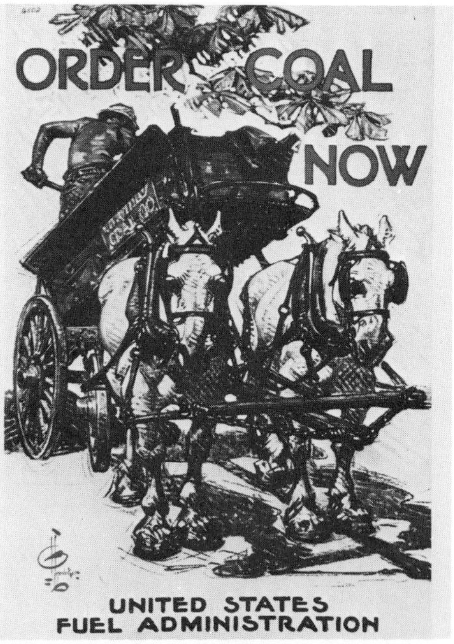

Joseph C. Leyendecker, poster for the U.S. Fuel Administration, 1917. A pictorial genre scene of a coal company delivery, painted in Leyendecker's choppy brush strokes, is a reminder to citizens that fuel orders should be placed early.

Joseph C. Leyendecker, poster celebrating a successful bond drive, 1917. Requested to honor the role of Boy Scouts in the Third Liberty Loan Campaign, Leyendecker combined basic visual symbols—Liberty clad in the flag, holding an imperial shield, and taking a "Be Prepared" sword from the Scout—that had patriotism building value with all levels of society.

J. Paul Verrees, poster promoting Victory gardens, 1918. Public action—the raising of one's own food—is tied directly to the defeat of the enemy. *Library of Congress, Washington, D.C., Poster Collection.*

The maverick from Munich

Ludwig Holwein (1874–1949) of Munich began his career as a graphic designer in 1906 after studying architecture. During the first five decades of the century, Holwein's graphic art evolved with changing social conditions. The Beggarstaff Brothers were his initial inspiration, and during the years before World War I, Holwein took great delight in reducing his images to flat shapes. Unlike the Beggarstaffs and his Berlin rival Bernhard, however, Holwein applied a rich range of texture and decorative pattern to his images. Many of these early posters were for clothing manufacturers and retail stores, and it seemed that Holwein never repeated himself. In the posters that he designed during World War I, Holwein began to combine his simple, powerful shapes with more naturalistic imagery. As evidenced in the 1914 Red Cross fund-raising poster, Holwein's work straddles the line between the symbolic poster philosophy of other Central Powers

Ludwig Holwein, poster for Marque MKZ men's clothing store, 1908. In his designs before World War I, Holwein delighted in playing complex flat patterns against each other and the flat background.

ROTE KREUZ-SAMMLUNG
1914
SAMMLUNG ZUGUNSTEN DER FREI-
WILLIGEN KRANKENPFLEGE IM KRIEGE

Ludwig Holwein, fundraising poster, 1914. A graphic symbol (the red cross) combines with a pictorial symbol (a wounded soldier) in an appeal with emotional power and visual attention-getting qualities. *Library of Congress, Washington, D.C., Poster Collection.*

graphic designers and the pictorial poster used by the Allies.

After the war, Holwein was much sought after by commercial accounts desiring his style, which was becoming more fluid and painterly. Frequently, figures were arranged on a flat white ground with colorful lettering placed around them.

After an unsuccessful 1923 attempt to seize power in the Munich *Putsch,* Adolf Hitler was sent to prison, where he spent his time writing *Mein Kampf* which set forth his political philosophy and plans to take over Germany. He wrote that propaganda, including the poster, "must be aimed at the emotions and only to a limited degree to the so-called intellect." Hitler advocated propaganda whose content level was directed toward the least educated in the audience using only essential, simple forms in stereotyped formulas. Hitler was convinced that the more artisticially designed posters used in Germany and Austria during World War I were less effective than the conceptually

Ludwig Holwein, poster for the Deutsche Lufthansa, 1936. A mythological winged being symbolizes the airline, German victory in the Berlin Olympics, and the triumph of Nazi movement. *Library of Congress, Washington, D.C., Poster Collection.*

Ludwig Holwein, concert poster, 1938. A Teutonic she-warrior looms upward because the light strikes her from below. *Library of Congress, Washington, D.C., Poster Collection.*

simpler, but more illustrative work from England and the United States. Hitler had an almost uncanny knack for visual propaganda. The swastika was adopted as the symbol for the Nazi party. Uniforms consisting of brown shirts with red armbands bearing a black swastika in a white circle began to appear throughout Germany as Nazi storm troopers grew in strength and numbers.

It seems almost inevitable, in retrospect, that the Nazi party would commission a steady stream of posters from Holwein, for the evolution of his work coincided closely with Hitler's concept of effective propaganda. As Hitler spoke in his passionate radio addresses to the nation about the "master race" of fair-haired German youth and the triumphant superiority of German athletes, Holwein posters carried these images all across the nation. Hitler's ideas gained visual presence, and the repetition of seeing the images over and over again reinforced them. As the Nazi dictatorship consolidated its power and the stormy holocaust of World War II approached, Holwein moved toward a bold imperial and militaristic style of tight, heavy forms and strong tonal contrasts.

Post-Cubist pictorial modernism

After World War I, the nations of Europe and North America sought a return to normalcy. The war machinery was turned toward peacetime needs, and a decade of unprecedented prosperity dawned for the victorious Allies. Faith in the machine

Ludwig Holwein, recruiting poster, early 1940s. In one of Holwein's last posters for the Nazis, a stern and somber soldier appears above the simple question, "And you?" *Library of Congress, Washington, D.C., Poster Collection.*

and technology was at an all-time high, and this ethic gained expression through art and design. Léger's celebration of mechanical, machine-made, and industrial forms became an important design resource, and the Cubist ideas of spatial organization and synthetic imagery inspired an important new direction in pictorial images. Among the graphic designers who incorporated Cubism directly into their work, an American working in London, E. McKnight Kauffer (1890–1954), and a Russian immigrant to Paris, A.M. Cassandre (pseudonym for Adlophe Jean-Marie Mouron, 1901–1968), achieved exceptional creative accomplishments.

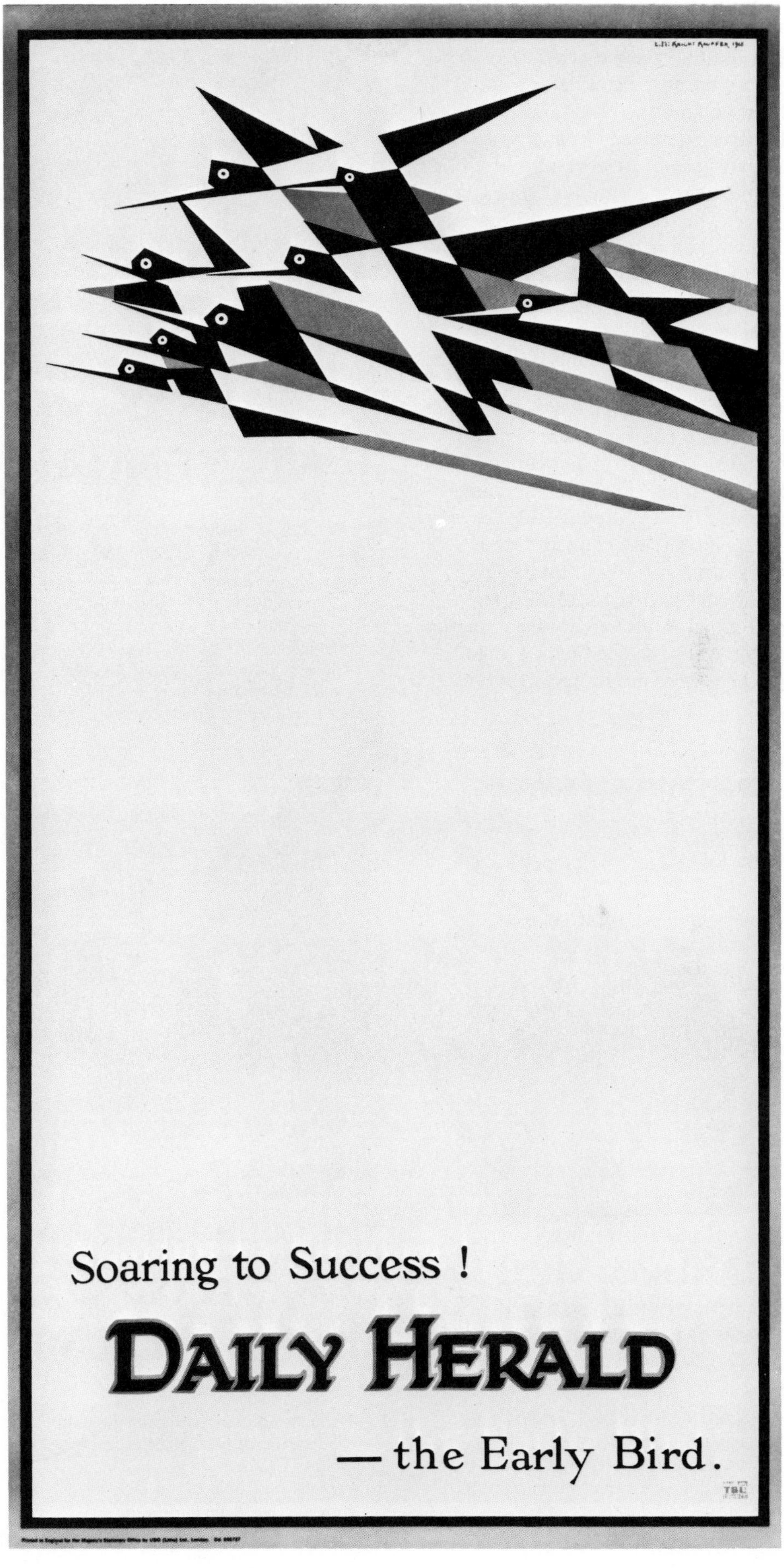

E. McKnight Kauffer, poster for the *Daily Herald,* 1918. Although it is somewhat flawed by the choice of type and its placement, this stunning and famous poster was a harbinger that the formal language of Cubism and Futurism could be used with strong communications impact in graphic design. *Courtesy of Her Majesty's Stationery Office, Norwich, England.*

Born in Great Falls, Montana, E. McKnight Kauffer's formal education was limited to eight years of grammar school because his itinerant fiddler father abandoned the family when Kauffer was three. At age twelve Kauffer began to work at odd jobs to supplement the family income. At age sixteen, he traveled to San Francisco and worked in a bookstore while taking night-school art classes and painting on weekends. Moving to New York late in 1912, Kauffer stopped in Chicago for several months to study at the Art Institute. While there, he saw the famous Armory Show, which traveled to Chicago from New York in 1913. This first American exposure to modern art caused a scandalous uproar. The 16 March 1913 *New York Times* headline screamed, "Cubists and Futurists Make Insanity Pay."

Twenty-two-year-old Kauffer responded intuitively to the strength of the work, decided his Chicago teachers were not on top of recent developments in art, and moved to Europe. After living in Munich and Paris, he journeyed to London in 1914 when war broke out. For the next quarter of a century, a steady stream of posters and other graphic design assignments enabled him to apply the invigorating principles of modern art, particularly Cubism, to the problems of visual communications. He designed one hundred forty-one posters for the London Underground Transport. The writer Aldous Huxley observed that, in contrast to the use of money and sex in advertising for everything from scents to sanitary plumbing, Kauffer "prefers the more difficult task of advertising products in terms of forms that are symbolical only to those particular products . . . He reveals his affinity with all artists who have ever aimed at expressiveness through simplification,

E. McKnight Kauffer, poster for the London Underground, 1924. Lyrical greens, tans, and grays capture the idyllic quality of the rural location. *Library of Congress, Washington, D.C., Poster Collection.*

E. McKnight Kauffer, book jacket for *Ulysses,* 1952. James Joyce employed stream-of-consciousness writing and created and distorted words. In Kauffer's cover design, both the huge *U* that fades into darkness and the red *L* that zips upward take on a visual identity separate from their function as letterforms. *Random House, New York.*

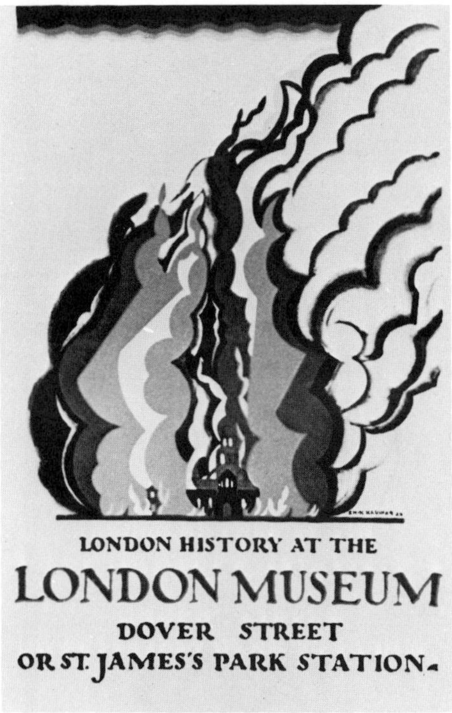

E. McKnight Kauffer, poster for the London Underground, 1922. To make a historical museum interesting, Kauffer selected a dramatic event—the burning of Parliament—and illustrated it with slashing red and orange shapes inspired by Cubism.

E. McKnight Kauffer, poster for the London Underground, 1924. Kauffer solved the problem of achieving graphic impact with a landscape subject on posters by developing a flat-shape illustration style that distills the essence of the subject into restful blue and green planes.

distortion, and transposition, and especially the Cubists,'' to produce ''not a copy, but a simplified, formalized and more expressive symbol.'' When World War II began, Kauffer returned to his native America, where he worked until his death in 1954.

At age fourteen, A. M. Cassandre migrated to Paris from Russia, where he had been born in the Ukraine to a Russian mother and French father. He studied at the Ecole des Beaux Arts and Académie Julian. His graphic design career began when he took a job with Hachard et Compagnie printing firm to earn money for art study and living expenses. From 1923 until 1936 he produced a stunning series of posters that helped revitalize French advertising art. Cassandre's bold, simple designs emphasize two dimensionality and are composed of broad, simplified planes of color. By simplifying his subjects into almost iconographic symbols, he moved very close to Synthetic Cubism. His love of letterforms is evidenced by an exceptional ability to integrate words and images into a total composition. For the Deberny and Peignot typefoundry, Cassandre designed typefaces that were daring innovations in their design qualities. During the late 1930, Cassandre worked in the United States for clients including *Harper's Bazaar,* Container Corporation of America, and N. W. Ayer. After returning to Paris in 1939, he turned to painting and design for the ballet and theater, which were his major involvements over the next three decades.

In addition to Kauffer and Cassandre, a number of other graphic de-

A. M. Cassandre, railway poster, 1927. In addition to being a magnificent abstract design, an intangible aspect of travel—the unknown experience and hope of a destination far in the future—is conveyed by this poster for the ''North Star'' night train from Paris to Amsterdam. *Reinhold Brown Poster Gallery, New York.*

A. M. Cassandre, poster for *L'Intransigeant,* 1925. The collage-inspired pictographic images depict Marianne, the symbolic voice of France, urgently shouting the news that is being received over the telegraph wires. In this masterpiece of composition, Cassandre cropped the client's name as it races out the upper right-hand corner, leaving the often-used shortened name. *Reinhold Brown Poster Gallery, New York.*

L'AMERIQUE DU SUD
PAR LE PAQUEBOT
"L'ATLANTIQUE"
(40000 T.)
COMPAGNIE DE NAVIGATION
SUD-ATLANTIQUE

A. M. Cassandre, poster for Dubonnet, 1932. Cinematic sequence is used in both word and image. DUBO (doubt), as the man eyes the glass uncertainly; DU BON (of some good), the beverage is tasted; and DUBONNET, the product is identified as the glass is refilled. For over twenty years this design appeared in formats ranging from scratch pads to billboards. *Museum of Modern Art, New York.*

signers and illustrators incorporated concepts and images from Cubism into their work.

Jean Carlu (b. 1900), a promising eighteen-year-old French architectural student, had been whipped under the wheels of a Paris trolley car, and his right arm was severed from his body. His survival was miraculous, and during long days of recovery he thought intensely about the world and his future. World War I had turned northern France into a vast burial ground. A grid of white crosses stretched for miles where villages and farms had flourished for centuries. France struggled for economic recovery in the face of devastation and hardship. Having to abandon his dream of joining his father and brother in the practice of architecture, young Carlu vowed to become an artist and apply his talents to the needs of his country. With much commitment and concentration, he taught his left hand the control and discipline that had been lost in the accident.

Like Cassandre and Kauffer, Carlu understood the modern movements and applied this knowledge to visual communication. Realizing the need for concise statements, Carlu approached pictorial modernism by combining telegraphic copy, powerful geometric forms and structure, and symbolic imagery. Ideas were represented by symbols created through the simplification of natural forms into almost pictographic silhouettes. Carlu made a dispassionate, objective analysis of the emotional value of visual elements. Then, he assembled them with almost scientific exactness. Tenseness and alertness were expressed by angles and lines; feelings of ease, relaxation, and comfort were transmitted by curves. Carlu sought to convey the essence of the message by avoiding the use of "two lines where one would do" or using "two ideas where one will deliver the message more forcefully." He believed that the visual presentation of product information should echo the technical achievements of engineers and product designers. To study the effectiveness of communications in the urban environment, Carlu conducted experiments with posters moving past spectators at varying speeds so that message legibility and impact could be documented.

In 1940 Carlu was in America completing an exhibition entitled "France at War" for the French Information Service display at the New York World's Fair. On 14 June 1940 German troops marched into Paris, and Carlu was stunned to learn that his country was capitulating to Hitler. He decided to remain in America for the duration of the war, but this sojourn lasted for thirteen years. Some of his finest work was created during this period, notably the posters designed for the American and Allied war efforts. Word and image are interlocked into terse messages of great power in his finest designs.

Paul Colin (b. 1892) started his career as a graphic designer in 1925 when an acquaintance from the trenches of World War I asked the thirty-three-year-old painter if he would like to become the graphics and set designer for the Theatre des Champs-Elysées in Paris. The most frequent design organization of Colin's program covers and posters is to place a figure or object centrally before a colored background. Then, type or lettering is placed above and/or below this image. These strong, central images are animated by a variety of techniques: creating a double image, often with different drawing techniques and scale changes; using the transparency of overlapping

A. M. Cassandre, poster for a steamship line, 1931. The ship image is constructed on a rectangle that echoes the rectangle of the poster's edges. By exaggerating the scale difference between the ship and tugboat, a monolithic quality is achieved. The severe geometry is softened by the smoke and fading reflection. *Reinhold Brown Poster Gallery, New York.*

A. M. Cassandre, Acier Noir typeface, 1936. In this unique design, each letter is half solid and half outline.

A. M. Cassandre, Peignot typeface, 1937. In this thick-and-thin sans serif, Cassandre's lower case mixes lower case with small capitals. Note the design of the ascenders and descenders.

A. M. Cassandre, Bifur typeface, 1929. About half of each letter is omitted. A linear shaded area restores the basic silhouette. Therefore, the eye is able to fill in the missing parts and read the characters.

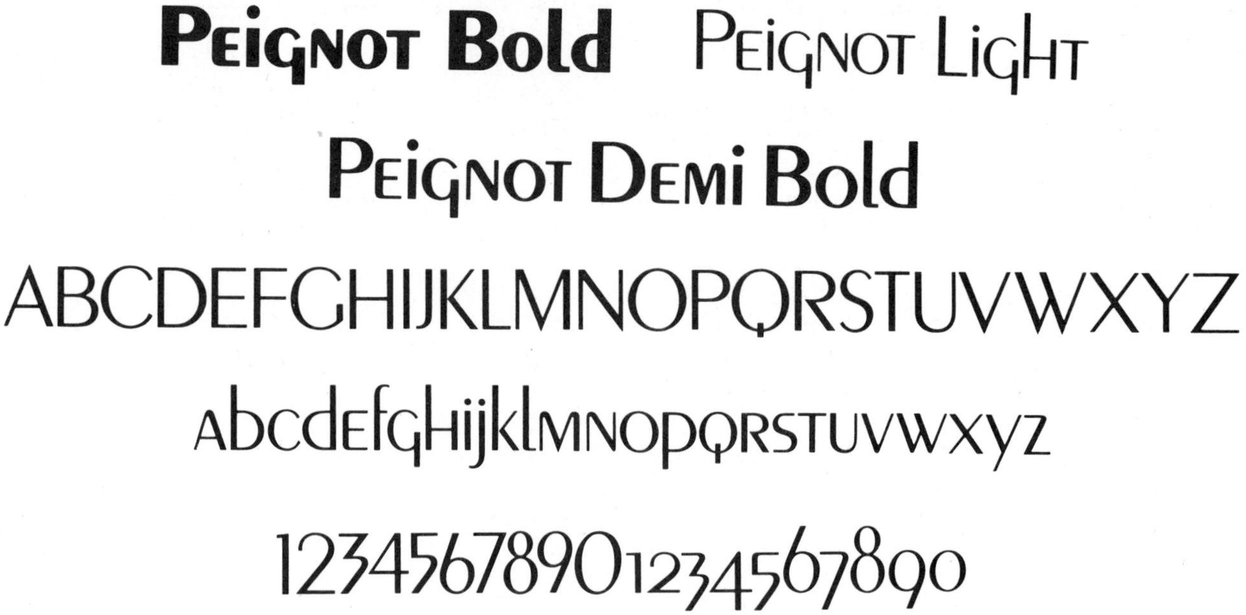

images as a means to make two things into one; or adding color shapes or bands behind or to the side of the central figure to counteract the static placement and create a less stable balance. The simple, sketchy quality of most of Colin's graphic designs enabled him to produce a substantial oeuvre. Estimates about the number of posters he created have ranged from over one thousand to as high as two thousand, and some sources credit him with a staggering eight hundred set designs. Colin is undoubtedly the most prolific and enduring designer of the Art Deco or pictorial modernism approach to graphic design. He produced propaganda posters during World War II until the fall of France, and new posters by Colin were still being commissioned, printed, and posted throughout Paris during the early 1970s.

A direct application of Cubism to graphic design was made by Austin Cooper (b. 1890) in England. In a series of three collage-inspired posters, he attempted to spark memories of the viewer's earlier continental visits by presenting fragments and glimpses of landmarks. Lively movement is achieved by shifting planes, sharp angles, and the superimposition of lettering and images. In 1924, Cooper made an interesting foray into the use of pure geometric shape and color to solve a communications problem for the London Electric Railway. A winter poster proclaimed that "it is warmer down below." Its summer counterpart promised that "it is cooler down below." The geometric forms, rising from the bottom to the top of each poster, change in a rainbow of colors from warm to cool to symbolize the temperature changes as one leaves the cold street in winter—or the hot street in summer—for the greater comfort of the underground railway.

In Vienna, Joseph Binder (1898–1972) studied at the Vienna School of Applied Art, which was under the direction of Alfred Roller, from 1922 until 1926. While still a student, Binder combined influences including Kolomon Moser and Cubism into a pictorial graphic design style with strong communicative power. Reducing natural images to

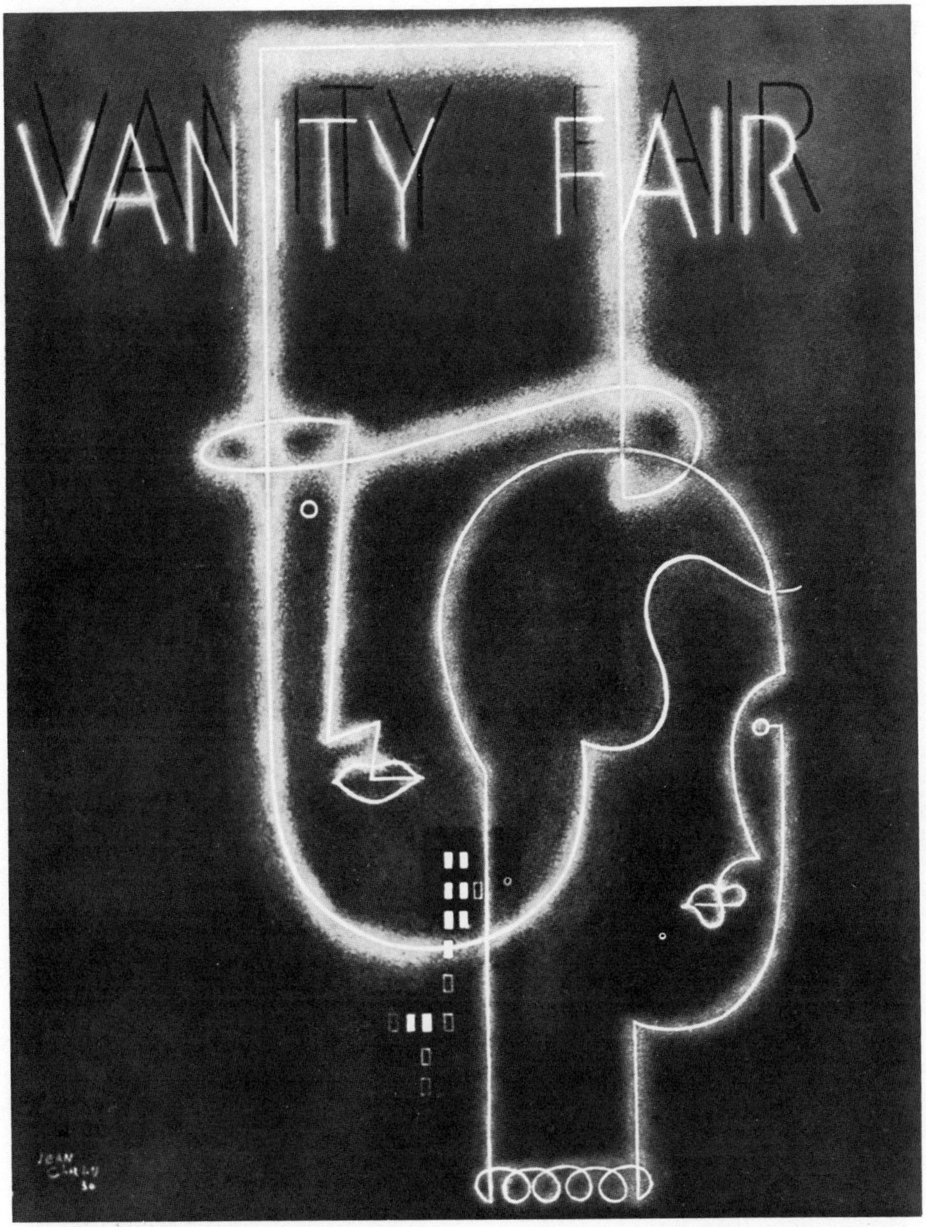

Jean Carlu, *Vanity Fair* cover, 1930. This stylized geometric drawing, expressed as the newly invented neon tube lighting, reflects its Cubist origin. The heads glow vibrantly in red and blue against the dark night sky.

Paul Colin, poster for the dancer Georges Pomies, 1932. The glowing red and orange figure of Pomies zigs to the right in counterpoint to his brown shadow, which zags to the left against the maroon background. A pulsating musical feeling is generated by the small contour-line white figure with its yellow companions.

basic forms and shapes like the cube, sphere, and cone and using two flat color shapes side by side to represent the light and shadow sides of a figure or object were hallmarks of his work.

His award-winning poster for the Vienna Music and Theater Festival is an early manifestation of what, in retrospect, became called Art Deco. This term, coined in the late 1960s as a name for the popular geometric styles of the 1920s, is an expression—not of a movement—but of the general aesthetic sensibility of the decade. The influences of Cubism, the Bauhaus, and Vienna commingled with *De Stijl,* Suprematism, and a mania for Egyptian, Aztec, and Assyrian motifs. Just as surely as Art Nouveau was a dominant design style at the turn of the century, Art Deco was a dominant design style in the decades between the two world wars. Streamlining, zigzag, modern, and decorative geometry; these terms express the simultaneous desires to express the modern era of the machine while still satisfying a passion for decoration.

Austin Cooper, poster for the Southern Railway, undated. The vocabulary of Cubism operates symbolically for visual communications purposes. Fun and excitement are conveyed by fragments of images and bright color.

Austin Cooper, posters for the London Electric Railway, 1924. Color and shape combine to express a concept. Winter or summer, the subway is more comfortable than surface transportation.

Joseph Binder, poster for the Vienna Music and Theater Festival, 1924. The figures are reduced to flat, geometric shapes, but the proportions and indication of a light and shadow plane retain a sense of naturalism.

Binder traveled widely and settled in New York City in 1935. As with so many emigrants to America, his style underwent changes, and he moved toward a highly refined and stylized naturalism in posters and billboards advertising throat lozenges, beer, travel, and public services.

In Germany between the world wars many graphic designers, like their other European counterparts, used color and plane to construct pictorial images. Artists such as Schulz-Neudamm, who is widely known for his promotional graphics for Universum-Film Aktiengesellschaft where he was staff designer for motion picture publicity, created exceptional work in this manner.

British designer Abram Games (b. 1914) was the last major graphic designer of the pictorial modernism philosophy. He began his career on the eve of World War II and became the most important British designer producing educational, instructional, and propaganda graphics during World War II. In writing about his philosophy, Games said "the message must be given quickly and vividly so that interest is subconsciously retained . . . The discipline of reason conditions the expression of design . . . The designer constructs, winds the spring. The viewer's eye is caught, the spring released." This hardworking designer sought to use commonplace images and forms organized in new ways to make the message more forceful and memorable. An example of this approach is his poster for the Emergency Blood Transfusion Service which asks the viewer, "If he should fall, is your blood there to save him?" Three ordinary images—a hand, a bottle, and a foot soldier—are combined into a

Schulz-Neudamm, poster for the film, *Metropolis,* 1926. While the Art Deco idiom often expressed an infatuation with the machine and an unbridled optimism in human progress, in this poster it turns darkly toward a future time when robots replace people. *The Museum of Modern Art, New York, Gift of Universum-Film Aktiengesellschaft.*

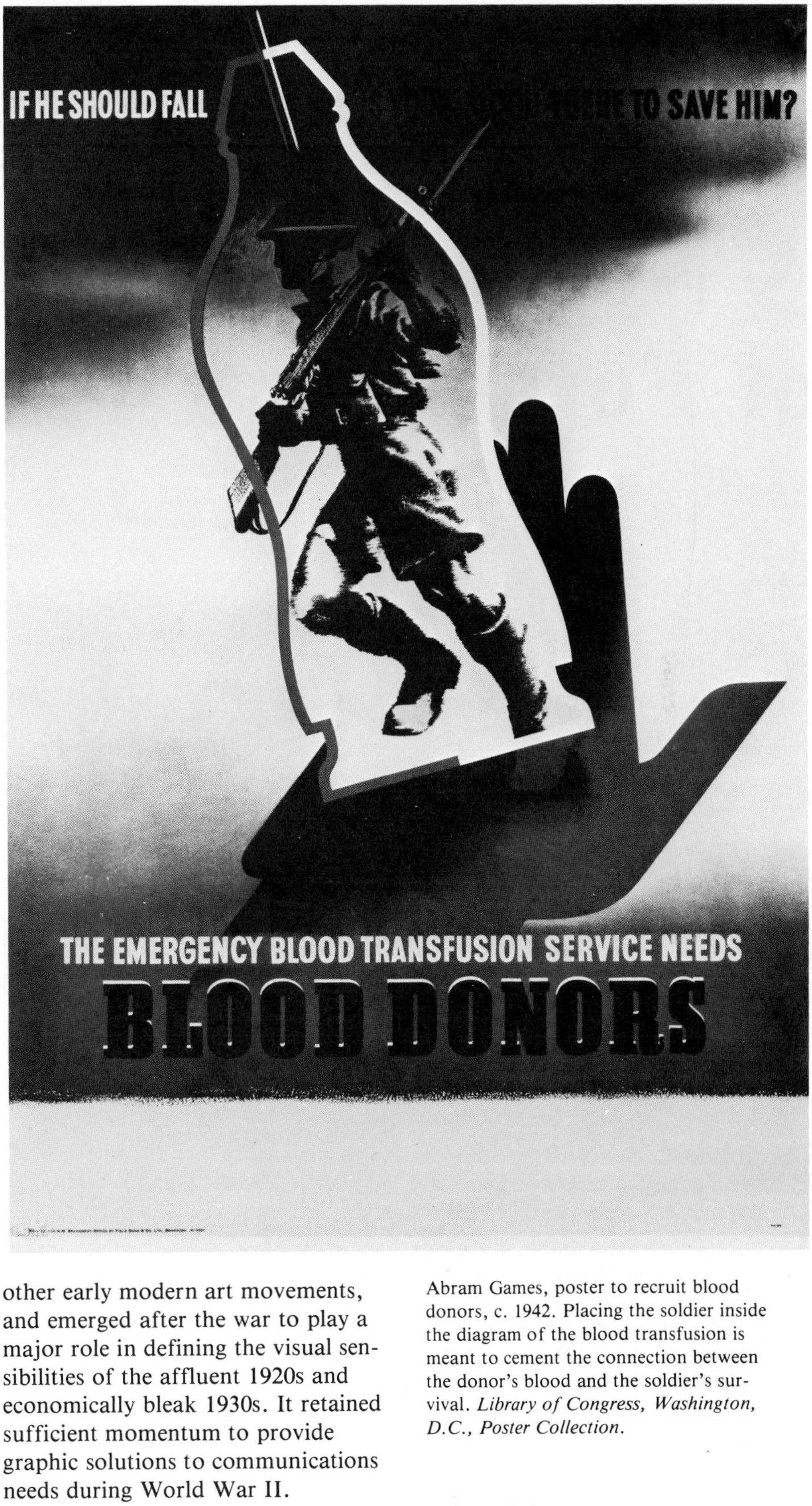

IF HE SHOULD FALL
TO SAVE HIM?
THE EMERGENCY BLOOD TRANSFUSION SERVICE NEEDS
BLOOD DONORS

Abram Games, poster to recruit blood donors, c. 1942. Placing the soldier inside the diagram of the blood transfusion is meant to cement the connection between the donor's blood and the soldier's survival. *Library of Congress, Washington, D.C., Poster Collection.*

compelling statement that provokes an emotional response from the observer.

European pictorial modernism was a designed approach to the creating of graphic illustrations that focused on the total integration of word and image. One of the most enduring currents of twentieth-century graphic design, pictorial modernism began with Bernhard's 1905 Priester matches poster, responded to the communications needs of World War I and the formal innovations of Cubism and other early modern art movements, and emerged after the war to play a major role in defining the visual sensibilities of the affluent 1920s and economically bleak 1930s. It retained sufficient momentum to provide graphic solutions to communications needs during World War II.

17

A New Language of Form

PICTORIAL MODERNISM WAS NOT the only major current of European graphic design between the wars. As McKauffer was pioneering the application of the planes of Synthetic Cubism to the poster in England, a more typographic and formal approach to graphic design was emerging in Holland and Russia where artists saw clearly the implications of Cubism. Visual art could move beyond the threshold of pictorial imagery into the invention of pure form. The shapes and ideas about composing space that developed in painting and sculpture were quickly applied to problems of design. It would be a mistake, however, to say that modern design is a stepchild of the fine arts. The Vienna Secession and Workshops, The Four Macs, Adolf Loos, Peter Behrens, and Frank Lloyd Wright were all moving a heartbeat ahead of modern painting in their consciousness of plastic volume and geometric form at the turn of the century. A spirit of innovation was present in all the visual arts, ideas were "in the air," and by the end of World War I, graphic designers, architects, and product designers were beginning to challenge prevailing ideas about form and function energetically.

Russian Suprematism and Constructivism

During the turbulence of World War I and the Russian Revolution, there was a brief flowering of creative art in Russia even as the Czar was overthrown, Russia was torn by civil war, and the Soviet Union was formed. This Russian art had an international influence on twentieth-century graphic design and typography. The decade, beginning in 1910 with Marinetti's Russian lectures, saw Russian artists absorb the new ideas of Cubism and Futurism with amazing speed and then move on to new innovations.

The Russian avant-garde saw suffi-

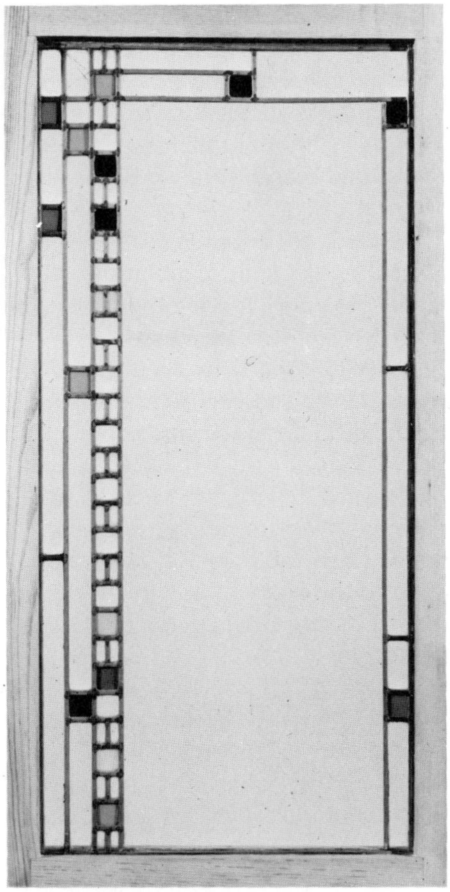

Frank Lloyd Wright, stained-glass window for the Coonley House, 1912. Before the turn of the century, Wright had begun to organize space into geometric planes. In this window brilliant square chips of red, orange, and blue create a vibrant counterpoint to the white planes separated by dark strips of lead. *The Hirshhorn Museum, Washington, D.C.*

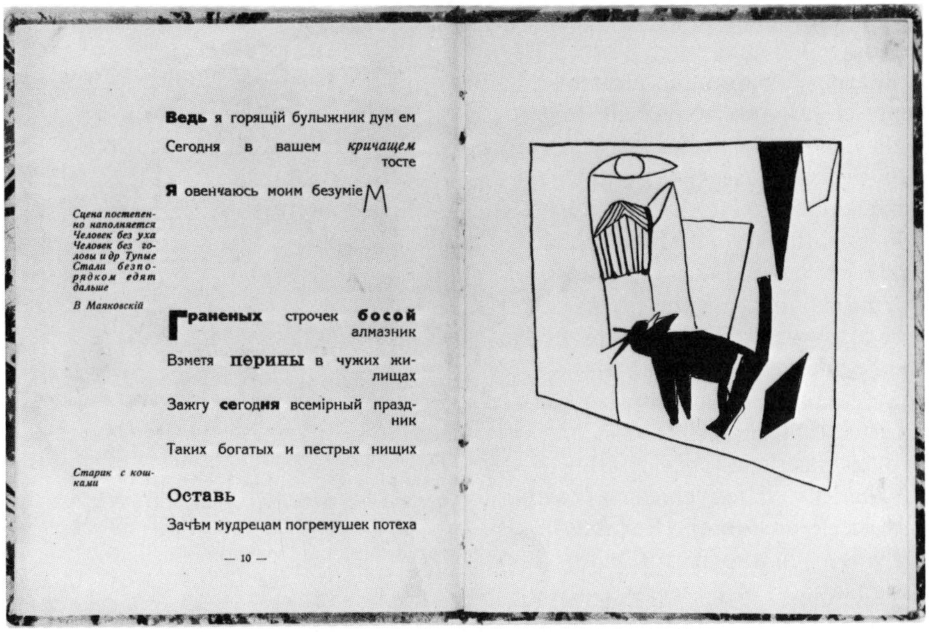

David and Vladimir Burliuk, pages from *Vladimir Mayakovsky—A Tragedy,* 1914. In an effort to relate visual form to meaning, Russian Futurist graphic design mixed type weights, sizes, and styles. *British Library, London.*

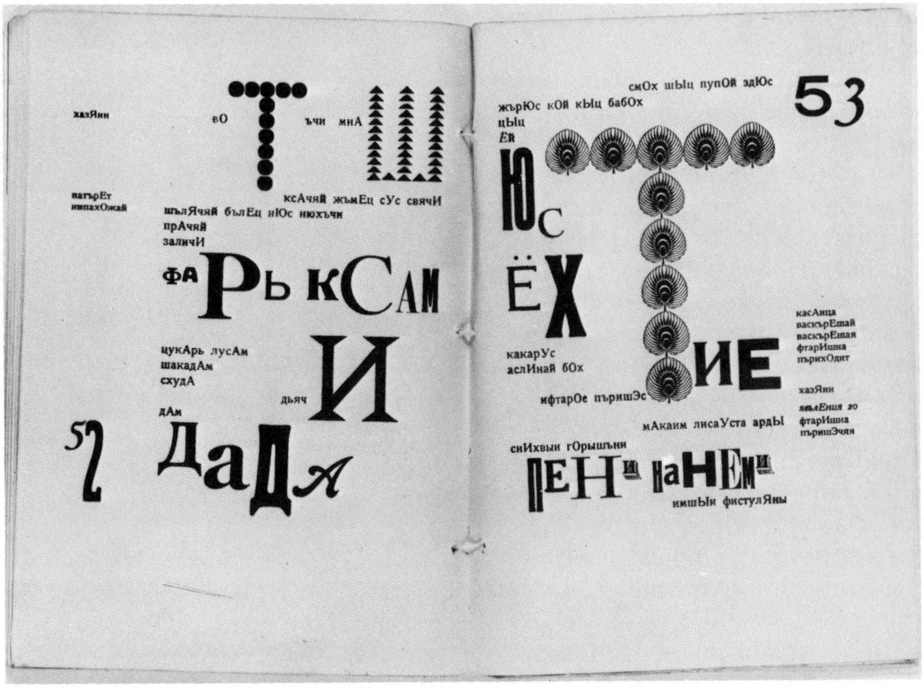

Ilya Zdanevich, pages from *Le-Dantyu as a Beacon,* 1923. The Burliuk brothers and the Dadaists inspired Zdanevich's design of his play, which was printed in Paris. Extreme mixing of elements and building letters from letterpress ornaments create lively movements on the pages. *The British Library, London.*

cient common traits in Cubism and Futurism to coin the term Cubo-Futurism. Experimentation in typography and design characterized the Futurist artists' books and periodicals presenting work by the visual and literary art community. Symbolically, the Russian Futurist books were a reaction against the values of Czarist Russia. The use of coarse paper, handicraft production methods, and handmade additions expressed the poverty of peasant society.

Kasimir Malevich (1878–1935) founded a painting style of basic forms and pure color that he called Suprematism. After working in the manner of Futurism and Cubism, Malevich created an elemental geometric abstraction that was new, nonobjective, and pure. Both utilitarian function and pictorial representation were rejected, for Malevich sought the supreme "expression of feeling, seeking no practical values, no ideas, no promised land." A logical thinker with lucid insights, Malevich realized that the essence of the art experience is the perceptual effect of color. To demonstrate this, in 1913 Malevich exhibited a black square painted on a white ground. He asserted that the feeling this contrast evoked was the essence of art.

The Russian movement was actually accelerated by the Revolution, for art was given a social role rarely assigned to it. The "leftist" artists had been opposed to the old order and its conservative visual art. In 1917 they turned their energies to a massive propaganda effort in support of the Bolsheviks. But by 1920, a deep ideological split developed concerning the role of the artist in the new communist state.

Some artists, like Malevich and Wassily Kandinsky (1866–1944), argued that art must remain an essentially spiritual activity apart from the utilitarian needs of society. "States, political and economic systems perish, ideas crumble, under the strain of ages . . . The realization of our perceptions of the world in the forms of space and time is the only aim of our pictorial and plastic art." Led by Vladimir Tatlin (1885–1953) and Alexander Rodchenko (1891–1956), twenty-five artists advanced the opposing viewpoint in 1921 when they renounced "art for art's sake" to devote themselves to industrial design, visual communications, and applied arts serving the new communist society. These Constructivists called on the artist to stop producing useless things and turn to the poster, for "such work now belongs to the duty of the artist as a citizen of the community who is clearing the field of the old rubbish in preparation for the new life." Tatlin turned from sculpture to the design of a stove that would give maximum heat from minimum fuel; Rodchenko forsook painting for graphic design and photojournalism.

An early attempt to formulate

Kasimir Malevich, *Black Square,* 1913. A new vision for visual art is as far removed as possible from the world of natural forms and appearances.

Kasimir Malevich, *Suprematist Composition,* 1915. Malevich saw the work of art as being a construction of concrete elements of color and shape. The visual form becomes the content, and expressive qualities develop from the intuitive organization of the forms and colors. *Stedelijk Museum, Amsterdam.*

Constructivist ideology was the 1922 brochure *Konstruktivizm* by Aleksei Gan (1893–1942). He criticized abstract painters for being unable to break their umbilical cord to traditional art, and boasted that Constructivism had moved from laboratory work to practical application. Gan wrote that tectonics, texture, and construction are the three principles of Constructivism. *Tectonics* represented the unification of communist ideology with visual form. *Texture* meant the nature of materials and how they are used in industrial production. *Construction* symbolized the creative process and search for laws of visual organization.

The Constructivist ideal was best realized by the painter, architect, graphic designer, and photographer El (Lazar Markovich) Lissitzky (1890–1941). This visionary with tireless energy and persistence profoundly influenced the course of graphic design. At age nineteen, after being turned down by the Petrograd Academy of Arts because of racial prejudice against Jews, Lissitzky turned to the study of architecture at the Darmstadt, Germany, School of Engineering and Architecture. The mathematical and structural properties of architecture became a basis for his art.

In 1919 Marc Chagall, principal of the art school in Vitebsk, asked Lissitzky to join the faculty. Malevich was teaching there and became a major influence on Lissitzky, who developed a painting style that he called PROUNS (an abbreviation for "projects for the establishment (affirmation) of a new art"). In contrast to the absolute flatness of Malevich's picture plane, PROUNS introduced three-dimensional illusions that both receded (negative depth) behind the picture plane (nought depth) and projected forward (positive depth) from the picture plane. Lissitzky called the PROUNS "an interchange station between painting and architecture." This indicates his synthesis of architectural concepts with painting; it also shows that the PROUNS would point the way to the application of modern painting concepts of form and space to applied design.

Lissitzky saw the October 1917 Russian Revolution as a new beginning for mankind. Communism and social engineering would create a new order; technology would provide for society's needs; and the artist/designer (he called himself a constructor) would forge a unity between art and technology by constructing a new world of objects to provide mankind with a richer society and environment.

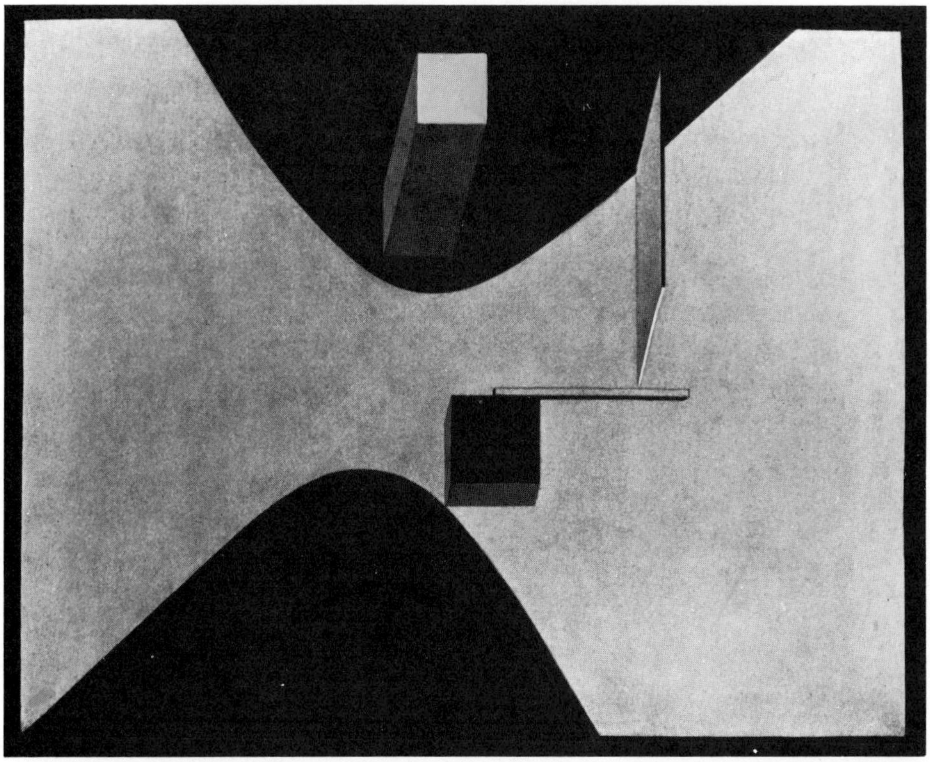

El Lissitzky, *PROUN 23,* no. 6, 1919. The visual ideas about balance, space, and form developed by Lissitzky in his oil paintings became the basis for his graphic design and architecture.

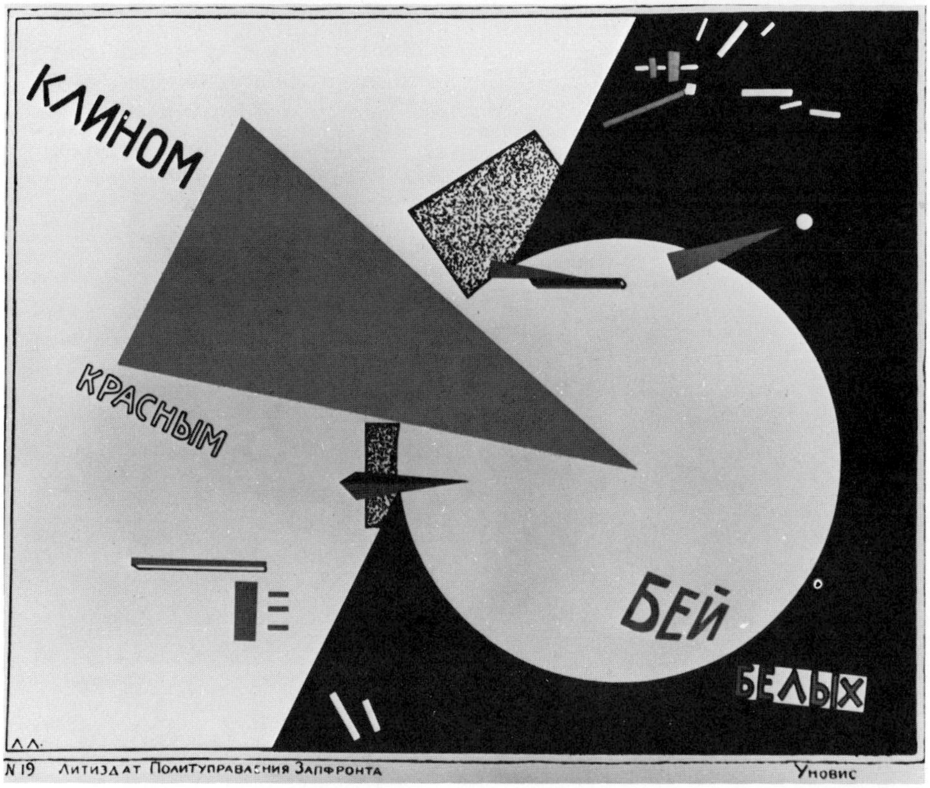

El Lissitzky, *Beat the Whites with the Red Wedge,* 1919. Suprematist design elements are transformed into political symbolism that even a semiliterate peasant can understand. In this poster, support for the "red" Bolshevik against the "white" forces of Kerenski is symbolized by a red wedge slashing into a white circle.

This idealism led him to put increasing emphasis on graphic design, as he moved from the private aesthetic experience of the museum into the mainstream of community life.

Rebelling against the constraints of metal typesetting, Lissitzky often used drafting instrument construction and pasteup to achieve his designs. In 1925, he correctly predicted that Gutenberg's system belonged to the past, and photomechanical processes would replace metal type and open new horizons for design as surely as radio had replaced the telegraph.

In 1921, Lissitzky moved to Berlin. At this time, postwar Germany had become a meeting ground for eastern and western advanced ideas in the aftermath of the world war and the Russian Revolution. His contacts included de Stijl, the Bauhaus, Dadaists, and other Constructivists. Access to excellent German printing facilities enabled his typographic ideas to develop rapidly. His tremendous energy and range of experimentation with photomontage, printmaking, graphic design, and painting enabled him to become the main conduit through which Suprematist and Constructivist ideas flowed into western Europe. Editorial and design assignments for several publications were important ways in which his ideas influenced a wider audience.

During the early 1920s, the Soviet government offered official encouragement to the new Russian art, and even sought to publicize it through an international journal. Editor Ilya Ehrenburg was joined by Lissitzky in creating the trilingual journal *Veshch*(Russian)/*Gegenstand* (German)/*Objet*(French). The title, *Object* in English, was chosen because the editors believed that art meant the creation of new objects, a process that was creating a new collective international style in Europe and Russia in the hands of young creative artists and designers. Realizing that a seven-year period of separation—while Russia was bled by the Revolution and Europe was wasted by war—had seen the evolution of similar

El Lissitzky, preparatory art for the first cover of *Veshch* ("Object"), 1921–22. Lissitzky often constructed his designs on a dynamic axis with asymmetric balance. Weight is often moved high on the page, and letterforms are constructed of geometric elements. Note the different letterform styles drawn for each of the three titles. *Van Abbemuseum, Eindhoven, Holland.*

El Lissitzky, title page for *Veshch* ("Object"), 1922. In this page layout, Lissitzky is groping for an organizational system of geometric structure and a way to treat type, geometric elements, and photographic images as elements in an organizational whole. He rapidly realized these goals during the following two years.

movements in art and design, Lissitzky and Ehrenburg saw *Veshch* as a meeting point for the new art and design of different nations. Also, Lissitzky's Berlin period enabled him to spread the message of Russian Constructivism through his frequent Bauhaus visits, important articles, and lectures. Major collaborations included the joint design and editing of a special double issue of *Merz* with Kurt Schwitters in 1924. The editors of *Broom,* a radical American magazine covering advanced literature and art, commissioned title pages and other graphics from Lissitzky. Advertisements and displays were commissioned by the Pelikan Ink Company.

As a graphic designer, Lissitzky did not decorate the book—he constructed the book by visually programming the total object. In *For the Voice,* a 1923 book of Vladimir Mayakovsky's poems, Lissitzky designed exclusively with typographic elements. Visual relationships and contrasts of elements, the relationship of forms to the negative space of the page, and an understanding of printing possibilities such as overlapping color were important in this work.

El Lissitzky, exploratory design for the *Veshch* ("Object") cover, 1921–22. Perhaps Lissitzky abandoned this concept because he felt that it was not achieving the unity of form that he sought in his graphic designs. *Van Abbemuseum, Eindhoven, Holland.*

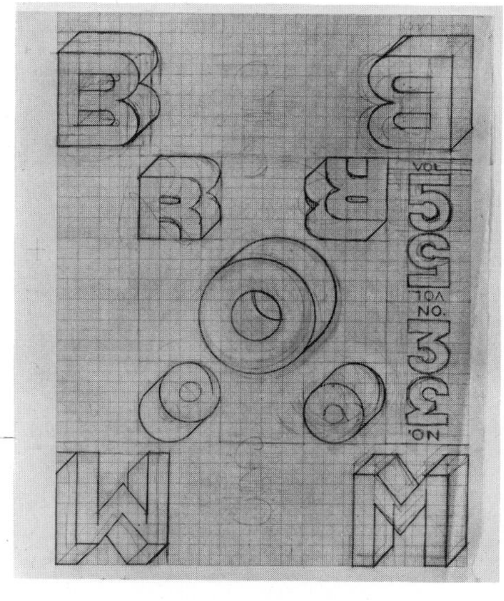

El Lissitzky, layout for a *Broom* cover, vol. 5, no. 3, 1922. By making his isometric perspective letterforms upside-down and backwards in the second presentation of the title, Lissitzky brings a subtle vitality to a rigorously symmetrical design. *Van Abbemuseum, Eindhoven, Holland.*

El Lissitzky, advertisement for Pelikan carbon paper, 1924. Typewriter type, the manufacturer's signature, and stamped letters expressive of the product's use combine with overlapping planes that relate to the sandwiching of material to produce a business letter with carbons.

El Lissitzky, poster for Pelikan Ink, 1924. This photogram was produced in the darkroom by composing the objects directly on the photographic paper, then making the exposure by flashing a light held to the left.

El Lissitzky, cover of *For the Voice* by Mayakovsky, 1923. In contrast to the *Veshch* cover, constructed on a diagonal axis, a rigid right angle is animated by the counterbalance of the *M* and circles.

Lissitzky pushed the potential of montage and photomontage for complex communications messages. Print composition and photographic images were used as building material to assemble pages, covers and posters.

One of the most influential graphic designs of the 1920s is the book, *The Isms of Art 1914–1924,* which Lissitzky edited with the Dadaist Hans Arp. The format that Lissitzky developed for this book is an important step toward the creation of a visual program, for organizing information. The three-column vertical grid structure used for the text, the three-column horizontal grid structure used for the title page, and the two-column structure of the contents page became an architectural framework for organizing the illustrated pages. Also, the way sans-serif typography and bars are handled is an early expression of the modernist style.

In 1923 he began an eighteen-year battle with tuberculosis. After returning to Russia in 1925, Lissitzky spent increasing amounts of time with large exhibition projects for the Soviet government in addition to publications, art direction, and some architectural design projects. In December 1941, six months after Germany invaded Russia, Lissitzky died. Through his social responsibility and commitment to his people, his mastery of technology to serve his goals, and his creative vision, El Lissitzky set a standard of excellence for the designer.

Alexander Rodchenko was an ardent Communist who brought an inventive spirit and willingness to experiment to typography, montage, and photography. His early interest in descriptive geometry led to an analytical precision and definition of form in his paintings. In 1921, Rodchenko abandoned painting and turned to visual communication, because his social views created a

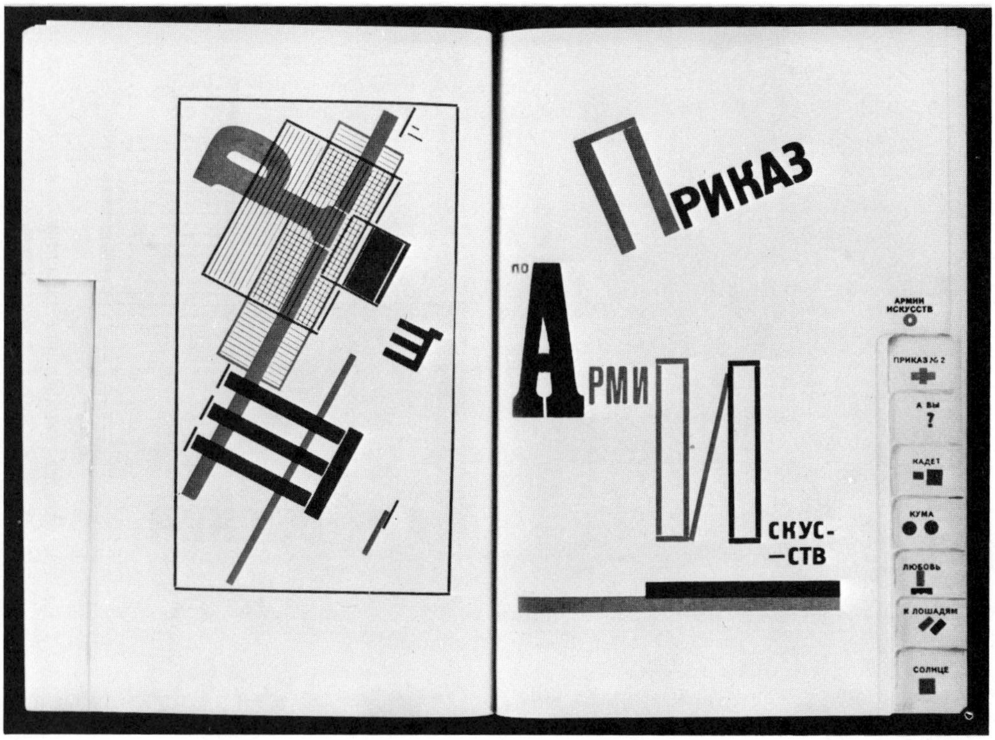

El Lissitzky, book cover for *The Isms of Art,* 1924. A complex group of typographic information is organized into a cohesive whole by the construction of structural relationships.

El Lissitzky, pages from *For the Voice* by Mayakovsky, 1923. An index of diecut tabs along the right-hand margin is used to make it easy for the reader to find a poem.

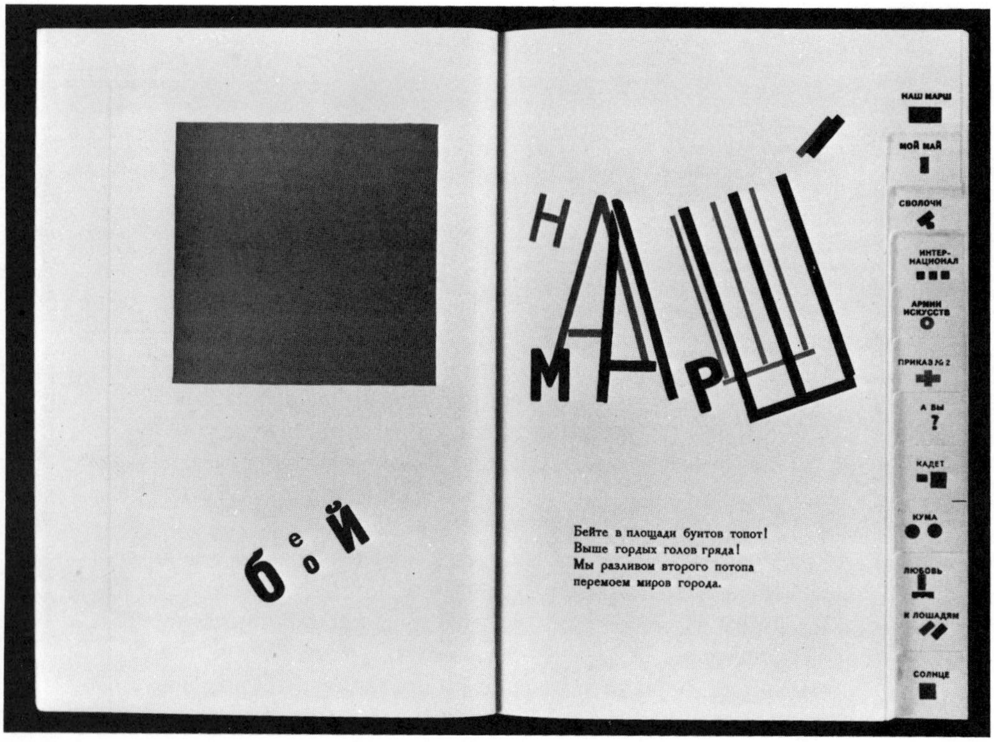

III

DIE KUNSTISMEN

HERAUSGEGEBEN VON EL LISSITZKY
UND HANS ARP

1924 1923 1922 1921 1920 1919 1918 1917 1916 1915 1914

LES ISMES DE L'ART

PUBLIÉS PAR EL LISSITZKY
ET HANS ARP

1924 1923 1922 1921 1920 1919 1918 1917 1916 1915 1914

THE ISMS OF ART

PUBLISHED BY EL LISSITZKY
AND HANS ARP

1924 1923 1922 1921 1920 1919 1918 1917 1916 1915 1914

EUGEN RENTSCH VERLAG
ERLENBACH-ZÜRICH, MÜNCHEN UND LEIPZIG
1925

El Lissitzky, pages from *For the Voice* by Mayakovsky, 1923. Using only the images and forms found in the typesetter's case, Lissitzky tried to interpret the poems in the same way "a violin accompanies a piano."

El Lissitzky, title page for *The Isms of Art,* 1924. The graphic spirit achieved by medium weight sans-serif type, mathematical division of the space, white areas, and the bold rules established a typographic standard for the modern movement.

sense of responsibility to larger society instead of to personal expression. Collaborating closely with the gifted writer, Mayakovsky, Rodchenko produced graphic designs with strong geometric construction, large areas of pure color, and concise legible lettering. His heavy sans-serif handlettering became the source for the bold sans-serif types that are widely used in the Soviet Union.

In 1923, Rodchenko began to design a magazine for all fields of the creative arts entitled *Novyi lef* (''Left front of the Arts''). A design style based on strong, static horizontal and vertical forms placed in machine-rhythm relationships emerged. Overprinting, kiss registration, and photomontage were regularly employed in *Novyi lef.* Rodchenko delighted in contrasting bold, blocky type and hard-edge shapes against the softer forms and edges of photomon-

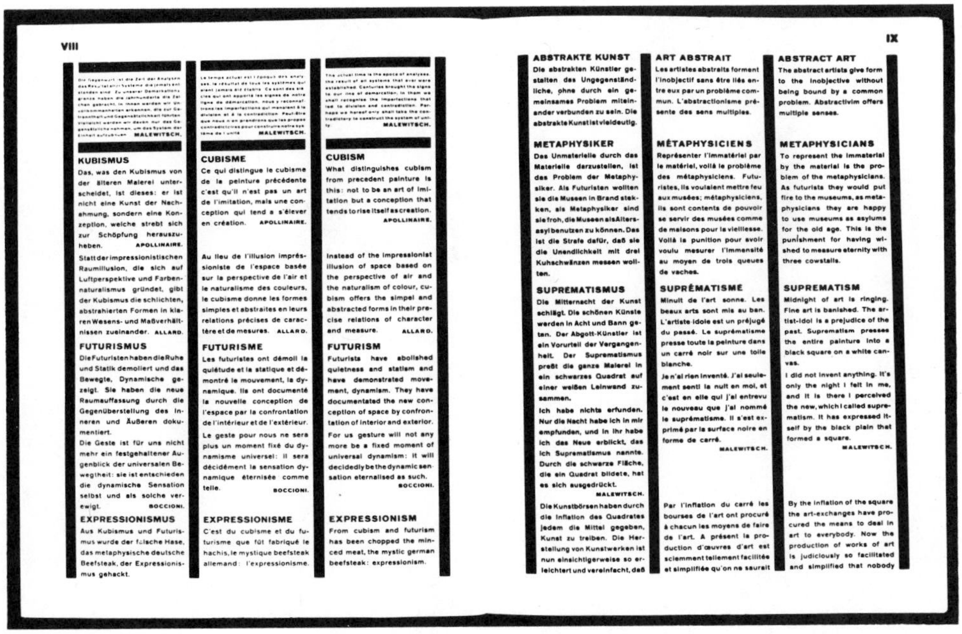

El Lissitzky, text format for *The Isms of Art,* 1924. The rigorous verticals separate the German, French, and English texts. The horizontal bars around the statement of the left hand page serve to emphasize this important introductory quotation.

El Lissitzky, exhibition poster, 1929. In this stark, powerful image, the youth of a collective society are cloned into an anonymous double portrait. They hover over the exhibition structure designed by Lissitzky. The image gives equal stature to the female portrait. In a formerly male dominant society, this is a significant symbolic communication.

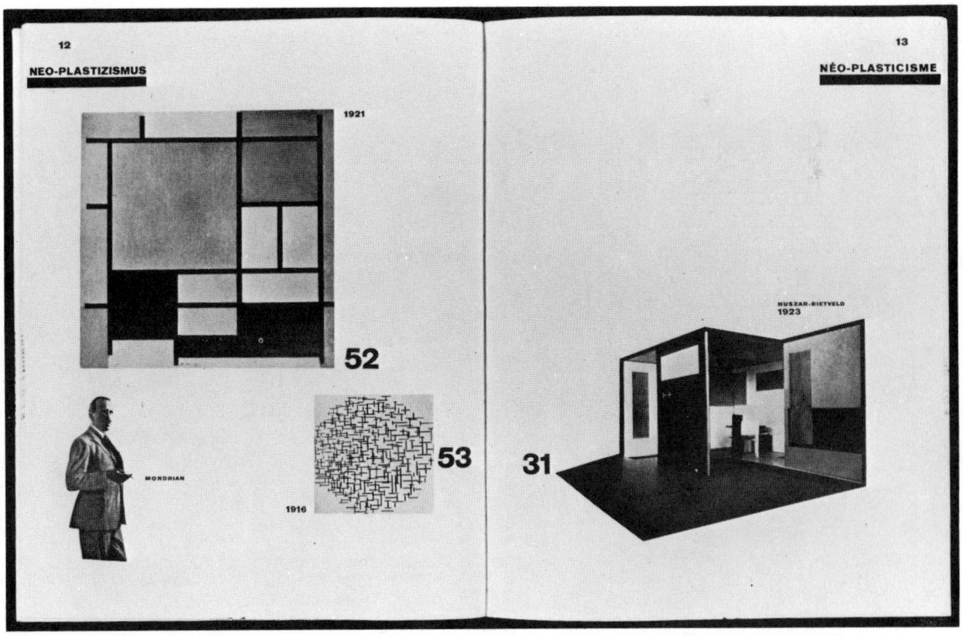

El Lissitzky, pictorial spread from *The Isms of Art,* 1924. In the forty-eight-page pictorial portfolio, the grid systems of the preceding typographic pages are echoed in the placement of the images. Asymmetrical balance, silhouette halftones, and a sensitive feeling for white space are other important design considerations. By using large bold sans-serif numbers to identify the pictures to the captions listed earlier, Lissitzky allows them to become compositional elements and expresses an attitude about number and letter as concrete form as well as verbal signal—an attitude adopted by many later twentieth-century graphic designers.

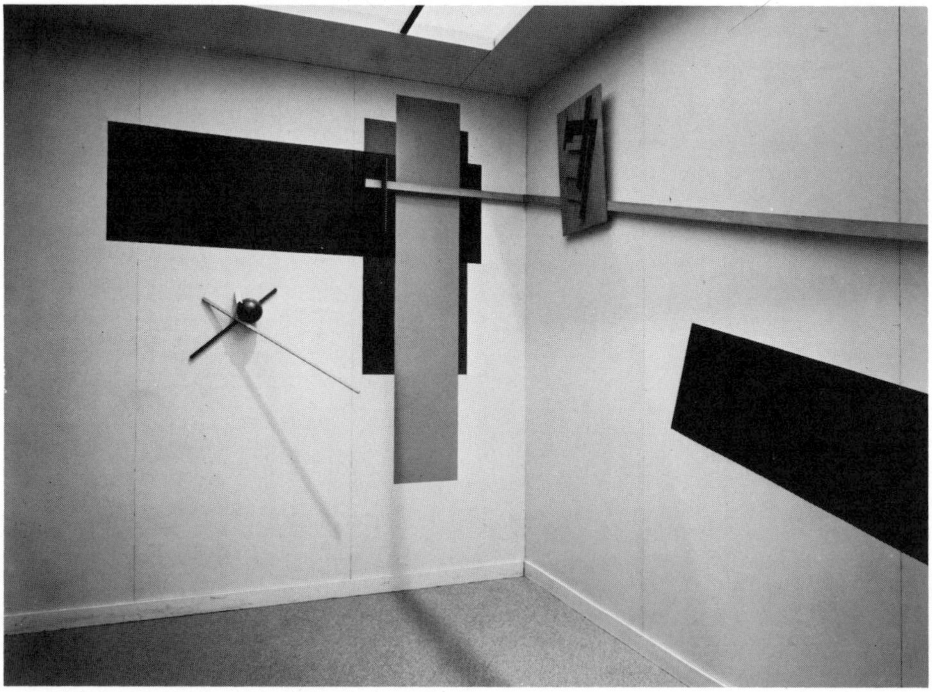

El Lissitzky, reconstruction of the 1923 PROUN room. The art of constructed relationships was transformed into the prototype of the "total environmental art experience." *Collection Van Abbemuseum, Eindhoven, Holland. Photograph courtesy of The Hirshhorn Museum, Washington, D.C.*

Alexander Rodchenko, cover for *Novyi lef* no. 1, 1923. Five thousand copies of this magazine, *Left Front of the Arts,* were printed. The logo was printed in kiss registration with the top half of the letterforms red and the bottom half black.

El Lissitzky, exhibition design for Pressa, 1928. Light, sound, and movement became design elements in Lissitzky's later exhibitions. In this example, the belts symbolic of web printing were in continuous movement.

Alexander Rodchenko, cover for *Novyi lef* no. 2, 1923. This magazine cover is one of Rodchenko's early efforts to forge a new illustration technique using photomontage. A red cross-out overprinting the montage negates the old order; young children emerging above the circle containing an old capitalist symbolize the new society. *Alma H. Law Collection, New York, N.Y.*

Alexander Rodchenko, cover for *Novyi lef* no. 3, 1923. Using a fountain pen as a bomb, a biplane bearing the magazine logo assaults a gorilla representing the old traditional arts of the Czarist regime. *Alma H. Law Collection, New York, N.Y.*

tages. His interest in photomontage was a conscious effort to innovate a new illustration technique appropriate to the twentieth-century rationalist era. The beginning of Russian photomontage coincided with the development of montage in film—a new conceptual approach to assembling cinematic information—and shared some of its vocabulary. Showing simultaneous action; superimposing images; using extreme closeups and perspective images, often together; and rhythmic repetition of an image: these are some of the common techniques. The concept of serial painting—a series or sequence of independent works unified by common elements or an underlying structure—was applied to graphic design by Rodchenko. In 1924, his series of ten covers for the Jim Dollar *Mess Mend* books used a standard, geometric format printed in black and a second color. The title, number, and photomontage elements changed with each edition and express the unique content of each book. The standardized elements bring consistency and economy to the whole series. Each design did not have to be developed from ground zero.

Georgy (1900–1933) and Vladimir (b. 1900) Stenberg were talented brothers who collaborated on theatrical designs and film posters. Mindful of the reproduction difficulties with photographs at the time, they made meticulously realistic drawings for their posters by enlarging film-frame images using projection and grid methods. These three-dimensional illusions were contrasted with flat forms in dynamic, well-designed posters with strong graphic communications qualities.

During the early years after the 1917 Revolution, the Soviet government tolerated the advanced art while more urgent problems commanded its attention. But by 1922 the government, having turned hostile, accused advanced artists of "capitalist cosmopolitanism" and advocated social realist painting. Although Constructivism lingered as an influence in Soviet graphic and industrial design, painters like Malevich who did not leave the country drifted into poverty and obscurity. Some artists vanished into the Gulag. The innovations of this artistic flowering had their further development in the West. Such is the nature of the creative spirit, however, that in spite of strong official disapproval innovative graphic design in the Constructivist tradition continued to appear from time to time. Such an example is the work of S. Telingater (1903–1969). A dash of Dada randomness was often mixed into his Constructivist designs, and a witty originality informed his use of typography and montage elements.

Alexander Rodchenko, photomontage of V. I. Lenin, 1937. Lenin looms above the crowd as a larger-than-life father figure, yet his hand makes symbolic contact with the masses. The "podium" is a *Pravda* newspaper whose headline proclaims "Peace! Bread! Land!" *Museum of Modern Art, Oxford, England.*

Alexander Rodchenko, paperback book covers, 1924. The series of ten covers for Jim Dollar ''Mess Mend'' books used a standard geometric format printed in black and a second color. The title, number, and photomontage elements changed. Consistency was achieved through standardization; the uniqueness of each book was expressed. *Ex Libris, New York.*

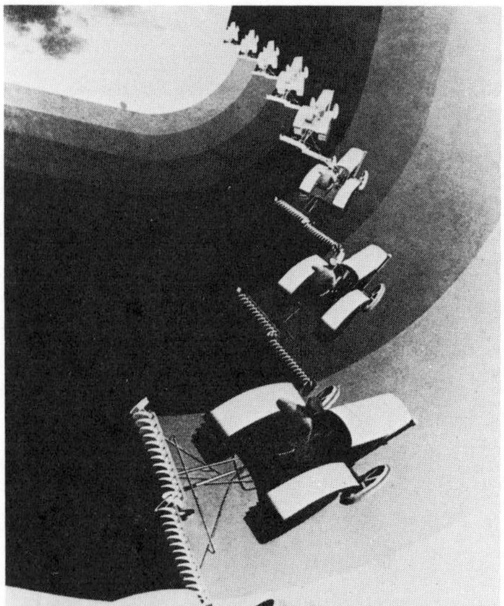

Georgy and Vladimir Stenberg, *To the Fallow Ground,* poster, 1928. Geometric archs combine with meticulous pencil drawings of tractors drawn from above. Agricultural productivity is symbolized.

S. Telingater, covers for *Slovo Predstaliaetsia Kirsanovu* (''The Word Belongs to Kirsanov'') by K. Kirsanov, 1930. The author's whimsy is reflected in Telingater's rollicking typography that changes tune, tempo, and key as it flows down the page. *Ex Libris, New York.*

The De Stijl *movement*

The late summer of 1917 marked the formation of the *De Stijl* movement and journal in the Netherlands. The painters Piet Mondrian (1872–1944) and Bart van der Leck (1876–1958), the architect J. J. P. Oud (1890–1963), and others joined the founder and guiding spirit, Théo van Doesburg (1883–1931) in this group. Of the members, van der Leck appears to have been the first to paint flat, geometric shapes of pure color. In addition, van der Leck was creating graphic designs with simple black bars organizing the space and using flat shaped images before the movement formed.

Mondrian's paintings are the wellspring from which *De Stijl's* philosophy and visual forms developed. Mondrian had evolved from traditional landscape painting to a symbolic style, influenced by Van Gogh, that expressed the forces of nature, when he first saw Cubist paintings in 1910. Over the next few years, Mondrian purged his art of all representative elements and evolved Cubism into a pure, geometric abstraction. He felt that the Cubists had not accepted the logical consequences of its discoveries; this was the evolution of abstraction toward its ultimate goal, the expression of pure reality. By 1917, Mondrian had reduced his visual vocabulary to the use of primary colors (red, yellow, and blue) with black and white, and shapes and forms were limited to straight lines, squares, and rectangles. Using these limited means, Mondrian constructed compositions of heroic asymmetric balance in which tension and balance of the elements reached an absolute harmony.

Mondrian believed that, in visual art, true reality "is attained through dynamic movement in equilibrium. Plastic art affirms that equilibrium can only be established through the balance of unequal but equivalent oppositions. The clarification of equilibrium through plastic art is of great importance for humanity . . . It is the task of art to express a clear vision of reality."

For a time, in 1917, paintings by Mondrian, van der Leck, and van Doesburg were virtually indistinguishable. In addition to the restricted visual vocabulary, the *De Stijl* artists sought an expression of the mathematical structure of the universe and the universal harmony of nature. They were deeply concerned with the spiritual and intellectual climate of their time and wished to express the "general consciousness of their age." They believed that the world war was sweeping away an old age. Science, technology, and political developments would usher in a new era of objectivity and collectivism. This attitude was "in the air" in Europe during World War I as philosophers, scientists, and artists realized that prewar values had lost their relevance. *De Stijl* sought the universal laws which govern visible

Théo van Doesburg, *Composition XI,* 1918. In the careful balancing of rectangles of primary color on a white field, a purity of form and visual harmony is achieved with an economy of means. The implications for modern design were staggering. *Collection The Solomon R. Guggenheim Museum, New York, photograph by Robert E. Mates.*

reality but are hidden by the outward appearance of things. Scientific theory, mechanical production, and the rhythms of the modern city formed from these universal laws.

In the Dutch language *schoon* means both pure and beautiful. For the *De Stijl* artists, beauty arises from the absolute purity of the work. Thus, the purification of art from representing the natural world, from a dependence on external values, and from the individual's subjective whims became paramount. The content of their work then became universal harmony, the order that pervades throughout the universe.

The modest journal, *De Stijl,* was edited by Théo van Doesburg from 1917 until his death in 1931. Primarily funded with his own limited funds, this publication spread the theory and philosophy of the movement to a larger audience. *De Stijl* advocated the absorption of pure art by applied art. The spirit of art could then permeate society through architecture, product and graphic design. Art

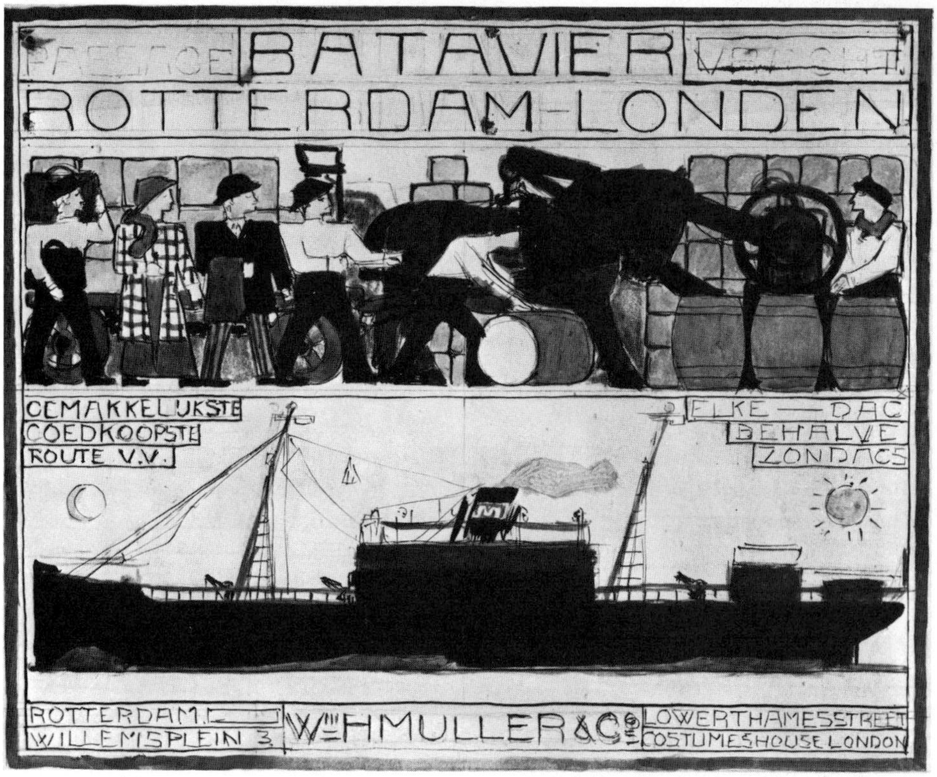

Bart van der Leck, layout for Batavier Line poster, 1915–16. In a series of layouts for this poster, van der Leck struggled to bring order to the design by dividing the space into rectangles. *Collection Rijksmuseum Kröller-Müller, Otterlo, Holland.*

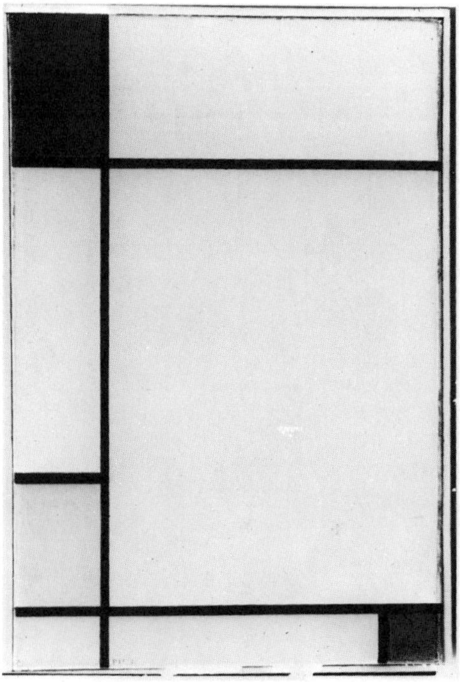

Piet Mondrian, *Composition in Red, Yellow, and Blue,* 1931. The search for universal harmony became the subject, and the concrete presence of painted form on canvas became the vehicle for expressing a new plastic reality. *Stedelijk Museum, Amsterdam.*

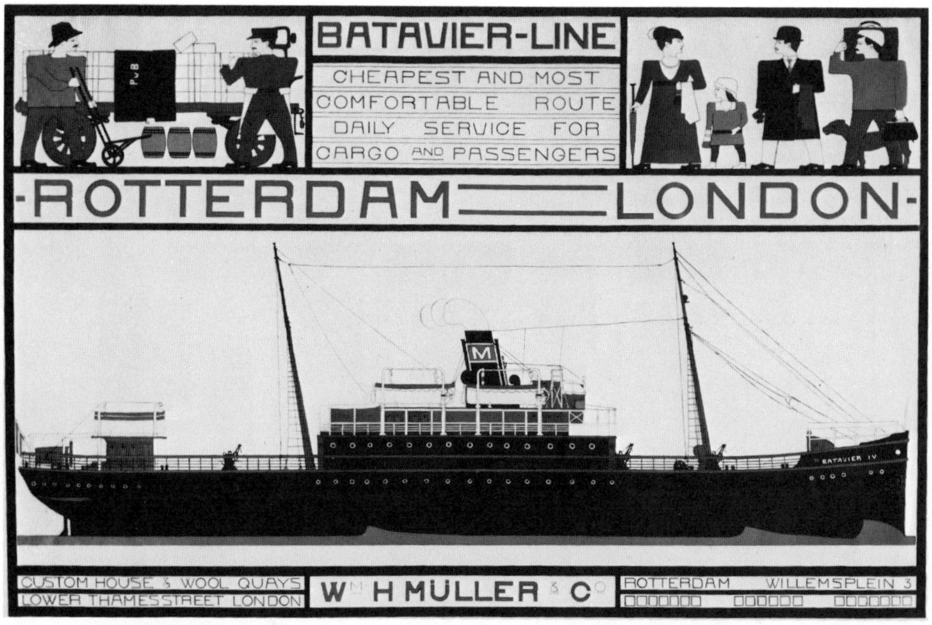

Bart van der Leck, poster for the Batavier Line, 1916. Flat shapes, heavy black lines dividing the space into boxes, and geometric sans-serif lettering all suggest that this might show the influence of de Stijl upon the poster. Only, van der Leck designed this poster one year before De Stijl was formed. *Collection Rijksmuseum Kröller-Müller, Otterlo, Holland.*

Vilmos Huszar, cover design for *De Stijl,* 1917. Van Doesburg designed this logo whose letters are constructed from an open grid of squares and rectangles, and Huszar combined it with his composition and type to create a concise rectangle in the center of the page. *Courtesy of Athenaeum-Polak & Van Gennep, Amsterdam.*

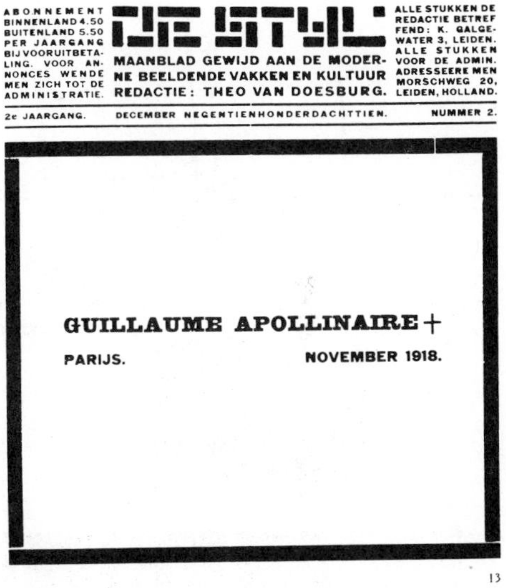

Vilmos Huszar, title pages for *De Stijl,* 1918. Huszar presented a beautiful study of positive and negative figure-ground spatial relationships and used restrained typography in the issue marking the death of Apollinaire. *Courtesy of Athenaeum-Polak & Van Gennep, Amsterdam.*

would not be subjugated to the level of the everyday object; the everyday object (and, through it, everyday life) would be elevated to the level of art. Beginning in the early 1920s, *De Stijl's* impact on architecture, industrial design, and typography began.

While Mondrian produced a body of paintings of incomparable spiritual and formal quality, van Doesburg's activities expanded to include architecture, sculpture, and typography. In 1921, van Doesburg moved to Weimar, Germany. Until 1923 he lived there and taught courses in *De Stijl* philosophy that were primarily attended by students from the Bauhaus.

Comprehending the liberating potential of Dada, van Doesburg invited Kurt Schwitters to Holland to campaign for Dada. They collaborated on typographic design projects, and van Doesburg began to explore Dada typography and poetry. In 1922, he convened an International Congress of Constructivists and Dadaists in Weimar. One of the Constructivists attending was El Lissitzky, who designed an issue of *De Stijl*.

The year 1924 marked the realization of *De Stijl* theory in architecture when Gerrit Rietveld designed the celebrated Schroeder house in Utrecht. The next year, Oud designed the Rotterdam cafe that became another architectural landmark.

In the typographic designs of van Doesburg and Vilmos Huszar (1884–1960), curved lines were eliminated and sans-serif typography was favored. Type was often composed in tight rectangular blocks. Asymmetrically balanced layouts were composed on an open implied grid. Red was favored as a second color in printing because of its graphic power to compete with black.

Théo van Doesburg, *An Alphabet,* 1919. This design uses the square as a rigorous module for the alphabet. A harmony of form is achieved. The banishing of curved and diagonal lines diminishes character uniqueness and legibility.

Théo van Doesburg, cover design for *Mecano,* no. 3, 1922. Under the pseudonymn I. K. Bonset, van Doesburg published experimental poetry and typography.

Théo van Doesburg, exhibition poster, 1920. Original lettering was executed in ink for reproduction to promote an international exhibition—*La Section d'Or, Cubists and Neo-Cubists.*

El Lissitzky's widow wrote years later that, during this period, periodicals sprouted like mushrooms, and like mushrooms they often had only a short existence. One such advanced publication was *i10*, edited by Arthur Lehning and published from January 1927 until July 1929. The title was chosen because publication began shortly before the tenth international. In *i10,* the *De Stijl* and Bauhaus ideals of integrating art with daily life were embraced. Realizing that social and cultural changes were necessary if this idealized vision was to come to fruition, Lehning expanded the content to include political material. The layout for the first issue was created by the Hungarian Constructivist Laszlo Moholy-Nagy (1895–1946), who then gave Lehning a crash course in typography and layout so that the

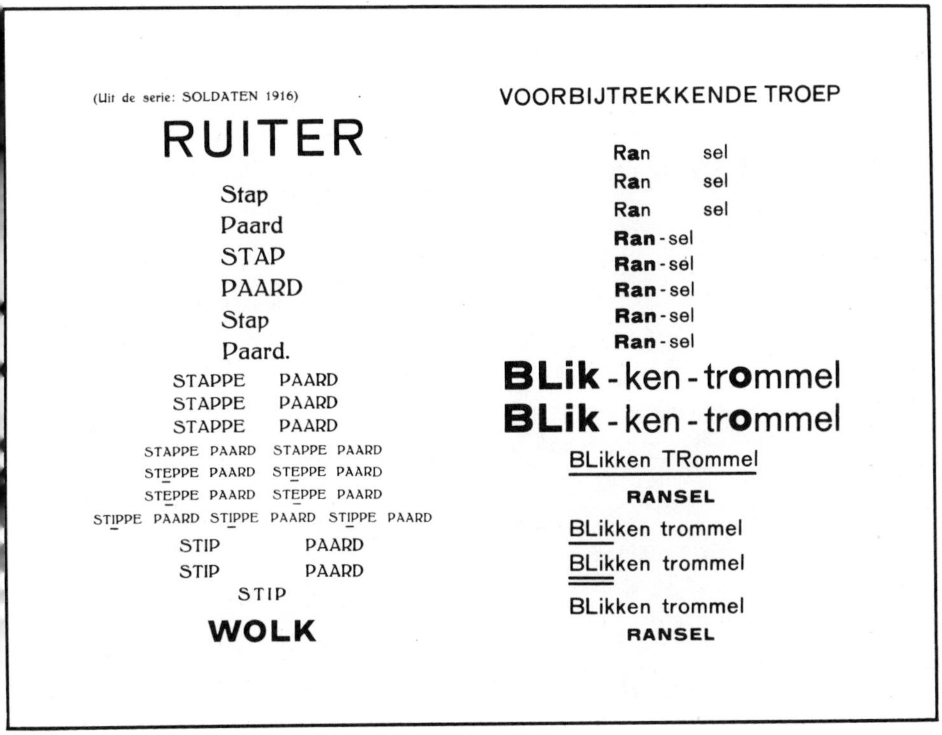

(Uit de serie: SOLDATEN 1916)

STAPPE PAARD
STAPPE PAARD
STAPPE PAARD
STAPPE PAARD STAPPE PAARD
STEPPE PAARD STEPPE PAARD
STEPPE PAARD STEPPE PAARD
STIPPE PAARD STIPPE PAARD STIPPE PAARD
STIP PAARD
STIP PAARD

VOORBIJTREKKENDE TROEP

BLik-ken-trommel
BLik-ken-trommel
BLikken TRommel

BLikken trommel
BLikken trommel
BLikken trommel

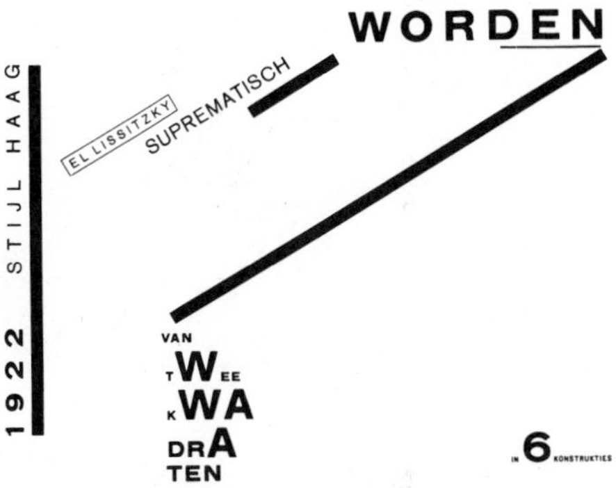

El Lissitzky, cover and page from *De Stijl,* 1922. van Doesburg invited Lissitzky to design and edit a double issue of *De Stijl* that reprinted "A Tale of Two Squares" in a Dutch version. *Courtesy of Athenaeum-Polak & Van Gennep, Amsterdam.*

DE STIJL
MAANDBLAD VOOR NIEUWE KUNST, WETENSCHAP EN KULTUUR. REDACTIE: THEO VAN DOESBURG. ABONNEMENT BINNENLAND F 6.-, BUITENLAND F 7.50 PER JAARGANG. ADRES VAN REDACTIE EN ADMINISTR. HAARLEMMERSTRAAT 73A LEIDEN (HOLLAND).
4e JAARGANG No. 11. NOVEMBER 1921.
LETTERKLANKBEELDEN (1921)
IV (in dissonanten)
X-Beelden (1920)
hé hé hé
hebt gij 't lichaamlijk ervaren
hebt gij 't lichaamlijk ervaren
hebt gij 't li CHAAM lijk er VA ren
— ruimte en
— tijd
verleden heden toekomst
het achterhierenginds
het doorelkaâr van 't niet en de verschijning
kleine verfrommelde almanak
die men ondersteboven leest
MIJN KLOK STAAT STIL
ZIG-ZAG
uitgekauwd sigaretteeindje op't
WITTE SERVET
vochtig bruin
ontbinding
GEEST
346
VRACHT AU TO MO BIEL
DWARS
trillend onvruchtbaar middelpunt
caricatuur der zwaarte
uomo electrico
rose en grauw en diep wijnrood
de scherven van de kosmos vind ik in m'n thee

Théo van Doesburg, Dada poetry from *De Stijl,* 1921. The size, weight, and style of type became part of the message. *Courtesy of Athenaeum-Polak & Van Gennep, Amsterdam.*

editor could handle this aspect of the publication. César Domela (b. 1900) assisted Moholy-Nagy with the cover design. (In 1980 Arthur Lehning stated that although this design has often been attributed to Domela, his recent discovery of Moholy-Nagy's layouts for the cover indicated major responsibility for this design should be credited to Moholy-Nagy.) It is one of the purest examples of *De Stijl* principles applied to typography. The printer was terribly upset by the complete disregard for the rules of typography by Moholy-Nagy and Domela, but eventually he came to understand and appreciate the design.

Because van Doesburg, with his phenomenal energy and wide ranging creativity, *was* the *De Stijl* movement, it is understandable that *De Stijl* as an organized movement did not survive

Gerrit Rietveld, the Schroeder House, Utrecht, 1924. The application of *De Stijl* principles to domestic architecture was so radical in 1924 that neighbors threw rocks. Classmates taunted the Schroeder children at school after the family moved into their new home. In the dining room photograph, note the use of industrial radiators, predating the integration of industrial equipment in domestic interiors (the high tech movement of the late 1970s) by a half century. *Courtesy, Stedelijk Museum, Amsterdam.*

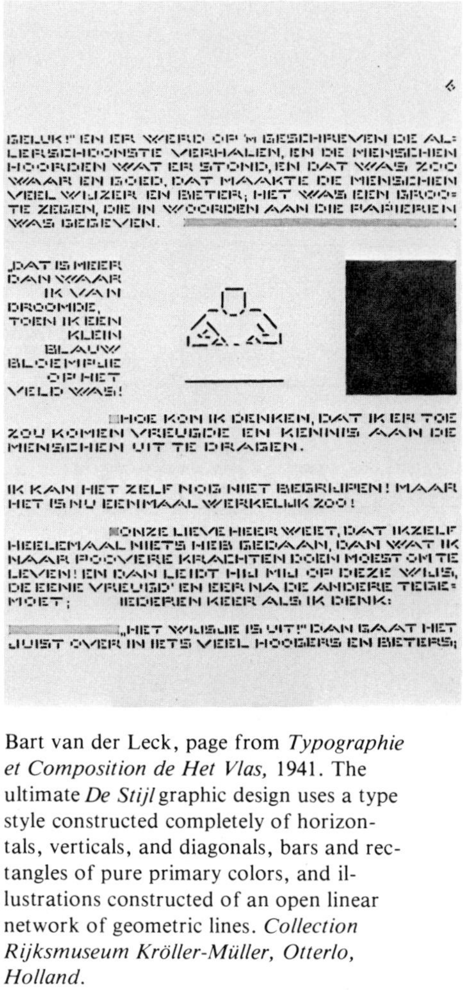

6

GELUK!" EN ER WERD OP 'M GESCHREVEN DE ALLERSCHOONSTE VERHALEN, EN DE MENSCHEN HOORDEN WAT ER STOND, EN DAT WAS ZOO WAAR EN GOED, DAT MAAKTE DE MENSCHEN VEEL WIJZER EN BETER; HET WAS EEN GROOTE ZEGEN, DIE IN WOORDEN AAN DIE PAPIEREN WAS GEGEVEN.

„DAT IS MEER DAN WAAR IK VAN DROOMDE, TOEN IK EEN KLEIN BLAUW BLOEMPJE OP HET VELD WAS!

HOE KON IK DENKEN, DAT IK ER TOE ZOU KOMEN VREUGDE EN KENNIS AAN DE MENSCHEN UIT TE DRAGEN.

IK KAN HET ZELF NOG NIET BEGRIJPEN! MAAR HET IS NU EENMAAL WERKELIJK ZOO!

ONZE LIEVE HEER WEET, DAT IKZELF HEELEMAAL NIETS HEB GEDAAN, DAN WAT IK NAAR POOVERE KRACHTEN DOEN MOEST OM TE LEVEN! EN DAN LEIDT HIJ MIJ OP DEZE WIJS, DE EENE VREUGD' EN EER NA DE ANDERE TEGEMOET; IEDEREN KEER ALS IK DENK:

„HET WIJSJE IS UIT!" DAN GAAT HET JUIST OVER IN IETS VEEL HOOGERS EN BETERS;

Bart van der Leck, page from *Typographie et Composition de Het Vlas,* 1941. The ultimate *De Stijl* graphic design uses a type style constructed completely of horizontals, verticals, and diagonals, bars and rectangles of pure primary colors, and illustrations constructed of an open linear network of geometric lines. *Collection Rijksmuseum Kröller-Müller, Otterlo, Holland.*

his untimely death in 1931 at age forty-seven. Mondrian had stopped contributing articles to the journal in 1924, after van Doesburg developed his theory of Elementarism which declared the diagonal to be a more dynamic compositional principle than horizontal and vertical construction.

The quest for a pure art of visual relationships that began in Holland and Russia has remained a major concern in the visual disciplines during the twentieth century. One of the dominant directions of graphic design has been the application of this geometric sensibility to bring order to the printed page.

Malevich and Mondrian used pure line, shape, and color to create a universe of harmoniously ordered, pure relationships. This was seen as a visionary prototype for a new world order. Mondrian wrote that art would "disappear in proportion as life gains in equilibrium." To unify social and human values, technology, and visual form became a goal for those who strived for a new architecture and graphic design.

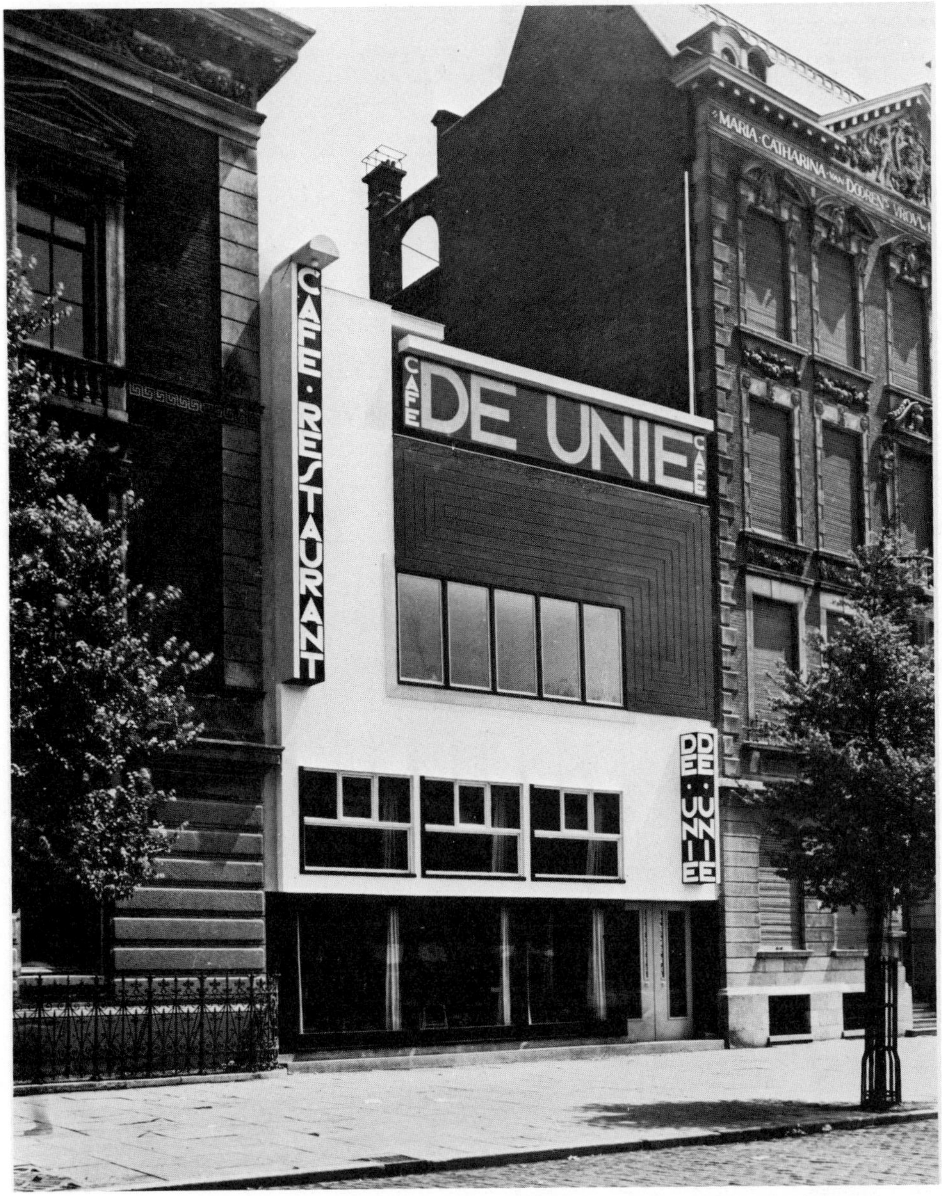

J. J. P. Oud, facade of the Café de Unie, Rotterdam, 1925. De Stijl's vision of order on an environmental scale is realized. Oud successfully resolved problems of structure, signage and identification. Architectural and graphic forms of contrasting value and scale are ordered into a harmonious balance. *Architectuur Museum, Amsterdam.*

Théo van Doesburg, advertisements and announcements from *De Stijl,* 1921. Five messages are unified by a system of open bars and sans-serif typography. *Courtesy of Athenaeum-Polak & Van Gennep, Amsterdam.*

i10
AMSTERDAM 1927
KANDINSKY
TOLSTOI
FILM
UTOPIE
SYNTHETISCHE KUNST
NIEUWE PHILOSOPHIE
GEEST EN TECHNIEK
MODERNE STAD
ARCHITECTUUR
MUZIEK
ARCHITECTUUR
TROTSKY
REPRODUCTIES
BEHNE
BIROEKOFF
TER BRAAK
BLOCH
KANDINSKY
DE LIGT
MOHOLY-NAGY
MONDRIAAN
OUD
PIJPER
VAN RAVESTEYN
ROLAND HOLST
1/1

Laszlo Moholy-Nagy, cover design for *i10,* 1927. Typography becomes concrete form and texture used with shape, line and measured interval in an asymmetrical balance that has clarity of communication and harmony of form.

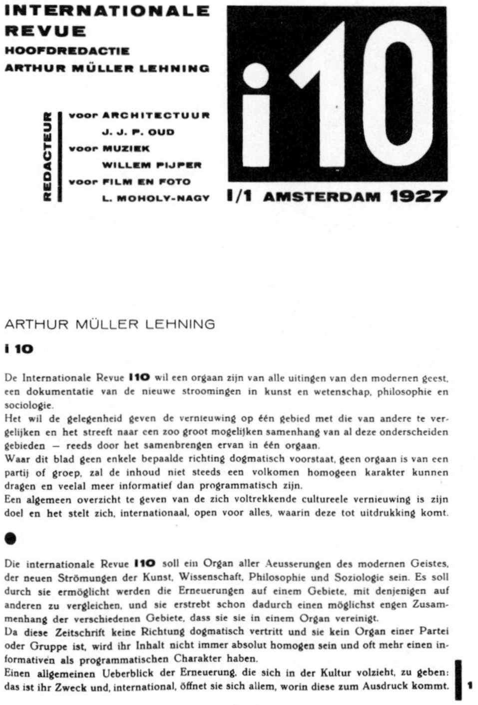

INTERNATIONALE REVUE
HOOFDREDACTIE
ARTHUR MÜLLER LEHNING

REDACTEUR
voor ARCHITECTUUR J. J. P. OUD
voor MUZIEK WILLEM PIJPER
voor FILM EN FOTO L. MOHOLY-NAGY

i10
I/1 AMSTERDAM 1927

ARTHUR MÜLLER LEHNING

i 10

De Internationale Revue **I10** wil een orgaan zijn van alle uitingen van den modernen geest, een dokumentatie van de nieuwe stroomingen in kunst en wetenschap, philosophie en sociologie.
Het wil de gelegenheid geven de vernieuwing op één gebied met die van andere te vergelijken en het streeft naar een zoo groot mogelijken samenhang van al deze onderscheiden gebieden — reeds door het samenbrengen ervan in één orgaan.
Waar dit blad geen enkele bepaalde richting dogmatisch voorstaat, geen orgaan is van een partij of groep, zal de inhoud niet steeds een volkomen homogeen karakter kunnen dragen en veelal meer informatief dan programmatisch zijn.
Een algemeen overzicht te geven van de zich voltrekkende cultureele vernieuwing is zijn doel en het stelt zich, internationaal, open voor alles, waarin deze tot uitdrukking komt.

●

Die internationale Revue **I10** soll ein Organ aller Aeusserungen des modernen Geistes, der neuen Strömungen der Kunst, Wissenschaft, Philosophie und Soziologie sein. Es soll durch sie ermöglicht werden die Erneuerungen auf einem Gebiete, mit denjenigen auf anderen zu vergleichen, und sie erstrebt schon dadurch einen möglichst engen Zusammenhang der verschiedenen Gebiete, dass sie sie in einem Organ vereinigt.
Da diese Zeitschrift keine Richtung dogmatisch vertritt und sie kein Organ einer Partei oder Gruppe ist, wird ihr Inhalt nicht immer absolut homogen sein und oft mehr einen informativen als programmatischen Charakter haben.
Einen allgemeinen Ueberblick der Erneuerung, die sich in der Kultur volzieht, zu geben: das ist ihr Zweck und, international, öffnet sie sich allem, worin diese zum Ausdruck kommt.

1

Laszlo Moholy-Nagy, title page for *i10,* 1927. Words running vertically, bold sans-serif type, set into Old Style text for emphasis, bullets for emphasis and bold bars by the page numbers; these are design ideas that upset the printer.

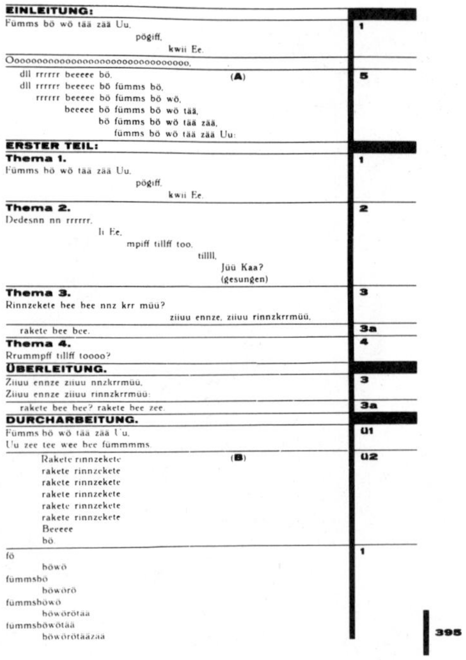

EINLEITUNG:
Fümms bö wö tää zää Uu, pögiff, kwii Ee. 1
Oooooooooooooooooooooooooooooooo,
dll rrrrrr beeeee bö. (**A**) 5
dll rrrrrr beeeee bö fümms bö,
rrrrrr beeeee bö fümms bö wö,
beeeee bö fümms bö wö tää,
bö fümms bö wö tää zää,
fümms bö wö tää zää Uu:

ERSTER TEIL:
Thema 1. 1
Fümms bö wö tää zää Uu, pögiff, kwii Ee.
Thema 2. 2
Dedesnn nn rrrrrr, Ii Ee, mpiff tillff too, tillll, Jüü Kaa? (gesungen)
Thema 3. 3
Rinnzekete bee bee nnz krr müü? ziiuu ennze, ziiuu rinnzkrrmüü,
rakete bee bee. 3a
Thema 4. 4
Rrummpff tillff toooo?

ÜBERLEITUNG.
Ziiuu ennze ziiuu nnzkrrmüü, 3
Ziiuu ennze ziiuu rinnzkrrmüü:
rakete bee bee? rakete bee zee. 3a

DURCHARBEITUNG.
Fümms bö wö tää zää Uu, U1
Uu zee tee wee bee fümmms.
Rakete rinnzekete (**B**) U2
rakete rinnzekete
rakete rinnzekete
rakete rinnzekete
rakete rinnzekete
rakete rinnzekete
Beeeee
bö.
fö 1
böwö
fümmsbö
böwörö
fümmsböwö
böwörötää
fümmsböwötää
böwörötääzää

395

Kurt Schwitters, *"Sonate in Urlauten,"* 1924 (reproduced in *i10,* 1927). This Dada poem/performance piece was packaged in a constructivist typographic format. Dada destroyed syntax and form; constructivism pointed the way to a reconstruction of the printed page.

Théo van Doesburg, cover for *De Stijl,* 1922. This format, with the logo and regular information asymmetrically balanced in the four corners of an implied rectangle, was used from 1921 until the last issue, which was published in 1932 after van Doesburg's death. Color was used, not as an afterthought or decoration, but as an important structural element. *Courtesy of Athenaeum-Polak & Van Gennep, Amsterdam.*

18

The Bauhaus and the New Typography

On the eve of World War in 1914, the Belgian Art Nouveau architect, Henri van de Velde, who directed the Weimar Arts and Crafts School, resigned his position to return to Belgium. Thirty-one-year-old Walter Gropius (1883–1969) was one of three recommendations he made to the Grand Duke of Saxe-Weimar as a possible replacement. During the war years the school was closed, and it was not until after the war that Gropius, who had already gained an international reputation for factory designs using glass and steel in new ways, was confirmed as the new director. It had been decided to merge the applied arts oriented Weimar Arts and Crafts School with a fine arts school, the Weimar Art Academy. Gropius was allowed to name the new school Das Staatliches Bauhaus, and it opened on 12 April 1919 at a time when Germany was in a state of terrible ferment. The catastrophic defeat in "the war to end all wars" led to stormy economic, political, and cultural strife. The prewar world of the Kaiser was dead, and a quest to construct a new social order pervaded all aspects of life.

The Bauhaus Manifesto, published in German newspapers, established the philosophy of the new school: "The complete building is the ultimate aim of all the visual arts. Once the noblest function of the fine arts was to embellish buildings; they were indispensable components of great architecture. Today the arts exist in isolation . . . architects, painters, and sculptors must learn anew the composite character of the building as an entity . . . The artist is an exalted craftsman. In rare moments of inspiration, transcending his conscious will, the grace of heaven may cause his work to blossom into art. But proficiency in his craft is essential to every artist. Therein lies the prime source of creative imagination."

Recognizing the common roots of both fine and applied visual arts, Gropius sought a new unity of art and technology as he enlisted a generation of artists in a struggle to solve problems of visual design created by industrialism. It was hoped that the artistically trained designer could "breathe a soul into the dead product of the machine," for Gropius believed that only the most brilliant ideas were good enough to justify multiplication by industry.

The Bauhaus was the logical consequence of a German concern for upgrading design in an industrial society that began in the opening years of the century. Architect and author Hermann Muthesius (1861–1927) played a key role in the 1907 founding of the Deutsche Werkbund in Munich. Vigorously concerned with elevating standards of design and public taste, the Werkbund attracted architects, artists, public and industry officials, educators, and critics to its ranks. While the English Arts and Crafts Movement believed that handicraft was superior to machine production, the Werkbund advocated that the differences between the two be recognized. Muthesius argued passionately for standardization and the value of the machine for design ends. He saw simplicity and exactness as being both a functional demand of machine manufacture and a symbolic aspect of twentieth-century industrial efficiency and power. The Werkbund effort attempted to forge a unity of artists and craftsmen with industry to elevate the functional and aesthetic qualities of mass production, particularly in low-cost consumer products.

Peter Behrens was a principal figure in the establishment of the Werkbund. In 1907, Gropius started his three-year assistantship in Peter Behrens' architectural office. Behrens' advocacy of a new objectivity and theories of proportion had a tremendous impact on the development of the youthful Gropius' thinking.

Henri van de Velde was also an important influence. During the 1890s, he declared that the engineer was the new architect and called for logical design using new technologies and materials of science: reinforced concrete, steel, aluminum, and linoleum.

Peter Behrens, poster for Deutsche Werkbund exhibition, 1914. Behrens called upon classical allegory to depict the designer as a torchbearer, in keeping with the Werkbund view that design was an enlightening and humanizing force in society. The subtitle reads, "Art in craft, industry and commerce . architecture." *Library of Congress, Washington, D.C., Poster Collection.*

The Bauhaus at Weimar

The Bauhaus years in Weimar (1919–24) were intensely visionary. Characterized by a utopian desire to create a new spiritual society, the early Bauhaus sought a new unity of artists and craftsmen to build for the future. Stained glass, wood, and metal workshops were taught by an artist and a craftsman and were organized along medieval *Bauhütte* lines—master, journeyman, apprentice. The Gothic cathedral represented a realization of man's longing for a spiritual beauty that went beyond utility and need, and it symbolized the integration of architecture, sculpture, painting, and crafts. Gropius was deeply interested in architecture's symbolic potential and the possibility of a universal design style as an integrated aspect of society.

Advanced ideas about form, color, and space were integrated into the design vocabulary when painters Paul Klee (1879–1940) and Wassily Kandinsky joined the staff in 1920 and 1922, respectively. Klee assimilated modern visual art with the work of primitive cultures and children, to create drawings and paintings that are charged visual communication. Kandinsky's belief in the autonomy and spiritual values of color and form had led to the courageous emancipation of his painting from the motif and representational elements. At the Bauhaus, no distinction was made between fine and applied art.

The heart of Bauhaus education was the preliminary course, initially established by Johannes Itten (1888–1967). His goals were to release each student's creative abilities, to develop an understanding of the physical nature of materials, and to teach the fundamental principles of design underlying all visual art. Itten put emphasis on visual contrasts and an analysis of Old Master paintings. Itten's methodology of direct experience sought to develop perceptual awareness, intellectual abilities, and emotional experience. In 1923 Itten left the Bauhaus because of disagreement about the conduct of this course. The Bauhaus was evolving from a concern for medievalism, expressionism, and handicraft toward more emphasis on rationalism and designing for the machine. Gropius began to consider Itten's mysticism to be an "otherworldliness" inconsistent with an emerging concern for an objective design language capable of overcoming the dangers of past styles and personal taste.

As early as the spring of 1919, Bauhaus teacher Lyonel Feininger (1871–1956) had become aware of *De Stijl* and began to make the Bauhaus community cognizant of this movement. The Bauhaus and *De Stijl* had similar aims, and in late 1920 van Doesburg moved to Weimar and established contacts with the Bauhaus. He desired a teaching position, but Gropius felt that van Doesburg was too dogmatic in its insistence on strict geometry and an impersonal style. He

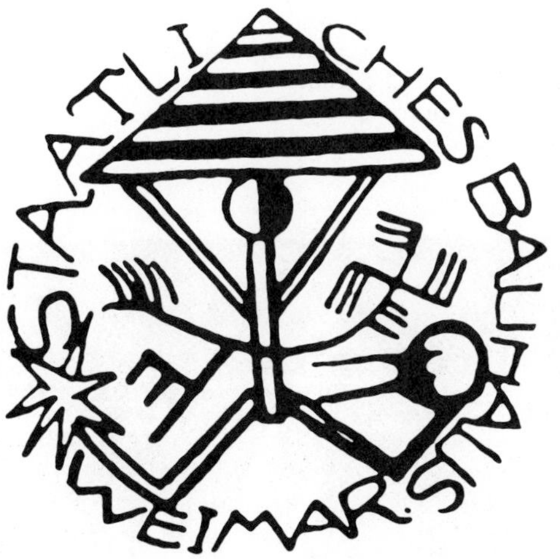

Attributed to Johannes Auerbach, first Bauhaus seal, 1919. The style and imagery of this seal expresses the medieval and craft affinities of the early Bauhaus. This design came from a student design competition.

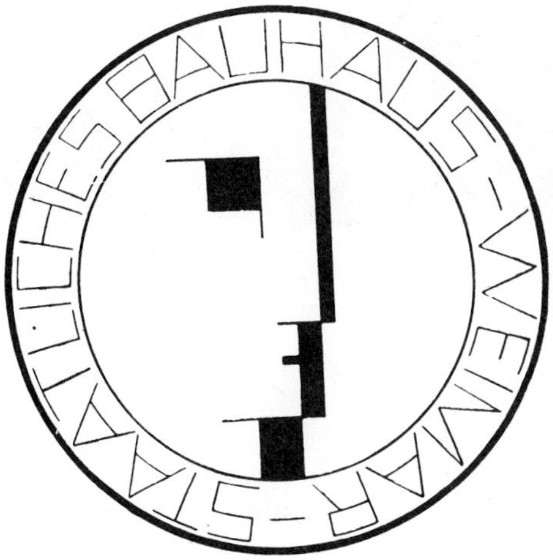

Oscar Schlemmer, later Bauhaus seal, 1922. Comparison of the two seals demonstrates how graphic designs can express ideas, for the later seal relates to the geometric style and design for mass production concepts that were emerging at the Bauhaus.

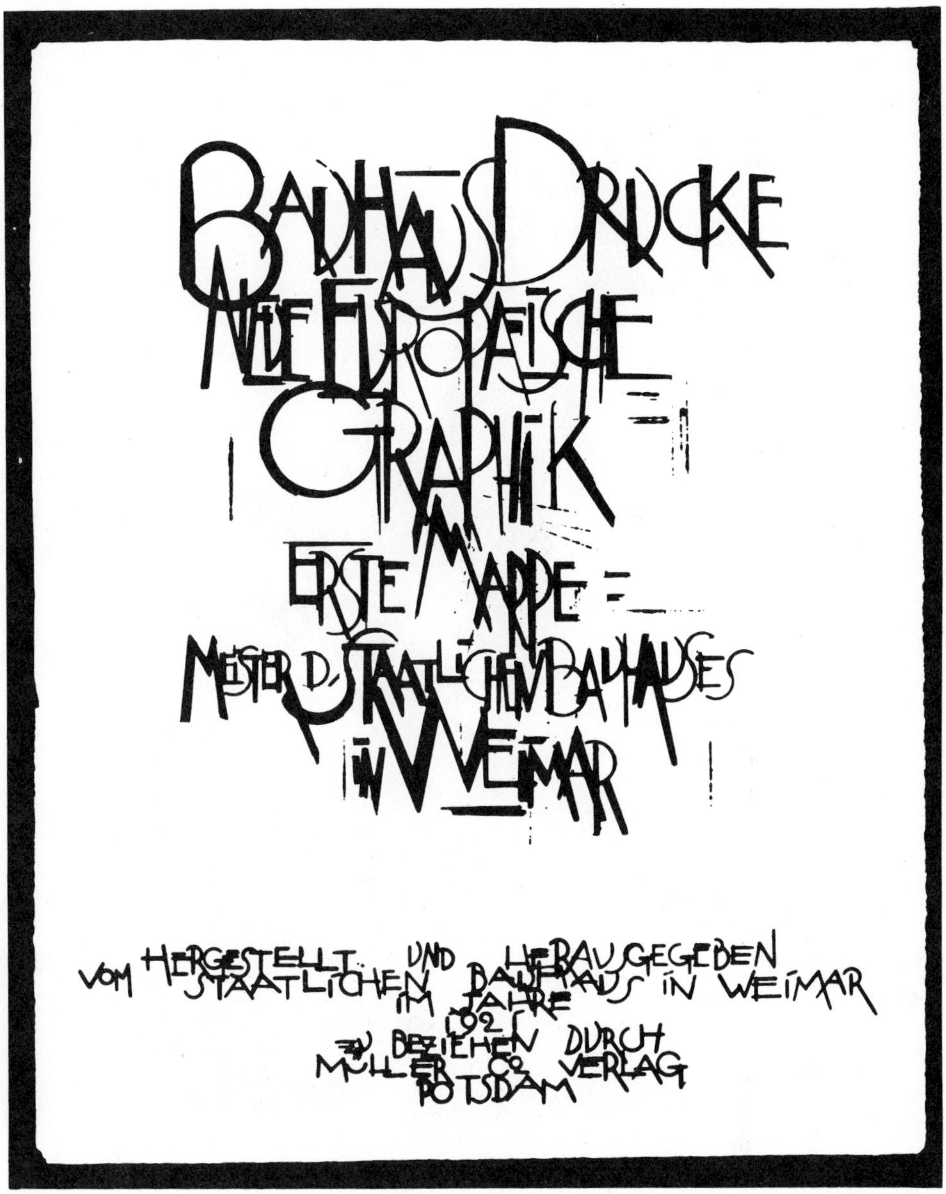

Lyonel Feininger, woodcut title page for *Europaische Graphik,* 1921. Graphic design during the early Bauhaus years reflected its expressionism and craft orientation. *The Museum of Modern Art, New York.*

believed that creating a Bauhaus style or imposing a style upon the students should be vigorously avoided. Even as an outsider, van Doesburg made a strong impact on the Bauhaus by allowing his home to become a meeting place for Bauhaus students and faculty and offering instruction in *De Stijl* principles. The furniture design and typography areas were especially influenced by *De Stijl.* This influence among faculty and students probably supported Gropius' efforts to lessen Itten's influence.

Continuing conflicts between the Bauhaus and the Thuringian government led the authorities to insist that a major exhibition be mounted by the Bauhaus to demonstrate its accomplishments. By this 1923 exhibition, which was attended by fifteen thousand people and brought international acclaim to the Bauhaus, romantic medievalism and expressionism were being replaced by an applied design emphasis to the point that Gropius changed the slogan "A Unity of Art and Handicraft" to "Art and Technology, a New Unity."

The impact of Laszlo Moholy-Nagy

In this same year, Itten's replacement as head of the preliminary course was the Hungarian Constructivist, Laszlo Moholy-Nagy. A restless experimenter, Moholy-Nagy explored painting, photography, film, sculpture, and graphic design.

Joost Schmidt, Bauhaus exhibition poster, 1923. Constructivism and a feeling of machine forms are echoed in this student poster design for the famous exhibition. *The Museum of Modern Art, New York.*

Laszlo Moholy-Nagy, *Photogram,* 1922. Light itself became a malleable medium for generating design and form. *George Eastman House, Rochester, N.Y.*

New materials such as plexiglass, new techniques such as photomontage and the photogram, and visual means including kinetic motion, light, and transparency were encompassed by this extraordinary thinker. Young and articulate, Moholy-Nagy's presence on the faculty had a marked influence on the evolution of Bauhaus instruction and philosophy, and he became Gropius' "Prime Minister" at the Bauhaus as the director pushed for a new unity of art and technology.

Moholy-Nagy's passion for typography and photography inspired a Bauhaus interest in visual communications and led to important experiments in the unification of typography and photography. Moholy-Nagy saw graphic design, particularly the poster, as evolving toward the *typophoto.* He called this objective integration of word and image to communicate a message with immediacy "the new visual literature." The 1923 Pneumatik poster is an experimental typophoto.

In 1923 he wrote that photography's objective presentation of facts could free the viewer from depending on another person's interpretation. He saw photography influencing poster design—which needs instantaneous communication—by techniques of enlargement, distortion, dropouts, double exposures, and montage. In typography he advocated emphatic contrasts and bold use of color. Absolute clarity of communication without preconceived aesthetic notions was stressed.

Gropius and Moholy-Nagy collaborated as editors for *Staatliches Bauhaus in Weimar, 1919–1923,* the first publication of the Bauhaus press. This record of the first years was designed by Moholy-Nagy and the cover was designed by a student, Herbert Bayer (b. 1900). Moholy-Nagy contributed an important statement about typography to this volume. He said that "typography is a tool of communication. It must be communication in its most intense form. The emphasis must be on absolute clarity . . . Legibility—communication must never be impaired by an *a priori* esthetics. Letters must never be forced into a preconceived framework, for instance a square.'' In graphic design, he advocated ''an uninhibited use of all linear directions (therefore not only horizontal articulation). We use all typefaces, type sizes, geometric forms, colors, etc. We want to create a new language of typography whose elasticity, variability, and freshness of typographical composition [are] exclusively dictated by the inner law of expression and the optical effect.''

In 1922–23, Moholy-Nagy ordered three paintings from a sign company. These were executed from his graph-paper layouts in colors selected from the firm's procelain enamel color-chart. This was in keeping with his theory that the essence of art and design was the concept, not the execution, and that the two could be separated. Moholy-Nagy acted on this belief beginning in 1929 when he re-

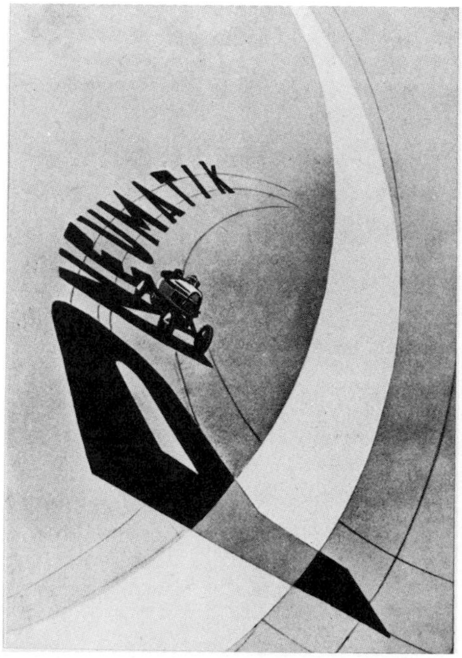

Laszlo Moholy-Nagy, poster for tires, 1923. The integration of letterforms, photography, and design elements into an immediate and unified communication was realized. *The Museum of Modern Art, New York.*

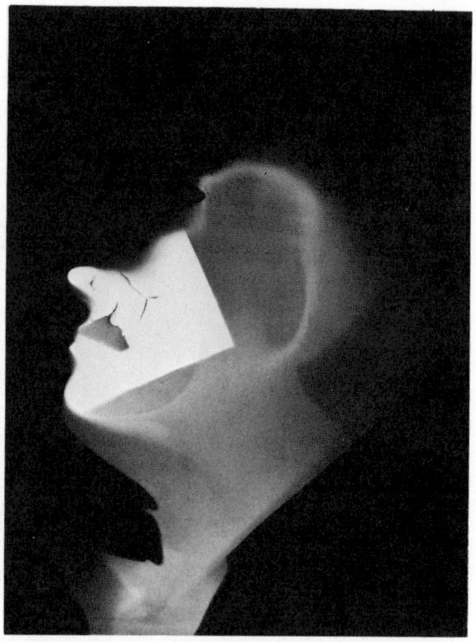

Laszlo Moholy-Nagy, *Self-portrait,* 1924. In this photogram made with torn paper, tone becomes the visual means for forming an image. *George Eastman House, Rochester, N.Y.*

tained an assistant, Gyorgy Kepes (b. 1906), to complete the execution of Moholy-Nagy's design commissions.

As a still photographer, Moholy-Nagy used the camera as a tool for design. Conventional compositional ideas yielded to unexpected organization, primarily through the use of light (and sometimes shadows) to design the space. The normal viewpoint was replaced by worm's-eye, bird's-eye, extreme closeup, and angled viewpoints. An application of the new language of vision to forms seen in the world characterizes his regular photographic work. Texture, light and dark interplay, and repetition are qualities of photographs such as *Chairs at Margate*. Moholy-Nagy antagonized the Bauhaus painters by proclaiming the ultimate victory of photography over painting.

In 1922 he began to experiment with photograms; the following year he began his *photoplastics*. Moholy-Nagy saw the photogram as representing an essence of photography. Without a camera, an artist can capture a patterned interplay of light and dark on a sheet of light-sensitive paper. The objects used by Moholy-Nagy to create photograms were chosen for their light-modulating properties, and

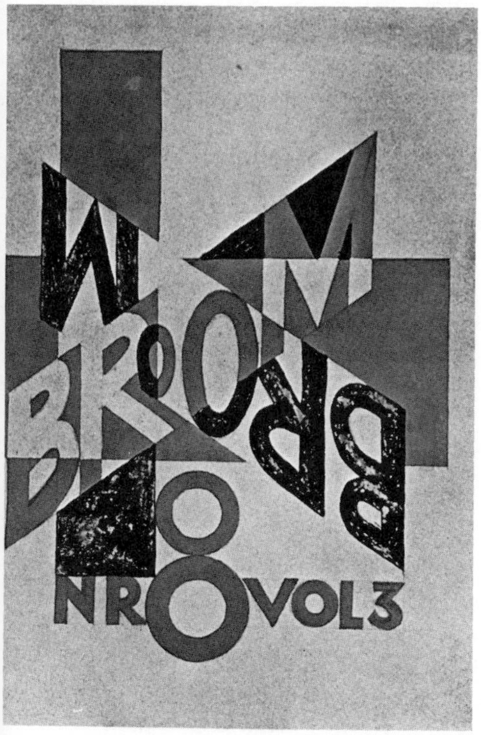

Laszlo Moholy-Nagy, proposed title page for *Broom,* 1923. This design for the avant-garde magazine shows how thoroughly Moholy-Nagy understood the new visual design vocabulary of Cubism and Lissitzky.

Laszlo Moholy-Nagy, *The World Foundation,* 1927. In this satirical photoplastic, Moholy-Nagy shows ''quack-clacking super-geese (pelicans)'' observing ''the simplicity of the world constructed as a leg show.'' *George Eastman House, Rochester, N.Y.*

any reference to the objects forming the black, white, and gray patterns or to the external world vanished in an expression of abstract pattern.

Moholy-Nagy saw his photoplastics, not as a collage technique, but as a forming process to arrive at a new expression that could become both more creative and more functional than straightforward imitative photography. Photoplastics could be humorous, visionary, moving, or insightful. Usually, these had drawn additions, complex associations and unexpected juxtapositions.

The Bauhaus at Dessau

Tension between the Bauhaus and the Thuringian government that had existed from the beginning intensified when a new, more conservative government came to power and tried to impose unacceptable conditions on the Bauhaus. On 26 December 1924, the director and masters all signed a letter of resignation effective on 1 April 1925, when their contracts expired. Two weeks later the students signed a letter to the government informing it that they would leave with the masters. Gropius negotiated relocating the Bauhaus with Dr. Fritz Hesse, the mayor of the little provincial town of Dessau. A new building complex was constructed and the curriculum was reorganized. In April 1925 some of the equipment was moved with faculty and students from Weimar to Dessau, and work began immediately in temporary facilities.

During the Dessau period (1925–32), the Bauhaus identity and philosophy came into full fruition. The *De Stijl* and Constructivist underpinnings were obvious, but Bauhaus did not merely copy these movements. Rather, clearly understood formal principles evolved that could be applied intelligently to design problems. The Bauhaus Corporation, a business organization to handle the sale of

Herbert Bayer, cover design, first Bauhaus book, 1923. Geometrically constructed letterforms are compressed into a square. *The Museum of Modern Art, New York.*

Laszlo Moholy-Nagy, title page, first Bauhaus book, 1923. The page structure is based on a rhythmic series of right angles. Stripes are applied to two words to create a second typographic plane. *The Museum of Modern Art, New York.*

Laszlo Moholy-Nagy, *Chairs at Margate,* 1935. Juxtaposition of two images is explored by Moholy-Nagy to create a contrast of pattern and texture and to introduce a process of time and change into the two-dimensional image. *George Eastman House, Rochester, N.Y.*

Walter Gropius, the Dessau Bauhaus building, 1925–26. Considered a landmark in the history of architecture, the Bauhaus building was a series of parts—workshop, classroom, dormitory, and administrative structures—unified into a whole. *The Museum of Modern Art, New York.*

workshop prototypes to industry, was created. Ideas flowed from the Bauhaus in abundance to impact twentieth century life and design: product design, steel furniture, functional architecture, and typography. The masters were now called professors and the medieval-inspired master, journeyman, and apprentice system was abandoned. In 1926 the Bauhaus was titled *Hochschule fur Gestaltung* ("High school for Form") and the influential *Bauhaus* magazine began publication.

This magazine, and the series of thirteen Bauhaus books, all except two of which were designed by Moholy-Nagy, became important vehicles for disseminating advanced ideas about art theory and its application to architecture and design. Klee, van Doesburg, Mondrian, Gropius, and Moholy-Nagy were editors or authors of volumes in the series.

Five former students were appointed masters, including: Josef Albers (1888–1976), who taught a systematic preliminary course investigating the constructive qualities of materials; Marcel Breuer

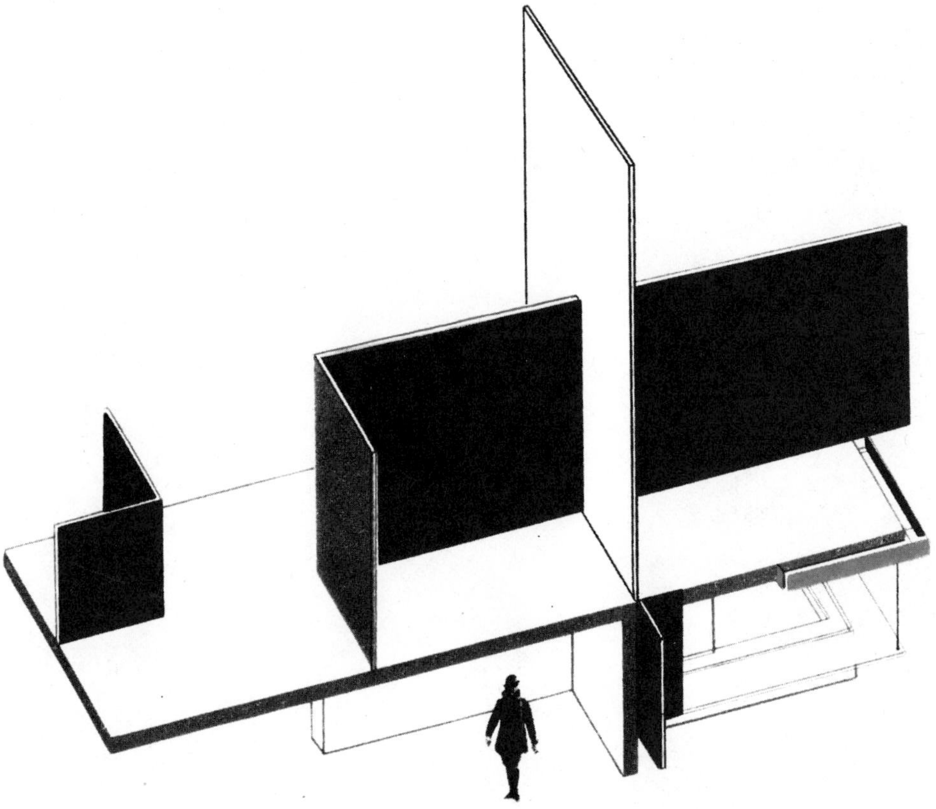

Herbert Bayer, proposed streetcar station and newsstand, 1924. Designed for economical mass production, this structure combines an open waiting area, newsstand, and rooftop advertising panels into a concise modular unit. *The Museum of Modern Art, New York.*

Herbert Bayer, cover for *Bauhaus* magazine, 1928. A page of typography joins the designer's tools and the basic geometric forms in a photographic still life. This design, which was composed in front of the camera instead of at a drawing board, achieves an integration of typography and photography that is rarely seen. *Bauhaus Archiv, Berlin.*

Laszlo Moholy-Nagy, brochure cover for *Fourteen Bauhaus Books,* 1929. Two photoprints of metal type collaged together create an unusual spatial configuration. Blue ink is printed on the upper numeral fourteen. *Bauhaus Archiv, Berlin.*

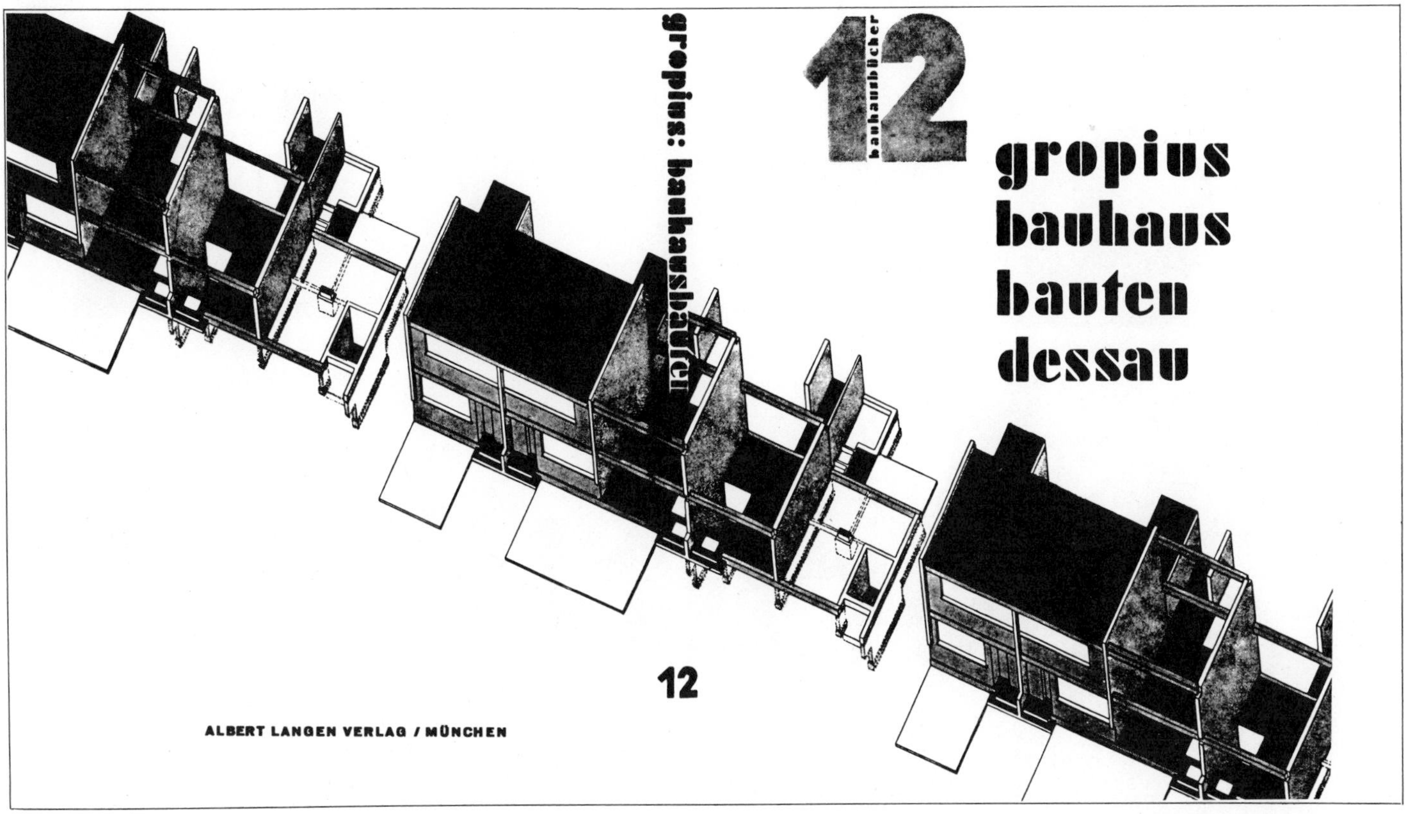

Laszlo Moholy-Nagy, dust jacket for *Bauhaus Book 12,* 1925. Printed on architect's translucent tracing paper in red and black ink, this design presented Gropius' modular housing concept in a slashing diagonal. This use of industrial fabrication methods for domestic housing combined economy and social purpose with structural functionalism and aesthetics. *Bauhaus Archiv, Berlin.*

Laszlo Moholy-Nagy, dust jacket for *Bauhaus Book 14,* 1929. To convey the properties of modern architecture, Moholy-Nagy photographed typography on transparent material and casting a shadow upon a red plane. *Bauhaus Archiv, Berlin.*

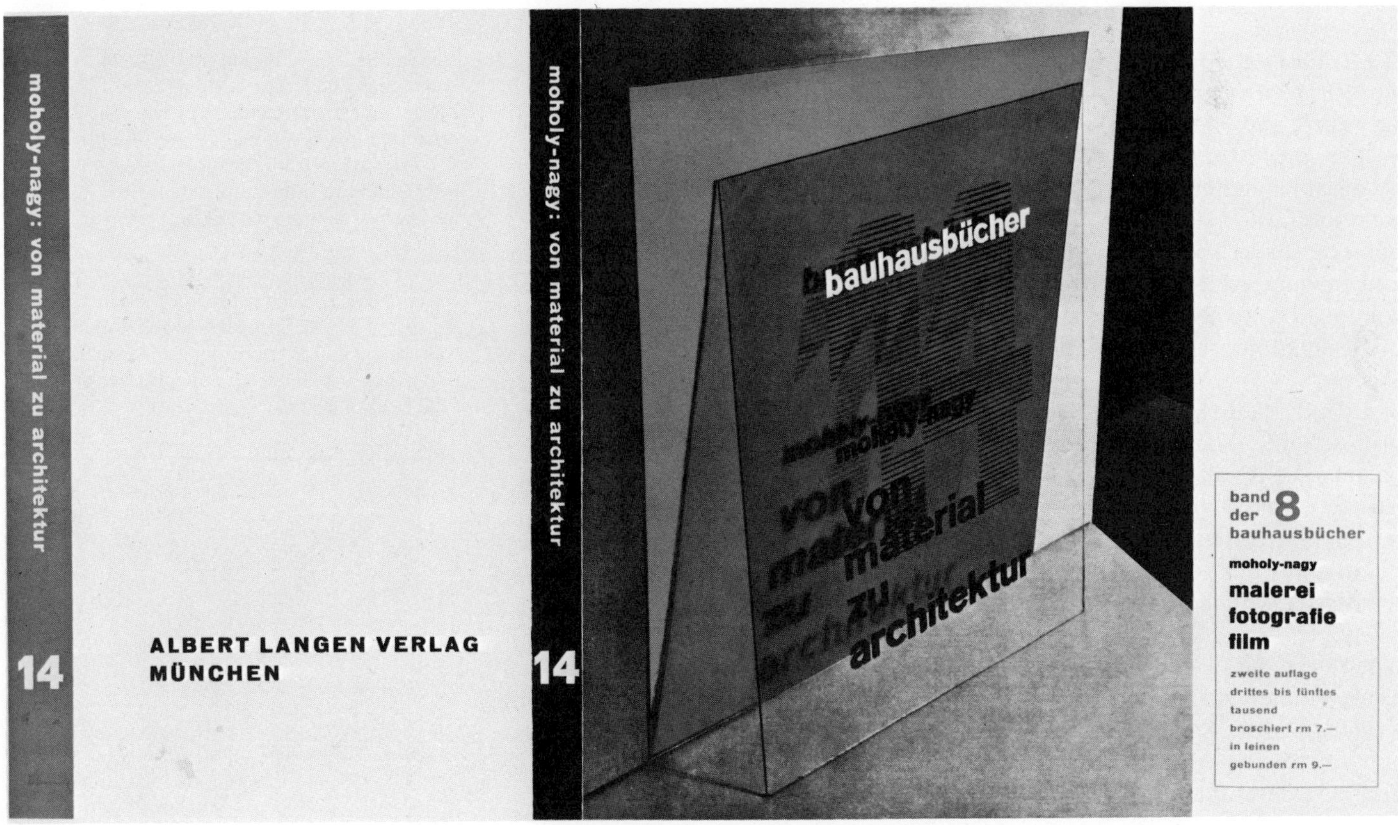

ANHALTISCHER
KUNSTVEREIN
JOHANNISSTR. 13
GEMÄLDE AQUARELLE
KANDINSKY
JUBILÄUMS-AUSSTELLUNG
zum
60.
GEBURTSTAG
Geöffnet:
Wochentags: 2-5 nachm.
Mittwoch u. Sonntag 11-1
Eintritt:
Mitglieder: Frei
Nichtmitglieder: 50 Pfg.

Herbert Bayer, exhibition poster, 1926. A communications hierarchy developed from careful analysis of content. Typography is organized in a functional progression of size and weight from the most important information to supporting details. *Museum of Modern Art, New York.*

(1902–1981), the head of the furniture workshop, who invented tubular steel furniture; and Herbert Bayer, who became professor of the newly added typography and graphic design workshop. In Weimar, Gropius had observed Bayer's interest in graphics and encouraged it with an occasional commission, so Bayer's typographic preoccupation preceded the move to Dessau.

In addition to soliciting printing orders from Dessau businesses to help balance the Bauhaus budget, Bayer led the workshop in dramatic innovation in typographic design along functional and Constructivist lines. Sans-serif fonts were used almost exclusively, and Bayer designed a universal type that reduced the alphabet to clear, simple, and rationally constructed forms. Arguing that we print and write with two alphabets (capitals and lowercase) that are incompatible in design, and that two totally different signs (capital A and small a), are used to express the same spoken sound, Bayer omitted capital letters in 1925. He experimented with flush left, ragged right typesetting without justification of letterspacing. Extreme contrasts of type size and weight were used to establish a hierarchy of emphasis determined by an objective assessment of the relative importance of the words. Bars, rules, points, and squares were used to subdivide the space, to unify diverse elements, and to call attention to important elements. Elementary forms and the use of black with one bright pure hue were favored. Open composition on an implied grid and a system of sizes for type, rules, and pictorial images brought unity to the designs. Dynamic composition with strong horizontals and verticals characterize Bayer's Bauhaus period.

Herbert Bayer, extended field of vision concept, 1938. Bayer dissolved the static walls of exhibition rooms by using exhibition panels planned to use the observer's total field of vision.

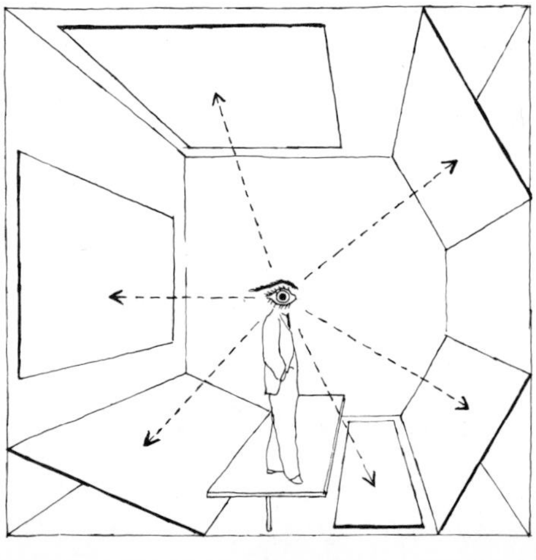

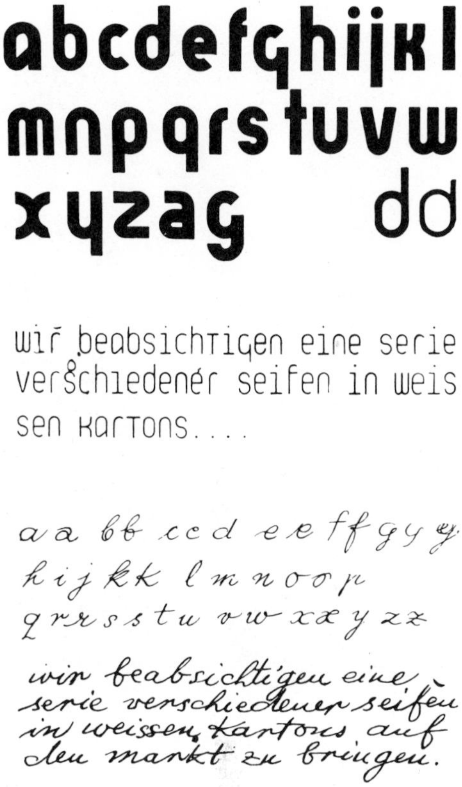

abcdefghijkl
mnpqrstuvw
xyzag dd
wir beabsichtigen eine serie verschiedener seifen in weis sen kartons....
wir beabsichtigen eine serie verschiedener seifen in weissen kartons auf den markt zu bringen.

Herbert Bayer, universal alphabet, 1925. This experiment in reducing the alphabet to one set of geometrically constructed characters has differences between letterforms maximized for greater legibility. The lower forms show different weights. Later, Bayer developed variations such as the condensed bold, typewriter, and handwriting style shown here. *The Museum of Modern Art, N.Y.*

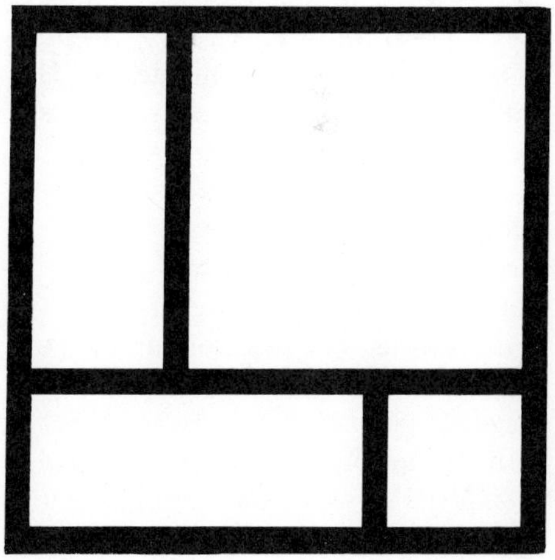

Herbert Bayer, symbol for the Kraus stained-glass workshop, 1923. A square is divided by a horizontal line into two rectangles. The top rectangle has the 3 to 5 ratio of the golden mean. Each rectangle formed is then divided with a vertical to form a square and a smaller rectangle. A harmony of proportion and balance is achieved with minimal means. *Herbert Bayer, © 1967, Reinhold.*

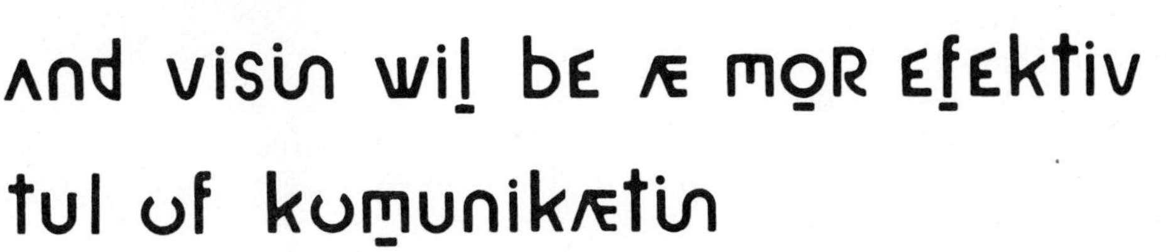

Herbert Bayer, phonetic symbols for syllables, 1959. The linguistic possibilities for the future evolution of the alphabet was explored through the invention of ligatures that could stand for sounds created by combinations of letterforms. *Herbert Bayer © 1967, Reinhold.*

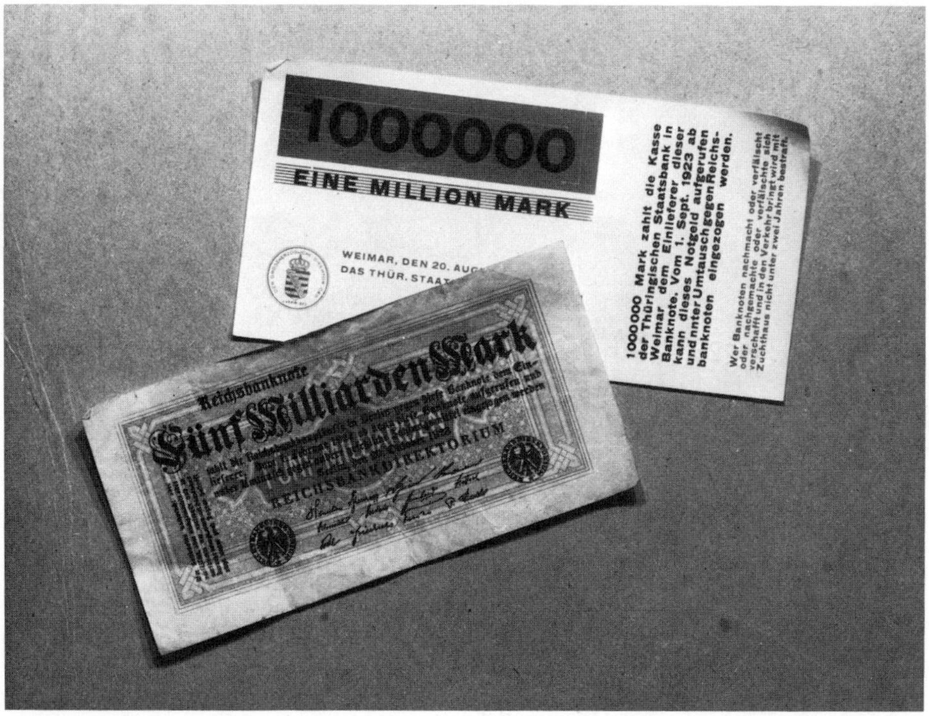

Herbert Bayer, banknote for the State Bank of Thuringia, 1923. Germany's rampant postwar inflation necessitated banknotes of large denomination. Bayer's new design—shown here with the design it replaced—overprinted red with black to minimize the possibility of photomechanical duplication. *The Museum of Modern Art, New York.*

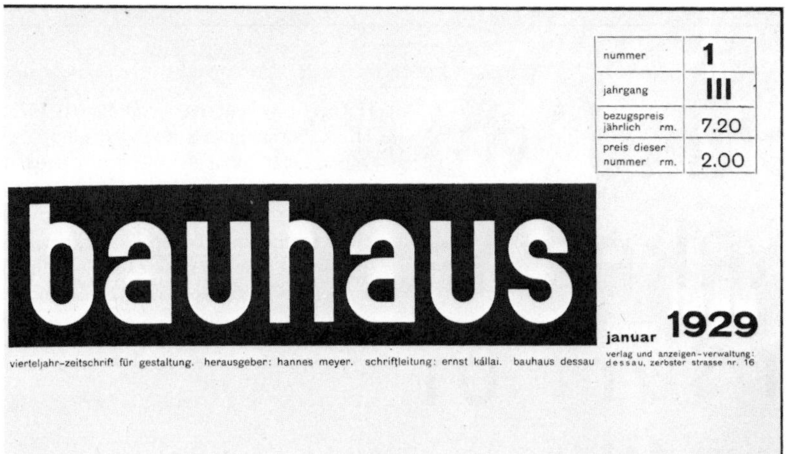

Joost Schmidt, *bauhaus* magazine cover, 1929. The format designed by Schmidt for the magazine allowed effective use of different sizes and shapes of images in the lower two-thirds of the cover. *Bauhaus Archiv, Berlin.*

The final years of the Bauhaus

In 1928, Walter Gropius resigned his post to resume private architectural practice. At the same time Bayer and Moholy-Nagy both left for Berlin, where graphic design and typography figured prominently in the activities of each. Former student Joost Schmidt (1893–1948) followed Bayer as master of typography and graphic design. He moved away from strict constructivist ideas and brought in a larger variety of type fonts. Exhibition design was outstanding under Schmidt, who brought unity to this form through standardized panels and grid system organization. The directorship of the Bauhaus was assumed by Hannes Meyer (1889–1954), a Swiss architect with strong socialist beliefs, who had been hired to set up the architectural program in 1927. By 1930, conflicts with the municipal authorities forced Meyer's resignation. Mies van der Rohe (1886–1969), a prominent Berlin architect whose design dictum "less is more" became a major attitude in twentieth-century architecture, became director.

In 1931 the Nazi party dominated the Dessau City Council and canceled Bauhaus faculty contracts in 1932. Mies tried to run the Bauhaus in an empty telephone factory in Berlin-Steglitz, but Nazi harassment made continuance untenable. The Gestapo demanded that "Cultural Bolsheviks" be removed from the school and replaced with Nazi sympathizers. The faculty voted to dissolve the Bauhaus, and it closed on 10 August 1933 with a notice to students that faculty would be available for consultation if needed. Thus ended the most important design school in this century. The growing cloud of Nazi persecution led many Bauhaus faculty members to join the flight of intellectuals and artists to America. In 1937 Gropius and Marcel Breuer were teaching architecture at Harvard University, and Moholy-Nagy established the New Bauhaus (now the Institute of Design) in Chicago. A year later Herbert Bayer began the American phase of his design career. This Atlantic exodus was to have significant impact on American design after World War II.

The Bauhaus accomplishments and influences transcend its fourteen-year life, thirty-three faculty members, and about one thousand two hundred fifty students. It created a viable, modern design style that has influenced architecture, product design, and visual communications. A modernist approach to visual education was developed, and the faculty's class preparation and teaching methods have made a major contribution to visual theory. In dissolving fine and applied art boundaries, the Bauhaus tried to bring art into a close relationship with life by design, which was seen as a vehicle for social change and cultural revitalization.

Years later Herbert Bayer wrote:

for the future
the bauhaus gave us assurance
in facing the perplexities of
work;
it gave us the know-how to
work.
a foundation in the crafts,
an invaluable heritage of timeless principles
as applied to the creative
process.
it expressed again that we are
not to impose aesthetics
on the things we use, to the
structures we live in,
but that purpose and form must
be seen as one.
that direction emerges when one
considers
concrete demands,
special conditions, inherent
character
of a given problem.
but never losing perspective
that one is, after all,
an artist. . . .

the bauhaus existed for a short
span of time
but the potentials,
inherent in its principles
have only begun to be realized.
its sources of design remain
forever full
of changing possibilities. . . .

Joost Schmidt, exhibition for the Industrial Association of Canned Goods Manufacturers, 1930. Aided by the metal, sculpture, and cabinet-making workshops, Schmidt led the printing and exhibition design students in creating functional and restrained exhibitions organized on an imaginary grid system. *Bauhaus Archiv, Berlin.*

Jan Tschichold and die neue typographie

Although much of the creative innovation in graphic design during the first decades of the twentieth century occurred as part of the modern art movements, several designers, working independently of these movements or the Bauhaus, made significant achievements in developing what has been called "the new typography." Each of these designers was aware of new innovations in form and visual theory and applied these insights to graphic design.

The person most responsible for developing theories about the application of Constructivist ideas to typography and introducing this new typography to a wide audience was Jan Tschichold (1902–1974). The son of a designer and sign painter in Leipzig, Germany, Tschichold developed an early interest in calligraphy, studied at the Leipzig Academy, and joined the design staff of Insel Verlag. In August 1923, twenty-one-year-old Tschichold attended the first Bauhaus exhibition in Weimar and was deeply impressed. He rapidly assimilated the new design concepts of the Bauhaus and the Russian Constructivists into his work and became an excellent practitioner of the new typography.

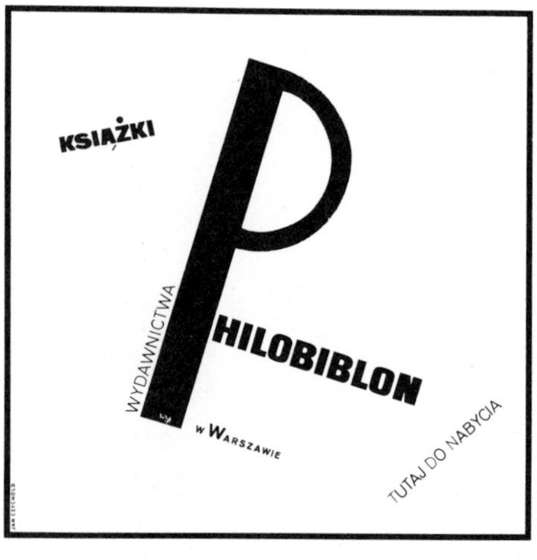

Jan Tschichold, display poster for a publisher, 1924. This poster is one of Tschichold's earliest attempts to apply the design principles he was learning from the modern movement. Printed in black and gold, it advises that "Books by Philobiblon are available here."

Jan Tschichold, advertisement for the Leipzig Trade Fair, 1922. Symmetry and historical letterforms characterized Tschichold's youthful work, as demonstrated by this hand-lettered advertisement.

Through articles and books written during the 1920s, he explained and demonstrated asymmetrical typography to a wide audience of printers, typesetters, and designers.

His 1928 book, *Die Neue Typographie,* vigorously advocated the new ideas. Disgusted with "degenerate typefaces and arrangements," he sought to sweep the slate clean and find a new typography that would express the spirit, life, and visual sensibility of its day. An objective was lucid design by the most straightforward means.

The radical new typography rejected decoration in favor of rational design planned solely for communications function. Functionalism, however, is not completely synonymous with the new typography. Tschichold observed that although plain utilitarianism and modern design have much in common, the modern movement sought spiritual content and a beauty more closely bound to the materials used, "but whose horizons lie far beyond." Tschichold felt that symmetrical organization was artificial because pure form came before the meaning of the words. By contrast, dynamic asymmetrical design of contrasting elements expressed the new age of the machine. Sans-serif type, in a range of weights (light, medium, bold, extra bold, italic) and sizes (condensed, normal, expanded), was declared *the* modern face. Its wide range of colors in the black and white scale allowed the expressive, abstract image sought by modern design. Stripped of unessential elements, sans serif reduces the alphabet to its basic elementary shapes. Designs were constructed on an underlying geometric grid. Rules, bars, and boxes were often used for structure, balance, and emphasis. The precision and objectivity of photography was preferred for illustration. Tschichold showed how the modern art movement could relate to graphic design by synthesizing his practical understanding of typography and its traditions with the new experiments.

Jan Tschichold, poster for the film, *Die Hose,* 1927. A slashing angle splits the space into red and white areas. The title and photograph are balanced asymmetrically, and the typography is designed to align with the angle.

VORZUGS-ANGEBOT

Im VERLAG DES BILDUNGSVERBANDES der Deutschen Buchdrucker, Berlin SW 61, Dreibundstr. 5, erscheint demnächst:

JAN TSCHICHOLD

Lehrer an der Meisterschule für Deutschlands Buchdrucker in München

DIE NEUE TYPOGRAPHIE

Handbuch für die gesamte Fachwelt und die drucksachenverbrauchenden Kreise

Das Problem der neuen gestaltenden Typographie hat eine lebhafte Diskussion bei allen Beteiligten hervorgerufen. Wir glauben dem Bedürfnis, die aufgeworfenen Fragen ausführlich behandelt zu sehen, zu entsprechen, wenn wir jetzt ein Handbuch der **NEUEN TYPOGRAPHIE** herausbringen.

Es kam dem Verfasser, einem ihrer bekanntesten Vertreter, in diesem Buche zunächst darauf an, den engen Zusammenhang der neuen Typographie mit dem **Gesamtkomplex heutigen Lebens** aufzuzeigen und zu beweisen, daß die neue Typographie ein ebenso notwendiger Ausdruck einer neuen Gesinnung ist wie die neue Baukunst und alles Neue, das mit unserer Zeit anbricht. Diese geschichtliche Notwendigkeit der neuen Typographie belegt weiterhin eine kritische Darstellung der **alten Typographie**. Die Entwicklung der **neuen Malerei,** die für alles Neue unserer Zeit geistig bahnbrechend gewesen ist, wird in einem reich illustrierten Aufsatz des Buches leicht faßlich dargestellt. Ein kurzer Abschnitt „**Zur Geschichte der neuen Typographie**" leitet zu dem wichtigsten Teile des Buches, den **Grundbegriffen der neuen Typographie** über. Diese werden klar herausgeschält, richtige und falsche Beispiele einander gegenübergestellt. Zwei weitere Artikel behandeln „**Photographie und Typographie**" und „**Neue Typographie und Normung**".

Der Hauptwert des Buches für den Praktiker besteht in dem zweiten Teil „**Typographische Hauptformen**" (siehe das nebenstehende Inhaltsverzeichnis). Es fehlte bisher an einem Werke, das wie dieses Buch die schon bei einfachen Satzaufgaben auftauchenden gestalterischen Fragen in gebührender Ausführlichkeit behandelte. Jeder Teilabschnitt enthält neben **allgemeinen typographischen Regeln** vor allem die Abbildungen aller in Betracht kommenden **Normblätter** des Deutschen Normenausschusses, alle andern (z. B. postalischen) **Vorschriften** und zahlreiche Beispiele, Gegenbeispiele und Schemen.

Für jeden Buchdrucker, insbesondere jeden Akzidenzsetzer, wird „Die neue Typographie" ein **unentbehrliches Handbuch** sein. Von nicht geringerer Bedeutung ist es für Reklamefachleute, Gebrauchsgraphiker, Kaufleute, Photographen, Architekten, Ingenieure und Schriftsteller, also für alle, die mit dem Buchdruck in Berührung kommen.

INHALT DES BUCHES

typ. tschichold

Das Buch enthält über 125 Abbildungen, von denen etwa ein Viertel zweifarbig gedruckt ist, und umfaßt gegen 200 Seiten auf gutem Kunstdruckpapier. Es erscheint im Format DIN A5 (148×210 mm) und ist biegsam in Ganzleinen gebunden.

Preis bei Vorbestellung bis 1. Juni 1928: **5.00** RM
durch den Buchhandel nur zum Preise von **6.50** RM

Bestellschein umstehend

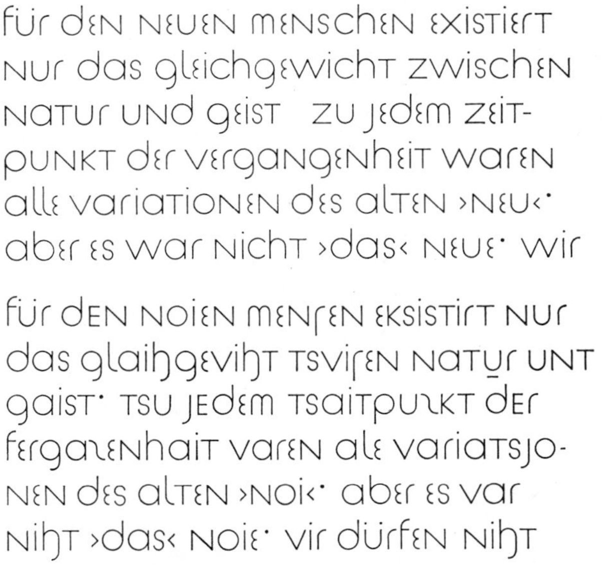

für den neuen menschen existiert nur das gleichgewicht zwischen natur und geist zu jedem zeitpunkt der vergangenheit waren alle variationen des alten ›neu‹· aber es war nicht ›das‹ neue· wir
für den noien mensen eksistirt nur das glaihgeviht tsvisen natur unt gaist· tsu jedem tsaitpunkt der fergangenhait varen ale variatsjonen des alten ›noi‹· aber es var niht ›das‹ noie· vir dürfen niht

Jan Tschichold, geometrically constructed universal alphabet, 1926–29. Tschichold's experiment in pure alphabetical form, shown with the phonetic variation, has an interesting rhythm created by the compressed *e* in contrast to the open color of the other characters.

Jan Tschichold, brochure for his book, *Die Neue Typographie,* 1928. Printed in black on yellow, this brochure functioned as a remarkable didactic example of the principles Tschichold was advocating.

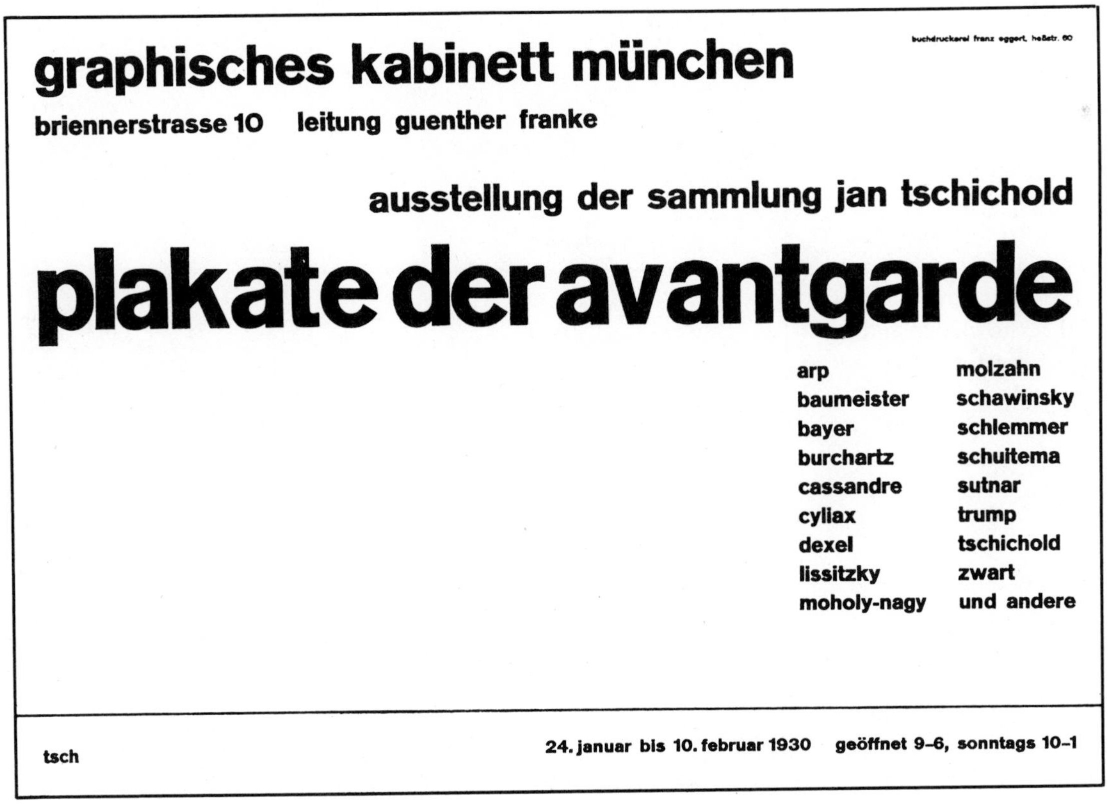

buchdruckerei franz eggert, hessstr. 60
graphisches kabinett münchen
briennerstrasse 10 leitung guenther franke
ausstellung der sammlung jan tschichold
plakate der avantgarde
arp
baumeister
bayer
burchartz
cassandre
cyliax
dexel
lissitzky
moholy-nagy
molzahn
schawinsky
schlemmer
schuitema
sutnar
trump
tschichold
zwart
und andere
tsch
24. januar bis 10. februar 1930 geöffnet 9–6, sonntags 10–1

Jan Tschichold, exhibition poster, 1930. Typography alone became the visual material for building a strong communication in this poster for an exhibition of posters by the European avant-garde.

Jan Tschichold, advertisement, 1932. Asymmetric balance, a grid system, and a sequential progression of type weight and size determined by the importance of the words to the overall communication are aspects of this design.

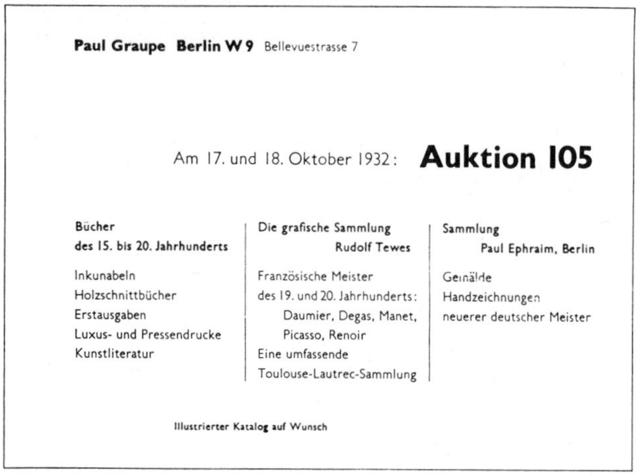

In March 1933, armed Nazis entered Tschichold's flat in Munich and arrested him and his wife. Accused of being a "cultural Bolshevik" and creating "un-German" typography, he was denied his teaching position in Munich. After six weeks of "protective custody," Tschichold was released and emigrated with his wife and four-year-old son to Basel, Switzerland, where he worked primarily as a book designer.

During the 1930s, Tschichold began to turn away from the new typography and to use Roman, Egyptian, and script styles in his designs. The new typography had been a reaction against the chaos and anarchy in German (and Swiss) typography around 1923, and he now felt that it reached a point where further development was not possible.

In 1946 he wrote that the new typography's "impatient attitude conforms to the German bent for the absolute, and its military will to regulate and its claim to absolute power reflect those fearful components of the German character which set loose Hitler's power and the Second World War."

Tschichold began to feel that the graphic designer should work in a humanist tradition that spans the ages and draws from the knowledge and accomplishments of master typographers of the past. He continued to feel that the new typography was suitable for publicizing industrial products and communication about contemporary painting and architecture. However, it was folly to use it for a book of Baroque poetry, for example, and he called reading long pages of sans serif "genuine torture."

During the 1940s, particularly with his work as typographer for Penguin Books in London from 1947–49, Tschichold led an international revival of traditional typography. While much of his later work used symmetrical organization and classical

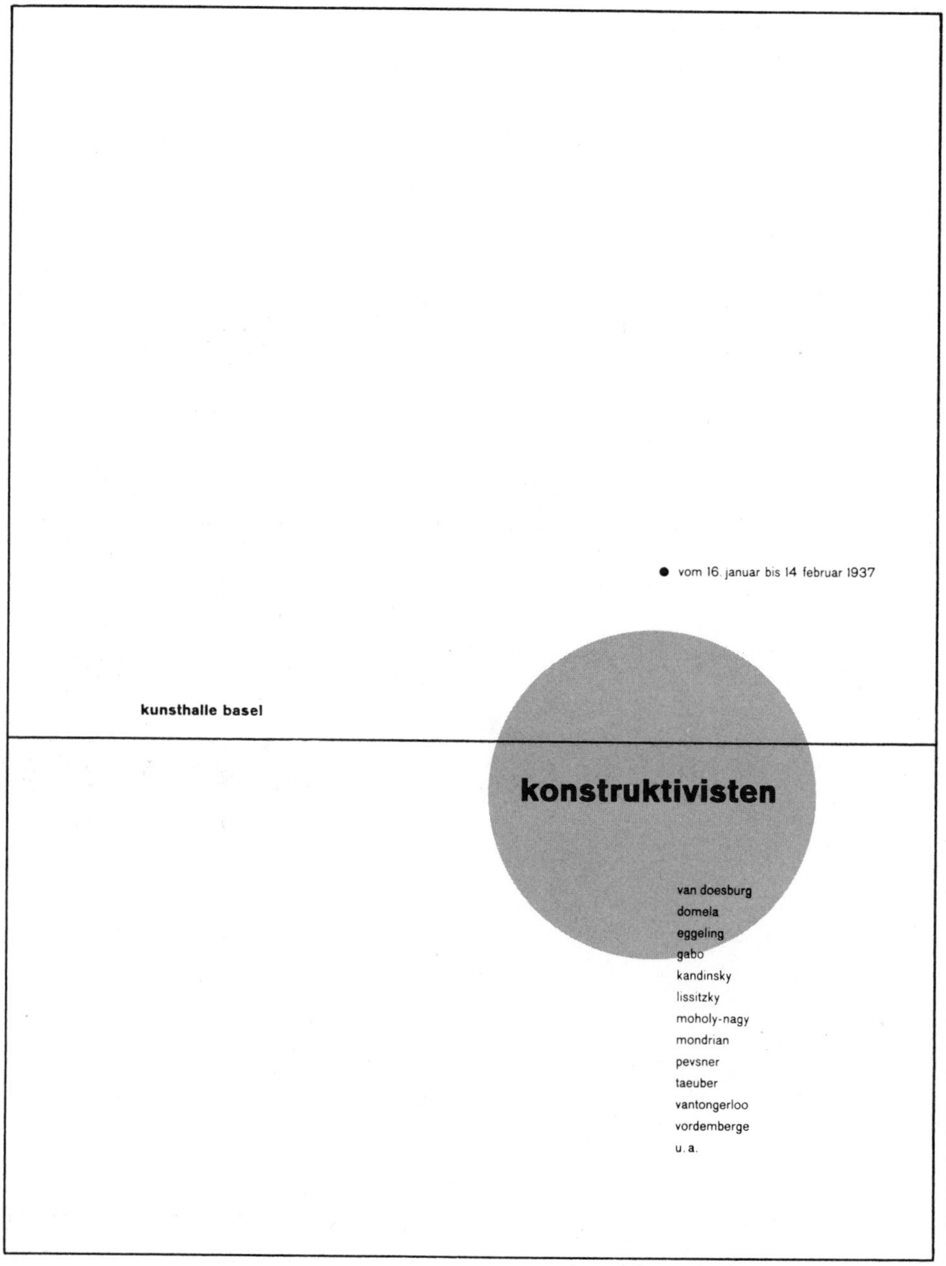

Jan Tschichold, exhibition poster, 1937. Printed in black type and a sand-colored circle, this poster has an economy of means and perfection of balance appropriate to its subject.

serif type styles, he advocated freedom of thought and artistic expression.

He even endorsed the occasional use of ornamental typography as having "a refreshing effect, like a flower in rocky terrain." He observed that perhaps a person must first lose his freedom (as he did) before one could discover its true value.

Tschichold continued to design and write in Switzerland until his death in 1972. Because he saw the value of the new typography as a striving for purification, clarity, and simplicity of means, Tschichold was able to bring typographic expression for the twentieth century to fruition. His revival of classical typography restored the humanist tradition of book design, and he made an indelible mark upon graphic design.

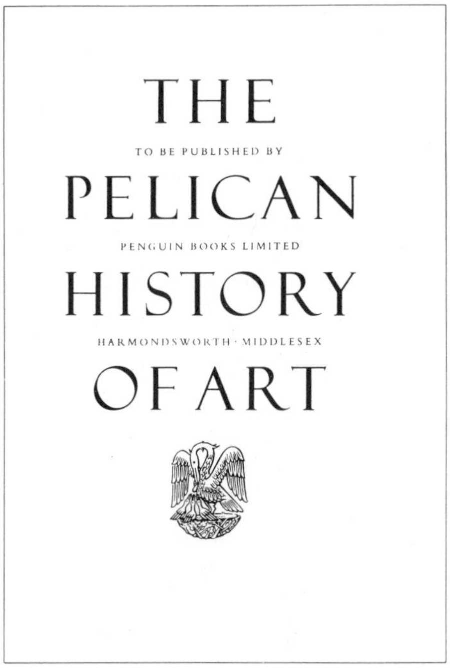

Jan Tschichold, brochure cover, 1947. The classical symmetry of this design has a power and subtlety that rivals Roman inscriptions and the best work of Baskerville and Bodoni.

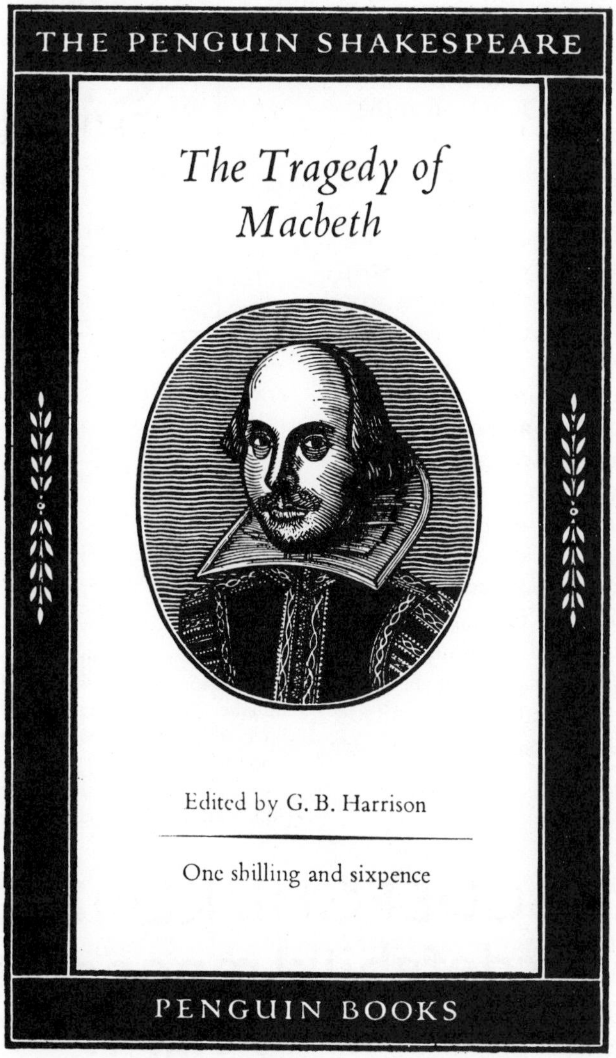

Jan Tschichold, paperback book cover, 1950. The format for the Penguin Shakespeare series illustrates Tschichold's philosophy, after World War II, that the graphic designer should draw upon the whole history of design to create solutions that express the content. *Courtesy of Ms. Jan Tschichold.*

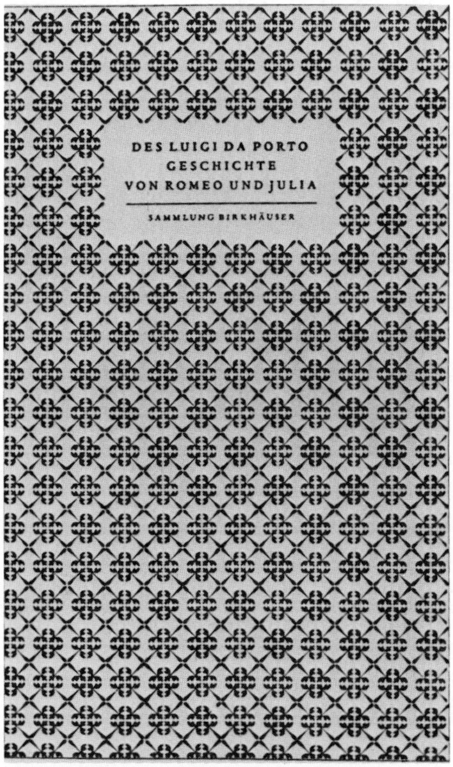

Jan Tschichold, typographic cover design for a paperback book, 1944. Printed on off-white paper in an alternating black and brick-red pattern, this design composed of typographic ornaments evidences that the master of the new typography has become a master in the classical tradition.

Typeface design for the twentieth century

The passion for the new typography created a spate of sans-serif styles during the 1920s. An early twentieth-century English sans serif, Johnston's Railway Type, was commissioned from calligrapher and designer Edward Johnston in 1916 for the exclusive use of the London Underground. Basing his shapes on classical forms from antiquity, Johnston sought the simplest possible design of the basic form of each alphabet character. This typeface is still in use for signage and graphics for the London Underground, and it inspired the Gill Sans series, which was designed by Johnston's friend and former student, Eric Gill (1882–1940), and issued from 1928–30. This type family, which eventually included fourteen styles, does not have an extremely mechanical appearance because its proportions stem from the roman tradition.

An architectural apprentice dropout tutored by Johnston at the turn of the century, Eric Gill was a complex and colorful figure who defies categorization in the history of graphic design. His activities encompassed stonemasonry, carving inscriptions for monuments, sculpture, wood engraving, typeface design, lettering, graphic design, and extensive writing. In 1903 he became an independent letter-cutter and monumental mason. Four years later, after joining a community of craftsmen at Ditchling in Sussex, he had his first printing experience at the St. Dominic's Press of Hilary Pepler. His conversion to Catholicism in 1913 intensified his belief that work had spiritual value, and the artist and craftsman served a human need for beauty and dignity.

Around 1925, in spite of his earlier polemics against machine manufacture, he was persuaded by Stanley Morison (1889–1967) of the Monotype Corporation to accept the challenge of type design. His first style, Perpetua, is an antique roman face inspired by the inscription on Trajan's column but subtly redesigned to accommodate the needs of typecasting and printing.

His embrace of historical influences—including the Trajan capitals, medieval manuscripts, the Incunabula, Baskerville and

FORASMUCH AS MANY HAVE TAKEN IN HAND TO SET FORTH IN ORDER A DECLARATION OF THOSE THINGS WHICH ARE MOST SURELY BELIEVED AMONG US, EVEN AS THEY DELIVERED them unto us, which from the beginning were eyewitnesses, and ministers of the word; It seemed good to me also, having had perfect understanding of all things from the very first, to write unto thee in order, most excellent Theophilus, That thou mightest know the certainty of those things, wherein thou hast been instructed.

THERE WAS IN THE DAYS OF HEROD, THE KING OF JUDÆA, A CERTAIN PRIEST NAMED ZACHARIAS, OF THE COURSE OF ABIA: AND HIS WIFE WAS OF THE DAUGHTERS OF Aaron, and her name was Elisabeth. And they were both righteous before God, walking in all the commandments and

131

Eric Gill, page from *The Four Gospels,* 1931. Descending sizes of type, all capitals on opening lines, unjustified right-hand margins, starlike bullets as paragraph separators (not shown here), and capital initials integrated with illustrations are forged into a unified whole in one of Gill's most original book designs.

Edward Johnston, Johnston's Railway Type, 1916. To express the essence of the alphabet, Johnston made the *O* a perfect circle. The capital *M* is a square with the center strokes meeting in the square's exact middle. All of the letterforms have a similar elemental design.

ABCDEFGHIJKLMNOPQRSTUVWXYZ
abcdefghijklmnopqrstuvwxyz
&£1234567890.,;:-!?'‘"“/()

Caslon—threatened to make him a historicist; his highly original vision and opinions enabled him to be an innovator who transcended the strong historical influence of much of his work. His work for *The Four Gospels* demonstrates this synthesis of old and new. The Golden Cockerel type that Gill created for this book is a revitalized roman incorporating both Old Style and Transitional qualities. His woodcut illustrations have an archaic, almost medieval quality. However, his total design integration of illustration, capitals, headings, and text into a dynamic whole is strikingly modern.

In his book, *Essay on Typography,* Gill first advanced the concept of unequal line lengths in typographic design. He argued that the uneven wordspacing of justified lines posed a greater legibility and design problem than the use of equal wordspacing and a ragged right margin. From late 1928 until his death, he was involved in the firm Hague and Gill, Printers, which used a hand press, hand-set type, handmade paper, and types exclusively designed by Gill for the press. This was not, however, a private press in the Arts and Crafts tradition. According to Gill a private press "prints solely what it chooses to print, whereas a public press prints what its customers demand of it."

A number of geometrically constructed sans-serif typefaces were designed in Germany during the 1920s. The most successful is the Futura series of fifteen alphabets (including four italics and two unusual display styles) designed by Paul Renner (1878–1956). As a teacher and designer, Renner fought tirelessly for the notion that designers should not just preserve and pass on to the next generation unchanged the inheritance that they had been given; each generation must try to solve problems that were inherited and attempt to create a contemporary form that is true to its own time.

A tremendous admiration for Rudolf Koch and Edward Johnston proved to be the catalyst that launched the career of a major twentieth-century calligrapher and

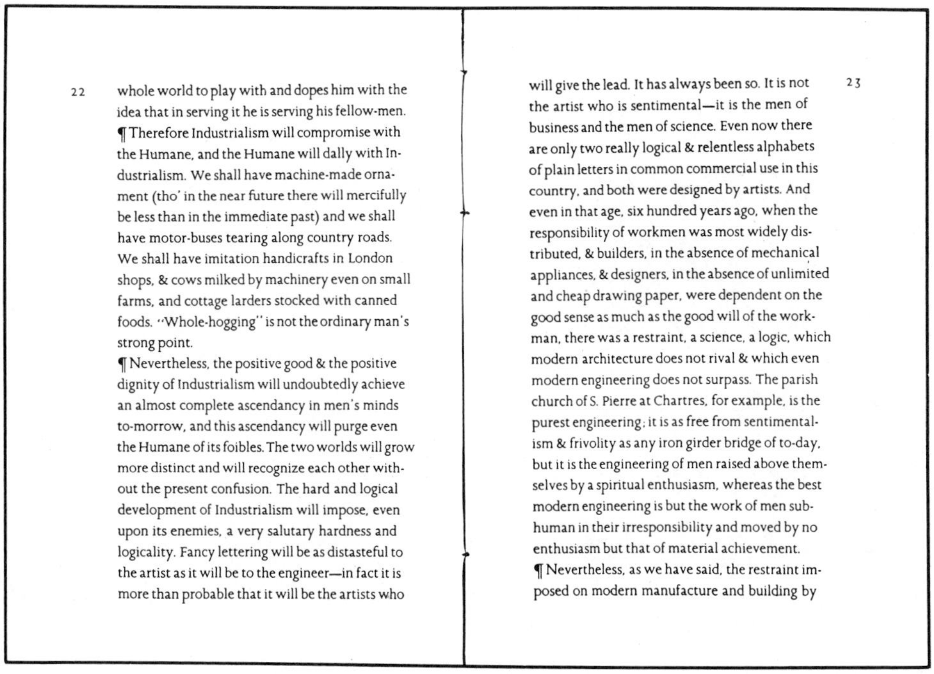
22 whole world to play with and dopes him with the idea that in serving it he is serving his fellow-men.
¶ Therefore Industrialism will compromise with the Humane, and the Humane will dally with Industrialism. We shall have machine-made ornament (tho' in the near future there will mercifully be less than in the immediate past) and we shall have motor-buses tearing along country roads. We shall have imitation handicrafts in London shops, & cows milked by machinery even on small farms, and cottage larders stocked with canned foods. "Whole-hogging" is not the ordinary man's strong point.
¶ Nevertheless, the positive good & the positive dignity of Industrialism will undoubtedly achieve an almost complete ascendancy in men's minds to-morrow, and this ascendancy will purge even the Humane of its foibles. The two worlds will grow more distinct and will recognize each other without the present confusion. The hard and logical development of Industrialism will impose, even upon its enemies, a very salutary hardness and logicality. Fancy lettering will be as distasteful to the artist as it will be to the engineer—in fact it is more than probable that it will be the artists who

will give the lead. It has always been so. It is not the artist who is sentimental—it is the men of business and the men of science. Even now there are only two really logical & relentless alphabets of plain letters in common commercial use in this country, and both were designed by artists. And even in that age, six hundred years ago, when the responsibility of workmen was most widely distributed, & builders, in the absence of mechanical appliances, & designers, in the absence of unlimited and cheap drawing paper, were dependent on the good sense as much as the good will of the workman, there was a restraint, a science, a logic, which modern architecture does not rival & which even modern engineering does not surpass. The parish church of S. Pierre at Chartres, for example, is the purest engineering; it is as free from sentimentalism & frivolity as any iron girder bridge of to-day, but it is the engineering of men raised above themselves by a spiritual enthusiasm, whereas the best modern engineering is but the work of men subhuman in their irresponsibility and moved by no enthusiasm but that of material achievement.
¶ Nevertheless, as we have said, the restraint imposed on modern manufacture and building by 23

Eric Gill, pages from *Essay on Typography,* 1931. In this highly personal and poetic little volume, Gill spoke of industrialism, humanism, letterforms, and legibility. It demonstrated his belief in the merit of typographic composition with unjustified lines.

futura

in zeichnung und schnitt gleich vollkommen, besteht vor der strengsten kritik. der typograph läßt sich nicht mehr durch schlagwörter verleiten. seine augen sind geschärft, und mit den künstlern der gegenwart teilt er den sinn für reine, große form. der knappen, ehrlichen gestaltung zuliebe verzichtet er gerne auf jeden dekor. er sucht nach einer schrift von zuchtvoller schönheit, die dem gedanken des typendruckes vollkommenen und reinen ausdruck verleiht. unsere zeit will höchstleistungen. rücksichtslos verwirft sie alles mittelmäßige. sie will eine bessere schrift. schriftkunst und schrifttechnik haben ihr bestes getan. die exakten, edlen formen der futura sind in gewissenhafter arbeit so vollkommen durchgebildet, daß die reinheit der schlichten linie allein überzeugt. die aufgabe war schwer, aber sie wurde gelöst. der typograph verfügt jetzt über eine schrift, die der besten kunst unserer zeit ebenbürtig ist

Paul Renner, folder for Futura, 1927. The initial version of Futura released by the Bauer foundry in Germany was more abstract than the version that came to America. The structural relationships in this layout are typical of the new typography.

FUTURA Light
FUTURA Light italic
FUTURA Book
FUTURA Medium
FUTURA Medium Italic
FUTURA Demibold
FUTURA Demibold italic
FUTURA Bold
FUTURA Bold italic
FUTURA Bold condensed
Futura Display
Futura Black
FUTURA INLINE

Paul Renner, Futura typefaces, 1927–30. The extensive range of sizes and weights provided the necessary graphic material for printers and designers who adopted the new typography.

Palatino
Palatino Italic
Palatino Semibold
Palatino Bold

Melior
Melior Italic
Melior Semibold
Melior Bold Condensed

Optima
Optima Italic
Optima Semi Bold

Hermann Zapf, the typefaces Palatino, 1950; Melior, 1952; and Optima, 1958. These alphabets have a harmony and elegance seldom achieved in typeface design.

typeface designer, Hermann Zapf (b. 1918). A native of Nuremberg, Germany, Zapf entered the graphic arts as an apprentice photo retoucher at age sixteen. A year later he started his study of calligraphy after acquiring a copy of Koch's *Das Schreiben als Kunstfertigkeit,* a manual on calligraphy. Four years of disciplined self-education followed, and at age twenty-one Zapf's first typographic involvement began when he entered Koch's printing firm. Later that year, Zapf became a freelance book and typographic designer, and at age twenty-two the first of his more than fifty typefaces was designed and cut for the Stempel foundry. Zapf developed an extraordinary sensitivity to letterforms in his activities as a calligrapher, typeface designer, typographer, and graphic designer. Zapf sees typeface design as "one of the most visible visual expressions of an age."

Zapf's triumvirate of typefaces designed during the late 1940s and the 1950s are widely regarded as major type designs of the century. Palatino (1950) is a roman style with broad letters, strong serifs, and elegant proportions somewhat reminiscent of Venetian faces. Melior (1952) is a modern style that departs from earlier models

Rudolf Koch, announcement for Kabel type, c. 1928. Koch's entry into the geometric sans-serif style of the 1920s and 1930s is enlivened by unexpected design subtleties. The ornamental design—composed of straight lines—is typical of the period. *Houghton Library, Harvard University, Cambridge, Mass.*

Hermann Zapf, page from *Manuale Typographicum,* 1968. The energy of Parandowski's quotation about the power of the printed word to "govern time and space" inspired this graphic field of tension radiating from the central cluster.

Hermann Zapf, page from *Manuale Typographicum,* 1968. Using his Michelangelo typeface, Zapf organized this page with classical symmetry and exquisite intervals between letters. The subtle shadow relief of the ruled lines suggests an inscriptional quality.

ALLIED TO THE FINE ARTS & TYPES HAVE ALWAYS REFLECTED THE TASTE * OR FEELING OF THEIR TIME
DANIEL B. UPDIKE * TYPOGRAPHY IS CLOSELY
ABCD
EFGHI
JKLM
NOPQ
RSTV
WXYZ

through its vertical stress and squared forms. Optima (1958), a thick and thin sans serif with tapered strokes, is one of the most original type designs of the second half of the twentieth-century. While his typeface designs are based on a deep understanding of the past, they are original inventions designed with a full understanding of the technologies of the twentieth century. To the complex and technically demanding craft of typeface design, Zapf brings the spiritual awareness of the poet who is capable of inventing new forms to express the current century and to preserve it for posterity.

In the area of book design, Zapf's two editions of *Manuale Typographicum,* published in 1954 and 1968, are outstanding contributions to the art of the book. Encompassing eighteen languages and more than a hundred typefaces, these two volumes consist of quotations about the art of typography. Zapf created a full-page typographic expression for each quotation selected.

Stanley Morison, typographic advisor to the British Monotype Corporation and the Cambridge University Press, supervised the design of a major twentieth-century newspaper and magazine typeface commissioned by *The Times* of London in 1931. Named Times New Roman, this typeface with short ascenders and descenders and sharp, small serifs was introduced in the 3 October 1932 edition of London's newspaper of record. The typographic appearance of one of the world's preeminent newspapers was radically changed overnight, and the traditionally conservative readers warmly applauded the legibility and clarity of the new typeface. Times New Roman went on to become one of the most widely used typefaces of the twentieth century. Its popularity had been attributed to its remarkable legibility, handsome visual qualities, and the economy achieved by moderately condensed letterforms. By making the stems and curves slightly thicker than most roman-style letterforms, the designers gave Times New Roman a touch of the robust color that is associated with types like Caslon.

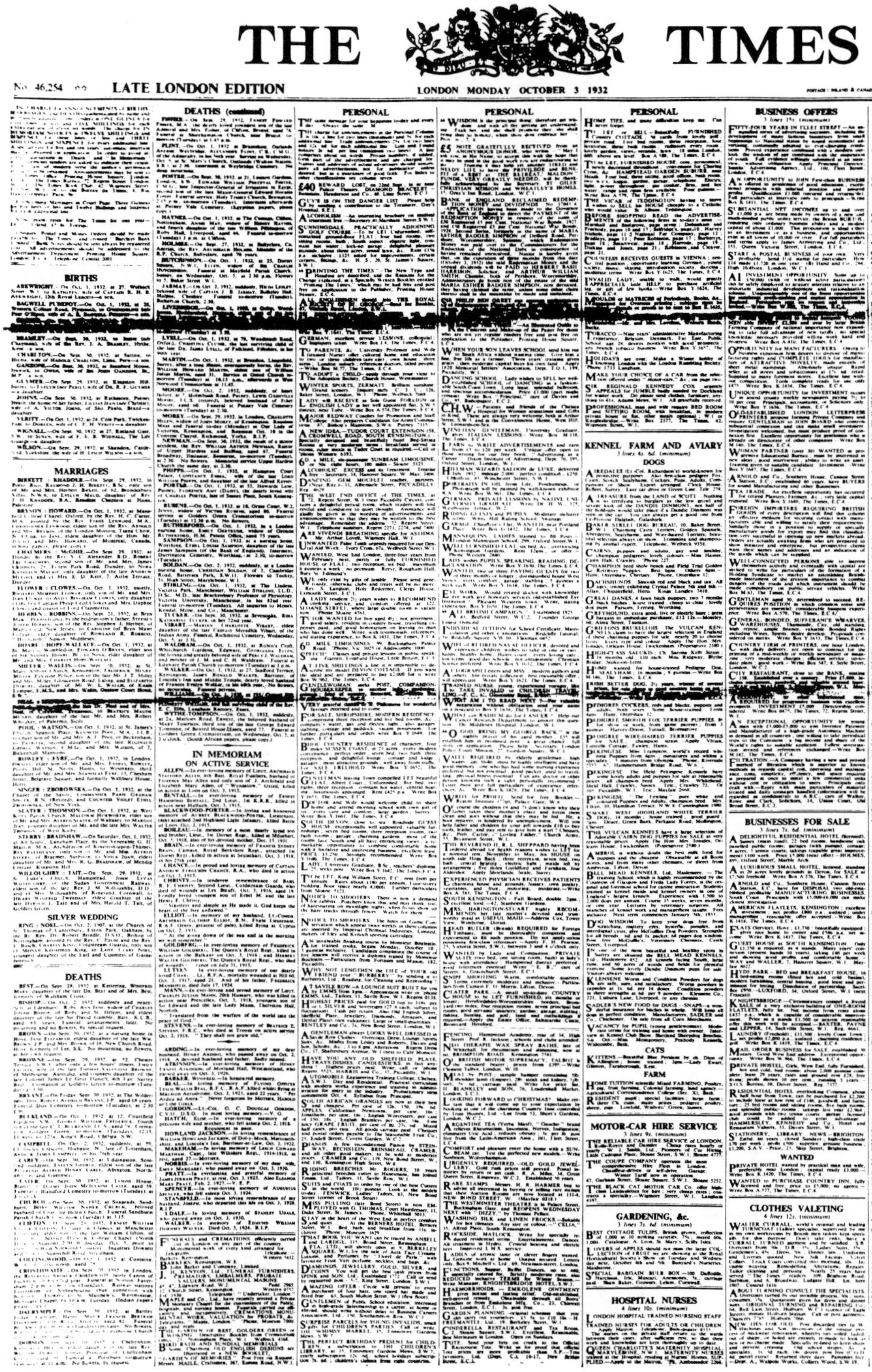
THE TIMES

No. 46,254 LATE LONDON EDITION LONDON MONDAY OCTOBER 3 1932 PRICE 2d

BIRTHS

MARRIAGES

SILVER WEDDING

DEATHS

DEATHS (continued)

IN MEMORIAM

ON ACTIVE SERVICE

PERSONAL

KENNEL FARM AND AVIARY

DOGS

CATS

FARM

MOTOR-CAR HIRE SERVICE

GARDENING, &c.

HOSPITAL NURSES

BUSINESS OFFERS

BUSINESSES FOR SALE

WANTED

CLOTHES VALETING

CLUB ANNOUNCEMENTS

CHEPSTOW RACE CLUB.

HELLENIC TRAVELLERS CLUB

SOCIETIES

INVESTMENTS AND LOANS

DIRECTORS AND PARTNERS

ROAD TRANSPORT

CLASSIFIED ADVERTISEMENTS INDEX

Stanley Morison (typographic advisor), *The Times,* 3 October 1932. Even the gothic masthead that had been used for one hundred twenty years fell victim to the redesign that introduced Times New Roman. *Courtesy of* The Times *of London.*

The Isotype movement

The important movement toward developing a "world language without words" began in the 1920s, continued into the 1940s, and still has important influences today. The *Isotype* concept involves the use of elementary pictographs to convey information. The originator of this effort was Vienna sociologist Otto Neurath (1882–1945). As a child, Neurath marveled at the way ideas and factual information could be conveyed by visual means. Egyptian wall frescoes in the Vienna Museum and diagrams and illustrations in his father's books fired his imagination.

Neurath felt that the social and economic changes following World War I demanded clear communication to assist public understanding of important social issues relating to housing, health, and economics. A system of elementary pictographs to present complex data, particularly statistical data, was developed. His charts were completely functional and shorn of decorative qualities. Neurath has ties with the new typography movement, for Tschichold assisted the group briefly in the late 1920s, and Paul Renner's new Futura typeface was adopted for Isotype designs immediately after it became available.

Originally called the *Vienna method,* the name Isotype (International System of Typographic Picture Education) was selected after Neurath moved to Holland in 1934. A vital group was the Transformation Team headed by scientist and mathematician Marie Reidemeister (1898–1959). Vast quantities of verbal and numerical data compiled by statisticians and researchers was converted into layout form by the Transformation Team. The layouts were handed over to graphic artists for execution of the finished format.

One problem was the need to produce large quantities of symbols for charts. Initially, the pictographs were individually drawn or cut from paper. After woodcut artist Gerd Arntz—whose constructivist-inspired prints included archetypal geometric figures—joined the group in 1928, he designed most of the pictographs. Often reduced as small as one-half-centimeter tall, these pictographs were designed to express subtleties such as drunk man, unemployed man, or emigrant man. The pictographs were cut on linoleum blocks by Arntz, printed on a letterpress, then pasted into the finished artwork. After 1940, when the Isotype group fled to England, pictographs were duplicated by means of type-high letterpress line blocks. Because of their Germanic background, Neurath and Reidemeister were interned briefly, then were allowed to resume their work in England. In 1942, Neurath and Reidemeister were married.

Important among Neurath's many assistants was Rudolph Modley, who came to America during the 1930s and established Pictorial Statistics, Inc., which later became The Pictographic Corporation. This organization became the North American branch of the Isotypes movement.

The Isotype group's contribution to visual communications is the set of conventions they developed to formalize the use of pictorial language. This includes a pictorial syntax (a system of connecting images to create an ordered structure and meaning) and the design of simplified pictographs. The impact of their work upon post–World War II graphic design includes research toward the development of universal visual language systems and the extensive use of pictographs in signage and information systems.

The prototype for the modern map

The London Underground also sponsored a major graphic design innovation when it made a trial printing of a new subway system map in 1933. Draftsman Henry C. Beck (b. 1903) submitted an unsolicited design proposal which replaced geographic fidelity with a diagrammatic interpretation. The central portion of the map with complex interchanges between routes was enlarged in proportion to outlying areas. Meandering geographic lines were codified into horizontals, verticals, and forty-five-degree diagonals. Bright color coding identified and separated the routes. Although cautious about the value of Beck's proposal, the publicity department printed the trial run and invited public response. When the public found it to be extremely functional, it was developed throughout the system. In preparing the camera-ready art for the first trial printing of his map, Beck handlettered over two thousand four hundred characters in Johnson's Railway Gothic! Beck's development and revisions of the London Underground maps over twenty-seven years has made a significant contribution to the visual presentation of diagrams and networks.

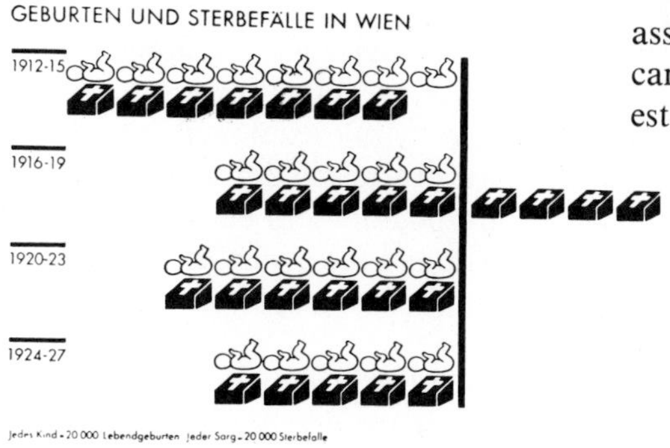

Otto Neurath and the Vienna Method, chart, "Births and Deaths in Vienna," c. 1928. Neurath called the Isotype a "language picture" which enabled the reader to make connections. In this chart, for example, the impact of World War I on mortality and births becomes dramatically evident.

Gerd Arntz, pictographs for Isotypes, early 1930s. These images show how simplified form and nuances of form bring communicative immediacy to Isotype images.

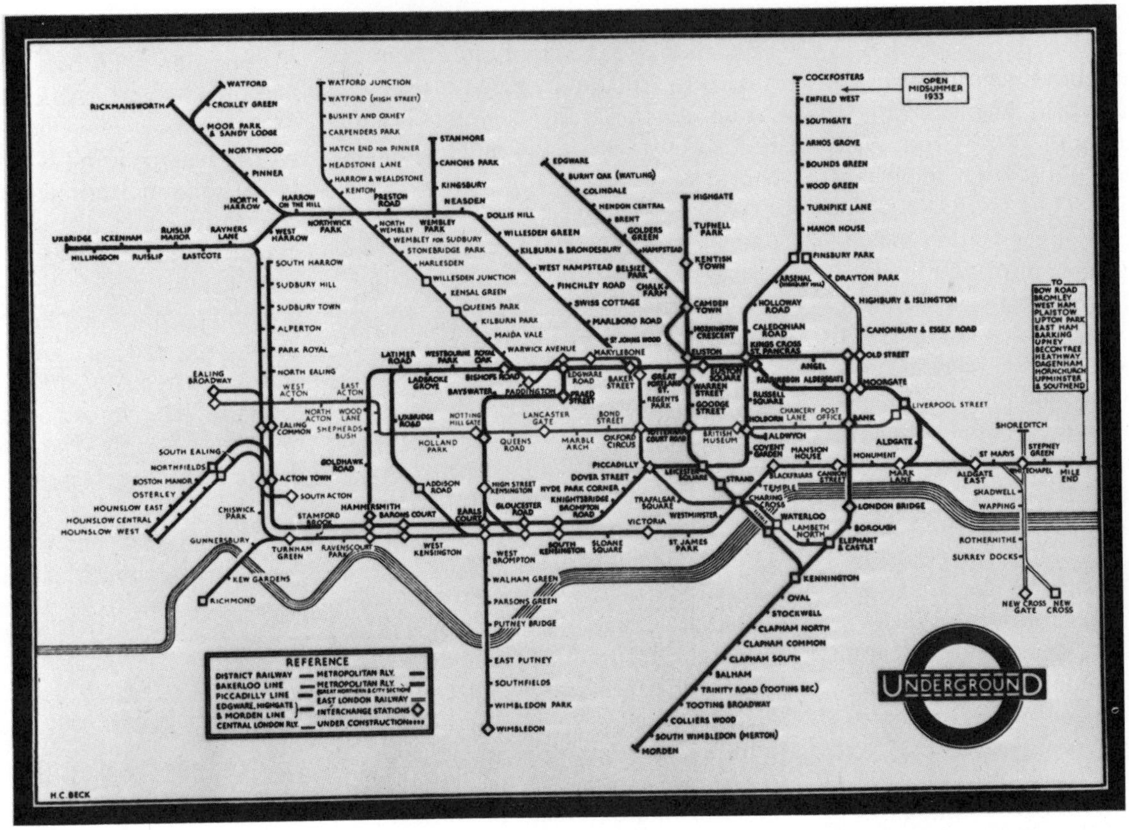

Henry C. Beck, map for the London Underground, 1933. By depicting a schematic concept of the subway lines rather than a conventional map, Beck simplified the communication of information for the subway rider.

Independent Voices of the New Typography

The Dutch designer, Piet Zwart (1885–1977), created a synthesis from two apparently contradictory influences; the Dada movement's playful vitality and the functionalism and formal clarity of *De Stijl*. By the time Zwart began graphic design projects at age thirty-six, he had designed furniture and interiors, worked as an assistant to the architect Jan Wils, and experienced contact with the *De Stijl* movement. Zwart never joined this movement because, although he agreed with its basic philosophy, he believed *De Stijl* to be too dogmatic and restrictive in its views. However, his interior design projects moved toward a functionalism and clarity of form after his communication with *De Stijl* artists began in 1919.

When, by happenstance, Zwart received his first typographic commissions, he rejected both traditional symmetrical layout and *De Stijl's* insistence on strict horizontals and verticals. After making a rough layout, Zwart would order words, rules, and symbols from a typesetter and playfully manipulate them on the surface to develop the design. The fluid nature of collage technique joined with a conscious concern for functional communication. Zwart designed the space as a "field of tension" brought alive by rhythmic composition, vigorous contrasts of size and weight, and a dynamic interplay between black form and white page.

Piet Zwart, personal logo, 1927.

Rejecting the dull grayness of conventional typographic design, Zwart's work became dynamic and arrestive. He fractured tradition by taking a new look at the material from which graphic designs are made, just as painters like Picasso and Matisse had taken a new look at the material from which a painting is made. Perhaps his "amateur" status, having no formal training in typography or graphic design, was an asset for he was uninhibited by rules and methods of traditional professional practice. The need for typography to be in harmony with its era and the available production methods were important concerns for Zwart.

Realizing that twentieth-century mass printing made typographic design an important and influential cultural force, Zwart had a strong sense of social responsibility and was concerned for the reader. The function of time as an aspect of the reader's experience was considered as Zwart planned his page designs. He realized that twentieth-century man

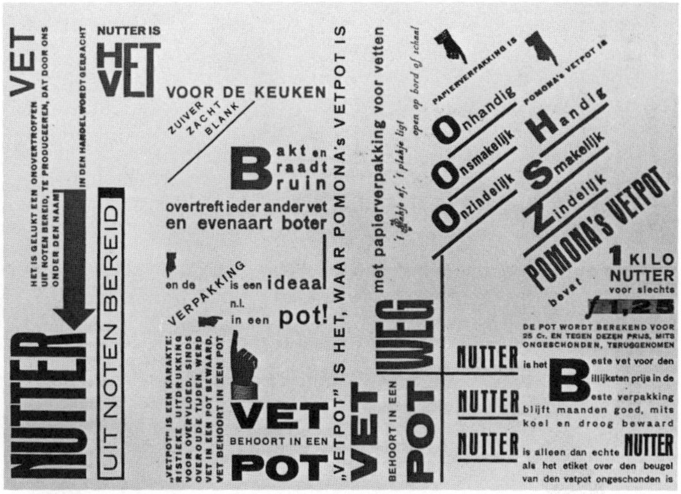

Piet Zwart, folder, 1924. Order is achieved in a complex communication by the rhythmic repetition of diagonals, words, letters, rules, and the dingbat hand.

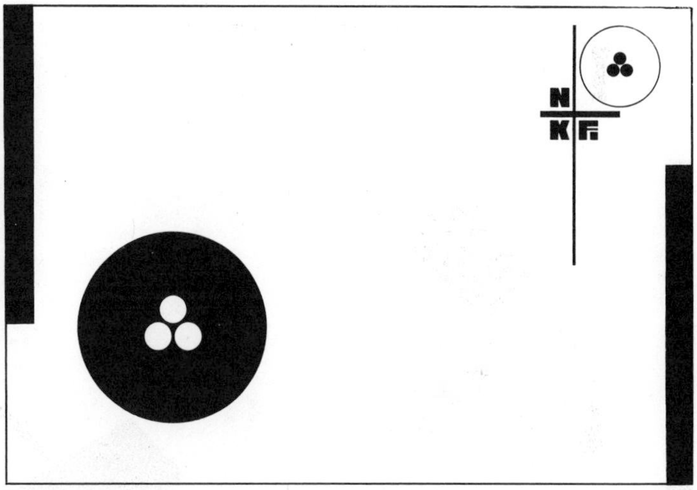

Piet Zwart, advertisement for the Laga Company, 1923. In Zwart's first advertising commissions, which came from this flooring manufacturer, the influence of *De Stijl* principles is evident.

Piet Zwart, front and back covers for an N. V. Nederlandsche Kabelfabriek (NKF) cableworks catalogue, 1928. The logo designed by Zwart for NKF is shown in these opening pages used alone and with the company initials. The black bars on the upper left-hand and lower right-hand edges function as compositional elements and protect the page from becoming dirty during repeated handling. *Courtesy of N. V. Nederlandsche Kabelfabriek, Delft.*

was bombarded with communications and could not afford the luxury of wading through masses of reading matter. Brief slogans with large letters in bold type and diagonal lines were used to attract the attention of the reader, who could quickly grasp the main idea or content and then decide whether to read further. Explanatory matter was organized to make it easy to isolate essential information from secondary material.

Zwart's activities over a long and illustrious career have included photography, product and interior design, and teaching. Zwart once called himself a *Typotekt*. This amusing play on words to express the fact that he was an architect who had become a typographic designer has a deeper meaning, for it expresses the working process of the new typography. The way that Zwart (as well as Lissitzky, Bayer, and Tschichold) constructed a design from the material of the typecase is analogous to the manner in which an architect's design is constructed from glass, steel, and concrete.

Another Dutch artist, Hendrik N. Werkman (1882–1945) of Groningen, is noted for his experimentation with type, ink, and ink rollers for purely artistic expression. After his large printing company floundered during the economic dislocations following World War I, Werkman—whose avocation was painting—established a small job-printing firm. Beginning in 1923, he used type, rules, printing ink, brayers, and a small press to produce one-of-a-kind compositions called *druksels* ("prints"). Also, he began publication of *the next call,* a small magazine of typographic experiments and texts, in 1923. The printing press became a "layout pad" as Werkman

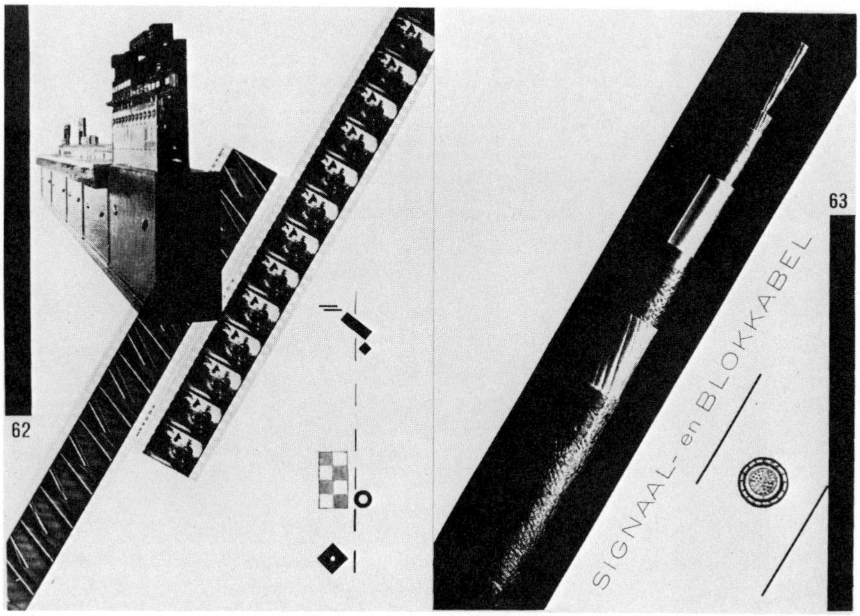

Piet Zwart, pages from the NKF cable-works catalogue, 1928. This layout demonstrates Zwart's uninhibited use of photographs as compositional shapes.

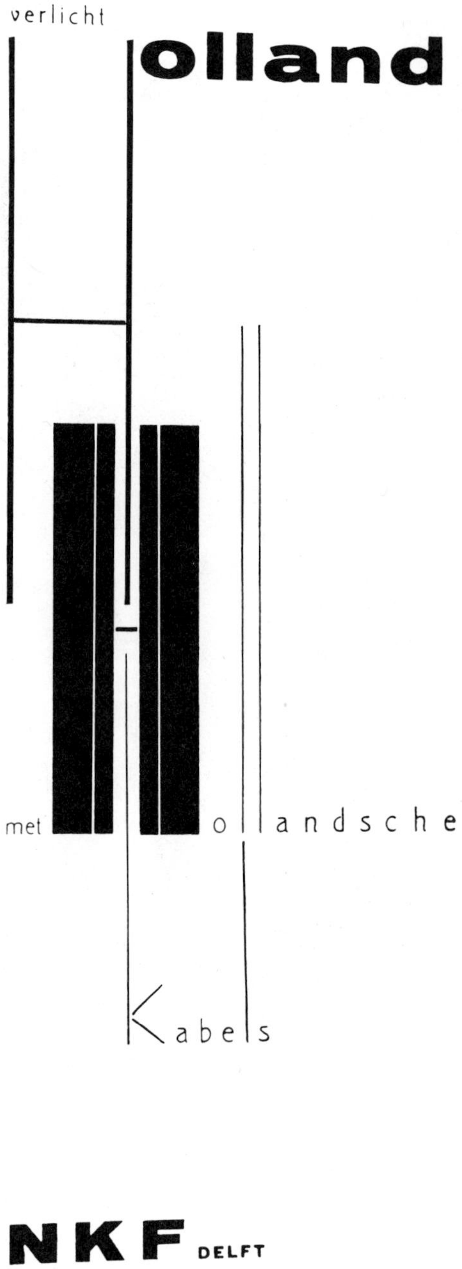

Piet Zwart, advertisement for the NKF cableworks, 1926. Structured on dynamic verticals, this design is an example of how Zwart, functioning as his own copywriter, would develop a simultaneous visual/verbal solution to the client's communications problem.

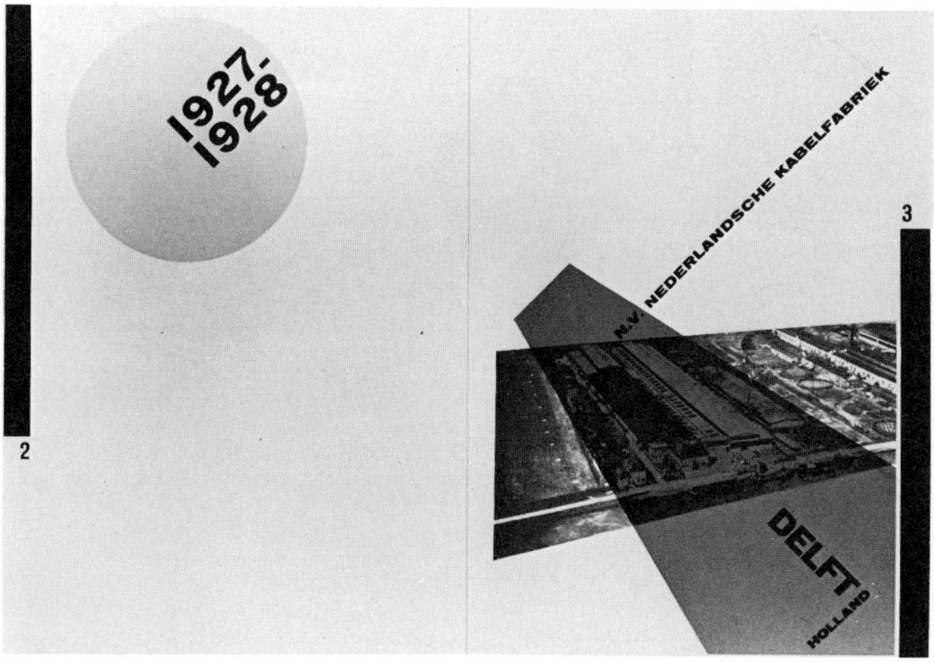

Piet Zwart, pages from the NKF cable-works catalogue, 1928. In a stunning use of asymmetrical balance, the date (printed over a yellow circle) is balanced against a red wedge crossing a blue halftone photograph of the NKF plant. The NKF plant area, overprinted by the red wedge, becomes a purple halftone on a red background.

composed wood type, blocks of wood, and even parts of an old lock directly on the letterpress bed. He loved printing and took joy in beautiful paper, textures of wood, and the unique qualities of each nicked and dented piece of wood type. His process of building a design from ready-made components can be com-

Piet Zwart, type specimen brochure page for N. V. Druckerei Trio, 1930. The primary colors of *De Stijl* and the playful randomness of Dada composition combine as Zwart demonstrates that this printing firm has a large variety of type styles and sizes. *Courtesy of Trio NV Drukkerij, The Hague.*

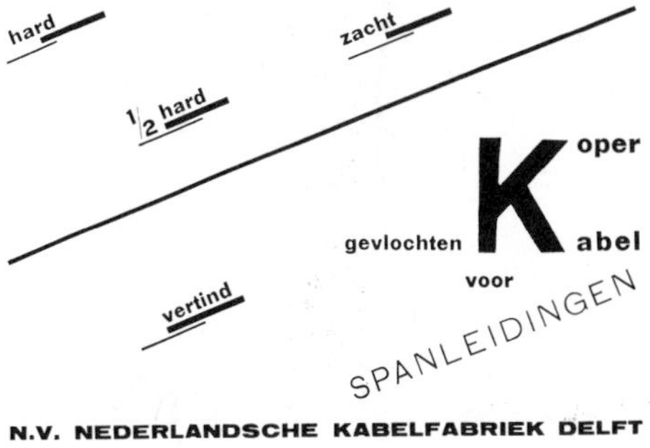

Piet Zwart, advertisement for NKF, 1931. This design, with its diagonal type and rules, inspired the "type and stripe" fad of the late 1970s. *Courtesy of NKF, Delft.*

H. N. Werkman, cover for *the next call 4,* 1924. The texture of fine deckle-edge paper and the coarseness of pitted old type brought a tactile physical presence to this work.

Piet Zwart, page from a publisher's brochure, 1931. Zwart moves the reader forward in no uncertain terms toward the information on the pages that follow in this direct and uninhibited use of "visual flow." *Courtesy of Nijgh and Van Ditmar, 's Gravenhage, The Netherlands.*

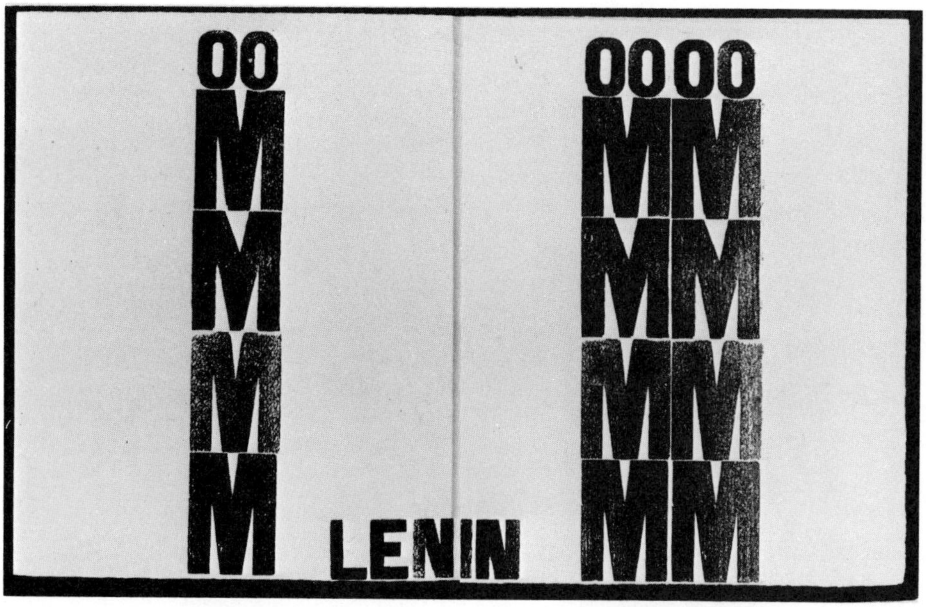

H. N. Werkman, pages from *the next call 4,* 1924. In tribute upon the death of Lenin, solemn totems composed of *M*s and *O*s suggest a silent crowd of mourners.

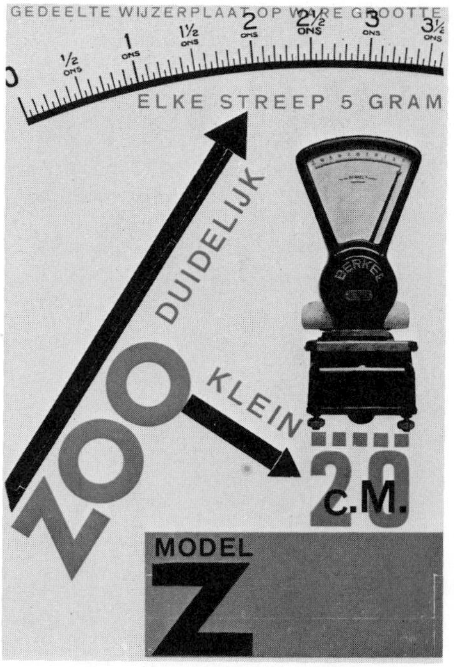

Paul Schuitema, brochure cover for the Berkel Model Z scales, before 1929. Arrows moving from the large word *ZOO* ("So") create a double headline: "So clear—every dash 5 grams," and "So small—20 centimeters [wide]." This brochure is printed letterpress from typographic material assembled on the press bed from Schuitema's layout. *The Museum of Modern Art, New York, Philip Johnson.*

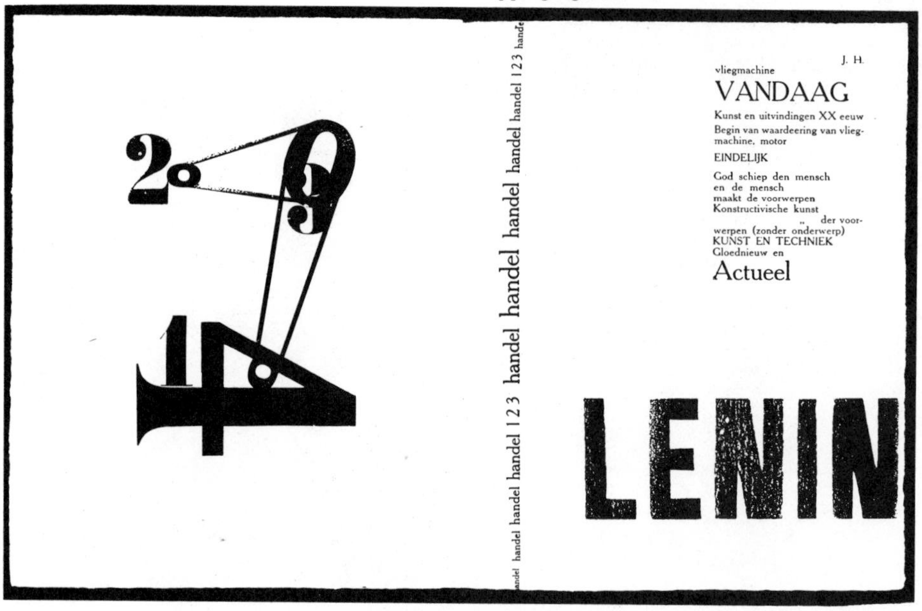

H. N. Werkman, pages from *the next call 4,* 1924. Composed directly on the press bed, the configuration on the left was achieved by multiple printings with overlapping figures.

pared to the creative process of the Dadaist, particularly in photomontage. Like Lissitzky, he explored type as concrete visual form as well as alphabet communication.

As time went on, Werkman used the brayer to lay areas of flat color directly on the paper and drew with the brayer edge. Stencils became increasingly important to his working process because he could more readily control composition and shape. A few days before the battle of liberation moved through Groningen in April 1945, Werkman was murdered by the Nazis, and much of his work was destroyed during the battle.

Another important Dutch graphic designer from Groningen province, Paul Schuitema (b. 1897) was educated as a painter during World War I, then turned to graphic design for the Berkel company in the early 1920s. He made significant use of overprinting and objective photography integrated with typography in his work. For thirty years he taught at the Royal Academy in the Hague.

In Czechoslovakia, Ladislav Sutnar (1897–1976) became the leading supporter and practitioner of functional design. He advocated the Bauhaus ideal and the application of design principles to every aspect of contemporary life. In addition to graphics, this prolific Prague designer created toys, furniture, silverware, dishes, and fabrics. The publishing house Druzstevni Prace retained Sutnar as design director. His book jackets and editorial design developed an organizational simplicity and typographic clarity giving strong graphic impact to the communication. Sutnar served as professor of design at the progressive State School for Graphic Arts from the middle of the 1920s until he emigrated to the United States in April 1939. This was one

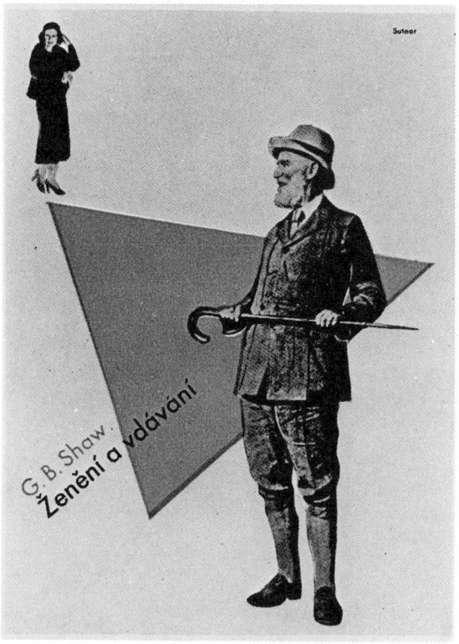

Ladislav Sutnar, cover design for *Zeneni a vdavani,* 1929. The red triangle creates a strong focal point, unifies the two silhouetted photographs, and becomes the main structural element in a delicately balanced asymmetrical composition.

Ladislav Sutnar, cover design for *Clovek nikdy nevi,* 1929. This is a superb example of Sutnar's ability to combine photography and geometric forms for highly original composition.

month after Hitler had summoned Czechoslovakia's leaders to Berlin and informed them that Prague would be destroyed from the air unless additional Czech territory was surrendered to him. In New York, Sutnar became a vital force in the evolution of modern design in the United States.

An important contribution to the use of photography as a graphic communications tool was made by Swiss designer/photographer Herbert Matter (b. 1907). While studying painting in Paris under Fernand Léger, Matter became interested in photography and design. In the early 1930s he worked with Deberny and Peignot typefoundry as a photographer and typographic designer and assisted Cassandre on posters. At age twenty-five, Matter returned to his native Switzerland and began to design posters for the Swiss National Tourist Office. Like Lazlo Moholy-Nagy, Matter thoroughly understood visual organization and techniques, such as collage and montage, of the modern movement, and applied this knowledge to photography and graphic design. His posters of the 1930s use montage, dynamic scale changes, and effective integration of typography and illustration. Photographic images become pictorial symbols removed from their normal relationships and composed in a new relationship.

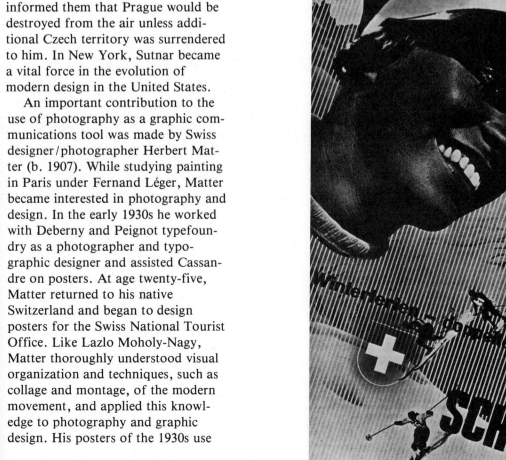

Matter pioneered extreme contrasts of scale and the integration of color with black-and-white photography. In the 1934 poster for Engelberg, the black-and-white mountain and cable car emerge from a pool of airbrushed blue. Half of the word Engelberg appears white reversed out of the blue, and half is printed in brown. A pale

Herbert Matter, travel poster for Switzerland, 1934. The dynamic shift of the composition at an angle conveys a sense of movement appropriate to winter sports. Matter had an unusual ability to combine black-and-white photography with tone. Here, for example, a screen tint under the large head introduces a skin tone, the airbrushed color around the two Swiss crosses is red, and the sky area is pale blue.

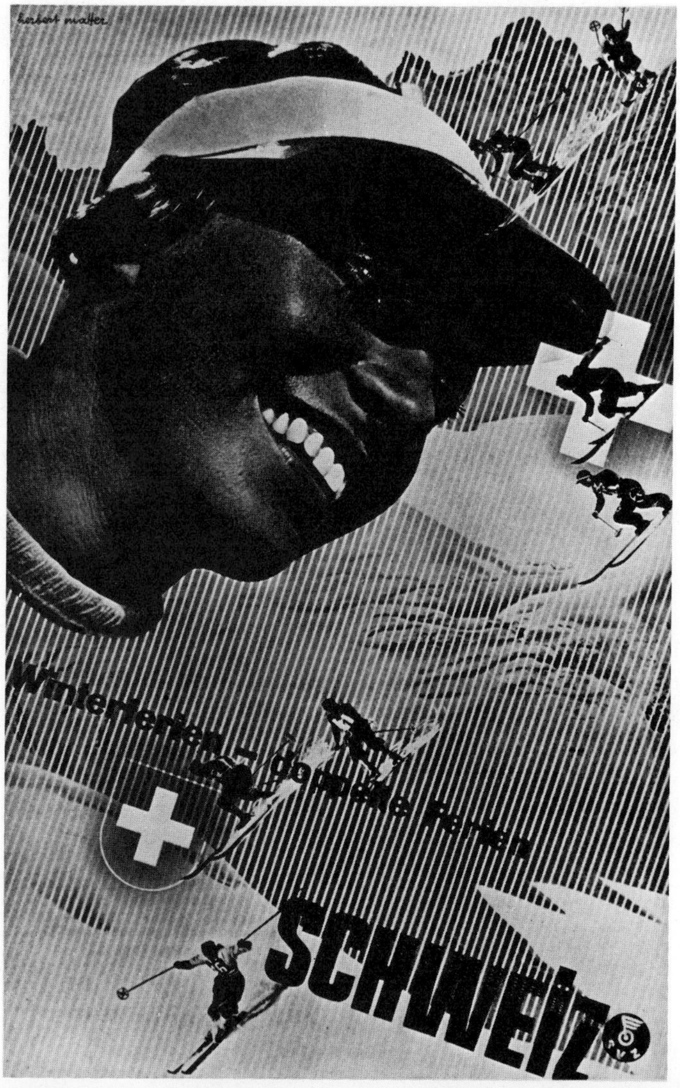

Herbert Matter, poster for Engelberg, 1934. Contrast of space and scale is achieved by the juxtaposition of the extreme closeup of the face and mittened hand and the deep vista of the cable car and mountain.

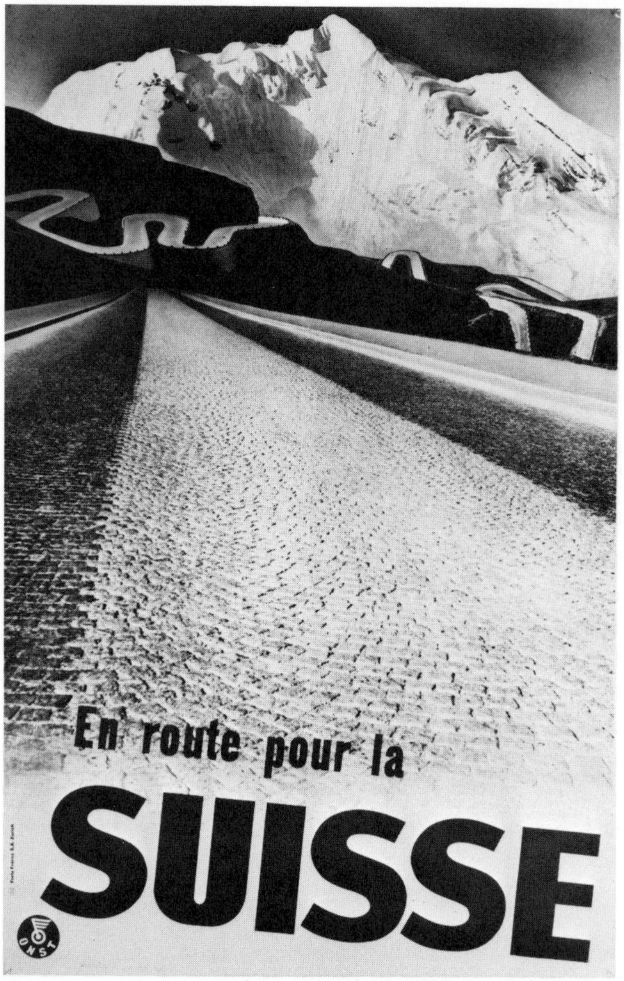

Herbert Matter, poster for the Swiss Tourist Office, 1935. The black-and-white photograph, placed between the flat blue sky and the red typography, has an internal spatial dynamic that captures a feeling of the mountain heights.

brown screen tint over the girl's face effectively introduces a feeling of color. In Matter's 1935 Swiss travel poster that proclaims that all roads lead to Switzerland, three levels of photographic information combine in a breathtaking expression of space. In the foreground, a cobblestone road photographed from ground level thrusts back into the space. Its motion is stopped by a ridge bearing the famous Swiss roadway that twists and winds over the mountains. Finally, a majestic mountain peak soars up against the blue sky.

Another innovator in the use of photography in graphic design during the 1930s was Walter Herdig (b. 1908) of Zurich, Switzerland. In publicity materials for Swiss resorts, Herdig achieved design vitality through the selection and cropping of photographic images. In designs for the St. Moritz ski resort, Herdig created a graphic unity through the consistent application of a stylized sun symbol and a gestural logotype.

The Polish designer Henryk Berlewi (1894–1967) was decisively influenced by Lissitzky's 1920 Warsaw lectures. In 1922–23 he worked in Germany and began to evolve his *mechano-faktura* theory. Believing that modern art was filled with illusionistic pitfalls, he mechanized painting and graphic design into a constructed abstraction that abolished any illusion of three dimensions. This was accomplished by mathematical placement of simple geometric forms on a ground. The mechanization of art was seen as an expression of industrial society.

In 1924 Berlewi opened a Warsaw advertising firm, called Roklama

Walter Herdig, brochure cover for St. Moritz, 1936. The closeup detailed view of the flowers combines with a panoramic vista of the mountains for a dynamic spatial composition. The trademark sun becomes part of the photograph.

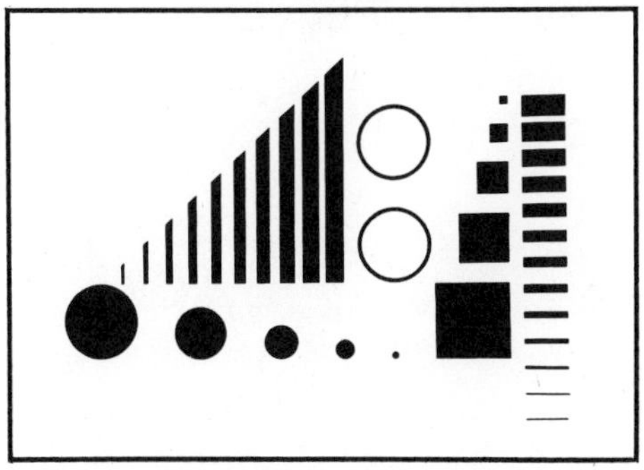

Henryk Berlewi, *Dynamic Contrasts,* Mechano-faktur composition, 1924. The "reading" of this graphic composition is intended to begin with the thin line in the lower right hand corner and follow the changing volume of forms, ending with the two outline circles.

Walter Herdig, brochure cover for St. Moritz, 1936. Dynamic angular composition and the judicious use of open space projects the thrills of skiing.

Henryk Berlewi, Plutos Chocolates brochure, page 6, 1925. The writer, Aleksander Wat, closely collaborated with the designer to integrate visual form with the copy. Printed in red and black on yellow paper, this Suprematist inspired design is composed on an implied cross that divides the page into quadrants.

Henryk Berlewi, exhibition poster, 1925. This early application of Mechano-faktur principles to graphic design is for an exhibition of Mechano-faktur works held from March 14–25, 1925. The Austro-Daimler automobile showrooms in Warsaw were selected for the presentation, and Berlewi saw the poster as a functional manifesto.

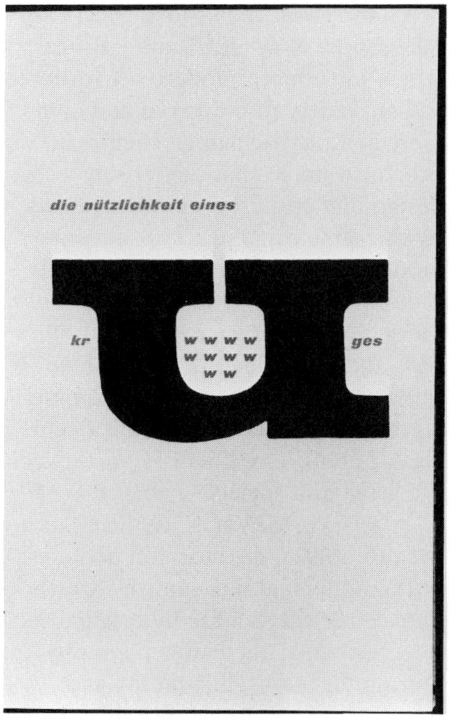

Willem Sandberg, page from *experimenta typografica,* 1956. In speaking of the utility of jugs, Sandberg transformed the *u* in *Kruges* ("jugs") into a vessel filled with blue letters.

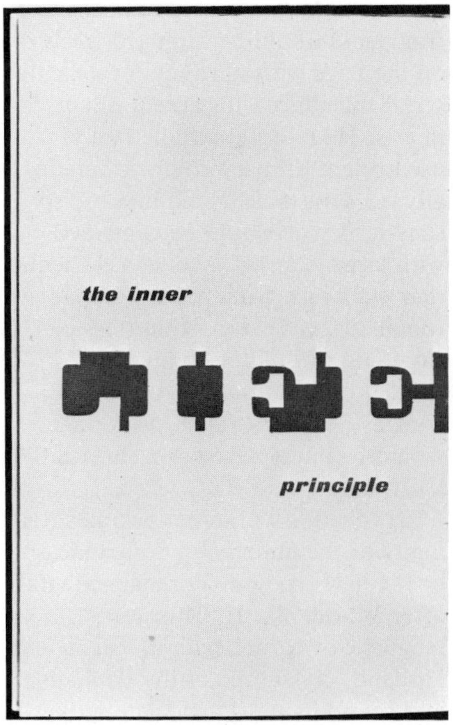

Willem Sandberg, page from *experimenta typografica,* 1956. Sandberg's sensitive exploration of the negative space between letterforms became enormously influential upon a generation of designers.

Mechano, with the Futurist poets Aleksander Wat and Stanley Brucz, which introduced modern art forms to Polish society in industrial and commercial advertisements. Their brochure stated that advertising design and costs should be governed by the same principles that govern modern industry and the laws of economy. Advertising copy was reorganized for conciseness and impact and visual layout was adapted to this text. Berlewi hoped that commercial advertising could become a vehicle for abolishing the division between the artist and society.

After World War II, Willem Sandberg (b. 1897), director and designer at the municipal museums in Amsterdam, emerged as a highly original practitioner of the new typography. During the war, while hiding and working for the Resistance, he created his *experimenta typographica.* This series of probing typographic explorations of form and space inspired his later work.

Sandberg was an explorer. In some projects, he used text settings that were completely unjustified. Sentence fragments would be arranged freely on the page with ultrabold or delicate script introduced for accent or emphasis. He rejected symmetry and used bright primary colors dramatically. Contrasts delighted him. Crisp sans-serif type would be combined with large letterform collage elements that were torn from paper and had rough edges. Text in exhibition catalogues would be printed on coarse, brown wrapping paper. In contrast, coated enamel stock pages would be interspersed as a surface for halftones.

Sandberg's work demonstrates that many of the underlying design ideas of the new typography remained vital after World War II. This new language of form began in Russia and Holland, crystalized at the Bauhaus, and found its most articulate spokesman in Jan Tschichold. The rational and scientific sensibilities of the twentieth century gained a graphic expression. Instead of being a constriction upon creativity, the new typography enabled designers of vision to develop visual communications that were functional and expressive. Aspects of the new typography continue to be important influences in the late twentieth century.

Willem Sandberg, cover for a museum journal, 1963. The white negative areas around the *m* and *j* are as important as these red letterforms. The torn edges contrast dynamically against the crisp type and razor-edged blue bar, which has an *E* torn from it. This allows white space to flow into the bar keeping it from separating from the whole.

Willem Sandberg, pages from *Keywords,* 1966. Contrasts of scale (large/small), color (red/yellow/blue/black), and edge (torn/sharp) are used in this asymmetrically balanced layout. Forms are pushed toward the edges of the page, and the implied horizontal movement created by lines of type through the lower middle help establish a unity. *Stedelijk Museum, Amsterdam.*

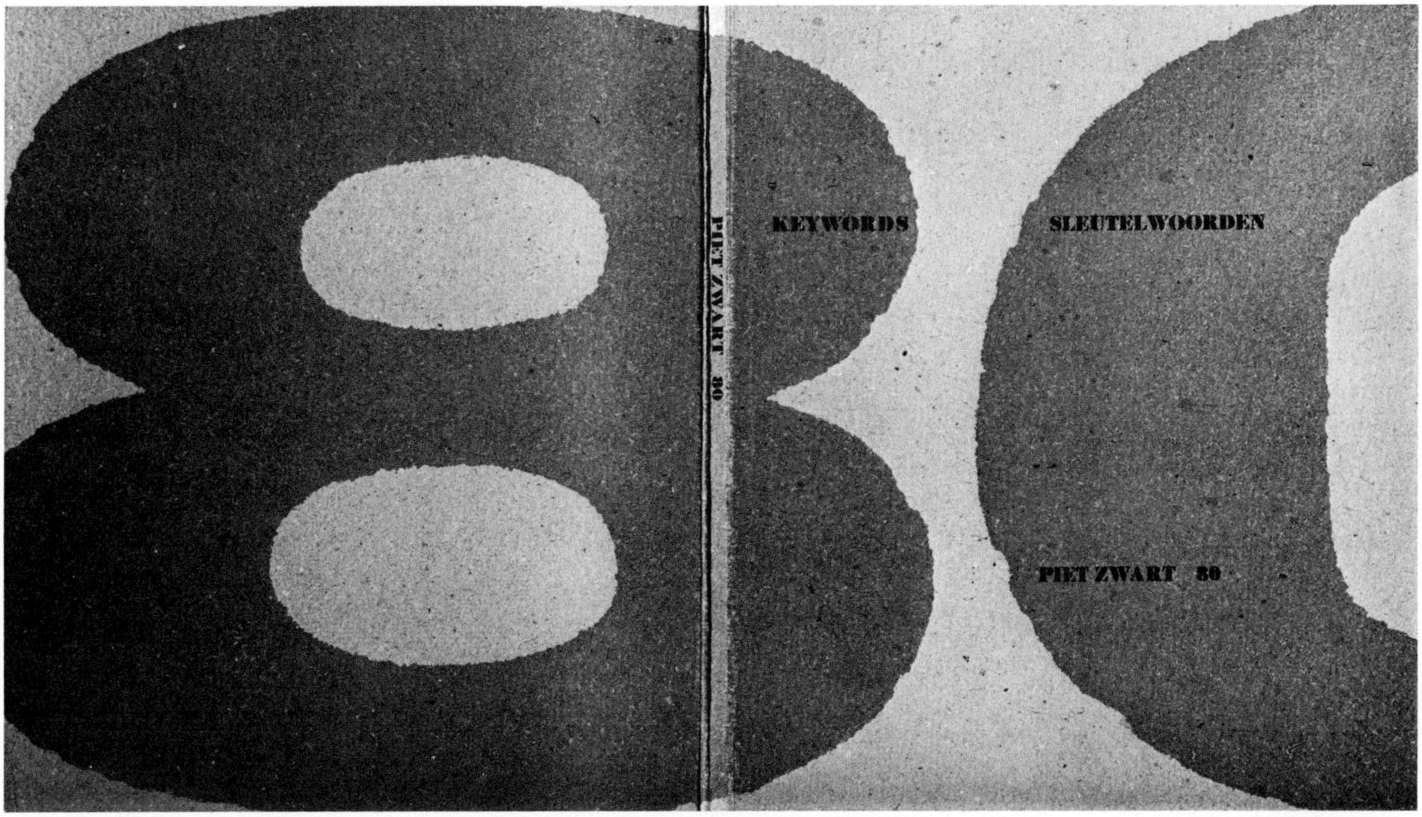

Willem Sandberg, cover for *Keywords,* 1966. In this commemorative booklet honoring Piet Zwart's eightieth birthday, the numerals are enlarged and cropped so that the front cover becomes a design interplay of positive and negative shapes. Sandberg delighted in texture and appearance of coarse papers like the stock used here. *Stedelijk Museum, Amsterdam.*

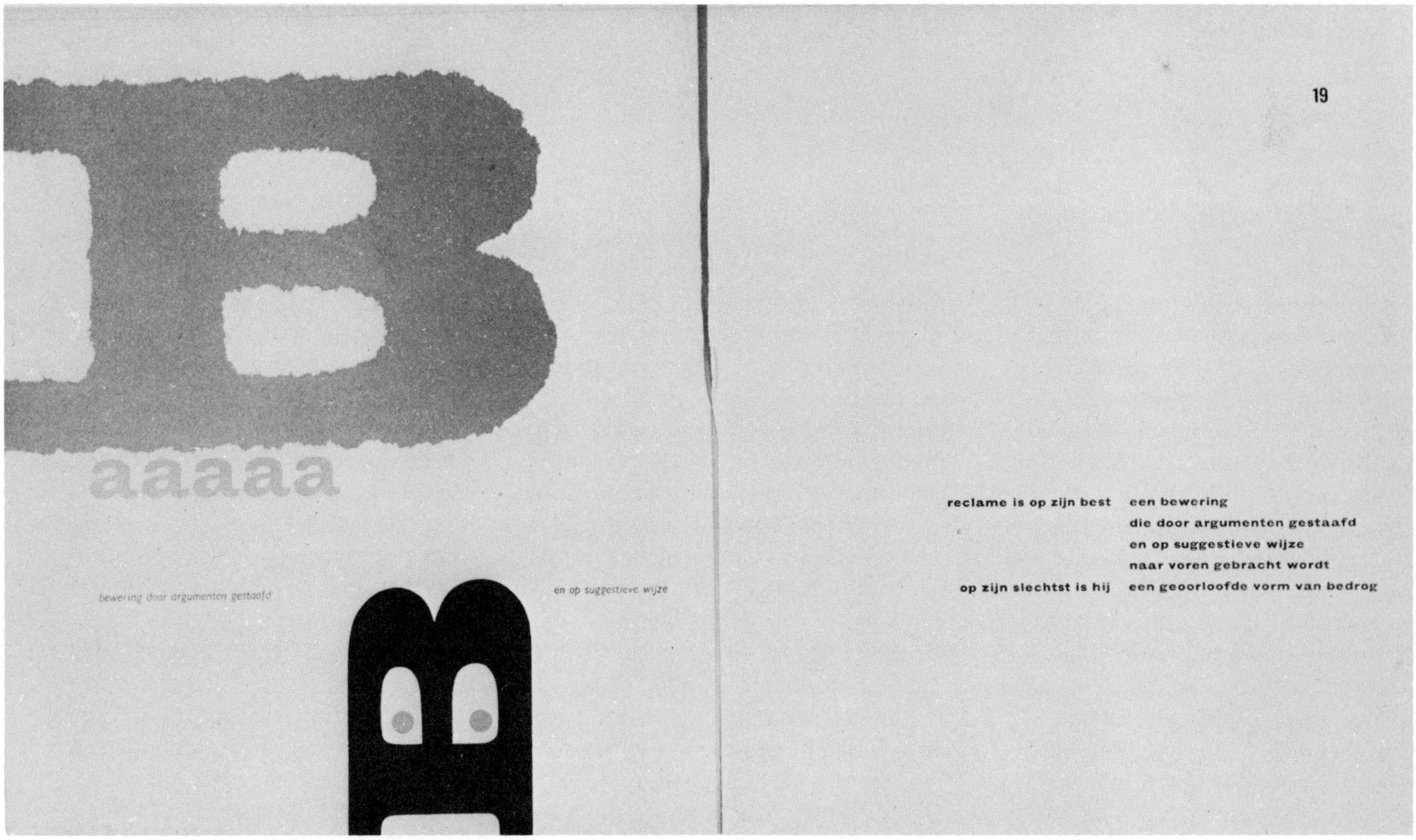

19

The Modern Movement in America

THE MODERN MOVEMENT DID NOT gain an early foothold in the United States. The fabled 1913 Armory Show, which generated a storm of protest when it introduced modern art in America, was not followed by public acceptance of modern art or design. The vitality and inventiveness of the advanced European concepts did not become a significant influence in American design until the 1930s. As the billboards in the 1936 Atlanta street scene photographed by Walker Evans (1903–1975) demonstrates, Depression Era graphic design in America was dominated by traditional illustration.

One of the leading exceptions to this rule is Lester Beall (1903–1969), a Kansas City native who moved to Chicago and earned a doctorate in art history in 1926. Beall was a self-taught graphic designer. His extensive reading and curious intellect formed the primary basis for his professional development. After gaining experience as a designer in Chicago, Beall moved his studio to New York in 1935. In the challenging social and economic environment of the Depression Era, Beall attempted to develop visual forms that were strong, direct, and exciting. Beall understood the new typography of Tschichold and the Dada movement's random organization, intuitive placement of elements, and role of chance in the creative process. Admiring the strong character and form of nineteenth-century American wood types, Beall delighted in incorporating these forms into his work of this period. Often, flat planes of color and elementary signs such as arrows were combined with photography as Beall sought visual contrast and a rich level of information content. Of particular note is Beall's poster campaign of the late 1930s for the Rural Electrification Administration, which was a Federal agency charged with bringing electricity to the rural areas of America.

In 1951, Beall moved his studio from New York City to his country

Walker Evans, *Untitled,* 1936. Evans' Atlanta photograph contrasting decaying homes and Depression Era movie posters demonstrates the gap that often exists between reality and graphic fantasy. *Library of Congress, Washington, D.C.*

home at Dumbarton Farms in Connecticut. In this new environment and in response to client and social changes, Beall became increasingly involved in the emerging corporate design movement of the 1950s and 1960s.

Immigrants to America

A migratory process began slowly, then reached a crescendo by the late 1930s, as cultural leaders from Europe—many graphic designers included—came to America. The design language that they brought with them and the changes that the American experience imposed upon their work, forms the next phase of the development of American graphic design in this century.

It is a curious coincidence that the first three individuals to bring European modernism to American graphic design were Russian-born, French-educated immigrants who worked in editorial design for fashion magazines. Erté (pseudonym for Romain de Tirtoff) was a Russian admiral's son, born in St. Petersburg in 1892. A prominent Paris illustrator and set designer who worked in the Art Deco manner, Erté was signed to an exclusive contract from 1924 until 1937 to design covers and fashion illustrations for *Harper's Bazaar* magazine. Erté's covers projected a sophisticated, continental image on the newsstand. Renowned for his fashion designs, set designs, illustrations, and graphics, Erté combined the stylized drawing of pictorial modernism with an exotic decorativeness of Persian complexity.

The first art director trained in the modern sensibility to handle the graphic destiny of a major American periodical was Dr. Mehemed Fehmy Agha (1896–1978). Born in the Ukraine to Turkish parents, Agha studied art in Kiev and received advanced degrees in languages in Paris. After working in Paris as a graphic artist, he had moved to Berlin and was there in 1928 when he met Condé Nast, who had come to close down

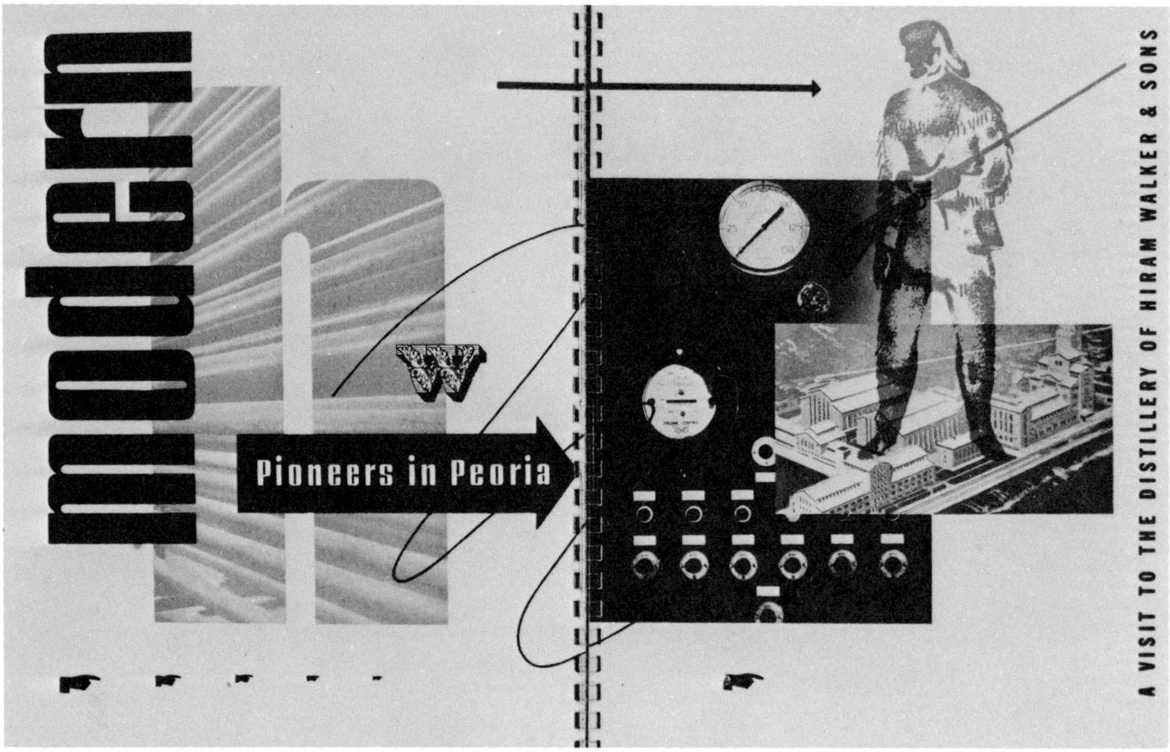

Lester Beall, title pages from a promotional brochure, c. 1935. Wood type contrasts with geometric sans-serif type and photography contrasts with drawing in this beautifully constructed layout. The strong horizontal movement is braked by a repetition of verticals.

Lester Beall, poster for the Rural Electrification Administration, c. 1937. The red and white stripes of the American flag are echoed in the "stripes" of the fence. *Library of Congress, Washington, D.C., Poster Collection.*

Lester Beall, poster for the Rural Electrification Administration, c. 1940. Dizzying diagonals establish an unstable composition that is stabilized by the rural tower bearing an aircraft beacon. *Library of Congress, Washington, D.C., Poster Collection.*

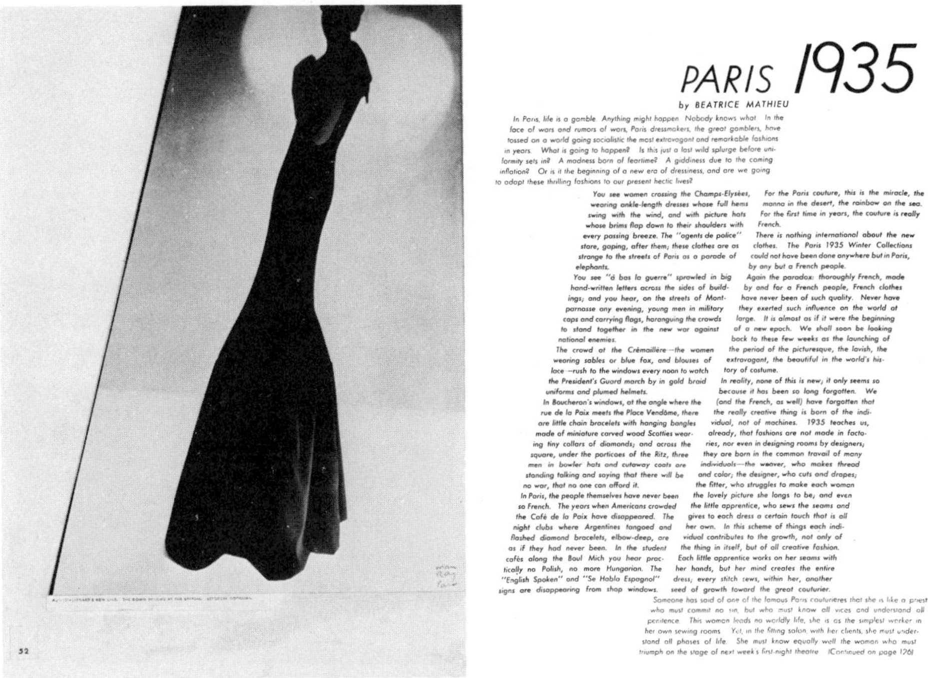

PARIS 1935

by BEATRICE MATHIEU

In Paris, life is a gamble. Anything might happen. Nobody knows what. In the face of wars and rumors of wars, Paris dressmakers, the great gamblers, have tossed on a world going socialistic the most extravagant and remarkable fashions in years. What is going to happen? Is this just a last wild splurge before uniformity sets in? A madness born of feartime? A giddiness due to the coming inflation? Or is it the beginning of a new era of dressiness, and are we going to adopt these thrilling fashions to our present hectic lives?

You see women crossing the Champs-Elysèes, wearing ankle-length dresses whose full hems swing with the wind, and with picture hats whose brims flap down to their shoulders with every passing breeze. The "agents de police" stare, gaping, after them; these clothes are as strange to the streets of Paris as a parade of elephants.

You see "à bas la guerre" sprawled in big hand-written letters across the sides of buildings; and you hear, on the streets of Montparnasse any evening, young men in military caps and carrying flags, haranguing the crowds to stand together in the new war against national enemies.

The crowd at the Crémaillère—the women wearing sables or blue fox, and blouses of lace—rush to the windows every noon to watch the President's Guard march by in gold braid uniforms and plumed helmets.

In Boucheron's windows, at the angle where the rue de la Paix meets the Place Vendôme, there are little chain bracelets with hanging bangles made of miniature carved wood Scotties wearing tiny collars of diamonds; and across the square, under the porticoes of the Ritz, three men in bowler hats and cutaway coats are standing talking and saying that there will be no war, that no one can afford it.

In Paris, the people themselves have never been so French. The years when Americans crowded the Café de la Paix have disappeared. The night clubs where Argentines tangoed and flashed diamond bracelets, elbow-deep, are as if they had never been. In the student cafès along the Boul Mich you hear practically no Polish, no more Hungarian. The "English Spoken" and "Se Habla Espagnol" signs are disappearing from shop windows.

For the Paris couture, this is the miracle, the manna in the desert, the rainbow on the sea. For the first time in years, the couture is really French.

There is nothing international about the new clothes. The Paris 1935 Winter Collections could not have been done anywhere but in Paris, by any but a French people.

Again the paradox: thoroughly French, made by and for a French people, French clothes have never been of such quality. Never have they exerted such influence on the world at large. It is almost as if it were the beginning of a new epoch. We shall soon be looking back to these few weeks as the launching of the period of the picturesque, the lavish, the extravagant, the beautiful in the world's history of costume.

In reality, none of this is new; it only seems so because it has been so long forgotten. We (and the French, as well) have forgotten that the really creative thing is born of the individual, not of machines. 1935 teaches us, already, that fashions are not made in factories, nor even in designing rooms by designers; they are born in the common travail of many individuals—the weaver, who makes thread and color; the designer, who cuts and drapes; the fitter, who struggles to make each woman the lovely picture she longs to be; and even the little apprentice, who sews the seams and gives to each dress a certain touch that is all her own. In this scheme of things each individual contributes to the growth, not only of the thing in itself, but of all creative fashion. Each little apprentice works on her seams with her hands, but her mind creates the entire dress; every stitch sews, within her, another seed of growth toward the great couturier.

Someone has said of one of the famous Paris couturières that she is like a priest who must commit no sin, but who must know all vices and understand all penitence. This woman leads no worldly life, she is as the simplest worker in her own sewing rooms. Yet, in the fitting salon, with her clients, she must understand all phases of life. She must know equally well the woman who must triumph on the stage of next week's first-night theatre (Continued on page 126)

Alexey Brodovich (art director) and Man Ray (photographer), pages from *Harper's Bazaar,* 1934. The figure's oblique thrust inspired Brodovich to construct a dynamic typographic page from several sizes and weights of geometric sans-serif types.

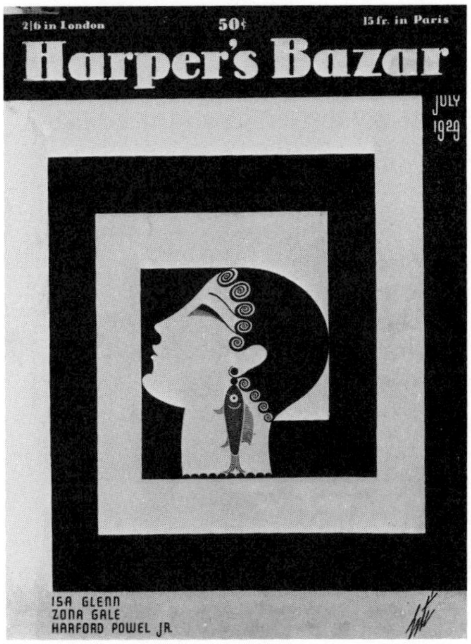

Erté, *Harper's Bazaar* cover, 1929. Bold blue and white shapes are accented by the stylized fish earring printed in scarlet.

the unprofitable Berlin edition of *Vogue* magazine. Nast was seeking a new art director for the American *Vogue.* Impressed with Agha's graphics, Nast persuaded the thirty-two-year-old Agha to come to New York and become *Vogue*'s art director. Energetic and uncompromising, Agha soon took over design responsibilities for *Vanity Fair* and *House & Garden* as well.

At the rival *Harper's Bazaar,* which had been purchased by newspaperman William Randolph Hearst in 1913 and revitalized through the use of photography, Carmel Snow became the editor in 1933. She was keenly interested in the visual aspects of the magazine and hired Hungarian Martin Munkacsi (1896–1963) as a staff photographer. Traditional conventions of editorial photography were slapped in the face by Munkacsi's fresh approaches.

Munkacsi was one of a new breed of editorial and advertising photographers who combined the visual dynamic learned from innovators, such as Moholy-Nagy and Man Ray, with the whole new approach to photography made possible by the new miniature camera, the 35mm Leica. This new camera combined with faster films of higher resolution

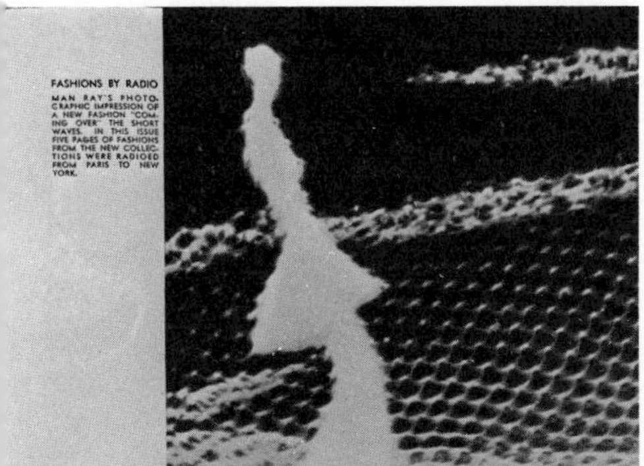

FASHIONS BY RADIO
MAN RAY'S PHOTOGRAPHIC IMPRESSION OF A NEW FASHION "COMING OVER" THE SHORT WAVES. IN THIS ISSUE FIVE PAGES OF FASHIONS FROM THE NEW COLLECTIONS WERE RADIOED FROM PARIS TO NEW YORK.
ALL COLLECTIONS VIOLENTLY PICTURESQUE
LOOK 1880 ONE MINUTE, 1950 THE NEXT
THE MOST FANTASTIC MODERN MATERIALS
STIFF AS INFANTAS IN THE EVENING
EVERYONE IS CUTTING WHOOPSY BANGS
DO NOT BELIEVE THAT DERRIERES ARE FLAT
CROWNS ZOOM HIGH AS HUSSARS
WONDERFUL NEW SHADE OF VIOLET BLUE

Alexey Brodovich (art director) and Man Ray (photographer), page from *Harper's Bazaar,* 1934. The forms and texture of the experimental photograph are amplified and complemented by the typographic design.

Martin Munkacsi, editorial photograph from *Harper's Bazaar,* 1934. Rejecting the conventions of the studio, Munkacsi allowed outside locations and the natural movements of his models to suggest innovative possibilities.

to make photography truly an extension of the photographer's vision. Invented by an employee of the Leitz Company of Germany in 1913, the introduction of this small portable camera (with a fast f/3.4-aperture lens, focal plane shutter, and a film advance that simultaneously cocked the shutter) was delayed by World War I.

After attending an exhibition in Paris of the work of Alexey Brodovich (1898–1971), Snow invited him to come to New York and art-direct *Harper's Bazaar,* where he remained from 1934 until 1958.

Brodovich, with a passion for white space and love of razor-sharp type on clear, open pages, rethought the approach to editorial design. He sought "a musical feeling" in the flow of text and pictures. The rhythmic environment of open space balancing text was energized by the art and photography he commissioned from such innovators as Salvador Dali, Henri Cartier-Bresson, and Man Ray. Brodovich taught designers how to use photography. His cropping, enlarging, and juxtaposing of images, and his exquisite selection from contact sheets were all done with extraordinary intuitive judgment.

Perhaps because of the strong pictorial quality of his designs, Joseph Binder received wide acclaim when he migrated to America. He arrived in 1934 for a series of lectures and workshops, and, touched by the response to his work, he settled in New York the following year. In America Binder's style became more refined, partly because he had begun to use the airbrush to achieve highly finished forms. His strong Cubist influence yielded to a stylized realism. Binder was an ideal choice to create the 1939 New York World's Fair poster. His refined, simple forms, with the sphere and obelisk symbols of the fair, the spotlights, and modern transportation symbols, signifies America's hesitant move into modernism and global power. As can be seen in his 1939 poster for iced coffee, traces of Cubism remain. Two-dimensional planes undergird and support the illustrative content. During his Vienna period, Binder had constructed images from planes. Now, the subject matter became dominant, and the design qualities subordinate.

Joseph Binder, poster for the New York World's Fair, 1939. The trylon and perisphere—emblems of the fair—combine with spotlights, a skyline, and modern transportation images to symbolize America's coming of age on the eve of World War II. World events would soon force the United States to cast aside its provincialism and neutrality. *Library of Congress, Washington, D.C., Poster Collection.*

Alexey Brodovich, poster for *Martini,* 1926. Before emigrating to America, Brodovich had achieved a thorough understanding of modern design in his French posters. *Museum of Modern Art, New York.*

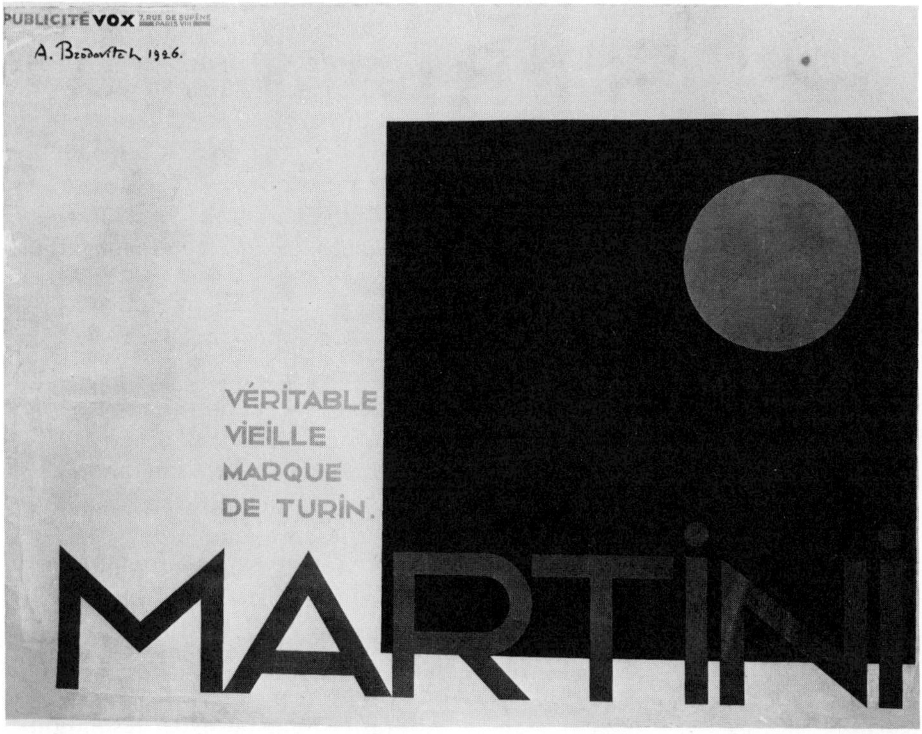

Joseph Binder, poster for A & P Coffee, 1939. Flat shapes and airbrushed modulations create strong value contrasts requiring the viewer to "fill-in" the details of Binder's edited naturalism.

The Works Progress Administration poster project

As part of the New Deal of President Franklin Delano Roosevelt, the Federal government created the Works Progress Administration (WPA) in 1935. Direct relief for the unemployed was replaced by work opportunities, and billions of dollars were pumped into the economy as an average of over two million workers were paid from fifteen to ninety dollars per month from 1935 until 1941. Jobs were designed to "help men keep their chins up and their hands in." A poster project was included among the various cultural programs in the WPA Federal Art Project. From 1935 until 1939, when the Federal Art Projects were abolished, over two million copies of approximately thirty-five thousand designs were produced. Most of the designs were silkscreened, and sculptors and painters joined unemployed illustrators and graphic designers in the studios.

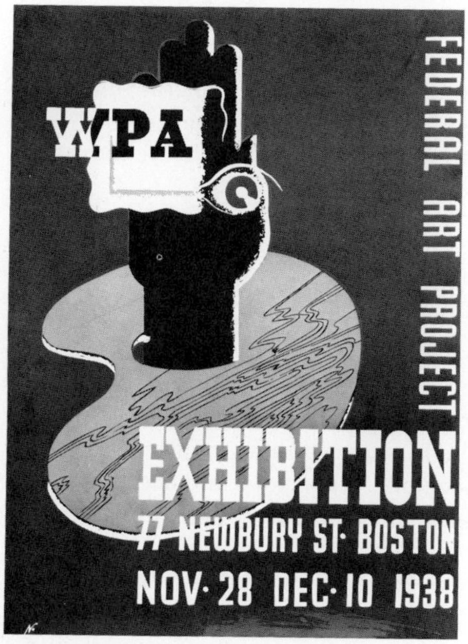

Works Progress Administration (WPA) poster, 1938. Often designed by artists who would rather be painting than producing graphics, the WPA posters combined elements of pictorial modernism with other graphic forms such as the slab-serif lettering shown here. *Library of Congress, Washington, D.C., Poster Collection.*

The natural, flat color qualities of silkscreen printing combined with Bauhaus, European pictorial modernism, and Constructivist influences to produce a surprisingly modern result in contrast to the dominance of naturalistic illustration in much American mass media graphics of the era. Government-sponsored cultural events, including theatrical performances and art exhibitions, were primary subjects for the poster project. Public service communication—health issues, crime prevention, housing, education—were other frequent subjects. Typography was often approached from an aesthetic viewpoint and used as both compositional element and message communication.

The flight from fascism

The rising tide of Nazism in Europe created the greatest transnational migration of intellectual and creative talent in history. European scientists, authors, architects, artists, and designers left Europe for the haven of North America during the late 1930s, for they realized that freedom of inquiry and expression was in grave danger on the European continent. The artists included Max Ernst, Marcel Duchamp, and Piet Mondrian. As mentioned earlier, the Nazis closed the Bauhaus in 1933. Faculty, students, and alumni dispersed throughout the world and made modern design a truly international movement. Walter Gropius, Mies van der Rohe, and Marcel Breuer transplanted the functionalist architectural movement to American shores, and Herbert Bayer and Laszlo Moholy-Nagy brought their innovative approaches to graphic design. Other graphic designers who came to America and made significant contributions to design in this country include Herbert Matter, Jean Carlu, Ladislav Sutnar, and Will Burtin.

Sponsored by the Association of Arts and Industries, Laszlo Moholy-Nagy arrived in Chicago in 1937 and established the New Bauhaus. This closed after one year due to inadequate financial support, but Moholy-Nagy managed to open the School of Design in 1939, backed more with imagination and spirit than economic resources. The primary source of financial support came from Moholy-Nagy and other faculty members, many of whom agreed to teach without pay if necessary. Moholy-Nagy was not the only one of the transplanted European designers who experienced difficulty in the effort to transplant their creative work into the new world; both Carlu and Bayer found it difficult to find clients who comprehended their work during their first months in America.

Chicago had an enlightened architectural heritage stemming from the work of Louis Sullivan, who designed early highrise buildings in that city, and Frank Lloyd Wright. A group of Chicago citizens arranged for Mies van der Rohe to come to Chicago and join the architectural faculty of the Armour Institute of Technology (now Illinois Institute of Technology).

A patron of design

A major figure in the development of the modern design movement in America beginning in the 1930s was a Chicago industrialist, Walter P. Paepcke (1896–1960), who founded the Container Corporation of America in 1926. At a time when most products were shipped in wooden containers, Paepcke pioneered the manufacture of paperboard and corrugated fiber containers. Acquisitions and expansion enabled Container Corporation to become a national company and the nation's largest producer of packaging materials. Paepcke was unique among the captains of industry of his generation, for he recognized that design could serve both a pragmatic business function and become a major cultural thrust by the corporation. In 1936, Paepcke hired Egbert Jacobson (1890–1966) to become the first director of Container Corporation's new department of design. As with the design program for AEG by Peter Behrens early in the century, Container Corporation's new logo and its implementation was based on two in-

Egbert Jacobson, logo for Container Corporation, 1936. This logical symbol combining the major product and suggesting the national scope of the firm was innovative for its time.

A. M. Cassandre, advertisement for Container Corporation, 1938. A strong statement, "Research, experience, and talent focused on advanced paperboard packaging," is given near hypnotic graphic impact.

A. M. Cassandre, cover for *Harper's Bazaar,* 1939. A pink perfume bottle forms the nose, lipstick creates a mouth, and a puff of powder colors a cheek in an almost textbook demonstration of simultaneity.

gredients: the visual design abilities of the designer and a supportive client. Jacobson had an extensive background as a color expert, and this knowledge was put to use as mill and factory interiors were transformed from drab industrial grays and browns to bright colors. A new trademark was designed, and graphic materials such as stationery and invoices were redesigned with a consistent format using Futura type and a standard color combination of black and tan (of the shipping carton variety).

Paepcke was an advocate and patron of design. He had maintained a long-standing interest in the Bauhaus, which may have been a response to the experiments with paper materials and structures. Moved by Moholy-Nagy's commitment and determination, Paepcke provided the moral and financial support needed by the Institute of Design to survive. By the time of Moholy-Nagy's tragic early death from leukemia on 24 November 1946, the Institute was on a firm educational and organizational footing.

Beginning in May 1937, A. M. Cassandre was commissioned to create a series of advertisements for Container Corporation that turned the conventions of American advertising upside down. The traditional headline and body copy were replaced by a dominant visual that extended a simple statement about Container Corporation. In contrast to the long-winded copywriting of the 1930s, many of these advertisements only had a dozen words. These communications separated Container Corporation from the general din of advertising.

During the late 1930s, Cassandre was commissioned to design covers for *Harper's Bazaar* by Alexey Brodovich. When Cassandre decided to return to Paris in 1939, Container Corporation continued his general approach by commissioning advertisements from other artists and designers of international statue including Herbert Bayer (who was retained as a consulting designer by Jacobson), Fernand Léger, Man Ray, Herbert Matter, and Jean Carlu.

From Budapest, Hungary, Albert Kner (1899–1976) headed for Chicago after arriving in America in 1940. Moholy-Nagy had informed his fellow countryman of Chicago's receptive climate toward design, and Kner had been impressed by the Container Corporation's advertising campaign. Paepcke hired Kner as Container Corporation's first staff package designer. For over two decades, Kner headed the Design and Market Research Laboratory. Scientific research methods were applied to marketing, to evaluating the sales effectiveness of packaging, and to the development of new packaging products and structures. The laboratory pioneered the Ocular camera which takes a continuous sequence of photographs as a person's eye movement traces over a design.

The war years

While World War I was primarily fought in trenches removed from the urban population, World War II was fought with lightning invasions by mechanized divisions and aerial bombardment of industry and cities. The trauma of this war disrupted the ability of many governments to produce graphic propaganda. In the United States, a diverse group of painters, illustrators, and designers received commissions from the U. S. Office of War Information.

In 1941, as America's entry into the global conflict became increasingly inevitable, the Federal government held a poster competition on the subject of production as America's colossal defense buildup began. Jean Carlu won first prize with one of the finest designs of his career. Over a hundred thousand of these posters were produced for distribution throughout the country, and Carlu was recognized with a top award by the New York Art Director's Club Exhibition.

Intense feelings about Hitler, Pearl Harbor, and the war seemed to pull powerful communications from the graphic designers, illustrators, and fine artists commissioned to create posters for the Office of War Information. Illustrator John Atherton (b. 1900), whose credits included numerous *Saturday Evening Post* covers, penetrated to the heart of the problem of careless talk, gossip, and discussion of troop movements as a source of enemy information. Joseph Binder's 1941 poster for the U. S. Army Air Corps is potent in its simplicity and beauty of design. E. McKnight Kauffer was commissioned to design stunningly simple posters to boost the morale of the occupied Allies. In the poster for Greece bearing the Greek headline that translates "We Fight for the Liberty of All," a classical Greek head is combined with an American flag to make a powerful graphic symbol. The angry social realist Ben Shahn (1898–1969), whose powerful style of awkward shapes had addressed social and economic injustice during the depression, reached a larger audience in posters conveying Nazi brutality.

Jean Carlu, poster promoting productivity, 1941. Visual and verbal elements are inseparably interlocked into an intense universal symbol of work. *Library of Congress, Washington, D.C., Poster Collection.*

John Atherton, poster for the U.S. Office of War Information, 1943. The placement of the two-part headline implies a rectangle within the space. This symmetry is animated by the white cross that is pushed to the left. *Library of Congress, Washington, D.C., Poster Collection.*

Joseph Binder, poster for the U.S. Army Air Corps, 1941. A symbolic suggestion of great depth is achieved by the scale change between the close-up aircraft wing and the formation of aircraft.

E. McKnight Kauffer, poster supporting the Greek resistance, 1940. Kauffer managed to unite two unlike symbolic forms, a flag and a classical head, into a unified whole. *Library of Congress, Washington, D.C., Poster Collection.*

The posters that Herbert Bayer produced during and after the war were surprising in their illustrative qualities compared to his ardent insistence on Constructivism during his Dessau Bauhaus period. Sensitive to his new audience and oriented toward communications problem solving, Bayer moved into an almost pictographic illustration style which was combined with the hierarchy of information and the strong underlying composition that he pioneered at Dessau. In his early 1940s poster promoting egg production, the large white egg centered against the black sky becomes a strong focal point. The headline to the left balances the flaming town to the right, and the diagonal subheading echoes the diagonal shadow cast by the egg.

When one compares Bayer's 1949 poster for polio research with the 1926 poster for the Kandinsky Jubilee Exhibition, one finds that these two graphic designs are worlds apart. The Kandinsky poster was designed by a twenty-six-year-old typography teacher at a young school optimistically hoping to rebuild a new social order by design. The polio research poster is the work of a forty-eight-year-old designer living in a foreign land, who had seen the death of twenty-six million people in Europe during World War II. The Dessau Bauhaus had been closed for political reasons; now it sat in mute testament to the hopes and dreams of a generation, locked behind the "iron curtain" that had divided Europe after the war. The photography and typography of his Bauhaus period have yielded to handpainted illustration and handlettering, but the commitment to functional communication, the integration of letterforms and imagery, and the asymmetrical balance remain constant.

During World War II, Container Corporation innovated new uses for

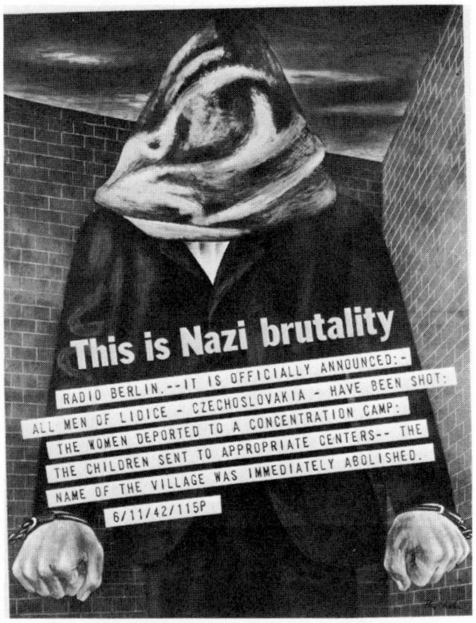

Ben Shahn, poster for the U.S. Office of War Information, 1943. A combination of graphic devices brings communicative power to this poster: the prisonlike closing of the space with a wall, the hood masking the victim's identity, the simple, straightforward headline, and the factual urgency of the telegraphic message. *The Museum of Modern Art, New York, Gift of The Office of War Information.*

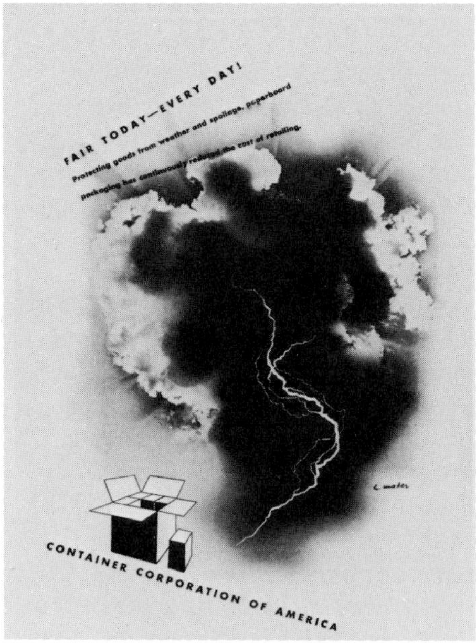

Herbert Matter, advertisement for Container Corporation, 1942. A dramatic thunderstorm ripped by lightning reinforces the copy concept that paperboard packaging protects goods from weather and spoilage. The lightning becomes a strong focal point that unites the two areas of typography by becoming a visual connector.

Herbert Bayer, poster to encourage egg production, c. 1943. The primary colors of De Stijl are used in altered form. The headline is blue, the flames are red, and the area to the left of the egg is a muted yellow. *Library of Congress, Washington, D.C., Poster Collection.*

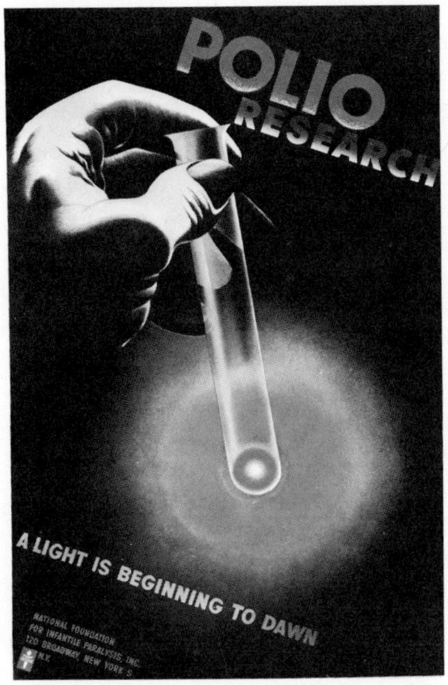

Herbert Bayer, poster supporting Polio Research, 1949. The diagonal shaft of the test tube leads the eye from the red-and-blue headline to the flowing yellow light that is beginning to dawn. This links the elements in the same manner as the thick black bars of his Bauhaus work. *Library of Congress, Washington, D.C., Poster Collection.*

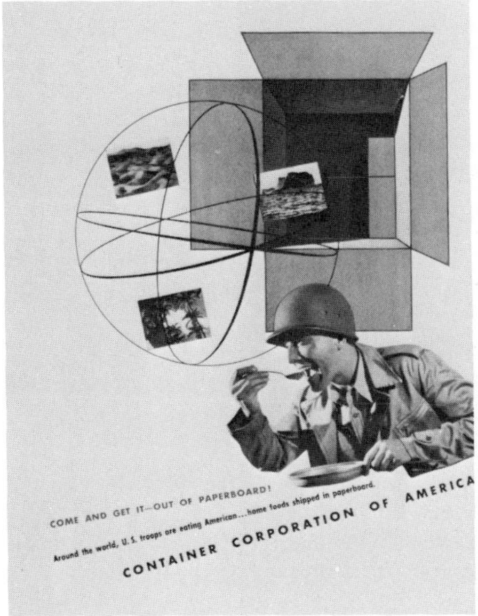

Herbert Matter, advertisement for Container Corporation, 1943. In this "paperboard goes to war" advertisement, a unified complex of images telegraphs global scope, paperboard boxes, and food for our troops.

U. S. supplies, packed in paper, speed the liberation of The Netherlands and colonies
CONTAINER CORPORATION OF AMERICA

Willem de Kooning, advertisement, *The Netherlands,* for Container Corporation, 1945. Once selected to visualize their native lands or states, the fine artists participating in these campaigns were given the freedom of their artistic convictions.

paperboard packaging, which freed metals and other strategic materials for the war effort. A "Paperboard Goes to War" advertising campaign continued the design experimentation and excellence of the earlier institutional advertisements. Each advertisement showed a specific use of a Container Corporation product in the war effort. Herbert Bayer, Jean Carlu, and Herbert Matter joined Jacobson in creating powerful telegraphic statements that went directly to the essence of the communications problem using strong visuals and two or three lines of typography whose angled thrust picked up diagonal compositional lines from the illustration or montage. The next series of Container Corporation advertisements commemorated the twenty-eight allied nations who were fighting together during World War II. The final documents ending the war in the Pacific were signed on 2 September 1945, and the list of countries was completed the following spring.

After the war

Seeking another institutional advertising campaign using fine art, Container Corporation decided to honor the states by commissioning paintings from a native artist from each of the then forty-eight states. Under each full-color painting, there appeared a simple copy line; for example, "IOWA—annual purchases: 1 $\frac{3}{4}$ billion—mostly packaged," followed by the Container Corporation logotype. Both the nations and states series served to advance a Bauhaus ideal; the union of art with life. Artists were commissioned to express visually their homeland or state, and these works of art were reproduced as part of the pragmatic need of Container Corporation to speak to its diverse audiences.

After completion of the series of advertisements commemorating the states, Walter Paepcke conceived what is perhaps the most brilliant institutional campaign in the history of advertising. Paepcke and his wife Elizabeth were attending the Great Books discussion group conducted in Chicago by Robert M. Hutchins and Mortimer Adler. These two scholars were also editing the series, Great Books of the Western World, which included two volumes discussing the ideas contained in the series. Paepcke approached Adler with the possibility of a series of institutional advertisements presenting the great ideas of western man. Each would have an artist's graphic interpretation of a great idea provided by Adler and his colleagues. Walter and Elizabeth Paepcke joined Egbert Jacobson and Herbert Bayer as a jury to select the visual artists who would be asked to bring graphic actualization to abstract concepts. Beginning in February 1950, this unprecedented institutional campaign transcended the bounds of advertising as ideas about liberty, justice, and human rights were conveyed to an audience of "business men, investors, prospective employees, and leaders of public opinion." The effectiveness of the campaign arose from the fact that it separated Container Corporation from its army of competitors. It made Container Corporation appear somehow different to its diverse publics,

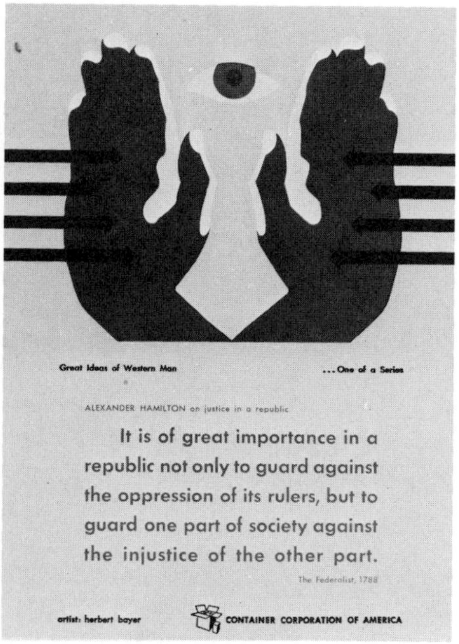

Herbert Bayer, "Great Ideas" advertisement for Container Corporation, 1954. Protection from injustice and oppression is expressed with immediacy by the blue and white hands warding off black arrows penetrating into the yellow page.

Herbert Bayer, "Great Ideas" advertisement for Container Corporation, 1960. Theodore Roosevelt's admonition that the "love of soft living and the get-rich-quick theory of life" were threats to America found expression in a collage of images of affluence and decadence.

for a company whose management spends a portion of its advertising budget conveying great ideas presented visually by outstanding artists and designers must possess positive social and cultural qualities. And this campaign has continued for over three decades.

Alexey Brodovich grew in skill and assurance as an editorial designer through the 1940s and 1950s. He showed remarkable skill at identifying and assisting new talent. Photographers Richard Avedon (b. 1923) and Irving Penn (b. 1917) both received early commissions and advice from Brodovich. Art Kane (b. 1925) was another Brodovich protegé. Kane worked as a photo retoucher and art director of *Seventeen* magazine before turning to photography. He is a master of symbolism, multiple exposure, and the reduction of photography to essential images needed to convey the essence of content with compelling conviction.

During the early 1950s, Brodovich designed the short-lived visual arts magazine *Portfolio.* At the height of his graphic powers, Brodovich gave this publication an elegance and visual flow that has seldom been matched. The pacing, cropping of images, and use of color and texture were extraordinary. Large images, dynamic space, and inserts on colored or textured papers changed the tactile and perceptual experience of reading a magazine.

Herbert Matter had arrived in the United States in 1936. In addition to his freelance design commissions for Container Corporation of America during the war, Matter received design and photographic assignments from many clients, including *Vogue, Fortune* and *Harper's Bazaar.* In 1946 Matter began a twenty-year period as graphic design and photography consultant to the Knoll Associates furniture design and manufacturing firm, and produced some of his finest work for this design-oriented client.

The 1948 advertisement in black and yellow for molded plastic chairs by Eero Saarinen is remarkable in its dynamic composition. Biomorphic

Alexey Brodovich, cover for *Portfolio,* 1951. Screen tints are used to produce the illusion that translucent rectangles of pink and blue-gray have been placed on the stencil logo slashing down the black cover.

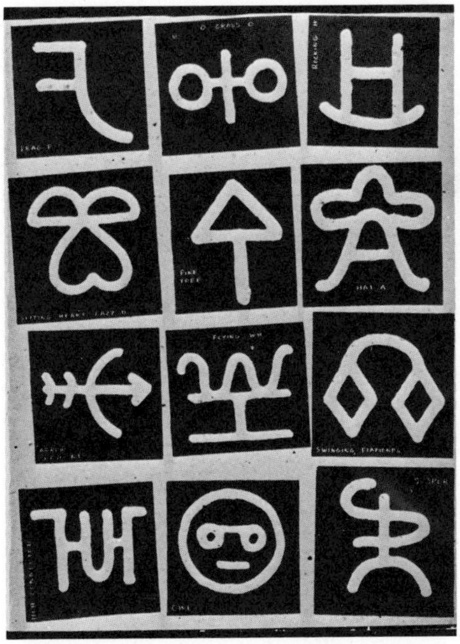

Alexey Brodovich, pages from *Portfolio,* 1951. Brodovich's mastery of contrast is seen in the scale change between the small scattered cattlebrands around the well-stamped bull and the large cattlebrands of the first page of the portfolio. Also, rough-textured paper contrasts with slick, coated white stock.

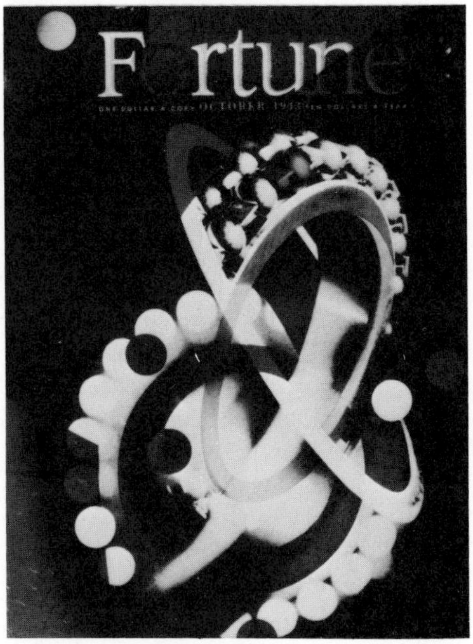

Herbert Matter, cover for *Fortune,* 1943. A photograph, a photogram, and graphic shapes combine to express industrial precision and machine engineering.

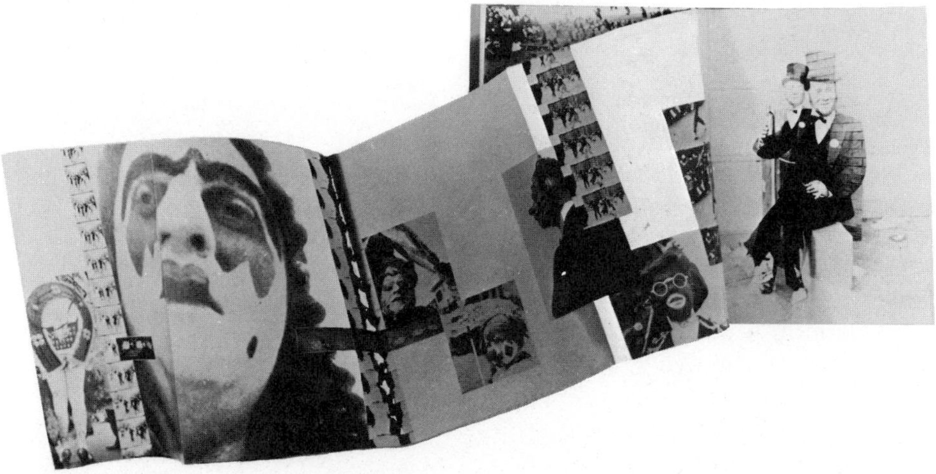

Alexey Brodovich, foldout photographic essay from *Portfolio,* 1951. Stretching about 138 centimeters (4 ½ feet), this layout of images from the Mummer's Parade is punctuated with vertical columns of film strips. Graphic design only rarely becomes this sequential and kinetic.

shapes were quite fashionable during the late 1940s and early 1950s in painting, furniture, and other design forms. Considered sophisticated and the ultimate expression of modernism circa 1950, biomorphic design became trapped in this time frame and is now associated with the sensibilities of the period. It is a tribute to Matter's strong sense of design fundamentals that the advertising series he created for Saarinen furniture has maintained a design vitality long after the forms of the era have become dated.

During the 1950s, Matter turned toward more purely photographic solutions after a quarter of a century of integration of graphic and photographic elements. His ability to convey concepts with images is shown in the 1956 folder unveiling a new line of molded plastic pedestal furniture. A strange object wrapped in paper appears on the cover of the brochure, printed in full color on translucent paper. Underneath, the reader finds a Saarinen pedestal chair bearing a fashionable model. The surprise value of this sequence grows out of the unexpected new furniture with just one pedestal leg. The viewer, first seeing the cover, does not recognize the shape of the traditional four-legged chair. These photographs were also

Herbert Matter, advertisement for Knoll Associates, 1948. Photographs of organic chair components combine with yellow flat-shaped "shadows" in an advertisement that has the energy of a Calder mobile.

used as advertisements on two consecutive right-hand pages of magazines.

With his powerful shapes and well-defined subjects, Joseph Binder remained a force on the American design scene until the 1960s. His ubiquitous military recruiting posters, which were among the last manifestations of pictorial modernism, were ingrained into the American consciousness during the 1950s. The geometric and symbolic shapes of pictorial modernism were converted into monolithic masses that became symbols of military might and the technological accomplishments of a new era of sophisticated weaponry.

Born to Italian and Swiss parents, George Giusti (b. 1908) worked in both Italy and Switzerland before coming to New York City in 1938 and opening a design office. Giusti's great gift as a graphic designer has been an ability to reduce forms and images to a simplified, minimal essence. His images become iconographic and symbolic. Giusti uses freehand drawing and includes evidence of process in his work. An image painted in trans-

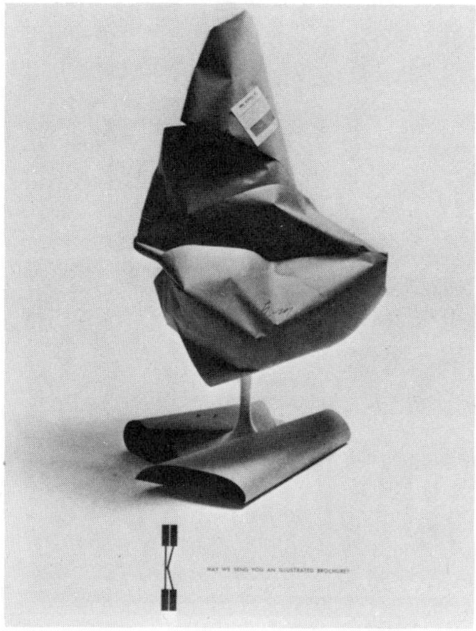

Herbert Matter, brochure covers introducing a Knoll chair, 1956. On the translucent cover, the warm browns of the kraft paper are keyed to the orange logo. On the inner cover, the crisp black and white of the girl's clothing and the white chair are accented with a red logo, cushion, and lipstick.

parent dyes will have areas of flooded and blotted color, and his three-dimensional illustrations often include the bolts or other fasteners used to assemble the elements. For all of their simplicity, Giusti's images retain a human warmth. Beginning in the 1940s and continuing well into the 1960s, Giusti received frequent commissions from *Holiday* and *Fortune* magazines for cover designs. *Holiday,* a travel publication, called upon Giusti to capture the essence of Rome or Germany or England for special features. *Fortune* commissioned Giusti to summarize subjects as complex as the trucking industry with elemental graphic images. The bold, iconographic quality of Giusti's images were used frequently in advertising campaigns, particularly industrial ones.

Joseph Binder, recruiting poster for the U.S. Navy, c. 1954. Traces of Cassandre's steamship posters remain, but the strength expressed is more powerful and forbidding. *Library of Congress, Washington, D.C., Poster Collection.*

Ladislav Sutnar came to New York in 1939 as design director for the Czechoslovakian Pavilion at the New York World's Fair and remained to continue his career. A close association with Sweet's Catalog Service enabled Sutnar to place an indelible mark upon the design of industrial

George Giusti, cover for *Holiday,* 1960. Part Cubism and part expressionism, this simplified and colorful design strikes to the heart of the legend of Romulus, the founder of Rome, and his twin Remus. Reputedly, the pair were raised by a wolf.

product information. Since 1906 Sweet's had provided a compendium of architectural and industrial product information.

Working closely with Sweet's research director, Sutnar defined informational design as a synthesis of function, flow, and form. Function is utilitarian need with a definite purpose: to make information easy to find, read, comprehend, and recall.

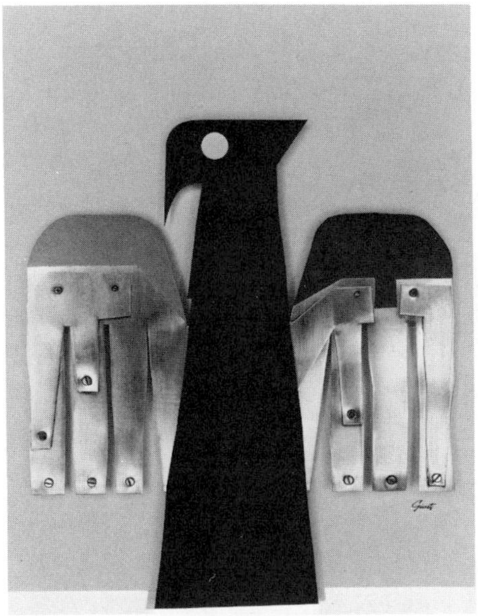

George Giusti, cover for *Holiday,* 1964. This three-dimensional construction of painted and unpainted metal symbolizes the imperial German eagle for a special issue on that country.

Ladislav Sutnar, Sweet's Catalog Service symbol, 1942. Disarmingly simple and possessing a beautifully harmonious figure-ground relationship, this symbol established the typographic character for Sweet's printed material. A registered trademark of McGraw-Hill, Inc., used by permission.

Ladislav Sutnar, title page for *Catalog Design Progress,* 1950. Bars and rectangles containing type become compositional elements to be balanced in dynamic equilibrium.

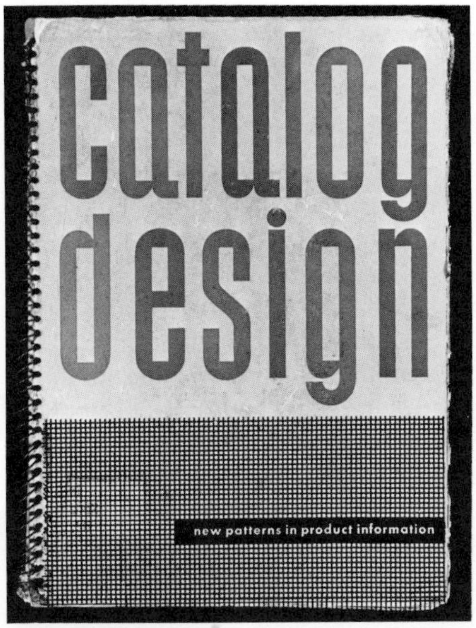

Ladislav Sutnar, cover for *Catalog Design,* 1944. This book presented Sutnar's emerging philosophy of structuring information in a logical and consistent manner. The geometrically constructed letterforms are alternated in blue and orange, and the grid pattern is printed in black.

Flow is the logical sequence of information. Sutnar felt the basic unit to be, not the page, but the "visual unit" which is the double-page spread. He rejected traditional margins because they are rigid containers that create barriers to visual flow. He employed bleeds extensively.

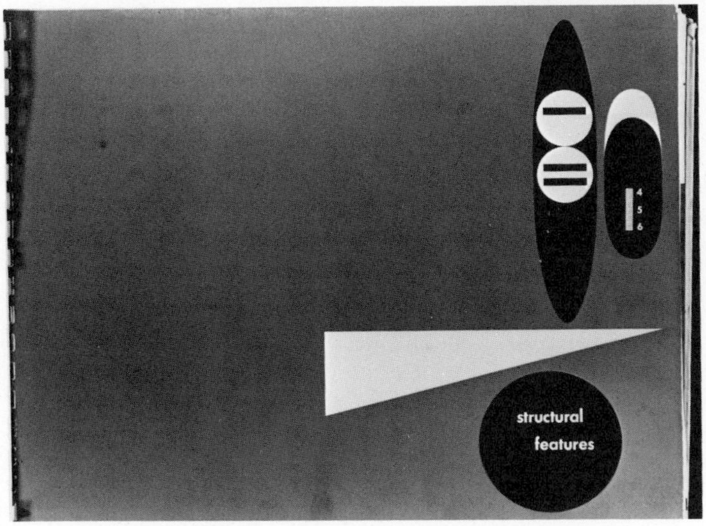

Ladislav Sutnar, section divider page from *Catalog Design Progress,* 1950. The coding on the ovals, following a system throughout the book, indicate that this is part one, section two, topics four, five, and six: structural features. The triangle points the reader forward.

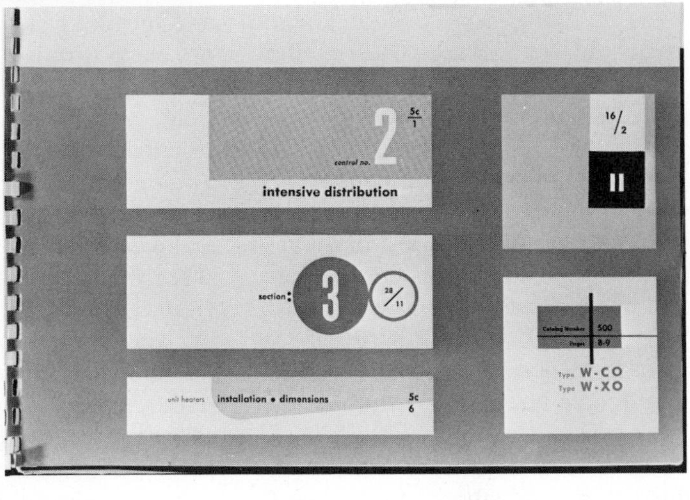

Ladislav Sutnar, page from *Catalog Design Progress,* 1950. These designs demonstrate how systems of identifying information can use line, shape, color, and type to create "visual traffic signs" in the upper right-hand corner, each visual unit's point of entrance, to assist the user in the search for information.

Ladislav Sutnar, page from *Catalog Design Progress,* 1950. The construction of page layouts for an electron tubes catalogue is shown. A consistent, horizontal band and three-column grid were the unifying graphic theme of this particular catalogue.

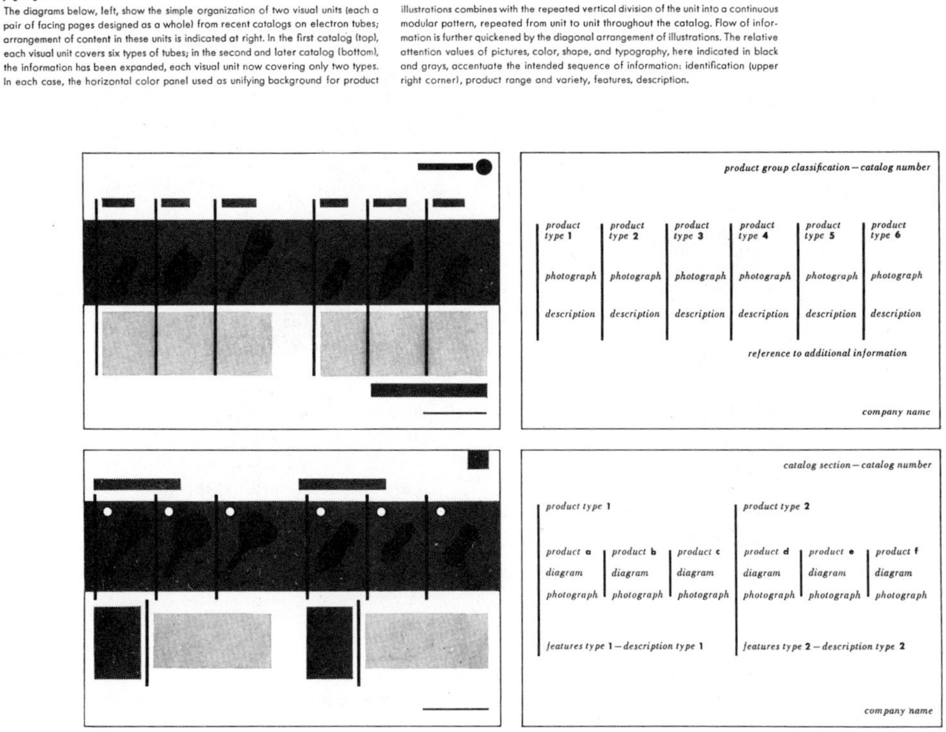
page organization—continued >
The diagrams below, left, show the simple organization of two visual units (each a pair of facing pages designed as a whole) from recent catalogs on electron tubes; arrangement of content in these units is indicated at right. In the first catalog (top), each visual unit covers six types of tubes; in the second and later catalog (bottom), the information has been expanded, each visual unit now covering only two types. In each case, the horizontal color panel used as unifying background for product illustrations combines with the repeated vertical division of the unit into a continuous modular pattern, repeated from unit to unit throughout the catalog. Flow of information is further quickened by the diagonal arrangement of illustrations. The relative attention values of pictures, color, shape, and typography, here indicated in black and grays, accentuate the intended sequence of information: identification (upper right corner), product range and variety, features, description.
product group classification—catalog number
product type 1
product type 2
product type 3
product type 4
product type 5
product type 6
photograph
description
reference to additional information
company name
catalog section—catalog number
product type 1
product type 2
product a
product b
product c
product d
product e
product f
diagram
photograph
features type 1—description type 1
features type 2—description type 2
company name

He used shape, line, and color, not as decorative elements, but as functional elements to direct the eye as it moved through the design seeking information. Careful construction of the visual flow allows the designer to pull diverse information into a clear sequence for precise use.

As Sutnar approached problems of form, static and uniform arrangements of catalogue information gave way to dynamic information patterns and clear, rational organization. Symmetrical typography was discarded because it lacked a relationship to the functional flow of information. Visual articulation of type—underlining, size and weight contrasts, spacing, color, and reversing—was used to aid searching, scanning, and reading. A simple visualization language with emphasis upon graphic charts, diagrams, and pictures was used to clarify complex information and save reader's time. The upper right-hand corner, which Sutnar considered the visual entry point for each layout, was used for identifying information. Optical unity was achieved by a systematic use of signs, shapes, and color. As design of *Sweet's Catalog* became more functional, the writing style became more compact and factual, using brief concise statements.

Design for science

A major graphic design accomplishment of the late 1940s and 1950s and an important milestone in the visual presentation of data was the publication of the *World Geo-Graphic Atlas* by Container Corporation in 1953. In an introduction, Paepcke spoke of a need for "a better understanding of other peoples and nations." Herbert Bayer was the designer and editor of this volume and labored for five years on the project. Once again, Paepcke had behaved in a manner unlike the conventional businessman. A corporation had published, for the information of its clients and suppliers, plus distribution to libraries and museums, a three hundred sixty-eight-page book filled with one hundred twenty full-page maps of the world supported by one thousand two hundred diagrams, graphs, charts, symbols, and other graphic communications about the planet earth. Bayer assembled information that cut across the scientific disciplines including geography, astronomy, climatology, economics, and sociology. This information is presented through symbols, charts, and diagrams. Bayer was ahead of his time in his effort to inventory earth resources and study the planet earth as interlocking geophysical and life systems. Visual design was used to make man and his world more understandable. The final section of the *World Geo-Graphic Atlas* discusses the conservation of resources. Population growth and the depletion of earth resources were addressed, then Bayer called for careful management and development of earth resources, international cooperation, and increased agricultural productivity.

In 1938, Will Burtin (1908–1972) came to the United States from Germany where he had trained as a typographer, studied design, and practiced as an exhibition and graphic designer. He designed for the American war effort, then art-directed *Fortune* magazine from 1945 until 1949. Next, Burtin turned to full-time consultation, notably for the Upjohn Pharmaceutical Company. He created graphics with simple, direct images capturing the essence of the content. His most important contribution was made in the visualization of scientific processes.

Burtin believed that visual communications should be based on four principal realities: of man, as measure and measurer; of light, color, and texture; of space, time, and motion; and of science. Man, according to Burtin, is the most important consideration of a designer. As measure, the "dimensions of his hands, his eyes, his entire body" become the standard against which any design is assessed. As measurer, Burtin believed that the individual's "emotional, physical, and intellectual response" and understanding of the information communicated

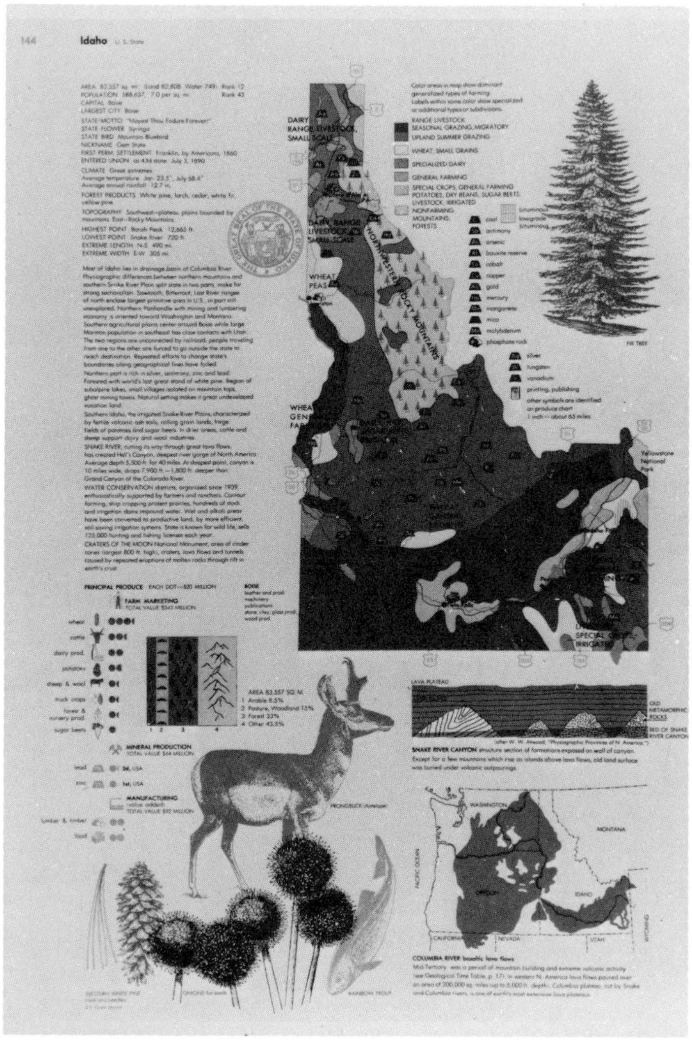

Herbert Bayer, page from the *World Geo-Graphic Atlas,* 1953. Color coding, symbols, cross-sections, and illustrations were used by Bayer to provide a visual inventory of earth resources.

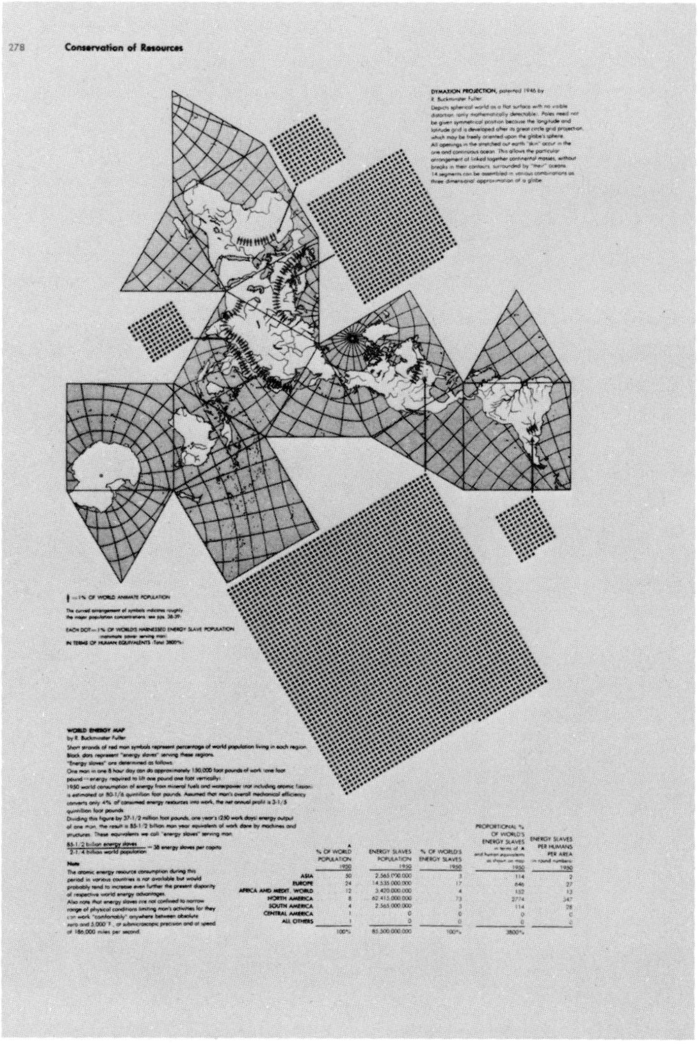

Herbert Bayer, page from the *World Geo-Graphic Atlas,* 1953. Bayer used R. Buckminster Fuller's Dymaxion Projection, a map that shows the globe in two dimensions without distortion, as a base for pictographs representing population and rectangles of black dots symbolizing energy consumption. Immediate comparisons can be made between population and energy use.

should be the yardstick used to measure or evaluate a visual communications design. Burtin saw science and the scientific method as having great value when applied to all areas of people's social and psychological life, including art. He believed that science allows people "to see the workings of nature, makes transparent the solid, and gives substance to the invisible." Burtin saw the designer as the "communicator, link, interpreter, and inspirer" who is able to make comprehendable the knowledge of science.

Through graphic and exhibition design, Burtin made scientific knowledge visible. His model of a Uranium-235 atom contained ninety-two miniature electric lights on fine steel rods that rotated around the nucleus representing electrons. Enclosed in a translucent, blue sphere, the physical and kinetic qualities of the atom were articulated. Burtin's most ambitious presentation of scientific process was his 1958 Upjohn Cell Exhibit. This 7.3-meter(24-feet)-in-diameter model of half a human red blood cell was enlarged about a million times. The viewer physically entered and walked inside to view the minute structures that make up the fundamental biological unit of human life. Developed from fuzzy microphotographs and numerous consultations with scientists, Burtin's graphic articulation of cell structures and processes had great educational value.

Many of the design nomads who brought European design concepts to the United States arrived virtually penniless and with minimal possessions. But they were armed with talent, ideas, and a strong belief in design as a valuable human activity that could contribute to the improvement of human communication and the human condition. The American experience was greatly enriched by their presence.

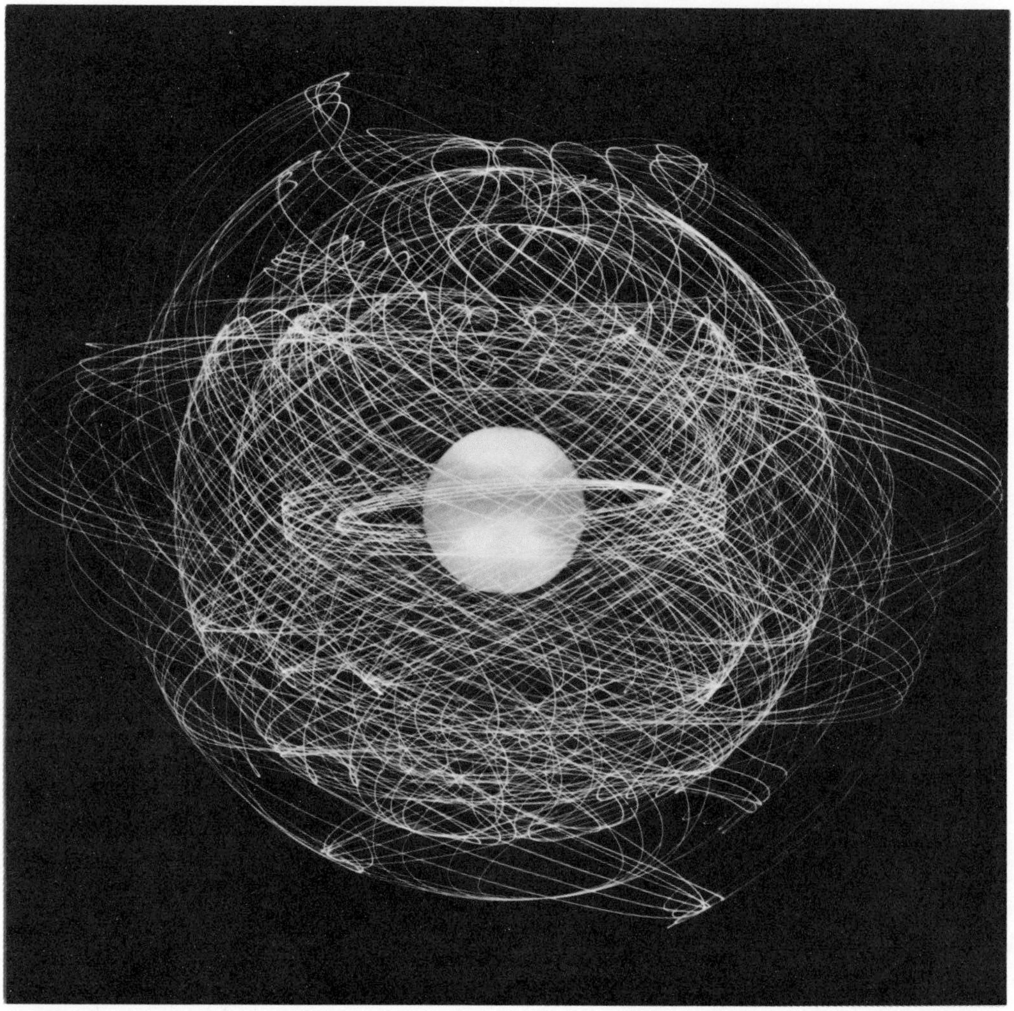

Will Burtin, exhibition of the Uranium-235 atom. Time-lapse photography created a two dimensional expression of Burtin's three-dimensional model.

Will Burtin, Upjohn Cell exhibition, 1958. The plastic model was imbued with life through the use of moving, pulsating lights glowing through the structure.

20

The International Typographic Style

DURING THE 1950s, A DESIGN STYLE emerged from Switzerland that has been called Swiss design or, more appropriately, the International Typographic Style. The objective clarity of this design movement won converts throughout the world. Its approach to graphic design remained a major force for more than twenty years, a period of vitality longer than most twentieth-century artistic movements. Detractors of the international typographic style complain that it is based on formula and results in a sameness of solution. Advocates argue that the purity of means and legibility of communication enable the designer to achieve a timeless perfection of form, and they point to the inventive range of solutions by leading practitioners as evidence that neither formula nor sameness is indigenous to the style, except in the hands of lesser talents.

The visual characteristics of this international style include: a visual unity of design achieved by asymmetrical organization of the elements of the design on a mathematically drawn grid; the use of sans-serif type (particularly Helvetica after its introduction in 1957); typography set in a flush-left and ragged-right margin configuration; objective photography and copy that present visual and verbal information in a clear and factual manner, free from the exaggerated claims of much propaganda and commercial advertising. More important than the visual appearance of their work is the attitude that the early pioneers of this movement developed toward their profession. Design is defined as a socially useful and important activity. Personal expression and eccentric solutions are rejected in favor of a more universal and scientific approach to design problem solving. The designer defines his role not as an artist, but as an objective conduit for spreading important information between components of society. Clarity and order is the ideal. The initiators of this style believe that sans-serif typography expresses the spirit of the present age, and that mathematical grids are the most legible and harmonious means for structuring information.

Ernest Keller, poster for an exhibition, 1931. Dynamic diagonals and a mathematically constructed image appropriately express modern architecture. *Kunstgewerbemuseum der Stadt Zurich, Switzerland.*

Pioneers of the Swiss movement

More than any other individual, the quality and discipline found in the Swiss design movement can be traced to Ernst Keller (1891–1968). In 1918, Keller was twenty-seven when he joined the Zurich *Kunstgewerbeschule* ("School of Applied Art") to teach the advertising layout course. From this modest beginning, Keller developed a thorough professional course in design and typography and headed the program until 1956. In teaching and his own creative projects in lettering, trademarks, and poster design, Keller established a standard of excellence over the course of four decades. Rather than espouse a specific style, Keller advocated that the solution to the design problem should emerge from the content. The range of his work encompasses diverse solutions. His 1931 poster for an exhibition of Walter Gropius' architecture has a geometric pictographic hand holding a trowel. Quite different is the 1948 exhibition poster with almost medieval overtones and rigorous symmetrical balance. A gentle and unassuming man, Keller initiated a climate of excellence in Swiss graphic design that continues over a quarter of a century after his death.

The roots of the International Typography Style grew from *De Stijl*, the Bauhaus, and the new typography of the 1920s and 1930s. Two principal links between the earlier Constructivist graphic design and the new movement that formed after World War II are two Swiss designers who studied at the Bauhaus, Théo Ballmer (1902–1965) and Max Bill (b. 1908).

An original application of *De Stijl* principles to graphic design using an arithmetic grid of horizontal and vertical alignments was made by Théo Ballmer in 1928. Born in Lausanne, Switzerland, Ballmer studied design in high school and worked for a printing firm there before journeying to Zurich to study under Ernst Keller. In 1928 Ballmer's poster designs achieved a high degree of formal harmony as he used an ordered grid to construct visual forms. In the *buro* poster, both the black work and its red "reflection" are carefully developed on the underlying grid. The other lettering on this poster shows an understanding of van Doesburg's experiments with geometric letterforms. However, Ballmer's lettering is more refined and graceful. While the grid in the *buro* poster used to build the forms is invisible, in the *norm* poster the grid becomes the visual subject. Ballmer studied briefly at the Dessau Bauhaus under Klee, Gropius, and Meyer during the late 1920s. In 1931, Ballmer joined the faculty of the *Kunstgewerbeschule* in Basel, where he remained for over thirty years. During the course of the 1930s, Ballmer's work became increasingly il-

Ernst Keller, poster for an exhibition, 1948. The medieval town crest and rough-hewn letterforms with calligraphic slashed serifs projects a traditional old world feeling appropriate to the nature of the exhibition. *Kunstgewerbemuseum der Stadt Zurich, Switzerland.*

Théo Ballmer, poster for *buro,* 1928. Traces of the grid of squares used to construct this poster remain as the thin white lines between the letterforms. *Reinhold Brown Gallery, New York.*

Théo Ballmer, poster for *norm,* 1928. Unlike the asymmetrical horizontals and verticals of Mondrian's paintings, Ballmer used a structure of absolute mathematical construction. *Reinhold Brown Gallery, New York.*

lustrative; his most innovative work was created in the late 1920s.

Max Bill attended the Bauhaus from 1927 until 1929 and studied with Gropius, Meyer, Moholy-Nagy, Josef Albers, and Kandinsky. Bill moved to Zurich and began a career in his native land that has encompassed painting, sculpture, and architecture as well as product, exhibition, and graphic design. It was in 1931, when he embraced the concepts of Art Concret, that Bill began to find his way clearly. Eleven months before his death, Théo van Doesburg formulated a *Manifesto of Art Concret* in April 1930, which called for a universal art of absolute clarity. The visually controlled arithmetical construction of the painting would be completely created from pure, visual elements, that is, planes and colors. These pure elements, which have no meaning other than themselves, result in a painting that has no meaning except itself. Of course, graphic design is the antithesis of this concept in the sense that, when a graphic design does not have symbolic or semantical meaning, it ceases to be a graphic communication and becomes fine art. But, as can be seen in Bill's poster designs, the aesthetics of Art Concret can be applied to the problems of graphic design. His layouts are constructed of elemental geometric elements organized with absolute order.

Max Bill, poster for a Christmas exhibition and sale, 1940. Dynamic positive and negative shapes and an exquisite visual harmony are created by the repetition of star shapes and the careful alignment of points and edges. *Reinhold Brown Gallery, New York.*

As the 1930s gave way to the war years, and Switzerland sat in splendid neutrality in the midst of a ravaged Europe, Bill played a major role in evolving a Constructivist ideal in graphic design. Mathematical proportion, geometric spatial division, and the use of Akzidenz Grotesque type (particularly the medium weight) are aspects of his work of this period. He explored the use of the ragged-right margin and indicated paragraphs by an interval of space instead of a paragraph indent in some of his 1940s book designs.

The evolution of Bill's art and design was based on the development of cohesive principles of visual organization. The linear division of space into harmonious parts; the use of modular grids; arithmetic and

Max Bill, typographic book jacket, 1942. Mathematical precision is achieved by the alignment of letterforms down the center of the page, which creates harmony and order in an informal asymmetric layout. Akzidenz Grotesk (Standard) typestyles reflect the functional geometry of the architecture in the book. During the 1950s this typestyle was widely used by Swiss designers.

Max Bill, exhibition poster, 1945. In carefully balancing diamond-shaped photographs on a grid, Bill almost creates the effect of an arrow exploding. That is, some of the diamonds that would make up a big wedge shape composed of photographs have been pulled out into the white ground to equalize the figure and ground. *Library of Congress, Washington, D. C., Poster Collection.*

Max Bill, exhibition poster, 1951. Bill used two sizes of type to form a cross, then repeated this configuration in smaller type. A hierarchy of information is established, and depth is implied by the descending sizes of typography. *Library of Congress, Washington, D. C., Poster Collection.*

Max Bill, exhibition poster, 1956. For an exhibition by three artists who were all working with geometric abstraction, Bill lined up three white squares bearing the artists' last names on a purple field. This poster is an example of the emerging Swiss concept of using the minimum means necessary to objectively present the information. *Library of Congress, Washington, D. C., Poster Collection.*

geometric progressions, permutations, and sequences; and the equalization of contrasting and complementary relationships into an ordered whole are important concerns. In 1949, he wrote that, "I am of the opinion that it is possible to develop an art largely on the basis of mathematical thinking."

In 1950, Bill became involved in the planning of the curriculum and buildings for the *Hochschule für Gestaltung* ("Institute of Design") in Ulm, Germany. This school, which operated until 1968, attempted to establish a center of research and training to address the design problems of the era and fill an educational need that had been lacking since the Bauhaus closed. Bill left the Ulm directorship in 1956, and the school evolved along scientific and methodological approaches to design problem solving.

In counterpoint to Max Bill's evolution toward a strong purist approach to graphic design during the 1930s and 1940s, there was also a strong tendency toward complexity in graphic design in this period. This is evidenced in the work of Lester Beall, for example.

In Swiss design during the same era, Max Huber (b. 1919) brought an extraordinary vitality and complexity to his work. After studying the formal ideas of the Bauhaus and experimenting with photomontage as a student at the Zurich School of Arts and Crafts, Huber moved south to Milan, Italy, and began his career. Returning to his native Switzerland during the darkest period of the war, Huber collaborated with Max Bill on exhibition design projects. After his return to Italy in1946, Huber produced dazzling graphics. Bright, pure hues were combined with photographs in intense, complex visual organizations. Huber took advantage of the transparency of printing inks by designing with forms and images that overlapped to create layers of information. Sometimes Huber's designs are pushed to the edge of chaos, but he always tries to use balance and alignment to maintain order in the midst of great complexity.

Max Huber, poster for Monza motocars, 1948. Typography racing back in perspective and arrows arcing forward give depth to the printed page.

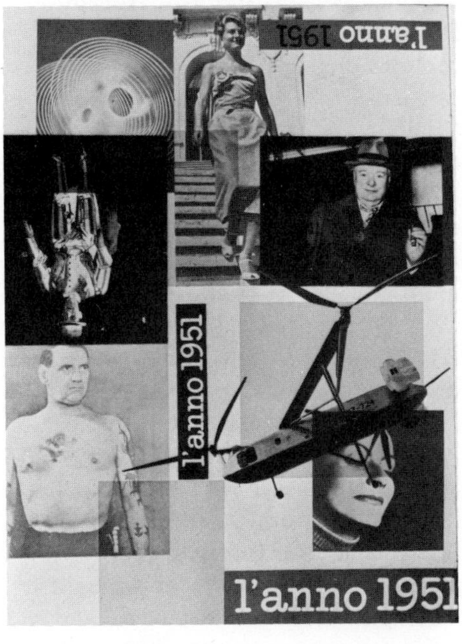

Max Huber, yearbook cover, 1951. An informal balance of halftones printed in red, black, and blue combine with yellow rectangles to turn the space into an energy-charged field.

Functional graphics for science

German-born Anton Stankowski (b. 1906) worked as a graphic designer in Zurich from 1929 until 1937, where he enjoyed close contacts with many of the leading artists and designers of Switzerland including Max Bill, Herbert Matter, and Richard P. Lohse. During his Zurich period, Stankowski was particularly innovative in photography, photomontage, and darkroom manipulation of images. Visual pattern and form were explored in his closeup photographs of common objects whose texture and detail were transformed into abstract images.

In 1937 Stankowski moved to Stuttgart, Germany, where he has been active as a painter and graphic designer for over four decades. Stankowski is involved in a dialogue between his painting and his design. Often ideas of color and form from his paintings find their way into his graphic designs. Conversely, his wide range of form experimentation in searching for design solutions often provides shapes and compositional ideas for his fine art.

World War II and military service, including a period as a prisoner of war after his capture by the Russians, interrupted Stankowski's career. After the war, his work started to crystallize into what was to become his major contribution to graphic design: the creation of visual forms to communicate invisible processes and physical forces. The abilities Stankowski brought to this search were a strong mastery of Constructivist design, an intellectual acumen for science and engineering, and a burning curiosity. Research and an intellectual comprehension of the subject preceded design, for only then can forms be invented that become symbols of unseen scientific and engineering concepts. Stankowski tackled the unseen, ranging from electromagnetic energy to the internal workings of a computer, and transformed the underlying concept for these forces into visual designs.

Anton Stankowski, trademark for Standard Elektrik Lorenz AG, 1953. A dynamic equilibrium is achieved by this asymmetric construction within an implied square that symbolizes telecommunications transmitting and receiving.

Anton Stankowski, calendar cover for Standard Elektrik Lorenz AG, 1957. This geometric configuration symbolizes transmission and radiation to signify the outward communication made possible by the client's radio and telephone products.

In 1968, the senate of the city of Berlin charged Stankowski and his studio with developing a comprehensive design program for that city. Consistent design standards for architectural signage, street signs, and publications were developed. Instead of designing a trademark or unique typographic logo for use as the unifying visual element, Stankowski developed a *tectonic element* that is consistently used on all material. This is a long horizontal line with a short vertical line rising from it. This element becomes a symbol for the divided city of Berlin. The vertical line represents the Berlin Wall that separates the Russian-occupied portion of the city from the rest of Berlin. The word "Berlin" is always placed in the right-hand side of the tectonic element set in medium Akzidenz Grotesque.

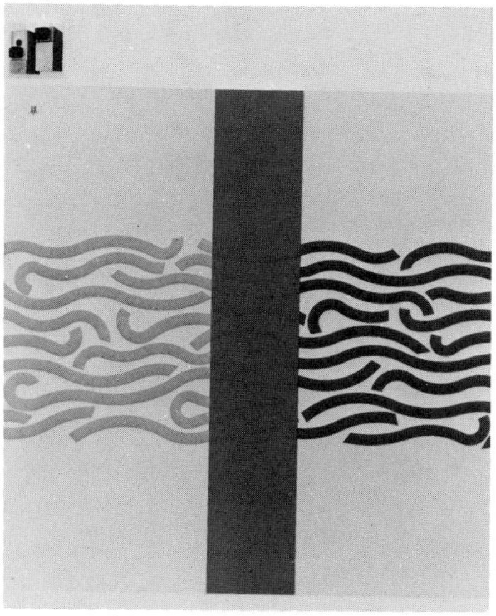

Anton Stankowski, image from a calendar for Viessmann. Cool blue curved elements change to a bright orange after passing through the red bar in the center of the page. This symbolizes the transfer of heat and energy in furnace boilers manufactured by Viessmann.

Anton Stankowski, cover for *Berlin Layout,* 1971. The red, yellow, and blue design on this cover is an image originally developed in Stankowski's painting.

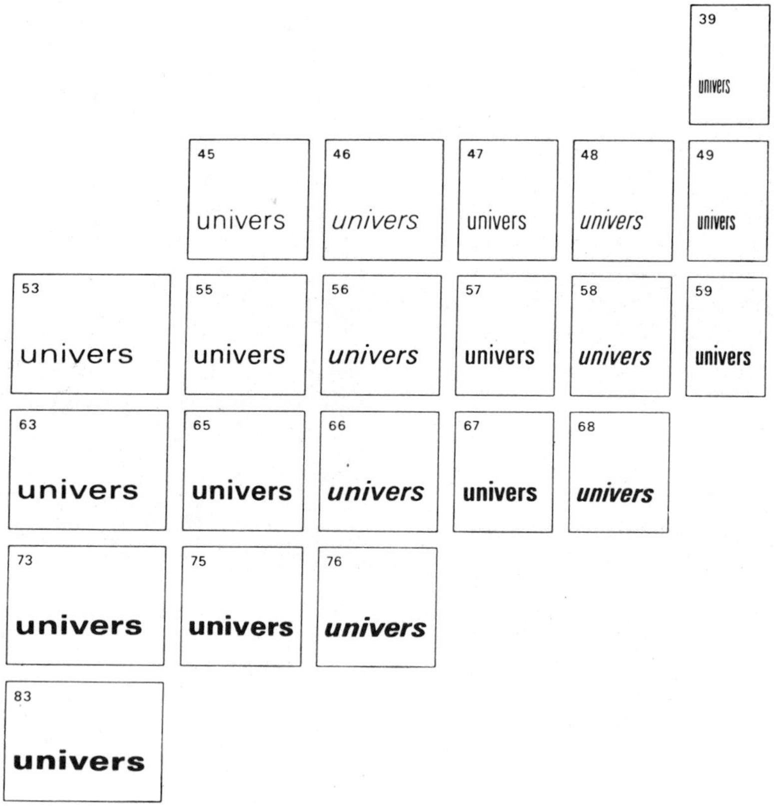

Adrian Frutiger, schematic diagram of twenty-one Univers styles, 1954. Starting with Univers 55, which has the proper black-and-white relationships for book setting, Frutiger expanded the forms moving leftward, condensed the forms moving to the right, and made the weights lighter toward the top and darker or bolder toward the bottom.

New Swiss sans-serif typefaces

The emerging International Typographic Style gained its alphabetical expression in several new sans-serif typestyles that were designed in the 1950s. The geometric sans-serif styles, mathematically constructed with drafting instruments during the 1920s and 1930s, were rejected in favor of new designs inspired by the nineteenth-century Akzidenz Grotesque fonts. In 1954 a young Swiss designer working in Paris, Adrian Frutiger (b. 1928), created a visually programmed family of twenty-one sans-serif fonts named Univers. The "palette" of typographic variations—limited to regular, italic, and bold in traditional typography—was expanded sevenfold. Conventional nomenclature was replaced by numbers. The normal or regular weight was called Univers 55. The family ranges from Univers 39 (light / extra condensed) to Univers 83 (expanded / extrabold). Because all twenty-one fonts have the same *x*-height and ascender and descender lengths, they form a uniform whole that can be used together with complete harmony. The size and weight of the capitals is closer to the size and weight of the lower-case characters; therefore, the color of a text setting is more uniform than that of most earlier typestyles. Frutiger labored for three years on Univers. To produce

Helvetica
Helvetica Italic
Helvetica Medium
Helvetica Bold
Helvetica Bold Condensed

Edouard Hoffman and Max Miedinger, Helvetica, 1961. The basic version of Helvetica released by the Stempel foundry in 1961 is shown with some of the variations developed later.

Bruno Pfäffli of Atelier Frutiger, composition with the letter *u*, c. 1960. The variety of contrasts that Adrian Frutiger achieved with his program of twenty-one variations of Univers, all of which can be used together to achieve dynamic contrasts of weight, tone, width, and direction, are shown in this composition.

the Univers family, the Deberny-Peigot foundry in Paris invested over two hundred thousand hours of machine engraving, retouching, and final hand punching to create the thirty-five thousand matrices needed to produce all twenty-one fonts in the full range of sizes.

In the middle 1950s, Edouard Hoffman of the HAAS type foundry in Switzerland decided that the Akzidenz Grotesque fonts should be refined and upgraded. Hoffman collaborated with Max Miedinger, who executed the designs, and their new sans serif with an even larger *x*-height than Univers was released as the New Haas Grotesque. When this design was produced in Germany by D. Stempel AG in 1961, the Germans shocked Hoffman by naming the face Helvetica, which is the traditional Latin name for Switzerland that appears on its postage stamps. Helvetica's well-defined forms and excellent rhythm of positive and negative shapes made it the most specified typeface internationally during the past quarter of a century. Because the various weights, italics, and widths were developed by different designers in several countries, the Helvetica family lacks the cohesiveness of Univers.

Design in Basel and Zurich

The further development of Swiss design occurred in two cities, Basel and Zurich, located 70 kilometers (about 50 miles) apart in northern Switzerland.

Fifteen-year-old Emil Ruder (1914–1970) began a four-year compositor's apprenticeship in 1929, and attended the Zurich School of Arts and Crafts when he was in his late twenties. In 1947 Ruder joined the faculty of the Basel School of Arts and Crafts (*Allegemeine Gewerbeschule*) as a typography teacher, and continued in this position for the rest of his life. Ruder called upon his students to strike a correct balance between form and function and taught that when type lost its communicative meaning it lost its purpose. Legibility and readability became dominant concerns. His classroom projects developed sensitivity to negative or unprinted spaces including the spaces between and inside letterforms. Ruder advocated systematic overall design and the use of a complex grid structure to bring all elements—typography, photography, illustration, diagrams, and charts—into harmony with each other while allowing for design variety. Problems of unifying type and image were addressed.

More then any other designer, Ruder realized the implications of Univers and the creative potential unleashed by the unity of proportion that allowed the intermixing of all twenty-one members of this type family. Ruder and his students exhaustively explored the contrasts, textures, and scale possibilities of the new face in both commissioned and experimental work.

After completing his education in Zurich and working as a staff designer for several studios, Armin Hofmann (b. 1920) began teaching graphic design at the Basel School of Arts and Crafts in 1947. At the same time, Hofmann opened a design studio in collaboration with his wife Dorothe. Hofmann has a deep sense of

Armin Hofmann, logotype for the Basel Civic Theater, 1954. This handlettered logotype anticipates the tight spacing and capital ligatures of phototypography. The control of the intervals of space between letterforms is masterful.

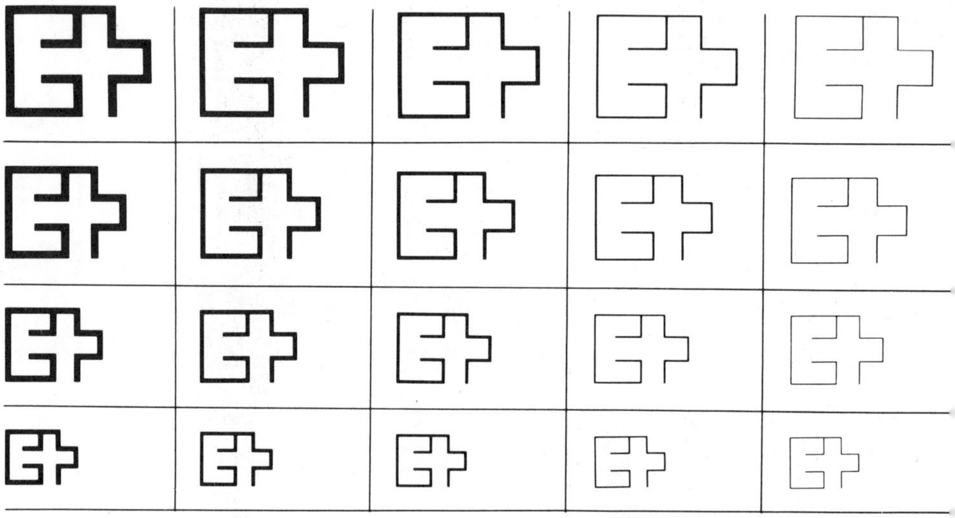

Armin Hofmann, trademark for the Swiss National Exhibition, Expo 1964. A memorable form is created by linking an E for Exhibition and the Swiss cross. The open bottom of the cross allows the white space of the page to flow into the symbol.

Armin Hofmann, poster for Herman Miller furniture, 1962. The shapes and silhouettes of Herman Miller chairs cascade through the space, anchored to the format and the type by the red logo at the top center.

Armin Hofmann, poster for the Basel theater production *Giselle,* 1959. Hofmann has used intense contrasts in this poster that combines an organic, kinetic, and soft photographic element with a geometric, static, and hard-edge typographic element.

aesthetic values which enables him to plumb deeply into the essence of form and apply this understanding to both teaching and designing. As time passed, Hofmann evolved a design philosophy based on the search for a graphic form language to replace traditional pictorial ideas with a contemporary aesthetic based on the fundamental, elemental nature of visual phenomena. In his work and in his teaching, Hofmann seeks a dynamic harmony where all the parts of a design are unified. He sees the relationship of contrasting elements as the means to breathe life into visual design. These contrasts include light to dark, curved lines to straight lines, form to counterform, and dynamic to static. Resolution is achieved when the creator brings the total into an absolute harmony. As with music, painting, or dance, design moves to a higher place of expression when this resolution is accomplished. Hofmann works in diverse areas, including posters, advertising, and logo design. His environmental graphics, which take the form of letterforms or abstract shapes based on letterforms, are often incised into molded concrete.

Swiss design began to coalesce into a unified international movement when the journal, *New Graphic Design,* began publication in 1959. The editors were four Zurich designers who played a major role in the evolution of the International Typographic Style: Richard P. Lohse (b. 1902), Josef Müller-Brockmann (b. 1914), Hans Neuburg (b. 1904), and Carlo L. Vivarelli (b. 1919). This

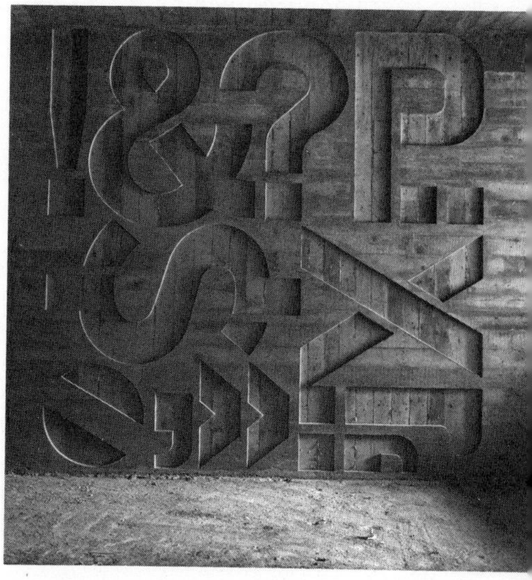

Armin Hofmann, exterior sculpture for the Disentis, Switzerland, high school. The altered direction of the boards of the molds used to cast the concrete relief produce a vigorous textural contrast.

Armin Hofmann, advertisements for Herman Miller furniture, 1962. Segments of the poster's sequence of forms are used to create an extraordinary dynamic relative to the usual layout of newspaper advertisements.

Herman Miller Collection
Verkauf ab 9. März
Contura SA Basel Aeschen vorstadt 4 Passage
Möbel unserer Zeit

Herman Miller Collection Möbel unserer Zeit
Verkauf ab 9. März Contura S.A. Basel, Aeschenvorstadt 4 Passage

Herman Miller Collection Möbel unserer Zeit
Verkauf ab 9. März Contura S.A. Basel, Aeschenvorstadt 4 Passage
2 x neu
calci-tonic
neu: jetzt als Brausetabletten
neu: die handliche Packung
Das moderne Aufbau-Tonikum mit Calcium-Sandoz + Vitamine C und D.
Schweizerische Spar- & Kreditbank
In Europa und Übersee
Schweizerische Bankgesellschaft
Hit z'obe kunnt d'Fasnachtszytig vo dr Nazi use!
Forschung und Technik

Das grosse Revirement in einem grossen Verband
7. Kantonal-Turnfest beider Basel
Der erste Waffenlauf der Saison
Herman Miller Collection Möbel unserer Zeit
Verkauf ab 9. März Contura S.A. Basel, Aeschenvorstadt 4 Passage

trilingual periodical began to present the philosophy and accomplishments of the Swiss movement to an international audience. Its format and typography were a living expression of the order and refinement achieved by the Swiss designers.

Emerging as a leading theorist and practitioner of the movement, Josef Müller-Brockmann sought an absolute and universal graphic expression through an objective and impersonal presentation communicating to the audience without the interference of the designer's subjective feelings and devoid of propagandistic techniques of persuasion. A measure of his success can be gauged by observing the visual power and impact of his work. Posters created by Müller-Brockmann in the 1950s are as fresh and contemporary as the latest fashion and communicate their message with a remarkable intensity and clarity. His photographic posters treat the image as a symbol. In his celebrated concert posters, the language of Constructivism creates a visual equivalency to the structural harmony of the music to be performed.

The *der Film* exhibition poster of 1960 is one of Müller-Brockmann's masterpieces. It demonstrates the universal design harmony achieved by mathematical spatial division. The poster is in the three-to-five ratio of the golden mean, considered the most beautifully proportioned rectangle

Armin Hofmann, poster for an exhibition of lace, 1969. The wonderful black surrounding the photograph and typography turns this poster into a strong focal point on the street. Hofmann is a master at reducing a design to its essentials.

Carlo L. Vivarelli, visual identifier for Swiss television, 1958. Seeking essences, Vivarelli unified two universal symbols, the Swiss cross and the abbreviation "TV" for television, into a simple design. The angle at the bottom of the *T* unifies it with the form of the *V* and serves to make the mark unique.

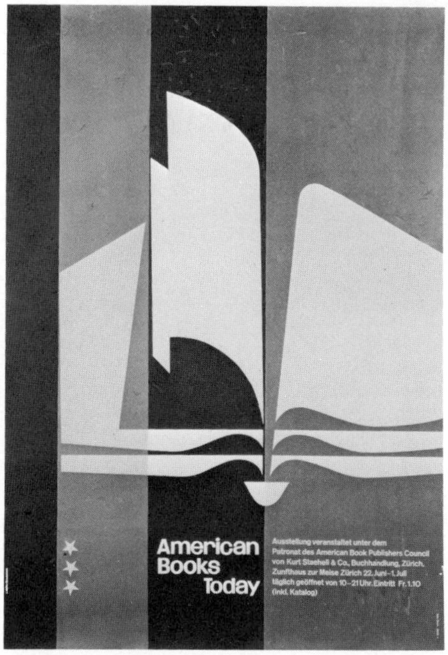

Josef Müller-Brockmann, poster for an exhibition, *American books today,* 1953. In this early poster, the white curvilinear shapes forming the book counter the rigid red and blue vertical stripes.

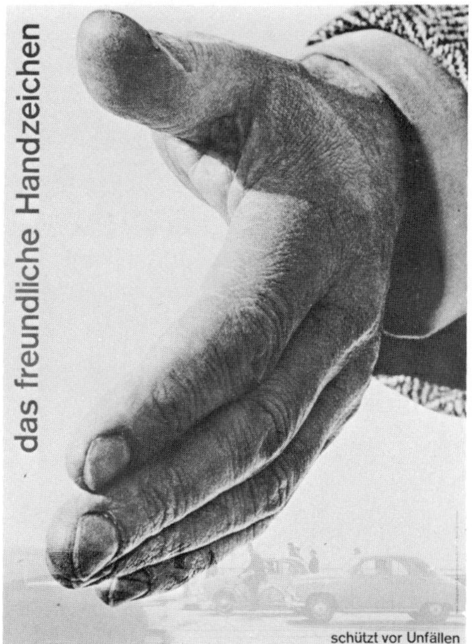

Carlo L. Vivarelli, poster, *For the Elderly,* 1949. The exquisite juxtaposition of a photograph that is organic, human, and textured, with typography that is sharp and geometric enables the contrast between these elements to intensify the meaning of each. The angle of illumination on the face contributes a dramatic impact in this poster conceived to create an awareness of the elderly and their problems.

Carlo L. Vivarelli, magazine cover design, 1958. The mathematical structure of the organizational grid serves as a statement of the scientific and functional design philosophy of the innovators of the Swiss design movement.

Josef Müller-Brockmann, poster for the Swiss Auto Club, 1954. *The friendly handsign* (shown in a huge black-and-white photograph) *protects from accidents* (symbolized by the traffic scene overprinted in red). This is a superb example of Müller-Brockmann's objective use of photography as information.

since Greek times. This rectangle is divided into fifteen squares or modules (three across the horizontal dimension and five down the vertical dimension). The top nine modules form a square, the title fills three units, and three are below the title. *Film* occupies two units, and the secondary typographic information aligns with the front edge of the *F* in *Film*. This design organization grew out of functional communication needs. The title projects clearly at great distances against the field of black. The overlapping of *Film* in front of *der* is a typographic equivalent to the cinematic techniques of overlapping images and dissolving from one image to another. For all its elemental simplicity, this poster successfully combines effective communication of information, expression of the content, and visual harmony. Through his writing, teaching, and example of his work, Müller-Brockmann is the Swiss designer whose impact was most influential as this national movement grew beyond Swiss borders.

In a country with such outstanding design schools as Switzerland, Siegfried Odermatt (b. 1926) is a rarity: the self-educated graphic designer. Originally he planned to become a photographer, but after working in photographic studios for several years Odermatt turned to design and typography. After a period of employment in several advertising agencies, Odermatt opened his own studio in 1950.

Working for corporate clients in the areas of trademark development, informational graphics, advertising, and packaging, Odermatt played a

Hans Neuburg, pages from *New Graphic Design,* 7, 1960. The layout of this article about an exhibition design by Max Bill demonstrates the asymmetrical balance and use of white space by the founders of the international typographic style.

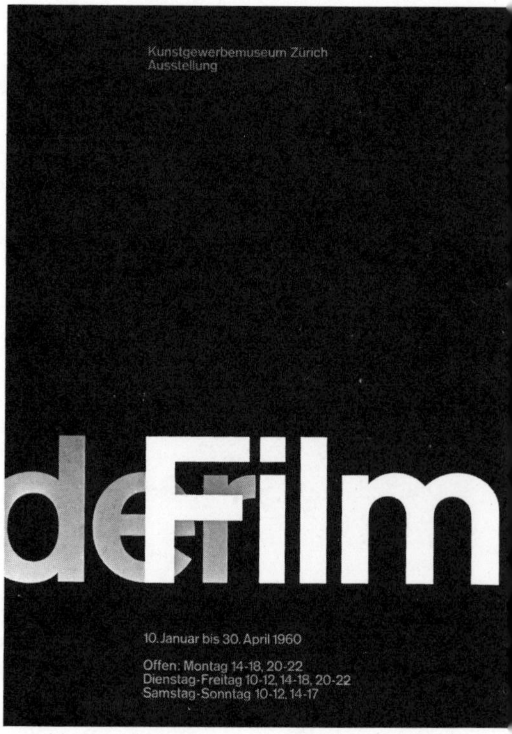

Josef Müller-Brockman, exhibition poster, *Of the film,* 1960. The elementary simplicity of this poster's graphic power is remarkable. Against a black field, the word *Film* is white, the word *der* is gray, and the other typography is red.

major role in defining the International Typographic Style as applied to the communications of business and industry. He combined the clean, efficient presentation of information with a dynamic visual quality. Straightforward photography is used with drama and impact. Ordinary images are turned into convincing and engaging photographs through the careful use of cropping and lighting with attention to shape and texture as qualities that cause an image to reach out from the page. Odermatt expresses originality through the idea, not through visual style. Graphic design is always seen as an instrument of communication, and the visual tools used are typography, photography, and constructive drawing.

Much of Odermatt's work is purely typographic, and he is willing to take great liberties with the traditions of typography. It is his belief that a one-color typographic design can achieve

Hans Neuburg, pages from *New Graphic Design,* 13, 1962. Entries in a trademark design competition are organized on a grid of squares with intervals of space which create an overall movement from upper left to lower right.

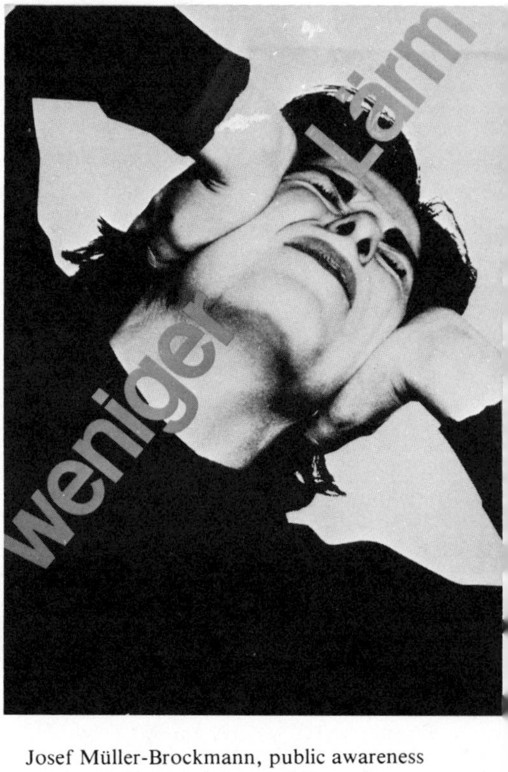

Josef Müller-Brockmann, public awareness poster, 1960. To heighten public awareness of noise pollution, the red type shouts "less noise," and the photograph graphically depicts the discomfort of noise pollution.

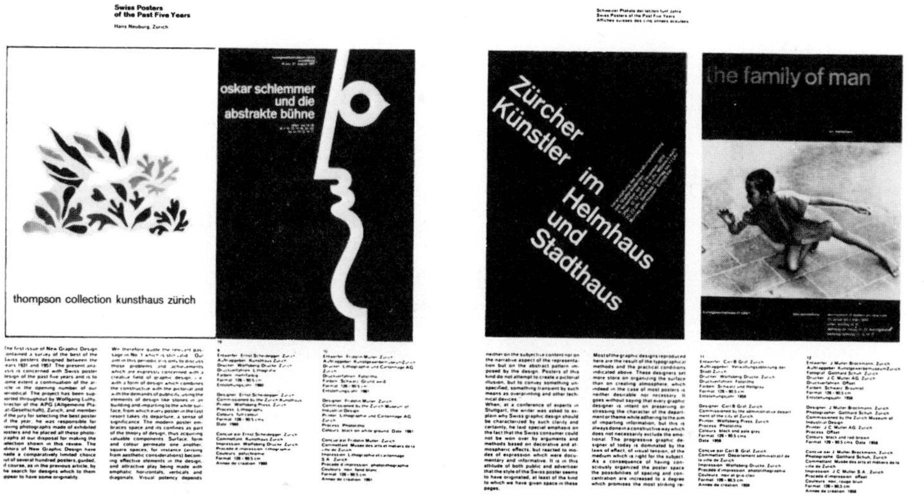

Hans Neuburg, pages from *New Graphic Design,* 16, 1963. The four-column grid used for this journal allowed a tremendous variety of page designs. In this survey of posters, the tone of the images creates horizontal movement across the pages.

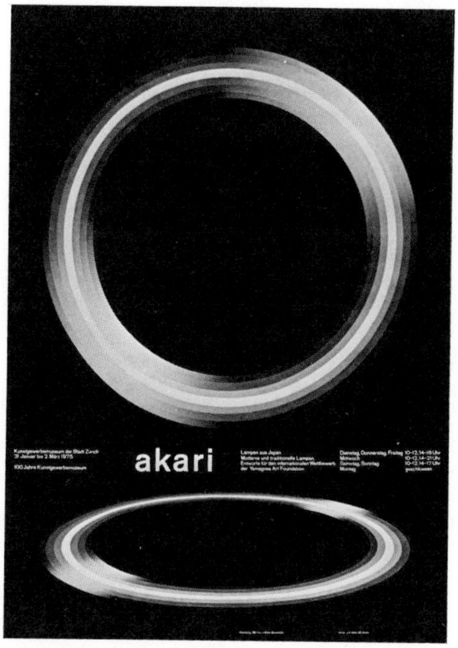

Josef Müller-Brockmann, poster for an exhibition of lamps, 1975. The modulated and glowing multicolor disks symbolize the radiant energy of lighting fixtures.

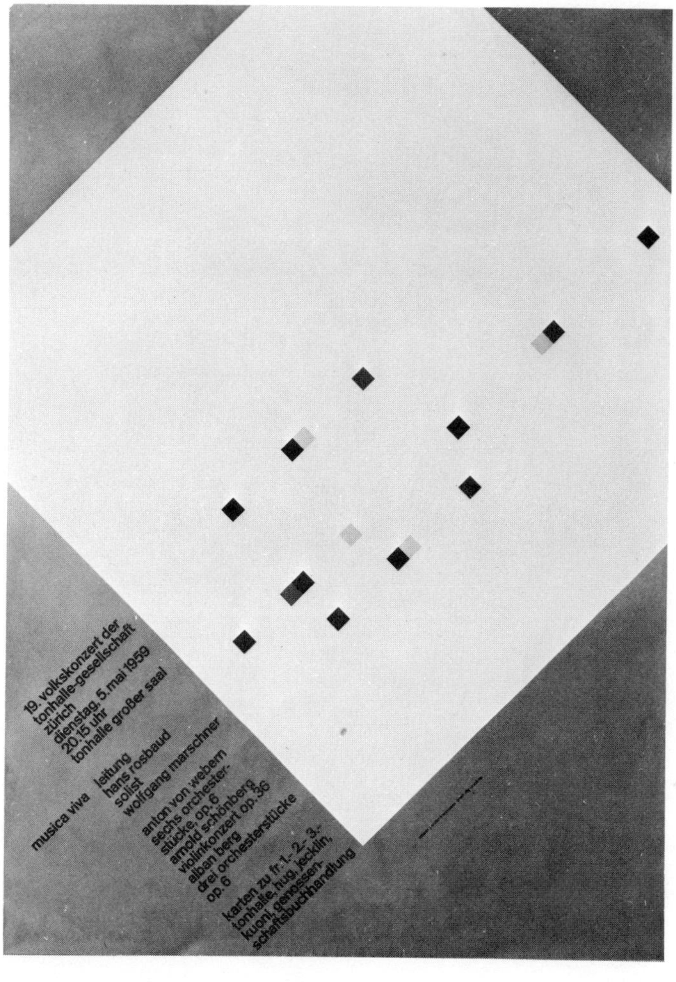

Josef Müller-Brockmann, poster for musica viva concert, 1972. The red, yellow, and blue squares march in musical rhythm on the tilted white diamond. The use of a grid puts typography and shapes in harmonious juxtaposition.

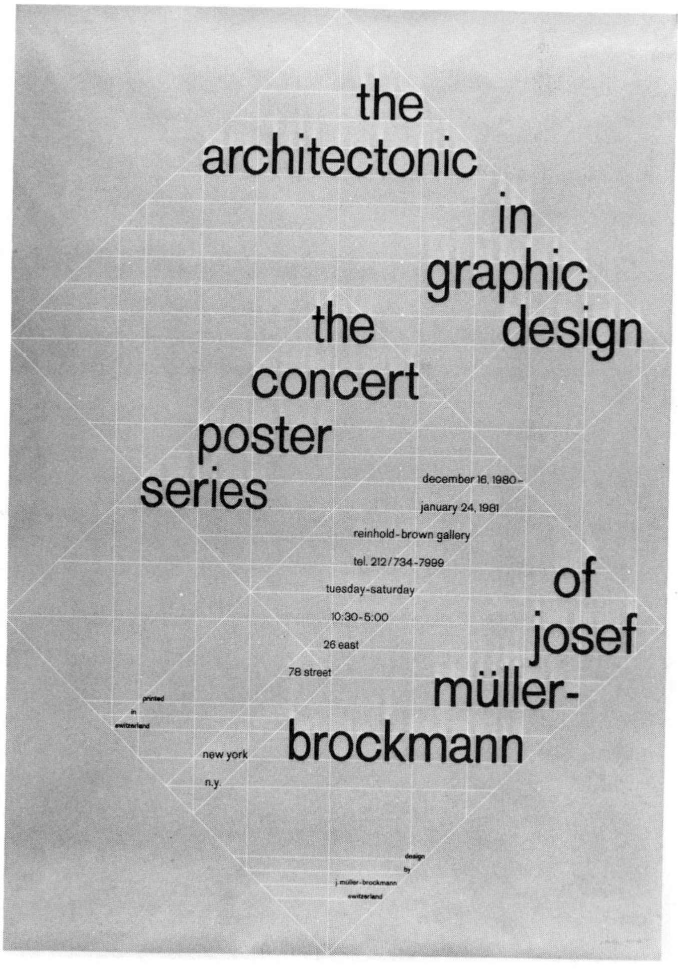

Josef Müller-Brockmann, exhibition poster, 1980. The grid, always underlying Müller-Brockmann's designs, becomes visible as a major element in this poster.

the visual impact and power of full-color graphics through the strength of the concept and the manipulation of visual form, space, shape, and tone. By his fresh and original manipulations of the graphic elements, Odermatt has made a mockery of those designers who say that there are only so many ways to divide and organize the space of the printed page. Unlike many Swiss designers, an element of the playful and the uninhibited appears in Odermatt's work. A young designer who joined his studio in the early 1960s, Rosmarie Tissi, also has a strong playful element in her work. In 1968 Tissi became an equal partner with Odermatt in the studio Odermatt & Tissi. This studio loosened the boundries of the International Typographic Style and introduced elements of chance, the development of surprising and inventive forms, and intuitive visual organization into the vocabulary of graphic design. This phase of the studio's development marked the beginning of a break with the traditions of Swiss design and will be discussed in a later chapter.

During the post-World War II era, there was a growing spirit of internationalism. Increased trade resulted in multinational corporations that were active in as many as a hundred different countries. The speed and pace of communications were turning the world into a "global village." There was a need for communicative clarity, multilingual formats to transcend language barriers, and elementary pictographs and glyphs to enable people from around the world to comprehend signs and information. The new graphic design developed in Switzerland helped fill these needs. The fundamental concepts and approach developed in Switzerland began to spread throughout the world.

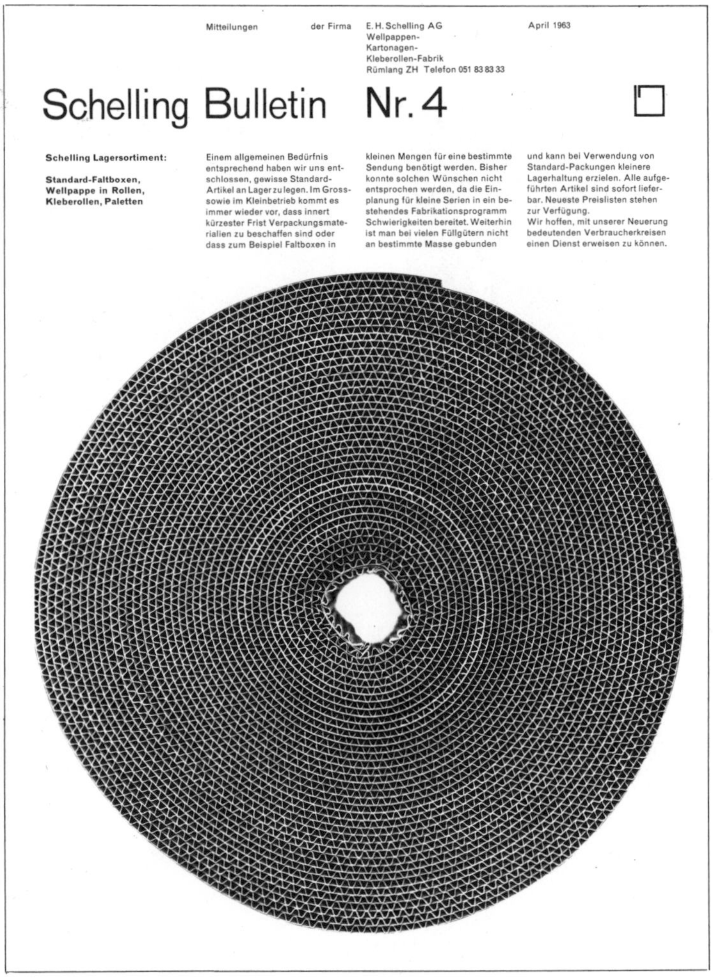
Mitteilungen der Firma E. H. Schelling AG Wellpappen- Kartonagen- Kleberollen-Fabrik Rümlang ZH Telefon 051 83 83 33

April 1963

Schelling Bulletin Nr. 4

Schelling Lagersortiment:

Standard-Faltboxen, Wellpappe in Rollen, Kleberollen, Paletten

Einem allgemeinen Bedürfnis entsprechend haben wir uns entschlossen, gewisse Standard-Artikel an Lager zu legen. Im Gross- sowie im Kleinbetrieb kommt es immer wieder vor, dass innert kürzester Frist Verpackungsmaterialien zu beschaffen sind oder dass zum Beispiel Faltboxen in kleinen Mengen für eine bestimmte Sendung benötigt werden. Bisher konnte solchen Wünschen nicht entsprochen werden, da die Einplanung für kleine Serien in ein bestehendes Fabrikationsprogramm Schwierigkeiten bereitet. Weiterhin ist man bei vielen Füllgütern nicht an bestimmte Masse gebunden und kann bei Verwendung von Standard-Packungen kleinere Lagerhaltung erzielen. Alle aufgeführten Artikel sind sofort lieferbar. Neueste Preislisten stehen zur Verfügung.
Wir hoffen, mit unserer Neuerung bedeutenden Verbraucherkreisen einen Dienst erweisen zu können.

Siegfried Odermatt, cover and inside pages for Schelling Bulletin, No. 4, 1963. In this folder for a manufacturer of paperboard and packaging, Odermatt's layout unifies typography with product photography through the use of a four-column grid.

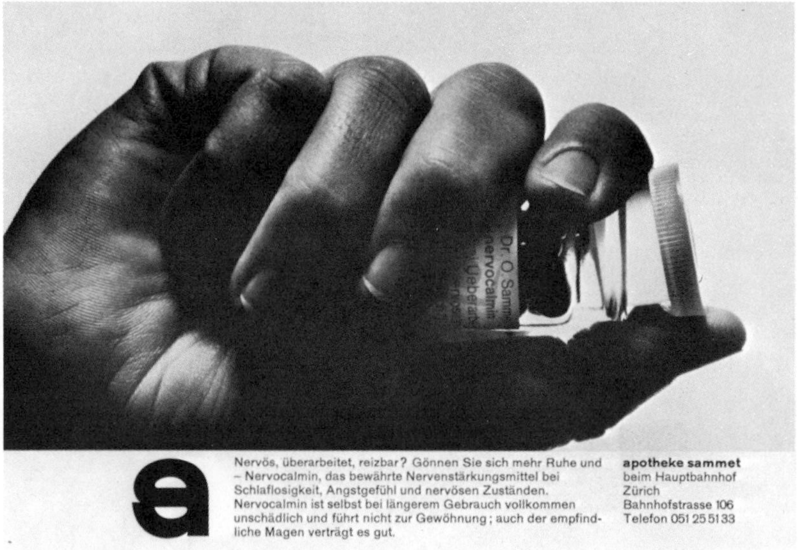

Siegfried Odermatt, advertisement for Apotheke Sammet, 1957. Odermatt's advertisements for this pharmacy's private label medicines used large, arresting closeup photography. Note Odermatt's trademark which clones the initials of the client's name.

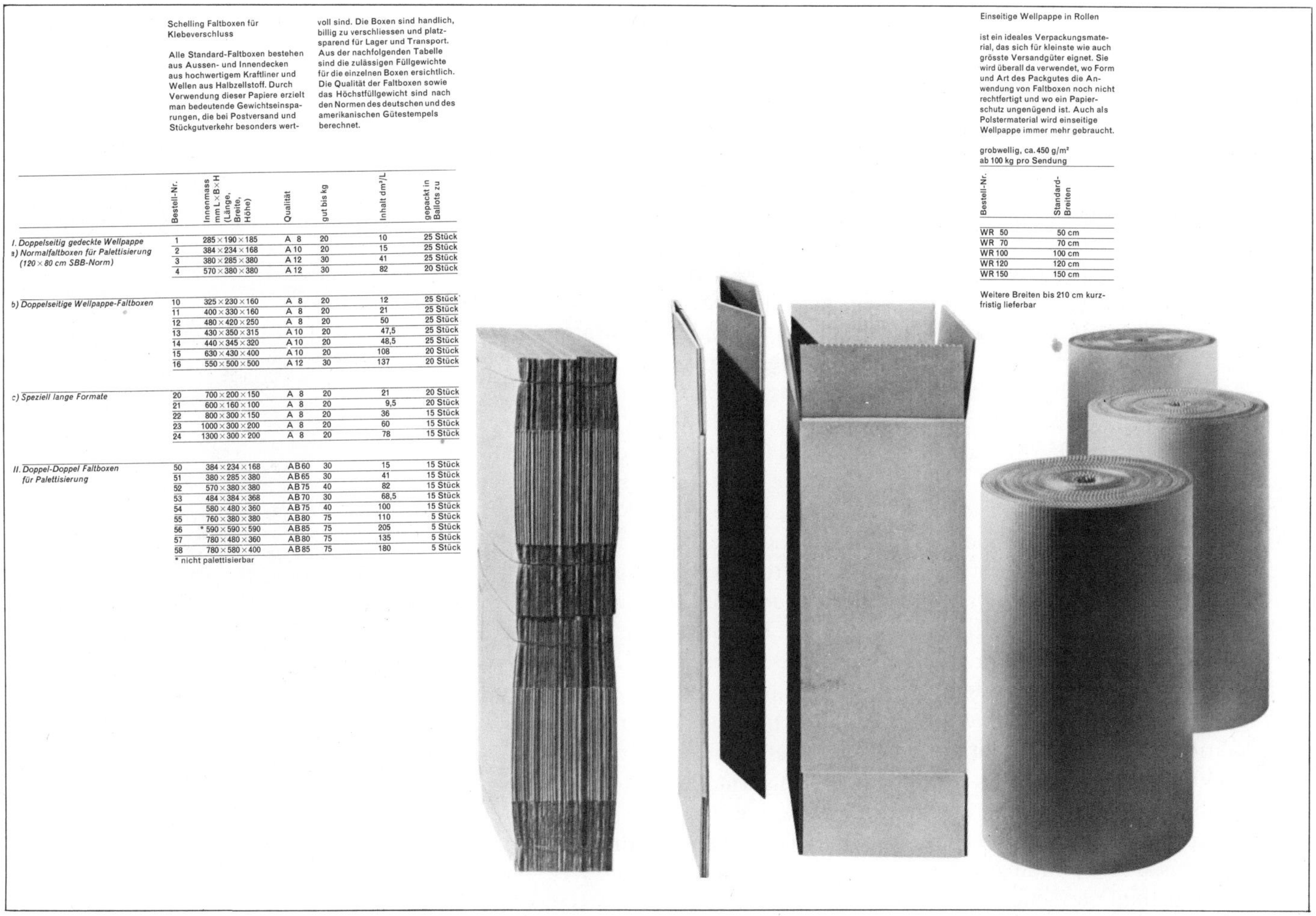

Schelling Faltboxen für Klebeverschluss

Alle Standard-Faltboxen bestehen aus Aussen- und Innendecken aus hochwertigem Kraftliner und Wellen aus Halbzellstoff. Durch Verwendung dieser Papiere erzielt man bedeutende Gewichtseinsparungen, die bei Postversand und Stückgutverkehr besonders wertvoll sind. Die Boxen sind handlich, billig zu verschliessen und platzsparend für Lager und Transport. Aus der nachfolgenden Tabelle sind die zulässigen Füllgewichte für die einzelnen Boxen ersichtlich. Die Qualität der Faltboxen sowie das Höchstfüllgewicht sind nach den Normen des deutschen und des amerikanischen Gütestempels berechnet.

	Bestell-Nr.	Innenmass mm L × B × H (Länge, Breite, Höhe)	Qualität	gut bis kg	Inhalt dm³/L	gepackt in Ballots zu
I. Doppelseitig gedeckte Wellpappe a) Normalfaltboxen für Palettisierung (120 × 80 cm SBB-Norm)	1	285 × 190 × 185	A 8	20	10	25 Stück
	2	384 × 234 × 168	A 10	20	15	25 Stück
	3	380 × 285 × 380	A 12	30	41	25 Stück
	4	570 × 380 × 380	A 12	30	82	20 Stück
b) Doppelseitige Wellpappe-Faltboxen	10	325 × 230 × 160	A 8	20	12	25 Stück
	11	400 × 330 × 160	A 8	20	21	25 Stück
	12	480 × 420 × 250	A 8	20	50	25 Stück
	13	430 × 350 × 315	A 10	20	47,5	25 Stück
	14	440 × 345 × 320	A 10	20	48,5	25 Stück
	15	630 × 430 × 400	A 10	20	108	20 Stück
	16	550 × 500 × 500	A 12	30	137	20 Stück
c) Speziell lange Formate	20	700 × 200 × 150	A 8	20	21	20 Stück
	21	600 × 160 × 100	A 8	20	9,5	20 Stück
	22	800 × 300 × 150	A 8	20	36	15 Stück
	23	1000 × 300 × 200	A 8	20	60	15 Stück
	24	1300 × 300 × 200	A 8	20	78	15 Stück
II. Doppel-Doppel Faltboxen für Palettisierung	50	384 × 234 × 168	AB 60	30	15	15 Stück
	51	380 × 285 × 380	AB 65	30	41	15 Stück
	52	570 × 380 × 380	AB 75	40	82	15 Stück
	53	484 × 384 × 368	AB 70	30	68,5	15 Stück
	54	580 × 480 × 360	AB 75	40	100	15 Stück
	55	760 × 380 × 380	AB 80	75	110	5 Stück
	56	* 590 × 590 × 590	AB 85	75	205	5 Stück
	57	780 × 480 × 360	AB 80	75	135	5 Stück
	58	780 × 580 × 400	AB 85	75	180	5 Stück

* nicht palettisierbar

Einseitige Wellpappe in Rollen

ist ein ideales Verpackungsmaterial, das sich für kleinste wie auch grösste Versandgüter eignet. Sie wird überall da verwendet, wo Form und Art des Packgutes die Anwendung von Faltboxen noch nicht rechtfertigt und wo ein Papierschutz ungenügend ist. Auch als Polstermaterial wird einseitige Wellpappe immer mehr gebraucht.

grobwellig, ca. 450 g/m²
ab 100 kg pro Sendung

Bestell-Nr.	Standard-Breiten
WR 50	50 cm
WR 70	70 cm
WR 100	100 cm
WR 120	120 cm
WR 150	150 cm

Weitere Breiten bis 210 cm kurzfristig lieferbar

Rosemarie Tissi, advertisement for Univac, 1965. A dynamic and arresting image is created by the careful cropping and placement of two telephone receivers.

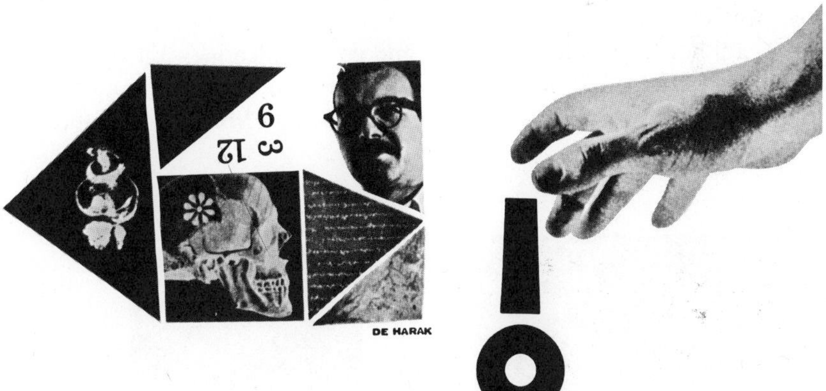

Rudolph de Harak, illustration for *Esquire,* 1956. A hand reaching into the page to take the exclamation mark combines with a dynamic complex of pictures and triangles to suggest several aspects of an article on psychological testing.

The International Typographic Style in America

One of the earliest American designers to be aware of the potential of Swiss design was Rudolph de Harak (b. 1926), a self-taught graphic designer from California who began his career in Los Angeles in 1946. Four years later de Harak moved to New York, and in 1952 he formed his own design studio. During the 1950s de Harak took great delight in bringing structural order to his work. His ability to compose with simple graphic elements is demonstrated in the 1956 *Esquire* magazine illustration, where photographs and simple geometric shapes combine to express the content of an article on psychological testing.

De Harak's evolution has been a continuing quest for communications clarity and visual order, which are the qualities he regards as vital to effective graphic design. He recognized these qualities in Swiss design during the late 1950s and began to apply aspects of the movement to his work. Grid structures and asymmetrical balance were used. Responding to the legibility and formal perfection of Akzidenz Grotesk before it was available in the United States, de Harak obtained specimen sheets from European foundries so that he could assemble headlines for his designs. These combine purity of form with elemental images expressive of the content. A series of album covers for Westminster Records evoked a conceptual, mental image of the structure of the sounds in the music of the composer.

During the early 1960s, de Harak initiated a series of over three hundred fifty book jackets for McGraw-Hill Publishers that were designed using a common typographic system and grid. The subject of each book was articulated by visual configurations which ranged from elemental pictographs to abstract geometric structures. Because this large series of paperback books covered academic subject areas including psychology, sociology, management, and mathematics, de Harak's approach appropriately expressed a high intellectual content. This series altered the course of book-jacket design in the United States.

A sustained level of quality and imagination has been maintained by the graphic design group at the Massachusetts Institute of Technology. A graphic design program, which enables all members of the university community to benefit from free, professional graphic design assistance on their publications and publicity material, was established at this university in the early 1950s. This was a very early recognition of the cultural and communicative value of design by an American university, and there developed an MIT design approach

Rudolph de Harak, cover for *Personality and Psychotherapy,* 1964. Vertical lines of orange, green, and purple form an elusive dualistic head to communicate the intangible and complex aspects of personality.

Rudolph de Harak, album cover for Bach Concertos, 1961. The mathematical perfection of Bach's music is evoked by a complex optical illusion with four quadrants.

Rudolph de Harak, album cover for percussion music, 1961. The fluid gesture seems to be a graphic record of the movement of a musician's hand beating a percussion rhythm.

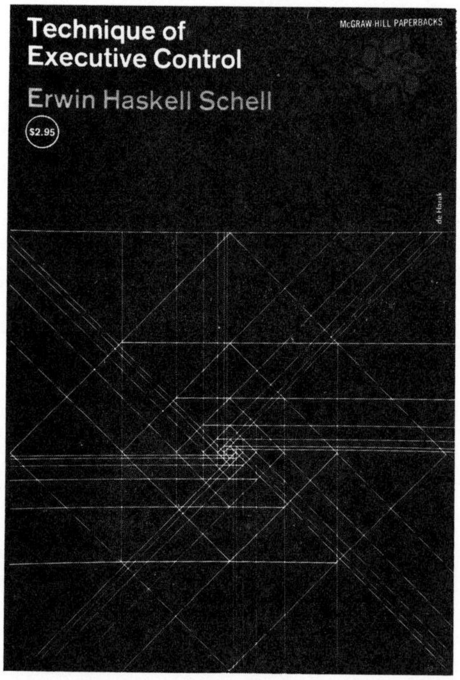

Rudolph de Harak, cover for *Technique of Executive Control,* 1964. The geometric structure, with its concentration of lines in the center, symbolizes centralization of management authority.

Jacqueline S. Casey, announcement for the Ocean Engineering program, 1967. A classic typographic grid sits above an x-ray of a chambered nautilus shell superimposed upon a wavelike repetition of fluid shapes.

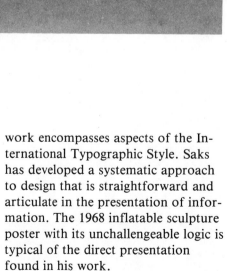

Dietmar Winkler, poster for a computer-programming course, 1969. The word "cobol" is constructed of elemental forms and repeated in red, white, and blue segments against a black background.

based on a commitment to the grid and the sans-serif typography of the International Typographic Style. The MIT staff was innovative in the use of designed letterforms and manipulated words as vehicles to express content. This approach evolved in the work of Jacqueline S. Casey (b. 1927), director of the Design Services Office; Ralph Coburn (b. 1923); and Dietmar Winkler (b. 1938), a German-trained designer who worked with Casey and Coburn from 1966 until 1971. The most visible of the work by the Design Services Office is the production of small posters announcing concerts, speakers, seminars, exhibitions, and courses on the university campus. These frequently used solid-colored backgrounds. While photography is sometimes employed, most of their solutions are typographic. In a sense, letterforms become illustrations, for the design and arrangement of the letters in key words frequently becomes the dominant image.

Arnold Saks (b. 1931) is prominent among the American designers whose work encompasses aspects of the International Typographic Style. Saks has developed a systematic approach to design that is straightforward and articulate in the presentation of information. The 1968 inflatable sculpture poster with its unchallengeable logic is typical of the direct presentation found in his work.

The Swiss design, which outgrew its native boundaries to become truly international, was particularly useful as a design approach when a diverse body of informational materials, ranging from signage to publicity, needed to be unified into a coherent body. The growing awareness of design as a logical tool for large organizations after World War II caused a growth in corporate design and visual identification systems. During the middle 1960s, the development of corporate design and the International Typographic Style were linked into one movement, to be discussed in a later chapter.

Jacqueline S. Casey, poster for an exhibition, 1970. The word "six" is constructed from six geometric shapes, and it became a potent visual configuration when posted.

Jacqueline C. Casey, poster for an open house, 1974. Stencil letterforms announce the open house, and the open *O* does double duty as a concrete symbol of the opening of the campus.

Arnold Saks, poster for the Jewish Museum, 1968. This sequence of bars that bend and expand as they move up the page becomes a symbol for the action of energy upon pliable materials. The essence of inflatable sculpture is articulated on the printed page.

Ralph Coburn, poster for the MIT jazz band, 1972. A staccato repetition of the letterforms of the word "jazz" begins to establish musical sequences that animate the space.

21

The New York School

As we have seen, the first wave of modern design in America was imported by talented imigrants from Europe seeking to escape the political climate of totalitarianism. These individuals brought Americans a first-hand introduction to the European avant-garde. Just as Paris had been the most democratic city in the world with great receptivity to new ideas and images during the late nineteenth and early twentieth centuries, New York City assumed that role during the middle twentieth century. The arts flourished. It may have been that these cultural incubators nurtured innovators because the climate existed to enable creative individuals to realize their potential. Or, the climate that existed may have been a magnet that attracted individuals of great talent and potential. In either case, New York became the cultural center of the world in the middle of the twentieth century, and graphic design innovation ranked high among its accomplishments. During the 1940s, the first steps toward an original American approach to design were made. While borrowing freely from the language of form developed by European designers, Americans developed attitudes and invented forms that added to the tradition of graphic design. European design was theoretical and highly structured; American design was pragmatic, intuitive, and more informal in its approach to organizing space.

Although European in origin, unique aspects of American culture and society dictated its own approach to modern design. The United States is an egalitarian society with pragmatic attitudes and values, limited artistic traditions, and a diverse ethnic heritage. Emphasis was placed upon the expression of ideas and an open, direct presentation of information. In this highly competitive society, novelty of technique and originality of concept were much prized, and designers sought simultaneously to solve communica-

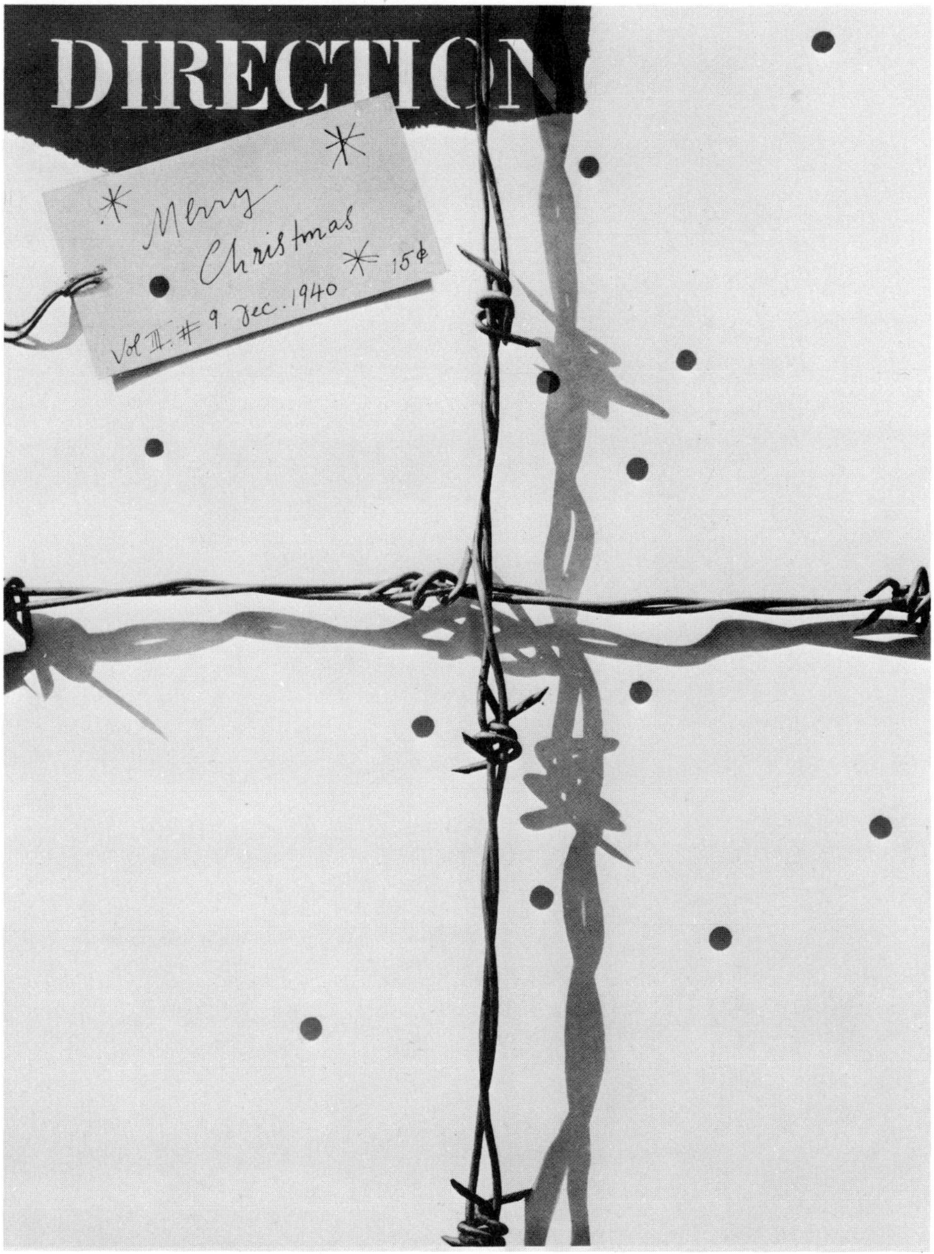

Paul Rand, cover for *Direction* magazine, 1940. This design, created when Rand was twenty-six years old, indicates the important role that contrast plays in his work. Communicatively, a Christmas package wrapped with barbed wire instead of ribbon is a grim reminder as the world hurled deeper into global war. The handwritten Christmas tag on a crisp rectangle contrasts sharply with the mechanical stencil lettering of the logo on a torn edge collage element.

Paul Rand, *Jazzways* yearbook cover, 1946. Collage technique, elemental symbolic forms, and dynamic composition were graphic qualities of Rand's work in the late 1930s and 1940s.

tions problems and satisfy a need for personal expression. This era of American graphic design—beginning with strong European roots during the 1940s, gaining international prominence for its original viewpoints in the 1950s, and continuing today—has been called the American School of Graphic Expressionism by designer Herb Lubalin.

Perhaps more than any other American designer, Paul Rand (b. 1914) initiated this American approach to modern design. When he was twenty-three years old, Rand began the first phase of his design career as a promotional and editorial designer for *Apparel Arts, Esquire, Ken, Coronet,* and *Glass Packer.* His magazine covers broke with the traditions of American publication design. A strong understanding of the modern movement, particularly the works of Klee, Kandinsky, and the Cubists, led Rand to an understanding that freely invented shapes could have a self-contained life, both symbolic and expressive, as a visual tool for communications. His ability to manipulate visual form (shape, color, space, line, value) and skillful analysis of communications content, reducing it to a symbolic essence without being sterile or dull, allowed Rand to become widely influential while still in his twenties. The playful, visually dynamic, and unexpected often find their way into his work. He seized upon collage and montage as a means to bring concepts, images, textures, and even objects into a cohesive whole. *Thoughts on Design,* his 1946 book illustrated with over eighty examples of his work, inspired a generation of designers.

From 1941 until 1954 Paul Rand worked at the Weintraub advertising agency applying his design approach to advertisements. His collaborations with Bill Bernbach became a prototype for the art/copy team working closely together to create a synergistic visual-verbal integration. The campaign they created for Ohrbach's department store for over two years

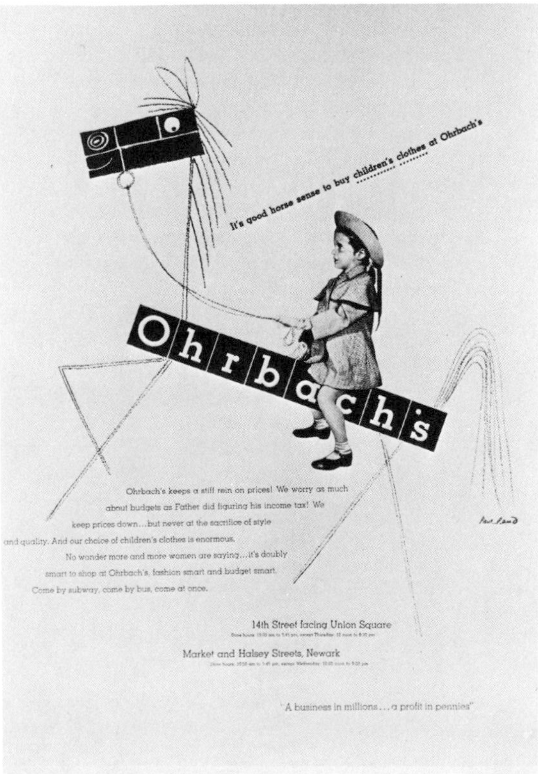

Paul Rand, advertisement for Ohrbach's, 1946. A combination of elements—the logotype, photograph, decorative drawing, and type—are playfully combined into a unity. The image visually reinforces the headline.

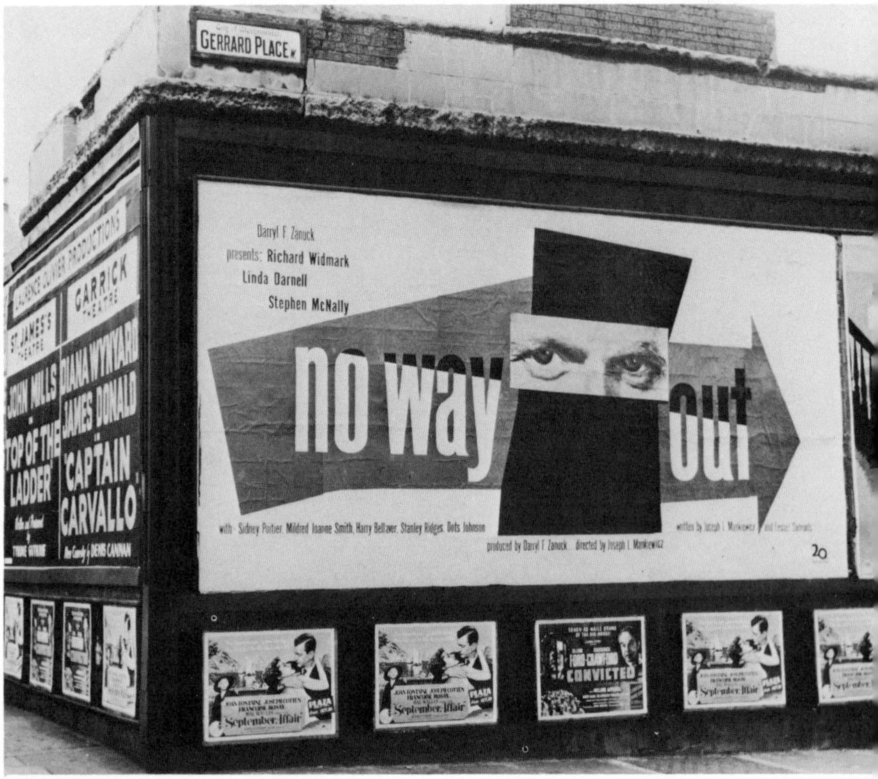

Paul Rand, poster for the film, *No Way Out,* 1950. Rand's design language—integrating photography, typography and graphic shapes and surrounding active form with passive white space—is in marked contrast to the conventional film posters shown in this photograph.

Paul Rand, monograph cover, 1953. An exuberance of shape and whimsical images have been recurring themes in Rand's advertisements and children's books.

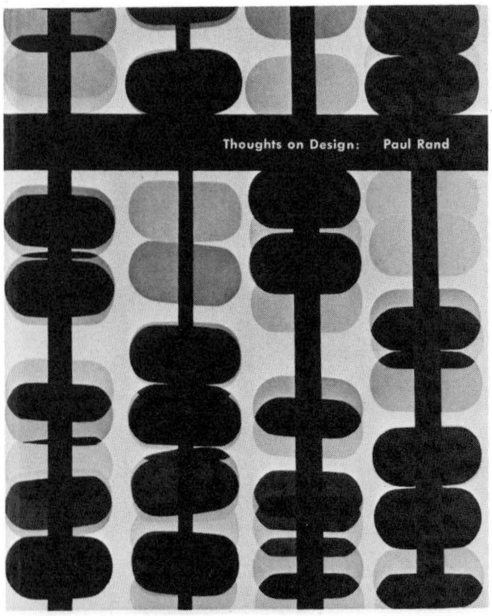

Paul Rand, cover for *Thoughts on Design,* 1947. A photogram was created by making several exposures of an abacus placed on photographic paper in the darkroom. It becomes a metaphor of the design process—moving elements around to compose space—and provides a visual record of this process.

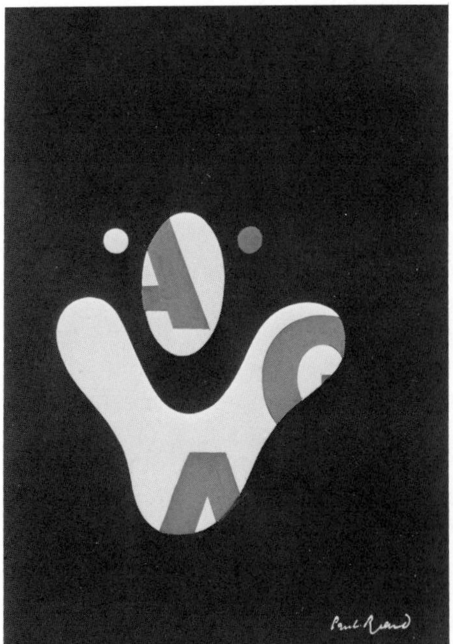

Paul Rand, cover design for the American Institute of Graphic Arts, 1968. A red "A. Eye. G. A." plays hide-and-seek against the green background as a pictographic clown face plays hide-and-seek with an organic abstraction. Design becomes play, and the Futurist concept of simultaneity is evoked.

featured entertaining puns and wordplay supported by Rand's whimsical integration of photography, drawing, and logo. After leaving the agency, Rand became an independent designer with increasing emphasis upon trademark and corporate design.

Paul Rand understands the value of ordinary, universally understood signs and symbols as tools for translating ideas into visual communications. To engage the audience successfully and communicate memorably, he knows that the designer's alteration, juxtaposition, or interpretation is necessary to make the ordinary into something extraordinary. Sensual visual contrasts mark his work. Playing red against green, organic shape against geometric type, photographic tone against flat color, cut or torn edges with sharp forms, and the textural pattern of type against white margins are some of the contrasts in which he delights. He has been willing to take risks by exploring ideas that have not been proven. For all his visual inventiveness, Rand defines design as the integration of form and function for effective communication. The cultural role of the designer is defined as upgrading rather than serving the least common denominator of public taste.

During the early period of Rand's career, he made forays into the vocabulary of modern art but never parted from an immediate accessibility of image. This was a major hallmark of his contribution. Perhaps there is a limit to how far a designer can follow the modern painter into the uncharted realm of pure form and subjective expression without losing the vital foothold on public communication.

During a design career in a life cut tragically short by illness, Alvin Lustig (1915–1955) incorporated his subjective vision and private symbols into graphic design. Born in Colorado, Lustig bounced between east and west coasts and between architecture, graphic design, and interior design. At age twenty-one, Lustig operated a graphic design and printing business from the rear of a Los Angeles drugstore. On projects for the Ward Ritchie Press, Lustig created abstract geometric designs using type rules and ornaments.

Sensing that Lustig's work was created by "an artist who might possess a touch of genius," publisher James Laughton of New Directions in New York began to commission book and jacket designs from him. As New Directions published books of outstanding literary quality, Lustig's design approach—searching for symbols to capture the essence of the contents and treating form and content as one—was extremely successful with the caliber of audience that reads quality literature. Lustig believed in the importance of painting to design and design education and considered the artist's pure research into private symbols to be the wellspring for the public symbols created by the designer. By 1950 Lustig was becoming increasingly involved in design education, but his eyesight had begun to fail, and he was totally blind by the autumn of 1954. In the face of this overwhelming tragedy for an artist, Lustig continued to teach and design until his death the following

Alvin Lustig, cover for *A Season in Hell* by Arthur Rimbaud, 1945. Sharp black-and-white biomorphic figures on a deep red field suggest the French poet's spiritual descent into hell, and his failures in love and art. *Courtesy of Elaine Lustig Cohen.*

Alvin Lustig, cover for *27 Wagons Full of Cotton* by Tennessee Williams, 1949. A delicate magnolia flower brutally nailed to rough siding: these contradictory photographic symbols represent the underlying violence and hatred behind the civilized façade in human affairs. Lustig understood the frail human spirit and brutal environmental forces articulated in Williams' plays. *Courtesy of Elaine Lustig Cohen.*

Alvin Lustig, cover for *3 Tragedies* by Federico Garcia Lorca, 1949. In this stunning montage of five photographic images, the author's name and title become objects photographed in the world. *Courtesy of Elaine Lustig Cohen.*

Alvin Lustig, cover for *Camino Real* by Tennessee Williams, 1952. The typographic, posterlike title contrasts crisply with the graffiti-marred wall upon which it is posted. *Courtesy of Elaine Lustig Cohen.*

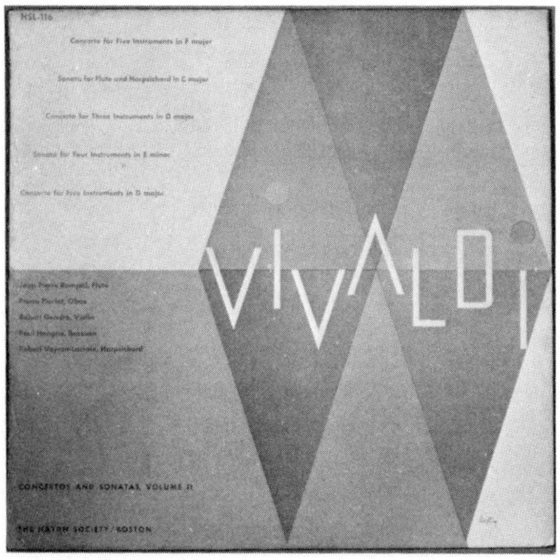

Alvin Lustig, album cover for Vivaldi, 1951. Moving like music notes along the median line, the abstracted letters forming the Italian composer's name echo the background triangular shapes. *Courtesy of Elaine Lustig Cohen.*

December. One is compelled to wonder what the impact of this perceptive man upon design and visual education might have been had he lived a normal lifespan.

Alvin Lustig, album cover for Mozart, 1951. An intricate visual structure becomes a graphic equivalent for the sound structures in Mozart's music. *Courtesy of Elaine Lustig Cohen.*

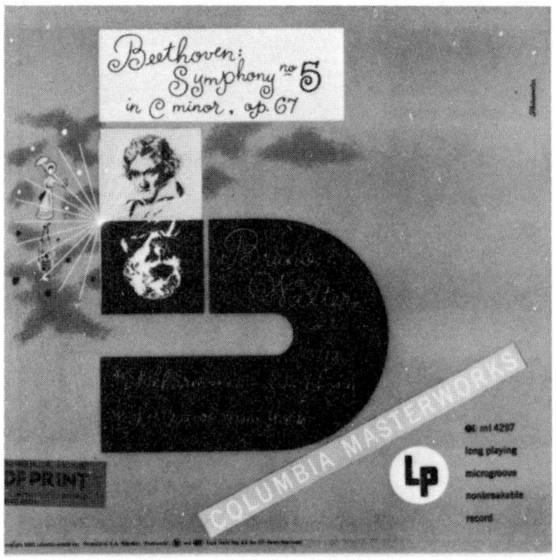

Alex Steinweiss, album cover for Beethoven's Symphony No. 5, 1949. A big "5" constructed of geometric elements, casual script writing, positive and negative images of the composer, a pink bar, and a white circle on a blue background; these elements are typical of the vocabulary Steinweiss used in hundreds of album designs during the 1940s. *Courtesy of CBS Records.*

In 1940, twenty-four-year-old Alex Steinweiss (b. 1916) was named art director of Columbia Records. The modern design sensibilities of the 1940s were applied to record album design as Steinweiss searched for visual forms and shapes to express music. Steinweiss had an informal approach to space. Elements were placed casually on the field with an informal balance that sometimes bordered on a random scattering of forms. Steinweiss initiated a commitment to quality and appropriate expression of the musical content that continues over four decades later at Columbia Records and throughout the musical recording industry.

Bradbury Thompson (b. 1911) emerged as one of the most influential graphic designers in post-war America. After graduation from Washburn College in his hometown of Topeka, Kansas, in 1934, Thompson worked for printing firms there for several years before moving to New York.

His designs for Westvaco Inspirations from 1939 until 1961 had tremendous impact. His thorough knowledge of printing and typesetting, combined with an adventurous spirit of experimentation, allowed him to expand the range of design possibilities. A four-color publication demonstrating printing papers, Westvaco Inspirations used letterpress plates of art and illustration borrowed from advertising agencies and museums. With a limited budget for new plates or artwork, Thompson used the typecase and printshop as his "canvas, easel, and second studio." Four-color process plates would be taken apart and used to create designs and often overprinted to create new colors. Large, bold organic and geometric shapes were used to bring graphic and symbolic power to the page. He discovered and explored the potential of eighteenth- and nineteenth-century engravings as design resources. Letterforms were often enlarged to great size and used as design elements or to create visual patterns and movements. Thompson achieved a rare mastery of complex organization, form, and visual flow.

During the 1960s and 1970s, he turned increasingly to a classical approach to book and editorial format design. Readability, formal harmony, and a sensitive use of Old Style typefaces have marked this work for periodicals such as *Smithsonian* and *ARTnews,* postage stamps, and a steady flow of books.

The sensibilities of the New York School were carried to Los Angeles by

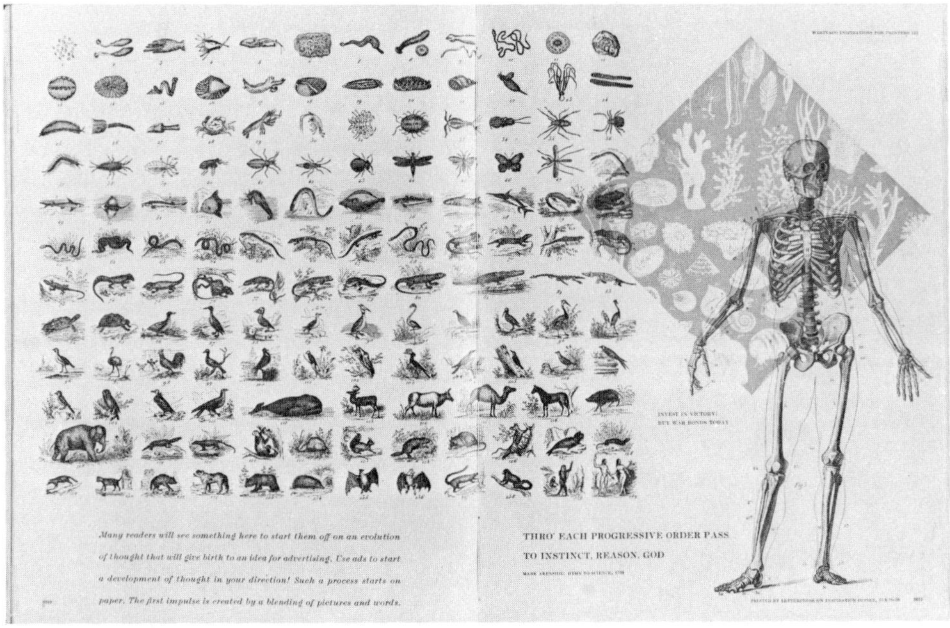

Bradbury Thompson, pages from *Westvaco Inspirations,* 151, 1945. The vast storehouse of printed images that had passed into the public domain was deftly probed and became part of the graphic design vocabulary.

Bradbury Thompson, pages from *Westvaco Inspirations,* 186, 1951. For the opening spread of an issue exploring the theme, enlarging upon printing, that covered ideas such as enlarging halftone dots, Thompson composed this spirited collage.

Saul Bass (b. 1921). This native New Yorker was educated and worked in his home city until 1950, when he moved to California. Two years later, he opened his own studio. Paul Rand's use of shape and asymmetric balance during the 1940s was an important inspiration for Bass. But while Rand's carefully orchestrated compositions used complex contrasts of shape, color, and texture, Bass frequently reduced the graphic design to a single dominant image, usually centered in the space.

Bass has a remarkable ability to identify the nucleus of a design problem. This is then expressed with images that become glyphs, or elemental pictorial signs, that possess great graphic power. Bass stripped visual complexity from American graphic design and reduced the communication to a simple pictographic image. But this is not the elemental graphics of Constructivism. Chunky forms are cut from paper with scissors or drawn with a brush. Freely drawn, decorative letterforms are as likely to be used in his work as typography or handwriting. There is a robust energy about his forms, and an almost casual quality about their execution. While images are simplified to a minimal statement, they lack the exactitude of measurement or construction that could make them rigid.

The motion picture had long used traditional portraiture of actors and actresses in promoting films. Producer/director Otto Preminger commissioned Bass to create unified graphic materials for his films beginning in the 1950s encompassing a logo, theater posters, advertising, and animated film titles.

The first comprehensive design program for a film unifying both print and media graphics was the 1955 design program for Preminger's *The Man with the Golden Arm.* For this film about drug addiction, Bass developed a thick pictographic arm that thrusts downward into a rectangle composed of slablike bars, then bracketed the arm with the name of the film. The titles for this motion picture broke new ground. Accompanied by staccato jazz music, a single white bar thrust down onto the screen, followed by three more. When all four reached the center of the screen, typography appeared listing the featured performers. All of these elements except one bar, retained for continuity, faded. Then, four bars swept in from the top, bottom, and sides to frame the film-title typography which suddenly appeared. This kinetic sequence of animated bars and typography continued in perfect synchronization to the throbbing wail of jazz music through the credits. Finally, the bars thrust into the space and transformed into the pictographic arm of the logo. Bass became the acknowledged master of the film title. He pioneered an organic process of forms that appear,

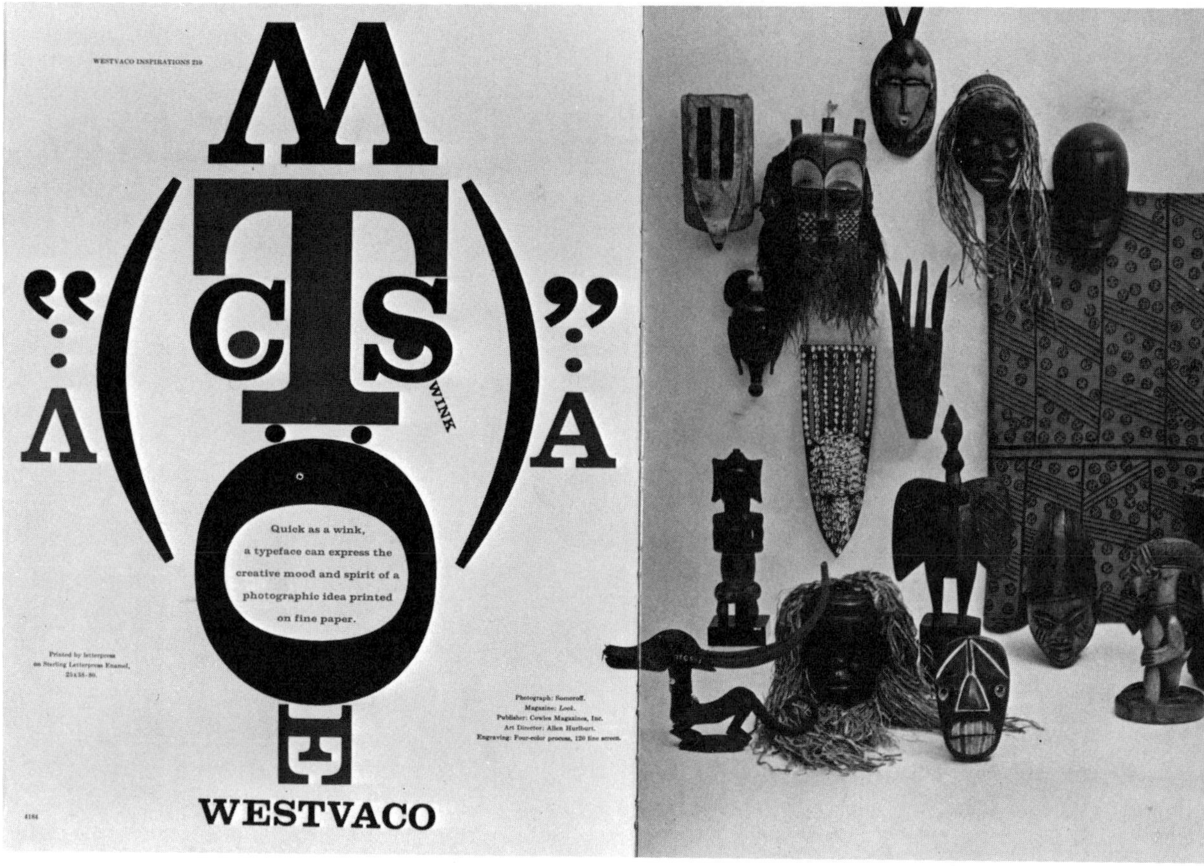
WINK
Quick as a wink,
a typeface can express the
creative mood and spirit of a
photographic idea printed
on fine paper.
Printed by letterpress
on Sterling Letterpress Enamel,
25x38-80.
Photograph: Somoroff.
Magazine: Look.
Publisher: Cowles Magazines, Inc.
Art Director: Allen Hurlburt.
Engraving: Four-color process, 120 line screen.
WESTVACO

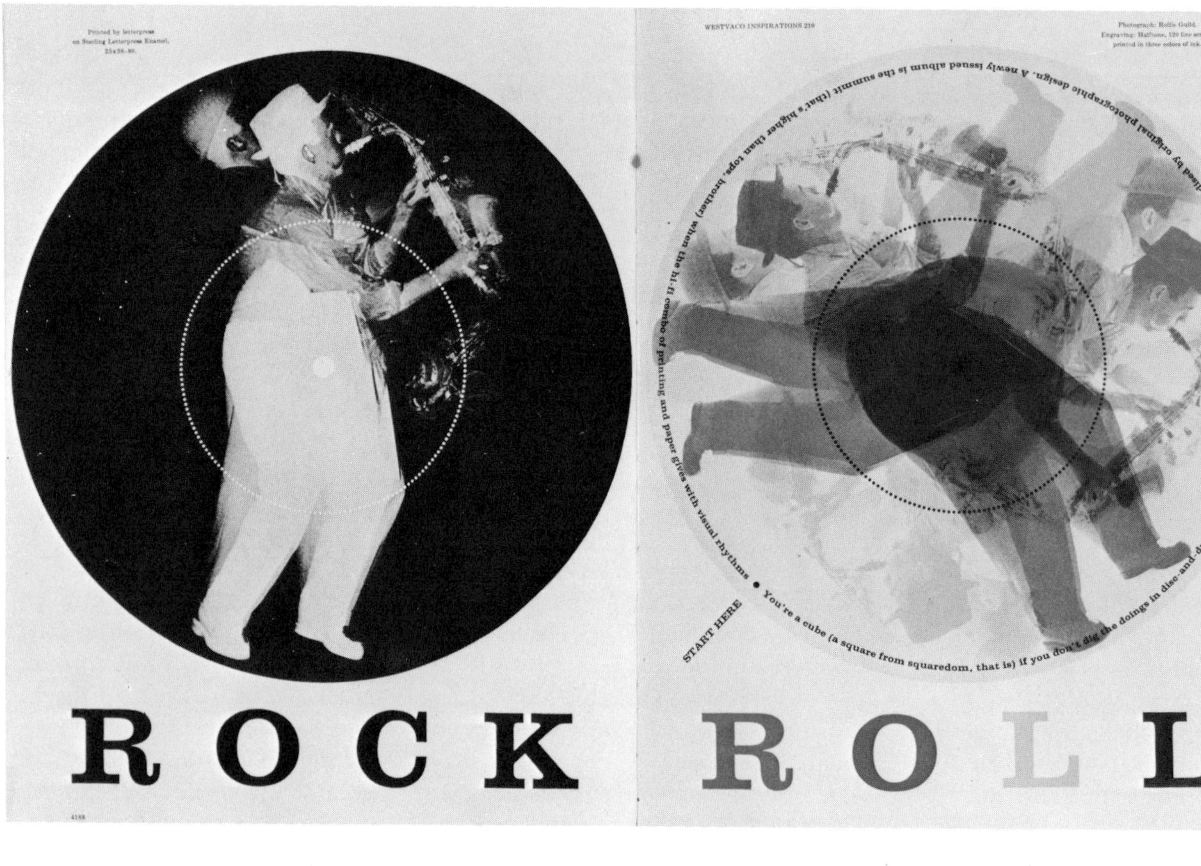
START HERE
You're a cube (a square from squaredom, that is) if you don't dig the doings in disc-and dungaree circles. Fact is, the cats are real gone about platters merchandised by original photographic design. A newly issued album is the summit (that's higher than tops, brother) when the hi-fi combo of printing and paper gives with visual rhythms
ROCK
ROLL

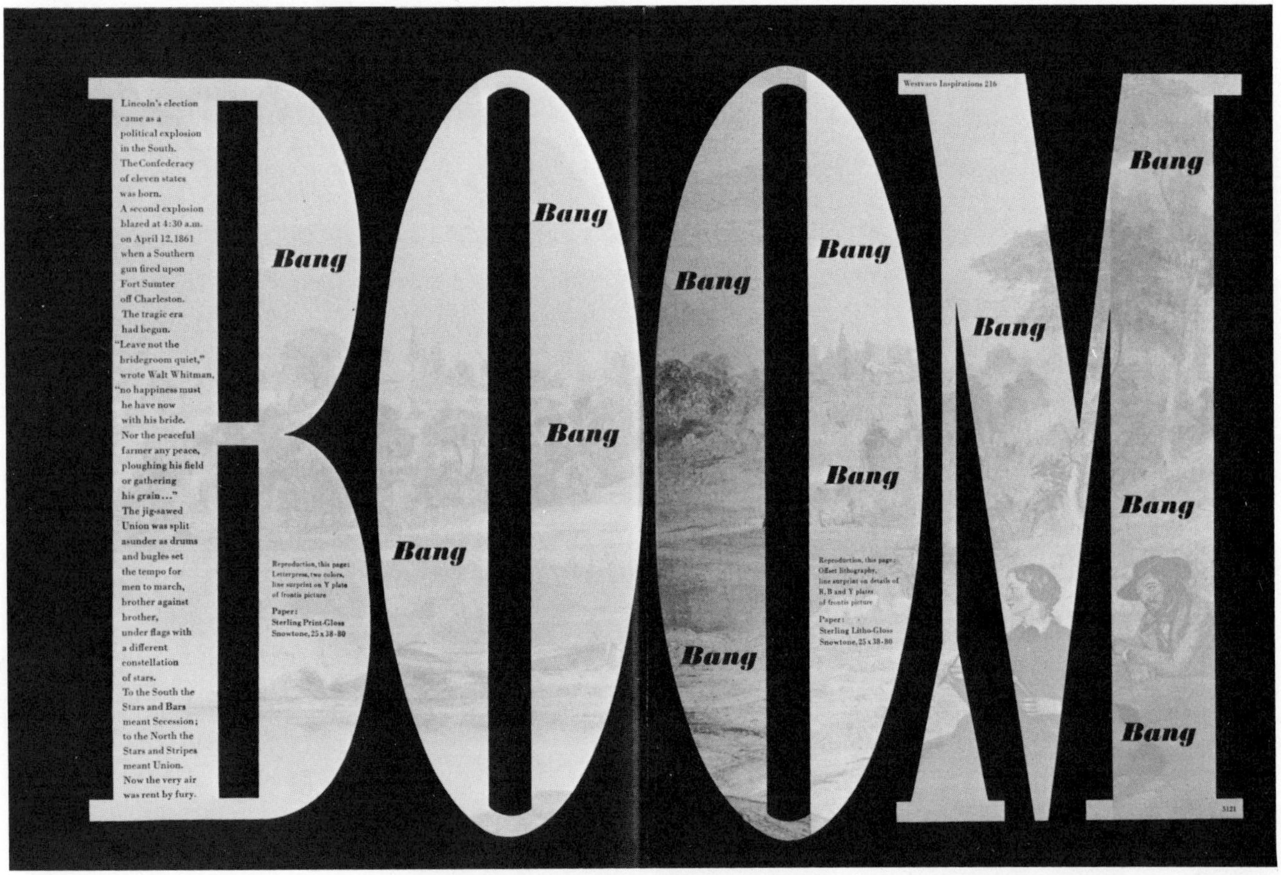

Bradbury Thompson, pages from *Westvaco Inspirations,* 216, 1961. The final issue discussed the American Civil War. Thompson used complex typography to express the subject matter. In this spread, a painting reproduced on the preceding pages is printed in yellow and black, blue and red, red, and red and yellow as it moves across the page behind the letterforms.

Bradbury Thompson, pages from *Westvaco Inspirations,* 210, 1958. Letterforms from the word "Westvaco" are used to construct a winking face expressing the stylized geometry of the African masks in Somoroff's photograph. The photograph, loaned for use as a printing specimen, was a given. Thompson's creative response was typographic. (Opposite, above)

Bradbury Thompson, pages from *Westvaco Inspirations,* 210, 1958. Starting with a multiple exposure photograph of a saxophone player, Thompson reversed it out of a black circle on the left and overprinted it in primary colors on the right.

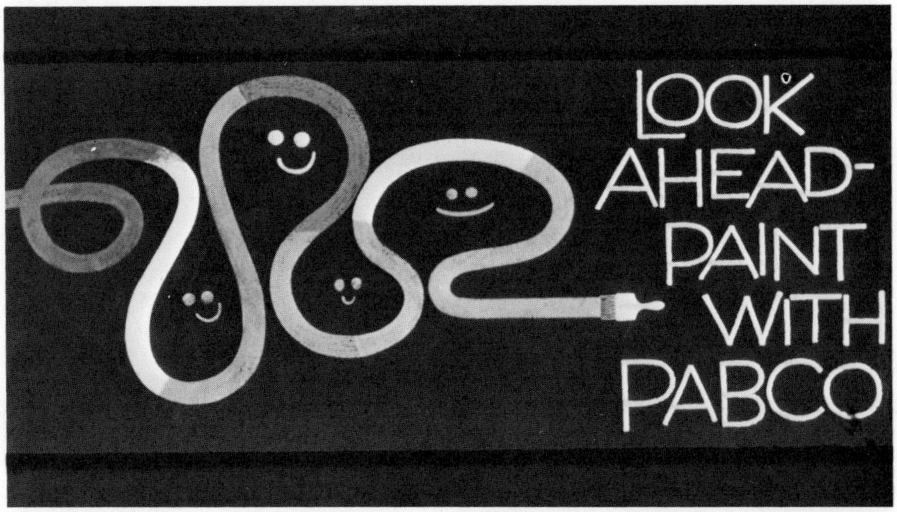

Saul Bass, billboard for Pabco Paints early 1950s. The process of painting is reduced to a multicolored stripe. The happy people who look ahead by using quality paint are articulated by three simple marks.

Saul Bass, symbol for *The Man with the Golden Arm,* 1955. This consistent and memorable visual identifier was flexible enough for uses ranging from minute newspaper advertisements to large-scale posters.

FRANK SINATRA · ELEANOR PARKER · KIM NOVAK
THE MAN WITH THE
GOLDEN ARM
Produced & Directed by Otto Preminger, Released by United Artists

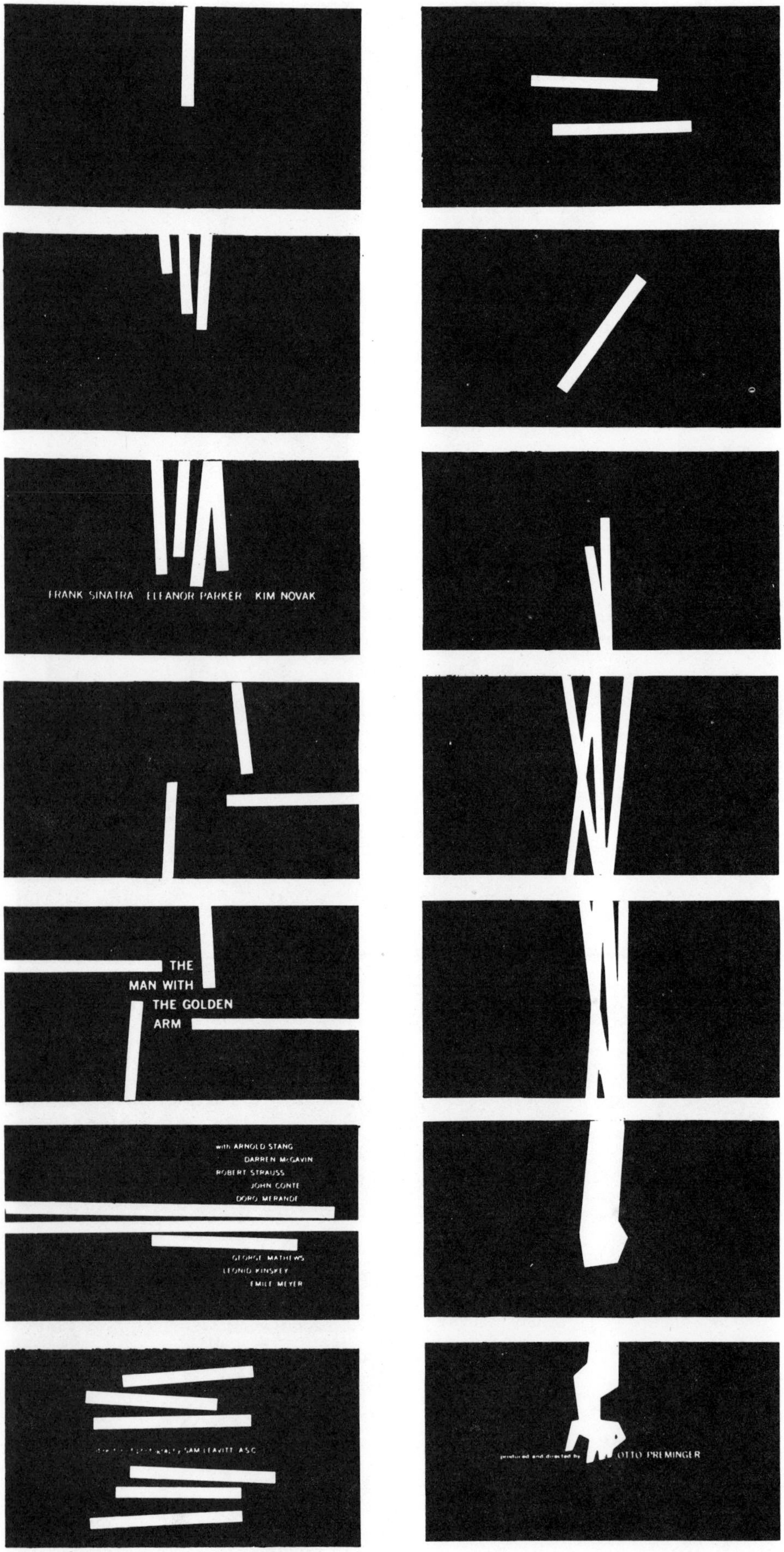
FRANK SINATRA ELEANOR PARKER KIM NOVAK
THE
MAN WITH
THE GOLDEN
ARM
with ARNOLD STANG
DARREN McGAVIN
ROBERT STRAUSS
JOHN CONTE
DORO MERANDE
GEORGE MATHEWS
LEONID KINSKEY
EMILE MEYER
SAM LEAVITT A.S.C.
produced and directed by OTTO PREMINGER

Saul Bass, film titles for *The Man with the Golden Arm,* 1955. Abstract graphic elements created a spare, gaunt intensity that reflected the character of the film. Graphic design for film was revolutionized.

Saul Bass, poster for the movie, *Exodus,* 1960. The trauma of Israel's birth is expressed by two levels of reality: the two-dimensional logo; and the moment frozen by photography when this image is being engulfed in flames.

Saul Bass, trade advertisement for *Exodus,* 1960. To communicate that Exodus was all wrapped-up or "in the can," a film can was wrapped in a Hebrew newspaper, tied, and labeled with a tag bearing the logo.

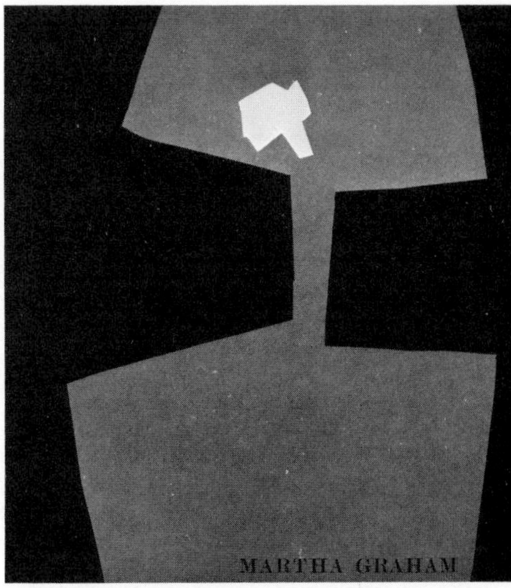

George Tscherny, dance program cover, 1958. At first glance, this appears as a beautiful color study in positive and negative space. Then, the viewer realizes that with two pieces of cut paper, Tscherny has captured the renowned modern dancer, Martha Graham, in one of her classic poses.

disintegrate, reform, and transform in time and space. This combination, recombination, and synthesis of form was carried over into the area of printed graphics.

An exceptional example of the design program by Bass can be seen in the 1960 graphics of the movie *Exodus.* Bass created a powerful pictograph of arms reaching upward and struggling for a rifle. This conveyed the violence and strife connected with the birth of the nation of Israel. This mark was used in a comprehensive publicity program, including newspaper, magazine, and trade advertisements; posters and film titles; and even stationery, shipping labels, and other routine printed matter. Each individual item was approached as a unique communications problem. Diversity was achieved while the strong graphic qualities of the mark insured continuity.

In addition to the film graphics that made him famous, Bass has created numerous corporate identity programs. He has directed a number of films ranging from the outstanding *Why Man Creates,* that uses a kaleidoscope of film techniques probing the nature of human creativity, to a feature length motion picture.

George Tscherny (b. 1924) is a native of Budapest, Hungary, who emigrated to the United States as a child and received his visual education there. Tscherny served as head of the graphic design department for George Nelson & Associates before opening his own design office in 1956. For a quarter of a century, Tscherny has functioned as an independent designer, which is somewhat unique in a profession where partnerships, large staffs, and staff positions are the norm. The particular gift that this intuitive and sensitive man brings to the design process is an ability to seize the essence of the subject and express it in stunningly simple terms. The results are elegant and to the point; other designers have found his designs so disarmingly simple and appropriate that "why didn't I think of this?" is a common reaction. Tscherny's vocabulary of techniques for solving design problems includes the purely typographic, photography, simple calligraphic brush drawing, and the bold, simple shapes that he delights in cutting from colored papers. Regardless of technique, Tscherny's process of reducing complex content to an elemental graphic symbol expressing the underlying order or basic form of the subject is constant.

George Tscherny, exhibition catalogue covers, 1961. José de Rivera is a Constructivist sculptor whose parabolic curves twist and bend in space. Tscherny expressed this quality by photographing type which he had bent and twisted.

Saul Bass, *8th San Francisco International Film Festival,* poster, 1964. The white space separating the two black squares also becomes the film-editing bar holding colorful shots of the flags from participating countries.

George Tscherny, promotional poster for a printing paper, 1975. Even the richness of New York City's architectural clutter yields to Tscherny's simplifying process in this photographic study of contrasts.

An editorial design revolution

Alexey Brodovich taught editorial design classes at his home and then at the New School for Social Research during the 1940s and early 1950s. The seeds for an expansive design-oriented period of editorial graphics were sown in Brodovich's classes. One of his students, Otto Storch (b. 1913), wrote later that "Brodovich would dump photostats, type proofs, colored pieces of paper, and someone's shoe lace, if it became untied, on a long table together with rubber cement. He would fold his arms and with a sad expression challenge us to do something brilliant." Brodovich's students learned to examine each problem thoroughly, develop a solution from this understanding, then search for a brilliant visual presentation. The impact of Brodovich upon a generation of editorial designers and photographers who came into their own during the 1950s was phenomenal, and editorial design experienced one of its greatest eras.

An art director at Dell publishing, Storch was unhappy with the level of subject matter in his assignments, and he had developed a keen interest in the design of *Harper's Bazaar* by Brodovich. He joined the art directors, photographers, fashion and general illustrators, and packaging, set, and typographic designers who gathered to learn from the master. After class one evening, Brodovich reviewed Storch's portfolio and advised him to quit his job because Storch showed potential but his position didn't. A seven-year period of freelancing followed, then Storch joined the McCall's Corporation as assistant art director for *Better Living Magazine.* In 1953, Storch was named art director of *McCall's.* A major publication for women, *McCall's* was having circulation problems. A new editor named Herbert Mayes was brought in to revitalize the magazine in the late 1950s. Storch was given a free hand to upgrade the graphics in 1958, and an astounding visual approach developed. Typography was unified with photography by designing it to lock tightly into the photographic image. Scale was explored in the large-format publication. Headlines often became part of the illustration. For example, the article title "Why Mommy Can't Read" was written on a pair of glasses, which were then photographed. Full-bleed double-page photographs were designed with preplanned areas for the type. In other pages, type would become the illustration. In one case, a tight rectangle of over sixty capital Baskerville *Z*'s linked with the title, "Bored of Education," for an article discussing how some children found school so dull that it put them to sleep. Small objects became large graphics. Subjects including a beautiful ear of fresh summer corn in the food section of the magazine and a closeup of a woman's lips as she put on lipstick were presented as full, double-page layouts. Storch and the

M
onroe? Just a slob, really: an untidy divinity – in the sense that a banana split or cherry jubilee is untidy but divine.
Her slippery lips, her overspilling blondness and sliding brassiere straps, the rhythmic writhing of restless poundage wriggling for room inside roomless décolletage—such are her emblems, those caricaturable flauntings that, one would have supposed, made her at once world-recognizable. However, in what is said to be real life, the Monroe is not easily identified. She maneuvers New York streets unmolested by stares, signals for taxis that do not stop, is served orange juice at a sidewalk Nedick's by an attendant unaware that the customer is the subject of some of his more ambitious ambitions: indeed, more often than otherwise one has to be told Monroe is Monroe, for she seems, casually glanced, merely another specimen of the American geisha, the expense-account darling, those cabaret-cuties whose careers progress from tinted hair at twelve to a confiscated husband or three at twenty. But true to type as aspects of the Monroe are, she is not genuinely of the genre, she is too untough to be, moreover she is capable of sensitive concentration always the secret of making any talent work, which hers does: the character she performs, a waif-figure of saucy pathos, is sound and convincing charm: very understandably so, since there is small difference between her screen image and the impression she
85

Alexey Brodovich (designer) and Richard Avedon (photographer), page from *Observations* by Richard Avedon and Truman Capote, 1959. The organic softness of figure and feathers contrasts markedly with the erect elegance of the Bodoni italic type. Unity is achieved by the similar placement of each page's focal point: the expressive head and the initial *M*. *Simon and Schuster.*

Otto Storch (art director) and Paul Dome (photographer), pages from *McCall's*, 1961. These introductory pages to a feature on frozen foods unify typography and photography into a cohesive structure. *Courtesy of Otto Storch.*

photographers who worked with him went to great pains to produce photographic essays that were unexpected and poetic. Foods and fashions were often shot on location instead of in the studio. For an article on breakfasts around the world, Storch photographed the foods on the wing of a transatlantic airplane.

Storch ranks high among the innovators of the period. His philosophy that idea, copy, art, and typography should be inseparable in editorial design was very influential on both editorial and advertising graphics.

After gaining experience in studios and an advertising agency, Vienna-born Henry Wolf (b. 1925) became art director of *Esquire* in 1953. Like Storch, Wolf studied under Brodovich, and he redesigned *Esquire's* format with greater emphasis on the use of white space and large photographs. When Brodovich retired as art director of *Harper's Bazaar* in 1958, Wolf had the honor of replacing the master. Wolf felt that he had a rare privilege to make the magazine visually beautiful. Experimenting with typography, Wolf would make it very large to fill the page on one spread and then use petite headlines on other pages. The sophistication and inventiveness of photography commissioned by *Harper's Bazaar* under Wolf's tenure was extraordinary. In 1961, Wolf left *Bazaar* to design the new *Show* magazine, a short-lived periodical that explored new design territory as a result of Wolf's conceptually imaginative and visually elegant art direction. Among the other editorial art directors of this wonderful era of magazine design, Allen Hulbert art-directed *Look* magazine from 1953 until 1968 and brought relevance, intelligence, and a keen sense of scale to this publication. Some of the photographic essays used in *Look* during the 1960s raised editorial design and photography to a high aesthetic level.

Otto Storch became very involved with photography. In 1967, after nearly fifteen years as art director of *McCall's,* he resigned to concentrate on full-time editorial and advertising photography. Success had made *McCall's* management more conservative, and opposition to creative layout was building. Also, there were broader factors at work in the publications industry that were to end the era of large pages of lavish photography, and design dominating content. In the late 1960s the two-decade period of ever-growing affluence in America was yielding to inflation and economic problems. At the same time, public concerns about the Vietnam War, environmental problems, the rights of minorities and women, and a host of other issues produced a need for a different kind of publication.

A higher information content was demanded by the public, and skyrocketing postal rates, paper shortages, and escalating paper and printing costs shrunk the large-format periodicals (*McCall's* and *Esquire,* for example, were 33.4 by 25.5 centimeters, or 13 $\frac{1}{8}$ by 10 $\frac{1}{8}$ inches) to a fairly standard format size of 27.5 by 21 centimeters (11 by 8 $\frac{1}{2}$ inches). Others, including *Life, Look,* and *The Saturday Evening Post,* ceased publication.

Henry Wolf, cover for *Esquire,* 1958. To express the "Americanization of Paris," Wolf photographed a packet of "instant red wine" to symbolize satirically the creeping spread of American technology, customs, and conveniences.

Otto Storch (art director and photographer), pages from *McCall's,* 1965. For an article on breakfasts around the world, Storch photographed food on the wing of an international jet liner. *Courtesy of Otto Storch.*

the forty-winks reducing plan

This is a plan for growing slimmer and shapelier. It involves a diet—the only way to lose pounds is to take in fewer calories. It involves exercise—the most effective way to slough off inches is by toning muscles. But this plan has a third ingredient, which supplies what most plans lack—a feeling of comfort and well-being while you lose. The secret: a half-hour nap every afternoon. Your first reaction may be one of disbelief. You've probably always heard that sleeping puts on weight, but this is not true—nothing adds weight except eating. What rest can do for most people is reduce the compulsion to eat. Tired and tense, you feel you need the midmorning pastry or midafternoon sandwich for energy to keep going; rested and relaxed, you're less likely to want it. Perhaps a nap seems out of the question—you could never find the time, or you couldn't fall asleep in the middle of the day. These are common problems; but often, both can be solved. Some women may choose a time while the children are in school or while the baby, too, naps. Others may enlist the cooperation of another family member or exchange services with a neighbor. It may mean cutting down on the time you spend over coffee in the morning or perusing the newspaper, so your work gets done a little earlier. It will certainly take some juggling, and it won't be a cinch for most women, who are pretty overwhelmed with household chores; but for many, we believe it can be managed. As for your imagined inability to fall asleep, that can be remedied. The exercises on pages 78 to 81 should relax and just pleasantly tire your body, and the yawning trick described on page 80 is near magic. (No reason you shouldn't use it at night, too.) We know it's easy to prepare all sorts of plans and assume, impractically, that all women have the time to follow them. But we feel this plan has such special merit that we hope it can be tried out by a majority of our readers. Here's what we propose: At a given time each afternoon, muffle the telephone, and retire to your bedroom. Spend about twenty minutes doing the nonstrenuous exercises, and be sure to do them in order. Then pull down the shades; go through the yawning routine; and sleep or, at least, doze for the balance of the hour. Practice this for one week: at the end of that time, we predict you'll be noticeably slimmer and prettier, and you will have no gnawing hunger pangs as you follow the diet on page 192.

Otto Storch (art director) and Dan Wynn (photographer), pages from *McCall's,* 1961. Typography bends under the weight of the sleeping woman with the elasticity of a soft mattress. *Courtesy of Otto Storch.*

Henry Wolf, cover for *Harper's Bazaar,* 1959. This refracted image is typical of the imaginative visual solutions Wolf brought to ordinary design problems. A subtle touch is the way the logo is refracted, too.

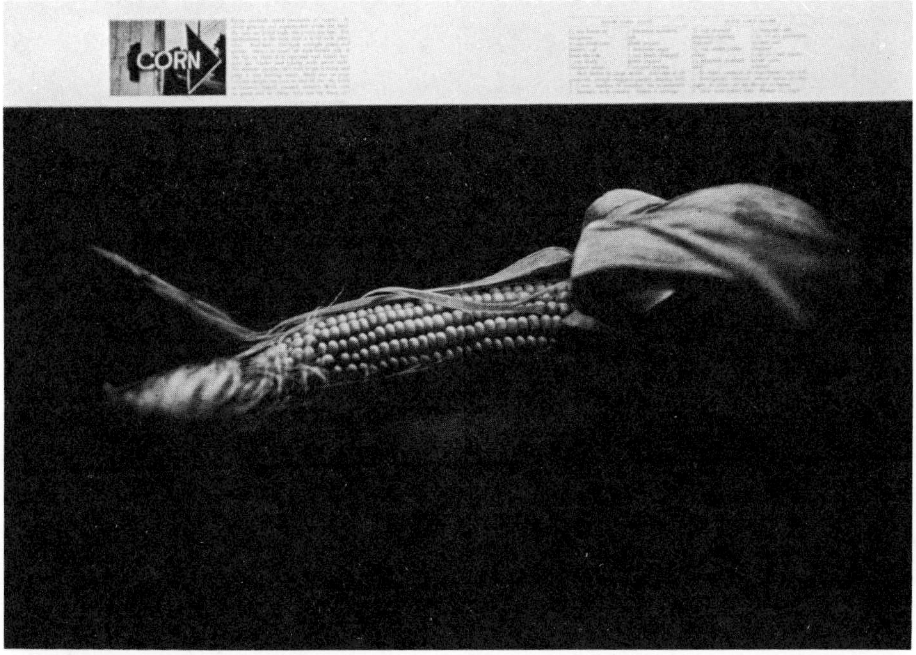

Otto Storch (art director and photographer), pages from McCall's, 1965. The soft beauty of an ear of corn fills the pages. The title for this feature is a photograph of a handmade sign from a roadside market. *Courtesy of Otto Storch.*

Henry Wolf, cover for *Harper's Bazaar,* 1959. The colors of the peacock feather are picked up by the eye makeup in this arresting juxtaposition of forms.

Otto Storch (art director) and Allen Arbus (photographer), pages from *McCall's,* 1959. Typography sprinkles from the hand and foot of moving models. By photographing the model wearing a red dress against a black background, and a model in a black-and-white outfit against a red background, a dynamic color effect is achieved. *Courtesy of Otto Storch.*

Henry Wolf, cover for *Show,* 1963. On this Valentine's Day cover, Wolf has used an x-ray machine to locate the model's graphic red heart. The red heart on the white rectangle makes a strong focal point against the high contrast black photograph and deep blue background.

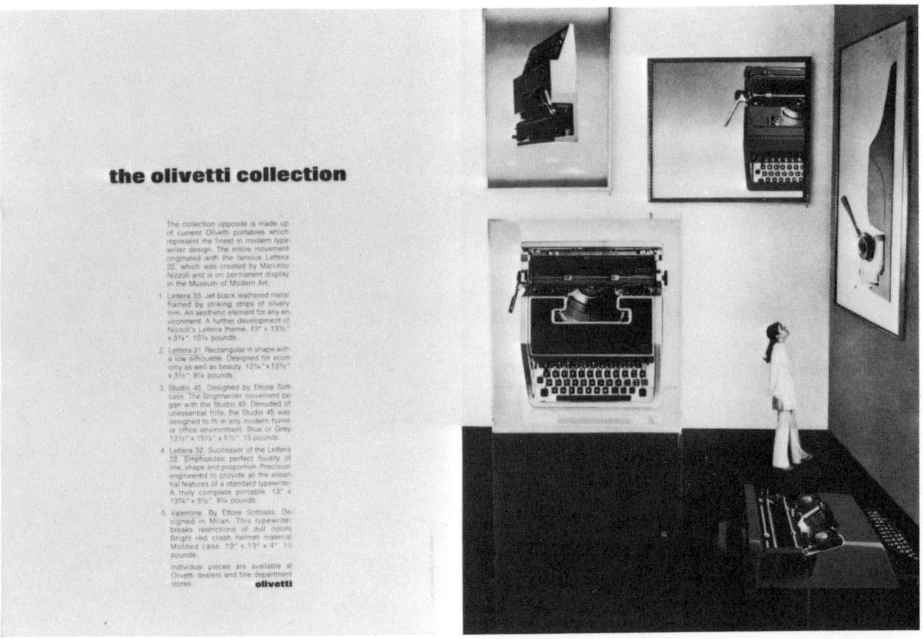

Henry Wolf, advertisement for Olivetti, 1960s. In a surreal art gallery, the industrial design of typewriters is honored for its artistic quality.

The new advertising

The 1940s were a lackluster decade for advertising. A pile-driver repetition of slogans, movie star testimonials, and exaggerated claims were mainstays of the decade, punctuated by occasional design excellence. On 1 June 1949, a new advertising agency, Doyle Dane Bernbach, opened its doors at 350 Madison Avenue in New York City with a staff of thirteen and less than a half million dollars in client accounts. Copywriter Bill Bernbach (b. 1911) was the partner with responsibility for the creative area, and his initial staff consisted of art director Bob Gage and copywriter Phyllis Robinson.

Doyle Dane Bernbach "took the exclamation mark out of advertising" as they talked intelligently to consumers. For each campaign a strategy would be developed surrounding any important advantage, useful difference, or superior feature of the product. In order to break through the indifference of consumers who are bombarded by perpetual commercial messages, Bernbach sought an imaginative "package" for this information. It is here that Bernbach made his major contribution, for Bernbach's team integrated words and images in a new way. In the past, a copywriter would write a headline and body copy. These would be sent to the art director, who then made a layout. In the Bernbach approach, a synergistic relationship between visual and verbal components is established. Paul Rand's bellwether approach to advertising in the 1940s integrated words and phrases provided by copywriters in a freer organization with visual metaphors and puns seldom seen in advertising; Bernbach and his colleagues smashed through the boundaries separating verbal and visual communications and evolved the visual/verbal syntax: word and image are fused into a conceptual expression of an idea so that they become completely interdependent.

This new advertising saw a new working relationship as writers and art directors worked as "creative teams." In addition to Bob Gage, Bill Taubin, Helmut Krone (b. 1925), Len Sirowitz (b. 1932), and Bert Steinhauser rank among the art directors who have produced outstanding creative work in collaboration with Doyle Dane Bernbach copywriters. Because concept becomes dominant, the design of many Doyle Dane Bernbach advertisements is reduced to the basic elements necessary to convey the message: a large arresting visual image, a concise headline of bold weight, and body copy that stakes its claim with factual and often entertaining writing instead of puffery and meaningless superlatives. Often the visual organization is symmetrical, for design arrangement is not allowed to distract from the straightforward presentation of an idea.

Doyle Dane Bernbach became a training ground for "the new advertising." Many writers and art directors who developed there participated in spin-off agencies as the boutique agency, a small shop with emphasis on creativity rather than full marketing services, challenged the dominance of the monolithic multimillion dollar agencies during the flowering of advertising creativity in the 1960s. The notion of the advertising superstar was fed by a proliferation of awards, competitions, professional periodicals, and annuals.

Bob Gage (art director), Bill Bernbach and Judy Protas (writers), department store advertisement, 1958. Words and picture combine in an arresting and effective presentation of a "catty lady" who discovers that high fashion at lower prices is the reason an acquaintance dresses so well. *Courtesy of Doyle Dane Bernbach, New York, N.Y.*

Len Sirowitz (art director) and Leon Meadow (copywriter), eye-care industry institutional advertisement, 1963. By photographing typography out of focus to graphically communicate vision problems, Sirowitz turned typography into an illustration.

Charlie Piccirillo (art director) and Judy Protas (writer), back to school advertisement for Ohrbach's, 1962. The clichés of conventional seasonal advertising yielded to a direct presentation of the joys and sorrows of everyday life. White space effectively focuses the reader's attention toward the headline and image in the crowded newspaper page.

Bert Steinhauser (art director) and Chuck Kollewe (writer), political action advertisement, 1967. A powerful participatory challenge to the reader, combined with a listing of congressmen who voted for and against the rat extermination bill, was so persuasive that the art director received a letter from President Lyndon B. Johnson after the bill was passed.

Helmut Krone (art director) and Julian Koenig (writer), motorcar advertisement, 1960. By making an economical automobile lovable and replacing the exaggerated claims and superlatives of advertising with straightforward facts, ''strange little cars with their beetle shapes'' were successfully marketed to a public that had come to accept luxury and horsepower as status symbols.

Bill Taupin (art director) and Judy Protas (writer), subway poster, c. 1965. The stereotypes of mass communication were replaced by real people, and the taboos against ethnic and racial subject matter began to fall during the 1960s.

The first regular television broadcasting had started in 1941, and immediately after World War II it began its spectacular growth as an advertising medium. By the early 1960s, it became the second largest medium (after newspapers) in terms of total advertising revenue and the largest medium in major national advertising budgets. Print art directors began to turn toward the design of television commercials. At its best, this ubiquitous communication form began to expand public understanding of cinematic form as techniques from experimental film were incorporated. At their worst, television commercials became a bane upon the public consciousness.

Since the ''new advertising'' developed at the same time as the ''new journalism,'' a spate of comparisons was inevitable. The new journalism of writers like Tom Wolfe (b. 1931) replaced journalism's traditional objectivity with subjective responses as a component part of reportage. The journalist experienced as a participant rather than as a dispassionate observer. The new advertising continued advertising's orientation toward persuasive selling techniques and subjective emotional appeals. But the techniques used became more honest, literate, and tasteful.

American typographic expressionism

A playful, graphic design trend that began in the 1950s and continued into the 1960s among New York graphic designers was an interest in figurative typography. This took many forms. Letterforms became objects; objects became letterforms. Gene Federico (b. 1919) was one of the first graphic designers who delighted in using letterforms as images. Another approach to figurative typography used the visual properties of the words themselves, or their organization in the space, to express an idea. Don Egensteiner's "Tonnage" advertisement is an example of the visual organization of type taking on connotative meaning. Typography was sometimes scratched, torn, bent, and vibrated to express a concept or introduce the unexpected into the printed page.

Gene Federico (art director), advertisement for *Woman's Day,* 1953. In this double-page advertisement from the *New Yorker* magazine, the perfectly round *O* of the Futura typeface provides bicycle wheels in this early example of figurative typography.

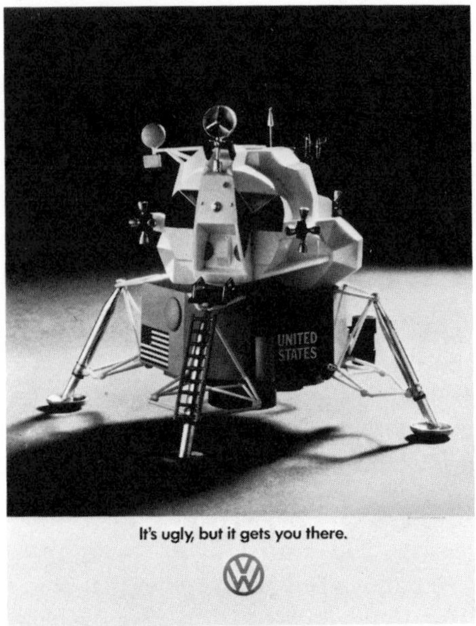

Jim Brown (art director) and Larry Levenson (writer), motorcar advertisement, 1969. Appearing in newspapers all across America immediately after the lunar landing, this advertisement gained its phenomenal impact from the continuity with the earlier advertisements. It reinforces the concept that the Volkswagen is a homely but well-engineered, reliable vehicle by a visual metaphor between a car and the space vehicle.

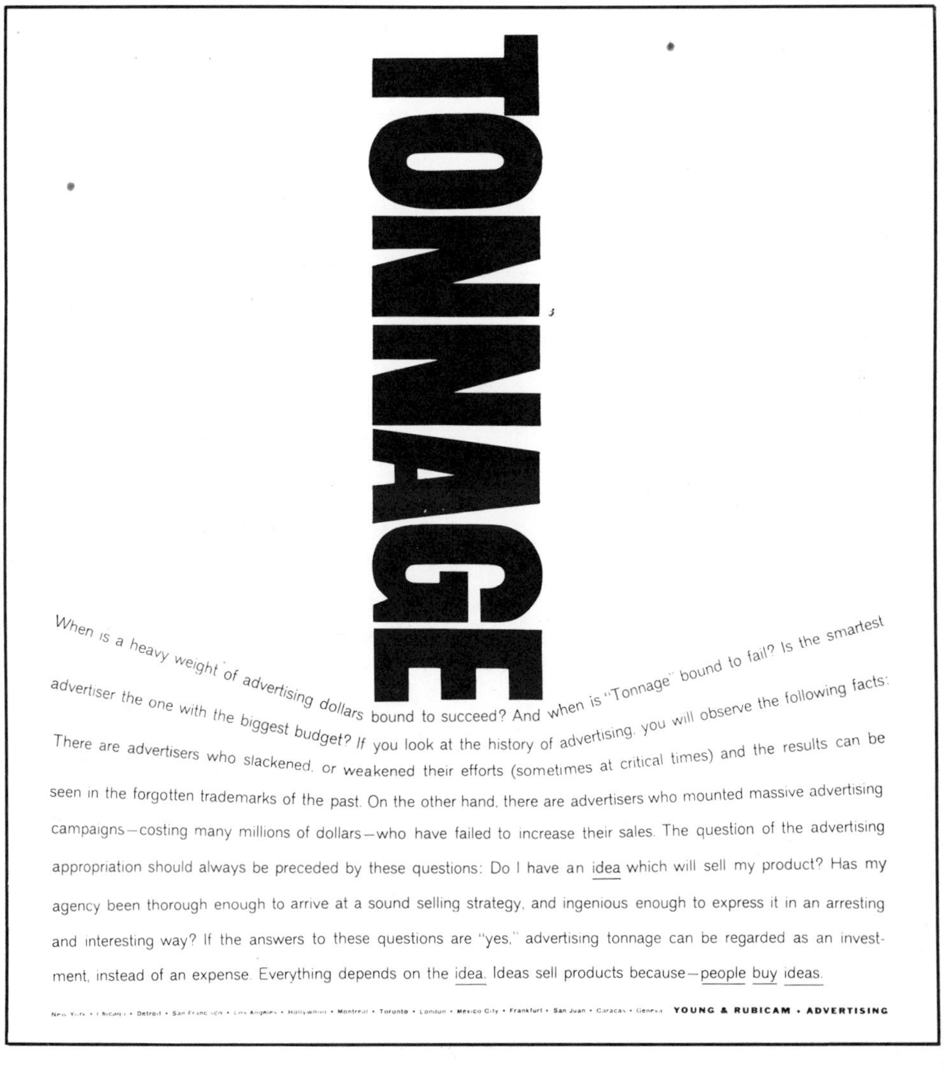

Don Egensteiner (art director), advertisement for Young and Rubicam Advertising, 1960. The heavy, one word headline crashes into the body copy to accomplish a major communications objective: to gain attention. *Courtesy of Young and Rubicam.*

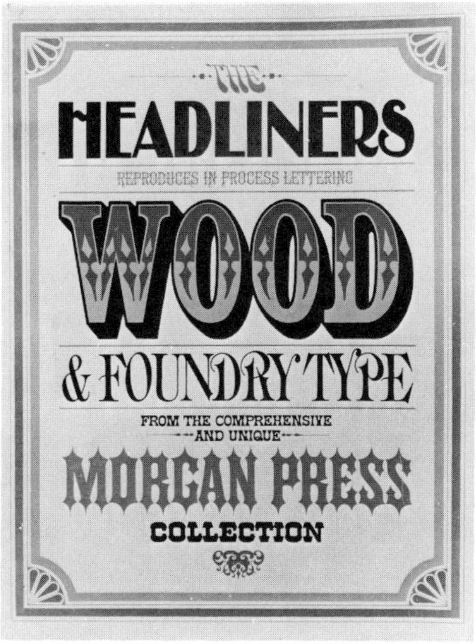

John Alcorn, cover for a phototype specimen booklet, 1964. The symmetrical mixture of decorative fonts paraphrases the nineteenth-century wood-type poster, but the spacing and use of color is innovative.

Herb Lubalin, poster announcing the Stettler typeface, 1965. Marriage, "the most licentious of human institutions," becomes an illustration through the joined *R*s.

Another typographic trend that began slowly in the 1950s was a reexamination of the nineteenth-century decorative and novelty typography which had been rejected for many decades under the influence of the modern movement. This revival of interest was inspired by Robert M. Jones, art director of RCA Victor Records, who established a private press named The Glad Hand Press in 1953. Jones had a fondness for colonial and nineteenth-century printing, and exercised this interest in hundreds of pieces of graphic ephemera produced at the press. In addition, Jones often set typography for his record album designs using wood type acquired for the press. Jones' interest inspired a revival of discarded typographic forms and a lessening of prejudice toward the decorative and outmoded.

Phototypography, the setting of type by exposing negatives of alphabet characters to photographic paper, was attempted as early as 1893 with limited results. During the 1920s inventors in England and America moved closer to success.

The year 1925 saw the quiet dawning of a new era of typography with the public announcement of the Thothmic photographic composing machine invented by E. K. Hunter and J. R. C. August of London, England. A keyboard produced a punched tape to control a long, master opaque film with transparent letterforms. As the letter moved in position in front of a lens, it was exposed to photographic paper by a beam of light. The Thothmic symbolized a graphic revolution whose full implications were not realized for nearly a half century. Commercially viable photographic display typesetting in the United States began when the Photolettering firm was established in 1936. It was headed by Edward Rondthaler (b. 1905), who had been instrumental in perfecting the Rutherford Photolettering Machine. Phototypography had the potential to replace the rigid quality of metal type with a dynamic new flexibility. But for over two decades it was used as an alternative method to set type with some production advantages and disadvantages. A major advantage of phototype was a radical reduction in the cost of introducing new typestyles. The expansion of phototype on a large scale during the 1960s was accompanied by new designs and the reissue of old designs. The introduction of the Morgan Press collection of nineteenth-century type by Headliners Process Lettering in a specimen book by John Alcorn (b. 1935) was one of many phototype collections that made the Victorian faces widely available. Graphic designers were able to rethink the value of outmoded forms and incorporate them in their work.

A typographic genius was needed to define the aesthetic potential of phototypography by understanding its new flexibility and exploring the possibilities for graphic expression that it opened.

A generalist *ne plus ultra* whose achievements include advertising and editorial design, symbol and typeface design, posters and packaging, Herb Lubalin (1918–1981) has been hailed as "the typographic genuis of his time." Lubalin's rare gifts as a graphic designer began to emerge in the 1950s. The two main thrusts of American graphic design—the visual/verbal concept orientation of Doyle Dane Bernbach and the trends toward figurative and more structured typography—unified in Lubalin's work. From a visual standpoint, space and surface became his primary considerations. Rules and the proper practice of typography were abandoned by Lubalin, who looked at alphabet characters as both visual form and message communication.

Discontent with the rigid limitations of metal type, Lubalin started cutting apart his type proofs with a razor blade and reassembling them. Type was compressed until letters joined into ligatures, type was enlarged to unexpected sizes, and letterforms were joined, overlapped, and enlarged. Capital *O*'s became receptacles for images. The traditional separation between word and image collapsed for Lubalin: words and letters could become images; images could become a word or a letter. Photographs of objects, including a rock and a bakery roll, replaced the word in a headline. This typographic play engages the reader and requires participation. Lubalin practiced design, not as an art form or craft created in a vacuum, but as a means to give visual form to a concept or a message. In his most innovative work, concept and visual form are yoked into a oneness that has been called a *typogram,* meaning a brief visual typographic poem. Making type talk, Lubalin's wit and strong message orientation enabled him to transform words such as *Marriage* and *Mother and Child* into ideographic typograms about the subject.

Herb Lubalin, proposed logo for a publication, 1967. In this masterpiece of figurative typography, the ampersand enfolds and protects the "child" in a visual metaphor for motherly love.

Herb Lubalin, poster announcing the Lincoln Gothic typeface, 1965. The brilliant red suspenders became a capital *M* against the yellow background.

When the decade of the 1960s opened, most display typography was the hand-set cold metal type of Gutenberg's day. But this five-hundred-year-old craft was being rendered obsolete by phototype. By the end of the decade, metal type was virtually a thing of the past. More than any other graphic designer, Lubalin explored the creative potential of phototypography and how the fixed relationships of letterforms marching upon square blocks of metal were being exploded by phototype's dynamic and elastic qualities. In phototype systems, letterspace can be compressed to extinction, and forms can overlap. The range of available type sizes expanded, and type can be set to any size required by the layout or enlarged to huge sizes without losing sharpness. Special lenses can be used to expand, condense, italicize, backslant, or outline letterforms. Lubalin incorporated these possibilities into his work, not just as technical or design ends in themselves, but as potent means to intensify the printed image and express content. During the metal type era, hundreds of thousands of dollars were invested in the deployment of a new typestyle. Punches and matrices had to be manufactured for every size of hand-set and hot metal keyboard type. Then, each typesetting firm had to purchase a large stock of metal type in each size and variation of roman, bold, italic, and so on to meet client requests. Phototypography reduced this implementation cost to simple film fonts, and a proliferation of typeface designs to rival the Victorian era began. An extreme thick and thin modern style typeface, designed by Lubalin in collaboration with lettering artist John Pistilli, was used on the call for entries for a National Typeface Design Competition in 1965. This competition was sponsored by the Visual Graphics Corporation, a fledgling manufacturer of an economical display phototypesetter widely adopted by design studios for internal typesetting. Lubalin's posters demonstrating the design potential of the dozen winning designs spurred the awareness of phototypography and its design potential. When his detractors wondered whether his typography suffered a decline in legibility because of the tightness of spaces and overlap of forms, Lubalin responded that "sometimes you have to compromise legibility to achieve impact."

Lubalin also turned toward editorial design during the 1960s and made a major contribution to this area. A host of editorial redesigns, including two for the ill-fated *Saturday Evening Post,* accompanied his collaboration with erstwhile publisher Ralph Ginzburg on a series of magazines. Launched in 1962 with a massive, direct-mail compaign, a hardbound quarterly journal called *Eros* was billed as the magazine of love. Its ninety-six-page, advertising-free format allowed Lubalin to explore scale, white space, and visual flow. In a photographic essay about President John Kennedy, scale changes, ranging from a double-page bleed photograph to pages jammed with eight or nine photographs, established a lively pace. Believing that typeface selection should express the content and be governed by the visual configuration of the words, Lubalin used a variety of display types in *Eros* including giant condensed sans serif, novelty faces, and delicate Old Style romans. Although the visual and written content of *Eros* was tame in comparison to the explicit material permitted a decade later, Ginzburg was tried and convicted of sending obscene material through the mails.

Herb Lubalin, poster announcing the Davida Bold typeface, 1965. Printed in black, magenta, red, and orange, the four stanzas of the Peter Piper "tongue-twister" share a common capital *P*.

In 1967 Ginzburg established *Fact* magazine featuring explosive editorial exposés of hallowed institutions and sacred cows: Lubalin's brilliant, graphic treatment on a frugal production budget harbingered the restrained economics of inflationary 1970s pub-

WE ALL LOVE JACK

by Faye Emerson

First there were the "jumpers." It began with the primaries, when John F. Kennedy was fighting desperately for the nomination a lot of Americans thought he was too young, too Catholic, and too rich to deserve. His political advisers and the press, alert to any straw in the wind, began to notice an odd reaction in the crowds. An increasing number of young women seemed to be traveling by pogo sticks and when Mr. Kennedy approached, they bounced in the air like lady jumping jacks. They shrieked ecstatically, threw kisses and waved madly at their hero.

Then there were the "touchers." These were for the most part respectable, mature women who, with incredible determination and stamina, fought their way close to Mr. Kennedy, patted him gently and retired dazed and happy. They didn't even ask for his autograph.

As the phenomenon of female reaction to the candidate became more pronounced, there was a good deal of discussion as to just what it all meant. The political wise men shook their heads gravely and the press viewed with suspicion, if not outright alarm. No one had seen anything quite like it before in politics. This was not the fond father figure of Eisenhower. It wasn't even like the "friend-protector" magic of F. D. R. No, this was much more personal. And there was something for all the girls. His boyish appeal made mothers and grandmothers want to look after him, see that he got a haircut and a good meal. Wives all over the country daydreamed themselves into Jackie's shoes. Teen-agers forgot about Fabian, and the very young set thought Caroline was the luckiest little girl in the world. Glamorous movie stars stumbled over their sables to stand near him, even when there wasn't a camera in sight. An astonishing number of ladies in café society suddenly recalled intimate little friendships with "Jack," and a few hinted discreetly at even more tender relationships—pre-Jackie, of course.

The press and the politicians were puzzled. What did it mean to the candidate? "It's nice to be loved," they said, "but is it dignified?" What would it do to the so-called "image" that had been so carefully presented? Were the women voters listening with cool intelligence to Mr. Kennedy speak of taxes, tariffs and treaties? Were they moved by the call of the New Frontier, or was it just "that old feeling"? And most important of all, would this surge of emotion sweep the ladies into the voting booths? Would love pull the right lever?

Well, the answers to all these questions are now purely academic. How much influence the lovelorn ladies had on the election will be found in the history books eventually, but in the meantime, the romance is still on. The females of this country have a crush on J.F.K. They dig him. His shining armor may be a little battered, but it doesn't hide his sex appeal.

5

Herb Lubalin, page from *Eros,* 1962. This opening spread from a pictorial essay demonstrates several aspects of Lubalin's design approach: the intensity of the page, overlapping letterforms, the compression of space between the words, and the squeezing of words and images into a rectangle.

Herb Lubalin, title page for an *Eros* pictorial essay, 1962. The typographic configuration is typical of Lubalin's daring use of printing techniques. The body copy is in process blue, the ornaments are magenta, *The* is green made by overprinting process yellow and blue, and *Cigar Box* is a bright red achieved by overprinting process magenta and yellow.

lishing. Lacking an adequate budget to hire ten different illustrators or photographers to visualize each article, Lubalin commissioned a guest illustrator to do all the work in each issue. He placed these full-page images opposite each article's title page, which was designed in a Times Roman format so constant that the type could be specified and ordered from the typographer with foolproof accuracy.

Ginzburg and Lubalin closed out the decade with the square format

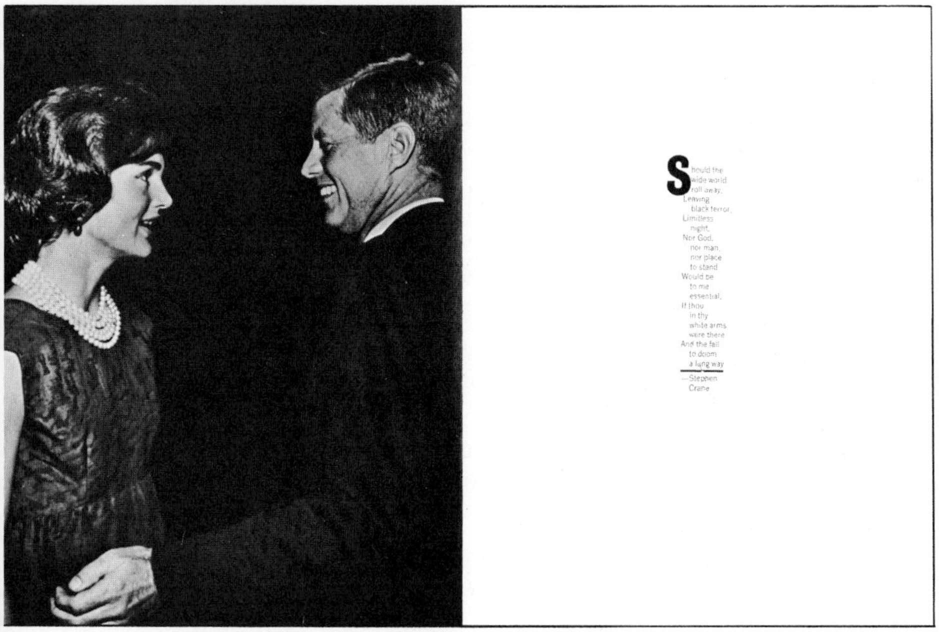

Should the
wide world
roll away,
Leaving
black terror,
Limitless
night,
Nor God,
nor man,
nor place
to stand
Would be
to me
essential,
If thou
in thy
white arms
were there
And the fall
to doom
a long way
—Stephen
Crane

Herb Lubalin, pages from *Eros,* 1962. The pictorial essay closed with a photograph of the young president and his wife opposite a quotation from Stephen Crane which became a chilling forewarning. President Kennedy was assassinated the following year.

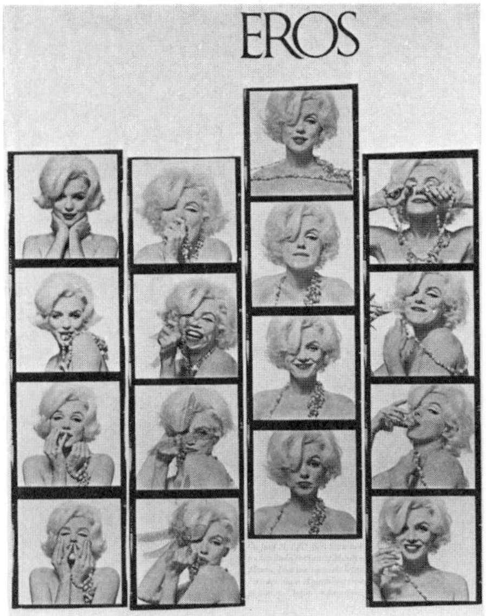

Herb Lubalin (designer) and Bert Stern (photographer), cover for *Eros,* 1962. The grid of images formed by strips of photographic transparencies is violated by one which shifts upward to align with the logo and headline.

Herb Lubalin (designer) and Bert Stern (photographer), pages from *Eros,* 1962. An expansive vitality is created by enlarging a transparency that had been crossed out with a marker by Marilyn Monroe. A totem of images from the same shooting session balance it on the opposite page.

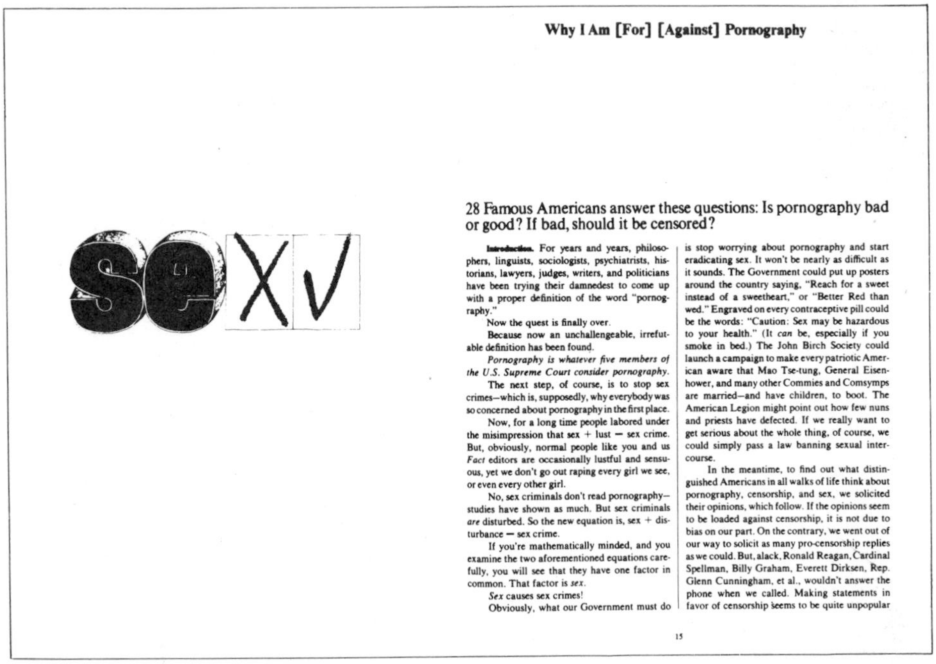

Why I Am [For] [Against] Pornography

28 Famous Americans answer these questions: Is pornography bad or good? If bad, should it be censored?

Introduction. For years and years, philosophers, linguists, sociologists, psychiatrists, historians, lawyers, judges, writers, and politicians have been trying their damnedest to come up with a proper definition of the word "pornography."

Now the quest is finally over.

Because now an unchallengeable, irrefutable definition has been found.

Pornography is whatever five members of the U.S. Supreme Court consider pornography.

The next step, of course, is to stop sex crimes—which is, supposedly, why everybody was so concerned about pornography in the first place.

Now, for a long time people labored under the misimpression that sex + lust — sex crime. But, obviously, normal people like you and us *Fact* editors are occasionally lustful and sensuous, yet we don't go out raping every girl we see, or even every other girl.

No, sex criminals don't read pornography—studies have shown as much. But sex criminals *are* disturbed. So the new equation is, sex + disturbance — sex crime.

If you're mathematically minded, and you examine the two aforementioned equations carefully, you will see that they have one factor in common. That factor is *sex*.

Sex causes sex crimes!

Obviously, what our Government must do is stop worrying about pornography and start eradicating sex. It won't be nearly as difficult as it sounds. The Government could put up posters around the country saying, "Reach for a sweet instead of a sweetheart," or "Better Red than wed." Engraved on every contraceptive pill could be the words: "Caution: Sex may be hazardous to your health." (It *can* be, especially if you smoke in bed.) The John Birch Society could launch a campaign to make every patriotic American aware that Mao Tse-tung, General Eisenhower, and many other Commies and Comsymps are married—and have children, to boot. The American Legion might point out how few nuns and priests have defected. If we really want to get serious about the whole thing, of course, we could simply pass a law banning sexual intercourse.

In the meantime, to find out what distinguished Americans in all walks of life think about pornography, censorship, and sex, we solicited their opinions, which follow. If the opinions seem to be loaded against censorship, it is not due to bias on our part. On the contrary, we went out of our way to solicit as many pro-censorship replies as we could. But, alack, Ronald Reagan, Cardinal Spellman, Billy Graham, Everett Dirksen, Rep. Glenn Cunningham, et al., wouldn't answer the phone when we called. Making statements in favor of censorship seems to be quite unpopular

15

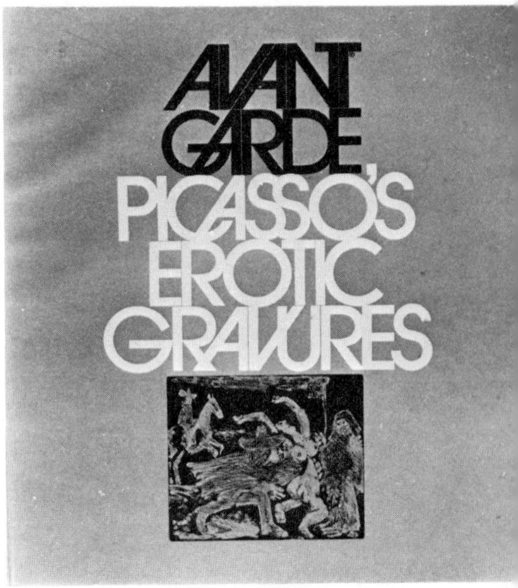

Herb Lubalin (designer) and Pablo Picasso (lithographer), title page for *Avant Garde,* 1960. The *Avant Garde* logo became a typeface filled with extraordinary ligatures as shown in this heading for a special issue devoted to Pablo Picasso's erotic lithographs.

Avant Garde, a lavishly visual periodical that published visual essays, fiction, and reportage. Born amidst the social upheavals of civil rights, women's liberation, sexual freedom, and antiwar protest, this magazine became one of Lubalin's most innovative achievements. Lubalin's layouts have a strong underlying geometric structure.

Herb Lubalin, pages from *Fact* magazine, 1967. Design economy was achieved by the standardized format using Times Roman Bold title and Times New Roman subtitle. The guest illustrator who created line drawings for every article in this issue was Etienne Delessert. The ''illustration'' for this article is an example of Lubalin's conceptual and figurative solutions.

Herb Lubalin, advertisement for an antiwar poster competition, 1967. Unity and impact, rarely achieved in purely typographic design, results from complex information being compressed into a rectangle surrounding the bright blue headline with the typographic power of brass knuckles.

However, this is not the classical geometry of the Basel and Zurich designers; it is the exuberant and optimistic order of the expansive American character unencumbered by a sense of tradition or any thought that there are limitations that cannot be overcome. The logotype for *Avant Garde,* composed of tightly integrated capital ligatures, was developed into a family of typefaces bearing the same name.

By 1970 typeface design began to occupy more of Lubalin's time. As a graphic designer, Lubalin stated his task as projecting a message from a surface using three interdependent means of expression: photography, illustration, and letterforms. As time passed, Lubalin's love for letterforms and the satisfaction he drew from working with them grew. Although photography and, more recently, illustration have been recognized as art forms, this status still eludes the typographic designer. Perhaps the all pervasive presence of alphabet communication in industrialized cultures makes people immune to their potent aesthetic qualities, and the imposition of technical process between the mind and eye of the artist and the final work defies the traditional notion of art as precious artifact.

As the design of new typefaces increased, design piracy became a vital issue. Original typeface designs requiring hundreds of hours of work could now be photocopied by unscrupulous operators who produced instant film fonts but did not pay designers a royalty or commission. To enable designers to be adequately compensated for their designs while licensing and making master fonts available to all manufacturers, Lubalin joined with phototypography pioneer Edward Rondthaler and typographer Aaron Burns in establishing the International Typeface Corporation in 1970. Thirty-

Herb Lubalin, proposed logo for use by New York City, 1966. The isometric perspective implied by the forty-five-degree angles creates a dynamic tension between two and three dimensionality; the relationships between the black shapes surrounding the white letterforms create an ambiguous interplay between figure and ground. *Courtesy of Herb Lubalin.*

Herb Lubalin, logo for *Family Circle* magazine, 1967. Through a visual linking and overlapping process, Lubalin created a strong unified logo from two words.

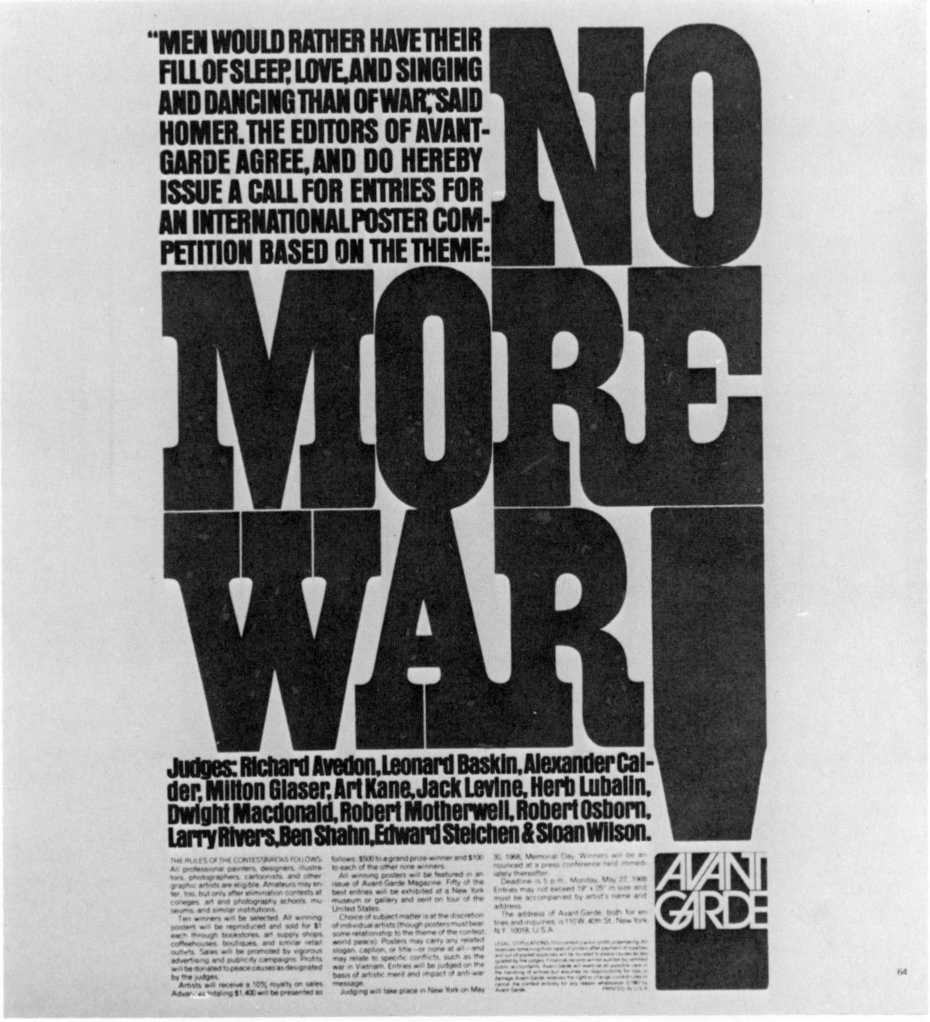

Herb Lubalin, Ice Capades logo, 1967. Both an ice skate and the qualities of nineteenth-century engraving are evoked by this figurative and illustrative logo.

Herb Lubalin, type specimen pages from *U&lc,* 1978. These two specimens demonstrate the structural diversity of Lubalin's approach to layout. An informal layout gains cohesiveness by the large words pinwheeling around an implied central axis; interest is added to the specimens tightly packed into a square by the huge quotation marks hanging in the generous margins above and below.

four fully developed type families and about sixty additional display faces were developed and licensed during ITC's first decade. Tightness of fit, a design tendency that began with phototypography, was an important concern. As with the Helvetica fonts, emphasis was placed on a large *x*-height. Short ascenders and descenders allowed tighter linespacing. With Lubalin as design director, ITC began a journal, *U & lc,* to publicize and demonstrate its designs. Lubalin said that after over three decades of designing for clients, he was now his own client. The complex, dynamic style that he gave this tabloid-size newsprint publication as well as the popularity of ITC typefaces had a major impact on typographic design of the 1970s.

From the time that Lubalin left his position as vice president and creative director of the Sudler and Hennessey advertising agency in 1964, he formed partnerships and associations with a number of associates including graphic designers Ernie Smith and Alan Peckolick (b. 1940) and lettering artists Tony DiSpigna (b. 1943) and Tom Carnase. These artists have demonstrated stylistic affinities with Lubalin while achieving unique creative solutions to a diverse range of problems.

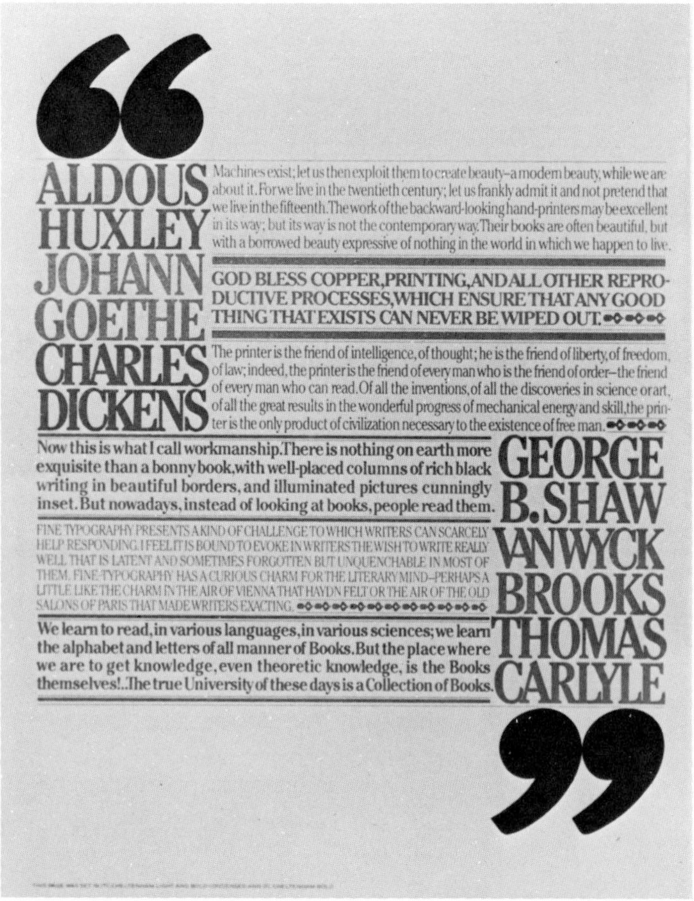

ALDOUS HUXLEY

Machines exist; let us then exploit them to create beauty–a modern beauty, while we are about it. For we live in the twentieth century; let us frankly admit it and not pretend that we live in the fifteenth. The work of the backward-looking hand-printers may be excellent in its way; but its way is not the contemporary way. Their books are often beautiful, but with a borrowed beauty expressive of nothing in the world in which we happen to live.

JOHANN GOETHE

GOD BLESS COPPER, PRINTING, AND ALL OTHER REPRODUCTIVE PROCESSES, WHICH ENSURE THAT ANY GOOD THING THAT EXISTS CAN NEVER BE WIPED OUT.

CHARLES DICKENS

The printer is the friend of intelligence, of thought; he is the friend of liberty, of freedom, of law; indeed, the printer is the friend of every man who is the friend of order–the friend of every man who can read. Of all the inventions, of all the discoveries in science or art, of all the great results in the wonderful progress of mechanical energy and skill, the printer is the only product of civilization necessary to the existence of free man.

GEORGE B. SHAW

Now this is what I call workmanship. There is nothing on earth more exquisite than a bonny book, with well-placed columns of rich black writing in beautiful borders, and illuminated pictures cunningly inset. But nowadays, instead of looking at books, people read them.

VAN WYCK BROOKS

FINE TYPOGRAPHY PRESENTS A KIND OF CHALLENGE TO WHICH WRITERS CAN SCARCELY HELP RESPONDING. I FEEL IT IS BOUND TO EVOKE IN WRITERS THE WISH TO WRITE REALLY WELL THAT IS LATENT AND SOMETIMES FORGOTTEN BUT UNQUENCHABLE IN MOST OF THEM. FINE TYPOGRAPHY HAS A CURIOUS CHARM FOR THE LITERARY MIND–PERHAPS A LITTLE LIKE THE CHARM IN THE AIR OF VIENNA THAT HAYDN FELT OR THE AIR OF THE OLD SALONS OF PARIS THAT MADE WRITERS EXACTING.

THOMAS CARLYLE

We learn to read, in various languages, in various sciences; we learn the alphabet and letters of all manner of Books. But the place where we are to get knowledge, even theoretic knowledge, is the Books themselves!..The true University of these days is a Collection of Books.

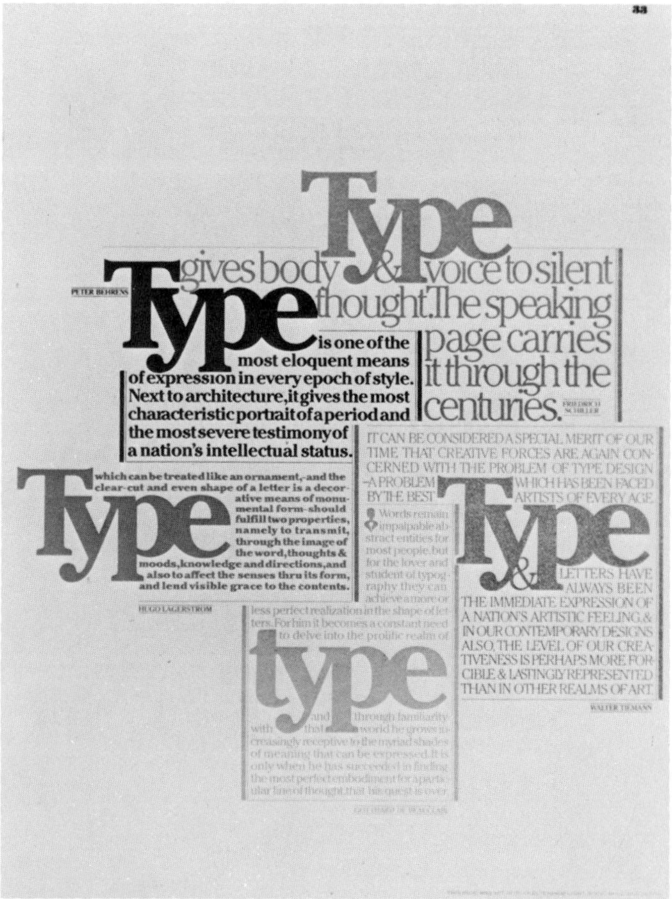

PETER BEHRENS

Type is one of the most eloquent means of expression in every epoch of style. Next to architecture, it gives the most characteristic portrait of a period and the most severe testimony of a nation's intellectual status.

Type gives body & voice to silent thought. The speaking page carries it through the centuries.

FRIEDRICH SCHILLER

Type which can be treated like an ornament,-and the clear-cut and even shape of a letter is a decorative means of monumental form-should fulfill two properties, namely to transmit, through the image of the word, thoughts & moods, knowledge and directions, and also to affect the senses thru its form, and lend visible grace to the contents.

HUGO LAGERSTROM

IT CAN BE CONSIDERED A SPECIAL MERIT OF OUR TIME THAT CREATIVE FORCES ARE AGAIN CONCERNED WITH THE PROBLEM OF TYPE DESIGN –A PROBLEM WHICH HAS BEEN FACED BY THE BEST ARTISTS OF EVERY AGE. Type & LETTERS HAVE ALWAYS BEEN THE IMMEDIATE EXPRESSION OF A NATION'S ARTISTIC FEELING & IN OUR CONTEMPORARY DESIGNS ALSO, THE LEVEL OF OUR CREATIVENESS IS PERHAPS MORE FORCIBLE & LASTINGLY REPRESENTED THAN IN OTHER REALMS OF ART.

WALTER TIEMANN

Words remain impalpable abstract entities for most people, but for the lover and student of typography they can achieve a more or less perfect realization in the shape of letters. For him it becomes a constant need to delve into the prolific realm of type and with that through familiarity world he grows increasingly receptive to the myriad shades of meaning that can be expressed. It is only when he has succeeded in finding the most perfect embodiment for a particular line of thought that his quest is over.

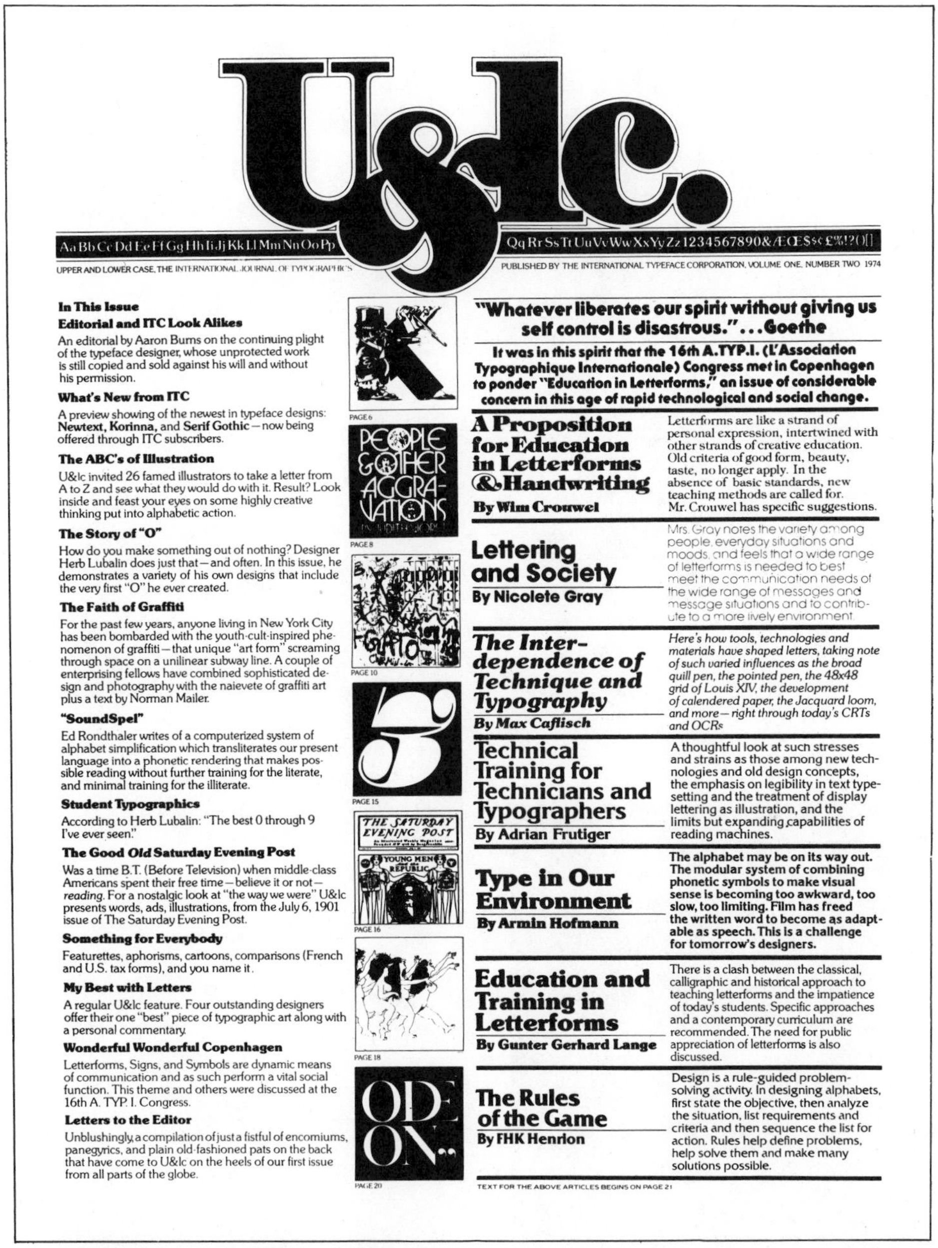

U&lc.

Aa Bb Cc Dd Ee Ff Gg Hh Ii Jj Kk Ll Mm Nn Oo Pp Qq Rr Ss Tt Uu Vv Ww Xx Yy Zz 1234567890&ÆŒ$¢£%!?()[]

UPPER AND LOWER CASE, THE INTERNATIONAL JOURNAL OF TYPOGRAPHICS

PUBLISHED BY THE INTERNATIONAL TYPEFACE CORPORATION, VOLUME ONE, NUMBER TWO 1974

In This Issue

Editorial and ITC Look Alikes
An editorial by Aaron Burns on the continuing plight of the typeface designer, whose unprotected work is still copied and sold against his will and without his permission.

What's New from ITC
A preview showing of the newest in typeface designs: **Newtext, Korinna,** and **Serif Gothic**—now being offered through ITC subscribers.

The ABC's of Illustration
U&lc invited 26 famed illustrators to take a letter from A to Z and see what they would do with it. Result? Look inside and feast your eyes on some highly creative thinking put into alphabetic action.

The Story of "O"
How do you make something out of nothing? Designer Herb Lubalin does just that—and often. In this issue, he demonstrates a variety of his own designs that include the very first "O" he ever created.

The Faith of Graffiti
For the past few years, anyone living in New York City has been bombarded with the youth-cult-inspired phenomenon of graffiti—that unique "art form" screaming through space on a unilinear subway line. A couple of enterprising fellows have combined sophisticated design and photography with the naievete of graffiti art plus a text by Norman Mailer.

"SoundSpel"
Ed Rondthaler writes of a computerized system of alphabet simplification which transliterates our present language into a phonetic rendering that makes possible reading without further training for the literate, and minimal training for the illiterate.

Student Typographics
According to Herb Lubalin: "The best 0 through 9 I've ever seen."

The Good *Old* Saturday Evening Post
Was a time B.T. (Before Television) when middle-class Americans spent their free time—believe it or not—*reading*. For a nostalgic look at "the way we were" U&lc presents words, ads, illustrations, from the July 6, 1901 issue of The Saturday Evening Post.

Something for Everybody
Featurettes, aphorisms, cartoons, comparisons (French and U.S. tax forms), and you name it.

My Best with Letters
A regular U&lc feature. Four outstanding designers offer their one "best" piece of typographic art along with a personal commentary.

Wonderful Wonderful Copenhagen
Letterforms, Signs, and Symbols are dynamic means of communication and as such perform a vital social function. This theme and others were discussed at the 16th A. TYP. I. Congress.

Letters to the Editor
Unblushingly, a compilation of just a fistful of encomiums, panegyrics, and plain old-fashioned pats on the back that have come to U&lc on the heels of our first issue from all parts of the globe.

PAGE 6 · PEOPLE GOTHER AGGRAVATIONS · PAGE 8 · PAGE 10 · PAGE 15 · THE SATURDAY EVENING POST · YOUNG MEN REPUBLIC · PAGE 16 · PAGE 18 · ODE ON.. · PAGE 20

"Whatever liberates our spirit without giving us self control is disastrous."...Goethe

It was in this spirit that the 16th A.TYP.I. (L'Association Typographique Internationale) Congress met in Copenhagen to ponder "Education in Letterforms," an issue of considerable concern in this age of rapid technological and social change.

A Proposition for Education in Letterforms (&)Handwriting
By Wim Crouwel
Letterforms are like a strand of personal expression, intertwined with other strands of creative education. Old criteria of good form, beauty, taste, no longer apply. In the absence of basic standards, new teaching methods are called for. Mr. Crouwel has specific suggestions.

Lettering and Society
By Nicolete Gray
Mrs. Gray notes the variety among people, everyday situations and moods, and feels that a wide range of letterforms is needed to best meet the communication needs of the wide range of messages and message situations and to contribute to a more lively environment.

The Interdependence of Technique and Typography
By Max Caflisch
Here's how tools, technologies and materials have shaped letters, taking note of such varied influences as the broad quill pen, the pointed pen, the 48x48 grid of Louis XIV, the development of calendered paper, the Jacquard loom, and more—right through today's CRTs and OCRs.

Technical Training for Technicians and Typographers
By Adrian Frutiger
A thoughtful look at such stresses and strains as those among new technologies and old design concepts, the emphasis on legibility in text typesetting and the treatment of display lettering as illustration, and the limits but expanding capabilities of reading machines.

Type in Our Environment
By Armin Hofmann
The alphabet may be on its way out. The modular system of combining phonetic symbols to make visual sense is becoming too awkward, too slow, too limiting. Film has freed the written word to become as adaptable as speech. This is a challenge for tomorrow's designers.

Education and Training in Letterforms
By Gunter Gerhard Lange
There is a clash between the classical, calligraphic and historical approach to teaching letterforms and the impatience of today's students. Specific approaches and a contemporary curriculum are recommended. The need for public appreciation of letterforms is also discussed.

The Rules of the Game
By FHK Henrion
Design is a rule-guided problem-solving activity. In designing alphabets, first state the objective, then analyze the situation, list requirements and criteria and then sequence the list for action. Rules help define problems, help solve them and make many solutions possible.

TEXT FOR THE ABOVE ARTICLES BEGINS ON PAGE 21

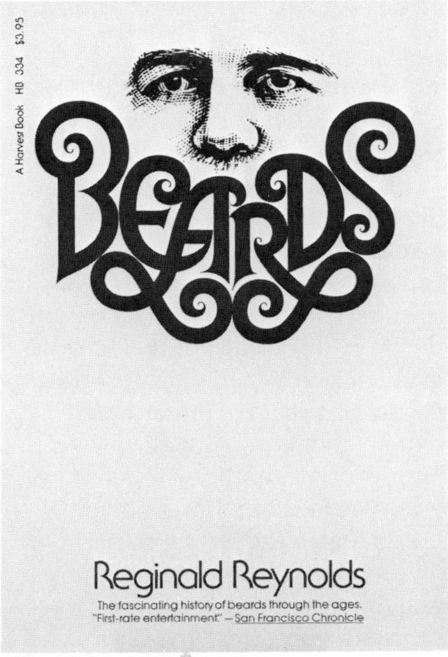

A Harvest Book HB 334 $3.95
BEARDS
Reginald Reynolds
The fascinating history of beards through the ages.
"First-rate entertainment." —San Francisco Chronicle

Alan Peckolick, book jacket for *Beards,* 1975. The figurative typography and the Futurist concept of simultaneity are unified in this book jacket. The title *Beards* becomes a beard.

Herb Lubalin, cover for *U&lc,* 1974. This cover format demonstrates Lubalin's ability to organize complex information. Fifty-nine typographic units, seven illustrations, and sixteen rules for a total of eighty-two separate elements are integrated into an information-filled page.

PBS

PUBLIC BROADCASTING SERVICE

Ernie Smith, logo for the Public Broadcasting Service, 1971. One altered edge and a slightly displaced dot is all that was required to bring a human and symbolic quality to these distinctive initials.

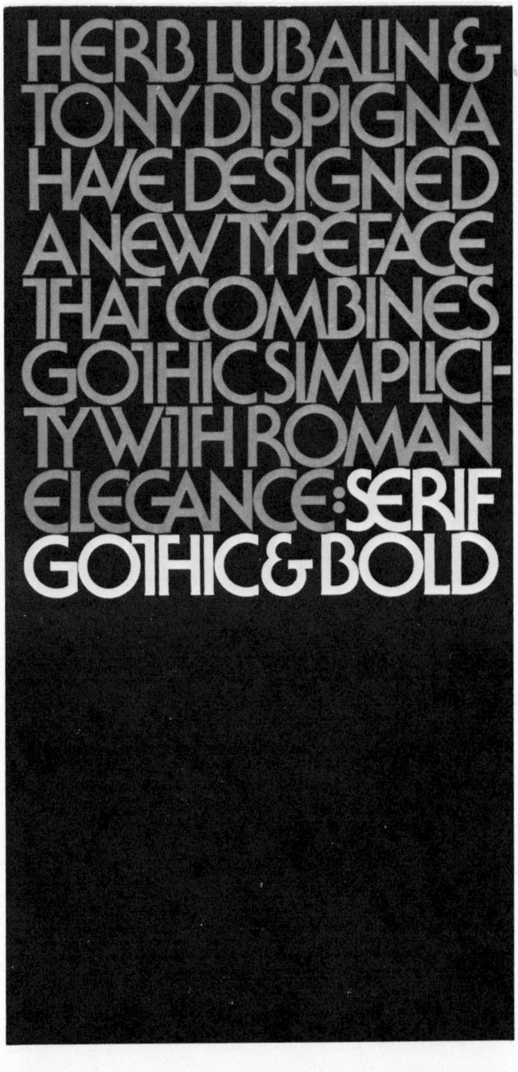

HERB LUBALIN & TONY DI SPIGNA HAVE DESIGNED A NEW TYPEFACE THAT COMBINES GOTHIC SIMPLICITY WITH ROMAN ELEGANCE: SERIF GOTHIC & BOLD

Herb Lubalin and Tony DiSpigna, Serif Gothic and Bold typestyle, 1972. A hint of serifs brings distinction to this somewhat rotund, geometrically constructed style. A range of alternate characters and capital ligatures supports the spatial maneuvering and compression in which Lubalin takes great delight, as demonstrated in this specimen folder.

George Lois

Among the young art directors and copywriters who passed through Doyle Dane Bernbach during the late 1950s, George Lois (b. 1932) became the enfant terrible of American mass communications. Lois' energetic efforts to sell his work, resulting in such legendary tactics as climbing out on the three-story ledge of the A. Goodman & Company president's office demanding that his poster be accepted, combined with a tendency to push concepts to the very limit of propriety, earned him this reputation. Lois adopted the Bernbach philosophy that fully integrated visual/verbal concepts were vital to successful message conveyance. Lois wrote that an art director must treat words "with the same reverence that he accords graphics, because the verbal and visual elements of modern communication are as indivisible as words and music in a song." His designs are deceptively simple and singlemindedly direct. Backgrounds are usually stripped away to enable the content-bearing verbal and pictorial images to interact unhampered. This he learned at Bernbach, which was Lois' third agency. At age twenty-eight, he left Bernbach to cofound Papert, Koenig and Lois, which grew to forty million dollars a year in billing in seven short years. On three subsequent occasions, Lois left an agency partnership to form yet another advertising agency.

In 1962, *Esquire* was in serious trouble. If any two consecutive issues lost money on newsstand sales, *Esquire* would have to fold. It had been *the* man's magazine in America, but the younger audience was now reading *Playboy,* which had been started by former *Esquire* staff member Hugh Hefner in 1960. *Esquire* editor Harold Hayes asked Lois to develop effective cover designs for the literate but nearly bankrupt magazine. Lois felt that design—a harmony of elements—had no place on a magazine cover. He opted for the cover as a *statement* that captured the reader with a spirited comment on one of the major articles inside. Over the next decade

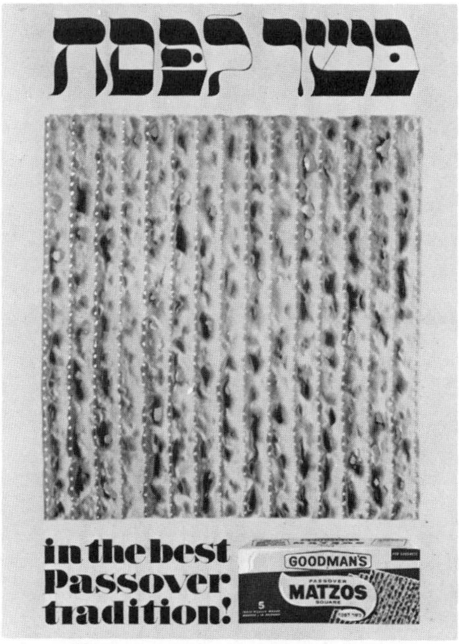

George Lois, subway poster for Goodman's Matzos, 1960. The scale change of the enlarged cracker created an arresting and unexpected image.

George Lois, advertisement for Coldene, 1961. In contrast to the coarse hard-sell advertising of most over-the-counter pharmaceutical products, a simple black page with twelve words becomes a midnight exchange between concerned parents.

Lois designed over ninety-two covers, mostly in collaboration with photographer Carl Fischer (b. 1924). These covers helped capture the audience, and by 1967 *Esquire* turned a three-million-dollar profit.

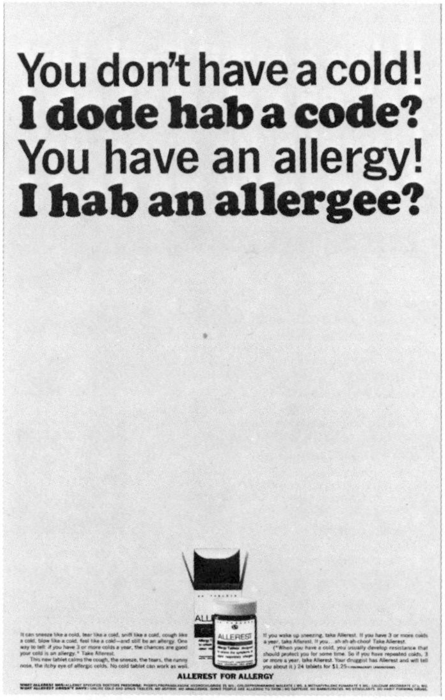

George Lois, advertisement for Allerest, 1961. Figurative typography and eccentric spelling combine to make type talk in the voice of an allergy sufferer.

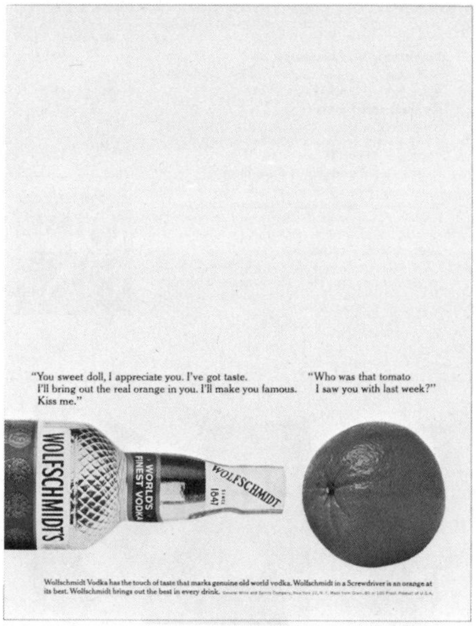

George Lois, advertisement for Wolfschmidt's, 1962. Blatant symbolism and outrageous humor combine in an inventive technique. Continuity developed, for the preceding week's advertisement had the loquacious bottle talking to a tomato.

Lois felt that Fischer was one of the few photographers who understood ideas. Their collaborative efforts created covers that challenged,

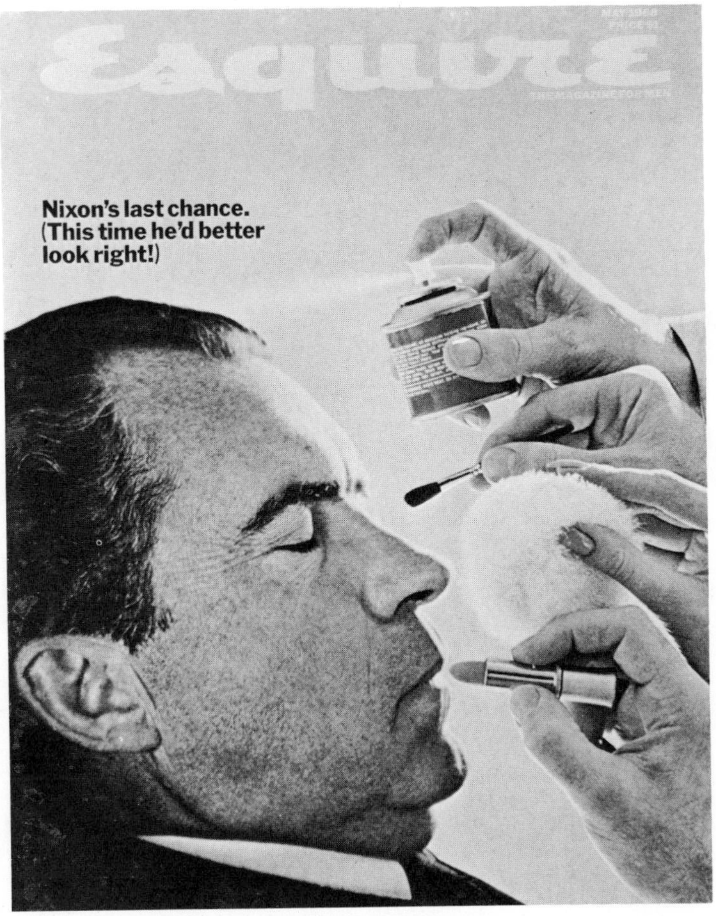

George Lois (designer) and Carl Fischer (photographer), *Esquire* cover, May 1968. This composite photograph of presidential candidate, Richard M. Nixon, being made up for a television appearance is typical of Lois' audacity.

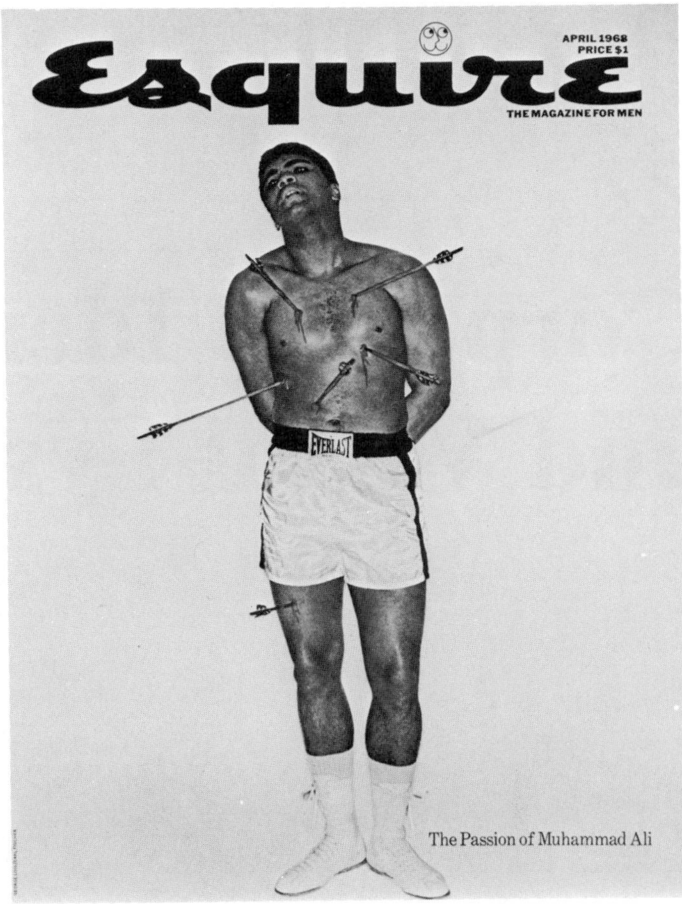

George Lois (designer) and Carl Fischer (photographer), *Esquire* cover, May 1968. Paraphrasing paintings depicting Saint Sebastian as a beautiful young man whose body is pierced with arrows enabled Lois to imply that Muhammad Ali is a modern-day martyr.

shocked, and often provoked the audience. Unexpected combinations of images and photographic montage techniques served to intensify an event or make a satirical statement. The 24 November 1963 murder of Presidential assassin Lee Harvey Oswald, witnessed by millions on television, was visualized by showing a young boy watching this event on television while eating a hamburger with a cola. The terror of the Vietnam War was presented by a solid black cover with large white Bodoni letters proclaiming "Oh my God—we hit a little girl." Lois pulled this quote from an article telling the "true story of M Company from Fort Dix to Vietnam." Lois' skills in persuading people to participate in photographs resulted in powerful images. Lieutenant Calley, placed on trial for his alleged role in the killing of over one hundred children, women, and old men in the Vietnam village of My Lai, was photographed posing with a group of oriental children. In 1968 Lois persuaded Muhammad Ali, who had been stripped of his World Heavyweight Championship title because as a conscientious objector he refused military service, to pose for an *Esquire* cover as Saint Sebastian, the legendary Christian martyr condemned by Roman Emperor Diocletian and shot by archers. As Richard Nixon mounted his second presidential campaign in 1968, Lois combined a stock photograph of the candidate with Fischer's photograph of four hands applying makeup. This concept grew out of Lois' recollection of the 1960 presidential campaign when Nixon lost the race to John F. Kennedy partly because Nixon's "five o'clock shadow made him look evil." Lois received a call from one of Nixon's staff, who called Lois an (expletive deleted) because the lipstick was "an attack on Nixon's masculinity."

An ability to stay closely in touch with one's times is a vital requirement for someone in visual communications, and many of Lois' most innovative concepts have grown from his ability to understand and respond to the people and events of his era.

22

Corporate Identity and Visual Systems

THE TECHNOLOGICAL ADVANCES during World War II were staggering. As productive capacity turned toward consumer goods, many people believed that the outlook for the capitalist economic structure could be unending economic expansion and prosperity. "Good design is good business" became a rallying cry among the graphic design community during the 1950s. Prosperity and technological development seem closely linked to the increasingly important corporations, and these large industrial and commercial organizations were becoming aware of the need to develop a corporate image and identity among various sectors of the public. Design was seen as a major way to shape a reputation for quality and reliability.

The use of visual marks for identification has, of course, been in existence for centuries. In medieval times, proprietary marks were compulsory as a means of enabling the guilds to control trade. By the 1700s virtually every trader and dealer had a trademark or stamp. The arrival of the industrial revolution with mass manufacturing and marketing caused visual identification and trademarks to gain in value and importance. But the visual identification systems that began during the 1950s went far beyond the trademark or symbol. By unifying all communications from a given organization into a consistent design system, the corporation could establish a cohesive image to aid in realizing identifiable goals. The national and multinational scope of many corporations made a cohesive image difficult to maintain, and a systematic approach became almost essential.

Pintori at Olivetti

The pioneering efforts toward corporate visual identity were accomplished by strong individual designers who put their personal imprint upon the designed image of their client. This was the case with Peter Behrens at AEG, and a similar process began at the Olivetti Corporation in 1936 after Adriano Olivetti, son of the founder of this Italian typewriter company, hired twenty-four-year-old Giovanni Pintori (b. 1912) to join the publicity department. For a thirty-one-year period, Pintori put his personal stamp upon the graphic images of Olivetti. The logotype that Pintori designed for the firm in 1947 consisted of the name in lowercase sans-serif letters slightly letterspaced. Identity was achieved, not through the use of this logo in a design program, but through the general visual appearance of promotional graphics.

There is a casual and almost relaxed quality to the organization of space in Pintori's designs. And yet, extremely complex designs have a feeling of simplicity because of his ability to organize small elements into unified structures through a repetition of size and visual rhythms. This complexity of form was well suited to Olivetti's publicity needs during the 1940s and 1950s, for the firm sought a high-technology image to promote advanced industrial design and engineering features in their typewriters and business machines. Pintori was particularly adept at using simplified graphic shapes to visualize the mechanisms and processes of Olivetti products. Often, he would construct abstract configurations that suggested the function or purpose of the product being advertised. Olivetti's corporate graphic design under Pintori was not an isolated phenomenon, for this firm has received international recognition for its commitment to design excellence in product design, architecture, and publicity. From its inception in 1908 when it was founded by Camillo Olivetti, it has had a dual commitment to humanist ideals and technological progress. As a matter of corporate policy, design has been seen as a vital component in addressing both goals.

Giovanni Pintori, poster for the Olivetti Elettrosumma 22, 1956. This informal structure of brightly colored cubes with numerals suggests the adding and mathematical building process that takes place when one uses this calculating machine.

Giovanni Pintori, poster for the Olivetti 82 Diaspron, c. 1958. A schematic diagram demonstrating the mechanical action of the typewriter key combines with a photograph of the machine to communicate two levels of information about the product.

Design at CBS

The Columbia Broadcasting System of New York City moved to the forefront in corporate identity design as a result of two vital assets: CBS President Frank Stanton, who understood art and design and its potential in corporate affairs; and William Golden (1911–1959), an art director at CBS for almost two decades, and a brilliant graphic designer with uncompromising visual standards and keen insight into the communications process. The effectiveness of the CBS corporate identity does not depend on a regimented design program or application of a specific style to all of the corporation's communications. Rather, it was the quality and intelligence of each design solution that has enabled CBS to establish an ongoing and successful corporate identity.

By the late 1940s, a corporate philosophy and approach to advertising was emerging. Advertisements designed by Golden for CBS Television and for CBS Radio by Lou Dorfsman (b. 1918), a young art director who joined CBS in 1946, combined simplicity of idea with a straightforward and provocative visual presentation. Typography and image were arranged in well-ordered relationships using white space as a design element.

In a lecture at a design conference, Golden called upon designers to have a sense of responsibility and a rational understanding of the function of their work. He declared the word "design" to be a verb "in the sense that we design something to be communicated to someone," and the designer's primary function is ensuring that the message is accurately and adequately communicated.

Painters including Feliks Topolski, René Bouche, and Ben Shahn were commissioned by Golden to create illustrations for CBS advertisements. Golden's integrity and willingness to allow these artists freedom encouraged them to accept these commissions and resulted in a high artistic level relative to newspaper and trade publication advertisements of the period. A classic example of this approach is the 1957 "The Big Push" advertisement. It appeared in business and advertising trade publications during a booming economy. The text reveals that Americans will purchase more than during any other summer in history and recommends television advertising during this big summer sales push. The provocative headline, amplified by Ben Shahn's Klee-like drawing of shopping carts, lends dignity and taste to a commercial message.

Golden designed one of the most successful trademarks of the twentieth century for CBS. When the pictographic CBS eye first appeared as an on-air logo on 16 November 1951, it was superimposed over a cloud-filled sky and projected an almost surreal sense of an eye in the sky. After one year, Golden suggested to Frank Stanton that they might abandon the eye and seek another logo. Stanton reminded Golden of the old adage that "just when you're beginning to get bored with what you have done is probably the time it is beginning to be noticed by your audience." The eye remained. In applying this trademark to the corporation's multitude of printed material, from shipping labels to press releases, care and concern

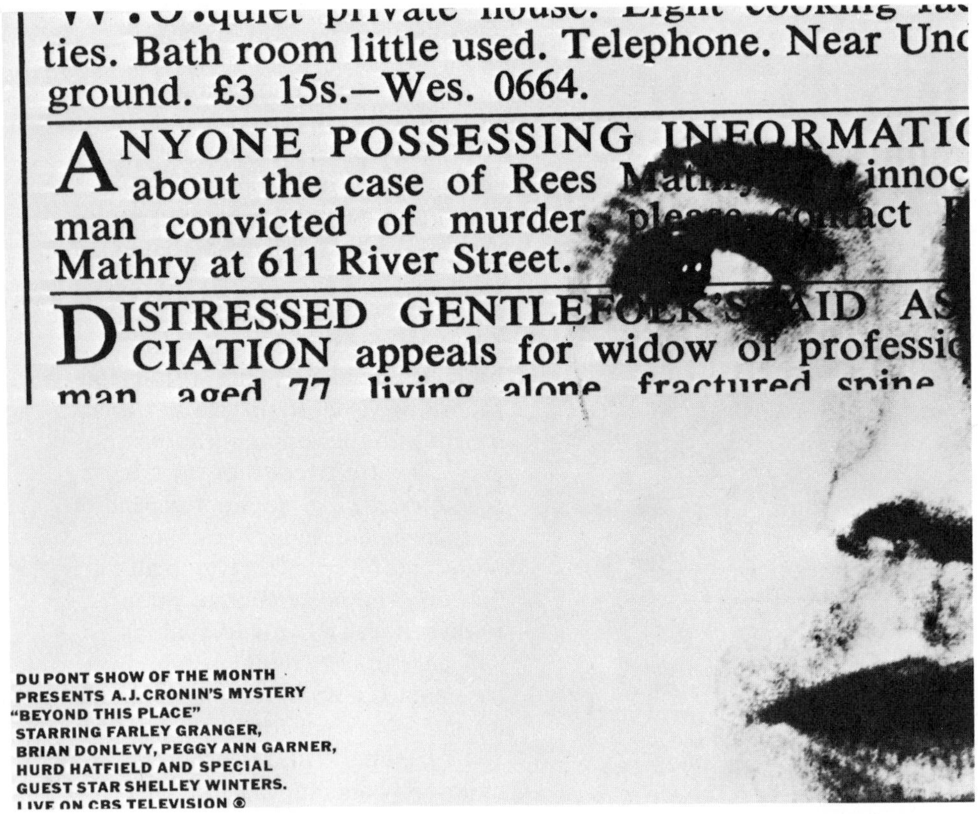

William Golden, program kit cover for DuPont Show of the Month, 1957. Classified advertising typography overlapping the actor's face, with his eyes cut to the left, conveys the essence of this mystery drama.

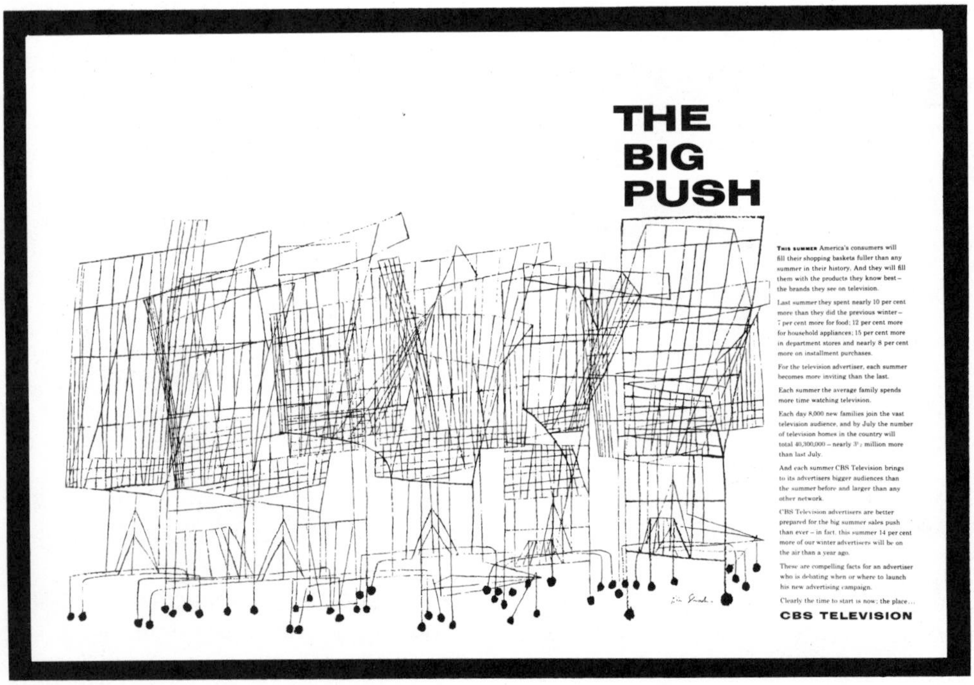

William Golden (designer) and Ben Shahn (illustrator), trade advertisement for CBS Television, 1957. Textured shopping carts and text type unify into a horizontal band. This tonal complexity contrasts with a bold headline in the white space above, and the staccato repetition of the black wheels and logotype across the bottom.

William Golden, symbol for CBS Television, 1951. Two circles and two arcs construct a pictographic eye. Translucent and hovering in the sky, it symbolizes the awesome power of images projected through the air into every home.

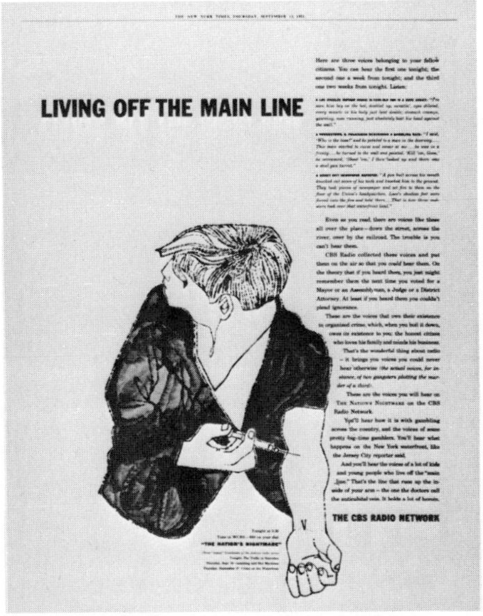

Lou Dorfsman, program advertisement for CBS Radio, 1951. This early advertisement shows the open, direct presentation that has characterized all of Dorfsman's work.

Lou Dorfsman (designer) and Edward Sorel (illustrator), advertisement for a CBS special program, 1964. To overcome the graphic jungle of the American newspaper, Dorfsman's program ads are simple and direct, but executed with distinction.

Lou Dorfsman, advertisement for CBS Television, 1962. Two ordinary symbols—an American flag and a rocket launch—combine into an extraordinary image to announce CBS's coverage of the first American orbital space flight. The photograph of the rocket transforms the flat flag into a deep space.

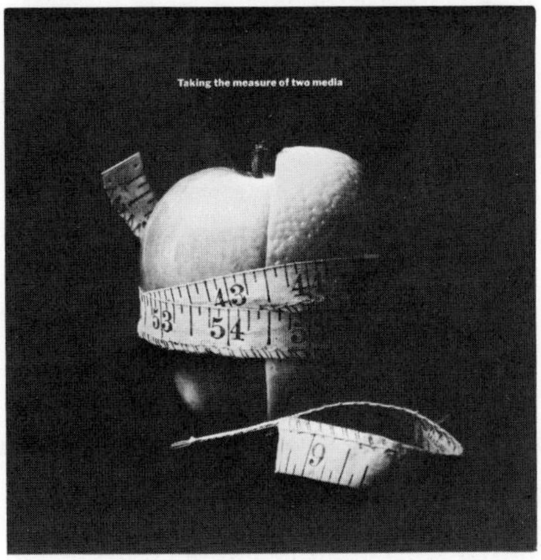

Lou Dorfsman, sales presentation cover. An old adage, "It's like comparing apples and oranges," received photographic illustration on the cover of a brochure discussing the relative costs and effectiveness of two media of communications.

were applied to even the most modest graphic designs. Dogmatic consistency in using the CBS trademark was not considered necessary. It was used in print with a variety of different company signatures, Golden and his staff avoided forcing it where it doesn't belong, and even in printed advertising it is omitted whenever it conflicts with the rest of the design. The effectiveness of the CBS symbol demonstrated to the larger management community that a contemporary graphic mark could compete successfully with traditional illustrative or alphabetical trademarks.

Stanton's recognition of the importance of design resulted in designers being given executive and administrative authority. In 1951, Golden was named creative director in charge of advertising and sales promotion for the CBS Television Network, and in 1954, Dorfsman was named director of advertising and promotion for the CBS Radio Network. Because advertising is created by internal graphic designers instead of advertising agencies, a unified philosophy and design approach between advertising and other graphics can be maintained.

After Golden's sudden death at age forty-eight, Dorfsman became the creative director of CBS Television. As art director of the CBS Radio Network during the 1950s, Dorfsman had forged a design approach that combined a pragmatic sense of effective communication with intuitive and imaginative problem solving. Dorfsman represents no single philosophic use of certain typefaces, spatial layouts, or the same illustrators and photographic approaches. Rather, it is the overall quality of problem solving and standards of visual organization during his three decades with CBS that enabled him to project a quality image for the corporation. Dorfsman was named director of design for the entire CBS Corporation in 1964, and vice president in 1968. This was in keeping with Stanton's philosophy that design is a vital area that should be managed by professionals.

When CBS constructed a new highrise headquarters building in 1966 designed by Eero Saarinen, Dorfsman designed all aspects of the typographic information right down to the numerals on the wall clocks, numbers on elevator buttons, exit signs, and elevator inspection certificates. (The last two items required Fire Department and City Building Inspection approval before they could replace the required but graphically inferior stan-

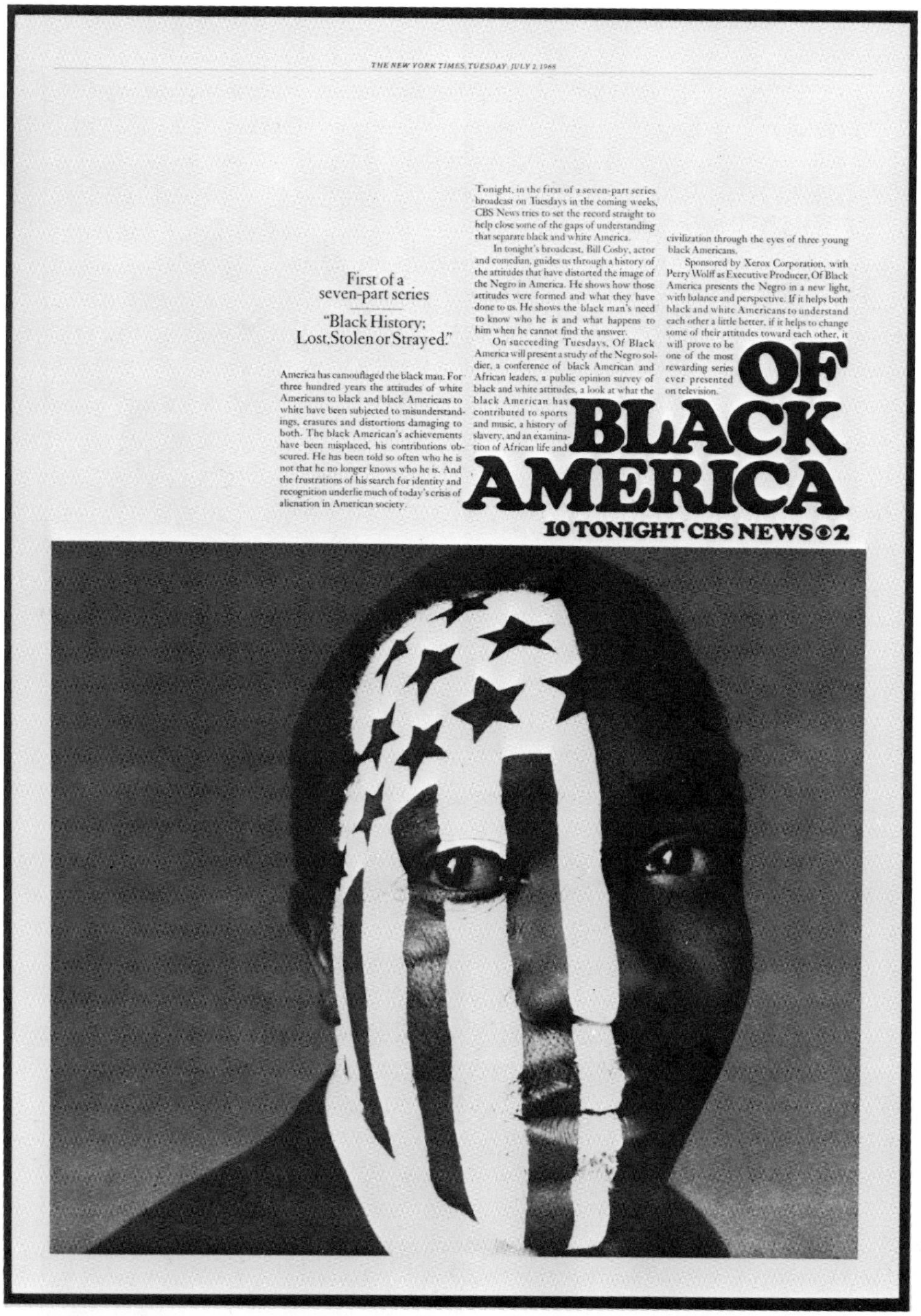

Lou Dorfsman, advertisement for a program series, 1968. Combining two images into one gained tremendous shock value and readership for an important news program series.

dard.) Dorfsman has applied his graphic design sense to film, computer animation in the production of promotional spots, informational materials, and title sequences used by the network. The CBS approach to corporate image and design is not dependent on a system or style but on the management policy toward design and the creative abilities of its design personnel. The strength of this approach is a varying and dynamic corporate design that can shift with company needs and evolving sensibilities; the potential danger is that should management policy or design staff move into less insightful hands there is no "fall-back" position.

The CIBA corporate design program

An early effort toward a comprehensive international corporate design program was launched by CIBA in the early 1950s. Originating as a small Basel, Switzerland, dyehouse in 1859, this firm organized as a stock company named Society for Chemical Industry in Basel in 1884. The name CIBA was derived from its initials as the firm grew from a small manufacturer of brilliant chemical dyes into a global chemicals, plastics, and pharmaceuticals firm.

In mid-1951, James K. Fogleman (b. 1919) was hired as design director of an American subsidiary, CIBA Pharmaceutical Products Incorporated of Summit, New Jersey, and he began to evolve a design program. The lengthy corporate name was reduced to CIBA, consistently printed in an outline Egyptian type style. A range of three typefaces was used for product identification; Fogleman believed that this variety of style and weight was necessary for design flexibility. In 1953, Fogleman persuaded CIBA in Summit to adopt a standardized, square format for promotional material. In addition to the recognition value of the infrequently used shape, economy was a key factor in its adoption. Artwork could be used throughout a series and "gang runs" of promotional materials for several products significantly reduced production costs.

In a talk before a 1953 international conference of CIBA employees, Fogleman spoke of the "need for integrated design, or a controlled visual expression of corporate personality, which plays a large role in achieving *corporate identity.*" Speaking before the management committee in Basel, he called for "a sense of unity, clarity or singleness of viewpoint" and argued that "policies are necessary which will, after a period, tie together into a unified or corporate expression of the company's character and personality." CIBA's Basel headquarters became concerned about the need for a uniform corporate identity, and a logo designed by Fritz Beuhler of

Paul Rand, package designs for IBM products. A strong corporate identification was established with this design series, starting in the late 1950s. The repeated pattern of capital letters are printed in blue, green, and magenta on the black package fronts. The handwritten product names are white, and the package tops and sides are blue.

sultants, such as Paul Rand, and internal staff design departments whose managers have authority for maintaining the corporate visual identity, has produced an evolving design program while maintaining a continuing level of quality.

As a result of a 1959 study of the "public faces" of the Westinghouse Corporation, a decision to redesign the "Circle W" trademark was made. Paul Rand was commissioned to symbolically incorporate the nature of the company's business in a new mark that would be simple, memorable, and distinct. No specific signs or symbols, but several relevant graphic forms are evoked that relate to areas of Westinghouse involvement: wires and plugs, electronic diagrams and circuitry, and molecular structures. Rand also developed a typeface for Westinghouse and applied these new elements to packaging, signage, and advertising.

Rand's redesign of the trademark for the American Broadcasting Company also demonstrated his ability to reduce the information to its simple essence while achieving a memorable and unique image.

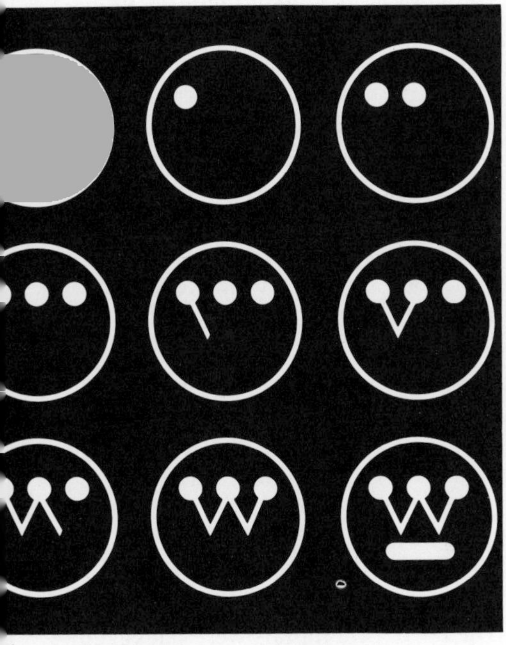

Paul Rand, trademark for Westinghouse, 1960. This design, evocative of electronic diagrams and circuitry, is depicted as it might be constructed in an animated film sequence.

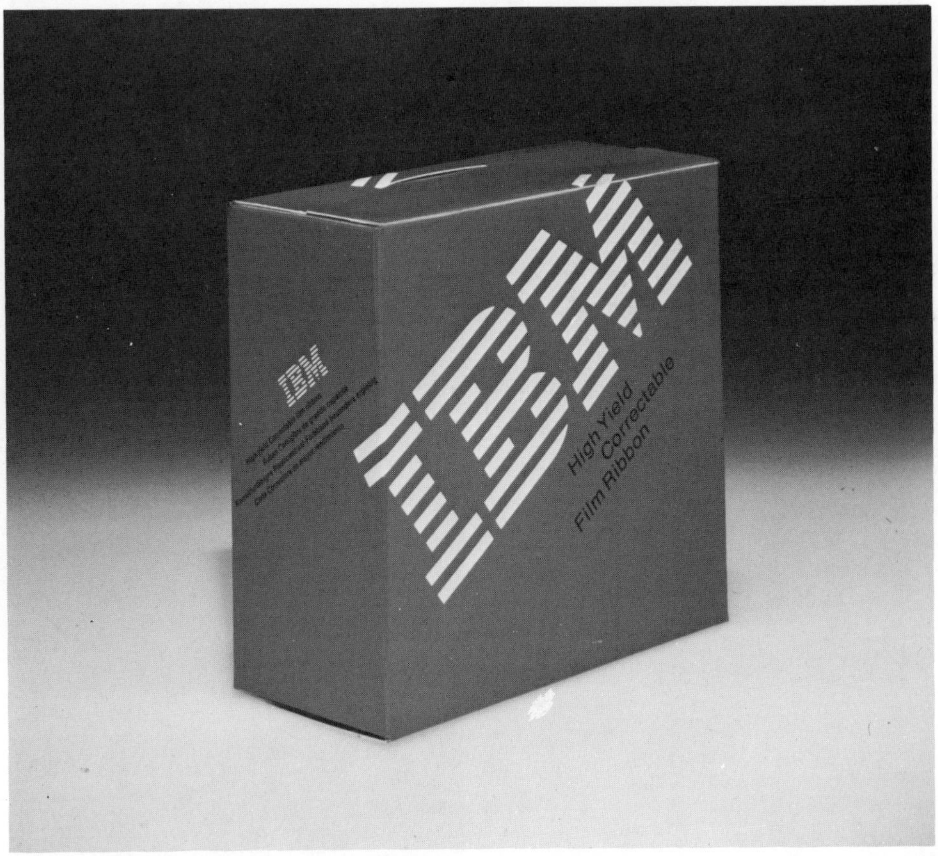

Paul Rand, package design for IBM, 1975. After two decades, the original packaging design program is being replaced with this updated design using the eight-stripe logo.

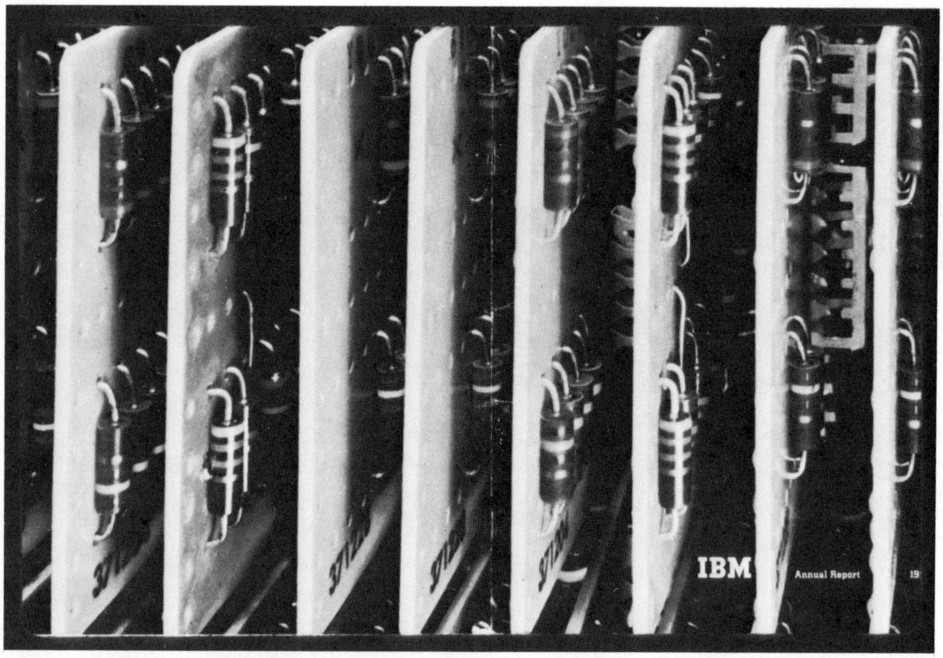

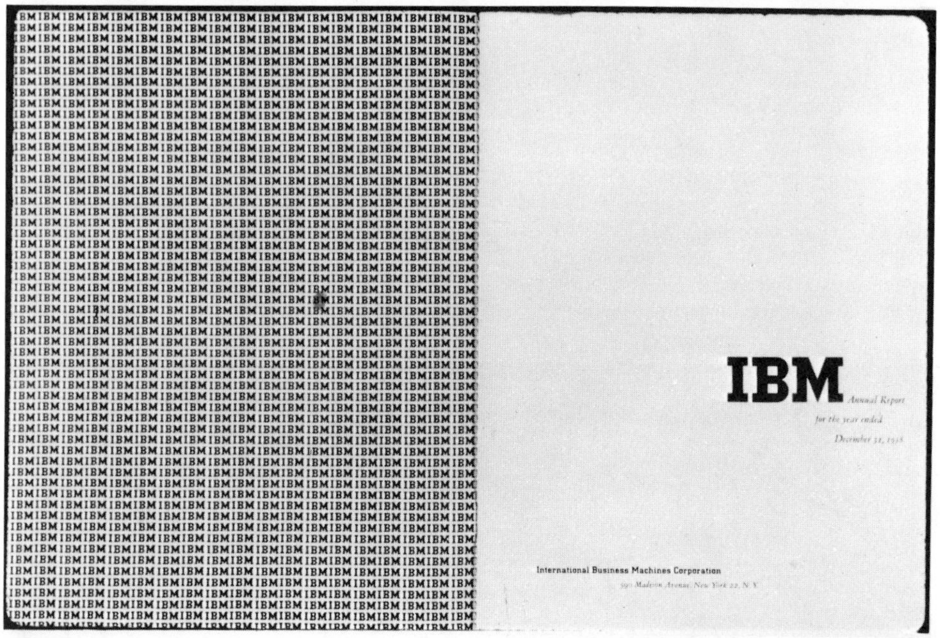

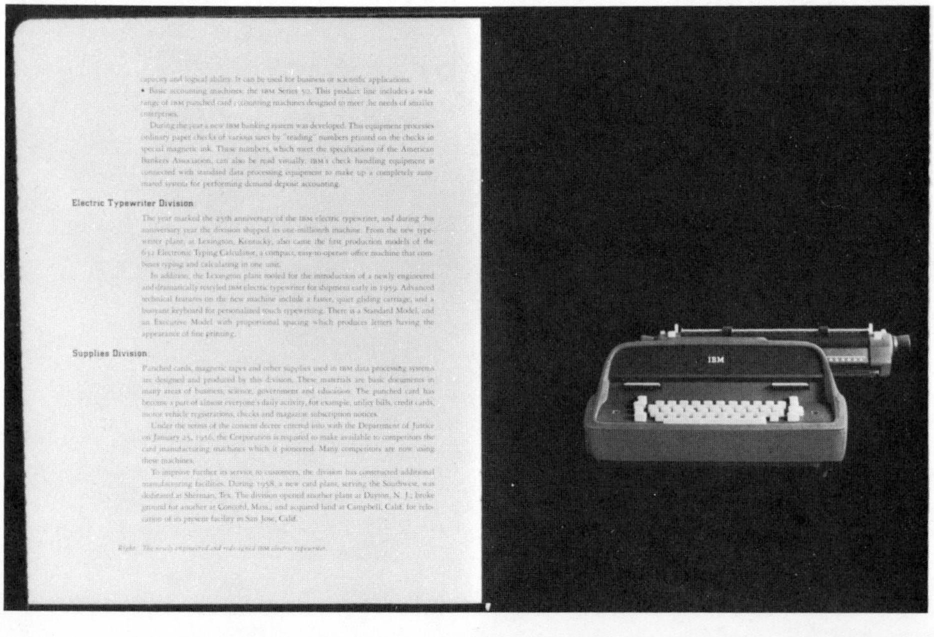

Paul Rand, annual report for IBM, 1958. Some of the trend-setting design qualities of this annual report include closeup photography of electronic components that almost become abstract patterns, simple dramatic photographs of products and people, and a typographic system combining clarity with restrained elegance.

Lester Beall's forty-five-year career had almost single-handedly launched the modern movement in American design during the late 1920s and early 1930s. During the last two decades of this distinguished career, Beall did pioneering work in corporate identity. In programs for many corporations, including Martin Marietta, Connecticut General Life Insurance, and International Paper Company, Beall blazed the trail in the development of the corporate identity manual. The scope of an organization like the International Paper Company, the largest paper manufacturer in the world with farflung facilities, required consistency in the design of everything from vehicles and signs to calling cards and invoices. Beall developed a manual that specifically prescribed the uses and forbidden abuses of the trademark. If a plant manager in a small town retained a signpainter to paint the trademark and name on a truck, for example, the corporate design manual specified the exact proportions and placement. The International Paper Company trademark was controversial in the design community when it first appeared. The letters *I* and *P* are distorted to make a tree symbol, and critics questioned whether letterforms should be altered to this extreme. The continuing viability of this mark since its inception in 1960 indicates that Beall's critics were overly cautious.

Container Corporation updated its image with a new corporate logo in 1957 developed by the design staff under Director Ralph Eckerstrom. The corporate initials were packaged in a rectangle which had two corners shaved at a forty-five-degree angle to imply an isometric box. Eckerstrom stated the requirements of a corporate identification program: "As a function of management, design must be an integrated part of overall company operation and directly related to the company's business and sales activities. It must have continuity as a creative force. It must reflect total corporate character. Unless it meets these requirements, the company image it seeks to create will never coalesce into a unified whole, but will remain a mosaic of unrelated fragments.''

John Massey (b. 1931) joined Container Corporation in 1957 and became the director of design in 1964. Under his direction, corporate design and the International Typographic Style merged into one design continuity. Visual identification and the design of systems in general and design in Chicago in particular were broadly influenced by Massey. At Container Corporation, Massey adopted Helvetica as the corporate typeface, and developed standardized grids for all signage and publications. A strong advocate of design consistency and unity, as early as 1961 Massey used thematic and visual continuity in such diverse communications materials as the annual report to stockholders and trade advertising. Under his direction, the Great Ideas of Western Man advertising campaign, which had undergone pendulum swings of typographic style during the 1950s, entered a two-decade period of typographic continuity. In 1966 Container Corporation established the Center for Advanced Research in Design, an independent design studio that worked on advanced and experimental projects and received commissions from other organizations. For example, the center developed a comprehensive visual identification system for Atlantic Richfield, a major oil company whose name changed to Arco.

Convinced that designers have a social role, Massey conceived and directed a series of cultural posters for the cities of Chicago, New York, and San Francisco which served to make the citizens more aware of the cultural resources of their cities. Active as a painter and printmaker, Massey explores ''geometric patterns and volumes as they relate to the order of the universe.'' This sense of order, and the bringing of a wholeness to a sphere of activity, strongly informs Massey's work as a corporate design manager.

Paul Rand, trademark for the American Broadcasting Company, 1965. The continuing legacy of the Bauhaus and Herbert Bayer's universal alphabet informs this trademark in which each letterform is reduced to its most elemental configuration.

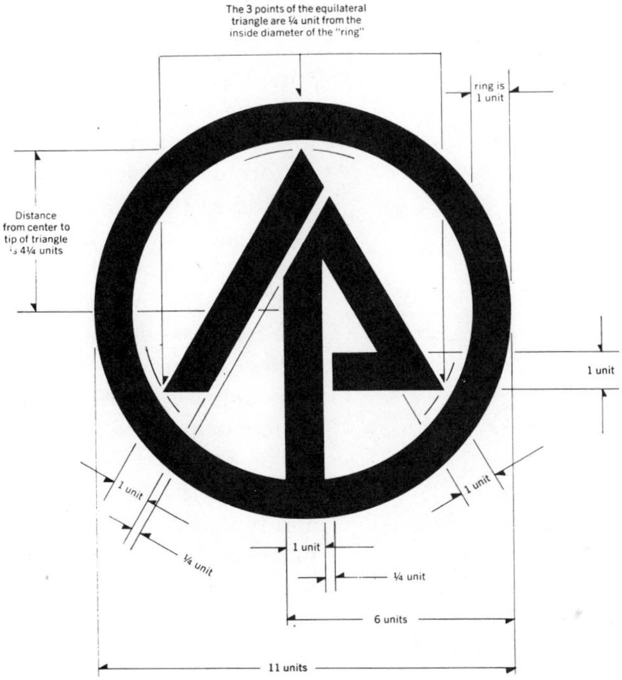

Lester Beall, logo for International Paper Company, 1960. Initials, tree, and upward arrow combine in a mark whose fundamental simplicity—an isometric triangle in a circle—assures a timeless harmony.

Ralph Eckerstrom, trademark for Container Corporation, 1957. Because this flat image changes into an isometric optical illusion, it symbolizes packaging while provoking visual interest.

Chermayeff & Geismar Associates

In 1957, three youthful designers established the firm of Brownjohn, Chermayeff, and Geismar in New York City. By calling this firm a "design office" instead of an "art studio," they reflected their attitudes toward design and the design process. Robert Brownjohn (1925–1970) had studied painting and design under Moholy-Nagy and architecture under the distinguished architect-teacher Serge Chermayeff; Ivan Chermayeff (b. 1932), son of Serge Chermayeff, had worked as an assistant to Alvin Lustig and as a record album designer; and his close friend from graduate school, Tom Geismar (b. 1931) had served two years with the United States Army as an exhibition designer and then freelanced.

Their initial contribution to American graphic design sprang from a strong aesthetic background and an understanding of the major ideas of European modern art that had been reinforced by their contacts with the elder Chermayeff, Moholy-Nagy, and Lustig. A communicative immediacy, a strong sense of form, and a vitality and freshness characterized their work in the early months of the partnership. In typographic collages for a variety of projects, including a record-album cover for Beethoven's *Eroica,* Chermayeff combined texture, color, and typeforms in unexpected combinations, and he combined images and symbols with an almost surreal sense of dislocation in New Directions

The great and glorious masterpiece of man is to live to the point.
All other things–to reign, to hoard, to build–are, at most, but inconsiderable props and appendages.
Michel de Montaigne, Essays, 1588
Container Corporation of America
Great Ideas of Western Man . . .
one of a series
CCA

John Massey, advertisement in the "Great Ideas" series, 1964. Hanging below a great slab of blue-gray like an unerring plumb bob, a heart (feeling) and an eye (perception) symbolize the spirit and awareness of the person who lives to the point.

Ivan Chermayeff, album cover for Beethoven's *Eroica,* 1957. Through the trial and error collage method, Chermayeff presented each letter as a visual element that began to take on uncommon and unexpected relationships with the other letterforms in the word.

Robert Brownjohn, album cover for Machito and his orchestra, 1959. A visual pattern of abstract bits is formed by repeating the bottom portion of letterforms that have been broken into fragments by a stencil lettering effect.

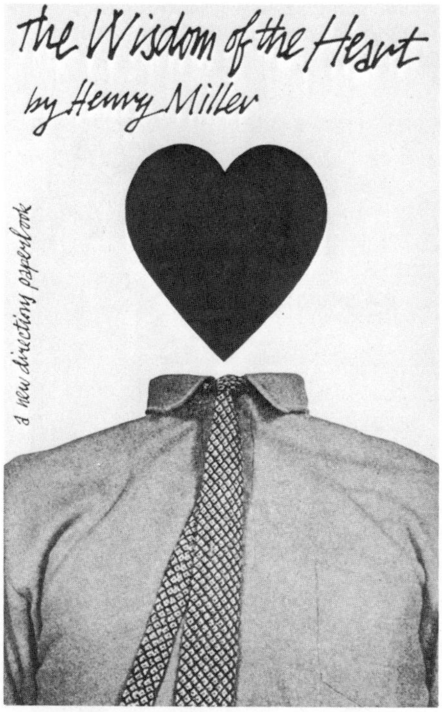

Ivan Chermayeff, cover for *The Wisdom of the Heart* by Henry Miller, 1959. The author's verbal metaphor becomes a powerful visual metaphor through the unexpected juxtaposition of a graphic symbol and a photographic image.

book jackets. Brownjohn's typographic solutions, such as the record-album cover for Manchito and his orchestra, used color repetition and unusual letterforms to express the subject matter. The growing reputation of this firm during its first three years was based on the outstanding artistic quality of their book-jacket and record-album designs. A particularly fine sense of both typographic and art history, developed in educational backgrounds that opened horizons, enabled these young designers to chart a course based on problem solving. Solutions grow out of the needs of the client and the limitations of the problem in hand.

An organizational and project management expertise necessary to handle large multicomponent projects became evident in 1958 when Brownjohn, Chermayeff, and Geismar were commissioned to design a major exhibition for the United States Pavilion at the Brussels World's Fair. The scale and character of the American urban environment was presented, not by duplicating a typical street scene, but through an environmental-scale, three-dimensional, typographic assemblage expressing the vitality and spirit of the city.

In 1960 Brownjohn left the partnership and moved to England, where he made significant contributions to British graphic design, especially in the area of film titles. Particularly inventive was the title design for the motion picture *Goldfinger*. Brownjohn's typographic designs for the credits were made as 35mm color slides. These were projected upon a moving human body filmed in real time. This integration of two-dimensional graphics with figurative cinematography launched a number of other experimental titling efforts.

Brownjohn, Chermayeff, and Geismar, American Pavilion, Brussels World's Fair, 1958. Fragments of signage and a seemingly random placement of planes in space successfully communicate a sense of place.

Chermayeff & Geismar Associates, typeface and signage for The Chase Manhattan Bank, 1960. The application of graphics to architecture requires consideration of the texture and surface of building materials, integration of signage and architectural form, and the effects of distance on legibility.

The partnership was renamed Chermayeff & Geismar Associates, and they moved into the forefront of the corporate identification movement with a comprehensive visual image program for the Chase Manhattan Bank of New York. Chase Manhattan's new logo was composed of four geometric wedges rotating around a

Chermayeff & Geismar Associates, The Chase Manhattan Bank corporate identity program, 1960. Consistent use of the logo, color, and new typeface began to build recognition value through the process of visual redundancy.

Chermayeff & Geismar Associates, Mobil Service Station exhibition, 1964. A predominance of cylinder forms and a thematic repetition of circular bands brings design order to a type of retail outlet long noted for visual pollution and clutter.

central square to form an external octagon shape. It was an abstract form unto itself, free from alphabetical, pictographic, or figurative connotations. Although it does have general overtones of security or protection because the four elements confine the square, this service mark demonstrated that a completely abstract form could successfully function as a visual identifier for a large organization. A distinctive sans-serif typeface was designed for use with the logo. The selection of an expanded letter grew out of Chermayeff & Geismar's study of the client's design and communications problems. Signage in the city is often seen by pedestrians at extreme angles. When an extended letterform is optically condensed by viewing at an extreme angle, it still retains its character recognition. The uncommon presence of the expanded sans-serif form in the Chase Manhattan corporate design system launched a fashion for this kind of letterform during the first half of the 1960s. Consistency and uniformity in the application of both logo and letterform enabled redundancy, in a sense, to become a third identifying element.

The Chase Manhattan Bank corporate identification system became a prototype for the genre. It led many corporate managers to seriously evaluate their corporate image and the need for an effective and unique visual identifier. The rapid recognition value gained by the Chase Manhattan mark indicated that a successful logo could, in effect, become an additional character in the inventory of symbolic forms that every person carries in his memory. Tom Geismar observed that a symbol must be memorable and have "some barb to it

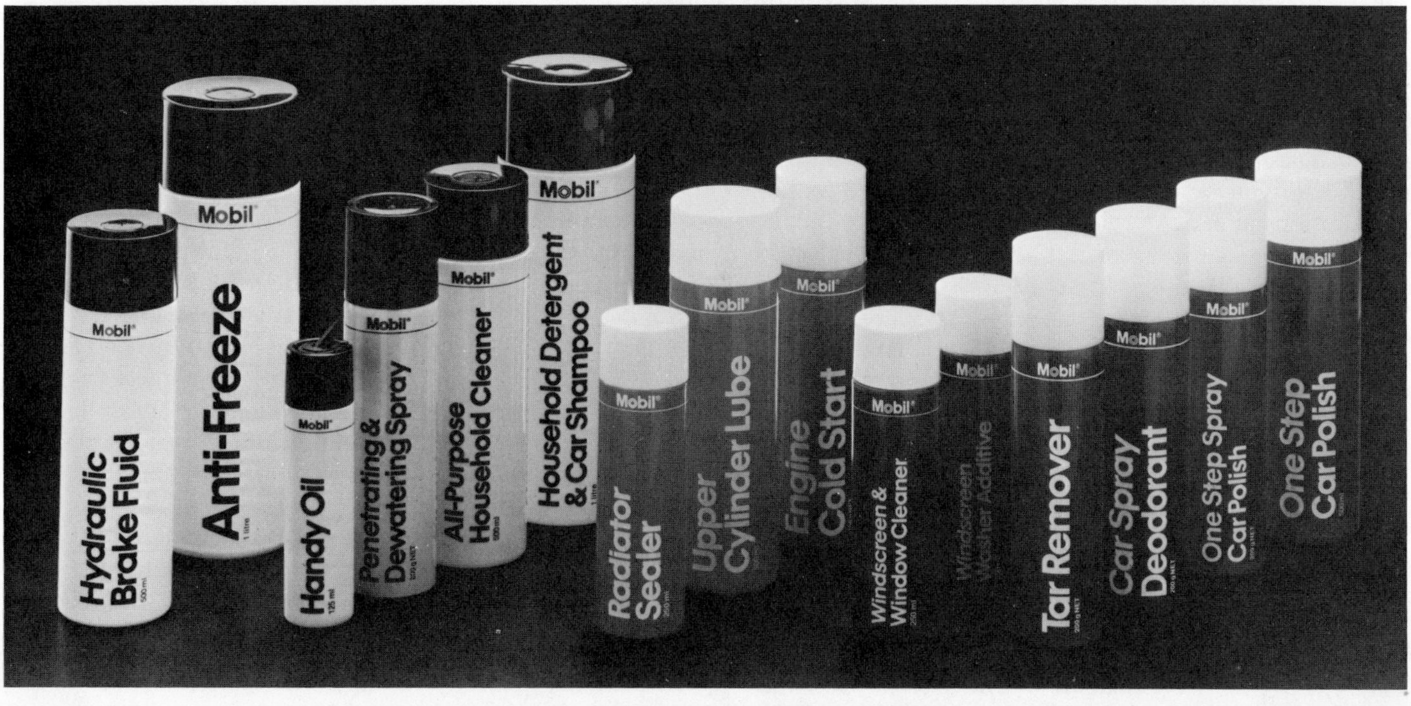

Chermayeff & Geismar Associates, packaging for Mobil, from 1975. The "aesthetic of the functional" is realized through absolute simplicity, typographic clarity, and strict adherence to a grid system. *Courtesy of Chermayeff & Geismar Associates.*

Chermayeff & Geismar Associates, Mobil Oil logo, 1964. The old pictorial trademark, a red flying horse, was discarded in favor of a simple and direct presentation of a memorable word.

Ivan Chermayeff, poster for the National Park Service Museum of Immigration, 1974. By painting these replicas of the Statue of Liberty in a range of hues expressive of the range of skin tones of the human family, a sense of the broad ethnic heritage of the American people is conveyed.

that will make it stick in your mind.'' At the same time, it must be ''attractive, pleasant, and appropriate. The challenge is to combine all those things into something simple.''

In addition to corporate identification, Chermayeff & Geismar Associates have developed innovative exhibition techniques. They call one of their techniques the ''supermarket principle.'' A large variety of objects are clustered in a manner that will communicate an insight. At the 1976 Nation of Nations exhibition in Washington, D.C., installed for the United States Bicentennial, for example, an exhibition of diverse spinning wheels brought to America from European countries—from Scandinavia to the Balkans—communicated the cultural variety and diversity of the peoples who ventured across an ocean seeking a better life. By stacking illuminated logos and signs identifying several American corporations in many foreign countries and languages, the concept of global trade was projected.

One of their most far-reaching corporate design programs was for Mobil Oil, a multinational corporation operating in over a hundred countries. The logotype, executed in an elemental geometric sans-serif typeface designed for Mobil, is the ultimate in simplicity. The word ''Mobil'' is executed in five vertical strokes, the angle of the *M,* and two circles. The name became the trademark; the round, red *O* separated this word from the visual presentation of other words. This emphasis on the circle is projected as a visual theme throughout the identification program.

Chermayeff & Geismar have produced over one hundred corporate design programs. In addition, the office continues to accept a steady stream of smaller projects, such as posters, requiring immediate, innovative solutions. This enables the senior staff to continually sharpen their creative problem-solving abilities on an almost daily basis. There is no limit to the vocabulary of forms they are willing to draw upon in their problem-solving approach to searching for appropriate and effective solutions. The range spans from advanced, artistic form to popular iconography and even tourist souvenirs, such as the replicas of the Statue of Liberty used in an American Museum of Immigration poster. The notion of an ''office style'' is rejected in favor of the philosophy of allowing the solution to evolve from the problem, an attitude which has been held by Chermayeff & Geismar since 1957.

The design system for the XIX Olympiad in Mexico

By the late 1960s, currents in graphic design, including corporate identification programs and the International Typographic Style, were fostering the idea of comprehensive design systems. An awareness developed that comprehensive planning for large organizations or events was not only functional and desirable, but actually necessary if large numbers of people were to be accommodated. This becomes particularly true in international events including World's Fairs and Olympics, where an international and multilingual audience must be directed and informed. Among many outstanding design programs that have been developed, the design program for the XIX Olympiad, held in Mexico City in 1968, is significant for its comprehensiveness and creativity.

Peter Murdoch (structures) and Lance Wyman (graphics), directional and facilities environmental signage, 1968. Murdoch's preliminary studies show the modular components that were assembled into units throughout the city.

tickets, postage stamps, and film titles and spots.

For the exterior environmental signage system, Wyman and Murdoch collaborated on the development of a complete system of functional components that were modular and had interchangeable parts. These combined directional and identification signage with mailboxes, telephones, water fountains, and so on. Color was used in both decorative and pragmatic ways. For example, the rainbow of colors used to identify major routes on the official map was painted on the curbs of the corresponding streets. A person who wished to travel from his or her hotel on Avenue Universidad to the footraces at the stadium on the Avenue de Los Insurgents Sur (identified by a pictograph of a foot) followed the purple line along Avenue Universidad until it crossed the red line at the intersection with the Avenue de Los Insurgents Sur. Turning right, the person could follow the red line along the curve until arriving at the stadium, where a large footrace pictograph announced the sporting event held in that location. This design system was so effective that *The New York Times* proclaimed, "You can be illiterate in all languages so long as you are not colorblind."

The Olympic concept in antiquity embraced the physical and intellectual unity of the whole man. In an effort to restore this concept, cultural events were added to the program requiring a set of pictographic representations for nineteen cultural events. To immediately separate cultural from athletic events, the cultural symbols were placed in the silhouetted shape formed by the *68* of the logo. Wyman's goal was to create a design system that was completely unified, easily understood by people of all language backgrounds, and flexible enough to meet a vast range of applications. Measured in terms of

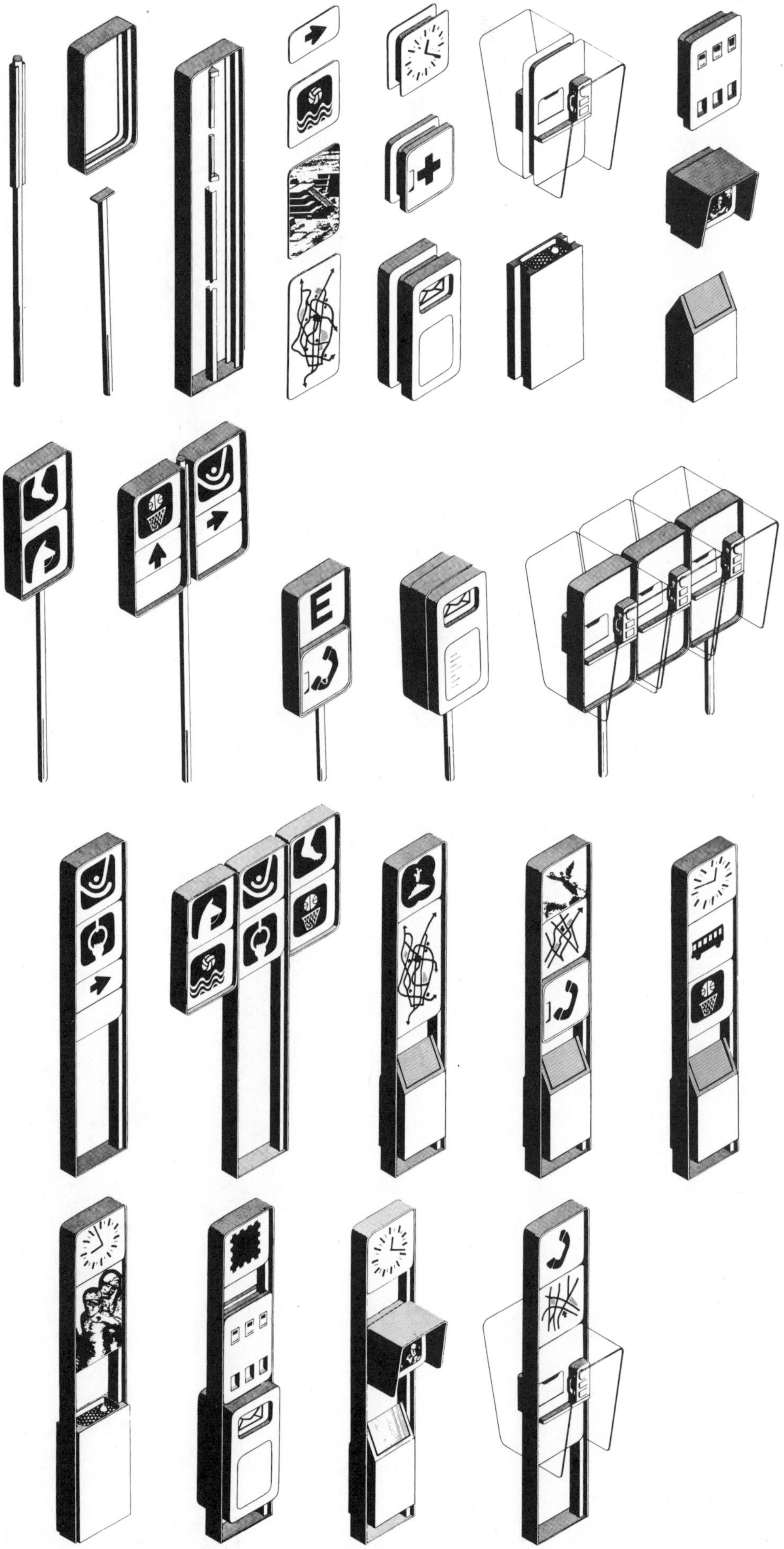

Peter Murdoch (structure) and Lance Wyman (graphics), information kiosk, 1968. Thirty of these information kiosks were wrapped in brightly colored images and placed in strategic locations around Mexico City.

graphic originality, innovative functional application, and its value to thousands of visitors to the XIX Olympiad, the graphic design system developed by Wyman and his associates in Mexico must be judged as one of the most successful in the evolution of visual identification.

After completion of the two-year Olympiad project in Mexico City, Lance Wyman returned to New York City and reestablished his design firm. The expertise gained on the Mexican project has been put to good use, for comprehensive design programs for many projects including shopping plazas and a municipal zoo have been included in his firm's diverse activities.

Lance Wyman and Beatrice Cole, tickets for the XIX Olympiad, 1968. The tickets were coded in a universal visual language of colors and symbols. The top portion identifies the sport (by pictograph) and location, and the bottom portion identifies the date and time. These are color-coded to the day of the week and coordinated with the program of events. The middle portion is coded to the color of the seating area and uses pictographs to identify the gate, ramp, row, and seat.

MEXICO 68
AZTECA 68
OCT. 14
2
1
55
$3.00
1
$3.00
OCT. 14
P.M.
P.M.

MEXICO 68
PALACIO 68
OCT. 15
25
2
29
$100.00
25
$100.00
OCT. 15
A.M.
A.M.

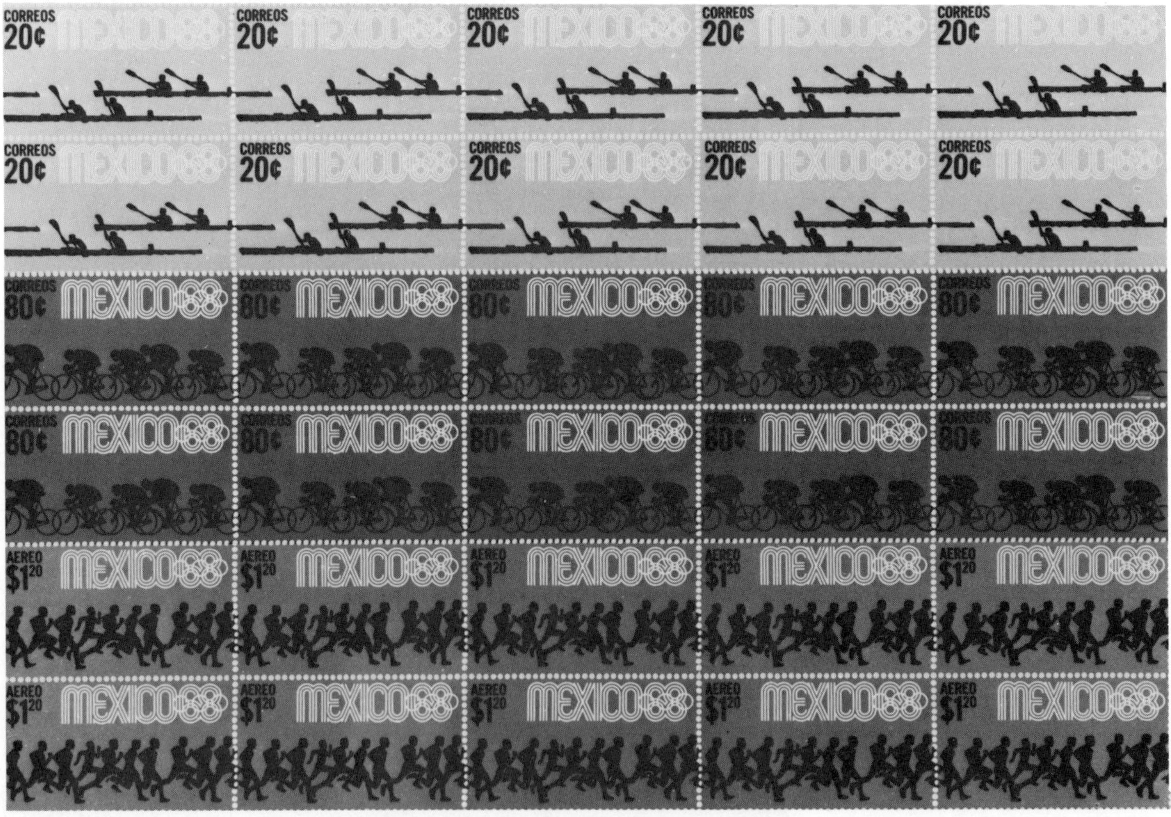

Lance Wyman, Olympic postage stamps, 1967–68. A series of stamps depicted silhouette figures engaged in different sports and printed over brilliant color backgrounds. The images were designed to flow from stamp to stamp in a continuous design.

The Federal Design Improvement Program

In May 1974, the United States Government responded to the growing awareness of design as an effective tool for fulfilling organizational objectives by initiating the Federal Design Improvement Program. This was coordinated by the Architectural and Environmental Arts Program (later renamed the Design Arts Program) of the National Endowment for the Arts. All aspects of design including architecture, interior space planning, landscaping, and graphic design were upgraded under the program. The Graphics Improvement Program, under the direction of Jerome Perlmutter, set forth to improve the quality of visual communications and the ability of governmental agencies to communicate effectively to its citizens. The first graphic standards system to be completed for a federal department or agency was the proposal for the Department of Labor developed by John Massey and the Center for Advanced Research in Design. Outmoded, unresponsive, and impersonal images; a lack of uniform and effective communications policies; and insufficient image continuity: these were some of the problems identified by the case study. The goals that Massey set for the new design program were: "uniformity of identification; a standard of quality; a more systematic and economic template for publication design; a closer relationship between graphic design (as a means) and program development (as an end) so that the proposed graphics system will become an effective tool in assisting the department to achieve program objectives."

A graphic standards manual was published. It projected a cohesive, visual identification and publication format system. In addition to a unity of identification, the establishment of standards for format sizes, typography, grid systems, paper specifications, and colors realized tremendous economies in material and time. These standards, however, were carefully structured so that the creativity and

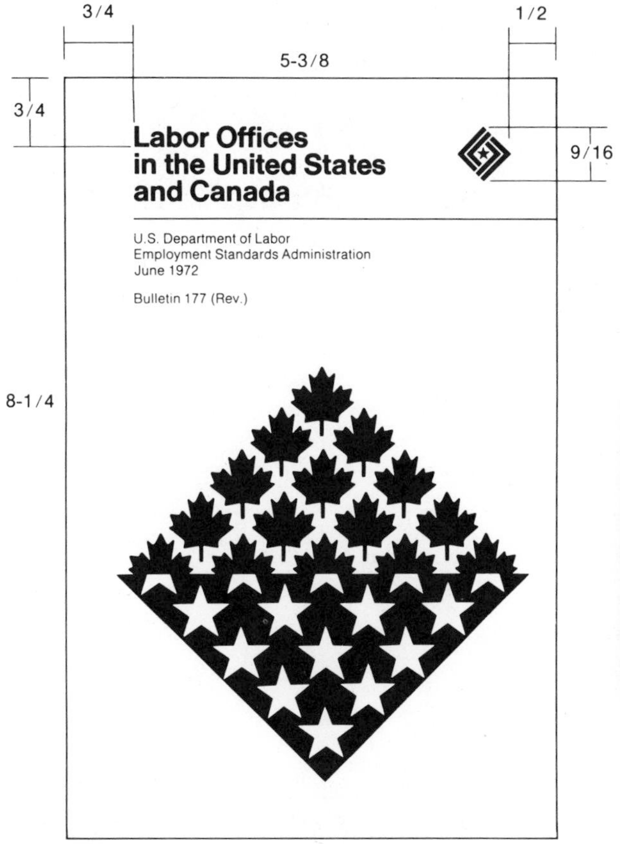

John Massey, images from the U.S. Department of Labor Graphic Standards Manual, 1974. These representative images from the system include the communications mark, typographic formats for standard publication covers, a publication grid system, and a prototype from the signage system.

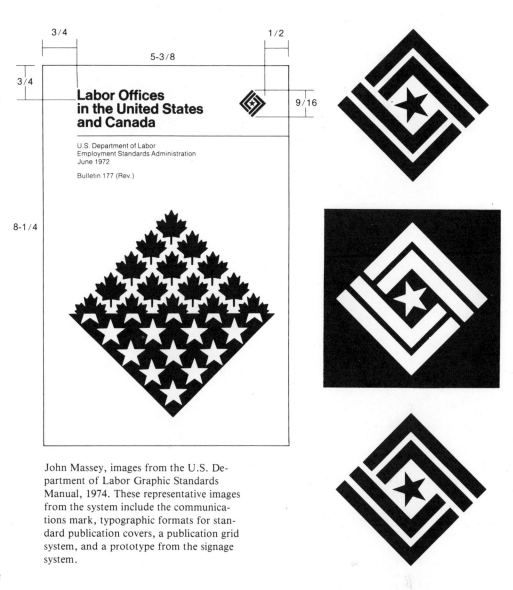

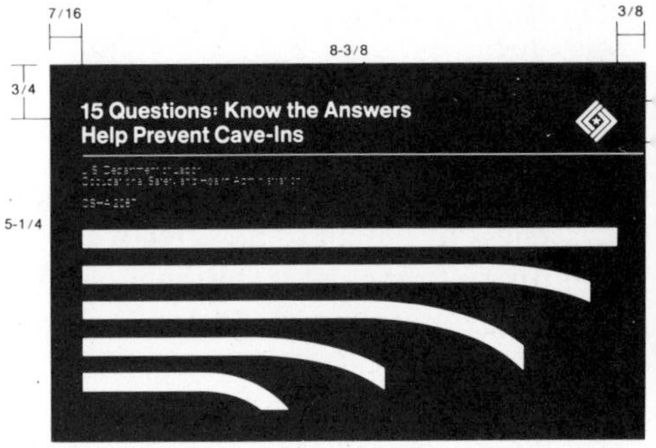

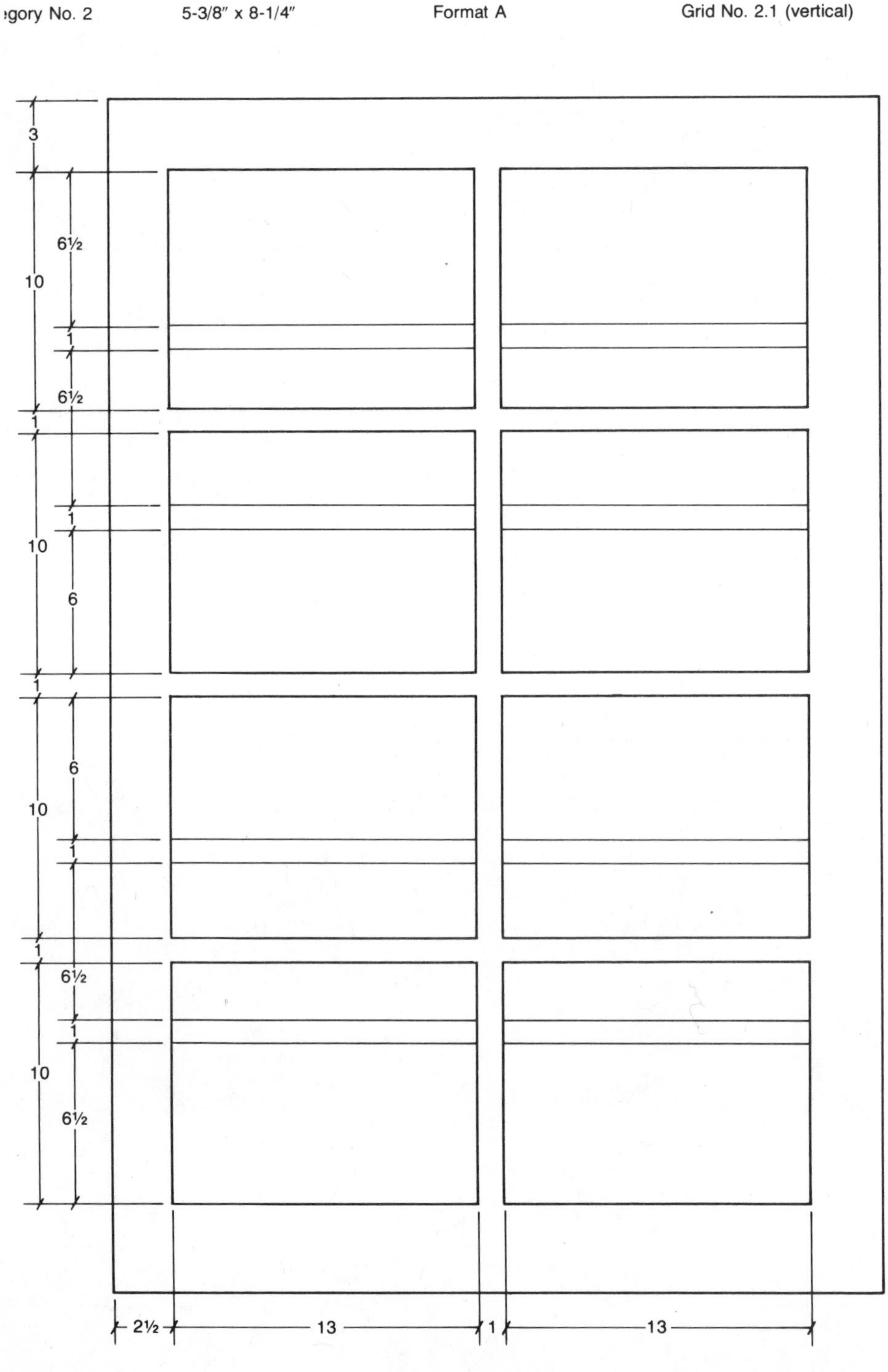

responsiveness to each communications project would not be seriously hampered. With the mechanics of the printing and format predetermined, Department of Labor staff designers were free to devote their time to the creative aspects of the problem at hand.

The Department of Labor communications mark was composed of two interlocking letters *L*, forming a diamond configuration around a star. By designing the letterforms with a striped effect, Massey effectively expressed the stars-and-stripes visual theme of the American flag. A set of publication format sizes provided economy of production and minimized paper waste. A series of grid systems for these publication formats and uniform typographic specifications ensured consistency of graphic style. Routine printed materials, including stationery, envelopes, and forms, were given consistent standardized formats.

The design vocabulary that had been developed through the evolution of the search for corporate identification in the private sector and the sensibilities of the International Typographic Style was now used to bring graphic excellence to the public sector. At least thirty-nine different Federal departments and agencies initiated visual identification programs, and many of the leading designers in America were called upon to develop them.

Transportation signage symbols

With each major international event, including the Olympics, and as major airports and other transportation facilities handling international travelers were constructed, graphic designers were commissioned to create a set of pictographs as part of an overall signage program to communicate important information and directions quickly and simply. The development of these sign and symbol systems involved considerable time and expense, and near duplication of effort often occurred. In 1974, the United States Department of Transportation commissioned the American Institute of Graphic Arts (AIGA), the nation's oldest professional graphic design organization, to create a master set of thirty-four passenger- and pedestrian-oriented symbols for use in transportation-related facilities. A consistent and interrelated group of symbols bridging language barriers and simplifying basic messages at domestic and international transportation facilities was sought. The first step was the compilation and inventory of symbol systems developed for individual transportation facilities and international events.

A committee of five prominent graphic designers, headed by Thomas H. Geismar, acted as evaluators and advisors on the project. The Department of Transportation provided the AIGA with a list of message areas. Examples, manuals, and research from around the world were gathered and compiled. Prior solutions to the thirty-four subject areas were evaluated by each member of the advisory committee, then the committee attempted to determine the best approach to each symbol. Some existing symbols were determined to be adequate for inclusion in a system; in other subject categories a totally new glyph was needed. The final set of symbols was designed and drawn by the outstanding design partnership of Roger Cook (b. 1930) and Don Shanosky (b. 1937); Cook and Shanosky Associates of Princeton, New Jersey. Clarity of image was the overriding goal. The resulting symbol system combined overall harmony with a visual consistency of line, shapes, weights, and forms. This effort represented an important first step toward the goal of unified and effective graphic communications transcending cultural and language barriers in a shrinking world. A two hundred eighty-eight-page book published by the Department of Transportation provides invaluable information about the design process and evaluation used to arrive at the system.

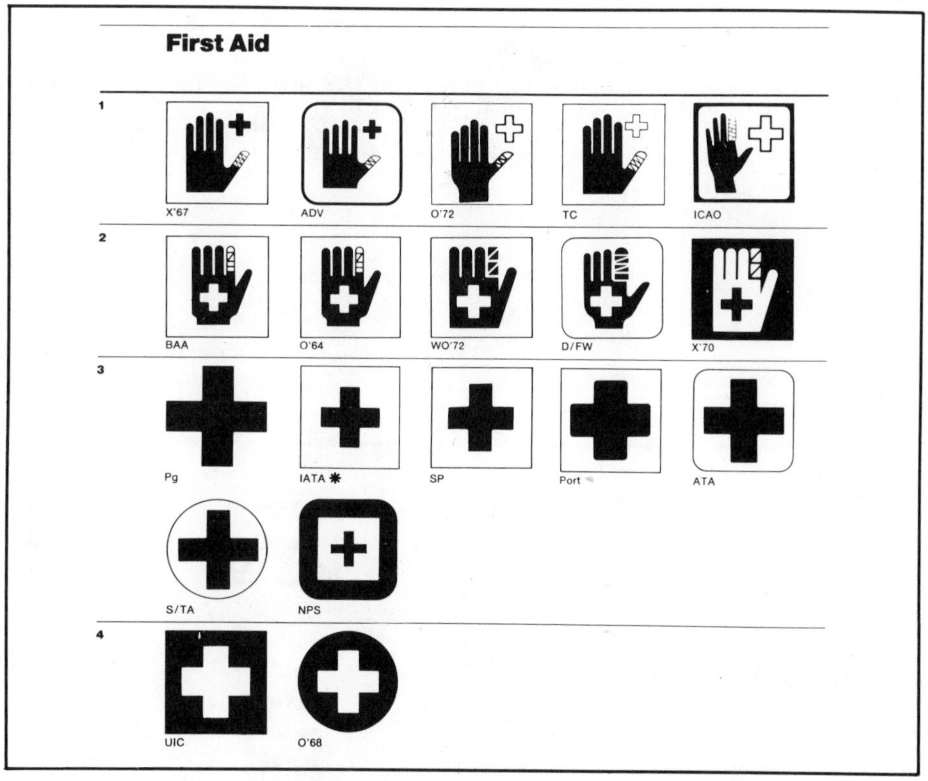

These nineteen First Aid symbols from various systems throughout the world were evaluated for their semantic, syntactic, and pragmatic values by the committee. Then, a summary recommendation by the advisory committee was used by Cook and Shanosky for guidance in developing the final symbol.

Roger Cook and Don Shanosky, signage symbol system for the U.S. Department of Transportation, 1974. The thirty-four symbols were introduced to a wide audience by this black, red, and tan poster. (Overleaf)

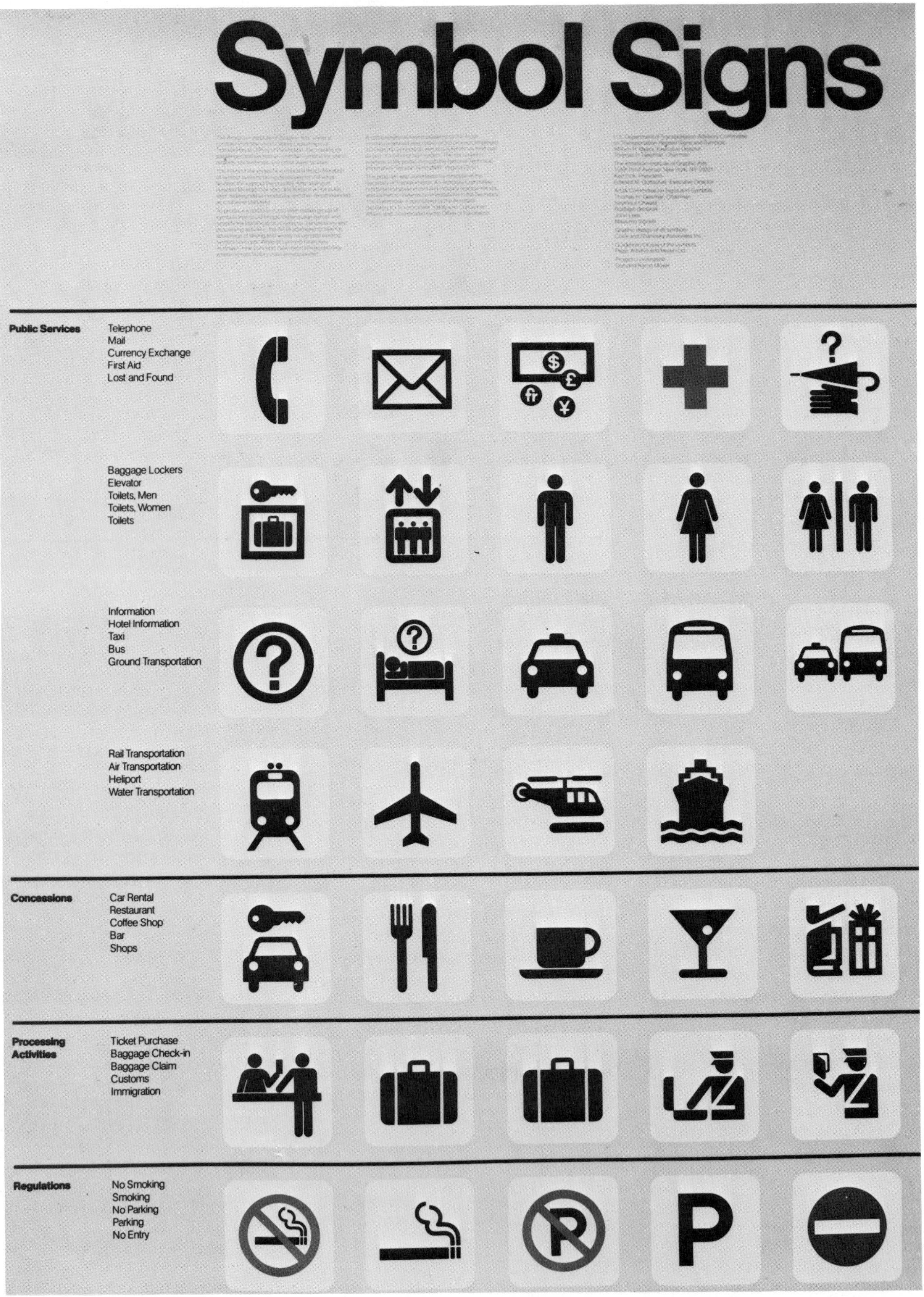

Symbol Signs
Public Services
Telephone
Mail
Currency Exchange
First Aid
Lost and Found
Baggage Lockers
Elevator
Toilets, Men
Toilets, Women
Toilets
Information
Hotel Information
Taxi
Bus
Ground Transportation
Rail Transportation
Air Transportation
Heliport
Water Transportation
Concessions
Car Rental
Restaurant
Coffee Shop
Bar
Shops
Processing Activities
Ticket Purchase
Baggage Check-in
Baggage Claim
Customs
Immigration
Regulations
No Smoking
Smoking
No Parking
Parking
No Entry

23

The Conceptual Image

SENSING THAT TRADITIONAL NARRATIVE illustration did not address the needs of the times, the graphic artists of pictorial modernism who emerged after World War I reinvented the communicative image to express the age of the machine and the advanced visual ideas of the period. In a similar quest for new forms and images, the decades after World War II saw the development of the conceptual image in graphic design. Images conveyed, not merely narrative information, but ideas and concepts. Mental content joined perceived content as motif. The illustrator interpreting a writer's text yielded to the graphic imagist making a statement. Instead of scooping out a rectangle of illusionistic space on a printed page, this new breed of image makers was concerned with the total design of the space and the integration of word and image. In the exploding information culture of the second half of the twentieth century, the entire history of visual arts was available to the graphic artist as a library of forms and possible images. In particular, inspiration was gained from the advances of twentieth-century art movements: the spatial configurations of Cubism; the juxtapositions, dislocations, and scale changes of Surrealism; the pure color loosened from natural reference of Expressionism and Fauvism; and the retreading of mass-media images of Pop Art. As graphic artists had greater opportunity for self-expression, they created more personal images and pioneered individual styles and techniques. The traditional boundaries between the fine arts and public visual communications became blurred.

The creation of conceptual images became a significant design approach in Poland, the United States, Germany, and even Cuba. It also cropped up around the world in the work of individuals whose search for relevant and effective images in the post–World War II era led them toward the conceptual image. In the

Armando Testa, poster for Pirelli, 1954. The strength of a bull elephant is bestowed upon the tire by the surrealist technique of image combination.

Armando Testa, poster for an exhibition of rubber and plastics, 1972. A hand holding a plastic ball is a direct and appropriate image for this trade exhibition. When one realizes that the hand itself is made of synthetic materials, the impact is intensified.

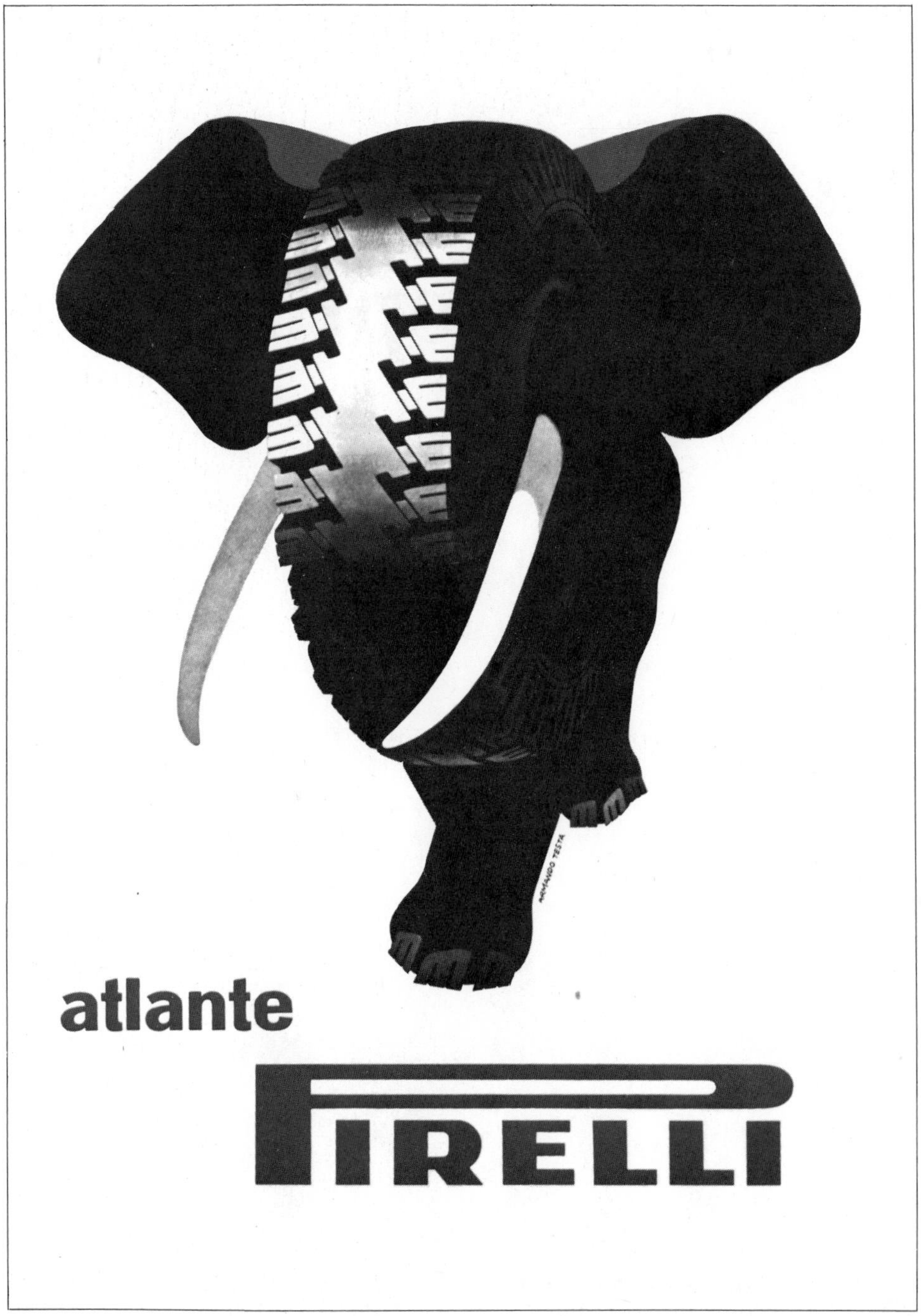

most original work of the Italian graphic designer Armando Testa (b. 1917), for example, metaphysical combinations are used to convey elemental truths about the subject. Testa was an abstract painter until after the war, when he established a graphic design studio in his native Turin. In his 1950s publicity campaigns for Pirelli tires which had an international impact upon graphic design thinking, Testa called upon the vocabulary of Surrealism by combining the image of a tire with symbols of immediately recognizable qualities. In his posters and advertisements the image is the primary means of communication, and he reduces the verbal content to a few words or just the product name. In more recent years, Testa has effectively used more subtle contradictions, such as images made of artificial materials, as a means of injecting unexpected elements into graphic design.

The Polish poster

The violence of World War II swept over Europe on 1 September 1939 with Hitler's lightning invasion of Poland from the north, south, and west without a declaration of war. Seventeen days later, Soviet troops invaded Poland from the east, and a six-year period of devastation followed. Poland emerged from the war with enormous population losses, devastated industry, a wrecked agriculture, and the capital city of Warsaw almost completely eradicated. Printing and graphic design, like so many aspects of Polish society and culture, had ceased to exist. It is a monumental tribute to the resilience of the human spirit that from this devastation, an internationally renowned Polish school of poster art emerged.

In the Communist society established in Poland after the war, the clients are state-controlled institutions and industry. Graphic designers join filmmakers, writers, and fine artists in the Polish Union of Artists, which establishes standards and sets fees.

Entry into the union comes after completion of the educational program at either the Warsaw or the Krakow Academy of Art. Entry standards for these schools are rigorous, and the number of graduates produced is carefully controlled to equal the need for design.

The earliest Polish poster artist to emerge after the war was Tadeusz Trepkowski (1914–1956). During the first decade after the devastation, Trepkowski expressed the tragic memories and aspirations for the future that were deeply fixed in the national psyche. Trepkowski's approach involved reducing the imagery and words until the content was distilled into its most simple statement. The famous 1953 antiwar poster contains just one word, "No!" A few simple shapes to symbolize a devastated city superimposed over a silhouette of a falling bomb say the rest. Henryk Tomaszewski (b. 1914) became the spiritual head of Polish graphic design after Trepkowski's untimely death and has been an important impetus for the movement from his position as professor at the Warsaw Academy of Fine Arts.

The poster has become a source of great national pride in Poland, and its role in the cultural life of the nation is unique. Electronic broadcasting lacks the frequency and diversity of western nations, and in a communist country the din of economic competition is less pronounced. Therefore, posters for cultural events, the circus, movies, and politics become important communications. In 1964, the Warsaw International Poster Biennial began, and Muzeum Plakatu—the world's first museum devoted exclusively to the art of the poster—was established in Wilanow near Warsaw.

During the 1950s, the Polish poster began to receive international attention. The aesthetically pleasing style that was predominant was an escape from the somber world of tragedy and remembrance into a bright decorative world of color and shape. In an almost casual collage approach, designs were created from torn and cut pieces of colored paper, then printed by the silkscreen process.

Tadeusz Trepkowski, antiwar poster, 1953. Trepkowski reduced his passionate statement to one word and simple but emotion laden images.

Henryk Tomaszewski, poster for a play, *Marie and Napoleon,* 1964. Tomaszewski led Polish graphic design toward a colorful and artistic expression.

Jerzy Flisak, cinema poster for *Rzeczpospolita Babska,* undated. Bright red, pink, orange, yellow, and green project the festive quality of the 1950s Polish poster. *Library of Congress, Washington, D.C., Poster Collection.*

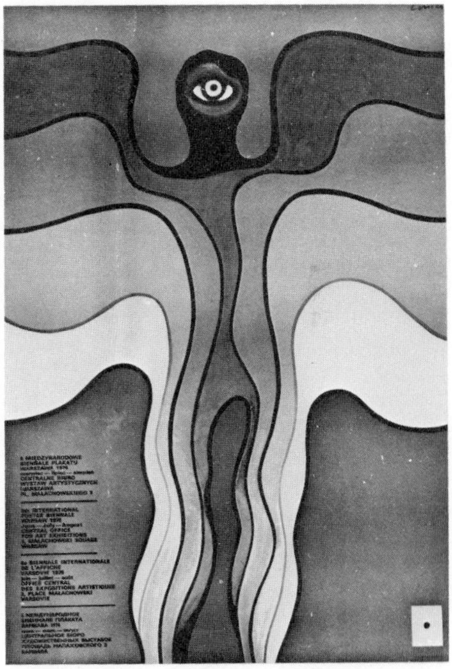

Jan Lenica, poster for the Warsaw Poster Biennale, 1976. Meandering arabesques isolate a series of bands ranging from yellow to dark green while metamorphosizing into a winged being.

Typical of this style is the film poster for *Rzeczpospolita Babska* by Jerzy Flisak (b. 1930). The symbolic female figure has a pink doll-like head with round, rouged cheeks and a heart-shaped mouth.

An extraordinary range of graphic inventiveness was achieved by a generation of Polish poster artists who came into prominence during the

1960s. Also famous for his experimental animated films, Jan Lenica (b. 1928) pushed the collage style toward a less innocuous and more menacing communication. In the 1963 poster for the film *Iwans Kindheit,* a pattern of shapes torn from paper with modulated washes of blackish brown tone establishes a lively rhythm of positive and negative interplay. Suddenly, two spiky forms with the killer instincts of a Venus flytrap begin to close and trap a butterfly. During the middle 1960s, Lenica arrived at a poster style using flowing, stylized contour lines that weave through the space and divide it into colored zones which form an image.

The third major tendency in Polish posters, after the expressions of a collective national conscience by Trepkowski and the sunlight of the informal, colorful collages, started to evolve during the 1960s and reached a crescendo during the 1970s. This was a tendency toward the metaphysical and Surrealism as a darker, more somber side of the national character was addressed. It has been speculated that this represented either a subtle reaction to the social constraints of the dictatorial regime or a despair and yearning for the autonomy that has so often been denied the Polish nation during its history. One of the first graphic designers to incorporate this new metaphysical sensitivity into his work was Franciszek Starowiejski (b. 1930). In his 1962 poster for the Warsaw Drama Theater, a serpent hovers in space coiling around two circles that become shaking hands. This enigmatic image was a harbinger of things to come in Starowiejski's work, which sometimes tends toward the gall-bladder-and-maggot school of graphics, and in the work of a number of other Polish graphic designers.

In counterpoint to this more philosophic bent in the Polish poster, the circus poster has flourished as a lighthearted expression of the magic and charm of this traditional entertainment. Approximately a dozen Polish circus posters per year are selected by a jury of artists and published by the Graphic Arts Publishers in Warsaw. This poster tradition did not begin until 1962, when concern for the mediocre quality of some circus publicity inspired the program. Each poster only bears the word *cyrk* ("circus"). WAG prints strips of typographic information giving full particulars for the specific engagement which are posted under the poster image on kiosks and walls.

Lenica and Starowiejski were joined in their break with the mainstream of Polish poster design by several others of the emerging generation who realized that a danger existed; the Polish poster could fossilize into an academic national style. This potential danger has been avoided as designers, including Waldemar Swierzy (b. 1931), arrived at unique personal visions. Approaching graphic design with a painterly viewpoint, Swierzy draws upon both twentieth-century art and folk art for inspiration. This prolific artist, who has created over a thousand posters with virtuoso skill, uses a wide variety of media. He often incorporates acrylics, crayon, pencil, and watercolor into a design. In his famous poster for the American rock musician Jimi Hendrix, Swierzy animated the large portrait with swirling energetic gestures that give the impression that the artist

Franciszek Starowiejski, poster for the Warsaw Drama Theater, 1962. The cube drawn in perspective centered below the snake is crucial, for it transforms the flat page into deep space, forcing the strange complex above it to float. *Library of Congress, Washington, D.C., Poster Collection.*

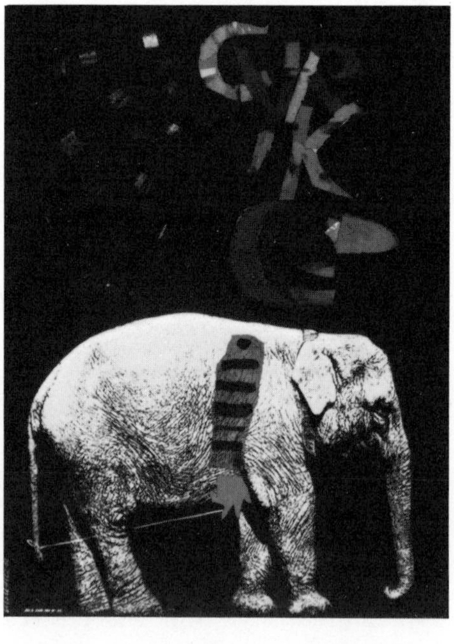

Roman Cieslewicz, poster for the circus, 1962. Bright collage elements superimpose the word Cyrk and a clown upon a high-contrast photograph of an elephant.

Waldemar Swierzy, poster for Jimi Hendrix, 1974. The electric vitality of the gestures on the cobalt blue portrait suggest the vigorous energy of hard rock music.

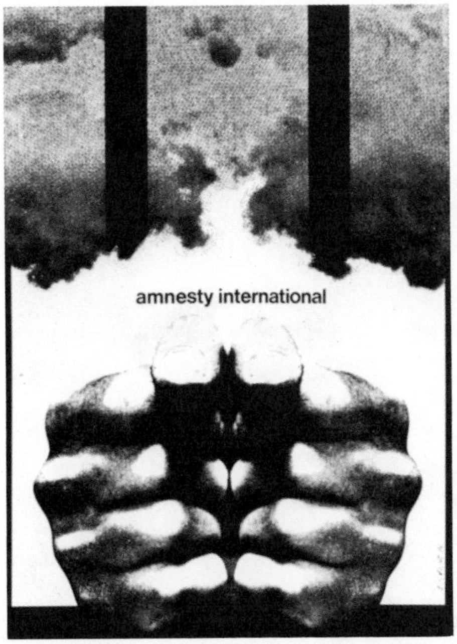

Roman Cieslewicz, poster for Amnesty International, 1975. A monumental statement about anonymous victims of political persecution emerges from the massive, totemlike image.

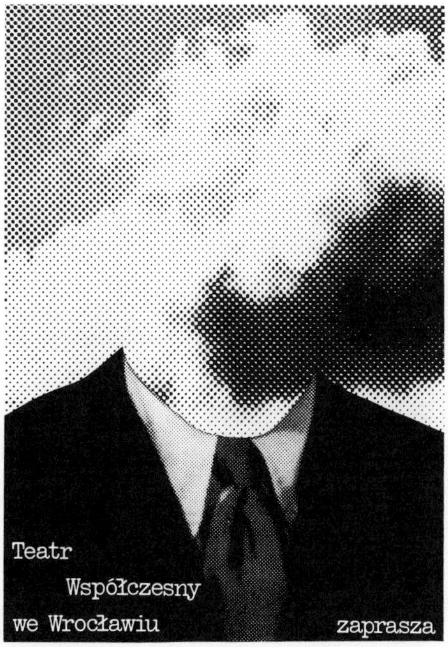

Roman Cieslewicz, poster for the Krackow Temporary Theater, 1974. In this surreal image, the tradition of hunting for an image in the clouds proves fruitless if the viewer seeks to complete the portrait.

defaced an immaculately rendered portrait by drawing graffitilike gestures into the wet paint with the brush handle. The spontaneous quality of much of his work is deceptive, for Swierzy generally devotes three weeks to each poster and sometimes executes a poster five or more times before being satisfied with the results.

An exiled Polish poster artist, Roman Cieslewicz (b. 1930), has been living in Paris since the 1960s. Closely associated with the Polish avant-garde theater, Cieslewicz has taken the poster, a public art form, and transformed it into a metaphysical medium to express profound ideas that would be difficult to articulate verbally. Cieslewicz's techniques include collage, montage, and halftone images enlarged to a scale that turns the dots into a tactile texture setting up an interplay between two levels of information; the image and the dots that create it. The tilt toward the metaphysical in Polish posters found its strongest expression in Cieslewicz's work.

The tradition of excellence, bolstered by the strong educational system, may insure a continuing poster art form in Poland. Inventiveness is being demonstrated by younger graphic designers entering the profession. (And profession is the right word in Poland, for the commercial artist is accorded the status of more traditional disciplines like architecture and medicine in that country). Marek Freudenreich (b. 1939) and Andrzej Klimowski (b. 1949) are among the new generation of emerging graphic designers who are producing superb work.

The Polish poster designers have accomplished something that is rare in the history of visual arts. A group of individual artists have been given the freedom to express their personal attitudes, graphic explorations, and even their private fantasies. Concurrent with this accomplishment, the social and cultural life of a nation has been focused and crystalized.

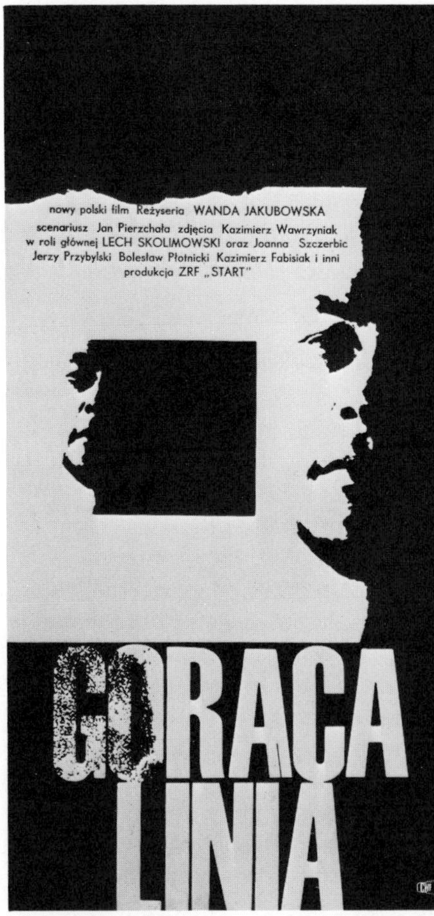

Marek Freudenreich, poster for a new Polish film, *Goraca Linia,* undated. Scale change takes on an inventive quality, for the two sizes of the high-contrast image introduces depth to a flat one color design. *Library of Congress, Washington, D.C., Poster Collection.*

Andrzej Klimowski, poster for the American film, *Nashville,* 1976. Four white lines zip in to the ear of the young singer poised before the stripes of an American flag, calling attention to the musical character of this movie. *Library of Congress, Washington, D.C., Poster Collection.*

American conceptual images

During the 1950s, the "Golden Age of American Illustration," the half century when heavy illustration ruled American graphic design, was drawing to a close. (*Heavy illustration* is a prevalent term of the 1950s communications industry used to denote traditional realistic painting, in contrast to *light illustration,* the decorative and humorous illustration popular during that decade.) Improvements in paper, printing, and photography caused the illustrator's edge over photography to decline rapidly. An ability to exaggerate value contrasts, intensify color, and make imagery crisper than life to compensate for the loss in reproduction, had enabled illustrators to create more convincing images during the first half of the century. But now, improvements in photographic materials and processes enabled photography to expand its range of lighting conditions and image fidelity. The death of illustration was somberly predicted as photography made rapid inroads into its traditional market. But as photography stole illustration's traditional function—the creation of narrative and descriptive images—a new approach to illustration emerged.

The primary wellspring of this more conceptual approach to illustration began with a group of young New York graphic artists. Art students Seymour Chwast (b. 1931), Milton Glaser (b. 1929), Reynolds Ruffins (b. 1930), and Edward Sorel (b. 1929) banded together and shared a loft studio. Upon graduation in 1951, Glaser received a Fulbright Scholarship to study etching under Giorgio Morandi in Italy, and the other three friends found employment in New York, in advertising and publishing. To solicit freelance assignments, a joint publication called *The Push Pin Almanac* was published bimonthly featuring interesting editorial material from old almanacs illustrated by the group. When Glaser returned from Europe in August 1954, the Push Pin Studio was formed.

Milton Glaser, poster for The Shadowlight Theatre, 1964. A dictionary of strange characters unleashed from Glaser's ink bottle are halftones reversed from the background. The scumble and tonality of his ink washes lend a kind of graphic detail to these vague spirits.

After a time, Ruffins left the studio and became a prominent decorative and children's-book illustrator. In 1958, Sorel started free-lancing and emerged as a major political satirist of his generation. Chwast and Glaser maintained a collaborative studio for over two decades. *The Push Pin Almanac* became the *Push Pin Graphic,* and this experimental magazine provided a forum for developing new ideas. Their philosophy, techniques, and personal visions had a major impact. Graphic design has often been fragmented into component parts of image making and layout or design. Like turn-of-the-century graphic designers Mucha and Bradley, Glaser and Chwast united these components into a total communication conveying the individual vision of the creator. Using visual art history from Renaissance painting to comic books as a data bank of form, images, and visual ideas, the Push Pin artists freely paraphrased and incorporated a multiplicity of inspirations into their work. However, these resources were reinvented into new and unexpected forms.

Milton Glaser's singular genius is hard to categorize, for over the course of several decades he ''reinvented himself as a creative force'' by exploring new graphic techniques and new motifs. During the 1960s, Glaser created images of flat shapes formed by thin, black ink contour lines with color added by adhesive color films. This almost schematic drawing style echoed the simple iconography of comic books, the flowing curvilinear drawing of Persian and Art Nouveau arabesques, the flat color of the Japanese print and Matisse cutouts, and the dynamic of contemporary Pop Art. As with other graphic designers whose work captured and expressed the sensibilities of the time, Glaser was widely imitated. Only his ability to maintain a steady stream of innovative conceptual solutions, along with his restless exploration of different techniques, prevented Glaser from being consumed by his followers.

While the forms created by this technique are formed by the edge, another approach developed by Glaser evolved from the mass. Inspired by oriental calligraphic brush drawing and Picasso aquatints, Glaser began making gestural silhouette wash drawings in the late 1950s that tease the viewer by only suggesting the subject; this asks the viewer to ''fill in'' the details from his or her own imagination. An example of this is the 1964 *Shadowlight Theatre* poster for a performance of a contemporary interpretation of the Balinese shadow play. Against a rich black field, the figures are printed in a ''split font;'' that is, the ink font or reservoir on the printing press is filled with more than one color of ink. These are blended by the ink rollers of the press. The baroque figures of the *Shadowlight Theater* poster take on an eerie glow as the color flickers from yellow-green to red to brown.

For Glaser, geometric forms, words, and numbers are not merely abstract signs, but tangible entities with an object-life that allows them to be interpreted as motifs just as figures and inanimate objects are interpreted by an artist. This original approach to sign and symbol is seen in the 1968 *One Print One Painting* exhibition poster, in which an isometric cube comes alive with the magical ability to warp and bend the large numerals. In the rejected poster design for the Museum of Modern Art's Dada and Surrealism exhibition, the words themselves take on a metaphysical afterlife as objects. ''Dada'' is impaled through the tabletop to hover over its wayward offspring, ''Surrealism.'' Like the art movements it projects, this design defies rational interpretation. Perhaps the officials of the museum did not understand it.

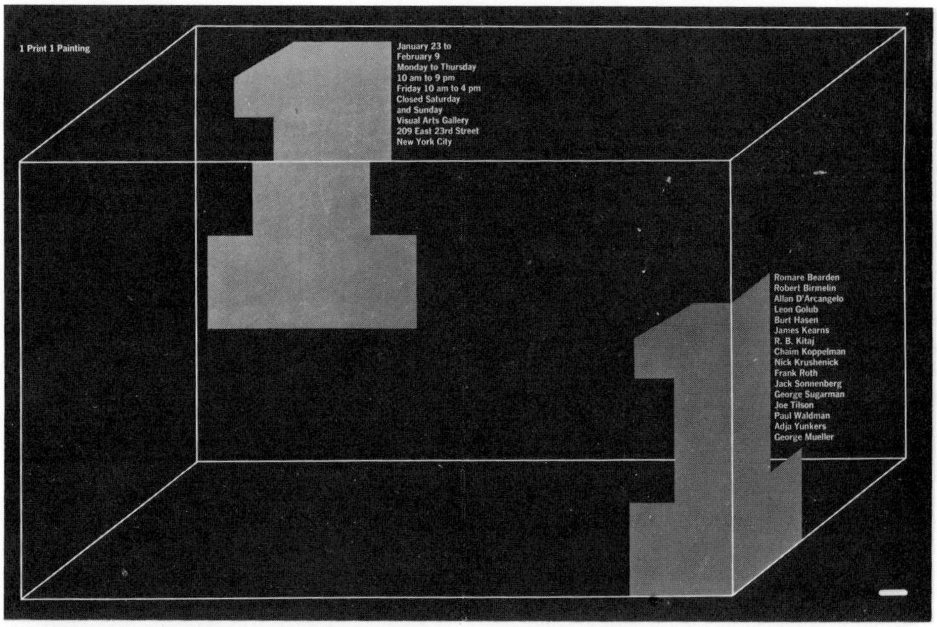

Milton Glaser, poster for *One Print, One Painting* exhibition, 1968. The dense purple-black field is created by overprinting the deep blue of the numerals and the red of the typography, which makes the thin white line of the isometric box glow vividly. *Library of Congress, Washington, D.C., Poster Collection.*

Milton Glaser, poster for a Dada and Surrealism exhibition, 1968. The smaller table isolates the word ''real'' from the longer word ''Surrealism.'' Context and scale change, plus the objectlike quality of the words, paraphrase the visual conventions of these movements.

In graphic designs for music, including concert posters and record albums, Glaser has achieved a singular ability to combine his personal vision with the essence of the content. When Gertrude Stein complained to young Pablo Picasso that the portrait he painted of her during the winter of 1905–06 did not look like her, he reportedly advised her that in time, it would. To this day, the public image of Gertrude Stein is contained in Picasso's portrait, and so it is with Glaser's iconographic image of the folk-rock singer Bob Dylan. A photographer related to Glaser that while on assignment on the Amazon River, he stopped at a remote Indian

Milton Glaser, record album cover for *The Sound of Harlem,* 1964. In this early example of Glaser's contour line and flat color period, the figures become weightless shapes unbothered by the force of gravity and free to move and flow in musical rhythm. *Courtesy of CBS Records; John Berg, Art Director.*

Milton Glaser, poster for Bob Dylan, 1967. This famous image of the popular folk singer, presented as a black silhouette with brightly colored hair patterns inspired by Islamic design, became the graphic icon for a generation.

village where this poster was hanging on the wall in one of the huts. Nearly six million copies of the poster were produced for inclusion in a best-selling record album, which enables it to rival Flagg's Uncle Sam poster as one of the most seen and reproduced graphic icons in the collective American experience.

In contrast to the simplicity of the Dylan cover, Glaser's interpretation of Johann Sebastian Bach is extremely complex. Glaser writes that his personal associations, "particularly in terms of the music's structure and geometry—were details from an Islamic rug, a series of geometric references including grids, overlapping discs, and a variety of perspective lines. Reference to certain natural forms—leaves, trees, and landscapes—point to pastoral aspects in Bach's work."

Milton Glaser, poster for Johann Sebastian Bach. Although separated by a black gulf, the landscape and portrait are unified graphically by the diagonal lines. In addition, the shape of Bach's head and neck repeats the silhouette of the tree.

Milton Glaser, poster for Poppy Records, 1968. Symbolizing an independent new recording company seeking to break through the monolithic conventions of the recording industry, Glaser's brilliant orange and red poppy blooms forth from a granite cube.

Perhaps the vision of Chwast is even more personal than Glaser's. Often using the technique of linear drawing with adhesive color films to overlay flat color, Chwast's images are vastly different. Echoes of children's art, primitive art, and comic books appear in his imaginative reinventions of the world. Chwast's color is frontal and intense. In contrast to Glaser's spatial depth, an absolute flatness is maintained. Chwast has been called a typographic genius. His innocent vision, love of Victorian and figurative letterforms, and ability to integrate figurative and alphabetical information has enabled Chwast to produce unexpected design solutions. In his 1968 announcement of Electra Production's move to a new location, each letterform in the word lumbers across the space endowed with its own form of transpor-

Milton Glaser, record album cover for Jan Hammer, 1975. Snakes and planets inhabit a primeval landscape painted on the chipboard back of a tracing paper tablet.

Seymour Chwast, moving announcement for Elektra Productions, c. 1965. Walking, riding, or propelled by locomotive power, the client's name travels to its new location.

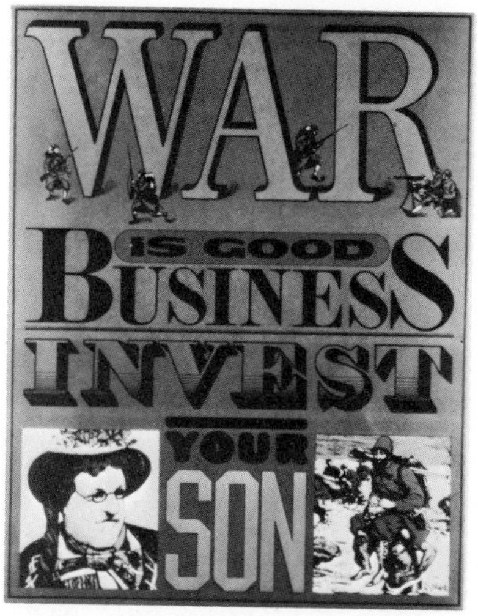

Seymour Chwast, graphic statement about war, 1967. Red, orange, lavender, and blue letterforms pull Victorian typography into a twentieth-century context. The copy line uses the propaganda technique of the positive endorsement that evokes a negative response in the viewer.

tation. The nineteenth-century wood-type poster with its multiplicity of typestyles has been revived by Chwast and invigorated with bright color and illustrations to allow its graphic complexity to speak to the citizens of yet another century. With a layout style that is outrageously uninhibited, Chwast continued the *Push Pin Graphic* after his partnership with Glaser was dissolved. For instance, the special issue on chickens has an opening page with a background of chicken images flipping to and fro in the wide margin to the left and bottom of the page.

Both Chwast and Glaser developed a number of novelty typefaces. Often, these began as lettering for assignments, then were developed into full alphabets. An excellent example of this is Chwast's Artone ink package that uses an Art Nouveau-inspired initial letter that seems to drip and run with a bulging fluidity expressing the character of the product.

The Push Pin Studio hired other designers and illustrators in addition to Glaser and Chwast, and a number of younger individuals, who worked for the studio and then moved on to freelance or to other positions, expanded the range and base of what became known as the "Push Pin Style." This so-called style is less a matter of a set of visual conventions, or a unity of visual techniques or images, as it is an attitude about visual communications, an openness to try new forms and techniques, and an ability to integrate word and image into a decorative whole.

An enormously influential young graphic designer in the late 1960s and early 1970s, Barry Zaid (b. 1939) joined Push Pin for a few years during this period. A Canadian who majored in first architecture then English during college before becoming a self-taught graphic designer and illustrator, Zaid worked in Toronto then London before joining Push Pin Studio. As a graphic archeologist who based his work upon a thorough study of the graphic vernacular of bygone eras, Zaid became an important force upon the revivalism and historicism that was prevalent in graphic design during this period. Zaid was particularly prominent in the revival of the Art Deco decorative geometric forms of the 1920s, and made a

Seymour Chwast, title page for the *Push Pin Graphic,* 1976. Chwast's playful layouts achieve a rare humor through unexpected visual arrangements and images.

Seymour Chwast, package for Artone ink, 1964. Seldom has a letterform expressed the physical properties of a product more appropriately. *Courtesy of Seymour Chwast.*

Seymour Chwast, poster against the Vietnam War, 1968. In this multicolor linoleum-cut illustration, the trivial is used to convey powerful antiwar feelings.

Seymour Chwast, package for Love Drops candies, 1974. A light-hearted line of Push Pin Candies showed just how decorative and appealing packages could be.

Barry Zaid, billboard for the 7-Up Beverage, 1969. To create a nostalgic reminder of summer leisure, Zaid began with a Victorian chromolithograph, then painted a bottle in the little girl's hand and added a sign and the lettering.

Barry Zaid, cover for the Australian *Vogue* magazine, 1971. The rotund geometric forms of Leger and pictorial modernism are evoked.

James McMullan, poster for *Anna Christie,* 1976. McMullan often calls attention to the physical properties of the medium. For example, the red background behind the figure changes into painterly strokes that become lettering.

Barry Zaid, book cover for *Art Deco* by Bevis Hillier, 1970. In this orange, green, and black cover, the decorative geometry of the 1920s is reinvented in the context of the sensibilities of a half century later.

number of forays into Victorian graphics. Zaid's work, however, did not merely mimic the nostalgic forms of his motifs. His sense of spatial organization, scale, and color were of his own time.

Among other illustrators who worked at Push Pin before leaving to freelance, James McMullan (b. 1934) revived watercolor, a medium that had declined from a position second only to oil paint as a medium for fine art and illustration, and restored it as a means of graphic expression. McMullan achieved prominence during the 1960s for energetic ink line and watercolor illustrations that often combined multiple images with significant changes in spatial depth and image size and scale. Moving into the 1970s, McMullan's watercolor technique became increasingly masterly, and he developed a photo-documentary approach of sharply increased detail and realism. At the same time, however, a concern for total design asserted itself, and McMullan began to make fluid lettering an important part of his images. In McMullan's 1977 poster for Eugene O'Neil's play *Anna Christie,* the intimate spatial level of the figure sitting in an interior is superimposed over an ocean scene; the dual image combines to communicate the locale

Paul Davis, poster for the play, *For Colored Girls . . .*, 1977. The title is appropriately written in a graffiti rainbow of colors behind the sensitive portrait. The theater and its address, executed in the mosaic tiles of New York subway signs, establishes the locale.

of the play while creating an engaging spatial interplay.

Another Push Pin alumnus who moved into a total design approach is Paul Davis (b. 1938). Davis first appeared in the *Push Pin Graphic* with a series of primitive figures painted on rough, wood panels with targets superimposed on them. From this beginning, Davis moved toward a painting style of minute detail that drew upon primitive Colonial American art as a resource. Davis evolved into a master of meticulous naturalism in which the solid shapes of his forms project a convincing weight and volume. Like McMullan, Davis often became involved in a painterly integration of image and words.

The Push Pin school of graphic illustration and design presented an alternative to the heavy illustration of the past, the mathematical and objective typographic and photographic orientation of the International Typographic Style, and the formal concerns of the New York School. Warm, friendly, and accessible, Push Pin design projects vitality with its unashamed allusions to other art and its lush color.

Although not formally associated with the Push Pin Studio at any point of his career, a graphic designer who turned to illustration is Richard Hess (b. 1934). He developed a rendering style somewhat allied to that of Paul Davis. Hess has more of a tendency toward Surrealism than Davis, and often drew upon the spatial manipulations of René Magritte. An understanding of the folklore and imagery of nineteenth-century America enabled Hess to produce a number of images that thoroughly captured the essence of this earlier period.

The Push Pin Studio group did not maintain a monopoly on the concep-

Richard Hess, record album cover for Charles Ives, 1974. The complex format used on Victorian era circus posters enables Hess to depict many images from the composer's era. *Courtesy of Columbia Records; Henrietta Condak, Art Director.*

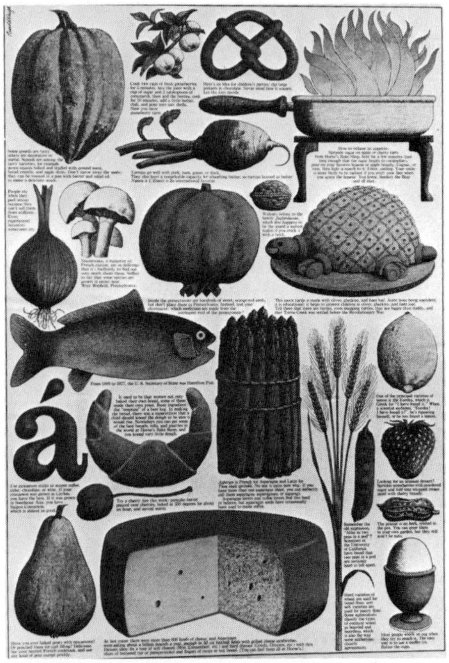

Arnold Varga, newspaper advertisement for Joseph P. Horne, c. 1966. The joys of cooking and pleasures of Horne's gourmet shop are conveyed by this full color newspaper advertisement. When printed in the newspaper, a small Horne byline appeared at the bottom of the page.

tual image in America, for a number of independent voices forged uniquely personal approaches to communications problem solving while combining the traditional conceptualization and layout role of the graphic designer with the image-making role of the illustrator. One such person who practically reinvented the retail newspaper advertisement, Arnold Varga (b. 1926), entered the field in 1946. Beginning in the middle 1950s, Varga's newspaper advertisements for two Pittsburgh, Pennsylvania, department stores—Joseph P. Horne & Co. and Cox's—indicated that this usually pedestrian form of visual design could be turned into memorable image-building communications. Many of his ads used white space and headlines carefully integrated with large simple illustrations to break through the monotonous gray of the newspaper page. Varga is particularly noted for the lighthearted, entertaining copy in his advertisements. A multiple-image picture and caption approach, such as the gourmet shop advertisement for Joseph P. Horne, achieved notable public response. People actually offered to buy this advertisement to hang on their walls!

Michael Doret (b. 1946) first became known during the late 1960s for his innovative forms and skill in creating lettering. Designing and rendering letterforms is important in Doret's designs. But as his work evolved, he defined it as just one component of his graphic design approach. The use of color as a creative tool became just as important; and he takes particular delight in unexpected color combinations and juxtapositions. Alphabet forms, his geometric shapes that contain them, and pictorial elements are combined in Doret's complex page designs. Part illustrator, part designer, and part lettering artist, Doret's color is almost always composed of screen tints of process color stripped in photomechanically by the printer. Early works used a prominent black plate of ruled lines, images, and lettering. As time passed, this containment contour vanished from Doret's vocabulary, and his designs are constructed of flat color shapes and tones whose edges join without a separating line. In magazine and book covers, lettering for the title or subject is so completely unified with elemental symbolic images that it would be impossible to separate them.

Michael Doret, cover for *Time* magazine, 1979. The 1930s red gasoline pump has a circular orange, blue, and white lamp that becomes the *O* in the word "oil." This pump symbolizes the oil industry; the black splatter of oil behind it suggests the crisis of supply and price.

John Berg (art director and designer), cover for the *William Tell Overture,* 1963. As happened in "the new advertising," complex visual organization has been replaced by the simple presentation of a concept. *Courtesy of CBS Records.*

John Berg (art director) and Nick Fasciano (illustrator), album cover for Chicago, 1974. Images of nineteenth-century Chicago from the stockyards to the great fire are executed in handtooled leatherwork. *Courtesy of CBS Records.*

John Crocker (artist and designer), album cover for the violin music of Schubert, 1968. A sheet of music erupts into graphic flourishes that become a visual interpretation of the music. *Courtesy of CBS Records.*

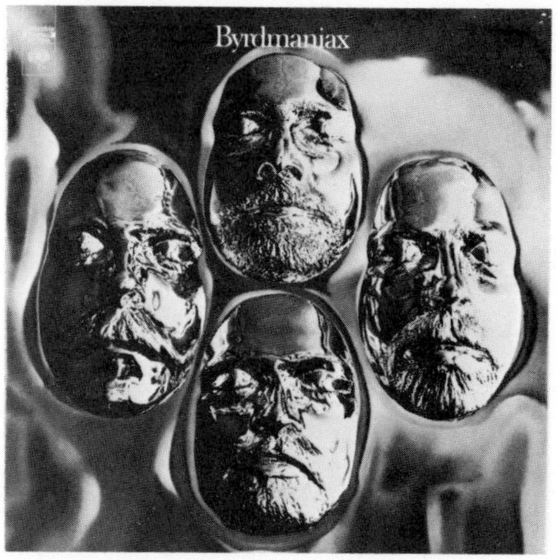

John Berg (art director) and Virginia Team (designer), album cover for the Byrds, 1971. An enigmatic image transcends normal portraiture as masklike faces emerge from the surface of an oily fluid. *Courtesy of CBS Records.*

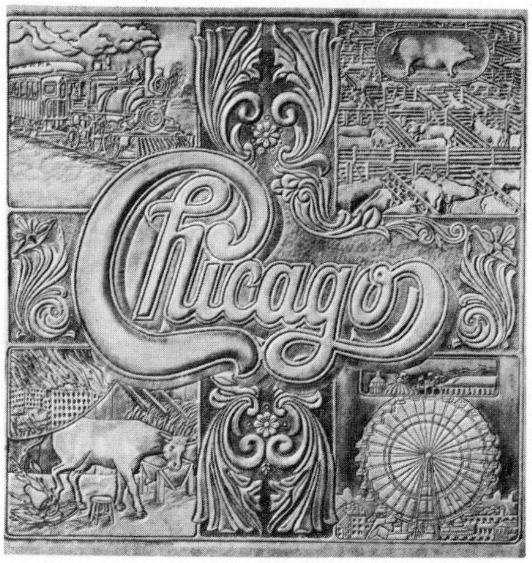

The conceptual image is not the exclusive providence of the illustrator/designer, for art directors called upon the entire range of image-making possibilities in their search for means to convey concepts and ideas. This is particularly true in the work of graphic designers in the musical recording industry. In terms of consistency and quality, Columbia Records established an early leadership in record album design and has maintained it for over four decades. This conceptual image emerged as a significant direction in album design during the early 1960s after John Berg (b. 1932) joined Columbia Records. Instead of a photograph of the musicians performing or a portrait of the composer, Berg communicated the *William Tell Overture* in 1963 with a large color photograph of an apple with a target painted upon it. An ability to zigzag with the qualities of music and the sensibilities of the potential audience ranging from the teenage subculture to the sophisticated audience of opera and classical music characterizes the work of Berg and other designers of album covers.

The concept of corporate identification of consistent image is totally irrelevant in the musical industry, for the reputation and longevity of the firm manufacturing the record is seldom a factor for the audience. The specific recording artist or musical selections are the overriding concerns of buyers. Sometimes a sense of corporate identity (in the broadest sense of the word) is created for a series of albums by a given composer or group. For example, John Berg has designed a large series of album covers by the musical group Chicago that features a logotype in lettering reminiscent of bold nineteenth-century Victorian scripts. This logo has appeared as a handpainted sign on wood, a chocolate bar, tactile leathercraft, a wall sign being painted by sign painters, and even as the shape of a highrise building in a bird's-eye view illustration.

The poster mania

In contrast to postwar Polish posters, which were patronized by governmental agencies as a national cultural form, the poster craze that erupted in the United States during the 1960s was a grass roots movement fostered by a climate of social activism. The civil rights movement, the vast public protest against the Vietnam War, the early stirrings of the Women's Liberation movement, and a search for alternative lifestyles figured into the social upheavals of the decade. The posters of the period were posted on apartment walls more frequently than they were posted in the streets. These posters made statements about social viewpoints instead of advertising commercial messages.

The first wave of poster culture popped from the Hippie subculture centered in the Haight-Ashbury section of San Francisco. Emphasis was upon antiestablishment values, rock music, and experimentation with psychedelic drugs. The graphics movement that expressed this cultural climate drew from a number of resources: the flowing sinuous curves of Art Nouveau, intense optical color vibration associated with the brief Op Art movement popularized by a Museum of Modern Art Exhibition, and the recycling of images from popular culture or by manipulation (such as reducing continuous tone images to high contrast black and white) that was prevalent in Pop Art.

Most of the initial artists in this movement were largely self-taught, and their primary clients were rock-and-roll concerts and dances. These dances were intense perceptual experiences of loud music and light shows that dissolved the environment with throbbing fields of projected color and bursting strobes. This experience was paralleled graphically in posters using swirling forms and lettering warped and bent to the edge of illegibility. It was reported that respectable, intelligent businessmen were unable to decipher the lettering on these posters, yet they communicated well enough to fill

Wes Wilson, poster for the Buffalo Springfield/Steve Miller Blues Band concert, 1967. Printed in intense contrasting colors, this poster uses letterforms that are variants of Alfred Roller's Art Nouveau alphabets. When printed in the original vibrating colors, the message was deciphered rather than read by the viewer. *Library of Congress, Washington, D.C., Poster Collection, Bill Graham Bequest.*

Victor Moscoso, poster for a Big Brother and the Holding Company concert, 1966. This long-haired hippie with his pinwheel eyes, top hat, and giant cigarette represented a cult figure of the era.

auditoriums with a younger generation. Wes Wilson was the original innovator of this style and created many of the stronger images. Kelly/Mouse Studios and Victor Moscoso, the only major artist of the movement with formal art training, were other prominent members of this brief movement.

Some aspects of the psychedelic poster movement were used in the wildly popular poster art of New York designer Peter Max (b. 1937). He created a series of posters during the late 1960s that combined the Art Nouveau qualities of psychedelic poster art with a more accessible image and less strident color. His most famous image, the 1970 *Love* graphic, combined the fluid organic line of Art Nouveau with the hard, black contour of the comic book. In his finest work, Max experimented with images and printing techniques. The 1970 *Toulouse-Lautrec* poster, adapted from a book jacket designed by Max

Peter Max, "Love" poster, 1970. Max's split-font printing resulted in the word and linear drawing being purple dissolving to blue, and the background fades from green to yellow to orange to pink.

for a biography of the tragic Post-Impressionist, used turn-of-the-century lettering superimposed over the hat. A photograph of a bacchanal scene is printed in the letterforms using two split-fount impressions. Cool colors are printed as a halftone; the reverse of this image is then printed in warm colors for a strange graphic effect created on the printing press.

By the early 1970s, the poster mania reached its peak. As with the rats in Albert Camus' allegorical novel, *The Plague,* it was almost as though people suddenly realized one day that they were gone. American poster art of inventive quality retreated to the university campus, which is one of the few surviving pedestrian environments in America. Since universities have a large number

Peter Max, "Toulouse-Lautrec" poster, 1970. Red, yellow, and purple lettering contains a period image that suggests the Post-Impressionist painter's bohemian lifestyle.

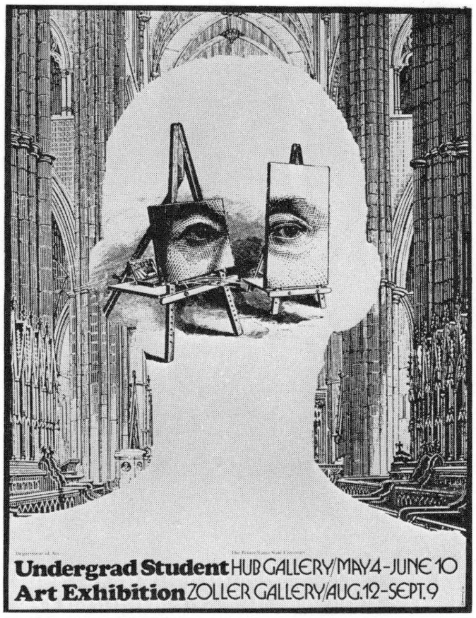

Lanny Sommese, poster for a student art exhibition, 1979. Easels and eyes create a compelling image in the white silhouette of a head cut from an engraved interior.

of events, this makes the campus an ideal poster communications environment.

A number of prominent poster designers emerged from among university design faculties. For instance, Lanny Sommese (b. 1944) became a prolific poster designer at an eastern university during the 1970s. Drawn images were executed in a free, casual manner more reminiscent of European printmaking and graphic illustration than American sources. Often, these images were drawn small, then greatly enlarged, which radically changed the image and line quality. During his graduate study, Sommese photographed hundreds of wood engravings from nineteenth-century science magazines. These are used in surreal collages.

David Lance Goines (b. 1945) proves that even in the late twentieth-century era of overspecialization, it is possible for the individual artist or craftsman to define a personal direction and operate as an independent creative force having total control over his or her work. The eldest of eight children, this Oregon native had an early interest in calligraphy which blossomed into a serious study after he entered the University of California at Berkeley. Goines was expelled from the university at age nineteen for his participation in the Free Speech Movement. He learned graphic arts as an apprentice pressman at the radical Berkeley Free Press, where he wrote, printed, and bound a book on calligraphy. A year in London was followed by a return to Berkeley to open a graphic design studio down the street from his former employers. When the Berkeley Free Press failed in 1971, Goines managed to acquire it. He renamed it the Saint Heironymous Press and continued to print and publish books while developing his poster style. Offset lithography and graphic design are unified and become a medium for personal expression and public communications in his hands. He designs, illustrates, and letters posters, makes the negatives and plates, then operates the press to print the edition. This thoughtful and scholarly designer has evolved a highly personal style that integrates diverse sources of inspiration. Symmetrical composition, simplified line drawing, quiet planes of flat color, and subtle stripes rimming the contours of his forms are characteristics of his poster style.

David Lance Goines, poster for a classical film screening, 1973. Celtic ornaments are reinvented as bold, flat imagery. The pale color embracing the edges of images and letterforms became a graphic "trademark" in Goines' posters. *Library of Congress, Washington, D.C., Poster Collection.*

David Lance Goines, poster for a classical film screening, 1973. Most of Goines' posters have a directness of image and composition; his poetic sense of color and sensitive drawing imbue them with graphic distinctiveness. *Library of Congress, Washington, D.C., Poster Collection.*

The German visual poets

Poetry was once defined as bringing together unlike things to create a new experience or evoke an unexpected emotional response. In West Germany beginning in the 1960s and continuing on into the 1980s, there emerged a poetic approach to graphic design based on photography and the manipulation of photographic images through collage and montage. Editorial and promotional materials including book and album covers, magazine design, and posters for concerts, television, and radio proved to be the areas of communication providing a receptive audience and clients for these poets who stretched time, merged and floated objects, and fractured and fragmented images in a sometimes disturbing but always engaging manner. The conservative, traditional, and expected were rejected by these graphic designers who defined the design process, not as form arrangements or construction, but as the invention of unexpected images to convey ideas or feelings.

A master of this movement is Gunther Kieser (b. 1930), who began his freelance career in 1952. This brilliant imagist has consistently demonstrated an ability to invent unexpected visual content to solve communications problems. Kieser brings together images or ideas to create a new vitality, new arrangement, or synthesis of disparate objects. Kieser's poetic visual statements always have a rational basis that links expressive forms to communicative content; it is this ability that separates him from design practitioners who use fantasy or Surrealism as ends rather than means. An expansive quality is often present in Kieser's designs. Sometimes this is achieved by scale. In other designs, color or value contrast brings this quality to his work. In the late 1970s and early 1980s, Kieser began to construct fictitious objects that are convincingly real. The viewer stops in his or her tracks to study the huge posters bearing color photographs of Kieser's private visions to determine if he or she is having delusions.

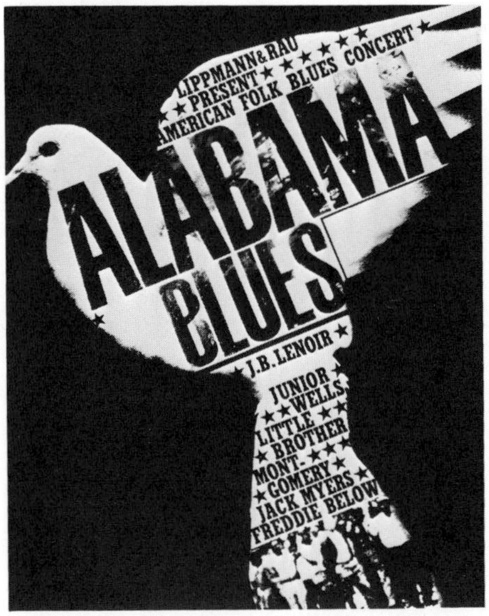

Gunther Kieser, concert poster for Alabama Blues, 1966. In this stark black-and-white poster, a dove with typography inspired by nineteenth-century woodtype becomes a potent symbol of the longing for freedom and justice contained in the folk blues music.

Gunther Kieser (designer) and Hartmann (photographer), poster for Berlin Jazz Days, 1975. By photographing this 119.5-centimeter (about 4-foot) tall portrait ripping through the graphics of a bygone era, Kieser conveys the historical roots of jazz. A powerful *trompe l'oeil* effect of a poster peeling from the wall to reveal a presence beneath is created.

Gunther Kieser (designer) and Hartmann (photographer), poster for the Frankfurt Jazz Festival, 1978. Kieser almost convinces us that a moss-covered tree stump can grow in the shape of a trumpet. It sprouts a new branch with the same inevitability as the annual return of the jazz festival.

Launched in Munich in 1959, the German periodical *Twen,* whose name, derived by chopping the last two letters from the English word "twenty," signified the age group of sophisticated postteenagers to whom the magazine was addressed, featured excellent photography used in dynamic layouts by art director Willy Fleckhouse. With a genius for cropping images and using typography and white space in unexpected ways, Fleckhouse made the bold, uninhibited pages of *Twen* a milestone in editorial design. While the Brodovich tradition of editorial design was undoubtedly a resource for Fleckhouse, the dynamic of scale, space, and poetic images found in *Twen* created a provocative and original format.

One of the most innovative studios in late twentieth-century design is the Grafik & Foto group of Frankfurt, Germany. Gunter Rambow (b. 1938) and Gerhard Lienemeyer (b. 1936) began their collaboration in 1960; in 1973, Michael van de Sand (b. 1945)

Willy Fleckhouse (art director), cover for *Twen,* 1970. Graphic communications often become political symbols in the struggle between alternative value systems and generations.

Willy Fleckhouse (art director), pages from *Twen,* 1970. Sensitive cropping, a full-page photographic symbol, and white space create a dynamic and expansive layout.

joined the group. In their graphic designs, the medium of photography is manipulated, massaged, montaged, and airbrushed to convert the ordinary into the extraordinary. Everyday images are combined or dislocated, then printed as straightforward, documentary black-and-white images. Theirs is an original metaphysical statement of poetry and profundity. Sometimes the manipulation occurs through the creation of objects or events designed and constructed to be photographed, as in the 1978 *Baumeister Solness* poster. Scaffolding surrounds and obscures a seated figure with a placard for the theater and play mounted on the front. In a series of posters commissioned by the Frankfurt book publisher S. Fischer-Verlag for distribution yearly beginning in 1976, the book has been used as a symbolic object altered and transformed to make a statement about this communications form. The book as a means of communicating with vast numbers of people was symbolized by a huge book emerging from a crowd scene, and the book as a door or window opening upon a world of new knowledge was symbolized by turning the cover of the book into a door one year and a window the following year.

Gunter Rambow, Gerhard Lienemeyer, and Michael van de Sand, poster for S. Fischer-Verlag, 1976. The portability of the book is conveyed in memorable fashion by this book jacket that has come to life.

These metaphysical and symbolic advertisements carried no verbal information except the logo and name of the client. The audience of educated editors and publishers were given memorable and thought-provoking visual phenomena rather than a sales message.

Sometimes collage or montage is the means used to create new graphic

Gunter Rambow, Gerhard Lienemeyer, and Michael van de Sand, poster for the play, *Baumeister Solmess,* 1978. The caged figure is surrounded by liliputian people who are responsible for his imprisonment.

reality; in other projects the team of Rambow, Lienemeyer, and van de Sand rephotographs images that have been altered or combined. In the 1980 poster for the play *Die Hamlet-*

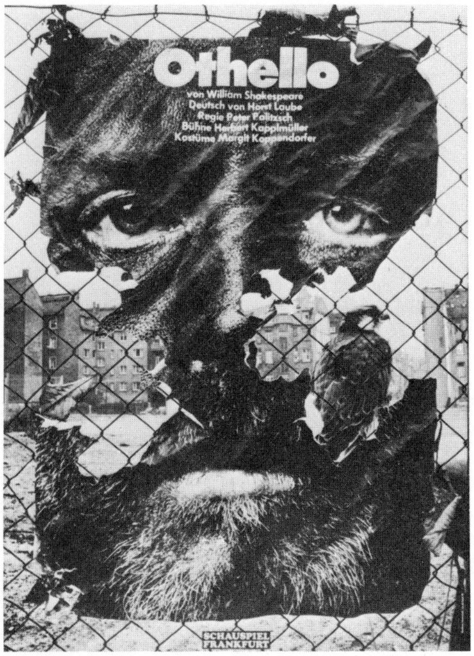

Gunter Rambow, Gerhard Lienemeyer, and Michael van de Sand, poster for the play *Othello,* 1978. Winner of the first prize at the eight Warsaw Poster Biennale, this baffling image projects the great pathos of Shakespeare's tragedy.

Gunter Rambow, Gerhard Lienemeyer, and Michael van de Sand, poster for S. Fischer-Verlag, 1980. The book and reading as a "window on the world" gains intensity from the luminous sunlight streaming from this volume.

Gunter Rambow, Gerhard Lienemeyer, and Michael van De Sand, poster for the play, *Die Hamletmaschine,* 1980. A chilling sense of anonymity is produced by this self-inflicted act of vandalism.

Gunter Rambow, Gerhard Lienemeyer, and Michael van de Sand, poster for the play *Antigone,* 1978. Pathos and isolation are conveyed by the burning chair photographed from a low vantage point at dusk.

machine, a photograph of the wall is superimposed under the photograph of the man standing before the wall before the top photograph was ripped. The final rephotographed image presents the viewer with a perplexing impossibility. This image seems to be capable of self-destruction; a figure seems to possess the existential ability to negate itself.

A number of other practitioners of the imagist approach to graphic design include Hans Hillman (b. 1925), whose illustrations frequently combine two images in the manner of Salvador Dali's simultaneous image technique, and Holger Matthies (b. 1940), whose bold images are often manipulated. For example, a high contrast photograph of an actress is superimposed over a photogram of a leaf in one opera poster, and a gun pointing at the spectator wears sunglasses in a promotional piece.

The Cuban poster

On New Year's Day of 1959, President Fulgencio Batista fled the island nation of Cuba, conceding political control of the country to the well-armed revolutionary force led by Fidel Castro (b. 1927). Over the course of the next two years, a Marxist course was charted, leading to a complete breakdown in diplomatic ties with the United States and to a close association with the Soviet Union and other communist nations. The creative arts had been virtually ignored under the Batista regime. A series of three meetings in June 1961 enabled artists and writers to meet with governmental leaders to forge a mutual understanding. At the final meeting on June 30, Dr. Castro delivered his lengthy address, "Words to the Intellectuals," that established governmental policy toward the creative arts. Castro assured the artists and writers "that freedom of form must be respected," but freedom of content was seen as a more subtle and complex matter. As a guide, Castro advised the assembly that artists and intellectuals "can find within the Revolution a place to work and create, a place where their creative spirit, even though they are not revolutionary writers and artists, has the opportunity and freedom to be expressed. This means: within the Revolution, everything; against the Revolution, nothing." The creative community was told that each person could "express freely the ideas he wants to express," but that "we will always evaluate his creation from the revolutionary point of view."

Since the Castro government defined "the good, the useful, and the beautiful" in the context of whatever is "noble, useful, and beautiful" for "the great majority of the people—that is, the oppressed and exploited classes," it comes as no surprise that popular art forms and propaganda media, rather then the traditional fine arts, were developed. Film and theater, posters and leaflets, songs and poetry: these are the arts that were encouraged. The traditional arts of painting and sculpture are relatively inefficient in reaching large numbers of people with a revolutionary message.

When artists and writers are admitted to the union, they receive salaries, work space, and materials. Graphic designers produce their work for a variety of government agencies with specific missions. Important leaders of Cuban graphic design include Raul Martinez, a painter who creates illustrative designs, and Felix Beltran (b. 1938), who was educated in New York during the late 1950s and early 1960s. Beltran has served as art director for COR (Commission for Revolutionary Action), which creates internal ideological propaganda. Commemorative days and past leaders are often used to maintain public consciousness of the revolution. The cultural life of the island has not been neglected, and a host of bureaus and institutes have responsibility for motion pictures, musical and theatrical events, publishing, and exhibition programs. Emphasis is upon outreach. Unlike many countries where cultural programs are only available to the urban population, a serious attempt is made to reach the rural areas and posters are widely distributed. Posters for films are lively, happy affairs printed in multicolor silkscreen using an uninhibited palette of bright colors. Most Cuban posters are small; 55 by 34 centimeters ($21\frac{1}{2} \times 13\frac{1}{2}$ inches) is the standard format size.

Propaganda materials for export throughout the Third World are produced by OSPAAAL (Organization of Solidarity with Asia, Africa, and Latin America). Posters and leaflets by OSPAAAL support revolutionary activity and build public consciousness for the ideological points of view. OSPAAAL posters are printed offset and use elemental symbolic images that can be readily comprehended by people of diverse nationalities, languages, and cultural backgrounds. The Castro government sees itself as being involved in an ideological war with "Yankee Imperialism" for the hearts and minds of people in the emerging Third World countries of Latin America, Asia, and Africa. Ideas are the weapons, and the poster is a major vehicle in the struggle. The media selection is a good one, for many Third World nations do not have widely developed electronic communications. The poster is used with the intensity and frequency of the European posters of World War I.

Raul Martinez, poster celebrating the Cuban people, c. 1970. Leaders and workers are cheerfully depicted in a comic-book drawing style and bright, intense color.

Poster for COR, 1967. Clouds parting to reveal a glimpse of the orange sun symbolize the ill-fated 26 July 1953 assault on the Santiago army barracks which launched the Cuban revolution.

Rich color is used on posters to bring vitality and beauty to the drab urban slums of overpopulated cities. The eye of the beholder is tantalized while revolutionary consciousness is formed through repeated exposure. The international distribution of OSPAAAL graphics is evidenced by the presence of Arabic, English, French, and Spanish typography on each poster.

Myth and reality have been unified in a powerful graphic symbol based on the image of Ernesto ("Che") Guevara. A leader of the Cuban revolution, Guevara left Cuba in the mid-1960s to lead a group of guerillas in the South American country of Bolivia. On 9 October 1967, he was gunned down in the jungle village of Higuera. Graphic designers have converted Che's image into a symbolic icon representing struggle against oppression throughout the Third World. Che's image has been reduced to a depersonalized stereotype. The look

of high contrast photography conveys the fallen guerilla wearing a beard and a beret with a star. His head tilts slightly upward. One of the most reproduced images of the late twentieth century, Che's effigy has been used in a carefully controlled manner to become a universal symbol of a struggle for liberation. This "trademark" becomes everyman; and its potency transcends Che and South America. A specific person, Ernesto Guevara, has been graphically converted into the mythic hero or savior who sacrifices his life so that others might live.

Lacking artistic traditions, Cuban graphic designers have assimilated a variety of resources. In the ideological war, the graphic styles from America have been converted into propaganda weapons in the battle for the hearts and minds of people. These include Pop Art, the psychedelic poster, and the formal vocabulary of American graphic designers including Saul Bass, Peter Max, and Milton Glaser. Graphic design from eastern European nations, particularly the Polish poster, provides another important resource. The "heroic worker" school of romanticized realism of the Soviet Union and China is avoided. The icon, ideograph, and telegraphic message are far more effective in developing nations.

Poster for "Day of the Heroic Guerrilla," 1968. The iconographic image of Che Guevara transforms into a map of South America in a radiating image meant to symbolize revolutionary victory. *Library of Congress, Washington, D.C., Poster Collection.*

24

A Global Dialogue

In 1966, the German graphic designer Olaf Leu wrote that German design no longer had any national attributes. Observing that while some might favor this development, Leu also acknowledged that others regret it. The purist geometry from Switzerland and the uninhibited freedom of American design coexisted as dominant influences upon German design as well as design activity around the globe. A period of international dialogue had begun. Just as events in Southeast Asia or the Middle East directly affect Europe, the Americas, and Japan, conceptual innovation and visual invention spread like wildfire. An international culture embracing the fine arts, performing arts, and design spans national boundaries.

Postwar graphic design in Japan

Japan, an island nation lying off the east coast of Asia, has over one hundred five million people and a population density of about seven hundred twenty-nine persons per square mile. Eighty percent of the island consists of rugged uninhabitable mountains, and both food and fuel have to be imported. Japan retained an isolated and feudal society until the middle of the nineteenth century, then its rapid industrial development throughout the course of the twentieth century, particularly during the decades since World War II, is a major testament to the will and energy of the Japanese people. During this postwar period of rapid industrial expansion and the assimilation of western social patterns and lifestyles, the philosophic problem facing the Japanese graphic designer was how to retain national traditions while incorporating western influences. The tree-planting poster by Ryuichi Yamashiro (b. 1920) demonstrates just how successfully this could be accomplished.

The twentieth-century design move-

Ryuichi Yamashiro, poster for a tree-planting campaign, 1961. The Japanese characters for tree, grove, and forest are repeated to form a forest. Eastern calligraphy and spatial concerns unite with a Western communications concept. *Library of Congress, Washington, D.C., Poster Collection.*

ment had not been well received in Japan before the 1950s; the 1931 effort to incorporate Bauhaus concepts into the curriculum at the Shin School of Design and Architecture in Tokyo had a short life. One of the students during that period, Yusaka Kamekura (b. 1915), apprenticed to an architect then worked as art director for several Japanese cultural magazines from 1937 until 1948. During the postwar recovery period, Kamekura emerged as a design leader so influential that he has earned the name "Boss" in Japanese design circles. Under his leadership, Japanese graphic designers dispelled the widely held belief that visual communications must be hand-drawn, and the notion of applied arts' inferiority to fine art faded as Japanese designers established their professional status.

European Constructivism became the major source for the new Japanese design movement. However, the systematic organization and strong theoretical foundation of European Constructivism was tempered by a traditional Japanese inclination toward intuitive problem solving and a heritage of simplified emblematic form. Instead of the relational asymmetrical balance of European Constructivism, Japanese designers are more prone to central placement and the organization of space around a median axis. This reflects the compositional traditions of many Japanese arts and crafts. An important design inspiration for the Japanese graphic designer is the traditional family symbol or crest, the *mon,* which has been in use for a thousand years. The simplified designs of flowers, birds, animals, plants, and household objects contained in a circle were applied to all belongings and worn on clothing.

Kamekura charted the course of this new Japanese movement through the vitality and strength of his creative work, his leadership in founding the Japan Advertising Art Club to bring professionalism and focus to the new discipline, and through the establishment of the Japan Design Center in 1960. Kamekura became managing director of this organization, which brought Japan's leading graphic designers together with industry.

Technical discipline, a thorough understanding of printing techniques, and careful construction of the visual elements characterize Kamekura's work. International attention focused on Japan for the 1964 Olympics, and the logo and posters created by Kamekura for these events received international acclaim and established Japan as a center of creative design activity.

An imaginative approach to photographic design was developed by Masuda Tadashi (b. 1922). While still a student, he was drafted under the Student Mobilization Law and spent three years in the Japanese Navy during World War II. Afterwards he joined the prominent Dentsu Advertising Agency. A growing involvement in photographic illustration to solve

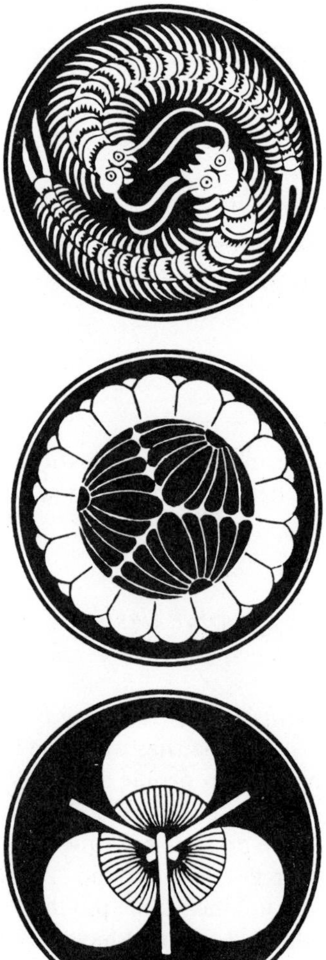

The traditional Japanese crests have a direct frontal presentation of a simplified image executed in a refined use of line and space. Similar qualities are found in the work of many Japanese graphic designers.

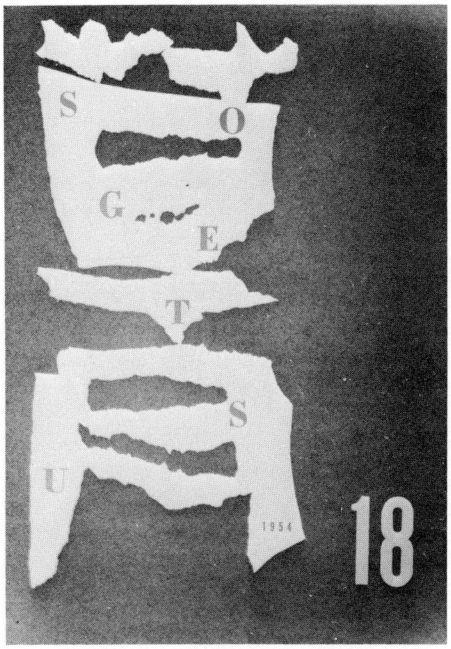

Yusaku Kamekura, booklet cover, 1954. Calligraphic characters torn from paper bearing Bodoni letterforms, spelling out the same word, exemplifies the early synthesis of Oriental and Occidental forms by Kamekura.

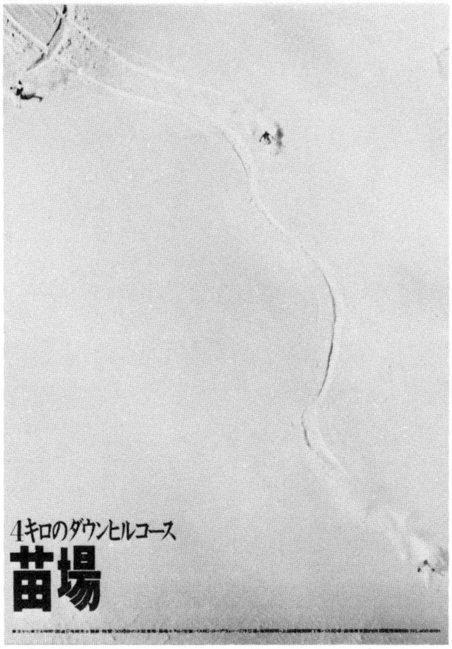

Yusaku Kamekura (designer) and Saburo Kitai (photographer), poster for a ski resort, 1968. The bird's-eye view and indeterminate space express the concept of small man in big nature that is found in traditional Oriental painting.

Yusaku Kamekura (designer) and Osamu Hayasaki (photographer), Tokyo Olympics poster, 1964. One of series depicting various events, this poster's meticulously planned and lighted photograph becomes the ultimate emblematic expression of the footrace.

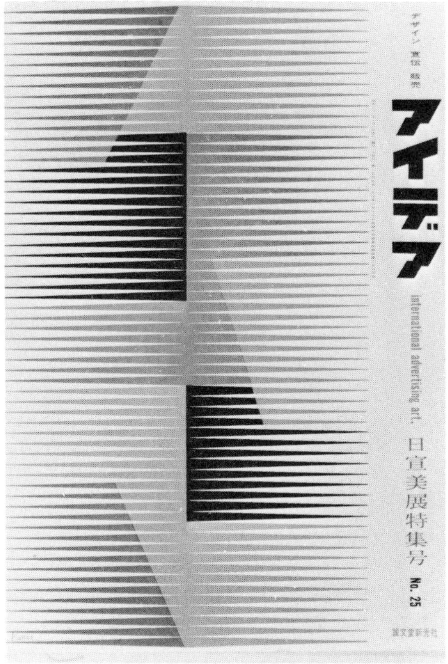

Yusaku Kamekura, magazine cover, 1957. Resonant wedges of black, red, and purple create kinetic rhythms up the page. The kiss registration demonstrates the disciplined skill of Japanese printers.

Yusaku Kamekura, Tokyo Olympics logo and poster, 1964. Three ordinary symbols—the red sun of the Japanese flag, the Olympic rings, and the words, "Tokyo 1964"—are combined to create an immediate and compelling communication.

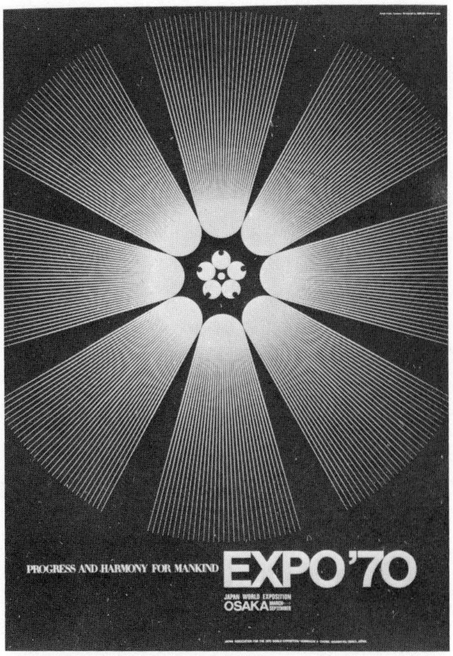

Yusaku Kamekura, poster for the Osaka World Exposition, 1970. Japanese designers' imaginations are constantly tested by the need to invent new sun images as part of the heritage of "the land of the rising sun."

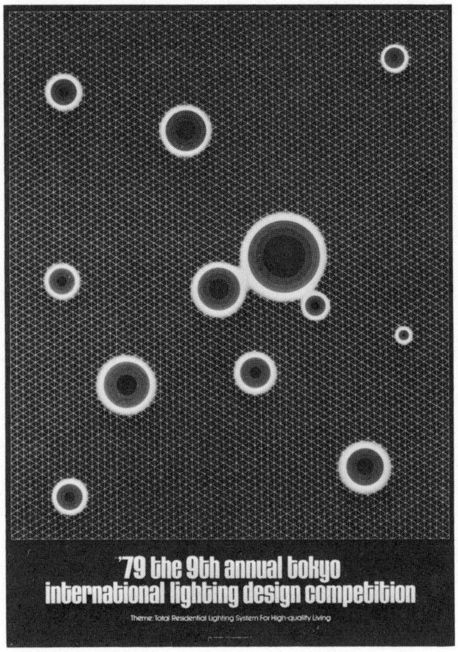

Yusaku Kamekura, lighting design competition poster, 1979. Against a rigid geometric field, orbs of black, purple, blue, green, yellow, and white concentric rings glow in a wonderful expression of luminosity.

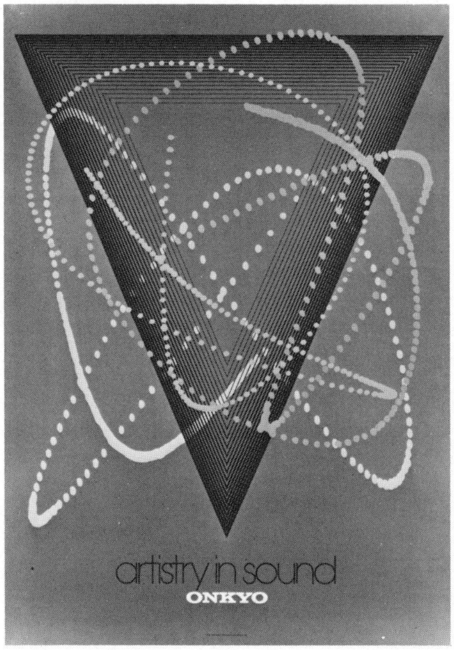

Yusaka Kamekura, poster for a stereo manufacturer, 1980. Technical perfection in delivering exuberant sound is symbolized by bright yellow, pink, and blue traceries darting around a mathematically constructed black triangle on a deep blue field.

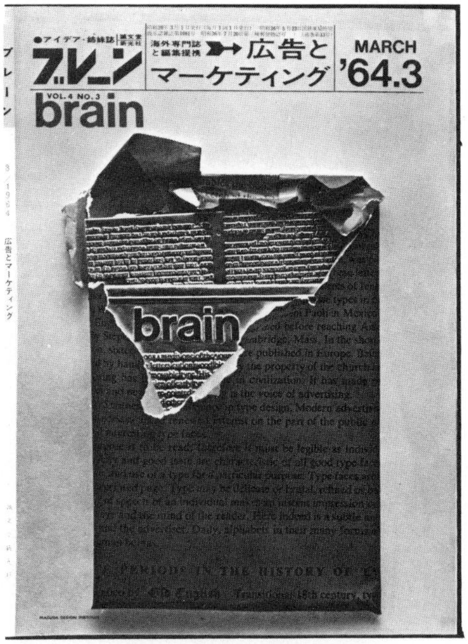

Masuda Tadashi (designer) and Doki Mitsuo (photographer), cover for *Brain* magazine, 1964. To illustrate an article on typography, metal printing plates are wrapped in typographic printed proofs which are torn to reveal the contents.

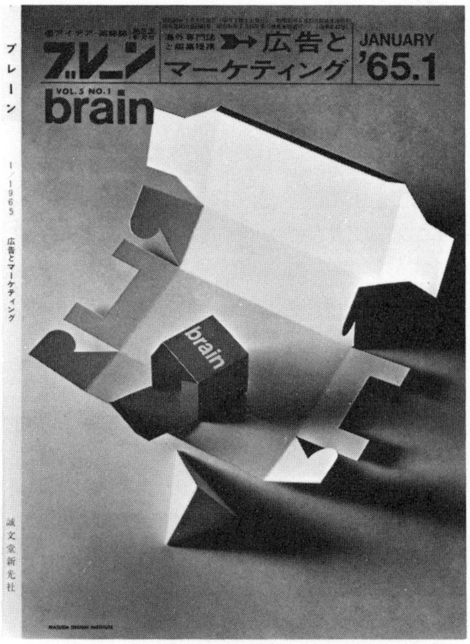

Masuda Tadashi (designer) and Doki Mitsuo (photographer), cover for *Brain* magazine, 1965. Creativity and the birth of ideas are expressed by boxes which have opened to reveal boxes. The concept is supported by exquisite placement and lighting in the photograph.

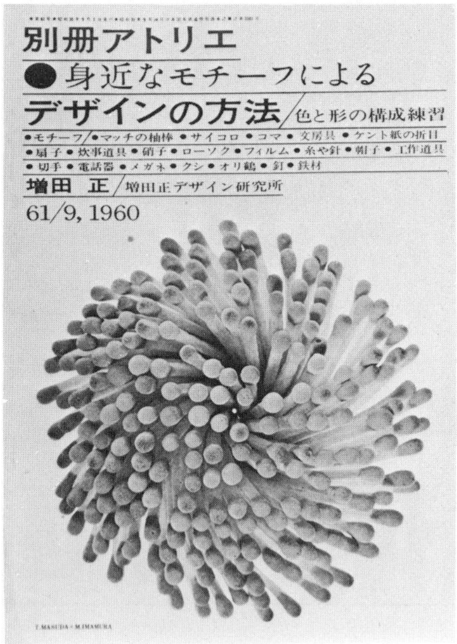

Masuda Tadashi (designer) and Imamura Masaaki (photographer), advertisement for Atorie Sha, 1960. Imaginative photography transforms pedestrian matches into a wonderful graphic blossom.

graphic design problems, combined with his interest in collaborative and team design, culminated in the establishment of the Masuda Tadashi Design Institute in 1958. At the institute, fresh new solutions, unexpected combinations, and new ways of seeing things were explored as individual personalities worked in a group to seek the best possible solution to the problem. Masuda Tadashi holds that a balance between artistic and social responsibilities must be maintained, for graphic communications have an economic and cultural impact and influence a people's lifestyle. Many art directors and graphic designers view photographers and illustrators as subcontractors—button and pencil pushers—on call to give form to the designer's concepts. Masuda Tadashi's collaborative approach allowed brilliant, creative solutions to emerge from dialogue and teamwork. The placement of typography on, above, or below the photograph is usually done with great sensitivity. A favored layout approach is to design a structure of fine, ruled lines as a vessel to contain the typographic information. Color was used very effectively. Bright colored backgrounds were sometimes contrasted against objects

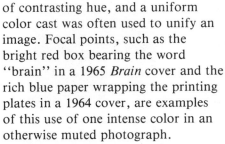

Tadanori Yokoo, poster for Koshimaki Osen, 1966. East and West meet in a virtual catalogue of images and techniques.

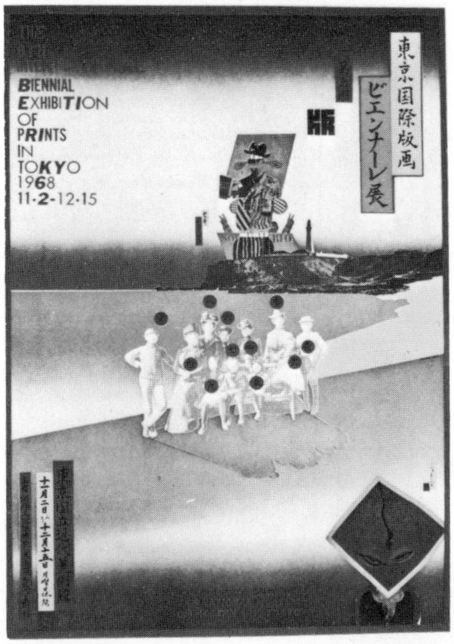

Tadanori Yokoo, poster for a printmaking exhibition, 1968. As Yokoo began to open his densely packed spaces and expand his range of printing techniques, he moved from Pop Art to personal statement.

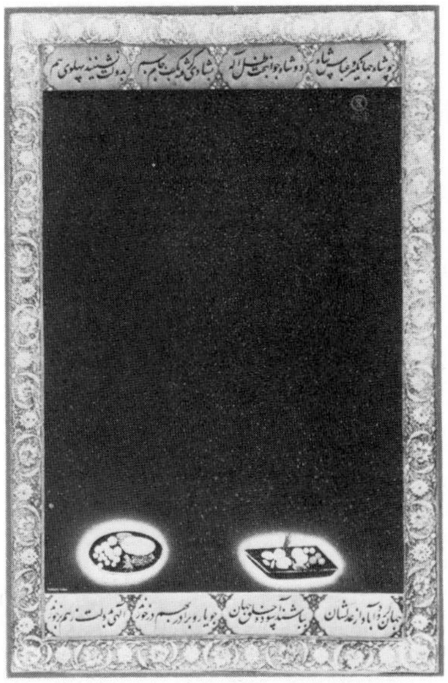

Tadanori Yokoo, exhibition poster, 1973. The reds, blues, and golds of a Persian carpet frame an enigmatic black rectangle, where two plates of food hover inexplicably.

of contrasting hue, and a uniform color cast was often used to unify an image. Focal points, such as the bright red box bearing the word ''brain'' in a 1965 *Brain* cover and the rich blue paper wrapping the printing plates in a 1964 cover, are examples of this use of one intense color in an otherwise muted photograph.

Poles apart from the order and simplicity found in the works of Kamekura and Tadashi, Tadanori Yokoo (b. 1936) stands a generation apart from these designers and their philosophy. In 1960, twenty-four-year-old Yokoo joined the Japan Design Center, but four years later he left for freelance design. His design vocabulary rejects the order and logic of Constructivism. In its place, the restless vitality of Dada and a fascination with mass media, popular art, and comic books are resources. During the middle 1960s, Yokoo used the comic book technique of black line drawing as a vessel to contain flat areas of photomechanical color. Photographic elements would often be collaged into the designs, and traditional Japanese images were translated into the Pop Art idiom.

During the late 1960s and into the 1970s, Yokoo's design vocabulary and range of art and printing techniques became increasingly uninhibited. Nudes are painted with fluorescent paint then photographed under ultraviolet light, a samurai warrior in front of a rear-projected image of the Arch of Triumph in Paris raises his foot to reveal a portrait painted on his sole, and collaged butterflies flutter daintily above the lava flow from an erupting volcano. The *Sixth International Biennial Exhibition of Prints in Tokyo* poster combines a variety of techniques: a halftone group portrait in pink; a sky with an airbrushed brown band across the top and a red one at the horizon; calligraphic writing on vertical bands as found in earlier oriental art; and a monumental, montaged figure towers over the lighthouse on the bank across the water. During the decade of the 1970s, Yokoo's work often moved toward unexpected and even mystical images. The artist often speaks for a generation; Yokoo expresses the passions and curiosity of a Japanese generation that grew up with American mass popular culture and electronic media; television, movies, radio, and records. Shifting values and a rejection of tradition find symbolic expression in Yokoo's uninhibited graphics, and he gained a reputation not unlike the ''cult figure'' status attained by certain rock musicians in the western industrial democracies. The advanced technology of the late twentieth century creates a cultural milieu of simultaneity: ancient and modern cultures; eastern and western thought; handicraft and industrial production; past, present, and future blur into a continuum of information and visual form. Perhaps more than any other visual artist of his generation, Yokoo is in tune with this phenomenon and translates it into his work.

An independent French innovator

During the 1960s, both literary and graphic design communities throughout the world were astounded and delighted by the experimental typography of French designer Robert Massin (b. 1925), who designed editions of poetry and plays for Editions Gallimard in Paris. As a young man, Massin apprenticed in sculpture, engraving, and letter-cutting under his father. Rather than seek formal design training, he learned graphic design under typographic designer

ionesco
LA CANTATRICE CHAUVE
suivie d'une scène inédite. Interprétations *typographique* de Massin et *photo-graphique* d'Henry Cohen d'après la mise en scène de Nicolas Bataille Éditions Gallimard

Robert Massin, cover and double-page spreads from *La Cantatrice Chauve* (''The Bald Soprano'') by Eugene Ionesco, 1964. Henry Cohen's high-contrast photographs of the actors combine with Massin's highly original typographic treatment and dynamic layouts to create visual vitality, tension, and confusion appropriate to the play. The pictorial directness of the comic book is combined with the expressive letterforms of Futurist poetry. *Editions Gallimard.*

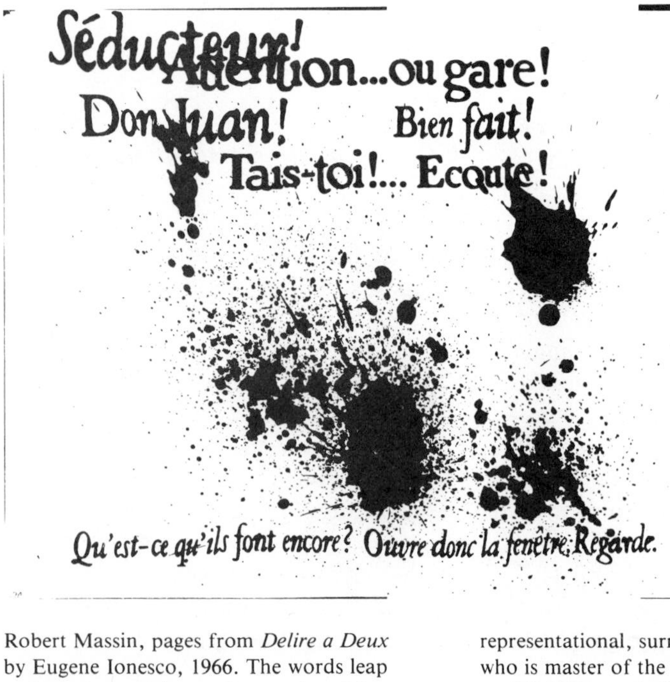

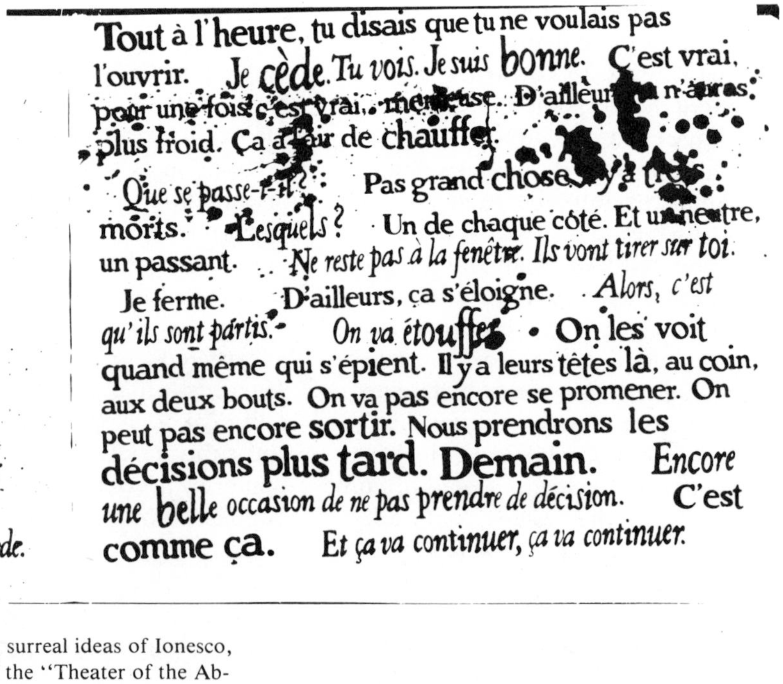

Robert Massin, pages from *Delire a Deux* by Eugene Ionesco, 1966. The words leap and run and overlap and smear into ink blots in a calligraphic homage to the nonrepresentational, surreal ideas of Ionesco, who is master of the ''Theater of the Absurd.'' *Editions Gallimard.*

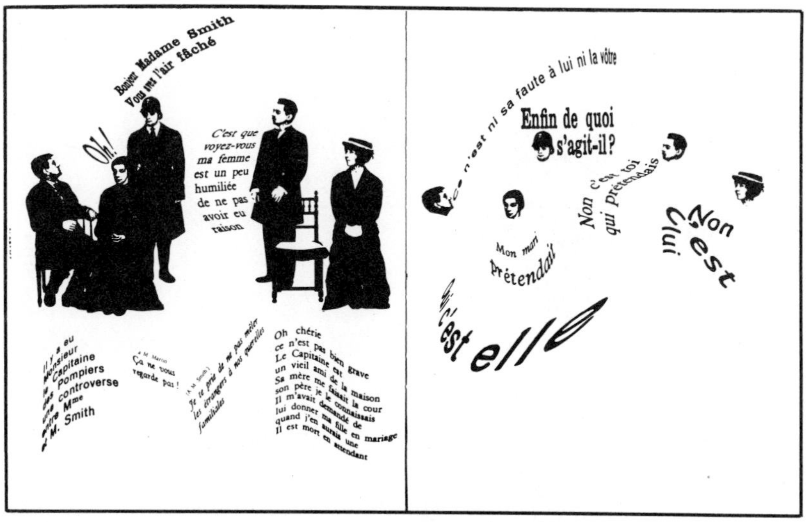

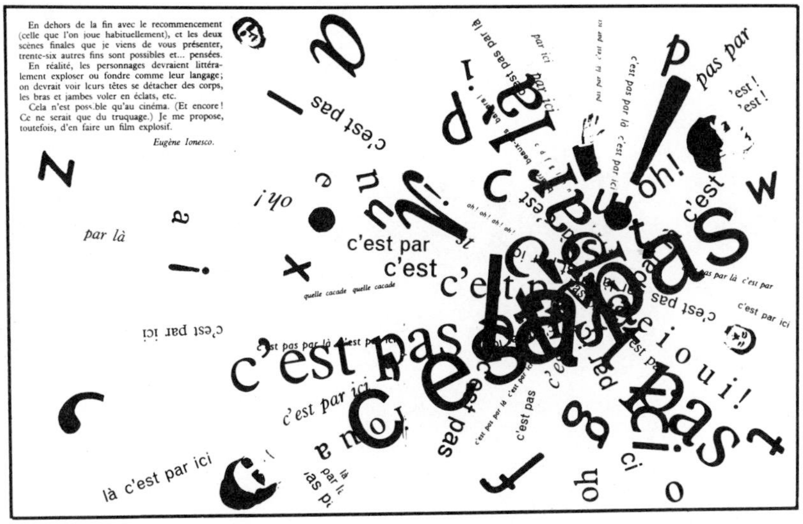

Pierre Faucheux. His work has affinities, in its dynamic configurations and use of letterforms as concrete visual form, with Futurist and Dada typography. But his intensification of both narrative literary content and visual form into a cohesive unity that expresses the author's meaning is uniquely original. His work for Ionesco's plays combines the pictorial conventions of the comic book with the sequencing and visual flow of the cinema. His many years of research into letterforms and their history led to the important book, *Letter and Image,* which explores the pictorial and graphic properties of alphabet design through the ages.

The British contribution to international design

The postwar English design community sat between the formal clarity of the International Typographic Style on one side and the graphic expressionism from New York on the other. Avoiding the pitfalls of becoming a colony to these pervasive international influences was successfully achieved by outstanding English designers. Herbert Spencer (b. 1924) became an important voice in renewing British graphic design after the trauma of World War II through his writing, teaching, and graphic design practice. Spencer's thorough understanding of modern art and design was translated into a rare typographic sensitivity and structural vitality. American designer Saul Bass provided strong inspiration for British graphic designers. His direct approach to problem solving, subtle sense of humor, and the wholesome vitality of his forms had great appeal to the British sensibility.

The locus of postwar British design has been a design partnership that began in 1962 when Alan Fletcher (b. 1931), Colin Forbes (b. 1928) and Bob Gill formed the studio Fletcher, Forbes, and Gill. In 1965 the name was changed to Crosby, Fletcher, Forbes after Gill left the partnership and architect Theo Crosby (b. 1925) joined the firm. Exhibition design, historic conservation, and industrial design were added to the studio's activities, and offices opened in Zurich and New York to handle continental and North American assignments. As additional partners were added, the name of the studio was changed to Pentagram, but continued growth made even this five-pronged name obsolete, for Pentagram had ten part-

Alan Fletcher, Colin Forbes, and Bob Gill, cover for *Graphis,* 1965. Asked to design a cover for this magazine carrying an article about their work, the studio mailed this parcel containing the material for the article from London to Zurich with separate instructions requesting that it be returned unopened. When it arrived back in London, a color photograph was made documenting its journey through the postal system. The package which carried the work to the publication became the package (cover) that carried the work (contents) to *Graphis* readers.

Alan Fletcher, bus poster for Pirelli slippers, 1965. The bus passengers supply the heads and shoulders for the photographic bodies wearing Pirelli slippers. This gave the client twice as many square feet of advertising space as he purchased.

ners and fifty employees by 1980.

This group has not developed a unified style or philosophy of design. Rather, the intelligence and appropriateness of their design solutions, which grow out of the needs of the problem, are the hallmark of Pentagram design. An ability to evaluate the problem thoroughly and invent a dynamic visual solution became evident in the mid-1960s in such design solutions as Allen Fletcher's 1965 bus poster for Pirelli slippers which used the bus passengers as part of the design. Thorough evaluation of the communications problem and the specific nature of the environmental conditions under which the design was to appear combined with wit and willingness to try the unexpected. This, perhaps, summarizes the essence of the Pentagram approach to graphic design.

In the best English tradition, Pentagram combines a sense of the contemporary with a strong historical understanding. Their design solutions range from clean geometric forms in corporate identity systems to a warm historicism in packaging design and graphics for smaller clients. Even the vernacular of Pop Art is called upon when appropriate. Conceptual, visual, and often expressive of British wit, the attitudes that the partners in this studio brought to graphic design enabled Britain to establish an international presence in graphic design just as it did at the turn of the century and in the years after World War I.

Alan Fletcher and Georg Staehelin, logo for an exclusive boutique, 1968. By assembling ornamented initials from five different Renaissance designs, an unexpected graphic expression of the name is conveyed.

Colin Forbes, symbol for the Zinc Development Association Die Casting Conference, 1966. Pentagram solutions seem to appear magically from the requirements of the problem. An opportunity to render the year of a conference in the male and female components of a die-casting mold occurs only once each decade.

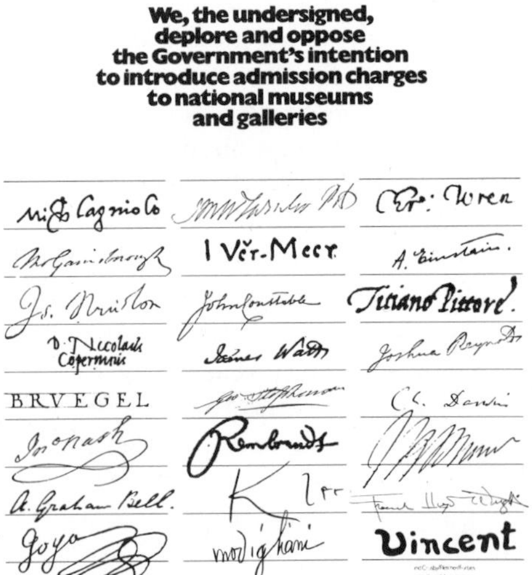

We, the undersigned,
deplore and oppose
the Government's intention
to introduce admission charges
to national museums
and galleries
I Ver-Meer
Titiano Pittore
BRVEGEL
Rembrandt
Vincent
Write in protest to your MP
and send for the petition forms to
Campaign Against Museum Admission Charges
221 Camden High Street
London NW1 7BU

Colin Forbes, poster for a campaign against museum charges, 1970. A standard petition was being circulated to protest the proposal to charge admission to public museums. A slight change in the petition wording and two dozen famous signatures turned an ordinary document into an extraordinary and memorable poster.

Brooks Baker & Fulford Limited, 3 Princes Street, London W1. 01-629 7916. J. Baker (Managing), R. Brooks (USA), L. Fulford, J. McKeand

Alan Fletcher, stationery for a film company, 1968. A "corporate identity program" for a firm whose main product is the creativity of the three partners uses an unconventional photograph of the group. The white shirts become the sheet of paper. By dividing the image, Fletcher designed business cards for the three partners using the same full-color separations.

Editorial design after the fall

Soothsayers predicted the death of the magazine as a communications form during the 1960s. The demise of major, mass audience periodicals and economic problems for the industry indicated that the era of the large format and visual essay magazines was rapidly fading. However, a new breed of periodical with smaller formats and addressing the specific interests of a specialized audience emerged and thrived. Advertisers who wished to reach the specific audience of these more specialized magazines bought advertising space. This new editorial climate, with more emphasis on content, longer text, and less opportunity for lavish visual treatment, necessitated a new approach to editorial design. Layout became more controlled, and the use of a consistent typographic format and grid—undoubtedly under the influence of the International Typographic Style—became the norm.

The harbinger for the future evolution of the magazine as a graphic communications form can be found in the work of art director Peter Palazzo, who was design editor of the *New York Herald Tribune* from 1962 until 1965. Palazzo received considerable acclaim for his overall typographic design of this newspaper, the editorial design approach of the *Book Week Supplement* and the *New York* magazine, and the conceptual power of many of the images he commissioned. In the weekly *New York* magazine section, Palazzo established a three-column grid and a consistent size and style for article titles, which were always bracketed by a thick ruled line above and a thin rule below. Palazzo made a little white space go a long way: a band of space across the top of an editorial spread here, a vacant left hand column with the title at the top there, and an illustration containing open spaces on another page. The total effect existed somewhere between the newspaper—with its dominant masses of text—and the magazine design of the period—with engaging visuals and ample white space. After the *New York Herald Tribune* ceased publication in April 1967, the *New York* supplement continued as a well-known city magazine.

A new breed of editorial art directors emerged who were as much editors as designers and helped shape the editorial viewpoint and philosophy of the publications. The prototype for this new editorial designer is Dugald Stermer, who left a studio job in Texas in 1965 to return to his native California and become art director of *Ramparts* magazine. Public opposition to the Vietnam War and concern for a host of other social and en-

Peter Palazzo (art director), cover for *New York*, 1965. For a special issue discussing women's problems and their desire for greater freedom and equality, Palazzo applied eye shadow and mascara to the Statue of Liberty.

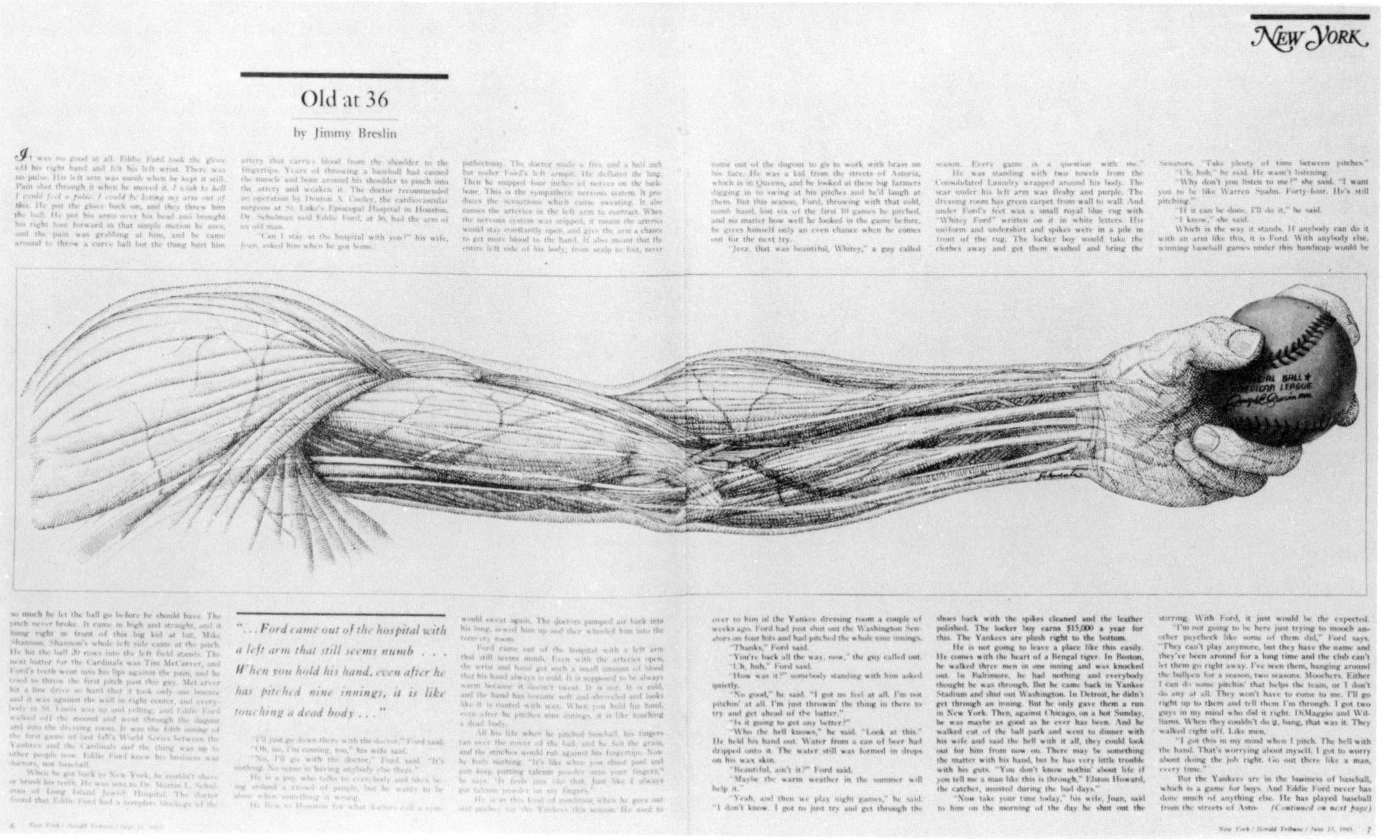

Peter Palazzo (art director), editorial design for *New York,* 1965. Palazzo combined a transparent anatomical drawing of an arm with a photograph of a baseball to express the arm problems of a leading major league pitcher.

Dugald Stermer (art director), cover for *Ramparts,* 1967. Because the editors' names are clearly visible on the burning draft cards, this act of civil disobedience took on the quality of a "self-documented" crime.

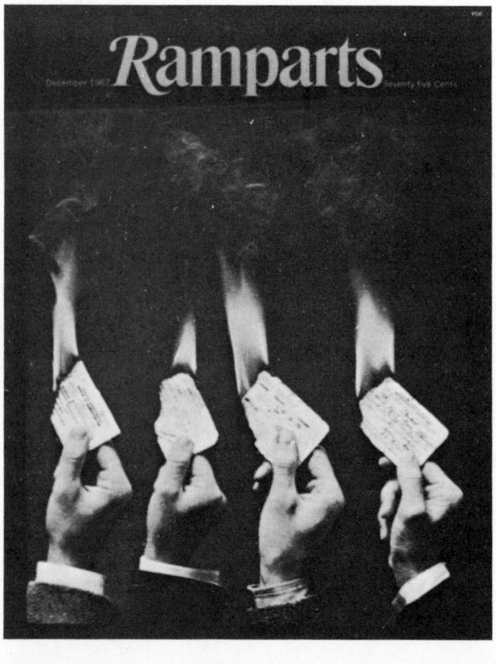

vironmental issues was exploding, and *Ramparts* became the journal of record for the movement. Stermer developed a format using Times Roman typography with capital initials, two columns of text on the page, and centered titles and headings. The dignity and readability of classical, traditional typography packaged the most radical periodical of the era. It was in the use of images, which were often full-page illustrations or photographs on covers and at the beginning of the articles, that Stermer made a major contribution to graphic design. He did not commission images to illustrate the article or topic: he used images as a separate communication to provide "information, direction, and purpose" separate from the printed word. Stermer and editors Warren Hinkle, Robert Scheer, and Sol Stern came perilously close to being indicted for conspiracy as a result of the December 1967 cover design. Many young Americans were burning their Selective Service registration cards as a matter of conscience; this cover depicted four hands holding burning "draft" cards of the four above-mentioned persons. In a country that constitutionally guarantees freedom of speech, this may be the only case on record when the state attempted to convict an art director and subpoenaed him to testify before a grand jury as a result

Dugald Stermer (art director) and Carl Fischer (photographer), cover for *Ramparts,* 1967. With the black-and-white intensity and lost-and-found forms of a Rembrandt etching, this universal indictment of man's inhumanity to man gains a sudden immediacy through the presence of American soldiers at the crucifixion scene.

of art-directing. Convincing arguments by attorney Edward Bennet Williams persuaded the grand jury not to indict the four.

After five years with *Ramparts,* Stermer left the magazine to write a book on Cuban revolutionary graphic design, then established a freelance practice in San Francisco. In addition to art-directing *Oceans* magazine, Stermer cofounded Public Interest Communications in 1973. This nonprofit advertising agency only serves clients working in behalf of the public interest. Stermer faced a difficult problem in creating advertising for nonprofit and community clients. Instead of the "saturation bombing" of media repetition typical of much commercial advertising, community interest clients often have limited funds for purchasing media space or time. Stermer developed an effective approach to the need to effectively convey a lot of information in a limited space. An example is the Delancey Street Foundation advertisement that demonstrates how an editorial approach using lengthy copy, an engag-

Bea Feitler, cover for *Ms.* magazine, 1972. Social conventions and standard design thinking were challenged by this unique, completely typographic magazine cover. The traditional holiday greeting, normally expressing good will to men, is directed toward people. The notion that magazine covers must be pictorial to attract attention is overcome by the use of close-value color. The typography is lime green against a fluorescent pink background that projected brightly from the newsstands.

Bea Feitler, pages from *Ms.* magazine, 1972. This layout demonstrates Feitler's ability to use typography and decoration as a direct expression of the content.

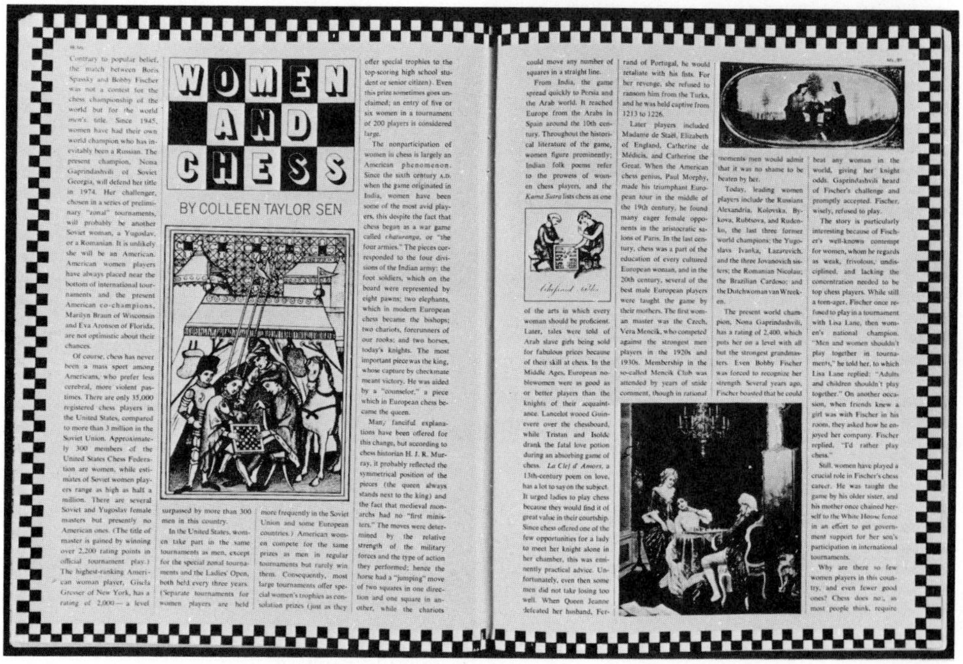

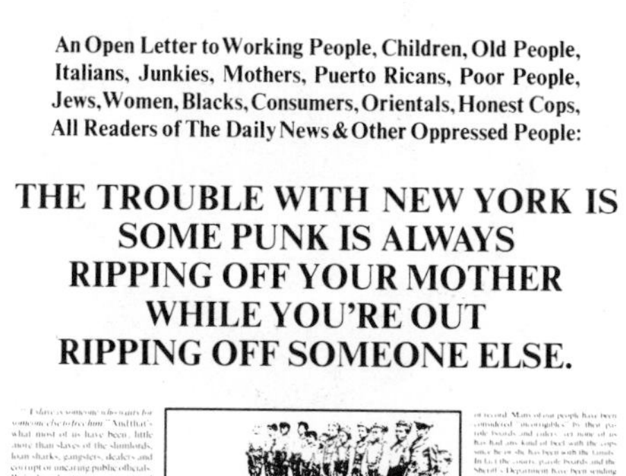

Dugald Stermer (designer and writer), advertisement for the Delancey Street Foundation, 1980. The provocative headline and straightforward, symmetrical editorial feeling of the page invites readership.

Bea Feitler, pages from *Ms.* magazine, 1972. Typography functions as illustration. By visually relating a stencil sans-serif type style to the ruled bars, Feiter was able to use it successfully with slab-serif type. The bars order the page into three zones: headline, and the beginning of two articles, each of which is set in a different text face for separation.

ing headline, and carefully selected spot illustration can provoke interest and motivate the reader.

Stermer is an outstanding example of the graphic designer with strong environmental and political convictions who is able to use his professional abilities in the service of deeply held beliefs without making ethical compromises.

In contrast to the consistent format adopted by Stermer, the design of *Ms.* magazine by Bea Feitler depended heavily upon the diversity of typographic style and scale to bring vitality and expression to this journal of the movement for equal rights and opportunities for women. Feitler has an original approach to typography and design depending, not on consistency of style, but on a finely tuned ability to make appropriate choices uninhibited by current fashion or standard typographic practice. In a single issue of *Ms.* magazine, Feitler's graphic range included fifteenth-century French Renaissance Garamond with ornamental initials, simple geometric sans-serif types, and novelty and illustrated letterforms. All were carefully used to express the content of an article. After her tenure at *Ms.,* Feitler became active as a freelance book designer who sometimes received contractual royalties in an industry where designers, unlike authors, normally work for a fixed fee. In addition, Feitler is a consultant designer to periodicals, the recording industry, and other clients.

A number of currents—the conceptual approach to cover design pioneered by George Lois, the role of art director expanding into editorial matters as defined by Dugald Stermer, and the growing interest in nostalgia, ephemera, and popular culture partly inspired by 1960s Pop Art—dovetailed in the work of Mike Salisbury (b. 1941). In 1967 Salisbury became the art director of *West,* the Sunday supplement of the *Los Angeles Times.* For a period of five years, until the newspaper terminated this outstanding periodical citing inadequate advertising revenue to meet production costs as the reason, Salisbury made *West* a vital expression of California culture. The visual delights of popular artifacts, ranging from orange-crate labels to blue jeans advertising to customized cars, were featured in editorial spreads researched by Salisbury and designed with a combination of randomness and order in original layouts that intensified the pages of *West.*

In 1974, Salisbury redesigned the entire format of *Rolling Stone,* a rock-music newspaper that was repositioned as a tabloid magazine. The element of surprise became the primary design tool used by Salisbury to give *Rolling Stone* a visual energy. Typography was used differently for each article in an issue, and the range of illustrations and photographic approaches knew no bounds. In addition to defining *Rolling Stone's* format, Salisbury established an uninhibited, somewhat "funky" design approach that influenced the layout of many popular, specialized, and regional periodicals for a decade. Salisbury also worked as a consultant designer or art director for *Oui, City,* and *New West.* By the early 1980s, over a half billion copies of magazines had been distributed with covers or concepts created by him.

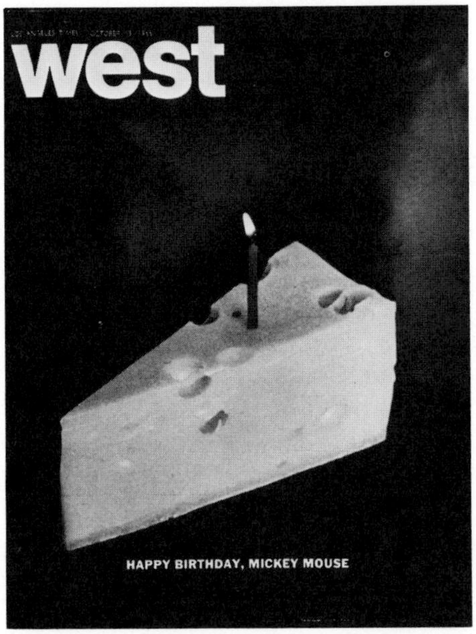

Mike Salisbury (art director) and Rod Dyer (photographer), cover for *West,* 1968. Salisbury's first conceptual cover for *West* simply presented a slice of birthday cheese for a renowned mouse.

Mike Salisbury, cover for *West,* 1971. The passing of the Ed Sullivan television show after more than twenty years on the air inspired this image of the CBS eye shedding a tear.

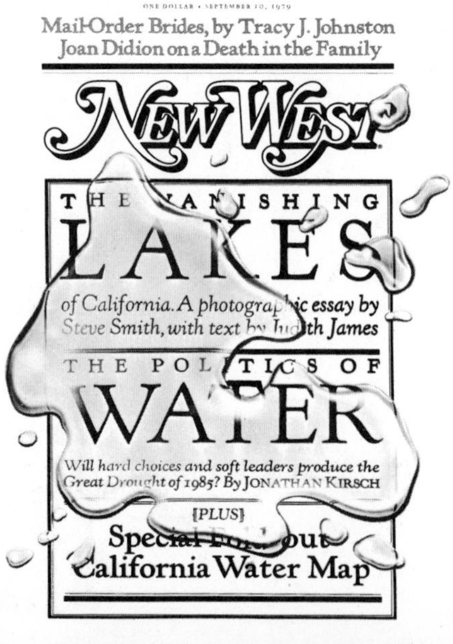

Mike Salisbury, cover for *New West,* 1979. A typographic cover about serious water supply issues gains visual impact through the *trompe l'oeil* realism of water spilled onto the type.

ROLLING STONE, JUNE 6, 1974

VISIONS OF COLDCHISEL EYES

THE INNER TRUTH ABOUT BRONC BUSTERS, STEER WRESTLERS, TEAM ROPERS, CALF ROPERS AND BULL RIDERS

By DOUGLAS KENT HALL

Imagine. The Hilton Inn wanted to be rodeo cowboy headquarters. They actually bid for the chance to house cowboys during the ten-day-long National Finals Rodeo in Oklahoma City. And to cinch the deal, they even offered a cowboy discount on room rates. So the NFR filled the Hilton Inn to overflowing (literally) with the world's top cowboys, rodeo producers and stock contractors.

Which might have been a mistake, I tell myself as I come in from Will Rogers International Airport. Because, even glimpsed briefly from the Northwest Expressway, the Hilton, bulging with all that rodeo energy, looks weak and ill-fated. The whole place has about it the feeling of fragility that comes with flimsy prefabricated cardboard and single-strength glass.

I make my way through a lobby filled with big expensive felt hats. There are two messages waiting for me at the desk. The first is from Larry Mahan, the World's Champion All-Around Cowboy.

Freak, I've gone to a cocktail party. See you later. Bull.

The second is an invitation — unsigned, unexplained — to come to Room 212.

My room is on the fifth floor. When I step off the elevator, I see a tall, whiskey-eyed bulldogger trying to snuff out a cigar in the ashtray fixed to the wall between the two elevator doors. He steadies himself, takes aim and drives so hard with his cigar that the screws rip out of the wall and the ashtray rattles to the floor, spewing out ashes and filter tips. A bell rings, a red arrow lights up; the big dogger drops the smoldering remains of his cigar on the carpet and stumbles into the car. . . . Only a gentle foreshadowing of what

—Continued

Mike Salisbury, pages from *Rolling Stone,* 1974. Salisbury used a typographic style mixing diverse faces that are contained in shapes, plaques, and boxes. The full two-page photograph brought lively graphic pacing to *Rolling Stone*'s information-filled pages.

Mike Salisbury, pages from *West,* late 1960s. The art director becomes a visual historian. Salisbury researched and selected the old Levi's advertisements and products for a pictorial essay.

The pair of pants stretched across the top of the page was known as "Spring Bottoms," a popular style around the turn of the century, resurrected recently in the form of bellbottoms. The brown Levi's with the deep pockets were styled for women. A few years ago the company wanted to reintroduce that style, but found that they couldn't afford the kind of work necessary in the stitching. The Levi's at right, dating from the 1920s, were the first to have the distinctive gull-wing design on the back pocket, and were the last model to have the belt in the back. The boy getting in the car marked the first ad in the 1950s where Levi's were promoted as "leisure wear" (as opposed to "western gear") and aimed at kids. The $500 check at far left was written on oilcloth attached to the leather trademark label from a pair of Levi's. Note that the check DID clear the bank. The metal buttons at left are another trademark and date from the days when Levi Strauss had a lock on the idea. The company's annual catalogues (bottom left) used to be opulently illustrated affairs. The Koveralls which kept kids clean were an integral part of the Levi's line until the '30s. The company recently found that — as with the brown Levi's — the expense in workmanship made it impossible to reintroduce the line at competitive prices. The folder at lower right is a pair of blue Levi's. Ingeniously folded, it opens to show the complete overalls line from the late 1910s. The "Evolution" folder and the two tags at right represent Levi's emphasis on workclothes.

Supermannerism and supergraphics

Like so many art history labels, Supermannerism was first used as a disparaging term. Mannerism is the art-history term generally used to label the stylish art of the 1500s, that broke with the natural and harmonious beauty of the High Renaissance. This word, generally describing a departure from the norm that takes liberties with the classical vocabulary of form, was elevated to Supermannerism by the advocates of the purist modern movement to describe the young bulls who were invading the architectural profession with decorative and intricate design ideas during the 1960s. By 1970, the term Post-Modernism came into use to label the work of artists and designers who were breaking with the International Style. A general feeling developed that the Modern era was drawing to a close in art, design, politics, and literature. The social, economic, and environmental awareness of the period caused many to feel that the modern aesthetic was no longer relevant to what was rapidly becoming a postindustrial society of shrinking resources. New technologies and new social concerns always push innovators in all areas of creative endeavors to seek new solutions and new forms to express the needs and feelings of the era.

In the 1960s the application of graphic designs to architecture in large-scale environmental graphics extended the formal concepts of Art Concret and the International Typographic Style. Supergraphics is the popular name for the bold geometric shapes of bright color, giant Helvetica letterforms, and huge pictographs that warp walls, bend corners, and flow from the floor to the wall and across the ceiling. Supergraphics can expand or contract space as its scale changes relative to the architecture. Psychological as well as decorative values were addressed as designers created forms to enliven dismal institutional architecture, reverse or shorten the perspective of endless hallways, and bring vitality and color to the built environment. Initially supergraphics were linked to the so-called Supermannerist architectural movement.

A reaction against the machine aesthetic and simple geometric forms stripped of ornament used in the International Style of Mies van der Rohe and Walter Gropius, Supermannerism drew upon an expanded design vocabulary that embraced the Pop Art notion of changing the scale and context of materials and objects. It introduced zigzag diagonals into the cool formal vocabulary of the right angle and pure rectangle.

The most controversial and original of the Supermannerist architects is Philadelphia-born Robert Venturi (b. 1925). He looked at the vulgar and disdained urban landscape of billboards, electric signs, and pedestrian buildings and found a vitality and functional purpose there. He urged designers to learn from Las Vegas. Venturi saw the building not as sculptured form, but as a component of an urban traffic/communication/interior/exterior environmental system. Uncommon uses and juxtaposition of materials, graphic elements from the commercial roadside strip, billboards, and environmental-scale lettering were freely added to Venturi's vocabulary of architecture. Perhaps the large graphic wall decorations of his 1962 diner-inspired Grand's Restaurant in West Philadelphia (now destroyed) were the impetus for the Supergraphics concept. Venturi sees graphic communications and new

Robert Venturi, interior of Grand's Restaurant, 1962. Giant stencil letterforms, repeated in mirror image on the opposite wall, alter the scale and space of the environment. *Photograph by Lawrence S. Williams*

Robert Venturi, competition model for the Football Hall of Fame, 1967. A vast kinetic electronic graphics display dominates the building. Information replaced the structure as the dominant "subject" of architecture. *Photograph by George Pohl*

Barbara Stauffacher Solomon, supergraphics for Sea Ranch, 1966. Vibrant primary colors, Helvetica letterforms, arcs, and slashing diagonals form a brilliant counterpoint to the architectural structure and the brilliant California sunshine streaming through the windows.

technologies as important tools for architecture. His proposal for the Football Hall of Fame used a giant, kinetic graphic, illuminated sign that would have been visible for miles on the approaching interstate highway.

The Supermannerist architect Charles W. Moore (b. 1925) designed a large condominium project at Gualala, California, in the middle 1960s. He called upon graphic designer Barbara Stauffacher Solomon (b. 1932) to bring the walls and ceilings of this large architectural project to life through the application of color and shape. Solomon, a San Francisco native and painter who had studied graphic design at the Basel School of Arts and Crafts during the late 1950s, used a vocabulary of pure hue and elementary shape in compositions that transformed the totality of the space. In 1970, the American Institute of Architects presented its medal to Solomon for "bold, fresh, and exciting designs clearly illustrating the importance of rational but vigorous graphics in bringing order to the urban scene."

Both the name, Supergraphics, and the idea caught the public's fancy, and soon Supergraphics were being incorporated into corporate identification systems, decorating shops and boutiques, and brightening factory and school environments.

Post-Modernism

As architecture, the slowest moving and most permanent design discipline, lumbered into the 1970s, architects began to seek a new humanism that called upon clients and users as partners in an advocacy design process. The expanding range of formal possibilities continued, and an ethic of energy conservation emerged. Graphic design, the fastest moving and most ephemeral design discipline, was never dominated by the International Typographic Style the way architecture was dominated by the International Style of Architecture. The design trends that have been labeled Post-Modernism are primarily the work of individuals trained in the Swiss style who have enlarged the formal vocabulary. Some of the approaches include: using contrasting type weights, sometimes in the same word; establishing a grid then violating it; and defining the overall space as a field of tension much as Piet Zwart had done a half century earlier. Rules and bars are commonly used with type on a diagonal, and Dada photomontage techniques are sometimes employed. Often, the functional elements of the 1920s new typography are used as decorative elements. Intuition and play have reentered the design process.

The main thrust of the International Typographic Style was toward neutral and objective typography. The playful, unexpected, or disorganized were rarely allowed to encroach upon the cool clarity and almost scientific objectivity of its major practitioners. One of the earliest "straws in the wind" to indicate that a younger generation of graphic designers was starting to break with the International Typographic Style is the 1964 advertisement for the printer E. Lutz & Company by Rosemarie Tissi, who had joined the studio of Seigfried Odermatt. Different kinds of copy, printed by the client—headlines, text, halftones, and solids—are illustrated by elemental symbols. Instead of lining these images in boxes like soldiers in perfect order as one might expect from a Swiss designer, the five images appear if they have been intuitively and randomly placed in a pile. The ruled lines forming the edges of the squares upon which these images rest have lost-and-found edges that force the viewer to fill in the missing lines. In a 1966 advertising campaign for the Univac Computer Company, typography was pushed up to the top of the page and the photography or graphic diagrams in the large white area below were composed with dynamic angular movements in contrast to the Mondrian-like insistence on horizontal and vertical organization usually found in the International Typographic Style.

In 1966, Odermatt designed a trademark for the Union Safe Company that is the antithesis of Swiss design, for the letterforms in the word "Union" are jammed together to form a compact unit suggesting the sturdy strength of the product. In the process, legibility declines. In full-page newspaper advertisements for Union, placed during prestigious

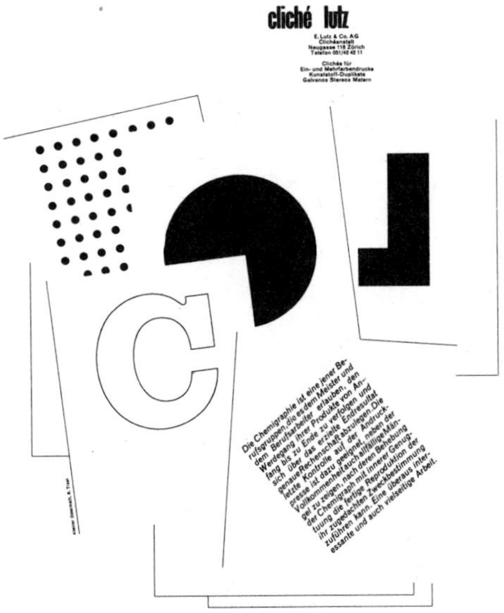

Rosemarie Tissi, advertisement for E. Lutz & Company, 1964. The space comes to life through subtle shifts and angles which throw the page into a state of suspended animation.

Siegfried Odermatt, advertisement for Union, 1968. Overlapping and cropping the logo printed in black and blue-gray brings the vitality and impact of pure form to the newspaper page.

Siegfried Odermatt, advertisement for Union, 1969. The white logo on a red background is folded and bent into a pure expression of dynamic form.

banking conferences, Odermatt treated this logo as pure form to be manipulated visually, creating a plastic dynamic on the newspaper page. Strong, graphic impact, a playful sense of form, and unexpected manipulation of space have always been used in the context of finding a logical and effective solution to a design problem in the work of Odermatt and Tissi. When Odermatt and Tissi have turned their talents toward typeface design, their originality of form has produced unexpected letterforms, as can be seen in Tissi's 1980 advertisement for Englersatz AG which features her typefaces.

Another Swiss designer with a strong interest in complexity of form is Steff Geissbuhler (b. 1942), who joined the Geigy pharmaceutical company in the middle 1960s. In a capabilities brochure for the publicity department, Geissbuhler symbolized the richness and complexity of Geigy publicity by a typographic configuration that became a circular tunnel moving back into space. Geissbuhler moved to Philadelphia and established an independent design practice before joining Chermayeff & Geismar

Rosemarie Tissi, advertisement for Englersatz AG, printers, 1980. The whimsical geometric shapes of Tissi's novel typeface designs engage the viewer with their texture and dimension.

Associates as a partner. Geissbuhler's complexity of form is never used as an end in itself; the dynamic of multiple components forming a whole grows from the fundamental content of the design problem at hand.

In 1964, young Wolfgang Weingart (b. 1941), who had already completed a three-year apprenticeship in typography and studied art, arrived in Basel from southeastern Germany to study with Emil Ruder. After Ruder's death, Weingart joined Armin Hofmann on the faculty of the Basel School in 1968. Initially Weingart had worked under the influence of Ruder, Hofmann, and Müller-Brockmann. When he began to teach, however, he determined that he must teach type in a different way than the approach of his mentors. Weingart began to question the typography of absolute order and cleanness. He wondered if perhaps the International Style had become so refined and proliferated throughout the world that it had reached an anemic phase. Rejecting the right angle as an organizing principle, Weingart achieved a joyous and intuitive design with a richness of visual effects. Ideology and rules collapsed in the face of his boundless energy. A restless experimenter, Weingart draws upon broad technical knowledge and a willingness to ex-

Steff Geissbuhler, poster for Blazer financial services, 1974. One of a sequence of five posters used as decorative-functional wall displays, this poster suggests travel by kinetic repetition of forms moving across the space.

Steff Geissbuhler, brochure cover for Geigy, 1965. In this swirling typographic configuration, legibility is sacrificed for dynamic visual organization.

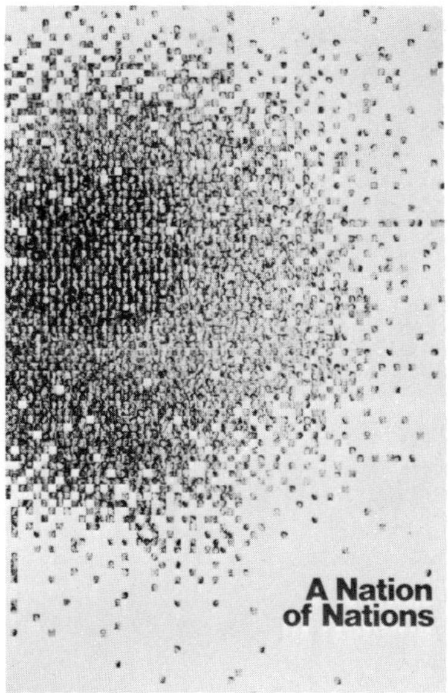

Steff Geissbuhler, poster for the Nation of Nations Exhibition, 1976. To symbolize America as a nation of immigrants, Geissbuhler composed hundreds of portrait photographs of immigrants to America into a complex configuration that seems to expand and contract in space.

plore the untried. He "heated up" the intensity of the page.

From 1968 until 1974, Weingart worked with lead type and letterpress systems. He consciously sought to breathe a new spirit into the typography of order and neatness by questioning the premises, rules, and surface appearances that were hardening the innovations of the Swiss masters into an academic style in the hands of their followers. The most time-honored traditions of typography and visual language systems were rethought. Why must paragraphs be indicated by indents? What other ways could be invented to divide text visually? Why not change weights in mid-word? To emphasize an important word in a headline Weingart would often reverse it from a chunky, black rectangle. The use of wide letterspacing, discarded in the fetish for tight type that accompanied the revolution from metal to photographic typographic systems in the 1960s, was revived by Weingart. Responding to a request to identify the kind of typographic design he created, Weingart's list included sunshine type, bunny type, ant type, five-minute type, typewriter type, and "for-the-people" type. This sense of humor and expressive use of language metaphor to define his work finds close parallels in his typographic invention.

As his students from America returned there to teach and practice, Weingart's influence began to filter into an American design profession

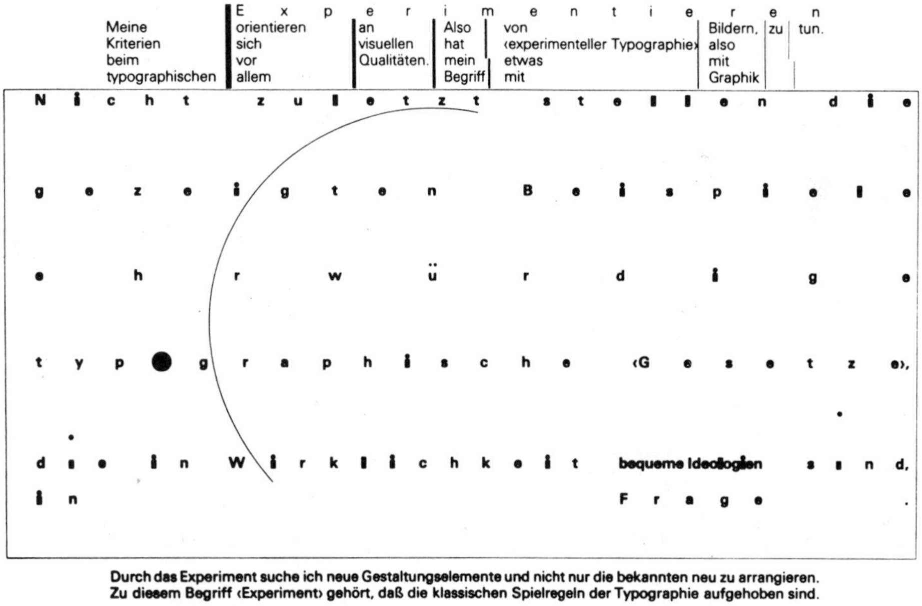

Wolfgang Weingart, experimental text setting, 1969. As Weingart began to test the concepts of the International Typographic Style in the late 1960s, even traditional concepts about wordspacing and letterspacing that date to the medieval manuscript were called into question.

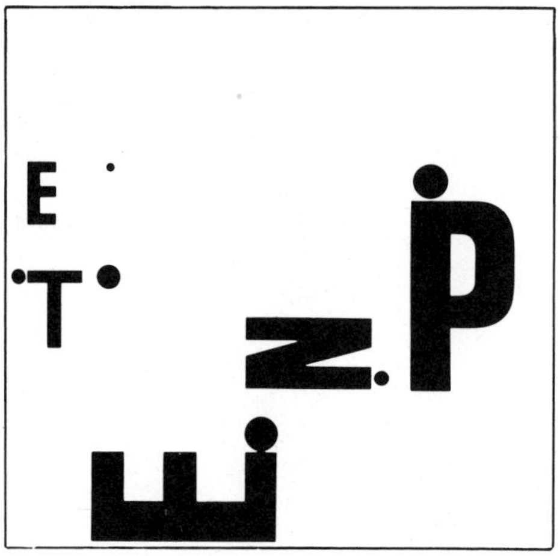

that had become restless with the redundancy of corporate systems using Helvetica but did not have clear vision of where to go next. By the late 1970s, type and stripe (the use of a repetition of rules, often short and diagonal and sometimes of varying weights), letterspaced Helvetica or

Wolfgang Weingart, typographic experiments, 1971. The top composition is a form exploration relating bullets to letterforms. The listing of four German words explores inverted lowercase *m* forms to make a *B* and *e*. Colons and apostrophes combine to form accented *u* letterforms.

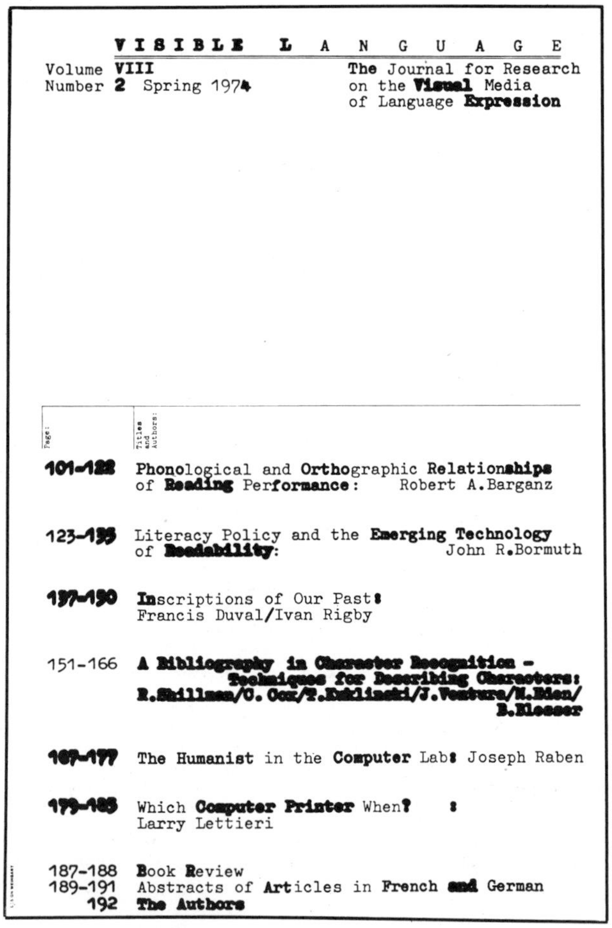
VISIBLE LANGUAGE

Volume VIII
Number 2 Spring 1974

The Journal for Research on the Visual Media of Language Expression

Page: Titles and Authors:

101–122 Phonological and Orthographic Relationships of Reading Performance: Robert A. Barganz

123–135 Literacy Policy and the Emerging Technology of Readability: John R. Bormuth

137–150 Inscriptions of Our Past: Francis Duval/Ivan Rigby

151–166 A Bibliography in Character Recognition – Techniques for Describing Characters: R. Shillman/C. Cox/T. Kuklinski/J. Ventura/M. Eden/B. Blesser

167–177 The Humanist in the Computer Lab: Joseph Raben

179–185 Which Computer Printer When? : Larry Lettieri

187–188 Book Review
189–191 Abstracts of Articles in French and German
192 The Authors

Wolfgang Weingart, cover design for *Visible Language,* 1974. Even the lowly typewriter is explored by Weingart. Weight changes are achieved by swelling the letterforms with varying degrees of overexposure. Collaged together, these varying weights create a tactile rhythm.

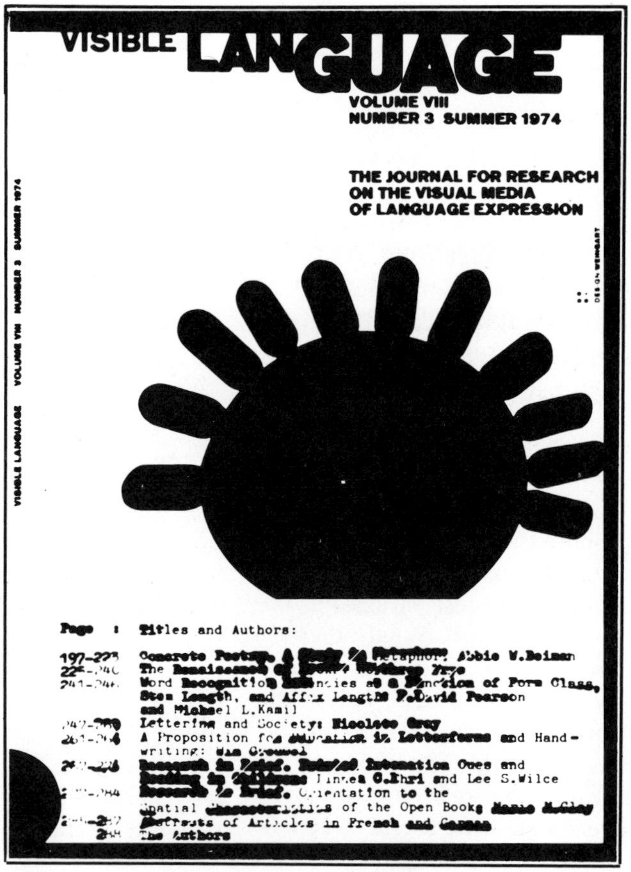

Wolfgang Weingart, covers for *Visible Language,* 1974. Modulated and warped by overexposure, scratched and defaced, the collage of typewriter type listing the contents teeters on the brink of illegibility. But it is, in fact, an expressive graphic image; the real contents listing is inside the magazine. The sun image symbolizes the summer issue.

Wolfgang Weingart, announcement from *Typographische Monatsblaetter,* 1974. This advertisement is an early example of Weingart's involvement in overlapping collage images and complex dropouts. Numbers and arrows rather than the standard left to right and top to bottom sequencing are used to direct the reader through the page.

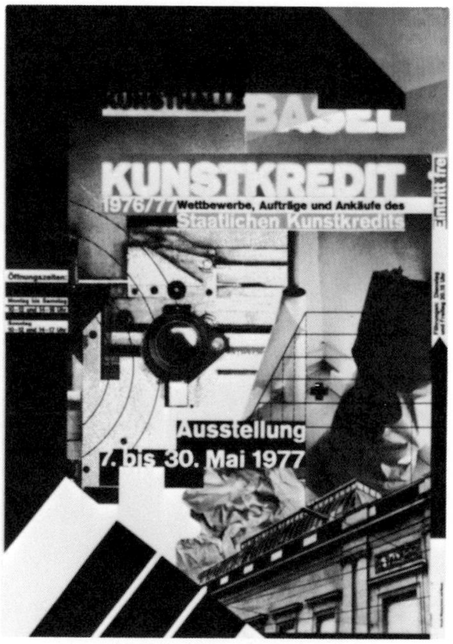

Wolfgang Weingart, poster for an art exhibition, 1977. A kaleidoscope of shifting images and forms calls into play experience of the museum and its art.

Univers, bold step-shapes, ruled lines that outline the random edge of uneven columns of type, diagonal type, and type reversed out of a series of bars were design devices used by American designers in the late 1970s that had been explored by Weingart in the early 1970s.

But by the mid-1970s, Weingart was off in a new direction when he turned his attention toward offset printing and film systems. The printer's camera was used to alter images and the unique properties of the film image were explored. Weingart began to move away from purely typographic design and embraced collage as a medium for visual com-

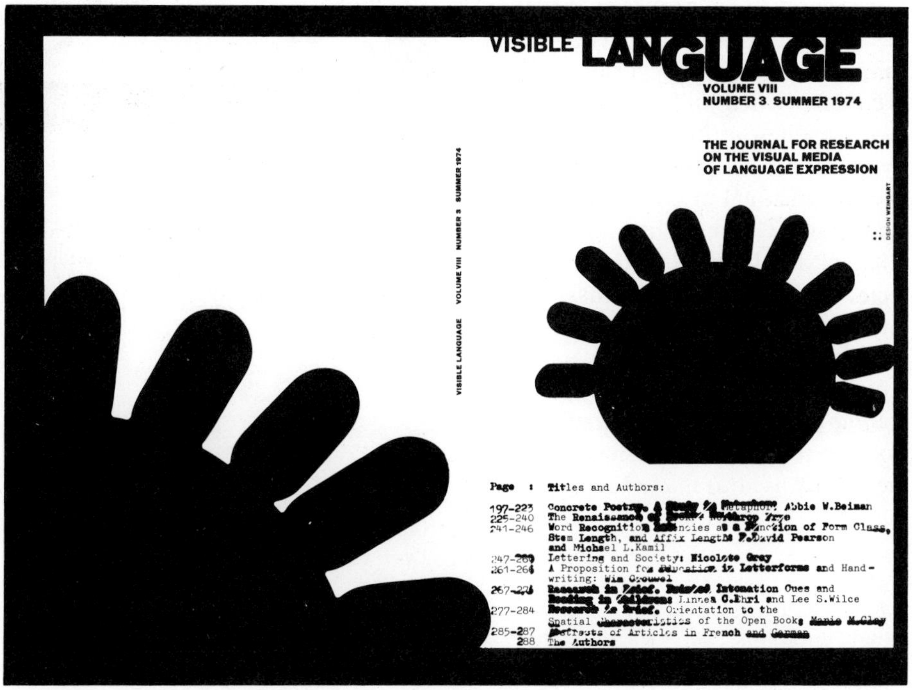

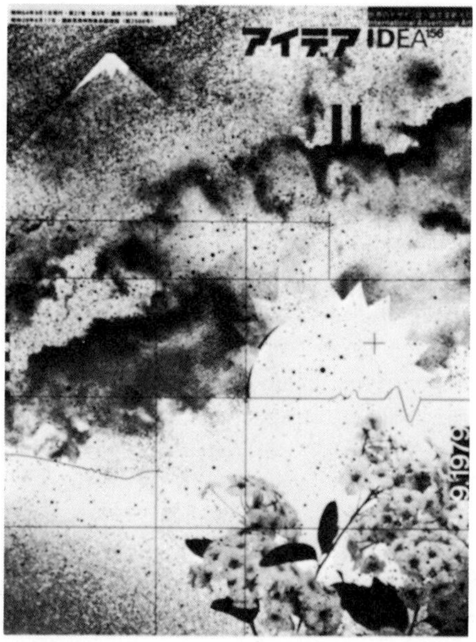

Wolfgang Weingart, cover for the Japanese design magazine *Idea,* 1979. Although he had never visited Japan, Weingart combined imagery evocative of his impressions of that land: snowcapped Mount Fujiyama, rolling fog, industry, a rising sun, earthquakes, and fragile blossoms (which are a halftone made by flowers directly in an engraver's camera).

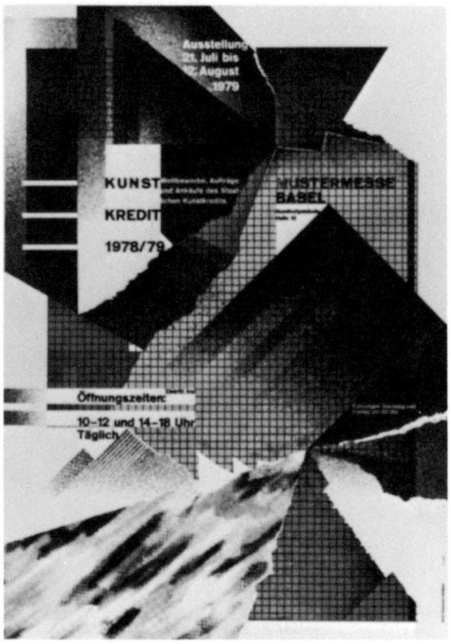

Wolfgang Weingart, poster for an exhibition, 1979. Many film positives and negatives were exposed to create this dynamic composition contrasting mechanical grids with tonal fades, and crisp right-angle edges with soft torn edges.

munication. A new technique—the sandwiching or layering of images and type that have been photographed as film positives—enabled Weingart to juxtapose textures with images, overlap complex visual information, and unify typography with pictorial images in unprecedented ways. Particular delight is taken in the graphic qualities of enlarged halftone dots and the moiré patterns that are produced when these dot patterns are overlapped, then shifted against each other. His design process involves multiple film positives and masks that are stacked, arranged, then exposed with careful registration to produce one negative which goes to the printer. Weingart advocates the "Gutenberg approach" to graphic communications: the designer, like the early typographic printers, should strive to maintain an involvement in all aspects of the process (including concept, typesetting, prepress production, and printing) to ensure the realization of his vision. This remarkable experimenter continues to move forward. Acceptance of the new always lags behind the progress of the innovator. By the time homogenized versions of Weingart's innovations were assimilated into the mainstream of graphic design, he had moved on to new explorations.

In the late autumn of 1973 Weingart traveled to America and delivered presentations at eight prominent design schools. His new design sensibility fell on fertile soil. A more intuitive and free design approach entered the American profession from the bottom up and began to filter into the mainstream in the late 1970s as students who had been exposed to these new ideas completed their apprenticeships and moved into graphic design and art director positions.

Around 1800 the Spanish painter and printmaker Francisco Goya proclaimed, "Vitality! Ideal proportion and classical beauty be damned!" A similar attitude might be said to be held by the graphic designers who emerged in the 1970s.

April Greiman (b. 1948) established a studio in Los Angeles after studying with Weingart in Basel. Weingart observed that "April Greiman took the ideas developed at Basel in a new direction, particularly in her use of color and photography. All things are possible in America!" While Greiman draws from the design vocabulary developed at Basel, using forms like the step-rule at the bottom of the Luxe logotype which was inspired by the step-pattern of the stairways in ruins at an archeological site that Weingart visited on his travels, she evolved a new attitude toward space. Typographic design has been the most two dimensional of all the visual disciplines; Greiman introduced a sense of depth to the typographic page. Overlapping forms, diagonal lines that imply perspective or reverse perspective, gestured strokes that move back in space, overlap, or move behind geometric elements, and floating forms that cast shadows are the means used to make forms move

April Greiman, masthead for *Luxe,* 1978. The step-rule, mixture of letterspaced and italic type, and isolation of each letter as an independent form reflect Greiman's Basel heritage.

April Greiman and Jayme Odgers (co-designers), poster for an exhibition, 1979. In an intricate and masterful manipulation of space, a stunning range of graphic and photographic forms move and flow in illusionistic space, where solid forms become flat and flat forms float in space.

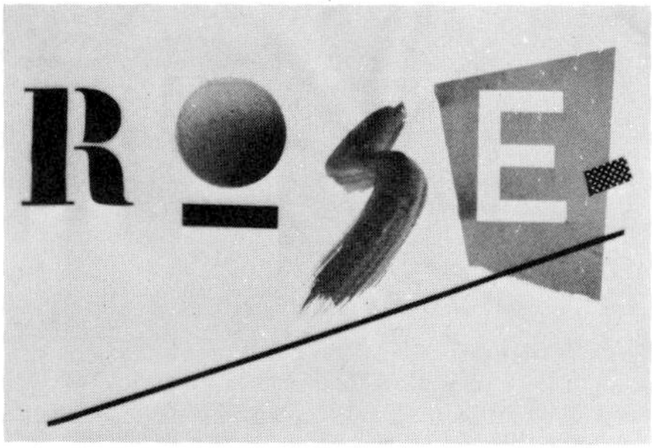

April Grieman, exploratory logo for Rose, 1979. A stencil letter, a floating sphere, a gestural brushstroke, and a letterform cut from a collage element combine to form an extraordinary graphic image.

April Greiman (designer) and Jayme Odgers (photographer), section graphics for the *Cal Arts Bulletin,* 1979. The rectangles and type, overlapping and underlapping the photograph, set up a visual dialogue with the forms in the image, bringing graphic and photographic worlds into a harmonious whole.

April Greiman, advertisement for China Club, 1980. Overlapping forms and movements in and out of space dissolve the flat typographic page.

April Greiman (designer) and Jayme Odgers (photographer), section graphics for the *Cal Arts Bulletin,* 1979. The cliché cube, cone, and cylinder of art school graphics suddenly spring to life as metaphysical forms in a new environment and new space.

forward and backward from the surface of the printed page. Greiman's typographic space operates with the same governing principle defined by El Lissitzky in his PROUN paintings but never applied to his typographic designs.

Strong tactile qualities are found in Greiman's work, as textures including enlarged halftone screens and repetitive patterns of dots or ruled lines contrast with broad flat shapes of color or tone. The intuitive dispersal of numerous elements could collapse into disorder, but a "point-counterpoint" organizational system maintains order by pulling the eye into the page through dominant elements which quickly give way to other elements as the viewer moves through the richness of form on the page.

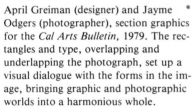

In collaboration with the photographer Jayme Odgers (b. 1939), Greiman moved photographic illustration into a new realm of dynamic space. Graphic elements become part of the "real space" of photographs. Wide angle photographs by Odgers with extreme depth of field have objects thrusting into the picture space from the peripheral edges. Multiple exposure and the incorporation of abstract light patterns into naturalistic photographs implies the fundamental nature of photography as a documentary and artistic medium created by light waves.

Many leading American graphic designers who had developed strong personal design vocabularies began to test their precepts against the more exploratory design attitudes that were emerging. For example, Kenneth Hiebert (b. 1930) retained the harmonious balance that he had achieved through much experience designing with grid systems. But in designs such as the art/design/play poster, he introduced texture, a wider range of typefaces, and shifted forms on his grid.

Post-Modernism sent shockwaves through the design establishment as it challenged the order and clarity of design, particularly corporate design. Design forms have political and social meaning. Why did Post-Modernism gain such a foothold among the generation of American designers who emerged in the 1970s? Perhaps the International Typographic Style had been so thoroughly refined and explored and had received so much acceptance that a feeling existed that the time for a change had come. The 1970s had been called the "me generation" because the social protest—antiwar, civil rights, women's liberation, and environmental concerns—of the late 1960s had given way to more self-absorbed personal involvements. The intuitive and playful aspects of Post-Modernism reflects this personal involvement; the designer places a form in space because it "feels" right rather than to fulfill a rational communicative need. As radically different as a psychedelic poster and a corporate design manual might be, both are *corporate* design, i.e., for or relating to a unified body made up of individuals. Much Post-Modernist design becomes subjective and even eccentric; the designer becomes an artist performing before an audience as surely as a mime troop in the park, and the audience either responds or passes on. As has happened in many past decades, a younger generation responded positively to the outstanding designers of this new movement.

Kenneth Hiebert, poster for an exhibition and symposium, 1979. A formal, underlying grid structure is implied, but a playful intuitive process of form exploration enabled the designer to establish unexpected relationships.

Epilogue

At the time of this writing, human affairs are undergoing a new revolution comparable to the industrial revolution that launched the machine age. Electronic circuitry, microprocessors, and computer-generated imagery threaten to radically alter our culture's images, communications processes, and the very nature of work itself. Graphic design, like many other spheres of human activity, is undergoing profound changes. The graphic design community is responding to this new age of electronic circuitry by an involvement in media graphics, systems design, and computer graphics. The tools—as has happened so often in the past—are changing with the relentless advance of

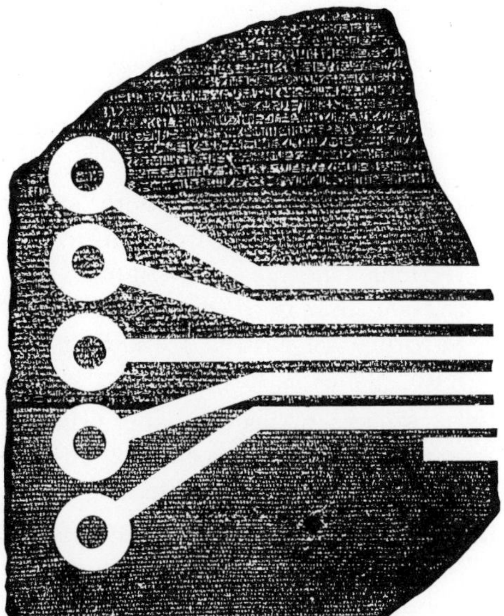

technology, but the essence of graphic design remains unchanged. That essence is an ability to translate ideas and concepts into visual form and to bring order to information.

The need for clear and imaginative visual communications to relate people to their cultural, economic, and social lives has never been greater. Graphic designers have a responsibility to adapt new technology and to express the *zeitgeist* of their times by inventing new forms and new ways of expressing ideas. The poster and the book, vital communications tools of the industrial revolution, will survive the new age of electronic technology as major art forms; the written word remains.

Glossary

AFFICHEURS. Workers who adhere posters to the walls and billboards of French cities.

ALPHABET. A set of visual letters or characters, arranged in an order fixed by custom, that are used to represent the sounds of a spoken language.

AMBROTYPE. A photographic negative on a glass plate that can be seen as a positive image when placed in front of black cloth and viewed at an angle that allows the emulsion surface to reflect light toward the viewer.

AUTOMATISM. Used by the Surrealists to denote suspension of the conscious mind so that subconscious thoughts and images could be released.

BLOCK BOOKS. Books in which the entire text and illustrations for each page are printed from a hand-carved wood block.

BOUSTROPHEDON. Writing with alternating lines written in opposite directions. One line is written from left to right, then in the next line the letterforms are written from right to left.

BROADSHEET. A sheet of paper printed on one or both sides and folded for distribution as a pamphlet.

BROADSIDE. A sizeable sheet of paper printed on one side—frequently, to publicize an official proclamation or controversy—and handed out or posted.

BRONZE SCRIPT. A stage in the evolution of Chinese calligraphy. Beginning during the Shang dynasty (1766–1123 B.C.), these refined redesigns of the earlier bone-and-shell script were engraved on bronze vessels.

CALLIGRAMME. A poem in which the words are arranged to form a visual design, figure, or pictograph relating to the content.

CALOTYPE (from the Greek; "beautiful impression"). Talbot's early photographic process using paper sensitized with silver iodide; brushed with a solution of silver nitrate, acetic acid, and gallic acid; and developed after exposure to light using a solution of silver nitrite and gallic acid.

CAMERA LUCIDA (Latin; "light chamber"). An instrument that projects an external object or scene onto a surface by means of mirrors or prisms so that the image formed can be traced.

CAMERA OBSCURA. (Latin; "darkroom"). A dark chamber, box, or room into which light is admitted by an aperture or lens. This light falls upon the opposite surface and forms an image of external objects which can be traced or photographed.

CANCELLARESCA. A cursive manuscript handwriting style with sweeping ascenders and descenders that originated at the Vatican in the fifteenth century.

CAPITALIS MONUMENTALIS (Latin; "monumental capitals"). Formal, inscriptional letterforms that were carved on monuments and tombs during the Roman Empire.

CAPITALIS QUADRATA (Latin; "square capitals"). The everyday writing version of Roman capitals that were made with thick and thin strokes of a reed pen. The name derives from the fact that wide letterforms such as *M* were exactly square.

CAPITALIS RUSTICA (Latin; "rustic capitals"). A Roman writing style whose letterforms are condensed to conserve space. The pen is held at an almost vertical angle to make the vertical strokes thin and the horizontal strokes thick.

CAPITALS. The larger set of letterforms, in the dual alphabet system, that date from the Roman Empire and are used for initials and emphasis.

CARPET PAGES. Ornamental pages in medieval manuscripts so named because their complex decorations resemble the design patterns of carpets.

CHAP BOOK STYLE. A graphic design style of the late 1890s that minimized ornament, used ruled boxes to divide the space, and adopted the Caslon types, wide letterspacing, and crude woodcuts of Colonial printing.

CHÉRETTE. The lively, uninhibited young women drawn by Jules Chéret that became archetypes for the modern, liberated woman.

CHI-RHO. A Christian symbol and monogram composed of the first two letters, *chi* (*X*) and *rho* (*P*), of the Greek word for Christ.

CHROMOLITHOGRAPHY. Lithographic printing in which inks of various colors are overprinted in exact registration to create a multicolor or full-color image.

CLASSICAL STYLE. The structure or visual forms prevalent in the ancient Greek and Roman worlds.

CODEX. A Roman manuscript book made of rectangular leaves that are folded and stitched together along one edge so that the pages can be turned by the reader.

COLD TYPE. Type which is composed by strike-on or photographic devices that do not involve cast metal types.

COLOPHON. An inscription at the end of a manuscript or book that contains facts about its production; an identification of artists, designers, or printers, and specifications of the typefaces and papers used.

CONSTRUCTION. The act or process of building; used in Aleksei Gan's theory of Constructivism to symbolize the creative process and the search for laws of visual organization.

CONSTRUCTIVISM. A nonfigurative art movement that began in Moscow around 1920 as a secession from Suprematism. It was concerned with the visual organization of geometric planes, the use of modern industrial materials (glass, plastic, and so on), and the application of artistic creation to social needs.

COPISTI. The letterer or copyist who wrote the text in medieval manuscript books.

CORANTOS. Common name for the early two-page English newspaper, adapted from the Middle French word for running to denote "running news."

CRIBLÉ. A background pattern in a woodcut or engraving that is formed by small white dots which are made by tapping a metal tool into the surface of the printing plate.

CUBISM. A French modern art movement that began about 1906. It expressed natural form in terms of lines, simplified planes, and elementary geometric forms.

CUBOFUTURISM. Term coined by the Russian avant-garde during the second decade of the twentieth century to describe their painting style that was strongly influenced by both Cubism and Futurism.

CUNEIFORM. Sumerian writing style of wedge-shaped characters that are pressed into damp clay with a stylus.

DADA. A movement in European arts during the World War I decade that used purposeful irrationality and the negation of concepts of beauty and social organization to protest war and bourgeoise society.

DAGUERREOTYPE. An early photographic process in which a silver-coated copper plate is made light sensitive by the action of iodine (or iodine and bromide). After the plate is exposed in a camera, the latent image is made visible through the chemical interaction of mercury vapor with the light-sensitive silver compounds.

DECALCOMANIA. The process or technique of transferring images or designs from one substrate or surface to another.

DEMOTIC (Greek; "popular, common"). An abstract Egyptian writing style that evolved from the hieratic script around 400 B.C. and was widely used for commercial and legal transactions.

DIMINUENDO. A gradual decrease in size or intensity of a series of graphic elements in a design.

DRUKSELS. Term used by H. N. Werkman for his one-of-a-kind typographic compositions that were created on a printing press.

EDUBBA. The tablet house or writing school where young boys in ancient Mesopotamia learned cuneiform.

EGYPTIAN TYPE. Type styles characterized by thick, slab serifs and a general evenness of weight in the strokes of the letterforms.

ENGRAVING. The art or technique of printing from an image that is incised into the surface of the printing plate.

EX LIBRIS (Latin; "from the library"). This phrase, used before the name of a book owner on a bookplate pasted into the front of volumes to show ownership, has come to mean the bookplate itself.

EXEMPLAR. In early printing, the manuscript copy used as a guide for typesetting, woodblock illustrations, and page design.

EXPRESSIONISM. Art that seeks to depict, not the objective reality perceived by the artist, but the subjective emotional response of the artist to objects and events.

FAT FACES. Extremely bold roman typefaces from the early 19th century characterized by thick strokes having a one-to-two-and-a-half or one-to-two relationship with the capital height.

FAUVISM. An early twentieth-century painting movement characterized by vivid color, a free treatment of form, and composition based on the interaction of planes and shapes of contrasting colors.

FLEURONS. (See printer's flowers).

FORMSCHNEIDER. The medieval craftsman who carved or cut the artist's or designer's image into the woodblock.

FRAKTUR. A sixteenth-century German style of letterforms that incorporated curved strokes to soften the angularity of earlier Gothic styles.

FRISKET. A frame containing a windowed sheet of parchment that is hinged to a hand printing press to protect the portions of a sheet of paper that are not to be printed.

FRONTISPIECE. An ornamental figure or illustration on the first page of a book, usually facing the title page.

FROTTAGE. The technique of recording textures or images by placing a sheet of paper over a textured or relief surface, then rubbing the back of the paper with a pencil or crayon.

FUTURISM. A literature, art, and music movement that began in Italy in 1910 and was characterized by a violent rejection of traditional forms and an effort to express the dynamic energy and speed of the machine age.

GILLOTAGE. An early method of using photographic transfer processes to convert images into relief plates for letterpress printing.

GRAPHIC DESIGNER. An artist who specializes in the design of visual communications. Originally used to designate designers of typography and printing, it now refers to a wide range of information design activity.

HALFTONE SCREEN. A fine grid of ruled lines on a glass plate. When a continuous tone subject is photographed through the halftone screen, the image is broken into tiny black dots of varying sizes. After these dot patterns are printed, the viewer's eye blends them into the continuous tone image.

HALF-UNCIAL. A lettering style dating from the third century, so named because the letterforms are constructed on four horizontal guidelines, one-half uncial (the Roman inch) apart. More cursive strokes, ascenders, and descenders were introduced.

HEAVY ILLUSTRATION. The illustration approach of the first half of the twentieth century which used a full tonal rendition of natural form to depict narrative subject matter.

HIERATIC. A cursive script writing that represented a simplification of hieroglyphics. It was developed and used by ancient Egyptian priests.

HIEROGLYPHICS. A writing system developed in ancient Egypt that used pictographs to represent words and sounds.

HISTORICISM. The use of, and strong reliance upon, earlier historical styles in art and design.

HOT TYPE. General term for type which is cast from molten metal.

HUMANISM. A cultural and intellectual movement of the Renaissance which followed the rediscovery of the ancient Greek and Roman cultures. A concern for people and their potential for self-actualization replaced the focus upon supernaturalism found in the preceding medieval period.

IDEOGRAPH. A sign or character that represents an idea or concept.

ILLUMINATED MANUSCRIPT. Technically, a handmade book of the medieval period that is embellished with precious metals, especially gold leaf, that reflect light in a luminous manner. This term is sometimes used to denote any handwritten manuscript book of the medieval period.

ILLUMINATED PRINTING. Printing that has color or other embellishments applied by hand.

INTERLACE. Surface decoration consisting of a number of ribbons or straps woven together to create a symmetrical design.

INTERNATIONAL GOTHIC STYLE. A manner of depicting the human figure with elongated proportions that was prevalent from the twelfth century to the fifteenth century in the various European countries.

ISOTYPE. A pictographic symbol designed to represent a fixed number or amount of the depicted subject and used in the construction of graphic statistical data.

JUGENDSTIL. (German; "youth style") The late 19th and early 20th Century German decorative style of art nouveau.

KOMMERZ (see *Merz*).

LACERTINES. Interlaces having stylized animate form, frequently suggestive of lizard forms.

LI. A three-legged pottery vessel used in ancient China; the Chinese calligraphic character for this vessel.

LIGATURE. A character composed of two or more letterforms which are joined into a single graphic configuration.

LIGHT ILLUSTRATION. The decorative and less realistic illustration style that came into prominence in the 1950s.

LINOTYPE MACHINE. The first keyboard-operated typesetting machine. Invented by Ottmar Mergenthaler in 1886, this linecasting machine assembled circulating matrices into lines. These matrices were filled with molten lead to cast a slug that could print a line of type by letterpress.

LITHOGRAPHY. Process of printing multiple impressions from an oil-based image applied to a flat stone surface that is moistened before the image is inked. Invented by Aloys Senefelder in 1796, lithography works on the chemical principle that oil and water will not mix.

LOGOGRAM. A letter, sign, or symbol used to represent an entire word without having phonetic representation; for example, $ stands for dollar.

MECHANO-FAKTURA. A theory of visual art and design advanced by Henryk Berlewi in Warsaw in the early 1920s. Rejecting illusions of any kind, Berlewi called for an absolutely flat visual art composed of mechanically constructed planes that did not overlap. Repetition, rhythm, and interval were important concerns.

MERZ. Name given to his collage style of Dada paintings and constructions by Kurt Schwitters, adopted from a fragment of the word *Kommerz* ("commerce") in one of his compositions.

MODERN. Of or pertaining to the present or recent past, in contrast to ancient times. In the graphic arts, this term was adopted to describe the new typographic styles developed in the late eighteenth century that have regular shape construction, extreme contrasts of thick and thin strokes, precisely constructed forms, and straight hairline serifs.

NEGATIVE. An image in which the light areas of the subject appear dark and the dark areas appear light; that is, the values are reversed from normal appearances.

PAPIER MÂCHÉ. A material composed of paper pulp or shreds and glue or paste that is malleable when wet, but becomes hard and stiff when dry.

PARCHMENT. Animal skins that are dried and processed to become a substrate for writing.

PETROGLYPH. An elemental sign or pictograph carved or drawn on rock.

PHONOGRAM. A visual character or sign that represents a sound.

PHOTOGENIC DRAWING. A drawing made by tracing the image projected by a camera lucida or camera obscura.

PHOTOGRAM. A photographic image produced by placing transparent, translucent, and/or opaque objects between light-sensitive photographic paper and a light source, after which the latent image is developed.

PHOTOGRAPHY. The art and technique of using the camera to record optical images on light-sensitive materials.

PHOTOPLASTICS. Term coined by Laszlo Moholy-Nagy to describe his photographic collages, which he saw as the result of a new forming process that opened unexplored avenues of creativity and communication.

PICTOGRAPH. An elementary picture sign that represents the object or word depicted.

PIED DE ROI. A now obsolete measurement containing twelve French inches (equivalent to 12.7892 English or American inches), adopted by François Ambroise Didot as the basis for his typographic measuring system.

POSITIVE. An image or rendition in which light values of the subject depicted appear light and dark values of the subject appear dark.

POUCE. A now obsolete unit of French measurement that is slightly longer than an inch.

PRINTER'S DEVIL. An apprentice in a printing establishment, so called because he often became black with ink from cleaning types and presses.

PRINTER'S FLOWERS. Metal type ornaments, usually stylized or abstract floral or leaf shapes, used to decorate and enliven printing.

PROUN. Term used by El Lissitzky to describe his painting style, formed from the Russian initials of the phrase, "Projects for the establishment (affirmation) of a new art."

PUB-SET. Advertising typography that is set by the publication rather than supplied by the client or his advertising agency.

RAS SHAMRA SCRIPT. A 32-character alphabetical cuneiform script discovered on clay tablets excavated near the Syrian village of Ras Shamra from 1929 to 1936.

RAYOGRAPH. Name given to photogram experiments by the photographer, Man Ray.

REBUS WRITING. The use of pictures and/or pictographs to represent words and syllables which have the same or similar sound as the objects depicted.

RECTO. The side of a leaf in a manuscript or book that is to be read first; the right-hand page.

REGULAR STYLE. The final stage in the evolution of Chinese calligraphy, which has been in continuous use for nearly two thousand years.

RELIEF PRINTING. The duplication of an image by carving or making a printing surface that has the image to be printed raised. Ink is applied to the raised image, then transferred to a sheet of paper by pressing it against the printing surface.

ROTULUS. A roll made from sheets of papyrus pasted together from a writing scroll, frequently about 9 inches (23 centimeters) high and up to about 35 feet (10.7 meters) long, used extensively in the ancient Greek and Roman world.

SANS SERIF TYPE. Type styles characterized by the absence of serifs.

SCHADOGRAPHS. The photographer Christian Shad used this term for his abstract photogram compositions beginning in 1918.

SCRAP. Album cards printed in the Victorian Era for collectors of printed ephemera.

SCRIPTORIUM. The writing room of a medieval monastery where manuscript books were produced.

SCRITTORI. The head of the medieval scriptorium, a learned scribe who had overall responsibility for the editorial and graphic production of manuscripts.

SEMI-UNICAL. An alternative name for half-unicals.

Sezessionstil. (German; "secession style") Austrian style of art nouveau that began when the Vienna Secession was formed in 1897.

Simultaneity. The quality or state of two things occurring at the same instant; for example, imagery that can be read as two forms or views.

Sinaitic script. An alphabetical writing style found in inscriptions from Sinaitic mines that may form a link from Egyptian hieroglyphs to the Phoenician alphabet.

Solarization. The reversal of the denser areas of a photographic image by exposing the light-sensitive film or paper to either an intense or a long continuous source of illumination during the normal development process.

Stele. An inscribed or carved stone slab or pillar used for commemorative purposes.

Stereotyping. The process of making a solid metal duplicate called a stereotype of a relief printing plate by pressing a malleable material (papier mâché, clay, or plaster) against the original, then using the resulting mold to cast a duplicate from molten metal.

Stile Liberty. Italian name for art nouveau, refers to the decorative fabrics marketed by the London department store, Liberty and Co.

Substrate. The base or surface which contains or carries visual information.

Sui generis (Latin; "of its own kind"). The writing script of about one hundred characters which are pictographic signs devoid of any remaining pictorial meaning, dating from about 2000 B.C. in ancient Phoenicia.

Surrealism. An art movement originating in Paris during the 1920s that called upon intuition, dreams, and stream-of-consciousness thought as sources for art and literature. This movement developed a vocabulary of unnatural juxtapositions, fantastic imagery, and absurdity.

Talbotype. An alternate name for calotype.

Tectonic element. A form or design element that is mathematically or geometrically constructed.

Tectonics. The art or science of construction; used by Aleksei Gan in his theory of constructivism to represent the establishment of design or construction methods that would be consistent and appropriate to Communist ideology and social needs.

Textur. Lettering style of the Gothic era that is written by making the upright vertical strokes, then adding strong diagonal strokes to form all connecting elements and the tops and bottoms of verticals.

Texture. The tactile or visual surface qualities of a material; used in Aleksei Gan's theory or Constructivism to signify the nature of materials and how they are used in industrial production.

Tintypes. A positive photographic image, common in the later nineteenth century, which has a photographic emulsion applied to a thin metal plate having a darkened surface, usually black enamel. After exposure and development, the viewer sees the remaining emulsion as light values against the black background.

Toy books. Used in the middle nineteenth century to denote picture books for preschool children.

Transitional roman. Eighteenth century typestyles characterized by sharp serifs, increased contrast between thick and thin strokes, and a strong vertical stress.

Turba scriptorium (Latin; "crowd of scribes").

Tympan. On a hand-printing press, a sheet of material in a wooden frame that holds the sheet of paper to be printed. This provides "padding" behind the paper when it is pressed upon the type by the impression plate.

Typogram. A concise typographic communication in which the message and visual configuration are joined into an expressive unity.

Typography. The art and technique of printing from raised alphabet characters cast on metal blocks; now used for other processes, such as photocomposition.

Typophoto. Term used by Laszlo Moholy-Nagy to describe "a new visual literature" involving the objective integration of words and images for rapid, immediate communication.

Typotekt. Term used by Piet Zwart that expresses the relationship between the graphic designer who constructed a design with the material from a typecase and the construction approach of the architect.

Uncials. A rounded, freely drawn manuscript writing style used as early as the third century in ancient Greece, so named because it was frequently written on guidelines one uncia (the Roman inch) apart.

Wood engraving. A relief printing surface on a block of wood, cut upon the end grain and characterized by fine line work giving an appearance of tone, used to print designs and illustrations by letterpress.

Woodcut. A relief printing surface cut into a block of wood, with the grain of the wood, that bears a raised illustration or design, that is made by cutting away the areas that do not print.

Verso. The side of the leaf in a manuscript or book that is read second; the left-hand page.

Vortographs. Photographs having jewellike abstract kaleidoscope patterns, created by Alvin Langdon Colburn beginning in 1917, which are considered to be the first nonobjective photographic images.

X-height. The height of lower case letters without ascenders or descenders in a type style or font, normally measured on the lower case *x*.

Xylotypography. Technical term for relief printing from a raised wooden surface.

Ziggurat. Ancient Mesopotamian temples consisting of a tall pyramidal structure constructed as a series of stepped-back levels becoming progressively smaller as they move toward the shrine at the top.

Bibliography

Books

Adlmann, Jan Ernst. *Vienna Moderne: 1898–1918.* Houston: University of Houston, 1979.

Alexander, J. J. G. *Italian Renaissance Illuminations.* London: Chatto & Windus, 1977.

Allen, Thomas George. *The Book of the Dead or Going Forth by Day.* Chicago: The University of Chicago Press, 1974.

Anscombe, Isabelle, and Gere, Charlotte. *Arts and Crafts in Britain and America.* London: Academy Editions, 1978.

Apollinaire, Guillaume. *The Cubist Painters, Aesthetic Meditations, 1913.* New York: Wittenborn, 1962.

——. *Calligrammes.* Paris: Editions Gallimard, 1925.

Apollonio, Umbro, ed. *Futurist Manifestos.* New York: Viking Press, 1973.

Arts and Crafts Exhibition Society. *Arts and Crafts Essays.* London: Longmans Green and Company, 1893.

Arwas, Victor. *Belle Epoque Posters and Graphics.* New York: Rizzoli, 1978.

Ashbee, Charles R. *An Endeavor towards the Teaching of John Ruskin and William Morris.* London: Edward Arnold, 1901.

Aslin, Elizabeth. *The Aesthetic Movement: Prelude to Art Nouveau.* London: Elek Books, 1969.

Backhouse, Janet. *The Illuminated Manuscript.* Oxford: Phaidon Press Limited, 1979.

Bann, Stephen, ed. *The Tradition of Constructivism.* New York: Viking Press, 1974.

Barron, Stephanie, and Tuchman, Maurice, eds. *The Avant Garde in Russia 1910–1930.* Los Angeles: Los Angeles County Museum of Art, 1980.

Baljeu, Joost. *Théo van Doesburg*. New York: Macmillan, 1974.

Baxandall, Lee. *Radical Perspectives in the Arts*. Middlesex: Penguin Books, Ltd., 1972.

Bayer, Herbert; Gropius, Walter; and Gropius, Ise, eds. *Bauhaus, 1919–1928.* Boston: Branford, 1952.

Bayer, Herbert. *Herbert Bayer painter designer architect.* New York: Reinhold, 1967.

Beardsley, Aubrey. *The Early Work of Aubrey Beardsley.* London: John Lane, 1899.

———. *The Later Work of Aubrey Beardsley.* London: John Lane, 1900.

Bernard, Auguste. *Geoffroy Tory.* Translated by George B. Ives. New York: Houghton Mifflin, 1909.

Berry, W. Turner; Johnson, A. F.; and Jaspert, W. P. *The Encyclopaedia of Type Faces.* London: Blandford, 1958.

Binder, Carla, ed. *Joseph Binder.* Vienna: Anton Schroll & Co., 1976.

Bliss, Douglas Percy. *A History of Wood-Engraving.* London: J. M. Dent and Sons, 1928.

Bojko, Szymon. *New Graphic Design in Revolutionary Russia.* London: Lund Humphries, 1972.

Bowlt, John E., ed. and trans. *Russian Art of the Avant-garde Theory and Criticism 1902–1934.* New York: Viking, 1976.

Brady, Elizabeth. *Eric Gill: Twentieth Century Book Designer.* Metuchen: The Scarecrow Press, 1974.

Breitkopf, Johannes G. I. *Versuch den Ursprung der Spielkarten, Die Einführung des Leinenpapieres, und den Anfang der Holzschneidekunst in Europa.* Leipsig, 1784.

Brewer, Roy. *Eric Gill: The Man Who Loved Letters.* London: Frederick Muller Ltd., 1973.

Broos, Kees. *Piet Zwart.* The Hague: Gemeentemuseum, 1973.

Brown, Robert K., and Reinhold, Susan. *The Poster Art of A. M. Cassandre.* New York: E. P. Dutton, 1979.

Budge, Sir E. A. Wallis, Kt. *The Dwellers on the Nile.* New York: Benjamin Blom, Inc., 1972.

———. *The Book of the Dead.* London, 1909.

———. *The Rosetta Stone in The British Museum.* New York: AMS Press Inc., 1976.

Carter, Harry, trans. *Fournier on Typefounding.* New York: Lenox Hill, 1972.

Carter, Thomas Francis. *The Invention of Printing in China and its Spread Westward.* 2d ed. New York: Ronald Press, 1955.

Cassou, Jean, and Leymarie, Jean. *Fernand Léger: Drawings and Gouaches.* Greenwich: New York Graphic Society, 1973.

Cate, Phillip Dennis, and Hitchings, Sinclair Hamilton. *The Color Revolution.* Santa Barbara and Salt Lake City: Peregrine Smith, 1978.

Chibbett, David. *The History of Japanese Printing and Book Illustration.* Tokyo: Kodansha, 1977.

Compton, Susan P. *The World Backwards: Russian Futurist Books 1912–16.* London: British Museum Publications, 1978.

Cooper, Austin. *Making a Poster.* London: The Studio, Ltd., 1938.

Crane, Arnold H. *Man Ray Photo Graphics.* Milwaukee: Milwaukee Art Center, 1973.

Crane, Walter. *Line and Form.* London: G. Bell & Sons, Ltd., 1900.

Crane, Walter. *The Bases of Design.* London: George Bell and Sons, 1898.

Damase, Jacques. *Revolution Typographique.* Geneve: Galerie Motte, 1966.

D'Ancona, P., and Aeschlimann, E. *The Art of Illumination.* London: Phaidon Press Ltd., 1969.

Darracott, Joseph. *The First World War in Posters.* New York: Dover, 1974.

Delevoy, Robert L; Culot, Maurice; and Brunhammer, Yvonne. *Guimard, Horta, van de Velde.* Paris: Musée des Arts Decoratifs, 1971.

De Rache, André, ed. *Joan Miró.* Brussels: Gemeentelijke Casino, 1971.

DeVinne, Theodore L. *The Invention of Printing.* New York: Francis Hart & Co., 1876.

———. *A Treatise on Title-pages.* 1901. Reprint. New York: Haskell House, 1972.

Didot, A. Ambroise Firmin. *Essai sur la typographie.* Paris, 1851.

Diringer, David. *The Alphabet,* 2 vols. New York: Funk and Wagnalls, 1968.

Dodgson, Campbell. *Catalog of Early German and Flemish Woodcuts, Vol. I and II.* London: British Museum, 1903.

Durant, Stuart. *Victorian Ornamental Design.* London: Academy Editions, 1972; and New York: St. Martin's Press, 1972.

Dürer, Albrecht. *Of the Just Shaping of Letters.* Translated by R. T. Nichol. New York: Dover, 1965.

———. *Underweisung der Messung mit dem Zirckel und Richtscheyt.* Nuremberg, 1525.

Elliott, David. *Rodchenko and the Arts of Revolutionary Russian.* New York: Pantheon, 1979.

Enyeart, James. *Bruguiere, His Photographs and His Life.* New York: Knopf, 1977.

Ernst, Max. *Une Semaine De Bonté.* New York: Dover, 1976.

Ferebee, Ann. *A History of Design from the Victorian*

Era to the Present. New York: Van Nostrand Reinhold, 1970.

Fournier, Pierre Simon. *Manuel Typographique, Vol. I & II.* Paris, 1764 and 1768.

Franciscono, Marcel. *Walter Gropius and the Creation of the Bauhaus in Weimar: The Ideals and Artistic Theories of its Founding Years.* Urbana: University of Illinois Press, 1971.

Franklin V, Benjamin. *Boston Printers, Publishers, and Booksellers: 1640–1800.* Boston: G. K. Hall, 1980.

Frutiger, Adrian. *Type Sign Symbol.* Zurich: Editions ABC, 1980.

Freeman, Dr. Larry. *Louis Prang: Color Lithographer.* Watkins Glen, New York: Century House, 1971.

Fry, Edward F. *Cubism.* London: Thames and Hudson, 1966; and New York: Oxford University Press, 1978.

Gallo, Max. *The Poster in History.* Concise ed. Milan: Arnoldo Mondadori Editore, 1975.

Geelhaar, Christian. *Paul Klee and the Bauhaus.* Greenwich: New York Graphic Society, 1973.

Gerhardus, Maly and Dietfried. *Symbolism and Art Nouveau.* Oxford: Phaidon Press Limited, 1979.

Gerstner, Karl. *Designing Programmes.* Teufen: Verlag Arthur Niggli AG, 1968.

Gill, Eric. *An Essay on Typography.* London: Sheed and Ward, 1931.

Gillon, Edmund V., Jr. *Art Nouveau: An Anthology of Design and Illustration from* The Studio. New York: Dover, 1969.

Givler, William. *Masterworks in Wood: The Woodcut Print.* Portland: Portland Art Museum, 1976.

Glaser, Milton. *Milton Glaser: Graphic Design.* Woodstock: The Overlook Press, 1973.

———. *The Milton Glaser Poster Book.* New York: Harmony Books, 1977.

Gluck, Felix. *World Graphic Design Fifty Years of Advertising Art.* New York: Watson Guptill, 1969.

Gorb, Peter, ed. *Living by Design: Pentagram.* London: Lund Humphries, and New York: Whitney Library of Design, 1978.

Gray, Camilla. *The Great Experiment: Russian Art 1863–1922.* New York: Abrams, 1962.

Gray, Nicolete. *Nineteenth Century Ornamented Typefaces.* Berkeley and Los Angeles: University of California Press, 1976.

Grayson, A. Kirk, and Redford, Donald B. *Papyrus and Tablet.* Englewood Cliffs: Prentice-Hall, Inc., 1973.

Graziosi, Paolo. *Paleolithic Art.* New York: McGraw-Hill, 1960.

Gress, Edmund. *The Art and Practice of Typography.* New York: Oswald, 1917.

Habasque, Guy. *Cubism.* Paris: Skira, 1959.

Haebler, Konrad. *Incunabula: Original Leaves Traced by Konrad Haeber.* Munich: Werss and Company, 1927.

Haenlein, Carl-Albrecht. *Dada Photomontagen.* Hannover: Kestner-Gesellschaft, 1979.

Hanks, David A. *The Decorative Designs of Frank Lloyd Wright.* New York: E. P. Dutton, 1979.

Hansard, Thomas C. *Typographia: A Historical Sketch of the Origin and Progress of Printing . . .* London: Baldwin, Cradock, and Joy, 1825.

Hassall, A. G. and W. O. *The Douce Apocalypse.* New York: Thomas Yoseloff, 1961.

Hausmann, Raoul, and Schwitters, Kurt. *PIN.* London: Gaberbocchus Press, 1962.

Herdeg, Walter, *Film & TV Graphics.* Zurich: The Graphis Press, 1967.

———. *Film & TV Graphics 2.* Zurich: The Graphis Press, 1976.

Hillier, Bevis. *100 Years of Posters.* New York: Harper & Row, 1972.

Hind, Arthur M. *An Introduction to a History of Woodcut.* New York: Dover, 1963.

Holloway, Owen E. *French Rococo Book Illustration.* New York: Transatlantic Arts Inc., 1969.

Hollstein, F. W. H. *German Engravings Etchings and Woodcuts CA. 1400–1700.* Amsterdam: Menno Hertzberger, 1962.

Huss, Richard E. *The Development of Printer's Mechanical Typesetting Methods 1822–1925.* Charlottesville: University Press of Virginia, 1973.

Huelsenbeck, Richard. *Memoirs of a Dada Drummer.* New York: Viking Press, 1969.

Hurlburt, Allen. *Layout: The Design of the Printed Page.* New York: Watson-Guptill, 1977.

Hutchison, Harold F. *The Poster.* New York: Viking, 1968.

Hutt, Allen. *Fournier, the Compleat Typographer.* London: Frederick Muller, Ltd., 1972.

Hüttinger, Eduard. *Max Bill.* Zurich: ABC edition, 1978.

Huyghe, René. *Larousse Encyclopedia of Prehistoric and Ancient Art.* New York: Prometheus Press, 1962.

Itten, Johannes. *Design and Form: The Basic Course at the Bauhaus.* New York: Reinhold, 1964.

Jaffe, Hans L. C. *De Stijl.* New York: Harry N. Abrams, 1971.

Jaffé, H. L. C., et al. *Mondrian und De Stijl.* Obenmarspforten: Galerie Gmurzynska, 1979.

Johnson, Fridolf. *A Treasury of Bookplates from the Renaissance to the Present.* New York: Dover, 1977.

Julien, Edouard. *The Posters of Toulouse-Lautrec.* Monte-Carlo: Andre Sauret, 1966.

Karginov, German. *Rodchenko.* London: Thames and Hudson, 1979.

Kaster, Joseph. *Wings of the Falcon*. New York: Holt, Rinehart and Winston, 1968.

Keay, Carolyn. *American Posters of the Turn of the Century*. London: Academy Editions, 1975.

Klee, Paul. *Pedagogical Sketchbook*. New York: Praeger, 1953.

Koschatzky, Walter, and Kossatz, Horst-Herbert. *Ornamental Posters of the Vienna Secession*. New York: St. Martin's Press, 1974.

Kostelanetz, Richard, ed. *Moholy-Nagy*. New York: Praeger, 1970.

Kraus, Theodor. *Pompeii and Herculaneum: The Living Cities of the Dead*. New York: Abrams, 1975.

Kurth, Dr. Willi. *The Complete Woodcuts of Albrecht Dürer*. New York: Crown, 1946.

le Bé, Pierre. *Modeles de lettres de Pierre le Bé*. Paris, 1601.

Lehmann-Haupt, Hellmut. *Gutenberg and the Master of the Playing Cards*. New Haven: Yale University Press, 1966.

——. *The Book in America*. New York: Bowker, 1951.

Levarie, Norma. *The Art & History of Books*. New York: James H. Heineman, Inc., 1968.

Lewis, John. *Typography/Basic Principles*. New York: Reinhold, 1966.

Lippard, Lucy R., ed. *Dadas on Art*. Englewood Cliffs: Prentice-Hall, 1971.

Lissitzky-Kuppers, Sophie. *El Lissitzky—Life•Letters•Texts*. Greenwich: New York Graphic Society, 1968.

Little, Roger. *Guillaume Apollinaire*. London: Athlone Press, 1976.

Lois, George, and Pitts, Bill. *The Art of Advertising: George Lois on Mass Communications*. New York: Abrams, 1977.

Lönberg-Holm, K., and Sutnar, Ladislav. *Catalog Design*. New York: Sweet's Catalog Service, 1944.

——. *Catalog Design Progress*. New York: Sweet's Catalog Service, 1950.

Lowance, Mason I., Jr., and Bumgardner, Georgia B., eds. *Massachusetts Broadsides of the American Revolution*. Amherst: University of Massachusetts Press, 1976.

Lowry, Martin. *The World of Aldus Manutius*. Ithaca: Cornell University Press, 1979.

Mackmurdo, Arthur H., ed. *The Century Guild Hobby Horse*. London: 1884–88.

Margolin, Victor. *The Golden Age of the American Poster*. New York: Ballentine Books, 1976.

Marinetti, Filippo T. *Marinetti: Selected Writings*. Edited by R. W. Flint. New York: Farrar, Straus, and Giroux, 1971.

Martin, Marianne W. *Futurist Art and Theory 1909–1915*. Oxford: Clarendon Press, 1968.

Martinet, Jan. *H. N. Werkman: 'Druksel' Prints and General Printed Matter*. Amsterdam: Stedelijk Museum, 1977.

——. *Hendrik Werkman: The Next Call*. Utrecht: uitgeverij Reflex, 1978.

Marzio, Peter C. *The Democratic Art*. Boston: David R. Godine, 1979.

McClinton, Katharine Morrison. *The Chromolithographs of Louis Prang*. New York: Clarkson N. Potter, Inc., 1973.

McCrillis, John O. C. *Printer's Abecedarium*. Boston: Godine, 1974.

McLean, Ruari. *Jan Tschichold: Typographer*. Boston: David R. Godine, 1975.

McLuhan, Marshall. *The Gutenberg Galaxy*. Toronto: The University of Toronto Press, 1962.

——. *The Mechanical Bride*. New York: Vanguard Press, 1951.

——. *Understanding Media: The Extensions of Man*. New York: McGraw-Hill, 1964.

McMurtrie, Douglas C. *The Book: The Story of Printing and Bookmaking*. New York: Oxford University Press, 1943.

——. *Modern Typography and Layout*. Chicago: Eyncourt Press, 1929.

Menten, Theodore. *Advertising Art in the Art Deco Style*. New York: Dover, 1975.

Metzl, Ervine. *The Poster: Its History and Its Art*. New York: Watson–Guptill, 1963.

Michalowski, Kazimierz. *Art of Ancient Egypt*. New York: Abrams, 1978.

Michaud, Guy. *Mallarmé*. New York: New York University Press, 1965.

Moholy-Nagy, Sibyl. *Moholy-Nagy: Experiment in Totality*. Cambridge: M. I. T. Press, 1969.

Mondrian, Piet. *Plastic Art and Pure Plastic Art*. New York: Wittenborn, 1951.

Moran, James. *Stanley Morison His Typographic Achievement*. London: Lund Humphries, and New York: Hastings House, 1971.

Morison, Stanley. *German Incunabula in the British Museum*. New York: Hacker Art Books, 1975.

——, and Day, Kenneth. *The Typographic Book 1450–1935*. London: Ernest Benn Limited, and Chicago: The University of Chicago Press, 1963.

Mortimer, Ruth. *French 16th Century Books (Vol. I & II)*. Cambridge: The Belknap Press of Harvard University Press, 1964.

Mott, Frank Luther. *A History of American Magazines*. Cambridge: Belknap Press of Harvard University, 1957.

Mucha, Juri. *Alphonse Mucha*. New York: St. Martin's Press, 1971.

Muir, Percy. *Victorian Illustrated Books*. New York:

Praeger Publishers, 1971.

Müller, Fridolin, ed. *Piet Zwart*. Teufen: Verlag Arthur Niggli AG, 1966.

Muther, Richard. *German Book Illustration of the Gothic Period and the Early Renaissance (1460–1530)*. Metuchen, N. J.: The Scarecrow Press, Inc., 1972.

Mutherich, Florentine, and Gaehde, Joachim E. *Carolingian Painting*. New York: George Braziller, 1976.

Naylor, Gillian. *The Arts and Crafts Movement*. Cambridge: The M.I.T. Press, 1971.

Nebehay, Christian M. *Ver Sacrum 1898–1903*. Rizzoli, New York, 1977.

Nesbitt, Alexander. *The History and Technique of Lettering*. New York: Dover, 1950.

Newell, Kenneth B. *Pattern Poetry: A Historical Critique from the Alexandrian Greeks to Dylan Thomas*. Boston: Marlborough House, 1976.

Newhall, Beaumont. *The History of Photography*. New York: Museum of Modern Art, 1964.

Nordenfalk, Carl. *Celtic and Anglo-Saxon Painting*. New York: George Braziller, 1977.

Overy, Paul. *De Stijl*. London: Studio Vista, 1969.

Panofsky, Erwin. *The Life and Art of Albrecht Dürer*. Princeton: Princeton University Press, 1955.

Papanek, Victor. *Design for the Real World*. New York: Pantheon Books, 1970.

Pardoe, F. E. *John Baskerville of Birmingham: Letter-Founder and Printer*. London: Frederick Muller Limited, 1975.

Parrot, Andre. *The Arts of Assyria*. New York: Golden Press, 1961.

Passuth, Krisztina, and Senter, Terence A. *L. Moholy-Nagy*. London: Arts Council of Great Britain, 1980.

Petrie, Sir W. M. Flinders. *Buttons and Design Scarabs*. Guildfold: Biddles Limited, 1974.

———. *Scarabs and Cylinders with Names*. Guildford: Biddles Limited, 1974.

Pognon, Edmond. *Les Tres Riches Heures de Duc de Berry Fifteenth Century Manuscript*. Fribourg: Productions Liber SA, 1979.

Pollack, Peter. *The Picture History of Photography*. New York: Abrams, 1969.

Rand, Paul. *Thoughts on Design*. New York: Van Nostrand Reinhold, 1970.

Read, Brian. *Aubrey Beardsley*. New York: Bonanza, 1968.

Read, Herbert. *A Concise History of Modern Painting*. New York: Praeger, 1959.

Richards, J. M., and Pevsner, Nikolaus, eds. *The Anti-Rationalists*. Cambridge: The Architectural Press, 1973.

Ricketts, Charles. *A Defence of the Revival of Printing*. London: Ballantyne Press, 1909.

Rosenbaum, Robert. *Cubism and Twentieth-Century Art*. New York: Abrams, 1966.

Rossiter, Evelyn. *The Book of the Dead*. Fribourg-Geneve: Productions Liber SA and Editions Minerva SA, 1979.

Rossiter, Henry Preston. *Albrecht Dürer: Master Printmaker*. Boston: Museum of Fine Arts, 1971.

Rubinger, Krystyna; Bojko, Szymon; and Bowlt, John E., et al. *Women-Artists of the Russian Avantgarde, 1910–1930*. Koln: Galerie Gmurzynska, 1980.

Rye, Jane. *Futurism*. London: Studio Vista, 1972.

Sainton, Roger. *Art Nouveau Posters and Graphics*. New York: Rizzoli, 1977.

Schlemmer, Oscar. *Man*. Cambridge: M. I. T. Press, 1971; and London: Lund Humphries, 1971.

Schmalenbach, Werner. *Fernand Léger*. New York: Abrams, 1976.

Schuster, Peter-Klaus, ed. *Peter Behrens und Nurnberg*. Munich: Prestel-Verlag, 1980.

Schwartz, Arturo. *Man Ray: The Rigour of Imagination*. New York: Rizzoli, 1972.

Selz, Peter, and Constantine, Mildred, eds. *Art Nouveau*. New York: The Museum of Modern Art, 1959.

Seuphor, Michel. *Piet Mondrian*. New York: Abrams, 1956.

Sharp, Dennis. *Henri van de Velde, Theatres 1904–1914*. London: The Architectural Association, 1974.

Shove, Raymond H. *Cheap Book Production in the United States, 1870 to 1891*. Urbana: University of Illinois Library, 1937.

Siepmann, Eckhard. *Montage: John Heartfield*. Berlin: Elefanten Press Galerie, 1977.

Speaight, Robert. *The Life of Eric Gill*. London: Methuen, 1966.

Spencer, Herbert. *Pioneers of Modern Typography*. New York: Hastings House, 1970; and London: Lund Humphries, 1970.

Stankowski, Anton. *Bildpläne*. Stuttgart: Edition Cantz, 1979.

———. *Visual Presentation of Invisible Processes*. Teufen: Verlag Arthur Niggli AG, 1966.

Steegmuller, Francis. *Apollinaire, Poet among the Painters*. Freeport: Books for Libraries Press, 1971.

Steinitz, Kate Trauman. *Kurt Schwitters: A Portrait from Life*. Berkeley and Los Angeles: University of California Press, 1968.

Stern, Madeleine B. *Publishers for Mass Entertainment in Nineteenth Century America*. Boston: G. K. Hall, 1980.

Strauss, Walter L. *The German Single-Leaf Woodcut, 1550–1600*. New York: Abaris Books, Inc., 1975.

Strommenger, Eva. *5000 Years of Mesopotamian Art*. New York: Abrams, 1964.

Sutton, J. and Bartram, A. *An Atlas of Typeforms*. New

York: Hastings House, 1968.

Sylvester, David. *Magritte.* New York: Praeger, 1969.

Tadashi, Masuda. *Works of the Masuda Tadashi Design Institute.* Tokyo: Seibundo Shinkosha, 1966.

Talbot, Charles W., ed. *Dürer in America: His Graphic Work.* New York: Macmillan, 1971.

Talbot, William Henry Fox. *The Pencil of Nature.* London: Longman, Brown, Green and Longmans, 1844.

Taylor, John Russell. *The Art Nouveau Book in Britain.* Edinburgh: Paul Harris Publishing, 1979.

Tebbel, John. *The American Magazine: A Compact History.* New York: Hawthorne Books, 1969.

Thomson, Oliver. *Mass Persuasion in History.* Edinburgh: Paul Harris Publishing, 1977.

Thompson, Susan Otis. *American Book Design and William Morris.* New York: R. R. Bowker Company, 1977.

Thorp, Joseph. *Eric Gill.* London: Jonathan Cape, 1929.

Triggs, Oscar Lovell. *Chapters in the History of the Arts and Crafts Movement.* Chicago, 1902. Reprint. New York: Arno Press, 1979.

Tschichold, Jan. *Asymmetric Typography.* English ed. New York: Reinhold, 1967.

——. *Designing Books,* English ed. New York: Wittenborn, Schultz, Inc., 1951.

——. *Die Neue Typographie.* Berlin: Verlag des Bildungsverbandes der Deutschen Buchdrucker, 1928.

Updike, Daniel Berkeley. *Printing Types: Their History, Forms and Use.* Cambridge: Harvard University Press, 1937.

van Doesburg, Théo ed. *De Stijl, Vol. I–VII 1917–1931.* Reprint. Amsterdam: Athenaeum, 1968.

Verneuil, M. M. P.; Auriol, G.; and Mucha, A. *Combinaisons Ornementales.* Paris: Librairie Centrale des Beaux Arts, undated.

Weber, Wilhelm. *Peter Behrens.* Berlin: Pfalzgalerie Kaiserslautern, 1966.

Weitzmann, Kurt. *Late Antique and Early Christian Book Illumination.* New York: George Braziller, 1977.

Williams, John. *Early Spanish Manuscript Illumination.* New York: George Braziller, 1977.

Wilson, Adrian. *The Making of the Nuremberg Chronicle.* Amsterdam: Nico Israel, 1976.

Zapf, Hermann. *Manuale Typographicum.* Frankfurt and New York: Z-Presse, 1968.

Major periodicals

Communication Arts: Vol. 1 No. 1, 1959–Vol. 23 No. 3, 1981.

Graphis: Vol. 1 No. 1, 1944–Vol. 37 No. 214, 1981.

Print: Vol. 1 No. 1, 1940–Vol. 35 No. 4, 1981.

Novum Grebrauchsgraphik (formerly *Grebrauchsgraphik*): Vol. 7 No. 1, 1930–Vol. 52 No. 8, 1981.

Visible Language (formerly *The Journal of Typographic Research*): Vol. 1 No. 1, 1967–Vol. 14 No. 4, 1981.

Index

Illustrations are indicated in *italics* at the end of each entry.